Biographical
Dictionary
of
American Labor

Biographical Dictionary of American Labor

EDITOR-IN-CHIEF
GARY M FINK

Greenwood Press
Westport, Connecticut • London, England

Library of Congress Cataloging in Publication Data
Main entry under title:

Biographical dictionary of American labor.

Rev. ed. of: Biographical dictionary of American
labor leaders. 1974.
Bibliography: p.
Includes index.
1. Labor and laboring classes—United States—Biography 2. Trade-unions—United States—Officials and
employees—Biography. I. Fink, Gary M II. Biographical
dictionary of American labor leaders.
HD8073.A1B56 1984   331.88′092′2 [B]   84-4687
ISBN 0-313-22865-5 (lib. bdg.)

Library of Congress Catalog Card Number: 84-4687
ISBN: 0-313-22865-5

First published in 1984

Greenwood Press
A division of Congressional Information Service, Inc.
88 Post Road West, Westport, Connecticut 06881

Printed in the United States of America

10 9 8 7 6 5 4 3 2 1

Contents

Illustrations

Contributors
(to Second Edition)

Steve Babson, Wayne State University

Barbara Bartkowiak, Wisconsin Rapids, Wisconsin

Jon Bloom, Tamiment Library, New York University

Dennis C. Dickerson, Williams College

Robert Fitrakis, Wayne State University

Gilbert J. Gall, Tennessee State University

Joseph Y. Garrison, Atlanta, Georgia

John W. Hevener, Ohio State University, Lima

Christopher Johnson, Wayne State University

Bruce L. Larson, Mankato State University

Stephen H. Norwood, Columbia University

Faye Phillips, Troup County Historical Society and Archives, La Grange,
    Georgia

Merl E. Reed, Georgia State University

Donald G. Sofchalk, Mankato State University

Marie Tedesco, Atlanta, Georgia

Sharon Trusilo, Carnegie-Mellon University

Seth Wigderson, University of Michigan, Dearborn

Gay Zieger, Detroit, Michigan

Robert H. Zieger, Wayne State University

Consultants (As Identified in the First Edition)

Advisory Editor
Milton Cantor, Professor of History, University of Massachusetts, Amherst

Consultant Editors
Albert A. Blum, Professor of Labor History, Michigan State University

David Brody, Professor of History, University of California, Davis

Melvyn Dubofsky, Professor of History, State University of New York at Binghamton

Sidney Fine, Andrew Dickson White Professor of History, University of Michigan

Walter Galenson, Professor of Economics and Industrial Relations, Cornell University

Morris A. Horowitz, Professor of Economics and Chairman of the Department, Northeastern University, Boston

Vernon H. Jensen, Professor of Industrial and Labor Relations, Emeritus, New York State School of Industrial and Labor Relations, Cornell University

Charles P. Larrowe, Professor of Economics, Michigan State University

Bruce Laurie, Professor of History, University of Massachusetts, Amherst

David Montgomery, Associate Professor of History, University of Pittsburgh

Maurice F. Neufeld, Professor of Industrial and Labor Relations, New York State School of Industrial and Labor Relations, Cornell University

Edward Pessen, Distinguished Professor of History, Baruch College and the Graduate Center, The City University of New York

Howard Quint, Professor of History, University of Massachusetts, Amherst

Leon Stein, Editor, *Justice*

Philip Taft, Professor Emeritus, Brown University

Leo Troy, Professor of Economics, Rutgers University

Warren R. Van Tine, Assistant Professor of History, Ohio State University

Preface to Second Edition

This volume constitutes an expanded and updated version of the *Biographical Dictionary of American Labor Leaders* published in 1974. Two hundred thirty-four new sketches have been added to the approximately five hundred contained in the first edition. Several of the original sketches were completely rewritten because of the availability of additional biographical information, and the remaining sketches were updated and revised where appropriate. Similarly, the biographical references listed at the end of each sketch were updated and the location of personal papers identified. Finally, an extended introduction has been added, providing a quantitative and qualitative analysis of American labor leaders. The introduction should be helpful to the user of the *Dictionary* in placing individual sketches into a broader context.

The title of this edition has been altered slightly to reflect the broader criteria applied in the selection of new biographical subjects. As was true of the first edition, no claim is made—explicitly or implicitly—that the subjects contained in this volume constitute the most significant figures in the world of American labor, either historically or contemporaneously; but they are meant to be representative of the great diversity that has existed (and still exists) among trade union leaders, political radicals, intellectuals, and the like. Although numerous trade unionists have been added, the emphasis on orthodox trade union leaders in the original publication was not continued in the selection of subjects for this edition. Instead, a greater effort has been made to reflect the diversity that has always existed in American working-class movements.

The number of women included has been substantially expanded, and several labor reformers, such as Jane Addams and Florence Kelley, have been added along with female radicals and trade unionists. The diversity of the radical Left should also be reflected better with the inclusion of John Reed, the Haymarket martyrs, Sacco and Vanzetti, among others. Alice and Staughton Lynd's *Rank and File*, along with other oral histories, has made it feasible to include profiles of several rank-and-file leaders. Similarly, a small number of labor publicists, intellectuals, and academicians have been included for the first time in this volume. Unfortunately, the effort to expand the coverage of black Americans and other minorities was less successful.

A major effort was made to expand the coverage of labor leaders during the last quarter of the nineteenth century. This crucially important period in the history of American labor was characterized by great turbulence and industrial warfare as the American economy went through the labor pains of industrialization and the birth of the modern American labor movement. David Montgomery and Philip Foner alerted me to a series of biographical profiles published in the Chicago *Workingman's Advocate* during 1873–1874, and Sharon Trusilo compiled biographical information on a substantial number of the early leaders of the Amalgamated Association of Iron, Steel and Tin Workers. The biographical sketches that resulted are not always complete, but the information thus acquired was considered important enough to warrant inclusion. Similarly, it was decided to include several of the sketches first published in 1887 by George E. McNeill in *The Labor Movement: The Problem of To-Day*. McNeill is identified as the author of those sketches, which have been edited slightly to conform to the style used in this volume.

Robert H. Zieger and Merl E. Reed read portions of the introduction and offered many useful suggestions. Les Hough and his staff at the Southern Labor Archives were very helpful in locating biographical information. The College of Arts and Sciences, Georgia State University, provided release time from teaching which facilitated completion of the manuscript. My gratitude to the contributors identified earlier will be obvious to anyone who uses this volume. Finally, at this point, I have customarily thanked my wife, Mary B. Fink, for her constructive criticism, editing, and proofreading. In this case, however, she had nothing to do with the preparation of this volume. After a lengthy hiatus, she has resumed her own teaching career; her insights, wisdom, and sharp editorial pencil will be missed.

Gary M Fink
  Atlanta, Ga.   June 1983

Preface to First Edition

This volume contains career biographies of approximately five hundred men and women who have had a significant impact on the American labor movement. It is made up of a diverse and interesting group. An eye-setter in a doll factory, a steelworker, and a pioneer aviator exemplify the variety of occupations of those included. Diversity also characterizes their socioeconomic backgrounds and their career patterns. There are, for example, biographical sketches of a Supreme Court justice, a state governor, several cabinet officers, senators, congressmen, ambassadors, and mayors. The volume also includes those whose trade union careers ended in disgrace or in prison, and a few who lived out their final days as destitute residents of skid row. Some of the individuals included are well known, but many others are unknown to all but the most dedicated students of the American labor movement.

The first major task in writing this *Biographical Dictionary* was selecting the five hundred figures to be included from the thousands of men and women who led or were closely associated with the labor movement in the United States. It was not an easy task, and the decisions that were made undoubtedly will not satisfy everyone, if indeed anyone! Nevertheless the number of leaders included had to be limited, and criteria were established to guide and facilitate the selection process. It was determined that each individual included in the *Biographical Dictionary* should have had a substantial impact on the American labor movement in one way or another. However, labor leaders whose significance was limited to local, state, or regional organizations were included as well as leaders of national or international unions. It was also considered important to include a broad sampling of leaders from different eras, from as many different industries, crafts, and trades as possible, and from among those women, Afro-Americans, and Chicanos whose contributions to the labor movement have been largely ignored until recently. Although the emphasis was on leaders of the trade union movement, an effort was made to include a representative group of labor-oriented radicals, politicians, editors, staff members, lawyers, reformers, and intellectuals.

In some cases those originally selected for inclusion had to be dropped because sufficient biographical information was lacking. Biographies of persons like Alfred Phelps, Homer Call, and Michael Casey certainly qualified for inclusion, but they were deleted because basic biographical information .was unavailable and other comparable leaders could be substituted in their place. But in some instances, most of them concerning early-nineteenth-century leaders, such substitutions were not possible or advisable.

Without the availability of *Who's Who in Labor*, published in cooperation with the American Federation of Labor in 1946, and Solon DeLeon's *The American Labor Who's Who*, published in 1925, the task of collecting basic biographical information would have been enormously more difficult. Many labor leaders were reticent individuals who shunned publicity. Few of them made a major effort to save personal papers or to record the significant events in their lives for posterity. Moreover, in our efforts to acquire biographical information, only a few of the many international unions responded to our correspondence. In some instances, the individuals themselves were uncertain about specific details of their lives. For example, after several conflicting birthdates were discovered for one leader, it was learned that he himself was unsure of the precise date. Samuel Gompers, who was uncertain as to whether he had 12 or 14 children, further illustrates the problem.

The Biographical Dictionary of American Labor Leaders is the second in a projected series of biographical dictionaries to be published by Greenwood Press. The first was Robert Sobel's *Biographical Directory of the United States Executive Branch, 1774–1971*.

The general format and style used in the Sobel *Directory* were followed in this volume. The biographies include significant dates in the subject's life; relevant family information, including father's occupation; religious and political preferences when known; trade-union affiliations; and offices held, both public and private. Each biography also includes bibliographical references to guide the reader who desires more detailed information. The vast majority of references cited contain additional information on the subject of the biography; in the few cases where published material dealing with the subject does not exist, sources were given that provide useful background information. In writing the sketches, an effort was made to maintain a uniform length, but, owing to the availability of information, some variance inevitably occurred. In no case should the length of the sketch be taken as an indication of relative importance. Some of the individuals included in the *Dictionary* were involved in a great variety of union, reform, and political movements. Although this lengthened their biographies, it does not necessarily increase their significance.

Numerous individuals contributed in a variety of ways to the completion of this volume. With only minor changes, the sketches of James Davis, William Doak, Martin Durkin, Arthur Goldberg, and William Wilson were taken from the Sobel *Directory*. The scholars listed on the Consultant Editors page reviewed preliminary lists of labor leaders in their areas of specialized interest and read the finished sketches. C. L. Coburn, UAW; Stanley L. Johnson, Illinois AFL-

CIO; David Selden, AFT; Al Shipka, Greater Youngstown AFL-CIO; Lazare Teper, ILGWU; Catharine B. Williams, ACWA; and Elmer T. Kehrer, John Wright, and Charles C. Mathias, Atlanta AFL-CIO, all responded generously to requests for assistance.

The following individuals either reviewed preliminary lists, previewed selected sketches, or contributed information: Louis Cantor, Jules Chametsky, Helen Elwell, Wayne Flint, Harvey Friedman, Ernesto Galarza, George Green, Alice Kessler Harris, Mark Kahn, Daniel Leab, David B. Lipsky, Garth Mangum, F. Ray Marshall, Mark Perlman, James R. Prickett, Ronald Radosh, Mark Reisler, Stephen Vladeck, and Merle W. Wells. Those of us in Atlanta owe a special thanks to Jane Hobson and her reference department staff at the Georgia State University Library. The Georgia State University School of Arts and Science and Joseph O. Baylen, Chairman of the Department of History, assisted the editor by providing release time from teaching and research assistance. Mary B. Fink read and revised many of the sketches, did much of the proofreading, and aided in drawing up the appendices. Finally, Robert Hagelstein of the Greenwood Press provided valuable ideas and advice, useful criticism, and timely encouragement.

Gary M Fink
  Atlanta, Ga.

January 1974

Milton Cantor
  Amherst, Mass.

Introduction: The American Labor Leader in the Twentieth Century: Quantitative and Qualitative Portraits

PART 1: SOURCES AND METHODOLOGY

Numerous writers interested in the history and development of the American labor movement have turned, from time to time, to an examination of the leadership of that movement. Biographies, autobiographies, memoirs, and biographical directories provide a wealth of both quantitative and qualitative information about those who assumed a leadership role in working-class organizations and activities. Moreover, four collective biographies of unusual quality have appeared in recent years to illuminate the character of labor leadership at particular times in American history. These include Edward Pessen's *Most Uncommon Jacksonians: The Radical Leaders of the Early Labor Movement* (1967), Ray Boston's *British Chartists in America, 1839–1900* (1971), David Montgomery's *Beyond Equality: Labor and the Radical Republicans, 1862–1872* (1967), and Warren R. Van Tine's *The Making of the Labor Bureaucrat: Union Leadership in the United States, 1870–1920* (1973). These studies are firmly grounded in the nineteenth century when the number of labor leaders was limited and biographical data were difficult to acquire. As a consequence, with the exception of the Van Tine study, none of the authors employed a statistically based quantitative analysis.

Students of twentieth-century labor leadership confront a much different problem. Instead of a dearth of information, the researcher in the modern period must contend with a rich abundance of biographical information. Labor directories published in 1925, 1946, and 1976 contain basic biographical data on nearly ten thousand labor leaders. Institutional histories, union publications, labor newspapers, and a wide variety of reference sources contain additional information on labor leaders and the nature of labor leadership.

In the pages that follow, a sampling of that information was used to provide a broad, evolving statistical portrait of American labor leaders with which the individual sketches might be compared. Four sample years were employed: 1900, 1925, 1946, and 1976. Although these years were chosen primarily because of

the availability of biographical directories, they do provide a generational ge-
nealogy of twentieth-century labor leadership.

Just as the directories dictated the sample years, they also influenced the
selection of variables to be considered. Different authors, questionnaires, and
objectives created considerable variance in these directories. Nevertheless, enough
consistency existed in the type of information contained to permit the examination
of 19 significant variables. Those variables tended to fall into three distinct
classifications: institutional characteristics, basic biographical traits, and sociopolitical associations. The institutional variables examined were union type
(professional, white collar, craft, transportation, service, government, industrial,
needle trades); union position (national federation official, state/regional federation official, local federation official, international union official, state/regional
union official, local union official, national staff position, state-regional staff
position, local staff position, lawyer, editor/publicist, educator, economist/stat-
istician); age, age when assuming union position or years in organized labor,
and years in organized labor when assuming union position. Originally, it was
hoped that enough information would be available to identify the age at which
union leaders acquired their first union position, but reliable information on this
prospective variable was simply too sketchy to permit confident generalization.

The personal biographical variables studied were sex; occupation of father
(professional, business, white collar, military, farmer, blue collar); marital status;
age at marrige; number of children; city of birth (large, medium, small); city of
residence (large, medium, small); region of birth (New England, Mid-Atlantic,
Midwest, Border, South, Mountain States, Far West, Foreign); region of residence (same as region of birth); education (college, business/vocational, secondary, elementary, self-educated). Only the 1976 directory contained information
on the occupation of mother and spouse. Such information proved extremely
difficult to obtain for the other sample years and consequently was not included.

Three sociopolitical variables were analyzed: civic activity index (high, medium, low); religious preference (Protestant, Catholic, Jewish, other); political
preference (Democrat, Republican, Socialist, labor/progressive, nonpartisan).

The absence of reliable information of sufficient quality to permit valid statistical analysis forced the elimination of two other sociopolitical variables: ethnic
background and racial composition.

As noted earlier, the character of the samples for the four years examined in
this analysis varied considerably. Because of this, a brief description of the data
base from which the samples were drawn should help the reader to understand
and to evaluate critically the statistical information contained in the essay that
follows.

1900

The 1900 sample was the only one not drawn from a biographical directory.
Because of the difficulty in acquiring biographical data on these early labor

leaders, no effort was made to construct a random sample. Instead, the availability of information became the principal criterion for inclusion. Drawing from a variety of sources, including this *Dictionary*, information was coded for 80 male leaders. Although a variety of biases undoubtedly crept into the sample because of the manner in which it was drawn, enough consistency exists between it and other sample years to permit the researcher to employ it with confidence. Most important, the sample, collectively, conforms to what we know subjectively about labor leaders of that period. The summary statistics for the 1900 sample (Table 3), for example, agree in most respects with the results of Warren Van Tine's analysis of biographical characteristics of labor leaders in the late nineteenth century.

Another problem with the 1900 sample is its exclusive concentration on white males. There were few women or blacks in leadership positions at this time, however, and biographical information on those few was difficult to obtain. Finally, over 60 percent of the individuals included in the sample were national-level leaders, and, among the others, several were destined to become national leaders.

1925

The 1925 sample was drawn entirely from the *American Labor Who's Who* edited by Solon DeLeon (q.v.).* The son of Daniel DeLeon (q.v.), Solon identified himself with the Communist Workers' party in 1925 and his volume contains a large number of radicals, among them 43 Communists. Nevertheless, the volume is indexed by organization and occupation which made it easy to separate the institutional union leaders from the educators, journalists, radicals, and other reformers associated with the labor movement but not leaders of organized labor in the strictest sense.

DeLeon's directory contains 846 regular labor leaders. Of that number, 22 were orthodox female leaders and another 18 were associated with the Women's Trade Union League (WTUL). Thus regular trade union women constituted only 2.6 percent of the total, and when the WTUL women are included the percentage is still only 4.7. Because a sampling of these female unionists would have been too small to analyze effectively, it was decided to supplement the list by the addition of several other female union leaders about whom biographical information is available. Thus two samples were created: a 20 percent sample of male leaders and another sample containing all the females included in the trade union group plus those from the supplemental list. Only ten black leaders were listed in DeLeon's volume, and, of those, individuals such as W.E.B. Du Bois, James Weldon Johnson, and Walter F. White had only a tenuous connection with the labor movement. Thus any quantitative analysis of black leaders was virtually impossible.

*q.v. indicates that a biographical sketch of the individual identified is contained in this volume.

DeLeon's volume also contains an urban-metropolitan, northeastern bias. Of the approximately fifteen hundred biographical sketches, nearly 25 percent resided in New York. Thus a sample group of labor leaders drawn from *American Labor Who's Who* cannot be considered representative of the labor movement as a whole. The degree of distortion, however, appears to be minimal, especially when only trade union leaders are considered, and does not seriously compromise its utility for the purposes of this essay.

1946 and 1976

The *Who's Who in Labor* published in 1946 and again in 1976 contains by far the most comprehensive data used in this study. The 1946 book contains over four thousand sketches and the 1976 edition nearly three thousand. The labor movement actively assisted in the collection of data for both volumes, and the questionnaires used in both instances were quite elaborate. Union leaders at various levels controlled the distribution of the questionnaires to constituent unions, and, while discrimination on an individual basis undoubtedly occurred, no consistent bias was detected. Both volumes appear to be quite representative of the labor movement as a whole. The volumes are well balanced between local, state, and national leaders, and women and minorities are represented in approximately the same ratio that they appear in the ranks of labor leadership as a whole. Once again, separate samples were drawn for men and women. One hundred women were included in each female sample (approximately half of those listed) and a 10 percent sample was used for males. Although the volume appears to contain a representative number of black leaders, in many instances they were impossible to identify, and those who were identifiable represented too small a group to subject to quantitative analysis. While easier to identify, Chicanos and other minorities presented a similar problem.

Much of the biographical information collected from those sources consists of categorical, nominal-level data. As a result, the range of quantative procedures that could be employed was limited largely to descriptive statistics. Along with such standard statistical measures as percentage, mean, mode, median, and standard deviation, crosstabulation tables were constructed and a variety of measures of association used, depending on the questions asked and the nature of the data. Each of the variables included in the analysis was tested as both a dependent and an independent variable, and, where appropriate, the results of those analyses are reported in the text.

After initial analysis, it was decided to treat male and female leaders separately. This was done, in part, because the number of women in the ranks of labor leadership through the entire period was so small (never more than 5 percent of the total) that a stratified sample procedure was necessary to produce a statistically significant group. Moreover, the biographical variables of female leaders were so distinctive from those of their male counterparts that it represented something of a bimodal distribution. This female distinctiveness would have been lost in

a more integrated analysis and would have distorted to some extent the biographical characteristics of the predominantly male leaders.

The initial analysis of the 1946 sample also revealed a bimodal distribution.
In this case the two groups that appeared represented distinctiveness in many of
the variables separating labor leaders affiliated with the American Federation of
Labor (AFL) and the Congress of Industrial Organizations (CIO). These differences are discussed in detail in part 4 of the introduction.

The Creation of Composite Labor Leaders

The results of the quantitative analysis employed in this study are reported in
the following pages in tables and charts. In addition to reporting and analyzing
these figures, an effort has been made to combine the objective results of the
quantitative analysis with a more subjective discussion of leadership characteristics derived from a synthesis of the experiences of actual labor leaders. This
was done through the creation of composite or representative labor leaders illustrative of the various time periods and subgroups. The obvious alternative
was to select real labor leaders who closely resembled the statistical portraits.
The attempt to do this, however, necessitated numerous qualifications and ultimately was awkward and often confusing. Creating fictional labor leaders who
conformed precisely to the statistical results identified in Tables 1, 3, and 4 (thus
the first such fictional leader was born in 1859, was married at age 25, had two
children, and so on) proved, in this respect at least, clearer and more efficient.

For good reason, historians have avoided imaginative re-creations related to
their topic or subject. The dangers inherent in such flights of literary imagination
are obvious to any reader of historical fiction. Nevertheless, in an impersonal
analysis of a statistical table, the fundamental humanity of the people represented
often tends to get lost in the jumble of figures and percentages. Moreover,
statistical analyses, like snapshots, freeze time at a particular moment in history
and, as such, fail to reflect adequately the dynamics of change over time. The
development of composite representative labor leaders, it is hoped, will com-
pensate for this by combining the normative facts of the labor leaders' existence
with an understanding and appreciation of the external influences—also a composite of actual experiences and influences—that did so much to condition their
thinking and mold their lives.

PART 2: THE AMERICAN MALE LABOR LEADER

The following, a statistically derived analysis of biographical variables, provides an overview of changes in the character of American labor leadership
during the first 75 years of the twentieth century. For reasons already discussed,
this analysis is confined to male leaders whose biographical characteristics are
divided into three broad categories: institutional traits; personal, biographical
characteristics; and social/political commitments. Composite labor leaders have

Table 1
Institutional Variables, 1900–1976 (Summary Statistics)

Variables	1900	1925	1946	1976
Age	41.6	48.6	45.9	53.7
Age when Assuming Union Position	34.4	40.9	40.6	44.6
Years in Organized Labor	19.0	25.9	16.7	27.8
Years in Organized Labor for Position	12.4	18.3	11.5	18.9

been created from the summary statistics for the 1900, 1925, and 1976 sample years. Because the 1946 sample contained a bimodal distribution, it was impossible to construct the portrait of a single, composite labor leader. The statistical characteristics of AFL and CIO leaders and the development of model leaders for the 1946 sample group will be included in part 4.

Institutional Variables

The four institutional variables used in this analysis are age, age when assuming primary union position, years in organized labor, and years in organized labor when acquiring primary union position. The summary statistics listed in Table 1 reveal, as might be expected, that the average age and experience of labor leaders increased steadily through the years surveyed; interesting variations, however, do occur.

The average age of the male labor leader in the United States increased by a little over 12 years during the first 75 years of the twentieth century, from 41.6 to 53.7 years. The only notable break in the increasingly advanced age of labor leaders occurred as a result of the turbulent years of the 1930s when the division of the labor movement led to the organization of numerous dual unions as well as a great many new unions. Had the leadership of the maverick movement, the Congress of Industrial Organizations, been excluded, the age levels in 1946 would have been almost identical to those listed for 1925 (see Figure 1). That the average age of labor leaders in the older, better-established AFL did not increase perceptibly evidences a still substantial influx of new leaders into that organization as it moved to meet the challenge of the CIO.

While the average age of labor leaders increased by over 12 years during the period studied, the age at which those leaders assumed their primary position increased by 10 years, the length of time in organized labor by 8 years, and the time spent in organized labor before acquiring their union position by only 6 years. These rather confusing statistics reveal significant changes that occurred in labor leadership. One of the more obvious is that the labor leader of 1976 entered the work force and the labor movement at an older age than his 1900 counterpart. Subtracting the years in organized labor from the average age of labor leaders during the four sample periods reveals that the average labor leader

Figure 1

Comparative Ages of AFL and CIO Leaders, 1900–1976
Summary Statistics

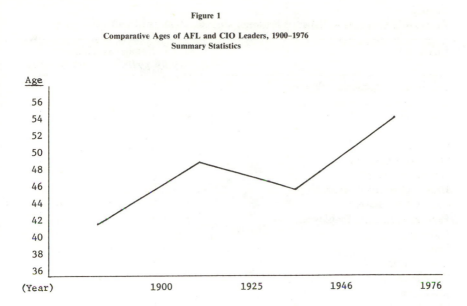

in 1900 first joined a labor union at age 21. His counterpart in 1976 was nearly four years older when acquiring his first membership card. This also correlates highly with the increased level of education evident in Table 3. The tenure of union leaders on the job, which increased substantially during the period, similarly influenced these statistics. Leadership changes in several national unions were compared during the 1900–1910 period with those in the decade of the 1960s. This survey revealed that on an average there were 1.75 changes in leadership during the earlier period and only 0.57 in the latter years (see Table 2).

Finally, the relatively small increase in the fourth variable, the number of years spent in labor before acquiring a primary union position, especially between the 1925 and 1976 samples, suggests that mobility within the labor movement remained relatively stable after diminishing sharply during the first quarter of the century. The 1946 figures for this variable once again reflect the drastic changes introduced by the labor upheaval of the 1930s; and, as a consequence, must be considered a deviation from the general trend.

To summarize, then, the general tendency within the labor movement during the twentieth century was for labor leaders to have entered the ranks of organized labor at an increasingly later age. Consequently, by 1976, the average labor leader was considerably older when acquiring his primary union position than had been his counterpart in 1900. Moreover, he was more experienced, having spent more time in the labor movement before assuming a leadership position, although the experience level, measured by years, increased only half as much as the age level. Finally, it is also clear that the tenure in office of labor leaders

Table 2
Leadership Changes in Selected National Unions, 1900–1910 and 1960–1970

Union	Number of Changes	
	1900–1910	*1960–1970*
Bakery & Confectionery Workers	1	0
Boilermakers	2	1
Bricklayers	3	1
Carpenters	1	0
Electrical Workers	2	1
Operating Engineers	5	1
Garment Workers	1	0
Ladies' Garment Workers	5	1
Glass Bottle Blowers	0	0
Hotel & Restaurant Employees	0	0
Laborers	3	0
Lathers	4	1
Letter Carriers	2	2
Longshoremen	1	1
Machinists	0	2
Maintenance of Way Employees	1	0
Meat Cutters	1	0
Mine Workers	1	0
Musicians	1	0
Plumbers	2	0
Printing Pressmen	2	0
Railroad Trainmen	1	1
Railroad Carmen	3	1
Railway Conductors	1	2
Retail Clerks	1	1
Teamsters	2	0
Textile Workers	2	0
Typographers	1	0
Total Number of Changes	49	16
Average Number of Changes	1.75	.57

Source: Gary M Fink, ed., *Labor Unions* (1977), App. 4.

in the later period was much longer than it had been for leaders in the early years of the new century, thus restricting the ability of younger men to rise to the higher echelons of labor leadership.

Composite Labor Leader Profile No. 1
Gordon Mahoney: A Labor Leader for a New Century

As men of his age are wont to do, Gordon Mahoney, a 41-year-old labor activist reflected about the course of his life and reassessed his present commitments as a new century dawned upon the American horizon on January 1, 1900. Born of Roman Catholic, working-class parents in a small midwestern town two years before the outbreak of the Civil War, he was destined to grow to maturity in an environment almost as turbulent as the one into which he was born. The future labor leader attended public schools until forced to suspend his education and enter the work force during the depression of the 1870s, thus ending his formal schooling in the eighth grade. Like his father before him, young Mahoney eventually entered the molders' trade and served an apprenticeship before acquiring the status of a journeyman laborer and joining the Iron Molders' Union of America in 1881.

That the young iron molder should have joined the union of his craft is not surprising. The Iron Molders' Union, one of the oldest and most influential labor organizations in the United States, had produced one of the nation's most respected nineteenth-century labor leaders, William Sylvis (q.v.), the memory of whom was still revered in the Mahoney household. Aside from this heritage of craft identification and pride, Mahoney had come to maturity during one of the more volatile periods in the history of the American working class. The outbreak of the Molly Maguire Riots and the Great Railroad Strike of 1877 had occurred shortly after he entered the labor force and did much to stimulate his thinking about labor issues. Furthermore, accelerated industrialization, waves of new immigrant and migrant workers, employer arrogance, and the introduction of technological change in methods of production at an unprecedented rate had confronted skilled workers in America with challenges that could only be met through collective action.

In 1885, at age 25, Mahoney married Mary Sullivan, an Irish working-class woman who eventually bore two children while devoting her time and energies to family and household duties. His marriage and subsequent family responsibilities led Mahoney to reassess his employment situation, and this in turn further stimulated his interest in union matters.

The dramatic victory of the Noble Order of the Knights of Labor over the Jay Gould-controlled Wabash Railroad later in the same year further excited the young molder's concern about labor affairs. Victory over the famous—or infamous—railroad baron excited workers everywhere and by the year's end membership topped the 700,000 figure. Like many other molders, Mahoney joined a mixed assembly of the Knights in his area during this period even though the national leadership of the Iron Molders resisted affiliation.

In many ways the following year was even more traumatic. The eight-hour-day campaign, which had been going on for several years, came to a climax in 1886 with the aborted May Day general strike and the Haymarket Square Riot that did so much to influence the thinking of trade unionists of the day. After what was considered a decade of labor violence, public opinion turned sharply against labor and the labor movement, a resentment soon felt in legislative chambers as well as Statehouses and courthouses across the nation. Moreover, in a second confrontation with Jay Gould, the Knights of Labor lost, diminishing the aura of invincibility that had enveloped it earlier. Other lost strikes soon precipitated a rapid decline in the fortunes of the Noble Order, which wiped out most of its previous membership gains. As a consequence, Mahoney, like many other trade unionists, followed with great interest the meeting of trade union leaders in Columbus, Ohio, in December that resulted in the organization of the American Federation of Labor. Representatives of the iron molders attended the meeting, and the Iron Molders' Union became a charter member of the new federation.

After having been a member of his union for 12 years, Mahoney was elected to the executive board of his local in 1888—his first union office—and 2 years later became a full-time union employee, serving as the local's business agent and president. In 1893, at age 34, he was elected a vice-president of the national union and left the small town in which he had been born and bred to establish residence in Chicago.

As his involvement in union affairs increased, Mahoney's commitment to the concept of industry-wide bargaining grew. In 1890 the Iron Molders' Union had succeeded in negotiating a contract with the Stove Founders' National Defense Association, a national employers' association, but two other employer groups, the National Stove Manufacturers' Association and the National Founders' Association resisted union bargaining overtures and persisted in their devotion to the open-shop method of employment. As a result, the last decade of the nineteenth century was a period of virtual industrial warfare for many molders, a condition that the depression of the 1890s, which further weakened labor's bargaining position, did nothing to alleviate. The end product of all of this was a marked increase in labor militancy. Meanwhile, the deployment of state and federal troops to crush strikes in Homestead, Pennsylvania, and nearby Pullman, Illinois, further alienated many trade unionists, like Mahoney, from the mainstream of American society.

It was in this frame of mind that Mahoney, as a representative of the Iron Molders' Union, attended his first AFL convention in 1894. The previous year Socialist delegates had introduced a comprehensive political platform which affiliated unions were asked to study and be prepared to vote on the following year. During the 1894 meeting, every plank of the Socialist platform was adopted except the controversial Plank 10 which would have committed the AFL to the public ownership of the means of production and distribution. Like so many others in attendance, Mahoney voted against Plank 10, fearing it would further exacerbate an already hostile public opinion, but voted for John McBride (q.v.), a Socialist delegate from the United Mine Workers, who successfully challenged Samuel Gompers's (q.v.) reelection to the AFL presidency.

Mahoney's seemingly irrational voting behavior reflected a growing frustration and disillusionment with the established leadership of the labor movement and the prevailing socioeconomic order on the one hand, and an inbred sense of caution and an unwillingness to burn too many bridges on the other. Official governmental hostility toward organized labor convinced Mahoney that the labor movement should take a more active political role, if for no other reason than as a matter of self-defense. Nevertheless, he distrusted both established parties, leaving the factionalized Socialists the best available option to the labor movement, although Mahoney would eagerly have supported any movement to establish an independent labor party.

By 1900, he was beginning to rethink many of his earlier assumptions. The economy had recovered from the depression signaled by the Panic of 1893, and the labor movement was in the midst of a remarkable period of growth. Increased prosperity qualified employer hostility to organized labor as many businessmen began to reassess the whole idea of collective bargaining and trade agreements. Moreover, a developing reform movement at the state and local levels held the promise of a more sympathetic governmental attitude toward labor.

Along with these contemporary influences, Mahoney's working-class background and his 20-year association with organized labor had resulted in the development of an increasingly coherent philosophy of trade unionism. To some extent he had absorbed the skilled craftsman's disdain for unskilled, industrial workers, and the failed strikes at Homestead and Pullman further convinced him that such workers were difficult if not impossible to organize into effective unions. A year later he would enthusiastically endorse Samuel Gompers's declaration of craft autonomy as the cornerstone of the American labor movement.

Mahoney's respect for Gompers had grown tremendously after John McBride's disastrous year as AFL president, and in 1895 the Molders' vice-president had enthusiastically voted to return Gompers to the federation's helm. Meanwhile, Mahoney continued to support the Socialists politically and viewed the emergence of Eugene Debs (q.v.) to the head of the radical movement as a positive development. Nevertheless, many of his more conservative trade union associates aligned themselves with the progressive wings of one of the major politicial parties, and the continued denunciation of the Socialist movement by the Catholic clergy created psychological strains that dampened his enthusiasm for radical politics.

Family affairs also created problems in the Mahoney household. Mahoney was determined that his son, now 14, would attain a better education than had been possible for him, and he wanted his 12-year-old daughter to grow to maturity in a neighborhood with better marriage opportunities than existed in the rather shabby working-class district in which they now lived. The major problems, of course, were financial. Mahoney's salary as a national union vice-president was little more than he could have earned as an iron molder, and the tenure of union officials, as he well knew, tended to be quite short. Given these circumstances, Mahoney quietly assessed employment opportunities outside the molders' craft and the trade union movement while also speculating about his chances of being elevated to the union presidency. Clearly, during his years as a trade union leader, Mahoney had unconsciously assimilated middle-class values and aspirations while still retaining a working-class wage.

Biographical Variables

The major biographical variables considered in this study (see Table 3) are the father's occupation, education, city and region of birth and city and region of residence, marital status, age at marriage, and number of children. An examination of these variables should provide some indication of social mobility, geographical mobility, and family circumstances.

The figures reflecting their fathers' occupations in Table 3 suggest that the socioeconomic background of American labor leaders in the twentieth century changed far less than might have been anticipated. Indeed, when the two bottom categories—farmer and blue collar—are combined, the percentages are surprisingly consistent throughout the period: 71.7 (1900), 73.8 (1925), 68.1 (1946), 72.8 (1976). That the vast majority of labor leaders had their roots in the working class is obvious. The comparable percentages reflecting a middle-class background are 28.1 (1900), 26.4 (1925), 31.8 (1946), and 27.2 (1976). Two obvious inconsistencies appear in the general pattern. One is the very low percentage of farmers in the 1925 sample. As noted earlier, this sample had a northeastern, urban-metropolitan bias that probably distorted the blue collar-farmer ratio. Conversely, the white-collar categories for 1925 appear quite consistent with the pattern for other sample years. The other inconsistency appears in the figures for 1946 and reflects the large number of middle-class reformers and radicals who joined the labor movement—primarily the CIO—during the turbulent 1930s.

To the extent that patterns and trends are identifiable in these figures, it can be observed that the percentages of labor leaders born to professional-level fathers increased slightly, although the relative percentages remained very low. Similarly, the percentage of labor leaders born into lower-level, middle-class circumstances also reflects a slight increase. Conversely, the number of labor leaders with a family business background decreased. The subjective evidence indicates that the businesses represented here were small, fragile concerns, the failure of which often landed the operator's children into working-class occupations at an early age.

If labor leadership can be considered a middle-class occupation—and it meets virtually every accepted criterion—then the conclusion appears obvious that the labor movement constituted an escalator that elevated its leadership into a higher socioeconomic class. That this upward social mobility became permanent is clear from a survey of the children of labor leaders, very few of whom reverted back to working-class status. The children of labor leaders generally attained at least one and in many cases two levels of education higher than their fathers. The female children generally married in the middle class, while the males entered into a variety of middle-class occupations. A substantial number of the male children were attracted to professional careers. The legal profession attracted the most, with teaching second, and a substantial number followed their fathers' footsteps into the labor bureaucracy.

The data on the educational level of labor leaders produced rather confusing

Table 3
Biographical Variables, 1900–1976 (Summary Statistics in Percentages)

Biographical Variables	1900	1925	1946	1976
Occupation of Father				
Professional	4.3	3.7	5.7	6.3
Business	19.6	15.9	9.4	11.0
White Collar	4.3	6.5	16.4	9.4
Military	—	—	0.3	0.5
Farmer	21.7	9.3	22.5	13.6
Blue Collar	50.0	64.5	45.6	59.2
Marital Status				
Married	88.6	N/A*	92.2	92.8
Single	11.5	N/A	7.8	7.2
Age at Marriage (Averages)	25.0	N/A	26.3	25.4
Number of Children (Averages)	2.32	N/A	2.05	2.59
City of Birth				
Large	16.3	35.4	21.1	25.5
Medium	32.7	20.3	19.3	25.5
Small	51.0	44.3	59.5	49.0
City of Residence				
Large	67.1	61.7	35.0	41.8
Medium	30.4	27.5	48.1	43.0
Small	2.5	3.3	16.9	14.4
Region of Birth				
New England	7.5	10.3	6.9	8.4
Mid-Atlantic	23.7	23.1	15.0	20.7
Midwest	22.5	23.9	30.3	30.7
Border	2.5	8.5	13.9	12.7
South	2.5	5.1	7.8	21.1
Mountain States	1.2	—	2.2	1.6
Far West	—	2.6	2.8	2.8
Foreign	40.0	26.5	20.3	2.0
Region of Residence				
New England	7.5	5.0	10.0	4.5
Mid-Atlantic	32.5	35.0	18.9	19.8
Midwest	35.0	25.8	32.2	28.4
Border	15.0	23.5	12.1	19.0
South	—	5.8	6.7	12.7
Mountain States	5.0	5.0	3.3	2.6
Far West	1.2	10.8	10.8	10.1
Canadian	—	—	5.8	3.0
Education				
College	10.5	5.5	16.4	41.3
Business/Vocational	1.3	0.9	7.4	10.2
Secondary	14.5	23.6	41.8	47.7
Elementary	48.7	58.2	34.4	0.4
Self-Educated	25.0	11.8	—	0.4

* = Not Available

results. The effort here was to ascertain the highest level of education attained. The criteria used was not completion of a degree—elementary, secondary or college—but significant matriculation at a particular level. Thus, the individual who spent at least two years in college was considered college educated. The data could be misleading. When a labor leader reported having spent two years or more at a particular school, for example, there was often no way of determining whether he was a full-time or a part-time student. Confidence in the data, moreover, is further compromised by the unusually high percentage of college-educated leaders identified in the 1900 sample (10.5 percent) and the correspondingly smaller number in the 1925 group (5.5 percent). The pattern of those reporting a secondary-level education conforms more closely to what might be expected. Despite these inconsistencies, however, it can be safely concluded that labor leaders, throughout the period, were substantially better educated than the population at large and that their level of educational attainment was increasing somewhat more rapidly than that of the population generally. A direct comparison between these data and those reported in the *Statistical Abstract of the United States* is not possible because of the different criteria used and the changes introduced by the U.S. Census Department in the way in which it reported educational attainment between 1900 and 1970. Nevertheless, general levels of educational attainment and the rate of increase are rather easy to ascertain.

While comparative educational levels generally may have remained fairly static during this period, an advanced level of education appears to have become increasingly important to a rise in the ranks of labor leadership. Indeed, by 1976 the staffs of international unions and national federations—the best-educated segment of the labor movement—were beginning to supply an increasing number of national union leaders. Perhaps the most dramatic example of this trend is reflected by the two highest offices in the AFL-CIO: president and secretary-treasurer. Neither Lane Kirkland (q.v.), president, nor Thomas Donahue (q.v.), secretary-treasurer, rose from the ranks of their respective unions. Both are well educated—Kirkland received a B.S. from Georgetown University's School of Foreign Service and Donahue earned the LL.B. from Fordham University Law School, both had held staff positions for international unions before joining the AFL-CIO staff, both had served as executive assistants to AFL-CIO president George Meany (q.v.). Although this rise to the heights of labor leadership is still far from typical, it does appear to be the wave of the future. The top leadership positions in several national unions are now being filled by people who never worked in the trade organized by the union. They are college graduates, several with professional degrees, who joined the headquarters staff and quickly rose into executive position. (See, for example, the sketches of Sol Chaiken, John Sweeney, and Murray Finley.)

Entry into and advancement in the labor bureaucracy also required a willingness to leave the town and, in many cases, the region in which one was born. By all available evidence, labor leaders were an unusually *geographically* mobile group of people even within a very mobile society. The traditional rise to an executive position in a national union involved a person who had worked his or her way up through the union bureaucracy from the local and state or regional level to the national level. Along the way, he or she changed residence several times but generally the tendency was to move from small towns to larger and larger cities. The figures reflecting city of residence in Table 3 are somewhat deceptive in that the samples for 1946 and 1976 contained many more local and state leaders than comparable samples for 1900 and 1925. Yet, the trend seems obvious: most labor leaders were born in a small town and resided in a much larger city. Clearly, small-town America provided a majority of the leaders of the American labor movement. Most of those small towns were located in either the Midwest or Mid-Atlantic states, not coincidentally the best-organized sections in the nation.

In an effort to determine which sections of the nation supplied labor leaders and which sections used them, the figures for region of birth and region of residence were combined for the four sample years. As the results listed in Table 4 clearly demonstrate, immigrants accounted for the largest positive increase in labor leadership. Indeed, 40 percent of all American labor leaders in 1900 were foreign born and as late as 1946 one out of every five labor leaders was still of foreign birth. (The foreign leaders listed in the region of residence column resided in Canada.) The only domestic sections of the nation that supplied an excess of labor leaders were the South and New England. The largest users were the far western and Mid-Atlantic states. A careful examination of the figures in Table 2 suggests that most of the foreign-born leaders tended to locate in the midwestern and Mid-Atlantic states. By 1976, however, both of those sections were supplying more labor leaders than they used. Conversely, the large increases in the Rocky Mountain and far western states resulted from an internal migration from other sections of the nation. Clearly, the majority of labor leaders in these two sections were born outside that region, an imbalance that remained fairly constant. The substantial increase in the figures for the border states reflects the migration of national union headquarters and labor leaders to the Washington, D.C., area.

The family situation of labor leaders through the four periods examined remained remarkably stable. The average labor leader throughout the period married at age 25 and had two children. There was a very slight decrease in the number of single leaders, but there is no perceptible trend in the other two variables. What is obvious, however, is that the labor leader married later and had fewer children than the population at large.

Both continuity and change are obvious in the biographical variables considered in this study. Surprising continuity existed in the socioeconomic origins of twentieth-century labor leaders. Almost as many labor leaders in 1976 had their roots in the working class as their counterparts in 1900. That the labor bureaucracy provided a social and economic escalator out of the working class

Table 4
Region of Birth and Residence, 1900–1976 (in Percentages)

Region	Birth	Residence	Change
New England	33.1	27.0	− 6.1
Midwest	107.4	121.4	+ 14.0
Mid-Atlantic	82.5	106.2	+ 23.7
Border	37.6	58.7	+ 21.1
South	36.5	25.2	− 11.3
Mountain States	5.0	15.9	+ 10.9
Far West	8.3	32.9	+ 24.6
Foreign	88.8	8.8	− 80.0

also remained quite consistent throughout the period. Small families and late marriages continued as a social cost exacted from those who aspired to careers in the American labor movement.

Change was obvious in the degree of education attained by labor leaders. At the beginning of the century nearly half the labor leaders considered had attained less than a grammar school education. By 1976 a majority had attended college. The declining number of foreign-born leaders, who had invested the labor movement with an element of philosophical and cultural diversity, also constituted a significant change. While geographical mobility remained a constant, the influence of the small town had begun to decline by 1976. Certainly, the small-town culture into which most early leaders had been born and bred must have had an impact on their later social and political behavior.

Composite Labor Leader Profile No. 2
Arthur George: A Labor Leader during the Lean Years

Born and raised in a small, midwestern railroad town, Arthur George celebrated his forty-ninth birthday in 1925. The eldest of five children, he had entered the labor force in 1890 after the death of his father who, for several years, had operated a small blacksmith shop. Although family financial contingencies precipitated the move, George left school with few regrets after completing the eighth grade. He had grown increasingly restless in the classroom and had already informed his parents that he had no desire to continue his education, a decision he would later regret.

A new machine shop on the Milwaukee Railroad had opened nearby, and he soon acquired a position as an apprentice machinist. While he had never been enthusiastic about labor unions, he reconsidered his position after being laid off during the depression of the midnineties. Moreover, he sympathized with the workers at Homestead, Pennsylvania, and Pullman, Illinois, whose strikes had been crushed through governmental intervention. The use of government force in these instances not only violated the young machinist's sense of fair play but suggested to him an insensitivity to the plight of working people who, as he well knew, had legitimate grievances. As a consequence of all of this, his attitude toward organized labor changed, and in 1899, he joined the local lodge of the International Association of Machinists (IAM) that had been organized in his shop. In affiliating with a union at this time, George joined thousands of other workers, primarily skilled, who swelled the ranks of organized labor at the turn of the century. Between 1897 and 1904, IAM membership increased from 14,000 to 55,700, and this simply reflected what was happening in other trades. AFL membership during the same period rose from 264,800 to 1,676,200.

These good years for organized labor came to a sudden halt in 1904 when employers launched a nationwide open-shop offensive in an effort to crush the labor movement. So-called citizens' alliances sprang up everywhere, encouraging employers to break relations with organized labor and often providing assistance to those who did so. While the IAM held its own in this conflict, new membership advances came to a virtual standstill. Between 1904 and 1912, the IAM enrolled only four thousand new machinists into its ranks.

It was during these years that Arthur George began to play an active role in the affairs of his local lodge. By 1912 he had served in virtually every local union office. In the Machinist elections of 1912, George aligned himself with the socialist faction which supported greater local autonomy, industrial unionism, and William H. Johnston's (q.v.) candidacy for the IAM presidency. Johnston succeeded in ousting the incumbent James O'Connell (q.v.), a more conservative, pure-and-simple trade unionist, and George was rewarded for his support with appointment to the position of international organizer, a grand lodge position.

The failure of the open-shop offensive to roll back union gains, the wartime prosperity, and the decision to admit unskilled workers employed in the machine industry all stimulated a new IAM membership surge that by 1916 had reached over 100,000. And this was merely a prelude. By 1920 the IAM had enrolled nearly a third of a million workers, making it the third largest AFL affiliate.

In 1917 George ran successfully for the presidency of IAM District 7 in Milwaukee. During that year he was elected an IAM vice-president and as such became a member of the national union's executive council. Moving his family to Milwaukee, however, disrupted a comfortable, small-town lifestyle. George had married Agnes Henderson, the daughter of a local farmer, in 1901, and they had two children, now ages 14 and 12. After the children reached school age, Agnes became increasingly restless and began to devote more time to the affairs of the IAM's women's auxiliary, and before George's elevation to the District 7 presidency had herself been elected president of the local's auxiliary group. She also took an active interest in civic and church affairs as well as a variety of social activities.

Although the war years had been good for organized labor, they were not particularly good for workers who found that their real wages had failed to keep pace with steady increases in the cost of living. After the signing of the Armistice in November 1918, working-class frustration and anger burst forth in a wave of strikes that threatened to paralyze the American economy. Alarmed by the gains made by organized labor during the war, employers were determined to resist further advances. In this endeavor, employers soon found a willing ally in government at all levels. An emerging red scare, which the federal government had helped to ignite, created a climate detrimental to the labor movement, and most postwar strikes were lost, destroying promising union initiatives in such important industries as steel and meatpacking. Moreover, employers launched a renewed open-shop offensive under the moniker of the "American Plan" which, unlike its predecessor earlier in the century, succeeded in rolling back many of the labor movement's previous gains.

George viewed these events with alarm. The labor movement, it seemed, was being attacked on all fronts and could count very few victories in this increasingly one-sided contest with militant employers. Court decisions undermined the very legitimacy of organized labor, while state and federal legislators debated bills drastically restricting the activities of organized workers. Like many other unions, the Machinists had been involved in a number of postwar confrontations with employers. A major strike against the American Can Company failed in 1920, and two years later a disastrous national strike by railroad shop craftsmen almost destroyed labor organization in what had previously been a machinist stronghold. By 1923, as membership fell to prewar levels, the IAM had lost nearly two-thirds of the gains it had registered by 1920.

In common with many labor leaders, George came to the conclusion that labor could never effectively exercise its economic power as long as government, including state and federal courts, continued to align itself with employers. The obvious solution was to change the character of government, but in this endeavor, neither of the major political parties could be trusted. Businessmen firmly controlled the Republican party and the Wilson administration's attacks on organized labor in the postwar years permitted little optimism about the sensitivity of the Democrats to economic justice or industrial democracy. Meanwhile, the divided Socialists had lost their most influential leader, Eugene Debs, and did not appear to have any chance of electoral success. This dilemma was resolved when the railroad brotherhoods convinced Senator Robert La Follette to head a third-party effort. George had found his candidate. He knew and respected La Follette and ultimately convinced himself that the famous Wisconsin progressive was electable. Although La Follette ran surprisingly well for a third-party candidate, garnering 16 percent of the popular vote, George was dejected and disillusioned. Labor had attemped to exercise its potential economic and political power and had failed in both instances. From the perspective of 1925, George could find little evidence that anything was going to change in the foreseeable future. These were indeed "lean years" for the labor movement.

Table 5
Sociopolitical Variables, 1900–1976 (Summary Statistics in Percentages)

Sociopolitical Variables	1900	1925	1946	1976
Civic Activity Index				
High	46.2	42.5	24.2	28.0
Medium	40.0	34.2	43.8	39.8
Low	13.7	23.3	32.0	32.1
Religious Preference				
Protestant	29.2	N/A	56.5	N/A
Catholic	52.1	N/A	35.1	N/A
Jewish	16.7	5.4	5.3	N/A
Other	2.1	N/A	3.1	N/A
Political Preference				
Democrat	21.3	13.7	69.4	N/A
Republican	21.3	11.2	13.4	N/A
Socialist	37.7	27.5	8.1	N/A
Progressive/Labor	11.5	25.0	.5	N/A
Nonpartisan	8.2	21.0	8.6	N/A

Social and Political Variables

The three social and political variables studied were civic activity, religious preference, and political preference. The data for these were the least consistent and least reliable of any of the variables examined. Only about half of those surveyed responded to questions about their religious and political preferences, and many no doubt failed to identify civic activities in which they were involved. The 1925 directory did not include religious preference, and both religious and political preferences were left out of the 1976 volume. As a consequence, generalizations drawn from the available data should be treated with a degree of skepticism (see Table 5).

Of the three sociopolitical variables examined, civic activity is the least conclusive. The objective here was to measure the extent to which labor leaders were involved in reform or civic activities outside the labor movement. The questionnaires used in the biographical directories of 1925, 1946, and 1976 all included a category for civic or public affairs, but the nature of those associations changed significantly over time. Moreover World Wars I and II created many new channels for public service that, for the most part, were not available to leaders in the 1900 and 1976 samples. In coding this material an effort was made to eliminate purely social or fraternal organizations, but the line between social and service groups is a fine one.

A civic activity index was constructed for each sample period. A high rating on the index indicates the individual was involved in five or more activities, a medium rating, two to four, and a low rating, one or none. The quantitative data thus reveals that leaders of local and state central bodies along with Jewish leaders were the most likely to be actively involved in a variety of social and civic activities outside the labor movement. The index of activity is higher in the 1900 and 1925 samples than in the later periods. This seems to lend support to the general observation that, in the earlier years of the labor movement, labor leaders tended to be involved in a wide variety of reformist activities but as organized labor became more established and entrenched the range of outside activities diminished as organizational affairs absorbed more of the average union leader's time.

As noted earlier these conclusions must be viewed with some skepticism. Much of the civic activity in the earlier samples revolved around a variety of immigrant assistance, mutual aid, and ethnic associational activities. The high index rating of Jewish leaders, to some extent at least, is a reflection of this characteristic. Finally, based on the secondary literature, it appears that these civic and reform associations were more meaningful to people in the earlier period and were much more working class in their orientation than the civic/ reform associations of labor leaders in the later sample periods, which had a much broader, essentially middle-class membership that often involved passive rather than active participation.

Ultimately, however, the quantity of civic activity is probably less important than the quality. It was one thing for a labor leader in the 1976 sample to belong to the National Association for the Advancement of Colored People (NAACP) and quite another for the 1925 leader to have joined. The NAACP membership of an Atlanta, Georgia, leader in 1946 had a different significance than that of a comparable figure in Madison, Wisconsin. The quantitative scale used in this analysis simply does not provide any measure of intensity of activity and that could well be more important than the quantity.

The most significant change appearing in the religious preference category is that labor leaders who were predominantly Catholic in 1900 had been succeeded by those who were mostly Protestant by 1946. The relative percentage of Jewish leaders also declined through the years, although their actual numbers remained fairly constant. The 1946 sample does not reveal any discernible differences between the AFL and CIO with regard to religious affiliation. The CIO had a slightly larger percentage of Catholics, while the AFL had slightly higher percentages of Protestants and Jews. Throughout the period under survey, Jewish leaders were concentrated in the various needle trades.

In many ways, the political preference category was the most intriguing and interesting of the variables examined. If one can equate political conservatism with allegiance to one of the two established parties, the influence of Franklin D. Roosevelt and the New Deal becomes readily apparent. In 1925 only 24.9 percent of the leaders examined identified themselves with the Democratic or Republican parties. By 1946, 82.8 percent associated themselves with one of the established parties, nearly 70 percent with Roosevelt's Democratic party.

The 1925 figures, of course, were influenced by Robert La Follette's Progressive party candidacy in 1924. This probably also accounts for the unusually large number of nonpartisan identifications in 1925. Nevertheless, the number of labor leaders in the 1900 and 1925 samples who were committed to Socialist or Independent labor politics remained quite consistent: 49.2 percent in 1900 and 52.5 percent in 1925. By 1946 that percentage had fallen to 8.6. Clearly during the first quarter of the twentieth century, a constituency for third-party labor politics existed within the ranks of labor leadership in the United States.

The survey of social and political variables suggests that the degree of civic activity of labor leaders declined as labor unions became more entrenched. This decreased social activity also appears to have had a political manifestation in the increasingly conservative politics practiced by labor leaders. While the nonpartisanship supposedly espoused by both the AFL and the CIO, and later the AFL-CIO, was practiced by relatively few labor activists, labor leaders, who exhibited a distinct tendency toward radical politics in the early years of the century, had by midcentury become a faction within the Democratic party. Finally the thesis concerning the Catholic church's conservatizing influence is not supported by the data provided here. Instead, the predominantly Catholic labor leaders of 1900 exhibited a much higher degree of political radicalism than the more Protestant leadership of 1946. The data suggests, at least, that religious influences on the development of the labor movement's trade union philosophy probably have been exaggerated. The political preferences of 19 of the 25 Catholics in the 1900 sample are known. Of those, 37 percent were Democrat, 11 percent Republican, 32 percent Socialist, 16 percent Progressive/Labor, and 5 percent nonpartisan.

Composite Labor Leader Profile No. 3
Thomas Miller: Labor Bureaucrat as Labor Leader

On June 17, 1976, Thomas Miller celebrated two anniversaries. It was the fifty-fourth anniversary of his birth and the twenty-eighth anniversary of his affiliation with organized labor. An unusual labor leader in many respects, Miller had never resided anywhere other than his hometown of Madison, Wisconsin, with the exception of a three-year tour of duty in the Air Force during World War II. His father, who for many years worked for the Ray-O-Vac Battery plant in Madison, had joined AFL federal Local 19587 shortly after it had been organized in 1934 and thereafter played an active role in union affairs. Thus trade unionism was never foreign to the younger Miller's thinking or experience. As he grew to maturity he had observed with interest the great organizing drives of the 1930s, the sit-down strikes, and the fratricidal conflict between the AFL and the CIO. Like his father, Thomas sympathized with the AFL in this struggle while at the same time hoping for labor unity.

After attending the Madison public schools, Miller enrolled in the University of Wisconsin's School of Public Administration. His education, however, was interrupted by the war and a difficult period of adjustment after the war. In 1947, he married Louise Simpson, and the following year graduated with a B.S. in public administration. Shortly thereafter, he took a job as an examiner with the Wisconsin State Civil Service Department and joined the Madison local of the American Federation of State, County and Municipal Employees (AFSCME). Arnold Zander (q.v.), who had organized the local in 1933, was one of the founders of AFSCME and had served as its president from its chartering in 1935.

Although venerating Zander, Miller did not take an active role in union activities for several years. Embarrassed by charges of communist influence in the labor movement during a period of increased anti-radical sentiment, his discomfiture grew when the CIO expelled ten "communist dominated" international unions at midcentury. Moreover, the junior senator from Wisconsin, Joseph R. McCarthy, was emerging as one of the leaders of the anti-Communist hysteria. Given all of this, the young war veteran decided to devote most of his spare time to uncontroversial civic activities and to his growing family. He also spent much time worrying about being recalled to active duty during the Korean War.

Had it not been for a growing schism within AFSCME's ranks, Miller would probably never have become actively involved in the affairs of his local union. To some extent, AFSCME's problems were a by-product of its dynamic growth. The union had been an unqualified success almost from the beginning, and during the 1950s, when most labor unions were experiencing hard times, AFSCME continued to grow at an accelerated pace. A membership of fifty thousand at the end of World War II had doubled by the time of the AFL-CIO merger in 1955 and by the midsixties had topped the quarter-million mark. This rapid growth brought with it internal tensions and, ultimately, disagreements over tactics and strategy. From its inception, AFSCME under Zander's leadership had emphasized the extension of the civil service and improvements in the merit system primarily through administrative and legislative lobbying. By the midfifties, however, an insurgency led by Jerry Wurf (q.v.) was making its influence felt at all levels of the national union. The Wurf faction advocated union recognition, collective bargaining, union dues checkoff, and signed agreements.

As much out of loyalty to Zander as philosophical principle, Miller supported the established leadership in this controversy and was disturbed when Wurf defeated Zander in the union elections of 1964. Nevertheless, because of the nature of public employee unionism, there was an unusual degree of local autonomy in AFSCME, and in 1967, Miller successfully campaigned for the presidency of his local union with the objective of maintaining the low-key Zander approach. Ultimately, however, he recognized the advantages of Wurf's policies and slowly began to move his local in that direction.

Because of his opposition to the Wurf faction and his late entry into the ranks of labor activism, Miller realized that he probably had no future in the AFSCME hierarchy. Thus he was relatively content to manage the affairs of his local and look after family responsibilities. The oldest of his three children was about to enter college and would have created a severe financial strain but for the salary of his wife, Louise, a public school teacher. Although he considered himself progressive on the issue, few of his trade union colleagues had working wives, and it bothered him that Louise had to work even though she was firmly committed to her career. Indeed, many things bothered this middle-aged labor leader. He agreed with Louise's fervent support of the Equal Rights Amendment, but she was beginning to adopt many feminist positions that he found unsettling. Other social issues disturbed him even more. A strong civil rights advocate for many years, he was alarmed by the emergence of the black power movement and the destructive urban riots of the 1960s. In a similar vein, he doubted the wisdom of American involvement in Southeast Asia but thought many of the anti-war protestors naive and simplistic. At this particular moment, however, he was more concerned about the student revolt taking place on campuses across the nation. A daily witness to the unsettling events occurring on the campus of the University of Wisconsin, he wondered about the wisdom of sending his impressionable young son into such an environment. But if the draft was to be avoided, he had to be enrolled in college.

Meanwhile, most of Miller's working hours were taken up by politics in one form or another. He spent his days adjusting grievances, lobbying various state agencies, negotiating new contracts, and closely monitoring state politics. Although himself a Democrat, he attempted to maintain a nonpartison public posture that would permit him to work effectively with legislators and administrators from either party.

As he reflected back on the occasion of his fifty-fourth birthday, Miller speculated as to how little his life had changed as a result of leaving the state government bureaucracy and entering the labor bureaucracy. Perhaps the greatest change was that while a civil servant he had worked 8 hours a day, 40 hours a week. At 54, he was working 10 to 12 hours a day, 6 days a week. This, he thought, was about all he had in common with those labor leaders who had struggled to build the movement in the early years of the century. Those pioneers had rarely been considered respectable members of the community, and their greatest conflicts revolved around the issue of union recognition. Much had changed since then. The legitimacy of organized labor and collective bargaining was then firmly established in law, labor-management relations had become formalized, and government often sat as a third party—formally or informally—in contract negotiations. Yet, while so much had changed, much still remained the same. As earlier, the greatest problem confronting labor was getting people organized and keeping them organized. Of late, union membership as a percentage of the total work force had steadily declined as technology eroded the industrial labor base upon which the labor movement had been rebuilt during the 1930s. Meanwhile, the service industry work force, which had grown dramatically in the years following World War II, proved highly resistant to union organization. Although his own union, AFSCME, had grown dramatically during these years, much of that membership was still confined to the shrinking blue-collar sector of its jurisdiction. Clearly, AFSCME had been less successful in organizing its potentially huge pool of white-collar workers. The American economy, Miller recognized, had changed substantially since World War II, but the labor movement had not. What labor needed, he concluded, was a new John L. Lewis (q.v.), capable of leading the movement in new directions.

Union Position

The level of union leadership—national, state/regional, and local—was examined in an effort to discover what variables, if any, distinguished labor leaders at different levels of union leadership. The result of that analysis, simply stated, was that none of the variables examined proved a very good predictor of the leadership level of any particular individual. To be sure, local leaders were somewhat younger and less experienced than national leaders, but these differences were not as great as might be expected. Similarly, the remaining variables failed to reveal any dramatic or consistent differences, although interesting variations did occur from sample to sample (see Table 19 in the appendix to the introduction).

In an effort to measure the discriminating qualities of the variables more precisely, all were reduced to dichotomous variables. Local, state, and regional leaders were combined into one group and crosstabulated against national union leaders. The phi measure of association was employed to compare those two groups of labor leaders. The results of that analysis are reported in Table 6.

Political preferences revealed the greatest mean difference between labor leaders at the two levels of leadership studied. National union leaders were much more likely to identify with one of the two established parties than union officials at a lower level, a much greater percentage of whom associated themselves with the Socialist party or an independent labor party. Clearly, union leaders of all levels were moving toward a more homogeneous position on this variable through the years considered.

Second to political preference, the occupation of the spouse, available only for the 1976 sample, most distinguished between labor leaders at the national and state or local level. In this case, local labor leaders were more likely to have a spouse employed outside the home than national leaders.

Several institutional variables also distinguished between labor leaders at various levels. National leaders tended to be older, more experienced in the labor movement, and to have acquired their positions at an older age than comparable state and local leaders. Differences in these variables were most consistent and persistent of all of these variables analyzed.

Religious preference also distinguished between union officials at the national and local levels during the early years of the period studied. National leaders were more likely to be Catholic than the predominant Protestants at the local level, but like political preference, the distinctiveness of religious identification

Table 6
Crosstabulations by Union Position, 1900–1976

Variable	1900	1925	1946	1976	X
Political Preference	.485	.197	.084	N/A	.255
Occupation of Spouse	N/A	N/A	N/A	.156	.156
Years in Organized Labor	.200	.030	.188	.169	.147
Years in Organized Labor for Position	.105	.089	.025	.256	.119
Religious Preference	.170	N/A	.054	N/A	.112
Age	.027	.050	.179	.151	.102
City of Birth	− .054	.002	− .025	.174	.097
Age Assumed Union Position	.052	.091	.025	.201	.092
Marital Status	.323	N/A	− .106	.050	.089
Civic Activity Index	N/A	.125	.036	.033	.065
Age at Marriage	.027	N/A	.111	.024	.053
Occupation of Father	.313	− .108	.015	− .027	.048
Number of Children	.132	N/A	− .038	.032	.042
Occupation of Mother	N/A	N.A	N.A	.011	.011
Region of Birth	.096	− .034	.098	− .117	.011
Education	.003	− .173	.050	.159	.010
Average	.153	.090	.074	.111	.084
					(.107)

diminished through the years. In this case the large percentage of Catholic union leaders at the national level declined while the distribution at the state and local level remained fairly constant.

Beyond those variables discussed above, few differences separated labor leaders at the two levels considered. The place of birth, socioeconomic origins, education, and degree of civic involvement of labor leaders at all levels were quite similar. Indeed, considering the low phi levels on all the variables considered, it is clear that labor leaders were much more similar than they were different.

Nevertheless, to the degree that distinctiveness is discernible, differences between labor leaders at the two levels analyzed were greatest in 1900 and then gradually diminished through 1946 before the trend was reversed in 1976. Most of the significant differences in the 1976 sample derived from institutional variables, reflecting the relative stability of the labor movement between 1946 and 1976.

PART 3: THE FEMALE LABOR LEADER

The most striking differences to appear among the individuals surveyed in this analysis of twentieth-century American labor leaders separated males and females in the various samples. In addition to the contrasts that existed within the variables analyzed, it should be kept in mind that the relatively small number of women who appeared in the ranks of labor leadership remained the greatest disparity between the sexes during the period studied. Over and above this, substantial differences appeared in almost every variable considered.

Differences within the institutional setting are especially apparent. Women who assumed leadership roles tended to be concentrated in a relatively few types of unions, at the city and state federation level, or in the local units of national and international unions. They also tended to be younger and less experienced than their male counterparts. Moreover, substantial social costs were exacted from those women who aspired to even these modest positions of influence in the labor movement. For many, a career in labor leadership required a better education and a willingness to forgo marriage and family. Perhaps because of their commitment to social reform, they were less conservative than male leaders and more likely to support progressive political causes (see Table 11).

Institutional Variables

As noted, women tended to be concentrated in particular unions within the labor movement. In part, this resulted from occupational segregation, but differences within individual unions also appear to have contributed to the comparative isolation of those women who did rise into leadership ranks. Nearly 25 percent of the women in leadership roles in 1925 represented professional or white-collar unions, with the largest group coming from the American Federation of Teachers. The needle trades contributed another 25 percent, and the Women's Trade Union League (WTUL) and the telephone operators associated with the International Brotherhood of Electrical Workers provided 20 and 11 percent respectively. Although variations in these patterns occurred in the two remaining sample periods, the general trend remained quite consistent. In 1946, for example, 48 percent of the women in leadership positions came from professional or white-collar unions. The comparable figure for the 1976 sample was 45 percent (see Table 7). Similarly, the needle trades provided 16 and 11 percent respectively. Concentration also appeared with respect to union positions, with a substantial majority of women either serving a leadership role in a local union or being associated with local or state federations of labor, often as the recording secretary (see Table 8).

The average age of women labor leaders increased from 42 years in 1925 to 48 in 1976. As was true of the male group, the average age of women fell slightly in the 1946 sample, a reflection of the tremendous growth of the labor movement in the preceding years. Likewise, the experience level, derived from the length of association with organized labor, increased from an average of 14.4 years in 1925 to 19 years in 1976, again with a substantial decline in 1946. The average woman member in 1925 had joined a labor union in 1911 and acquired her primary union position in 1917. Her counterpart in 1976 had joined a union in 1957 and had spent nearly 13 years in the labor movement before acquiring her primary union position in 1970. Thus mobility in the labor movement slowed from 6 years in 1925 to 13 years a half century later.

Table 7
Women by Union Type, 1925–1976 (in Percentages)

Union Type	1925	1946	1976
Professional	17.9	11.0	20.0
White Collar	—	25.0	11.0
Government Service	5.4	12.0	14.0
Craft	1.8	13.0	10.0
Telephone Operators	10.7	—	—
Transportation	—	3.0	2.0
Industrial	1.8	14.0	10.0
Service	—	6.0	5.0
Needle Trades	26.8	16.0	11.0
Federation Official	1.8	—	15.0
Staff	14.3	—	—
Women's Trade Union League	19.6	—	—

Table 8
Women by Union Position, 1925–1976 (in Percentages)

Union Position	1925	1946	1976
National Federation Official	—	—	3.0
State/Regional Federation Official	2.0	2.0	7.0
Local Federation Official	43.1	6.0	7.0
National Union Official	11.8	11.0	22.0
State/Regional Union Official	7.8	15.0	10.0
Local Union Official	17.6	46.0	32.0
National Union Staff	—	12.0	18.0
State/Regional Union Staff	2.0	4.0	—
Local Union Staff	7.8	3.0	—
Editor/Publicist	5.9	—	1.0
Other	2.0	—	—

Table 9
Women Labor Leaders: Institutional Variables, 1925–1976 (Averages)

Institutional Variables	1925	1946	1976
Age	42.0	39.1	48.1
Age when Assuming Union Position	N/A	N/A	41.7
Years in Organized Labor	14.4	10.7	19.0
Years in Organized Labor for Position	6.0	N/A	12.7

Composite Labor Leader Profile No. 4
Kate F. Douglas: Female Labor Leader during the Lean Years

Born in Carterville, Illinois, on May 8, 1896, Kate F. Douglas was approaching her thirtieth birthday as she walked a picket line in Chicago during the early winter of 1925. The light snow swirling around her ankles as she walked evoked nostalgic memories of a happy childhood spent on a small, family farm in southern Illinois. As she had on other occasions, she wondered if she should go back, get married, and raise a family as had so many of her former girlfriends at Carterville High School from which she had graduated in 1914. To do so, however, would be difficult. Over the past ten years, her life style had changed dramatically, and she would be loath to abandon the crusade to which she had given most of her adult years.

Shortly after graduating from high school, Douglas took a job as a telephone operator in nearby Herrin, Illinois, and joined the telephone operators' department of the International Brotherhood of Electrical Workers (IBEW). Although unhappy with the second-class membership accorded telephone operators in the IBEW, she realized it was the only real option available. Low wages, long hours, and poor working conditions had convinced her of the necessity of union organization and collective bargaining. At the same time, however, the discriminatory practices of male-dominated trade unions awakened her to the necessity of organizing by sex as well as class. Consequently, she joined the National Women's Trade Union League (WTUL) and actively participated in its efforts to improve the conditions of female workers. In this respect, she took an especially active role in the campaign to secure an eight-hour day law for women workers in Illinois.

In 1920, Douglas left her job as a telephone operator and became a full-time organizer for the IBEW's telephone operators' department. The following year she attended Bryn Mawr Summer School for Women in Industry, where her knowledge of industrial affairs grew along with her commitment to trade unionism.

The postwar years, however, were bad years for the labor movement in general and the telephone operators' department in particular. The organization of telephone operators had increased dramatically after the government assumed control of the communications industry during World War I, but when federal authorities returned the telephone companies to private control, an anti-union offensive and the introduction of company unions on a massive scale quickly eroded union strength in the industry. By 1924, only Chicago and Montana had managed to maintain independent organizations of telephone operators.

Even though she had been elected to the executive board of the telephone operators' department in 1921, Douglas realized that the union could no longer afford to maintain a staff of paid organizers, so she resigned her position in 1924 and accepted an appointment as a field representative for the WTUL. A year earlier, she had been elected vice-president of the Illinois branch of the WTUL. While still committed to the organization of telephone operators, Douglas was excited about her new position with its greater range of activities. It would also permit her to play a more active role in politics where she could work for protective legislation for women workers. A staunch supporter of Robert La Follette's Progressive party candidacy in 1924, she retained a strong interest in progressive, reform politics for the remainder of her life.

Although an active communicant in the Methodist church, much of Douglas's social life revolved around trade-union affairs. She particularly enjoyed the short courses, seminars, and lectures sponsored by the WTUL. Although often accompanied on these occasions by male friends and associates, she avoided any long-term romantic involvement. Most men, she discovered, had very definite ideas about the role of women and after 12 years of self-sufficiency and independence, she doubted she could or would conform to such expectations. Besides, there was still so much to do.

Biographical Variables

Based on their fathers' occupations, women labor leaders were much more likely to have been born into middle-class circumstances than their male associates. When combining the professional, business, and white-collar occupational categories (see Table 10), approximately half the women sampled were born into middle-class families and only in 1946 were more than a third of the women products of the working class (40.5 percent). The unusually high percentage of middle-class occupations in 1925 was influenced by a large number of WTUL members in the sample, almost all of whom came from affluent, middle-class families. When the WTUL women are removed from the 1925 sample, it more closely resembles the other sample years. The general trend among women labor leaders was toward a more working-class base. Women deriving from the two highest categories, professional and business, steadily declined from 46.5 percent in 1925 to 32.1 percent in 1946, and 22.9 percent in 1976. In this variable, at least, women appear to have been moving toward a closer approximation of the socioeconomic origins of male leaders.

Women labor leaders, historically, were also much better educated than men, although, once again, the educational gap between the sexes diminished through the years. In 1925, 28.6 percent of the women and 70 percent of the men had less than a secondary education. By 1976, no women and only 0.8 percent of the men fit this category. Conversely, 39.3 percent of the women in the 1925 sample were college-educated as opposed to 5.5 percent of the males. The comparable figures for the 1976 sample were 64.8 percent for women and 41.3 percent for men.

The most consistent differences between male and female leaders, however,

Table 10
Women Labor Leaders: Biographical Variables, 1925–1976 (in Percentages)

Biographical Variables	1925	1946	1976
Occupation of Father			
Professional	16.3	7.1	8.3
Business	30.2	25.0	14.6
White Collar	14.0	8.3	25.0
Farmer	9.3	19.0	22.9
Blue Collar	30.2	40.5	29.2
Occupation of Spouse			
Professional	N/A	N/A	24.4
Business	N/A	N/A	9.8
White Collar	N/A	N/A	36.6
Farmer	N/A	N/A	2.4
Blue Collar	N/A	N/A	26.8
Occupation of Mother			
Professional	N/A	N/A	7.8
Business	N/A	N/A	9.8
White Collar	N/A	N/A	31.4
Farmer	N/A	N/A	—
Blue Collar	N/A	N/A	—
Housewife	N/A	N/A	64.7
Marital Status			
Married	21.8	56.0	57.0
Unmarried	78.2	44.0	43.0
Age at Marriage (Averages)	N/A	24.8	23.7
Number of Children (Averages)	N/A	0.6	1.4
City of Birth			
Large	45.5	22.6	29.3
Medium	25.0	16.1	27.2
Small	29.5	61.3	43.5

Table 10 (Continued)
Women Labor Leaders: Biographical Variables, 1925–1976 (in Percentages)

Biographical Variables	1925	1946	1976
City of Residence			
Large	82.1	47.0	47.5
Medium	17.9	37.0	41.4
Small	—	16.0	11.1
Region of Birth			
New England	9.1	9.0	15.2
Mid-Atlantic	18.2	19.0	18.5
Midwest	25.5	26.0	26.1
Border	14.5	10.0	14.1
South	5.5	19.0	14.1
Mountain States	1.8	5.0	2.2
Far West	3.6	3.0	4.3
Foreign	21.8	9.0	5.4
Region of Residence			
New England	8.9	7.0	12.3
Mid-Atlantic	37.5	26.0	20.6
Midwest	26.8	26.0	20.6
Border	17.9	12.0	20.6
South	3.6	15.0	10.3
Mountain States	1.8	3.0	6.2
Far West	3.6	10.0	8.2
Canada	—	1.0	1.0
Education			
College	39.3	36.8	64.8
Business/Vocational	8.9	17.9	15.4
Secondary	23.2	34.7	19.8
Elementary	23.2	10.5	—
Self-Educated	5.4	—	—

were associated with marriage and family. Women were much less likely to be married and had fewer children than either male labor leaders or the female population at large. Moreover, those women who married did so at younger ages and, based on information available from the 1976 sample, were more likely to have been divorced or widowed than comparable males. Clearly, for many women, marriage and a family were incompatible with a trade-union career.

No substantial differences between women and men existed with regard to either region of birth or region of residence. To a slight degree, however, women were born in and resided in slightly larger cities than the average male leader. Women were also somewhat more likely to have been born in the South or the border states than the predominant male leader.

Composite Labor Leader Profile No. 5
Rose Brown Hudson: CIO Leader and Social Activist

Unlike a majority of women who had attained leadership in the American labor movement by the midtwentieth century, Rose Brown Hudson was born in a large city—Chicago—to working-class parents. Her father, a tool and die maker, had for many years been a member of the International Association of Machinists. Thus for Hudson, trade unionism was neither strange nor unfamiliar but rather something that, ever since she could remember, had been a part of her life.

Thirty-nine years old at the end of World War II, Hudson had spent most of her adult years living through either economic depression or war. Her experiences in both situations thus served to reinforce an already existent commitment to the necessity of social reform and union organization.

After completing an elementary education in the Chicago public schools, Hudson graduated from J. Sterling Morton High School in Cicero, Illinois, in 1925. A devoted evangelical Lutheran, she then enrolled in the business school at Valparaiso University, concentrating on a course in secretarial science. She left Valparaiso in 1927, taking an office job in a small business firm, a position she held until the business went into bankruptcy in 1930. Unable to find another secretarial position, she secured employment at a Westinghouse electrical fixtures assembly plant where, after the passage of the National Industrial Recovery Act in 1933, with its provisions for union recognition and collective bargaining, she joined a newly organized federal labor union of electrical workers. Shortly thereafter, she was elected recording secretary of the local. Federal unions of radio and electrical workers bolted from the AFL in 1936, after being ordered to affiliate with the International Brotherhood of Electrical Workers, and organized their own national union—the United Electrical, Radio and Machine Workers of America—and successfully petitioned for a CIO charter.

Meanwhile, Rose married George Hudson, a structural steelworker, in 1932. The Hudson's had their first and only child in 1936. After the birth of their young son, they moved to Indianapolis where she took a job as secretary to Powers Hapgood (q.v.), a CIO regional director. Much to the annoyance of her CIO supervisors, Hudson helped organize a local of the United Office and Professional Workers of America, comprised of CIO office workers, shortly after the national union had been chartered in 1937. Once again, she was elected to the position of recording secretary. In 1939 she became a local representative to the Indianapolis Industrial Union Council and six months later was appointed secretary of the council.

Confined primarily to clerical positions within the labor movement, Rose, like many of her female counterparts, sought challenges in other avenues. She became an active member of the National Association for the Advancement of Colored

People, the Young Women's Christian Association, and the American National Red Cross. She also took an interest in politics, eventually assuming the position of executive secretary of the CIO's Political Action Committee in Indianapolis. Although her father had been a committed Socialist, Hudson eventually aligned herself with the Democratic party and became an active member of the party's women's bureau in Indianapolis. Hudson, however, received her greatest satisfaction from her writings on labor and related topics. She was a contributor to several union publications and wrote numerous articles for general circulation newspapers, depicting the conditions of working women and the contributions of the labor movement generally.

Hudson's concern about the position of women in the working class grew during the war and postwar years. The number of women in the labor force increased dramatically during World War II, and it became obvious that many of those women were going to remain in the work force in the postwar years. Few of them, however, were organized, and even fewer had been permitted to play any substantial leadership role in the labor movement. Because of its horizontal, industrial-union structure, the CIO organized women on an equal basis with men, but, as Hudson knew well, within the CIO bureaucracy women served primarily in staff-support positions, and she doubted the situation was any better in the AFL. Thus, along with her commitment to labor unionism, by midcentury Hudson was also becoming an active feminist.

Sociopolitical Variables

Women, as a group, tended to be the most socially active leaders in the American labor movement. They were involved in a variety of civic and reform organizations, such as the American National Red Cross and the American Civil Liberties Union, as well as consumer groups, ethnic clubs, and church activities. If there is a discernible trend, however, it was for women to become less involved in outside activities as they became more entrenched in the labor movement. In this respect, women exhibited the same general tendency as male leaders.

The most obvious discrepancy in the figures listed in Table 11 is the apparent dip in the civic activity index in 1946. It would appear that as a result of the intense labor organizing and union-building activity during the depression and war years of the 1930s and early 1940s, women, like men, devoted relatively little time to social and civic activities outside the labor movement.

Only in the 1946 sample were the religious preferences of women labor leaders identified. Based on that data, women were overwhelmingly Protestant in their religious affiliations, much more so than their male associates, a greater percentage of whom were Catholic. Based on percentages, there were also nearly twice as many Jewish women as Jewish men in the ranks of labor leadership.

Politically, women generally assumed a position on the left wing of the labor movement and remained the most progressive element in the ranks of organized labor during the period surveyed. In 1925 only 22 percent of the women sampled

Table 11
Women Labor Leaders: Sociopolitical Variables, 1925–1976 (in Percentages)

Sociopolitical Variables	1925	1946	1976
Civic Activity Index			
High	58.9	22.0	36.0
Medium	28.6	34.0	39.0
Low	12.5	44.0	25.0
Religious Preference			
Protestant	N/A	67.7	N/A
Catholic	N/A	16.1	N/A
Jewish	N/A	11.3	N/A
Other	N/A	4.8	N/A
Political Preference			
Democrat	14.8	66.7	N/A
Republican	7.4	3.5	N/A
Socialist	40.7	14.0	N/A
Progressive/Labor	37.0	10.5	N/A

identified with one of the two established parties; the remainder either identified with the Socialist party (41 percent) or an independent labor ticket—in this case, La Follette's Progressive party (37 percent). While their identification with the Democratic party increased as a result of New Deal labor policies during the 1930s, many women in the 1946 sample still retained a strong commitment to progressive politics either through support of the socialist cause or a commitment to the organization of an independent labor ticket.

Composite Labor Leader Profile No. 6
Jane Durkin Rutledge: Professional and Union Activist

Born on September 14, 1928, in Mendota, Illinois, Jane Durkin Rutledge celebrated her forty-eighth birthday as she contemplated the reopening of the public schools for the new school year. This would be the sixth year that she had failed to meet classes at the beginning of a new school year, and she wondered whether she had made a mistake when she accepted a full-time position with the American Federation of Teachers (AFT). Certainly, she missed the class-room, which she had found rewarding, yet she also knew that the job she was doing for the union was very important to her profession.

Rutledge completed her elementary and secondary education in Mendota, a small, rural community where her father worked as a clerk in the local branch of the U.S. Post Office. After graduating from high school, she enrolled in the foreign language program at Northern Illinois University in De Kalb, where she earned a B.A. in Spanish and Portuguese. In 1950 she accepted a job as a Spanish teacher in La Salle-Peru Township High School. She immediately joined several professional associations, including the American Association of Teachers of Spanish and Portuguese and the American Council of Foreign Language Teachers. She also joined the local classroom teachers' unit of the National Education Association. Eventually, however, she came to the conclusion that the administrator-dominated NEA simply had failed to promote improvements aggressively in either the classroom situation or in the economic benefits accorded teachers in her school district. Consequently, in October 1957, she joined Local 1243 of the American Federation of Teachers. Always an activist, Rutledge quickly became involved in the affairs of Local 1243 and soon was being elected to minor offices within the union.

Shortly after graduating from college, Jane had married Harry Rutledge, who was also a public school teacher and an active unionist. The Rutledges' only child, a girl, died shortly after birth in 1956. Although they talked about adopting a child, both decided to return to college and pursue the master's degree, and they ultimately became so involved in graduate courses, professional activities, and union affairs that they never seriously pursued the idea of another child.

In 1962, Rutledge was elected a vice-president of Local 1243 and executive secretary of the Northern La Salle, Bureau and Putnam County Labor Council's political action committee. The following year, she took a short leave of absence to lobby both local and state representatives in the interest of legislation beneficial to teachers and to the public school system. Her largely successful efforts in this endeavor led to her elevation to the presidency of Local 1243 in 1965. Thereafter, her union career blossomed quickly. She was elected vice-president of the Illinois Federation of Teachers the following year, and in 1970 became the president of the Illinois branch of the AFT and a member of the national union's executive council.

An accomplished teacher-lobbyist, Rutledge found herself spending more and more time at the state capitol in Springfield, and this, along with divergent career patterns, created tensions in her marriage. Her husband, Harry, had been appointed a high school principal in 1965 and of necessity had dropped his affiliation with the AFT. Moreover, after serving in an administrative position for a time, he came to the conclusion that there were no essential conflicts of interest between teachers and administrators. His wife unequivocally rejected that assumption, and it became a point of contention between them. Still, a return to classroom teaching, she believed, would largely resolve her marital problems. She was reluctant, however, to forfeit a promising career in the labor movement to molify her increasingly obstinate husband.

Crosstabulations

In an effort to identify more clearly the differences between male and female leaders in the American labor movement, all of the biographical characteristics studied were reduced to dichotomous variables. Crosstabulation tables were

Table 12
Crosstabulations by Sex, 1925–1976 (in Percentages)

Variable	1925	1946	1976	X̄
Marital Status	N/A	.421	.430	.426
Education	.490	.288	.269	.349
Number of Children	N/A	.365	.326	.346
Occupation of Spouse	N/A	N/A	.278	.278
Occupation of Mother	N/A	N/A	.216	.216
Political Preference	.228	.203	N/A	.216
Occupation of Father	.323	.087	.176	.195
Age when Assuming Union Position	.498	.043	.013	.184
Years in Organized Labor for Position	.289	.043	.164	.165
Age	.267	.123	.096	.162
Years in Organized Labor	.155	.106	.216	.159
Civic Activity Index	.348	.083	.043	.158
Age at Marriage	N/A	.095	.182	.138
Religious Preference	N/A	.090	N/A	.090
Region of Birth	.079	.063	.073	.072
Primary Union Position	.018	.047	.080	.048
City of Birth	.043	.025	.030	.033

constructed and the phi measure of association used to differentiate between men and women in leadership positions. The result of that procedure is reflected in Table 12.

The variable that most distinguished between male and female leaders was marital status, with women far less likely to be married than men. As might be expected, because so many of the females in the sample were single, women as a group had substantially fewer children than men. When considering only the married women in the samples, however, the data reveal that women still had fewer children than their male associates in the labor movement or women in the population generally.

Women also were substantially better educated and were born into families of a higher socioeconomic status than male leaders. Moreover, based on evidence available in the 1976 sample, women tended to be married to men with higher status occupation than the spouses of the male leaders, a substantial majority of whom were housewives. The mothers of female labor leaders, similarly, were more likely to have pursued careers outside the home.

The political preferences of male and female labor leaders reveal another significant difference. Women were less likely than men to support either of the two established political parties and among those who did, women were much less likely to be affiliated with the Republican party. At least through 1946, Socialists and third-party advocates had a substantial following among women in the leadership hierarchy of the labor movement. Along similar lines, women tended to be much more active in reform and civic affairs outside the labor movement than comparable males, although differences on this variable diminished as the Women's Trade Union League's influence declined during the 1930s and 1940s.

Clear differences between men and women labor leaders were also apparent among institutional variables considered. As noted earlier, occupational segregation contributed to a concentration of women labor leaders in white-collar and professional-type unions along with the needle trades and various federation offices. Other institutional variables reflecting significant differences between the sexes included age, length of association with organized labor, and the age at which males and females assumed leadership positions in the labor movement. Women were generally younger, had been union members for shorter periods of time, and assumed union office at younger ages than the average male.

Few statistically significant differences existed between men and women on the remaining variables. Thus, it would be very difficult to predict the sex of labor leaders based on their age at marriage, religious preference, city or region of birth, or their primary union position.

To summarize then, substantial differences on several biographical variables distinguished between men and women in the labor movement. Even more important, however, the very small percentage of women who acquired union leadership positions, even in female-dominated occupations, remained the most significant difference between male and female leaders. Unfortunately, that imbalance does not appear to have declined significantly during the first 75 years of the twentieth century.

PART 4: RIVAL UNIONISM: AFL AND CIO LEADERS

The division of the labor movement during the 1930s into rival federations was one of the most interesting and significant episodes in the history of American labor. Given the more sympathetic attitude toward labor exhibited by Franklin D. Roosevelt and the members of his administration, labor leaders agreed that the time had arrived to organize the mass production workers in American industry. Nevertheless, great differences existed over precisely how this was to be accomplished. Most AFL leaders, including President William Green (q.v.) and his allies among the building trades' unions, advocated the organization of mass production workers through the traditional, vertical, craft unionism format that, for the most part, had been followed since the founding of the AFL in 1886. In his so-called Scranton Declaration in 1901, Samuel Gompers declared that craft autonomy was the cornerstone upon which the American labor movement would be built, and this remained AFL policy into the 1930s. The voices of dissent, which had always existed, however, found a dynamic leader during the 1930s in the person of John L. Lewis (q.v.), the head of the United Mine Workers of America. Along with several other dissident AFL leaders, Lewis advocated a policy of horizontal, industrial unionism to organize mass production workers. Differences over the issue, among other disagreements, eventually split the labor movement and Lewis assumed leadership of the newly organized CIO. Ultimately, the workers in the mass production industries decided the issue by overwhelmingly endorsing the horizontal organizing strategy, thus elevating the CIO to the status of a full-fledged rival to the AFL.

Besides the organizing issue, AFL and CIO leaders also exhibited different attitudes toward social issues, politics, and the role of the labor movement in national and international affairs. In the analysis that follows, the biographical characteristics of rival AFL and CIO leaders are examined in an effort to determine the extent to which they may reflect or have contributed to this very traumatic period in the history of the American labor movement.

Institutional Variables

AFL and CIO male leaders exhibited striking differences in variables associated with institutional affiliation and leadership characteristics. Over half of the AFL sample consisted of leaders of craft unions (specifically, those of the craft, transportation, and service categories as demonstrated in Table 13), while 75 percent of the CIO sample represented industrial unions. CIO leaders were also eight years younger than their AFL counterparts and had been union members only half as long.

Standard deviations for the CIO sample were consistently smaller than those for the AFL, reflecting a much more homogenous sample on these variables among CIO leaders. Conversely, the growth of the labor movement during the 1930s produced an influx of new, younger labor leaders into the AFL that resulted in a bimodal distribution. The differences between the younger and older groups in the AFL were almost as great as the differences between the AFL and CIO.

AFL and CIO women also differed significantly, although the contrast is not as striking as that existing between male leaders. The AFL female leader was seven years younger than her male associates but seven years older than CIO women. Similarly, she had been affiliated with the labor movement for six years longer than the average CIO woman but eight years less than the AFL male leader. AFL women leaders, however, were older and had been union members longer than CIO males. The type of union with which they were affiliated marked the greatest difference between women for both federations and their male associates. Whereas AFL men were predominantly craft unionists and CIO men industrial unionists, the women of both groups tended to be associated with white-collar unions (including professionals and those in government service) with a substantial number representing the needle trades (see Table 13.)

AFL and CIO women also tended to occupy different union positions. Only 7.6 percent of the AFL women held staff positions while 34.1 percent of the CIO women served in a staff capacity. Similarly, 17 percent of the AFL women held a national union post as compared to only 4.5 percent of the CIO. In part this was a product of differences between the large industrial unions of the CIO and the small specialized unions of the AFL which facilitated greater female involvement in leadership roles. These considerations aside, however, the AFL clearly provided more opportunities than the CIO for women who aspired to leadership roles in the labor movement.

Table 13
Men and Women AFL and CIO Leaders by Union Type (in Percentages)

Union Type	Men		Women	
	AFL	CIO	AFL	CIO
Professional	2.5	7.1	13.2	9.1
White Collar	5.1	7.1	22.6	25.0
Craft	48.5	0.6	18.9	4.5
Transportation	11.2	3.2	1.9	4.5
Service	2.0	3.9	9.4	2.3
Government Service	13.3	1.3	15.1	9.1
Industrial	9.7	74.0	—	31.8
Needle Trades	7.7	2.6	18.9	13.6

Table 14
Men and Women AFL and CIO Leaders by Union Position (in Percentages)

Union Position	Men		Women	
	AFL	CIO	AFL	CIO
National Federation Official	1.0	1.9	—	—
State/Regional Federation Official	6.0	7.1	1.9	2.3
Local Federation Official	8.5	7.8	5.7	6.8
National Union Official	17.6	13.0	17.0	4.5
State/Regional Union Official	16.1	20.1	11.3	15.9
Local Union Official	45.2	44.2	54.7	36.4
National Staff Official	1.5	1.9	5.7	20.5
State/Regional Union Staff Official	0.5	—	—	9.1
Local Staff Official	—	1.3	1.9	4.5
Editor/Educator	3.5	2.6	1.9	—

Table 15
Men and Women AFL and CIO Leaders: Institutional Variables (Averages)

Institutional Variables	Men		Women	
	AFL	CIO	AFL	CIO
Age	49.6	41.2	42.7	35.1
Age when Assuming Union Position	N/A	N/A	N/A	N/A
Years in Organized Labor	21.1	10.7	12.9	7.8
Years in Organized Labor for Position	N/A	N/A	N/A	N/A

Composite Labor Leader Profile No. 7
Robert Johnson: AFL Craft Unionist

Born in La Prairie, Illinois, on November 5, 1896, Robert Johnson celebrated his fiftieth birthday as he prepared to go to the polls and vote in the midterm elections of 1946. Like his father before him, Johnson, a vice-president of the International Brotherhood of Electrical Workers (IBEW), voted a straight Democratic ticket but feared that this would not be a good year for his party. To some extent, he blamed this on the CIO which, he believed, had tarnished the party and the labor movement with its Communist sympathies and advocacy of left-wing causes. The Republicans, campaigning on a red-baiting, anti-labor platform, seemed to have attracted a sympathetic public ear. Johnson worried that this was simply the beginning of another anti-union campaign similar to the one that had followed World War I.

Johnson vividly remembered the short-lived but intense red scare of the early 1920s that quickly dissolved into a national open-shop campaign, eventually threatening even the well-established building trades' unions before it gradually lost momentum. He had first joined the IBEW during these years and found it difficult to recall many pleasant memories of the period to which historians would later refer as the lean years.

Johnson had graduated from high school in Chicago where his father, a teamster, had moved shortly after the turn of the century. Shortly thereafter, the younger Johnson worked at a variety of odd jobs before becoming an apprentice electrician. Before he could finish his training, however, he found himself in uniform and on a troop ship bound for France as the United States intervened in the European war that had been going on for three years. After the war, Johnson joined IBEW Local 134 in Chicago and completed his apprenticeship in 1924. Two months before the stock market crashed in New York in 1929, he was elected an IBEW Local 134 inspector and thereafter served in a variety of local union offices before being elected a Brotherhood vice-president and executive council member in 1936.

These were difficult years for building trades' workers. The construction industry, which experienced a boom during the early postwar years, had already fallen into decline by 1926–1927. Even before the Great Depression struck the national economy, unemployment in the construction trades topped 25 percent, and by 1933, only two of every ten building trades' workers were regularly employed in their trades. Johnson's diminishing salary as Local 134's business manager was the only thing permitting him to keep his expanding household together during these years. He had married Grace Anderson in 1922 and they now had two sons. Further complicating the Johnson's financial situation, Robert's father lost his job, and he and Robert's mother had moved into the younger Johnson's home in an effort to pool resources and cut expenses during the hard times of these years.

Besides the problems posed by the depression and the slow recovery of the construction industry, Johnson, like many other craft unionists, also had to contend with the challenge of industrial unionism. With the organization of the CIO, once-sacred jurisdictional boundaries were threatened as the trade union movement confronted the militant and surprisingly successful organizing initiatives made by the new industrial unions. Although the CIO's effort to challenge the AFL in the building trades failed dismally, hundreds of skilled workers and hundreds of thousands of semiskilled and unskilled workers, over which unions like the IBEW had claimed jurisdiction, were rapidly being unionized by the CIO. For his part, Johnson worried most about the inroads being made by the Telephone Workers' Organizing Committee and the United Electrical, Radio and Machine Workers of America, both of which were organizing workers previously claimed by the IBEW. To meet this challenge, the IBEW, at Johnson's suggestion, created a class B membership to facilitate the organization of workers in utility and manufacturing plants. Class B members would pay lower initiation fees and reduced per capita taxes, but they were excluded from death and pension benefits and were limited in voting to one vote per local as opposed to the one vote cast by each class A member. Although Johnson considered this a major concession to industrial workers in the IBEW jurisdiction, they obviously resented the stigma attached to second-class membership and rejected the IBEW for CIO unions. Nevertheless, the Brotherhood continued to grow, especially with the development of the preparedness and mobilization efforts that accompanied American intervention in World War II. A membership that had grown to 200,000 by 1941 leaped to 360,000 by 1946.

Jurisdictional conflicts subsided somewhat during the war, and Johnson devoted an increasing percentage of his time to a variety of government agencies in which he served. Service on the National Defense Mediation Board and the War Production Board was especially sensitive and time-consuming, and he gradually devoted less and less time to such traditional union activities as organizing and bargaining.

The war altered his domestic life as drastically as it had his trade union affairs. Both of his sons were in uniform, serving in the armed forces overseas, and his wife spent several hours each day as a Red Cross volunteer. Even more disconcerting, she continued to talk of accompanying a Red Cross mission abroad even though he had pointedly discouraged such a venture.

With the war's end, Johnson's family life regained a degree of normality, although it would never return to the prewar state. He and Agnes continued to mourn the death of their youngest son in France, but rather than bringing the two closer together, this tragedy had, if anything, the opposite effect. They had seen little of each other during the preceding several years and had grown further apart. She was becoming more independent and assertive and less willing to accept his unilateral decisions. He concluded that this was probably the product of a menopausal reaction, but still it bothered him and consultation with their local Presbyterian minister had not helped. Moreover, their oldest son was having difficulties readjusting to civilian life after the war and was a constant source of concern.

Meanwhile, the end of the war abroad did not end the conflict in the American labor movement but rather reintensified it. Moreover, employers seemed more militant and reluctant to make concessions at the bargaining table. Adding to these complexities, the death of President Franklin Roosevelt, whom Johnson revered, and the succession of the little-known Harry Truman had clouded the political situation.

By the summer of 1946, however, all of this had become of secondary concern. Charges of mismanagement and corruption in his Chicago office had begun to surface and had to be confronted. Johnson knew that his record was clean and was confident that his associates in the Chicago office were honest, but the Chicago building trades had been scandalized in the past by corruption and now everyone was suspect. He speculated that someone was preparing to challenge him in the union's elections in December and that this was the source of the unsubstantiated charges against him. As Johnson worried about all of this, he came to the conclusion that the labor movement's successes during the past decade had brought about as many problems as it had solved, and he wondered if there was not an easier way to earn a living.

Biographical Variables

The socioeconomic origins of AFL and CIO leaders were quite similar, although CIO leaders had a substantially greater probability of being born into urban working-class families than their AFL rivals; AFL leaders were more likely to have been the sons of farmers. As demonstrated in Table 16, 34 percent of the AFL leaders and 28 percent of the CIO leaders were sons of fathers with white-collar occupations. The greatest dissimilarity in this variable occurs among AFL and CIO women. Nearly 50 percent of the CIO sample were products of the middle class while less than 30 percent of the women in the AFL sample listed white-collar occupations for their fathers. As with the male samples, many more AFL women were products of rural America. This is also clearly revealed in the region of birth. Over half of the AFL women listed their region of birth as the Midwest or the South; only 34 percent of the CIO women were born in those regions. Women in both samples were much more likely to have been born in the South than male leaders. The significance of this is unclear, although it does contradict the stereotypical characterization of southern women. Finally, the figures on region of birth also indicate that both AFL males and females were more likely to be foreign born than their CIO counterparts.

With regard to family characteristics, males in the AFL were more likely to be married than in the CIO, but, conversely, CIO women were married at a substantially greater percentage than their AFL counterparts. CIO men and women were married at a slightly younger age and had fewer children than those in the AFL, while AFL leaders of both sexes were more likely to have been born in a small town. Meanwhile CIO leaders were much more likely to reside in a large city, a reflection of the CIO's strength among workers in mass production in-

Table 16
Men and Women AFL and CIO Leaders: Biographical Variables (in Percentages)

Biographical Variables	Men		Women	
	AFL	CIO	AFL	CIO
Occupation of Father				
Professional	7.4	3.9	7.1	7.7
Business	8.0	11.6	16.7	28.2
White Collar	18.4	12.4	4.8	12.8
Military	0.6	—	—	—
Farmer	25.8	18.6	31.0	7.7
Blue Collar	39.9	53.5	40.5	43.6
Marital Status				
Married	96.5	86.8	45.3	68.2
Single	3.5	13.2	54.7	31.8
Age at Marriage (Averages)	26.1	26.4	25.8	24.1
Number of Children (Averages)	2.20	1.86	0.49	0.68
City of Birth				
Large	17.3	26.8	20.4	26.8
Medium	19.1	20.3	10.2	17.1
Small	63.6	52.9	69.4	56.1
City of Residence				
Large	28.1	43.5	37.7	56.8
Medium	49.2	47.4	41.5	31.8
Small	22.6	9.1	20.8	11.4
Region of Birth				
New England	5.5	9.1	3.8	13.6
Mid-Atlantic	7.5	24.7	11.3	29.5
Midwest	34.2	25.3	34.0	18.2
Border	14.6	13.6	13.2	6.8
Mountain States	2.5	1.9	1.9	9.1
Far West	3.0	2.6	5.7	—
Foreign	23.6	17.5	11.3	6.8
Region of Residence				
New England	7.5	3.8	13.6	9.1
Mid-Atlantic	13.1	27.3	17.0	38.6
Midwest	33.7	39.1	24.5	29.5
Border	14.1	10.4	17.0	4.5
South	7.5	5.8	17.0	11.4
Mountain States	4.0	1.9	3.8	2.3
Far West	12.6	7.8	15.1	4.5
Foreign	7.5	3.9	1.9	—
Education				
College	12.7	21.6	32.7	41.5
Business/Vocational	6.1	9.4	19.2	17.1
Secondary	42.5	40.3	32.7	36.6
Self-Educated	—	—	—	—

dustries. CIO leaders were substantially better educated than those in the AFL sample, reflecting, in part at least, the younger age of CIO leaders, their later entry into the labor movement, and the substantial number of radicals and reformers who enlisted in the CIO cause.

Ultimately, the most surprising outcome of this analysis was not the dissimilarities revealed between AFL and CIO leaders but rather their similarities. To some extent the differences that do appear can be attributed to the substantially younger ages of CIO leaders of both sexes. As was true of the institutional variables, the younger group of AFL leaders were more similar to the CIO leaders than they were to the older AFL leaders in the sample.

Composite Labor Leader Profile No. 8
William Roy: CIO Industrial Unionist

Reading the *Detroit Free Press* on the morning of November 7, 1946, William Roy mourned the extent of the liberal defeat in the midterm elections held the previous day. He had campaigned vigorously for liberal candidates and had had some successes, but the Republicans won an overwhelming victory nationally and would now control both houses of Congress for the first time since 1928. After more than a decade of turbulence, Roy should have grown accustomed to adversity and discord; instead, he found himself yearning for a more stable, orderly existence. The conservative victory along with the increased militancy of the work force, tense industrial relations, and continuing union factionalism, however, promised little more stability in the future than had existed in the past.

Born in New Straitsville, Ohio, on September 12, 1905, Roy had had an uneventful childhood. His father, a coal miner and active member of the United Mine Workers, had instilled in his young son a respect for labor and the labor movement. Roy attended the public schools of New Straitsville, graduating from high school in 1923. Although a serious student who had excelled in athletics as well as his studies, Roy's hopes of going to college faded as the coal industry fell into an increasingly deep depression that reduced his father to a part-time laborer. The younger Roy's search for work eventually took him to Toledo where he secured employment as an apprentice tool and die maker in a Chrysler Corporation DeSoto plant. The young machinist excelled at his job and before the end of the decade he had been promoted to foreman of the tool and die department. Although he worked steadily during the early years of the depression, many of his friends and fellow workers did not, and this along with predepression concerns about speed ups, poor working conditions, and seasonal layoffs, reinforced Roy's belief in the necessity of union organization.

Despite the anxieties and insecurities caused by the depression, on June 15, 1931, Roy married Helen Thompson, whose father also worked in the DeSoto plant. They were married in the Methodist church and eventually had two children, both of whom were destined to secure a college education.

The enactment of the National Industrial Recovery Act in 1933 with its Section 7(a) provisions for union recognition and collective bargaining seemingly provided the opportunity for which Roy and his friends had been waiting. They quickly organized a local in the DeSoto plant and requested an AFL federal labor union charter. Elected the first president of the local, Roy attended a meeting in Detroit in June 1934, where delegates representing federal labor unions of automobile workers organized the National Council of Automobile Workers' Union. Although pleased with the chartering of a national council, the automobile workers persisted in their demands for the chartering of an international union of automobile workers.

Meanwhile, the automobile manufacturers remained adamantly anti-union. In response to the collective bargaining provisions of NIRA, they organized company unions on a large scale. The Roosevelt administration's reluctance to enforce the labor provisions of Section 7(a) inspired further employer resistance in the industry. This, along with the failure of several strikes during the summer of 1934, brought the organizing initiatives in the automobile industry to a virtual halt. It was in this atmosphere that William Green (q.v.), AFL president, issued a limited industrial union charter to the United Automobile Workers of America (UAW) in August 1935.

Although the chartering of a national union of automobile workers fulfilled one of Roy's life-long dreams, the AFL's limited jurisdictional grant, which among others excluded employees of die, tool, and machinery manufacturers, offended him. As a result, Roy joined other disgruntled delegates at the second UAW national convention in ousting Francis Dillon, the AFL-appointed president of the union, replacing him with Homer Martin (q.v.). Roy also supported the decision to join the Committee for Industrial Organization (CIO), a move that led to the AFL's suspension of the UAW charter in 1936 and its revocation two years later. An ad hoc extralegal AFL committee, the CIO had been founded to promote the organization of mass production workers into industrial unions. Because industrial organization, which both Roy and his father before him enthusiastically supported, would have disrupted the cherished jurisdictional claims of the predominant AFL craft unions, the CIO-affiliated unions were suspended by the AFL executive council. Under the leadership of the UMW's John L. Lewis (q.v.), the leaders of the suspended unions then converted the Committee for Industrial Organization into the Congress of Industrial Organizations, a full-fledged rival to the AFL.

Affiliation with the militant CIO proved a shrewd move for the UAW. Obviously pleased with the CIO affiliation and emboldened by the enactment of the National Labor Relations Act, automobile workers began joining the UAW in unprecedented numbers. Relieved of all the petty jurisdictional squabbles that had disrupted organizing efforts within the AFL, UAW officials could finally turn their full attention to organizing the automobile industry. The sit-down strike quickly proved the most effective weapon to accomplish this goal. Following the example of automobile workers in Flint, Michigan, who used the sit-down tactic to bring officials of the General Motors Corporation to the bargaining table, members of Local 227, following Roy's lead, sat down at the Chrysler Corporation's DeSoto plant in Toledo. Similar strikes at other Chrysler facilities soon brought union recognition.

With the achievement of the primary objective of union recognition, Roy turned his attention to collective bargaining and to the increasingly fractious internal politics of the UAW. Although generally left wing in his political sympathies, he distrusted the Communist faction in the UAW and by 1946 had joined the moderate, Reuther Caucus. He had been elected a regional director in 1942, a position that brought with it membership on the UAW executive board, and six years later would become one of the UAW's three vice-presidents as the Reuther faction consolidated its control of the UAW.

The outbreak of war in Europe shortly after the UAW had gained recognition at Chrysler and the preparedness and mobilization effort in the United States finally ended the depression and very quickly turned a labor surplus into a labor shortage. Although the labor movement consolidated and expanded upon its previous organizing gains during the war, union officials found their membership restless and rebellious. The no-strike pledge made by union officials during the war and the federal government's "Little Steel Formula," which limited wage increases, created much of this unhappiness. Like many other union leaders during the war, Roy found himself confronted with numerous job actions and wildcat strikes that demanded immediate attention.

Worker militancy steadily increased in the months following the formal end of hostilities as the government attempted to maintain wage and price controls during the reconversion of the economy from wartime to peacetime production. And this was only one of the problems with which Roy had to contend. His wife, Helen, who had taken a job in a defense plant during the war, decided to continue working after the war, a development he had neither foreseen nor encouraged. Still, his salary as a UAW district official was modest and his children would soon be entering high school. Moreover, given the volatile political situation within the UAW, his position in the union was none too secure.

Despite all of these problems, Roy, as he entered middle age, had few regrets about the way he had spent the past 20 years. They had been exciting, dynamic times, and he had participated in some of the most important events of the previous two decades. But he, like many other CIO leaders, had reached an age at which order, stability, and respectability were becoming increasingly important. Rather than the labor agitator he had been in the past, he now longed for recognition as a labor statesman.

Sociopolitical Variables

The greatest disparity between AFL and CIO leaders among sociopolitical variables occurred in the political preference category. Although both groups, including the female unionists, were overwhelmingly Democratic in their political loyalties, significant differences appeared. One AFL leader out of five voted

Table 17
Men and Women AFL and CIO Leaders: Sociopolitical Variables (in Percentages)

Sociopolitical Variables	Men		Women	
	AFL	CIO	AFL	CIO
Civic Activity				
High	30.0	17.4	18.9	27.3
Medium	38.7	51.6	32.1	34.0
Low	31.2	31.2	49.1	38.6
Religious Preference				
Protestant	57.2	54.5	70.6	61.6
Catholic	34.0	37.6	14.7	19.2
Jewish	6.3	4.0	11.8	11.5
Other	2.5	4.0	2.9	7.7
Political Preference				
Democrat	66.1	73.9	65.4	65.6
Republican	21.7	2.2	7.7	—
Socialist	5.2	12.0	—	27.6
Progressive/Labor	0.9	—	23.1	—
Nonpartisan	6.1	12.0	3.8	6.9

Republican while only 2.2 percent of the CIO sample identified with the GOP (see Table 17). Women were far less inclined toward the Republican party than men. No CIO woman supported the Republicans and only 7.7 percent of the AFL women did so. On the other end of the political spectrum, twice as many CIO male leaders identified themselves as Socialist or nonpartisan as the AFL group. But the most surprising discrepancy occurred among the women of both groups; they were much more likely to support a third-party effort than their male associates. But the women in the two samples differed substantially among themselves. Over a quarter of the CIO women identified themselves as Socialists while nearly as many AFL women fell into the Progressive/Labor column. Because of the anti-Socialist bias in the AFL, federation women probably found it more politic to identify themselves with progressive political causes or a labor party (i.e., the Liberal party) than with the moribund Socialists.

Among the other sociopolitical variables, few significant differences appeared. AFL males and CIO females tended to be the most active in civic affairs and the greatest difference among religious preferences occurred between males and females rather than between the AFL and CIO. Women were much more inclined to be Protestant or Jewish than the males. Indeed, the percentage of Jewish women in both groups was almost twice as high as that for men. To some extent, this reflects the concentration of women in the needle trades with its heavily Jewish labor force.

In an effort to identify the differences between AFL and CIO leaders more sharply, all of the elements were reduced to dichotomous variables and crosstabulated using AFL or CIO affiliation as the dependent variable. The phi measure of association was again used to distinguish between the two groups (AFL and

Table 18
Crosstabulations of AFL and CIO Leaders

Variable	Phi
Union Type	.80
Years in Organized Labor	.33
Age	.32
Education	.12
Political Preference	.12
City of Birth	.11
Civic Activity Index	.06
Age at Marriage	.06
Region of Birth	.05
Marital Status	.04
Religious Preference	.04
Occupation of Father	.00

CIO) being compared. The higher the phi statistic, the greater the differences between the AFL and CIO samples.

As can be observed in Table 18, the institutional variables had by far the most discriminating power. AFL leaders were much more likely to be identified with craft-type unions, to be older, and to have been associated with organized labor longer than their CIO counterparts. The other variables that revealed a degree of discriminating power were education, political preference, and city of birth. In this case the CIO leaders were better educated, less conservative in their politics, and less likely to have been born in a small town than comparable AFL leaders.

More interesting than the variables that separated AFL and CIO leaders are those that revealed little or no discriminating power. Most striking in this respect was the virtually identical socioeconomic origins (occupation of father) of labor leaders from both groups. Similarly, no statistically significant differences appeared in either the civic activity index, religious preference, region of birth, or marital status of AFL and CIO leaders.

Everything considered, then, the most obvious conclusion to be drawn from this analysis is that AFL and CIO leaders were much more alike than they were different. Moreover, the dissimilarities that do appear were primarily institutional in character, and their discriminating quality, as a result, would gradually disappear with the passage of time. Thus ideological conflicts, personal rivalries, and differences over organizing tactics still provide the best explanation for the division of the labor movement during the 1930s. This also explains why labor unity could be achieved so easily once the discordant personalities were removed from the scene and differences over organizing tactics ceased to be a divisive issue. Simply stated, the CIO, over the years, became increasingly conservative socially and politically, while the AFL, during those same years, abandoned its previous position on industrial unionism as well as its earlier anti-statist political passivity.

PART 5: THE LABOR LEADER AS BUSINESS UNIONIST: A QUALITATIVE PROFILE

Warren Van Tine, in his interesting analysis of the bureaucratization of the labor movement, identified four images self-consciously used by labor leaders at various times. The labor union as a *democracy* evolved naturally from a society that ascribed to the principles of freedom and liberty, but it also served to sanctify the existing leadership of the labor movement with a cloak of legitimacy. The union as *fraternity* emphasized brotherhood and a sense of mutual interests that could be mobilized when challenges arose to the existence and security of the union. It then assumed the image of an *army* protecting the sovereignty, integrity, and survival of the organization. The image of the union as fraternity, then, suggests a latent sense of class identity that could be transformed into militant class consciousness when, under attack, the union assumed the guise of an army.

The fourth image, the union as a *business*, soon came to be distinguished by the term "business unionism." William Habar, a student of the American labor movement, defined business unionism as the use of a labor union "as a business institution paying dividends in the form of higher wages, shorter hours, better working conditions and greater control over those factors which endanger the security of the job ... [and] embodying a philosophy which is essentially opportunistic" (*Labor Relations and Productivity in the Building Trades*, 1956).

Business unionism grew directly from the pure and simple, job-conscious trade unionism favored by Samuel Gompers and like-minded leaders. The labor movement, they argued, should concentrate on such immediate concerns as wages, hours of labor, and working conditions. In Gompers's words, the labor movement should concentrate its energies on acquiring "more, more, more, NOW" for the trade union member.

Union leaders hoped to establish control over the supply of labor through the closed shop, which provided that only union workers could be hired on a particular job. When this situation existed, a potential employer contacted the union, and it supplied the necessary number of workers on a defined contractual basis. Thus, although rhetorically paying homage to the concept of the free market and the free enterprise system, labor leaders, like their business counterparts, sought to establish a monopoly on the supply of labor and sell it to the consumers of labor in the "free" market place of the capitalist economy.

Although all four images—the union as a business, fraternity, democracy, and army—were used, the business metaphor increasingly became the predominant way in which labor leaders saw their organizations as the union movement grew and matured during the early years of the twentieth century. The inclination of labor leaders to view their organizations as business institutions and themselves as businessmen obviously conflicted with the visage of labor leaders generally held in the public mind.

To much of the public, the labor leader was apparently visualized as a grim, somewhat sinister-looking individual, portly in stature, and attired in a rumpled, ill-fitting suit with tie slightly askew. Ashes fell aimlessly from the long, ever-present cigar clamped securely between the humorless but generously gapped teeth of this coarse, uncultured, and unlettered man, whose lack of sophistication was starkly revealed by his blunt, profane language spoken in the working-class accents of distant cities. In short, the popular stereotype of the labor leader involved something of a combined portrait in caricature of George Meany and James R. Hoffa.

Characteristic of most stereotypes, the above description contains a kernel of truth but, in reality, distorts more than it informs. But for the accident of circumstances, many of the nation's premier labor leaders might well have been respected businessmen rather than "contentious" labor leaders. (With a few exceptions sketches of all the labor leaders mentioned in part 5 are contained in this volume.)

Peter Arthur, the seminal figure in the early history of the Brotherhood of Locomotive Engineers, became a railroad engineer only after the cartage business he founded in Schenectady, New York, went bankrupt. Martin Irons, the radically inclined Knights of Labor leader of the unsuccessful southwestern railroad strike of 1886, twice tried, without success, to establish a grocery business. Another leader of the Knights, Charles Litchman, was a co-owner of a shoe factory that failed during the depression of 1873, and Gordon Chapman, long-time secretary-treasurer of the American Federation of State, County and Municipal Employees, owned and managed an advertising firm before devoting his energies to organized labor. These examples could be multiplied many times over.

The ease with which numerous labor leaders switched sides of the bargaining table also dramatically illustrates the close affinity between businessmen and the leaders of labor. John Jarrett, one of the early leaders of the Amalgamated Association of Iron and Steel Workers (forerunner of the United Steelworkers), left the labor movement in 1883 and, as a lobbyist for the Tin Plate Association, succeeded in gaining a high tariff duty on Welsh plate in the McKinley Tariff Act of 1890. A life-long Republican, his reward for supporting the McKinley-Hobart ticket in the campaign of 1896 was an appointment as American consul in Birmingham, England. While serving in this post, he studied the Welsh tin plate industry and, upon returning to the United States, served as an official in the Tin Plate and Sheet Steel Trade Association for eight years. Thereafter, he successfully founded his own tin plate business in Pittsburgh. P. H. Morrisey resigned the presidency of the Brotherhood of Railway Trainmen to accept a similar position in the American Railway Employees and Investors Association, an organization that lobbied various legislative bodies in the interest of the railroad industry. John Alpine resigned his presidency of the United Association of Plumbers and Steam Fitters of the United States and Canada and an AFL vice-presidency to become assistant to the president for labor relations of the Grinell Company, a manufacturer of sprinkler fixtures. He also served as chairman of the labor relations committee of the National Automatic Sprinkler and Fire Control Association.

A friend and confidant of Samuel Gompers, Edward F. McGrady, Typographical union official and labor leader in Massachusetts, left the labor movement in 1937 to become a vice-president of the Radio Corporation of America, a position he held until 1959. Gustave M. Bugniazet resigned a seat on the AFL executive council and the influential office of secretary-treasurer of the International Brotherhood of Electrical Workers to enter the insurance business, eventually assuming the presidency of the American Standard Life Insurance Company.

After becoming victims of inter-union rivalries in the turbulent early years of the United Automobile Workers Union, both Richard Frankensteen and Homer Martin pursued careers in the business world. Frankensteen became assistant general manager and labor relations consultant for Allen Industries in Detroit, and Martin, after a stint as a Michigan farmer, joined the Tulare and Kings County (Calif.) Employers Council as a labor counselor. Thomas L. Lewis, president of the United Mine Workers from 1908 to 1911, became a labor advisor to an anti-union West Virginia coal operators' association after his failure to regain union office in the elections of 1912.

Along similar lines, a number of union leaders began small businesses after losing union positions. Frederick Turner, a long-time leader of the Knights of Labor, became a grocer; George Addes of the Automobile Workers, a tavern operator, and Jack Lawrenson of the National Maritime Union operated a moving and trucking business. Other labor leaders proved to be adept entrepreneurs in real estate. Thomas A. Devyr, a radical nineteenth-century Chartist, acquired a sizeable fortune through successful real estate speculations in New York City and used much of the money to subsidize the radical press. The aforementioned Peter Arthur invested wisely in Cleveland real estate as did William Maloney, a long-term president of the International Union of Operating Engineers, in Chicago. Indeed, Maloney was so successful it sometimes proved an embarrassment. Many of those unfamiliar with Maloney's investments, but all too familiar with the propensity for corruption in the Chicago labor movement, inevitably assumed Maloney's good fortune was tainted by graft and corruption. Meanwhile, Maloney did little to quiet his critics by buying and occupying a huge mansion in Chicago's fashionable West End. After Teamster president Dave Beck's disastrous appearances before the Senate Select Committee on Improper Activities in the Labor or Management Field in 1957, the committee's chief counsel, Robert F. Kennedy, declared, "He [Beck] was dead. All that was needed was someone to push him over and make him lie down as dead men should.'' Indeed Beck's career as a labor leader came to an end when he decided against running for reelection in 1957, but he was far from dead. As he later explained, Beck decided to stop making money for the Teamsters and start making it for himself. Within a short time, he owned a $450,000 warehouse, a $900,000 motel, a $375,000 restaurant and office building, a $250,000 retail store, and a $135,000 tavern. When his wife died in 1961, she left a $2 million estate. Later, Beck earned about $150,000 annually while spending 30 months at McNeil Island Federal Penitentiary after conviction for federal income tax evasion.

As might be expected of a group of individuals so adaptable to the business world, labor leaders themselves often emphasized their similarity of function with businessmen rather than their differences. Dave Beck once stated: ''I run this office just like a business—just like an oil company or a railroad; our business is selling labor.'' Thomas Gleason, the head of the International Longshoremen's Association, exhibited the same attitude while further illustrating the evolution of a labor leader. ''I am a union man by a freak,'' he stated. ''I was working for a company seventeen years and I was a superintendent of a steamship company. And because I refused to work alongside of scabs in 1932, I was blackballed and lost my home . . . and that is how I got into the union business.'' James C. Petrillo of the American Federation of Musicians evidences a similar career pattern. ''If I was a good trumpet player,'' he explained, ''I wouldn't be here. I got desperate. I hadda look for a job. I went into the union business.''

The business orientation of labor leaders is also suggested by the frequency of which they attended business colleges in their early years. James B. Carey, who at various times served as president of both major electrical appliance unions and as general secretary-treasurer of the Congress of Industrial Organizations (CIO), attended the University of Pennsylvania's Wharton School of Finance and Commerce for two years. I. W. Abel of the United Steelworkers and former presidents Alvanley Johnston of the International Association of Machinists and Thomas Rickert of the United Garment Workers are other examples of union officials who received training in business schools.

Sociological Characteristics

The parallels between labor leaders and businessmen, while obvious and intriguing, should not be exaggerated. Sociologically, the two groups differed in many ways. An examination of the geographic and socioeconomic origins, education, and religious affiliation of labor leaders illustrates these differences as well as the areas of similarity.

The labor leader was much more likely to have been of foreign birth than the average businessman. Of the approximately 750 labor leaders listed in this volume, approximately one-third were of foreign birth. Jewish immigrants from southern and eastern Europe, along with a smaller number of Italians, dominated union organization and leadership in the needle trades. Irish immigrants played an important role in the building trades' unions and, along with other immigrants from the British Isles, were especially prominent in mining unions and in the metal trades.

Although many of these immigrants arrived on American soil while still children, others were accomplished agitators and organizers before emigrating. British Chartism, revolutionary activities in nineteenth-century Europe, Jewish radicalism in eastern Europe, and the Irish Revolution were the training schools for many of the men and women who would eventually assume positions of leadership in the American labor movement. Moreover, many well-educated, highly skilled immigrants left Europe because prevailing patterns of discrimination threatened to stifle their creative energies, while others left to avoid the military draft which, in many cases, was also rife with discriminatory practices. Thus many of the immigrants who assumed leadership positions in the American labor movement had skills and an education at least equivalent to most native-born leaders.

The early careers of Max Zaritsky and David Dubinsky illustrate this point. Zaritsky was born in Petrikov, Russia, in 1885, the son of a rabbi and wealthy lumberman. After completing a secondary education, young Zaritsky, still in his early teens, was placed in charge of one of his father's saw mills. Discharged after instituting a number of labor reforms including a five-day work week, he moved to Vilna at age 15 and earned his living by tutoring the children of wealthy families. A three-day pogrom against students, liberals, intellectuals, and Jews, which he witnessed in Kiev in 1905, led to his decision to emigrate to the United States. Arriving in Boston in 1907, he took a job in a millinery shop and joined a forerunner of the United Hatters, Cap and Millinery Workers' Union. By 1919, he was elected international president of the union and served in that capacity until his retirement in 1950.

David Dubinsky was born in Brest-Litovsk, Russian Poland, in 1892. After attending a Zionist school, he became an apprentice in his father's Lodz bakery at age 11. Three years later, he became a master baker, joined the local bakers' union and was elected assistant secretary. As a result of the abortive revolution of 1905, a wave of repression bringing mass arrests to union agitators caught up the 15-year-old Dubinsky. After his release, he was elected secretary of the bakers' union and quickly organized a strike in which he dramatically picketed his father's bakery. Since his father approved of the cause for which he was agitating, however, the picketing was a symbolic act. Dubinsky was once again arrested and released, after a bribe was paid by his father, with the understanding that he leave Lodz. Nevertheless, the irrepressible Dubinsky soon returned to Lodz and once again became involved in radical activities. This time authorities arrested and sentenced him to exile in Siberia, although he spent 18 months in the Lodz prison until reaching the age for exile.

Dubinsky escaped during the long trek to Siberia and for several months lived under an assumed name until his father gained amnesty for him in 1910. Shortly thereafter he emigrated, arriving in New York City in 1911. Upon his arrival, he joined the Socialist party, registered in a night school, and took a job in the garment industry, eventually becoming a skilled cutter. He joined Garment Cutters Local 10 of the International Ladies' Garment Workers' Union, over which he eventually presided for nearly four decades.

The socioeconomic origins of American labor leaders are as varied and colorful as the leaders themselves. Unlike most business leaders, a majority of labor leaders derived from working- or lower-class parents. Such influential American labor leaders as Samuel Gompers, Philip Murray, John L. Lewis, and George Meany were all working-class products. But just as some business leaders were products of working-class parents, a surprising number of labor leaders were born into the middle class and sometimes the upper class. Some of these sons and daughters of the middle class forsook promising careers in the professions or in white-collar positions to pursue work as manual laborers. As might be anticipated, varied reasons explain this voluntary descent to lower steps on the accepted social ladder. In broad terms, however, boredom with middle-class occupations, adventurism, personal pyschological needs, and ideological convictions appear to have been the most important motivations for so masochistically violating the Horatio Alger ethic.

The single most easily identifiable group of labor leaders to derive from the upper rungs of the socioeconomic ladder were the women who entered the labor movement during the early years of the twentieth century. The ranks of the Women's Trade Union League, first organized in 1903, were filled with college-educated women—bright, talented, and frustrated women bored with their assigned role in American society. Refusing to conform, some, like Jane Addams and Lillian Wald, became pioneers in the settlement house movement; others walked picket lines, organized the unorganized, and utilized their manifold talents in support of the labor movement and in the quest for social justice.

Although perhaps more dramatic than others, Maud Younger's career is probably more typical than atypical of this group of labor and social reformers. Younger was born in San Francisco in 1870, the daughter of an affluent pioneer family that had settled in California in 1848. Her father was a highly successful dentist who later established a fashionable practice in Paris. Her mother, who died when Maud was 12, left her a substantial fortune inherited from her maternal grandfather.

During her early years, Ms. Younger played the role of a young San Francisco socialite. She attended private schools, played the organ at the Episcopalian church, was an active participant in San Francisco's social life, and made occasional sojourns to Europe.

All of this changed, however, at age 31 when, on the way to visit her father in Paris, she asked to spend a few days at the College Settlement in New York City "to see the slums." When she left the settlement house five years later, she was an enthusiastic advocate of trade unionism and protective labor legislation for women and children. In order to understand better the problems of working women, she took a job as a waitress in a New York restaurant chain and became an active member of the Waitresses' Union. Upon returning to San Francisco, she once again secured employment as a waitress and launched a successful campaign to organize a waitresses' union in San Francisco. Popularily known as the "millionaire waitress," she not only succeeded in organizing a union but was elected its president for three terms and served as its delegate to the Central Trades and Labor Council.

Thereafter, Maud Younger's reform agenda began to grow as she joined the Women's Trade Union League, the National Consumers' League, and the Women's Suffrage Association. She ended her career in the 1930s as a strong advocate of the Equal Rights Amendment.

Women, however, were not the only labor leaders to spring from affluent circumstances. Harry Bridges, the controversial founder and leader of the International Longshoremen's and Warehousemen's Union, had a career not unlike that of Maud Younger. Bridges was born in Australia in 1901, the son of a prosperous Melbourne realtor. After attending Catholic schools and completing a high school education, he was expected to join his father and, as the eldest son, become the heir apparent to the family business. Nevertheless, he found his first job, that of collecting rent from oftentimes poor or destitute tenants, distasteful, and eventually convinced his father that he was not suited to the real estate business. He then acquired a job as a clerk in a stationery store, but, while this job did not offend his sense of social justice, he soon became bored with it. Meanwhile, he read the adventures of Jack London (*Sea Wolf*) from which he imbibed both a romantic attachment to the sea and the seeds of a radical ideology. Thus at age 16 he began a career as a merchant seaman and later as a San Francisco longshoreman, occupations he pursued until devoting his energies exclusively to the West Coast labor movement.

A similar career pattern was followed by Powers Hapgood, an influential figure in the United Mine Workers Union and the CIO. The son of the president and manager of a large cooperative canning firm in Indianapolis, Hapgood completed grammar school in Indianapolis, attended a private academy in Massachusetts, and graduated from Harvard University in 1921. After acquiring one of the best educations the United States had to offer, Hapgood worked in an iron mine in Minnesota, on the Northern Pacific Railroad, in a Montana sugar beet factory, and in the coal mines of Montana, Colorado, and Pennsylvania. He joined the United Mine Workers and eventually became an organizer in the Central Pennsylvania district. Following the unsuccessful national coal strike of 1922, he traveled abroad working in the mines of Wales, France, Germany, and Siberia, studying the working conditions and the political radicalism of European workers.

Upon his return to the United States in 1926, Hapgood resumed work in the Pennsylvania coal mines and joined a group of union reformers opposing John L. Lewis's autocratic control of the United Mine Workers. As a result of these activities, he was drummed out of the union, and, along with two other agitators, took a job with his father's canning firm. When his two companions were fired for spreading disaffection among the workers and disrupting the cooperative experiment, Hapgood also quit and worked as an organizer for several unions during the next few years. Reconciled with John L. Lewis during the midthirties, he became a CIO organizer and participated in the successful efforts to unionize the rubber, automobile, steel, shoe, and farm implement industries. He spent the remainder of his life in the CIO bureaucracy.

Another group of labor leaders with middle-class origins sprang from the labor movement itself. They were the sons and daughters of union officials. Indeed, some union organizations appear almost as family enterprises in which the son assumes control of the business upon the death or retirement of the father. When William Hutcheson retired as president of the Brotherhood of Carpenters in 1952, a position he had held since 1915, his son Maurice replaced him. Similarly, John H. Lyons, Jr., succeeded his father as president of the International Association of Bridge, Structural and Ornamental Iron Workers, and Lawrence M. Raftery of the Brotherhood of Painters saw his son replace him as president of the union. Frank Feeney, Jr., served as secretary-treasurer of the Elevator Constructors, a union over which his father presided. Such examples of nepotism admittedly are unusual, but even such respected leaders as Samuel Gompers, John L. Lewis, and George Meany put close relatives on the payroll. In some instances, this practice bordered on corruption. James R. Hoffa, for example, not only hired his son's law firm as the Teamsters' legal counsel but also placed his wife on the union payroll as president of the Ladies' Auxiliary at $40,000 a year.

Among those labor leaders of middle-class origin, however, a majority neither entered working-class occupations voluntarily nor were they relatives of union officials. They were the sons and daughters of stable and relatively affluent parents who had suddenly fallen upon hard times. As a result, the children became manual laborers and found the union bureaucracy the most immediate and available avenue of escape. Among the most common circumstances were the failure of a small businessman or contractor, the unexpected loss of professional, managerial, or executive employment, or the death or disability of the family breadwinner. In these cases secondary and sometimes grammar school education ceased and all thoughts of college training evaporated as family members, especially older male children, entered the labor force in an effort to relieve financial stringencies.

As a group, businessmen achieved a higher degree of education than labor leaders, but differences in this area often resulted from unfortunate circumstances. Actually a surprising number of labor leaders attended colleges, universities, and business or commercial schools. The more common educational experience occurred, however, when the individual dropped out prior to graduating from high school because of the family financial situation. Later, many of these individuals attended night school to complete a secondary education or enrolled in a vocational or technical school.

Although the average labor leader had a limited education, many in labor's ranks acquired a comparatively advanced degree of education. Arnold Zander received the doctor of philosophy degree in public administration prior to his founding of the American Federation of State, County and Municipal Employees Union, which he served as president for nearly three decades. Ernesto Galarza, an active participant in the long struggle to organize farm and migratory workers, received a Ph.D. in economics from Columbia University. A number of union leaders held the masters degree. Albert Shanker and David Selden of the American Federation of Teachers, Emery Bacon and Elmer Cope of the United Steelworkers, John Driscol of the Mine, Mill and Smelter Workers and later the Connecticut AFL-CIO, and Elmer T. Kehrer of the AFL-CIO civil rights department are a few examples of labor leaders holding masters degrees.

Finally, a surprising number of trade union leaders successfully passed state bar exams. Ralph Helstein of the United Packinghouse Workers attended the University of Minnesota Law School and practiced law in Minneapolis before entering the ranks of union leadership. Terence V. Powderly and Frank Morrison, prominent in the Knights of Labor and the AFL, respectively, both practiced law. Such international union presidents as Woodruff Randolph of the Typographers, Edward Brown of the Electrical Workers, Oscar Nelson of the Post Office Clerks, Willard Townsend of the Transport Workers, Patrick Gorman of the Amalgamated Meat Cutters, Matthew Woll (and his son Jay) of the Photoengravers, Herman Kenin of the American Federation of Musicians, and Selma Borchardt of the American Federation of Teachers were all qualified to practice law.

As is true of similar organizations, the staff bureaucracies maintained by most international unions contain the most educated people in the labor movement. In some cases the unions subsidize the advanced education of their staffers, and in other cases they recruit trained people whether or not they have any association with the trade union movement or the particular industry concerned. As a consequence, the educational gap between labor and business organizations has diminished significantly in recent years as the labor movement has recruited more and more college-trained staff members.

Substantial differences in religious affiliations also separated labor and business leaders. The labor leader was much more likely to be Catholic or Jewish; the businessman, Protestant. Among those who were Protestants, moreover, there was a much greater tendency for labor leaders to be affiliated with the Baptist or Methodist churches than the Presbyterian or Episcopalian ties common to businessmen. The labor leader also appears, rhetorically at least, to have been less religious than the typical business leader, who perhaps found religious affiliations more useful in secular affairs than did the labor leader. Nevertheless, the religious convictions of labor leaders, especially Catholics and Jews, probably had a greater impact on the trade union movement than the businessman's religiosity had on industrial affairs.

Career Patterns

Labor leaders, as a group, were highly ambitious, upwardly mobile individuals, very similar to their business counterparts. The labor movement provided the elevator they used in their rise up the socioeconomic scale, but the union was not always the first vehicle chosen to satisfy their drive for success. The possibility of professional baseball careers attracted such figures as George Meany, Guy Brown of the Locomotive Engineers, and Louis Stulberg of the International Ladies' Garment Workers' Union. After two years as a semiprofessional catcher, Meany decided he had a brighter future in plumbing than baseball. Both Brown and Stulberg played professional baseball, the latter spending two years with the Memphis Chicks of the Southern Association.

The first ambition of Richard Frankensteen of the Automobile Workers was to be a composer. He wrote and staged three plays while attending college and, along with his father, composed *Gypsy Moon*, an operetta performed on stage several times. He eventually resolved upon a career as a high school athletic coach. By his own account, he paid his way through the University of Dayton playing tackle on the university's football team and received the Award of Honor as the outstanding man in his 1932 graduating class. Frankensteen finished his formal schooling at a time when the Great Depression was most severe, thus frustrating his hopes of becoming a coach. Financial necessity forced him to take a job in a Dodge assembly plant in Detroit, where he soon became involved in the labor movement and began to study law at the University of Detroit night school.

Homer Martin, the first president of the United Automobile Workers, was a national hop, step, and jump champion and qualified for the United States Olympic team in 1924. Later he attended a Baptist theological seminary in Kansas City and in 1931 accepted a Baptist ministry. His pro-labor sentiments, however, offended influential members of his congregation, and he soon found himself working in a Chevrolet assembly plant in Kansas City. Indeed, the ministry seems to have been almost as attractive as athletics to many future labor leaders. John Eklund, one-time president of the American Federation of Teachers, held a Methodist pastorate prior to becoming a labor leader, and such labor-associated figures as Abraham J. Muste and Norman Thomas held pulpits before devoting their energies to radical causes.

Perhaps Thomas Hagerty was the most unusual cleric to become actively involved in the labor movement. Hagerty completed seminary training in the Roman Catholic faith in 1895 and, after completing an apprenticeship in Chicago, served two parishes in Texas and then one in New Mexico. A convert to socialism, he attempted to rationalize the apparent contradictions in Marxist and Catholic dogma. Shortly after being transferred to Our Lady of Sorrows Church in Las Vegas, New Mexico, in 1901, he became associated with the Western Federation of Miners and the American Labor Union, a western rival of the

AFL. Along with Eugene V. Debs, the noted Socialist leader, he toured western mining camps in 1902, recruiting members for the American Labor Union and the Socialist party. The following year he served as a Socialist party lecturer. Becoming increasingly radical, he began to criticize the right-wing Socialists who advocated a gradualist, democratic approach to the cooperative commonwealth. In 1905, he was one of the founders of the Industrial Workers of the World (IWW) and participated in the drafting of the *Industrial Union Manifesto*. During the founding convention of the IWW, he served as secretary of the constitution committee, writing the influential preamble of the IWW constitution. A few months afterward, however, for unknown reasons he suddenly dropped out of both the radical union movement and the Catholic church. Later, under the alias Ricardo Moreno, Hagerty taught Spanish in Chicago and conducted a small oculist practice before descending into poverty, becoming a derelict on Chicago's skid row.

Other future labor leaders pursued a variety of careers prior to devoting their lives to the labor movement. Leland S. Buckmaster of the Rubber Workers took employment with the Firestone Tire and Rubber Company after losing a teaching job. Uriah S. Stephens, a co-founder of the Knights of Labor, also taught school prior to his involvement with the labor movement. David Selden, president of the American Federation of Teachers, devoted his energies exclusively to organized labor only after failing in his pursuit of a serious writing career and frustration in founding an experimental college. Mary "Mother" Jones, the famous angel of the coal miners, devoted her life to wifely chores and motherhood until a yellow fever epidemic in Memphis took her husband and four children. She then began a dressmaking business that was destroyed by the historic Chicago fire of 1871. After this disaster she found solace in a Knights of Labor assembly hall, and launched her career as a labor agitator and organizer. Willard Townsend studied premedicine for two years at the University of Toronto before transferring to the Royal College of Science in Toronto from which he received a degree in chemistry. Finding few opportunities for black chemists, he took a job as a redcap in the North Western Railway terminal in Chicago and a few years later organized the Brotherhood of Red Caps, the predecessor of the United Transport Service Employees of America.

If some individuals entered the labor movement only after experiencing frustration or abandoning earlier career choices, others used the labor movement to launch careers in politics and government. One-time labor leaders have served in all branches and at all levels of government, both appointive and elective. At the national level, former labor leaders have lived in the White House, served on the U.S. Supreme Court, as cabinet members, especially in the Department of Labor but also in other departments of government, as ambassadors, as presidential advisors, and in both houses of the Congress. On the state level, they lived in gubernatorial mansions, served in state legislatures, and held a variety of positions in state government. Locally, union leaders were elected mayors of such cities as San Francisco, Detroit, St. Paul, Milwaukee, and Newark, served on city councils, and received appointments to a variety of public boards and agencies.

While not always the first or last career choice of talented and ambitious young men and women, the labor movement nevertheless produced its own versions of the Horatio Alger success story. Like the proverbial poor immigrant boy who made good in America by taking advantage of the business opportunities presented by the American economic system, the labor movement also provided a vehicle to elevate an individual into the realm of wealth, respectability, status, and power. The previously mentioned Peter Arthur is one such figure. Born Peter McArthur in Paisley, Scotland, in 1831, the future labor leader emigrated to the United States 11 years later. While acquiring a few years of formal education, he lived and worked on an uncle's farm in upstate New York. Later, after working as an independent farm worker and unsuccessfully attempting to inaugurate a business enterprise, Arthur at age 18 became an engine wiper of the New York Central Railroad. Within a few years he became an engineer. A charter member of the Brotherhood of Locomotive Engineers organized in 1863, Arthur was elected its president in 1874, a position he held until his death. While he built the Locomotive Engineers into a solid, respected union, Arthur also acquired a considerable fortune through successful real estate speculations in Cleveland.

Although not an immigrant himself, the career of George L. Berry of the Printing Pressmen provides an even more dramatic illustration of the labor success story. Berry was born in Lee Valley, Tennessee, the son of an influential political figure who had served as a state legislator and state judge. At age 9, tragedy struck and young George was placed in a Baptist orphanage after the sudden death of his parents. He found orphanage life unappealing and ran away after a few months, settling in Jackson, Mississippi, where he earned his livelihood as a newsboy for the Jackson *Evening News*. When war with Spain erupted in 1898, he enlisted in the U.S. Army's Third Mississippi Regiment. Upon receiving his discharge, he became a printing pressman and, while working at the *Globe-Democrat* in St. Louis, Missouri, joined the union of his trade. Prospecting in Nevada soon attracted him, however, making his stay in St. Louis short. As a result of several successful mining ventures, he acquired a sizeable bank account and financial independence before moving on to San Francisco.

When the members of the San Francisco local of the Printing Pressmen selected a delegate to attend the national Pressmen's convention meeting in Brighton Beach, New York, in 1907, they chose Berry, according to a story that might well be apocryphal, because he was the only member of the local with the resources to finance his own trip. Whatever the circumstances of his selection, he obviously made a favorable impression; before the convention adjourned, he had been elected international president and served in that capacity until his death in 1948. During that period, he attended numerous international trade union conferences, served as a major in the U.S. Army Corps of Engineers during World War I (and was always addressed thereafter as Major Berry), ran unsuccessfully for governor of Tennessee, lost the Democratic vice presidential nomination in 1924 by two votes, served as a U.S. senator from Tennessee from 1937 to 1939, published a newspaper, ran a cattle ranch, manufactured cigarette wrappers, founded a bank, and organized and led the movement creating Pressmen's Home, Tennessee, an extensive union establishment, including a trade school, retirement home, cemetery, and a variety of other facilities.

Not all labor leaders climbed the success ladder without losing their footing and occasionally falling, however. One of the more tragic stories belongs to Peter J. McGuire, the founder of the United Brotherhood of Carpenters, a founder and vice-president of the AFL and usually credited as the "father" of the Labor Day holiday. After leading the Carpenters' union through the first two decades of its existence, in 1902 he was expelled from the union he had created, the victim of embezzlement charges contrived by ambitious union bureaucrats eager to succeed him. He lived out his last days in poverty—dishonored, discredited, and forgotten.

A similar fate befell Martin Irons of the Knights of Labor. After the failure of the 1886 railroad strike, Irons became a convenient scapegoat for government and railroad leaders who claimed he perpetrated the strike and for Knights of Labor leaders who blamed him for its failure. The unfortunate Irons spent his remaining 15 years living in abject poverty. Blacklisted and unable to work at his trade, he constantly was hounded by self-righteous defenders of established order and slandered by an official congressional investigating committee. Despite the myopic insensitivity of their contemporaries, both McGuire and Irons became labor heroes in death, and monuments were built honoring their contributions to the labor movement. Perhaps history will be less kind to those labor leaders who ended their labor careers in prison. Teamsters' leaders Dave Beck, James R. Hoffa, and Roy Williams and W. A. "Tony" Boyle of the United Mine Workers are but recent examples of labor leaders who abused the trust and confidence placed in them.

The lawless propensity of some labor leaders perhaps inevitably resulted from the pervasive cynicism regarding the law that existed in certain labor circles. For too long the law had been used by anti-union employers as a convenient tool to crush union organization. The law lost its aura of moral authority as a result of frequent perversions of justice. Until recently, labor leaders often lived and worked in an environment characterized by fear, repression, and violence. In their attempts to resist or break union organizations, employers, often with official sanction, instigated much of the violence against labor leaders. During the late nineteenth and early twentieth centuries, a variety of union-breaking organizations, usually thinly disguised as private detective agencies, attempted the intimidation of union members and organizers. The report on violations of civil liberties of the Senate Civil Liberties Committee chaired by Senator Robert La Follette in the midthirties graphically documented the violence anti-union employers committed against union leaders and members.

Aside from the frontal assault of employers, union leaders faced potential violence from other quarters. At various times the underworld has exercised considerable influence in unions such as the longshoremen on the East Coast and in the building trades unions of such cities as New York, Chicago, and San Francisco. Whether attempting to resist racketeer influence or striving to eliminate it, a violent struggle usually ensued. Factional struggles often have been equally lethal. Such fraticidal conflicts resulted from struggles for power within the union, ideological conflicts for union control, or dual unionism.

From Homestead to Ludlow to River Rouge, the literature of American labor history abounds with examples of employer anti-union violence; consequently, only a few illustrative examples of other forms of violence are presented here. Anti-union violence was especially common against radical unionists who rejected the capitalist economic system. Frank Little of the Industrial Workers of the World, whose organizing activities in Butte, Montana, and whose opposition to American intervention in World War I offended local protectors of Americanism, died at the hands of vigilantes on the night of August 1, 1917. Michael Donnelly, the first president of the Amalgamated Meat Cutters and Butcher Workmen, twice received severe beatings as a result of his reform activities in the then corruption-ridden Chicago Federation of Labor. Along with a growing alcoholic addiction, the beatings apparently contributed to severe mental derangement. Unknown assailants physically maimed both Walter and Victor Reuther of the United Automobile Workers. Joseph Yablonski's temerity in opposing the existing leadership of the United Mine Workers cost him, his wife, and his daughter their lives. Finally, James C. Petrillo of the American Federation of Musicians worried about his safety so much that he never went anywhere without burly bodyguards and a bulletproof automobile.

The financial rewards that accompanied success in the labor business provided some compensation for the hazards labor leaders encountered. Yet, in relative terms, the salaries of most union executives fell well below those of comparable officials in the business world. As late as the mid-1960s, for example, 80 percent of the presidents of national and international unions received less than $20,000 per year. Inflation, of course, has driven the salary figure upward in recent years, but even the usually high salary paid the Teamsters' president, $225,000 a year, would be considered modest by industry standards.

Modest salaries, however, were sometimes supplemented by generous expense accounts, a variety of fringe benefits, and enviable retirement benefits. David McDonald, former president of the United Steelworkers had access to two Cadillacs, a chauffeur, and four bodyguards. Moreover, the Steelworkers maintained a suite in Washington's Madison Hotel for his convenience when visiting the nation's capital. Dave Beck sold his $163,000 home in the plush Sheridan Beach district of Seattle—complete with artificial waterfalls and projection room—to the Teamsters Union and then leased it rent free. James Cross of the Bakery and Confectionary Union charged Cadillacs, air conditioners, luggage, and a variety of other items to his union. He also put a pretty, young brunette (with an arrest record for prostitution) on the Bakers' payroll as an organizer. When investigating Cross's affairs, the McClellan Committee asked the young woman what Cross was paying her for; she pleaded the Fifth Amendment.

Retirement benefits, in many instances, were also very generous. Union officials sometimes retired at full salary or at two-thirds of salary. When Joseph Curran of the National Maritime Union retired in 1973, he acquired an annual pension equal to two-thirds of his average salary, which could be taken in a lump sum based on actuarial estimates, plus severance pay equal to one month's salary for each year of service. Curran's pension settlement, however, was modest compared to James Hoffa. Hoffa accepted $1.7 million in lieu of a pension upon his retirement from the Teamsters Union.

The Character of the Modern Labor Movement

Drastic changes have altered the American labor movement since its founding in 1886. By midcentury, the small, neophyte labor organizations of the late nineteenth and early twentieth centuries had become large, powerful institutions. Union membership grew rapidly even though a substantial majority of American workers remained unorganized. By 1970 approximately 20 million American workers held union membership cards. The largest international union, the Brotherhood of Teamsters, had a membership in excess of 2,000,000; the Auto Workers, 1,350,000; the Steelworkers, 1,200,000; the International Brotherhood of Electrical Workers, 977,295; and the Machinists, 900,000.

Over the years, many of the most successful labor organizations exhibited the same centralizing tendencies first manifested by American industry. Just as industry integrated vertically and horizontally during the late nineteenth century, labor unions did much the same during the twentieth century. The United Brotherhood of Carpenters and Joiners provides an excellent example of vertical integration in the labor movement. As its name implies, the union began by simply organizing carpenters; then it added joiners. It gradually broadened its jurisdictional claims, however, to include "anything made of wood," and "then anything that ever was made of wood." Finally, a revised Brotherhood constitution permitted international officers "to issue charters to auxiliary unions composed of persons working at any industry where organization would be a benefit to the brotherhood."

Exemplified by combinations, mergers, and amalgamations, the horizontal integration of the labor movement has also been a constant process. In some instances this process, which was greatly accelerated by the AFL-CIO merger, produced its own version of the conglomerate structure. The International Brotherhood of Teamsters, which expanded its jurisdictional claims to include any unorganized worker, provides the best current example of a labor conglomerate. Such varied occupational groups as brewery workers, college teachers, farm laborers, retail clerks, and taxicab drivers all hold teamster membership cards.

Increased union membership also augmented the wealth and financial stability of organized labor. Complying with the union financial provisions of the Labor-Management Reporting and Disclosure Act, American labor unions in 1970 reported assets totaling $2.574 billion and liabilities of only $254 million. Larger international unions such as the Teamsters, Steelworkers, and Auto Workers reported annual receipts in the neighborhood of $50 million. Due to this large cash flow, most national and international unions maintained extensive investment portfolios. In 1964, for example, the United Auto Workers had an investment portfolio totaling $75,588,586.83, and by 1983 union officials founded a strike fund totaling nearly $500 million, an acute embarrassment given the depressed state of the industry and rampant unemployment.

International unions also owned and managed banks, office buildings, and other real estate, and a variety of insurance, pension, and welfare funds. In some instances the health and retirement funds constituted millions of dollars. The International Ladies' Garment Workers' Union's health and welfare retirement funds totaled $167,108,274 as early as 1955. As a result of the United Mine Workers' strikes of 1946 and 1948, the union won a royalty on every ton of coal mined to finance its welfare and retirement funds. The agreement permitted the Mine Workers' union to build a financial empire. The funds were used to construct a chain of hospitals in southern Appalachia and by 1969 over $2.5 billion had been disbursed in retirement and medical benefits.

The changing character of the labor movement and the growing financial resources of international unions greatly altered the role and function of union leaders. Ceasing, in any strict sense, to be organizers, labor leaders have become administrators of large bureaucracies and managers of huge and varied enterprises. Indeed, the unions themselves have become large employers of labor. International union offices are staffed by managers, auditors, accountants, lawyers, stenographers, clerks, organizers, custodians, and a variety of other occupational groups. Moreover, local unions, district councils, and other subdivisions maintain their own staffs.

Besides administering large staffs, the modern labor leader is also responsible for the receipt and disbursement of union funds. The varied functions of the former president of the Amalgamated Clothing Workers, Jacob S. Potofsky, graphically illustrates the wide range of responsibility exercised by labor leaders. At the time of his retirement in 1972, Potofsky served as president of the Amalgamated Insurance Company, chairman of the board of the Amalgamated Insurance Fund, chairman of the board of the Amalgamated Bank of New York, president of Amalgamated Dwellings, Inc., treasurer of the Amalgamated Housing Corporation, director of the Hillman Housing Corporation, and president of the Sidney Hillman Foundation. In addition to these union responsibilities, he was also a member of a number of private and public boards and agencies. Thus many American labor leaders not only thought like businessmen and acted like businessmen, but by the middle of the twentieth century, had in reality become businessmen.

FOR FURTHER READING

Students who desire to pursue a study of the character of American labor leadership should consult the four collective biographies cited in part 1 of this introduction and authored by Edward Pessen, Ray Boston, David Montgomery, and Warren Van Tine. For individual labor leaders, the biographical references listed at the end of each sketch should prove useful. Profiles of labor leaders are also contained in Charles A. Madison, *American Labor Leaders: Personalities and Forces in the Labor Movement* (1950); Bruce M. Minton and John Stuart, *Men Who Lead Labor* (1937); and Frederick C. Giffin, *Six Who Protested: Radical Opposition to the First World War* (1977). Benjamin Stolberg's *Tailor's Progress: The Story of a Famous Union and the Men Who Made It* (1944) contains profiles of several of the early leaders of the International Ladies' Garment Workers' Union.

Among the more critical evaluations of American labor leadership—usually from the left—are Harold Seidman, *The Labor Czars* (1938); William Z. Foster, *Misleaders of Labor* (1927); C. Wright Mills, *The New Men of Power: America's Labor Leaders* (1948). Reflections of rank-and-file leaders are included in Alice and Staughton Lynd, eds., *Rank and File: Personal Histories by Working-Class Organizers* (1973); and radical profiles are contained in Philip S. Foner, ed., *The Autobiographies of the Haymarket Martyrs* (1969).

The nature of labor leadership has been examined by Lois MacDonald, *Leadership Dynamics and the Trade Union Leader* (1959); Eli Ginsberg, *The Labor Leader: An Exploratory Study* (1948); and David Brody, "Career Leadership and American Trade Unions," in Frederick C. Jaher, ed., *The Age of Industrialism in America: Essays in Social Structure and Cultural Values* (1968).

Different aspects of labor leadership are covered in Lorin Lee Cary, "Middle-Echelon Labor Leaders and the Union-Building Process," in Merl E. Reed et al., *Southern Workers and Their Unions: 1880–1975* (1981); Alvin W. Gouldner, "Attitudes of 'Progressive' Trade-Union Leaders," *American Journal of Sociology* (March 1947); Moses Rischin, "From Gompers to Hillman: Labor Goes Middle Class," *Antioch Review* (June 1953); Pitirim Sorokin, "Leaders of Labor and Radical Movements in the United States and Foreign Countries," *American Journal of Sociology* (November 1927); Louis Stark, "Problems of Labor Leaders," *Annals of the American Academy of Political and Social Science* (March 1936).

The influence of intellectuals on the labor movement is examined by H. L. Wilensky, *The Intellectual in Labor Unions* (1956); and Joel S. Denker, *Unions and Universities: The Rise of the New Labor Leader* (1981).

For an analysis of labor leadership during the 1930s and 1940s which largely parallels the account provided in part 4 of the introduction to this volume, see Walter Licht and Hal Seth Barron, "Labor's Men: A Collective Biography of Union Officialdom during the New Deal Years," *Labor History* (Fall 1978).

APPENDIX TO INTRODUCTION

Table 19
Union Position, 1900–1976 (in Percentages)

Section 1

Institutional Variables	1900	1925	1946	AFL 1946	CIO 1946	1976
AGE						
National	42.6	49.4	49.9	54.0	43.6	56.8
State/Regional	43.2	47.1	44.6	49.1	39.9	52.7
Local	35.4	48.8	45.0	48.2	40.9	51.9
AGE WHEN ASSUMING UNION POSITION						
National	34.3	41.1	N/A*	N/A	N/A	48.2
State/Regional	34.6	41.5	N/A	N/A	N/A	44.1
Local	33.4	42.3	N/A	N/A	N/A	42.2
YEARS IN ORGANIZED LABOR						
National	20.7	27.9	22.3	27.6	14.4	31.9
State/Regional	18.8	19.8	16.2	20.6	10.9	27.2
Local	13.1	24.1	14.9	19.0	9.8	24.7
YEARS IN ORGANIZED LABOR FOR POSITION						
National	13.6	20.3	N/A	N/A	N/A	23.0
State/Regional	10.8	13.7	N/A	N/A	N/A	18.6
Local	10.4	17.6	N/A	N/A	N/A	15.6

Section 2

Biographical Variables	1900	1925	1946	AFL 1946	CIO 1946	1976
OCCUPATION OF FATHER						
Professional						
National	3.8	3.2	4.0	3.3	5.3	7.0
State/Regional	—	—	5.2	5.1	5.4	4.8
Local	—	7.1	6.0	8.3	3.1	4.2

* = Not Available

Table 19| (Continued)

Biographical Variables	1900	1925	1946	AFL 1946	CIO 1946	1976
Business						
National	11.5	19.0	12.0	16.7	5.3	8.5
State/Regional	33.3	18.2	13.0	7.7	18.9	2.4
Local	30.0	—	6.0	4.8	7.8	15.4
White Collar						
National	—	6.3	12.0	16.7	5.3	11.3
State/Regional	33.3	9.1	13.0	15.4	10.8	9.5
Local	—	7.1	19.2	21.4	14.1	6.9
Farmer						
National	26.9	11.1	40.0	43.3	36.8	16.9
State/Regional	—	4.5	18.2	23.1	13.5	23.8
Local	10.0	7.1	18.5	20.2	15.6	11.1
Blue Collar						
National	57.7	60.3	32.0	20.0	47.4	56.3
State/Regional	33.3	68.2	50.6	48.7	51.4	59.5
Local	60.0	78.6	50.3	45.2	59.4	62.5
MARITAL STATUS						
Married						
National	95.2	N/A	90.3	94.6	87.0	92.0
State/Regional	55.6	N/A	93.1	100.0	85.7	90.6
Local	84.6	N/A	94.1	98.1	88.5	91.8
Unmarried						
National	4.8	N/A	9.7	5.4	13.0	8.0
State/Regional	44.4	N/A	6.9	0.0	14.3	9.4
Local	15.4	N/A	5.9	1.9	11.6	8.2
NUMBER OF CHILDREN (AVERAGES)						
National	2.52	N/A	1.74	2.11	1.30	2.70
State/Regional	1.88	N/A	2.23	2.68	1.79	2.72
Local	3.00	N/A	2.14	2.22	2.08	2.32
AGE AT MARRIAGE (AVERAGES)						
National	24.9	N/A	27.3	26.5	28.8	25.7
State/Regional	19.7	N/A	25.4	25.5	25.4	23.4
Local	24.1	N/A	26.2	26.1	26.2	26.1
CITY OF BIRTH						
Large						
National	18.8	39.2	18.5	21.1	15.8	32.6
State/Regional	—	7.1	25.7	21.1	31.4	19.4
Local	22.2	40.0	18.9	12.9	26.7	17.3
Medium						
National	28.1	17.6	18.5	21.1	15.8	29.5
State/Regional	20.0	21.4	20.3	18.4	22.9	22.6
Local	44.4	40.0	20.7	19.4	22.7	23.5
Small						
National	53.1	43.1	63.0	57.6	68.4	37.9
State/Regional	80.0	71.4	54.1	60.5	45.7	58.1
Local	33.3	20.0	60.4	67.7	50.7	59.2

Biographical Variables	1900	1925	1946	AFL 1946	CIO 1946	1976
(REGION OF BIRTH)						
New England						
National	6.1	12.3	4.8	2.7	8.7	5.5
State/Regional	—	4.8	6.9	4.5	9.5	3.3
Local	14.3	14.3	7.9	6.5	10.0	13.3
Mid-Atlantic						
National	26.5	30.1	16.1	5.4	30.4	20.9
State/Regional	9.1	9.5	12.6	4.5	21.4	16.4
Local	35.7	14.3	15.8	9.3	25.0	19.4
Midwest						
National	22.4	23.3	35.5	37.8	34.8	34.1
State/Regional	36.4	38.1	25.3	36.4	14.3	27.9
Local	14.3	21.4	28.4	31.8	23.7	28.6
Border						
National	2.0	6.8	12.9	18.9	4.3	14.3
State/Regional	—	4.8	16.1	13.6	19.0	11.5
Local	—	7.4	13.2	13.1	13.7	10.2
South						
National	4.1	4.1	8.1	8.1	4.3	17.6
State/Regional	—	4.8	6.9	6.8	4.8	29.5
Local	—	14.3	8.90	11.2	6.3	22.4
Mountain States						
National	2.0	—	1.6	—	4.3	2.2
State/Regional	—	—	3.4	4.5	2.4	4.9
Local	—	—	1.6	1.9	1.2	—
Far West						
National	—	2.7	3.2	5.4	—	2.2
State/Regional	—	4.8	3.4	—	7.1	1.6
Local	—	—	2.6	3.7	1.2	4.1
Foreign						
National	36.7	20.5	17.7	21.6	13.0	3.3
State/Regional	54.5	33.3	25.3	29.5	21.5	4.9
Local	35.7	28.6	21.6	22.4	17.5	2.0
EDUCATION						
College						
National	8.5	2.9	17.6	12.5	26.3	52.5
State/Regional	9.1	10.0	23.1	7.1	42.9	38.3
Local	—	7.7	9.1	10.2	7.9	—
Business/Vocational						
National	—	1.5	11.8	12.5	10.5	11.2
State/Regional	—	—	2.6	4.8	—	8.3
Local	8.3	—	8.0	5.1	11.8	33.0
Secondary						
National	14.9	19.1	43.1	37.5	52.6	35.0
State/Regional	18.2	25.0	35.9	42.9	28.6	51.7
Local	8.3	15.5	46.9	46.9	46.1	9.9

71

Table 19 (Continued)

Sociopolitical Variables	1900	1925	1946	AFL 1946	CIO 1946	1976
Elementary						
National	48.9	61.8	27.5	37.5	10.5	—
State/Regional	45.5	50.0	38.5	45.2	28.6	1.7
Local	58.3	76.9	36.0	37.8	34.2	57.1
Self-Educated						
National	27.7	14.7	—	—	—	1.2
State/Regional	27.3	15.0	—	—	—	—
Local	25.0	—	—	—	—	—

Section 3

Sociopolitical Variables	1900	1925	1946	AFL 1946	CIO 1946	1976
CIVIC ACTIVITY INDEX						
High						
National	40.8	12.1	7.3	21.6	13.0	11.9
State/Regional	54.5	36.4	12.5	13.7	12.0	23.1
Local	35.7	26.7	18.5	22.5	13.7	22.4
Medium						
National	42.9	35.1	34.6	32.4	30.4	31.2
State/Regional	45.5	36.4	33.3	34.2	30.9	30.7
Local	42.9	33.3	29.0	24.2	36.2	32.6
Low						
National	16.3	52.7	58.3	45.9	56.5	57.0
State/Regional	—	27.3	54.0	52.3	57.1	46.2
Local	21.4	40.0	52.7	53.2	49.9	44.9
RELIGIOUS PREFERENCE						
Protestant						
National	36.7	N/A	63.4	63.3	63.6	N/A
State/Regional	—	N/A	48.4	50.0	46.2	N/A
Local	33.3	N/A	56.2	56.6	54.1	N/A
Catholic						
National	50.0	N/A	31.7	33.3	27.3	N/A
State/Regional	83.3	N/A	40.3	41.7	38.5	N/A
Local	44.4	N/A	35.6	32.5	41.0	N/A
Jewish						
National	10.0	N/A	2.4	3.3	—	N/A
State/Regional	16.7	N/A	4.8	2.8	7.7	N/A
Local	22.2	N/A	6.2	8.4	3.3	N/A
Other						
National	3.3	N/A	2.4	—	9.1	N/A
State/Regional	—	N/A	6.5	5.6	7.7	N/A
Local	—	N/A	2.1	2.4	1.6	N/A
POLITICAL PREFERENCE						
Democrat						
National	31.4	17.5	61.5	60.9	62.5	N/A

Sociopolitical Variables	1900	1925	1946	AFL 1946	CIO 1946	1976
State/Regional	—	11.1	68.8	65.4	71.4	N/A
Local	18.2	14.3	71.8	67.8	78.0	N/A
Republican						
National	31.4	12.5	12.8	21.7	—	N/A
State/Regional	11.1	5.6	10.4	19.2	—	N/A
Local	9.1	14.3	15.5	23.7	4.0	N/A
Socialist						
National	20.0	17.5	12.8	8.7	18.8	N/A
State/Regional	55.6	22.2	12.5	7.7	19.0	N/A
Local	9.1	14.3	15.5	23.7	4.0	N/A
Progressive/Labor						
National	5.7	22.5	—	—	—	N/A
State/Regional	33.3	38.9	—	—	—	N/A
Local	9.1	21.4	0.9	1.7	—	N/A
Nonpartisan						
National	11.4	30.0	12.8	8.7	18.8	N/A
State/Regional	—	22.2	8.3	7.7	9.5	N/A
Local	9.1	7.1	6.4	3.4	10.0	N/A

Table 20
Union Type: Institutional Variables, 1900–1976 (Averages)

Variable	1900	1925	1946	1976
Age				
White Collar	35.0	46.5	45.6	51.2
Craft	42.0	50.5	48.4	54.2
Industrial	35.8	45.6	42.9	53.3
Needle Trades	36.8	42.9	48.8	59.6
Age when Assuming Union Position				
White Collar	34.8	40.0	N/A	43.5
Craft	33.7	42.2	N/A	45.5
Industrial	34.0	41.2	N/A	45.0
Needle Trades	29.8	34.9	N/A	44.4
Years in Organized Labor				
White Collar	9.5	23.8	12.1	24.1
Craft	19.9	27.6	21.6	28.8
Industrial	17.3	26.7	11.9	26.5
Needle Trades	12.6	18.0	23.5	36.7
Years in Organized Labor for Position				
White Collar	8.8	17.4	N/A	16.7
Craft	12.4	19.2	N/A	20.3
Industrial	14.9	22.7	N/A	18.1
Needle Trades	5.8	11.1	N/A	21.7

Table 21
Union Type: Biographical Variables, 1900–1976 (in Percentages)

Variable	1900	1925	1946	1976
OCCUPATION OF FATHER				
Professional				
White Collar	—	—	8.9	16.0
Craft	3.2	2.8	6.0	5.0
Industrial	—	—	1.8	—
Needle Trades	—	9.1	21.4	7.7
Business				
White Collar	66.7	14.3	23.2	12.0
Craft	19.4	15.3	6.0	11.2
Industrial	—	11.1	7.3	8.5
Needle Trades	—	27.3	—	15.4
White Collar				
White Collar	—	7.1	25.0	16.0
Craft	3.2	6.9	17.2	5.0
Industrial	—	—	10.0	6.4
Needle Trades	33.3	9.1	28.6	15.4
Farmer				
White Collar	—	7.1	16.1	10.0
Craft	32.3	9.7	27.6	15.0
Industrial	—	—	23.6	23.4
Needle Trades	—	18.2	—	7.7
Blue Collar				
White Collar	33.3	71.4	26.8	46.0
Craft	41.9	65.3	42.2	62.5
Industrial	100.0	88.9	57.3	61.7
Needle Trades	66.7	36.4	50.0	53.8
MARITAL STATUS				
White Collar				
Married	50.0	N/A	90.8	82.1
Single	50.0	N/A	9.2	17.9
Craft				
Married	91.8	N/A	93.5	92.8
Single	8.2	N/A	6.5	7.2
Industrial				
Married	100.0	N/A	91.0	95.7
Single	0.0	N/A	9.0	4.3
Needle Trades				
Married	80.0	N/A	94.1	100.0
Single	20.0	N/A	5.9	0.0
NUMBER OF CHILDREN (AVERAGES)				
White Collar	0.50	N/A	1.80	2.39
Craft	2.14	N/A	1.99	2.69
Industrial	5.67	N/A	2.11	2.44
Needle Trades	3.50	N/A	1.90	2.16

Table 21 (Continued)

Variable	1900	1925	1946	1976
CITY OF BIRTH				
Large				
White Collar	—	28.6	24.6	36.4
Craft	20.6	34.5	18.3	20.2
Industrial	—	16.7	23.0	16.2
Needle Trades	—	100.0	14.3	47.1
Medium				
White Collar	66.7	14.3	24.6	25.8
Craft	26.5	21.8	15.9	26.6
Industrial	28.6	33.3	18.9	25.0
Needle Trades	—	—	42.9	23.5
Small				
White Collar	33.3	57.1	50.8	37.9
Craft	52.9	43.6	65.9	53.2
Industrial	71.4	50.0	58.2	58.8
Needle Trades	100.0	0.0	42.9	29.4
REGION OF BIRTH				
New England				
White Collar	25.0	—	9.2	12.9
Craft	7.4	14.3	6.4	4.4
Industrial	—	22.2	7.5	8.6
Needle Trades	—	7.1	—	15.8
Mid-Atlantic				
White Collar	—	6.7	18.5	27.4
Craft	29.6	26.9	6.4	11.4
Industrial	11.1	22.2	24.1	17.1
Needle Trades	—	14.3	5.3	47.4
Midwest				
White Collar	50.0	40.0	32.3	25.8
Craft	20.4	23.1	36.4	32.5
Industrial	33.3	33.3	26.3	28.6
Needle Trades	20.0	7.1	10.5	5.3
Border				
White Collar	—	20.0	9.2	9.7
Craft	3.7	7.7	16.4	13.2
Industrial	—	11.1	15.0	15.7
Needle Trades	—	—	5.3	—
South				
White Collar	—	13.3	4.6	9.7
Craft	1.9	5.1	11.4	27.2
Industrial	11.1	—	6.8	21.4
Needle Trades	—	—	—	10.4
West*				
White Collar	—	13.3	9.3	11.3

*Mountain states and Far West states have been combined.

Table 21 (Continued)

Variable	1900	1925	1946	1976
Craft	—	1.3	3.5	4.4
Industrial	11.1	—	4.5	2.8
Needle Trades	—	—	5.3	—
Foreign				
White Collar	25.0	6.7	16.9	3.2
Craft	37.0	21.8	19.3	7.0
Industrial	33.3	33.3	15.8	5.8
Needle Trades	80.0	71.4	73.7	21.1
EDUCATION				
College				
White Collar	—	16.7	48.3	68.9
Craft	11.5	2.7	7.3	33.3
Industrial	—	—	10.4	27.9
Needle Trades	—	7.7	23.1	60.0
Business/Vocational				
White Collar	—	8.3	8.6	9.8
Craft	1.9	—	4.8	12.1
Industrial	—	—	10.4	8.2
Needle Trades	—	—	—	6.7
Secondary				
White Collar	50.0	33.3	29.3	21.3
Craft	13.5	18.7	46.8	53.5
Industrial	11.1	11.1	43.2	62.3
Needle Trades	33.3	53.8	46.2	33.3
Elementary				
White Collar	50.0	33.3	13.8	—
Craft	50.0	68.0	41.1	—
Industrial	44.4	66.7	36.0	1.6
Needle Trades	33.3	23.1	30.8	—
Self-Educated				
White Collar	—	8.3	—	—
Craft	23.1	10.7	—	1.0
Industrial	44.4	22.2	—	—
Needle Trades	33.3	15.4	—	—

Table 22
Union Type: Sociopolitical Variables, 1900–1976 (in Percentages)

Variable	1900	1925	1946	1976
CIVIC ACTIVITY INDEX				
High				
White Collar	25.0	33.3	21.6	19.1
Craft	38.9	20.0	14.3	20.1
Industrial	66.7	33.3	14.4	20.0
Needle Trades	40.0	20.0	31.6	52.6
Medium				
White Collar	75.0	20.0	33.9	33.9
Craft	40.7	37.5	28.6	28.9
Industrial	33.3	22.2	30.9	28.5
Needle Trades	60.0	40.0	26.3	15.8
Low				
White Collar	—	46.7	44.6	47.0
Craft	20.4	42.5	57.1	50.9
Industrial	—	44.4	54.9	51.4
Needle Trades	—	40.0	42.1	31.7
POLITICAL PREFERENCE				
Democrat				
White Collar	100.0	20.0	51.6	N/A
Craft	21.4	13.5	72.7	N/A
Industrial	16.7	—	80.8	N/A
Needle Trades	50.0	18.2	35.7	N/A
Republican				
White Collar	—	—	22.6	N/A
Craft	26.1	17.3	18.2	N/A
Industrial	33.3	—	5.5	N/A
Needle Trades	—	—	7.1	
Socialist				
White Collar	—	40.0	12.9	N/A
Craft	31.0	17.3	1.1	N/A
Industrial	50.0	33.3	5.5	N/A
Needle Trades	50.0	63.6	42.9	N/A
Progressive/Labor				
White Collar	—	30.0	—	
Craft	9.5	28.8	—	N/A
Industrial	—	16.7	—	N/A
Needle Trades	—	9.1	7.1	N/A
Nonpartisan				
White Collar	—	10.0	12.9	N/A
Craft	11.9	21.1	8.0	N/A
Industrial	—	50.0	8.2	N/A
Needle Trades	—	9.1	7.1	N/A

Table 22 (Continued)

Variable	1900	1925	1946	1976
RELIGIOUS PREFERENCE				
Protestant				
White Collar	—	N/A	59.5	N/A
Craft	33.3	N/A	64.4	N/A
Industrial	50.0	N/A	53.5	N/A
Needle Trades	20.0	N/A	21.4	N/A
Catholic				
White Collar	100.0	N/A	33.3	N/A
Craft	57.6	N/A	31.7	N/A
Industrial	50.0	N/A	40.4	N/A
Needle Trades	—	N/A	14.3	N/A
Jewish				
White Collar	—	N/A	7.1	N/A
Craft	6.1	N/A	—	N/A
Industrial	—	N/A	—	N/A
Needle Trades	80.0	N/A	64.3	
Other				
White Collar	—	N/A	—	N/A
Craft	3.0	N/A	3.8	N/A
Industrial	—	N/A	4.0	N/A
Needle Trades	—	N/A	—	N/A

BIOGRAPHIES

BIOGRAPHIES

A

ABEL, Iorwith Wilber (1908–). Born in Magnolia, Ohio, August 11, 1908; son of John, a blacksmith, and Mary Ann (Jones) Abel; Lutheran; married Bernice N. Joseph on June 27, 1930; three children; graduated from Magnolia (Ohio) High School and Canton Actual Business College; went to work as a molder in 1925; helped organize the first Congress of Industrial Organizations (CIO) local at Canton Timkin Roller Bearing in 1936 and served as its president; participated in the "Little Steel" strike of 1937; after serving as a union staff representative, elected director of the Canton District of the United Steelworkers of America (USWA) in 1942; served as a panel member on the War Labor Board during World War II; was an active member of the CIO Political Action Committee and the Ohio CIO Council; after the death of Philip Murray (q.v.) in 1952, elected secretary-treasurer of the USWA, succeeding David J. McDonald (q.v.) who became president; after loyally supporting McDonald for the next decade, became disturbed by his soft bargaining approach to the steel industry; aware of members' dissatisfaction with recent contracts that substituted fringe benefits for wage increases and ignored local issues, decided to challenge McDonald for the USWA presidency in 1965; unpretentious, a former steel-worker who had moved up through the union hierarchy, was an excellent candidate to run against an incumbent under fire for allegedly losing sight of rank-and-file interests; promising to revive militant bargaining, to seek a general wage increase, and to restore rank-and-file control over basic union policy, and with the backing of several key USWA district directors, won by a ten thousand-vote margin; elected an American Federation of Labor (AFL)-CIO vice-president and executive council member in 1965; was chosen president of the AFL-CIO industrial union department in 1968; as USWA president, tolerated dissent by staff and unfettered debate of controversial issues at conventions; encouraged greater participation by nonwhites in union affairs and in leadership positions, and acted to eliminate racial job discrimination in steel industry; presided over mergers of the International Union of Mine, Mill and Smelter Workers with District 50, Allied and Technical Workers; working through the USWA executive board beginning in 1967, sought a means of ending the boom-bust cycle created by stockpiling of steel in anticipation of steel strikes; instrumental in signing in March 1973, by the USWA and the basic steel firms of a milestone experimental negotiating agreement providing for binding arbitration of unresolved national contract issues, thus precluding industry-wide strikes for the life of the four-year agreement; appointed an alternate representative of the U.S. delegation to the United Nations in 1967; served on the National Advisory Commission on Civil Disorders; appointed to the pay board of the National Stabilization Program in 1971, but resigned in 1972 in protest against board policy; participated in several international labor conferences; a fervent Democrat; was close to the Lyndon B. Johnson administration and helped nominate Hubert H. Humphrey as Democratic presidential candidate in 1968, but refused to support Democratic presidential candidate Senator George S. McGovern in 1972; retired union positions in 1977; Lloyd Ulman, *The Government of the Steelworkers' Union* (1962); John Herling, *Right to Challenge: People and Power in the Steelworkers Union* (1972); *Who's Who in Labor* (1946); *Current Biography* (1965); Nelson Lichtenstein, ed., *Political Profiles: The Johnson Years* (1976); Eleanora W. Schoenebaum, ed., *Profiles of an Era: The Nixon-Ford Years* (1979); *Biography News*, November 1974.

Donald G. Sofchalk

ADDAMS, Jane   (1860–1935). Born in Cedarville, Ill., on September 6, 1860; daughter of John Huy, a prosperous miller, banker, and state senator, and Sarah (Weber) Addams; Presbyterian; never married; attended public schools and then enrolled in the Rockford (Ill.) Female Seminary in 1877, earning the B.A. degree in 1882; enrolled in the Woman's Medical College of Pennsylvania but poor health forced her withdrawal; toured Europe with her stepmother, 1883–1885; during 1885–1887, she lived in Baltimore, Md., where she attended lectures and engaged in sporadic charity work in black neighborhoods; returned to Europe in 1887 and during this trip an idea for a settlement house that had long intrigued her began to take shape, especially after a visit to Toynbee Hall in London in 1888; along with her traveling companion, Ellen Gates Starr, she rented a decaying mansion on the corner of Polk and Halsted streets in Chicago, Ill., and launched her famous Hull House experiment which by 1905 had become "the finest aggregation of buildings devoted to working-class education and recreation in the United States"; meanwhile, the investigation of tenement conditions, child labor, and sweatshops, which she had either participated in or inspired, led to the enactment of Illinois's first factory inspection act in 1893; her fervent support of the labor movement along with her concern for immigrant welfare, protective women and child labor reform, factory and occupational safety, and compulsory education sometimes alienated wealthy benefactors who provided much of the necessary financial support for Hull House programs; although labor reform, particularly for women and children, constituted her primary interest, she was involved in a great variety of other reformist causes; she was the first woman to be elected president of the National Conference on Charities and Correction in 1909; became the president of the National Federation of Settlements in 1911, a post she held until her death; served as first vice-president of the National American Woman Suffrage Association, 1911–1914; was one of the founders of the National Association for the Advancement of Colored People in 1909; attended the Budapest convention of the International Woman Suffrage Alliance in 1913; helped organize and was elected chairman of the Woman's Peace party in the United States in 1915 and later that same year was elected president of the International Congress of Women at The Hague; was the first president of the Women's International League for Peace and Freedom, 1919; was one of the founders of the American Civil Liberties Union in 1920; was a co-recipient of the Nobel Peace Prize in 1931; a labor reformer, a feminist, a pacifist, and a civil libertarian, her influence, by the 1920s, transcended national boundaries; only the Daughters of the American Revolution, the American Legion, and other right-wing organizations appeared immune to her appeal; a progressive who seconded Theodore Roosevelt's Progressive party nomination for president in 1912, she was a political independent who supported Herbert Hoover in 1928 and 1932; authored numerous books and articles including *Twenty Years at Hull-House* (1910) and *Second Twenty Years* (1935); died in Chicago on May 21, 1935; Jane Addams's Papers, Swarthmore College Peace Collection; *Notable American Women*, Vol. 1; *Dictionary of American Biography*, Vol. 21; Allen F. Davis, *Spearheads for Reform: The Social Settlements and the Progressive Movement, 1890–1914* (1967); John C. Farrell, *Beloved Lady: A History of Jane Addams' Ideas on Reform and Peace* (1967).

ADDES, George P. (1910–   ). Born in La Crosse, Wis., August 26, 1910; son of Nicholas, a maintenance worker, and Mary Addes; Roman Catholic; married Victoria Rose Joseph on September 16, 1933; completed two years of high school; secured employment with the Willys-Overland Company in Toledo, Ohio, in 1923; later completed one year at the Wayne University Law School; joined an American Federation of Labor federal labor union in Toledo in 1933, which shortly thereafter became a local of the United Automobile, Aircraft, and Agricultural Implement Workers of America (UAW) and soon elected financial secretary of the local; involved in the 1934 Auto-Lite strike and the 1935 Chevrolet strike in Toledo; elected secretary-treasurer of the UAW in 1936 and served in that capacity until 1947; served on the Congress of Industrial Organizations (CIO) executive board and was a member of the CIO Political Action Committee; during World War II, served as a special labor mediator for the National War Labor Board; was one of the principal leaders of the left-wing, Addes-Rolland J. Thomas (q.v.)-Richard Leonard (q.v.) faction of the UAW that was defeated by Walter P. Reuther's (q.v.) faction in the union elections of 1947; defeated for reelection as secretary–treasurer in 1947; left trade union activities and became a tavern operator; supported the Democratic party; Jack Stieber, *Governing the UAW* (1962); Frank Cormier and William J. Eaton, *Reuther* (1970); Jean Gould and Lorena Hickok, *Walter Reuther: Labor's Rugged Individualist* (1972); Sidney Fine, *The Automobile Under the Blue Eagle: Labor, Management, and the Automobile Manufacturing Code* (1963); Victor G. Reuther, *The Brothers Reuther and the Story of the UAW: A Memoir* (1976); George P. Addes Interview, Walter P. Reuther Library, Wayne State University; Roger Keeran, *The Communist Party and the Auto Workers Unions* (1980); Harvey A. Levenstein, *Communism, Anticommunism, and the CIO* (1981).

ALLEN, William L. (1896-1971). Born in Comnock, Ontario, Canada, April 17, 1896; son of Gerard, a teamster, and Mary (Cripps) Allen; married Ruth Delilah Smithburg on July 15, 1932; one child; left school in 1908 to begin a career as a telegrapher, starting as a messenger and shortly thereafter became a Morse operator; served with Canadian forces in France and Belgium during World War I; after the war, resumed his occupation as a telegrapher and joined the Canadian branch of the Commercial Telegraphers Union (CTU), which represented all Western Union employees except those in New York City; during the 1920s, opposed efforts of those CTU members on the Canadian National General Committee to disaffiliate with the CTU and form an independent union; became chairman of the Western District of the CTU's Canadian Division No. 43 in 1928, and in this capacity served as local chairman, organizer, and international representative in Canada; also elected international secretary-treasurer of the CTU in 1928, serving until 1941, when elected international president of the CTU; attended several American Federation of Labor (AFL) conventions and served as a delegate to the Trades and Labor Congress convention in Canada in 1928; was a member of the AFL committees on education, transportation, and postwar planning; led the CTU in strikes against United Press in 1950 and Western Union in 1952; served as the editor of the *Commercial Telegraphers Journal*, 1928–1941; retired from union positions in 1963; died in Sun City Center, Fla., October 26, 1971; Vidkunn Ulriksson, *The Telegraphers: Their Craft and Their Unions* (1953); *Current Biography* (1953); *Who's Who in Labor* (1946).

ALPINE, John P. (1868–1947). Born in Boston, Mass., ca. 1868; Roman Catholic; married; three children; attended the public schools of Boston and served a trade apprenticeship, eventually joining Boston Gas Fitters' Union Local 175 of the United Association of Plumbers and Steam Fitters of the United States and Canada (UA); after serving Local 175 in several capacities, including that of president, and after being president of the Building Trades Council of Boston and Vicinity for several years, became a member of the general executive board of the UA and, in 1904, was elected a vice-president, representing gas fitters; served as a special UA organizer, 1904–1906; in a close election, was selected as international president of the UA in 1906; as president, noted for the vigorous and effective introduction and administration of a radically new system of internal union government that had been drawn up shortly before his election, the strengthening of the union's organizing staff, and substantial gains in membership; was elected an American Federation of Labor vice-president and executive council member in 1908; was a member of the board of governors of the American Construction Council, presided over by Franklin D. Roosevelt; during World War I, served with Secretary of War Newton D. Baker on a commission that supervised labor relations at cantonments and aviation fields, with Assistant Secretary of Navy Franklin D. Roosevelt on a commission that oversaw labor relations at naval operations on shore, and with the War Policies Board as a labor advisor; served as a labor advisor to the American delegation to the Paris Peace Conference in 1919; resigned union positions in 1919 to become an assistant to the president of the Grinell Company, Inc., a manufacturer of automatic sprinklers, and in 1920 also became chairman of the labor relations committee of the National Automatic Sprinkler and Fire Control Association; appointed as a special assistant to the Secretary of Labor in 1931 and placed in charge of the Federal Employment Service; attempted, with limited success, to find employment for the growing numbers of unemployed; politically a Republican; died in New York City, April 21, 1947; Martin Segal, *The Rise of the United Association: National Unionism in the Pipe Trades, 1884–1924* (1970); Philip Taft, *The A.F. of L. in the Time of Gompers* (1957); *The New York Times*, April 22, 1947.

AMERINGER, Oscar   (1870–1943). Born in Achstetten, Germany, on August 4, 1870; the son of a cabinet maker, he attended Catholic parochial schools in Germany for seven years after which he became an apprentice in his father's shop; although raised a Roman Catholic, he later became a member of the Unitarian church; married Lulu Wood in 1903 and, after the failure of that marriage, Freda Hogan, the daughter of an Arkansas Socialist, in 1930; three children (first marriage); emigrated to the United States in 1886; went first to Cincinnati, Ohio, where he secured work as a cabinet maker and almost immediately joined a mixed assembly of the Knights of Labor; became a Knights of Labor organizer shortly thereafter and soon lost his job as a result; traveled extensively around the United States while performing as a musician, 1887–1890; returned to Germany in 1890 and stayed there for five years studying art at Munich; after returning to the United States in 1896, he resumed his music career and, in 1903, joined the American Federation of Musicians; founded and/or worked as editor of several labor newspapers, including *The Labor World*, 1904–1906, the *National Rip Saw*, 1904–1912, the *Oklahoma Pioneer*, 1907–1909, the *Oklahoma Leader*, 1920–1924, and the *Milwaukee Leader*, 1917–1919; actively involved in Socialist affairs from his arrival in the United States, he went to Milwaukee, Wis., in 1910, where he worked in Victor Berger's (q.v.) successful campaign for the U.S. Congress; thereafter, he became a Socialist state organizer and later Milwaukee County organizer; was an unsuccessful Socialist candidate for governor of Wisconsin in 1912 and for the U.S. Congress from Wisconsin's 2nd District in 1918; edited the *Illinois Miner* during the 1920s; one of the most remarkable labor newspapers ever published in the United States, the *Illinois Miner* was sponsored by rebellious District 12 of the United Mine Workers of America; was involved in the anti-John L. Lewis (q.v.) Reorganized United Mine Workers Union during the late 1920s; remained active in Socialist and trade union affairs during the turbulent 1930s; one of the best Socialist editors in the United States, his colorful writing style and the absence of the stultifying jargon that marred the writing of so many Marxist editors attracted a large readership in and out of the Socialist movement; authored the autobiographical *If You Don't Weaken* (1940), and *Socialism, What It Is and How to Get It* (1930); died in Oklahoma City, Okla., on November 5, 1943; *Dictionary of American Biography,* Suppl. 3; *Dictionary of Wisconsin Biography* (1960); Solon DeLeon, ed., *American Labor Who's Who* (1925); Sally M. Miller, *Victor Berger and the Promise of Constructive Socialism, 1910–1920* (1973); McAlister Coleman, *Men and Coal* (1943); Donald D. Egbert and Stow Persons, eds., *Socialism in American Life* (1952); Oscar Ameringer Papers, Walter P. Reuther Library, Wayne State University; Philip S. Foner, *American Socialism and Black Americans from the Age of Jackson to World War II* (1977).

ANDERSON, Mary   (1872–1964). Born in Lidköping, Sweden, August 27, 1872; daughter of Magnus, a farmer, and Matilda Anderson; Lutheran; received a grammar school education in Sweden prior to emigrating to the United States in 1889; secured her first job in the United States as a dishwasher at a Michigan lumber camp; after holding various jobs, found employment around 1891 as a stitcher in a West Pullman, Ill., shoe factory; in 1894 joined the International Boot and Shoe Workers' Union (BSWU), while working for Schwab's in Chicago, Ill.; served as president of Stitchers Local 94, 1895–1910; was the only woman on the BSWU executive board for 11 years; served as the BSWU delegate to the Chicago Federation of Labor; joined the Chicago Women's Trade Union League (WTUL) about 1903; quit factory work in 1910 to become the Chicago WTUL representative to the United Garment Workers Union; during 1910–1913 served as an investigator to ensure that the agreement ending the Hart, Schaffner, and Marx strike of 1910 was carried out; while associated with the Chicago WTUL, served as a delegate to the Union Label League; was an organizer for the national WTUL, 1913–1920; participated in investigations of the 1913 copper miners' strike in Calumet, Mich., and the 1916 spar miners' strike in Rosiclare, Ill.; began a government career in 1916 when appointed assistant director of the Women in Industry Service of the U.S. Department of Labor and replaced Mary Van Kleeck (q.v.) as director in 1919; served in the Women in Industry Section of the Advisory Committee of the Council of National Defense and on the Women in Industry Section of the Ordnance Department during World War I; was director of the permanent Women's Bureau of the U.S. Department of Labor, 1920–1944; as a WTUL delegate, attended the labor conferences of the 1919 Paris Peace Conference, the 1919 First International Congress of Working Women in Washington, D.C., the 1923 Third International Congress of Working Women in Vienna, and the 1928 Pan-Pacific Union Conference in Honolulu, Hawaii;

was the unofficial United States delegate to the 1931 International Labor Organization Conference in Geneva; appointed by President Franklin D. Roosevelt as an advisor to the U.S. delegation to the Technical Tripartite Conference on the Textile Industry; retired official positions in 1944; authored *Woman at Work: The Autobiography of Mary Anderson as told to Mary N. Winslow* (1951); died in Washington, D.C., January 30, 1964; Mary Anderson Papers, Schlesinger Library, Radcliffe College; Gladys Boone, *The Women's Trade Union Leagues in Great Britain and the United States* (1942); *AFL-CIO News*, February 8, 1964; *Current Biography* (1940); G. M. Horne, "Mary Anderson and the Development of Protective Legislation for Women in the United States, 1890–1938" (Ph.D. diss., 1972); *Notable American Women*, Vol. 4; Philip S. Foner, *Women and the American Labor Movement from World War I to the Present* (1980).

Marie Tedesco

ANDREWS, Emmet Charles (1916–1981). Born in San Francisco, Calif., on August 3, 1916; son of Lincoln and Ada (Tiernan) Andrews; married Elizabeth Lucille Byrne on April 8, 1938; one child; after completing an elementary and secondary school education in the public schools of San Francisco, he became a clerk for the U.S. Post Office in San Francisco in 1936 and joined Local 2 of the National Federation of Postal Clerks; served as secretary and then president of Local 2, 1938–1955, before being appointed a national vice-president for the San Francisco region in 1955; was elected a full-time vice-president in 1962; moved to national union headquarters in Washington, D.C., in 1966 after being elected an executive aid; became administrative aid of the clerk craft in 1971 following the merger of postal unions creating the American Postal Workers Union (APWU); was elected APWU industrial relations director in 1972; re-elected to this position in 1974 and 1976, he represented the APWU in grievance and equal opportunity cases before the Civil Service Commission and served on the union's negotiating committee; was appointed by the executive board to fill the unexpired term of APWU president Francis Filbey (q.v.) who died in 1977; was elected to a full two-year term in 1978; negotiated a new contract with the U.S. government in 1978, thus avoiding a strike and a looming confrontation with the federal government; was elected an American Federation of Labor-Congress of Industrial Organizations (AFL-CIO) vice-president and member of the executive council in 1978; defeated for reelection in 1980, in part because of unhappiness over the 1978 contract; he resigned from the AFL-CIO executive council in 1981; a Democrat; died in Walnut Creek, Calif., on November 11, 1981; *The New York Times*, November 12, 1981; *AFL-CIO News*, May 28, 1977; *Who's Who in America, 1980–1981*.

ANTONINI, LUIGI (1883–1968). Born in Vallata Irpina, Avellino, Italy, September 11, 1883; son of Pietro Valeriano, a school teacher, and Maria Francesca (Netta) Antonini; Roman Catholic; married Jennie Costanzo on October 24, 1909; graduated from secondary school in Tortona, Italy, then served as a sergeant in the Italian Army for four years; emigrated to the United States in 1908 and worked in a New York cigar factory for two years; worked in a piano factory, 1910–1912; became a dress presser in 1913 and joined the International Ladies' Garment Workers' Union (ILGWU); was one of the founders and initial executive board members of the Italian Chamber of Labor in 1913; became an organizer for ILGWU Local 25 in 1916; was instrumental in the organization of Italian Dressmakers Local 89, ILGWU, and served as its general secretary; one of the founders and vice-chairman of the Anti-Fascisti Alliance in 1922; during the controversy over organizing strategy in the mid-1930s, favored industrial organization and supported the efforts of ILGWU president David Dubinsky (q.v.) to mediate the conflict between the American Federation of Labor (AFL) and the Congress of Industrial Organizations (CIO); was elected president of the Italian-American Labor Council in 1941; served on a variety of public and private boards and agencies during World War II; following the war, served on the AFL delegation appointed to investigate the rebuilding of the Italian labor movement and to reestablish Italian-American labor relations; was first vice-president of the ILGWU, 1934–1967; was chairman of the American Labor party, 1936–1942, and was one of the founders of the Liberal party of New York in 1944; was a long-time editor of *L'Operaia*, an Italian-language magazine sponsored by Local 25; retired from union activities in 1968; died in New York City, December 29, 1968; John Stuart Crawford, *Luigi Antonini: His Influence on Italian American Relations* (1950); Benjamin Stolberg, *Tailor's Progress: The Story of a Famous Union and the Men Who Made It* (1944); Louis Levine, *The Women's Garment Workers: A History of the International Ladies' Garment Workers' Union* (1924); *ILGWU Report and Proceedings* (1971).

ARONS, Milton   (1917–1977). Born in Newark, N.J., on January 3, 1917; son of Max and Hannah Arons, both garment workers; divorced; after graduating from high school, he attended night classes at New York University before becoming involved in union affairs; served as an organizer for the International Union of Mine, Mill and Smelter Workers, the International Fur and Leather Workers Union, the United Steelworkers of America, and the Amalgamated Clothing Workers of America (ACWA), 1933–1943; served with the U.S. Maritime Service during World War II, 1943–1946; joined the ACWA in 1946 as a senior administrative assistant; served as a labor consultant to the Special Technical Assistance Mission to Denmark, 1951, and Norway, 1952, for the U.S. Economic Cooperation Administration; was appointed director of organization for the Community and Social Agency Employees Union in 1952, serving until being appointed administrative director of the Amalgamated Laundry Workers Health Center in New York City in 1954; became administrative director of the Union Health Center, International Ladies' Garment Workers' Union (ILGWU), in 1961; the Union Health Center, established in 1914, provides health services to the members of 27 ILGWU affiliates, including diagnostic and therapeutic care in most specialties, and has a staff of two hundred employees and an annual budget of $2 million; was also active in a variety of public health groups, serving as a consultant to the Albert Einstein College of Medicine and as a member of the steering committee of the New York City Comprehensive Health Planning Agency; was a founder of the Group Health Association of America in 1959 and from 1954 to 1959 served as a trustee of the American Labor Health Association; died in New York City on June 23, 1977; *Who's Who in Labor* (1976); *The New York Times*, June 24, 1977.

ARTHUR, Peter M. (1831–1903). Born in Paisley, Scotland, in 1831; emigrated to the United States in 1842; settled in New York state, working there on an uncle's farm; received little formal education; bought a horse while still a teenager and began an unsuccessful carting business in Schenectady, N.Y.; became an engine wiper in 1849 on a line which was soon incorporated into the New York Central Railroad; soon thereafter became a locomotive engineer; was a charter member of the Brotherhood of Locomotive Engineers (BLE) in 1863; elected grand chief engineer in 1874 and held this office until his death; was a conservative trade unionist who believed in the mutuality of interests between labor and capital; seldom called strikes, preferring to resolve disputes through conciliation and arbitration; while president, converted BLE from a largely benevolent and insurance society to an economic-oriented trade union; as grand chief engineer, staunchly defended the independence of the BLE and refused to affiliate with such organizations as the Knights of Labor, the American Federation of Labor, or the American Railroad Union; acquired considerable wealth through successful real-estate speculations in Cleveland; was an associate editor of *The Labor Movement: The Problem of Today* (1887); died in Winnipeg, Canada, July 17, 1903; Reed C. Richardson, *The Locomotive Engineer, 1863–1963: A Century of Railway Labor Relations and Work Rules* (1963); *Dictionary of American Biography*, Vol. 1; *Encyclopedia of Social Sciences*, Vol. 2.

ARYWITZ, Sigmund (1914–1975). Born in Buffalo, N.Y., in 1914; married; completed his elementary and secondary schooling in Buffalo and then enrolled in New York State Teachers College at Buffalo, also attended the University of Buffalo and City College of New York; while attending college, he worked at various odd jobs, including a butcher shop and a sportswriter for the *Buffalo Evening News*; served with the U.S. Army Medical Corps during World War II; after the war, he joined the International Ladies' Garment Workers' Union (ILGWU) and in 1947 was placed on the international staff as an organizer; moved to California and was appointed West Coast director of education for the ILGWU, a position he held for 15 years; led the campaign to defeat a state right-to-work referendum in 1958; was appointed California state labor commissioner by California governor Edmund G. Brown, Sr., in 1959, serving until 1967; was elected executive secretary-treasurer of the Los Angeles County American Federation of Labor-Congress of Industrial Organizations (AFL-CIO) in 1967; was a strong supporter of the organizing efforts of the United Farm Workers in

California vineyards and lettuce fields; as head of the Los Angeles AFL-CIO, he was especially active in promoting programs for senior citizens, women's rights, occupational safety, ecology, and energy conservation; was also an avid supporter of cultural arts programs; a Democrat; died in Los Angeles on September 9, 1975; *AFL-CIO News*, September 13, 1975; *The New York Times*, September 10, 1975.

AZPEITIA, Mario (1899–   ). Born in Key West, Fla., November 22, 1899; son of Armando H. and Andrea (Esquinaldo) Azpeitia; Roman Catholic; married Rosalia Ciccarello on October 30, 1967; five children; attended San Carlos School in Key West, then eventually took a job in the cigar-making industry; joined Local 500 of the Cigarmakers' International Union (CMIU) in 1935; elected general secretary of Local 500 in 1941, serving in that capacity until 1949; elected international president of the CMIU in 1949, beginning a long and continuing term of service in that position; represented the CMIU at the annual conventions of the American Federation of Labor (AFL), 1949–1955, and the AFL-Congress of Industrial Organizations (CIO) since 1955; served on numerous AFL and AFL-CIO committees; a member of the Florida State Society in Washington, D.C., and Centro Español and Circulo Cubano in Tampa, Fla.; *Who's Who in America, 1958–1959.*

Merl E. Reed

B

BACON, Emery F.   (1909–   ). Born in Indianapolis, Ind., May 1, 1909; son of Frank, an attorney, and Laura (Claason) Bacon; Presbyterian; married Helen Hotham in 1936; two children; attended Wooster College for a short time and later received a B.A. (1931) and an M.A. (1942) from the University of Pittsburgh; became a reporter for the McKeesport (Pa.) *Daily News* after receiving the B.A.; was a junior executive in business for a while during the early 1930s; became associated with the labor movement as a volunteer organizer for the Amalgamated Association of Iron, Steel, and Tin Workers during 1934–1935; became business manager and head of the classics department at a private Pennsylvania preparatory school in 1939, and saved it from bankruptcy; was a delegate at the founding convention of the United Steelworkers of America (USWA) in 1942; one of several intellectuals in the USWA and had a reputation of being a "practical realist"; was selected to head a program of worker education begun by USWA president Philip Murray (q.v.); in 1945 launched the union's pioneering Summer Labor Institutes for local union officers and rank-and-file members at regular colleges and universities; started at the Pennsylvania State University, by the 1950s the program was regularly held every summer at from 20 to 30 campuses across the United States and in Canada, offering sessions in labor history, economics, collective bargaining, and current issues like poverty and automation; guided start in 1962 of a 12-week resident program at a few state universities offering steelworkers credit courses; believed that the institutes offered participants a means of increasing their ability to deal with "bread and butter" union matters and of participating more effectively in wider community affairs; was instrumental in initiating, in 1947, the USWA's highly successful scholarship program for the sons and daughters of steelworkers; union districts and larger locals provided an increasing number of scholarships, awarded on a competitive basis, for attendance at any accredited college or university; by 1961 a total of $700,000 in scholarships had been awarded; resigned as education director in 1964 to accept the post of assistant to the president of West Virginia University; a Democrat; ran unsuccessfully for Congress from Pennsylvania's

27th Congressional District; Lloyd Ulman, *The Government of the Steelworkers' Union* (1962); *Steel Labor* (May 1961, April 1965).

Donald G. Sofchalk

BAER, Fred William   (1884–1946). Born in Kansas City, Mo., August 16, 1884; son of William Henry, a superintendent in a factory school, and Jenny Louise Baer; married Grace Marie Morgan on August 5, 1930; completed grammar school, then joined a fire fighters' survey group in Sonora, Calif.; joined the Kansas City Fire Department in 1907 and became a driver of the first motorized vehicle used in Kansas City; became a fire department lieutenant in 1917; retired from active service in 1919; organized Kansas City firemen into an American Federation of Labor (AFL) federal labor union in 1917 and was elected president of the federal local; participated in the organizational convention of the International Association of Fire Fighters (IAFF) called by AFL president Samuel Gompers (q.v.) in 1918; served as president of Kansas City Local 42 of the IAFF, 1918–1919; elected a vice-president in charge of the IAFF's third district in 1918; elected international president of the IAFF in 1919, serving in that capacity until 1946; was actively involved in the organization of fire fighters in cities throughout the United States and in the campaign for an eight-hour day for firemen; was credited with building the IAFF from an infant organization in 1919 to a mature trade union with a membership of 40,000 fire fighters in 1945; politically a Democrat; edited *The Fire Fighter* for several years beginning in 1919; died in Topeka, Kans., May 15, 1946; James J. Gibbons, *The International Association of Fire Fighters* (1944); *The American Federationist* (June 1946); *The New York Times*, May 17, 1946; *Who's Who in Labor* (1946).

BAER, John Miller   (1886–1970). Born in Black Creek, Wis., on March 29, 1886; son of John Mason, a homesteader and postmaster, and Elizabeth Caroline (Riley) Baer, a national vice-president of the Women's Relief Corps; Congregationalist; married Estelle G. Kennedy on December 28, 1910; three children; B.A., Lawrence University, Appleton, Wis., 1909; Federal School of Art, Minneapolis, Minn., and National School of Art, Washington, D.C.: track worker and civil engineer for the Northern Pacific Railroad, 1909–1910; settled in Beach, N.D., where he engaged in business and agricultural activities, 1910–1915; was city engineer and served as postmaster from 1913 to 1915; at the same time he cartooned for farm papers and humor magazines such as *Jim Jam Jems*; moved to Fargo, N.D., in 1916, where he became publicity director for the Nonpartisan League (NPL), a strong farm political protest movement that began in North Dakota and spread into 13 midwestern and western states; his cartoons and editorial writing appeared in the *Nonpartisan Leader*, the official NPL newspaper, and the *Fargo Courier-News*, a farm weekly; in 1917 Baer was drafted by the league to run for the U.S. Congress from North Dakota when a vacancy occurred; elected at age 31, he was the youngest member of Congress; reelected as a progressive Republican in 1918; in 1920 he lost the congressional race, but his work as the "Congressman-cartoonist" had already begun; in 1921 he permanently joined the staff of *Labor*, the organ of the railroad unions, where his career spanned 50 years; known as the "dean of labor cartoonists," he produced over fifteen thousand cartoons for *Labor*, the NPL *Leader*, and other publications including the Hearst papers edited by Arthur Brisbane; a crusader for the cooperative efforts of farmers and laborers, Baer claimed birth of the caricature, "Big Biz"; his sharp-witted cartoons and journalistic efforts had broad impact; one early 1931 cartoon, showing farmers and workers demanding a "New Deal," helped later to popularize the Roosevelt program; another, in 1920, labelled the "Appropriation Pie," illustrating how over 90 percent of the federal budget went for past and future wars, was one of the most widely reproduced cartoons ever published; from 1935, he served for many years as publicity director of the American Federation of Labor (AFL) and later the AFL-Congress of Industrial Organizations (CIO) union label trades department where he used his talents as cartoonist and writer to promote union products and services; he also designed many labor and nonlabor symbols and trademarks, including the revised official seal of the AFL-CIO, the first United Nations emblem, and the Pan American World Airways symbol; the huge symbol of clasped hands on the lobby floor of the AFL-CIO headquarters building in Washington, D.C., is Baer's design; a colorful personality, he was well known in Washington political and congressional circles; he contributed over 300 cartoons free for liberal congressional candidates over the years; registered as a Democrat in 1960; member of the National Press Club; authored his "Baerfacts" column, a feature used for many years by the International Labor Press Association; died in Washington, D.C., on February 18, 1970; *Biographical Directory of the American Congress, 1774–1971* (1971); Robert L. Morlan, *Political Prairie Fire: The Nonpartisan League, 1915–1922* (1955); Bill G. Reid, "John Miller Baer: Nonpartisan League Cartoonist and Congressman," *North Dakota History* (Winter 1977); *Electrical Workers Journal* (January 1967); *Labor,* March 7, 1970; Solon DeLeon, ed., *The American Labor Who's Who* (1925).

Bruce L. Larson

BAGLEY, Sarah G.   (fl. 1806–1847). Born in Candia, N.H., on April 29, 1806; daughter of Nathan, a farmer and businessman, and Rhoda (Witham) Bagley; secured employment in 1837 as an operative in a Hamilton Manufacturing Company cotton mill in Lowell, Mass., in 1844, organized the Lowell Female Labor Reform Association (LFLRA), an auxiliary of the New England Workingmen's Association; led the campaign to collect 2,000 signatures on a petition to a Massachusetts legislative committee investigating wages, working conditions, and worker demands for a ten-hour day; appeared before the committee as a witness for the workers in 1845; actively involved in the organization of female workers in the mills of Dover, Nashua, and Manchester, N.H., and Waltham and Fall River, Mass.; criticized factory owners and the management-oriented mill-girls' magazine, the *Lowell Offering*, in a series entitled *Factory*

Tracts, published in 1845; was a LFLRA delegate to three New England Work-ingmen's Association conventions in 1845 and served as corresponding secretary; was one of the founders of the Lowell Industrial Reform Lyceum; served on the LFLRA's publication committee; later was a frequent contributor and, for a short time, the chief editor of the *Voice of Industry* after the LFLRA acquired it from the Workingmen's Association in 1846; in 1846, was a delegate to the National Industrial Congress in Boston and the National Reform Convention in Worcester; developed an interest in utopian social philosophies, particularly those of Charles Fourier and George Ripley, and was elected vice-president of the Lowell Union of Associationists; replaced as president of the LFLRA by Mary Emerson in 1847 and appointed superintendent of the Lowell Telegraph Office, becoming the country's first female telegraph operator; returned to the mills briefly in 1848 and thereafter little is known about her later life; John Andrews and W.D.P. Bliss, "History of Women in Trade Unions," *Report on Conditions of Woman and Child Wage-Earners in the United States*, Vol. 10 (1911); *Notable American Women,* Vol. 1; Madeleine B. Stern, *We the Women* (1962); Eleanor Flexner, *Century of Struggle: The Women's Rights Movement in the U.S.* (1959); Hannah Josephson, *The Golden Threads: New England's Mill Girls–and Magnates* (1949); Thomas Dublin, *Women at Work: The Transformation of Work and Community in Lowell, Massachusetts, 1826–1860* (1979); Helena Wright, "Sarah G. Bagley: A Biographical Note," *Labor History* (Summer 1979); Philip S. Foner, *Women and the American Labor Movement from Colonial Times to the Eve of World War I* (1979).

BAKER, E.R.P.   (fl. 1844–1874). Born in Fairfield County, Ohio, on February 1, 1834; spent much of his early life on a farm where he labored during the summer while working in saw mills during the winter months; although having few opportunities for formal education, he was a voracious reader who at age 12 was admitted to Otterview University in Westerville, Ohio; forced to leave the university after one term because of poor health, he later enrolled at Ohio State University and then Union Law School in Poland, Ohio; moved to Cleveland, Ohio, in 1857, and there was admitted to the bar in the states of Ohio and Indiana; moved to Lancaster, Ohio, in 1858, where he purchased a farm and became a farmer; opened a drug store in Thomasville somewhat later while still involved in farming; was the Democratic nominee for a seat in the state legislature in 1873 and was subsequently elected; although never directly connected with the trade union movement, he was an energetic champion of the working class in the state legislature and received the enthusiastic political support of workers; introduced mine safety legislation in the Ohio legislature and, despite the vigorous opposition of the coal operator's lobby, successfully guided it through the legislative process; succeeded in having Andrew Roy (q.v.) named inspector of mines under the new legislation; supported the principles identified in the preamble and platform of the Industrial Congress and was the workingmen's candidate for Ohio secretary of state in 1874; Chicago *Workingman's Advocate*, May 2, 1974.

BALDANZI, George   (1907–1972). Born in Black Diamond, Pa., January 23, 1907; son of Natale, a miner and blacksmith, and Clelia (Rutilli) Baldanzi; married Lena Parenti on February 25, 1932; one child; completed grammar school, then began working in the Pennsylvania coal fields; eventually secured employment as a textile dyer in Paterson, N.J.; organized and became the first president, 1933–1936, of the Federation of Dyers, Finishers, Printers, and Bleachers of America, a subfederation of the United Textile Workers of America (UTW); was one of the principal UTW advocates of affiliation with the Congress of Industrial Organizations (CIO); associated with the UTW-Textile Workers Organizing Committee (TWOC) campaigns in the late 1930s; became president of the UTW-TWOC in 1938; after the UTW-TWOC was reorganized into the Textile Workers Union of America (TWU) in 1939, was elected executive vice-president, serving until 1952; was a member of the CIO executive board and was the CIO representative on a five-member labor delegation visiting Italy in 1944; served as the chairman of the committee on constitution which, during the CIO's Eleventh Constitutional Convention, held in 1949, sponsored successful resolutions requiring officials of CIO unions to take non-Communist oaths; disillusioned with the failures of the TWU to organize the textile workers of the South; therefore, challenged President Emil Reive (q.v.) for the TWU presidency in 1952, but lost; relieved of international offices after his defeat, and eventually led a small group of textile workers back into the American Federation of Labor; served as director of organization for the UTW, 1952–1953; was a regional director of the Eastern Conference of Teamsters, International Brotherhood of Teamsters, 1953–1955; elected international president of the UTW, and a vice-president of the United Italian-American Labor Council in 1958; appointed a member of the U.S. Secretary of Commerce's Textile Advisory Committee in 1959; named chairman of the Passaic County (N.J.) Area Redevelopment Board in 1963; died in Hawthorne, N.J., April 22, 1972; Walter Galenson, *The CIO Challenge to the AFL: A History of the American Labor Movement, 1935–1941* (1960); Herbert J. Lahne, *The Cotton Mill Workers* (1944); *Who's Who in Labor* (1946); *National Cyclopaedia of American Biography*, Vol. 60.

BARKAN, Alexander Elias   (1909–   ). Born in Bayonne, N.J., August 8, 1909; son of Jacob and Rachel (Perelmen) Barkan; married Helen Stickno, a Textile Workers Union of America (TWU) organizer, on May 10, 1942; two children; was graduated from the University of Chicago in 1933 and then taught high school in Bayonne, N.J., until 1937; joined the Congress of Industrial Organizations' (CIO) Textile Workers Organizing Committee in 1937; became an organizer for the TWU in 1938 and served as a subregional director, 1938–1942; served with the U.S. Navy during World War II, 1942–1945; became veterans' director of the CIO community service committee in 1945; elected executive director of the New Jersey CIO Council in 1946; became political action director of the TWU in 1948, serving in that capacity until 1955; appointed assistant director of the American Federation of Labor (AFL)-CIO Committee on Political Education (COPE) in 1955 and deputy director in 1957; became the director of COPE after the death of James L. McDevitt (q.v.) in 1963, and directed its highly successful efforts during the 1964 national elections; was dispatched by AFL-CIO president George Meany (q.v.) to work full-time for Hubert Humphrey's nomination as the Democratic party presidential candidate in 1968; a quiet, unostentatious administrator; created a computerized voter registration information bank during his directorship of COPE and made an effort to expand COPE's activities and influence in suburban areas; identifies himself as nonpartisan, but usually supports liberal Democratic candidates for public office; Terry Catchpole, *How to Cope with COPE: The Political Operations of Organized Labor* (1968); Joseph C. Goulden, *Meany* (1972); *The American Federationist* (April 1957); *AFL-CIO News*, August 17, 1963.

BARKER, Mary Cornelia   (1879–1963). Born in Atlanta, Ga., on January 20, 1879; daughter of Thomas Nathaniel, a teacher, and Dora Elizabeth (Lovejoy) Barker, a teacher; Methodist; never married; attended public schools in Rockmart, Ga., before enrolling in Agnes Scott Institute, Decatur, Ga., in 1894; graduated in 1900 and accepted a one-year appointment as a teacher in Stockbridge, Ga.; a year later she completed a similar one-year appointment in McDonough, Ga., before spending two years at the Decatur Orphans Home; accepted a job with the Atlanta public school system in 1904 and remained a classroom teacher until 1922 when she became principal of the Ivey Street School; one year later, she was appointed principal of John B. Gordon School, a position she held until 1944; was a founding member of the Atlanta Public School Teachers' Association in 1905; was influential in the association's decision to affiliate with the American Federation of Teachers (AFT) in 1919, becoming Local 89; was one of five Local 89 delegates to the Atlanta Federation of Trades, the American Federation of Labor's city central body; was elected president of Local 89 in 1921, serving in that capacity until 1923; during her two years as president of Local 89, she continued to press for salary increases, a tenure law, and continuing education for teachers; vigorously supported the AFT's campaign for a child labor amendment to the U.S. Constitution; served as a Local 89 representative to the national AFT convention in 1923 and two years later was elected national president; inheriting an organization confronting both internal conflicts and external challenges, she restored a sense of order and unity during her six-year presidency and reversed a declining membership that had seriously weakened the AFT during the early 1920s; during her presidency, the AFT also adopted a legislative program, including smaller classes, improved compensation, improved classroom facilities, the abolition of "factory standards" of production for schools, and increased academic freedom for teachers; along with her concern for teachers, she also maintained a long-term interest in the welfare of southern working women and became a member of the organizing committee of the Southern Summer School for Women Workers in Industry in 1926; chaired the school's central committee from 1927 to 1944; an influential leader in Atlanta's biracial movement, she was a member of the Atlanta Urban League, the Committee on Interracial Cooperation, and the American Civil Liberties Union; meanwhile, she encouraged black teachers to form their own union and agitate for an equal salary schedule with white teachers; an active civil libertarian, among other causes, she became active in the campaign to free Angelo Herdon, a black Communist convicted under Atlanta's 1866 insurrection law; wrote numerous articles, including "The Public-School Teachers Awakes," *The Labor World*, May 1, 1931; poor health forced her to retire from most formal activities in 1944 although she retained an active interest in social causes until her death in Atlanta on September 15, 1963; Mary C. Barker Papers, Emory University, Special Collections; Joseph W. Newman, "A History of the Atlanta Public School Teachers' Association, Local 89 of the American Federation of Teachers, 1919–1956" (Ph.D. diss., 1978); Wayne J. Urban, "Organized Teachers and Educational Reform during the Progressive Era," *History of Education Quarterly* (Spring 1976); William E. Eaton, *The American Federation of Teachers, 1916–1961* (1975); *Notable American Women*, Vol. 4; Joseph W. Newman, "Mary C. Barker and the Atlanta Teachers' Union," in Merl E. Reed et al., *Southern Workers and Their Unions, 1880–1975* (1981).

BARNES, John Mahlon   (1866–1934). Born in Lancaster, Pa., June 22, 1866; the son of a bootmaker; was orphaned at an early age and resided at the Soldiers' Orphan School in Mt. Joy, Pa., 1875–1882; took Chautauqua correspondence courses, 1883–1885; joined the Knights of Labor in 1884; maintained his membership until 1887 and then joined the Cigarmakers' International Union (CMIU); served as secretary to numerous CMIU locals, 1887–1922; joined the Socialist Labor party in 1891 and in 1899 switched to the Socialist party; served as national secretary, 1906, campaign director, 1912, and wrote the Socialist party platform in 1917; favored industrial unionism, the Socialist platform, and an independent labor party and was a constant critic and antagonist of Samuel Gompers (q.v.); was instrumental in defeating Gompers's bid for reelection as president of the American Federation of Labor (AFL) in 1894; ran against Gompers at the 1896 CMIU convention for election as AFL delegate, but withdrew before election; at 1904 AFL convention introduced an unsuccessful amendment to the AFL constitution that would have prohibited a lobbying committee on the grounds that both national parties served as "tools of the capitalist class" and that lobbying produced poor results; was elected national secretary of the CMIU in 1905, serving until 1911; sponsored an unsuccessful anti-Gompers resolution at a CMIU convention that would have denied union membership to anyone holding membership in the National Civic Federation, a resolution protesting the arrest of Mexican anarchists in Los Angeles in 1907, which led the AFL executive council to demand a congressional investigation and to appeal for justice to President William H. Taft; unsuccessfully opposed Gompers's proposed American Alliance for Labor and Democracy at the 1917 AFL convention; became the director of the American Freedom Foundation after it was organized in 1919; served as business manager of *New Day*, 1920–1921; died in Washington, D.C., in 1934; Solon DeLeon, ed., *The American Labor Who's Who* (1925); Samuel Gompers, *Seventy Years of Life and Labor: An Autobiography* (1925); Philip Taft, *The A.F. of L. in the Time of Gompers* (1957); Bernard Mandel, *Samuel Gompers: A Biography* (1963).

Merl E. Reed

BARNUM, Gertrude   (1866–1948). Born in Chester, Ill., September 29, 1866; daughter of William J., an attorney and circuit court judge, and Clara Letitia (Hyde) Barnum; attended Chicago grammar schools and Evanston (Ill.) Township High School, then the University of Wisconsin, 1891–1892; served as a social worker in Chicago's Hull House, ca. 1889–1896; was chief social worker at Henry Booth House, Chicago, 1902–1903; joined the National Women's Trade Union League (WTUL) in 1903 and served as national secretary, 1903–1904; was a WTUL national organizer, 1903–1913; directed several strikes in 1905, including the Fall River, Mass., strike of female textile operatives, the corset workers' strike in Aurora, Ill., and the laundry workers' strike in Troy, N.Y.; served as an arbitrator and agent for the International Ladies' Garment Workers' Union (ILGWU), 1911–1916; toured the Middle West for the ILGWU during the 1911 Cleveland garment workers' strike in an unsuccessful effort to persuade wholesale and retail merchants to boycott Cleveland goods; helped direct an ILGWU strike in Boston and publicized and solicited funds for the New York white-goods workers' strike during 1913; was a special agent for President Woodrow Wilson's U.S. Commission on Industrial Relations in 1914; assistant director of investigative services in the U.S. Department of Labor, 1918–1919; retired in 1919; died in Los Angeles, Calif., June 17, 1948; *Notable American Women*, Vol. 1 (1971); Louis Levine, *The Women's Garment Workers: A History of the International Ladies' Garment Workers' Union* (1924); Gladys Boone, *The Women's Trade Union Leagues in Great Britain and the United States of America* (1942).

Marie Tedesco

BARONDESS, Joseph   (1867–1928). Born in Kamenets-Podolsk, Russia, July 3, 1867; son of Judah Samuel, a rabbi, and Feige (Goldman) Barondess; Jewish; married Amma Zifels in 1885; four children; acquired an orthodox Jewish education, then emigrated to England at an early age and soon became involved in the British trade union movement; emigrated to the United States in 1888 and gained employment as a kneepants–maker in New York City; attended the night school of the New York University Law School while working in the garment industry; became a union organizer during the 1890s and was involved in the organization of the Cloakmakers' Union, the Hebrew Actors' Union, the Ladies' Garment Workers' Union, and the Hebrew-American Typographical Union; led a cloakmakers' strike in 1890 that brought him to the forefront of union organizing in the New York needle trades; arrested in 1891 as a result of organizing activities and, while free on bail, fled to Canada; returned to the United States and, after spending a few weeks in jail, was granted a pardon by governor of New York; led an unsuccessful general strike of New York cloakmakers in 1895 that largely destroyed the union; was a strong, zealous, and impetuous personality, and consequently at the center of most of the divisive ideological struggles in the New York labor movement during the 1890s; participated in the founding of the International Ladies' Garment Workers' Union in 1900; became a committed Zionist in 1903 and involved in several Zionist organizations; was a founding member of the American Jewish Congress and served on its delegation to the 1919 Paris Peace Conference, which was instrumental in having a clause providing for Jewish minority rights incorporated into the treaty; appointed to the New York City Board of Education in 1910 and served two four-year terms; during his later years he became an insurance broker; politically a Socialist; translated and wrote an introduction to Frank B. Copley's *The Impeachment of President Israels* (1916); died in New York City, June 19, 1928; Benjamin Stolberg, *Tailor's Progress: The Story of a Famous Union and the Men Who Made It* (1944); Louis Levine, *The Women's Garment Workers: A History of the International Ladies' Garment Workers' Union* (1924); Melech Epstein, *Profiles of Eleven* (1965) and *Jewish Labor in the U.S.A., 1914–1952*, 2 Vols. (1953); Aaron Antonovsky, trans., *The Early Jewish Labor Movement in the United States* (1961).

BARRETT, Francis Grover   (1892–1971). Born in Rutland, Vt., November 25, 1892; son of John James, a hotelman, and Theresa (Hanley) Barrett; Roman Catholic; married Frances Elizabeth Stamm on June 30, 1925; three children; received his primary education at St. Peter's School in Rutland and enrolled in the extension division of the Knights of Columbus school in New York City from which he received the equivalent of a high school education; took employment in 1911 in the Vermont printing industry and two years later, at age 21, became an apprentice typographer in New York City; joined the International Typographical Union (ITU) in 1913; served in the U.S. Navy, 1917–1919; after being discharged from the Navy, he secured employment in a New York City printing plant and shortly thereafter obtained his journeyman's card; served as a New York City delegate to the ITU's national convention in Indianapolis in 1927; a few years later, he became a linotype operator for the Fairchild Publishing Company of New York City and continued in that employment until 1932; elected second vice–president of the ITU in 1932; led a successful pressmen's sit-down strike—one of the few conducted by an American Federation of Labor–affiliated union—in Springfield, Ohio, in 1937, and then conducted a successful organizing campaign in Dayton, Ohio; appointed an advisor by Secretary of Labor Frances

Perkins to the American labor delegation to the International Labor Organization conference in Geneva, Switzerland, in 1937; was elected first vice–president of the ITU in 1938; after losing a bid for reelection in 1940, he returned to his former job as a linotype operator for the Fairchild Publishing Company and continued in that employment until 1949 when he ran successfully as a Progressive in the ITU's two–party electoral system for the presidency of New York Typographical Union Local 6, one of the oldest and the largest ITU local unions with a membership in excess of twelve thousand by 1960; appointed to the U.S. Department of Labor Conference on Industrial Safety in 1950; was defeated for reelection by the Conservative party candidate in 1951 and again returned to his job as a linotype operator before regaining the ITU Local 6 presidency in 1953 and continuing in office until his retirement in 1961; served on the New York City Unemployment Insurance Advisory Council, 1959–1960; was a highly successful organizer who unionized hundreds of printing shops during his union career; an equally effective negotiator, he obtained substantial increases in the union wage scale, improvements in medical and welfare benefits, and additional paid holidays during his tenure as Local 6 president; was a proponent of unity and cooperation among unions in the New York printing industry and had his efforts rewarded by a new spirit of solidarity among New York printing trades unions; after retiring, he became chairman of the seven hundred-unit housing cooperative in Woodside, N.Y., that Local 6 had sponsored under his administration and continued in that capacity until 1969; affiliated with the Democratic party in New York City; the recipient of numerous labor awards, he was also a frequent contributor to the labor press; died in Colorado Springs, Colo., on July 27, 1971; *National Cyclopaedia of American Biography*, Vol. 56; Seymour M. Lipset et al., *Union Democracy: The Internal Politics of the International Typographical Union* (1956); *The New York Times*, July 28, 1971.

BARRY, Leonora Marie Kearney   (1849–1923). Born at Kearney, County Cork, Ireland, on August 13, 1849; daughter of John, a farmer, and Honor Granger Brown Kearney; Roman Catholic; married William E. Barry, a painter, on November 30, 1871, and after his death in 1881, Obadiah Read Lake, a printer, on April 17, 1890; three children; immigrated with her family to the United States in 1852, settling on a farm in St. Lawrence County, N.Y.; after attending local public schools in Pierrepont, N.Y., she received a year of private instruction and, at age 16, qualified for a teacher's certificate; for several years thereafter, she taught in rural, upstate New York schools; after her marriage in 1871, she gave birth to three children and devoted her energies to domestic affairs; with the death of her husband ten years later, she was confronted with the problem of earning, with limited skills, a livelihood for her family; ultimately, she took a job as an unskilled worker in a clothing plant; distressed by poor working conditions and low wages, in 1894 she joined a local assembly of the Knights of Labor, which consisted of fifteen hundred women and quickly assumed a leadership role in the organization, rising to the post of master workman;

served as a delegate to District Assembly 65 in Albany, N.Y., in 1886 and was selected as one of District Assembly 65's five delegates to the Knights of Labor national convention meeting in Richmond later in that year; after the Knights of Labor created a women's department in 1886, she was appointed a general investigator of the department; thereafter, she traveled extensively around the country, organizing women workers and, when necessary, serving as a trouble-shooter for the Knights of Labor leadership; was influential in the campaign that resulted in the passage of Pennsylvania's first factory inspection act in 1889; after her second marriage in 1890, she withdrew from her labor work and devoted much of her energy to temperance and women's suffrage affairs; died in Minooka, Ill., on July 18, 1923; *Notable American Women*, Vol. 1; *Who's Who in America*, 1914–1915; Eleanor Flexner, *Century of Struggle: The Women's Rights Movement in the U.S.* (1959); Philip S. Foner, *Women and the American Labor Movement from Colonial Times to the Eve of World War I* (1979).

BARRY, Thomas B.   (fl. 1852–1888). Born in Cohoes, N.Y., July 17, 1852; received little formal education before beginning work in a knitting mill in 1860 at age 8; joined a short-lived carders' union in 1867 and shortly thereafter became an apprentice axe-polisher but was blacklisted two years later for union organizing activities; joined the Noble Order of the Knights of Labor (K of L) in the early 1880s and was appointed an organizer; elected to the Michigan state legislature on the Democratic-Greenback ticket in 1884 while residing in Saginaw County, Mich.; sponsored several pro-labor bills as a legislator, including a ten-hour bill; led a largely unsuccessful but widely publicized strike of Saginaw Valley lumber workers when mill owners refused to institute the ten-hour day without wage reductions; as a result of activities associated with the strike, was arrested six times with total bail exceeding $20,000; elected to the executive committee of the K of L in 1885; sent to Chicago, Ill., to lead an eight-hour strike in the stockyards in 1886, but Grand Master Workman Terence Powderly (q.v.) called the strike unauthorized and ordered it stopped; after the crushing of the strike, Barry increasingly criticized Powderly's "autocratic" leadership and sacrifice of rank-and-file interests; was therefore expelled from K of L in 1888 by Powderly's supporters; subsequently attempted to organize dissident K of L unionists into a Brotherhood of United Labor, but with little success outside Barry's home state of Michigan; Norman J. Ware, *The Labor Movement in the United States, 1860–1895* (1929); Gerald N. Grob, *Workers and Utopia: A Study of Ideological Conflict in the American Labor Movement, 1865–1900* (1961); Doris B. McLaughlin, *Michigan Labor: A Brief History from 1818 to the Present* (1970); Harry J. Carman, Henry David, and Paul N. Guthrie, eds., *The Path I Trod: The Autobiography of Terence V. Powderly* (1940).

BASKIN, Joseph   (1880–1952). Born in Minsk, Russia, October 20, 1880; son of Nachim Mendel, a Hebrew teacher, and Rose Baskin; Jewish; married Mary Plotkin in 1918; two children; studied at various yeshivas in Russia and attended a school in Vilna, Lithuania, for higher Talmudic learning; at age of 16, became active in Bund, a general union of Jewish workers; went to Geneva, Switzerland, in 1899 on a Baron de Hirsch scholarship and attended College de Genève, 1899–1900; studied electrical engineering at the University of Lausanne, 1901, and the electrical school at the University of Nancy, France, 1905; graduated with degree in electrical engineering in 1905; founded and became publisher of the Bund's Yiddish daily *Folks Zeitung* in Vilna; arrested, along with other newspaper staff members, in 1907, for anti-government activities; emigrated to the United States later that year and took job in a Cleveland, Ohio, automobile plant; employed by the Westinghouse Electrical Company in Pittsburgh, Pa., 1908–1913; appointed assistant secretary of Workmen's Circle in 1914 and general secretary in 1916, serving until 1952; edited Workmen's Circle publication *The Friend*, 1924–1952; organized Workmen's Circle educational, medical, and social service departments during his administration; also established a home for the aged and elementary and intermediate Yiddish schools; politically a Socialist; died in New York City, June 26, 1952; Melech Epstein, *Jewish Labor in the U.S.A., 1914–1952,*. 2 Vols. (1953); Hyman J. Fliegel, *The Life and Times of Max Pine: A History of the Jewish Labor Movement in the U.S.A. during the Last Part of the 19th Century and the First Part of the 20th Century* (1959); *Who's Who in World Jewry* (1955); Solon DeLeon, ed., *The American Labor Who's Who* (1925); *The New York Times*, June 27, 1952.

BATES, Harry Clay   (1882–1969). Born in Denton, Tex., November 22, 1882; son of Jefferson Davis, a businessman, and Minnie Smith Bates; Roman Catholic; married Marguerite Roddy on July 29, 1932; shortly after graduating from high school in Denton, became an apprentice bricklayer and joined Waco, Tex., Local 9 of the Bricklayers, Masons and Plasterers International Union of America (BMPIU) in 1900; elected president of Dallas, Tex., Local 5 in 1910 and served until 1916; between 1914 and 1922 was president of the Texas Conference of Bricklayers, Masons and Plasterers; served as president of the Joint Labor Legislative Board of Texas, 1916–1922; was elected an international vice-president of the BMPIU in 1920 and treasurer four years later; elected the first vice-president of the BMPIU in 1928 and in 1935 became international president of the union; elected an American Federation of Labor (AFL) vice-president and member of the executive council in 1935; appointed chairman of the standing AFL housing committee that aimed to provide information and sponsor housing legislation in the United States Congress; served during World War II as labor advisor to the War Production Board and was a member of the Wage Adjustment Board; was a member of the 1942 AFL negotiating committee to discuss merger with the Congress of Industrial Organizations (CIO); was an AFL delegate to the British Trades Union Congress in 1949; served as a member of President Harry S. Truman's Wage Stabilization Board, created during the Korean War in 1950; reappointed to the board after its 1951 reorganization; one of three AFL delegates to the AFL-CIO unity committee that reached agreement in 1955 on merger; served as a delegate to the 1958 meeting of the International Labor Organization conference in Geneva; retired from union affairs in 1967; politically a Democrat; authored *Bricklayers' Century of Craftsmanship* (1955); died in Golden Beach, Fla., April 4, 1969; Philip Taft, *The A.F. of L. from the Death of Gompers to the Merger* (1959); Walter Galenson, *The CIO Challenge to the AFL: A History of the American Labor Movement, 1935–1941* (1960); *AFL-CIO News,* April 12, 1969; *Who's Who in Labor* (1946).

BECK, Dave   (1894–   ). Born in Stockton, Calif., June 16, 1894; son of Lemuel, a carpet cleaner, and Mary (Tierney) Beck; Presbyterian; married Dorothy E. Leschander in 1918 and remarried after her death in 1961; one child; forced by a family financial crisis to leave high school before graduation; later took extension courses from the University of Washington; secured a job as a laundry worker and joined Seattle, Wash., Local 24 of the Laundry Workers International Union; worked for a short period as an inside laundry worker, then became a driver of a company laundry wagon; became a charter member of Seattle Laundry and Dye Drivers Local 566, chartered by the International Brotherhood of Teamsters, Chauffeurs, Warehousemen and Helpers (IBT) in 1917; served with the Naval Aviation Service as a machinists' mate in England during World War I; resumed work after the war as a laundry driver and was elected to the executive board of Local 566; elected president of IBT Joint Council 28 in 1923 and secretary-treasurer of Local 566 in 1925; appointed a full-time IBT general organizer for the Northwest and elected president of Local 566 in 1927; appointed to the Washington Board of Prison Terms and Paroles in 1935; organized and became the president of the Western Conference of Teamsters in 1937; became an international vice-president in 1940 and in 1947 elected to the newly created position of executive vice-president; appointed a regent of the University of Washington in 1945; served as an American Federation of Labor (AFL) fraternal delegate to the British Trades Union Congress in 1949; elected international president of the IBT after the retirement of Daniel Tobin (q.v.) in 1952; became an AFL vice-president and executive council member in 1953; declined to seek reelection in 1957 because of his investigation by the McClellan Committee of the U.S. Senate; expelled from AFL-Congress of Industrial Organization's executive council for refusing to answer McClellan committee questions regarding corruption and the embezzlement of union funds; served a 30-month prison term, 1962–1965, after being convicted for filing a false federal income tax return; became a successful real-estate entrepreneur in Seattle, Wash., following his retirement from union affairs; usually supported the Republican party; Donald Garnel, *The Rise of Teamster Power in the West* (1972); Sam Romer, *The International Brotherhood of Teamsters: Its Government and Structure* (1962); Robert D. Leiter, *The Teamsters Union: A Study of Its Economic Impact* (1957); *Current Biography* (1949).

BEHNCKE, David Lewis   (1897–1953). Born in rural Wisconsin in 1897; son of a farmer; married Gladys May Henson in 1925; two children; ended formal education in 1913 and ran away from home; joined the U.S. Army prior to World War I, hoping to become a pilot; participated in General John J. Pershing's expedition against Pancho Villa in 1916; became a pilot during World War I but, because of the lack of formal education, failed to become a career military flier; after World War I, joined with other former service fliers to form a flying circus that specialized in stunt flying; after a year of barnstorming, organized a short-lived air-freight express service; was forced by 1925 to sell the business, losing both his airfield and his planes; became Northwest Airlines' first pilot in 1926; served a one-year tour with the U.S. Army during 1927; became a United Air Lines pilot in 1928, and in 1930 and 1931 emerged as the spokesman for United pilots in a major wage dispute; led the formation in 1931 of a new union, the Air Line Pilots Association (ALPA), and, despite the reservations of many pilots, obtained an international union charter for ALPA from the American Federation of Labor; deliberately avoided collective bargaining for many years, successfully lobbying instead for a federal pilot pay formula based on seniority, speed, miles, and hours flown (Decision No. 83 of the National Labor Board, May 10, 1934, enacted into law in the Air Mail Act of 1934), and also for the inclusion of air transportation within the Railway Labor Act (achieved under Title II of the Act, April 10, 1936); initiated collective bargaining in 1938; signed the first ALPA contract with American Airlines on May 15, 1939, and within a few years with all other carriers; successfully led post–World War II ALPA campaign to improve and extend Decision No. 83 pay formula (including addition of "gross weight pay" in 1947) to larger four-engine aircraft; proved unable to delegate authority adequately for needs of expanding ALPA and was increasingly deaf to rank-and-file attitudes; recalled from ALPA presidency by the union's board of directors in 1951; declined an offer of president emeritus status and lifetime salary, instead waging a bitter but unsuccessful legal battle to regain control of the ALPA; politically a Democrat; died in Chicago, Ill., April 14, 1953; George E. Hopkins, *The Airline Pilots: A Study in Elite Unionization* (1971); Oscar Leiding, *A Story of the Origin and Progression of the Air Line Pilots Association and of Its Key Figure and Organizer, 1930–1944* (1945); *Who's Who in Labor* (1946); Harold M. Levinson et al., *Collective Bargaining and Technological Change in American Transportation* (1971).

BEIRNE, Joseph A.   (1911–1974). Born in Jersey City, N.J., February 16, 1911; son of Irish immigrants Michael Joseph, a railroad engineer, and Annie T. (Giblin) Beirne; Roman Catholic; married Anne Mary Abahaze on July 2, 1933; three children; left high school after two years and went to work as an office boy; resumed high school education in the evening after gaining employment in 1928 as a utility boy in the inspection department of the Western Electric Company in Jersey City, N.J.; completed three years of college work by taking evening courses at St. Peter's College and New York University; became president of the employees association of Western Electric's New York distribution department in 1937 and during the same year helped establish the National Association of Telephone Equipment Workers; credited with transforming a company union into an economic-oriented trade union; elected vice-president of the National Federation of Telephone Workers in 1940, president in 1943; elected as a Democrat to the city council of Fairview, N.J., 1939–1945; served on the U.S. Board of War Communication during World War II; negotiated the first national contract with the American Telephone and Telegraph Company in 1946; became president of the reorganized Communications Workers of America (CWA) in 1947 and transformed it from a loose federation of autonomous, independent unions into a strong, centralized union; led the CWA into the Congress of Industrial Organizations (CIO) in 1949 and became a CIO vice-president; designated one of the CIO representatives on the Wage Stabilization Board in 1951; became a vice-president, executive council member, and chairman of the standing committee on community relations after the American Federation of Labor-CIO merger in 1955; appointed a Public Broadcasting Corporation Director in 1968 and a member of the National Committee on Productivity in 1970; served as member of numerous public and private boards and agencies; a Democrat; authored *New Horizons for American Labor* (1962) and *Challenge to Labor: New Roles for American Trade Unions* (1969); retired in 1974; died in Washington, D.C., on September 2, 1974; Jack Barbash, *Unions and Telephones: The Story of the Communications Workers of America* (1952); *Current Biography* (1946); *Who's Who in Labor* (1946); *AFL-CIO News*, September 7, 1974; Thomas R. Brooks, *Communication Workers of America: The Story of a Union* (1977).

BELLAMY, Edward   (1850–1898). Born in Chicopee Falls, Mass., on March 26, 1850; son of Rufus King, a Baptist minister, and Maria Louisa (Putnam) Bellamy; Baptist; married Emma Sanderson in 1882; was educated in the Chicopee Falls schools and spent a short time at Union College; spent a year in Europe, primarily Germany, in 1868, at age 18; during his travels in Europe, his interest in social reform began to develop; after returning to the United States, he studied law and was admitted to the bar but never enthusiastically practiced law; was always more interested in writing and first turned to journalism, the *Springfield Union, New York Evening Post,* and in 1880, became co-owner (with his brother) of the *Springfield Daily News,* before devoting most of his time to a literary career; of the many novels he wrote, *Looking Backward* (1888) was by far the most influential; his vision of a utopian socialism attracted a national and international audience, but it received its most enthusiastic reception from urban workers who were suffering through the rigors of accelerated industrialization; "Bellamy Clubs" sprang up in the working–class districts of American cities, reflecting the disillusionment of workers with American society, and their hopes for a better future; in 1891 Bellamy founded the *New Nation* in Boston, Mass., to promote his Socialist dream but tuberculosis forced him to conserve his energies most of which were spent completing *Equality* (1897), the sequel to *Looking Backward;* authored *The Duke of Stockbridge* (1879), *Dr. Heiden-*

hoff's Process (1880), *Mrs. Ludington's Sister* (1884), and *The Blind Man's World and Other Stories* (1898), a collection of his short stories published after his death; died in Chicopee Falls on May 22, 1898; *Dictionary of American Biography*, Vol. 2; *Who Was Who*, historical volume; Christine McHugh, "Edward Bellamy and the Populists: The Agrarian Response to Utopia, 1888–1898" (Ph.D. diss., 1977); R. Jackson Wilson, "Experience and Utopia: The Making of Edward Bellamy's *Looking Backward*," *Journal of American Studies* (1977).

BELLANCA, Dorothy Jacobs   (1894–1946). Born in Zemel, Russian Latvia (now part of the Soviet Union), August 10, 1894; daughter of Harry, a tailor, and Bernice Edith (Levinson) Jacobs; Jewish; emigrated to the United States in 1900; married August Bellanca, an Amalgamated Clothing Workers of America (ACWA) organizer, in August 1918; attended the public schools of Baltimore, Md., until age 13, then hired in a Baltimore men's clothing factory as a buttonhole maker; helped to found United Garment Workers of America Local 170 and led it into the ACWA in 1914; elected a delegate and secretary to the Baltimore Joint Board, ACWA, in 1915; elected to the ACWA general executive board in 1916 and served until her marriage in 1918; headed the short-lived women's bureau of the ACWA, 1924–1926; served on the ACWA executive board, 1934–1946, and during this time was the ACWA's only woman vice-president; was a member of the Congress of Industrial Organizations' Textile Workers Organizing Committee, 1937–1938; served as a labor advisor to regional conferences of the International Labor Organization, 1939, 1941; participated in various organizing drives and strikes, notably the 1930 Philadelphia organizing campaign, 1932–1934, and the shirt workers' organizing drives in New York, New Jersey, Connecticut, and Pennsylvania; was appointed to the General Advisory Commission on Maternal and Child Welfare in 1938; member of the New York commissions on discrimination in employment, 1941, 1943; served on several industrial commissions responsible for establishing minimum wage rates after enactment of the Fair Labor Standards Act; was a political activist and helped organize the American Labor party (ALP) in 1936; was an unsuccessful candidate for the U.S. Congress on the ALP ticket in 1938; served as state vice-president of the ALP in 1940 and 1944; died in New York City, August 10, 1946; Dorothy J. Bellanca Papers, Catherwood Library, Cornell University; *Notable American Women*, Vol. 1 (1971); *Who's Who in Labor* (1946).

BELSKY, Joseph   (1902–1976). Born in Odessa, Russia, on March 22, 1902; son of Abraham, a carpenter, and Yetta Belsky, a homemaker; Jewish; married Kate Lasky, a homemaker, on December 22, 1923; two children; emigrated with his family to the United States in 1904, settling in New York City where he attended public elementary schools and completed his high school education at Pace Institute; joined Hebrew Butcher Workers Union, Local 234, of the Amalgamated Meat Cutters and Butcher Workmen of North America (AMCBW) in 1928; was elected secretary-treasurer of Local 234 in 1926 and retained that position for nearly a half century; during his long career as the chief administrative officer of Local 234, its membership in the New York-New Jersey area increased from 540 in 1923 to 60,000 in 1972; was elected an AMCBW international vice-president in 1937; an active participant in New York politics during the 1930s and 1940s, he ran unsuccessfully for the New York State Senate on the American Labor party ticket in 1938; was one of the founders of the Liberal party of New York and ran unsuccessfully on its ticket for city-wide councilman in 1940; under his direction Local 234 sponsored six low-cost housing cooperatives built in Brooklyn, the Bronx, and Utica, New York, with the objective of making a contribution to the community in which union members lived and worked (the housing provided was not restricted to union members); after the retirement of Thomas J. Lloyd (q.v.) in 1972, he became international president of the AMCBW by virtue of being the senior vice-president and later in the same year was elected to a full four-year term; retired from union offices in 1976; led a union drive, 1974–1975, to raise $500,000 to build a nonsectarian medical center near Jerusalem; dedicated in 1976, the facility was named the Joseph Belsky Medical Center; authored *I, the Union* (1952); died in New York City on September 27, 1976; *The New York Times*, September 28, 1976; *AFL-CIO News*, October 2, 1976; *Who's Who in Labor* (1946, 1976).

BENSON, Herman   (1915–   ). Born in New York City on July 9, 1915; son of Samuel, a real-estate manager, and Lillian Benson; Jewish; married Revella Sholiton on April 2, 1946; two children; attended public schools and, for two years, City College of New York; later completed a B.A. at Empire State College, State University of New York; joined the Young People's Socialist League and campaigned for Norman Thomas (q.v.) for president in 1932; during the 1930s worked as a laborer and as an adult educator under the Works Progress Administration; also worked in doll and toy factories, and, from 1940, as a machinist; meanwhile, he joined the Trotskyist faction inside the Socialist party, 1936–1937, and left the Socialist party with the Trotskyists; became a member of the "Shachtmanite" Workers' party when it was formed in 1940; was a toolmaker and active member of the Congress of Industrial Organizations' United Auto Workers, United Electrical Workers, and United Rubber Workers unions in New York and Detroit, Mich., during the 1940s; ran for mayor of Detroit on a nonpartisan, left-wing ticket in 1947, receiving about 5 percent of the vote; was labor editor of *Labor Action*, 1949–1958, and also contributed articles on labor to *Dissent, Labor History, Liberation, The New International, The Progressive,* and *The Reporter*; in the late 1950s, he became concerned with the problems of union democracy and due process for individual union members, and with the help of Norman Thomas launched *Union Democracy in Action* to publicize the efforts of union members fighting for democracy within their unions; after the murders of Dow Wilson and Lloyd Green, reformers in the West Coast painters union, about whom Benson had written, he organized the Citizens' Committee for Investigation of the Wilson-Green Murders, calling for a federal investigation; between 1967 and 1973, he served as aide to Frank Schonfeld, secretary-treasurer of Painters District Council 9, New York, as managing editor of its monthly paper, *District Council 9 Newsletter*, and editor of its daily strike bulletin in the spring of 1968; since 1969, he has served as executive director of the Association of Union Democracy (AUD), a nonprofit foundation devoted to promoting the principles and practices of internal union democracy; has edited the AUD publication *Union Democracy Review* since 1972; author of *Democratic Rights for Union Members: A Guide to Internal Union Democracy* (1979); a long-time member of the Workers' Defense League and the American Civil Liberties Union; Herman Benson Papers, Walter Reuther Archives, Wayne State University.

Jon Bloom

BERGER, Victor Luitpold   (1860–1929). Born in Nieder-Rehbach, Austria, February 28, 1860; son of Ignatz, a farmer and innkeeper, and Julia Berger; married Meta Schlichting on December 4, 1897; two children; attended the Gymnasium at Leutschau and the universities of Budapest and Vienna; emigrated to the United States in 1878 and settled near Bridgeport, Conn.; worked there as a metal polisher, boiler mender, and salesman; moved to Milwaukee, Wis., in 1880 and taught German in public schools for ten years; edited the *Milwaukee Daily Vorwaerts*, 1892–1898; became editor of the *Social Democratic Herald* in 1900 and continued in that capacity after the *Herald* became a daily in 1911 and was renamed the *Milwaukee Leader*; served as its editor until his death; joined the International Typographical Union and was a delegate to several American Federation of Labor (AFL) conventions where he was one of the leading Socialist critics of established AFL leaders and policies; one of the founders of the Social Democratic party of America in 1897 and the Socialist party of America (SPA) in 1901; served as a member of the national executive board of the SPA from its founding until 1923; ran unsuccessfully for mayor of Milwaukee in 1904; elected a Milwaukee alderman-at-large in 1910 and later that year elected to the U.S. Congress, the first Socialist to be seated in Congress; reelected in 1918, but denied his seat because of his opposition to United States' involvement in World War I; reelected three more times but denied his seat each time; tried and convicted in 1921 on a number of charges growing out of an indictment for anti-war speeches and sentenced to 20 years, but the conviction was overturned by the U.S. Supreme Court; reelected to Congress in 1922 and served three consecutive terms before being defeated for reelection in 1928; died in Milwaukee, Wis., August 7, 1929; David A. Shannon, *The Socialist Party of America: A History* (1955); James Weinstein, *The Decline of Socialism in America, 1912–1925* (1967); Sally M. Miller, *Victor Berger and the Promise of Constructive Socialism, 1910–1920* (1973); *Dictionary of Wisconsin Biography* (1960); *Dictionary of American Biography*, Vol. 21; Philip S. Foner, *American Socialism and Black Americans from the Age of Jackson to World War II* (1977).

BERRY, George Leonard (1882–1948). Born in Lee Valley, Hawkins County, Tenn., September 12, 1882; son of Thomas Jefferson, a judge and legislator, and Cornelia (Trent) Berry; Baptist; married Marie Margaret Gehres on August 6, 1907; attended the public schools of Hawkins County, Tenn., before being orphaned in 1888; ran away from a Baptist orphanage at age 9 and became a newsboy for the Jackson (Miss.) *Evening News*; served with the Third Mississippi Regiment of the U.S. Army during the Spanish-American War; employed in the pressroom of the St. Louis *Globe-Democrat* after the war, and in 1899 joined the International Printing Pressmen's and Assistant's Union of North America (IPPAUNA); became involved in several successful mining ventures in Nevada, 1903–1904, and acquired a degree of financial independence; in 1907 was a San Francisco delegate to the national convention of the IPPAUNA in Brighton Beach, N.Y., and elected international president of the IPPAUNA; was an American Federation of Labor (AFL) delegate to the British Trades Union Congress in 1910 and two years later attended the International Printers Congress in Stuttgart, Germany, and the International Economic Conference in Zurich, Switzerland; commissioned a major in the U.S. Army Corps of Engineers during World War I and served with the American Expeditionary Force in France; appointed a labor advisor on the American commission to the treaty negotiations ending World War I; was one of the founders of the American Legion; became a vice-president and member of the AFL executive council in 1935; was a conservative trade unionist and did not advocate militant strike activity, but preferred to resolve industrial disputes through conciliation and arbitration; was a Democrat and ran unsuccessfully for governor of Tennessee in 1914; lost the Democratic vice presidential nomination in 1924 by a narrow margin; was chairman of the labor division during the Democratic National Convention of 1928; was a member of the National Labor Board of the National Recovery Administration, 1933–1935; was instrumental in organizing labor's Nonpartisan League to support the reelection of Franklin D. Roosevelt in 1936; appointed a U.S. Senator from Tennessee on May 6, 1937, to fill the vacancy caused by the death of the incumbent and served until January 16, 1939; other than trade union activities, was involved in several business enterprises, including newspaper publishing, cattle raising, manufacturing cigarette wrappers, and banking; organized and led the movement creating Pressmen's Home, Tenn.; authored *Labor Conditions Abroad* (1912); died in Pressmen's Home, December 4, 1948; Elizabeth F. Baker, *Printers and Technology: A History of the International Printing Pressmen and Assistants' Union* (1957); Philip Taft, *The A.F. of L. from the Death of Gompers to the Merger* (1959); *Current Biography* (1948); *National Cyclopaedia of American Biography*, Vol. 36; *Dictionary of American Biography*, Suppl. 4.

BIEBER, Owen Frederick (1929–   ). Born in North Dorr, Mich., on December 28, 1929; son of Alfred F. and Minnie (Schwartz) Bieber; Roman Catholic; married Shirley M. Van Woerkom on November 25, 1950; five children; attended Visitation Elementary and Catholic Central High School in Grand Rapids, Mich.; went to work as an auto seat boarder wire bender at McInerney Spring and Wire Company, Grand Rapids; joined Local 687 of the United Automobile, Aircraft and Agricultural Implement Workers of America (UAW) where his father had been on the organizing drive and served as a department steward; rose within the local; elected shop steward, 1949, executive board, 1951, bargaining committee, 1955, vice-president, 1955, and president, 1956; assigned as part-time regional organizer, Region 1-D (Western Michigan), 1961; full-time international representative, 1962; serviced General Motors and Chrysler plants, 1964–1972; elected regional director in 1974 at special convention when current regional director resigned due to ill health; reelected at 1977 UAW convention; elected UAW vice-president in 1980 and appointed director of the General Motors department; chosen as the presidential candidate of the administration caucus in November 1982 and elected UAW president at the 1983 convention; was a liberal, Kent County (Grand Rapids) Democratic party precinct delegate, 1960–1980, and chairman of the Kent County Democratic party, 1964–1966; was named "Labor's Man of the Year" by the Kent County American Federation of Labor-Congress of Industrial Organizations Council in 1961; served on numerous civic and church committees; was active in labor education and voter registration drives; served three years on the board of directors of Project Rehab; was a member of Michigan League for Human Services and the Personnel and Labor Advisory Council, Grand Valley State College; was a member of the board of directors, West Michigan Comprehensive Health Planning Unit, the State Health Advisory Board, and the State Mental Health Board; a member of the National Association for the Advancement of Colored People and the National Urban League; in 1982, he led the UAW in negotiating a new contract with General Motors which included numerous concessions; under rank-and-file pressure, the negotiations were twice broken off and the final contract was approved by a 52 to 48 percent vote; his selection as the administration caucus's presidential candidate culminates a transition in the UAW's leadership—he is the first president who was not associated with the earlier pioneering years of the UAW; *Detroit News*, November 13, 1982; *Flint Journal*, November 13, 1982; *News from the UAW*, July 23, 1980; *Detroit Free Press*, November 13, 1982.

                                                                    Seth Wigderson

BIEMILLER, Andrew John   (1906–1982). Born in Sandusky, Ohio, July 23, 1906; son of Andrew Frederick and Pearl (Weber) Biemiller; Society of Friends; married Hannah Periot Morris on December 20, 1929; two children; attended public schools; received a B.A. degree from Cornell University in 1926 and did postgraduate work at the University of Pennsylvania, 1928–1931; served as an instructor in history at Syracuse University, 1926–1928, and the University of Pennsylvania, 1929–1931; moved to Milwaukee, Wis., in 1932 and became a reporter for the *Milwaukee Leader*; served as a labor relations counselor and an organizer for the Milwaukee Federation of Trade Councils and the Wisconsin

State Federation of Labor, 1932–1942; elected to the Wisconsin State Assembly as a Socialist-Progressive in 1936 and served as a floor leader, 1939–1941; appointed assistant to the vice-chairman for labor production of the War Production Board in 1941, serving until 1944; elected as a Democrat to the Seventy-ninth Congress, 1945–1946, and the Eighty-first Congress, 1949–1950, but was defeated for reelection in both instances; served as a special assistant to the U.S. Secretary of Interior, 1951–1952, and thereafter became a public relations counselor in Washington, D.C.; shortly after being defeated for election to Congress in 1952, became a legislative lobbyist for the American Federation of Labor (AFL) and in 1956 was appointed director of the AFL-Congress of Industrial Organizations' legislative department; considered a resourceful and effective legislative lobbyist; actively involved in the enactment of civil rights legislation and in the socioeconomic reform measures passed during the 1960s; a member of numerous public and private agencies and boards; was a Socialist early in his career, but later supported Democratic candidates; retired in 1978; died in Bethesda, Md., on April 3, 1982; Joseph C. Goulden, *Meany* (1972); Terry Catchpole, *How to Cope with COPE: The Political Operations of Organized Labor* (1968); *Fortune* (February 1969); *AFL-CIO News*, December 2, 1978, April 10, 1982; *The New York Times*, April 4, 1982.

BILLINGS, Warren Knox   (1893–1972). Born in Middletown, N.Y., in 1893; son of a carpenter, who died shortly after Billings's birth, and a mother who took in washing and ironing to provide support for her nine children; married; moved with his family to Brooklyn, N.Y., after the death of his father in 1895 and worked in his brother-in-law's dairy while attending Brooklyn P.S. 144 from which he graduated in 1905; thereafter he drifted about, working at one time as a shoe lining cutter and at another time as a streetcar conductor; dismissed from the latter job for pocketing fares, he then lost his savings in a crap game and settled into a routine of odd jobs and occasional vagrancy; eventually made his way to San Francisco where, in 1913, he acquired a job as a shoe lining cutter at the Frank and Hyman Shoe Company which was then being struck by the Boot and Shoe Workers Union; hired by the company to spy on the strikers, he instead became a double agent, reporting to Industrial Workers of the World and Socialist leaders through the intermediary of Thomas J. Mooney (q.v.); after successfully disrupting several company operations, he was involved in an argument with a plant guard which led to an accidental shooting for which he was arrested on charges of assault with a deadly weapon; after spending nearly three months in jail, the charges against him were dropped, and he was released; was later elected president of the San Francisco Boot and Shoe Workers local union; after his release from jail, he moved in with the Mooneys; along with Mooney, he became involved in a violent electrical workers' strike against the Pacific Gas and Electric Company and was eventually arrested and charged with possession of dynamite; was convicted of conspiracy to dynamite Pacific Gas and Electric Company property and was sentenced to two years in Folsom Penitentiary; was released in time to be arrested along with Mooney for complicity in a San Francisco Preparedness Day Parade bombing which killed ten people; was tried in September 1916, found guilty, and sentenced to life imprisonment; although little evidence existed linking either Billings or Mooney to the crime and perjured testimony had clearly been used to convict them, all appeals for a retrial were denied; Billings's sentence was commuted in October 1939 and in 1961 he was officially pardoned by the governor of California; after his release, he opened a small jewelry shop in San Francisco where he applied the watchmaking and watch repair skills he had learned in prison and lived a life of relative obscurity; died on September 4, 1972; Mooney-Billings Papers in the Bancroft Library, University of California, Berkeley; Richard H. Frost, *The Mooney Case* (1968); Henry T. Hunt, *The Case of Thomas J. Mooney and Warren K. Billings* (1929); Ernest J. Hopkins, *What Happened in the Mooney Case* (1932); Curt Gentry, *Frame-Up: The Incredible Case of Tom Mooney and Warren Billings* (1967); Solon DeLeon, ed., *American Labor Who's Who* (1925); *The New York Times*, September 5, 1972.

BIRTHRIGHT, William Clark   (1887–1970). Born in Helena, Ark., May 27, 1887; son of William Conwell, a machinist, and Margaret Ellen (Linebaugh) Birthright; Presbyterian; married Birdie Lee Huss on June 29, 1910; one child; attended the public schools of Nashville, Tenn.; adopted the barber's profession in Nashville at age 17 and joined Local 35 of the Journeymen Barbers' International Union of America (JBIUA); elected vice-president of Local 35 in 1907 and selected as a delegate to the Nashville Trades and Labor Council; served as secretary of the Tennessee State Federation of Labor, 1916–1931; appointed secretary of the Tennessee Nonpartisan Political Campaign Committee in 1920; served as an American Federation of Labor (AFL) field representative, 1918–1921, and a JBIUA field representative, 1921–1930; became a member of the JBIUA executive board in 1924; appointed along with Francis Gorman (q.v.) of the United Textile Workers of America and Paul Smith of the AFL to head a drive to organize southern textile workers in 1930; after serving for seven years as general secretary–treasurer of the JBIUA, elected general president in 1937; was an AFL fraternal delegate to the British Trades Union Congress in 1937; was elected a vice-president and member of the AFL executive council in 1940; elected international president of the renamed Journeymen Barbers, Hairdressers and Cosmetologists' International Union of America (JBHCIU) in 1941; frequently served as an AFL mediator in jurisdictional disputes; selected as chairman of the Marion County (Ind.) Selective Service Board and of the Indiana State Personnel Board in 1946; was one of three AFL delegates on the Wage Stabilization Board established by President Harry S. Truman during the Korean War; became a member of the AFL-Congress of Industrial Organizations (CIO) executive council after the 1955 merger and served until 1965; appointed chairman of the AFL-CIO standing committee on public relations and publicity in 1955; usually supported Democratic candidates; retired from union affairs in 1963 and was named president emeritus of the JBHCIU; died in Indianapolis, Ind., April 18, 1970; W. Scott Hall, *The Journeymen Barbers' International Union of America* (1936); *National Cyclopaedia of American Biography*, Vol. G; *AFL-CIO News*, April 25, 1970; *Who's Who in Labor* (1946).

BISNO, Abraham   (1866–1929). Born in Belaya Tserkov, Russia, in 1866; son of Herschel, a tailor, and Malke Bisno; Jewish; married Tillie Regent in 1890 and, after that marriage ended in divorce, Sarah in 1892; six children; received little formal education; was apprenticed to a tailor at age 11; emigrated with family to the United States in 1881, living successively in Atlanta, Ga., Chattanooga, Tenn., and, in 1882, Chicago, Ill.; began work as a tailor shortly after immigrating; was one of the founders of the Workingmen's Educational Society in 1888; helped organize and became the first president of the Chicago Cloak Makers' Union in 1890; served as a factory inspector under Florence Kelley (q.v.) during John Peter Altgeld's governorship of Illinois; was associated with John R. Commons's (q.v.) investigation of immigrant conditions in American industry; a vigorous critic of the conciliation method of resolving industrial disputes that was written into the "Protocol of Peace," which ended the 1910 New York garment strike, and advocated strict arbitration as an alternative; elected chief clerk of the New York Joint Board of Cloakmakers, a division of the International Ladies' Garment Workers' Union (ILGWU), in 1911 and general manager the following year; his proposed reforms encountered opposition from both garment manufacturers and the international officers of the ILGWU and therefore was forced out as chief clerk in 1913 and replaced by Dr. Isaac A. Hourwich; served as chief clerk of the Chicago Joint Board of Cloakmakers, 1915–1917; retired from union affairs after 1917 and became a Chicago realtor; authored *Abraham Bisno: Union Pioneer* (1967); died in Chicago, Ill., December 1, 1929; Benjamin Stolberg, *Tailor's Progress: The Story of a Famous Union and the Men Who Made It* (1944); Louis Levine, *The Women's Garment Workers: A History of the International Ladies' Garment Workers' Union* (1924).

BITTNER, Van Amberg   (1885–1949). Born in Bridgeport, Pa., March 20, 1885; son of Charles, a coal miner, and Emma Ann (Henck) Bittner; Lutheran; married Bertha Mae Walter on June 8, 1911; one child; started working in the mines at age 11 while continuing to attend school; was graduated from high school in Vanderbilt, Pa.; joined the United Mine Workers of America (UMWA) shortly after beginning to work in the mines and in 1901, at age 16, was elected president of his local; became a vice-president of UMWA District 5 in 1908 and three years later was elected District president; became a UMWA international representative and organized locals in Tennessee, Alabama, and West Virginia; elected president of UMWA District 17 as a result of organizing activities in West Virginia; served on the Appalachian Coal Conference between 1933 and 1942; associated with the organizing activities of the Steel Workers Organizing Committee (SWOC) in 1935 and assigned the task of organizing steelworkers in the western Great Lakes area; one of the signers of the SWOC contract with the United States Steel Corporation in 1937; appointed chairman of the Packinghouse Workers Organizing Committee in 1937; involved in the successful effort to organize farm equipment workers; led the successful drive to organize the Bethlehem Steel Corporation in 1941; became an assistant to the president of the United Steelworkers of America after it was formed from the SWOC; resigned as president of UMWA District 17 in 1942 as a result of conflicts between the Congress of Industrial Organizations (CIO) and UMWA president John L. Lewis (q.v.); appointed to the West Virginia State Planning Board in 1942; during World War II, served as a labor advisor to the Office of Emergency Management and Production Management and as a member of the National War Labor Board; served as vice-chairman of the CIO's Political Action Committee; appointed national director of the CIO southern organization drive in 1946; a self-described independent in politics, but usually supported the Democratic party; died in Pittsburgh, Pa., July 19, 1949; Van A. Bittner Papers, West Virginia University Library; Robert R. R. Brooks, *As Steel Goes,. . . Unionism in a Basic Industry* (1940); Lloyd Ulman, *The Government of the Steel Workers' Union* (1962); *Current Biography* (1947); *National Cyclopaedia of American Biography* Vol. 37; Melvyn Dubofsky and Warren Van Tine, *John L. Lewis: A Biography* (1977).

BLANKENHORN, Ann Washington Craton (1891–   ). Born in Provincetown, Mass., on September 1, 1891; married Heber H. Blankenhorn (q.v.), a labor publicist and reformer, in 1936; graduated from George Washington University with a B.A. in 1915; worked as a case investigator/adoption supervisor for the Bureau of Children's Guardians in rural Virginia, 1916–1918; became field supervisor for the Bureau of Labor Statistics, in 1919, as well as secretary and employment counselor for the New York Child Labor Committee; attended Columbia Graduate School of Social Sciences, 1922–1924, and participated in educational program research on the clothing and textile industry under the joint auspices of Columbia's economics department and the research department of the Amalgamated Clothing Workers of America; worked as a caseworker for the disaster relief staff of the American Red Cross, 1926–1931; began gathering materials for a book on American industrial villages for the Institute of Social and Religious Research in 1930; served on the staff of the Temporary Emergency Relief Committee in New York City in 1932; left her job as an editor for the Agricultural Adjustment Administration in 1937 to work on a manuscript describing social conditions in the towns and cities of coal mining areas; after the 1956 death of her husband, she attempted to complete his memoirs at her Alexandria, Va., home; over the years, she published several articles on social and economic conditions in various industries, particularly as they pertained to women and children; her publications appeared in *Advance, Labor Age,* and *New York*

Nation; Ann Washington Craton Blankenhorn Papers, Walter Reuther Archives, Wayne State University.

Gilbert J. Gall

BLANKENHORN, Heber H. (1884–1956). Born in Orreville, Ohio, on March 26, 1884; son of Henry, a physician, and Emma (Amstutz) Blankenhorn; married Mary Dewhurst in 1913, divorced in 1925; remarried to Ann Washington Craton (q.v.) in 1936; no children; graduated from Wooster College in Ohio with a B.A. in 1905; taught English in public schools after a year's travel in Europe; moved to New York City where he graduated from Columbia University with an M.A. in 1910; became a reporter and later assistant editor for the *New York Evening Sun*, 1910–1917, where he first encountered the struggles of the labor movement; worked in the New York offices of the Committee on Public Information and organized and headed an American propaganda leafleting mission for the American Expeditionary Force in World War I; returned to New York where he became co-director of the Bureau of Industrial Research, 1919–1923; served as secretary of the Commission of Inquiry of the Interchurch World Movement and prepared that organization's influential report on the steel strike of 1919; hired as publicity director for the Amalgamated Clothing Workers of America (ACWA) in 1921; conducted economic research for the United Mine Workers' nationalization research committee, 1922–1924; became foreign correspondent for the railway brotherhood's journal *Labor*, 1924–1932; returned to the United States in 1933 and joined the public relations staff of the National Recovery Administration; later assistant to Senator Robert F. Wagner (chairman of the National Labor Board); employed as an industrial economist in the first and second National Labor Relations Boards, 1934–1947; interested Senator Robert M. La Follette, Jr., in investigating anti-union practices of employers in 1936, hoping to aid politically the nascent industrial union movement and help establish the National Labor Relations Act; served as head of the National Labor Relations Board (NLRB) as liaison and chief planner for the La Follette committee from 1936 to 1940 and authored the committee's report on industrial munitions; directed the special NLRB investigation into the anti-union policies of the Ford Motor Company's service department in 1941; from 1942 to 1946, he again saw war service in charge of European propaganda leaflet operations; returned to the NLRB in 1947 where he lobbied against the passage of the Taft-Hartley Act, resigning from government service in protest upon its passage; persuaded by the United Auto Workers to conduct a private investigation into the attempted assassinations of Walter and Victor Reuther (q.v.), 1949–1950; briefly resumed his stint as foreign correspondent for *Labor* in the early 1950s; retired to work on his uncompleted memoirs; died in Washington, D.C., on January 1,1956; compiled and edited Interchurch World Movement's *Public Opinion and the Steel Strike* (1921); authored Interchurch World Movement's *Report on the Steel Strike of 1919* (1920), *Adventures in Propaganda: Letters from an Intelligence Officer in France* (1919), and *The Strike for Union* (1924);

Heber H. Blankenhorn Papers, Walter Reuther Archives, Wayne State University; Gilbert J. Gall, "Heber Blankenhorn, the La Follette Committee, and the Irony of Industrial Repression," *Labor History* (Spring 1982).

Gilbert J. Gall

BLOOR, Ella Reeve   (1862–1951). Born near Mariners' Harbor, Staten Island, N.Y., July 8, 1862; daughter of Charles, a drugstore owner, and Harriet Amanda (Disbrow) Reeve; married Andrew Omholt in 1932 after earlier marriages to Lucien Ware and Louis Cohen ended in divorce; attended public schools in New York City and Bridgeton, N.J., and a private school in Bridgeton until age 14; became associated with the labor movement for the first time around 1884–1885 by joining a mixed local of the Knights of Labor; became a member of the Prohibition party in 1887 and organized and served as president of a Women's Christian Temperance Union branch in Woodbury, N.J.; participated in the Philadelphia Amalgamated Association of Street and Electric Railway Employes' strike in the early 1890s; was influenced by Eugene V. Debs (q.v.) and joined the Social Democracy of America in 1897, and was elected secretary of its Brooklyn branch; joined the Socialist Labor party (SLP) around 1900 and became an SLP organizer for Essex County, N.J.; elected to the general executive board of the Socialist Trade and Labor Alliance in 1900; became disenchanted with the SLP's theoretical approach and joined the Socialist party of America (SPA) in 1902; served as an SPA state organizer for Pennsylvania and Delaware, 1902, 1905, Connecticut, 1905–1910, and Ohio, 1910; nominated by the SPA for secretary of state of Connecticut in 1908; called "Mother" Bloor, worked as an organizer with Pennsylvania coal miners during the 1902 coal strike, with Ohio miners in the early 1900s and again in 1914–1915, and with Colorado miners in 1914; did relief work during the 1913 Calumet, Mich., copper strike; spent several months organizing for the United Cloth Hat and Cap Makers' Union in New York, New England, St. Louis, Mo., and Philadelphia, Pa., in 1917; was nominated for lieutenant governor of New York on the SPA ticket in 1919; worked as an organizer for the Workers' Defense Union; while an organizer in Kansas City, Mo., in 1919, quit the SPA and formed a branch of the Communist Labor party (CLP); became national organizer for the Eastern Division of the CLP in 1919; when the CLP merged with the Communist party of America (CPA) in 1922, became a CPA member; was a delegate to both the Red International of Labor Unions and the Third World Congress of the Communist International meeting in Moscow in 1921; helped form and was a field organizer for the Workers' party, Los Angeles, Calif., in 1921; was a delegate from the Central Labor Council of Minneapolis, Minn., to the Second Red International Labor Union Congress, Moscow, 1922; served as a national organizer for the International Defense, 1921–1924; was an organizer for the United Front Committee of Textile Workers in several cities, 1925–1927; worked as an organizer for the United Farmers' League in North and South Dakota and cooperated with the Farmers' Holiday Association during the Iowa dairy farmers strike in 1932;

was a member of the CPA's national committee and was chairman of its Women's Commission, 1932–1948; authored *We Are Many: An Autobiography of Ella Reeve Bloor* (1940); died in Quakertown, Pa., August 10, 1951; James Weinstein, *The Decline of Socialism in America, 1912–1925* (1967); John L. Shover, *Cornbelt Rebellion: The Farmers Holiday Association* (1965); Andrew Sinclair, *The Emancipation of the American Woman* (1965); Theodore Draper, *The Roots of American Communism* (1957); *Dictionary of American Biography*, Suppl. 5; *Notable American Women*, Vol. 4.

BLUMBERG, Hyman   (1885–1968). Born in Legum, Russian Lithuania (now part of the Soviet Union), November 25, 1885; son of Moses, a clothing worker, and Hannah (Herman) Blumberg; Jewish; married Bessie Simon on October 20, 1907; two children; emigrated with family to the United States in 1890; left school at age 12 and began work in the men's garment industry in Baltimore; began union organizing activities while employed as a pocketmaker and in 1909 was selected chairman of District Council 3 of the United Garment Workers Union of America (UGW); in 1914 helped organize the Amalgamated Clothing Workers of America (ACWA) and led members of his local out of UGW and into the new union; elected an ACWA vice-president in 1916; moved to New York City in 1922, becoming manager of the New York Joint Board and assuming responsibility for ACWA organizing activities in the eastern United States; served on the Men's Clothing Code Authority of the National Recovery Administration, 1933–1935; was a member of the Apparel Industry Committee of the Wage and Hour Division of the United States Department of Labor; served as the Congress of Industrial Organizations' labor advisor to the International Labor Organization's conference in Geneva in 1938; was manager of the Amalgamated Laundry Workers' Joint Board, 1939–1941, the Boston Joint Board, and the Shirt and Leisure-wear Joint Board of New York City; elected executive vice-president of the ACWA in 1946; was the general supervisor of the social insurance programs initiated by the ACWA; served as New York State secretary of the American Labor party (ALP) from 1944 to 1946 and then became state chairman; along with the ACWA, withdrew from the ALP in 1948 and thereafter usually supported candidates of the Democratic party; died in New York City, October 17, 1968; Harry A. Cobrin, *The Men's Clothing Industry: Colonial through Modern Times* (1970); Hyman Bookbinder, *History of the ACWA* (1950); Matthew Josephson, *Sidney Hillan: Statesman of American Labor* (1952).

BOMMARITO, Peter   (1915–   ). Born in Detroit, Mich., on May 17, 1915; married; a few years after graduating from high school, he became a web fabric machine operator at a U.S. Rubber Company plant in Akron, Ohio; joined Local 101 of the United Rubber, Cork, Linoleum & Plastic Workers of America (URW) in 1940; elected a shift committeeman in 1940, serving in that capacity until 1942 when he enlisted in the U.S. Marine Corps; served in the Pacific, including Guadalcanal, during World War II; returning to his employment with the U.S. Rubber Company after the war, he was elected treasurer and an executive board member of Local 101 in 1948; was elected vice-president of Local 101 in 1955 and president two years later; elected an international vice-president in 1960, served until 1966, when he was elected international president of the URW; elected as American Federation of Labor-Congress of Industrial Organizations (AFL-CIO) vice-president and executive council member in 1969; appointed vice-president of the AFL-CIO industrial union department; was active in a number of civil affairs including the Committee for National Health Insurance and the advisory board of the Salvation Army; during his presidency he created considerable controversy and opposition by centralizing bargaining among the four biggest companies in the rubber industry—Goodyear, Firestone, Uniroyal, and B. F. Goodrich; led a 140-day strike in 1976 which produced a 36 percent increase in wages and benefits over the three-year period of the contract and an advantageous cost-of-living adjustment; despite the favorable contract terms, opposition to centralized bargaining continued and, in 1978, he was opposed for reelection; although winning 61 percent of the vote, much of the opposition came from the fifty-eight thousand workers employed by the industry's "big four" producers; stilled much of the criticism by negotiating a very favorable contract after the 1978 elections and then retired in 1981; *Who's Who in Labor* (1976); *Business Week*, September 18, October 30, 1978; Eleanora W. Schoenebaum, ed., *Profiles of an Era: The Nixon-Ford Years (1979); Who's Who in America, 1980–1981*.

BONADIO, Frank (1904–   ). Born in Pittsburgh, Pa., on March 19, 1904; son of Felice and Amelia (Torchia) Bonadio; Roman Catholic; married Carmela Doccolo on June 1, 1930; three children; after completing his primary and secondary education, he served an apprenticeship and became a journeyman in Baltimore, Md., Local 122 of the International Sheet Metal Workers Union (ISMW) in 1929; became business manager of Local 122 in 1936, serving in that capacity until 1948; was an international representative for the ISMW, 1948–1954; elected vice-president and treasurer of the Baltimore Building and Construction Trades Council in 1941 and served two terms; was a member of the National Joint Board for the Settlement of Jurisdictional Disputes, 1949–1954; was elected an international vice-president of the ISMW in 1956; became the secretary-treasurer of the American Federation of Labor-Congress of Industrial Organizations (AFL-CIO) building and construction trades department (BCTD) in 1954; was elected president of the BCTD in 1971; a Democrat; retired AFL-CIO position on June 1, 1974; *AFL-CIO News*, May 11, 1974; *Who's Who in America, 1974–1975*.

BORCHARDT, Selma Munter (1895–1968). Born in Washington, D.C., December 1, 1895 (birthdate has also been listed as December 1, 1900 and December 1, 1899); daughter of Newman and Sara (Munter) Borchardt; attended Washington, D.C., public schools; received a B.S. degree in education from

Syracuse University in 1919, and a B.A. in 1922; received an LL.B. from Washington College of Law in 1933 and an M.A. from Catholic University in 1937; was a member of the Washington, D.C., and U.S. Supreme Court bars; joined Local 8 of the American Federation of Teachers (AFT) in 1923; served Local 8 as vice-president and legislative chairman, 1922–1924; was an AFT representative to the Women's Joint Congressional Committee, 1927–1958; served as secretary of the American Federation of Labor (AFL) committee on education, 1929–1955, and after the AFL-Congress of Industrial Organizations' (CIO) merger, served in the same capacity in the AFL-CIO; was the AFT's Washington and congressional legislative representative; along with Florence Hanson, helped investigate Communist influence in AFT Local 5 in New York in 1935, and later in the same year recommended that Local 5's charter be withdrawn; was the director and vice-president of the World Federation of Education Associations, 1927–1947; was a member of the U.S. National Committee on the United Nations Educational, Scientific, and Cultural Organization; authored numerous books and articles on labor and education; retired union positions in 1962; died in Washington, D.C., January 30, 1968; Selma M. Borchardt Papers, Walter Reuther Library, Wayne State University; Solon DeLeon, ed., *The American Labor Who's Who* (1925); *Who's Who in Labor* (1946); *AFL-CIO News*, February 3, 1968; *Notable American Women*, Vol. 4.

Marie Tedesco

BOWEN, William J. (1868–1948). Born in Albany, N.Y., in 1868; son of Thomas B. and Margaret (Doran) Bowen; married; two children; after attending the grammar schools of Albany, N.Y., became an apprentice bricklayer at age 13; joined Albany Local 6 of the Bricklayers, Masons and Plasterers International Union (BMPIU) in 1890; served as business manager of Local 6 in 1891 and president in 1895; appointed assistant general secretary in 1900 and became first vice-president of the BMPIU a year later; was elected international president in 1904; inheriting a union that was financially insolvent, restored the financial integrity and stability of the BMPIU during the first few years of his presidency; guided the BMPIU in establishing a death benefit fund in 1910 and a relief fund in 1914; led the BMPIU into the American Federation of Labor (AFL) in 1916; served on the labor commission established by President Woodrow Wilson during World War I; was an AFL fraternal delegate to the British Trades Union Congress in 1918; was president when the BMPIU sponsored the construction of a brick plant in El Paso, Tex., to counter building contractors' efforts to constrict supplies to union contractors in the post–World War I period; became president emeritus of BMPIU in 1928, but remained as chairman of the board of trustees; was a conservative trade unionist and was a vigorous critic of Communist elements in the labor movement; died in New York City, July 27, 1948; *The American Federationist* (November 1940); Harry Clay Bates, *Bricklayers' Century of Craftsmanship* (1955); *The New York Times*, July 29, 1948.

BOWER, Andrew Park (1869–1949). Born in Apollo, Pa., May 14, 1869; son of Charles Columbus, a potter and itinerant school teacher, and Philippa Ann (Park) Bower; Baptist; married Maud E. Weightman on April 10, 1893; two children; left school after completing the fifth grade in the public schools of Reading, Pa.; later attended night school and a business college where he studied commercial law; joined the Cigarmakers' International Union of America (CMIU) in 1886; elected secretary-treasurer of Reading Local 286 of the CMIU in 1904 and served until his death; served as secretary-treasurer of the Federated Trades Council of Reading, 1906–1948; elected a vice-president of the Pennsylvania State Federation of Labor in 1909 and served in that capacity for nearly 40 years; during World War I, served on the judicial exemption board and on the state employment board; was a director of the Cooperative League, 1921–1925, and vice-president, 1921–1924; served as secretary-treasurer of the Cigarmakers' Co-operative Association, 1920–1948; was elected president of the CMIU in 1942 after serving as a vice-president for more than 20 years; served on several county agencies during World War II; retired union positions in 1948; politically a Socialist; edited the *Cigarmakers' Official Journal*, 1942–1948; died in Reading, Pa., October 24, 1949; *National Cyclopaedia of American Biography*, Vol. 38; Solon DeLeon, ed., *The American Labor Who's Who* (1925); *Who's Who in Labor* (1946).

BOYCE, Edward (1863–1941). Born in County Donegal, Ireland, on November 8, 1863; educated in an Irish Catholic school; married Eleanor Day, an Idaho teacher, on May 14, 1901; emigrated to the United States in 1882; after working briefly as a railway construction laborer in Wisconsin, went to Leadville, Colo., to work in the mines and in 1884 joined the Knights of Labor; then drifted to the Coeur d'Alene mining district of Idaho and to Butte, Mont., working as a laborer and hard-rock miner; returning to the Coeur d'Alene in 1888, became recording secretary of the Wardner Miners' Union; helped lead the violent Coeur D'Alene strike of 1892; as a result, convicted of contempt of court, jailed for several months, and blacklisted; after prospecting in the Bitter Root Mountains in 1893, obtained employment again in the Coeur D'Alene mines; represented the Wardner Union at the second convention (1894) of the Western Federation of Miners (WFM) and was elected to the WFM executive board; the next year, appointed general WFM organizer, travelled extensively establishing several new local unions; meanwhile, benefiting from the alliance of Idaho Populists and the WFM, elected to the legislature, in which he served one term, failing in an attempt to have the practice of blacklisting outlawed; in 1896, while still employed as a miner, elected president of WFM; arranged for the affiliation of his union with the American Federation of Labor (AFL); but soon, smarting from AFL president Sam Gompers's (q.v.) refusal to give striking miners in Colorado financial aid, concluded that intensified class warfare between western hard-rock miners and the operators made trade unionism obsolete and vigorously debated the point with Gompers; successfully urged the 1897 WFM convention to reject trade unionism in principle, in favor of militant industrial unionism and to disaffiliate from the AFL; instrumental in 1898 in the founding of the Western Labor Union (later the American Labor Union) as a regional alternative to the AFL; during 1899–1900, established the *Miner's Magazine* as the WFM official organ; meanwhile became an associate of Socialist leader Eugene Debs (q.v.), and shortly moved into the Socialist camp; advised the 1902 WFM convention to embrace "socialism without equivocation" and it endorsed the Socialist party platform; also urged the WFM to work toward the goal of substituting union ownership of mines for the wage system by gradually buying up mining properties; but at the same convention, Boyce—disillusioned by mismanagement in some WFM locals, the opposition to him in the powerful Butte Miners' Union No. 1, and a dwindling union treasury—resigned his presidency; despite his disillusionment, he had led the WFM, the most radical union to that point in American history, to the apogee of its membership and influence; after 1902, although continuing to attend WFM conventions for a few years, supporting the WFM's role in founding the Industrial Workers of the World in 1905, and testifying on behalf of William D. Haywood (q.v.) and other WFM leaders (at their 1907 trial on charges of having arranged for the murder of a former Idaho governor), Boyce played no important role in the labor movement; in 1909, along with his wife, Eleanor, née Day, who had become wealthy from her investments in a highly profitable Idaho silver mine, and other members of the Day family, bought the exclusive Portland Hotel in Oregon, which Boyce managed from 1910 to 1930; died in Portland, Ore., on December 24, 1941, leaving an estate of slightly over $1 million; Vernon H. Jensen, *Heritage of Conflict: Labor Relations in the Nonferrous Metals Industry up to 1930* (1950); John H. M. Laslett, *Labor and the Left: A Study of Socialism and Radical Influences in the American Labor Movement, 1881–1924* (1970); John Fahey, "Ed Boyce and the Western Federation of Miners," *Idaho Yesterdays* (Fall 1981).

Donald G. Sofchalk

BOYLE, William Anthony   (1904–   ). Born in Bald Butte, Mont., December 1, 1904; son of James P., a miner, and Catherine (Mallin) Boyle; married Ethel V. Williams on June 3, 1928; one child; attended schools in Montana and Idaho and then began working as a coal miner; joined the United Mine Workers of America (UMWA); elected president of UMWA District 27, Montana, serving until 1948; served as regional director in four western states for the Congress of Industrial Organizations and for UMWA District 50; represented the UMWA on several government and industry committees during World War II; was an assistant to UMWA president John L. Lewis (q.v.), 1948–1960; during this period, also served on the coal industry's Joint Review Board and Joint Industry Safety Committee; served as an international UMWA vice-president, 1960–1963, acting president, 1962–1963, and elected international president in 1963; was a member of the executive committee and board of directors prior to his election as a vice-president of the National Coal Policy Conference; was opposed for the

UMWA presidency in 1969 by Joseph A. Yablonski (q.v.), who represented Miners for Democracy, a rank-and-file insurgent group; reelected by a two-to-one margin in a bitterly contested election; shortly thereafter Yablonski, his wife, and daughter were murdered in their Clarksville, Pa., home; was defeated for reelection by Arnold Miller (q.v.) in 1972 after the U.S. Department of Labor obtained a court order invalidating the 1969 election; attempted suicide with an overdose of drugs in September 1973; was indicted and convicted of using union funds for illegal political contributions and began serving a three-year sentence in the federal prison in Springfield, Mo., in December 1973; in the same month, was indicted and later convicted of conspiring to murder Yablonski (See Yablonski's sketch); *United Mine Workers Journal*, February 15, 1963; *Current Biography* (1971); *Who's Who in America, 1972–1973; The New York Times*, September 7, 1973; Brit Hume, *Death in the Mines* (1971); Stuart Brown, *Man Named Tony: The True Story of the Yablonski Murders* (1976); Arthur H. Lewis, *Murder by Contract: The People versus Tough Tony* (1975); Joseph E. Finley, *The Corrupt Kingdom: The Rise and Fall of the United Mine Workers* (1972).

John W. Hevener

BRENNAN, Peter Joseph   (1918–   ). Born in New York City, May 24, 1918; son of John, an ironworker and member of the teamsters' union, and Agnes (Moore) Brennan; Roman Catholic; married Josephine Brickley in 1940; three children; graduated from high school in New York City; received the B.S. degree in business administration from City College of New York; while in college, became an apprentice painter and joined Local 1456 of the Brotherhood of Painters, Decorators and Paperhangers of America; joined the U.S. Navy during World War II and served on a submarine in the Pacific; returned to the painting trade after the war and became the acting business agent of Local 1456; elected business agent of Local 1456 in 1947; appointed maintenance chairman of the Construction Trades Council of Greater New York in 1951 and, in 1957, elected president of the council; served as vice-president of the New York State American Federation of Labor-Congress of Industrial Organizations; was severely criticized by civil rights leaders who accused him of maintaining discriminatory hiring practices in the New York building trades; gained national publicity in 1970 when he organized New York construction workers in support of President Richard M. Nixon's Southeast Asian war policies and led them in a violent confrontation with anti-war protesters; nominated U.S. Secretary of Labor in 1972 and took office in 1973, serving until 1977; although identified as a Democrat, has often supported Republican candidates, including Governor Nelson Rockefeller of New York and President Richard Nixon in 1968 and 1972; Joseph C. Goulden, *Meany* (1972); *Current Biography* (1973); *New York Post*, December 9, 1972; *Washington Post*, November 30, 1972.

BRESLAW, Joseph   (1887–1957). Born in Miskifky, Russia, April 18, 1887; son of Israel, a merchant, and Marie (Burdman) Breslaw; Jewish; married Rosa

Saslaw on January 3, 1908; three children; received some formal education in Russian schools; emigrated to the United States in 1907; first took employment as a shoe worker and then in 1909 hired as a cloak presser; joined Cloak, Skirt and Dress Pressers Local 35 of the International Ladies' Garment Workers' Union (ILGWU); elected to the executive board of Local 35 in 1914 and shortly thereafter became the business agent of the union; elected manager and secretary-treasurer of Local 35 in 1916; elected an ILGWU vice-president in 1922; forced out of the union as a result of a reform movement conducted by Morris Sigman (q.v.) in 1925 but regained ILGWU positions in 1929; usually considered to be on the right wing of union politics; was a craft-conscious trade unionist who opposed the efforts to lead the ILGWU into the Congress of Industrial Organizations (CIO); attracted a large number of loyal followers within the ILGWU who provided him with considerable power within the union; served the ILGWU in a variety of capacities, including chairman of the ILGWU Union Health Center for several years and permanent treasurer of Unity House, the union's summer resort in the Poconos; was a strong advocate and supporter of the State of Israel and was chairman of the American Trade Union Council for Histadrut, the Israeli labor organization; was a member of the American Labor party and for a time served as a member of its state executive committee; authored *A Cloakmaker Looks at Stolberg's "Tailor's Progress"*; died in New York City, July 3, 1957; Louis Levine, *The Women's Garment Workers: A History of the International Ladies' Garment Workers' Union* (1924); Benjamin Stolberg, *Tailor's Progress: The Story of a Famous Union and the Men Who Made It* (1944); Melech Epstein, *Jewish Labor in the U.S.A., 1914–1952*, 2 Vols. (1953); *Who's Who in Labor* (1946).

BREWER, Roy Martin   (1909–   ). Born in Cairo, Hall County, Neb., August 9, 1909; son of Martin M., a blacksmith and mechanic, and Lottie (Woodworth) Brewer; Christian church; married Alyce J. Auhl on July 9, 1929; two children; graduated from high school in Grand Island, Neb., in 1926 and took a job as a projectionist, continuing in that occupation until 1933; joined Local 586 of the International Alliance of Theatrical Stage Employees and Motion Picture Machine Operators of the United States and Canada (IATSE) in 1927; elected vice-president of the Nebraska State Federation of Labor (NSFL) in 1928; served as president of the NSFL, 1933–1934, 1937–1943; was president of IATSE Local 586 for 15 years and secretary of the Grand Island Central Labor Union for 4 years; served as Labor Compliance Officer for the National Recovery Administration in Nebraska, 1934–1935; during World War II, was a member of the Nebraska Defense Council and chief of the plant community facilities division of the Office of Labor Production, War Production Board; during 1945 to 1953, served as an international representative of the IATSE, assigned to resolve jurisdictional conflict in Hollywood, Calif., movie studios; became president of the American Federation of Labor's Hollywood Film Council in 1947; was a vociferous anti-Communist and strongly supported the House Committee on Un-American Activities' investigations of alleged Communist activity in the motion-picture industry; became manager of branch operations for Allied Artists Productions in 1953 and during 1966–1967 served as assistant vice-president and studio manager; was manager of production development for the IATSE in 1965; usually supported the Democratic party; *Current Biography* (1953); *International Motion Picture and Television Almanac, 1952–1953*; *Who's Who in Labor* (1946); *Who's Who in America, 1972–1973*.

BRIDGES, Harry Alfred Renton   (1901–   ). Born in Melbourne, Australia, July 28, 1901; son of Alfred Earnest, a prosperous realtor, and Julia (Dorgan) Bridges; reared as a Roman Catholic; married Noriko (Nikki) Sawada in 1956 after two previous marriages, to Agnes Brown in 1923 and to Nancy Fenton Berdecio in 1946, ended in divorce; three children; completed a secondary school education at St. Brennan's Parochial School in Melbourne in 1917, then became a clerk in a retail stationery store; quit his job after a short time and began a five-year period as a merchant seaman; emigrated to the United States in 1920 and the following year joined the Industrial Workers of the World, serving as an organizer; became a longshoreman in San Francisco in 1922; began organizing San Francisco longshoremen for the International Longshoremen's Association (ILA) in 1933 and between 1933 and 1935 helped edit *The Waterfront Worker*; led the longshore strike in San Francisco in 1934 that evolved into the famous San Francisco General Strike; organized the Maritime Federation of the Pacific in 1935; led most Pacific coast locals of the ILA into the Congress of Industrial Organizations (CIO) under the auspices of the newly organized International Longshoremen's and Warehousemen's Union (ILWU) in 1937; became CIO regional director for the Pacific Coast and a member of the national CIO executive board; began a long fight to stay in United States after Secretary of Labor Frances Perkins issued a warrant for his deportation in 1939; later, the U.S. House of Representatives voted 330 to 42 to deport him but the Senate refused to act; in 1942, was ordered deported by U.S. Attorney General Francis Biddle, but the U.S. Supreme Court invalidated the order; in 1949, was indicted and convicted of perjury for swearing during his naturalization hearing that he was not a member of the Communist party; sentenced to a prison term of five years for perjury and of two years for criminally conspiring to obstruct the naturalization laws, but the conviction was overturned by the U.S. Court of Appeals, and in 1953, the U.S. Supreme Court ruled that the statute of limitations had expired on the matter; found not guilty of a charge of civil conspiracy to obstruct the naturalization laws by a U.S. District Court in 1955; led a long but successful strike of West Coast longshoremen in 1948; after lengthy negotiations, signed contracts with the Pacific Maritime Association in 1960 that suspended ILWU-negotiated work rules, allowing a reduced work force on the docks as called for by mechanization and automation; in return, got a multimillion dollar trust fund to be used for retirement pensions and no-layoff guarantees for registered workers; led a 135-day strike of West Coast longshoremen in 1971–1972;

retired in 1979; Charles P. Larrowe, *Harry Bridges: The Rise and Fall of Radical Labor in the U.S.* (1972), and *Shape-Up and Hiring Hall: A Comparison of Hiring Methods and Labor Relations on the New York and Seattle Waterfronts* (1955); Maud Russell, *Men along the Shore* (1966); Charles A. Madison, *American Labor Leaders: Personalities and Forces in the Labor Movement* (1950); Harvey Schwartz, "Harry Bridges and the Scholars Looking at History's Verdict," *California History* (1980); Nelson Lichtenstein, *Labor's War at Home: The CIO in World War II* (1982); Harvey A. Levenstein, *Communism, Anticommunism, and the CIO* (1981).

BROCKHAUSEN, Frederick Carl   (1858–1929). Born in Fredericia, Denmark, on May 20, 1858; attended public schools in Fredericia, and then in 1877 became a journeyman cigarmaker; joined the cigarmakers' union and affiliated with the Socialist party before immigrating to the United States in 1879; lived in Chippewa Falls and St. Paul, Minn., before settling permanently in Milwaukee, Wis., in 1894; meanwhile, he had joined the Cigar Makers' Union in St. Paul in 1890; was active in the People's party campaign during the mid-1890s and then in 1897 joined the Milwaukee branch of the Social Democracy of America; elected to the Wisconsin state legislature in 1905, serving until 1912; one of the founders of the Wisconsin State Federation of Labor, he served it as an unpaid legislative representative and secretary-treasurer, 1900–1912; was active in the movement to secure a state workmen's compensation law, a campaign that finally succeeded in 1911; although entering the cigar-making business in 1912, he remained committed to the labor movement and served as chairman of the labor committee of the Wisconsin State Council of Defense during World War I; served on the board of trustees of the Milwaukee County Institutions, 1921–1929; died in Milwaukee on June 16, 1929; F. Brockhausen Papers, Wisconsin State Historical Society; Frederick I. Olson, "The Milwaukee Socialists, 1897–1941" (Ph.D. diss., 1952); *Milwaukee Leader*, June 17, 1929; *Dictionary of Wisconsin Biography* (1960).

BROPHY, John   (1883–1963). Born in St. Helens, Lancashire, England, on November 6, 1883; son of Patrick, a coal miner, and Mary (Dagnall) Brophy; Roman Catholic; married Anita Anstead on August 13, 1918; two children; attended primary school in St. Helens and the public schools of Philipsburg, Pa.; later studied at Brookwood Labor College; emigrated with family to the Pennsylvania coal-mining region in 1892; at age 12, began a 21-year period working in the mines of Pennsylvania, Iowa, Michigan, and Illinois; joined the United Mine Workers of America (UMWA) in 1899 and after serving as a local union president, was president of District 2, UMWA, central Pennsylvania, 1916–1926; was a leading exponent of public ownership of coal mines, and from 1921 to 1923 served on the UMWA's nationalization research committee, expounding the case for nationalization in several pamphlets; when seventy-five thousand formerly non-union central Pennsylvania miners responded to the 1922 national coal strike, Brophy urged that no wage agreement be signed until operators owning both union and non-union mines signed for both; however, on August 15, John L. Lewis (q.v.) approved the Cleveland settlement that abandoned the District 2 non-union miners and, on January 19, 1923, called off the non-union miners' strike; defied the international officers and continued to support the strike by soliciting funds and borrowing heavily; however, finally conceded defeat in August 1923; for the remainder of the 1920s, criticized Lewis's "No Backward Step" policy of forcing high wages on northern union operators while simultaneously neglecting organizing efforts in the southern non-union fields, thus causing operators to shift production from their northern union mines to their southern non-union mines; in 1926, founded along with several other critics of Lewis the "Save the Union" committee, which sponsored Brophy's candidacy against Lewis in the UMWA elections of 1926; was defeated by a margin of 170,000 to 60,000 votes amidst charges of fraud and election abuses; supported the 1930 call for a Springfield, Ill., convention to reorganize the union, but bolted the organization when the corruption-tainted Frank Farrington (q.v.) was seated; worked as a salesman for Columbia Conserve Company, Indianapolis, Ind., 1930–1933; after a reconciliation with Lewis, served as a UMWA organizer, 1933–1935, and national director of the Congress of Industrial Organizations (CIO), 1935–1939; after participating in the effort to organize steel and auto workers, became national director of the CIO's department of industrial union councils in 1951; politically an independent; authored *A Miner's Life* (1964); John Brophy Papers, Catholic University of America; retired in 1961 and died in Falls Church, Va., February 20, 1963; *United Mine Workers Journal*, March 1, 1963; Walter Galenson, *The CIO Challenge to the AFL: A History of the American Labor Movement, 1935–1941* (1960); *AFL-CIO News*, February 23, 1963; M. Camilla Mullow, "John Brophy, Militant Labor Leader and Reformer: The CIO Years" (Ph.D. diss., 1966); Joseph E. Finley, *The Corrupt Kingdom: The Rise and Fall of the United Mine Workers* (1972); Melvyn Dubofsky and Warren Van Tine, *John L. Lewis: A Biography* (1977).

John W. Hevener

BROUN, Heywood Campbell   (1888–1939). Born in Brooklyn, N.Y., December 7, 1888; son of Heywood Cox, a small businessman, and Henriette (Brose) Broun; an Episcopalian early in his life, but converted to Roman Catholicism during the 1930s; married Ruth Hale on June 6, 1917, and, after a divorce in 1933, Constantina Maria Incoronata Fruscella on January 9, 1935; two children; completed his elementary and secondary education in New York City; attended Harvard University, 1906–1910, but failed to receive a degree; in 1908, while a student at Harvard, began working as a reporter on the *New York Morning Telegraph*, and continued to 1912; after traveling to China and Japan with a theatrical company, became a reporter and columnist for the *New York Tribune* in 1912; served as a correspondent with the American Expeditionary Force in France during 1917 and was replaced because of his criticism of War

Department inefficiencies; switched to the *New York World* in 1921 and began a widely read column entitled, "It Seems to Me"; was highly critical of government actions during the red scare following World War I; became involved in the Sacco-Vanzetti (q.v.) controversy and was eventually fired by the *New York World* for stridently defending them; joined the Scripps-Howard newspaper chain in 1928; ran for the U.S. Congress from New York on the Socialist party ticket in 1930; was one of the founders and served as vice-president of the New York Newspaper Guild in 1933; later in 1933, was instrumental in organizing the American Newspaper Guild (ANG) and was elected its first president; led the ANG through its early formative period when it faced strong opposition from publishers, who allegedly received government aid and assistance in their efforts to crush the new union; led the ANG into the American Federation of Labor in 1936, but switched to affiliation with the Congress of Industrial Organizations in 1937; also wrote regularly for the *Nation* and the *New Republic*; founded his own literary weekly, *Connecticut Nutmeg* (later *Broun's Nutmeg*) during the 1930s; authored 12 books, including *Pieces of Hate and Other Enthusiasms* (1922), *The Boy Grew Older* (1922), and *Gandle Follows His Nose* (1926); died in New York City, December 18, 1939; Daniel J. Leab, *A Union of Individuals: The Formation of the American Newspaper Guild, 1933–1935* (1970); Bruce Minton and John Stuart, *Men Who Lead Labor* (1937); Walter Galenson, *The CIO Challenge to the AFL: A History of the American Labor Movement, 1935–1941* (1960); *Dictionary of American Biography*, Suppl. 2; Richard O'Connor, *Heywood Broun: A Biography* (1975).

BROWN, Edward J.   (1893–1950). Born in Chicago, Ill., November 20, 1893; son of John J. and Katherine (Shaughnessy) Brown; married Jean E. Duffy on October 2, 1915; no children; graduated from high school and then began an apprenticeship as an electrician in 1911, soon joining Chicago, Ill., Local 282 of the International Brotherhood of Electrical Workers (IBEW); served as chief electrician for Robert White and Company, Chicago, 1925–1929; received an LL.B. degree from the Chicago Law School in 1927; became an IBEW special representative in 1930, and during his ten years in that position, was especially active in organizing electricians in Milwaukee, Wis.; served as a member of the IBEW executive council, 1937–1940; was a University of Wisconsin regent, 1935–1938; appointed IBEW president by the executive council in 1940 to replace Daniel W. Tracy (q.v.), who resigned after being appointed Assistant U.S. Secretary of Labor; elected president of the IBEW in 1941; appointed to the National Defense Mediation Board during World War II; was a member of the American Federation of Labor international labor relations committee; after being defeated for reelection in 1946 by Daniel Tracy, was expelled from the IBEW as a result of charges related to his conduct as business manager of the Milwaukee local; left the labor movement, and conducted a law practice in Wisconsin and Washington, D.C., serving as a consultant to the Fuqua Insurance Company; died in Washington, D.C., January 31, 1950; Philip Taft, *The A.F.*

of L. from the Death of Gompers to the Merger (1959); Walter Galenson, *The CIO Challenge to the AFL: A History of the American Labor Movement, 1935–1941* (1960); *The New York Times,* February 2, 1950.

BROWN, Guy Linden   (1893–   ). Born in Boone, Iowa, August 22, 1893; son of Linden Forest, a minister, and Georgia Anna (Blackburn) Brown; Methodist; married Bernice Jackson on December 17, 1908; four children; attended the public schools of Ellston, Iowa; played professional baseball for a short time; entered railroad service as a fireman on the Chicago and North Western Railroad in 1909; became an engineer in 1914 and remained active in railroad service until 1945; joined the Brotherhood of Locomotive Engineers (BLE) and was elected local chairman of Division 860, Boone, Iowa, in 1939; was BLE general chairman for the Chicago and North Western Railroad, 1945–1947; elected second alternate grand chief engineer in 1947, assistant grand chief engineer in 1949, first assistant grand chief engineer in 1950, and grand chief engineer in 1953; retired union offices in 1960; Reed C. Richardson, *The Locomotive Engineer, 1863–1963: A Century of Railway Labor Relations and Work Rules* (1963); *Who's Who in Railroading* (1959); *Who's Who in America, 1958–1959*; *Labor,* August 8, 1953, May 28, 1960.

BROWN, Harvey Winfield   (1883–1956). Born in Dow, Pa., October 28, 1883; son of William Washington, a farmer, and Catherine Brown; Protestant; married Emma C. Abbott on December 1, 1911; one child; attended elementary school in Pottsville, Pa.; apprenticed as a machinist in 1900 and worked at the craft until 1911; joined the International Association of Machinists (IAM) in 1905; served as business agent for the Wilkes-Barre, Pa., local, 1911–1915; was an IAM international organizer, 1915–1916, and business agent for the Newark, N.J., machinists' local, 1916–1921; served as a delegate to the American Federation of Labor (AFL) conventions in 1919 and 1921; was elected an IAM vice-president in 1921; served as acting president during the illness of President Arthur Wharton (q.v.), 1938–1939; served as IAM president, 1940–1948; was elected an AFL vice-president and executive council member in 1941; as IAM leader, responded to the challenge of the Congress of Industrial Organizations and took advantage of New Deal labor legislation, National Labor Relations Board certification machinery, and general recovery and wartime prosperity; transformed the IAM from a predominantly railroad-machinist craft orientation to an industrial union heavily concentrated in the airframe and general manufacturing industries and launched aggressive organizing drives that added hundreds of thousands of new members; was a bellicose leader and exerted strong national control over dissident autonomy-minded locals; also engaged in a bitter conflict with IAM secretary-treasurer Emmet Davison (1916–1943); embroiled in an embittered, expensive, and perhaps unnecessary jurisdictional struggle with the carpenters and operating engineers and ultimately withdrew the union's affiliation from the AFL in protest of its jurisdictional treatment of the IAM; after two adverse rulings by the National Labor Relations Board, the IAM executive council in 1948 ordered the racial exclusion clause removed from local's secret ritual, an action upheld by the national convention the following year; became a vice-president of the Union Labor Bank and Trust Company in Indianapolis, Ind., in 1924; politically nonpartisan; died in Harrisburg, Pa., September 4, 1956; Mark Perlman, *The Machinists: A New Study in American Trade Unionism* (1961), and *Democracy in the International Association of Machinists* (1962); Solon DeLeon, ed., *The American Labor Who's Who* (1925); *Who's Who in Labor* (1946).

John W. Hevener

BROWN, Henry ("Hank") Stanley (1920–   ). Born in Pittsburgh, Pa., October 24, 1920; son of Stanley J., a coal miner, and Sophie Brown; Roman Catholic, married Sophie E. Wigman in 1939; three children; attended the primary and secondary schools of Pennsylvania and was a student at San Antonio (Junior) College, 1950–1951, St. Mary's University, 1952, and Harvard University, 1956; joined Plumbers and Pipefitters Local 142 of the United Association of Plumbers and Steam Fitters of the United States and Canada and served it as business manager, 1940–1953, 1959–1961; was educational director of the Texas State Federation of Labor (TSFL), 1953–1959; after the American Federation of Labor-Congress of Industrial Organizations' (AFL-CIO) merger in Texas, was elected president of the Texas AFL-CIO in 1961, serving in that capacity until 1971; worked to improve conditions of Texas's low-paid Mexican and black workers, and increased their union memberships by one-third between 1961 and 1968; persuaded the Texas AFL-CIO Council to contribute $100,000 to support families of striking Mexican-American farm workers; as head of the Texas AFL-CIO Committee on Political Education, promoted a liberal-labor-Mexican-black political alliance in the early 1960s and challenged the conservative wing of the Texas Democratic party with liberal candidates for state and national office; lobbied in the Texas legislature against increased auto insurance rates; increased the state AFL-CIO budget to $500,000 by raising the tax on each union member from 8¢ to 25¢; one-third of budget went to equal opportunity activities and another large share to community service; was a frequent critic in the 1960s of Governor John Connally's conservative position on the repeal of Section 14b of the Taft-Hartley Act, medical care for the elderly, the war on poverty, bracero programs, state minimum wage laws, and minority job discrimination; served during his career as vice-president of the TSFL, president of the Texas Pipe Trades Association, executive secretary of the Texas Building and Construction Trades Council, vice-president of the San Antonio Building Trades Council, and on advisory committees for several state and national agencies and charitable organizations; politically a Democrat; *Who's Who in America, 1972–1973*; *Business Week,* June 22, 1968; *AFL-CIO News,* June 5, 1965.

Merl E. Reed

BROWN, Irving Joseph (1911–   ). Born in New York City, November 20, 1911; son of Ralph, a Teamster union official, and Fannie (Singer) Brown;

married Lillie Clara Smith on March 13, 1934; one child; received a B.A. degree in economics from New York University in 1932 and took postgraduate courses for two years at Columbia University; participated in the efforts to organize the automobile industry, 1934–1937 and was physically attacked and savagely beaten by representatives of the Ford Motor Company; became a national American Federation of Labor (AFL) organizer in 1936 and served in that capacity until 1942; after being recommended by AFL, appointed as one of the labor representatives on the War Production Board in 1942; was a member of the International Association of Machinists and elected to the executive committee of the International Metalworkers Federation in 1945; became director of the labor and management division of the branch of the United States Foreign Economic Administration designed to administer labor policy in occupied areas following World War II; resigned from the position because of his disagreement with official U.S. policy of limiting union organization in Germany to the local and factory levels; became the AFL's European representative in October 1945, and later was named AFL representative on the European Recovery Program trade union advisory board; was one of the founders of the International Confederation of Free Trade Unions (ICFTU) in 1949, which seceded from the Communist-dominated World Federation of Trade Unions; served as the ICFTU representative to the 1951 labor conference in Karachi, Pakistan, that created the first non-Communist regional union organization in Asia; was named ICFTU representative to the United Nations in 1962; was appointed director of the African-American Labor Center, an AFL-Congress of Industrial Organizations' (CIO) agency designed to support non-Communist unions in Africa, in 1965; appointed director of the AFL-CIO department of international affairs in 1982; was a determined anti-Communist and devoted much of his trade union career to the promotion of a "free" trade union movement in Western Europe; Ronald Radosh, *American Labor and United States Foreign Policy: The Cold War in the Unions from Gompers to Lovestone* (1969); Joseph C. Goulden, *Meany* (1972); Philip Taft, *The A.F. of L. from the Death of Gompers to the Merger* (1959); *Current Biography* (1951).

BRYSON, Hugh   (1914–   ). Born on an Illinois farm, October 4, 1914; son of Hugh E., a farmer, and Josie W. (Gaffney) Bryson; married Abigail Alvarez on June 23, 1945; was graduated from high school and then attended a business college in 1932; joined the National Marine Cooks' and Stewards' Association (NMCSA) and served successively as assistant secretary, dispatcher, patrolman, and ship's delegate; was vice-president of the San Francisco branch of Labor's Nonpartisan League in 1939; elected to the executive board of the San Francisco Industrial Union Council, Congress of Industrial Organizations (CIO) in 1942 and vice-president in 1946; served as a vice-president of the California State Industrial Union Council, CIO, 1944–1946; elected president of the NMCSA in 1946; after the NMCSA was expelled from the CIO for alleged Communist domination in 1949, was indicted and convicted of perjury for filing a non-Communist affidavit under the provisions of the Taft-Hartley Act; the NMCSA rapidly deteriorated as a result of Bryson's imprisonment and its expulsion from the CIO and was absorbed by Harry Lundeberg's (q.v.) Sailors' Union of the Pacific; identified himself as a Democrat, but strongly supported the candidacy of Henry A. Wallace on the Progressive party ticket in 1948 and was the principal architect of the Independent Progressive party of California which was modeled after the American Labor party in New York; edited the NMCSA organ, *Voice*, 1944–1951; authored *History of the Study of Ideological Conflict in the American Labor Movement, 1865–1900* (1961); *Dictionary of American Biography*, Vol. 3.

BUCHANAN, Joseph Ray   (1851–1924). Born in Hannibal, Mo., December 6, 1851; son of Robert Sylvester and Mary Ellen (Holt) Buchanan; married Lucy A. Clise on December 16, 1879; employed in a variety of occupations after leaving the public schools of Hannibal; obtained work on a Hannibal newspaper in 1876 and learned the typesetting trade; moved to Denver, Colo., in 1878, becoming, in turn, a typesetter and then managing editor of a daily newspaper, the proprietor of an unsuccessful printing office, and a prospector; joined the International Typographical Union (ITU) in 1878; moved to Leadville, Colo., in 1879, but threats against his life growing out of his support of striking miners forced him to return to Denver the following year; served as the Denver delegate to the national ITU convention in 1882; joined the Noble Order of the Knights of Labor (K of L) during the same year and, along with Samuel H. Laverty, began publishing the *Labor Enquirer*, a weekly labor newspaper; named Rocky Mountain representative of the International Workingmen's Association the following year; led a successful strike of Union Pacific shopmen in 1884 and later the same year won a national reputation by leading successful strikes against railroads controlled by Jay Gould; unsuccessfully attempted as a member of the general executive board of the K of L to mediate the growing differences between the K of L and trade unions, 1884–1886; led a secessionist movement in 1886 after being expelled from the K of L as a result of differences with the Order's leader, Terence Powderly (q.v.) over the expulsion of the Cigarmakers' International Union; moved to Chicago, Ill., in 1887, and attempted to gain amnesty for the men convicted of the Haymarket Square bombings; moved to Montclair, N.J., in 1888 and failed in two attempts to be elected to the U.S. Congress; served as labor editor of the *New York Evening Journal*, 1904–1915; was a member of the conciliation council of the U.S. Department of Labor, 1918–1921; one of the organizers of the People's party in 1892 and served on its national committee in 1892, 1896, and 1900; was a Socialist and had at one time been a member of the Socialist Labor party; authored *The Story of a Labor Agitator* (1903); died in Montclair, N.J., September 13, 1924; Norman J. Ware, *The Labor Movement in the United States, 1860–1895* (1929); Gerald N. Grob, *Workers and Utopia: A Study of Ideological Conflict in the American Labor Movement, 1865–1900* (1961); *Dictionary of American Biography*, Vol. 30.

BUCKLEY, Leo Jerome   (1899–1956). Born in Lewiston, Me., February 4, 1899; son of Michael Horace and Margaret (Moriarty) Buckley; Roman Catholic; married Elizabeth Ray on April 18, 1940; one child; completed grammar school; became an apprentice in the stereotype trade and later became an electrotyper; joined New York Local 1 of the International Stereotypers' and Electrotypers' Union of North America (SEUNA); after serving as vice-president of Local 1, 1932–1938, was elected international president of the SEUNA in 1938; served during World War II on the newspaper commission of the War Labor Board, the printing division of the War Production Board, and as a member of Industrial Division 49 of the Wage and Hour Board; served as chairman of the board of governors of the Allied Printing Trades Association and on the board of directors of the Union Labor Life Insurance Company; died in New York City, June 10, 1956; *Who Was Who in America*, Vol. 3; *The New York Times*, June 11, 1956.

BUCKMASTER, Leland Stanford   (1894–1967). Born in Geneva, Ind., March 30, 1894; son of William Vance, a farmer and contractor, and Elizabeth (Thatcher) Buckmaster; Protestant; married Olive Beatrice Shimp on May 11, 1920; four children; was graduated from high school and then attended Tri-State College in Angola, Ind., majoring in teacher education; taught in rural Indiana schools, 1913–1917; served with the U.S. Army during World War I; employed as a tin finisher and builder with the Firestone Tire and Rubber Company, Akron, Ohio, 1919–1937; joined American Federation of Labor (AFL) Federal Union 18321 in 1933 and served as shop committeeman, member of the executive board and president; when the federal local was converted to Local 7 of the United Rubber Workers of America (URWA) (now the United Rubber, Cork, Linoleum and Plastic Workers of America), was elected president and served until 1941; became a member of the URWA general executive board in 1936 and was elected a URWA vice-president in 1941 and international president in 1945; was considered a conservative anti-Communist in the internal ideological conflicts of the union during the 1940s; removed as president in 1949 by the general executive board of the URWA for "malfeasance in office," a charge growing from his conflicts with the leadership of a Pottstown, Pa., local, but was returned to office four months later when reelected by delegates to the annual convention; was a member of the united labor policy committee organized by the AFL, CIO, and independent unions to develop uniform policies on issues affecting labor during the Korean War; was one of the major advocates of a merger between the AFL and CIO; after the 1955 merger, was elected an AFL-CIO vice-president and executive council member, serving until 1962; retired as president of the URWA in 1960; politically a Democrat; died in Henderson, Ky., January 2, 1967; Harold S. Roberts, *The Rubber Workers: Labor Organization and Collective Bargaining in the Rubber Industry* (1944); *Fortune* (July 1951); *Who's Who in Labor* (1946); *The New York Times*, January 4, 1967.

BUGNIAZET, Gustave M.   (1878–1960). Born in New York City in 1878; Roman Catholic; married Mary Doyle and remarried after her death in 1953; six children (three of them stepchildren); became an apprentice electrician after completing a grammar school education; joined Local 419 of the International Brotherhood of Electrical Workers (IBEW) in 1902, and for five years served the local as business manager; later transferred his membership to IBEW Local 98 in Philadelphia, Pa.; was elected an IBEW vice-president in 1911, serving until 1925; served during World War I as a member of the adjustment board of the U.S. Railroad Administration; appointed the IBEW's national legislative representative in Washington, D.C., in 1918; served as an assistant to both the president and secretary of the IBEW prior to being elected international secretary of the Brotherhood in 1925; was elected a vice-president and member of the American Federation of Labor (AFL) executive council in 1930, serving until 1946 when a fourth vice-president; was a member of the AFL committee that in 1936–1937 attempted to resolve the differences with the Committee on Industrial Organization (CIO); was appointed to the AFL committee on social insurance in 1939; was appointed as an AFL alternate to the Combined War Labor Board formed by the AFL and the CIO at the request of President Franklin D. Roosevelt in 1942; served on numerous AFL ad hoc and standing committees, and as secretary of the Electrical Workers' Benefit Fund which administered the IBEW's insurance program; edited the *Journal of Electrical Workers and Operators,* 1925–1947; retired from union positions in 1947 and entered private business, serving for a time as president of the American Standard Life Insurance Company; died in Washington, D.C., March 25, 1960; Philip Taft, *The A.F. of L. from the Death of Gompers to the Merger* (1959); Walter Galenson, *The CIO Challenge to the AFL: A History of the American Labor Movement, 1935– 1941* (1960); Solon DeLeon, ed., *The American Labor Who's Who* (1925); *Labor,* April 2, 1960.

BURKE, John Patrick   (1884–1966). Born in North Duxbury, Vt., on April 21, 1884; the son of a farm family that moved to Franklin, N.H., in 1896; Roman Catholic; married Bessie Leon in 1921; no children; graduated from high school in Franklin and subsequently took courses at the Rand School of Social Sciences in New York City; worked in a hosiery mill and as a carpenter as a youth; also traveled to Europe on a cattle boat; employed at the International Paper Company mill in Franklin; helped organize the Franklin local of pulp workers and attended the first convention of the International Brotherhood of Pulp, Sulphite, and Paper Mill Workers (IBPSPMW), which met in Portland, Me., in 1909; was elected fourth vice-president of the IBPSPMW in 1914 and was elected president-secretary in 1917; reelected consecutively until his retirement in 1965; led the IBPSPMW through its disastrous strikes of the 1920s and through the heavy membership losses of the early depression years; eagerly grasped the opportunity for revival during the New Deal period and supported industrial unionism in the American Federation of Labor; during the 1930s and 1940s, IBPSPMW under his direction expanded to the South, the Northwest, and into paper converting; membership grew from about 5,000 in 1933 to over

175,000 by 1960; pulp and paper workers made substantial gains in wages, fringe benefits, and reduced hours in this period; defection of 20,000 West Coast members in 1964 marred his last year in office; resigned as president-secretary on January 11, 1965, due to poor health; named president emeritus; a Socialist and Socialist party candidate for governor of New Hampshire in 1914, he voted for Robert M. La Follette in 1924 and for Norman Thomas in 1940; died in Miami Beach, Fla., on April 22, 1966; *United Paper*, May 6, 1966; Keith Emory Voelker, "The History of the International Brotherhood of Pulp, Sulphite, and Paper Mill Workers from 1906 to 1929" (Ph.D. diss., 1969); Robert H. Zieger, *Rebuilding the Pulp and Paper Workers' Union, 1933–1941* (1984).

Robert H. Zieger

BURKE, Walter James (1911–   ). Born in Antioch, Ill., September 14, 1911; son of Anthony Frederick, a printer, and Margaret Luella Burke; Roman Catholic; married Aletha Phyllis Luff on August 12, 1939; five children; was graduated from Waukegan (Ill.) Township High School; taught printing in high school, 1930–1932; moved to Fond du Lac, Wis., and worked as an inspector in a metal-fabricating plant, 1932–1937; became president meanwhile of Lodge 1935, Amalgamated Association of Iron, Steel, and Tin Workers; employed on the staff of the Steel Workers Organizing Committee, 1937–1939; served as secretary-treasurer of the Wisconsin Congress of Industrial Organizations' Industrial Union Council, 1939–1941; during World War II, was a panel member of the Chicago Regional War Labor Board; was a member of the United Steelworkers of America (USWA) wage inequities committee during the 1940s and helped revise the entire wage structure in basic steel; became director of USWA District 32 (Milwaukee, Wis., area) in 1948 and was reelected to that position several times; was one of several district directors opposed to David McDonald's (q.v.) administration and managed Joseph Molony's (q.v.) 1955 campaign for international vice-president; was teamed on a slate with I. W. Abel (q.v.) and Molony in 1965 and was elected international secretary-treasurer; was reelected in 1969 and 1973; authored and played a major role in gaining adoption of a graduated dues increase that was accepted by a special convention in 1968 and made possible a strike fund; became a vice-president of the American Federation of Labor-CIO industrial union department in 1965; represented American unions at the 75th anniversary convention of the German Metalworkers Federation in 1966; served on numerous governmental commissions; was chairman of a special committee to direct USWA community action programs aimed at stabilizing employment and creating new jobs in communities threatened by plant shutdowns; politically a Democrat; John Herling, *Right to Challenge: People and Power in the Steelworkers Union* (1972); *Who's Who in America, 1972–1973*.

Donald G. Sofchalk

BURNS, Matthew James (1887–1967). Born in Appleton, Wis., November 6, 1887; son of Andrew Byrnes, a farmer, and Mary (Davey) Burns; Roman

Catholic; married Sarah Elvira Hendricksen in 1912; four children; completed a grammar school education in Appleton and later took courses from the Funk and Wagnalls Correspondence School; began work in the pulp and paper mills of Kaukauna, Wis., in 1901; joined the Kaukauna Local 20 of the International Brotherhood of Paper Makers (IBPM) in 1902; served as an IBPM general organizer, 1920–1922; elected international secretary of the IBPM in 1922, serving in that capacity until 1928; elected international IBPM president in 1929, serving until 1940; joined the International Brotherhood of Pulp, Sulphite and Paper Mill Workers in 1940; served during World War II as a labor economist, an alternate member of the Overall Appeals Board, and assistant director, pulp and paper division, of the War Production Board; reelected president of the IBPM in 1943 and served until his retirement in 1947; edited the *Paper Makers' Journal,* 1922–1928; politically a Democrat; authored *History of the International Brotherhood of Paper Makers* (1922); died in Albany, N.Y., June 15, 1967; Harry E. Graham, *The Paper Rebellion: Development and Upheaval in Pulp and Paper Unionism* (1970); *AFL-CIO News,* June 24, 1967; *Who's Who in Labor* (1946).

BURNS, Thomas F. (1906–   ). Born in Holyoke, Mass., June 19, 1906; son of Thomas F., a loom fixer, and Elizabeth Burns; Roman Catholic; married Maude M. Walton on July 25, 1925; three children; completed one year of high school, then left school to work full time as an employee of the Fisk Tire and Rubber Corporation at Chicopee Falls, Mass.; was one of the principal organizers of American Federation of Labor (AFL) federal Union 18363 at the Fisk plant in 1933; became president and business agent of Fisk Local 18363; served as an AFL organizer, 1934–1935; was one of the leading critics of AFL domination of the United Rubber Workers of America (URWA), which had been chartered by the AFL in 1935, and led the movement toward autonomy; was elected a URWA vice-president in 1935 and became a member of the general executive board; was a staunch advocate of industrial unionism and supported the URWA's affiliation with the Congress of Industrial Organizations (CIO) in 1936; during World War II was chief of the Office of Price Management's labor disputes section, a labor consultant to the National Defense Advisory Committee, and a deputy vice-chairman of the labor products division of the War Production Board; served as an assistant to the chairman of the CIO's Political Action Committee; Harold S. Roberts, *The Rubber Workers: Labor Organization and Collective Bargaining in the Rubber Industry* (1944); *Who's Who in Labor* (1946).

BYRON, Robert (c. 1880–1959). Born in Lynwood, Scotland, ca. 1880; the son of a coal miner and active trade unionist; Protestant; married; one child; emigrated with his parents to the United States in 1888, after his father had been blacklisted in Scotland because of union organizing activities; attended the public schools of Springfield, Ill.; at age 15 began to work in the coal mines around Springfield; in 1897 was hired in a sheet metal works and, three years later, became one of the founders of Springfield Local 84 of the Sheet Metal Workers' International Association (SMWIA); served Local 84 as recording and financial secretary; was an active participant in local and state labor organizations, serving as secretary of the Springfield Federation of Labor, business agent of the Springfield Building Trades Council, and a delegate to the Illinois State Federation of Labor; became an international representative for the SMWIA in 1908 and was assigned an organizing jurisdiction ranging from Pittsburgh, Pa., to the Pacific coast and from Alaska to the Gulf of Mexico; was appointed international president of the SMWIA in 1939 and was subsequently reelected to the post until his death; substantially increased the membership of the SMWIA during his incumbency and helped negotiate collective bargaining agreements providing higher wages, better working conditions, and a variety of fringe benefits; was a vice-president of the American Federation of Labor (AFL) building and metal trades departments; served as a delegate to over 50 AFL and AFL-Congress of Industrial Organizations' national conventions, and represented the AFL at meetings of the International Labor Organization and the International Confederation of Free Trade Unions; died in Northbrook, Ill., May 30, 1959; *Labor,* June 6, 1959; *The New York Times*, May 31, 1959; *American Federation of Labor Weekly News Service*, January 21, 1939.

C

CADDY, Samuel Hubert   (1883–1959). Born at Short Health, Staffordshire, England, December 9, 1883; son of Henry, a coal miner, and Amy (Davenport) Caddy; Methodist; married Dorothy Eva Johnston on September 2, 1919; two children; attended elementary school for five years and then, at age 9, began attending school six hours a day and working five hours in a mine, hand-turning a ventilation fan, then driving a mine pony, and finally, at age 15, becoming a full-time coal loader; emigrated to Halifax, Nova Scotia, in 1905; obtaining a series of mining jobs, worked his way across Canada, saving $1,400; used part of money to help educate his sister; dragged a supply sled 375 miles into the Alaskan gold fields with three companions and spent 23 months prospecting, making one $7,000 strike; joined the United Mine Workers of America (UMWA) in 1907 by transferring from the British Miners Union; settled near Seattle, Wash., in 1909 and worked there in coal mines; became an active union organizer; beginning in 1918, represented District 10 on the UMWA international executive board for five years, and then served as a UMWA international representive for ten years; from 1918 to 1933, organized local unions in Oklahoma, West Virginia, Indiana, Pennsylvania, and Kentucky; shortly before the passage of the National Industrial Recovery Act in June 1933, was sent by President John L. Lewis (q.v.) to organize UMWA District 30 in eastern Kentucky, where the UMWA had all but evaporated after World War I; solidly organized the twenty-five thousand miners of District 30 within five weeks, in contrast to the prolonged and violent union campaign in nearby Harlan County, Ky.; in 1934, was appointed by Lewis as president of District 30 and as a member of the UMWA international executive board and served for 25 years until his death in 1959; as a result of the complicated course of the UMWA's relationship with the rival Congress of Industrial Organizations (CIO) and the American Federation of Labor (AFL), was the only man in Kentucky history to serve for two years as president of the Kentucky State Federation of Labor, AFL, and three years as president of the Kentucky Industrial Union Council, CIO; served from 1933 to 1945 on various federal government coal boards; active for a quarter of a century in Kentucky Democratic politics and served on a governor's committee to reorganize state government; fought before the state legislature and congressional committees for better mine safety laws, improved mine ventilation, rock dusting, more mine mechanization, improved hospitalization, pensions, and security benefits for miners, against the use of black powder for blasting, and for his pet project, the chain of seven UMWA hospitals in eastern Kentucky; known as "the grand old man of Kentucky labor," he died in Lexington, Ky., January 24, 1959; *United Mine Workers Journal*, February 1, 1959; *Who's Who in Labor* (1946).

John W. Hevener

CAHAN, Abraham   (1860–1951). Born in Podberezye, Russian Lithuania (now part of the Soviet Union), July 7, 1860; son of Shachno, a storekeeper and Hebrew teacher, and Sarah C. Cahan; Jewish; married Anna Braunstein in 1887; was graduated from the Teachers' Seminary in Vilna in 1881 and became a teacher in a Jewish elementary school; participated in revolutionary activities, and therefore was forced to flee Russia in 1882 and emigrated to the United States; was a vigorous participant in the organization of immigrant Jewish workers and in the founding of a variety of Jewish trade unions; helped found the Jewish Socialist periodicals *Neue Zeit* in 1886 and *Arbeiter-Zeitung* in 1890; served as editor of the *Arbeiter-Zeitung*, 1891–1894; edited *Zukunft*, a Yiddish periodical, 1894–1897; became the first editor of the *Jewish Daily Forward* in 1897; associated with Lincoln Steffens's *Commercial Advertiser* as a police reporter, 1898–1902; was a moderate Socialist and represented the American Socialist movement at numerous international Socialist congresses; resumed editorship of the *Daily Forward* in 1902; authored numerous books and articles, including *The Rise of David Levinsky* (1917) and *Bletter von Mein Leben*, 5 Vols. (1926–1931); died in New York City, August 31, 1951; Moses Rischin, *The Promised City; New York's Jews, 1870–1914* (1962); Ronald Sanders, *The Downtown Jews: Portraits of an Immigrant Generation* (1969); Melech Epstein, *Profiles of Eleven* (1965) and *Jewish Labor in the U.S.A., 1914–1952*, 2 Vols. (1953); *Dictionary of American Biography*, Suppl. 5.

CAIRNS, Thomas Francis   (1875–1949). Born in Durhamshire, England, in 1875; son of John, a clerical worker, and Jane (Gibney) Cairns; Presbyterian; married Melvina Koon on June 14, 1899; two children; attended high school in England and took a mining engineering course at Scranton (Pa.) Correspondence School; emigrated to the United States, settling in Scranton; joined the United Mine Workers of America (UMWA) there; UMWA president John Mitchell (q.v.) appointed him as an international organizer in 1902; participated in the founding of the West Virginia State Federation of Labor (WVSFL) in 1903; became a member of the UMWA international executive board in 1908, representing District 17, Kanawha District of West Virginia; served as president of District 17, UMWA, 1912–1917, during the violent Kanawha Valley coal strike of 1912–1913; served as an American Federation of Labor (AFL) district representative and organizer, 1938–1949; when the officials of the WVSFL refused to execute the AFL's order to expel the UMWA and other Congress of Industrial Organizations' (CIO) affiliates in August 1937, they were expelled from the AFL and founded the rival West Virginia State Industrial Union Council, CIO; headed, along with William Kirk, another AFL organizer, 53-delegate "loyalist" faction that reorganized the WVSFL; in December 1937, AFL President William Green (q.v.) appointed William J. Dillon as acting president of the WVSFL and he in turn appointed Cairns acting secretary-treasurer; elected president of the WVSFL during the reorganization convention in 1938, serving until 1945; transferred his local union affiliation from the UMWA to the International Brotherhood of Teamsters' Local 175, Charleston, W.Va., in 1938 and five years later affiliated with the Federal Labor Union of Enamel Workers Local 23055, Dunbar, W.Va.; provided, together with Secretary-Treasurer Volney Andrews (1938–1953), efficient and stable, but rather unimaginative, caretaker leadership of the WVSFL; as president, concentrated on adding to membership, which increased from eleven thousand to eighteen thousand, and on affiliation of craft locals, but ignored opportunities for labor legislation and public education; followed a highly controversial political policy of endorsing candidates who were anti-CIO (for example, Republican gubernatorial candidate Chapman Revercomb in 1940 rather than Democrat Matthew M. Neely, who possessed an excellent, though pro-CIO, labor record); kept in office throughout World War II only out of deference to "Uncle Tom's" 53 years of service to labor; finally, in 1945, was unseated by critics who, in a bitter election, bestowed the office on Eugene Carter, a reluctant but able Charleston teamster; Cairns was named honorary chairman for life; died in Charleston, W.Va., March 22, 1949; *Who's Who in Labor* (1946); *The New York Times*, March 23, 1949; Evelyn L. K. Harris and Frank J. Krebs, *From Humble Beginnings: West Virginia State Federation of Labor, 1903–1957* (1960).

John W. Hevener

CALVIN, William Austin   (1898–1962). Born in St. John, New Brunswick, Canada, February 5, 1898; son of John, a boilermaker, and Agnes (Kelly) Calvin; Methodist; married Iranell Marian Jester on April 12, 1936; three children; completed elementary school in New Brunswick; employed as a boilermaker by the Canadian Pacific Railroad, and a Baltimore, Md., firm; joined the International Brotherhood of Boilermakers, Iron Shipbuilders, and Helpers of America (IBB) in 1914; joined the Canadian Army in 1915, not returning to civilian life until 1919 due to a combat wound; emigrated to Florida and went to work as a boilermaker for the Seaboard Airline Railroad; elected chairman of his local shop committee in 1921 and became president of District Lodge 40 in 1924; in 1929 elected a vice-president of the IBB; served as secretary-treasurer of the American Federation of Labor (AFL) metal trades department, 1933–1940; served on several government boards during the 1930s and 1940s, including the National

Recovery Administration's Industrial Relations Committee for Shipbuilding; helped draft the Merchant Marine Act of 1936, which gave the Maritime Commission comprehensive regulatory powers; left his union position in 1951 to become a full-time labor specialist for the National Production Authority; returned to the IBB in 1953 as assistant to President Charles J. MacGowan (q.v.); replaced MacGowan as president the following year and was elected to that office in 1957 and reelected in 1961; was elected a vice-president and executive council member of the AFL in 1961; was a member of the Railway Labor Executives' Association; visited Latin America as a labor specialist on behalf of the U.S. State Department in 1958; was an AFL-Congress of Industrial Organizations' fraternal delegate to the Indian National Trade Union Congress in 1959; was an active proponent of nuclear-powered merchant vessels, serving as a director of the Fund for Peaceful Atomic Development, Inc., a nonprofit group set up in 1954 to support President Dwight D. Eisenhower's atoms-for-peace program; died in Kansas City, Kans., January 27, 1962; *The New York Times*, December 21, 1954, January 28, 1962; *Journal of the International Brotherhood of Boilermakers, Iron Shipbuilders, and Blacksmiths* (March 1962).

Donald G. Sofchalk

CAMERON, Andrew Carr   (1836–1890). Born in Berwick-on-Tweed, England, September 28, 1836; son of a Scots printer; worked in his father's printing shop after receiving a limited elementary education; emigrated with parents to the United States in 1851, settling near Chicago, Ill.; joined the International Typographical Union while working for a Chicago newspaper; as a result of a printers' strike in 1864, became the editor of the newly established *Workingman's Advocate*, which served as the official organ of the Chicago Trades Assembly and later the National Labor Union (NLU); elected president of the Chicago Trades Assembly in 1866 and served for four years; also elected president of the Grand Eight Hour League and the Illinois State Labor Association; was one of the founders of the NLU and served as an organizer and as chairman of the NLU platform committee for six years; was an NLU delegate to the Fourth Congress of the International Workingmen's Association (IWA) in Basle in 1869, but became hostile to the IWA after it moved its headquarters to the United States; was prominently identified with the cause of independent labor political action and deliberately kept himself out of the limelight in the Industrial Congress, which he helped organize; discontinued publication of the *Workingman's Advocate* in 1880 and then was editor until his death of the *Inland Printer*; died in Chicago, Ill., May 28, 1890; David Montgomery, *Beyond Equality: Labor and the Radical Republicans, 1862–1872* (1967); Norman J. Ware, *The Labor Movement in the United States, 1860–1895* (1929); *Dictionary of American Biography*, Vol. 3; John R. Commons et al., *History of Labour in the United States*, Vol. 2 (1918).

CAMPBELL, Patrick J.   (1918–   ). Born in New York City on July 22, 1918; son of Peter James, an employee on the Inter-Borough Railroad, and Mary

Campbell, a homemaker; Roman Catholic; after completing his formal education in New York City, he served an apprenticeship as a carpenter; served as a staff sergeant in the U.S. Air Force during World War II, 1941–1945; after the war he joined Local 964, Rockford County, N.Y., of the United Brotherhood of Carpenters and Joiners of America (UBC); was elected president of Local 964 in 1954, serving in that position until 1969; served on the UBC organizing staff, 1955–1957, and as a general representative, 1957–1966; was appointed assistant to the UBC general president in 1966; was elected to the UBC's general executive board in 1966 and became second vice-president of the international union in 1974; also was elected a vice-president of the New York State American Federation of Labor-Congress of Industrial Organizations (AFL-CIO) in 1970 and vice-president of the New York State Building Trades Council in the same year; succeeded to the presidency of the UBC after the retirement of William Konyha (q.v.) in 1982; *AFL-CIO News*, October 23, 1982; *Who's Who in Labor* (1976).

CANNON, Joseph D.   (1871–1952). Born in Locust Gap, Pa., October 26, 1871; son of John, a coal miner, and Bridgid (Early) Cannon; married Laura G. Cannon on August 16, 1911; completed primary school and then began work in the mines; in 1899 joined the Western Federation of Miners (WFM); involved in the efforts to organize copper workers in Arizona in 1906–1908, 1917, and served as president of the Bisbee (Ariz.) Miners' Union and the Arizona State Federation of Labor; served as an organizer for the WFM (name changed to International Union of Mine, Mill and Smelter Workers in 1916), 1907–1920; was a member of the executive board of the WFM, 1911–1912; served as a director of the Cooperative League of the U.S.A., 1918–1920; was a member of the executive board of the American Federation of Labor mining department, 1914–1920; participated in the efforts to organize the steel industry, 1919–1920, 1936–1937, and served as an organizer and business representative for unions in the cleaning and dyeing, paper box, and doll industries; joined the Congress of Industrial Organizations (CIO) in 1937 and became a field representative; served as the chairman of the CIO's Distillery Workers' Organizing Committee; served as Kentucky regional CIO director until his retirement in 1946 from union affairs; was an active Socialist and ran for the U.S. Congress from Arizona on the Socialist party ticket in 1906 and 1908, for the U.S. Senate from New York in 1916, and for governor of New York in 1920; joined the American Labor party shortly after it was organized in New York in 1936; died in New York City, January 4, 1952; Vernon H. Jensen, *Heritage of Conflict: Labor Relations in the Nonferrous Metals Industry up to 1930* (1950); Erma Angevine, *In League with the Future* (1959); Solon DeLeon, ed., *The American Labor Who's Who* (1925).

CAPETILLO, Luisa   (1880–1922). Born in Arecibo, Puerto Rico, about 1880; daughter of a construction worker and a domestic servant; while still an adolescent, she became the mistress of Manuel Ledesma, the son of her mother's aristocratic employer, and bore him two children; unhappy with her position in life she dissolved her relationship with Ledesma, although in the tradition of the Puerto Rican upper class, he had provided support for her, her mother, and her two children; worked at various times in both the textile and tobacco industries of Puerto Rico; somewhat later, she was employed by a factory owner to read to his employees while they worked; this stimulated an older commitment to learning, which had provided her with the ability to read and write, and she began to expand her reading into syndicalist and anarchist literature; thereafter, she soon became involved in the emerging Puerto Rican labor movement; became a member of the Free Federation of Puerto Rican Workers in 1907 and participated in a strike at an Arecibo factory; soon thereafter, she became a union organizer and then a reporter for *Workers' Union*, a labor newspaper; always a feminist as well as a trade unionist, she sponsored a resolution at the 1908 convention of the Free Federation calling for woman's suffrage regardless of literacy (a reform that was not achieved until 1930); founded *La Mujer* ("Woman") in 1910, a feminist magazine; was arrested for wearing pants in public but was later released; authored *My Opinion on the Liberties, Rights and Obligations of the Puerto Rican Woman* in 1911; for the remainder of her life, she traveled extensively throughout Central and North America supporting feminist and female labor causes; died in Puerto Rico in 1922; *Ms* (January 1975); Angel Quintero Rivera, *Workers' Struggle in Puerto Rico: A Documentary History* (1976); Miles Galvin, *The Organized Labor Movement in Puerto Rico* (1979).

CAREY, James Barron   (1911–1973). Born in Philadelphia, Pa., August 12, 1911; son of John, a paymaster at the U.S. Mint, and Margaret (Loughery) Carey; Roman Catholic; married Margaret McCormick on January 8, 1938; two children; was graduated from high school in Glassboro, N.J.; worked in a Philco Corporation radio laboratory in Philadelphia while attending the night school of Drexel Institute; studied electrical engineering from 1929 to 1931, then attended the University of Pennsylvania's Wharton (evening) School of Finance and Commerce, 1931–1932; helped organize the workers in the Philco Corporation plant where he was employed and led a successful strike for union recognition; became a general American Federation of Labor (AFL) organizer in 1934; became president of Radio and Television Workers federal Union 18368, Philadelphia, in 1935; elected president of the National Radio and Allied Trades Council the same year and unsuccessfully sought an AFL charter; elected president of the newly organized United Electrical, Radio and Machine Workers of America (UE) in March 1935; was an advocate of industrial unionism and led his union into the Congress of Industrial Organizations (CIO) six months later; was a staunch anti-Communist and was defeated for reelection to the UE presidency in 1941 by a left-wing coalition of delegates; elected national secretary of the CIO in 1938 and general secretary-treasurer in 1942; served during World War II as an associate member of the National Defense Mediation Board and as a member of the Production Planning Board of the Office of Production Management; attended the 1945 London and Paris conferences that resulted in the organization of the World Federation of Trade Unions; appointed to the Presidential Commission on Civil Rights in 1946; in 1949 assumed the presidency of the newly chartered International Union of Electrical, Radio and Machine Workers (IUE) after the UE was expelled from the CIO because of alleged Communist domination; was a member of the AFL-CIO unity committee that negotiated the merger of the two organizations in 1955; became an AFL-CIO vice-president and executive council member, and was appointed secretary-general of the industrial union department; resigned as president of the IUE after his 1965 reelection was successfully challenged by Paul Jennings (q.v.); left the IUE and became a labor liaison representative of the United Nations Association; was a Democrat and a member of the national board of Americans for Democratic Action; died in Silver Spring, Md., September 1, 1973; James B. Carey Papers, Walter Reuther Library, Wayne State University; Philip Taft, *The A.F. of L. from the Death of Gompers to the Merger* (1959); Walter Galenson, *The CIO Challenge to the AFL: A History of the American Labor Movement, 1935–1941* (1960); Max M. Kampelman, *The Communist Party vs. the C.I.O.: A Study in Power Politics* (1957); *Current Biography* (1951); *AFL-CIO News*, September 16, 1973; Carey Interview, Columbia Oral History Collection; Nelson Lichtenstein, *Labor's War at Home: The CIO in World War II* (1982); Harvey A. Levenstein, *Communism, Anticommunism, and the CIO* (1981).

CARLTON, Albert A. (fl. 1847–1886). Born in Lynn, Mass., in 1847; at the age of 10 years he began work in a shoe shop, to add to the income of his father's family; he worked at his trade until July 16, 1865, when at the age of 17 he enlisted for the war; after meritorious services in the army, he returned to Lynn and entered the shops as a shoe cutter; he displayed an early interest in labor organization, and was a member of the first cutters' unions, also of the Knights of St. Crispin, he was prominently identified with the Lynn Workingmen's Association, whose purposes were political; in 1877 he joined the Knights of Labor, as a member of Local Assembly 1715; he at once displayed ability as an organizer, and was chosen master workman of the district at its first session, an office from which he retired in Lowell, January 19, 1886, having rendered distinguished services as an organizer of the Order; on his retirement he was presented with a gold watch and chain as a testimonial; he was elected delegate to the General Assembly at Detroit, 1879, but was unable to attend, owing to the lack of funds in the treasury; he served in General Assemblies at Cincinnati, Philadelphia, Hamilton, Cleveland, and Richmond; in January 1886, his conspicuous ability as a public speaker gained him an appointment at the hands of the executive board as general lecturer for the Order; in this latter position he traveled extensively, and delivered a large number of speeches; George E. McNeill, *The Labor Movement: The Problem of To-Day* (1887); Gerald N. Grob, *Workers and Utopia: A Study of Ideological Conflict in the American Labor Movement,*

1865–1900 (1961); Norman J. Ware, *The Labor Movement in the United States, 1860–1895* (1929).

George E. McNeill

CARROLL, Thomas Claude   (1894–1960). Born in Donalds, S.C., May 22, 1894; son of Samuel Harvey, a railroad section foreman, and Ida Mae Smith; Methodist; married Marie E. Smith in 1914 and remarried after her death; was graduated from high school and then worked in a variety of railroad jobs—clerk, brakeman, conductor, section foreman—on the Piedmont, Alabama Railroad, 1913–1919; joined the Brotherhood of Maintenance of Way Employees (BMWE) during this period; hired by the Louisville and Nashville Railroad as a section hand and yard foreman in 1919; elected general chairman for the Dixie (southeastern) Federation of the BMWE in 1919, serving until 1925; served as president of the International Association of General Chairmen, BMWE, 1920–1922; elected secretary of the grand lodge executive board in 1922, serving until 1925; served as a grand lodge vice-president for the southeastern region and as a member of the grand lodge executive board during the period 1925–1947; was appointed national legislative representative in Washington, D.C., in 1926, serving in that capacity for several years; elected grand lodge president in 1947; along with the leaders of other nonoperating railroad unions, negotiated shortly after taking office a 40-hour week at 48-hours' pay; also negotiated several wage increases and a variety of fringe benefits; became president emeritus in 1958, after successfully negotiating the first contract to include a national job-stabilization agreement with carriers; was a Democrat; died in Bradenton, Fla., in September 1960; Denver Willard Hertel, *History of the Brotherhood of Maintenance of Way Employees: Its Birth and Growth, 1877–1955* (1955); Brotherhood of Maintenance of Way Employees, *Pictorial History, 1877–1951* (1952); *Who's Who in Labor* (1946); *Labor*, October 8, 1960.

CARTER, William Samuel   (1859–1923). Born in Austin, Tex., August 11, 1859; son of Samuel Miles and Margaret Frances (Oliphant) Carter; married Mary Evelyn Gorsuch on December 26, 1880, and, after her death in 1892, Julia I. Cross on November 27, 1902; attended the public schools of Williamson County, Tex., and then the Agricultural and Mechanical College of Texas for two years; worked for a time as a cowboy before becoming a fireman on a southwestern railroad in 1879; worked during 1879–1894 as a baggageman, fireman, and engineer on several different railroads in the United States and Mexico; joined the Brotherhood of Locomotive Firemen and Enginemen (BLFE); became editor and manager of the *Brotherhood of Locomotive Firemen and Enginemen's Magazine* in 1894 and served until 1904; elected general secretary-treasurer of the BLFE in 1904 and president in 1909; appointed director of the division of labor of the U.S. Railway Administration during World War I; retired from the presidency of the BLFE in 1922 and was appointed manager of the newly organized research department; an opponent of compulsory arbitration, but was an essentially conservative trade unionist who advocated mediation and arbitration as an alternative to strikes; supported the Democratic party; died in Baltimore, Md., March 15, 1923; Brotherhood of Locomotive Firemen and Enginemen, *An Historical Sketch of the Brotherhood* (1937); *Dictionary of American Biography*, Vol. 3.

CASHEN, Thomas Cecil   (1879–1959). Born in South Thompson, Ohio, September 15, 1879; son of John, a farmer, and Sarah (McKee) Cashen; Roman Catholic; married Marie Burhenne on September 7, 1905; one child; was graduated from high school in Cleveland, Ohio, then hired as a locomotive fireman on the Lake Shore and Michigan Southern Railroad in 1899; operated a grocery and retail meat market, 1902–1906; became a switchman on the New York Central Railroad in 1906; joined the Switchmen's Union of North America (SUNA) in 1907; served as the SUNA chairman for the western district of the New York Central Railroad for ten years, then elected to the grand board of directors of the SUNA in 1918; elected a SUNA vice-president in 1919 and served in that capacity until elected international president in 1921; served during World War II as a member of the advisory board of the Office of War Mobilization and Reconversion; served as director of the Labor Cooperative Education and Publishing Society in Washington, D.C., a director of the Union Labor Life Insurance Company of New York, and as president of the Railway Labor Executives' Association; retired as international president of the SUNA in 1947; was a Democrat; died in Skokie, Ill., in March 1959; Solon DeLeon, ed., *The American Labor Who's Who* (1925); *Who's Who in Labor* (1946); *Who Was Who in America*, Vol. 3.

CENERAZZO, Walter William   (1913–1968). Born in Somerville, Mass., on July 21, 1913; son of Anthony Peter, a contractor, and Mary (Buonsanto) Cenerazzo; Roman Catholic; married Marian Evelyn Harding on July 4, 1941; no children; attended Catholic parochial schools and public schools in Somerville; ended his formal education before finishing high school and took a job as a printer's devil in a newspaper composing room; after serving apprenticeship, he became a journeyman typographer and joined the International Typographical Union (ITU); became an organizer for the ITU in 1932 and the American Federation of Labor (AFL) in 1937; organized the Seafood Workers Union of Gloucester, Mass., in 1938, and served as its business agent until 1941; organized the employees of Waltham Watch Company in Waltham, Mass., for the International Jewelry Workers Union (IJWU) in 1941, becoming the new local's president and business agent; two years later the Waltham local, the Waltham Watch Workers Union, seceded from the IJWU and became an independent; organized the Hamilton Watch Workers Union in Lancaster, Pa., and the Elgin National Watch Workers Union in Elgin, Ill., uniting them with the Waltham Watch Workers Union into a new international union, the American Watch Workers Union (AWWU), which remained independent as a result of the AFL's refusal to grant it a charter in the same jurisdiction as the IJWU; the AWWU was the first union to organize the entire American jeweled watch industry; Cenerazzo served as president of the AWWU until 1958; was internationally known in the labor movement for developing an advanced code of ethics for labor unions; unlike most of the larger AFL unions, the AWWU adopted and strictly adhered to a code of ethics, which included provisions for financial disclosure, membership referenda, and democratic union elections; an effective negotiator, he regularly secured higher wages, improved working conditions and fringe benefits without resorting to strikes; led a long but largely unsuccessful effort to raise tariffs on imported watches that were undermining the industry in the United States; after the Waltham Watch Company was forced into bankruptcy in 1948, he helped secure a federal Reconstruction Finance Corporation loan which allowed the company to stay in operation until 1954, permitting its fifteen hundred employees to secure other employment; left the labor movement in 1958 and devoted his attention thereafter to various business interests which included the Marion Village Motor Inn in Camden, Me., which he had owned and operated since 1952, and Schoolhouse Togs, a Rockport, Me., firm which he also owned that specialized in garment assembly; an active participant in local civic affairs, he also served as a labor-management consultant to several presidents; died in Portland, Me., on May 12, 1968; *National Cyclopaedia of American Biography*, Vol. 55; *Who's Who in America*, Vol. 19.

CHAIKEN, Sol C.   (1918–   ). Born in New York City on January 9, 1918; son of Sam, a cloak maker, and Beckie (Schechtman) Chaiken, a dressmaker; Jewish; married Rosalind Bryon, a teacher, on August 31, 1940; four children; after attending public elementary schools in New York City, he enrolled at Townsend Harris High School for the academically gifted, graduating in 1934; entered Brooklyn Law School in 1938 after earning the baccalaureate degree at City College of New York; was awarded the LL.B. in 1940 and passed the New York bar exam the following year; shortly after receiving his law degree, he took a job as an organizer for the International Ladies' Garment Workers' Union (ILGWU) Local 178 in Fall River, Mass.; a few months later was appointed business agent for Local 281, covering Boston and Lowell, Mass.: entered the U.S. Air Force in 1943 and served with distinction in the South Pacific before receiving his discharge in 1946; after the war, was appointed business manager of ILGWU Local 226 in Springfield and, in 1948, was named manager of the western Massachusetts district of the ILGWU's Northeast department; served as the director of the ILGWU's lower Southeast region from 1955 to 1959, a region composed of Texas, Arkansas, Oklahoma, and Louisiana; was appointed assistant manager of the ninety-five thousand-member Northeast department in 1959 and associate director six years later; elected an ILGWU international vice-president in 1965 and international secretary-treasurer in 1973; assumed the ILGWU presidency in 1975; a dynamic union leader with strong rank-and-file support, he immediately set about reforming and modernizing the management of the ILGWU whose membership and influence had declined precipitantly during the 1970s; among the changes he instituted were (1) the conclusion of the piecework rate system of garment worker compensation which had retarded the introduction of labor-saving technology, (2) the introduction of computerized data processing and other modern management techniques within ILGWU national headquarters, (3) a massive union label advertising campaign, (4) a major union organizing drive in the South, (5) and an intensive effort to promote better labor-management cooperation in attacking the critical problems confronting the American garment industry; was a delegate to the International Labour Organization's World Employment Conference in 1976; served as a labor representative to the Commission for Security and Cooperation in Europe in 1977; an active participant in numerous civic, social, and policy organizations, including the Trilateral Commission, the Brookings Institute, Workmen's Circle, the National Committee for Labor Israel, the Jewish Labor Committee, Freedom House, and the National Urban Coalition; a liberal Democrat, he seconded Jimmy Carter's nomination for a second term in 1980; *Current Biography* (1981); *New York Post*, June 7, 1975; *Forbes*, January 23, 1978; *Who's Who in Labor* (1976); Sol C. Chaiken Papers, ILGWU Archives.

CHAMBERLAIN, Edwin M. (fl. 1835–1872). Born in Cambridge, Mass., on November 7, 1835; son of David, a wealthy tavern keeper; his mother was a direct descendant of Solomon Martin who had settled in Virginia in 1636; married; two children; attended school and worked at his father's tavern-hotel throughout much of his youth and early adulthood; enlisted in the army during the Civil War and raised a battery of artillery for which he received a commission; at various times during the war, he served on the staff of General John McNeil of Missouri in the signal corps, and under Admiral David Farragut on board his flagship, the *Hartford*; after the war, he became commander of Post 7, G.A.R., Boston; having become involved in labor reform activities during the second half of the 1860s, he was selected a delegate to the first Labor Reform party political convention in Massachusetts in 1869; was nominated for governor of Massachusetts on the Labor Reform ticket; vigorously campaigned throughout the state and received 13,500 votes while losing the contest; was nominated for the same office again in 1871 (Wendell Phillips had been the party's nominee in the intervening year); in another losing campaign, he advocated monetary reform, a reduction in the hours of labor, factory legislation, and a variety of other labor reforms; became chairman of the Massachusetts Labor Reform state central committee in 1872; meanwhile, he was the steward of the Adams House, an elite Boston club; *Chicago Workingman's Advocate*, March 7, 1874; David Montgomery, *Beyond Equality: Labor and the Radical Republicans, 1862–1872* (1967).

CHAPMAN, Gordon Warner (1907–   ). Born in Tomah, Wis., September 5, 1907; son of Allie H. and Dora (Parshall) Chapman; Congregationalist;

married Ferne Everhardt on June 28, 1935; three children; was graduated from the University of Wisconsin's School of Commerce in 1931, then became the proprietor of an advertising firm, managing it until 1934; served as an assistant director of surplus commodity distribution for the Wisconsin Public Welfare Department, 1934–1936; joined Local 1 of the American Federation of State, County and Municipal Employees (AFSCME) shortly after it was organized and appointed national accountant of the AFSCME; elected secretary-treasurer of the international union in 1937, serving in that capacity until named executive assistant to AFSCME president Arnold S. Zander (q.v.) in 1945; after the office of executive assistant was eliminated in 1948, again elected secretary-treasurer; was a member of the International Confederation of Free Trade Unions' (ICFTU) delegation that studied trade union affairs in Asia in 1950; was a member of the ICFTU committee that studied working conditions and union organizations in Okinawa in 1956; resigned from his union positions in 1961 when appointed a special assistant to the Secretary of State to coordinate international labor affairs in the U.S. State Department, serving until 1962; again elected secretary-treasurer of the AFSCME in 1963; a Democrat; resigned union positions in 1966 because of failing health; Leo Kramer, *Labor's Paradox: The American Federation of State, County and Municipal Employees, AFL-CIO* (1962); *AFL-CIO News*, July 30, 1966; *Who's Who in Labor* (1946); Joseph C. Goulden, *Jerry Wurf: Labor's Last Angry Man* (1982).

CHAVEZ, Cesar Estrada   (1927–   ). Born near Yuma, Ariz., March 31, 1927; son of Librado, a small farmer, migrant worker, and union supporter; Roman Catholic; married Helen Favila; eight children; attended more than 30 elementary schools before completing the eighth grade; worked as a field laborer from an early age; served with the U.S. Navy during World War II, 1944–1945; joined the National Agricultural Workers' Union in 1946; associated with the Community Service Organization (CSO), 1952–1962, and served as California state organizer, 1953–1960, and general director, 1960–1962; resigned from the CSO when it refused to organize farm workers; believed that people should identify and solve their problems without outside help, and was a disciple of the principle of nonviolence; in 1962 moved to Delano, Calif., and formed there the National Farm Workers Association (NFW), which in two years became self-supporting with one thousand dues-paying members in seven counties; led minor strikes in 1965 involving rents at farm labor camps and wages in horticulture; shortly thereafter, joined Filipino workers in a strike against Coachella Valley table-grape growers, attracting nationwide support from civil rights workers, students, ministers, Walter P. Reuther (q.v.), Senator Robert F. Kennedy, and the U.S. Senate Subcommittee on Migratory Labor headed by Senator Harrison Williams; used unconventional tactics such as "following the grapes out of the fields" to shipping terminals, consumer boycotts, and the *peregrinación* (march) on Sacramento, Calif., in the spring of 1966; despite competition from the International Brotherhood of Teamsters (IBT), won contracts from Schenley,

DiGiorgio, and others; after the merger of the NFW and the Agricultural Workers Organizing Committee, became the leader of the resulting United Farm Workers Organizing Committee (UFWOC), American Federation of Labor-Congress of Industrial Organizations (AFL-CIO); began the "great grape boycott" in August 1967, which produced three-year contracts with major grape growers of the Coachella and San Joaquin Valleys in 1969–1970, establishing a two dollar minimum wage and union hiring halls; made control of pesticides a union goal in 1968; the AFL-CIO chartered United Farm Workers' Union (UFW), which had been organized from the UFWOC, next moved against lettuce growers but with only minimal success; faced serious internal problems in administering contracts, including the unpopularity of the hiring halls with the growers and many workers, his own alleged shortcomings as an administrator, the continuing difficulty of creating a union of farm workers, and the IBT's intervention; after the grape growers and Teamsters signed contracts eliminating the union hiring hall and recognizing the IBT, the UFW, receiving substantial support from the AFL-CIO and other outraged groups and individuals, eventually negotiated a jurisdictional agreement with the IBT, but the IBT failed to abide by the terms of the agreement; finally negotiated an agreement with the Teamsters in 1977, giving the UFW the sole right to organize field workers; the significance of this achievement, however, was compromised by internal dissention, punctuated by charges that he had disrupted the union staff by his advocacy of Synanon-type encounter sessions, holistic medical practices and faith healing, resulted in the resignation or firing of many of the UFW's most experienced leaders; meanwhile, membership fell from fifty thousand to thirty thousand and the hopes of organizing a truly national union of farm workers seemed more remote than ever; apparently supports the Democratic party although not a political activist; Cesar E. Chavez Papers, Walter Reuther Library, Wayne State University; Joan London and Henry Anderson, *So Shall Ye Reap: The Story of Cesar Chavez and the Farm Workers' Movement* (1970); John G. Dunne, *Delano: The Story of the California Grape Strike* (1967); George D. Horwitz, *La Causa: The California Grape Strike* (1970); *Current Biography* (1969); *New Republic*, May 19, 1973; *Newsweek*, December 14, 1981.

Merl E. Reed

CHESSER, Al H. (1914–   ). Born in Pettis County, Mo., on February 26, 1914; married; educated in the public schools of Sedalia, Mo.; after working at various jobs for several years, he became a brakeman and conductor on the Santa Fe Railway in 1914, continuing in that employment until 1956; joined Lodge 608 of the Brotherhood of Railroad Trainmen (BRT) and, in 1945, was elected its secretary-treasurer and legislative representative, serving in those positions until 1956; elected secretary of the BRT's Texas legislative board in 1952 and four years later became its chairman, serving in that capacity until 1962 when he became a BRT national legislative representative; after the merger of the BRT and three other railroad operating unions in 1968, creating the United

Transportation Union (UTU), he became the new union's national legislative director; elected president of the UTU in 1971; became a vice-president and member of the American Federation of Labor-Congress of Industrial Organizations executive council in 1972; elected chairman of the Congress of Railway Unions in 1972; an active member of several public and private boards and agencies, he served on the Amarillo Civil Service Commission, 1948–1954, the Texas Industrial Commission, 1950–1956, organized and chaired the Amarillo Labor Political Council, 1954–1956, the President's Consumer Advisory Council, 1964–1968, and, among others, the Task Force on Railroad Safety, created by the U.S. Department of Transportation's Federal Railroad Administration, the Transportation Study Group of the Domestic Affairs Task Force, the Greater Cleveland Growth Board, and the National Defense Executive Reserve of the Interstate Commerce Commission; a Democrat, he served on the board of directors of the National Democratic Committee; retired union positions in 1979; during his ten-year UTU presidency, union members gained 124 percent increases in wages and fringe benefits, greater job safety, and larger employer contributions to the employees' retirement fund; authored several pamphlets including *Project 70's* (1971), *Railroads and the Energy Crisis* (1974), and *Transportation and Energy* (1975); *Who's Who in Labor* (1976); *AFL-CIO News*, June 16, 1979.

CHEYFITZ, Edward Theodore   (1913–   ). Born in Montreal, Canada, September 13, 1913; son of Joseph, a plumber, and Faye (Stephenson) Cheyfitz, national chairwoman of the Congress of Industrial Organizations' (CIO) Women's Auxiliaries; married Julia Frank Pollock on June 26, 1936; one child; spent a year in the Soviet Union; was graduated from the University of Michigan in 1934 with a B.A. in engineering and went to work for the Doehler Die Casting Company in Toledo, Ohio; joined the National Association of Die Casting Workers (NADCW), a small union affiliated with the CIO; in the late 1930s, organized automobile and other industrial workers in the Toledo area and elected secretary of the Toledo Industrial Union Council, CIO; elected national executive secretary of the NADCW in 1939, and led a difficult campaign to organize the die casters in Cleveland, Ohio, and eastern New York State; became a member of the national CIO executive board and was a protégé of John L. Lewis (q.v.); with Lewis's support, ambitiously tried to create another large mass-production industrial union alongside of steel, placing the NADCW into a large union embracing all nonferrous metal production; after Lewis broke with the CIO in 1940, Cheyfitz continued to push the proposed merger of NADCW, aluminum workers, and the International Union of Mine, Mill and Smelter Workers (IUMMSW); realized that Communists would control the union and attempted unsuccessfully to block the merger; nevertheless, became the head of the die casters division within the IUMMSW in 1942; served in the U.S. Army Air Force during World War II and then returned to his IUMMSW post in 1945; sought to consolidate the conservative opposition to the growing power of the Communist faction on the union executive board; concluded that this was not possible and resigned to accept a job with Eric Johnson in the motion-picture industry; Vernon H. Jensen, *Nonferrous Metals Industry Unionism: 1932–1954* (1954); *Who's Who in Labor* (1946).

Donald G. Sofchalk

CHRISTMAN, Elisabeth   (1881–1975). Born in Chicago, Ill., on September 2, 1881; daughter of Henry, a musician, and Barbara (Guth) Christman, both German immigrants; Lutheran; attended German Lutheran schools until the age of 13, then was hired at the Eisendrath Glove Factory in Chicago; with Agnes Nestor (q.v.), helped form Operators Local 1 of the International Glove Workers Union (IGWU), and served as the local's chairman of shop stewards and treasurer, 1905–1911, and president, 1912–1917; was a delegate from the IGWU to the 1916 convention of the American Federation of Labor (AFL); served as secretary-treasurer of the IGWU, 1916–1931; elected an IGWU vice-president in 1931 and served until 1937 when the glove workers affiliated with the Amalgamated Clothing Workers of America; was a member of the executive board of the Chicago Women's Trade Union League (WTUL), 1910–1929; elected to the national executive board of the WTUL in 1919; served during World War I as chief of women field representatives for the National War Labor Board; became secretary-treasurer of the WTUL in 1921; appointed to the 1921 Unemployment Conference by President Warren G. Harding; was a member of the WTUL committee that unsuccessfully attempted to persuade the AFL to grant charters to women who were not admitted to their industries' unions; was a delegate to the third meeting of the International Congress of Working Women, meeting in Vienna in 1923; served as the WTUL national representative to the International Labor Organization conference in Geneva in 1931; along with Mary Dreier (q.v.) and Ethel Smith, was a WTUL representative to a committee to work with President Herbert Hoover's Organization on Unemployment Relief in 1933; became a member of the code authority for the leather and woolen knit glove industry of the National Industrial Recovery Administration in 1934; appointed by President Franklin D. Roosevelt to the Commission on Vocational Guidance in 1936; became a member of the advisory committee of the Women's Bureau in the U.S. Department of Labor in 1940; took a WTUL leave of absence, 1942–1943, to investigate for the Women's Bureau the problems resulting from the employment of women in war industries; edited the WTUL publication, *Life and Labor Bulletin*; was a Democrat; died in Delphi, Ind., on April 26, 1975; Gladys Boone, *The Women's Trade Union Leagues in Great Britain and the United States of America* (1942); Mary Anderson, *Woman at Work: The Autobiography of Mary Anderson as told to Mary Winslow* (1951); *Who's Who in Labor* (1946); *Current Biography* (1947); *Notable American Women*, Vol. 4; Philip S. Foner, *Women and the American Labor Movement from World War I to the Present* (1980).

Marie Tedesco

CHRISTOPHER, Paul Revere   (1910–1974). Born in Easley, S.C., on February 14, 1910; son of Clarence Erasker, a loom fixer and craft unionist, and

Mary Jane (Hamphill) Christopher; Methodist and Unitarian; married Mary Elizabeth Lybrand on August 13, 1932; two children; graduated from Parker High School, Greenville, S.C., in 1930; attended Clemson Agricultural College of South Carolina, majoring in industrial engineering for three semesters, 1930–1931, but was compelled by economic necessity to return to the textile mills of Greenville and Slater, S.C., where he had worked part-time since age 14; joined the United Textile Workers of America (UTWA) local at the Cleveland Cloth Mill in Shelby, N.C., early in 1933; became local president later that year and participated in the mill workers' organizing drive; accepted a position with the UTWA as organizer and technical advisor early in 1934; elected vice-president of the North Carolina Federation of Labor later that year; strongly supported Francis Gorman (q.v.) and UTWA rank-and-file antagonism over textile management's continued violations of the National Recovery Administration (NRA) Cotton Code; joined Gorman in a call for a general textile strike which began September 1, 1934; was designated by Gorman as strike coordinator for western North Carolina and, in that capacity, closed down numerous mills; after the strike failed, he continued organizing in the Carolinas and developed an interest in labor politics and social welfare work; despite his craft unionist upbringing and his own training as a weaver, he supported the concept of industrial unionism and joined Sidney Hillman (q.v.) and the Textile Workers Organizing Committee (TWOC) created by the Congress of Industrial Organizations (CIO) in 1937; organized in the Carolinas, Georgia, and Alabama and acted as technical advisor to other organizers brought in from the Northeast; remained with the TWOC despite the defection of Gorman and seven Rhode Island locals which returned to the American Federation of Labor (AFL) ranks in 1939; joined fellow organizers in a move to democratize the TWOC which led to the formation of the Textile Workers Union of America (TWUA); in May 1939, was appointed TWUA South Carolina director and elected a vice-president of the national TWUA; resigned from TWUA on September 7, 1940, in the wake of unfounded charges of misappropriation of TWUA district office finances leveled by Roy R. Lawrence, a union rival; moved to Tennessee in October 1940 and took a position as Tennessee CIO State Industrial Union Council secretary-treasurer; organized miners, food workers, refiners, and textile workers; was appointed CIO regional director for Tennessee in 1942; acted as special mediation representative for Region 4 of the National War Labor Board; led the Tennessee CIO in "Operation Dixie" from 1946 to 1952; advised various Tennessee industrial unions on organizing strategy and National Labor Relations Board (NLRB) certification procedures; headed the Tennessee Volunteer Organizing Committee movement, combatting management dilatory tactics spawned by the Taft-Hartley Act and working to minimize AFL raiding of newly certified CIO locals; was appointed CIO regional director for Region 4 (Tennessee, Kentucky, North Carolina, and Virginia) in 1953; supported the merger efforts of the AFL and CIO, and after the merger, he was appointed AFL-CIO director of Region 8 (Kentucky and Tennessee) in 1964; retained that position until his death; a

Democrat; died in Knoxville, Tenn., on February 27, 1974; Paul R. Christopher Papers, Southern Labor Archives, Georgia State University; Joseph Yates Garrison, "Paul Revere Christopher: Southern Labor Leader, 1910–1974" (Ph.D. diss., 1976); Lucy Randolph Mason, *To Win These Rights: A Personal Story of the CIO in the South* (1952); *Who's Who in Labor* (1946).

Joseph Y. Garrison

CHURCH, Samuel Morgan, Jr.   (1936–   ). Born in Matewan, W.Va., on September 20, 1936; the son of a disabled miner who became a barber; married Patti Church, a union secretary, on March 23, 1978, after the failure of an earlier marriage; four children (three by his first wife); moved with his family to Appalachia, Va., in 1944, where he attended public schools and graduated from Appalachia High School in 1954; enrolled at Berea College in Kentucky in 1955; but he left college after one year and moved to Baltimore, Md., where he secured a job as a maintenance mechanic in a Domino Sugar Company warehouse; joined the United Packinghouse Workers Union in 1956 and soon became a union activist, serving variously as safety committeeman, shop steward, and a reporter for the local's newspaper; fulfilled an earlier desire in 1965 when he took a job with the Clinchfield Coal Company; a short time later he became an electrician-mechanic with the Westmoreland Coal Company in Virginia; after joining the United Mine Workers of America (UMWA) in 1965, he quickly became active in the affairs of his local, serving as a mine committeeman, safety committeeman, financial secretary, and president; was elected a full-time UMWA field representative for District 28 in 1973 shortly after being discharged by the Westmoreland Coal Company after an altercation with his foreman (was later reinstated); after winning over 70 percent of the arbitration cases he handled as a field representative, he was reelected in 1975; although he had supported the incumbent, W. A. "Tony" Boyle (q.v.), in the UMWA elections of 1972, he joined the reform movement after evidence of Boyle's complicity in the murder of Joseph A. Yablonski (q.v.) became increasingly apparent; joined reform president Arnold Miller's (q.v.) headquarters' staff as an international representative in 1975 and a year later became deputy director of the UMWA contracts department; became Miller's executive assistant in October 1976; was elected to the UMWA's vice-presidency in 1977, during which he increasingly assumed the day-to-day management of the UMWA from the ailing Miller; elected to the UMWA presidency by the union's executive board after the retirement of Arnold Miller on November 16, 1979; inheriting the leadership of a union scarred by scandal, near bankruptcy, suffering from an epidemic of wildcat strikes, and constantly losing membership, he immediately set out to restore the historic union's earlier prestige and power; after a 2-month strike in 1981 and an earlier settlement rejected by the membership, he negotiated a 40-month contract that provided substantial benefits for the UMWA membership; defeated for reelection in 1982; *Current Biography* (1981); *News-*

week, April 28, 1980; *Industry Week*, March 9, 1981; *Business Week*, December 3, 1979.

CLARK, Hugh D.   (1913–   ). Born in Lamotte, Iowa, on May 18, 1913; son of John R., a businessman, and Leona (Donovan) Clark, a homemaker; Roman Catholic; married Rita Kay (Nagle) Clark in 1932; three children; graduated from Columbia Academy High School, Dubuque, in 1930; became an apprentice in the plumbing and pipe-fitting trade after graduating from high school and in 1940 joined Local 66, Dubuque, of the United Association of Journeymen and Apprentices of the Plumbing and Pipe Fitting Industry of the United States and Canada (UA); elected to the executive board of Local 66 in 1945; served as secretary-treasurer of the Iowa State Building Trades Council, 1950–1966; became business manager for Local 66 in 1954 and president of the Dubuque Federation of Labor, American Federation of Labor-Congress of Industrial Organizations (AFL-CIO), in 1960; elected president of the Iowa Federation of Labor, AFL-CIO, in 1966 and served in that capacity for 13 years before retiring in 1979; in addition to the political responsibilities associated with his office, he was active in a variety of civic affairs, including the Urban Renewal Board, the Governor's Committee on Employment of the Handicapped, and the Governor's Committee on Area Schools, State of Iowa; *Who's Who in Labor* (1976); *AFL-CIO News*, June 9, 1979.

CLARK, Jesse   (1901–   ). Born in Terre Haute, Ind., November 21, 1901; son of Stephen, a farmer, and Carrie (Towell) Clark; Methodist; married Mary Rosalie Ring on December 24, 1937; completed elementary school in 1915, then held various jobs before becoming a foreman in a Terre Haute spoke factory when only 15 years of age; after a short strike in the plant, left for a job with the Standard Wheel Works and Columbia Enameling and Stamping Mill in Terre Haute, and worked there until 1918; attended night schools, taking courses in business English and typing; employed by the Pennsylvania Railroad (PRR) in 1918 and worked in its car shops and signal department until 1921, when fired for "contrariness"; employed by the Cleveland, Cincinnati, Chicago and St. Louis Railway, 1921–1923; employed again in the signal department of the PRR during 1924–1935; meanwhile, had joined Terre Haute Lodge 142 of the Brotherhood of Railroad Signalmen of America (BRS) in 1919, and served as recording secretary during 1924–1928; was a member of the local grievance committee of Lodge 142, 1926–1928, and local chairman, 1928–1935; served as a member of the PRR joint reviewing board, 1930–1935; was BRS vice-general chairman for the PRR, 1932–1935, and general chairman, 1935–1939; served as assistant to the grand president of the BRS, 1939–1941; was elected vice-president of the BRS in 1941, secretary-treasurer in 1943, and president in 1945; while president, extended BRS organization throughout the United States and Canada and was an effective proponent of railroad safety, especially among signal workers; became president emeritus in 1967; was a self-professed independent, but usually supported Republican candidates for public office; Brotherhood of Railroad Signalmen of America, *50 Years of Railroad Signaling: A History of the Brotherhood of Railroad Signalmen of America* (n.d.); *Who's Who in Railroading* (1959); *Labor*, October 7, 1967.

CLARK, John   (1888–1967). Born in Sheffield, England, in 1888; married; emigrated to British Columbia, Canada, and in 1908 joined the Western Federation of Miners there; entered the United States; drove stagecoach in Arizona, ranched in Washington; settled during the 1920s in Great Falls, Mont., and worked there in a zinc refinery; in the early 1930s, tried panning gold for a living; became a United States citizen in 1936, and in same year elected secretary of Great Falls Local 16 of the International Union of Mine, Mill and Smelter Workers (IUMMSW); in the next decade played an increasingly important role at conventions of the IUMMSW; as a result of a shake-up in the union leadership in 1947, became vice-president, succeeding Maurice Travis (q.v.), who became president; opposed by the IUMMSW right-wing, Travis resigned at the 1947 convention and Clark was elected as a compromise candidate; was appointed a member of the executive board of the Congress of Industrial Organizations (CIO) in 1948; although not a left-winger, as president was allegedly under the influence of the Communist faction of the IUMMSW; during his presidency the union faced several crises: 14 of its top leaders (though not Clark) were tried for conspiring to falsify the Taft-Hartley Act non-Communist affadavit; more serious was the estrangement of the IUMMSW from the CIO; on good terms with CIO president Philip Murray (q.v.), but chose to defy the CIO demand that the IUMMSW purge its Communist leaders; the IUMMSW was expelled from CIO in 1950 and thus exposed to raiding by several rival unions; sought to end IUMMSW's isolation by initiating merger talks with various unions in the 1950s, including the United Steelworkers of America (USWA); was unsuccessful, but helped prepare the ground for the 1967 merger of the IUMMSW and the USWA; retired in 1963 and was named honorary president; died in Tucson, Ariz., February 26, 1967; Vernon H. Jensen, *Nonferrous Metals Industry Unionism, 1932–1954* (1954); *Mine-Mill Union* (March, April 1967); F. S. O'Brien, "The 'Communist-Dominated' Unions in the U.S. since 1950," *Labor History* (Spring 1968).

CLARK, Lewis J.   (1902–   ). Born in Centerville, Iowa, April 23, 1902; son of Thomas William Grant, a farmer, and Minerva (Taylor) Clark; married Alice Wilma Ruka on June 30, 1921; was graduated from high school and eventually was hired in the Wilson and Company meat packing plant in Cedar Rapids, Iowa; helped organize the employees of the Wilson plant into a union that affiliated with the Amalgamated Meat Cutters and Butcher Workmen of North America (AMCBWNA) in 1933; elected business manager of the Cedar Rapids local; after the Wilson local in Cedar Rapids seceded from the AMCBWNA in 1935, organized the Midwest Union of All Packing House Workers, which affiliated with the Packinghouse Workers Organizing Committee (PWOC) created by the Congress of Industrial Organizations (CIO) in 1937; served as an assistant CIO director for Iowa and Nebraska; appointed to the staff of the PWOC in 1940 and shortly thereafter named director of PWOC District 3; appointed vice-chairman of the PWOC in 1941; served for a period as PWOC secretary-treasurer and then elected president of the United Packinghouse Workers of America (UPWA), which replaced the PWOC in 1943; became secretary-treasurer of the UPWA after Ralph Helstein (q.v.); became president of the union in 1946; association with the UPWA ended when defeated for reelection in the union elections of 1950; a Democrat; David Brody, *The Butcher Workmen: A Study of Unionization* (1964); *Who's Who in Labor* (1946).

CLINE, Isaac   (fl. 1835–1884). Born in Winslow, N.J., January 12, 1835; when young, worked in window-glass factory; in early life, lived in Cincinnati, Millville and Winslow, N.J., Pittsburgh and Croton, Pa.; in 1852, went again to Pittsburgh; apprenticed to learn blowing window-glass; went to Wheeling, then again to Pittsburgh, where he joined first window-glass workers' organization, May 1858; to Croton, in 1859, where he worked until May 1861; formed a company of volunteers, joined 100th Pennsylvania, remained in service until July 27, 1865, serving with honorable distinction; became identified with Window-glass Blowers' Union in 1872; president of Artsman's Association; in 1881, chosen president of Local Assembly 300, and held office until retirement; in 1884, helped organize window-glass workers of Europe, and form Universal Federation of Window-glass Workers, being its first president; George E. McNeill, *The Labor Movement: The Problem of To-Day* (1887).

George E. McNeill

COEFIELD, John   (1869–1940). Born in Petroleum Center, Pa., June 18, 1869; son of John and Isabella (Wright) Coefield; married Ethel B. McKinnon; two children; was graduated from high school in Franklin, Pa., and then became a plumbers' apprentice, joining the United Association of Plumbers and Steam Fitters of the United States and Canada (UA); worked in various cities before settling in San Francisco, Calif., in 1903; became a leader in UA Local 442 and later served as business agent of the San Francisco Building Trades Council; elected first vice-president and a member of the UA executive board in 1911; elected president of the UA in 1919 and retained that position until his death; was able, while president, to unify the UA, which had become seriously divided during the administration of his predecessor, John Alpine (q.v.); was an American Federation of Labor (AFL) fraternal delegate to the British Trades Union Congress in 1927; elected an AFL vice-president and executive council member in 1929 and served as a vice-president of the AFL metal trades department; during the conflict between the craft union leaders and the Committee on Industrial Organization (CIO), was a strong critic of industrial organization and supported the suspension of the CIO unions; was a member of the AFL housing committee that cooperated with Congressman Henry Ellenbogen and Senator Robert F. Wagner in developing legislation creating the U.S. Housing Authority; died in Washington, D.C., February 8, 1940; Philip Taft, *The A.F. of L. from the Death of Gompers to the Merger* (1959); Martin Segal, *The Rise of the United Association: National Unionism in the Pipe Trades, 1884–1924* (1970); *Who's Who in America, 1938–1939.*

COHN, Fannia (1888–1962). (Considerable disagreement exists among standard biographical sources on several of the dates used in this sketch. The dates listed here generally conform to those used in *Who's Who in Labor* [1946].) Born in Minsk, Russia, April 5, 1888; daughter of Hyman Rozofsky and Anna Cohn; Jewish; received a private school education in Russia: was a member of the Social Revolutionary party in Russia, 1901–1904; emigrated to the United States in 1904 and a year later began work in a New York garment factory; joined the International Ladies' Garment Workers' Union (ILGWU) in 1909; served as a member of the executive board of Kimona, Wrappers and Housedress Workers Local 41, 1909–1914; was chairman of the executive board of Local 41, 1911–1914; moved to Chicago, Ill., in 1915 to organize and assist garment workers striking against the Herzog Garment Company; the strike resulted in the organization of ILGWU Local 59, and she served as president during 1915; was influential in the 1919 Chicago corset-makers' strike that gained a 40-hour week and increased wages; served as a general ILGWU organizer in Chicago, 1915–1916; elected the ILGWU's first woman vice-president in 1916 and served until 1925; became the executive secretary of the ILGWU's education department in 1918 and served in that capacity until 1961; was one of the co-founders of the Workers' Education Bureau and the Brookwood Labor College in 1921; served on the board of directors of the Labor Publication Society of Brookwood Labor College, 1926–1928; was vice-president of Brookwood Labor College, 1932–1937; retired from union affairs in 1961; died in New York City, December 24, 1962; Fannia Cohn Papers, ILGWU Archives; Benjamin Stolberg, *Tailor's Progress: The Story of a Famous Union and the Men Who Made It* (1944); Louis Levine, *The Women's Garment Workers: A History of the International Ladies' Garment Workers' Union* (1924); James Morris, *Conflict within the A.F.L.: A Study of Craft versus Industrial Unionism, 1901–1938* (1958); *ILGWU Report and Proceedings* (1965); R. C. Cohen, "Fannia Cohn and the International Ladies' Garment Workers' Union" (Ph.D. diss., 1976); *Notable American Women*, Vol. 4.

Marie Tedesco

COLLINS, Jennie (1828–1887). Born in Amoskeag, N.H., in 1828; orphaned as a child and brought up by a grandmother; as a young girl, worked as a mill hand in Lowell and Lawrence, Mass.; later worked as a vest maker and organized a soldiers' relief fund in Boston, Mass., in 1861; after 1865, became a labor agitator and was associated with the New England Labor Reform League;

advocated the eight-hour day and better working conditions for women; supported women's suffrage and in 1870 lectured to the Women's Suffrage Association in Washington, D.C.; established a center in Boston in 1870 that distributed food and clothing to impoverished working women; authored *Nature's Aristocracy, or Battles and Wounds in Time of Peace*; died in Brookline, Mass., July 20, 1887; David Montgomery, *Beyond Equality: Labor and the Radical Republicans, 1862–1872* (1967); *The Twentieth Century Biographical Dictionary of Notable Americans*, Vol. 2 (1968); *Notable American Women*, Vol. 1 (1971).

Marie Tedesco

COMMERFORD, John   (fl. 1830–1874). Reared in Brooklyn, N.Y.; while a young man, learned and practiced the chairmakers' trade there; supported the Robert Owen (q.v.) and George Henry Evans (q.v.) faction of the New York Working Men's party in 1830; shortly thereafter, became actively involved in the labor movement and elected president of the New York Chairmakers' and Gilders' Union Society; committed to antibanking and anti-paper-money reform and represented the fifteenth ward of New York City on the general committee of the "New York Workingmen Opposed to Paper Money and Banking and to all Licensed Monopolies," ca. 1832; chosen by the Chairmakers' and Gilders' Society as its delegate to the National Trades' Union in 1834; elected secretary of the National Trades' Union in 1834 and in subsequent sessions served as recording secretary and treasurer; was a leader in the agitation for prison labor reform and in 1834 headed the United Working Men's Association, an ephemeral organization concerned with the prison labor issue; in 1841, chaired a meeting of Albany, N.Y., workingmen advocating prison labor reform; became active in Democratic reform politics during the mid-1830s, and advocated Locofoco separation from the Democratic party; supported the Boston, Mass., and Philadelphia, Pa., ten-hour strikes of 1835; succeeded Ely Moore (q.v.) in 1835 as president of the General Trades' Union of New York, which under his leadership became a vigorous organization that stimulated the organization of journeymen societies; was instrumental in the founding of the General Trades' organ, the *Union*, and was its editor; increasingly turned to reformist activities after 1837; served in 1842 as president of the Free Trade Association, a John C. Calhoun-inspired organization; however, devoted most of his time and energy to the land-reform principles of George Henry Evans, and espoused them for the remainder of his life; became the proprietor of a chairmaking shop in 1842; was one of the founders, along with Evans, of the National Reform Association in 1844 and was nominated for Congress by the group; was a delegate to the New York City Industrial Congress in 1850; in 1859, attracted by the free homestead plank, switched from Democratic to the Republican party and became a Republican candidate for the New York Assembly; was a Republican candidate for Congress in 1860; as late as 1874, was still involved in the land reform movement; Walter E. Hugins, *Jacksonian Democracy and the Working Class: A Study of the New York Workingmen's Movement, 1829–1837* (1960); Edward Pessen, *Most Un-*

common Jacksonians: The Radical Leaders of the Early Labor Movement (1967); Philip S. Foner, *History of the Labor Movement in the United States*, Vol. 1 (1947); Helene S. Zahler, *Eastern Workingmen and National Land Policy, 1829–1862* (1941).

COMMONS, John Rogers (1862–1945). Born in Hollansburg, Ohio, on October 13, 1862; son of John, at various times a harnessmaker, journalist, editor, and Clarissa (Rogers) Commons, an Oberlin graduate and school teacher; Presbyterian; married Ella Brown Downey, an Oberlin classmate, on December 25, 1890; five children (only two of whom survived infancy); graduated from Winchester (Ohio) high school in 1882 and then enrolled at Oberlin College from which he received the B.A. in 1888; enrolled at Johns Hopkins University later that year to study under Richard Ely; left Hopkins before completing his Ph.D. and, in 1890, took an instructorship in economics at Wesleyan University, Conn., where he remained for one year; subsequently served on the faculties of Oberlin, 1891, Indiana University, 1892–1895, and Syracuse University, 1895–1899; his growing reputation for radicalism and his discomforture in the classroom were largely responsible for his lack of employment security during these years; during 1899–1900, he did freelance research for the Democratic National Campaign Committee; worked for the U.S. Industrial Commission, 1902–1904, writing a report on immigration and serving as an assistant to Ralph Easley of the National Civic Federation; by the early twentieth century he had become one of the leaders, along with such figures as Wesley C. Mitchell and Thorstein Veblen, of a new school of institutional economics, a nontheoretical, empirical approach to the study of economics which emphasized an evolutionary stage analysis of economic development in which the clash of institutions—labor unions, corporations, and so forth—constituted the central focus; attracted by his former professor, Richard Ely, he took a position in the department of political economy at the University of Wisconsin, where he was to remain until his retirement in 1932; became an active figure in Wisconsin's progressive movement, drafting the state's civil service law in 1905, public utility law in 1907, and workmen's compensation measure in 1911, among other significant pieces of legislation; founded and directed Milwaukee's Bureau of Economy and Efficiency, 1911–1913; served on the Wisconsin Industrial Commission, 1911–1913, of which he had been one of the principal founders; his reform activities, however, transcended state boundaries—he was a founder of the American Association for Labor Legislation in 1906, was involved in the Russell Sage Foundation's "Pittsburgh Survey" in 1906–1907, and served on the editorial board of the resultant *Survey Magazine*, and served on the U.S. Commission on Industrial Relations, 1913–1915; frequently testified before legislative bodies, especially the U.S. House Committee on Banking and Currency; was president of the National Consumers' League, 1923–1935; was the founder of the Wisconsin school of labor history, the first substantial effort to put the study of labor on a solid, scholarly foundation, which applied his emphasis on empiricism and institutional conflict to the study of labor; attracted a brilliant group of students who produced, under his direction, the ten-volume *Documentary History of American Industrial Society* (1910– 1911), and the four-volume *History of Labour in the United States* (1918, 1935); along with his students, he generally supported Samuel Gompers's (q.v.) emphasis on a conservative, decentralized, and craft-oriented trade union movement as the only practical form of union organization in the American environment; retired from the faculty of the University of Wisconsin in 1932; his many publications include *Social Reform and the Church* (1893), *The Distribution of Wealth* (1893), *Proportional Representation* (1896), *Races and Immigrants in America* (1907), *Legal Foundation of Capitalism* (1924), *Institutional Economics* (1934), and the posthumously published *The Economics of Collective Action* (1950); also wrote an autobiographical account, *Myself*, published in 1934; died during a visit to Raleigh, N.C., on March 11, 1945; *Dictionary of American Biography*, Suppl. 3; Lafayette G. Harter, *John R. Commons: His Assault on Laissez-Faire* (1962); Ben B. Seligman, *Main Currents in Modern Economics* (1962); *American Economic Review* (September 1945); John R. Commons Papers, State Historical Society of Wisconsin.

CONLON, Peter J.   (1869–1931). Born in Brooklyn, N.Y., September 23, 1869; son of a locomotive engineer; Roman Catholic; married; seven children; moved with family to Springfield, Ill.; attended elementary school there and later took Speakers' Service Bureau correspondence courses; at age 14, began work as a plumber, and during 1885–1889 was apprenticed as a machinist in the Cotton Belt Railroad shops, Pine Bluff, Ark.; moved to Kansas City, Kans., and in 1899 began working there for the Union Pacific Railroad; joined the Knights of Labor and for several years traveled around the West in boxcars, working and organizing local unions in every state west of the Mississippi River and in Mexico; nine months after the founding of the International Association of Machinists (IAM) in 1889, joined IAM Local Lodge 27 in Kansas City; helped form District Lodge 1 in 1894 and was elected district master machinist (president); was a delegate to the IAM's 1895 national convention and elected to the general executive board, serving until 1901; served as first vice-president of the IAM, 1901–1916; handled some of the IAM's most important strikes, and, during the Cincinnati, Ohio, eight-hour strike of 1916, arrested four times in three months for violating an anti-picketing ordinance; served during World War I as an assistant to Bert M. Jewell (q.v.), president of the American Federation of Labor's railway employees' department; served as an IAM general organizer, 1917–1921; was one of the IAM's eight general vice-presidents, 1921–1931; throughout his career, contributed regularly to the *Machinists' Monthly Journal*, particularly the popular "Memories of the Past" column; was an early supporter of the Populist party, but, after it collapsed in 1898, turned to Eugene V. Debs (q.v.) and the Socialist party and advocated a national referendum on congressional legislation and municipal ownership of public utilities; precluded because of deep Catholic faith from accepting Marxist doctrine of class conflict, but espoused "social consciousness," acknowledging the fatherhood of God but promulgating a radical interpretation of the brotherhood of man; served as chairman of the Progressive party in Virginia and vice-president of the Nonpartisan Voters' League of Arlington County, Va., during the 1920s; died in Washington, D.C., April 1, 1931; *Machinists' Monthly Journal* (May 1903, May 1931); Solon DeLeon, ed., *The American Labor Who's Who* (1925); Mark Perlman, *The Machinists: A New Study in American Trade Unionism* (1961); John H. M. Laslett, *Labor and the Left: A Study of Socialism and Radical Influences in the American Labor Movement, 1881–1924* (1970).

John W. Hevener

CONNORS, David M. (1914–1977). Born in Buffalo, N.Y., on June 2, 1914; son of Patrick, a common laborer, and Nelle Connors; married Carmella Connors in 1967 (second marriage); three children (three step children); graduated from South Park High School, Buffalo, in 1933; after completing his formal education, he secured employment as a longshoreman at the port of Buffalo and in 1935 joined Local 109 of the International Longshoremen's Association (ILA); served as president of Local 109, 1948–1960; was a member of the Buffalo Port Board, 1949–1955; organized the Buffalo Joint Council of Longshoremen in 1951; served as president of ILA Local 928, which he had helped organize, 1955–1964, and also helped organize and was elected president of ILA Local 2,000 in 1959; was elected an ILA international vice-president in 1958; was elected a vice-president of the Buffalo American Federation of Labor-Congress of Industrial Organizations (AFL-CIO) Council in 1968; active in Democratic party affairs, he was a member of the Erie County Democratic Committee; was given the Owen J. Kavanagh Award for "outstanding contributions to longshoremen in Buffalo and other ports" by the Buffalo Joint Council of Longshoremen in 1966; organized and served as president of ILA Local 2,000A, 1970–1974; died in Buffalo on June 14, 1977; *Who's Who in Labor* (1976); *The New York Times*, June 16, 1977.

CONWAY, Jack T. (1917–   ). Born in Detroit, Mich., on December 20, 1917; son of James B., a plumber, and Blanche Conway, a homemaker; married LuVerne Conway, an attorney, in 1939; three children; graduated from the University of Chicago in 1940 and attended the University of Washington, 1940–1942; secured employment in an aircraft factory in 1942 and joined Local 6 of the United Automobile, Aerospace and Agricultural Implement Workers of America (UAW); served in the U.S. Army during World War II; joined the staff of the UAW in 1946 and soon had become an administrative assistant to UAW president Walter Reuther (q.v.); still working with Reuther at the time of the American Federation of Labor-Congress of Industrial Organizations (AFL-CIO) merger, he followed Reuther into the AFL-CIO industrial union department (IUD), where he soon took over most of the administrative functions of the department; became the executive director of the AFL-CIO IUD in 1963 and sought to coordinate the bargaining practices of different unions representing workers in the same plant; introduced a computer-based information retrieval and analysis system to facilitate the bargaining activities of member unions in 1966; meanwhile, he had also been active in public affairs, being appointed deputy administrator of the Federal Housing and Home Finance Agency by President John F. Kennedy in 1961, and deputy director of the Office of Economic Opportunity (OEO) by President Lyndon B. Johnson in 1964; he served in both of these positions for one year; in 1968, he retired his union positions to become president of the Center for Community Change, a Ford Foundation-sponsored organization that promoted community action groups in low-income areas—an activity he had favored as an OEO director; was appointed president of Common Cause in 1971; returned to the labor movement in 1975 as the executive director of the American Federation of State, County and Municipal Employees; *Who's Who in Labor* (1976); Nelson Lichtenstein, ed., *Political Profiles: The Kennedy Years* (1976), and *Political Profiles: The Johnson Years* (1976).

COOK, Harry Herman   (1883–1972). Born in Wheeling, W.Va., February 28, 1883; son of a glass blower; married; left school in 1892 and began working in the glass industry; joined Wheeling Local 99 of the American Flint Glass Workers Union (AFGW) in 1901; moved to Bellaire, Ohio, and affiliated with AFGW Local 13 in 1903, serving it as an organizer, secretary, and president; was an official of the Ohio Valley Trade Council, 1906–1907; elected to the AFGW national executive board in 1912, serving until 1916; became national assistant secretary of the AFGW in 1916; after serving as first vice-president and executive board member for several years, elected national president of the AFGW in 1940; frequently represented the AFGW in American Federation of Labor (AFL) conventions and served on several committees, including the au-diting committee in 1923; both before and after the merger of the AFL and the Congress of Industrial Organizations in 1955, resisted suggestions of mergers between the AFGW and other unions in the glass industry; retired union positions in 1957 and was named president emeritus of AFGW; politically identified himself as an independent; died in Toledo, Ohio, May 28, 1972; Solon DeLeon, ed., *The American Labor Who's Who* (1925); *Who's Who in Labor* (1946); *AFL-CIO News*, June 15, 1957, June 3, 1972.

COPE, Elmer F.   (1903–1965). Born in Elwood, Ind., July 24, 1903; son of Gilbert, a steelworker, and Nora (Hall) Cope; Society of Friends; married Corrine Snyder on January 13, 1940; two children; shortly after going to work at age 16 in a Warren, Ohio, tin mill, joined the Amalgamated Association of Iron, Steel, and Tin Workers and became a grievance committeeman; later studied economics at Swarthmore College and received a B.A.; attended Brookwood Labor College, 1929–1930; was a member of the Conference for Progressive Labor Action, 1929–1934, and during this time period returned to work and union activity in Warren as a follower of A. J. Muste (q.v.); joined the Steel

Workers Organizing Committee in 1936 and was given the task of trying to organize Weirton Steel Company plants in West Virginia; served for a short time as director of District 27 (Canton, Ohio) of the United Steelworkers of America (USWA); served during World War II on the Fifth Regional National War Labor Board; meanwhile, received an M.A. degree from Western Reserve University; participated actively in the Congress of Industrial Organizations' (CIO) Political Action Committee; was a CIO delegate to the World Federation of Trade Unions (WFTU) in 1947, at time of the rift between the Communist and non-Communist affiliates of the WFTU; became one of three CIO representatives who withdrew the CIO from the WFTU and helped form the International Confederation of Free Trade Unions in 1949; subsequently, became director of economic and international affairs for the USWA; elected as the first secretary-treasurer of the newly formed Ohio American Federation of Labor (AFL)-CIO in 1958; played a key role in the state labor movement's defeat of a powerful effort, organized by chambers of commerce and smaller employers, to obtain an Ohio right-to-work law along lines of a law enacted in Indiana the previous year; opposed group called "Ohioans for Right-to-Work," which sought to amend the state constitution by referendum during the general election; by undertaking intensive voter registration and public relations campaigns, the Ohio AFL-CIO and municipal labor bodies defeated the amendment by almost two to one and also helped to defeat Republican Senator John W. Bricker, a foe of unions; due to ill health, stepped down as Ohio AFL-CIO secretary in 1963, and took a position as an educational consultant with the USWA; was a Democrat; died in Pittsburgh, Pa., May 26, 1965; Elmer F. Cope Papers, Ohio Historical Society; *Who's Who in Labor* (1946); Glen W. Miller and S. T. Ware, "Organized Labor in the Political Process: A Case Study of the Right-to-Work Campaign in Ohio," *Labor History* (Winter 1963).

Donald G. Sofchalk

COSGROVE, John Tam   (1873–1948). Born in Elizabeth, N.J., September 11, 1873; son of Patrick, a steamboat captain, and Dora (Toner) Cosgrove; Roman Catholic; married Katherine V. Hennessy on October 21, 1901; five children; graduated from St. Patrick's High School in Elizabeth, then began work as a carpenter and joined Local 167 of the United Brotherhood of Carpenters and Joiners of America (UBC) in 1892; helped to found both the Union County (N.J.) Central Trades and the New Jersey State Federation of Labor, and served as president of both central bodies; elected business agent of Local 167 in 1899 and served until 1915; was a principal organizer of the New Jersey Building and Construction Trades Council and served as its president from 1904 to 1915; became an unofficial labor adviser to Woodrow Wilson during his governorship of New Jersey and presidency of the United States; was influential in the passage of the federal workmen's compensation act; elected first general vice-president of the UBC in 1915, serving until 1929; forced by progressive blindness to cut short his union activities during the last ten years of his life; was a Democrat;

died in Elizabeth, N.J., November 3, 1948; Robert A. Christie, *Empire in Wood: A History of the Carpenters' Union* (1956); *The New York Times*, November 4, 1948; *Who's Who in Labor* (1946).

COULTER, Clarence Castrow   (1882–1948). Born in Venango County, Pa., June 4, 1882; son of William Harry, a farmer, and Sarah J. (Brown) Coulter; Protestant; married Sarah Fowler on April 9, 1930; two children; graduated from high school, then secured employment as a clerk in Washington, D.C., and joined Local 262 of the Retail Clerks International Protective Association (RCIA) in 1901; between 1901 and 1926, served as business agent and financial secretary of Local 262, financial secretary and vice-president of the Washington, D.C., Central Labor Union, vice-president of the District of Columbia Federation of Labor, and vice-president of the RCIA; was elected general secretary-treasurer (then the chief administrative officer) of the RCIA in 1926; strongly supported the American Federation of Labor's traditional craft-oriented organizing tactics, and suspended a number of New York RCIA locals opposing this policy; saw the suspended locals organize the rival United Retail, Wholesale and Department Store Employees of America, which affiliated with the Congress of Industrial Organizations in 1937; retired union positions in 1947 and was named secretary-treasurer emeritus; edited the RCIA organ, *Advocate*, 1926–1947; was a Democrat; died in Lafayette, Ind., in August 1948; George G. Kirstein, *Stores and Unions: A Study of the Growth of Unionism in Dry Goods and Department Stores* (1950); Michael Harrington, *The Retail Clerks* (1962); *Who's Who in Labor* (1946).

COUNTS, George Sylvester   (1889–1974). Born in Baldwin City, Kans., on December 9, 1889; son of James Wilson, a farmer, and Mertie Florella (Gamble) Counts; Methodist; married Lois Hazel on September 24, 1913; graduated from Baker University with a B.A. in 1911 and received the Ph.D. from the University of Chicago in 1916; after leaving Chicago, he accepted a job as the head of the Department of Education and director of the summer school at Delaware College in 1916; thereafter, he was professor of educational psychology, Harris Teachers' College, St. Louis, Mo., 1918–1919, professor of secondary education, Yale University, 1920–1926, professor of education, University of Chicago, 1926–1927, and professor of education, Teachers' College, Columbia University, 1927–1959; served as associate director of the International Institute, 1927–1932; was director of research for the American Historical Association-sponsored study of the teaching of social studies, 1931–1933; appointed to the educational policies committee of the National Education Association in 1936; won a bitter contest for the presidency of the American Federation of Teachers (AFT), which he had joined several years earlier, opposing a Communist-backed rival candidate; Communists were then ousted from the AFT executive board and two years later two New York City locals and one Philadelphia, Pa., union were expelled from the union as Communist-dominated; although many teachers sympathized with the Congress of Industrial Organizations, he succeeded in keeping the AFT securely within the American Federation of Labor fold; never held another union office after leaving the AFT presidency in 1943 but remained a vigorous supporter of trade unionism and was an active participant in labor political action; was an independent in politics; authored numerous books and articles, including *The Selective Character of American Secondary Education* (1922), *Principles of Education* (1924), *The Senior High School Curriculum* (1926), *Education in Soviet Russia* (1928), *Secondary Education and Industrialism* (1929), *The Social Foundations of Education* (1934), and *The Prospects of American Democracy* (1938); died in Belleville, Ill., in November 1974; *National Cyclopaedia of American Biography*, Vol. F; *AFL-CIO News*, November 23, 1974; Robert J. Braun, *Teachers and Power: The Story of the American Federation of Teachers* (1972); American Federation of Teachers, Commission on Education, *Organizing the Teaching Profession* (1955); Gerald L. Gutek, *George S. Counts and American Civilization: The Educator as Social Critic* (1984).

CROSSWAITH, Frank Rudolph   (1892–1965). Born in Frederiksted, St. Croix, Virgin Islands, July 16, 1892; son of William Ignatius, a painter, and Ann Eliza Crosswaith; Roman Catholic; married Alma E. Besard in January 1915; four children; Afro-American; emigrated to the United States while still in his teens and worked as an elevator operator while attending the Rand School of Social Science; after graduation began a long term of service as an organizer for the International Ladies' Garment Workers' Union; was a Socialist early in his career, and often ran for public office on the Socialist party ticket in New York; also served as a lecturer for the party and for the League for Industrial Democracy; actively involved in the organization of black workers in such occupations as elevator operators, elevator constructors, mechanics, laundry workers, and retail clerks; served as a special organizer for the Brotherhood of Sleeping Car Porters; was appointed by Mayor Fiorello La Guardia to the New York City Housing Authority in 1942; joined the American Labor party during the 1930s and became a member of the state executive board of the Liberal party, which was organized in 1944; served as the editor of the Negro Labor News Service for 12 years; was one of the organizers and became the chairman of the Negro Labor Committee, an association of unions with a predominantly black membership; authored *True Freedom for Negro and White Workers* and *Discrimination, Incorporated*; died in New York City, June 17, 1965; Benjamin Stolberg, *Tailor's Progress: The Story of a Famous Union and the Men Who Made It* (1944); *AFL-CIO News*, June 19, 1965; *The New York Times*, June 18, 1965; Irwin M. Marcus, "Frank Crosswaith: Black Socialist, Labor Leader and Reformer," *Negro History Bulletin* (1974); Philip S. Foner, *American Socialism and Black Americans from the Age of Jackson to World War II* (1977).

CROUCH-HAZLETT, Ida   (fl. 1875–1925). Born in Chicago, Ill., about 1875; both parents were college-educated teachers; married; attended elementary school in Monmouth, Ill., the Monticello Seminary in Godfrey, Ill., and Illinois State Normal School in Bloomington; also took courses at Stanford University, Chicago Municipal College, and the Chicago School of Social Sciences; after completing her normal school education, she worked as a special teacher in elocution in Illinois, Colorado, and Wyoming; during the period 1894–1900, she worked as a newspaper reporter in Chicago, Denver, and Leadville, Colo.; was a national organizer for the Woman Suffrage Association, 1896–1901; joined the Socialist party in 1901, became a state organizer for the party in Utah in 1901 and the following year ran for Congress on the Socialist ticket in Colorado, becoming the first female candidate for Congress; spent much of her time from 1902 to 1904 touring the country on behalf of the Socialist party; served as a Colorado delegate to the National Socialist convention in 1904; became the state organizer for Montana and edited the party-owned newspaper, *Montana News*, 1905–1910; joined the American Labor Union during these years and was associated with the Western Federation of Miners; was a Montana delegate to the national Socialist convention in 1908; after the *Montana News* was destroyed by factional disputes, she resumed her activities as an organizer and Socialist speaker, devoting much of her time to the South from 1914 to 1916; ended her activity as a Socialist organizer and lecturer in 1921; enrolled in the graduate school of New York University in 1925 in pursuit of the doctoral degree; *American Labor Who's Who* (1925); Ida Crouch-Hazlett Vita, Social Democratic Party Papers, Milwaukee County Historical Society, Milwaukee, Wis.

CRUIKSHANK, Nelson Hale   (1902–   ). Born in Bradner, Ohio, on June 21, 1902; son of Jesse Lincoln and Jessie Margaret (Wright) Cruikshank; Methodist; married Florence Crane on August 30, 1928; one child; attended Oberlin College and Ohio Wesleyan University before earning a master of divinity degree from the Union Theological Seminary in 1929; became the director of the social services department of the Brooklyn Federation of Churches after graduating, serving in that capacity until joining the American Federation of Labor (AFL) staff as a political strategist during the early 1940s; during the 1940s and early 1950s, he worked closely with the AFL secretary-treasurer, George Meany (q.v.), on a variety of matters; after the merger of the AFL and the Congress of Industrial Organizations (CIO) in 1955, he was appointed director of the newly organized department of social security; in this position, he campaigned successfully for changes in the social security program authorizing payments to the totally disabled regardless of age; following the achievement of this expansion of social security coverage, he immediately began lobbying for medical assistance for the elderly; medicare, as it came to be known, became a reality during Lyndon B. Johnson's administration in 1965, despite the vigorous opposition of the American Medical Association; retired from the AFL-CIO in 1965 and became the head of the National Council of Senior Citizens which had campaigned vigorously for medicare and continued to advocate other issues of concern to the elderly; a Democrat; *Who's Who in America, 1968–1969*; Nelson Lichtenstein, ed.,

Political Profiles: The Johnson Years (1976); Nelson H. Cruikshank Papers, State Historical Society of Wisconsin.

CRULL, John L.   (1901–   ). Born in Geneosea, Ill., August 4, 1901; son of William Albert, a carpenter, and Anna Pearl (Duncan) Crull; Christian church; married Lydia C. Stahlheber on August 8, 1923; two children; completed a high school education, then secured work as a carpenter and joined the United Brotherhood of Carpenters and Joiners of America; began working for the Southwestern Bell Telephone Company in Wichita, Kans., in 1936; was one of the organizers of the Southwestern Telephone Workers Union, which became Wichita Local 1261 of the National Federation of Telephone Workers (NFTW) in 1937; served as a special representative for Local 1261 during 1937–1943; became southern regional director of the NFTW and a member of the national executive board in 1943, serving until 1947; chosen first vice-president in 1947 of the Communications Workers of America (CWA), which had absorbed the NFTW; placed in charge of internal organization, and given responsibility for organizing non-CWA telephone workers who were represented by CWA representative units; became one of the seminal figures in the CWA; was a persistent, thorough, and conscientious union leader, and loyally carried out CWA policies even when in disagreement with them; served on the board of directors of the Council for Cooperative Development; was a Republican; retired union positions in 1967; Jack Barbash, *Unions and Telephones: The Story of the Communications Workers of America* (1952); *Who's Who in Labor* (1946); *AFL-CIO News*, February 18, 1967; Thomas R. Brooks, *Communication Workers of America: The Story of a Union* (1977).

CURRAN, Joseph Edwin   (1906–1981). Born in New York City, March 1, 1906; son of Eugene, a cook, and Ida (Cohan) Curran; Roman Catholic; married Retta Toble on October 19, 1939, and after her death in 1963, married Florence B. Stetler on April 1, 1965; one child; after being expelled from Westfield, N.J., parochial school in the seventh grade for irregular attendance, became in turn a caddy and a "factory monkey"; moved to New York City in 1921 and took a job as an office boy with the Gold Medal Flour Company; the following year, at age 16, began a 17-year period as a seaman; joined the International Seamen's Union (ISU) in 1935; led a wildcat strike of the S.S. *California*'s crew, whose eventual discharge led to a long East Coast strike and the organization of the National Maritime Union of America (NMU) as a rival to the ISU; was elected president of the NMU after its establishment in 1937; elected president of the Greater New York Industrial Union Council, Congress of Industrial Organizations (CIO), in 1940; elected a CIO vice-president in 1941; ran for Congress on the American Labor party ticket in 1940; served during World War II as a member of the advisory committee for the New York area of the War Manpower Commission; after the war, was a CIO delegate to the conferences in London and Paris that resulted in the organization of the World Federation of Trade

Unions; became a vice-president and executive council member of the newly merged American Federation of Labor and CIO; retired as president of the NMU in 1973; was accused of Communist leanings during his early trade union career, but eventually assumed a conservative position in the NMU's ideological conflicts; died in Boca Raton, Fla., August 14, 1981; Joseph P. Goldberg, *The Maritime Story: A Study in Labor-Management Relations* (1958); Walter Galenson, *The CIO Challenge to the AFL: A History of the American Labor Movement, 1935–1941* (1960); Charles P. Larrowe, *Harry Bridges: The Rise and Fall of Radical Labor in the U.S.* (1972); *Current Biography* (1945); *AFL-CIO News*, August 22, 1981; Eleanora W. Schoenebaum, ed., *Profiles of an Era: The Nixon-Ford Years* (1979); Harvey A. Levenstein, *Communism, Anticommunism, and the CIO* (1981).

D

DAILEY, Edward L.   (fl. 1855–1886). Born in Danvers, Mass., October 6, 1855; educated in common schools until age 11; admitted to Holten High School in Danvers; graduated there at 13; apprenticed and worked as a shoemaker, particularly as a laster; was a member of Knights of St. Crispin in Danvers and Lynn; one of the 16 who founded Lasters' Protective Union in Lynn, in 1879, which he named; was its first secretary, and member of its advisory board the first two years; was chosen general secretary of Lasters' Protective Union of New England in April 1885; unanimously reelected in 1886; author of petition to Massachusetts legislature of 1885 to abolish convict labor; was among the first to organize lasters' protective unions in shoe towns of Maine and New Hampshire; member of Local Assembly 715, Knights of Labor, since its organization; was a delegate to the American Federation of Labor annual convention in 1894 and during that meeting voted against the Socialist platform; George E. McNeill, *The Labor Movement: The Problem of To-Day* (1887); Gerald N. Grob, *Workers and Utopia: A Study of Ideological Conflict in the American Labor Movement, 1865–1900* (1961).

George E. McNeill

DALRYMPLE, Sherman Harrison   (1889–1962). Born in Walton, W.Va., April 4, 1889; son of Herbert Clarence and Eliza Eleanor (Atkinson) Dalrymple; married Esta Robinson on January 3, 1914, and, after her death, Grace Moomaw on October 2, 1928; one child; completed a grammar-school education in the public schools of Mt. Lebanon, W.Va., then began working in the rubber industry in 1909; was an oilfield worker, 1911–1914, before returning to employment in the rubber industry, 1914–1917; served successively during World War I as a private, corporal, sergeant, and second lieutenant in the U.S. Marine Corps and received the Fourragers and croix de guerre decorations; after the war, resumed work in the rubber industry; joined American Federation of Labor Federal Union 18319 of Goodrich Rubber Company workers and served as its president, 1934–1935; was elected president of the newly organized United Rubber Workers of

America (URWA) in 1935; led the URWA into the Congress of Industrial Organizations (CIO) in 1936 and became a CIO vice-president; led an anti-Communist campaign in the CIO in 1939; served during World War II on the Labor
Policy Advisory Committee of the National Defense Advisory Commission; was
a member of the CIO social security committee, the legislative committee, and
the Utility and Construction Workers Organizing Committee; retired as president
of URWA in 1945 as a result of his opposition to a strike against the Firestone
Tire and Rubber Company and the Goodyear Tire and Rubber Company; edited
the *United Rubber Worker* until his retirement; usually supported the Democratic
party; died in Downey, Calif., March 16, 1962; Harold S. Roberts, *The Rubber
Workers: Labor Organization and Collective Bargaining in the Rubber Industry*
(1944); Walter Galenson, *The CIO Challenge to the AFL: A History of the
American Labor Movement, 1935–1941* (1960); *The New York Times*, March
19, 1962.

DAMINO, Harry Orazio   (1893–1968). Born in Catania, Italy, on January
6, 1893; son of Thomas, a small businessman, and Catherine (Marmazza) Damino; Roman Catholic; married Elena Elizabeth Carciopolo on June 29, 1924;
three children; received his only formal education in the schools of Catania
before immigrating with his family to the United States in 1910, settling in New
York City; became a naturalized citizen in 1915; worked with his father in a
family-owned lumber business and became a skilled wood worker and furniture
maker; the family business was sold after the death of his father and poor business
conditions that accompanied the depression of 1919–1920; became a skilled eye
setter in a doll factory and soon had 14 apprentices working under him; appalled
by the terrible working conditions in the doll and toy industry, he soon launched
an organizing drive among doll workers that led to a series of strikes between
1926 and 1933, which ultimately resulted in the organization of Local 223,
Playthings and Novelty Workers of America after a 16-week strike in 1933; the
New York City-based union continued to grow during the 1930s and by 1940
the union had organized the 81 shops associated with the New York Stuffed Toy
Manufacturers Association and the New York Doll Manufacturers Association;
with the organization of Fleishacker and Baum Company in 1946, Local 223
had organized the entire industry in New York City; became assistant manager
of Local 223 in 1938 and ten years later became manager, a position he retained
until his death; was instrumental in the organization of a national union of toy
makers, the International Union of Doll and Toy Workers of the United States
and Canada in 1952 and was elected president of the new international union,
a position he held for the remainder of his life; after the merger of the American
Federation of Labor-Congress of Industrial Organizations (AFL-CIO) in 1955,
he was elected a vice-president and executive council member of the new federation; was elected a vice-president and executive council member of the AFL-
CIO maritime trades department in 1965; active in a variety of public and civic
affairs, he was appointed to the President's Committee for the Department of

Labor in 1962, was a member of the Italian-American Labor Council and the Italian-American Federation (which he served as director for several years); was also a trustee of the Italian and Parkway hospitals and was a member of the executive committee of Boys Town of Italy; a liberal Democrat in politics, from 1952 to 1962 he served as a vice-president of the Liberal party of New York; died in Rockville Centre, N.Y., on June 17, 1968; *National Cyclopaedia of American Biography*, Vol. 54; *AFL-CIO News*, June 22, 1968; *The New York Times*, June 19, 1968.

DANIEL, Franz E. (1904–1976). Born in Osceola, Mo., on April 4, 1904; son of George H., an attorney, and Josephine (Landis) Daniel, a homemaker; married and divorced; two children; graduated from Southwest Missouri State University High School in 1922; enrolled at the University of Wisconsin in 1924, earning the B.A. degree in 1927; pursued graduate studies at the Union Theological Seminary, 1927–1930; became an organizer for the Amalgamated Clothing Workers of America (ACWA) in 1933 and continued in that position until 1944; was involved in many of the major Congress of Industrial Organizations (CIO) organizing campaigns in the South during the 1930s and 1940s; served as an advisor to the United Textile Workers of America, 1934, and the United Auto Workers, 1939, 1941; was the assistant director of the southeastern district of the Textile Workers Organizing Committee, CIO, 1937–1939; served as the CIO representative to the United Labor Committee of Philadelphia, Pa., 1943–1944; was an international representative of the Marine and Shipbuilding Workers of America in Washington, D.C., 1945; served as the CIO district director in various parts of the United States, including South Carolina, 1946–1949, North Carolina, 1949–1952, and the Rocky Mountain region, 1951–1953; was appointed an assistant to CIO president Walter Reuther (q.v.) in 1953, serving until the 1955 merger of the American Federation of Labor (AFL)-CIO; appointed AFL-CIO assistant director of organizing in 1955, and served in that position until being transferred to the AFL-CIO industrial union department's organizing staff in 1963; retired union positions in 1969 and returned to Springfield, Mo., where he was active in Alcoholics Anonymous and served as vice-chairman of the Springfield Public Utility Commission; a Democrat, he was a delegate to the Democratic National Convention in 1976; died in Springfield, Mo., on August 19, 1976; *Who's Who in Labor* (1976); *AFL-CIO News*, August 28, 1976; Franz E. Daniel Papers, Walter Reuther Library, Wayne State University.

DAVIDSON, Roy Elton (1901–1964). Born in Fairmount, Ill., July 4, 1901; son of Frank A., a coal miner and farmer, and Sarah L. (Foster) Davidson; Presbyterian; married Cecil May Rinehart on October 31, 1920; four children; was graduated from Oakwood (Ill.) Township High School in 1917, then took courses at the University of Illinois and the University of Chicago and also became a fireman on the Illinois division of the New York Central Railroad; joined the Brotherhood of Locomotive Firemen and Enginemen (BLFE) in the summer of 1918; was appointed general chairman of the New York Central's Illinois division-Indiana Harbor Belt Railroad, BLFE, in 1922; although eligible for membership in the Brotherhood of Locomotive Engineers (BLE) after being promoted to engineer in 1921, remained active instead in the BLFE and did not join the BLE until 1937; became a member of the BLE division 682, Hammond, Ind., in 1937 and was appointed general chairman for the engineers of the Illinois division-Indiana Harbor Belt Railroad in 1941; was made assistant grand chief engineer for the Chicago area in 1947; was elected first assistant grand chief engineer in 1953 and, after the retirement of Guy L. Brown (q.v.) in 1960, was chosen BLE grand chief engineer; primarily involved during his incumbency with railroad management demands that unnecessary personnel be eliminated from train crews and that work rules be adjusted in response to the poor financial position of the nation's railroads; supported the Democratic party; died in Cleveland, Ohio, July 7, 1964; Reed C. Richardson, *The Locomotive Engineer, 1863–1963: A Century of Railway Labor Relations and Work Rules* (1963); *Current Biography* (1963); *Who's Who in Railroading* (1959).

DAVIS, Hal C.   (1914–1978). Born in Pittsburgh, Pa., on February 27, 1914; son of Harry J., assistant treasurer, Fischer Scientific Material Company, and Tillie M. (Reitzel) Davis; married Marion Davis, homemaker, in 1963; two children; attended Allegheny High School, 1927–1931; began his professional career in 1930 as a percussionist and musician on KDKA, the nation's first radio station; also worked for station WCAE and in theaters and nightclubs; served as a corporal in the U.S. Marine Corps during World War II; joined Local 60-471, American Federation of Musicians (AFM) and served as its president, 1949–1970; was a vice-president of the Pennsylvania State Federation of Labor, 1950–1955, and the Pennsylvania American Federation of Labor-Congress of Industrial Organizations (AFL-CIO) Council, 1955–1961; was elected an AFM vice-president and executive council member in 1963, and held that position until being elected international president of the AFM in 1970; elected to the executive council of the International Secretariat of Entertainment Trade Unions in 1970; served as president of the Inter-American Federation of Entertainment Workers, 1974; became a vice-president and executive council member of the AFL-CIO in 1975; elected a vice-president of the AFL-CIO department for professional employees at its founding convention in December 1977; was a presidential appointee on the National Council of the Arts and served as the director of the Associated Councils of the Arts; authored several articles in the National Association of Jazz Educators publication as well as various trade magazines; died in New York City in January 1978; *Who's Who in Labor* (1976); *AFL-CIO News*, January 14, 1978.

DAVIS, James John   (1873–1947). Born in Thedegar, South Wales, England, October 27, 1873; son of David James and Esther Ford (Nichols) Davis; Baptist; married Jean Rodenbaugh on November 26, 1914; five children; emi-

grated to the United States with parents in 1881, living first in Pittsburgh, Pa.,
and moving later to Sharon, Pa.; attended the public schools there and Sharon
Business College; apprenticed as a puddler in the steel industry at age 11, and
worked in Sharon, Pittsburgh, and Birmingham, Ala.; moved to Elwood, Ind.,
in 1893 and worked in steel and tin-plate mills; joined the Amalgamated Association of Iron, Steel, and Tin Workers of America and for a short time served
as international president of the union; was elected city clerk of Elwood in 1898,
serving until 1902; was recorder of Madison County, Ind., 1903–1907; moved
to Pittsburgh in 1907; was elected general director of the Loyal Order of Moose
in 1907, and, as chairman of its War Relief Commission, visited camps in the
United States, Canada, and Europe in 1918; appointed U.S. Secretary of Labor
by President Warren Harding in 1921 and reappointed by Presidents Calvin
Coolidge in 1925 and Herbert Hoover in 1929; made his most important contributions in the areas of increasing public works construction to provide employment, settling labor disputes, supplying low-cost housing for tenant workers,
providing machinery for securing restrictions on immigration in accordance with
the 1921 quota law, creating an Immigration Board of Review, and initiating
studies of mothers' pension, child dependency, and juvenile delinquency laws;
resigned from office on December 9, 1930, following his election to the U.S.
Senate as a Republican from Pennsylvania to fill the vacancy caused by Senate
refusal to seat William S. Vare; was reelected in 1932 and 1938, but ran unsuccessfully for reelection in 1944; was appointed by Vice President John N.
Garner to serve on a special Senate committee investigating the Tennessee Valley
Authority; coauthored *You and Your Job* (1927), and authored *The Iron Puddler*
(1922) and *Selective Immigration* (1926); died in Tacoma Park, Md., November
22, 1947; Andrew Sinclair, *The Available Man* (1965); Francis Russell, *The
Shadow of Blooming Grove: Warren G. Harding and His Times* (1968); *The
American Federationist* (December 1947); John B. Dudley, "James J. Davis:
Secretary of Labor under Three Presidents, 1921–1930" (Ph.D. diss., 1972).

DAVIS, Leon Julius   (1907–   ). Born near Pinsk, Russia, on November
21, 1907; son of Isaac and Hannah Davis; married Julia Gaberman, a social
worker, in 1930; two children; after emigrating to the United States in 1921 with
an older brother, he settled in Hartford, Conn., with an aunt and attended public
schools there before moving to New York City in 1927; worked in a dry cleaning
shop and attended Columbia School of Pharmacy for two years, leaving to
become a drugstore clerk; joined the small Medical Workers Union; was a founder
of the Pharmacists Union of Greater New York in 1932, which brought together
the Medical Workers and other small organizations of clerks; became a full-time
general organizer in 1936, when the Pharmacists Union became Local 1199 of
the Retail Clerks International Association, American Federation of Labor (AFL);
successfully conducted a seven-week-long strike in the winter of 1936–1937 for
the right of black pharmacists to work in Harlem drug stores; after Local 1199
bolted the AFL in 1937, joined the United Retail Employees of America, Con-

gress of Industrial Organizations (CIO), he was instrumental in organizing Whelan and Liggett's drugstore chains in New York; participated in the formation of the United Retail, Wholesale and Department Store Workers Union (RWDSU), CIO, in 1938; became president of Local 1199 after World War II and an international vice-president of the RWDSU in 1955; in the late 1950s, the six thousand-member Local 1199 set out to organize hospital workers, winning its first organizing victory at Montefiore Hospital in the Bronx in 1958; led a 46-day strike of thirty-five hundred workers in May 1959 against seven hospitals that refused to allow representation elections; jailed in 1962 for 30 days for contempt of court during a strike which was settled when Governor Nelson Rockefeller supported passage of state collective bargaining legislation for hospital workers; named Labor Man of the Year by New York City Central Labor Council in 1964; received Page One award of the American Newspaper Guild in 1965; spoke out against American intervention in Vietnam beginning in 1964 and worked to mobilize opposition to the war within the labor movement; became president of the newly organized National Union of Hospital and Health Care Employees in 1969, while continuing as president of the New York Drug and Hospital Union, renamed District 1199; the national union claimed a membership of 130,000 at the time of his retirement in 1982; *1199 Drug News*, June 1957; *1199 News*, March 1982; *Who's Who in Labor* (1976); Dan Marschall, "1199: For Dignity and Justice," *In These Times*, May 10–16, 1978; Leon Fink and Brian Greenberg, "Organizing Montefiore: Labor Militancy Meets a Progressive Health Empire," in *Health Care in America*, edited by Susan Reverby and David Rosner (1979); Philip S. Foner, *Women and the American Labor Movement from World War I to the Present* (1980).

Jon Bloom

DAVIS, Richard L.   (1864–1900). Born in Roanoke, Va., December 24, 1864; married; number of children unknown; Afro-American; received a "very fair education" in the Roanoke public schools becoming a "good reader" and a "good writer"; at age 8, began work in Roanoke tobacco factory for nine years; worked as a coal miner in the Kanawha and New River fields of West Virginia; moved to Rendville, a coal mining village in southeastern Ohio, in 1882, and worked intermittently as a miner and union organizer until his death; participated actively in the labor movement from age 18, first joining the Knights of Labor and then the United Mine Workers of America (UMWA); was chosen as a delegate to the UMWA's founding convention in 1890 and as a member of the executive board of District 6, UMWA, Ohio, serving until 1896; finished seventh in a field of 28 candidates for one of six vacancies on the international executive board, UMWA, in 1895; a year later, received the highest vote among 14 candidates for a position on the international executive board, the highest UMWA office yet held by a black; reelected with the second highest vote in 1897, but lost his bid for reelection in 1898; concentrated his organizing efforts on southeastern Ohio and was most responsible for bringing Ohio's black miners into the union; participated in organizing campaigns in the New River field of West Virginia and in McDonnell, Pa., in 1892, in the Pocahontas field of West Virginia in 1894, and in West Virginia and Alabama in 1897–1898; died in Rendville, Ohio, January 24, 1900; Herbert G. Gutman, "The Negro and the United Mine Workers of America: The Career and Letters of Richard L. Davis and Something of Their Meaning," in *The Negro and the American Labor Movement*, edited by Julius Jacobson (1968); Stephen Brier, "The Career of Richard L. Davis Reconsidered: Unpublished Correspondence from the *National Labor Tribune*," *Labor History* (Summer 1980).

John W. Hevener

DAVIS, Walter G. (1920–). Born in New York City on November 27, 1920; son of Harold F. and Daisy Davis; married Doris E. Nelson, a registered nurse, in 1950; three children; Afro-American; attended the New York High School of Commerce, 1933–1937; received a B.S. from Columbia University, which he attended during 1951–1956; also studied at Brooklyn Law School, 1956–1958, and Columbia's School of International Affairs; served as a master sergeant in the U.S. Army Corps of Engineers, 1943–1946; entered the labor movement after the war when he became a member of the United Transport Service Employees of America (UTSE); was president of UTSE Local 290, 1951–1958; elected international executive vice-president of the UTSE in 1961 and was placed in charge of all collective bargaining with railroads and airlines; joined the staff of the American Federation of Labor-Congress of Industrial Organizations (AFL-CIO) in 1961, becoming the assistant director of the department of civil rights; joined the American Newspaper Guild in 1964; entered government service briefly during 1965–1966, while serving as deputy director of the Equal Employment Opportunity Commission; returned to the AFL-CIO as director of the department of education in 1965; appointed director of the AFL-CIO department of community service activities in 1980—the department coordinates volunteer efforts of trade unions and their members on behalf of community agencies and maintains a close working relationship with such national service agencies as the Red Cross and the United Way; involved in a variety of civic activities, he was a member of the Black Trade Unionists Committee of the New York Central Labor Council, AFL-CIO, the Committee on Non-Traditional Study, 1971–1972, and the advisory committee of the Community College of the Air Force; was appointed to the panel of experts, Workers Education Bureau, International Labor Organization; became a member of the committee on credits, National Council on Education in 1974; was appointed a member of the committee on selection of the White House Fellows in 1975; became a member of the board of directors of the A. Philip Randolph Institute, 1964, and the board of trustees of the AFL-CIO Labor Studies Center in 1969; the recipient of numerous awards including the A. Philip Randolph Human Rights Award, and the U.S. Department of Labor's Award for Outstanding Service; wrote "Labor and the Schools: A Report" (1974), an AFL-CIO publication, and, for *The American Federationist*, "Labor Education and Effective Unions" (1967) as well as "The Slow Pace of Desegregation" (1962); *Who's Who in Labor* (1976); *AFL-CIO News*, May 10, 1980.

DEBS, Eugene Victor   (1855–1926). Born in Terre Haute, Ind., November 5, 1855; son of Jean Daniel, a small businessman, and Marguerite Marie Debs; married Katherine Metzel in 1885; left school at age 15 to work in a railroad enginehouse and two years later became a locomotive fireman; served for three years as secretary of the Terre Haute, Ind., local of the Brotherhood of Locomotive Firemen (BLF), then became associate editor of the *Firemen's Magazine* in 1878; elected grand secretary and treasurer of the BLF (renamed the Brotherhood of Locomotive Firemen and Enginemen in 1906) and editor-in-chief of the *Firemen's Magazine* in 1880; resigned his offices in the BLF in 1892 and began organizing the American Railway Union (ARU), designed to represent all railroad laborers in one industrial union; successfully led an ARU strike against the Great Northern Railroad in 1894, but saw the union crushed in a strike against the Pullman Palace Car Company later that year; arrested for his activities during the Pullman strike, charged with conspiring to obstruct the delivery of federal mail, and sentenced to six months in prison; incarcerated in the McHenry County Jail in Woodstock, Ill.; became a Socialist shortly after serving his six-month prison term and in 1897 was instrumental in the formation of the Social Democratic party; led his new party into a 1901 merger with the "Rochester Faction" of the Socialist Labor party, led by Morris Hillquit (q.v.), and Victor Berger's (q.v.) Wisconsin party organization, resulting in the formation of the Socialist party of America; joined with other radicals to form the Industrial Workers of the World in 1905; resigned three years later over differences concerning political action; opposed American involvement in World War I and was convicted for violating the Espionage Act; sentenced to ten years in prison on September 14, 1918, and incarcerated in the Federal Penitentiary in Atlanta, Ga.; pardoned by the executive order of President Warren G. Harding in 1921; despite his identification with the Socialist party during most of his life, first ran for political office as a Democrat and was elected to the Indiana legislature in 1885, serving one term; endorsed William Jennings Bryan in 1896; ran for president of the United States under the Socialist banner in 1900, 1904, 1908, 1912, and 1920; endorsed Robert M. La Follette's Progressive party candidacy in 1924; authored *Walls and Bars* (1927); writings and speeches collected in Bruce Rogers, ed., *Debs: His Life, Writings, and Speeches* (1908), Joseph M. Bernstein, ed., *Writings and Speeches of Eugene V. Debs* (1948), and Gene Tussey, ed., *Eugene V. Debs Speaks* (1970); died at Lindlahr Sanitarium, Ill., October 20, 1926; Ray Ginger, *The Bending Cross: A Biography of Eugene Victor Debs* (1949); H. Wayne Morgan, *Eugene V. Debs: Socialist for President* (1962); David Herreshoff, *American Disciples of Marx: From the Age of Jackson to the Progressive Era* (1967); Harold W. Currie, *Eugene V. Debs* (1976); Nick Salvatore, *Eugene V. Debs: Citizen and Socialist* (1982).

De CAUX, Leonard Howard   (1899–   ). Born in Westport, New Zealand, on October 14, 1899; son of Howard Percival, a missionary, and Helen Hammond De Caux; married Caroline Abrams on July 14, 1928; one child; educated at Harrow School in New Zealand; enlisted in the Royal Field Artillery during World War I; after the war he entered Hertford College, Oxford University, 1919–1921; emigrated to the United States in 1921, landing in Philadelphia; moved to New York City, where he worked as a busboy at a YWCA cafeteria and then as an office clerk for the Onyz Hosiery Corporation; after working for a time in New York City, he hired out as a gandydancer, moved west, and for a period of time "rode the rails" working as a common laborer and seeing the country; during his travels he became associated with several Industrial Workers of the World (IWW) activities but never became deeply involved in the affairs of the disintegrating radical movement; settled in Chicago in 1923, where he worked at various times as a factory operative, reporter, editor, and printer; blacklisted because of his radical beliefs and union organizing activities; was assistant editor of the *Illinois Miner* in 1925; returned to New York where he worked in basic industries and attended Brookwood College; after returning to Chicago, he worked in a variety of jobs while doing a series of articles for the IWW's *Industrial Solidarity* on working conditions in various industries; served as the assistant editor of the *Locomotive Engineers Journal*, 1926–1934; became the Washington correspondent for the *Federated Press* in 1934; was appointed national publicity director of the Committee for Industrial Organization (CIO) when it was organized in 1937; became the editor of the *CIO News* in 1937; forced to resign both of his CIO positions in 1947 because of his Communist associations, he spent the next two years traveling the country, repeating the travels he had made several years earlier, 1947–1948; after working in the Henry Wallace campaign in 1948, he moved to southern California; became a reporter for the *March of Labor*, a left-wing newspaper which sought to speak for leftists expelled from regular unions as well as those still in the unions; was called before the House Un-American Activities Committee (HUAC) in 1952; blacklisted after the HUAC hearing and because of his association with the *March of Labor*, he bounced from job to job before getting steady employment as a proofreader in a non-union printing plant in Chicago; discharged after once again being called before HUAC in 1954, he studied linotyping, became a skilled linotype operator and eventually gained some degree of job security as a member of the linotypers' union; authored the autobiographical *Labor Radical: From the Wobblies to CIO, A Personal History* (1970), and *The Living Spirit of the Wobblies* (1978); Harvey A. Levenstein, *Communism, Anticommunism, and the CIO* (1981); Bert Cochran, *Labor and Communism: The Conflict that Shaped American Unions* (1977); Melvyn Dubofsky and Warren Van Tine, *John L. Lewis: A Biography* (1977); Leonard De Caux Papers, Walter Reuther Library, Wayne State University.

DELANEY, George Philip   (1909–1972). Born in Washington, D.C., February 20, 1909; son of George Patrick and Agnes E. (Connery) Delaney; Roman

Catholic; married Margaret D. Mulholland in July 1947; four children; completed a secondary education, then attended St. Mary's College, and, during 1945–1946, Harvard University; became an apprentice molder at the U.S. Navy Yard in Washington, D.C., in 1928; joined the International Molders and Foundry Workers Union of North America (IMFWU) in 1928; served as an international representative for the IMFWU, 1938–1942; joined the U.S. Navy during World War II, 1942–1945; resumed his duties after the war as an IMFWU international representative, serving until 1948; served as a labor specialist for the Civilian Production Administration, 1946–1947; became an international affairs representative for the American Federation of Labor in 1948, serving until 1958; beginning in 1948, served as a United States worker delegate and a member of the governing board of the International Labor Organization (ILO); participated actively in the formation of the International Conference of Free Trade Unions in 1949; became director of organization for the International Union of Operating Engineers, but resigned upon appointment as special assistant for international labor affairs in the U.S. Department of Labor; served on the U.S. delegation to the ILO, 1963–1970; became the first director of the Office of Labor Affairs in the Agency for International Development; following his retirement from government service in 1970, served as the Washington representative of the International Longshoremen's Association; was a Democrat; died in Washington, D.C., February 9, 1972; *AFL-CIO News*, August 1, 1964, July 19, 1972; *Who's Who in America, 1972–1973*; Philip Taft, *The A.F. of L. from the Death of Gompers to the Merger* (1959).

DeLEON Daniel   (1852–1914). Born in Curaçao, Venezuela, December 14, 1852; son of Salomon, a surgeon in the Dutch colonial army, and Sara (Jesurun) DeLeon (DeLeon apparently fabricated much of the factual information concerning his youth. For this reason, the material presented here may not be entirely accurate); Jewish; married Sara Lobo on August 2, 1882, and, after her death, Bertha Canary on June 10, 1892; one child; educated in German gymnasiums; emigrated to the United States in 1874, settling in New York City; while teaching school in Westchester County, N.Y., attended classes in law and political science at Columbia University and in 1878 received the LL.B. degree; practiced law in Texas for a time and then returned to New York in 1883; won a prize lectureship in Latin American diplomacy at Columbia and held it for six years; supported Henry George's candidacy for mayor of New York City in 1886; joined the Knights of Labor (K of L) in 1888; became a member of the Socialist Labor party (SLP) in 1890 and was its candidate for governor of New York in 1891 and 1902; became editor of the SLP organ, *The People*, in 1892; led a secessionist movement from the K of L in 1895 and founded the Socialist Trade and Labor Alliance; involved in the organization of the Industrial Workers of the World (IWW) in 1905 and immediately merged his Socialist Trade and Labor Alliance with it; failed to obtain a seat at the IWW's 1908 convention because of his disruptive tactics and emphasis on political action, and thus organized the rival

Workers' International Industrial Union; with his doctrinaire, domineering, and egotistical manner, was one of the most controversial and divisive figures in the radical union movement; was known as an implacable opponent of the American Federation of Labor, and was a dual unionist with a strong commitment to radical politics: authored *Two Pages from Roman History* (1903), *What Means This Strike?* (1898), *Socialist Reconstruction of Society* (1905), and other tracts; died in New York City, May 11, 1914; Daniel DeLeon Papers, State Historical Society of Wisconsin; *Daniel DeLeon: The Man and His Work, A Symposium* (1919); Charles A. Madison, *Critics and Crusaders: A Century of American Protest* (1947); Melvyn Dubofsky, *We Shall Be All: A History of the Industrial Workers of the World* (1969); *Dictionary of American Biography*, Vol. 5; Carl Reeve, *The Life and Times of Daniel DeLeon* (1972); L. Glen Seretan, *Daniel DeLeon: The Odyssey of an American Marxist* (1978).

DeLEON, Solon   (1883–1975). Born in New York City on September 2, 1883; son of Daniel (q.v.), Marxist leader of the Socialist Labor party (SLP), and Sarah (Lobo) DeLeon; Jewish (although he was not aware of his parents' Jewish background until he was an adult); married Mabel Poole on March 12, 1927; three children; attended public schools and City College of New York, where he studied languages and sciences and received a B.A. in 1902; after working in Connecticut as a carpenter, house painter, and teacher in one- and two-room schools, he returned to New York in 1905 to work on the SLP publications *Daily People* and *Weekly People* as a reporter, rewrite man, and assistant editor; translated *The Sword of Honor or the Foundation of the French Revolution* by Eugene Sue and *Patriotism and the Worker* by Gustave Hervé for publication by the SLP publishing house, New York Labor News Co.; received an M.A. in economics from Columbia University in 1912 and a social work degree from the New York School of Social Work (then the New York School of Philanthropy) in 1913; was employed by the American Association for Labor Legislation as a field investigator, writer, and researcher, 1912–1920, while continuing to contribute to SLP publications under the pseudonym, Braset Marteau; but became politically and personally estranged from his father and the SLP and was expelled from the party in 1918; was briefly a member of the Socialist party of America, joining the Workers' Council group which became part of the Communist party in 1920; contributed to and helped to edit the *Advance*, the Amalgamated Clothing Workers of America's newspaper, 1919–1922; was director of the labor research department, Rand School of Social Science, during the 1920s, and edited *The American Labor Who's Who* (1925), the first compilation of data on American labor leaders, as well as the annual *American Labor Year Book* published by the Rand School; during the 1930s, he taught science and shop at the Walden School, a private progressive school in New York; was a nature and shop counselor at children's summer camps, and, as Bert Grant, wrote a science and nature column for the *New Pioneer*; was assistant research director for the National Maritime Union, 1943–1964; was also active in the Labor Research Association during the 1960s, and a regular contributor of articles and book reviews to its publication *Economic Notes*; was librarian and French instructor at Kittrell Junior College, a black college in North Carolina, 1965–1967; died in Ellenville, N.Y., on December 3, 1975; *Who's Who in Labor* (1946); *The New York Times*, December 4, 1975.

Jon Bloom

DELLUMS, Cottrell Laurence   (1900–   ). Born in Corsicana, Tex., on January 3, 1900; son of William Henry, a barber, and Emma (Anthony) Dellums; married Walter Lee Allen on March 25, 1927; one child (California Congressman Ronald V. Dellums); Afro-American; attended Frederick Douglass High School, 1915–1919; after graduating from high school, he taught for a short time before becoming a Pullman porter; along with A. Philip Randolph (q.v.), he was one of the founders of the Brotherhood of Sleeping Car Porters (BSCP) in 1925; served as vice-president and then president of the Oakland (Calif.) Division of the BSCP, 1929–1968; was elected an international vice-president of the BSCP in 1929, serving in that capacity until being elected international president in 1968; was a member of the state advisory board of the National Youth Administration; active in civic and civil rights activities, at various times he served on the President's Committee on Fair Employment Practices, was chairman of the Alameda County (Calif.) Labor's Nonpartisan League and a member of the state executive board, Labor's Nonpartisan League; was appointed one of the original members of the California Fair Employment Practices Commission and served as its president, 1951–1963; joined the National Association for the Advancement of Colored People (NAACP) in 1924 and served as western regional chairman, 1945–1968; was elected a vice-president and member of the American Federation of Labor-Congress of Industrial Organizations (AFL-CIO) executive council in 1974; a Democrat; *Who's Who in Labor* (1946, 1976); *AFL-CIO News*, August 10, 1974; Brailsford R. Brazeal, *The Brotherhood of Sleeping Car Porters: Its Origins and Development* (1946); Jervis Anderson, *A. Philip Randolph: A Biographical Portrait* (1972).

DELORENZO, Anthony J.   (1915–1978). Born in Stamford, Conn., on May 7, 1915; married Alice E. Wells; three children; after completing a secondary school education in Bristol, Conn., he secured employment in an electrical appliance plant and joined Local 260, United Electrical, Radio and Machine Workers of America in 1937; served as president and business agent of Local 260, 1940–1942; joined Local 626 of the United Automobile Workers Union in 1942 after securing employment in the New Departures Division, General Motors Corporation; joined the staff of Local 626 in 1944 and during 1945–1946 was chairman of the local's bargaining and strike committees; was appointed a UAW international representative in 1948, a position he retained for over 20 years; was elected director of UAW Region 9A in 1970 and became special assistant to UAW president Douglas Fraser (q.v.) in 1972; along with his union activities, he was also very active in Democratic party affairs, beginning with his election to the Democratic Town Committee of Bristol during the early 1950s and culminating with his election as chairman in 1961 and his service as a Democratic party national committee member from Connecticut; was a delegate to national Democratic conventions in 1956 and 1960; also served as a member of the board of directors of the Connecticut Blue Cross, the board of finance of the city of Bristol, and the Connecticut Fire and Safety Committee; died in New Britain, Conn., on June 29, 1978; *Who's Who in Labor* (1976); *The New York Times*, June 30, 1978.

DeLURY, John Joseph   (1904–1980). Born in New York City on September 30, 1904; son of John Joseph and Charlotte DeLury; Roman Catholic; married Margaret Theresa Donnelly on November 21, 1931; three children; attended Catholic parochial elementary schools and St. James High School in New York City; later took special courses at St. John's University but never graduated from either high school or college; left high school in 1921, at age 16, to help support his family—he had 12 siblings—and took a job as a Wall Street messenger; after working at various jobs for brokerage houses for 15 years, he became a dump laborer for the New York City Sanitation Department; organized Uniformed Sanitation Men's Association, Local 308, American Federation of State, County and Municipal Employees, in 1938, and was elected president and business agent of the new union, a position he was to hold for 40 years; a shrewd bargainer and astute political organizer, he built Local 308 into one of the most powerful and effective municipal locals in the United States; by the time of his retirement in 1978, he had nearly accomplished his long-term objective of equalizing the pay of sanitation workers with that of policemen and firemen; much of his success was built on a political power base of nearly 250,000 voters composed of the members, friends, and relatives of Local 308; was usually able to achieve collective bargaining objectives through negotiations but when neccessary called strikes such as in 1968 and 1975; a Democrat; died in Lauderdale Lakes, Fla., on February 12, 1980; *Who's Who in Labor* (1946); *The New York Times*, February 1–26, 1968, July 1–29, 1975, and February 13, 1980.

DENNIS, Charles Leslie   (1908–1978). Born in Beardstown, Ill., on June 21, 1908; son of Charles Eugene, a railroad brakeman, and Mae Anna (Preckwinkle) Dennis; married Harriet Huseby, also a member of the Railway Clerks, in 1950; four children; joined the Brotherhood of Railway, Airline and Steamship Clerks, Freight Handlers, Express and Station Employees (BRAC) as a freight handler on the Chicago and Northwestern Railroad after being fired as a biscuit factory worker when he tried to organize a union; became general chairman for Chicago and Northwestern System Board of Adjustment in 1940; appointed acting vice-president of the BRAC in 1957; two years later he was elected a grand lodge vice-president; elected president of the BRAC in 1963; elected an American Federation of Labor-Congress of Industrial Organizations (AFL-CIO) vice-president and executive council member in 1969; represented the AFL-CIO in a number of overseas missions; appointed chairman of the railroad retirement committee, Congress of Railway Unions, in 1969; appointed chairman of the Conference of Transportation Trades in 1968; was a labor member of the U.S. Railroad Retirement Committee, 1972–1974; was a member of the International Transportation Workers' Federation; retired from his BRAC presidency in 1976 and the following year retired from his other labor positions; died in Chicago, Ill., in September 1978; *Who's Who in Labor* (1976); *AFL-CIO News*, August 5, 1968.

DENNIS, Eugene (Francis Eugene Waldron)   (1905–1961). Born in Seattle, Wash., August 10, 1905; son of Francis X. and Nora (Vieg) Waldron; married Reggie Schneiderman; two children; after graduation from Franklin High School in Seattle, went to work as a salesman to earn enough money to enter the University of Washington; forced to leave the university after one term because of his father's illness; worked as an electrician, teamster, carpenter, lumberjack, and longshoreman; joined the Industrial Workers of the World and participated in the general strike in Seattle in 1919; joined the Communist party of America (CPA) in 1926 and became regular party employee assigned to teach economics at a Communist camp in Woodland, Wash.; spent several years in Europe and South Africa, and attended the Lenin Institute in the Soviet Union; returned to the United States in 1935 and resumed Communist organizing in Wisconsin; was elected to the Communist National Committee from Wisconsin in 1939; served for a short period as an organizer for the National Maritime Union during the late 1930s; was appointed general secretary of the CPA in 1945; convicted for contempt of Congress after failing to respond to a subpoena issued by the House Committee on Un-American Activities in 1947 and sentenced to one year in prison; later indicted and convicted of "teaching and advocating the overthrow of the Government by force and violence," and was imprisoned during 1951–1955; modified his ideological stance after the 1956 Russian invasion of Hungary, and thus increasingly came into conflict with hardline Communist William Z. Foster (q.v.); became national chairman of the CPA in 1959 and served until his death; died in New York City, January 31, 1961; Eugene Dennis Papers, State Historical Society of Wisconsin; Joseph R. Starobin, *American Communism in Crisis, 1943–1957* (1972); David A. Shannon, *The Decline of American Communism* (1959); Max M. Kampelman, *The Communist Party vs. the C.I.O.: A Study in Power Politics* (1957); *Current Biography* (1949); Bert Cochran, *Labor and Communism: The Conflict that Shaped American Unions* (1977); Harvey A. Levenstein, *Communism, Anticommunism, and the CIO* (1981); Joseph R. Starobin, *American Communism in Crisis, 1943–1957* (1972); Peggy Dennis, *Autobiography of an American Communist: A Personal View of Political Life, 1925–1975* (1977).

DeNUCCI, George   (1902–1979). Born in Italy on February 14, 1902; son of Vincent, a tailor, and Catherine DeNucci; Roman Catholic; married Lena

Vellani on October 16, 1929; one child; a high school graduate, he was a garment cutter by trade who was destined to play a leadership role in the Ohio labor movement for 50 years; served as the president of the Columbus (Ohio) Federation of Labor before joining the Amalgamated Clothing Workers of America in 1936; quickly became one of the Congress of Industrial Organizations' (CIO) most effective union leaders in Ohio and was elected president of the Columbus Industrial Union Council; during World War II he served as the secretary-treasurer of the Ohio State Industrial Union Council, executive secretary of the Columbus Industrial Union Council, and secretary-treasurer of the Ohio CIO Political Action Committee; also was a member of the war bond drive committee, a panel member of the War Manpower Commission, and the Ohio Postwar Planning Commission; after the war he was appointed a CIO regional director; after the merger of the American Federation of Labor (AFL) and the CIO, he joined the AFL-CIO staff as assistant director for Ohio and West Virginia; later he became a district organizing director for the United Steelworkers of America; was involved in many civic activities including the American Red Cross and the Urban League; a Democrat; died in Columbus, Ohio, on July 23, 1979; *AFL-CIO News*, July 29, 1979; *Who's Who in Labor* (1976); George DeNucci Papers, Ohio Historical Society.

DERWENT, Clarence   (1884–1959). Born in London, England, March 23, 1884; son of Charles, an actor, and Alice (Falk) Derwent; Society for Ethical Culture; attended St. Paul's School in London and the Birbeck Institute for instruction in acting; made his first stage appearance on September 1, 1902 at the Theatre Royal in Weymouth, England; performed minor roles in Shakespearean plays with the Frank Benson Company, 1902–1907; was associated with Horniman's Manchester Repertory Company, 1907–1909; made his London debut as Abergavenny in *Henry VIII* at His Majesty's Theatre in 1910; traveled to the United States in 1915, and, although remaining a British citizen, devoted most of his professional career to acting, directing, and producing in the United States; joined Actor's Equity Association (AEA) in 1925 and was chosen president in 1946, serving until 1952; served as AEA delegate to the meeting of the International Theatre Institute in Paris in 1947; was elected chairman of Experimental Theatre, Inc., in 1947; was also a member of the New York City Center of Music and Drama and the American Federation of Radio Artists; during his administration, brought about the AEA vote to boycott any performance in Washington, D.C., that denied admission to Americans of African descent; became president of the American National Theatre and Academy in 1952, serving until his death; authored *The Derwent Story: My First Fifty Years in the Theatre in England and America* (1953); died in New York City, August 6, 1959; *Current Biography* (1947); *Who's Who in the Theater* (1947); *Who's Who in Labor* (1946); *The New York Times*, August 7, 1959.

DEVYR, Thomas Ainge   (1805–1877). Born in County Donegal, Ireland, in 1805; married; had several children, one of whom belonged to the Shaker com-

munity of New Lebanon, N.Y.; acquired a limited formal education, then worked
as a peddler, writer, constable, and journalist; became an early convert to Chartist
reform; served as assistant editor, 1839–1840, of the *Northern Liberator* published in Newcastle-on-Tyne; named corresponding secretary of the Northern
Political Union; after organizing a secret, armed band of Chartist guerillas in
1840, was forced to flee Great Britain; emigrated to the United States, settling
in New York; became editor of the *Williamsburg* (N.Y.) *Democrat*, a Democratic
party newspaper, in 1840, but offended the party leaders with his radical principles and thus saw them withdraw vital support from the newspaper; became
an organizer for the Anti-Rent party in upstate New York shortly thereafter;
repeating the same paramilitary, guerilla tactics used in Newcastle, successfully
exposed the feudal conditions especially prevalent in the Hudson River Valley;
allied himself with George Henry Evans (q.v.) in the effort to revive the workingmen's movement in the form of the National Reform Association and the
National Reform party, which was organized in New York in 1844; attended
the New England ten-hour convention held in Faneuil Hall, Boston, in 1844,
and addressed the delegates regarding the advantages of land reform; was an
Albany, N.Y., delegate to the Industrial Congress in 1845; partly because of
his indiscretion, vanity, ungovernable temper, and dictatorial manner, caused
the dilution of the radical free soil principles that he advocated (termed Devyrism)
and their preemption by dissident Whigs and Democrats who organized the
Republican party; after exhausting his financial reserves in the Anti-Rent movement, accumulated a sizeable fortune through successful real estate speculations
and developments in New York and used most of that money to endow various
radical newspapers; supported the Republican party in 1860 because of its homestead plank; served as editor of the Fenian newspaper, *The Irish People*, 1865–
1866, and joined the editorial staff of the *Irish World* in 1877; remained a
spokesman and agitator for land reform until his death in Brooklyn, N.Y., in
1877; edited the New York periodicals *The National Reformer* and *The Anti-
Renter*; authored *Our Natural Rights* (1836) and *The Odd Book, or Chivalry in
Modern Days* (1882); Ray Boston, *British Chartists in America, 1839–1900*
(1971); Helene S. Zahler, *Eastern Workingmen and National Land Policy, 1829–
1862* (1941); Henry Christman, *Tin Horns and Calico* (1945).

DICKASON, Gladys Marie   (1903–1971). Born in Galena, Okla., on January 28, 1903; daughter of Simon, a stockraiser and realtor, and Linnie (Kel-
lerman) Dickason; associated with (and perhaps briefly married to) Arthur S.
Harrison, a New York building contractor; no children; graduated from high
school in 1918 and acquired a B.A. from the University of Oklahoma; earned
an M.A. in economics and political science from Columbia University in 1924;
taught at Hamilton Grange School, New York City, and later briefly attended
the London School of Economics; joined the Department of Economics, Sweet
Briar College, Virginia, in 1926; entered the doctoral program of Columbia
University in 1928 but did not complete the degree and returned to Sweet Briar

in 1929; became an instructor in political science at Hunter College in 1930; began working for the Amalgamated Clothing Workers of America (ACWA) in 1933 after serving on the industrial committee of the National Recovery Administration's Cotton Garment Code Authority, 1933–1934; named research director of the ACWA in 1935; while in this position, she advocated minimum wage standards for the Fair Labor Standards Act of 1938 and provided staff support for union cases before the War Labor Board; was an active participant in the organizing drives among garment workers during the 1930s; she was especially effective among the wives and daughters of southern industrial workers; her successful organizing campaign at Cluett, Peabody & Company, a four-year struggle which finally brought the nation's largest shirt manufacturer to the bargaining table in 1941, established her reputation as a tough, dedicated ACWA organizer; was elected an ACWA vice-president in 1946 and became assistant director of the Congress of Industrial Organization's "Operation Dixie" organizing campaign after World War II; shortly thereafter, she was appointed director of the ACWA's southern department; spearheaded a campaign to raise minimum wage rates, 1948–1949; traveled to Japan as a representative of the U.S. Army to study and talk to women in the Japanese labor movement; authored "Women in Labor Unions," American Academy of Political and Social Science *Annals* (May 1947); retired in 1963; died in New York City on August 31, 1971; *Notable American Women*, Vol. 4; *Fortune* (November 1946); *The New York Times*, September 1, 1971; *Advance*, September 17, 1971.

DOAK, William Nuckles   (1882–1933). Born near Rural Retreat, Va., December 12, 1882; son of Canaro Drayton and Elizabeth (Dutton) Doak; married Emma Maria Cricher in 1908; after attending the public schools of the area, studied at a business college at Bristol, Va.; worked for the Norfolk and Western Railroad at Bluefield, W.Va., in 1900; joined the Brotherhood of Railroad Trainmen (BRT) in 1904; served as secretary-treasurer of the southern association of general committees of the Order of Railroad Conductors and the BRT, 1909–1916; was general chairman for the Norfolk and Western systems, 1912–1916; after his election as a BRT vice-president in 1916, became the BRT's national legislative representative in Washington, D.C.; was appointed a member of the Railway Board of Adjustment Number One in 1918; served on the train service board of adjustment for southern and eastern territories, 1921–1928; was elected first vice-president of the BRT in 1922; ran unsuccessfully for the U.S. Senate from Virginia on the Republican party ticket in 1924; became assistant BRT president in 1927; was elected managing editor of *The Railroad Trainmen* and national legislative representative in 1928; was appointed U.S. Secretary of Labor by President Herbert Hoover in 1930, serving until 1933; devoted much attention during his incumbency to immigration laws and opposed labor reforms advocated by the labor movement; was politically a Republican; died in McLean, Va., October 23, 1933; Walter F. McCaleb, *Brotherhood of Railroad Trainmen, with Special Reference to the Life of Alexander F. Whitney* (1936); Irving Bernstein,

The Lean Years: A History of the American Worker, 1920–1933 (1960); Eugene Lyons, *Herbert Hoover: A Biography* (1964).

DOBBS, Farrel (1907–   ). Born in Queen City, Mo., July 25, 1907; son of a mechanical superintendent in a coal firm; married Marvel Scholl in April 1927; three children; graduated from high school in Minneapolis, Minn., in 1925; worked during the next several years for Western Electric, rising from a blue-collar job to a supervisory position; failed in an attempt to start a small business in 1932; secured a job as a truck driver and joined General Drivers Local 574 of the International Brotherhood of Teamsters, Chauffeurs, Ware-housemen, and Helpers of America (IBT); saw a small group of Trotskyists, led by Vincent R. Dunne (q.v.) and Carl Skoglund, use Local 574 to organize the coal yards, planning to make them the opening wedge for unionization of all general trucking, including helpers and inside workers; was influenced by Dunne and Skoglund to become a full-time organizer for Local 574; meanwhile, joined the Communist League, precursor of the Socialist Workers party (SWP); emerged as a brilliant unionist during Local 574's famous strikes of 1934 by displaying a keen sense of tactics he would soon apply to unionize highway drivers; was elected secretary-treasurer of Local 574 and in 1936 began organizing highway truckers throughout the upper Midwest; sought to establish an area-wide agree-ment providing uniform wages and working conditions; founded the North Cen-tral District Drivers' Council in 1937; by "leapfrogging" from organized terminal cities such as Minneapolis and Chicago to other key trucking centers, was able to secure a contract in 1938 covering 250,000 over-the-road drivers; resigned from the IBT after renewing the agreement in 1939; devoted most of his time to SWP activity after 1940; was convicted of violating the Smith Act, a 1940 sedition statute, in 1941; served as editor of *The Militant*, 1943–1948; ran as the SWP candidate for president of the United States in 1948; served as SWP national chairman, 1949–1953, and as national secretary until 1972; authored *Teamster Rebellion* (1972) and *Teamster Power* (1973); Ralph C. James and Estelle D. James, *Hoffa and the Teamsters: A Study of Union Power* (1965); Irving Bernstein, *Turbulent Years: A History of the American Worker, 1933–1941* (1969).

Donald G. Sofchalk

DOCKTER, Wallace John (1925–   ). Born in Drake, N.D., on May 1, 1925; son of Chris and Mary Dockter; Lutheran; married Grace E. Stradcutter, a secretary, in 1946; six children; graduated from Velva High School in 1943; served as an aviation electronics technician third class with the U.S. Navy during World War II, 1943–1946; attended DePauw University, Greencastle, Ind., Indiana State College, Terre Haute, and the University of Georgia, Athens, 1944; later attended the Labor Leadership Institute, 1966, 1968, 1974, and Bismarck Junior College Night School, 1971, 1973, 1974; worked as an electric and telephone construction worker, 1946–1949; joined Local 949, International

Brotherhood of Electrical Workers in 1947; became a telephone installer, repairman, central office tester, and switchman, 1949–1963; during this time he served the union in a number of positions, including delegate and financial secretary, Minot Central Labor Union, 1953–1963, union steward, 1958–1960, union unit chairman, 1957–1961, and secretary-treasurer of the North Dakota American Federation of Labor-Congress of Industrial Organizations (AFL-CIO) Council in 1963; joined Local 12 of the Office and Professional Employees International Union in 1973; appointed staff representative of the AFL-CIO department of organization and field services in May 1977; very active in a wide variety of civic organizations such as the Governor's Council on Human Resources and member of the board, YMCA, 1961; member of the State Advisory Council on Vocational Education, 1963–1966, director of the United Fund, board member on Status of Women Commission, 1963–1966; *Who's Who in Labor* (1976); *AFL-CIO News*, October 8, 1977.

DOHERTY, William Charles   (1902–   ). Born in Glendale, Ohio, February 23, 1902; son of Lawrence Michael, a railroader, and Catherine (Ryan) Doherty; Roman Catholic; married Gertrude Helen Dacey on February 23, 1925; nine children; was forced to leave school because of family illness and to begin work at an early age; while working as a telegraph messenger, attended the Cincinnati, Ohio, School of Telegraphy and graduated at age 16; appointed manager of the Postal Telegraph Office in Cincinnati in 1918; joined the Commercial Telegraphers Union in 1919; enlisted in the U.S. Army in 1919, after a telegraphers strike began in Cincinnati; participated in the occupation of Siberia following World War I; was blacklisted in the telegraph industry as a result of his union activities; eventually took the civil service examination as a letter carrier and began work with the Cincinnati Post Office in 1923; joined the National Association of Letter Carriers (NALC) in 1923; was elected financial secretary of NALC Branch 43 in 1926 and president in 1928; was chosen president of the Ohio State Letter Carriers Association in 1932; became an executive board member of the NALC in 1935 and was elected president in 1941; was chosen a vice-president and member of the executive council of the American Federation of Labor (AFL) in 1943; served as the AFL fraternal delegate to the British Trades Union Congress in 1945 and 1957; served as a vice-president and executive council member of the newly merged AFL-Congress of Industrial Organizations (CIO) in 1955; retired from union affairs in 1962, after leading the NALC in a successful U.S. Post Office Department national representation election; associated himself with many AFL and AFL-CIO foreign policy endeavors; was appointed U.S. Ambassador to Jamaica in 1962; was politically a Democrat; authored *Mailman U.S.A.* (1960); Philip Taft, *The A.F. of L. from the Death of Gompers to the Merger* (1959); *Who's Who in Labor* (1946); *Who's Who in America, 1964–1965*.

DONAHUE, Thomas Reilly   (1928–   ). Born in New York City on September 4, 1928; son of Thomas R. and Mary E. Donahue; Roman Catholic; after completing his elementary and secondary schooling, he enrolled in Manhattan College, earning a B.A. in labor relations in 1949; later enrolled in the Fordham University Law School from which he received the LL.B. in 1956; served as a seaman in the U.S. Navy, 1945–1946; became a part-time organizer for the Retail Clerks International Association in 1948; joined Local 32B of the Service Employees International Union (SEIU) in 1949; served as the SEIU director of education, 1949–1952; during the period of 1952 to 1957, he served as director of the contract department and assistant to SEIU president George Hardy; served as European labor program coordinator for the Free Europe Committee in Paris, 1957–1960; returned to the SEIU in 1960, serving as Hardy's executive assistant until 1967; appointed Assistant Secretary of Labor by President Lyndon B. Johnson in 1967 and was responsible for department's labor relations activities; elected executive secretary and first vice-president of the SEIU in 1969; became executive assistant to American Federation of Labor-Congress of Industrial Organizations (AFL-CIO) president George Meany (q.v.) in 1973; after Meany's retirement in 1979, he was elected secretary-treasurer of the AFL-CIO, replacing Lane Kirkland (q.v.) who was elevated to the AFL-CIO presidency; involved in a variety of civic activities including the Committee on Social Development, U.S. Catholic Conference, and service as a member of the board of directors and chairman of the executive committee of the Muscular Dystrophy Association; a Democrat; *Who's Who in Labor* (1976); *AFL-CIO News*, November 19, 1979.

DONNELLY, Michael   (fl. 1898–1916). Married; learned the butchers' trade and joined Sheep Butchers' Local 36 in South Omaha, Neb.; was elected the first international president of the Amalgamated Meat Cutters and Butcher Workmen of North America (AMCBWNA) in 1897; was a gifted organizer; along with Homer D. Call, was largely responsible for the early growth of the AMCBWNA; was an advocate of inclusive organization and attempted to organize packinghouse workers on an industrial basis; forced by undisciplined local leaders and rank-and-file pressures into a general strike of packinghouse workers in 1904 that nearly destroyed the AMCBWNA; led a bitter but somewhat more successful strike against the Cudahy Packing Company in Louisville, Ky., in 1905; unfairly became the scapegoat for the AMCBWNA's failures, but was nevertheless able to win reelection in 1906; severely beaten twice as a result of his reform activities in the Chicago (Ill.) Federation of Labor and this, along with a growing alcohol addiction, apparently caused increasing serious mental disorders; resigned as AMCBWNA president in 1907 and for several years disappeared from union activities; worked for a short time on several jobs, then in 1916 was employed by the AMCBWNA as an organizer; succeeded in organizing a local in Fort Worth, Tex., and commissioned as an American Federation of Labor organizer assigned to the Chicago area; however, disappeared before the commission was delivered, was never heard from again; in 1950 the AMCBWNA, which had voted him a $3,000 annual pension, attempted without success to locate him; advocated an independent labor party during his trade union career; David Brody, *The Butcher Workmen: A Study of Unionization* (1964); *The American Federation of Labor Weekly News Service*, April 11, 1950.

DONNELLY, Samuel Bratton   (1866–1946). Born in Concord, Pa., November 7, 1866; son of James M. and Hannah M. (Bratton) Donnelly; married; one child; graduated from high school in Lewistown, Pa., and attended the State Normal School at Shippensburg, Pa.; taught in rural Pennsylvania schools, 1883–1886; learned the printers' trade and became associated with various New Jersey and New York newspapers between 1886 and 1901; joined New York Typographical Union No. 6 and during 1895–1898 served as its president; was elected president of the International Typographical Union in 1898, but failed to win reelection in 1900; was appointed secretary of the National Civic Federation in 1901 and served for two years; became a member of the joint arbitration board of the New York Building Trades Employers Association in 1903, serving until 1908; was named to the New York Board of Education in 1901 by Mayor Seth Low and served until 1908; served as Public Printer in the administrations of Theodore Roosevelt and William Howard Taft, 1908–1913; was secretary of the New York Building Trades Employers Association, 1913–1923, and chairman of the board of control of the Allied Building Metal Industries, 1923–1931; retired in 1931 to a Monmouth County, N.J., farm; was a Republican; died in Neptune, N.J., January 26, 1946; George A. Stevens, *New York Typographical Union No. 6: A Study of a Modern Trade Union and Its Predecessors* (1913); Seymour Martin Lipset et al., *Union Democracy: The Internal Politics of the International Typographical Union* (1956); *Encyclopedia Americana*, Vol. 9.

DOUGLAS, Dr. Charles   (fl. 1831–1850). Born in New London, Conn., around the turn of the nineteenth century; traveled extensively throughout the world as a young man, and, although not himself a laborer, identified with the workingmen's cause at an early age; during 1831, established the *New England Artisan*, which was published in Pawtucket, R.I., and the New London *Political Observer and Workingman's Friend*, both of which championed the cause of labor; was elected first president of the New England Association of Farmers, Mechanics, and other Workingmen in 1832; favored an independent labor party, but usually supported the reform-wing of the Democratic party and ran in 1832 as the Democratic nominee for state senator from Connecticut's Seventh District; was one of the principal founders of the Boston Trades' Union, presiding over its initial meeting, helping to draft its constitution, and delivering a major address at its organizational convention in the spring of 1834; made his *New England Artisan* the official organ of the Boston Trades' Union; served as a Boston delegate to the formative meeting of the National Trades' Union (NTU) meeting in New York in 1834; despite the failure of the Boston Trades' Union, was elected as a special delegate to represent the women and child workers of Boston cotton factories at the NTU conference in Philadelphia, Pa., in 1836; after the

192

DOUGLASS, FREDERICK

decline of the labor movement and start of the depression in the wake of the Panic of 1837, continued to advocate labor reforms; addressed the state convention of the Friends of Industrial Reform in Boston; fervently supported public education throughout his career; Edward Pessen, *Most Uncommon Jacksonians: The Radical Leaders of the Early Labor Movement* (1967); John R. Commons et al., eds., *A Documentary History of American Industrial Society*, Vol. 6 (1910) and *History of Labour in the United States*, Vol. 1 (1918); Philip S. Foner, *History of the Labor Movement in the United States*, Vol. 1 (1947).

DOUGLASS, Frederick (1817–1895). Born Frederick Augustus Washington Bailey in Tuckahoe, Talbot County, Md., probably in February 1817; the son of an unknown white father and Harriet Bailey, a slave; Afro-American; married Anna Murray, a free black woman, in 1838; his early childhood, which resembled that of many slave children, was characterized by neglect, cruelty, and hard work; learned to read and write as a young man while working in Baltimore, Md., as a house servant; after his owner's death, he was returned to the Talbot County plantation where he worked as a field laborer; although arrested for conspiring to escape, an indulgent owner returned him to Baltimore where he learned the ship-caulking trade; successfully escaped his bondage on September 3, 1838, and went to New York; moved to New Bedford, Mass., where he worked as a common laborer; became involved in the activities of the Massachusetts Anti-Slavery Society in 1841 and soon became a popular anti-slavery orator; participated in the successful campaign in Rhode Island against a new constitution which would have disfranchised black voters; after the publication of his autobiographical *Narrative of the Life of Frederick Douglass* in 1845, he spent two years in England and Ireland, fearing that the publicity accompanying publication of his book would result in his reenslavement; returned to the United States in 1847 and arranged for the purchase of his freedom; began publication of the *North Star* in 1847, a newspaper designed for a black readership; meanwhile, he continued lecturing and agitating against slavery; assisted Harriet Beecher Stowe in establishing an industrial school for black youth; accused by the governor of Virginia of conspiring with John Brown, he fled to Canada after being indicted, remaining there for six months during 1859; after the outbreak of the Civil War, he assisted in the recruitment of black regiments from Massachusetts; after the war he turned his attention to the plight of the newly emancipated black worker and in 1868 became the vice-president of the National Colored Labor Union—a parallel organization to the National Labor Union—which sought to create a national organization of black trade unions; was appointed Secretary of the Santo Domingo Commission in 1871, serving until 1877; served as U.S. marshall, 1877–1881, and recorder of deeds, 1881–1886, of the District of Columbia; was U.S. minister to Haiti, 1889–1891; after the death of his first wife, he created a stir by marrying Helen Pitts, a Caucasian, on January 24, 1884; a Republican; authored, among other publications, *My Bondage and My Freedom* (1855), and *Life and Times of Frederick Douglass* (1881); died in

Washington, D.C., on February 20, 1895; Philip S. Foner, ed., *The Life and Writings of Frederick Douglass*, 4 Vols. (1976); *Dictionary of American Biography*, Vol. 5; *National Cyclopaedia of American Biography*, Vol. 2; F. M. Holland, *Frederick Douglass, the Colored Orator* (1891); C. W. Chesnutt, *Frederick Douglass* (1907).

DREIER, Mary Elisabeth   (1875–1963). Born in Brooklyn, N.Y., on September 26, 1875; daughter of Theodor, an iron broker, and Dorothea Adelheid (Dreier) Dreier; born into and raised in the German Evangelical faith, she joined the Presbyterian church in 1943; never married; no children; attended George Brackett's School in Brooklyn and later took courses at the New York School of Philanthropy, but much of her education came from private tutors; became a volunteer settlement house worker in Brooklyn in 1899; joined the New York Women's Trade Union League (WTUL) after it was organized in 1903 and from 1906 until 1914 was president of the New York league; participated in the dramatic New York garment workers strikes of 1909, 1910, 1913, and in 1909 was arrested for her picketing activities; investigated and wrote reports on police brutality against arrested strikers; along with Robert Wagner, Alfred E. Smith, and six others, she was a member of the New York State Investigating Commission which undertook an extensive study of working conditions in American industry after the tragic Triangle Shirtwaist Company fire of 1911 which resulted in the deaths of 146 trapped workers, most of whom were women and children; the commission, which met from 1911 to 1915, studied fire prevention, occupational diseases, hours and wages, and safety standards; served on the New York Board of Education, 1915; chaired New York City's Woman Suffrage party and the industrial section of the New York State Suffrage party; during World War I, she chaired the New York State Committee on Women in Industry of the Council of National Defense's Advisory Commission; chaired the New York Joint Legislative Conference, 1918–1922; served as secretary of the New York Conference for Unemployment Insurance and chairman of the New York State Conference for the Federal Child Labor Amendment; involved in numerous peace and law enforcement activities, she was a member of the Executive Committee for Law Enforcement, chairman of the WTUL's Outlawing of War Contracts Committee, and a member of the executive committee of the New York Council for Limitation of Armaments, 1921–1927; was a staunch supporter of Soviet-American friendship during the 1920s and 1930s and was later investigated by the FBI during the McCarthy period as a possible subversive; helped mobilize anti-Nazi sentiment in the United States during the 1930s; served as acting president of the New York WTUL, 1935; was a member of the executive board of the national WTUL; after World War II, she joined the anti-nuclear movement; a political progressive, she was a delegate-at-large to the Progressive party convention in 1912; supported Robert M. La Follette in 1924; campaigned for Franklin D. Roosevelt and the New Deal during the 1930s, and supported Henry A. Wallace in 1948; her most consistent political affiliations were with the

American Labor party and the Liberal party of New York; authored *Margaret Dreier Robins: Her Life, Letters, and Work* (1959); wrote numerous articles and flyers for labor and trade publications; died at Bar Harbor, Me., August 15, 1963; *Notable American Women*, Vol. 4; *National Cyclopaedia of American Biography*, Vol. 1; *Who's Who in Labor* (1946); Solon DeLeon, ed., *The American Labor Who's Who* (1925); *The New York Times*, August 19, 1963.

DRISCOLL, John J. (1911–   ). Born in Waterbury, Conn., December 11, 1911; son of William J., a clerk, and Mary Ellen Driscoll; Roman Catholic; attended the elementary and secondary schools of Waterbury, then matriculated at the Massachusetts Institute of Technology, 1929–1930; received the B.A. (1933) and M.A. (1934) degrees from Wesleyan University, and did graduate study at Brown University, 1934–1935; attended Harvard University Law School, 1935–1936; joined Local 251 of the International Union of Mine, Mill and Smelter Workers of America (IUMMSW) and served during the period 1937–1942 as secretary of Local 251; was a founder of the Connecticut State Industrial Union Council, and was elected its secretary-treasurer, serving until the merger of the American Federation of Labor (AFL) and Congress of Industrial Organizations (CIO) in Connecticut; proved an influential leader of IUMMSW's brass district in Connecticut, but ran unsuccessfully for the post of secretary-treasurer of IUMMSW in 1940; despite early support of IUMMSW president Reid Robinson (q.v.), grew increasingly critical of Robinson for allegedly coming under the influence of the Communist element in the international union; opposed Robinson unsuccessfully for the IUMMSW presidency in a bitterly contested election in 1942; helped to lead Connecticut-centered secessionist movement in 1947 that created the Provisional Metalworkers Council (PMC) as a rival organization; was elected chairman of the PMC and hoped to affiliate it with the International Union of Marine and Shipbuilding Workers of America; after the IUMMSW's expulsion from the CIO as a Communist-dominated union in 1950, affiliated PMC with the United Automobile, Aerospace, and Agricultural Implement Workers of America; was elected president of the newly merged Connecticut AFL-CIO, and remains in that post; devoted much of his time as leader of the Connecticut labor movement to political affairs, especially to lobbying for favorable legislation in the state legislature; was politically a Democrat; Vernon H. Jensen, *Nonferrous Metals Industry Unionism, 1932–1954* (1954); *Who's Who in Labor* (1946); Harvey A. Levenstein, *Communism, Anticommunism, and the CIO* (1981).

DROZAK, Frank P. (1927–   ). Born in Coy, Ala., on December 24, 1927; married; one child; began working as a boatswain in Mobile, Ala., and joined the Seafarers International Union (SIU) in 1944; served as an organizer in Mobile, 1953–1960; was an SIU international representative in Brooklyn, N.Y., in 1960, and in Philadelphia, Pa., in 1963; was Philadelphia port agent in 1964 and the following year was elected an SIU international vice-president;

was elected vice-president for contracts and contract enforcement in 1972; became executive vice-president of Atlantic, Gulf, Great Lakes and Inland Waterways District in 1976; after serving for a time as acting president during the illness of SIU president Paul Hall (q.v.), he became international president of the SIU in 1980; was elected president of the American Federation of Labor-Congress of Industrial Organizations (AFL-CIO) maritime trades department in 1976; before assuming the SIU presidency, he had been a member of the New York State Coastal Management Citizens' Advisory Committee and had held a variety of positions in the New Jersey State Federation of Labor; *Who's Who in Labor* (1976); *AFL-CIO News*, February 23, 1980, July 7 and 12, 1980.

DUBINSKY, David   (1892–1982). Born in Brest Litovsk, Russian Poland (now a part of the Soviet Union), February 22, 1892; son of Bezallel, a bakery owner, and Shaine (Wishinggrad) Dubnievski; Jewish; married Emma Goldberg in 1915; one child; ended formal schooling at age 11 and became a baker's apprentice, advancing to master baker four years later; after joining bakers' union in Lodz, Poland, participated in a successful strike against the city's Jewish bakeries, including his father's; was arrested as a labor agitator shortly thereafter, and spent 18 months in prison; was exiled to Chelyabinsk, Siberia, but escaped en route and lived under an assumed name until given amnesty in 1910; emigrated to the United States in 1911 and became a citizen the same year; learned the cloak cutting trade and joined Local 10 of the International Ladies' Garment Workers' Union (ILGWU); was elected successively between 1918 and 1920 to the executive board, vice-chairmanship, and chairmanship of Local 10; became a vice-president and member of the ILGWU executive board in 1922; was elected secretary-treasurer in 1929, at the time of ILGWU effort to rebuild itself after a disastrous Communist-led strike; was chosen president in 1932; served as a labor advisor to the National Recovery Administration, 1933–1935; became a vice-president of the American Federation of Labor (AFL) and a member of its executive council in 1935; was a delegate to the International Labor Organization conference in Geneva in 1935; served as a member of the AFL Committee for Industrial Organization (CIO); resigned from the AFL executive council after the suspension of CIO unions in 1937; opposed the establishment of a permanent CIO, and thus kept his union independent for a year-and-a-half before reaffiliating with the AFL in 1940; regained the AFL vice-presidency and membership on the executive council in 1945; participated in the founding of the International Confederation of Free Trade Unions; was a co-founder of the American Labor party, a vice-chairman of the Liberal party of New York, and a board member of Americans for Democratic Action; served on a large number of public and private boards and agencies, including the Labor League for Human Rights, the Jewish Labor Committee, and the Post-War Planning Committee; after retiring the positions of secretary-treasurer in 1959 and president in 1966, served as director of the ILGWU retiree service department; died in New York City on September 17, 1982; David Dubinsky Papers, ILGWU Archives; David Dubinsky and A. H. Raskin, *David Dubinsky: A Life of Labor* (1977); Max D. Danish, *The World of David Dubinsky* (1957); "David Dubinsky, the I.L.G.W.U. and the American Labor Movement," Special Supplement, *Labor History* (Spring 1968); Charles A. Madison, *American Labor Leaders: Personalities and Forces in the Labor Movement* (1950); John Dewey, *David Dubinsky: A Pictorial Review* (1951).

DUBROW, Evelyn   (1912–   ). Born in Garfield, N.J., on May 6, 1912; daughter of Isador J., a carpenter, and Kathryn (Kahan) Dubrow; married briefly and divorced, never remarried; after graduating from Passaic High School, she earned a degree in journalism at New York University; began her career doing press work for the police commissioner and editing *The Citizen*, an Italian-American weekly; joined the American Newspaper Guild (ANG) in 1935; became an organizer for the Textile Workers Organizing Committee in 1937, serving until 1940; served as education director of the New Jersey Textile Workers Union, 1940–1942; became secretary to the president of the New Jersey Industrial Union Council in 1943; was appointed assistant to the president of the New Jersey Industrial Union Council in 1944 as well as chairman of the women's division of the New Jersey Political Action Committee, Congress of Industrial Organizations (CIO); helped organize and served as secretary of the New Jersey ANG; assisted in the establishment of a number of labor and industrial schools; served as director of organization for Americans for Democratic Action, 1947–1956; appointed executive secretary of the political department, International Ladies' Garment Workers' Union (ILGWU) in 1956; became a Washington, D.C., legislative representative for the ILGWU in 1961; was elected an ILGWU vice-president in 1977; involved in a variety of civic and union affairs, she was a member of the National Association for the Advancement of Colored People and the Urban League, was a founding member of the National Consumer Federation, served as secretary-treasurer of the New Jersey Fair Employment Council, was a member of the industrial committee of the YWCA, the New Jersey State Education Advisory Committee, the American Labor Education Service, and the Coalition of Trade Union Women; supported the American Labor party and the Liberal party of New York during the 1930s and 1940s and thereafter supported the Democratic party; *Who's Who in Labor* (1946, 1976); Lydia Kleiner, "Oral History Interview with Evelyn Dubrow," *The 20th Century Trade Union Woman: Vehicle for Social Change*, Oral History Project (1978).

DuCHESSI, William Magno   (1914–1979). Born in Amsterdam, N.Y., on November 29, 1914; married; one child; left school at age 14 to take a job in a carpet factory in Amsterdam; when the Textile Workers Organizing Committee (TWOC) of the Congress of Industrial Organizations (CIO) initiated a drive to organize the factory, he joined the campaign and became a charter member of TWOC Local 1 in 1937; a short time later he joined the TWOC staff as an organizer and continued in that position when TWOC became the Textile Workers

Union of America (TWUA), CIO, in 1939; served as a petty officer in the U.S. Navy during World War II, 1944–1946; following the war, he rejoined the TWUA, serving as a county joint board manager in Oswego, N.Y., 1946–1948; became director of the TWUA's Maryland and West Virginia region in 1948 and then served as assistant director of the TWUA's upper South region, 1948–1955; became director of the carpet division in 1955; was elected an international vice-president and member of the TWUA's executive council in 1956; was appointed director of the TWUA's Committee on Political Education (COPE) in 1956 and in 1963 became the union's legislative director in Washington, D.C.; was elected international secretary-treasurer in 1972 and after the merger of the TWUA and the Amalgamated Clothing Workers of America, creating the Amalgamated Clothing and Textile Workers Union of America, he was elected executive vice-president of the new union; was a member of the American Federation of Labor (AFL)-CIO COPE operating committee and was a member of the executive board of the AFL-CIO's industrial union department; died in Washington, D.C., on May 19, 1979; *Who's Who in Labor* (1976); *AFL-CIO News*, May 26, 1979; *The New York Times*, May 22, 1979.

DUFFY, Frank   (1861–1955). Born in County Monaghan, Ireland, in 1861; Roman Catholic; married; at least three children; received a limited formal education in Ireland, then emigrated to the United States in 1881, settling in New York City; secured employment as a carpenter and soon became actively involved in trade union affairs; joined the Greater New York United Order of American Carpenters and Joiners and was elected the first president of its executive council; after the merger of the United Order and the United Brotherhood of Carpenters and Joiners of America (UBC) in 1888, became a member of UBC Local 478; served variously as Local 478's representative to the New York District Council, as financial secretary, and as president of its executive council, 1888–1901; served as business manager of Local 478, 1896–1898; was elected to the UBC executive council in 1900, and helped to effect the removal from office of UBC founder Peter J. McGuire (q.v.) in 1901; became secretary-general in 1901, and held that position for 48 years; was elected an American Federation of Labor (AFL) vice-president and executive council member in 1918, serving until 1940; was a member of the United States labor delegation to the 1919 Paris Peace Conference; was a conservative unionist, and a staunch ally of William Hutcheson (q.v.) who, during the 1930s and 1940s, established nearly total control of the UBC; usually supported the Republican party; retired union positions in 1950; died in Indianapolis, Ind., July 11, 1955; Robert A. Christie, *Empire in Wood: A History of the Carpenters' Union* (1956); Morris A. Horowitz, *The Structure and Government of the Carpenters' Union* (1962); *The American Federationist* (August 1955).

DUFFY, James Michael   (1889–1963). Born in Wheeling, W.Va., June 28, 1889; son of Michael, a potter, and Mary (McGarry) Duffy; Roman Catholic;

married Kathryn Geon on September 6, 1916; five children; after completing his formal education in the parochial schools of East Liverpool, Ohio, became an apprentice potter; joined Local 31 of the National Brotherhood of Operative Potters (NBOP) in 1909; served as a labor advisor on the Workmen's Compensation Committee for the state of Ohio; held a variety of offices in Local 31 and Buffalo Local 76 of the NBOP prior to being elected international president in 1927; was a member of the National Labor Advisory Board of the National Industrial Recovery Administration, 1933–1935; served as an American Federation of Labor (AFL) delegate to the International Labor Conference in Geneva in 1937 and later as an AFL representative on a Labor League of Human Rights visit to China; was appointed a labor representative on the Labor-Management Conference Committee established by President Harry S. Truman in 1945; served as an AFL delegate to the Inter-American Labor Conference held in Lima, Peru, in 1948; served as a vice-president of the AFL union label trades department, a member of the executive council of America's Wage Earners' Protective Conference, and a director of the Union Labor Life Insurance Company; also maintained membership in numerous public and private boards and agencies; retired union positions in 1953; died in East Liverpool, Ohio, in March 1963; *Who's Who in Labor* (1946); *AFL-CIO News*, March 9, 1963.

DULLZELL, Paul   (1879–1961). Born in Boston, Mass., June 15, 1879; son of Paul, an artist, and Alice (O'Neill) Dullzell; married Vivian Korwalski in August 1914; beginning as a child actor with little formal education, appeared in dramas, vaudeville, musical comedies, and motion pictures between 1879 and 1919; joined Actors' Equity Association (AEA) in 1913; after an actors' strike against the United Managers Protective Association in New York in 1919, devoted most of his time to union organizing activities; became assistant executive secretary of AEA in 1920; was named international executive secretary of Associated Actors and Artists of America (AAAA) in 1923; was elected executive secretary of AEA in 1928 and treasurer shortly thereafter; served during World War II as the director of United Theatrical War Activities; retired as executive secretary of AEA in 1948 because of poor health but remained treasurer until 1960; served as president of AAAA until 1961; also served as chairman of the executive committee of the Chorus Equity Association, president of the Theater Authority, and vice-president of the American Theatrical Wing; died in New York City, December 21, 1961; *Who's Who in Labor* (1946); *Who Was Who in America*, Vol. 3; *The New York Times*, December 22, 1961.

DUNCAN, James   (1857–1928). Born in Kincardine County, Scotland, May 5, 1857; son of David, a farmer, and Mary (Forbes) Duncan; Presbyterian; married Lillian M. Holman in January 1887; one child; after attending the common schools of Aberdeen, Scotland, for a short time, began serving an apprenticeship as a granite cutter; emigrated to the United States at the age of 23 in 1880; joined the New York local of the Granite Cutters' National Union, precursor of the Granite Cutters International Association (GCIA), in 1881; moved to Baltimore in 1885 and was elected secretary of the local union of granite cutters; attended the 1886 national trades' union convention, in which the American Federation of Labor (AFL) was organized to replace the Federation of Organized Trades and Labor Unions; was elected second vice-president of the AFL in 1894 and served on its executive council until his death; assumed the presidency of the GCIA in 1885; was later to become a close personal friend and confidant of Samuel Gompers (q.v.), but nominated John McBride (q.v.) for the AFL presidency in 1895; was a fraternal delegate to the British Trades Union Congress in 1898; became the first vice-president of the AFL in 1900; successfully led granite cutters in strike for an eight-hour day in 1900; represented the AFL at the 1911 International Secretariat Conference in Budapest; was named to the United States commission to study workmen's compensation legislation in 1913; was appointed Envoy Extraordinary to Russia in 1917; was a member of the American labor mission to the Paris Peace Conference in 1919; nominated for the AFL presidency after the death of Samuel Gompers, but was defeated by William Green (q.v.); edited the *Granite Cutters' Journal*, 1895–1928; was an independent in politics; died in Quincy, Mass., September 14, 1928; Philip Taft, *The A.F. of L. in the Time of Gompers* (1957); *Dictionary of American Biography*, Vol. 5; *Who's Who in America, 1928–1929*; *Granite Cutters' Journal* (October 1928).

DUNNE, Vincent Raymond   (1889–1970). Born in Kansas City, Kans., April 17, 1889; son of an Irish Catholic immigrant and a French Canadian; married Jennie Holm in 1914; two children; moved with family to Little Falls, Minn., and attended grade school there for a few years; beginning at age 14, roamed the West and South as a lumberjack and harvest worker; joined the Industrial Workers of the World; settled in Minneapolis, Minn., in 1910; drove a team, and later worked as a coal yard laborer and a weighmaster; under influence of a Swedish immigrant, Carl Skoglund, joined the Communist party in 1920; was meanwhile elected a delegate from a local American Federation of Labor union to the Minneapolis Central Labor Union; helped to found the Trotskyist Communist League of America in 1929; by 1934, along with brothers Miles and Grant and with Skoglund, led a small but dynamic Trotskyist group in Minneapolis-St. Paul; led this group to promote radical unionism by working through General Drivers 574, a local of the International Brotherhood of Teamsters, Chauffeurs, Warehousemen and Helpers of America (IBT) that had a vague jurisdiction; won a midwinter strike in the coal yards, then joined his colleagues, along with Farrel Dobbs (q.v.), in seeking to force recognition of Local 574 throughout general trucking, including helpers and inside workers; during the summer of 1934, led what was probably the most ingeniously conceived and effectively executed walkout of the early thirties; disrupted the powerful open-shop Citizens Alliance, as well as establishing a militant industrial-type union as a new force in teamster unionism; was elected a trustee of Local 574 (now

Local 544) and used the local to spark organization of general drivers throughout the state, to extend jurisdiction to warehouse and other jobs related to trucking, and to begin to unionize over-the-road drivers, a project carried through by Farrel Dobbs's Central States Drivers Council; saw IBT president Daniel Tobin (q.v.) alternately placate and harrass Local 574, and thus decided in 1941 to affiliate the local with the Congress of Industrial Organizations; shortly thereafter, allegedly at Tobin's instigation, was indicted by the Roosevelt Administration, as were the other Minneapolis Trotskyists, under the Smith Act, a 1940 sedition law; lost his appeal in 1943 and spent more than a year in a federal penitentiary; devoted himself subsequently to the affairs of the Socialist Workers party and to the study of Greek history and philosophy; died in Minneapolis, Minn., February 17, 1970; Irving Bernstein, *Turbulent Years: A History of the American Worker, 1933–1941* (1969); Farrel Dobbs, *Teamster Rebellion* (1972); *Minneapolis Daily Tribune*, February 20, 1970; Walter Galenson, *The CIO Challenge to the AFL: A History of the American Labor Movement, 1935–1941* (1960).

Donald G. Sofchalk

DUNWODY, Thomas Edgar   (1887–1959). Born in Lafayette, Ga., August 1, 1887; son of Thomas Jefferson, an architect, and Elizabeth (Massey) Dunwody; Presbyterian; married Norma Backus on September 3, 1914; no children; completed high school and one year of a college education; was publisher and editor of the St. Matthews (S.C.) *Recorder*, 1905–1907; became an apprentice printing pressman in 1907 and joined Atlanta Local 6 of the International Printing Pressmen's and Assistants' Union of North America (IPPAUNA); received his journeyman's card shortly thereafter, and moved to Chattanooga, Tenn.; became a pressroom foreman there and president of the IPPAUNA Chattanooga Local 165; became an instructor in the IPPAUNA Technical Trade School in Pressmen's Home, Tenn., in 1913; was appointed editor and manager of the IPPAUNA organ, *American Pressman*, in 1916, and continued in that capacity for 35 years; was named director of the IPPAUNA Technical Trade School in 1916, serving until 1951; served as assistant president during the illness of IPPAUNA president J. Herbert de la Rosa, 1951–1952; was elected president in 1952, serving until his death; was an authority on many technological aspects of printing and wrote numerous articles on various facets of the printing industry; was a Democrat; died in Knoxville, Tenn., May 2, 1959; Elizabeth F. Baker, *Printers and Technology: A History of the International Printing Pressmen and Assistants' Union* (1957); *American Pressman*, January 1953; *Who's Who in Labor* (1946).

DURKIN, Martin Patrick   (1894–1955). Born in Chicago, Ill., March 18, 1894; son of James J., an Irish immigrant and stationary fireman, and Mary Catherine (Higgins) Durkin; Roman Catholic; married Anna H. McNicholas on August 29, 1921; three children; received a grammar school education in parochial schools and for three years took evening courses in heating and ventilation at a technical school; became an apprentice steam fitter in Chicago Local 597 of the United Association of Journeymen and Apprentices of the Plumbing and Pipe Fitting Industry of the United States and Canada (UA) in 1911; became a journeyman plumber in 1915; served in France for two years in the Sixth Cavalry Corps during World War I; became a business manager of UA Local 597 in 1921; was elected a vice-president of the Chicago Building Trades Council in 1927; was appointed Illinois state director of labor in 1933, serving until 1941; contributed most importantly to the establishment of a state unemployment compensation system, to the formation of a state mediation and conciliation service, to the regulation of minimum wage and maximum hours for women and children, and to the enactment of safety legislation; became president of the International Association of Government Labor Officials in 1933 and served until 1955; became secretary-treasurer of the UA in 1941 and president in 1943; served during World War II as a member of the National War Labor Board; was appointed to the Defense Mobilization Board and to the National Security Resources Board in 1951; was named U.S. Secretary of Labor in the administration of Dwight D. Eisenhower in 1953, but resigned eight months later because of Eisenhower's refusal to support his suggestions for amending the Taft-Hartley Act; resumed UA presidency in 1953, serving until his death; served as a director of the Union Labor Life Insurance Company and the National Safety Council and was vice-president of the Catholic Conference on Industrial Problems; was politically a Democrat; died in Washington, D.C., November 13, 1955; Joseph C. Goulden, *Meany* (1972); David A. Frier, *Conflict of Interest in the Eisenhower Administration* (1969); *National Cyclopaedia of American Biography*, Vol. 45: *The American Federationist* (December 1952); *Dictionary of American Biography*, Suppl. 5.

DYCHE, John Alexander   (1867–1938). Born in Kovno, Russian Lithuania (now part of the Soviet Union) in 1867; Jewish; married; emigrated to England in 1887 and participated for 14 years in the British trade union movement; emigrated to the United States in 1901 and secured employment in the New York garment industry as a skirt maker; joined the newly organized International Ladies' Garment Workers' Union (ILGWU) and in 1904 was elected its international secretary-treasurer, serving until 1914; regarded, along with Abraham Rosenberg, as the dominant figure in the international union during this period; was a staunchly conservative business unionist and preferred arbitration and conciliation to militant strike activity; also emphasized the sanctity of contractual relations between employers and employees; strongly supported the Protocol of Peace signed in September 1910, providing for arbitration of labor-management disputes in the garment industry; because of his conservative trade union policies, aroused great opposition among the ILGWU's left-wing, Socialist factions that finally took control of the union in 1914; left the labor movement shortly after his defeat and became a small businessman in the garment industry; authored *Bolshevism in American Labor Unions* (1926); died in New York City in October 1938; Benjamin Stolberg, *Tailor's Progress: The Story of a Famous Union and* *the Men Who Made It* (1944); Louis Levine, *The Women's Garment Workers: A History of the International Ladies' Garment Workers' Union* (1924); L. P. Gartner, *Jewish Immigrants in England, 1870–1914* (1960); Julius H. Cohen, *They Builded Better than They Knew* (1946).

DYER, Josiah B.   (fl. 1843–1886). Born in the village of Cross, parish of Luxillian, county of Cornwall, England, January 5, 1843; joined Operative Stone-masons' (O.S.M.) Society of England and Wales, when between 17 and 18 years old; learned stone cutting on granite, freestone, and limestone; before coming to this country worked for John Freeman & Sons, of Penryn, Cornwall, for about eight years; landed at Castle Garden, in March 1971; worked at Fall River, Dix Island, East Cambridge, Boston, Graniteville, Ayer Junction, Lowell, Mass.; he was elected secretary of Granite Cutters' Union, November 1878, to fill unexpired term of T. H. Murch; his brother, J. Edward Dyer, was general secretary of the O.S.M. Society of England and Wales for about 11 years, and dying in office, the union erected a monument to his memory in Sheffield; he was born in a trade-union family, father and brothers being all union men; he was one of the charter members of the first Local Assembly of the Knights of Labor organized in Boston; as secretary of the Granite-cutters' Union, he moved with headquarters of union from Rockland to Boston, then to Westerly, R.I., Quincy, Mass., and Philadelphia; was one of the authors of the circular calling a conference of unhappy trade unionists in the Knights of Labor on May 18, 1886; led his union into the American Federation of Labor after it was organized in 1886; George E. McNeill, *The Labor Movement: The Problem of To-Day* (1887); Gerald N. Grob, *Workers and Utopia: A Study of Ideological Conflict in the American Labor Movement, 1865–1900* (1961).

George E. McNeill

E

EAMES, Thomas B. (1882–1949). Born in Williamstown, N.J., November 20, 1882; son of James, a painter and paperhanger, and Ellen (Vanaman) Eames; Baptist; married Estella Charlesworth on August 5, 1908; two children; attended the grammar schools of Millville, N.J.; served an apprenticeship as a glass bottle blower and in 1906 joined the Glass Bottle Blowers Association of the United States and Canada (GBBA); served the local union in various capacities and was then elected to the GBBA international executive board in 1922, on which he served until his death in 1949; was chosen somewhat later as international secretary of the GBBA, and also held that post until his death; proved an influential figure in the New Jersey labor movement; served briefly during the early 1930s as president of the New Jersey State Federation of Labor after having been a vice-president for several years; was appointed to the National Recovery Administration (NRA) board for New Jersey in 1933, serving until the NRA was declared unconstitutional in 1935; served as a delegate to several American Federation of Labor conventions; was politically nonpartisan; died in Philadelphia, Pa., September 6, 1949; Leo Troy, *Organized Labor in New Jersey* (1965); *The American Federationist* (October 1949); *The New York Times*, September 7, 1949; *Who's Who in Labor* (1946).

EASTON, John Bertham (1880–1961). Born in Allegheny County, Pa., September 26, 1880; son of William, a mine foreman and lumber calculator, and Anna Easton; Congregationalist; married Jane Elizabeth Thomas in 1902; two children; attended public school and evening school; started work as a flint glass worker in 1893; joined the American Flint Glass Workers' Union of North America (AFGW) in 1897, and maintained that affiliation until joining the United Steelworkers of America in 1941; settled permanently at Williamstown (near Parkersburg), W.Va.; became a member of the AFGW international executive board; was elected president of the Parkersburg Trades and Labor Council in 1920, serving in that capacity for several years; served as vice-president of the West Virginia State Federation of Labor (WVSFL), 1922–1924, and as president,

1924–1937; symbolized by his 1924 election the effort by craft affiliates to curb the WVSFL's growing domination by locals of the United Mine Workers of America (UMWA); defeated C. Frank Keeney (q.v.), president of UMWA District 17, on the second ballot; retained the loyalty of the northern miners while the southern faction, led by Keeney and William Blizzard, bolted the WVSFL in 1925, only to return in 1927; met the challenge of dual unionism by condemning the rival "Save the Union" campaign of John Brophy (q.v.) in 1926 and the Reorganized United Mine Workers and West Virginia Miners Union led by Frank Keeney in 1930–1931; found the WVSFL $3,575 in debt in 1924, but freed it from debt by 1929; served as a Republican member of the West Virginia House of Delegates, 1926–1928; entered the Republican primary election for Congress from the Fourth Congressional District in 1928 and 1930, but was defeated on both occasions; led the WVSFL in helping to elect Democrat Matthew Neely, an anti-injunction candidate, to the U.S. Senate in 1930 over James E. Jones, a coal operator favoring yellow-dog contracts; saw the WVSFL reach a nadir in terms of membership, finances, and influence in 1933, as a result of the Great Depression and the disintegration of the UMWA, but also witnessed its rebirth by 1934, as a result of the National Industrial Recovery Act and the revival of the UMWA; having met the challenge to the WVSFL posed by the depression and unemployment, came to experience the rivalry after 1935 of the American Federation of Labor (AFL)-Congress of Industrial Organizations (CIO); refused to obey the AFL order to the WVSFL to expel all CIO affiliates, and also refused to appear before the AFL executive council to explain this disobedience; after ensuing revocation of the charter of the WVSFL by the AFL executive council, obtained a CIO charter for it as the West Virginia State Industrial Union Council (WVAIUC); despite withdrawal of many craft locals by August 1938, to organize an AFL state organization, led the CIO body to add 112 locals with 21,602 members, a net gain of 15,988; remained president of the WVAIUC and regional CIO director until his retirement in 1952; died in Williamstown, W.Va., December 20, 1961; *Who's Who in Labor* (1946); Evelyn L. K. Harris and Frank J. Krebs, *From Humble Beginnings: West Virginia State Federation of Labor, 1903–1957* (1960); *Charleston* (W.Va.) *Gazette*, December 22, 1961.

John W. Hevener

EDELMAN, John W. (1893–1971). Born in Belleville, N.J., on June 27, 1893; son of John H., an architect, and Rachelle (Krimont) Edelman; married Kate Van Eaton on April 26, 1920; three children; spent his early years in England after the death of his father, and became involved in both trade union organizing and the Independent Labour party in his early teens; returned to the United States in 1916 and, during World War I, enlisted in the U.S. Army despite his pacifist beliefs; after the war, he worked for various newspapers, among them the *Reading* (Pa.) *Tribune*; served as Pennsylvania campaign manager for Sen. Robert M. La Follette's third-party presidential effort in 1924;

accepted a position as public relations and research director for the American Federation of Full-Fashioned Hosiery Workers (a subsidiary of the United Textile Workers Union) and edited its publication, *The Hosiery Worker*, in 1926; worked as Congress of Industrial Organizations (CIO) regional director for eastern Pennsylvania, 1937–1939, in which position he became a promoter of labor-sponsored low-cost housing; during World War II, he served in a number of government positions, among them assistant director of information for the U.S. Housing Authority, 1940–1941, labor and consumer consultant for the Council for National Defense, 1941–1942, and CIO liaison in the Office of Price Administration, 1942–1943; accepted a post with the Textile Workers' Union of America, CIO, in 1943 as director of its Washington office; from then until retirement in 1963, he served as chief legislative lobbyist for the union; during the 1960s, he became increasingly active in various consumer and senior citizens' groups, serving as president of the National Council of Senior Citizens in 1964; died at his home in Arlington, Va., on December 27, 1971; an autobiography, *Labor Lobbyist* (1974), was edited and published posthumously.

Gilbert J. Gall

EKLUND, John Manly   (1909–   ). Born in Burlington, Iowa, September 14, 1909; son of Carl Petrus, a Swedish immigrant and minister, and Laura Alvira (Malnburg) Eklund; Methodist; married Zara Frances Zerbst on September 9, 1934; three children; after graduating from high school in 1927, entered Bethany College in Lindsborg, Kans., and received a B.A. degree in 1931; coached athletics and taught English in Burdick (Kans.) High School, 1931–1933; took postgraduate courses at the University of Denver and studied at the Iliff School of Theology, 1933–1934; was pastor of the Methodist Episcopal Church at Oak Creek, Colo., in 1934–1935 and of the Lakewood (Colo.) Methodist Episcopal Church in 1936; received a Master of Theology degree from the Iliff School of Theology and an M.A degree in education from the University of Denver in 1936; was an English teacher and vocational guidance instructor in the Denver public school system, 1937–1946; became an appraiser in the Veterans Administration Guidance Center at the Opportunity School in Denver in 1946; was a founder of the Denver Federation of Teachers, and became its president and a vice-president of the American Federation of Teachers (AFT) in 1946; served on the executive board of the Colorado Federation of Teachers, 1946–1953; was elected national president of the AFT in 1948, serving in that capacity until 1952; served as an American Federation of Labor (AFL) delegate to the United Nations Educational, Scientific, and Cultural Organization (UNESCO) conferences in 1947, 1949, and 1951; served as a member of the labor advisory committee to UNESCO in 1949 and of the U.S. National Committee for UNESCO for several years beginning in 1951; belonged to the AFL committee on vocational education; was a member of the national board of Americans for Democratic Action, 1949–1954; served as a delegate to the White House Conference on Education in 1955; became, successively, director of adult

education, director of organization and education, and assistant to the president
of the National Farmers Union during the period 1954–1964; was named executive vice-president of the Farmers Union International Assistance Corporation;
a Democrat; authored *Tools for Peace* (1960); *Current Biography* (1949); *Who's
Who in America, 1968–1969*; Robert J. Braun, *Teachers and Power: The Story
of the American Federation of Teachers* (1972).

ELLICKSON, Katherine Pollak (1905–   ). Born in Yonkers, N.Y., on
September 1, 1905; daughter of Francis D., a lawyer who died when she was
11, and Inez (Cohen) Pollak, who was active in feminist, labor, and consumer
organizations; Jewish by birth, raised in Ethical Culture circles, a Unitarian in
later years; married John Chester Ellickson, an economist, in 1933; two children;
attended Ethical Culture School in New York City; graduated from Vassar in
1926 with a B.A. in economics; active in student socialist/laborite groups at
Vassar; did graduate work in politics and economics at Columbia University,
1928–1929; taught history at Ethical Culture School, 1926–1928, and tutored
under the auspices of the Women's Trade Union League, 1926–1927; taught,
counseled, and prepared materials for classes at Bryn Mawr Summer School for
Women Workers, 1927–1929, Brookwood Labor College, 1929–1932, and the
Federal Emergency Relief Administration's Southern Teachers' Training School
in 1934; traveled in Europe and the Soviet Union in 1932; spent 1934–1935 in
North Dakota, a sojourn necessitated by her husband's job, and used the time
to survey organizing prospects for the American Federation of Teachers; did
research for the Bureau of Labor Statistics on company unions in 1935; through
her association with economist David Saposs, she was chosen as chief assistant
by John Brophy (q.v.), first Congress of Industrial Organizations (CIO) director
of organization in 1935; ran the CIO's Washington office, 1935–1937, preparing
organizing materials, establishing office procedures, writing policy statements
and speeches for Brophy and, on occasion, John L. Lewis (q.v.); was laid off
in 1937; worked part-time with the division of economic research of the National
Labor Relations Board, Social Security Board, and Labor Bureau of the Middle
West, 1938–1942; was CIO associate director of research, 1942–1955, serving
as liaison with the research staffs of CIO affiliates and government bodies, notably
the Bureau of Labor Statistics; represented the CIO on government advisory
committees relating to social security, manpower, farm labor, and women and
children, and wrote and prepared material for CIO use in legislation, postwar
planning, and guaranteed annual wages; was assistant director of the American
Federation of Labor-CIO (AFL-CIO) social security department, 1955–1961,
specializing in old age, survivors, and disability insurance and medical insurance;
active in the 1960 presidential campaign; helped draft plans to establish the
President's Commission on the Status of Women and served as executive secretary of the commission, 1961–1963; retired from the AFL-CIO in 1961; worked
for the Committee on Equal Employment Opportunity, U.S. Department of
Labor, 1963–1964; volunteer worker and consultant in civic and consumer af-

fairs, beginning in 1966; a Socialist in the 1920s and 1930s, she supported the Democratic party from the New Deal onward; Katherine Pollak Ellickson Collection, Walter Reuther Library, Wayne State University; Ellickson Oral Interviews, Reuther Library.

Robert H. Zieger

ELLIS, Christine Stanich   (1908–   ). Born in Tinj, Yugoslavia, in 1908; daughter of a coal miner and union member; reared a Roman Catholic; married; emigrated with her family to the United States in 1913, settling in Jerome, Iowa; began working full-time after completing an elementary education; at age 15, in 1923, she went to Cleveland, Ohio, where she worked for the American Can Company; moved to Chicago, Ill., in 1924, where she obtained work as a sewing machine operator for Bauer and Black, a company that produced medical supplies and athletic supporters; joined the Communist party of America (CPA) in 1928; worked as a CPA organizer in Chicago in 1931 and a year later became a CPA organizer for District 10, comprising Texas, Oklahoma, Missouri, Arkansas, Nebraska, Kansas, and Iowa; moved to Gary, Ind., during the 1940s and became increasingly disillusioned with the CPA as an instrument of social change, although no less committed to social justice; became a vigorous critic of American involvement in the Korean War as a result of which the U.S. Department of Justice sought, unsuccessfully, to have her deported under the provisions of the McCarran Act; spent ten months in jail with no provisions for bail, 1952–1953; continued to reside in Gary, Ind., where during the summer of 1971 she took an active part in the Labor History Workshop; Alice Lynd and Staughton Lynd, eds., *Rank and File: Personal Histories by Working-Class Organizers* (1973).

ENGEL, George   (1836–1887). Born in Cassel, Germany, April 15, 1836; son of Conrad, a mason and bricklayer, who died 18 months after George's birth; married in 1868; after the death of his mother in 1848, he was maintained in a foster home for two years before apprenticing himself briefly to a shoemaker and then later to a painter in Frankfort; after completing his apprenticeship as a painter, he traveled extensively through central Europe working at his trade; after the failure of a small business enterprise in Rehna, Mecklenburg-Schwerin, he emigrated to the United States in 1873, settling in Philadelphia, Pa., where he first found work in a sugar refinery and later as a painter; after a year's sickness left him and his family destitute, he moved to Chicago, Ill., where he secured employment in a wagon factory and became associated with the Chicago branch of the International Workingmen's Association (IWA); became the proprietor of a toy store in 1876; after the failure of the IWA, he helped organize the Socialistic Labor party of North America in 1878; became associated with the International Working People's Association, the American branch of the Black International, in 1883; attended the meeting near the McCormick Harvesting plant outside Chicago that led to the Haymarket Square meeting on May 4, 1886; although he did not attend the Haymarket Square meeting, he was later charged with being an accessory to the murder of a policeman during the riot that accompanied the meeting; indicted, convicted, and on November 11, 1887, put to death in one of the more shocking displays of official and judicial malevolence in American history; Philip S. Foner, ed., *The Autobiographies of the Haymarket Martyrs* (1969); Lucy E. Parsons, *Life of Albert R. Parsons with Brief History of the Labor Movement in America: Also Sketches of the Lives of A. Spies, Geo. Engel, A. Fischer and Louis Lingg*, 2d ed. (1903); David Henry, *The History of the Haymarket Affair*, rev. ed. (1963).

ENGLISH, John Francis   (1889–1969). Born in Boston, Mass., April 14, 1889; son of James Patrick and Mary (Holland) English; Roman Catholic; married Gertrude Ann Kurvin and, after her death in 1930, Katherine E. Noonan on December 8, 1948; one child; ended formal schooling at age 15 and secured a job driving a horse-drawn coal wagon; joined Boston Local 68 of the International Brotherhood of Teamsters, Chauffeurs, Warehousemen and Helpers of America (IBT) in 1904; was elected business manager of Local 68 in 1910, serving until 1935; belonged to the Coast Artillery during World War I; after serving the Boston Teamsters' Joint Council for several years in a variety of capacities, was elected an international IBT vice-president in 1927; was an IBT auditor and general organizer, 1936–1946; after serving as acting general secretary-treasurer of the IBT for a year, was elected to that post in 1947 and served until his death; was chosen an American Federation of Labor-Congress of Industrial Organizations (AFL-CIO) vice-president and executive council member in 1957, but served only a short time before the IBT was expelled from the AFL-CIO; adamantly opposed Dave Beck (q.v.) during his ascendancy in the IBT, but became a loyal ally of Beck's successor, James R. Hoffa (q.v.); died in Miami Beach, Fla., February 3, 1969; Sam Romer, *The International Brotherhood of Teamsters: Its Government and Structure* (1962); Robert D. Leiter, *The Teamsters Union: A Study of Its Economic Impact* (1957); Ralph C. James and Estelle D. James, *Hoffa and the Teamsters: A Study of Union Power* (1965).

ENGLISH, William   (fl. 1828–1836). Self-described as a "mechanic, born to toil from early childhood [who] never. . . entered a school by the light of day"; became a journeyman shoemaker in Philadelphia, Pa.; was actively involved by the late 1820s in the Philadelphia Mechanics' Union of Trade Associations, a short-lived, ineffective union organization formed as a result of a house carpenters' strike in 1827; organized district meetings of the Philadelphia Working Men's party in 1828 to nominate candidates for the city council and state legislature; served during the same year as vice-president of the Mechanics' Library Company of Philadelphia, which published the *Mechanics' Free Press*; emerged as one of the principal leaders of the Working Men's party, 1829–1831; was elected recording secretary of the Philadelphia Trades' Union in 1834; was a Philadelphia delegate to the founding convention of the National Trades' Union (NTU), and served on committees responsible for drafting a constitution for a

"National Union of Trades"; declined the nomination for NTU president, but was elected recording secretary; was chosen president of the Philadelphia Trades' Union in 1835 and again in 1836; ran unsuccessfully for the Pennsylvania state senate on a workingmen's ticket in 1835; at the founding convention of the short-lived National Association of Cordwainers' meeting in New York City in the spring of 1836, was appointed to committees to draft rules of order for governing the convention and to draw up a plan of cooperation for the various cordwainer societies in the United States; used his talent as an orator to speak often in favor of the ten-hour day; was elected to the Pennsylvania House of Representatives as a "progressive" Democrat in 1836, thus ending his formal association with the labor movement, but attended the 1836 convention of the NTU as a special delegate; while serving in the state legislature, offended many of his supporters by voting in favor of a Pennsylvania charter for the Second Bank of the United States; William A. Sullivan, *The Industrial Workers in Pennsylvania, 1800–1840* (1955); Edward Pessen, *Most Uncommon Jacksonians: The Radical Leaders of the Early Labor Movement* (1967); John R. Commons et al., eds., *A Documentary History of American Industrial Society* Vols. 5, 6 (1910), and *History of Labour in the United States*, Vol. 1 (1918); Philip S. Foner, *History of the Labor Movement in the United States*, Vol. 1 (1947).

ERNST, Hugo   (1876–1954). Born in Varasdin, Austria-Hungary (now part of Yugoslavia), December 11, 1876; son of Dr. Ignatz, a rabbi, and Henriette (Schey) Ernst; Jewish; never married; left high school in 1892, at age 16, and took a job as a clerk and bookkeeper for a grain merchant; a year later, began a period of European travel meagerly financed by articles written for a hometown newspaper; after becoming involved in a nationalist movement, emigrated to the United States in 1900; worked for a short time as a reporter for a Croatian-language nationalist weekly newspaper; became a busboy at the St. George Hotel in Brooklyn, N.Y., in 1902 and worked as a waiter in St. Louis, Mo., during the 1904 Lewis and Clark Exposition; after moving to San Francisco, joined Local 30 of the Hotel and Restaurant Employees' International Alliance and Bartenders' International League of America (HREIABIL) in 1906; was elected secretary of Local 30 in 1910 and thereafter, under the provisions of the local's constitution, rotated in office between president and secretary every six months; was chosen an international HREIABIL vice-president for the Pacific coast in 1927; was elected general secretary-treasurer of the HREIABIL in 1939 and succeeded Edward Flore (q.v.) as international president in 1945; served as a delegate to the San Francisco Labor Council, 1910–1939; was a frequent delegate to the conventions of the California State Federation of Labor, and represented it at the American Federation of Labor (AFL) conventions of 1915 and 1935; was an AFL fraternal delegate to the British Trades Union Congress in 1944; named a vice-president of Americans for Democratic Action and the AFL Labor League for Political Education; was a Democrat; died in Cincinnati, Ohio, July 22, 1954; Matthew Josephson, *Union House, Union Bar: The History of the*

Hotel and Restaurant Employees and Bartenders International Union, AFL-CIO (1956); Jay Rubin and M. J. Obermeier, *Growth of a Union: The Life and Times of Edward Flore* (1943); *Who's Who in Labor* (1946).

ERVIN, Charles W.   (1865–1953). Born in Philadelphia, Pa., November 22, 1865; son of Alexander, a manufacturer and banker, and Elizabeth (McBride) Ervin; married Mary McKee on November 22, 1888; three children; received a grammar school education in the public schools of Philadelphia and later took reading courses in literature; worked as a youth in the wholesale grocery and coffee business; became an editorial writer for the *Philadelphia Daily News-Post*; joined the Socialist party of America in 1906, and in 1917 became editor-in-chief of the Socialist *New York Daily* and *Sunday Call*, serving until 1922; after running unsuccessfully on the Socialist party ticket for the U.S. House of Representatives and the Senate from Pennsylvania, became the Socialist candidate for governor of New York in 1918; was actively involved in the organization of needle trades workers from 1907 to his death; was appointed public relations advisor to the Amalgamated Clothing Workers of America (ACWA) in 1924; became an active member of the newly organized American Newspaper Guild; became associate editor of the ACWA organ, *The Advance*, in 1944; authored *The Story of the Constitution of the United States* (1946), and *Home-grown Liberal, Autobiography* (1954); died in Yonkers, N.Y., February 5, 1953; *Nation*, February 14, 1953; *Wilson Library Bulletin* (April 1953); *Who's Who in Labor* (1946).

ETTOR, Joseph James   (1885–1948). Born in Brooklyn, N.Y., October 6, 1885; son of a laborer; was of Italian descent; moved with his family to Chicago, Ill., and attended grade school there until starting work as a newsboy at age 12; worked at several other manual jobs, then went to San Francisco, Calif., ca. 1900 and became a skilled shipbuilder there; joined the Socialist party and became associated with the radical labor movement; became a West Coast organizer for the Industrial Workers of the World (IWW) in 1906; helped to organize and lead an Oregon lumberworkers' strike in 1907; because of fluency in several languages, proved especially effective in organizing southern European immigrant workers; elected a member of the IWW general executive board in 1909 and went east to organize steelworkers, coal miners, and textile workers; made his mark as one of the most able IWW leaders during the great Lawrence, Mass., textile strike of 1912; along with his colleague Arturo Giovannitti (q.v.), called in by local Wobblies and took command of the situation; engendered solidarity among the strikers through his ebullient personality and enthusiastic oratory; also made tactical innovations—a strike committee composed of representatives of ethnic groups and nonviolent demonstrations—that were crucial in the strike's success; although a dedicated syndicalist, kept the strike focused on the immediate goals of higher wages and nondiscriminatory rehiring of all strikers; midway in the strike, imprisoned without bail along with Giovannitti for allegedly plotting the shooting death of a woman striker; after spending a year in jail, acquitted of the murder charge, largely because of an IWW protest and legal defense campaign, conducted nationwide, that helped turn public opinion against the employers, who conceded to the strikers' demands; elected the IWW's second highest post—general organizer—in 1915; during the Minnesota iron miners' strike of 1916, went to the ranges to help organize a legal defense fund for IWW leaders indicted for murder; served meanwhile as one of several prominent Wobbly leaders who broke with general secretary William Haywood (q.v.) over his policy of centralizing administration and authority in the Chicago, Ill., headquarters; was among the 166 IWW leaders indicted in 1917 under the Espionage Act, but saw his case dropped for insufficient evidence; subsequently left the labor movement and ran a small vineyard at Cucamonga, Calif.; died there on February 19, 1948; Solon DeLeon, ed., *The American Labor Who's Who* (1925); *The Industrial Worker*, February 28, 1948; Melvyn Dubofsky, *We Shall Be All: A History of the Industrial Workers of the World* (1969).

Donald G. Sofchalk

EVANS, Christopher   (1841–1924). Born in England in 1841; emigrated to the United States in 1869 and worked in Mercer County, Pa.; immediately became active in the unionization of miners; by 1875 was an organizer for the Knights of Labor and started a local assembly in New Straitsville, Ohio, where he resided after 1877; with John McBride (q.v.), he formed the Ohio Miners' Amalgamated Association in 1882 and served as District 1's president, 1884–1885; agitated for a national miners' federation from 1883 until its formation in 1885 as the National Federation of Miners and Mine Laborers, and served as that union's executive secretary, 1885–1889; served as secretary to an arbitration and conciliation board established to prevent friction over the interpretation of an interstate agreement to prevail in central competitive coal fields in 1886; afterwards considered the originator of the joint conference system of settlement between miners and mine operators; was a member of the 1886 committee of the Federation of Organized Trades and Labor Unions that drew up a treaty with the Knights of Labor; was vice-president of the Thomas A. Armstrong Monumental Association in 1877 and president of District 10, National Progressive Union of Mine Laborers in 1889; served as secretary of the American Federation of Labor, 1889–1893, and secretary-treasurer after 1894; was statistician of the Miners' International Union for several years; authored *History of the United Mine Workers of America*, 2 Vols. (1918–1920); died in New Straitsville, Ohio, November 5, 1924; *The New York Times*, November 5, 1924; Andrew Roy, *A History of the Coal Miners of the United States* (1905); Howard B. Furer, ed. and comp., *The British in America, 1578–1970* (1972).

Sharon Trusilo

EVANS, Elizabeth Glendower   (1856–1937). Born in New Rochelle, N.Y., on February 28, 1856; daughter of Edward Harrison, an architect, and Sophia

(Mifflin) Gardiner; did not belong to an organized church but was a devout adherent to a personal, mystical religious belief; married Glendower Evans, a lawyer, on May 18, 1882; no children; educated in private schools and later took courses in philosophy at Radcliffe College; never remarried after the death of her husband in 1884, but was left in affluent circumstances which permitted her to devote a life to progressive causes and to finance reformist activities; appointed to the board of trustees of the Massachusetts reformatory system in 1886, serving in that capacity until 1914; became a leading advocate of the case-work approach to juvenile reform and to training programs; toured England for four months during the winter of 1908–1909, and returned a confirmed Socialist; became an active participant in the activities of the Women's Trade Union League (WTUL); at the behest of Florence Kelley (q.v.), representing the Consumers' League, she financed and led the campaign in Massachusetts to establish the first minimum wage law for women in the United States, 1911–1912; participated in a weavers' strike in Roxbury, Mass., in 1910, and walked the picket line and publicized police brutality during the Lawrence, Mass., textile strike of 1919; became a women's suffrage advocate after returning from England; joined the National American Women Suffrage Association and campaigned for the reform in the Midwest, Massachusetts, and Washington, D.C.; became a peace advocate after the outbreak of war in Europe in 1914 and in 1915 joined Jane Addams (q.v.) as an American delegate to the International Congress of Women at The Hague; concerned by the persecution of radicals and aliens in the United States after World War I, she became a national director of the American Civil Liberties Union; her defense of the rights of aliens and free speech led to her involvement in the Sacco-Vanzetti case; was one of the principal figures in the effort to save Sacco (q.v.) and Vanzetti (q.v.) from execution, provided much of the financial aid for their defense, and enlisted numerous liberals and intellectuals to the cause, including H. L Mencken, Samuel Eliot Morrison, Felix Frankfurter, and soon-to-be chief defense lawyer William G. Thompson; an active contributor to *La Follette's Magazine* and its successor, the *Progressive*, 1913–1935; her financial contribution helped to keep the magazine in print; authored articles on Louis Brandeis (*Survey*, 1931) and on William James (*Atlantic Monthly*, 1929); died in Brookline, Mass., on December 12, 1937; *Notable American Women*, Vol 3; *Biographical Cyclopaedia of American Women*, Vol. 2; *Who's Who in America, 1920–1921*; *The New York Times*, December 13, 1937.

EVANS, George Henry   (1805–1856). Born in Bromyard, Herefordshire, England, March 25, 1805; son of George and Sara (White) Evans; atheist; emigrated to the United States with his family in 1820; became a printer's apprentice in Ithaca, N.Y.; became the editor of *The Man*, published in Ithaca, in 1822; edited the *Working Man's Advocate*, published in New York City at various times from 1829 to 1845 and the *Daily Sentinel* and *Young America* during 1837–1853; participated in and editorially supported the various workingmen's parties developed in Philadelphia, New York, and New England; retired to a farm in New Jersey in 1837 and developed his principles of agrarianism, a social philosophy emphasizing natural rights and individualism; was a doctrinaire land reformer, firmly believing in everyone's inalienable right to a homestead of 160 acres; also opposed monopolies, slavery, imprisonment for debt, and sex discrimination; organized the National Reform Association in 1844 to promulgate his land reform ideas and was instrumental in convening a series of industrial congresses that met in various cities from 1846 to 1856 and brought together most of the country's influential reformers; served as secretary of the Boston Industrial Congress of 1846; authored *History of the Origin and Progress of the Working Men's Party* (1840); died in Granville, N.J., February 2, 1856; Norman J. Ware, *The Industrial Workers, 1840–1860* (1924); John R. Commons et al., *History of Labour in the United States*, Vol. 1 (1918); Walter E. Hugins, *Jacksonian Democracy and the Working Class: A Study of the New York Workingmen's Movement, 1829–1837* (1960); Edward Pessen, *Most Uncommon Jacksonians: The Radical Leaders of the Early Labor Movement* (1967); *Dictionary of American Biography*, Vol. 6.

F

FARQUHAR, John McCreath   (1832–1918). Born in Ayr, Scotland, April 17, 1832; son of John and Marion (McCreath) Farquhar; Presbyterian; married Jane Wood on September 11, 1862; attended Ayr Academy; emigrated to the United States while still a boy and settled in Buffalo, N.Y.; learned the printing trade; during the 1850s, studied law, ventured into publishing, and did organizational work for the National Typographical Union (NTU); elected president of the NTU in 1860 and served for three years; enlisted as a private in the U.S. Army and advanced to the rank of major; served as judge advocate and inspector in the Fourth Army Corps; awarded the Congressional Medal of Honor for bravery at the battle of Stone River, Tenn.; returned to Buffalo after the war and, while maintaining his union ties, opened a successful law practice; elected as a Republican to the United States Congress in 1884, serving three terms; declined renomination in 1890; served as a member of the United States Industrial Commission, 1898–1902; shortly after retiring from public life and his private law practice, died in Buffalo, N.Y., April 24, 1918; was a Republican; David Montgomery, *Beyond Equality: Labor and the Radical Republicans, 1862–1872* (1967); *Biographical Directory of the American Congress, 1774–1971* (1971); *Who Was Who in America*, Vol. 1.

FARRINGTON, Frank   (1873–1939). Born in Fairburg, Ill., in 1873; son of a coal miner; married; three children; had no formal education; began working at age 9 in the mines at Streator, Ill.; joined the Knights of Labor in 1886 and later the United Mine Workers of America (UMWA); held several minor union offices before being elected president of District 12, UMWA, Illinois; served in that post from 1914 to August 30, 1926, when his three-year contract as a labor consultant with the Peabody Coal Company at a salary of $25,000 per year was disclosed; served on the UMWA international executive board for six years; was a conservative opponent of the Socialists in the Illinois UMWA prior to World War I, but supported the 1920 campaign of John H. Walker (q.v.), president of the Illinois State Federation of Labor, for governor of Illinois on the National

Farmer-Labor party ticket; was an able contract negotiator, invariably winning greater benefits for Illinois miners than surrounding districts won; was president of the most powerful autonomous union district and a personal enemy of John L. Lewis (q.v.); engaged in a continuing feud with Lewis throughout the first 11 years of Lewis's presidency; in 1917, along with John H. Walker, opposed the confirmation of Lewis as an international vice-president by the international executive board; revoked the charters of 24 local unions when between twenty-five thousand and seventy-five thousand Illinois miners revolted against his refusal to convene a wage scale convention in August 1919; was upheld in this action by Lewis and the international convention; made a national martyr of Alexander Howat (q.v.), president of the Kansas district, who got no support from Lewis in his imprisonment for violating the Kansas anti-strike law; was one of three UMWA delegates who supported Samuel Gompers (q.v.) in his 1921 contest with John L. Lewis for the American Federation of Labor presidency; employed Oscar Ameringer (q.v.), the famed ''Adam Coaldigger,'' to edit the *Illinois Miner*, an anti-Lewis organ, in 1922; supported Howat's nearly successful fight at the 1924 UMWA convention to destroy the Lewis machine by instituting rank-and-file election of international organizers; after supporting John Brophy's (q.v.) ''Save the Union'' campaign for the UMWA presidency in 1926, was discredited by Lewis's revelation of the Peabody Coal Company contract; involved in the 1930 convention of the Reorganized United Mine Workers; died in Streator, Ill., March 30, 1939; Solon DeLeon, ed., *The American Labor Who's Who* (1925); *The New York Times*, March 31, 1939; Selig Perlman and Philip Taft, *History of Labor in the United States, 1896–1932*, Vol. 4 (1935); Irving Bernstein, *The Lean Years: A History of the American Worker, 1920–1933* (1960); John H. M. Laslett, *Labor and the Left: A Study of Socialism and Radical Influences in the American Labor Movement, 1881–1924* (1970); McAlister Coleman, *Men and Coal* (1943); John Brophy, *A Miner's Life* (1964); Melvyn Dubofsky and Warren Van Tine, *John L. Lewis: A Biography* (1977).

John W. Hevener

FEENEY, Frank   (1870–1938). Born in New York City, April 22, 1870; son of a bricklayer; Roman Catholic; married; two children; completed grammar school in New York City before moving to Philadelphia, Pa.; acquired work as an elevator constructor, and became actively involved in the Philadelphia labor movement; beginning in 1896, served as a delegate to the annual conventions of the American Federation of Labor (AFL) until his death in 1938; was a founder of the International Union of Elevator Constructors (IUEC) in 1901, and served as its international president until his death; was an active and influential figure in the Philadelphia labor movement, serving as president of the Philadelphia Central Labor Union for seven years and also as president of the Philadelphia Building Trades Council for seven years; was an AFL fraternal delegate to the Canadian Trades and Labor Congress in 1905; participated actively in Republican party affairs in Philadelphia, and credited with organizing the labor movement in support of Boies Penrose's senatorial campaigns; served as chief of the Philadelphia Bureau of Elevator Inspection, 1908–1911, and as a supervising referee for the Pennsylvania Workmen's Compensation Bureau, 1919–1922; was a member of the Council of National Defense during World War I; served for many years as an official in the AFL building trades department; saw his son, Frank, Jr., serve as secretary-treasurer of the IUEC; died in Atlantic City, N.J., May 28, 1938, during son's tenure; Solon DeLeon, ed., *The American Labor Who's Who* (1925); *The American Federation of Labor Weekly News Service*, June 4, 1938.

FEHRENRATH, John   (fl. 1844–1878). Born in Rochester, N.Y., on June 29, 1844; the death of his mother in 1847 and the poverty of his father forced him to quit school in 1852, at age 8, and go to work at a woolen mill; although working from 6:00 A.M. to 7:00 P.M. each day, he attended night school and obtained the rudiments of a common school education; on April 11, 1857, he was apprenticed to a blacksmith; completing his apprenticeship on April 10, 1860, he moved to Peterboro, Ontario, where, disliking the blacksmith's trade, he secured an apprenticeship as a machinist; after completing this apprenticeship, he traveled to Cleveland, Ohio, on August 14, 1863, and a short time later found a job in a machine shop in Cincinnati, Ohio; in February 1864, he went to Evansville, Ind., where he gained employment in a machine shop and joined Local No. 6 of the Machinists and Blacksmiths Union; after moving to Indianapolis, Ind., later in the same year, he was elected vice-president of the Machinists and Blacksmiths Union No. 4; moved to Nashville, Tenn., in November 1864, where he was employed by the government on a U.S. military railroad; returned to Indianapolis in April 1865, took night courses at Purdue University while working as a machinist; elected special corresponding secretary of Machinists and Blacksmiths Union No. 4 in 1860, he opened a correspondence with various trade unions throughout Indiana with the objective of coordinating a statewide eight-hour movement; as a result, a convention was held in October 1866 at which the Indiana Grand Eight Hour League was organized and he was elected its secretary; was a delegate to the special session of the National Labor Union which convened in New York City in July 1868; returned to Rochester, N.Y., in 1870, where for six months he devoted his energies to the task of rebuilding Machinists and Blacksmiths Union No. 7; returned to Indianapolis in April 1871; was elected Local No. 4's delegate to the national convention of the Machinists and Blacksmiths Union which met in Cleveland in September 1871; was elected president of the national union at that meeting; during the following year he conducted a major organizing campaign which by the fall of 1872 had greatly increased the members and the number of locals organized by the Machinists and Blacksmiths Union—in 1870 the union had 28 unions represented at its national convention, two years later 132 local unions sent delegates; following the 1872 convention, he joined Martin A. Foran (q.v.) of the Coopers International Union and William Saffia and Harry Walls of the Iron Molders in the organization of the Industrial Labor Congress in Cleveland on July 14, 1873, of which he was elected president; was nominated by the Republican party for a seat in the Indiana state legislature in 1873 but lost; ran successfully for the same seat in 1876, serving until 1878 when he accepted a position in the Rutherford B. Hayes administration; *Chicago's Workingman's Advocate*, November 15, 1873; John R. Commons et al., *History of Labour in the United States*, Vol. 2 (1918); David Montgomery, *Beyond Equality: Labor and the Radical Republicans, 1862–1872* (1967).

FEINBERG, Israel   (1887–1952). Born in Berdichev, Ukraine, Russia, December 25, 1887; son of Hyman, a prosperous tailor, and Bertha Feinberg; Jewish; married Nellie Weissman in 1910; two children; acquired the equivalent of a high school education before beginning an apprenticeship in the tailor's trade at age 16; emigrated to England at the turn of the century and settled in Manchester; became an active participant in the British labor movement and organized a Jewish tailors' union in Manchester; emigrated to the United States in 1912 and, after finding employment as a cloak operator, joined Local 1 of the International Ladies' Garment Workers' Union (ILGWU); elected an official and executive board member of Local 1; became chairman of the New York Cloak Joint Board in 1919 and two years later elected general manager, serving until 1925; was a member of the New York Central Labor Council, 1918–1920; served as an ILGWU vice-president, 1922–1925 and 1928–1952; was an ILGWU general organizer in Canada, 1928–1931, and during 1931–1933 served as a supervisor of the ILGWU locals in Boston, Mass.; became West Coast regional director of the ILGWU in 1933 and assumed responsibility for the organization of garment workers in Los Angeles, Calif., San Francisco, Calif., Portland, Oreg., and Vancouver, Wash.; became general manager of the New York Joint Board of Cloak, Suit, Skirt and Reefer Makers Unions in 1934; took the initiative in establishing the ILGWU's first retirement fund in 1943; was a member of the board of directors of the Yiddish Science Institute and served as treasurer of the Central Yiddish Culture Organization; retired from union affairs in 1952; was a member of the Liberal party of New York; died in Los Angeles, Calif., September 16, 1952; Benjamin Stolberg, *Tailor's Progress: The Story of a Famous Union and the Men Who Made It* (1944); Louis Levine, *The Women's Garment Workers: A History of the International Ladies Garment Workers' Union* (1924); *ILGWU Report and Proceedings* (1953).

FEINSTONE, Morris   (1878–1943). Born in Warsaw, Russian Poland, in 1878; Jewish; married; two children; studied at the Warsaw Art School, and became a skilled carver, designer, and master draftsman; after imprisonment in Warsaw for participating in revolutionary activities, emigrated to Germany; moved somewhat later to England and secured employment as a woodcarver; joined the Woodcarver's Union in London and in 1895 elected its president; actively involved in the early organizing activities of the British Labour party in Birmingham; emigrated to the United States in 1910; secured employment in the New York umbrella industry and became a leader of the Umbrella Handle and Stick Makers' Union, as well as an active participant in the affairs of the United Hebrew Trades (UHT); became assistant secretary of the UHT in 1915 and, after the retirement of Max Pine (q.v.) in 1926, became executive secretary; represented the UHT on the executive board of the Central Trades and Labor Council of Greater New York for several years; strongly supported the movement to create a Jewish state in Palestine; was a member of the board of directors of the Hebrew Immigrant Sheltering Aid Society, chairman of the administrative committee of the National Labor Committee for Palestine, vice-chairman of the Jewish Labor Committee, and a member of the Forward Association, publisher of the *Jewish Labor Forward*; served as a member of the governing board of the Rand School of Social Science and of the *New Leader*, a Social-Democratic weekly labor newspaper; served during World War II as a panel member of the Regional War Labor Board and on the labor advisory board of the Office of Price Administration in New York City; as a Socialist and a long-time advocate of an independent labor party, became a leading proponent of the American Labor party; died in New York City, April 28, 1943; Hyman J. Fliegel, *The Life and Times of Max Pine: A History of the Jewish Labor Movement in the U.S.A. during the Last Part of the 19th Century and the First Part of the 20th Century* (1959); Melech Epstein, *Jewish Labor in the U.S.A., 1914–1952*, 2 Vols. (1953).

FELLER, Karl Franz   (1914–1981). Born in Dayton, Ohio, August 6, 1914; son of Karl John and Marie (Koch) Feller; Roman Catholic; married Virginia K. Snyder on October 9, 1937; five children; completed secondary school in Dayton, then became an apprentice brewer and joined Local 50 of the International Union of United Brewery, Flour, Cereal, and Soft Drink Workers of America (UBFCSDW) (now the International Union of United Brewery, Flour, Cereal, Soft Drink and Distillery Workers of America); worked as a brewer in Cincinnati, Ohio, Detroit, Mich., and Milan, Ohio, prior to returning to Dayton; elected president of Local 50, in Dayton, in 1939; elected business manager of Local 50 in 1940 and served as an organizer and trouble-shooter for the UBFCSDW in Ohio; founded the Ohio-Kentucky State Council of Brewery Syrup and Soft Drink Workers; served as a special UBFCSDW organizer, 1943–1945; became corresponding secretary of the UBFCSDW in 1945; as a result of a referendum vote in 1948, elected to the newly created office of international president, assuming office on January 1, 1949; was a member of the executive board of the Congress of Industrial Organizations (CIO) and, after the American Federation of Labor (AFL)-CIO merger, became a vice-president of the AFL-CIO industrial union department; named an AFL-CIO vice-president and executive council member in 1957, but expelled from the executive council in 1973 as a result of his holding merger discussions with the International Brotherhood of Teamsters, Chauffeurs, Warehousemen and Helpers; had been a consistent supporter of Walter P. Reuther (q.v.) on the AFL-CIO executive council, but his freedom of action was reduced by the weakness of his own union and the UBFCSDW's constant fear of encroachment by the powerful Teamsters; was politically a Democrat; died on February 5, 1981; Maurer, Fleisher & Associates, *Union with a Heart: International Union of United Brewery, Flour, Cereal, Soft Drink and Distillery Workers of America: 75 Years of a Great Union, 1886–1961* (1961); *Who's Who in America, 1972–1973*.

FENTON, Francis Patrick   (1895–1948). Born in Boston, Mass., March 11, 1895; son of John J., a union leader, and Catherine (Delaney) Fenton; Roman Catholic; married Christine Wilhelmina Tucker in 1923; five children; attended grammar school in Boston, then became a coal driver and joined Boston Local 68 of the International Brotherhood of Teamsters, Chauffeurs, Warehousemen and Helpers of America; later received an LL.B. degree from the Suffolk Law School; active during 1926–1939 in the Boston and Massachusetts labor movements, serving as an executive board member, vice-president, and president of the Boston Central Labor Union; also served during that period as president of the Workers Credit Union Bank, chairman of the resolutions committee of the Massachusetts State Federation of Labor, and president of the Board of Control of the Boston Trade Union College; was instrumental in gaining ratification in Massachusetts of the child labor amendment to the U.S. Constitution; after serving as an American Federation of Labor (AFL) organizer for the New England district, became director of organization for the AFL in 1939; served during World War II on a number of boards and agencies, including the National War Labor Board, the War Production Board, and the Office of Price Administration; was named international representative and permanent AFL representative to the International Labor Organization after the death of Robert J. Watt (q.v.) in 1947; served as a consultant on vocational education with the U.S. Department of Education; supported the Democratic party; died in Washington, D.C., August 9, 1948; *The American Federationist* (December 1947, September 1948); *Who's Who in Labor* (1946).

FERRAL, John   (fl. 1833–1850). Was a handloom weaver during the 1830s and became the most influential figure in the Philadelphia, Pa., labor movement, as well as a prominent figure in the national trade union movement; was the only non-New England delegate to the 1833 convention of the New England Association of Farmers, Mechanics and Other Working Men; attended the convention in order to study the New England labor movement; returned to Philadelphia and attempted to organize factory workers and farmers in the area around the city, hoping to effect a union (the Trades' Union of Pennsylvania) between city artisans, mechanics, and factory workers; became one of the principal figures in the Philadelphia Trades' Union and was a leader of the successful 1835 strike for the ten-hour day in Philadelphia; elected second vice-president of the National Trades' Union (NTU) at its inaugural convention in 1834 and, among other duties, served on a committee to prepare a statement regarding wages and hours; elected president of the NTU in 1835, serving until 1836; became corresponding secretary of the Philadelphia Trades' Union in 1837; believed in the inevitability of class conflict, and thus not only advocated militant trade union activity but also supported labor's involvement in politics; during the 1840s and 1850s, supported the land reform principles of George Henry Evans (q.v.); participated actively in the Pittsburgh Workingmen's Congress; was a delegate to the New York City Industrial Congress in 1850; Edward Pessen, *Most Uncommon Jacksonians: The Radical Leaders of the Early Labor Movement* (1967); William A. Sullivan, *The Industrial Workers in Pennsylvania, 1800–1840* (1955); John R. Commons et al., *A Documentary History of American Industrial Society*, Vols. 5, 6, 8 (1910–1911); Philip S. Foner, *History of the Labor Movement in the United States*, Vol. 1 (1947).

FIELDEN, Samuel   (1847–1923). Born in Todmorden, a town in the East Riding of Lancashire, England, on February 25, 1847; son of Abram, a steam-loom weaver, and Alice (Jackson) Fielden; Methodist; married in 1879; two children; learned to read while attending a small privately run school for six months and then began work in a cotton mill at age 8; worked in the mill for the following ten years while also attending a mill school part time; emigrated to the United States in 1868, settling briefly in Brooklyn, N.Y., where he attained work in a hat factory; shortly thereafter he moved to Providence, R.I., where he attained work in a textile mill; enticed by the prospect of farming, he traveled west in 1869, eventually settling in Chicago, Ill., where he secured employment on a dredge working on the Illinois and Michigan canal; traveled and worked in the South in 1870, where he observed the deplorable economic and social condition of the freedmen; returned to Chicago in the spring of 1871 and worked at various odd jobs during the next several years; returned to England for a visit and to fulfill a matrimonial engagement in 1879, and, upon his return to Chicago the following year, he became the proprietor of a small stone-hauling business; helped organize a short-lived teamsters' union in 1880; after taking an active role in a liberal league which supported the total separation of church and state, he joined the anarchist International Working People's Association in 1884 and soon became one of its more active speakers; was one of the speakers at the Haymarket Square meeting on May 4, 1886, which ended in the death of a policeman and several of the protestors; was arrested on May 5, tried, convicted, and sentenced to be executed on November 11, 1887; after appealing to the governor of Illinois for clemency, his sentence was commuted to life imprisonment and six years later Governor John P. Altgeld granted him an unconditional pardon; died in 1923; Philip S. Foner, ed., *The Autobiographies of the Haymarket Martyrs* (1969); David Henry, *The History of the Haymarket Affair*, rev. ed. (1963).

FILBEY, Francis Stuart   (1907–1977). Born in Wrightsville, Pa., on July 4, 1907; married Evelyn in 1926; two children; grew up in Baltimore, Md., and was educated at the Baltimore Polytechnic Institute, 1921–1924; began working as a postal clerk after completing his formal education and joined the National Federation of Post Office Clerks (NFPOC) in 1926; served as an officer in the Baltimore local of the NFPOC before being elevated to the presidency; was elected a national vice-president of the NFPOC and president of the Baltimore Federation of Labor, 1954–1959; elected president of the Metropolitan Baltimore Council of the American Federation of Labor-Congress of Industrial Organizations (AFL-CIO), 1959–1962; elected vice-president of the Maryland State and the District of Columbia AFL-CIO Councils in 1959; served as an administrative aide in the United Federation of Postal Clerks (UFPC), 1962–1969; elected national president of the UFPC in 1969; was instrumental in negotiating a merger of the UFPC, the National Postal Union, the Post Office and General Service Maintenance Employees, the Post Office Motor Vehicles Employees, and the Special Delivery Messengers, creating the American Postal Workers Union (APWU) in 1971; was elected president of the newly organized APWU in 1971; was elected an AFL-CIO vice-president and executive council member in 1974; became treasurer of the AFL-CIO's public employee department in 1976; active in a great variety of civic activities, he was a member of the Baltimore Equal Employment Opportunity Committee, the Mayor's Advisory Committee on Civil Defense, the Mayor's Advisory Committee on Housing and Enforcement of Urban Renewal, the Maryland Commission for Prevention and Treatment of Juvenile Delinquency, and numerous other public and private commissions, committees, associations, etc.; died in Towson, Md., on May 17, 1977; *Who's Who in Labor* (1976); *AFL-CIO News*, August 10, 1974, May 21, 1977; *The New York Times*, May 18, 1977.

FINCHER, Jonathan C.   (fl. 1858–1876). Born in Philadelphia, Pa., in 1830; worked as a machinist in Philadelphia; along with 13 fellow machinists, founded the first International Union of Machinists and Blacksmiths local unions in 1858; was among 21 delegates from 12 local unions in five cities and three states who convened in Philadelphia in the spring of 1859 to establish the national union that encompassed 57 locals and 2,828 members by late 1860; served as the union's national secretary-treasurer for several years, and established its monthly publication, the *Machinists' and Blacksmiths' International Journal*, in 1862; founded *Fincher's Trade Review* in 1863 and issued it weekly for the next three years; included Ira Steward (q.v.), Richard Trevellick (q.v.), and William H. Sylvis (q.v.) among its contributors, thus making *Fincher's Review* the most influential trade union publication of the era and one of the finest ever published in the United States; saw its circulation reach eleven thousand in 31 of 36 states and in five English cities by 1865; helped found the Philadelphia Trades' Assembly in 1863 and elected to its board of trustees; attending the National Labor Congresses in Baltimore in 1866 and in New York City in 1868, opposed currency reform and favored strong trade unions and eight-hour legislation attained by pressure on the two traditional parties; opposed labor's independent political action because it resulted in neglect of trade unions and fostered a new alliance of employers and employees; bolted the National Labor Union when it endorsed independent political action; established another Philadelphia labor paper, the *Welcome Workman*; published the Wilkes Barre, Pa., *Anthracite Monitor* in 1869; elected from Hazelton, Luzerne County, to the Pennsylvania legislature in 1876; with the support of John W. Morgan, a St. Clair miner-legislator, and John Siney (q.v.), a member of the Miners' National Association, helped exempt labor organizations from prosecution under Pennsylvania's conspiracy law; John R. Commons et al., *History of Labour in the United States*, Vol. 2 (1918); Edward Pinkowski, *John Siney: The Miners' Martyr* (1963); David Montgomery, *Beyond Equality: Labor and the Radical Republicans, 1862–1872* (1967).

John W. Hevener

FINLEY, Murray Howard   (1922–   ). Born in Syracuse, N.Y., on March 31, 1922; married Elaine Auerbach on July 14, 1946; two children; after completing his elementary and secondary schooling, he enrolled at the University of Michigan from which he received the B.A. degree in 1946; received the J.D. from the Northwestern University Law School in 1949; served as a sergeant in the U.S. Army, 1942–1945; after earning his law degree, he became the assistant regional attorney for the Amalgamated Clothing Workers of America (ACWA) in Chicago, Ill., in 1949; became the assistant manager of the Detroit, Mich., joint board (ACWA) in 1955 and in 1961 returned to Chicago as manager of the ACWA joint board there; elected an international vice-president of the ACWA in 1962; served as manager of the Midwest joint board, covering a nine-state area, 1964–1972; was elected general president of the ACWA after the resignation of Jacob S. Potofsky (q.v.) in 1972; was elected a vice-president and executive council member of the American Federation of Labor-Congress of Industrial Organizations (AFL-CIO) in 1973; after the amalgamation of the ACWA and the Textile Workers Union of America in 1976, he was elected president of the resulting Amalgamated Clothing and Textile Workers Union; involved in a variety of civic affairs, he was a member of the Committee for National Health Insurance, the Community Council of Greater New York, the board of directors of the A. Philip Randolph Institute, the African-American Labor Center, and honorable vice-chairman of the American Trade Union Council for Histadrut; *Advance* (June 1972); *Who's Who in America, 1982–1983; Who's Who in Labor* (1976); *AFL-CIO News*, June 10, 1972.

FISCHER, Adolph   (fl. 1850–1887). Born in Bremen, Germany; married in 1881; three children; after attending Bremen schools, he emigrated to the United States at age 15; upon reaching the United States, he traveled to Little Rock, Ark., to join his brother and entered an apprenticeship as a compositor in his brother's printing office; after completing his apprenticeship, he traveled extensively throughout the United States while working in printing offices; joined the German Typographical Union in St. Louis, Mo., in 1879; became a compositor in the offices of the *Arbeiter-Zeitung*, a German-language Socialist newspaper published in Chicago, Ill.; educated in socialism at his father's knee, he later became an anarchist and joined the International Working People's Association; was placed in charge of printing and distributing the handbills announcing the May 4 meeting at Haymarket Square to protest police violence at the McCormick plant two days earlier; after a bomb exploded at the Haymarket Square meeting, killing one policeman and wounding several others, he was arrested along with several other Chicago anarchists, tried, and convicted of murder; was executed on November 11, 1887; Philip S. Foner, ed., *The Autobiographies of the Haymarket Martyrs* (1969); Lucy E. Parsons, *Life of Albert R. Parsons with Brief History of the Labor Movement in America: Also Sketches of the Lives of A. Spies, Geo. Engel, A. Fischer and Louis Lingg*, 2d ed. (1903); David Henry, *The History of the Haymarket Affair*, rev. ed. (1963).

FISHER, Joseph A.   (1896–   ). Born in New York City, May 1, 1896; son of Joseph, a plumber, and Rose (Peters) Fisher; Roman Catholic; married Agnes B. Cosgrove on November 24, 1920; two children; was graduated from Holy Cross High School in Queens, N.Y., then attended the College of the City of New York; worked as an electrician in the New York City construction industry during 1912–1934; joined New York City Local 830 of the International Brotherhood of Electrical Workers in 1912; hired as an electrician with the Consolidated Edison Corporation in 1935; served as president of Local 830, 1937–1940; elected national president of the independent Utility Unions of America in 1941, serving until 1945; served as chairman of the joint council of the Brotherhood of Consolidated Edison Employees, 1941–1945; elected the first national president of the Utility Workers Union of America (UWUA), a new union chartered by the Congress of Industrial Organizations (CIO) in 1945; served on the executive board of the CIO, 1945–1955, and on the general board of the American Federation of Labor-CIO, 1955–1960; was largely responsible for building the UWUA into a well-organized, effective trade union and guiding it through its early formative years; retired as national president of the UWUA in 1960; *Who's Who in America, 1958–1959; Who's Who in Labor* (1946).

FITZGERALD, Albert J.   (1906–1982). Born in Lynn, Mass., in 1906; son of Irish immigrants; Roman Catholic; married; one child; after graduation from high school, became a lathe-turner in the motor department of the General Electric plant in Lynn; supported efforts to organize the plant, and appointed shop steward; later elected president of Lynn Local 201, United Electrical, Radio and Machine Workers of America (UE); elected district vice-president, district president, and secretary of the Massachusetts State Industrial Union Council, Congress of Industrial Organizations (CIO); elected general president of UE in 1941; denied any Communist affiliation, but usually allied with the left wing of the UE and of the labor movement nationally; became a CIO vice-president and member of the executive council; was a member of the CIO's Political Action Committee in 1943; led his union in a series of strikes in the immediate postwar period; supported Henry Wallace for president of the United States in 1948 and served as co-chairman of the Wallace for President Committee and chairman of the Wallace Labor Committee; served also as co-chairman of the Progressive party's national convention in 1948; during his presidency, the UE was expelled from the CIO in 1949 because of alleged Communist domination; the CIO chartered the International Union of Electrical, Radio and Machine Workers which soon became the largest union in the electrical industry; nevertheless, kept the UE a viable and effective trade union; along with other unions in the electrical industry, led the UE in a successful 95–day strike against General Electric in 1970; died in Boston, Mass., on April 3, 1982; Max M. Kampelman, *The Communist Party vs. the C.I.O.: A Study in Power Politics* (1957); *Current Biography* (1948); *Who's Who in Labor* (1946); F. S. O'Brien, "The 'Communist-Dominated' Unions in the U.S. since 1950," *Labor History* (Spring 1968); Albert Fitzgerald Interview, Pennsylvania State University, Labor Archives; Harvey A. Levenstein, *Communism, Anticommunism, and the CIO* (1981); *The New York Times*, April 4, 1982; Nelson Lichtenstein, *Labor's War at Home: The CIO in World War II* (1982).

FITZGERALD, Frank A. (1885–1951). Born in New York City, September 5, 1885; son of John, an operating engineer, and Catherine (Van Ness) Fitzgerald; Roman Catholic; married Mae Gardner on September 5, 1917; after graduating from high school, served an apprenticeship as a machinist; joined New Haven, Conn., Local 478 of the International Union of Operating Engineers (IUOE) in 1910; elected shortly thereafter as business agent of Local 478 and continued in that capacity for 20 years; elected to the IUOE board of trustees in 1916 and later served as board chairman; elected an IUOE vice-president in 1931, and later that same year filled the newly vacant office of general secretary-treasurer; during the depression of the 1930s, developed an elaborate listing service to inform unemployed engineers of government building projects and other employment opportunities; while serving as general secretary-treasurer, reorganized the various departments of the IUOE and established an efficient administrative governance system for the union that became a model for many other international unions; edited *The International Engineer*, 1931–1951; died in Washington, D.C., March 29, 1951; Garth L. Mangum, *The Operating Engineers: The Economic History of a Trade Union* (1964); *The American Federationist* (April 1951); *Who's Who in Labor* (1946).

FITZPATRICK, John (1871–1946). Born in Ireland, April 21, 1871; son of John, a small farmer and horseshoer, and Adelaide (Clarke) Fitzpatrick; Roman Catholic; married Katherine McCreash, a school teacher, on June 29, 1892; one child; attended grammar school in Ireland; emigrated to the United States in 1882, settling in Chicago, Ill.; became a journeyman horseshoer in 1886 and joined Local 4 of the International Journeymen Horseshoers' Union; elected president of the Chicago Federation of Labor (CFL) in 1901 and served one term; became a full-time CFL paid organizer in 1902; again elected president of the CFL in 1906, and served in that position for more than 40 years; led a movement to create a labor party in Illinois, and ran as its candidate for mayor of Chicago in 1918; headed a successful organizing drive in Chicago during World War I; was one of the leaders, along with William Z. Foster (q.v.), of the historic 1919 steel strike; assisted in the organization of Chicago packinghouse workers, garment workers, and teachers; belonged to the Regional Labor Board of the National Recovery Administration, 1933–1935; proved to be a vigorous and resourceful trade union leader and a diligent foe of racketeering and corruption in the Chicago labor movement; was a militant unionist, but opposed Communist efforts to infiltrate the labor movement during the 1920s and 1930s; long advocated an independent labor party, but usually supported Democratic candidates and served as vice-president of the Alfred E. Smith-for-President Union Labor League in 1928; enthusiastically admired President Franklin D. Roosevelt during the 1930s; died in Chicago, Ill., September 27, 1946; Barbara Warne Newell, *Chicago and the Labor Movement: Metropolitan Unionism in the 1930s* (1961); Eugene Staley, *History of the Illinois State Federation of Labor* (1930); David Brody, *Labor in Crisis: The Steel Strike of 1919* (1965); James Weinstein, *The Decline of Socialism in America, 1912–1925* (1967); *Dictionary of American Biography*, Suppl. 4.

FITZSIMMONS, Frank Edward   (1908–1981). Born in Jeannette, Pa., April 7, 1908; son of Frank, a brewery worker, and Ida May (Stahley) Fitzsimmons; after the death of his first wife, married Mary Patricia in 1952; two children; left school at age 17 because of his father's incapacitating illness; worked for a short while as a time clerk before securing employment as a bus driver for the Detroit Motor Company; later worked as a truck driver for the National Transit Corporation and the 3–C Highway Company; joined Detroit Local 299 of the International Brotherhood of Teamsters, Chauffeurs, Warehousemen and Helpers of America (IBT) in 1934; appointed business manager of Local 299 by the local's president, James R. Hoffa (q.v.), in 1937; elected vice-president of Local 299 in 1940 and three years later was appointed secretary-treasurer of the IBT's Michigan Conference; became an IBT executive board member and vice-president in 1961; elected in 1966 to the newly created office of general vice-president, a position created to provide a method of filling any vacancy that might occur in the union presidency; became president in 1967 when IBT president James R. Hoffa was imprisoned in the Lewisburg, Pa., Federal Penitentiary for jury tampering, conspiracy, and fraud; along with Walter P. Reuther (q.v.), helped organize the Alliance for Labor Action in 1969; appointed a member of President Richard M. Nixon's "Phase Two" pay board in 1971, and continued serving on the board after other labor leaders, led by American Federation of Labor-Congress of Industrial Organizations' president George Meany (q.v.), resigned to protest the administration's economic policies; elected president of the IBT in 1971; usually supported the Republican party; died in La Jolla, Calif., on May 6, 1981; Walter Sheridan, *The Fall and Rise of Jimmy Hoffa* (1972); Joseph C. Goulden, *Meany* (1972); *Current Biography* (1971); *The New York Times*, May 7, 1981; Steven Brill, *The Teamsters* (1978).

FLAUMENBAUM, Irving   (1909–1980). Born in Brooklyn, N.Y., on September 9, 1909; married; three children; a graduate of James Madison High School in Brooklyn, he attended the Columbia University College of Pharmacy, graduating in 1930; served in the New York National Guard, 1935–1937; after securing employment as a pharmacist in the Nassau County (N.Y.) Department of Social Services, he joined the Nassau Chapter of the New York State Civil Service Employees Association (CSEA); was elected president of the Nassau County CSEA in 1955 when it had a membership of fewer than one hundred and during the following 22 years built it into a large, powerful organization with a membership in excess of thirty thousand; was elected president of CSEA, Region 1, comprised of Nassau and Suffolk Counties, in 1973 and by 1977 had increased membership in the region to sixty thousand; when the CSEA merged with the American Federation of State, County and Municipal Employees (AFSCME) in 1977, he was elected an international vice-president of AFSCME; extremely active in a variety of civic activities in the Long Island area, he was a trustee of the United Fund Drive, Nassau and Suffolk Counties, chairman of the Nassau County Mental Health Fund Drive and Cancer Drive, board member, Central Island Mental Health Center, member of the Nassau County Committee on Priorities and Committee on Productivity, and a member of the advisory council, Nassau County Office of Manpower Development; died at Nassau County Medical Center on August 23, 1980; *Who's Who in Labor* (1976); *The New York Times*, August 24, 1980.

FLJOZDAL, Frederick Herman   (1868–1954). Born in Iceland, December 19, 1868; son of Arni Brynjolfson, a farmer and laborer, and Christine (Johnson) Fljozdal; Presbyterian; married Christina Nygren on August 24, 1893; six children; after receiving a grammar school education, emigrated to the United States in 1876; later took correspondence courses in common law and public speaking; began work as a laborer in 1888; was a farmer and justice of the peace, 1892–1898; served as a railroad construction foreman, 1898–1901; was a railroad section foreman during 1901–1915; joined the Brotherhood of Maintenance of Way Employees (BMWE) in 1902; served as secretary of BMWE Lodge 322 during 1902 and the following year elected president and local chairman; elected BMWE general chairman for the Canadian National Railway in 1905, serving until 1918; served as chairman of the BMWE's general chairman's association for the United States and Canada, 1910–1914; was secretary of the international executive board, 1915–1916, and chairman, 1916–1918; served as legislative representative in Washington, D.C., in 1918; elected a BMWE vice-president and member of the national committee in 1918; elected international president in 1922 and served until his retirement as president emeritus in 1940; served as a member of the executive committee of the Railway Labor Executives' Association and as a member of the editorial committee of the railroad newspaper, *Labor*; was an independent in politics; died in Detroit, Mich., December 16, 1954; Denver Willard Hertel, *History of the Brotherhood of Maintenance of Way Employees: Its Birth and Growth, 1877–1955* (1955); Brotherhood of Maintenance of Way Employees, *Pictorial History, 1877–1951* (1952); *Who's Who in Labor* (1946).

FLORE, Edward   (1877–1945). Born in Buffalo, N.Y., December 5, 1877; son of George, a German immigrant and saloon owner, and Catherine (Hassenfratz) Flore; Roman Catholic; married Mary Katherine Schneider on September 27, 1911; one child (died in infancy); left the public schools of Buffalo, N.Y., at age 16 and went to work as a bartender in his father's saloon; joined Bartenders' League Local 175 in 1900 and later the same year was elected recording secretary of the Buffalo local; elected a delegate to the Buffalo Central Labor Union in 1903; became a vice-president and member of the general executive board of the Hotel and Restaurant Employees' International Alliance and Bartenders' International League of America (HREIABIL) in 1905; elected international president of the HREIABIL in 1911 and held position for the remainder of his life; elected to the Erie County Board of Supervisors in 1908, serving until 1920; was an American Federation of Labor (AFL) fraternal delegate to the British Trades Union Congress in 1934; became an AFL vice-president and executive council member in 1937; remained loyal to the AFL, but supported the concept of industrial unionism and opposed the expulsion of the Committee on Industrial Organization unions from the AFL; served as an AFL delegate to the International Labor Organization's conference in Geneva in 1936; during his incumbency, saw the HREIABIL become one of the largest unions affiliated with the AFL; confronted as the major challenges during his presidency the long period of enforced prohibition and the recurring problems of graft and corruption, especially in locals in the New York and Chicago areas; was a Democrat; died in Buffalo, N.Y., September 27, 1945; Jay Rubin and M. J. Obermeier, *Growth of a Union: The Life and Times of Edward Flore* (1943); Matthew Josephson, *Union House, Union Bar: The History of the Hotel and Restaurant Employees and Bartenders International Union, AFL-CIO* (1956); *Current Biography* (1945); *Who's Who in Labor* (1946).

FLYNN, Elizabeth Gurley   (1890–1964). Born in Concord, N.H., August 7, 1890; daughter of immigrant Irish revolutionaries Thomas, a civil engineer, and Annie (Gurley) Flynn; married John A. Jones in January 1908; one child; joined the Industrial Workers of the World (IWW) in 1906 and a year later quit high school to devote full time to IWW activities; participated in the IWW free speech and assembly struggles in Missoula, Mont., and Spokane, Wash., 1908–1910; was active participant in the Lawrence, Mass., textile strike of 1912, the

Paterson, N.J., silk strike of 1913, the Mesabi Range miners' strike of 1916, and the Passaic, N.J., textile strike of 1926; after World War I, became a mediator between the IWW and the National Civil Liberties Bureau; was one of the founders of the Workers' Liberty Defense Union in 1918; involved during the next four years in defending those political and industrial prisoners arrested during the 1919–1920 red scare; was a founding member of the national committee of the American Civil Liberties Union in 1920; served as chairman of the International Labor Defense Committee, 1927–1930; joined the Communist party in 1937 and became a columnist for the party's organ, the *Daily Worker*; expelled from the American Civil Liberties Union national committee in 1940 because of her Communist party membership; convicted of teaching and advocating the overthrow of the government by force and violence and served a three-year prison sentence, 1955–1957; became the first woman to chair the Communist party's National Committee in 1961; authored *I Speak My Piece: Autobiography of the Rebel Girl* (1955); died in Moscow, USSR, September 5, 1964; Joseph R. Starobin, *American Communism in Crisis, 1943–1957* (1972); David A. Shannon, *The Decline of American Communism* (1959); Melvyn Dubofsky, *We Shall Be All: A History of the Industrial Workers of the World* (1969); *Current Biography* (1961); Rosalyn F. Baxandall, "Elizabeth Gurley Flynn: The Early Years," *Radical America* (1975); *Notable American Women*, Vol. 4.

Marie Tedesco

FORAN, Martin Ambrose   (1844–1921). Born in Choconut, Susquehanna County, Pa., November 11, 1844; son of James, a farmer and cooper, and Catherine (O'Donnell) Foran; married Kate Kavanaugh on December 29, 1868, and, after her death, Emma Kenny on December 20, 1893; two children; while in public school, learned the cooper's trade from his father; attended St. Joseph's College (Meadville, Pa.) for one year and then taught school for two years; served during the Civil War as a private in the Fourth Regiment, Pennsylvania Volunteer Cavalry, 1864–1865; resumed his apprenticeship as a cooper in Meadville after the war; moved to Cleveland, Ohio, in 1868 and quickly became leader of the local coopers' union; was one of the founders of the Coopers' International Union and served as its president for three years; edited the *Cooper's Journal* between 1870 and 1874; was a delegate to the Ohio Constitutional Convention of 1873; attended law school and admitted to the bar in 1874; served as prosecuting attorney for the city of Cleveland, 1875–1877; elected as a Democrat to the U.S. Congress in 1882 and served until 1889; as a Congressman, authored legislation preventing the importation of contract labor; became a judge in the Cleveland Court of Common Pleas in 1911 and served in that capacity until his death; was a Democrat; authored *The Other Side* (1886); died in Cleveland, Ohio, June 28, 1921; David Montgomery, *Beyond Equality: Labor and the Radical Republicans, 1862–1872* (1967); *National Cyclopaedia of American Biography*, Vol. 19; *Biographical Directory of the American Congress, 1774–1971* (1971).

FOSCO, Peter   (1892–1975). Born in Polish Russia on May 13, 1892; son of Vincent and Antonia Fosco; Roman Catholic; married Carmela Santucci on December 3, 1916; two children; received a common school education before emigrating to the United States in 1913, settling in Chicago, Ill., where he began his career as a common laborer; joined Local 2 of the Laborers' International Union of North America (LIU) and in 1916 was elected financial secretary of the local; was elected president of Local 2 in 1920, a position he held for the next 18 years; became manager of the LIU's Chicago region, encompassing nine states and two Canadian provinces, in 1936; elected general secretary-treasurer of the LIU in 1950; was elected general president of the LIU after the death of Joseph V. Moreschi (q.v.) in 1968; the following year he became an American Federation of Labor-Congress of Industrial Organizations (AFL-CIO) vice-president and executive council member; was elected first vice-president of the AFL-CIO building and construction trades department in 1969; an active participant in Chicago Democratic politics, he served as a Cook County Commissioner from 1938 to 1946; was named man of the year by the American Society in 1972; negotiated a merger with the National Association of Post Office and Postal Transportation Service Mail Handlers, Watchmen and Messengers during the early years of his presidential term; died in Chicago on October 26, 1975, and was succeeded in office by his son Angelo; *Who's Who in America, 1974–1975; AFL-CIO News*, November 1, 1975; *The New York Times*, October 27, 1975.

FOSTER, Frank K.   (1855–1909). Born in Palmer (Thorndike), Mass., December 18, 1855*; son of Charles Dwight and Jane Elizabeth (Burgess) Foster; married Lucretia Ella Ladd on May 22, 1879; was educated in common schools and at Monson Academy; learned the printer's trade at the office of the *Churchman*, Hartford, Conn., afterwards working as a compositor in various cities; his first connection with the labor movement was as a member of the Hartford Typographical Union, of which he was elected secretary; he went to Boston in 1880 and became president of the Cambridge Typographical Union; served the Cambridge union as a delegate to the international union at St. Louis and to the Federation of Trades Convention at Cleveland, Ohio; he was a delegate to this same body in 1883, representing the Boston Central Trades and Labor Union, and was chosen secretary; first joined the Knights of Labor as a member of Local Assembly 2006, and was elected delegate to convention of District 30, June 1882; elected secretary of District 30, 1883; delegate to General Assembly at Cincinnati, 1883; elected chairman of the executive board of the General Assembly at that session; served as delegate to General Assemblies at Philadelphia, Hamilton, Cleveland, and Richmond; member of executive board of District 30 since its inception; September 30, 1886, nominated for lieutenant governor of Massachusetts by the Democratic Convention at Worcester; founder and editor

*Date and place of birth was listed as Palmer, Mass., on December 19, 1854, in *Who Was Who*, Vol. 2.

of *Haverhill* (Mass.) *Daily and Weekly Laborer*; was a lecturer and Labor Day orator who spoke in 23 states; was editor and publisher of the *Liberator* beginning in 1886; was a member of the board of managers, Franklin Fund, in 1904; was a member of the examining committee of the Boston Public Library, 1904–1906; was a member of the Committee of 100, Boston Chamber of Commerce, and the New England Civic Federation; identified himself as an independent Democrat; authored *The Evolution of a Trade Unionist* (1901) and *The Karma of Labor* (1903); died in 1909; George E. McNeill, *The Labor Movement: The Problem of To-Day* (1887); *Who Was Who*, Vol. 2; Gerald N. Grob, *Workers and Utopia: A Study of Ideological Conflict in the American Labor Movement, 1865–1900* (1961).

George E. McNeill

FOSTER, William H.   (fl. 1847–1886). Born in Liverpool, England, May 3, 1847; taught school at age 15; went to learn the printing business, July 1, 1862, at Porta Down, County Armagh, Ireland, serving four years; finished his trade in Berylyton Steam Printing Works, Liverpool; became a journeyman, July 1, 1869; joined Liverpool Typographical Society as apprentice member; soon as had finished apprenticeship secured situation in Buxton, Derbyshire; came to America early in October 1873; stayed in Philadelphia four or five weeks; went to Cincinnati, worked on *Gazette* until the celebrated lockout on July 18, 1874; went to Philadelphia soon after; in June 1877, went to Cincinnati *Enquirer*; in 1878, elected president of Typographical Union 3; helped found and was secretary of Trades-Assembly, here acquired the title of the "Original Boycotter"; was leader in the successful efforts to make the *Enquirer, Sun, Gazette*, and *Commercial* union offices; February 14, 1880, with Patrick Caulfield, started the *Exponent*, one of the pioneer labor papers; about this time elected delegate to the Twenty-eighth Session of the International Typographical Union; chairman on committee for amalgamated unions, whose action finally culminated in the first trades union convention, at Pittsburgh, in November 1881, when he represented the Cincinnati Trades-Assembly; elected secretary of the convention, which selected Federation of Trades and Labor Unions of the United States and Canada as the title of the new organization; was secretary for two years and elected again at convention in Washington, 1885; in 1883, went to *Philadelphia Evening Call*, began active warfare against the non-union papers of that city; elected president of Typographical Union No. 2, in April 1884; was delegate from No. 2 to preliminary meeting of Central Labor Union, elected secretary; was one of the conveners of the trades union conference which met in Philadelphia on May 17, 1886 to discuss dissatisfaction with the Knights of Labor: John R. Commons et al., *History of Labour in the United States*, Vol. 2 (1918); George E. McNeill, *The Labor Movement: The Problem of To-Day* (1887).

George E. McNeill

FOSTER, William Zebulon   (1881–1961). Born in Taunton, Mass., February 25, 1881; son of James, an Irish railroad car washer, and Elizabeth (Mc-

Laughlin) Foster; married Esther Abramovitch on March 23, 1918; apprenticed to an artist in 1891 and learned the art crafts of modeling and stonecutting; quit art work in 1894 and for the next several years was employed as an industrial worker in a variety of occupations, including sailor, railroader, and homesteader; joined the Socialist party in 1900 but expelled nine years later for ideological reasons and joined the Industrial Workers of the World (IWW); traveled to Europe in 1910 as an IWW delegate to the Budapest meeting of the Trades Union Secretariat, but not seated and instead spent his time studying the labor movements of France and Germany; wrote the pamphlet *Syndicalism* in 1912, outlining the principles and programs of the Syndicalist League of North America; served as the league's national secretary; served as the business agent of a Chicago railway union in 1915; was a founder of the International Trade Union Educational League in 1917; served as secretary of the organizing committees that unionized packinghouse workers and steelworkers in the period 1917–1919; led the historic steel strike of 1919; founded the Trade Union Educational League in 1920 and served as its national secretary; along with Earl Browder, attended the congresses of the Communist International and Red International of Labor Unions in Moscow in 1921 and joined the Communist party of America (CPA)* shortly thereafter; was indicted but not convicted of criminal syndicalism in 1922; ran as the CPA candidate for president of the United States in 1924, 1928, and 1932; became national secretary of the CPA in 1930, and two years later was named national chairman, a position he held until 1957; ran for governor of New York as a CPA candidate in 1930; as a result of changes in ideological principles, replaced Earl Browder as the head of the CPA after a three-day policy conference in New York in 1945; retired as CPA national chairman emeritus in 1957; authored *The Great Steel Strike and Its Lessons* (1920); *The Russian Revolution* (1921); *Misleaders of Labor* (1927); *Towards Soviet America* (1932); *From Bryan to Stalin* (1937); and *Pages From a Worker's Life* (1939); died in Moscow, USSR, September 1, 1961; Theodore Draper, *American Communism and Soviet Russia* (1960), and *The Roots of American Communism* (1957); Joseph R. Starobin, *American Communism in Crisis, 1943–1957* (1972); David A. Shannon, *The Decline of American Communism* (1959); David Brody, *Labor in Crisis: The Steel Strike of 1919* (1965); *Current Biography* (1945); Arthur Zipser, *Workingclass Giant: The Life of William Z. Foster* (1981); Harvey A. Levenstein, *Communism, Anticommunism, and the CIO* (1981); Bert Cochran, *Labor and Communism: The Conflict that Shaped American Unions* (1977).

FOX, Martin   (1848–1907). Born in Cincinnati, Ohio, August 22, 1848; attended the Cincinnati public schools for several years, then became an apprentice molder at age 14; in 1864 as a journeyman, joined Local 3 of the International

---

*Over the years the name of the party was continually changing, and for short periods of time it simply ceased to exist. For the sake of conserving space and preserving clarity, this title is used throughout the sketch.

Molders Union of North America (IMUNA); elected a national trustee by the
IMUNA convention of 1878 and became increasingly influential in trade union
circles; appointed assistant to the president of the IMUNA in 1880 and elected
secretary by the 1886 convention; upon reaching IMUNA headquarters, found
a union beset by antagonistic employers and weakened by strike-prone locals;
after his election as union president in 1890, began to impose a centralized
authority on locals, enforcing it by executive board threats to withdraw the
charters of recalcitrant locals; having created a disciplined union, with a strike
fund, proceeded to negotiate an agreement with the Stove Founders' National
Defense Association to provide for "arbitration" of unresolved disputes by
conferences composed of union and employer representatives; saw this first pact
between a national union and a national trade association work surprisingly well
for many years although it was not really a mechanism for arbitration; encouraged
the machine founders to form a trade association, and in 1899 led the IMUNA
to negotiate an agreement with the National Founders' Association, although a
less satisfactory accord than the Stove Founders' agreement; refused, despite
pressure from many members, to oppose the introduction of labor-saving technology; led the IMUNA executive board to condemn the exclusion of black
molders from southern locals, and in 1900 created a separate Chattanooga local
in order to organize blacks; was an American Federation of Labor (AFL) fraternal
delegate to the British Trades Union Congress in 1897; was a member of the
Division of Conciliation and Mediation of the National Civic Federation, and
had a hand in the organization of the AFL metal trades department; forced by
ill health to resign as president in 1903; died in Cincinnati, Ohio, September
28, 1907; commemorated a few years later by a massive granite monument
erected by the IMUNA; *Iron Molders' Journal* (October 1907, August 1912);
Frank T. Stockton, *The International Molders Union of North America* (1921);
Philip Taft, *Organized Labor in American History* (1964).

Donald G. Sofchalk

FRAINA, Louis C. ("Lewis Corey")   (1892–1953). Born Luigi Carlo Fraina
in Galdo, Italy, on October 13, 1892; son of Antonio, an Italian worker with
republican views, and Louise (Fugacelli) Fraina, an illiterate peasant; married
Esther Nyesvishskaya, a Comintern employee he met in Moscow in 1920; one
child; emigrated with his family to the United States in 1895, settling in New
York City; formal schooling ended in 1907 after the death of his father; became
a cub reporter for the *New York Journal* after leaving school and soon began
writing for the *Daily People*, the Socialist Labor party (SLP) journal; was appointed organizational secretary of the SLP's New York office in 1909 at age
17; broke with the SLP and its leader, Daniel DeLeon (q.v.), in 1914 and became
the editor of the *New Review*, a theoretical journal supporting left-wing views
in the Socialist party; spent a month in jail in 1917 after criticizing United States
involvement in World War I in *The Socialist Attitude on the War*; edited the
New International in 1917 in which he became the first American Socialist to

support the ideas associated with Nikolai Lenin; resulting from his interest in the fine arts (a life-long avocation), he also edited the *Modern Dance Magazine* during this time; founded and led the Bolshevik Bureau of Information after the outbreak of the Russian revolution; meanwhile, the revolution interrupted plans he had, along with Leon Trotsky, Nikolai Bukharin, and Aleksendra Dollontai, to begin a new Socialist monthly, the *Class Struggle*; during the war years he continued his translation of the essays of Lenin and Trotsky which he published in 1918, the *Social Revolution in Germany* and *Proletarian Revolution in Russia*; at the same time he also published his own theoretical piece calling for mass action and the general strike, *Revolutionary Socialism*; edited the *Revolutionary Age* in 1918, a left-wing Socialist organ published in Boston in which he supported the Communist International; chaired the National Left-Wing Conference in 1919 which resulted in the division of the Socialist party and the creation of two Communist parties—the Communist Labor party and the Communist party of America (CPA); became the national editor and international secretary of the CPA; was a delegate to the Second Congress of the Communist International (Comintern) in 1920; disillusioned with the factionalism and in-fighting in the movement, he left the Communist party in 1922, moving to Mexico and taking some party funds with him—which did nothing to increase his stature in left-wing circles; returned to New York a year later and worked as a proofreader until 1929; changed his name to Lewis Corey and reemerged as a Socialist publicist and freelance writer, publishing *The House of Morgan* in 1931, and *The Decline of American Capitalism* in 1934; also served as associate editor of the *Encyclopedia of the Social Sciences*, 1931–1934; after reassociating himself with the Communist movement during the midthirties, he became disillusioned with the purges in the Soviet Union and by 1937 had become a critic of Soviet communism; after working briefly as a Works Progress Administration economist, he served as educational director of Local 22 of the International Ladies' Garment Workers' Union, 1937–1939; was one of the founders of the Union for Democratic Action (later Americans for Democratic Action) in 1940, and served as its research director; published *The Unfinished Task* in 1942 and during the same year became a professor of economics at Antioch College, where he also helped edit the *Antioch Review*; was associated with the Michigan Commonwealth Federation in 1944 which hoped to promote a Socialist revival after the war; in 1946, along with John Dewey, he was involved in transforming the federation into the National Educational Committee for a New Party, which he served as research director; wrote *Meat and Man* for the Amalgamated Butcher Workmen's Union in 1950 and a year later left Antioch to become the educational director for the union; during the red scare of the 1950s, he was investigated by the FBI and in 1952 was given a deportation order under the provisions of the McCarran Act; died in New York City on September 17, 1953, before the deportation order could be carried out; *Dictionary of American Biography*, Suppl. 5; Esther Corey, "Lewis Corey (Louis C. Fraina), 1892–1953: A Bibliography with Autobiographical Notes," *Labor History* (1963); Theodore Draper, *The*

Roots of American Communism (1957); Paul Buhle, "Lewis Corey" (M.A. thesis, 1968); Lee Baxandall, *Proletarian Writers of the Thirties* (1968).

FRANKENSTEEN, Richard Truman   (1907–   ). Born in Detroit, Mich., March 6, 1907; son of Harold L., a singer and composer, and Grace (Smith) Frankensteen; Episcopalian; married Grace Thelma Callahan on April 30, 1932; three children; graduated from the University of Dayton, Ohio, in 1932; after failing to secure employment as a high school teacher and coach, took a job on a Dodge assembly line in Detroit while attending law school at the University of Detroit; elected employee representative and then president of a company union that was reorganized in 1935 into the independent Automotive Industrial Workers Association and eventually amalgamated with the United Automobile, Aircraft and Agricultural Implement Workers of America (UAW); was elected a UAW vice-president in 1937; negotiated the first national contract with the Chrysler Corporation; gained national publicity after being severely beaten, along with Walter Reuther (q.v.), by Ford servicemen in the "Battle of the Overpass" at Ford's River Rouge plant; ran unsuccessfully for the Detroit Common Council in 1937; served on the Michigan Emergency Relief Committee, 1937–1938; became the national director of aircraft organization for the Congress of Industrial Organizations in 1941; appointed director of the UAW's political action and legislative activities; during World War II, served on the War Production Board and National War Labor Board; acted as chairman of the Michigan delegation to the 1944 Democratic National Convention; ran unsuccessfully for mayor of Detroit in 1945; aligned himself with the George Addes (q.v.)-Richard Leonard (q.v.)-Rolland J. Thomas (q.v.) faction in the internal politics of the UAW; retired from union affairs after the Reuther faction consolidated its control of the UAW; became the assistant general manager and labor relations consultant for Allen Industries, Inc., Detroit, in 1950; was a Democrat; authored several pamphlets on labor in the aircraft industry and co-authored the operetta, *Gypsy Moon*; Jack Stieber, *Governing the UAW* (1962); Sidney Fine, *Sit-Down: The General Motors Strike of 1936–1937* (1969); and *The Automobile under the Blue Eagle: Labor, Management, and the Automobile Manufacturing Code* (1963); Frank Cormier and William J. Eaton, *Reuther* (1970); Roger Keeran, *The Communist Party and the Auto Workers Unions* (1980); Nelson Lichtenstein, *Labor's War at Home: The CIO in World War II* (1982); Harvey A. Levenstein, *Communism, Anticommunism, and the CIO* (1981).

FRASER, Douglas Andrew   (1916–   ). Born in Glasgow, Scotland, on December 18, 1916; son of Douglas, an electrician, and Sara (Andrew) Fraser; married Winifred Davis, a psychology professor at Wayne State University, on July 28, 1967; two children; left school during his senior year at Chadsey High School in Detroit, Mich., and took a job on an automobile assembly line; after losing that job and a subsequent assembly line job for union organizing activities, he secured a permanent job as a metal finisher in the Chrysler Corporation's

DeSoto plant; joined Local 227 of the United Automobile, Aerospace and Agricultural Implement Workers of America (UAW) and by 1943 had been elected
president of the local; served for two years in the U.S. Army during World War
II, rising to the rank of sergeant; returning to the UAW at the time of an intense
internal struggle for power between factions loyal to R. J. Thomas (q.v.) and
Walter Reuther (q.v.), he sided with Thomas who was defeated; nevertheless,
Reuther was impressed by the young auto worker and union leader and appointed
him a UAW international representative in 1947; while working in the UAW's
Chrysler department, he was actively involved in negotiating a successful conclusion to a 104–day strike in 1950 and once again attracted the favorable
attention of UAW president Walter Reuther; became Reuther's administrative
assistant in 1951; elected co-director of UAW Region 1A in 1959 and as a
delegate-at-large to the executive board in 1962; negotiated a precedent-setting
contract with Chrysler in 1964 that included a wage increase, higher pension
benefits, longer vacations, and early retirement; won wage parity for American
Chrysler workers with Canadian workers in a contract negotiated in 1967; elected
a UAW vice-president in 1970; after the death of Reuther in May 1970, he
announced his candidacy for the UAW presidency but later withdrew his name
when it appeared that Leonard Woodcock (q.v.) had the support of a majority
on the UAW executive board; thereafter, he continued serving as one of six
UAW vice-presidents and, in that position, chaired the job training and development department, directed the progressional organizing, skilled trades, and
technical departments, and chaired the Michigan Community Action Program
Council, the political arm of the UAW; led a successful nine-day strike against
Chrysler in 1973, winning a comprehensive health program, increased retirement
benefits and restrictions on compulsory overtime; was elected UAW president
in 1977; became a member of the board of directors of the Chrysler Corporation
in 1980 as a result of extended contract negotiations during which the UAW
reduced its demands on the financially troubled corporation and agreed to join
with company officials in seeking government-guaranteed loans to revitalize the
once-powerful corporation; a resourceful and skilled negotiator whose popularity
among the union's rank and file permitted him to mediate acrimonious disputes
between black and white automobile workers as well as skilled and unskilled
workers; resigned from office in 1983 as required by the UAW constitution;
Who's Who in Labor (1976); *Biography News* (1975); *Time*, May 30, 1977; *The
New York Times*, September 10, 1964, May 20, 1977; *Current Biography* (October 1977).

FRASER, Harry Wilson   (1884–1950). Born in Topeka, Kans., June 7, 1884;
son of Lewis Peter, a salesman, and Lavara Virginia (Weltner) Fraser; Baptist;
married Lillian Elizabeth Spane on September 8, 1905; after attending the public
schools of Topeka, served as a clerk in the general offices of several different
railroads headquartered either in Topeka or in Pueblo, Colo., 1900–1907; promoted to conductor in 1909; joined Local 300 of the Order of Railway Conductors

of America (ORC) and served as the local's chairman of adjustment and as secretary of the general committee on adjustment for the Atchison, Topeka, and Santa Fe Railway; appointed secretary to the ORC president in 1929; became chief clerk in 1932, deputy president in 1934, vice-president in 1938, and president of the ORC in 1941; named a railroad labor member of the War Manpower Commission in 1943; became a trustee and secretary of the National Planning Association in 1945; elected chairman of the Railway Labor Executives' Association in 1947; served as a delegate-advisor to the 1944 International Labor Organization conference in Philadelphia and was a delegate to the 1947 and 1948 meetings of the Inland Transport Committee held in Geneva, Switzerland, and San Francisco, Calif., respectively; died in Chicago, Ill., May 13, 1950; *National Cyclopaedia of American Biography*, Vol. 39; *Railway Age*, Vol. 128; *Who's Who in Labor* (1946); *Labor*, May 20, 1950.

FRAYNE, Hugh   (1869–1934). Born in Scranton, Pa., November 8, 1869; son of Michael, an Irish immigrant, and Grace (Decon) Frayne; married Mary E. Cawley on November 8, 1888; three children; became a breaker boy in the anthracite mine fields of Pennsylvania at age 8 and continued in that employment for four years; apprenticed to a sheet-metal worker in 1882 and became a journeyman working at the trade until 1900; joined the Knights of Labor during the 1880s; became a charter member of the Amalgamated Sheet Metal Workers International Alliance in 1892 and served as a general vice-president from 1900 to 1904; appointed a general organizer of the American Federation of Labor (AFL) in 1901; placed in charge of the AFL's Philadelphia, Pa., office from 1907 to 1910, and of the New York office from 1910 until his death; served as the AFL fraternal delegate to the Canadian Trades and Labor Congress in 1908; became a vice-president and director of the National Committee on Prisons and Prison Labor and was an officer in various other public boards and agencies; was a close associate of AFL president Samuel Gompers (q.v.), and identified with the more conservative wing of the American labor movement; appointed chairman of the labor division of the War Industries Board during World War I and, as a result of his service, awarded the Distinguished Service Medal by Congress in 1923; was a nonpartisan in politics; authored several pamphlets on trade union subjects; died in New York City, July 13, 1934; Philip Taft, *The A.F. of L. in the Time of Gompers* (1957), and *The A.F. of L. from the Death of Gompers to the Merger* (1959); *Dictionary of American Biography*, Suppl. 1; *Who's Who in America, 1934–1935*.

FREY, John Philip   (1871–1957). Born in Mankato, Minn., February 24, 1871; son of Leopold, a manufacturer, and Julia Philomen (Beaudry) Frey; married Nellie Josephine Higgins on June 10, 1891; three children; received his education in the public schools of Mankato, Minn.; secured employment as an iron molder in Worcester, Mass., in 1887; elected president of the Worcester local of the International Molders and Foundry Workers Union of North America

(IMFWU) in 1893 and served until 1898; elected treasurer of the New England conference board of the IMFWU in 1898; elected a vice-president of the Massachusetts State Federation of Labor in 1899; became a vice-president of the IMFWU in 1900; served as an American Federation of Labor (AFL) fraternal delegate to the British Trades Union Congress in 1909, the Inter-Allied Labor and Socialist Conference in London in 1918, and the Pan-American Federation of Labor in 1921; served as president of the Norwood, Ohio, Board of Education, 1918–1922; elected president of the Ohio State Federation of Labor in 1924 and secretary-treasurer in 1927; served as chairman of the board of the National Bureau of Economic Research, 1918–1927, and as an executive board member of the Workers Education Bureau, 1923–1928; appointed to several government boards and agencies, including the Federal Commission to Investigate Scientific Management in 1927, the labor advisory board of the National Recovery Administration in 1933, and the Federal Commission on Apprentice Training and the shipbuilding stabilization committee of the War Production Board during World War II; served as a labor expert of the U.S. delegation to the 1927 International Economic Conference in Geneva; elected president of the metal trades department of the AFL in 1934, serving in that capacity until his retirement in 1950; served as a lieutenant colonel in the U.S. Army Specialist Reserve during World War II; was a conservative trade unionist, strongly supporting the apolitical, craft-conscious policies of the AFL; edited the *Iron Molders' Journal*, 1903–1927; was a Republican; authored several books, including *An American Molder in Europe* (1911), *The Labor Injunction* (1922), *Calamity of Prosperity* (1930), *Bakers Domination* (1933), *Calamity of Recovery* (1934), and *Craft Unions of Ancient and Modern Times* (1944); retired from union affairs in 1950; died in Washington, D.C., November 29, 1957; John P. Frey Papers, Library of Congress; Philip Taft, *The A.F. of L. from the Death of Gompers to the Merger* (1959); Frank T. Stockton, *The International Molders Union of North America* (1921); Walter Galenson, *The CIO Challenge to the AFL: A History of the American Labor Movement, 1935–1941* (1960); *National Cyclopaedia of American Biography*, Vol. 47.

FRIEDRICK, Jacob F.   (1892–1978). Born in Perjamos, Hungary (now Periam, Rumania), on January 31, 1892; father was a government woodsman and tanner; married Agnes J. Piechowiak in 1913; two children; after the death of his first wife in 1968 he married Eleanor Raasch in 1974; family emigrated to the United States in 1905, settling in Milwaukee, Wis., where he attended public schools; studied the machinist's trade at the Milwaukee Trade and Technical School; forced to leave school by the depression of 1907–1908; worked at International Harvester, 1909–1910, where he was injured on the job; worked at automotive and machine shops in Omaha, Neb., Milwaukee, Indianapolis, Ind., and Chicago, Ill., 1910–1913; joined Lodge 66 of the International Association of Machinists (IAM) in Milwaukee and in 1915 was elected secretary of Machinists District Board; elected Lodge 66 president in 1918; took an active role in the World War I-era labor unrest, on at least two occasions losing a job because of his involvement in strikes and demonstrations (1918 and 1919); elected business agent for IAM District Lodge No. 10 in 1919, which he held until 1929; helped establish the Milwaukee Labor College, a night school for workers, 1921–1922, and taught parliamentary law and public speaking; in 1925 he worked with John R. Commons (q.v.), Selig Perlman (q.v.), Elizabeth Brandeis, and others in establishing the School for Workers in Industry at the University of Wisconsin; helped Commons prepare a model unemployment compensation bill in 1920, a version of which was adopted by the Wisconsin legislature in 1932; named recording secretary of Federated Trades Council of Milwaukee in 1921; became labor editor and reporter for the *Milwaukee Leader* in 1929, serving until 1935; in that year, he became a general organizer for the Federated Trades Council; was American Federation of Labor regional director for Wisconsin, 1945–1951; served as secretary-treasurer, 1951–1959, and president, 1959–1969, of the Milwaukee County Labor Council; was a member of the Wisconsin Unemployment Advisory Committee, 1932–1974; was a member of the Socialist party, 1919–1942, and active in the Farmer-Labor Progressive Federation during the 1930s and 1940s; after World War II, he supported the Democratic party; was a member of the Wisconsin University Board of Regents, 1960–1969, serving as president during 1961–1962; urged the Milwaukee school board to promote racial integration in public schools in 1965 and thereafter worked through a local citizen's committee to improve race relations; died in Milwaukee on April 8, 1978; *Milwaukee Journal*, May 7–11, 1972, and April 8, 1978; *Milwaukee Labor Press*, April 13, 1978; *Wisconsin Labor AFL-CIO Bicentennial Edition, 1975–1976*; Thomas W. Gavett, *Development of the Labor Movement in Milwaukee* (1965).

Barbara Bartkowiak

FURUSETH, Andrew (Anders Andreassen Nilsen) (1854–1938). Born in Romedal, Hedmarken, Norway, March 12, 1854; son of Andreas, a farmer, and Marthe (Jensdatter) Nilsen; Protestant; never married; forced by the impoverished condition of his family to leave home at age 8; supported himself by working as a farm laborer while continuing his education; began working full-time in 1870 and, three years later, became a merchant seaman; after 1880, shipped out primarily from ports along the West Coast of the United States; joined and in 1887 became secretary of the Sailors' Union of the Pacific; became the legislative representative of seamen's unions in Washington, D.C., in 1894 and also served as a legislative representative of the American Federation of Labor (AFL); was an AFL fraternal delegate to the British Trades Union Congress in 1908; conducted a 21–year struggle to change the legal status of sailors, and saw enactment of the La Follette Seamen's Act of 1915 as the product of this struggle; became president of the International Seamen's Union in 1908 and served until his death in 1938; helped negotiate an end to the San Francisco, Calif., General Strike of 1934; refused to support a wildcat strike of West Coast seamen led by Joseph

Curran (q.v.), thus leading to the organization of the secessionist National Maritime Union of America in 1937; died in Washington, D.C., January 22, 1938; Silas B. Axtell, ed., *A Symposium on Andrew Furuseth* (1945); Paul S. Taylor, *The Sailors' Union of the Pacific* (1923); *Dictionary of American Biography*, Suppl. 2; Hyman G. Weintraub, *Andrew Furuseth: Emancipator of the Seamen* (1959); Library of Congress, *Andrew Furuseth, A Bibliographical List* (1942).

G

GAINOR, Edward Joseph (1870–1947). Born in Greencastle, Ind., August 1, 1870; son of a railroad roadmaster; Roman Catholic; married; one child; after graduating from high school, secured work as a puddler and heater in an iron rolling mill in 1889; joined Muncie, Ind., Lodge 4 of the Amalgamated Association of Iron, Steel, and Tin Workers and served as secretary of the lodge during 1890–1892; became a U.S. Postal Service letter carrier in 1897 and joined Muncie Branch 98 of the National Association of Letter Carriers (NALC); served on the national executive board of the NALC, 1901–1902; elected a vice-president of the NALC in 1905 and served until his election as president in 1914; acted as an American Federation of Labor (AFL) fraternal delegate to the British Trades Union Congress in 1924; elected an AFL vice-president and member of the executive council in 1935; served as NALC delegate to the annual conventions of the AFL, 1917–1943; retired NALC presidency in 1941; regarded legislation providing for reduced working hours, improved retirement benefits, and large increases in the NALC's membership as his major contributions; was a Democrat; served as a delegate to the National Democratic Convention of 1920; edited *The Postal Record* for several years; retired all union positions in 1943; died in Washington, D.C., November 10, 1947; William C. Doherty, *Mailman U.S.A.* (1960); *The American Federationist* (June 1941, December 1947); Solon De-Leon, ed., *The American Labor Who's Who* (1925); *The American Federation of Labor Weekly News-Service*, August 26, 1941.

GALARZA, Ernesto (1905–   ). Born in Jalcocotan, Nayarit, Mexico, August 15, 1905; son of migrant-worker parents; emigrated with his family to the United States at age 6; married Mae Taylor, a teacher, in December 1929; two children; after completing his primary and secondary school education in Sacramento, Calif., received the B.A. degree from Occidental College in 1927, the M.A. from Stanford University in 1929, and the Ph.D. from Columbia University in 1944; served as co-principal of Gardner School, Jamaica, Long Island, N.Y., 1932–1936; as a result of employment during his youth as a farm worker, cannery worker, and packing shed laborer, evidenced an early interest in the organization of agricultural laborers; served as specialist in education for the Pan-American Union, 1936–1946, and as chief of its division of labor and social information, 1940–1946; was director of research and education and a field organizer for the National Farm Labor Union in Florida, Louisiana, Texas, Arizona, and California, 1947–1955; served in a similar capacity for the National Agriculture Workers Union (NAWU), 1955–1960; led the strikes of San Joaquin tomato pickers in 1950 and Imperial Valley canteloupe pickers in 1951, exposing the evils of the wetback system; helped organize Louisiana sugar-cane workers and strawberry pickers, 1953–1954; waged a vigorous but fruitless campaign against the government functionaries, agricultural employers, and labor unions that supported or acquiesced in the passage of right-to-work laws restricting agricultural workers and that tolerated abuses of the *bracero* system; used a research grant from the Fund for the Republic to investigate the *bracero* program in 1955, and wrote *Strangers in Our Fields*, described as ''one of the outstanding successes of Galarza's career''; after serving in 1960 as an organizer for the Amalgamated Meatcutters and Butcher Workmen of North America, which had absorbed the NAWU into its newly created agricultural department, withdrew from the labor movement; led the San José Mexican-American community in demanding a Congressional investigation of the Chualar disaster (an accident in which 32 *braceros* were killed in a truck-train collision) in 1963; was a counsel to the House of Representatives' Committee on Education and Labor and in that capacity wrote a report on the *bracero* program that was later published as *Merchants of Labor*; served as program analyst of the Economic and Youth Opportunity Agency, Office of Economic Opportunity, in Los Angeles, Calif.; acted as a consultant to the government of Bolivia, the Ford Foundation, the Whitney Foundation, the U.S. Civil Rights Commission, and other bodies; chaired the National Committee of ''La Raza Unida''; held research and visiting professorships at Notre Dame University and San Jose State College; was appointed regents professor at the University of California, San Diego; authored *Spiders in the House and Workers in the Field* (1970), *Barrio Boy* (1971), and other works; Joan London and Henry Anderson, *So Shall Ye Reap: The Story of Cesar Chavez and the Farm Workers' Movement* (1970); *Who's Who in America, 1950–1951*.

Merl E. Reed

GARRETSON, Austin Bruce   (1856–1931). Born in Winterset, Iowa, September 14, 1856; son of Nathan, a lawyer, and Hannah Garretson; Society of Friends; married Marie Ream on September 2, 1878; three children; graduated from high school in Osceola, Iowa, then apprenticed to a wheelwright; obtained employment as a brakeman on a spur line of the Chicago, Burlington, and Quincy Railroad; promoted to conductor somewhat later and moved to Denison, Tex.; employed there by several railroads as a conductor; joined Division 53 of the Order of Railway Conductors (ORC) in 1884; elected grand senior conductor in

1887; elected grand chief conductor and president in 1906, serving until 1919; helped convert the ORC from a benevolent and fraternal organization into an economic-oriented trade union; chaired the committee of four operating railroad brotherhoods whose negotiations with management representatives eventually led to the enactment of the Adamson Act in 1917, establishing the eight-hour day for railroad workers; served on the Federal Commission on Industrial Relations, 1912–1915; after World War I, strongly advocated the Plumb Plan of government ownership of railroads; retired in 1919, but continued serving as an advisor to the organization until his death; edited the *Railway Conductor* for several years before his 1919 retirement; died in Cedar Rapids, Iowa, February 27, 1931; Edwin C. Robbins, *Railway Conductors: A Study in Organized Labor* (1914); *Dictionary of American Biography*, Suppl. 1; *Encyclopedia of Social Sciences*, Vol. 6.

GEORGE, Henry   (1839–1897). Born in Philadelphia, Pa., on September 2, 1839; son of Richard Samuel Henry, a book publisher and custom house clerk, and Catherine (Pratt Vallance) George, a school teacher; Methodist; married Annie Corsina Fox on December 3, 1861; four children; after a few years of education attained primarily in private schools, he left school at age 13 and became an errand boy for Samuel Asbury and Company; during the next several years, he traveled extensively first as a foremast boy on an East Indian freighter and then in the United States in search of employment; much of the latter time was spent on the West Coast; during these years of irregular employment, frequent destitution, and unsuccessful business ventures—usually either printing/publishing shops or mining speculations—he began to develop the ideas that would later be expanded in his highly influential writings; joined the Eureka (Calif.) Typographical Union in 1858; served consecutively as a printer, reporter, editorial writer, and managing editor of the *San Francisco Times*, 1866–1868; became the editor of the *Oakland Transcript*, a Democratic newspaper, in 1868, and the following year ran unsuccessfully for the California legislature as a Democrat; published *Our Land and Land Policy*, a pamphlet in which he anticipated the land, rent, and monopoly theories that he would later popularize in *Progress and Poverty* (1879); meanwhile, his pattern of irregular employment and unsuccessful publishing ventures continued; after the publication of *Progress and Poverty*, in which he sought to explain the existence of poverty in the midst of abundance, he spent much of his time espousing and promoting his idea of a ''single tax'' on unearned land values; after publication of *The Irish Land Question* in 1881, he traveled to Ireland as a correspondent for the *New York Irish World*; his writing soon gained him an international reputation and during the next several years he conducted frequent lecture tours in England and, in 1890, in Australia; was a candidate for mayor of New York City on a union labor ticket in 1884 and while losing to the Democratic candidate ran well ahead of the Republican candidate, Theodore Roosevelt; the single-tax reform became very popular during the late years of the nineteenth century and up to World

War I; students of Henry George clubs and single-tax leagues were organized throughout the country—most of them in working-class districts—to promote the reform but legislatures refused to consider the tax method, and efforts to get the proposal on the ballot through the initiative procedure were largely unsuccessful; George campaigned for William Jennings Bryan in 1896, and the following year, although in poor health, once again ran for mayor of New York City, this time as an independent Democrat; died during the campaign on October 2, 1897; also authored *Social Problems* (1883), *Protection or Free Trade* (1886), *The Science of Political Economy* (1897), *An Open Letter to the Pope* (1891), *The Condition of Labor* (1892), *A Perplexed Philosopher* (1892), and the autobiographical *The Life of Henry George* (1900); L. F. Post, *The Prophet of San Francisco: Personal Memories and Interpretations of Henry George* (1930); R. A. Sawyer, *Henry George and the Single Tax* (1926); *Dictionary of American Biography*, Vol. 7; Bernard Newton, "Henry George and Henry M. Hyndman: The Forging of an Untenable Alliance, 1882–83," *American Journal of Economics and Sociology* (1976); Will Lissner, "On the Centenary of Progress and Poverty," *American Journal of Economics and Sociology* (1979).

GEORGE, Leo E.   (1888–1967). Born in Medford, Wis., January 3, 1888; son of James, a farmer, and Mary H. (Atkins) George; Christian church; married Edith Simmons; three children; completed high school in Westfield, Pa., and later took courses at a teachers college; after entering the U.S. Postal Service in 1906, joined Local 1 of the National Federation of Post Office Clerks (NFPOC), formerly the Chicago Post Office Clerks' Union, a division of the United National Association of Post Office Clerks; elected financial secretary and a member of the executive board of Local 1 in 1918, serving until 1921; discharged from the postal service in 1920 for union activities and for publishing critical accounts of the postal service; later reinstated, but retired to work full time at union activities; served as a delegate to the Chicago Federation of Labor and the Illinois State Federation of Labor; elected vice-president of the NFPOC in 1921 and acting international president in 1923; elected general NFPOC president in 1923 and served in that capacity until 1956; served as president of the American Federation of Labor Government Employees Council; retired from union activities in 1956; died in Mount Rainier, Md., in November 1967; Karl Baarslag, *History of the National Federation of Post Office Clerks* (1945); *Who's Who in Labor* (1946); *AFL-CIO News* November 18, 1967.

GEORGINE, Robert A.   (1932–   ). Born in Chicago, Ill., on July 18, 1932; son of Silvio and Rose Georgine; Roman Catholic; married Mary Rita Greener in 1960; four children; attended DePaul Academy, Chicago, 1946–1950, DePaul University, 1950–1954, and the University of Illinois, 1954–1956; served in the U.S. Army, 1955–1957; became a journeyman with the Wood, Wire and Metal Lathers International Union (WWMLIU), Local 74, Chicago, in 1953; during the period 1956–1964, he served in a variety of offices in Local 74 including the presidency; appointed an international representative for the WWMLIU in 1964 and two years later became the assistant to the general president; was elected general president of the WWMLIU in 1930, serving for two years; elected secretary-treasurer of the building and construction trades department (BCTD), American Federation of Labor-Congress of Industrial Organizations (AFL-CIO), in 1971; after the retirement of the incumbent, Frank Bonadio (q.v.), in 1974, he was elected president of the BCTD; an active participant on several boards and agencies, he was a member of the Building Research Advisory Board, the construction advisory committee of the Federal Energy Administration, the Advisory Council on Employment Welfare and Pension Benefit Plans, the Collective Bargaining Committee in Construction, and the building technical advisory committee of the National Bureau of Standards; *AFL-CIO News*, May 11, 1974; *Who's Who in Labor* (1976).

GERMANO, Joseph Samuel   (1904–   ). Born in Chicago, Ill., February 12, 1904; son of Samuel Joseph, a railroad maintenance worker, and Maria (Albano) Germano; Roman Catholic; married Mary E. Alesia on April 15, 1923; two children; graduated from high school; employed as a steelworker for the Youngstown Sheet and Tube Company in South Chicago during the 1930s; helped organize and became president of Lodge 56, Amalgamated Association of Iron, Steel, and Tin Workers (AA); was a member of the AA rank-and-file faction preparing the way at the union's 1936 convention for cooperation with the Steel Workers Organizing Committee (SWOC) to unionize the industry; served as an organizer, 1936–1938, and as subdistrict director, 1938–1940, for the SWOC in the Chicago area; appointed director of United Steelworkers of America (USWA) District 31 in 1940; elected to that office in 1942 and reelected from 1945 through 1969; as director of the largest USWA district, became a powerful member of the international executive board; through his support, was instrumental in I. W. Abel's (q.v.) decision to run against President David J. McDonald (q.v.) in 1965; managed the Abel campaign that unseated McDonald; has been one of the most influential labor leaders in Illinois and has been a member of the Cook County Industrial Union Council and a vice-president of the state's American Federation of Labor-Congress of Industrial Organizations' council; has actively involved himself in political affairs, promoting USWA subdistricts as organizational bases for committees on political education activity in Chicago; has worked closely with Democratic party organizations in Cook County and Springfield, Ill., and has frequently supported liberal candidates, such as Paul Douglas, and liberal causes, such as preservation of the Indiana Dunes lakeshore; was a founding member of the USWA national civil rights committee, and has worked for the implementation of civil rights programs in Chicago; retired as director of District 31 in 1973; J. David Greenstone, *Labor in American Politics* (1969);

John Herling, *Right to Challenge: People and Power in the Steelworkers Union* (1972); *Who's Who in Labor* (1946); *Who's Who in the Midwest, 1972–1973*.

Donald G. Sofchalk

GERMER, Adolph F. (1881–1966). Born in Welan, Germany, January 15, 1881; son of a coal miner; Lutheran; married Vivian Marks; no children; attended public and Lutheran parochial schools in Braceville, Ill., and studied with the International Correspondence School and La Salle Extension University; emigrated to the United States in 1888, settling in Illinois; began working at age 11 as a coal miner at Staunton, Ill.; joined the United Mine Workers of America (UMWA) in 1894; elected secretary-treasurer of UMWA Local 728 in 1906 and state legislative committeeman and vice-president, Belleville Subdistrict of District 12, UMWA, in 1907; served as secretary-treasurer of Belleville Subdistrict, 1908–1912; was a UMWA international representative in the Colorado coal strike of 1913–1914; elected vice-president of District 12 in 1915, but expelled from the union a year later; joined the Socialist party in 1900, and served as national secretary of the party, 1916–1919; was the only prominent Socialist among the Illinois miners to sign the party's anti-war declaration; convicted along with four party colleagues under the Espionage Act for obstructing the draft and sentenced to 20 years imprisonment in 1919, but saw the U.S. Supreme Court reverse the decision two years later on a technicality; served as a national organizer for the Socialist party, 1919–1920, and as secretary of the Massachusetts Socialist party in 1922; while working in the California oilfields, joined and served as international organizer for the Oil Field, Gas Well, and Refinery Workers Union, 1923–1925; was a Socialist party organizer in 1925; signed the February 15, 1930, call for the Springfield convention of the Reorganized United Mine Workers of America and elected vice-president of the organization; did most of the work for the new union, speaking in Indiana, Ohio, West Virginia, and Illinois because of President Alexander Howat's (q.v.) alcoholism; was physically attacked by John L. Lewis's (q.v.) supporters at Royalton, Ill., on April 18, 1930; edited the *Rockford* (Ill.) *Labor News*, 1931–1935; through the intervention of John L. Lewis, was appointed labor representative on the National Recovery Administration Regional Compliance Board in Chicago, Ill., in 1934; named by Lewis as the Congress of Industrial Organizations' (CIO) first field representative in November 1935; between then and March 1937, helped organize auto workers, rubber workers, and oil workers; helped establish the United Rubber Workers' journal, *The Rubber Worker*; served as regional director of the Michigan CIO, 1937–1939; founded Michigan labor's Nonpartisan League, the CIO's political arm; founded the Michigan Industrial Union Council, the CIO's state labor federation, in 1938 and twice elected its president; established the *Michigan CIO News*; appointed regional director of the New York CIO in 1939 and later served as regional director for the CIO in the Rocky Mountain and Pacific states; died in Rockford, Ill., May 26, 1966; Adolph F. Germer Papers, State Historical Society of Wisconsin; Lorin Lee Cary, "Institutionalized Conservatism in the

Early C.I.O.: Adolph Germer, a Case Study,'' *Labor History* (Fall 1972); John
H. M. Laslett, *Labor and the Left: A Study of Socialism and Radical Influences
in the American Labor Movement, 1881–1924* (1970); Irving Bernstein, *The
Lean Years: A History of the American Worker, 1920–1933* (1960); *United Mine
Workers Journal*, June 15, 1966; Solon DeLeon, ed., *The American Labor Who's
Who* (1925); *The New York Times*, May 28, 1966; Lorin Lee Cary, "Adolph
Germer and the 1890's Depression," *Illinois State Historical Society Journal*
(1975); Melvyn Dubofsky and Warren Van Tine, *John L. Lewis: A Biography*
(1977).

John W. Hevener

GIBBONS, Harold J. (1910–   ). Born in Taylor, Pa., April 10, 1910;
son of an Irish immigrant, Patrick Thomas, a coal miner, and Bridget Gibbons;
married Ann Cutler on September 8, 1938; two children; quit school before
finishing high school but later took correspondence courses; after the death of
his father in 1926, moved with his family (he was the youngest of 23 children)
to Chicago, Ill.; worked there during the next five years as a cook, a ware-
houseman, and a construction laborer; won a summer scholarship to the University of Wisconsin's School for Workers in 1933; returned to Chicago later
that year as a teacher in one of the workers' education projects sponsored by
the Works Progress Administration (WPA); after joining the American Federation
of Teachers (AFT), organized WPA teachers in Chicago into an AFT local; was
elected an AFT vice-president in 1934; became a Congress of Industrial Organizations' (CIO) organizer in 1936 and was instrumental in efforts to organize
Chicago taxicab drivers; joined the CIO Textile Workers Organizing Committee
in 1938 and became a Midwest organizer; joined St. Louis Local 543 of the
United Retail, Wholesale and Department Store Employees of America
(URWDSE) in 1940 and a year later became its secretary-treasurer; served the
URWDSE as an international representative, as a director of the St. Louis Joint
Council, and as a member of the international executive board; was a member
of the Region 7 panel of the War Labor Board during World War II; was
discontented with the national administration of the URWDSE; thus, having built
Local 543 into a large and influential St. Louis union, merged it with Local 688
of the International Brotherhood of Teamsters, Chauffeurs, Warehousemen and
Helpers of America (IBT) in 1949; was elected secretary-treasurer of Local 688
and president of Teamsters' Joint Council 13; became secretary-treasurer of the
newly organized Central Conference of Teamsters in 1954; elected an IBT vice-
president and became an executive assistant to IBT president James R. Hoffa
(q.v.) in 1957; became director of the Central Conference of Teamsters in 1971;
as a liberal, reform-minded union leader, has often antagonized the more conservative members of the IBT executive board, especially through his endorsement of the candidacy of George McGovern on the Democratic party ticket in
1972; was relieved of his directorship of the Central Conference of Teamsters
in 1972 as a consequence of this antagonism; was a Socialist early in his career,

but later described himself as an independent, although usually supporting liberal Democratic candidates; Arnold Rose, *Union Solidarity: The Internal Cohesion of a Labor Union* (1952); Walter Sheridan, *The Fall and Rise of Jimmy Hoffa* (1972); Ralph C. James and Estelle D. James, *Hoffa and the Teamsters: A Study of Union Power* (1965); *The Nation*, March 23, 1957; Steven Brill, *The Teamsters* (1978).

GIBSON, Everett G.   (1903–   ). Born in Wallingford, Conn., December 28, 1903; son of George Gluster, a laundryman, and Clara (Stearns) Gibson; Reformed Episcopalian; married Katherine Lewis on June 10, 1928; one child; completed grammar school in Huntington, N.Y.; secured employment with the U.S. Postal Service, then joined Local 2 of the National Federation of Post Office Motor Vehicle Employees (NFPOMVE) in 1925; served as Local 2's president for eight years and as president of the Greater New York Conference of Affiliated Postal Employees for three years; served as national NFPOMVE vice-president and secretary prior to his election as national president in 1945; became the NFPOMVE legislative representative in Washington, D.C., in 1945; a Republican; Karl Baarslag, *History of the National Federation of Post Office Clerks* (1945); William C. Doherty, *Mailman U.S.A.* (1960); *Who's Who in Labor* (1946).

GIBSON, John Willard   (1910–   ). Born in Harrisburg, Ill., August 23, 1910; son of John Joseph, an English immigrant coal miner, and Nellie (Guard) Gibson; Methodist; married Jennie Pacotti on May 12, 1934; two children; after attending public schools in several cities, entered the coal mines of Taylorville, Ill., at age 16; worked alternately during the next several years in the Detroit, Mich., automobile shops and the Taylorville mines; joined the United Mine Workers of America in 1926; became a salesman for a Detroit dairy company in 1934 and soon began organizing Local 83 of the United Dairy Workers; joined the United Retail, Wholesale and Department Store Employees of America in 1937; attended Wayne State University during 1936–1937; served as vice-president of the Michigan State Industrial Union Council (IUC), Congress of Industrial Organizations (CIO), and assistant CIO director for the state of Michigan, 1937–1938; elected secretary-treasurer of the Michigan IUC in 1939, serving until 1941; appointed chairman of the Michigan Department of Labor and Industry in 1941, serving until his election as president of the Michigan IUC in 1943; served during World War II on the Michigan division of the War Production Board, the Office of Price Administration, and the War Manpower Commission; was a member of the Michigan Committee for Fair Employment Practices; appointed a special assistant to U.S. Secretary of Labor Louis B. Schwellenbach in 1945, thus beginning a career in government service; became one of three assistant secretaries of labor in the reorganized Department of Labor in 1946; appointed chairman of the Displaced Persons Commission in 1950; authored two handbooks, *Workmen's Compensation* and *Industrial Safety*, a number of pamphlets; politically a Democrat; *Current Biography* (1947); *Who's Who in Labor* (1946); *Who's Who in America, 1950–1951*.

GILBERT, Henry E.   (1906–   ). Born in Ethel, Mo., October 5, 1906; son of Henry H., a farmer and delivery wagon operator, and Irene R. (Windle) Gilbert; Presbyterian; married Alice Marie Iman on December 26, 1925; one child; graduated from high school in 1925 and attended Cleveland College in 1943; secured employment in the signal department of the Atchison, Topeka, and Santa Fe Railroad in 1925; became a locomotive fireman in 1926 and served in that capacity on the Alton Railroad during 1926–1935; joined Chicago, Ill., Lodge 707 of the Brotherhood of Locomotive Firemen and Enginemen (BLFE) in 1927 and served successively as secretary-treasurer, as a member of the grievance committee, as a general organizer, and, in 1931, as president of Lodge 707; became a locomotive engineman in 1935; was a member of the executive board of the BLFE legislative board for the state of Illinois; served as an assistant in the office of the BLFE president, 1942–1946; became a member of the BLFE executive board in 1944 and three years later elected vice-president; elected BLFE president in 1953; during his incumbency, led a long struggle to prevent the elimination of firemen in diesel locomotives; became assistant president of the newly organized United Transportation Union in 1969; retired union positions in 1972; Brotherhood of Locomotive Firemen and Enginemen, "Historical Sketch, 1873–1947," *Brotherhood of Locomotive Firemen and Enginemen's Magazine* (1947); *Time*, July 26, 1963; *Who's Who in Railroading* (1959).

GILLMORE, Frank   (1867–1943). Born in New York City, May 14, 1867; son of Parker, an author and naturalist, and Emily (Thorne) Gillmore; Episcopalian; married Laura MacGillivray on July 30, 1896; two children; educated in England at the Chiswick Collegiate School; launched an acting career in 1879 and played for three years in the provinces of England; performed on the London stage for five years; returned to the United States in 1892 after having acquired a reputation as an excellent leading man; participated in the 1912 organizational meetings resulting in the creation of Actors' Equity Association (AEA); became a member of the board of governors and chairman of the contract committee of AEA in 1913; elected to the newly created office of AEA executive secretary in 1918; as a proponent of affiliation with the American Federation of Labor, actively involved in chartering the Associated Actors and Artists of America (AAAA) in 1919; led a successful 30–day strike of actors in 1919; elected president of AAAA, AEA, and Chorus Equity in 1928; retired as president of AEA and Chorus Equity in 1937 to devote full time to the affairs of AAAA; was one of the principal architects of unionization among actors and artists in the United States and is credited with having achieved significant improvements in the wage scales and working conditions of performers; was a Democrat; died in New York City, March 29, 1943; Murray Ross, *Stars and Strikes: Unionization* *of Hollywood* (1941); Alfred Harding, *The Revolt of the Actors* (1929); *The American Federationist* (April 1943).

GILMARTIN, Daniel   (1911–1981). Born in Ireland on September 22, 1911; son of Roger, a tailor, and Margaret (Judge) Gilmartin, a homemaker; Roman Catholic; married Kathleen Gaffney, a homemaker, in 1935; six children; obtained his elementary and secondary education in Ireland before immigrating to the United States; settling in New York City, he took a job with the Independent Subway System and was involved in the efforts to organize the Transport Workers Union of America (TWU) in 1934; affiliated with the New York City Local 100, TWU, he rose through various union posts from shop steward to section chairman; participated in a sit-down strike in the early 1940s to win seniority rights; was elected to Local 100's executive board in 1945; became a full-time TWU organizer in 1948; was elected vice-president of Local 100 in 1950; served as his union's legislative representative in Albany, N.Y., during the 1950s when he frustrated efforts by TWU opponents to divide TWU's jurisdiction into smaller craft unions; also helped achieve social security coverage for Transport Authority workers; elected an international vice-president of TWU in 1955; elected president of Local 100 in 1960; led the union in the successful 1966 New York City transit strike which paralyzed public transportation for 12 days and resulted in his arrest, along with eight other union leaders, for violating New York's Condon-Wadlin Law prohibiting strikes by public employees; an active participant in the civil rights movement of the 1960s, he marched in Selma, Ala., during the protests there in 1965; an aggressive negotiator for improved benefits and working conditions, he was also credited with having "the sense of humor of a leprechaun"; a Democrat, he served as a presidential elector in New York in 1964; retired as president of Local 100 in 1974 but retained his position as a UTW vice-president; died in Venice, Fla., on September 15 1981; *Who's Who in Labor* (1976); *The New York Times*, September 16, 1981.

GINGOLD, David Reuben   (1896–1980). Born in Volcovisk, Russian Poland, on December 10, 1896; son of Jacob, a storekeeper, and Sylvia Gingold, a homemaker; Jewish; married Sarah, a homemaker, in 1914; three children; attended elementary and high school in Volcovisk before immigrating to the United States; joined Local 20, Waterproof Garment Workers Union, International Ladies' Garment Workers' Union (ILGWU), in 1913; elected to several Local 20 offices, including the executive board in 1922, vice-chairman in 1923, and manager in 1924, a position he held until 1930; served as an ILGWU international vice-president, 1925–1929; was the ILGWU's Pennsylvania state supervisor and then served as an ILGWU general organizer, 1933–1935; appointed superintendent of the ILGWU's cotton garment and miscellaneous trades department in 1935, serving until 1943; appointed director of the ILGWU's Northeast department in 1943 and two years later was elected an international vice-president; was credited with building the Northeast department into the

ILGWU's largest department; retired union positions in 1977; served as an officer in numerous Jewish organizations, including Workmen's Circle, the Jewish Labor Committee, the National Committee for Labor Israel, and the American ORT Federation; was associated with the New York Liberal party; died in New York City on December 17, 1980; *Justice* (December 1980); *Who's Who in Labor* (1946, 1976); *The New York Times*, December 18, 1980; David R. Gingold Interview, ILGWU Archives.

GIOVANNITTI, Arturo   (1884–1959). Born in Campobasso, Italy, January 7, 1884; son of a physician; married; three children; after attending college, emigrated to the United States at age 16; worked at various manual and clerical jobs until 1905; rejected his Roman Catholic heritage and attended a Protestant seminary; went to New York City ca. 1908 and became secretary of the Italian Socialist Federation and editor of its newspaper, *Il Proletario*; began to write poetry during this period; concerned about the fate of Italian workers, became an advocate of revolutionary syndicalism and joined the Industrial Workers of the World (IWW) in 1912 to help in the great Lawrence, Mass., textile strike; was a brilliant orator with a romantic air, and proved very effective as a leader of the immigrant strikers; jailed on charges of plotting the murder of a striker; while in jail, penned "The Walker," a brilliant piece of verse that made him famous as the workers' poet; eventually acquitted of the murder charge along with his colleague, Joseph Ettor (q.v.), after an international defense campaign elicited the support of even American Federation of Labor unionists; helped lead the ill-fated Akron tire strike of 1913; involved with several top Wobbly organizers in protest against William Haywood's (q.v.) centralizing policy, and thus resigned from the IWW in 1916; indicted the next year as part of a U.S. government crackdown on the IWW, but saw his case dropped in 1919; continued to work for the welfare of immigrant workers during the 1920s as an organizer for the International Ladies' Garment Workers' Union and as foreign language editor of *Advance*, the Amalgamated Clothing Workers' journal; was a founder, in 1923, of the Anti-Fascist Alliance of America that exposed and denounced Mussolini's regime; continued as an active Socialist party leader and unionist, often speaking at labor rallies, until his health failed in the 1940s; died in New York City, December 31, 1959; see *The Collected Poems of Arturo Giovannitti* (1962); Solon DeLeon, ed., *The American Labor Who's Who* (1925); Joyce L. Kornbluh, *Rebel Voices: An I.W.W. Anthology* (1964); Luciana J. Iorizzo and Salvatore Mondello, *The Italian-Americans* (1971), *Dictionary of American Biography*, Suppl. 6.

Donald G. Sofchalk

GIVENS, Paul A.   (1891–1968). Born in Indianapolis, Ind., October 11, 1891; son of Albert S. and Anna E. Givens; married Martha C. Prather on September 11, 1911; one child; after completing a high school education, became an apprentice stone cutter and in 1909 joined the Indianapolis local of the Journeymen

252   GLEASON, THOMAS WILLIAM

Stone Cutters Association of North America (JSCA); served his local union in several capacities and also actively involved in the Indianapolis Central Labor Union and Building Trades Council; elected JSCA secretary and general president in 1937, serving in that capacity until 1957; was a JSCA delegate to the national conventions of the American Federation of Labor, 1937–1957, and served as a member of several AFL committees; served during World War II as a member of the Sixth Regional Panel of the War Labor Board; retired union positions in 1957; died in Indianapolis, Ind., in September 1968; *Who's Who in Labor* (1946); *AFL-CIO News*, September 21, 1968.

GLEASON, Thomas William   (1900–   ). Born in New York City, November 8, 1900; son of Thomas W., a dockworker, and Mary Ann (Quinn) Gleason; Roman Catholic; married Emma Martin in 1923; three children; quit school in the seventh grade at age 15 to begin work on the New York docks; joined the International Longshoremen's Association (ILA) in 1919; after having risen to the position of dock superintendent, discharged in 1932 for honoring a union picket line and returned to the waterfront as a longshoreman and checker; appointed business manager of ILA Checkers' Local 1 in 1934 and later elected president of the local; appointed a full-time ILA organizer in 1947; often found himself in opposition to the policies and decisions of ILA president Joseph P. Ryan (q.v.); was thus fired frequently from his union positions, only to be rehired because of rank-and-file pressures; participated in the 1951 strike that tied up the port of New York and precipitated a governmental investigation of waterfront racketeering; as a result of the corruption revealed by these investigations the ILA was expelled from the American Federation of Labor (AFL) and ILA president Ryan resigned; after his friend William V. Bradley replaced him, Ryan was appointed to the newly created office of general organizer; became an ILA vice-president and elected president of the ILA's Atlantic Coast District in 1961; elected ILA president in 1963; appointed to the Maritime Advisory Committee in 1964; led a successful strike of longshoremen on the Atlantic and Gulf port docks in 1965; served as a member of the Joint Maritime Committee and the New York City Council of Port Direction and Promotion; became an AFL-Congress of Industrial Organizations vice-president and executive council member in 1969; a Democrat; Maud Russell, *Men along the Shore* (1966); Charles P. Larrowe, *Harry Bridges: The Rise and Fall of Radical Labor in the U.S.* (1972); *Current Biography* (1966).

GOLD, Ben   (1898–   ). Born in Bessarabia, Russia, September 8, 1898; son of Israel, a watchmaker and jeweler, and Sarah (Droll) Gold; Jewish; married Sadie Algus in 1929; emigrated to the United States in 1910 and, after working for a short time at a variety of occupations, was employed as an operator in a fur shop; joined the Furriers Union of the United States and Canada in 1912 (which became the International Fur Workers Union of the United States and Canada [IFWU] the following year), and later the same year became an assistant shop chairman during a furriers' strike; while working as an operator, attended the Manhattan Preparatory School at night in order to pursue a frustrated ambition to enter law school; joined the Socialist party in 1916; elected to the New York Furriers' Joint Board in 1919; affiliated with the Communist faction after the 1919 split in the Socialist party; was a leader of IFWU's left wing and was suspended from the union in 1924; reinstated later in the year in a unity effort; served as the manager of the New York Furriers' Joint Board, 1925–1929; was one of the leaders of a largely unsuccessful general strike of New York fur workers in 1926; along with other members of the New York Joint Board, was expelled from the IFWU as a Communist after the general strike; elected secretary of the Communist-organized Needle Trades Workers Industrial Union in 1928; in 1935 reinstated in IFWU after it and the Fur Workers Industrial Union division of the Needle Trades Workers Industrial Union merged; elected manager of the New York Fur Workers Joint Council in 1935 and served until 1937 when he was elected president of the IFWU; led IFWU into the CIO in 1937; in 1939 became the president of the International Fur and Leather Workers Union of the United States and Canada (IFLWU), created by the merger of the National Leather Workers Association and the IFWU; supported the candidacy of Henry A. Wallace for president of the United States in 1948; after the IFLWU was expelled from the CIO as a Communist-dominated union, announced his resignation from the Communist party in 1950 in order to comply with the non-Communist provisions of the Taft-Hartley Act; indicted for perjury in 1954 in connection with his non-Communist affidavit; gave up his leadership position when the IFLWU merged with the Amalgamated Meat Cutters and Butcher Workmen of North America in 1955; ran for the New York State Assembly in 1931 and 1936 and for president of the New York Board of Aldermen in 1933 on the Communist party ticket; Ben Gold Papers, Catherwood Library, Cornell University; Philip S. Foner, *The Fur and Leather Workers Union: A Story of Dramatic Struggles and Achievement* (1950); Max M. Kampelman, *The Communist Party vs. the C.I.O.: A Study in Power Politics* (1957); *Who's Who in Labor* (1946); Harvey A. Levenstein, *Communism, Anticommunism, and the CIO* (1981); Bert Cochran, *Labor and Communism: The Conflict that Shaped American Unions* (1977).

GOLDBERG, Arthur Joseph   (1908–   ). Born in Chicago, Ill., August 8, 1908; son of Joseph and Rebecca (Perlstein) Goldberg; Jewish; married Dorothy Kurgans on July 18, 1931; two children; attended the public schools of Chicago and studied at Crane Junior College of City College of Chicago, 1924–1926; while attending school, worked as a delivery boy for a Chicago shoe factory and labored with construction gangs; received the B.S.L. degree from Northwestern University in 1929, and during the same year was admitted to the Illinois bar; served as editor-in-chief of the *Illinois Law Review*, 1929–1930; was associated with the firm of Kamfner, Horowitz, Halligan, and Daniels, 1929–1931; earned the J.D. degree from Northwestern University in 1930; was an associate lawyer with Pritzker and Pritzker of Chicago, 1931–1933; opened his own law office in 1933; was a professor of law at the John Marshall Law School, 1939–1948; served as a special assistant in the Office of Strategic Services in 1942, and the following year was commissioned a captain in the U.S. Army, serving until 1945, when discharged with the rank of major; was a partner in the law office of Goldberg and Devoe, 1945–1947, and in 1947 became a senior partner in the law firm of Goldberg, Devoe, Shadur, and Mikva; became general counsel for the Congress of Industrial Organizations (CIO) and the United Steelworkers of America (USWA) in 1948; devoted considerable time and energy to the legal ramifications growing out of the Taft-Hartley Act; was one of the principal figures involved in the unity negotiations leading to the American Federation of Labor (AFL)-CIO merger in 1955; after the merger, served as a special counsel for the AFL-CIO; during David McDonald's (q.v.) USWA presidency, Goldberg assumed more and more of the basic decision-making power within the international union; was appointed U.S. Secretary of Labor by President John F. Kennedy in 1961; most important contributions were the fight against unemployment, creation of the Area Redevelopment Act of 1961, increasing the minimum wage, reorganization of the Office of Manpower Administration, formation of the President's Advisory Committee on Labor Management Policies, and work to eliminate racial discrimination in employment; appointed to the U.S. Supreme Court in 1962, serving until 1965 when appointed U.S. Ambassador to the United Nations; returned to private law practice in 1968 and ran unsuccessfully for governor of New York in 1970; authored *AFL-CIO: Labor United* (1956); Arthur J. Goldberg Papers, John F. Kennedy Library; John Herling, *Right to Challenge: People and Power in the Steelworkers Union* (1972); Joseph C. Goulden, *Meany* (1972); *Current Biography* (1949).

GOLDBLATT, Louis   (1910–   ). Born in New York City on June 5, 1910; son of Boris, a carpenter, and Tillie (Miller) Goldblatt, a garment maker; married Theresa Jaffe in 1940; three children; after graduating from Morris High School in New York City in 1926, he attended the College of the City of New York, 1926–1927, the University of California, Los Angeles, 1931, and the University of California, Berkeley, 1931–1933, from which he earned a B.A. before entering graduate school; with only a thesis required before completing his Ph.D., he dropped out of school and went to Hollywood, Calif., where he attempted to organize an industrial union in the motion picture industry; moved back to San Francisco in 1934 and took a warehouse job, joined Local 38-44 of the International Longshoremen's and Warehousemen's Union (ILWU), and became active in union affairs; after being discharged repeatedly for union activities, he was elected chairman of the ILWU's strike strategy committee in 1936; was appointed Congress of Industrial Organizations (CIO) director for northern California in 1937; the same year he was elected vice-president of Local 38-44, 1937–1940; after the organization of the California State Industrial Union Council, CIO, he was elected secretary, 1938–1941; returned to the ILWU as a staff organizer in 1942, working primarily in Chicago and New York; was elected international secretary-treasurer of the ILWU in 1943; served as secretary of the committee on maritime unity, 1946–1947; was one of the few California trade unionists to oppose the resettlement of Japanese-Americans during World War II, a position that was enormously valuable to the ILWU's successful organizing efforts in Hawaii; after the retirement of the union's controversial president, Harry Bridges (q.v.) in 1979, he was elected international president of the ILWU; an intellectual with a broad social vision, he had maintained a complementary, if not entirely comfortable, relationship with the volatile Bridges from the late 1930s; *Who's Who in Labor* (1976); Charles Larrowe, *Harry Bridges: The Rise and Fall of Radical Labor in the U.S.* (1972).

GOLDEN, Clinton Strong   (1888–1961). Born in Pottsville, Pa., November 16, 1888; son of Lazarus, a Baptist minister, and Lucy (Strong) Golden; married Dorothy Cleve on April 23, 1923; one child; when his father died in 1900, went to work in an iron mine and thus his formal education was ended; apprenticed as a machinist, but later worked several years as a railroad fireman and became active in the Brotherhood of Locomotive Firemen and Engineers; was a full-time representative for the International Association of Machinists, 1919–1922; served on the board of directors of Brookwood Labor College, 1923–1930, and as its field representative and business manager; helped found the Conference for Progressive Labor Action to promote industrial unionization; was an Amalgamated Clothing Workers of America organizer during 1933; served as senior mediator with the Pennsylvania Department of Labor and Industry in 1934; was appointed as regional director for the National Labor Relations Board in 1935 and prepared the unfair labor charge that culminated in the U.S. Supreme Court's historic *Jones and Laughlin* decision; was appointed director of the important northeastern region of the Steel Workers Organizing Committee (SWOC) in 1936; was the only major SWOC leader who had not been affiliated with the United Mine Workers of America, but was close to SWOC chairman Philip Murray (q.v.) and directed SWOC during Murray's illness in 1941; at the founding convention of the United Steelworkers of America (USWA) in 1942, was influential in the creation of an international executive board of regionally elected members; elected by the convention as an assistant to the international president (later vice-president); served as vice-chairman of both the War Production Board and the War Manpower Commission during World War II; was one of the few labor intellectuals with real influence in the trade union movement; believed that unions should play a greater role in socioeconomic affairs and tried to persuade management and organized labor that unions should share responsibility for maximizing productivity and participate in the distribution of profits; resigned as USWA vice-president in 1946; named chief labor advisor to the U.S. Mission to Aid Greece in 1947; served as consultant on European labor to the Economic Cooperation Administration; appointed executive director of the Harvard University trade union program and continued to lecture at Harvard and at many

labor education institutes until his retirement in 1959; avoided intra-union fac-
tionalism and was an independent in politics; co-authored *The Dynamics of
Industrial Democracy* (1942), and numerous articles; died in Philadelphia, Pa.,
June 12, 1961; Clinton S. Golden Papers, Pennsylvania State University, Labor
Archives; Thomas R. Brooks, *Clint: A Biography of a Labor Intellectual* (1978);
Robert R. R. Brooks, *As Steel Goes, . . . Unionism in a Basic Industry* (1940);
Current Biography (1948); Lloyd Ulman, *The Government of the Steelworkers'
Union* (1962).

Donald G. Sofchalk

GOLDFINGER, Nathaniel   (1916–1976). Born in New York City on August
20, 1916; son of Leo, a men's clothing worker, and Lena (Francis) Goldfinger,
a homemaker; Jewish; married Elizabeth Gordon, a secretary, in 1954; two
children; received the B.S. from the City College of New York (CCNY) in 1938
and took graduate courses at CCNY, New York University, the New School for
Social Research, and American University; served as research director for the
United Paperworkers of America, 1944–1950; appointed associate director of
research and secretary of the committee on economic policy for the Congress
of Industrial Organizations (CIO) in 1950; after the merger of the American
Federation of Labor (AFL) and the CIO in 1955, he was appointed economist
for the AFL-CIO department of research; was appointed assistant director of the
department in 1958 and, in 1963, became director; was a member of the advisory
committee of the Export-Import Bank, 1964–1969; was a member of President
Lyndon Johnson's Special Committee on East-West Trade in 1965; was a member
of the American Newspaper Guild, the American Economic Association, the
executive committee of the Joint Council on Economic Education, 1963–1976,
the National Bureau of Economic Research, 1963–1976, and, in 1974, he was
elected president of the Industrial Relations Research Association; served on
numerous government committees and panels and represented the AFL-CIO in
testimony before congressional committees; often referred to as ''labor's top
economist''; died in Silver Spring, Md., on July 22, 1976; *Who's Who in Labor*
(1976); *AFL-CIO News*, July 13, 1976.

GOLDMAN, Emma   (1869–1940). Born in Kovno, Lithuania, on June 27,
1869; daughter of Abraham, an impoverished merchant, and Taube Goldman;
Jewish; her marriage to Jacob Kershner in 1887 ended in divorce as did their
subsequent remarriage; married James Colton, a Welsh miner, in 1924 in order
to obtain English citizenship; was sent to Konigsberg, Prussia, in 1877 to live
with her maternal grandmother and received three years of formal education
there; moved with her family to St. Petersburg in 1882 where she went to work
in a glove factory to help support her family; emigrated with her sister to the
United States in 1885; settled in Rochester, N.Y., where she began working in
a clothing factory; also worked in a corset factory in New Haven, Conn., for a
time; disturbed by the injustices perpetrated at the Chicago, Ill., Haymarket

trials, she began to read socialist and anarchist literature avidly; became a devotee of *Die Freiheit*, a New York anarchist paper edited by Johann Most (q.v.), and in 1889 moved to New York City and joined Most and Alexander Berkman (with whom she was destined to have a long relationship), a young Russian anarchist who was later convicted of the attempted assassination of Henry C. Frick; meanwhile, she fully developed her latent talents as a public speaker and soon became a fixture on the platform of radical meetings; when she told a mass meeting of unemployed workers in New York to take bread if it was not given them, she was arrested for incitement to riot, convicted, and sentenced to a year in Blackwell's Island prison; after serving her prison sentence, she resumed her radical activities; toured England, Scotland, and Vienna in 1895, lecturing frequently and studying nursing at the Allgemeine Krankenhaus in Vienna—pursuing an interest she had developed in prison; upon her return to the United States, she once again participated in radical activities, speaking all over the United States; traveled to Europe again in 1899 where she met with numerous anarchist leaders; secured employment as a nurse upon her return to the United States in 1900; managed the lecture tour of the famous Russian anarchist Peter Kropotkin in the United States in 1901; founded and edited the anarchist monthly journal, *Mother Earth*, 1906–1917; continued to be a popular lecturer on radical causes, European literature, and theatre (of which she was rapidly becoming a nationally recognized authority), and, after 1916, birth control; after the outbreak of World War I in Europe, she quickly became involved in anti-preparedness, anti-war activities and in June 1917 was arrested and charged with obstructing the draft; as a result she served a two-year prison term; shortly after her release, federal authorities ordered her deportation to Russia, which was carried out in January 1920; quickly became disillusioned with the Soviet Union and spent the next several years traveling around Europe, living in different countries while lecturing and writing; the outbreak of civil war in Spain, like a magnet, attracted her to the loyalist cause; "Red Emma," "the most dangerous woman in the world," visited the United States only once, briefly during 1934, after her deportation; authored numerous books and articles including her autobiographical *Living My Life* (1931) as well as such books as *My Disillusionment in Russia* (1923), *What I Believe* (1908), *The Social Significance of the Modern Drama* (1914), and *My Further Disillusionment in Russia* (1924); died in London on May 14, 1940, and was buried near the graves of the Haymarket martyrs in Chicago; *Dictionary of American Biography*, Suppl. 2; Charles A. Madison, *Critics and Crusaders: A Century of American Protest* (1947); Rudolf Rocker, *Pioneers of American Freedom* (1949).

GOMPERS, Samuel   (1850–1924). Born in London, England, January 27, 1850; son of Solomon, a cigarmaker, and Sara (Rood) Gompers; Jewish; married Sophia Julian on January 28, 1866, and after her death Gertrude Gleaves Neuscheler in 1921; 12 or 14 children; attended a Jewish free school in London; emigrated with his family to the United States in 1863, settling in New York

City; furthered a limited formal education by attending night classes; while
working as a cigarmaker, joined Cigarmakers Local 15 in 1864 and in 1875 was
elected president of Local 144 of the Cigarmakers' International Union (CMIU),
serving until 1878; served as president of Local 144 again during the period
1880–1886; served as second vice-president of the CMIU, 1886–1896, and first
vice-president, 1896–1924; helped organize the Federation of Organized Trades
and Labor Unions and was its vice-president, 1881–1886; was one of the founders
of the American Federation of Labor (AFL) and the seminal figure in its early
years; served as president of the AFL during 1886–1895 and 1896–1924; was a
man of great personal integrity and brilliance and for 37 years provided the AFL
with strong and stable leadership, stressing business unionism, craft autonomy,
and voluntarism; was hostile to Eugene V. Debs (q.v.) and the American Railway
Union, which he believed to be a dual union; claimed he lacked authority to
order supporting strikes during the Pullman strike which ended in the destruction
of Debs's union; distrusting industrial unionism, joined with the AFL executive
council in proposing a settlement between the United Brewery Workers and two
AFL craft unions in a manner which would have virtually transformed the former
into a craft union; however, in 1906, fought moves to expel the United Brewery
Workers from the AFL; in the 1901 steel strike, was rightly suspicious of industrial union tendencies in the Amalgamated Association of Iron, Steel, and
Tin Workers, and although providing several AFL organizers, failed to negotiate
with J. P. Morgan along the lines favored by the Amalgamated Association,
refused to summon the executive council to aid the strike, and unsuccessfully
urged steelworker president T. J. Shaffer to accept a company offer compro-
mising the main strike issue, the union's demand for recognition; followed the
philosophy of the AFL crafts and usually ignored unskilled workers to guarantee
continued benefits for craft unionists; fearing failure, his support of the steel
strike of 1919 was considered cautious by many strikers who had looked for
greater encouragement; pursued a policy of voluntarism, opposing government-
sponsored workmen's compensation and old-age pensions except for government
employees, eight-hour laws, unemployment compensation, comprehensive health
insurance, independent political action, and compulsory arbitration; however,
favored child labor laws, immigration restriction, and legislative lobbying, supported an 1897 AFL resolution against discrimination against blacks over southern opposition and privately opposed discrimination, but by 1900 began
countenancing Jim Crow unionism and refused blacks charters as federated locals
when their affiliated unions would not grant jurisdiction; achieved significant
political accomplishments by 1917 with Congressional passage of the final proposals embodied in labor's Bill of Grievances, originally proposed in 1906;
protected labor's interests as a member of the Advisory Commission to the
Council of National Defense during World War I and founded the American
Alliance for Labor and Democracy to counter anti-war sentiments in the labor
movement; appointed to the American delegation at the Paris Peace Conference
in 1919; after the war, opposed sedition laws and pleaded for amnesty for political

prisoners, also espoused a philosophy of business-labor cooperation for industrial self-government; authored *Seventy Years of Life and Labor: An Autobiography*, 2 Vols. (1925), *American Labor and the War* (1919), and numerous essays and pamphlets; died in San Antonio, Tex., December 3, 1924, while returning from the inauguration of Mexican president Plutarco Calles; Samuel Gompers Letterbooks, Library of Congress; Bernard Mandel, *Samuel Gompers: A Biography* (1963); Philip Taft, *The A.F. of L. in the Time of Gompers* (1957); Stuart B. Kaufman, *Samuel Gompers and the Origins of the American Federation of Labor, 1848–1896* (1973); Philip S. Foner, *History of the Labor Movement in the United States*, Vol. 3 (1964); Rowland H. Harvey, *Samuel Gompers: Champion of the Toiling Masses* (1935); Harold C. Livesey, *Samuel Gompers and Organized Labor in America* (1978); Harvey Klehr, "Lenin on American Socialist Leaders and on Samuel Gompers," *Labor History* (Spring 1976); Robert H. Babcock, *Gompers in Canada: A Study in American Continentalism before the First World War* (1974).

Merl E. Reed

GOOGE, George Logan (1900–1961). Born in Palaky, Ga., July 25, 1900; son of Joseph George and Elizabeth (Youmans) Googe; Baptist; married Evelyn Elliott on December 4, 1928; two children; was graduated from high school in Waterboro, S.C., in 1921, and then attended the Printing Pressmen Trade School in Pressmen's Home, Tenn.; shortly after his graduation in 1922, joined the International Printing Pressmen's and Assistants' Union of North America (IPPAUNA); became a vice-president of the Georgia State Federation of Labor in 1925 and was elected president of the Trades and Labor Assembly of Savannah, Ga., in 1928; appointed southern representative of the American Federation of Labor (AFL) in 1928 and served in that capacity until 1949; served during World War II on the National Defense Labor Board, the President's Special Commission on Education, and the War Labor Board; appointed director of the AFL's 1946 southern organizing campaign; elected a vice-president of the IPPAUNA in 1948 and became secretary-treasurer in 1953; after the AFL-Congress of Industrial Organizations' merger in 1955, became a vice-president of the new labor federation's union label and service trades department; elected vice-president of the International Allied Printing Trades Association in 1956; was a Democrat; died in Pressmen's Home, Tenn., September 29, 1961; Elizabeth F. Baker, *Printers and Technology: A History of the International Printing Pressmen and Assistants' Union* (1957); F. Ray Marshall, *Labor in the South* (1967); *The American Federationist* (May 1952); *Current Biography* (1947).

GORMAN, Francis J. (1877–1975). Born in Bradford, England, in 1877; the son of a small-businessman who owned a public house patronized by the leaders of the Bradford wool workers union; Roman Catholic; married; seven children; emigrated with his family to the United States in 1890, settling in Providence, R.I., where at age 13 he began working as a sweeper in a woolen mill; joined the National Wool Sorters and Graders Union in 1910; became a member of the United Textile Workers of America (UTWA) in 1912 when the Providence wool sorters union affiliated with the UTWA; thereafter, he served his local union as president for 12 years while also serving as a legislative agent for the Rhode Island State Federation of Labor and president of the Providence Central Labor Union; became a UTWA organizer in 1913 and in 1922 was appointed an international representative; made his first organizing effort in the South in 1923, 1924; was elected an international vice-president of the UTWA in 1928; led the textile strike in Marion, N.C., in 1929, and, after no local clergyman would agree to do it, made the funeral oration for six striking workers who were killed during the conflict; thereafter led textile strikes in Elizabethton, Tenn., 1929, Danville, Va., 1931, Lawrence, Mass., 1932, and Pawtucket, R.I., in 1933; began agitating for a general strike in the textile industry in 1934 to protest numerous violations of the wage and hour provisions of the National Recovery Administration's Cotton Code; although the American Federation of Labor (AFL) executive council opposed the idea, the UTWA membership supported it and a strike was called for September 1, 1934; Gorman was appointed chairman of the special strike committee with headquarters in Washington, D.C.; after devising a highly organized plan for closing all of the nation's textile mills, he then organized "flying squadrons," composed of cavalcades of motorized UTWA members, which moved along the nation's highways, stopping at each textile mill along the way, calling the workers out, and shutting down operations; textile workers responded enthusiastically to the strike call and within a few days the giant industry had been virtually shut down; at one time nearly one-half million workers joined the strike making it the largest strike in American history to that time; nevertheless, the counteroffensive launched by textile manufacturers, the refusal of the AFL and most of its affiliated unions to support the strike, the use of local and state police power, particularly in the South, and the Roosevelt administration's compliant attitude toward the manufacturers ultimately doomed the strike which was officially ended on September 22, 1934; as usually happens in such cases, the leader of the strike was blamed for its defeat; nevertheless, he retained his vice-presidency in the UTWA, and after the resignation of incumbent president Thomas F. McMahon (q.v.) in 1937, he was elected international president of the UTWA; a strong advocate of industrial unionism, he took his union into the Congress of Industrial Organizations (CIO) when it was organized in 1937; although at first an enthusiastic supporter of the Textile Workers Organizing Committee (TWOC) created by the CIO and headed by Sidney Hillman (q.v.), by 1939 he recognized that the UTWA had become a mere appendage of the TWOC and this, along with a lagging organizing drive and the absence of called conventions where TWOC policy could be debated, led him to call a special convention of the UTWA on May 8, 1939, at which time he bolted the CIO and took seven of his original Rhode Island locals with him back into the AFL; after the AFL returned the UTWA charter, he became chairman of the international executive council and retained that position until he was reelected international president in 1946; after 1950, he served as editor of the *Textile Challenger*, the UTWA organ; was for many years the director of the UTWA research and education department and later spent much time in Washington, D.C., as the UTWA's legislative representative; died in Derry, N.H., on June 4, 1975; *New Republic*, October 3, 1934; *Textile Challenger* (August-September 1975); David B. Gracy II, interview with Francis J. Gorman, August 8, 1973, Southern Labor Archives, Georgia State University; John W. Kennedy, "The General Strike in the Textile Industry: September, 1934" (M.A. thesis, 1947); Joseph Yates Garrison, "Paul Revere Christopher, Southern Labor Leader: 1910–1974" (Ph.D. diss., 1976); Robert R. R. Brooks, "The United Textile Workers of America" (Ph.D. diss., 1935).

Joseph Y. Garrison

GORMAN, Patrick Emmet   (1892–1980). Born in Louisville, Ky., November 27, 1892; son of Maurice, a butcher and tanner, and Mary Ellen (Dwyer) Gorman; Roman Catholic; married Hattie Lee Dove on June 1, 1914; completed a high school education, and then began working as a butcher; joined Louisville Local 227 of the Amalgamated Meat Cutters and Butcher Workmen of North America (AMCBWNA) in 1911; served as business manager of Local 227, 1912–1920; was appointed a special AMCBWNA international organizer, 1917–1920; was graduated from the University of Louisville Law School, and then maintained a private law practice in Louisville, 1917–1920; elected president of the Louisville Union Trades and Labor Assembly in 1917, serving until 1919; served as a vice-president of the Kentucky Federation of Labor, 1918–1919; elected vice-president of the AMCBWNA in 1920 and served until becoming president in 1923; resigned as president in 1942 and became AMCBWNA secretary-treasurer (the chief administrative officer of the AMCBWNA); strongly supported industrial unionism, but opposed affiliation with the Congress of Industrial Organizations; was an American Federation of Labor fraternal delegate to the British Trades Union Congress in 1948; negotiated mergers between the AMCBWNA and the Fur and Leather Workers Union in 1955 and the United Packinghouse Workers of America in 1968; was an active participant in civic affairs, serving as a trustee of Roosevelt University, president of the Eugene V. Debs Foundation, and as an official of numerous other public and private organizations; recipient of numerous honors and awards; identified himself politically as an independent; edited the *Butcher Workman* for several years; died on September 3, 1980; David Brody, *The Butcher Workmen: A Study of Unionization* (1964); *Who's Who in Labor* (1946); *Who's Who in America, 1972–1973*.

GOSSER, Richard Thomas   (1900–1969). Born in Toledo, Ohio, December 13, 1900; son of James, a railroader, and Maizie Gosser; Roman Catholic; married Ruth Marie Bonnell on January 7, 1923; one child; completed grammar school and took courses in electrical engineering for three years; after an unstable childhood that included nearly two years in a Michigan reformatory, became an electrician's apprentice at the Willys-Overland Company in Toledo; joined Local 12, United Automobile, Aircraft and Agricultural Implement Workers of America (UAW) in 1935; served as chairman of the Willys-Overland unit of Local 12, 1937–1940; elected president of Local 12 in 1938 and served until 1942; appointed director of UAW Region 2B in 1942 and became a member of the international executive board; during World War II, was a member of the War Manpower Commission for the Toledo area and served on the Office of Price Administration's committee for civic advancement; served on the Congress of Industrial Organizations' Political Action Committee; elected one of two UAW vice-presidents in 1947 (later increased to four) and placed in charge of the skilled trades department; exonerated of charges of misusing union funds by the UAW executive board in 1950; relieved of many of his duties as a UAW vice-president in 1959 after a bitter dispute with UAW president Walter P. Reuther (q.v.) over the reorganization of the competitive shop department, which he headed and which supervised UAW organizing activities; became one of the foci of the Senate Crime Investigating Committee's (McClellan committee) investigation of the UAW in 1959; convicted of conspiring to defraud the government in a tax case in 1965 and sentenced to a three-year prison term; died in Toledo, Ohio, December 1, 1969; Jack Stieber, *Governing the UAW* (1962); Jean Gould and Lorena Hickok, *Walter Reuther: Labor's Rugged Individualist* (1972); Frank Cormier and William J. Eaton, *Reuther* (1970).

GRAHAM, James D. (1879–1951). Born in Greenock, Scotland, on February 2, 1879; son of Michael, a machinist, and Elizabeth (Denholm) Graham; married Jennie Whyatt in 1903; one child; attended high school and night school; joined the International Association of Machinists in 1896; later also was a member of the International Hod Carriers, Building and Common Laborers Union of America; was vice-president of the Montana State Federation of Labor during the 1920s; when the incumbent executive president of the federation vacated the office in 1929 under a cloud of mismanagement, he succeeded to the presidency; in 1931 he was elected president of the federation, an office he would hold for 30 years; attempted in 1930 to initiate a broad organizing campaign, including the Butte copper miners, and began lobbying for improvements in the state's inadequate worker protective laws; although the 1930 organizing effort was abortive, he renewed efforts during 1933–1934, which were successful; while promoting federal unions among lumber jacks, construction laborers, and other workers, cooperated closely with leaders of the International Union of Mine, Mill and Smelter Workers Union in reorganizing Butte Miners' Union No. 1, and also helped organize hard rock miners in the Coeur d'Alene district of Idaho; meanwhile, he was instrumental in securing passage of an eight-hour-day law for workers in strip mining, sugar refineries, and on federal hydroelectric construction projects; thus played a central role in the revitalization of the Montana labor movement; usually cooperated with American Federation of Labor president William Green (q.v.) but in a fashion protective of the interests of Montana unions; a life-long advocate of social insurance, direct democracy, and municipal ownership, he was a progressive who used those issues, as well as the principle of rewarding labor's political friends, as the basis for backing candidates; a staunch supporter of Senator Burton K. Wheeler, when Montana Democrats began to divide into pro-Wheeler and a liberal New Deal faction led by Senator James E. Murray, he ignored William Green's plea to endorse Murray; during the 1940s, he was instrumental in promoting the state federation's program of worker education and the study of labor economics in high schools and the state university; an outspoken anti-Communist, in 1950 he advocated expulsion of the Soviet Union from the United Nations in order to make it effective as a peacekeeping organization; died on June 9, 1951; *Who's Who in Labor* (1946); *Montana Labor News* (official organ of the Montana State Federation of Labor); Michael P. Malone and Richard B. Roeder, *Montana: A History of Two Centuries* (1976).

Donald G. Sofchalk

GRAHAM, Sylvester (1899–1970). Born in Sheridan, Mont., September 1, 1899; son of Thomas L., a rancher and miner, and Margaret Graham; Methodist; married Edith Miller on December 7, 1926; shortly after graduating from high school in Sheridan, Mont., joined the U.S. Army during World War I; began working in the mines around Butte, Mont., after the war; joined Butte Miners' Union No. 1 of the International Union of Mine, Mill and Smelter Workers (IUMMSW) in 1933; became an international organizer for the IUMMSW in 1936; elected secretary-treasurer of the Montana State Industrial Union Council, Congress of Industrial Organizations (CIO) in 1937, and elected president a year later, serving until 1942; became CIO sub-regional director for Montana and Wyoming in 1942; served as a member of the Montana State Apprenticeship Committee and the State Salvage Committee; served with the U.S. Army during World War II and then resumed his position with the CIO, continuing in that capacity until the American Federation of Labor (AFL)-CIO merger in 1955; became an AFL-CIO field representative in 1955, serving until 1964; died in Butte, Mont., December 25, 1970; *Who's Who in Labor* (1946); *AFL-CIO News*, January 10, 1970.

GRAY, Richard J. (1887–1966). Born in Albany, N.Y., December 6, 1887; son of William J., a bricklayer, and Hanora (Leahy) Gray; Roman Catholic; married Elizabeth Archambault in January 1911; three children; after attending the public schools of Albany, began work as a bricklayer; joined Local 6 of the Bricklayers, Masons and Plasterers International Union of America (BMPIU) in 1903; worked on the construction of the Panama Canal; served as president and then elected business manager of Local 6 in 1927; was an examiner for the New York State Education Department in 1927; served as international treasurer of the BMPIU, 1928–1936, and international secretary, 1936–1946; was a director of the Union Life Insurance Company, 1928–1937, and treasurer, 1937–1946;

was a staunch craft unionist and his vocal criticism of industrial unionism exacerbated relations between the American Federation of Labor (AFL) and the Committee on Industrial Organization (CIO) during the 1930s; served on the War Labor Board during World War II; elected president of the building and construction trades union department of the AFL in 1946; served as an AFL fraternal delegate to the British Trades Union Congress in 1951; his abrasive personality and conservative political, economic, and organizing policies alienated many of the union leaders affiliated with the AFL-CIO building and construction trades union department; was forced to resign as president in 1960; was a Republican and supported Dwight D. Eisenhower in 1952 and 1956; praised the work of Senator Joseph R. McCarthy during the early 1950s; died in Washington, D.C., May 1, 1966; Harry Clay Bates, *Bricklayers' Century of Craftsmanship* (1955); Philip Taft, *The A.F. of L. from the Death of Gompers to the Merger* (1959); *The New York Times*, May 3, 1966.

GREEN, John   (1896-1957). Born in Clydebank, Dumbartonshire, Scotland, November 15, 1896; son of Patrick and Mary Green; married Annie Allison Sievewright; four children; educated in Scotland; emigrated to the United States in 1923; hired as a sheet-metal worker at the New York Shipbuilding Corporation's yard in Camden, N.J.; helped organize a union in the Camden yard in 1933 and two years later was elected president of the newly organized Industrial Union of Marine and Shipbuilding Workers of America (IUMSWA); elected an international vice-president of the Congress of Industrial Organizations (CIO) in 1937; served as chairman of the CIO's United Railroad Workers of America; was a labor representative on the National Defense Advisory Committee in 1940; appointed to the management-labor policy committee of the War Manpower Commission in 1942; served as a CIO delegate to the World Trade Union Conference that met in 1945; retired as president of the IUMSWA in 1951; after the American Federation of Labor-CIO (AFL-CIO) merger in 1955, was appointed an AFL-CIO national representative for New Jersey; supported the Democratic party and was one of the founding members of Americans for Democratic Action; died in Audubon Park, N.J., February 19, 1957; Max M. Kampelman, *The Communist Party vs. the C.I.O.: A Study in Power Politics* (1957); *Who's Who in Labor* (1946); *The New York Times*, February 21, 1957.

GREEN, William   (1873–1952). Born in Coshocton, Ohio, March 3, 1873; son of Hugh and Jane (Oram) Green; Baptist; married Jennie Mobley on April 14, 1892; six children; received eight years of formal education; descended from English and Welsh coal-mining families; followed his father into the coal mines of Ohio at age 16; in 1891, became secretary of the Coshocton Progressive Miners Union, which later became a local of the United Mine Workers Union (UMWA); became a subdistrict president of the UMWA in 1900; became president of the Ohio District Mine Workers' Union in 1906; from 1910 to 1913, served two terms in the Ohio Senate where he wrote the state's workmen's compensation act, passed in 1911; served as Democratic floor leader during the second session; campaigned unsuccessfully for the presidency of the UMWA in 1910; began in 1912 a ten-year tenure as UMWA international secretary-treasurer; became a fourth vice-president and member of the executive council of the American Federation of Labor (AFL) in 1914; appointed by the AFL executive council to a five-man committee to represent labor at the international labor conferences held in connection with the Paris Peace Conference in 1919; following the death of Samuel Gompers (q.v.) in 1924, became president of the AFL and held that office until his death; during the early years of Franklin D. Roosevelt's administration, served on the advisory council of the President's Committee on Economic Security, was a member of the Labor Advisory Council of the National Recovery Administration, and served on the National Labor Board in 1934; elected to the governing board of the International Labor Organization in 1935 and served until 1937; broke with his former benefactor, John L. Lewis (q.v.), in 1935 over the issue of industrial unionism, and, acting in response to an executive council decision, ordered the expulsion of Committee on Industrial Organization (CIO) unions from the AFL in 1937; resigned from the UMWA the following year when threatened with expulsion; was a self-proclaimed advocate of labor unity, but was sometimes overwhelmed by stronger personalities on both the AFL executive council and among the leaders of the CIO; supported the mobilization effort during World War II in a variety of ways, and during the Korean War was a member of President Harry S. Truman's National Advisory Committee on Mobilization; was a member of numerous national and international boards and agencies and was associated with a variety of social and fraternal organizations; edited *The American Federationist* for many years and authored *Labor and Democracy* (1939); died in Coshocton, Ohio, November 21, 1952; William Green Papers, AFL-CIO Archives, George Meany Center for Labor Studies; Philip Taft, *The A.F. of L. from the Death of Gompers to the Merger* (1959); Max D. Danish, *William Green* (1952); Charles A. Madison, *American Labor Leaders: Personalities and Forces in the Labor Movement* (1950); *National Cyclopaedia of American Biography*, Vol. 41; *Dictionary of American Biography*, Suppl. 5; Melvyn Dubofsky and Warren Van Tine, *John L. Lewis: A Biography* (1977).

GREENBERG, Max   (1907–   ). Born in New York City, August 6, 1907; son of Isaac and Mollie (Biegel) Greenberg; Jewish; married Billie Garfinkle on September 21, 1929; two children; completed a secondary education, then became a retail clerk and in 1929 joined a retail men's furnishings union; was one of the principal organizers of New Jersey Local 108 of the Retail Clerks International Protective Association in 1936 and elected its first president, serving until 1954; led Local 108 into the newly organized United Retail, Wholesale and Department Store Employees of America (URWDSE) in 1937; served as a labor member of the New York regional panel of the War Labor Board, 1942–1946; elected an international vice-president of the URWDSE in 1946; was a member of the New Jersey Board of Mediation, 1949–1954; elected international president of the URWDSE in 1954 and during the same year became a member of the executive board of the Congress of Industrial Organizations (CIO); after the merger between the CIO and the American Federation of Labor (AFL) in 1955, became a member of the AFL-CIO general board; appointed to the labor advisory council of the President's Committee on Equal Employment Opportunity in 1964; named to the labor advisory council of the Office of Economic Opportunity in 1965; served as vice-president of the AFL-CIO industrial union department and on the administrative committee of the Committee on Political Education; elected an AFL-CIO vice-president and executive council member in 1967; a Democrat; *AFL-CIO News*, May 13, 1967; *Who's Who in America, 1972–1973*.

GREENE, Michael F.   (1884–1951). Born in Kilclohor, County Clare, Ireland, January 1, 1884; son of a Roman Catholic hatter; married Mary Daly; no children; emigrated with family to the United States in 1887 and settled in Danbury, Conn., and attended St. Peter's Parochial School there; left school and went to sea at age 13 and for the next four years worked at various occupations; became a hat makers' apprentice in 1901; joined the United Hatters of North America (UH) and in 1910 was elected president of UH Local 17 in Orange, N.J.; served as secretary-treasurer of Local 17, 1912–1918; elected international president of UH in 1918; was an American Federation of Labor (AFL) fraternal delegate to the British Trades Union Congress in 1925 and during the same year was a labor delegate to the International Labor Organization conference in Bern, Switzerland; was a member of the United States labor delegation to Italy in 1918; after negotiating a merger with Max Zaritsky (q.v.) of the United Cloth Hat and Cap Makers of North America, became the president of the amalgamated United Hatters, Cap and Millinery Workers' International Union in 1934 and served until 1936, when elected general secretary; during the conflict between the AFL and the Committee on Industrial Organization in the 1930s, supported the craft organization principle; died in Clearwater, N.J., October 20, 1951; Donald B. Robinson, *Spotlight on a Union: The Story of the United Hatters, Cap and Millinery Workers' International Union* (1948); Charles H. Green, *The Headwear Workers* (1944); Solon DeLeon, ed., *The American Labor Who's Who* (1925).

GREENE, Prince W.   (fl. 1897–1901). Early origins unknown; a weaver from Columbus, Ga., became a vice-president of the National Union of Textile Workers (NUTW) in 1897; was a strong supporter of Samuel Gompers' (q.v.) expulsion of Socialist and New England craft locals from the NUTW over the issue of industrial unionism; elected NUTW president in 1897 and reelected in 1898 and 1900; served as NUTW secretary-treasurer, 1900–1901, when the NUTW merged with the United Textile Workers of America (UTWA); served as the editor of the *Southern Unionist* and the *Phenix Gerard News*, the latter the official organ of the NUTW; in 1899, appointed as one of three special organizers for the South covering the Carolinas, Georgia, and Alabama by the American Federation of Labor (AFL) executive council; participated in the Augusta, Ga., textile strike of 1898–1899, achieving a 6 percent wage increase that placed Augusta mills above the competitive district wage rate; was a tireless organizer and formed AFL locals all over his territory during 1899—organizing textile workers in Macon, Ga., and Langley, Spartanburg, and Bath, S.C., a federated union in Macon, and a federation of trades in Augusta; along with Gompers, played an important personal role in the Danville, Va., strike of 1901; with the main issue the ten-hour day, correctly believed the Danville strike to be the key to organizing the mills of the southeastern Piedmont; was "determined to strike a blow for our women and children" while in Virginia and visited the commissioner of labor in May to complain about the textile millowners' violations of Virginia's ten-hour law; later, sent the commissioner documentary evidence of violations in the Danville mills; the NUTW lost the Danville strike because of rifts among local union leaders and their failure to follow policies outlined by Gompers and Greene; in Phenix City, Ala., Greene organized furniture employees (beamers and slashers), painters and decorators, retail clerks, ladies textile workers, carpenters, and a federal labor union; had as his main goal while NUTW president the establishment of a national textile-workers union, and therefore met with representatives of northern locals in 1899 seeking their reaffiliation with the NUTW; realized the southern union movement would fail without strong national support and hence requested that the AFL executive council persuade northern unions of mule spinners, weavers, the National Federation of Trade Unions, the carders, and the National Loom Fixers Association to unite with the NUTW into one big union; at the NUTW convention in 1900 persuaded delegates to pass resolutions favoring one international textile workers union although realized that southern dominance and his own leadership would end with such a merger; partly through Greene's efforts, the UTWA was formed in November 1901; *The American Federationist* (1899–1900); Melton A. McLaurin, *Paternalism and Protest: Southern Cotton Mill Workers and Organized Labor, 1875–1905* (1971).

Merl E. Reed

GRINER, John F. (1907–1974). Born in Camilla, Ga., August 7, 1907; son of Will and Dollier (Shiver) Griner; Baptist; married Claranell Nicholson on November 27, 1936; two children; was graduated from high school, then worked for several different railroads during 1925–1936, joining both the Order of Railroad Telegraphers and the American Train Dispatchers Association; during this period, attended and received the LL.B. degree from Columbus University, Washington, D.C.; served variously as the adjudicator, liaison officer, and labor relations officer for the U.S. Railroad Retirement Board, 1936–1962; elected national president of the American Federation of Government Employees (AFGE) in 1962; is credited with building the AFGE into a strong, stable trade union organization; was elected an American Federation of Labor-Congress of Industrial Organizations (AFL-CIO) vice-president and executive council member in 1967; served as an AFL-CIO fraternal delegate to the British Trades Union Congress in 1971; retired union positions in 1973; supported the Democratic party; died in Cairo, Ga., on April 22, 1974; *Who's Who in America, 1972–1973*; *AFL-CIO News*, April 27, 1974; *The New York Times*, April 23, 1974.

GROGAN, John Joseph   (1914–1968). Born in Hoboken, N.J., March 26, 1914; son of Irish immigrants, James J., a carpenter, and Catherine (May) Grogan; Roman Catholic; married Eileen McNulty on June 5, 1937; two children; graduated from high school in Jersey City, N.J., in 1932 and later attended Columbia University for one year; after high school, became a pipefitter's helper and joined the United Association of Journeymen and Apprentices of the Plumbing and Pipefitting Industry of the United States and Canada (UA); at age 19, became a UA shop steward; joined Local 15 of the newly organized Industrial Union of Marine and Shipbuilding Workers of America (IUMSWA) in 1936 and, later in the same year, elected secretary of Local 15; served as executive secretary of Local 15, 1937–1943, and as financial secretary, 1938–1939; became a member of the IUMSWA general executive board in 1941 and during the period 1941–1943 was national vice-president of the union; served on the national executive board of the Congress of Industrial Organizations (CIO), 1943–1955; elected president of the Hudson County (N.J.) Industrial Union Council, CIO, in 1943; served with the U.S. Army during World War II; served on a variety of federal and state governmental boards and agencies, including the U.S. Shipbuilding Stabilization Committee, the Labor-Management Advisory Committee, the U.S. Shipbuilding Commission, the War Labor Boards of New York and New Jersey and the Conciliation Service of the U.S. Department of Labor; served as an assemblyman in the New Jersey State Legislature, 1943–1947; became a city commissioner in Hoboken, N.J., and was appointed director of the city's Parks and Public Buildings Department in 1947; elected international president of the IUMSWA in 1951; elected mayor of Hoboken in 1953 and served until 1965; elected a vice-president and member of the executive council of the American Federation of Labor (AFL)-CIO in 1963; elected Hudson County clerk in 1963; was a member of the Democratic party; died in Jersey City, N.J., September 16, 1968; *Current Biography* (1951); *Who's Who in Labor* (1946); *AFL-CIO News*, October 12, 1963, September 21, 1968.

GROTTKAU, Paul   (1846–1898). Born in Berlin, Germany, in 1846; the son of affluent parents, he was trained as an architect; a student convert to Marxism, he became a follower of Ferdinand Lassalle; after having been involved in the German Socialist uprising of 1871 and the enactment of the anti-Socialist law in 1878, he emigrated to the United States, settling in Chicago, Ill., where, along with August Spies (q.v.), he edited the *Arbeiter-Zeitung*, 1878–1883; was an early advocate of militant trade union activities and abstention from politics;

broke with Spies after the 1883 Pittsburgh, Pa., meeting of the Revolutionary Socialist party which rejected collectivistic socialism in favor of communistic anarchism; assumed the editorship of the *Milwaukee Arbeiter Zeitung* in 1886 and quickly became one of the most influential leaders in Milwaukee's Socialist movement; was one of the leaders of the militant Milwaukee Central Labor Union which conducted the city's 1886 May Day strike for the eight-hour day; as a result of the accompanying Bay View riot, he was arrested and sentenced to one year in prison, but was able to appeal to the trial judge and was released after six weeks; while in prison, he ran unsuccessfully for mayor of Milwaukee in 1888; moved to San Francisco, Calif., the following year; was appointed, along with George E. McNeill (q.v.), to travel around the country in behalf of the eight-hour-day movement by the American Federation of Labor's executive council in 1890; a fiery orator and an effective editorialist, especially among German-language workers, he twice returned to Milwaukee (1895, 1898) to campaign for Social Democratic candidates; died on June 3, 1898; *Dictionary of Wisconsin Biography* (1960); Marvin Wachman, *The History of the Social-Democratic Party of Milwaukee, 1897–1910* (1945); John R. Commons et al., *History of Labour in the United States*, Vol. 2 (1918); Bayrd Still, *Milwaukee: The History of a City* (1948); Thomas W. Gavett, *Development of the Labor Movement in Milwaukee* (1965).

GUINAN, Matthew   (1910–   ). Born in County Offaly, Ireland, on October 14, 1910; son of John, a farmer and carpenter, and Bridget Guinan, a homemaker; Roman Catholic; married Margaret Glynn in 1935; three children; attended elementary and secondary schools in Offaly and Leix, Ireland; at age 18, he emigrated to the United States, arriving in New York City in 1929; became a trolley-car operator in 1933, working on the Kingsbridge line of the Third Avenue Railway; joined the Transport Workers Union of America (TWU) shortly after its founding in 1934; joined the drive to organize the Third Avenue Railway Corporation and led a successful union recognition strike in 1937; after serving for six years as a voluntary organizer, he became a paid TWU organizer in 1943; led the drive to eliminate Communists from the TWU in 1948 and the following year was elected president of the thirty-five thousand-member Local 100, the largest TWU local union; was elected TWU executive vice-president in 1952 and four years later also assumed the position as international secretary-treasurer; resigned his presidency of Local 100 in 1961 to devote all his time to international union affairs; along with international president Michael Quill (q.v.) and seven other TWU leaders, he was arrested for contempt of court in 1966 following the violation of court orders during a 12–day transit strike that paralyzed New York City; following the death of Quill in 1966, he assumed the international presidency and was elected to that office for a full term in 1969; became a member of the American Federation of Labor-Congress of Industrial Organizations (AFL-CIO) executive council and was elected an AFL-CIO vice-president in 1969; was also a vice-president of the AFL-CIO industrial union department and first vice-president of the New York City AFL-CIO; although exhibiting a much more subdued style of leadership than that of his flamboyant predecessor, he proved an equally adroit negotiator who periodically employed the threat of a strike to win bargaining concessions; retired union positions in 1979; L. H. Whittemore, *Man Who Ran the Subways: The Story of Mike Quill* (1968); *The New York Times*, December 30, 1969; *AFL-CIO News*, April 7, 1979; *Who's Who in Labor* (1976); *Current Biography* (September 1974).

H

HAAS, Francis Joseph (1889–1953). Born in Racine, Wis., on March 18, 1889; son of Peter F., a grocery store owner, and Mary (O'Day) Haas; Roman Catholic; received his early education in parochial and public schools; graduated from Racine High School and, in 1904, enrolled in St. Francis Seminary, Milwaukee, Wis., was ordained on June 11, 1913; served as an assistant in Holy Rosary parish, Milwaukee, 1913–1915; joined the faculty of St. Francis Seminary in 1915; entered the graduate school of the Catholic University of America in 1919, where he completed work for a Ph.D. in sociology in 1922; while at Catholic University, he came under the influence of Father John A. Ryan and soon absorbed Ryan's commitment to social justice and the labor movement; taught social science and literature at St. Francis Seminary, 1922–1931; was appointed director of the National Catholic School of Social Service in Washington, D.C., in 1931; was appointed to the Labor Advisory Board of the National Recovery Administration in 1933; was a member of the National Labor Board, 1933–1934, the Labor Policies Board of the Works Progress Administration, 1935–1938, and the Wisconsin Labor Relations Board, 1937–1939; served the U.S. Department of Labor as a special conciliator, 1935–1943, in which position he developed a national reputation as an effective mediator of industrial disputes; assisted in the settlement of over fifteen hundred labor-management disputes, including the Minneapolis teamsters' strike of 1934 and the equally volatile Allis-Chalmers strikes of 1938 and 1941; was also deeply committed to civil rights and equal employment opportunities for black workers; served as chairman of the President's Fair Employment Practices Committee in 1943; was a member of President Harry S. Truman's Committee on Civil Rights in 1947 and chaired the Michigan Advisory Committee on Civil Rights in 1949; throughout his nearly 20 years of government service, he continued his commitment to Catholic education; left the National Catholic School of Social Service in 1935 to become rector of St. Francis Seminary; was appointed the first dean of Catholic University's School of Social Science in 1937; was promoted to the rank of domestic prelate in 1943 and appointed bishop of Grand Rapids (Mich.); devoted most of his time thereafter to the duties and responsibilities of his episcopacy; authored *Man and Society* (1930), *Rights and Wrongs in Industry* (1933), *Jobs, Prices and Unions* (1941), *Catholics, Race and Law* (1947); died on August 29, 1953; *Dictionary of American Biography*, Suppl. 5; Thomas E. Blantz, "Francis J. Haas: Priest in Public Service" (Ph.D. diss., 1968); *Who's Who in Labor* (1946).

HAGERTY, Thomas J.   (fl. 1895–1920). Born ca. 1862; little is known of his life prior to finishing seminary training in the Roman Catholic faith in 1895; appointed assistant to the rector of St. Agatha's Church, Chicago, Ill., in 1895; assigned to St. Joseph's Church, Cleburne, Tex., in 1897, and appointed rector of Our Lady of Victory Church in Paris, Tex., in 1901; became a Socialist ca. 1892 and attempted to rationalize the apparent contradictions in Marxist and Catholic dogma; while a pastor in Texas, was closely associated with exploited Mexican railroad workers; found little Socialist literature available in Spanish and therefore translated several Socialist tracts from German, French, and English; transferred to Our Lady of Sorrows Church, Las Vegas, N.M., in 1901; shortly after arriving in New Mexico, became associated with the Western Federation of Miners and the American Labor Union (ALU) (originally, the Western Labor Union); during the summer of 1902, toured the mining camps of Colorado with Eugene V. Debs (q.v.), recruiting members for both the ALU and the Socialist party; suspended from his priestly duties in 1902, because of his radical views and his long absence from the Las Vegas parish; as a Catholic priest, was especially valuable to Socialists, whose appeal to Catholic workers was undermined by the church's anti-Socialist stance; was a skillful orator and served as a Socialist party lecturer during 1903, traversing much of the country arguing that the church should not interfere with the political convictions of its members; after the tour, wrote a series of pamphlets dealing with much the same subject; during 1903–1904, became increasingly radical and criticized in more and more vitriolic terms those right-wing Socialists who advocated boring from within the American Federation of Labor, gradualism, and revolution through the ballot box; as a result of his strident criticism of Socialist party leaders, his influence in the party declined precipitantly; helped draft the Industrial Union Manifesto which led to the founding of the Industrial Workers of the World (IWW); became editor of the *Voice of Labor*, a new publication of the ALU, in 1905, and used the columns of the short-lived monthly to champion industrial unionism; was an important participant in the inaugural convention of the IWW and served as secretary of the constitution committee and wrote the highly influential preamble to the IWW constitution; shortly after the IWW convention, unexplainedly dropped out of the radical union movement; lived under the name Ricardo Moreno and dissolved his connections with both the church and the IWW and for a time earned a living teaching Spanish and maintaining a small practice as an oculist; from 1920 to his death, apparently lived as a derelict on Chicago's skid row; Robert E. Doherty, "Thomas J. Hagerty, the Church, and Socialism," *Labor*

History (Winter 1962); Melvyn Dubofsky, *We Shall Be All: A History of the Industrial Workers of the World* (1969).

HAGGERTY, Cornelius Joseph   (1894–1971). Born in Boston, Mass., January 10, 1894; son of Daniel, a freight handler, and Nora (Driscoll) Haggerty; Roman Catholic; married Margaret Killeher on June 30, 1920; two children; completed elementary school in Boston and then began a short-lived singing career; became a lathers' apprentice in 1913 and two years later, after becoming a journeyman, joined Local 72 of the Wood, Wire and Metal Lathers International Union (WWMLIU); served with the U.S. Navy during World War I; moved to Los Angeles, Calif., in 1921 and affiliated with WWMLIU Local 42; served as a West Coast organizer for the WWMLIU and president of Local 42; elected secretary of the Los Angeles Building and Construction Trades Council in 1933; served as president of the California State Federation of Labor, 1937–1943, and secretary, 1943–1960; served during World War II on a variety of state and regional panels, including the War Manpower Commission, the Office of Price Administration, and the Civilian Defense Council; was a long-time vice-president of the WWMLIU; became president of the American Federation of Labor-Congress of Industrial Organizations' (AFL-CIO) building and construction trades department in 1960; in the inner councils of the AFL-CIO, often opposed the proposals and policies of the president of the industrial union department, Walter P. Reuther (q.v.); served on the California State Board of Education and as a regent of the University of California; retired from union affairs in 1970; usually supported the Democratic party; died in Palm Springs, Calif., October 10, 1971; Philip Taft, *Labor Politics American Style: The California State Federation of Labor* (1968); Louis B. Perry and Richard S. Perry, *A History of the Los Angeles Labor Movement, 1911–1941* (1963); *Who's Who in Labor* (1946).

HAGGERTY, John B.   (1884–1953). Born in St. Louis, Mo., in 1884; son of William R., an auditor, and Mary Haggerty; Roman Catholic; never married; completed a secondary school education in St. Louis, then became an apprentice in the printing industry; joined St. Louis Local 18 of the International Brotherhood of Bookbinders (IBB) and eventually served as its president; served as an international representative, international vice-president, and a member of the IBB executive council during the period 1916–1926; was an American Federation of Labor (AFL) fraternal delegate to the Trades and Labor Conference of Canada in 1929; elected international president of the IBB in 1926; served as a printing trades labor advisor to the National Recovery Administration, 1933–1935; was an AFL fraternal delegate to the British Trades Union Congress in 1937; during World War II, was a member of the labor advisory committee of the War Production Board; served for several years prior to his death as chairman of the board of governors of the International Allied Printing Trades Association; was a Democrat and a member of the Democratic National Committee's labor committee; died in Miami, Fla., March 4, 1953; *The American Federationist* (March 1953); *The New York Times,* March 5, 1953; *Who's Who in Labor* (1946).

HAIGLER, Carey Elbert   (1902–   ). Born in Ensley, Ala., on August 9, 1902; son of Frank Hampton, a foreman in a coal washery, and Mary Alma (Zeigler) Haigler; Methodist; married Sammie Louise Lusk on October 10, 1935; one child; attended high school for three years before dropping out of school and taking a job as a steelworker with the Tennessee Coal and Iron Company in Birmingham; joined Local 20 of the Amalgamated Association of Iron, Steel, and Tin Workers in 1934 and was eventually elected corresponding secretary and then president of the local; affiliated with the Steel Workers Organizing Committee (SWOC) after its organization in 1937, and became the SWOC representative in the Birmingham district; became a member of Local 1489 of the United Steelworkers of America (USWA) after it was chartered by the Congress of Industrial Organizations (CIO) in 1942; became a field representative and secretary-treasurer of the Alabama State Industrial Union Council, CIO, before being elected president of the state council in 1944, a postion he held until 1949; served as the regional director for the CIO in Alabama and as a member of the CIO's Political Action Committee; involved in a variety of public and private civic activities, he was a member of the Palestine for Jews Committee, the County War and Community Chest Committee and the Alabama chapter of the Southern Conference for Human Welfare; during his years as a state labor leader, his greatest contribution was in negotiating the difficult waters of racial division in the Alabama labor movement and convincing white workers that the organization of black workers was critical to their own best interests; a Democrat; Philip Taft, *Organizing Dixie: Alabama Workers in the Industrial Era* (1981); George G. Kundahl, Jr., "Organized Labor in Alabama State Politics" (Ph.D. diss., 1967); *Who's Who in Labor* (1946); Carey E. Haigler Papers, Southern Labor Archives, Georgia State University.

HALEY, Margaret Angela   (1861–1939). Born in Joliet, Ill., November 15, 1861; daughter of Michael, a stone-quarry and construction firm operator, and Elizabeth (Tiernan) Haley; Roman Catholic; attended grammar school at Channahon, Ill., and high school at St. Angela's Convent, Morris, Ill.; worked as a teacher in Dresden Heights, Joliet, and Lake, Ill., before securing a position at Henricks Elementary School, Chicago, Ill.; was an organizer of the Chicago Federation of Teachers (CFT) in 1897; was elected a CFT district vice-president in 1900; served as a full-time business agent of the CFT, 1901–1939; as a result of her persuasive arguments, the CFT affiliated with the Chicago Federation of Labor (CFL) in 1902; reorganized the National Federation of Teachers in 1901 and served as its president, 1901–ca. 1906; after the CFT was chartered as Local 1 of the American Federation of Teachers (AFT) in 1916, became the first national organizer of the AFT; withdrew the CFT from the AFT in 1917, after the Illinois Supreme Court upheld the Loeb rule that gave local school boards the right to refuse to hire, or to dismiss, teachers because of union membership; was instrumental in securing the state tenure law for teachers in 1917; served on the executive committee of the Labor party which ran John Fitzpatrick (q.v.) of the CFL for mayor of Chicago in 1919; was a constant agitator throughout career for the right of teachers to engage in union activities, and was a constant critic of corporations that failed to pay taxes on school lands they used; died in Chicago, Ill., January 5, 1939; *Notable American Women*, Vol. 2; Robert J. Braun, *Teachers and Power: The Story of the American Federation of Teachers* (1972); Robert L. Reid, ed., *Battleground: The Autobiography of Margaret A. Haley* (1982).

Marie Tedesco

HALL, Burton   (1929–   ). Born in South Orange, N.J., on November 16, 1929; son of Henry, a lawyer, and Harriet (Parsons) Hall, an astronomer and college professor; Presbyterian; attended public and Quaker grade schools, graduated from Williams College in 1951 and Yale Law School in 1954; was a member of the Food, Tobacco and Agricultural Workers Union in Camden, N.J., the International Longshoremen's and Warehousemen's Union, Local 11, and the International Association of Machinists, Local 751, on the West Coast, while in college and law school; served in the U.S. Army, 1954–1956; was admitted to the New York bar in 1957; worked as a lawyer for private firms and the Federal Aviation Agency before turning to labor law; from the 1960s, he has represented rank-and-file union members in relations with their unions in numerous cases involving such issues as restrictions on eligibility for running for union office, discipline against members for criticism of their leadership, and expulsion of union members for advocating radical political ideas; in his first such case, he successfully represented two members of the Steamfitters' Union who had been fined by their union for distributing leaflets at a union meeting, then barred from running for union office when they refused to pay the fine; has also represented union members against employers in discharge, discipline, and discrimination cases; was expelled from the Soviet Union in 1977 as a result of his attempts to file a petition for review of the criminal conviction of a Ukrainian political activist, Oleksander Serkhiyenko; his firm, Hall, Clifton and Schwartz, formed in 1980, is counsel for the New York Teamsters for a Democratic Union and for various local unions in New York, including the Drywall Tapers and Pointers (Painters Local 1974), Local 101 of the Transport Workers Union, and the United Staff Association (an affiliate of the New York State United Teachers); served on the national board of the Workers' Defense League during the 1960s and 1970s; edited *Autocracy and Insurgency in Organized Labor* (1972), a collection of articles and exchanges on issues of internal union democracy, many written by individuals who had been his clients over the previous eight years;

also contributed to *The Nation* and *New Politics* on labor and union democracy issues.

Jon Bloom

HALL, Paul   (1914–1980). Born in Alabama, August 21, 1914; married Rose; two children; attended the public schools of Alabama, then went to sea as an engine wiper in the early 1930s; was one of the founding members of the Seafarers International Union of North America (SIU) in 1938; served as an oiler on merchant ships during World War II; became a port patrolman after the war and elected the SIU's port agent in New York; elected first vice-president of the SIU in 1948 and became the SIU's chief officer for the Atlantic, Gulf, Great Lakes, and Inland Waters district; continuing to serve as secretary-treasurer for the Atlantic and Gulf district, became president of the SIU and president of the American Federation of Labor-Congress of Industrial Organizations' (AFL-CIO) maritime trades department in 1957; served as chief organizer of the International Brotherhood of Longshoremen, a newly chartered AFL international union that unsuccessfully attempted to supplant the International Longshoremen's Association after its expulsion from the AFL in 1953; elected an AFL-CIO vice-president and executive council member in 1962; along with Joseph Curran (q.v.), president of the National Maritime Union, established the short-lived International Maritime Workers Union to represent seamen working on American-owned ships flying the flags of Liberia, Panama, and Honduras; devoted much of his time and energy to eliminating Communist influence in maritime unions; usually supported Democratic candidates, but was a strong supporter of Republican president Richard M. Nixon; died in New York City on June 22, 1980; Joseph P. Goldberg, *The Maritime Story: A Study in Labor-Management Relations* (1958); Maud Russell, *Men along the Shore* (1966); *Current Biography* (1966); *AFL-CIO News*, June 28, 1980; *The New York Times*, June 23, 1980.

HALLBECK, Elroy Charles   (1902–1969). Born in Chicago, Ill., May 15, 1902; son of Charles August and Anna Marie (Hansen) Hallbeck; Unitarian; married Myrtle Elizabeth Montgomery on August 30, 1957; one child by a previous marriage; received a secondary education in the public schools of Chicago, then hired by the U.S. Postal Service in Chicago as a clerk in 1921; joined Local 1 of the National Federation of Postal Clerks (NFPC); elected president of Local 1 in 1934 after having served as secretary since 1926; elected a national vice-president of the NFPC in 1940 and served in that capacity until 1944 when he was appointed assistant national legislative director in Washington, D.C.; became national legislative director in 1946 and served in that capacity until his death; elected national president of the NFPC in 1960; negotiated a merger of the National Postal Transport Association, the United National Association of Post Office Craftsmen, and the NFPC in 1961 that created the United Federation of Postal Clerks (UFPC); elected chairman of the Government Employees Council, American Federation of Labor-Congress of Industrial Organizations in 1961;

was a member of the board of directors of the Union Life Insurance Company in New York City, and the Washington Arthritis and Rheumatism Foundation; attempting to negotiate the reunification of the UFPC and the National Postal Union at the time of his death; was a Democrat; died in Washington, D.C., January 14, 1969; *Who's Who in America, 1968–1969*; *AFL-CIO News,* January 18, 1964.

HANDLEY, John Joseph   (1876–1941). Born in Horicon, Wis., on August 5, 1876; received his early education in the public schools of Horicon and then served an apprenticeship as a machinist, joined the International Association of Machinists (IAM) in Rockford, Ill., as a journeyman in 1899; supported the eight-hour strike in Milwaukee, Wis., in 1901; was business agent and special organizer for Milwaukee District Lodge No. 10, IAM, 1902–1910; also served as business manager for IAM Lodge No. 66; was elected to the executive board of the Wisconsin State Federation of Labor (WSFL) in 1905, serving until 1907; was elected secretary-treasurer of the WSFL in 1912 and served in that capacity until his death (the office became a full-time, paid position in 1919); was instrumental in implementing the Wisconsin Workmen's Compensation Act of 1911; from 1919 to 1941 he was one of Wisconsin labor's major lobbyists in the state legislature, and in that capacity, he was a staunch advocate of old–age and widow's pensions, unemployment compensation, wage and hours laws, injunction reform, improved educational opportunities, and state recognition of collective bargaining rights; a Socialist who served in the administrations of Socialist mayors Emil Seidel (q.v.) and Daniel Hoan; during the New Deal years, he supported the creation of a progressive farmer-labor alliance that could influence the programs and policies of Robert M. La Follette's Progressive party in Wisconsin; died in Milwaukee on October 17, 1941; *Dictionary of Wisconsin Biography* (1960); Thomas W. Gavett, *Development of the Labor Movement in Milwaukee* (1965).

HAPGOOD, Mary Donovan   (1886–1973). Born in North Brookfield, Mass., on February 21, 1886; daughter of Dennis, a shoe worker, and Kate (Rice) Donovan, immigrants from Ireland; Roman Catholic; married Powers Hapgood (q.v.) on December 28, 1927; two children; principally known for her role in the defense of the Italian anarchists Sacco and Vanzetti (q.v.), which led Upton Sinclair to call her the ''Joan of Arc of the labor movement''; at age 7, three years after her mother's death, she was sent to Stafford, Conn., to live with an aunt who physically abused her; attended grammar school in Stafford and North Brookfield and high school in North Brookfield; entered the University of Michigan in 1906 as a devout Catholic; joined the Intercollegiate Socialist Society (ISS) in her third year, influenced by her brother Daniel, who had become a Socialist in the course of ten years spent in the West as a railroad worker, ranch hand, miner, and prospector; informed by Catholic authorities that she must resign from the ISS or leave the church; refused to do either and was excommunicated; joined the Socialist party in 1911; after graduating from Michigan in 1912, became a schoolteacher near North Brookfield; joined the Worcester (Mass.) Women's Trade Union League as a charter member in 1915, and served as its secretary-treasurer, 1915–1916; became a Massachusetts state factory inspector ca. 1917 and quickly developed a reputation for strict enforcement of labor laws; joined the Boston, Mass., local of the Stenographers', Bookkeepers', Accountants', and Office Employees' Union, serving as its delegate to the Boston Central Labor Union and to the Massachusetts Federation of Labor conventions of 1926–1927; traveled with her close friend James Larkin (founder of the Irish Transport and General Workers' Union) on American fund-raising campaigns for the Irish nationalist movement; was a leader of the Socialist and anti-clerical James Connolly Club of Boston, an Irish-American group; in 1921 went to Europe with Julia O'Connor (q.v.) to study labor conditions; her interest in the Sacco-Vanzetti case was first aroused in 1921 at a meeting addressed by Elizabeth Gurley Flynn (q.v.) and H.W.L. Dana; after 1924, she was a principal figure in the defense effort, serving as recording secretary of the Sacco-Vanzetti Defense Committee, 1924–1927; developed a strong emotional attachment to Bartolomeo Vanzetti, whom she often visited in prison (her daughter Barta is named for him); was fired as state factory inspector in April 1927 for allegedly spending work time on defense committee business; speaking on Boston Common shortly before the execution, was dragged from the platform by police when she called Governor Fuller a murderer; was arrested after having tried to place a placard critical of Judge Thayer before the caskets of Sacco and Vanzetti, and was sentenced to one year in prison for "inciting to riot" and "distributing anarchistic literature"; delivered the eulogy at the funeral of Sacco and Vanzetti; a bitter enemy of the Communists, who in 1926–1927 tried to wrest leadership of the Sacco-Vanzetti agitation from the defense committee, she was denounced by Mike Gold as "an obscure, spiteful female"; after the execution, became a dishwasher (as Vanzetti had once been) at Schrafft's in New York; served on the editorial board of the anti-fascist *Lantern*, 1927–1929, which grew out of the defense committee's bulletin; became active with her husband in the mine workers' insurgent movement in the Pennsylvania coal fields, and was jailed while leading a free-speech fight; was a Socialist party candidate for governor of Massachusetts in 1928, the first woman ever nominated for that office; moved to Lafayette, Colo., and wrote about the mines while her husband dug coal; in the 1930s moved to a farm near Indianapolis, Ind.; joined the staff of the Congress of Industrial Organizations' Textile Workers' Organizing Committee in 1937 and had charge of its central Massachusetts district; returned to Indiana, and was a contributor to the anti-fascist journal, *Controcorrente/Countercurrent*, established by Aldino Felicani in 1938; in the 1960s was active in the peace movement and Sacco-Vanzetti memorial activities; died in Indianapolis, on June 24, 1973; Mary Donovan Hapgood Papers, Lilly Library, Indiana University; Upton Sinclair, *Boston* (1928); Marion Denman Frankfurter and Gardner Jackson, eds.,

The Letters of Sacco and Vanzetti (1928); Jeannette Marks, *Thirteen Days* (1929); *Indianapolis Star,* June 27, 1973.

Stephen H. Norwood

HAPGOOD, Powers   (1899–1949). Born in Chicago, Ill., December 28, 1899; son of William Powers, president of Columbia Conserve Company, a canning factory operated under workers' management in Indianapolis, Ind., and Eleanor (Page) Hapgood; married Mary Donovan (q.v.), recording secretary of the Sacco-Vanzetti (q.v.) Defense Committee, Socialist party candidate for governor of Massachusetts in 1928, and textile workers' organizer for the Committee for Industrial Organization (CIO) in New England, on December 28, 1927; two children; attended grammar school and high school in Indianapolis and was graduated from Phillips Academy, Andover, Mass., in 1917; was graduated from Harvard University in 1921, finishing his course work in three years, with 1920–1921 spent studying the ''labor problem'' in a Minnesota iron mine, as a railroad section hand, as a teamster in Kansas, in a Montana sugar beet factory, and as a coal miner in Montana, Colorado, and Pennsylvania; joined the United Mine Workers of America (UMWA) and was an organizer for John Brophy's (q.v.) District 2, Central Pennsylvania, 1922–1924; led the non-union Somerset County, Pa., miners during the national coal strike of 1922 and was arrested a dozen times; worked in the coal mines of Wales, France, Germany, and the Soviet Union, 1924–1926; returned to Pennsylvania mines and joined the Socialist party; managed John Brophy's ''Save the Union'' campaign in 1926, an unsuccessful left-wing challenge to John L. Lewis's (q.v.) control of the UMWA; went to Boston in 1927 to take part in the last-ditch effort to save Sacco and Vanzetti, and worked as a docker; was arrested four times in the nine days preceding the execution and was imprisoned in an insane asylum; served on the editorial board of the *Lantern,* 1927–1929, the first English-language publication specifically devoted to combatting fascism; moved in 1928 to Wilkes-Barre, Pa., where he worked in an anthracite colliery and was jailed with his wife for ''inciting to riot'' after attempting to hold a meeting to defend three mine union dissidents accused of murder; after the couple's acquittal, they settled in Lafayette, Colo., where he worked as a miner and (after Lewis expelled him from the UMWA in 1929) as an assistant mining engineer; in 1930 joined with other anti-Lewis insurgents in founding the Illinois-based Reorganized UMWA, which disbanded after an unfavorable court ruling in 1931; unable to get a job in the mines, he worked for his father's Columbia Conserve Company from 1930 to 1933, but resigned in a dispute over his father's policies; was Socialist party candidate for governor of Indiana in 1932, and served on the party's national executive committee, 1932–1936; organized for the Amalgamated Clothing Workers in Kentucky in 1933; moved to Massachusetts, where he was business agent of the Gasoline Filling Station Workers' Union in Worcester, 1934–1935, and led the textile workers in central Massachusetts during their general strike in September 1934; sent by Norman Thomas (q.v.) in May 1935 to Arkansas to assist in the

organizing drive of the Southern Tenant Farmers' Union; with the founding of
the CIO, returned to work for John L. Lewis and became one of the CIO's
leading organizers; with Rose Pesotta (q.v.), Adolph Germer (q.v.), and Leo
Kyzycki (q.v.), was one of the "four horsemen" who helped lead the Akron,
Ohio, rubber workers to victory in the CIO's first test, the sit-down strike of
1936; worked for the Steel Workers' Organizing Committee in Ohio and Pennsylvania, and then went to Camden, N.J., to help the newly formed United
Electrical and Radio Workers' Union in its first big strike, against RCA Manufacturing Company, which was marked by exceptional police brutality and mass
arrests (including that of Hapgood); headed union committee to defend arrested
RCA strikers; organized gas and coke workers for the UMWA in the Northeast;
went to Flint, Mich., in January 1937 to help lead the auto workers' sit-down
strike; assigned to Fisher plants 1 and 2 in Saginaw, he helped plan the takeover
of Chevrolet plant 4, considered the strike's turning point; in February returned
to Boston to direct the New England CIO drive to organize five major industries,
devoting special attention to shoe workers; jailed in Lewiston, Me., where he
led a strike for union recognition against 19 shoe factories; served as national
director of the United Shoe Workers of America, 1937–1940; organized for the
Industrial Union of Marine Shipbuilders in the East Coast and Great Lakes ports,
1940–1941 and helped lead a strike in San Pedro, Calif.; in 1941 represented
the Farm Equipment Workers Organizing Committee in strike negotiations with
the International Harvester Company; was regional director of the Indiana CIO,
1941–1947, and served on the national committee of the American Civil Liberties
Union, 1930–1949; was the author of *In Non-Union Mines: The Diary of a Coal
Digger in Central Pennsylvania, August–September 1921* (1922) died of a heart
attack near Indianapolis on February 4, 1949; Powers Hapgood Papers, Lilly
Library, Indiana University; Rose Pesotta, *Bread upon the Waters* (1945); John
Bartlow Martin, *Indiana* (1947); John Brophy, *A Miner's Life* (1964); Kurt
Vonnegut, *Jailbird* (1979); Solon DeLeon, ed., *The American Labor Who's Who*
(1925); *Who's Who in Labor* (1946); *CIO News*, February 14, 1949; *The New
York Times*, February 5, 1949; Melvyn Dubofsky and Warren Van Tine, *John
L. Lewis: A Biography* (1977).

Stephen H. Norwood

HARRINGTON, Michael   (1928–   ). Born in St. Louis, Mo., on February 24, 1928; son of Edward H., a lawyer, and Catherine (Fitzgibbon) Harrington, a teacher; married Stephanie Gervis; two children; educated at St. Louis
University High School and earned the B.A. from Holy Cross University in
1947; attended Yale Law School, 1947–1948; received an M.A. from the University of Chicago in 1949; served as the associate editor of the *Catholic Worker*,
1951–1952; was a staff member of the Fund for the Republic's study of blacklisting in the entertainment industry, 1954–1956, and the trade union project,
1956–1962; organized a section of the Workers' Defense League, 1954–1956;
served as national chairman of the Young Socialists League, 1955–1958; was a

member of Sargent Shriver's Task Force on Poverty in 1964; was a co-organizer of the March on the Democratic Convention Movement in 1960; recruited by Walter Reuther (q.v.) as the keynote speaker for the founding convention of the Citizens' Crusade Against Poverty in 1965 and worked for the crusade to 1967; was a member of Negotiations Now, 1966–1967, Martin Luther King's advisory committee, 1965–1968, the national board of the American Civil Liberties Union, 1965, the national steering committee of the New Democratic Coalition, 1968, the national board of SANE, 1969–1970, and Democracy '76, 1976; was a visiting professor at the University of Illinois in 1970 and a faculty member of District 37, American Federation of State, County and Municipal Employees College, 1972; since 1973, has been a professor of political science at Queens College; served as the national chairman of the Socialist party, 1968–1972; was a participant in the split in the Socialist party over George McGovern's candidacy for president of the United States on the Democratic party ticket in 1972; was an active member of Labor for McGovern, a coalition that included the United Auto Workers, the American Federation of State, County and Municipal Employees, and the International Association of Machinists; was a founding member and national chairman of the Democratic Socialist Organizing Committee (DSOC), 1973–1982; became national chairman of Democratic Socialists of America, which emerged out of the merger of DSOC and the New American Movement in 1982; a member of the American Federation of Teachers; authored numerous books and articles, including *The Other America* (1962), *The Retail Clerks* (1962), *The Accidental Century* (1965), *Toward a Democratic Left* (1968), *Socialism* (1972), *Fragments of the Century* (1973), *The Twilight of Capitalism* (1976), *The Vast Majority* (1977), *Decade of Decision* (1980), *The Next America* (1981), and co-author of *Labor in a Free Society* (1959), *Unfinished Democracy* (1981), and co-editor of *The Seventies* (1972); Nelson Lichtenstein, ed., *Political Profiles: The Johnson Years* (1976).

Robert Fitrakis

HARRIS, David   (fl. 1837–1890). Born in England in 1837; served as president of the United Sons of Vulcan, 1874–1876; corresponded with David A. Plant and William Martin (q.v.) of the Roll Hands' Union about amalgamating with other ironworkers' unions and urged his union to adopt the idea; was active in the Amalgamated Association of Iron and Steel Workers; was boss puddler and assistant superintendent, Oliver Brothers Mill in the Woods Run district of Pittsburgh, Pa., 1880–1889; a member of Pittsburgh's Ninth Ward school board, 1882–1884; was a member of the Republican city executive committee in 1886; disappeared from the trade union scene in March 1890; *Pittsburgh City Directories: Vulcan Record*, 1874–1876; John William Bennett, "Iron Workers in Woods Run and Johnstown: The Union Era, 1865–1895" (Ph.D. diss., 1977).

Sharon Trusilo

HARRISON, George MacGregor   (1895–1968). Born in Lois, Mo., July 19, 1895; son of Louis Harvey, a merchant, and Mary Loga (Coppedge) Harrison;

Baptist; married Averil Mayo Hughes on October 16, 1912; three children; completed grammar school at age 14, then took a job on the Missouri Pacific Railroad; worked during 1909–1917 at various times as a yard clerk, distribution clerk, storekeeper, and mechanical valuation clerk; elected chairman of the St. Louis local of the Brotherhood of Railway and Steamship Clerks, Freight Handlers, Express and Station Employees (BRC) in 1917, serving until 1922; served as vice-president of the BRC, 1922–1928; elected grand president of the BRC in 1928; elected an American Federation of Labor (AFL) vice-president and executive council member in 1934; served as chairman of the Railway Labor Executives' Association, 1935–1940; served on the United States delegation of the American National Committee to the Third World Power Conference and as an American labor delegate to the International Labor Organization conference in Geneva in 1936 and Cuba in 1939; helped draft both the Railroad Retirement Act and the Social Security Act; chaired the AFL executive council subcommittee which attempted to mediate differences with the Committee for Industrial Organization (CIO) in 1935; not particularly sympathetic to the CIO, but opposed the AFL executive council's suspension of CIO affiliates as an unconstitutional exercise of authority; served on the advisory board of the National Youth Administration; served during World War II on the Joint Railroad Labor-Management Committee and the National Defense Mediation Board; served after the war on the President's Labor-Management Committee and was an advisor to the Council of Economic Advisors; served for many years as a director of the Workers' Education League of America and in 1948 became its president; became a vice-president and executive council member of the merged AFL-CIO in 1955; was appointed a member of the United States delegation to the United Nations in 1958; appointed to the President's Advisory Committee on Labor-Management Policy in 1961; was a member of numerous private and public boards and agencies, including the American Institute for Free Labor Development, the Afro-Asian Institute in Israel, and the Afro-American Labor Center; served as a trustee of both the Harry S. Truman and John F. Kennedy Library foundations; retired BRC presidency in 1963 and became chief executive officer; became president emeritus in 1965; was a Democrat; died in Cincinnati, Ohio, November 30, 1968; Harry Henig, *The Brotherhood of Railway Clerks* (1937); Philip Taft, *The A.F. of L from the Death of Gompers to the Merger* (1959); *Current Biography* (1949); *The American Federationist* (May 1941); *AFL-CIO News*, December 7, 1968.

HARTUNG, Albert Ferdinand   (1897–1973). Born in Cataract, Wis., June 18, 1897; son of Ernest and Minnie Hartung; married Farris Chapman on August 5, 1922, and Nina Calhoun on September 5, 1953; four children; attended the public schools of Cataract and eventually became a logger in the Pacific Northwest; in 1915 joined the Industrial Workers of the World; eventually joined an American Federation of Labor local union organized in Vernonia, Oreg., and in 1933 was elected president of the local; was a delegate to the founding convention of the International Woodworkers of America (IWA) in 1937, and served as president of Columbia River District Council 5, 1937–1941; was assistant director of organization for the IWA, 1941–1942; served during World War II with the lumber division of the War Production Board and the Office of Price Administration; also served on the West Coast Lumber Committee of the War Labor Board; became the Congress of Industrial Organizations' regional director for Oregon in 1942, serving until 1947; was first vice-president of the IWA during 1947–1951, then became international president; was a persistent critic of the Eisenhower administration's alleged anti-labor positions, and also refused to cooperate with the Kennedy administration's Committee on Equal Employment Opportunity by providing racial breakdowns of union membership; was a Democrat; retired IWA presidency in 1967; died in Portland, Oreg., in July 1973; *Who's Who in America, 1958–1959, 1972–1973*; *Who's Who in Labor* (1946); *CIO News* October 15, 1951; *ALF-CIO News*, July 28, 1973.

HAYES, Albert John   (1900–1981). Born in Milwaukee, Wis., February 14, 1900; son of Albert and Augusta (Wolter) Hayes; Lutheran; married Lillian M. Fink on February 25, 1921; one child; attended the public schools of Milwaukee, then began work in the railroad shops of Milwaukee as an apprentice machinist; joined the International Association of Machinists (IAM) in 1917; served during 1917–1934 as a local committeeman, local union officer, and as president of IAM District 7; appointed Grand Lodge representative in 1934, serving in that capacity until 1944; served on the War Labor Board during World War II; became an international vice-president in 1945 and was elected IAM president in 1949; led the IAM back into the American Federation of Labor (AFL) from which it had withdrawn in 1943 over a jurisdiction dispute with the United Brotherhood of Carpenters; served during 1950–1951 as a labor member of the National Security Board, the Advisory Committee to the Economic Stabilization Agency, and the Labor-Management Advisory Committee; became a special assistant to the Assistant Secretary of Defense in 1951; appointed chairman of the President's Commission on the Health Needs of the Nation in 1951; elected a vice-president and executive council member of the AFL in 1953; created much controversy in labor circles by advocating a plan of compulsory arbitration during testimony before the Senate Labor Committee in 1953; after the AFL-Congress of Industrial Organizations merger, he became a vice-president and executive council member of the new federation; retired union positions in 1965; died on August 20, 1981; Mark Perlman, *The Machinists: A New Study in American Trade Unionism* (1961), and *Democracy in the International Association of Machinists* (1962); *Current Biography* (1953); Albert J. Hayes, Columbia Oral History Collection; *AFL-CIO News*, August 22, 1981.

HAYES, Frank J.   (1882–1948). Born in What Cheer, Iowa, in 1882; son of a coal miner; Roman Catholic; unmarried; moved with family to Illinois in his youth; attended the public schools of Collinsville and Mt. Olive, Ill.; at age

13, began working as a coal miner; joined the United Mine Workers of America (UMWA) and held several local union offices; elected secretary-treasurer of the Belleville subdistrict of District 12, UMWA, Illinois, in 1904, when Adolph Germer (q.v.) served as subdistrict vice-president; with Germer, was among the most active Socialist leaders in the Illinois miners' movement; appointed to the executive board of District 12 in 1908; elected and served as international vice-president of the UMWA, 1910–1917; during his incumbency, directed the West Virginia coal strike of 1912–1913 and the violent Colorado coal strike of 1913–1914, which culminated in the Ludlow Massacre; after John P. White (q.v.) resigned as president to serve as labor consultant to the National Fuel Administration in 1917, elected as UMWA international president, serving until 1920; as president, had neither the taste nor talent for administration and, troubled by illness, turned most of his duties of office over to vice-president and acting president John L. Lewis (q.v.); resigned in 1920 and moved to Colorado, allegedly to seek a cure for alcoholism, meanwhile continuing as an UMWA international representative until his death; ran unsuccessfully for governor of Illinois on the Socialist party ticket in 1912, and in 1937–1938, after the Colorado miners were organized, elected for one term as lieutenant governor of Colorado on the Democratic ticket; was a labor poet and wrote strike songs and poems about Ludlow; died in Denver, Colo., June 10, 1948; George S. McGovern and Leonard F. Guttridge, *Great Coalfield War* (1972); *United Mine Workers Journal*, July 1, 1948.

John W. Hevener

HAYES, John W.   (1854–1942). Born in Philadelphia, Pa., December 26, 1854; son of Edward and Mary (Galbreath) Hayes; married Nellie A. Carlen in July 1882; when 9, was taken to Europe by parents, and remained several years; received no formal education; upon return, through financial reverses of family, went to work as brakeman on Pennsylvania railroad, served for eight years; settled in New Brunswick, N.J.; in 1878, while on duty was thrown on track and train passed over his right arm, necessitating amputation; compelled to seek other employment, became a telegraph operator; in 1883, was delegate to the Chicago Telegraphers' Convention, which ordered the great strike, in which he took a prominent part; upon failure of strike, went into grocery business and owned two large stores in New Brunswick; was one of the most prominent Knights of Labor in New Jersey, having joined it in 1874; in 1879, with the assistance of several others, he called the first New Jersey congress, and was its president for two terms; was elected general secretary of the Knights of Labor in 1888, serving until 1902; made charges of corruption against Knights of Labor leader Terence V. Powderly (q.v.) in 1893 which forced his resignation from the Knights; was elected grand master workman in 1902 and retained that position until 1906; was editor of the *Journal of the Knights of Labor* and the *National Labor Digest*; was president of the North Chesapeake Beach Land and Improvement Company; died on November 24, 1942; Gerald N. Grob, *Workers and*

Utopia: A Study of Ideological Conflict in the American Labor Movement, 1865–1900 (1961); Warren R. Van Tine, *The Making of the Labor Bureaucrat: Union Leadership in the United States, 1870–1920* (1973); George E. McNeill, *The Labor Movement: The Problem of To-Day* (1887); Norman J. Ware, *The Labor Movement in the United States, 1860–1895* (1929); *Who Was Who*, Vol. 2; John W. Hayes Papers, Catholic University of America.

George E. McNeill

HAYES, Maximilian Sebastian   (1866–1945). Born in Havana, Ohio, May 25, 1866; son of Joseph Maximilian Sebastian, a farmer, and Elizabeth (Borer) Hayes; reared a Roman Catholic; married Dora Schneider on December 11, 1900; one child; gained a grammar school education in the public schools of Ohio; became a printer's apprentice at age 13; joined the International Typographical Union (ITU) in 1884; was one of the founders of the *Cleveland Citizen*, which in 1892 became the official organ of the Cleveland Central Labor Union; served as the editor of the *Cleveland Citizen*, 1892–1939; was an influential figure in the Cleveland labor movement and served as a general organizer in the area for 15 years; was an American Federation of Labor (AFL) fraternal delegate to the British Trades Union Congress in 1903; was a long-time ITU delegate to the annual conventions of the AFL and was one of the leaders of the Socialist opposition to the AFL leadership; authored the Ohio Workmen's Compensation Law of 1911; unsuccessfully contested Samuel Gompers's (q.v.) re-election to the AFL presidency in 1912; was a member of the Ohio State Adjustment Board of the National Recovery Administration, 1933–1935; was a charter member of the Cleveland Metropolitan Housing Authority organized in 1933; spent much of his lifetime trying unsuccessfully to find a mutual basis of accord between Socialist principles and the American labor movement; identified with the Populist party until 1896, then the Socialist Labor party, 1896–1899, and finally the Socialist party of America after 1899; was a Socialist candidate for the U.S. Congress from Ohio in 1900, for secretary of state of Ohio in 1902, and for vice president of the United States on the Farmer-Labor ticket in 1920; died in Cleveland, Ohio, October 11, 1945; Philip Taft, *The A.F. of L. in the Time of Gompers* (1957); Lewis L. Lorwin, *The American Federation of Labor: History, Policies, and Prospects* (1933); James Weinstein, *The Decline of Socialism in America, 1912–1925* (1967); *Dictionary of American Biography*, Suppl. 3.

HAYWOOD, Allan Shaw   (1888–1953). Born in Yorkshire, England, on October 9, 1888; son of Arthur, a miner, and Ann Haywood; married Kate Dewsnap on May 31, 1909; three children; quit school, entered the mines, and joined the British Miners' Federation at age 13 in 1901; emigrated to the United States in 1906 and settled in Illinois where he continued as a coal miner and immediately joined the United Mine Workers of America (UMWA); becoming active in union affairs, during the next several years, he served successively as subdistrict vice-president, subdistrict president, and district executive board member of the

UMWA; served as a vice-president of the Illinois State Federation of Labor; was an advisor to the United Rubber Workers of America in 1936 and negotiated a contract with the Firestone Rubber Company, the first such agreement with a major producer in the rubber industry; served at various times as an organizer in the automobile, paper, gas, coke, chemical, department store, communications, packinghouse, and toy industries; appointed as the Congress of Industrial Organizations (CIO) regional director for New York City in 1937; between 1937–1939, he served as regional director of the Steel Workers' Organizing Committee, chairman of the Utility Workers' Organizing Committee, and president of the New York State Industrial Union Council, CIO; appointed CIO national director of organization in 1939 and served in that capacity until 1953; during World War II, he served as a member of the labor advisory committee to the Office of Price Mobilization and was a member of the advisory committee to the Council of National Defense; served as administrator of the Union of Federal Workers, 1941–1944; elected a CIO vice-president in 1942; was chairman of the Paper Workers Organizing Committee and a member of the Union of Railroad Workers Organizing Committee in 1944; was chairman of the Telephone Workers Organizing Committee which ultimately led to the chartering of the Communications Workers of America; was appointed head of the CIO department of industrial union councils in 1950; appointed to the newly created post of executive vice-president in 1951; a delegate to the 1949 London international trade union conference that established the International Confederation of Free Trade Unions as a rival to the Communist-dominated World Federation of Trade Unions; a popular personality in the labor movement who came to be known as Mr. CIO, he lost a bitterly contested election to Walter Reuther (q.v.) to succeed Philip Murray (q.v.) as president of the CIO in 1952; a Democrat; died in Wilkes-Barre, Pa., on February 21, 1953; Walter Galenson, *The CIO Challenge to the AFL: A History of the American Labor Movement, 1935–1941* (1960); *Current Biography* (1952); *Dictionary of American Biography*, Suppl. 5; *Who's Who in Labor* (1946); *CIO News*, March 2, 1953; Harvey A. Levenstein, *Communism, Anticommunism, and the CIO* (1981); Melvyn Dubofsky and Warren Van Tine, *John L. Lewis: A Biography* (1977); Thomas R. Brooks, *Communication Workers of America: The Story of a Union* (1977).

HAYWOOD, William Dudley   (1869–1928). Born in Salt Lake City, Utah, February 4, 1869; son of William Dudley, a pioneer and miner, who died in 1872; his mother was remarried to a miner; although his family was Episcopalian, he renounced the church; married Nevada Jane Minor in 1889; his formal education was interrupted by the necessity to hold odd jobs; subsequently read widely; at 15, went to work full-time as a miner, and for the next decade employed at several mines in Nevada and Utah; in 1894, moved his family to the mining town of Silver City, Idaho, and there joined and became an officer of a local of the recently formed Western Federation of Miners (WFM); elected a delegate to the 1898 WFM convention and came to the attention of President Edward

Boyce (q.v.); elected in 1899 to the WFM executive board; in 1900, elected secretary-treasurer of the WFM and moved to Denver, Colo.; had a major role in directing the bitter strikes at Telluride and Cripple Creek, Colo.; reacting to the exploitative policies of the mining corporations and to their adamant opposition to unions, evolved from a militant trade unionist into an advocate of revolutionary industrial unionism; in 1905, helped organize and chair the founding convention of the Industrial Workers of the World (IWW); jailed in 1906 along with WFM president Charles Moyer (q.v.) for the murder of a former Idaho governor, but acquitted in 1907; the case became a cause célèbre and Haywood became nationally known in labor and radical circles; purged by the moderates who dominated the WFM in 1908 and disgusted by the bickering of IWW factions, from 1908 to 1912 traveled throughout the country as an organizer and speaker for the Socialist party; became disillusioned with political socialism and rejoined the IWW as an active leader of the successful Lawrence, Mass., textile strike of 1912; elected general secretary (chief officer) of the IWW in 1915 and presided over Walter Nef's (q.v.) highly effective organizing drive of the Agricultural Workers Organization (AWO); taking advantage of the impetus and funds provided by the AWO, centralized authority in his office over organizing and altered the IWW's loose structure along the lines of separate industrial unions directly responsible to the Chicago, Ill., headquarters; his large stature, rugged features, and gruff manner seemed to personify the violent frontier milieu; but also concerned with all kinds of exploited workers; his obvious sincerity, courage, and commanding presence made him one of the most effective labor orators and agitators of the era; convicted in 1917 for violating the Espionage Act and, along with many other Wobblies, imprisoned; released in 1919 pending an appeal and agitated on behalf of his imprisoned colleagues; beguiled by the Bolshevik Revolution, jumped bail in 1921 to go to the Soviet Union and there reportedly managed a mining complex and later helped set up the International Labor Defense to aid jailed radicals and unionists; died in Moscow, USSR, May 18, 1928; *Bill Haywood's Book: The Autobiography of William D. Haywood* (1929); Joseph H. Conlin, *Big Bill Haywood and the Radical Union Movement* (1969); *Dictionary of American Biography*, Vol. 8; Bryan D. Palmer, " 'Big Bill' Haywood's Defection to Russia and the IWW: Two Letters," *Labor History* (Spring 1976); Frederick C. Giffin, *Six Who Protested: Radical Opposition to the First World War* (1977).

Donald G. Sofchalk

HEIGHTON, William   (fl. 1827–1830). Born in Oundle, Northamptonshire, England in 1800; emigrated to the United States as a youth and settled in Philadelphia, Pa.; received little formal education; hired as a cordwainer in Southwark, near Philadelphia; was a Ricardian Socialist who anticipated the labor theory of value popularized by the Marxists; wrote an influential pamphlet in 1827 that provided the organizational and theoretical inspiration for the Workingmen's movement in Philadelphia; was the principal founder of the Mechanics'

Union of Trade Associations in November 1827, conceiving it as a medium for political activity; became the chief editor of the Mechanics' Union newspaper, the *Mechanics Free Press*; after its candidates were defeated in the local elections of 1828, the Mechanics' Union, which had been instrumental in the founding of at least 15 new trade union societies, disbanded; was a vigorous advocate of public education and served as secretary of the Joint Committee of the City and County of Philadelphia that investigated public education in Philadelphia, 1829–1830; in 1830 ended his active association with the labor movement; authored "An ADDRESS to the Members of Trade Societies, and to the WORKING CLASSES GENERALLY" (1827), and "The Principles of Aristocratic Legislation" (1828); died in 1873; Louis H. Arky, "The Mechanics' Union of Trade Associations and the Formation of the Philadelphia Workingmen's Movement," *Pennsylvania Magazine of History and Biography* (April 1952); Edward Pessen, *Most Uncommon Jacksonians: The Radical Leaders of the Early Labor Movement* (1967); John R. Commons et al., *History of Labour in the United States,* Vol. 1 (1918).

HELFGOTT, Simon (1894–1957). Born in New York City, November 15, 1894; son of Louis Solomon and Sarah Hannah Helfgott; Jewish; married Esther Feinzig on June 10, 1922; two children; was graduated from high school, then became a debit insurance agent for the Metropolitan Life Insurance Company; joined New York Insurance Workers Local 30 of the United Office and Professional Workers of America (UOPWA); was chairman of the organizing committee and served on the executive board of Local 30; was a member of the executive board of the UOPWA and in 1949 elected president of Local 30; after the UOPWA was expelled from the Congress of Industrial Organizations (CIO) for alleged Communist domination, founded and became the first president of New York Industrial Insurance Employees Union Local 1706, which affiliated with the Insurance Workers of America International Union (IWAIU), chartered by the CIO in 1952; served as the vice-chairman of the Insurance and Allied Workers Organizing Committee and first vice-president of the IWAIU; retired because of ill health during the summer of 1957; a member of the American Labor party and later the Liberal party of New York; died in New York City, September 8, 1957; Harvey J. Clermont, *Organizing the Insurance Worker: A History of Labor Unions of Insurance Employees* (1966); *The New York Times,* September 9, 1957; *Who's Who in Labor* (1946); Joseph E. Finley, *White Collar Union: The Story of the OPEIU and Its People* (1975).

HELLER, George (1905–1955). Born in New York City, November 20, 1905; son of David and Frances Heller; Jewish; married Clara Mahr on June 3, 1934; two children; completed high school, then studied at the City College of New York, 1923–1925; began appearing in stage productions in 1926, performing as an actor, ballet dancer, and singer; was also a composer, director, and producer; shortly after its formation in 1937, joined the New York local of the

American Federation of Radio Artists (AFRA); elected executive secretary of AFRA's New York local shortly after joining; elected national executive secretary of AFRA in 1946; was a founder and the first national executive secretary of the Television Authority (TVA) in 1949; after the 1952 merger of the TVA and AFRA that created the American Federation of Radio and Television Artists (AFTRA), became the national executive secretary of the new union; negotiated the first successful union pension and welfare plan with the major television networks in 1954; served as first vice-president of the American Theatre Wing; was a member of the advisory council of the United Service Organization Camp Shows, Incorporated; was a Democrat; died in New York City, May 30, 1955; Allen E. Koenig, ed., *Broadcasting and Bargaining: Labor Relations in Radio and Television* (1970); *Fortune* (January 1951); *The New York Times,* May 31, 1955; *Who Was Who in America,* Vol. 3.

HELLER, Jacob J.   (1889–1948). Born in Russia, August 21, 1889; son of Mendel and Gutte Heller; Jewish; married Rose Ackerman on June 27, 1915; one child; studied at a yeshiva for the rabbinate before emigrating to the United States in 1906; shortly after entering United States, hired as a children's cloak-maker and joined Local 17 of the International Ladies' Garment Workers' Union (ILGWU); became manager of Local 17, ILGWU, in 1916; elected an ILGWU vice-president in 1920; was graduated from New York University's School of Commerce in 1923; was removed from union positions as a result of reforms instituted by ILGWU president Morris Sigman (q.v.) in 1925, and then opened an office in New York as an accountant and served as a business advisor to several unions; regained his union positions after Sigman's resignation in 1929; had an expansive view of the jurisdiction of Local 17, which kept him constantly embroiled in jurisdictional conflicts with other cloakmakers' locals; after the amalgamation of the reefermakers and cloakmakers in 1936, became the manager of the reefermakers' department of the New York Cloak Joint Board; was a conservative in the ILGWU's ideological conflicts and strongly supported the principle of craft organization, opposing efforts of the union's leadership to support the Congress of Industrial Organizations; became manager of the Liberal party of New York; authored *My Union My Life* and *Moment of Gloom*; died in New York City, September 25, 1948; Benjamin Stolberg, *Tailor's Progress: The Story of a Famous Union and the Men Who Made It* (1944); Louis Levine, *The Women's Garment Workers: A History of the International Ladies' Garment Workers' Union* (1924); *ILGWU Report and Proceedings* (1950).

HELSTEIN, Ralph   (1908–   ). Born in Duluth, Minn., December 11, 1908; son of Henry, a manufacturer, and Lena (Litman) Helstein; married Rachel Brin on January 2, 1939; two children; received the B.A. (1929) and LL.B. (1934) degrees from the University of Minnesota and then was admitted to the Minnesota bar in 1936; appointed labor compliance officer for the National Recovery Administration in Minnesota in 1934; conducted a private law practice in Minneapolis, Minn., 1936–1943; became general counsel for the Minnesota Industrial Union Council, Congress of Industrial Organizations (CIO), in 1939, serving until 1943; appointed general counsel for the United Packinghouse Workers of America (UPWA) in 1942; elected international president of the UPWA in 1946; became a member of the CIO executive board in 1946, serving until 1955; led a largely unsuccessful 82–day strike against the Swift, Wilson, Armour, and Cudahy meat-packing companies in 1948; as president, was credited with successfully negotiating a guaranteed work week, maintaining membership, and improving working conditions for UPWA members; elected an American Federation of Labor-CIO vice-president and executive council member in 1965, serving until 1969; after the merger of the UPWA and the Amalgamated Meat Cutters and Butcher Workmen of North America (AMCBWNA) in 1968, became a vice-president and special counsel of the new union; retired union positions in 1968–1969; elected president emeritus of the AMCBWNA after his retirement; a Democrat; David Brody, *The Butcher Workmen: A Study of Unionization* (1964); *Current Biography* (1948); *Who's Who in America, 1960–1961; Who's Who in Labor* (1946); *AFL-CIO News,* December 9, 1972.

HELT, Daniel Webster   (1883–1961). Born in Shamokin, Pa., September 24, 1883; son of Jeremiah M., a railroad worker, and Amanda E. (Hoover) Helt; Methodist; married Kate Peart Gilham on September 25, 1907; six children; attended public schools, beginning work as a slate picker at age 9; enlisted in the U.S. Marine Corps in 1901 and served with the Caribbean Squad until 1905; worked as a coal miner and carpenter prior to becoming a mechanic in the signal department of the Reading Railroad in 1910; joined Reading Lodge 26 of the Brotherhood of Railroad Signalmen (BRS) in 1910; elected as a Republican to the Pennsylvania House of Representatives in 1917 and served two terms; elected grand president of the BRS in 1917 shortly after becoming a railroad fireman; was one of the founders of both the Railway Labor Executives' Association and the railroad labor newspaper, *Labor*; as president of BRS, led a major organizing campaign in which the BRS unionized 95 percent of the workers in its jurisdiction; received a leave of absence from the BRS in 1934 shortly after being appointed a member of the National Railroad Adjustment Board; resigned as BRS president in 1936 and named grand vice-president; in 1948, resigned from the National Railroad Adjustment Board and named president emeritus after resigning his BRS positions; edited the *Signalman's Journal,* 1917–1934; authored *The Signalman and His Work* (1921); was a Republican early in his career, but later became disillusioned with the party and identified himself as an independent-progressive; died in Arlington Heights, Ill., October 21, 1961; Brotherhood of Railroad Signalmen of America, *50 Years of Railroad Signaling: A History of the Brotherhood of Railroad Signalmen of America* (n.d.); *Who's Who in Labor* (1946); *Labor,* August 14, 1948, October 28, 1961.

HENDERSON, Donald James   (1902–   ). Born in New York City, February 4, 1902; son of Daniel, a dairy farmer, and Jean (Crawford) Henderson;

married Florence McGee Thomas (second marriage) on October 10, 1943; three children; received the B.A. and M.A. degrees from Columbia University, and during the summer of 1925 attended the Geneva School of International Relations; joined the Railroad Telegraph Operators' Union in 1919, maintaining his membership until 1922; hired as a teacher at Columbia University and joined the American Federation of Teachers in 1926; dismissed by Columbia University in 1933 because his Communist party affiliation allegedly interferred with his teaching responsibilities; published the *Rural Worker* during the 1930s, and in 1935 organized the National Committee for Unity of Agricultural and Rural Workers; after the United Cannery, Agricultural, Packing and Allied Workers of America (UCAPAWA) was chartered by the Congress of Industrial Organizations (CIO) in 1937, elected its first president and built it into one of the largest CIO affiliates; negotiated a merger with the Southern Tenant Farmers' Union (STFU) in 1937, but conflicts with STFU leader H. L. Mitchell (q.v.) over local autonomy and communism led to a split in 1939 that weakened both unions; under his guidance, the UCAPAWA made its greatest advances in California where, in cooperation with Harry Bridges's (q.v.) International Longshoremen and Warehousemen's Union, seasonal workers were organized around a nucleus of permanently employed cannery workers; in 1946 the UCAPAWA was reorganized and renamed the Food, Tobacco, Agricultural and Allied Workers Union (FTA), symbolic of the growing emphasis upon the organization of processing workers, who were easier to organize; elected president of the FTA in 1946; his career in the postwar era was intimately affected by domestic Cold War passions; FTA membership declined to 22,590 by 1949; challenged CIO leaders by endorsing Henry Wallace for president of the United States in 1948, and by attending the World Federation of Trade Unions meeting after CIO withdrew from it; in order to avoid signing a non-Communist affidavit as required under the Taft-Hartley Act, resigned as president of the FTA in 1949 and became FTA national administrative director; however, the National Labor Relations Board refused to accept this change as a legitimate tactic; after an investigation conducted by the CIO's committee on Communism, he and the FTA were expelled from the CIO in 1950; ended his association with the trade union movement shortly thereafter; U.S. Department of Labor (Stuart M. Jamieson), *Labor Unionism in American Agriculture* (1945); Donald H. Grubbs, *Cry from the Cotton* (1971); Louis Cantor, *A Prologue to the Protest Movement: The Missouri Sharecropper Roadside Demonstration of 1939* (1969); Max M. Kampelman, *The Communist Party vs. the C.I.O.: A Study in Power Politics* (1957); *Who's Who in Labor* (1946); Bert Cochran, *Labor and Communism: The Conflict that Shaped American Unions* (1977); Harvey A. Levenstein, *Communism, Anticommunism, and the CIO* (1981).

Merl E. Reed

HENRY, Alice   (1857–1943). Born in Richmond, Australia, March 21, 1857; daughter of Charles Ferguson, an accountant, and Margaret (Walker) Henry, a seamstress; Unitarian; attended various public and private schools in Melbourne,

Australia; was a feature writer for the *Melbourne Argus* and its weekly, the *Australasian*, 1884–1904; journeyed to London in 1905 as the Melbourne representative to an English conference of charity organizations; emigrated to the United States in 1906; shortly after her arrival, at the invitation of Margaret Dreier Robins (q.v.), became the secretary of the Chicago, Ill., Women's Trade Union League (WTUL); headed the women's department of the Chicago-based *Union Labor Advocate*, 1908–1911; participated in an investigation of conditions among women brewery workers in Milwaukee, Wis., in 1910; edited the WTUL's monthly, *Life and Labor*, 1911–1915; served as a national WTUL organizer, 1918–1920; was an instructor at Bryn Mawr College summer school for women workers in 1921; headed the WTUL education department, 1920–1922, attended the International Workers' Education Conference held at Ruskin College, Oxford, England, in 1924; retired to Santa Barbara, Calif., in 1928 and returned to Melbourne in 1933; authored *The Trade Union Movement* (1915), *Women and the Labor Movement* (1923), and *Memoirs of Alice Henry* (1944); died in Melbourne, February 14, 1943; *Notable American Women* (1971); Mary E. Dreier, *Margaret Dreier Robins: Her Life, Letters and Work* (1950); Gladys Boone, *The Women's Trade Union Leagues in Great Britain and the United States of America* (1942).

Marie Tedesco

HERRICK, Elinore Morehouse   (1895–1964). Born in New York City on June 15, 1895; daughter of Daniel Webster, a Unitarian minister, and Martha Adelaide (Bird) Morehouse, a secretary and college registrar; Unitarian; married Horace Terhune Herrick in 1916 and divorced him in 1921; two children; family moved to Springfield, Mass., in her early childhood because of the illness of her father which resulted in his death in 1904; attended Technical High School and the MacDuffie School in Springfield; enrolled in Barnard College in 1913, majoring in economics, and also took courses in journalism at Columbia University; during this time she worked as a cub reporter for the *New York World*; left college in 1915; after her divorce in 1921, she was forced to take factory jobs; eventually rose to a supervisory position with the DuPont Corporation; was transferred to Old Hickory, Tenn., in 1923, where she became a production manager in the textile division of the DuPont Corporation plant; having reached the highest position available to a woman at DuPont, she moved to Ohio, where she enrolled in Antioch College in 1927; studied economics and labor relations with William L. Leiserson (q.v.), earning the B.A. degree in 1929; served as executive secretary of the New York Consumers' League, 1929–1934; retained her association with the Consumers' League after 1934 and at various times served as vice-president and as a member of its board of directors; helped draft and lobbied for state minimum wage and child-labor legislation; after the enactment of the minimum wage law in 1933, she served on New York's first minimum wage board; was appointed to the New York City Mediation Board in 1933; was appointed executive vice-chairman of the Regional Labor Board established by the National Labor Board created by the National Recovery Administration; after the enactment of the National Labor Relations Act in 1935, she became a regional director responsible for an area that included eastern New York, northern New Jersey, and Connecticut; was actively involved in the campaigns of the American Labor party in 1935 and served on its executive committee until 1940; resigned her position on the Regional Labor Board in 1942 and became director of personnel and labor relations for Todd Shipyards Corporation; after the war, she became director of personnel for the *New York Herald Tribune*; as she became further detached from the labor movement, her political sympathies increasingly reflected those of her new business associates; once a nominal Democrat and then an American Labor party activist, she now aligned herself with the Republican party, supported the Taft-Hartley Act, and joined the anti-Communist crusade; resigned her newspaper position in 1955 and died in Chapel Hill, N.C., on October 11, 1964; Elinore Herrick Papers, Schlesinger Library, Radcliffe College; *Notable American Women*, Vol. 4; *Current Biography* (1937); "Elinore Morehouse Herrick: Regional Labor Board Director of New York, 1933 to 1942" (M.A. thesis, 1967); *The New York Times*, October 12, 1964.

HICKEY, Thomas L. (1893–1963). Born in New York City in 1893; Roman Catholic; married; one child; began working after completing only a few years of formal education; during World War I, joined the U.S Army and served in France; after being discharged, hired as a coal-truck driver in New York City and in 1919 joined Local 807 of the International Brotherhood of Teamsters, Chauffeurs, Warehousemen and Helpers of America (IBT); after several unsuccessful campaigns for union office, elected secretary-treasurer of local 807 in 1936; became an IBT general organizer for New York City, a position that gave him great influence in the New York area; was appointed a vice-president and member of the IBT executive board in 1951 and was elected to that position with the support of James R. Hoffa (q.v.) a year later; acquired a reputation for unswerving honesty during the public scandals concerning IBT officials during the 1950s; became one of the major antagonists of James Hoffa in his attempts to consolidate his power in the IBT during the 1950s and was a cooperative witness before John L. McClellan's Senate Select Committee on Improper Practices in the Labor of Management Field in 1957; opposed Hoffa's election to the IBT presidency in 1957 and defeated for reelection as an IBT vice-president by Hoffa's supporters; dismissed as general IBT organizer for the New York area in 1958, but continued to serve as secretary-treasurer of Local 807; retired from union affairs in 1962; died in New York City, July 2, 1963; Sam Romer, *The International Brotherhood of Teamsters: Its Government and Structure* (1962); Robert D. Leiter, *The Teamsters Union: A Study of Its Economic Impact* (1957); Walter Sheridan, *The Fall and Rise of Jimmy Hoffa* (1972); Ralph C. James and Estelle D. James, *Hoffa and the Teamsters: A Study of Union Power* (1965); *Fortune* (October 1957).

HICKMAN, William Willis (1826–1881). Born in Wednesbury, Stafford-shire, England, in 1826; worked in iron mills from the age of 13; married in 1845; nine children; emigrated to Boston in 1846 and worked as a puddler for Gray and Company at their Old Mill Dam Rolling Mill until an 1848 strike; worked for a short time in Pennsylvania and then for 20 years in Pembroke, Me., where he organized a forge for the United Sons of Vulcan during the Civil War; in 1871 he moved to Bay View, Wis., and was a member of a forge there; served as fourth district deputy, United Sons of Vulcan, in 1875; retired from his mill position sometime after 1878, but retained ties with the Amalgamated Association of Iron and Steel Workers; appointed deputy sheriff of Milwaukee County, Wis., in 1878, and remained in that office until December 1880, when he was elected county coroner; died in Bay View from pneumonia in 1881; Amalgamated Association of Iron and Steel Workers, *Proceedings, 1881*.

                                                                Sharon Trusilo

HILL, Joe (Joel Emmanuel Hagglund) (1879–1915). Born in Gavle, Swe-den, October 7, 1879; son of Olaf, a railroad conductor, and Margareta Katarina Hagglund; raised in a conservative Lutheran family, all of whom played musical instruments in the home; became an accomplished amateur musician; was forced by his father's death to go to work in a rope factory at age 10; after his mother's death and the consequent disintegration of the family, emigrated to the United States in 1902; drifted around the country for several years working at various unskilled jobs and sporadically acting as a union organizer; in 1910, joined the San Pedro, Calif., local of the Industrial Workers of the World (IWW), soon becoming its secretary; was probably among a handful of Wobblies who in 1911 attempted to capture Baja California in support of Mexican revolutionaries; took name Joe Hill (sometimes Hillstrom) and participated in the San Pedro dock-worker's strike of 1912, during which the police arrested and tried to deport him; had no home, like most western Wobblies, and spent much time at the San Pedro Sailors' Rest Mission; there and while traveling, wrote the sardonic lyrics for the songs that made him famous; beginning in 1911, with "The Preacher and the Slave," his songs appeared in th IWW "Little Red Song Book"; although his lyrics best expressed the alienation of the homeless, migratory workers of the West, his songs dealt also with all major IWW groups, such as railway shopcraft workers, "Casey Jones—the Union Scab," and immigrant workers in the East, "John Golden and the Lawrence Strike"; in 1914, while living with a Swedish family in Salt Lake City, Utah, indicted for the murder of a grocer and his son; although the circumstantial evidence indicated his guilt, the pros-ecution was unable to obtain a positive identification of him as the murderer; although there was no specific evidence to prove that either the trial court or the Utah Supreme Court was influenced by Hill's IWW associations, the IWW charged that he had been framed by Utah authorities and the Mormons because he was a Wobbly; Hill's attorneys asked the Utah Pardon Board to commute his death sentence to life, but he only demanded a new trial; despite mass protest demonstrations and appeals on his behalf by the Swedish Minister to the United States and President Woodrow Wilson, Hill was executed by firing squad on November 19, 1915; one of his last requests was that his remains be taken out of state because, he said, "I don't want to be found dead in Utah"; at his funeral in Chicago, Ill., attended by thousands of workers, Wobbly orators claimed Hill as a martyr to the IWW cause; almost overnight he became a legendary labor hero; his songs continued to inspire rank-and-file union radicals, and some of them came to be recognized as folklore transcending their IWW origins; Vernon H. Jenson, "The Legend of Joe Hill," *Industrial and Labor Relations Review* (April 1951); Philip S. Foner, *The Case of Joe Hill* (1965); Gibbs M. Smith, *Joe Hill* (1969).

Donald G. Sofchalk

HILLMAN, Bessie Abramowitz   (1889–1970). Born near Grodno, Russia, on May 15, 1889; daughter of Emanuel, a merchant, and Sarah (Cherechevsky) Abramowitz; Jewish; married Sidney Hillman (q.v.) on May 3, 1916; two children; early education provided by tutors and, after emigrating to the United States in 1905, attended evening classes in the Chicago, Ill., public school system; began working in a Chicago garment factory at age 16 and was blacklisted after leading a protest against sweatshop working conditions; using an alias, obtained employment as a button sewer in the Hart, Schaffner and Marx factory in Chicago; later led a group of 16 women in protesting a reduction in piece rates which eventually evolved into the historic Chicago garment workers' strike of 1910; joined the Women's Trade Union League and participated in its efforts to support the garment workers' strike; served as the business agent for the Vestmakers Local 152 of Chicago, 1911–1916; after her 1916 marriage to Sidney Hillman, whom she had supported for the presidency of the Amalgamated Clothing Workers of America (ACWA) in 1914, she moved to New York City where, as a volunteer, she participated in organizing drives and continued her involvement in a variety of educational and civic activities; was appointed education director of the New York City Laundry Workers Joint Board, an ACWA affiliate, in 1937; during World War II, she was a member of the U.S. Department of Labor's Defense Advisory Committee on Women, served on the advisory board of the New York City Office of Price Administration, and on the Child Welfare Committee of New York; after her husband's death in 1946, she was elected an ACWA vice-president, continuing in that office until her death in 1970; during this time, she devoted much of her energy to ACWA educational activities; was also active in civil rights, child welfare, and peace movements; an advocate of equal rights for women, she represented the International Confederation of Free Trade Unions in the session of the United Nations' Commission on the Status of Women in 1962 and 1963; also served as a member of the American Labor Education Service, director of Pioneer Youth of America, and was a member of the Commission on the Status of Women appointed by John F. Kennedy in 1963; supported the American Labor party in New York City during the 1930s but then after the ACWA disassociated itself from the party, she became active in reform Democratic party activities; died in New York City on December 23, 1970; *National Cyclopaedia of American Biography*, Vol. 56; Matthew Josephson, *Sidney Hillman: Statesman of American Labor* (1952); George Soule, *Sidney Hillman: Labor Statesman* (1948); Jean Gould, *Sidney Hillman, Great American* (1952).

HILLMAN, Sidney   (1887–1946). Born in Zagare, Russian Lithuania (now part of the Soviet Union), March 23, 1887; son of Schmuel Gilman, a merchant, and Judith (Paikin) Hillman; Jewish; married Bessie Abramowitz in 1916; two children; studied to be a rabbi until age 15, then moved to Kovno, Russia, where he worked in a chemical laboratory and studied economics; spent eight months in prison after becoming involved in labor agitation; upon release, fled to England and in 1907 emigrated to the United States, settling in Chicago, Ill.; was a clerk for two years, then hired as a garment cutter and joined the United Garment Workers Union of America (UGW); participated in the 1910 strike against Hart, Schaffner and Marx in Chicago, beginning as a picket and becoming the leader of the strike; became chief clerk of the New York Cloakmakers' Union in 1914; led a group of unionists opposed to the leadership of the UGW and became president of the newly organized Amalgamated Clothing Workers of America (ACWA); was a member of the National Recovery Administration's Labor Advisory Board in 1933 and the National Industrial Recovery Board in 1935; served on the National Advisory Board of the National Youth Administration and the Textile Committee of the Fair Labor Standards Board; was one of the original leaders of the Congress of Industrial Organizations (CIO) and was elected first vice-president in 1937; served as chairman of the Textile Workers Organizing Committee; associated during World War II with the National Defense Advisory Committee in 1940, the Office of Production Management in 1941, and the War Production Board in 1942; served as labor advisor to President Franklin D. Roosevelt in 1943; appointed chairman of the CIO's Political Action Committee in 1943; had an essentially conservative trade union philosophy and was a strong advocate of labor-management cooperation; associated with the American Labor party and the Democratic party; died at his summer home in Point Lookout, Long Island, N.Y., July 10, 1946; Sidney Hillman Papers, Catherwood Library, Cornell University; Matthew Josephson, *Sidney Hillman: Statesman of American Labor* (1952); George Soule, *Sidney Hillman: Labor Statesman* (1948); Jean Gould, *Sidney Hillman, Great American* (1952); Melech Epstein, *Profiles of Eleven* (1965), and *Jewish Labor in the U.S.A., 1914–1952*, 2 Vols. (1953); *Dictionary of American Biography*, Suppl. 4.

HILLQUIT, Morris   (1869–1933). Born in Riga, Russian Latvia (now part of the Soviet Union), August 1, 1869; son of Benjamin, a school teacher, and Rebecca (Levene) Hillkowitz; Jewish; married Vera Levene on December 31, 1893; two children; attended the elementary and secondary schools of Russia and the United States, and was graduated from the New York Law School with an LL.B. degree in 1893; shortly after emigrating to the United States in 1886, began working in a New York City shirt factory; joined the Socialist Labor party (SLP) in 1890 and shortly thereafter joined the staff of the *Arbeiter-Zeitung*, a Yiddish-language newspaper; broke with SLP leader Daniel DeLeon (q.v.) over ideological and tactical questions in 1899 and became the leader of the "Rochester" faction of the SLP, which fused with the Social Democratic party in 1901 to form the Socialist party of America; was a member of the United Hebrew Trades and was involved in organizing garment workers in New York City during the 1890s; became a member of the International Socialist Bureau in 1904 and the following year was appointed a trustee of the Rand School of Social Science; was a member of the negotiating committee that secured a settlement in the 1910 cloakmakers' strike and led to the Protocol of Peace, which provided for conciliation machinery in labor disputes in the garment industry; became the International Ladies' Garment Workers' Union (ILGWU) general counsel in 1913, serving until 1933; involved in several significant legal cases involving left-wing activities, including the defense of Morris Sigman (q.v.) and other ILGWU leaders charged with murder in connection with the 1910 garment strike, and efforts to regain the seats of five Socialist assemblymen expelled from the New York state legislature in 1920; was an opponent of American involvement in World War I and founded the American Conference for Democracy and Terms of Peace in 1917; served as a legal advisor to the Soviet Government Bureau in the United States, 1918–1919; supported the Progressive party candidacy of Robert M. La Follette in 1924; was one of the leaders of the Socialist party, serving as a national committeeman from New York, 1901–1906, chairman of the national committee, 1913–1933, a member of the national executive committee, 1907–1912, 1916–1933, and national chairman in 1921; served as an American delegate to several international Socialist congresses from 1904 to 1931; authored *History of Socialism in the United States* (1903), *From Marx to Lenin* (1921), *Loose Leaves from a Busy Life* (1934), and other books and pamphlets; died in New York City, October 7, 1933; Morris Hillquit Papers, State Historical Society of Wisconsin; David A. Shannon, *The Socialist Party of America: A History* (1955); James Weinstein, *The Decline of Socialism in America, 1912–1925* (1967); Julius H. Cohen, *They Builded Better than They Knew* (1946); *National Cyclopaedia of American Biography*, Vol. 44; Melech Epstein, *Profiles of Eleven* (1965), and *Jewish Labor in the U.S.A., 1914–1952*, 2 Vols. (1953); Aaron Antonovsky, trans., *The Early Jewish Labor Movement in the United States* (1961); Richard W. Fox, "The Paradox of 'Progressive Socialism': The Case of Morris Hillquit, 1901–1914," *American Quarterly* (May 1974); Norman F. Pratt, "Morris Hillquit (1869–1933): A Political Biography of an American Jewish Socialist" (Ph.D. diss., 1977); Irwin Yellowitz, "Morris Hillquit: American Socialism and Jewish Concerns," *American Jewish History* (1978).

HINCHCLIFFE, John   (1822–1878). Born in Bradford, Yorkshire, England, in 1822; served an apprenticeship as a tailor and eventually became the proprietor of a small tailor shop; was an active participant in the Chartist movement before emigrating to the United States in 1847; worked for short periods as a tailor in New York City, Philadelphia, Pa., and St. Louis, Mo.; settled in Belleville, Ill., and admitted to the bar, quickly becoming prominent as editor of two Democratic newspapers; not a miner, but became one of the most prominent figures in the early efforts to organize miners; presided over the founding convention of the American Miners' Association in 1860 and became the editor of the association's journal, the *Weekly Miner*, in 1863; was an unsuccessful candidate for Congress on the Democratic ticket in 1862; lost the editorship of the *Weekly Miner* in 1865 as a result of a factional conflict that ultimately split the national union; represented the Railroad Men's Protective Union, the Printers' Union, the Machinery Molders' Union of St. Louis, and the Miners' Lodge of Illinois at the Baltimore, Md., Labor Congress of 1866 that resulted in the organization of the National Labor Union (NLU); was appointed spokesman of the NLU committee assigned to petition President Andrew Johnson for the eight-hour day; served as treasurer of the NLU, then elected a delegate to the Illinois Constitutional Convention in 1870, and there was able to secure a clause in the new constitution requiring the Illinois state legislature to enact a mine safety code; elected to the Illinois state senate in 1872, and led the efforts there to enact mine safety legislation; nominally a Democrat, but was a fervent anti-monopolist and very susceptible to third-party movements; died in St. Louis, Mo., in 1878; David Montgomery, *Beyond Equality: Labor and the Radical Republicans, 1862–1872* (1967); John R. Commons et al., *History of Labour in the United States*, Vol. 2 (1918); George E. McNeill, *The Labor Movement: The Problem of To-Day* (1887); Ray Boston, *British Chartists in America, 1839–1900* (1971); Clifton K. Yearley, Jr., *Britons in American Labor: A History of the Influence of the United Kingdom Immigrants on American Labor, 1820–1914* (1957).

HOCHMAN, Julius   (1892–1970). Born in Bessarabia, Russia, January 12, 1892; son of Samuel, a tailor, and Frieda Hochman; Jewish; married Celia Morris on October 1, 1916; one child; did not receive any formal education before being apprenticed to a tailor at age 11; emigrated with his family to the United States in 1907 and gained employment in the New York garment industry; earned his high school diploma by attending evening school and taking courses at the Rand School of Social Science while employed in the garment industry; joined Shirtmakers' Local 23 of the International Ladies' Garment Workers' Union (ILGWU) in 1910 and in 1913 transferred his membership to Waistmakers' Local 25; became assistant organizer of Local 25 in 1916; during the next several years, served as an ILGWU organizer in Chicago, Ill., Boston, Mass., Toronto and Montreal, Canada; became department manager for the Dressmakers' Union in 1921 and the following year was named general manager of the New York Dress Joint Board; resigned in 1923 because of his opposition to the amalgamation of the dressmakers' and cloakmakers' joint boards; attended Brookwood Labor College, 1923–1924; elected an ILGWU vice-president in 1925; became manager of the Joint Board of Waist and Dressmakers Unions in 1929; served as chairman of the ILGWU educational committee, as a vice-president of the Jewish Labor Committee and the New York Dress Institute, and as a director of the Organization for Rehabilitation Through Training; after leading a dressmakers' strike in 1958, left the Dress Joint Board and became the director of the ILGWU label department; retired from union affairs in 1962; was a member of the Liberal party of New York; authored *Why This Strike* (1936), *Industry Planning through Collective Bargaining* (1941), and *The Retirement Myth* (1950); died in New York City, March 17, 1970; Benjamin Stolberg, *Tailor's Progress: The Story of a Famous Union and the Men Who Made It* (1944); Louis Levine, *The Women's Garment Workers: A History of the International Ladies' Garment Workers' Union* (1924); "Remarkable Union—and Union Leader," *Reader's Digest* (April 1946); Jesse T. Carpenter, *Competition and Collective Bargaining in the Needle Trades, 1910–1967* (1972).

HOFFA, James Riddle (1913–1975?). Born in Brazil, Ind., February 14, 1913; son of John Cleveland, a coal driller, and Viola (Riddle) Hoffa; reared in the Christian church; married Josephine Poszywak on September 25, 1936; two children; completed the ninth grade in the public schools of Detroit, Mich., then took a full-time job as a department store stockboy; became a freight handler at a Kroger Grocery warehouse in 1930; along with four co-workers, organized American Federation of Labor Federal Labor Union 19341 in 1931; joined the International Brotherhood of Teamsters, Chauffeurs, Warehousemen and Helpers of America (IBT) in 1934 and took the membership of federal Local 19341 into IBT Local 299; during the same year, became a full-time organizer for IBT Joint Council 43; became business agent and in 1937 elected president of Local 299; along with Farrel Dobbs (q.v.), a Trotskyist teamster from Minneapolis, organized the Central States Drivers Council in 1937; became, successively, chairman and vice-president of the Central States Drivers Council, president of the Michigan Conference of Teamsters, examiner of IBT books, and in 1940, president of Teamsters Joint Council 43, Detroit, serving until 1946; elected an IBT vice-president in 1952 and president of the Central Conference of Teamsters in 1953; charged with attempting to bribe a U.S. Senate committee investigator in 1957, but acquitted; elected international president of the IBT in 1957; accelerated a centralization process within the IBT that permitted him to negotiate and sign the first national contract in the trucking industry in 1964; convicted, on separate charges, of jury tampering, fraud, and conspiracy in the disposition of union benefit funds in 1964; after exhausting appeals, entered Lewisburg, Pa., Federal Penitentiary in 1967 to begin serving a 13-year prison term; retired his IBT positions in 1971 and was named president emeritus and awarded $1.7 million in lieu of a pension; sentence commuted by President Richard M. Nixon in 1971 with the provision that he refrain from participating in union affairs until 1980;

usually supported Republican candidates; authored *The Trials of Jimmy Hoffa* (1970); disappeared mysteriously in July 1975 and in 1982 was officially declared dead; Walter Sheridan, *The Fall and Rise of Jimmy Hoffa* (1972); Ralph C. James and Estelle D. James, *Hoffa and the Teamsters: A Study of Union Power* (1965); Robert D. Leiter, *The Teamsters Union: A Study of Its Economic Impact* (1957); *Current Biography* (1972); *Newsweek*, August 18, 1975; Steven Brill, *The Teamsters* (1978).

HOFFMANN, Sal B.   (1899–1981). Born in Aversa, Italy, April 5, 1899; son of Leopoldo, an upholsterer, and Anna (Tornicaso) Hoffmann; Roman Catholic; married Frances Zeichner on June 2, 1920; three children; graduated from high school, then employed by the Bell Telephone Company and the Western Electric Company, 1917–1918; gained employment as an upholsterer and joined Philadelphia, Pa., Wholesale Upholsterers' Local 77 of the Upholsterers' International Union of North America (UIU) in 1919; served Local 77 as recording secretary and as an executive board member, 1920–1924, and business agent and business manager, 1924–1937; while serving as an UIU general organizer, 1929–1931, organized UIU Local 20 in Birmingham, Ala., in 1930; served as executive secretary of the Philadelphia Regional District Council, UIU, which he had been instrumental in founding, 1935–1937; elected international president of the UIU in 1937, a position he held until his death; during World War II, was a hearing officer for the National War Labor Board and a labor member of the War Production Board's advisory committee for the furniture industry; served on several American Federation of Labor (AFL) and AFL-Congress of Industrial Organizations' committees; was a vice-chairman of the Workers Defense League and a member of the national board of directors of Americans for Democratic Action; was a delegate to the White House Conference on Aging in 1961, chairman of the board of trustees of the Health and Welfare Fund, 1944–1971, and chairman of the board of governors of the National Pension Plan, 1953–1971; a Democrat; authored two pamphlets, *Work of a Business Agent* (1942), and *Trade Unions under War Conditions* (1943); died in Philadelphia, Pa., on January 9, 1981; Upholsterers' International Union Papers, Urban Archives, Temple University; *Who's Who in America, 1972–1973; Who's Who in Labor* (1946); *AFL-CIO News,* January 13, 1981.

HOLDERMAN, Carl   (1894–1959). Born in Hornell, N.Y., January 15, 1894; son of Matthias, a railroad worker, and Anna Marie Holderman, Episcopalian; married Beatrice Pauline on September 17, 1943; four children; completed two years of high school, then left school and took employment as a messenger and shop employee of the Erie Railroad; joined the American Federation of Hosiery Workers (AFHW) in 1918 after securing employment in the textile industry; became during subsequent years a national organizer and vice-president of the AFHW; was named by Sidney Hillman (q.v.) as a regional director of the Textile Workers Organizing Committee in 1937 and shortly thereafter became a vice-president of the Textile Workers Union of America; was one of the organizers of the Joint Board (of textile unions) for New Jersey in 1937, and served as its manager until 1940, when the Joint Board was divided into three regional groups; became the manager of the North Jersey Joint Board in 1940; was one of the organizers of the New Jersey Industrial Union Council, Congress of Industrial Organizations, and served as its treasurer, 1939–1940, secretary-treasurer, 1940–1945, director of the political action committee, 1944–1954, and its president between 1945–1954; served during World War II as a regional member of the Manpower Mobilization Committee, Alien Enemy Board, and War Labor Board; was appointed New Jersey commissioner of labor and industry in 1954; died in Newark, N.J., April 20, 1959; Leo Troy, *Organized Labor in New Jersey* (1965); *Who's Who in Labor* (1946).

HOLLANDER, Louis   (1893–1980). Born in Wadowice, Russian Poland, February 5, 1893; son of Hyman and Hannah Hollander; Jewish; married Mollie Bernstein on April 22, 1922; emigrated to the United States in 1903, settling in New York City; attended grammar school, then began working in a tailor shop in 1906 at age 13; later completed high school by taking evening courses; joined the United Garment Workers of America in 1908 and became a union organizer in 1912; was one of the founders of the Amalgamated Clothing Workers of America (ACWA) in 1914; held a variety of offices in the ACWA prior to beginning a long term of service as manager of the New York Joint Board, ACWA, in 1932; elected an ACWA vice-president in 1934; elected a city councilman from Brooklyn in 1937 and served a two-year term; was the chairman of the Kings County American Labor party, 1936–1942; elected president of the New York State Congress of Industrial Organizations' (CIO) Industrial Union Council in 1943 and served until the New York American Federation of Labor (AFL)-CIO merger in 1958; during World War II was a member of the New York Area War Manpower Commission and the New York State War Council; after the AFL-CIO merger in New York, became the chairman of the executive council of the New York State AFL-CIO; elected secretary-treasurer of the New York State AFL-CIO in 1962; was a co-chairman of the Jewish Labor Committee, a member of the advisory council of the New York State School of Industrial Relations, and a trustee of Cornell University; usually supported Democratic candidates; died in New York City on January 3, 1980; Matthew Josephson, *Sidney Hillman: Statesman of American Labor* (1952); Harry A. Cobrin, *The Men's Clothing Industry: Colonial through Modern Times* (1970); *Who's Who in Labor* (1946); *AFL-CIO News*, January 12, 1980.

HORN, Roy   (1872–1947). Born in Warsaw, Ill., March 10, 1872; son of John Henry, a carriage maker, and Leah Josephine (Shaw) Horn; Protestant; married; three children; completed grammar school, then went to work at age 14; joined the International Brotherhood of Blacksmiths, Drop Forgers and Helpers of America (IBBDFH) in 1901; by 1907, was business agent for the IBBDFH's

St. Louis District Council 31; two years later, became general vice-president of the IBBDFH; was a leader of the movement to federate the railway shop crafts for joint bargaining, which was vigorously resisted by some railroads; in 1912, was a delegate to the founding meeting of the Federation of Federations, which shortly thereafter became the railway employees' department of the American Federation of Labor (AFL); subsequently helped organize shop craftworkers in various parts of the country; in 1926, elected international president of the IBBDFH, thereby becoming a member of the recently established Railway Labor Executives' Association, which functioned as a policy-making body for legislative matters affecting railroad workers; during the controversy over the Committee for Industrial Organization's (CIO) industrial organizing campaigns, was a spokesman for the craft unionists and a staunch defender of their jurisdictions; at the 1936 AFL convention, spoke in favor of the suspension of the CIO and denied its contention that mass production workers could only be organized along industrial lines; by the 1940s, was second vice-president of the railway employees' department and first vice-president of the metal trades department of the AFL; was an independent in politics; widely respected among AFL leaders and employers; retired in 1947; died in St. Louis, Mo., November 22, 1947; Solon DeLeon, ed., *The American Labor Who's Who* (1925); *Who's Who in Labor* (1946); Walter Galenson, *The CIO Challenge to the AFL: A History of the American Labor Movement, 1935–1941* (1960); *The American Federationist* (December 1947).

Donald G. Sofchalk

HOUSEWRIGHT, James Talbertt   (1921–1977). Born in Wesco, Mo., on November 23, 1921; son of Thomas Austin and Nora (Asher) Housewright; Methodist; married Jane Housewright; four children; attended Hadley Vocational School, 1934–1937; was a sergeant in the U.S. Air Force during World War II, 1942–1945; joined Indianapolis, Ind., Local 725 of the Retail Clerks International Association (RCIA) in 1947; served as Local 725's secretary-treasurer, 1947–1953; became RCIA divisional organizing director in 1953, serving in that position until being appointed executive assistant to RCIA president James A. Suffridge (q.v.) in 1966; two years later after Suffridge retired, he was elected RCIA international president; elected an executive board member of the American Federation of Labor-Congress of Industrial Organizations (AFL-CIO) maritime trades department in 1968; elected an AFL-CIO vice-president and executive council member in 1972; appointed to the executive committee of the International Federation of Commercial, Clerical and Technical Employees in 1970; became a vice-president of the union label and service trades department, AFL-CIO, in 1973; elected to the executive board of the A. Philip Randolph Institute in 1972; became the first president of the AFL-CIO's newly organized food and beverage trades department in 1976; a young, vigorous union leader, he doubled the RCIA's membership during his tenure and, at the time of his death, was working on a merger with the Retail, Wholesale and Department Store Union and the Amalgamated Meat Cutters and Butcher Workmen of North America; died in Washington, D.C., on September 19, 1977; *Who's Who in Labor* (1976); *AFL-CIO News,* September 24, 1977; Michael Harrington, *The Retail Clerks* (1962); Albert A. Blum et al., *White-Collar Workers* (1971); *The New York Times*, September 20, 1977.

HOWARD, Asbury   (1907–   ). Born in Autaugoville, Ala., in 1907; married; two children; Baptist; Afro-American; became a "mule boy" in the Muscoda iron mine of the Tennessee Coal and Iron Company at Bessemer, Ala.; when the International Union of Mine, Mill and Smelter Workers (IUMMSW) moved into Alabama in 1933, he helped organize Local 123, of which he became recording secretary and, later, vice-president; (although black miners constituted 80 percent of IUMMSW membership in the Birmingham area, practice in locals was that the offices of president and financial secretary were reserved for whites and those of recording secretary and vice-president for blacks); in 1942 he was appointed IUMMSW representative for the South, and in 1950, southern regional director; elected an international vice-president of his union in 1953; ran an independent gas station, but continued active as a IUMMSW vice-president; he sought to eliminate racial discrimination in pay and seniority in the Birmingham ore mines and steel mills; during the 1950s when the United Steelworkers of America (USWA) tried to raid IUMMSW, he led a successful defense of the IUMMSW jurisdiction in the South; he was one of the IUMMSW officers indicted in 1956 for conspiracy to falsify the Taft-Hartley non-Communist affidavit, but due to insufficient evidence the charges against him were dismissed; he was involved in the merger negotiations with the USWA, and when the merger took place in 1967, became a USWA international representative, serving in the union's civil rights division; from the 1940s, when he was elected vice-president of the Bessemer, Ala., National Association for the Advancement of Colored People, Howard combined civil rights activism with his work in the labor movement; he helped organize and became president in 1951 of the Bessemer Voters' League, which increased black registration from 75 to 2,000 during the 1950s; as a consequence, he and his family were subjected to indictments and violent harassment; in 1957 his home was bombed; for having a civil rights poster reprinted during a voter registration campaign in 1959 in Bessemer, he was convicted of provoking "a breach of the peace" and while leaving the courtroom was savagely beaten by a mob; although IUMMSW appealed the case to the state supreme court, he spent six months on a convict chain gang; he led a IUMMSW contingent in the 1965 Selma-to-Montgomery march; in 1968 he succeeded in organizing aluminum workers in the Virgin Islands for the USWA; retired from the USWA in 1972 but remained active in civil rights; campaigned for Henry Wallace in 1948 and was elected to the Alabama state legislature in 1978; *The Negro History Bulletin* (February 1954); Jeffrey E. Fuller, "The Due Processing of Asbury Howard," *The Reporter*, April 16, 1959; John G. Spiese interview with Howard, March 1968, Labor Archives, Pennsylvania State University; Horace R. Cayton and George S. Mitchell, *Black Workers and the New Unions* (1939).

Donald G. Sofchalk

HOWARD, Charles Perry   (1879–1938). Born in Harvel, Ill., September 14, 1879; son of Lewis Pontius, a lawyer, and Mary M. (Williamson) Howard; married Margaret McPhail; no children; completed grammar school at age 13, then employed as a railroad worker, 1897–1899, and a miner, 1900–1903, prior to entering the printing trade; joined the Tacoma, Wash., local of the International Typographical Union (ITU) in 1907; transferred his membership to the Multnomah Typographical Union in Portland, Oreg., and became its president in 1914; served as president of the Portland Central Labor Council, 1916–1918; was Commissioner of Conciliation in the U.S. Department of Labor, 1918–1919; served as an ITU delegate to the American Federation of Labor (AFL), 1920–1922; edited the *Railway Maintenance of Way Employees' Journal*, 1919–1922; joined the Progressive party faction of the ITU's two-party system and was elected vice-president on that ticket in 1922; became ITU president when the incumbent, John McParland, died in 1923, but was defeated in the elections of 1924; elected ITU president in 1926 and served in that capacity for the remainder of his life, although defeated in the elections of 1938; was a proponent of industrial unionism and authored and sponsored two plans for industrial organization at AFL conventions in 1933 and 1934; joined other advocates of industrial unionism on the Committee for Industrial Organization (CIO) and became its secretary; although the ITU never affiliated with the CIO, it left the AFL after refusing to pay a special tax levied to fight the rival CIO; defeated for reelection in 1938, primarily because of his opposition to demands for additional local autonomy to deal with the problems of the depression; was a Republican; died in Colorado Springs, Colo., July 21, 1938; Seymour M. Lipset, et al., *Union Democracy: The Internal Politics of the International Typographical Union* (1956); Walter Galenson, *The CIO Challenge to the AFL: A History of the American Labor Movement, 1935–1941* (1960); *Dictionary of American Biography*, Suppl. 2; Melvyn Dubofsky and Warren Van Tine, *John L. Lewis: A Biography* (1977).

HOWARD, Robert   (fl. 1844–1886). Born in Northwich, Cheshire, England, of Irish parents, 1844 or 1845; at age 8, set to learn piecing in a Macclesfield silk mill; removed to Bollington, where he got work as a piecer; moved to Stockport, where he worked as a bobbin-boy, being then but 10 years old; at 15 he became a spinner; at 25, president of the Spinners' Union; declined offer as overseer, because he could not do the domineering required; prominent in the agitation for nine hours in textile industries; by conciliatory advice averted many strikes; in 1873, he immigrated to Fall River, Mass.; worked three years as spinner in the Flint Mill; in 1878 chosen secretary of the Fall River Spinners' Association; in 1879, chosen its permanent secretary; in 1880, elected to the

Massachusetts House of Representatives, receiving the nomination of both parties, where he was foremost among the supporters of labor legislation; declined a renomination; in 1882, his friends in England sent him a testimonial to show their appreciation of his services; in Rhode Island in 1883, began the agitation for a ten-hour workday for women and children; prevailed on Governor Bourne to recommend such legislation, which was enacted in 1885; also advocated the ten-hour day before the Maine Legislative Labor Committee; frequently advocated labor measures before Massachusetts legislative committees; in 1885, elected to state senate from Second Bristol District as a Democrat; also became associate editor of *Wade's Fibre and Fabric*; from 1881 to 1885, he was treasurer of the Federation of Trades and Labor Unions of the United States and Canada; was once secretary of the National Cottonspinners' Association; in May 1885, the Cottonspinners' Union of Fall River formed an assembly of the Knights of Labor, unanimously adopted his name and chose him as secretary. Howard, although a leader in labor matters, always commanded the respect of both political parties to an unusual degree; was one of the founders of the American Federation of Labor in 1886; John R. Commons et al., *History of Labour in the United States*, Vol. 2 (1918); George E. McNeill, *The Labor Movement: The Problem of To-Day* (1887); Norman J. Ware, *The Labor Movement in the United States, 1860–1895* (1929).

George E. McNeill

HOWAT, Alexander   (1876–1945). Born in Glasgow, Scotland, in 1876; married; emigrated to the United States; settled in Braidwood, Ill., growing up there with John Mitchell (q.v.), who admired the bellicose and impetuous youth; moved to Pittsburg, Kans., and joined the United Mine Workers of America (UMWA); served as president of District 14, UMWA, Kansas, 1906–1921; was a member of the Socialist party, and in 1914, the District 14 convention called for the establishment of a Socialist government "as the strong right arm of labor"; supported the National Farmer-Labor party in 1920; in the summer of 1921, organized Kansas miners' support for a Republican state administration to repeal the anti-strike legislation; provided a militant, strike-prone leadership that caused Kansans to complain that local "miners did far more picketing than mining"; sporadically defied both national union officials and Kansas state law; led two brief strikes during World War I and the immediate postwar period, which led the Kansas legislature to pass the 1920 Kansas Industrial Relations Act, which empowered a three-man industrial court to decide all labor disputes in industries affected with a public interest and to abolish strikes, picketing, and boycotts and the deduction of union dues; the 1920 and 1921 American Federation of Labor conventions and the 1920 District 14 convention encouraged defiance of the law, but when he led a 1921 strike and was arrested for refusing to testify before the industrial court, President John L. Lewis (q.v.) revoked the charters of District 14 and 81 local unions, half the district's locals, and appointed a provisional president to replace Howat; as a result, became a hero and martyr

to Kansas miners, the Kansas State Federation of Labor, and many city central
unions; after a district leadership purge, the national UMWA convention restored
the district's autonomy and toward the close of the 1920s he was reelected
president; along with Robert Harlin, District 10, Washington, opposed the in-
cumbents for reelection to the UMWA presidency and vice-presidency; participated in the Communist-tinged Progressive International Committee of Miners
in 1923; along with his Kansas followers, supported John Brophy's (q.v.) 1926
''Save the Union'' campaign for the union presidency and stumped the anthracite
region for the ticket; while again serving as District 14 president in 1930, elected
president of the Reorganized United Mine Workers and campaigned for support
in Missouri; became increasingly unstable and suffered from alcoholism, and
turned over most of his duties to Vice-President Adolph Germer (q.v.); refused
to appear before the international executive board and was expelled from the
union after Lewis revoked the District 14 charter and appointed a provisional
president; his union career destroyed, worked from 1930 to 1945 at various jobs
including a state border guard, editor of a Kansas labor paper, and a Pittsburg,
Kans., city employee; died in Pittsburg, Kans., December 10, 1945; *United
Mine Workers Journal*, January 1, 1946; *The New York Times*, December 11,
1945; Irving Bernstein, *The Lean Years: A History of the American Worker,
1920–1933* (1960); Marc Karson, ''Trade Unions in Kansas,'' in *Kansas: The
First Century*, ed. John D. Bright (1956); Selig Perlman and Philip Taft, *History
of Labor in the United States, 1896–1932*, Vol. 4 (1935); John H. M. Laslett,
*Labor and the Left: A Study of Socialism and Radical Influences in the American
Labor Movement, 1881–1924* (1970).

                                                                  John W. Hevener

HUBER, William   (fl. 1900–1912). A leader of the United Brotherhood of
Carpenters and Joiners (UBC) in New York City; elected general president of
the UBC in 1900; was one of the principal figures in the coterie of UBC leaders
who sought to depose the union's founder and executive leader, Peter J. McGuire
(q.v.); was assigned by the general executive board in 1901 to assist McGuire
in the administration of his duties as general secretary-treasurer, but found it
impossible to work with the ''brooding and recalcitrant McGuire''; presented
the charges of corruption that led to McGuire's dismissal from the UBC; allied
with Frank Duffy (q.v.) and using the cadre of paid organizers that he had
appointed, was able to build a powerful political machine within the UBC; his
power was limited by the institutional structure of the brotherhood and by the
local autonomy that had long existed within the union's structure; while president,
was able to expand gradually the jurisdictional claims of the UBC to include
''all that's made of wood'' and to have that jurisdiction recognized by the
American Federation of Labor (AFL); led the UBC campaign against the American Wood Workers Union and drew up the merger proposal that was accepted
in 1912; organized the UBC-dominated Structural Building Trades Alliance in
1902, a forerunner of the AFL building trades department; retired from the UBC

presidency in 1912 after nearly a decade of internecine conflicts with various members of the general executive board; while president, was a severe critic of racial discrimination within the UBC; also created the constitutional framework that converted the UBC from a confederation to a federation; the resulting centralization of power in the hands of the general officers of the UBC was used by William Hutcheson (q.v.) to establish near total control of the brotherhood; Robert A. Christie, *Empire in Wood: A History of the Carpenters Union* (1956); Philip Taft, *The A.F. of L. in the Time of Gompers* (1957).

HUDDELL, Arthur McIntire   (1869–1931). Born in Danvers, Mass., June 15, 1869; son of John, a shoemaker, and Caroline (McIntire) Huddell; Protestant; married Eliza Chase Dow on September 26, 1888; five children; completed grammar school in Salem, Mass., then went to work at age 13; worked as a coal-hoisting engineer during 1882–1896, then employed in the building trades; joined Boston, Mass., Local 4 of the International Union of Steam and Operating Engineers (IUSOE) (now the International Union of Operating Engineers) in 1898; elected president of Local 4 in 1902 and business agent in 1904; was an IUSOE vice-president during 1905–1910, and in 1910 ran unsuccessfully for the union presidency; served as an IUSOE organizer, 1907–1908; elected first vice-president of the IUSOE in 1916 and became international president in 1921 after the death of the incumbent, Milton Snellings; was a member of the Massachusetts Civil Service Commission, 1919–1922; was a strong advocate of international collective bargaining agreements negotiated directly between interstate businesses and international union officers; was the victim of an unsuccessful assassination attempt in Washington, D.C., in 1931; died five days later from the trauma of the blow while still hospitalized in Washington, D.C., on June 1, 1931; Garth L. Mangum, *The Operating Engineers: The Economic History of a Trade Union* (1964); Solon DeLeon, ed., *The American Labor Who's Who* (1925).

HUDSON, Hosea   (1898–   ). Born in Wilkes County, Ga., on April 12, 1898; son of Thomas, a common laborer and railroad maintenance worker, and Laura Camella (Smith) Hudson; reared a Baptist; married Sophie Scroggs in 1917 and Virginia Larue Marson in 1962; one child; Afro-American; educated intermittently until age 14, acquiring only the most rudimentary reading and writing skills; worked as a general farm laborer during his youth to provide some family support; became a sharecropper in 1918; took a job as a common laborer in a railroad roundhouse in Wilkes County in 1923; moved to Birmingham, Ala., in 1924, where he became an iron molder; appalled by the injustice perpetrated in the Scottsboro and Camp Hill cases, he joined the Communist Party of America (CPA) in 1931; became a full-time CPA worker in 1932 after losing his foundry job because of his political convictions; attended the national CPA meeting in New York City in 1933; participated in the CPA's National Training School in New York City in 1934; was a CPA organizer in Atlanta, Ga., 1934–1936;

returned to Birmingham, where he worked on Works Progress Administration projects, served as vice-president of the Birmingham and Jefferson County Workers' Alliance, and was recording secretary of the Steel Workers Organizing Committee Local 1489, 1937–1940; was elected president of Local 2815, United Steelworkers of America, in 1942, serving until 1947; during this time, he also served as chairman of Local 2815's grievance committee and was a delegate to the Birmingham Industrial Union Council, Congress of Industrial Organizations; served as vice-president of the Alabama People's Education Association, a CPA affiliate, 1944–1945; was expelled from the Birmingham Industrial Union Council in 1947 because of his Communist associations; lost his job and his local union offices and was blacklisted; organized the Bessemer, Ala., United Political Action Committee in 1950; worked for the CPA in Atlanta, 1951–1953; moved to New York City in 1954 and two years later secured employment as a restaurant janitor, a job he held until retiring in 1965; moved to Atlantic City, N.J., in 1965; toured the Soviet Union in 1971; authored *Black Workers in the Deep South* (1972); Nell Irving Painter, *The Narrative of Hosea Hudson: His Life as a Negro Communist in the South* (1979); Mark Naison, "Marxism and Black Radicalism in America: Notes on a Long (and Continuing) Journey," *Radical America* (1971); Theodore Draper, *American Communism and Soviet Russia* (1960).

HUERTA, Dolores Clara (1930–   ). Born in Dawson, New Mexico, on April 10, 1930; daughter of Juan and Alicia (Chavez) Fernandez; Roman Catholic; married Richard Huerta, an executive board member of the United Farm Workers of America, in 1949; seven children; in the early 1950s, met Fred Ross of the Community Service Organization (CSO) in Stockton, Calif., and assisted him in setting up CSO chapters; met Cesar Chavez (q.v.) in 1955 while working for the CSO and eventually became one of his most dedicated and effective associates in organizing farm workers; became a CSO lobbbyist in 1962; later that year quit the CSO and moved to Delano, Calif., to assist Chavez in organizing farm workers for the Farm Workers' Association; helped organize migrant workers in Stockton and Modesto, Calif., in 1964; joined the United Farm Workers' Organizing Committee (UFWOC) in 1964; helped the UFWOC negotiate a contract with the Delano grape growers in July 1970; participated in the 1970 lettuce boycott against Bud Antle Co. and Dow Chemical Co.; helped the United Farm Workers' Union (UFW) negotiate a contract with the lettuce growers in California; in 1970 and again in 1973, elected a vice-president of the UFW; Dolores C. Huerta Papers, Walter Reuther Library, Wayne State University; Mark Day, *Forty Acres: Cesar Chavez and the Farm Workers* (1971); Joan London and Henry Anderson, *So Shall Ye Reap: The Story of Cesar Chavez and the Farm Workers' Movement* (1970); *Ms.* (November 1976); *Who's Who in Labor* (1976);

Philip S. Foner, *Women and the American Labor Movement from World War I to the Present* (1980).

Marie Tedesco

HUGHES, Roy Orlo   (1887–   ). Born in Portland, N.D., September 24, 1887; son of Elijah, a blacksmith, and Maria Madeline (Olson) Hughes; Presbyterian; married Mary Ellen Penrod on November 26, 1912; three children; left school during his senior year at Mora High School, Mora, Minn., and hired as a machinist's helper on the Great Northern Railway in 1906; raised purebred Guernsey dairy cattle while continuing employment as a railroad worker, 1907–1928; joined the Northern Pacific Railroad as a brakeman in 1912, eventually becoming a conductor; joined Duluth, Minn., Division 336 of the Order of Railway Conductors (ORC) in 1916, and served successively as the division's legislative chairman, adjustment chairman, local chairman, and as a member of the general committee for the Northern Pacific; took employment as a conductor on the Chicago, Milwaukee, St. Paul and Pacific in 1925; gave up farming when transferred from Duluth to St. Paul, Minn., in 1928; elected secretary of the general committee for the Milwaukee Railroad in 1929 and three years later was named general chairman of the committee of adjustment; elected a vice-president and appointed grand trustee of the ORC in 1940; elected to the presidency of the ORC in 1950; acquired a reputation during the wage controversies of the 1940s and 1950s as a tough and effective bargainer; was an independent in politics; retired in 1958; *Current Biography* (1950); *Who's Who in Labor* (1946); *Labor*, June 14, 1958.

HUTCHESON, Maurice Albert   (1897–1983). Born in Saginaw County, Mich., May 7, 1897; son of William L. (q.v.), a union president, and Bessie Mae (King) Hutcheson; Methodist; married Ethel Hyatt on October 23, 1926; received a grammar school education in the public schools of Michigan; became a carpenter's apprentice in 1914 and joined the United Brotherhood of Carpenters and Joiners of America (UBC); served as a carpenter's mate in the U.S. Navy during World War I; worked as a journeyman carpenter, 1918–1928; appointed a UBC auditor in 1928, serving in that capacity until 1938; elected first general vice-president of the UBC in 1938; after the resignation of his father, William L., in 1952, became general president of the UBC; shortly after assuming the presidency of the UBC, took the Carpenters out of the American Federation of Labor (AFL) because displeased with the no-raiding agreement negotiated with the Congress of Industrial Organizations (CIO), but reaffiliated three weeks later; became an AFL vice-president and executive council member in 1953 and retained that position after the AFL-CIO merger in 1955; cited for contempt of Congress for refusing to answer questions before the McClellan Special Senate Committee in 1957, but was later pardoned by President Lyndon B. Johnson; convicted of bribing an Indiana state official to obtain advance information on highway routes in 1960 and sentenced to from 2 to 14 years in prison, but the conviction was overturned on appeal; as president of UBC, initiated multi-union agreements for union-label factory-built housing and restructured the UBC apprenticeship program in response to minority-group pressures; a Republican; retired union positions in 1972; died in Lakeland, Fla., in January 1983; Maxwell C. Raddock, *Portrait of an American Labor Leader: William L. Hutcheson* (1955); Robert A. Christie, *Empire in Wood: A History of the Carpenters' Union* (1956); Joseph C. Goulden, *Meany* (1972).

HUTCHESON, William Levi   (1874–1953). Born in Saginaw County, Mich., February 7, 1874; son of David Oliver, a Scottish immigrant, farmer, and ship carpenter, and Elizabeth (Culver) Hutcheson; Methodist; married Bessie May King on October 10, 1893; four children; apprenticed to his father as a carpenter in 1890; joined the United Brotherhood of Carpenters and Joiners of America (UBC) in 1902; four years later, became business agent for his local union; elected second vice-president of the UBC in 1913 and became president two years later; served during World War I on the War Labor Conference Committee appointed by President Woodrow Wilson to seek a way to eliminating labor-management conflicts during the war and was appointed to the War Labor Board that resulted from the committee's recommendations; elected to the American Federation of Labor (AFL) executive council in 1935 as tenth vice-president; was an AFL delegate to the International Labor Organization's conference in Chile in 1935; was an AFL fraternal delegate to the British Trades Union Congress in 1919 and 1926; resigned from the AFL executive council in 1936 over objections to the council's endorsement of New Deal legislation; returned to the executive council in 1940 and named first vice-president; was an opponent of the industrial unionism advocated by the Congress of Industrial Organizations, but favored craft-industrial unionism and was constantly embroiled in jurisdictional disputes by aggressively seeking to assume jurisdiction over any union member who had any connection with the woodworking industry; under his leadership, the UBC never conducted intensive organizing drives but instead preferred to let others organize the unorganized and then claim jurisdiction; resulting from these tactics, the membership of the UBC grew substantially during his incumbency; expanded and consolidated his near dictatorial control over a union that was increasingly plagued by unethical and corrupt activities; was a Republican and was placed in charge of the labor division of the national Republican party in 1932 and 1936; retired in December 1951, and was succeeded as UBC president by his son, Maurice (q.v.); died in Indianapolis, Ind., October 20, 1953; Maxwell C. Raddock, *Portrait of an American Labor Leader: William L. Hutcheson* (1955); Robert A. Christie, *Empire in Wood: A History of the Carpenters' Union* (1956); Morris A. Horowitz, *The Structure and Government of the Carpenters' Union* (1962); Charles A. Madison, *American Labor Leaders: Personalities and Forces in the Labor Movement* (1950); *National Cyclopaedia of American Biography*, Vol. G; *Dictionary of American Biography*, Suppl. 5.

HUTCHINS, Grace   (1885–1969). Born in Boston, Mass., on August 19, 1885; daughter of Edward Webster, a prominent and wealthy Boston attorney, and Susan Barnes (Hurd) Hutchins; reared an Episcopalian; never married; elementary and secondary schooling acquired at private schools after which she traveled around the world with her parents, 1898–1899; graduated from Bryn Mawr College with a B.A. in 1907; went to China as a missionary in 1912 and served as a teacher and principal of the Episcopal St. Hilda's School for Chinese Girls in Wuchang; after her return to the United States in 1916, she became involved in labor union activities; while teaching at a social training school in New York City, she joined the Socialist party to protest American involvement in World War I; continued her education at the New York School of Philanthropy, 1920–1921, where she studied labor problems, and Columbia University Teachers College, 1922–1923; inaugurated a friendship with Anna Rochester, a radical economist and historian, and shared a Greenwich Village apartment with her for the remainder of her life; joined the Fellowship of Reconciliation (FOR) and served as its business executive, 1925–1926, and press secretary, 1924–1926; was a contributing editor to the FOR's organ, *The World Tomorrow*, 1922–1924; along with Rochester, she attended the international FOR conference in Denmark in 1923 and thereafter traveled to Europe, the Far East, India, and the Soviet Union, 1926–1927; became a correspondent for the Federated Press after her return to the United States; arrested in 1927 during a Sacco-Vanzetti (q.v.) demonstration in Boston; appointed an investigator for the New York Department of Labor's Bureau of Women in Industry in 1927 but poor health forced her to resign after five months; one of the organizers of the Labor Research Association (LRA) in 1929, she remained a staff member until 1967; was one of the editors of the LRA's *Labor Facts Book*, a series of 17 volumes published annually; edited *Railroad Notes*, 1937–1962; wrote *Labor and Silk* in 1929 after participating in textile strikes in Paterson, N.J., in 1924 and New Bedford, Mass., in 1928; her major book, *Women Who Work*, first published in 1933, was reissued in 1934 and 1952; an active member of the Communist party, she ran unsuccessfully on the Communist party ticket in New York for city alderman, 1935, controller, 1936, and lieutenant governor, 1940; an affluent radical, she retained a generous allowance from her family when they were alive and inherited much of their estate when they died; as a result, she became one of the financial angels of radical causes; was elected treasurer of the Communist National Election Campaign Committee in 1936; was a major stockholder in the *Daily Worker*, 1950–1956; provided the bail money for Elizabeth Gurley Flynn (q.v.) and Alexander Trachtenberg ($10,000 and $5,000 respectively) when they were arrested in 1951 under the Smith Act; was a target of anti-Communist crusaders during the 1950s but continued to support radical causes; served as secretary of the Elizabeth Gurley Flynn Memorial Committee in 1964; died in New York City on July 15, 1969; Grace Hutchins Papers, University of Oregon Library; *Notable American Women*, Vol. 4; *The New York Times*, July 16, 1969; *Daily Worker*, July 17, 1969.

HYMAN, Louis   (1884–1963). Born in Witebask, Russia, June 17, 1884; son of Max, a storekeeper, and Ida (Ades) Hyman; Jewish; married Bella Press on May 20, 1925; one child; attended Hebrew schools in Russia and night schools in Great Britain and the United States; emigrated to Manchester, England, in 1903 and began work in a men's clothing factory; joined the British Socialist movement and became an influential figure in the Manchester trade union movement; emigrated to the United States in 1911 and a short time later joined Cloak and Suit Tailors Local 9 of the International Ladies' Garment Workers' Union (ILGWU); served as business agent, an executive board member, and president of Local 9; appointed a director of the ILGWU Union Health Centre in 1919; elected to the general executive board of the New York Joint Board in 1925; shortly thereafter, suspended, along with several other left-wing leaders, by ILGWU international officers; became chairman of the rival Joint Action Committee and led the unsuccessful garment strike of 1925–1926; became president of the Communist-controlled Needle Trades Workers Industrial Union; broke with the Communists after the Nazi-Soviet pact of 1939 and was readmitted to the ILGWU; elected manager of ILGWU Local 9 in 1942; became an ILGWU vice-president in 1949; died in New York City, October 12, 1963; Benjamin Stolberg, *Tailor's Progress: The Story of a Famous Union and the Men Who Made It* (1944); Harry Haskel, *A Leader of the Garment Workers: The Biography of Isidore Nagler* (1950); Louis Levine, *The Women's Garment Workers: A History of the International Ladies' Garment Workers' Union* (1924); *ILGWU Report and Proceedings* (1965).

I

IGLESIAS, Santiago   (1872–1939). Born in La Coruña, Spain, February 22, 1872; son of Manuel, a carpenter, and Joseta Pantin; Roman Catholic; married Justa Bocanegra in 1902; 11 children; left school at age 12 after the death of his father and was apprenticed to a carpenter; led a walkout of workers in 1884 protesting their employers' refusal to allow them to attend a Sunday protest meeting against sales taxes, then joined the Spanish section of the Socialist party; emigrated to Cuba in 1887 and, after gaining employment in a furniture factory, began organizing workers against the 12-hour day; after the outbreak of the Cuban war of independence in 1895, the workers' movement with which he was associated was suppressed and the following year he fled to Puerto Rico; served a prison sentence as a labor agitator, but avoided deportation to Spain; became a guide and interpreter to General John R. Brooke, who was in charge of the U.S. occupation of Puerto Rico; presided over the founding convention of the Puerto Rican Federation of Labor on October 20, 1898; convicted of conspiracy in 1900 and sentenced to four years in prison, but due to the intercession of American Federation of Labor (AFL) president Samuel Gompers (q.v.), whom he had met a year earlier, served only seven months; along with Gompers, was granted an interview with President Theodore Roosevelt in 1902 and as a result the U.S. administration in Puerto Rico was liberalized somewhat; served during 1900–1935 as president of the AFL-affiliated Federación Libre de Trabajadores de Puerto Rico and was an AFL organizer; organized the Puerto Rican Socialist party in 1915 and elected to the Puerto Rican senate two years later, serving until 1933; served as secretary of the Pan-American Federation of Labor, 1925–1939; elected the Puerto Rican representative to the United States Congress in 1933 and served until his death; was an advocate of statehood for Puerto Rico and he was shot and superficially wounded by a Puerto Rican nationalist in 1936; edited *Ensayo Obrero,* 1897–1899, *Porvenir Social,* 1899–1900, *Union Obrera,* 1903–1906, and *Justicia,* 1914–1925; authored *Quienes Somos* (1910), *Gobierno Proprio Para Quien?* (1914), *Luchas Emancipadoras* (1929); died in Washington, D.C., December 5, 1939; Lewis L. Lorwin, *Labor and Internationalism*

(1929); Rafael Alonso Torres, *Cuarenta Anos de Lucha Proletaria* (1939); *Dictionary of American Biography,* Suppl 2; William G. Whittaker, "The Santiago Iglesias Case, 1901–1902: Origins of American Trade Union Involvements in Puerto Rico," *The Americas* (April 1968); Angel Quintero Rivera, *Workers' Struggle in Puerto Rico: A Documentary History* (1976); Miles Galvin, *The Organized Labor Movement in Puerto Rico* (1979).

IRONS, Martin (1833–1900). Born in Dundee, Scotland, March 1, 1833; the son of moderately prosperous Scottish parents; married Mary Brown, from whom he was separated after she bore him seven children; emigrated to the United States in 1847; became a machinist's apprentice shortly after arriving in New York City; moved to Carrollton, La.; worked there as a machinist for several years, then opened an independent grocery, but soon was forced to sell out; moved to Lexington, Ky., and there led a successful strike of machinists for an eight-hour day; then lived in several Missouri cities including Kansas City, where he again unsuccessfully attempted to set up a business; settled in Sedalia, Mo., in 1885 and resumed work as a machinist; was one of the founders and elected master workman of Local Assembly 3476 of the Noble Order of the Knights of Labor (K of L) organized in Sedalia in 1885; was one of the founders of District Assembly 101 that brought together local assemblies of Missouri Pacific Railroad workers; led the historic (but unsuccessful) strike against the Jay Gould-controlled Missouri Pacific in 1886; after the strike, business and government leaders identified him as its sole perpetrator and the leaders of the K of L branded him as the sole cause of its failure; spent the last 15 years of his life living in poverty, blacklisted, and unable to practice his trade, hounded by insensitive and myopic defenders of the established order, and slandered by an official congressional investigating committee; died in Bruceville, Tex., November 17, 1900; Ruth A. Allen, *The Great Southwest Strike* (1942); Gerald N. Grob, *Workers and Utopia: A Study of Ideological Conflict in the American Labor Movement, 1865–1900* (1961); Norman J. Ware, *The Labor Movement in the United States, 1860–1895* (1929).

J

JARRETT, John   (1843–1918). Born in Elbow Vale, Monmouthshire, Wales, January 27, 1843; Congregationalist; married Margaret Price in 1869; two children; orphaned at age 12 and became an iron puddler; emigrated to eastern Pennsylvania in 1862 and joined the union of his trade, the Sons of Vulcan; returned to England ca. 1868, became active in the Amalgamated Ironworkers Association, and assimilated the cautious trade unionism of its founder, John Kane; emigrated to Pennsylvania again in 1872 and took a job at the Westerman Iron Works in Sharon; favored amalgamated unionism and participated, while serving as a vice-president of the Sons of Vulcan, in the formation of the Amalgamated Association of Iron and Steel Workers (AA) (later the Amalgamated Association of Iron, Steel, and Tin Workers of America) in 1875–1876; served as fifth district deputy, Sons of Vulcan, 1875; sixth district vice-president and trustee, 1876, and representative to the second joint committee on amalgamation in 1875; elected president of AA in 1880; chaired the 1881 convention of the Federation of Organized Trades and Labor Union, precursor of the American Federation of Labor, but withdrew the AA when the federation refused to endorse a high tariff; under his leadership, the AA became one of the foremost American unions, but its membership was largely confined to the iron mills of Allegheny County and the Ohio Valley; keenly aware of this, sought to create a disciplined rank and file and strongly urged circumspect use of the strike; in order to sustain AA wage scales, which were based on iron and steel prices, advocated protective tariffs and elimination of price competition through industrial consolidation; combined along with this job-conscious approach a broad concern about workers generally, the admission of blacks into AA, and equal pay for women; displayed however the typical trade unionist's fear of "new" immigrant labor; discouraged by internal bickering and opposed to the AA strikes of 1882, resigned in 1883; unsuccessfully sought appointment as head of the new U.S. Bureau of Labor Statistics in 1884; continued to support the labor movement during the next two decades and at same time devoted energy to establishing the tin-plate industry; was a lobbyist for the Tin Plate Association and secretary in 1887 and 1893; served as an employment agent for Carnegie Steel Company in 1893; was a consistent supporter of the Republican party; successfully lobbied Congress to include high duties on Welsh plate in the McKinley Tariff of 1890; was American Consul in Birmingham, England, 1889–1892, and there studied the Welsh tin-plate industry; was an executive of the tin-plate and sheet steel trade association, 1892–1900; subsequently, was in business in Pittsburgh; authored Chapter 11, "The Story of the Iron Workers," in George E. McNeill, ed., *The Labor Movement: The Problem of To-Day* (1887); see also his extensive testimony in U.S. Senate Committee on Education and Labor, *Report upon the Relations of Labor and Capital*, Vol. 1, *Testimony*, 48th Congress (1885); died in Pittsburgh, Pa., December 17, 1918; American Historical Society, *History of Pittsburgh and Environs: Biographical* (1922); John A. Fitch, *The Steel Workers* (1911).

Donald G. Sofchalk

JEFFREY, Mildred   (1911–   ). Born in Alton, Iowa, on December 29, 1911; daughter of Bert David, a pharmacist, and Bertha (Merritt) McWilliams, also a pharmacist; married Newman Jeffrey, an auto worker; two children; divorced in 1962; graduated from the University of Minnesota in 1933; earned an M.S. in social research at Bryn Mawr College in 1935; active in student political organizations and trade union work, especially in Philadelphia, Pa., textile factories; worked as a chicken plucker and textile operative; named education director of the Pennsylvania Joint Board of Shirt Workers, Amalgamated Clothing Workers of America, in 1935; worked as a newspaper reporter in Sheboygan, Wis.; moved to Detroit, Mich., in 1944 when her husband began work in an aircraft plant; served as first director of the United Automobile, Aerospace and Agricultural Implement Workers of America (UAW) women's department, 1945–1949, director of the UAW radio department, 1950–1955, community relations department, 1955–1972, and consumer affairs department, 1972–1976; throughout this period she served as a special assistant to UAW president Walter Reuther (q.v.); appointed by President John F. Kennedy to the National Commission on Youth Employment, 1961–1963, and by President Jimmy Carter to International Women's Year Commission, 1977; was a delegate to the National Women's Conference, Houston, Tex., in 1977; appointed by President Carter to the Advisory Committee for Women, 1978–1979; consultant to the Coalition of Labor Union Women in 1978; worked extensively with community and social action groups and served on boards of directors of many, including the Consumer Federation of America, the National Consumer League, the National Child Labor Committee, and the Commission on Race and Religion, National Council of Churches; became active in state and national Democratic party politics in 1948; was a precinct delegate to the Michigan State Democratic party from 1956; was chairman of the platform committee of the Michigan Democratic party, 1956–1964; was a delegate to the Democratic presidential nominating conventions from 1956 to 1976, and served on the rules committee, 1972, 1976, the credentials committee, 1978; elected to the Democratic National Convention Executive Committee, 1964–1972; was a founding member of the National Women's Political Caucus in 1972 and chairman of its Democratic Task Force, 1975–1976, and of the national organization, 1977–1979; was a member of the National Association for the Advancement of Colored People, the National Women's Caucus, the Women's Equity League, the National Organization for Women, the American Civil Liberties Union, Americans for Democratic Action, Democratic Socialists of America, the Women's International League for Peace and Freedom; has received many honors, including NOW Feminist of the Year Award, 1978, ADA Action Award, 1978, Eugene V. Debs Award, 1978; elected as a Democrat to the Wayne State University Board of Governors in 1975 and reelected in 1982; Mildred Jeffrey Papers, Walter P. Reuther Library, Wayne State University.

Gay Zieger

JENNINGS, Paul Joseph   (1918–   ). Born in Brooklyn, N.Y., March 19, 1918; married; two children; graduated from high school, then attended the Radio Corporation of America Institute and the Crown Heights Labor School; hired by the Brooklyn Edison Company and in 1938 was elected steward of the Independent Utility Workers; became an electronics technician for the Sperry-Rand Corporation in 1939; helped organize a United Electrical and Radio Workers of America (UE) local in the plant where he was employed and served at various times as shop steward, grievance chairman, shop chairman, and acting president of the local; served with the U.S. Navy during World War II; after the war, served successively as a member of his local's executive board, treasurer, and, in 1948, president; was one of the leaders of the UE conservative faction and joined James B. Carey (q.v.) in founding the International Union of Electrical, Radio and Machine Workers (IUE) after the UE was expelled from the Congress of Industrial Organizations (CIO) in 1949 for alleged Communist domination; elected executive secretary of IUE District 4 in 1950, and, after union districts were reorganized, became the executive secretary of District 3, comprising New York and New Jersey; served as a vice-president of both the New York City Industrial Union Council, CIO, and the New York State CIO Industrial Union Council; served as chairman of the American Federation of Labor-CIO (AFL-CIO) merger committees for the CIO councils of New York City and New York State; elected president of the IUE in 1965 by the union's executive board after a U.S. Department of Labor recount of IUE election returns revealed that the incumbent, James B. Carey, had been fraudulently declared the winner; served as a labor delegate to the Organization of Economic Cooperation and Development meeting in Germany in 1967; associated with numerous private organizations, including the National Urban League, which in 1967 honored him for his contributions to civil rights causes; served as a trustee of the University of the State of New York; a supporter of the Liberal party of New York; *Who's*

Who in America, 1972–1973; Current Biography (1969); *The New York Times*, April 6, 1965, October 27, 1969.

JESSUP, William J.   (fl. 1827–1873). Born in New York City, February 7, 1827; after the death of his mother about 1835, moved to Greenwich, Conn., where he attended a rural school for seven years and thereafter taught in the same school for two years; returned to New York City and secured employment with Harper Brothers publishers; worked for the publishing house for two years, then was attracted by the high wages in the shipbuilding industry and learned the ship joiners' trade; entered the labor movement by organizing a union of ship joiners in 1863; then mobilized successful union opposition to the Folger bill, which was introduced in the New York legislature the next year to declare strikes illegal conspiracies; became the most prominent figure in the labor organizations of New York City and state during the ensuing decade; was a strong supporter of the eight-hour movement and participated in the ship joiners' strike for shorter hours in 1866 and was active in organizing mass rallies and demonstrations that accompanied the city's general strike in 1872; was a ship joiner's delegate to the founding Baltimore Congress of the National Labor Union (NLU) in 1866 and served on the committee that drafted its constitution; elected vice-president from New York; cooperated closely with the International Workingmen's Association throughout the years of his activity; served frequently as president or secretary of both the Workingmen's Union of New York City and the State Workingmen's Assembly, and was regularly sent as a delegate from one of those bodies or the other to the congresses of the National Labor Union until 1870; supported the formation of a labor reform party for his own state and the greenback program of the NLU, but disassociated himself from the NLU after 1870 in protest against the growing prominence of middle-class reformers within it; in 1872, became both president and secretary of the ailing Carpenters' and Joiners' National Union and tried unsuccessfully to revive it; defeated for the presidency of the Workingmen's Assembly in 1873 and withdrew from the labor movment; David Montgomery, *Beyond Equality: Labor and the Radical Republicans, 1862–1872* (1967); Norman J. Ware, *The Labor Movement in the United States, 1860–1895* (1929); John R. Commons et al., *History of Labour in the United States,* Vol. 2 (1918); "William J. Jessup," an unidentified biographical sketch located in the Labor Collection, Biography and Papers, of the State Historical Society of Wisconsin.

JEWELL, Bert Mark   (1881–1968). Born in Brock, Neb., February 5, 1881; son of Charles James, a general construction contractor and farmer, and Ella Elizabeth (Adams) Jewell; Protestant; forced to leave school in 1897 before completing the eighth grade and for the next three years worked at a variety of occupations; became an apprentice boilermaker in High Springs, Fla., in 1900; completed his apprenticeship, then joined the International Brotherhood of Boiler Makers, Iron Ship Builders and Helpers of America (IBB) in 1905; traveled around the United States during 1905–1912, working as a boilermaker on various railroads and promoting trade unionism; established residence in Jacksonville, Fla., in 1912 and became IBB general chairman for the Seaboard Air Lines; was a leader of the Jacksonville Central Labor Union during 1912–1916; appointed an IBB general organizer in 1916 and organized the crews of shipyards and war activities plants during World War I; transferred to Washington, D.C., in 1918 and was assigned to represent the IBB in all war-related activities; became president of the railroad employees department of the American Federation of Labor (AFL) in 1918, and in that capacity coordinated the activities of AFL-affiliated railroad unions for the following three decades; was one of the principal negotiators for the nonoperating railroad unions during his incumbency and proved to be a resourceful and effective bargainer; represented the Railway Labor Executives' Association at international conferences in Europe and was an AFL delegate to labor meetings in South America; retired from union affairs in 1946; in 1948 was named a labor advisor to the Economic Cooperation Administration, which administered the European Recovery Program, serving in both Washington, D.C., and Europe; died in Kansas City, Kans., in December 1968; Philip Taft, *The A.F of L. from the Death of Gompers to the Merger* (1959); *The American Federationist* (1946); *Who's Who in Labor* (1946); *Who's Who in America, 1958–1959; Labor,* December 1, 1951, December 14, 1968.

JIMERSON, Earl W. (1889–1957). Born in East St. Louis, Ill., September 2, 1889; son of Elijah W., a carpenter, and Mary Jimerson; Protestant; married Frances Laura Gutwald on July 4, 1911; graduated from grade school, then began working in a hide cellar at age 14; gained employment in the East St. Louis meat-packing industry, joining the Amalgamated Meat Cutters and Butcher Workmen of North America (AMCBWNA) in 1914; in 1914 became one of the founders of AMCBWNA Local 534, East St. Louis, Ill., serving it as secretary-treasurer and business representative, 1914–1918; served as president of the East St. Louis and St. Louis, Mo., Packing Trades Council, 1918–1920; elected vice-president of the AMCBWNA in 1920 and served in that capacity until elected international president in 1942; participated in the merger discussions between the AMCBWNA and the United Packinghouse Workers of America in 1956; represented the American Federation of Labor-Congress of Industrial Organizations (AFL-CIO) at the meetings of the International Confederation of Free Trade Unions in 1955; was a staunch advocate of the European Recovery Program, the state of Israel, and the elimination of the poll tax; was also strongly anti-Communist and a severe critic of the Taft-Hartley Act; along with Patrick E. Gorman (q.v.), the chief executive official of the AMCBWNA, built the union from the 5,000 members who survived a strike in 1921 to 350,000 members, the twelfth largest in the AFL-CIO at the time of his death; was a Democrat; edited the *East St. Louis Union News;* died in East St. Louis, Ill., October 5, 1957; David Brody, *The Butcher Workmen: A Study of Unionization* (1964);

Current Biography (1948); *Who's Who in Labor* (1946); *The New York Times*, October 6, 1957.

JOHNS, John S. (1915–   ). Born in Beaver Falls, Pa., March 4, 1915; son of George and Rose (Abraham) Johns; Syrian Orthodox; married Emma Dager on June 15, 1941; two children; his family moved to Canton, Ohio, in 1925 and there he attended high school and learned the shoe repair trade; went to work in the Republic Steel Corporation tin-plate mill in Canton in 1933; joined, in 1936, and soon became financial secretary of All Nations Local No. 1200 of the Steel Workers Organizing Committee (SWOC) at Republic; was very active in the "Little Steel" strike of 1937, and therefore not rehired; as a SWOC staff representative during 1940–1942, helped prepare for a crosscheck of Republic employees; served with the U.S. Army in the South Pacific, 1942–1945; resumed his position as a United Steelworkers of America (USWA) staff representative for District 27 (Canton) in 1946; served five successive terms as president of the Stark County Congress of Industrial Organizations' (CIO) Industrial Union Council; became the director of District 27 in 1952 after the resignation of I. W. Abel (q.v.), who became international secretary-treasurer; elected to that post a few months later and reelected for 20 years; helped negotiate the merger between the American Federation of Labor (AFL) and the CIO in Ohio, and was a vice-president of the Ohio AFL-CIO for nine years; was active in local and statewide CIO Political Action Committees and AFL-CIO Committee on Political Education campaigns; was a member of United Organized Labor of Ohio, a group that in 1958 thwarted a powerful effort to enact a right-to-work law; throughout his involvement in the labor movement, has been sensitive to the problems and needs of minorities; opposed in the 1930s and 1940s the practice of relegating immigrant steelworkers to lower-paying jobs; worked in the 1950s and 1960s to end job discrimination against black steelworkers and to open up clerical and leadership positions in the USWA to blacks; was one of several district directors dissatisfied with USWA president David J. McDonald's (q.v.) leadership and was the first director publicly to support Abel's candidacy in 1965; elected international USWA vice-president in 1973; appointed to the board of trustees of Kent State University in 1971; served on the Ohio State Democratic Executive Committee; *Who's Who in American Politics, 1971–1972;* John Herling, *Right to Challenge: People and Power in the Steelworkers Union* (1972); Oral Interview, Labor Archives, Pennsylvania State University.

Donald G. Sofchalk

JOHNSON, William David   (1881–1963). Born in Brookfield, Mo., October 18, 1881; son of Elijah and Margaret E. Johnson; Methodist; married Myrtle Maude Fisher on October 7, 1908; completed grammar school in Brookfield, then hired by the Hannibal and St. Louis Railroad in 1898; a few years later, moved to Texas and worked for the Santa Fe Railroad, joining the Brotherhood of Railroad Trainmen; promoted to conductor in 1904 and joined the Order of

Railway Conductors of America (ORC) in Temple, Tex.; moved to Silsbee, Tex., and became a charter member of ORC Division 480; served in various offices in his local division and in system committees, then was named to the ORC's Texas Legislative Board in 1918; served in that capacity for 23 years and during the last 13 was chairman of the board; elected an international vice-president in 1931 and became the ORC's national legislative representative in Washington, D.C.; during more than 30 years in Washington, became acquainted with many legislators, thus facilitating his lobbying activities; during those years, played a vital role not only in the enactment of railroad labor legislation, but also in legislation of general interest to the labor movement; at the time of his retirement in 1963, was widely acclaimed as "the dean of organized labor's legislative representatives"; was a Democrat; died in Washington, D.C., in July 1963; *Who's Who in Labor* (1946); *Labor*, August 3, 1963.

JOHNSTON, Alvanley   (1875–1951). Born in Seeley's Bay, Ontario, Canada, May 12, 1875; son of Scots immigrant parents, David, an educator, and Annie (Jarrell) Johnston; Episcopalian; married Maude Ethel Forsythe on June 6, 1917; two children; attended elementary schools of Seeley's Bay and at age 15 enrolled in Brookville Business College, Ontario, attending for two years; became a railroad employee in 1892 as a call boy for the Great Northern Railway Company in Grand Forks, N.D.; transferred to the master mechanics office in Barnesville, Minn., a year later as a clerk and stenographer; worked as a locomotive engineer on the Great Northern Railroad, 1897–1909; became general chairman of the Great Northern Railroad division of the Brotherhood of Locomotive Engineers (BLE) in 1909; elected assistant grand chief engineer of the BLE in 1918 and grand chief engineer in 1925; convicted for misappropriation of BLE funds in connection with the failure of a union bank in Cleveland, Ohio, in 1933, but was acquitted by a court of appeals; appointed labor consultant by President Franklin D. Roosevelt when the government seized the railroads in 1943; appointed to the Combined War Labor Board in 1943 as a railroad union representative; led the BLE in the 1946 nationwide railroad strike but was forced, after two days, to end the strike because of the threat of drastic punitive legislation; acquired nearly unlimited control of the BLE during his presidency; retired and became grand chief emeritus in 1950; supported the Republican party; died in Shaker Heights, Ohio, September 17, 1951; Reed C. Richardson, *The Locomotive Engineer, 1863–1963: A Century of Railway Labor Relations and the Work Rules* (1963); Arthur F. McClure, *The Truman Administration and the Problem of Postwar Labor, 1945–1948* (1969); *National Cyclopaedia of American Biography*, Vol. 40; *Current Biography* (1946).

JOHNSTON, William Hugh   (1874–1937). Born in Westville, Nova Scotia, Canada, December 30, 1874; son of Adam, a leader of the Shipwrights and Spar Makers' Union, and Jane (Murray) Johnston; Congregationalist; married Harriet J. Lunn on November 1, 1907; no children; emigrated with his family to the

United States in 1885, settling in Providence, R.I., and there completed a grammar school education; served a machinist apprenticeship at age 14 at the Rhode Island Locomotive Works and plied his trade at several New England machine shops; while an employee at the Jencks Manufacturing Company, Pawtucket, R.I., 1895–1897, helped perfect automatic knitting machines; worked from 1897 to 1901 on Armington and Sims high-speed engines and Greene and Rice and Sargent stationary engines; early in his career, joined the Knights of Labor, and in 1895, joined the International Association of Machinists (IAM) and helped organize Local Lodge 379 at the Jencks Manufacturing Company in Pawtucket; selected president of Local Lodge 147 at Rhode Island Locomotive Company, Providence, in 1901; was a delegate to the IAM national convention and elected president of District 19, New England in 1905; during 1906–1909, three times elected business agent for Local Lodge 147; in 1909 elected president and general organizer of District 44, comprising all machinists employed by the federal government; was backed by the Populist-Socialist progressive faction and defeated James O'Connell (q.v.) for the IAM presidency in 1911; reelected until July 1926, resigning then because suffering from partial paralysis; opposed O'Connell and most American Federation of Labor (AFL) leaders who favored pure-and-simple trade unionism; espoused industrial unionism, independent political action, and government intervention in the economy; served during World War I as a Wilson appointee on the National War Labor Board and accompanied AFL president Samuel Gompers's (q.v.) labor mission to France and Great Britain; after the war, along with railroad brotherhood leaders, helped organize the Plumb Plan League to promote government ownership of the railroads; helped organize the National Conference for Progressive Political Action in 1921, and in 1924, chaired the Cleveland convention that nominated Senators Robert M. La Follette and Burton K. Wheeler for president and vice president of the United States; following resignation as IAM president, served as vice-president of the Mount Vernon Savings Bank, and from 1933 to 1936, worked at the IAM's grand lodge office; died in Washington, D.C., March 26, 1937; Mark Perlman, *The Machinists: A New Study in American Trade Unionism* (1961); John H. M. Laslett, *Labor and the Left: A Study of Socialism and Radical Influences in the American Labor Movement, 1881–1924* (1970); *Dictionary of American Biography*, Suppl. 2; *Who Was Who in America*, Vol. 1; Solon DeLeon, ed., *The American Labor Who's Who* (1925).

John W. Hevener

JONES, Mary Harris ("Mother")   (1830–1930). Born in Cork, Ireland, May 1, 1830; daughter of Richard, a railway construction worker, and Helen (Harris) Jones; Roman Catholic; emigrated with her family to the United States in 1835, and later moved to Toronto, Canada; attended normal and convent schools in Toronto, then taught at a convent school in Monroe, Mich.; left teaching to enter the dress-making business in Chicago, Ill., but returned to her former profession after settling in Memphis, Tenn.; married an Iron Molders'

Union member in 1861, but after her husband and four children died in the 1867 Memphis yellow fever epidemic, returned to dressmaking in Chicago; found solace at a Knights of Labor hall when the 1871 Chicago fire destroyed her dress-making business and began attending meetings regularly; first became involved in labor strikes during the 1877 Baltimore and Ohio railroad strike in Pittsburgh, Pa.; became in the 1890s an organizer for the United Mine Workers of America (UMWA), and thereafter gained fame as an agitator for coal miners, particularly in West Virginia; helped organize the Northern (Fairmont) fields and the New River camps in West Virginia, 1902–1903; and was active in the 1903–1904 Colorado coal miners' strikes; quit the UMWA after disagreeing with President John Mitchell's (q.v.) endorsement of a Northern fields' settlement, believing it exploited the Southern miners; left Colorado and ventured farther west, working with striking Southern Pacific Railway machinists; also agitated in favor of the Western Federation of Miners' copper strikes in Arizona in 1910; rejoined the UMWA in 1911 and became active in the 1912–1913 West Virginia coal strikes; returned to Colorado when trouble again broke out in the coal fields, 1913–1914; although arrested and removed from the coal fields three times, witnessed the 1914 Ludlow Massacre and publicized it through speeches and testimony before the House Mines and Mining Committee in 1914; was involved subsequently in the New York City streetcar and garment workers' strikes, 1915–1916, and the steel strike of 1919; was a delegate to the 1921 Pan-American Federation of Labor conference in Mexico City; was active throughout her career in publicizing the evils of child labor and led a children's march from the textile mills of Kensington, Pa., to the Oyster Bay, N.Y., home of President Theodore Roosevelt in 1903; worked in textile mills in Alabama and South Carolina to observe working conditions of child laborers during 1903–1905; was rather inconsistent in her political affiliations, supporting various parties throughout her life; helped found the Social Democratic party in 1898, was an organizer of the Industrial Workers of the World in 1905, campaigned for the Democratic party in 1916, and in 1924 supported the Farmer-Labor party; authored *Autobiography of Mother Jones*, which was edited by Mary Parton in 1925; died in Silver Spring, Md., November 30, 1930; Mary Jones Papers, Catholic University of America; *Notable American Women* (1971); *Dictionary of American Biography*, Vol. 10; Elsie Gluck, *John Mitchell: Miner* (1929); George S. McGovern and Leonard F. Guttridge, *The Great Coalfield War* (1972); Ralph Chaplin, *Wobbly: The Rough-and-Tumble Story of an American Radical* (1948); Dale Fetherling, *Mother Jones, the Miner's Angel: A Portrait* (1974); Philip S. Foner, *Women and the American Labor Movement from Colonial Times to the Eve of World War I* (1979).

Marie Tedesco

JONES, Thomas P. (fl. 1826–1874). Born in Aberammon, Glenmorgan, South Wales, on March 24, 1826; married his cousin, Phoebe Jones, on December 12, 1846; one of five children in his family, he was left fatherless at age 3 and went to work turning a lathe at age 10; about six months later, he became an errand boy in a shoe store, where he remained for two years, 1836–1838; secured employment as a ''puller up'' at the Hartford Mills in Ebbwvale, Monmouthshire, in 1838 and gradually rose to the position of helper by the time he was 14 years of age; severely burned in an industrial accident which incapacitated him for some time, he was given charge of a furnace in 1844 at age 18, and retained this position for two years; migrated to Monkland, near Glasgow, Scotland, in 1846, where he obtained employment in an iron works as a knobler; during his four years of employment in Monkland, he became interested in unionism and participated in several strikes; when several fellow workers failed to keep their pledge to refrain from work for less than a stipulated wage, he moved to Glasgow where he secured employment in the Govan Bar Iron Works; was prominent in the organization of the Govan Bar Iron Works Co-Operative Association in 1857, a successful consumer cooperative; as a result of depressed economic conditions in and around Glasgow, he emigrated to the United States in 1862, arriving in New York City and gradually making his way westward until reaching Newburgh, Ohio, where he gained employment as a heater's helper; when his Newburgh employers offered him a job at their new mills in Chicago, he moved there; helped organize a heater's union at the Bridgeport, South Chicago, mills in which he was employed and was elected secretary of the new union; discharged because of his union activities, he could not find work in his trade and so went to work on a farm for two years; through the influence of Hugh McLaughlin (q.v.) he obtained work as a laborer at the North Chicago Mills in 1869, where he remained for two years working as a puddler and then a heater; helped organize Friendship Lodge No. 1 of Chicago, a local heaters' union of which he was elected president; interested in the organization of a national union, he opened a correspondence with prominent union heaters throughout the country which resulted in the call for a national convention to be held on August 31, 1872; at this meeting, the Heater's National Union was organized, and he was elected its first president; was reelected the following year; represented the Heater's National Union at the Industrial Congress held in Cleveland, Ohio, in 1873 and was appointed deputy of the Industrial Congress for the State of Illinois; *Chicago Workingman's Advocate*, February 14, 1874.

K

KASTEN, Frank   (1878–1946). Born in Dolton, Ill., January 13, 1878; son of Louis, a brickmaker, and Caroline (Gese) Kasten; Lutheran; married Margaret Morford on November 2, 1914; two children; completed public grammar school in Dolton, then at age 15 became a brickmaker; joined Local 3 of the United Brick and Clay Workers of America (UBCW) and served as president of the local, 1907–1912; elected business manager of UBCW District 1 in Chicago, Ill., in 1912, serving until 1916; elected general president of the UBCW in 1916 and served in that capacity until his death; led a long and divisive strike of brick and clay workers at Brazil, Ind., that demonstrated his leadership qualities and the determination of the UBCW workers in its jurisdiction; served as UBCW delegate to the conventions of the American Federation of Labor (AFL), 1913–1946, and during this period served on several AFL committees; served as mayor of Blue Island, Ill., 1929–1935; was a Republican; died in Chicago, Ill., December 12, 1946; *The American Federationist* (January 1947); Solon DeLeon, ed., *The American Labor Who's Who* (1925); *Who's Who in Labor* (1946).

KAUFMAN, Morris (David Horodok)   (1884–1960). Born in Minsk, Russia, in September 1884; son of a cattle and poultry slaughterer; Jewish; married; two children; self-educated; began work at age 14 as a grocery clerk; worked as a bank clerk, 1900–1902; emigrated to the United States in 1902 and for a year worked as a cigarmaker; became a fur worker in 1904 and joined the New York Fur Workers' Union; became a member of the executive board of the Fur Workers' Union in 1905 and two years later elected secretary; served as secretary of the New York branch of The Bund, 1906–1907; joined the International Fur Workers Union of the United States and Canada (IFWU) when it was organized in 1913; served as business agent of the New York Joint Board of Fur Workers, 1916–1917, and manager, 1917–1921; elected a vice-president of the IFWU in 1917 and president the following year; defeated for the IFWU presidency by a left-wing coalition in 1925, but reelected in 1929, serving until 1932; continued working in the fur industry after the IFWU was taken over by a left-wing faction led by Ben Gold (q.v.); indicted and convicted in 1935 of conspiring with employers to raise wages, fix prices, and eliminate competition, receiving a suspended three-year sentence; became a manager of the Muskrat Division of the Fur Dressers Factor Corporation; retired from the fur business in 1953; supported the Socialist party during the early years of his trade union activity; died in New York City, July 7, 1960; Morris Kaufman Papers, Catherwood Library, Cornell University; Philip S. Foner, *The Fur and Leather Workers Union: A Story of Dramatic Struggles and Achievement* (1950); Solon DeLeon, ed., *The American Labor Who's Who* (1925); *The New York Times*, July 8, 1960.

KAVANAGH, William Francis   (1878–1963). Born in Jersey City, N.J., September 2, 1878; son of James, an operating engineer, and Mary (Ryan) Kavanagh; Roman Catholic; married Alice Josephine Woods on April 22, 1913, after the death of his first wife, Elizabeth McAuley, in 1911; eight children; attended parochial schools for four years, then was orphaned and during the next several years worked on an aunt's farm and in the textile industry; entered vaudeville in 1898 as a member of the Sheehan and Kavanagh song-and-dance team and later was a member of the Mobile Four quartet; became interested, after meeting Samuel Gompers (q.v.), in the labor movement and devoted much of the remainder of his life to that cause; organized Local 575 of the Hotel and Restaurant Employees' International Alliance and Bartenders' International League of America (HREIABIL) in 1903 and served as its president and business agent until 1945; served as an international representative and organizer for the HREI-ABIL, 1903–1945; served as president of the New Jersey Federation of Trades and Labor Unions prior to the organization of the New Jersey State Federation of Labor (NJSFL); was secretary of the NJSFL, 1927–1936; served as secretary-treasurer of the Union Label League of Jersey City, 1924–1945; elected president of the Central Labor Union of Hudson County, N.J., on two different occasions and served as its secretary-treasurer for more than 30 years prior to retiring from union affairs in 1945; served as a delegate to both the Federated Trades of New York and the Essex Trades Council of Essex County, N.J.; served as a civil defense worker during World War II; was for several years a delegate to the annual meetings of the Labor Institute at Rutgers University, which he had helped organize; was a member of the Nonpartisan League of New Jersey during the 1930s, but often supported Democratic candidates; died in Jersey City, N.J., October 11, 1963; *National Cyclopaedia of American Biography*, Vol. 49; *The New York Times*, October 13, 1963.

KAZAN, Abraham Eli   (1888–1971). Born in Kiev, Russia, December 15, 1888; the son of a Jewish businessman; married; three children; attended elementary and secondary schools in Russia; emigrated to the United States in 1903; later took courses at New York University and Brooklyn Polytechnic Institute; secured employment in the garment industry and joined cloak pressers' Local

35 of the International Ladies' Garment Workers' Union; served as bookkeeper and financial secretary of Local 35, 1912–1914, and secretary-treasurer, 1914–1919; joined the Amalgamated Clothing Workers of America (ACWA) in 1919 and became the director of its record department, serving until 1922; was secretary-treasurer of the New York Joint Board, ACWA, 1922–1923; appointed manager of the employment bureau of the New York Joint Board, ACWA, in 1924; became the president of the ACWA's Amalgamated Housing Corporation, a cooperative housing project, in 1927, and devoted much of the remainder of his life to the promotion of cooperative housing projects; served as president of the United Housing Foundation and of Community Services, both of which supplied information and technical services to cooperative housing projects and cooperative homeowners; was a director of the Cooperative League of the United States of America, 1931–1938, and elected to the same position again in 1958; died in New York City, December 21, 1971; Louis Levine, *The Women's Garment Workers: A History of the International Ladies' Garment Workers' Union* (1924); Erma Angevine, *In League with the Future* (1959); Solon DeLeon, ed., *The American Labor Who's Who* (1925).

KEARNEY, Denis   (1847–1907). Born in Oakmount, County Cork, Ireland; on February 1, 1847; Roman Catholic; married Mary Ann Leary in 1872; four children; the second son of seven children in his family, he went to sea at age 11; after 12 years at sea, during which he attained the rank of first officer on a coastal steamer, he settled in San Francisco, Calif., in 1870; ended his maritime days in 1872 when he bought a draying business; became a naturalized citizen of the United States in 1876; was associated with the Dreymen and Teamsters' Union and soon became a noted agitator and a volatile speaker; after being arrested for his agitation against big business magnates, local politicians, and Chinese immigrants, he was consistently acquitted by juries; organized the Workingmen's party of San Francisco in 1877 and became its president and the editor of its organ, the *Open Letter*; under his direction the Workingmen's party agitated against unemployment, monopoly land holdings, dishonest banking and railroad practices, and especially against Chinese labor competition; partially as a result of the anti-Chinese agitation in California, the federal Chinese exclusion act was passed in 1882; after the disintegration of the Workingmen's party, he supported General James B. Weaver on the Greenback ticket in 1880 and thereafter largely disappeared from public view; died in Alameda, Calif., on April 24, 1907; *Dictionary of American Biography*, Vol. 10; Philip Taft, *Labor Politics American Style: The California State Federation of Labor* (1968); Ira B. Cross, *A History of the Labor Movement in California* (1935).

KEATING, Edward   (1875–1965). Born in Kansas City, Kans., July 9, 1875; son of Stephen, a farmer, and Julia (O'Connor) Keating; Roman Catholic; married Margaret Sloan Medill on September 1, 1907, and, after her death in 1939, Eleanor Mary Connolly on May 3, 1941; after the death of his father, his family moved to Pueblo, Colo., in 1880 and Denver, Colo., in 1889; attended grammar school in the public schools of Colorado; worked as a "news butcher" on passenger trains running from Denver to the Aspen, Colo., mining camps, then became a copyholder of the *Denver Republican* in 1899; served as the Denver, Colo., city auditor, 1899–1901; was city editor of the *Denver Times*, 1902–1905, and editor of the *Rocky Mountain News*, 1906–1911; elected president of the International League of Press Clubs in 1906 and 1907; was president of the Colorado State Board of Land Commissioners, 1911–1913; purchased and became the editor of the *Pueblo Leader* in 1912; elected as a Democrat to the U.S. Congress in 1912 and served until defeated for reelection in 1918; while in Congress, was especially active in sponsoring child labor bills, minimum-wage laws for women and children in the District of Columbia, and in campaigning for the Adamson Act, which established the eight-hour day on railroads; voted against American entry into World War I; became the editor and manager of *Labor*, a newly established official weekly newspaper of the Associated Railroad Labor Organizations, in 1919; joined the International Typographical Union in 1919; retired as editor of *Labor* in 1953 and was named editor-manager emeritus; authored *The Story of Labor: The Gentleman from Colorado* (1965); was an independent Democrat; died in Washington, D.C., March 18, 1965; Philip Taft, *The A.F. of L. from the Death of Gompers to the Merger* (1959); *Biographical Directory of the American Congress, 1774–1971* (1971); *AFL-CIO News*, March 27, 1965; *Labor,* March 27, 1965; *American Federation of Labor News-Reporter*, April 10, 1953.

KEEFE, Daniel Joseph   (1852–1929). Born in Willowsprings, Ill., September 27, 1852; son of John, a teamster, and Catherine Keefe; Roman Catholic; married Ellen E. Conners in 1878 and, after her death, Emma L. Walker in 1904; left school at age 12 and worked as a teamster for his father; began working as a lumber handler and longshoreman in 1870; in 1882, was elected president of the Lumber Unloaders' Association, an organization of longshoremen that contracted with various shipping companies to load and unload vessels; was one of the founders in 1892 of the Lumber Handlers of the Great Lakes, whose jurisdiction was extended to all longshore work in 1893; after the name of the union had been changed to the International Longshoremen's Association (ILA), was elected its president in 1893, serving until 1908; assumed near dictatorial control of the ILA during his incumbency; served as a member of the Illinois State Board of Arbitration, 1897–1901; was a staunch supporter and active participant in the National Civic Federation organized in 1900; essentially a conservative trade unionist, but advocated the industrial method of organization for waterfront workers; served as an American Federation of Labor vice-president and executive council member, 1903–1908; campaigned for William Howard Taft in 1908 and was appointed Commissioner General of Immigration by President Theodore Roosevelt shortly before he left office, serving until 1913; served as a conciliation commissioner for the U.S. Department of Labor during World

War I; employed by the United States Shipping Board Merchant Fleet Corporation as a labor disputes mediator, 1921–1925; was a Republican; retired in 1925 and died in Elmhurst, Ill., January 2, 1929; Maud Russell, *Men along the Shore* (1966); Charles P. Larrowe, *Maritime Labor Relations on the Great Lakes* (1959); *Dictionary of American Biography*, Vol. 10.

KEENAN, Joseph Daniel   (1896–   ). Born in Chicago, Ill., November 5, 1896; son of Edward John, a teamster, and Minnie (Curtin) Kennan; Roman Catholic; married Myrtle Fietsch in 1920; two children; began working in 1914, at age 18, as an apprentice electrician; joined Local 134, International Brotherhood of Electrical Workers of America (IBEW) and completed his apprenticeship under its auspices in 1918; elected an IBEW Local 134 inspector in 1923 and three years later was elected recording secretary; elected secretary of the Chicago Federation of Labor, and, with the exception of government service during World War II, served in that capacity until 1948; during World War II, served as an American Federation of Labor (AFL) representative on both the National Defense Council and the Office of Production Management and was associate director of the War Production Board; appointed chief of the manpower division of the allied Control Commission for Germany in 1945; was named the first director of Labor's League for Political Education after its creation by the AFL in 1948; during the campaign and election of 1948, joined with Jack Kroll of the Congress of Industrial Organizations' (CIO) Political Action Committee to coordinate informally the political campaigns of the AFL and the CIO in behalf of Harry S. Truman's reelection effort; elected secretary-treasurer of the AFL building and construction trades department in 1951, serving until 1954; became the international secretary of the IBEW in 1954; elected an AFL vice-president and executive council member in 1955 and continued in that capacity after the AFL-CIO merger; was appointed a member of the Democratic National Committee's advisory committee on economic policy in 1957; has served on numerous public and private boards and agencies, including position as assistant to director of the Office of Civil Defense Mobilization; considered one of the AFL-CIO's premier labor politicians and developed considerable influence in the Democratic party in Chicago and in Washington, D.C.; retired union positions in 1976; Joseph C. Goulden, *Meany* (1972); Philip Taft, *The A.F. of L. from the Death of Gompers to the Merger* (1959); *Who's Who in Labor* (1946); *AFL-CIO News*, February 28, 1976.

KEENEY, C. Frank   (fl. 1912–1973). Born in Kanawha County, W.Va.; little is known about his childhood and early adult years; along with Mother Jones (q.v.) organized in 1912 the coal miners of Cabin Creek, W.Va., an area regular United Mine Workers of America (UMWA) organizers feared to enter; along with Fred Mooney (q.v.) and Lawrence Dwyer, a UMWA international organizer, established three years later an insurgent district, District 30, in the Cabin Creek area to protest alleged corruption and inefficiency on the part of

President Thomas Cairns (q.v.) and other officials of District 17, UMWA, West Virginia; after District 17 was reorganized by the international union in 1917, elected its president and served until 1924; within a year of becoming president, helped District 17 add ten thousand members, pay off a $35,000 debt, and show a treasury surplus of $25,000; in 1919, along with the governor of West Virginia, prevented a threatened union miners' march into nonunion territory that promised to result in violence; again in 1921, along with state and federal officials, prevented a second march; an attack by state policemen and Logan County deputies on a union tent colony at Sharples, W.Va., in 1922, however, ignited a march resulting in the "Battle of Blair Mountain," in which 3 deputies were killed and 40 miners wounded; indicted as a result of the conflict, but acquitted of treason and murder; while under indictment, elected president of the West Virginia State Federation of Labor (WVSFL); defeated for reelection by John Easton (q.v.) in a craft union movement to curb the power of the UMWA in the WVSFL; after his defeat, his UMWA supporters in southern West Virginia boycotted the WVSFL until 1927; along with Mooney, resigned his UMWA offices in 1924 to protest UMWA president John L. Lewis's (q.v.) attempt to enforce the Jacksonville scale in West Virginia, a policy they charged would destroy the union there; thereafter, the district was administered by provisional presidents Percy Tetlow (q.v.) and, later, Van A. Bittner (q.v.); moved to Illinois in 1926 to edit *The Coal Miner*, an official organ of John Brophy's (q.v.) "Save the Union" campaign; during 1927–1930, was first the proprietor of an orange drink stand and then an oil and gas speculator; in 1930, joined John H. Walker (q.v.), Frank Farrington (q.v.), Alexander Howat (q.v.), and Oscar Ameringer (q.v.) in the Reorganized United Mine Workers; after Walker reaffiliated with the regular UMWA and other leaders were expelled in 1931, founded his own West Virginia Miners' Union, which grew rapidly but destroyed itself with a strike during depressed conditions; became an American Federation of Labor organizer for the Progressive Mine Workers of America in 1938 and organized three West Virginia locals, all of which were destroyed by the UMWA's 1939 union shop agreement; thereafter, his career deteriorated, and his last known job was as a parking-lot attendant, according to relatives, still living in 1973; Evelyn L. K. Harris and Frank J. Krebs, *From Humble Beginnings: West Virginia State Federation of Labor, 1903–1957* (1960); J. W. Hess, ed., *Struggle in the Coal Fields: The Autobiography of Fred Mooney* (1967); Irving Bernstein, *The Lean Years: A History of the American Workers, 1920–1933* (1960); David A. Corbin, "Frank Keeney Is Our Leader, and We Shall Not Be Moved," in Gary M. Fink and Merl E. Reed, *Essays in Southern Labor History* (1977).

John W. Hevener

KEHEW, Mary Morton Kimball   (1859–1918). Born in Boston, Mass., September 8, 1859; daughter of Moses Day, a merchant and banker, and Susan (Tillinghast) Kimball; Unitarian; married William Brown Kehew, an oil merchant, on January 8, 1880; no children; received a private school education, including two years of study in Europe; in 1886, joined the Women's Educational and Industrial Union of Boston (WEIUB), an organization founded in 1877 to assist rural New England working girls adjust to urban life and to provide them with employment guidance; became a director of the organization in 1890 and two years later was elected WEIUB president, serving in that capacity until 1913; became acting president and chairman of the board of governors a year later, positions she retained until her death in 1918; during her years of WEIUB leadership, she gradually altered the original function of the organization, increasingly emphasizing vocational training and social reform; under her leadership, the WEIUB took an active role in the settlement house movement and spearheaded progressive reform in the Boston area; along with Mary Kenney, an American Federation of Labor (AFL) organizer, she used the facilities of the WEIUB to help found the Union for Industrial Progress in 1892, which worked to promote trade unionism among women workers; in subsequent years, unions of women bookbinders, laundry workers, and tobacco workers were organized in Boston; after the organization of the National Women's Trade Union League in 1903, she was elected the first president of the AFL-associated organization; spent many years lobbying for social reforms and monitoring the enforcement of those measures once legislated; was also active in promoting the collection of statistical and other empirical evidence related to the hours, wages, and working conditions of women workers in Boston; an ability to work effectively with politicians, reformers, labor leaders, and the social elite in Boston made her one of the most effective social reformers of the Progressive era; died in Boston on February 13, 1918; *Notable American Women*, Vol. 2; Gladys Boone, *The Women's Trade Union Leagues in Great Britain and the United States of America* (1942); *Boston Transcript*, February 13, 1918.

KEHRER, Elmer Thomas   (1921–   ). Born in Brighton, Mich., January 11, 1921; son of Charles, an autoworker, and Gertrude (Miller) Kehrer; Presbyterian; married Betty Hynson on October 4, 1952; received the B.A. degree from Olivet College and the M.A. from Yale University; joined the United Automobile, Aircraft, and Agricultural Implement Workers of America in 1937 and later affiliated with the American Newspaper Guild; became a field representative for the American Federation of Labor (AFL) Workers' Education Bureau in 1948; served as the assistant director of the International Ladies' Garment Workers' Union officer-training institute, 1950–1953, and as southern director, 1954–1964; was appointed southern director of the AFL-Congress of Industrial Organizations' civil rights department in 1965; in that capacity, directed programs to bring minority workers into the building trades of the South, including the recruiting and training of black construction workers in major southern cities in cooperation with local building trades unions and the U.S. Department of Labor; as chairman of the Georgia Democratic Party Forum, 1971–1972, successfully challenged the delegate selection process in Georgia for national conventions and promoted reforms of the state party structure; participated actively in the founding of the Southern Labor Archives at Georgia State University, Atlanta, Ga., particularly in encouraging organized labor's support of the project; is a member of several social and reform organizations, including Workmen's Circle, the Urban League, the National Association for the Advancement of Colored People, the A. Philip Randolph Institute, and the American Civil Liberties Union; is a board member of the Southern Regional Council, the Workers' Defense League, and the Georgia Council on Economic Education.

Merl E. Reed

KEIL, Edward A.   (fl. 1881–1886). Born in the United States, elected district deputy of the Amalgamated Association of Iron and Steel Workers (AA) in 1881 and 1885; was elected corresponding representative of the AA's Nonpareil Lodge, Pittsburgh, Pa., in 1881 and 1886–1887, president in 1882, and financial secretary, 1883, 1886; was one of the AA's national trustees, 1889–1891, and treasurer, 1891–1892; was a close friend of AA leader William Martin (q.v.); bass soloist and prominent lay leader of a neighborhood Presbyterian church; was a Republican; elected eleventh ward judge of elections in 1883; represented his ward on the Republican city executive committee in 1886; was elected president of the R. L. Martin Council of the Sovereigns of Industry in 1883; Amalgamated Association of Iron and Steel Workers, *Proceedings*, 1880–1892; John William Bennett, "Iron Workers in Woods Run and Johnstown: The Union Era, 1865–1895" (Ph.D. diss., 1977).

Sharon Trusilo

KELLEY, Florence   (1859–1932). Born in Philadelphia, Pa., on September 12, 1859; daughter of William D., a lawyer, judge, and congressman, and Caroline (Bartram) Kelley; Quaker; married Lazare Wischnewetzky, a doctor, on June 1, 1884; three children; although she attended Miss Longstreth's School for Girls and the Friends' Central School in Philadelphia for brief periods, much of her early education was acquired at home because of illness; entered Cornell University in 1876, earning her bachelor's degree in 1882; her senior thesis, "On Some Changes in the Legal Status of the Child since Blackstone" was published by the *International Review* in 1882; refused admission to the University of Pennsylvania graduate school because of her sex, she started evening classes for working girls at the Women's New Century Club in Philadelphia; while touring Europe in 1883, she learned that the University of Zurich accepted female students, and she enrolled there; while studying in Zurich, she associated with radical students and soon became a committed Socialist; returned to the United States in 1886 and immediately joined the Socialist Labor party (SLP); began an English translation of Friedrich Engels's *The Condition of the Working Class in England* in 1884 which was published in New York in 1887; while carrying on a correspondence with Engels that lasted several years, she also translated a Karl Marx address on free trade in 1888; was expelled from the SLP in 1887 for theoretical reasons; separated from her husband in 1891 and moved to Chicago, Ill.; resident of Hull House; began a long relationship with Jane Addams (q.v.), Julia Lathrop, and other settlement house reformers; was employed in 1892 by the Illinois Bureau of Labor Statistics to investigate sweatshop conditions in the garment industry and later in the same year was appointed by the federal labor commissioner to participate in a survey of city slums; appointed chief factory inspector of Illinois by Governor Peter Altgeld after she successfully lobbied for a factory act in the state legislature, limiting the working hours of women, prohibiting child labor, and regulating tenement sweatshops; took night classes at the Northwestern University Law School and was admitted to the bar after completing her degree in 1894; was not reappointed chief factory inspector after Altgeld left office and was replaced by a Republican; returned to her work and activities at Hull House; became general secretary of the National Consumers' League in 1899, a job she held for the remainder of her life; moved to New York City and took up residence at the Henry Street Settlement House in 1899, where she continued to devote much of her time and energy to protective labor legislation for women and children; along with Josephine Goldmark, she provided much of the documentation for the "Brandeis Brief" issued by Louis D. Brandeis in 1908; helped organize the New York Child Labor Committee in 1902 and the National Child Labor Committee in 1904; was also involved in the organization of the National Association for the Advancement of Colored People in 1909 and the Women's Industrial League for Peace and Freedom ten years later; served as a vice-president of the National Woman Suffrage Association for several years; a Socialist in politics, she joined the Intercollegiate Socialist Society in 1911 and served as its president, 1918–1920; among her many publications were "Our Toiling Children" (1889), and *Some Ethical Gains through Legislation* (1905); died in New York City, February 17, 1932; Kelley Family Papers, Columbia University; *Notable American Women*, Vol. 2; Josephine Goldmark, *Impatient Crusader: Florence Kelley's Life Story* (1953); Dorothy Rose Blumber, *Florence Kelley: The Making of a Social Pioneer* (1966).

KELSAY, Ray   (1888–1948). Born in Marion, Ind., July 8, 1888; son of Smith and Minerva (Morgan) Kelsay; Community church; married Martha Weaver on January 1, 1910; three children; finished elementary school, then went to work; in 1906 joined the Metal Polishers, Buffers, Platers, and Helpers International Union (MPBPHIU); shortly thereafter elected president of his local union; later elected president of the MPBPHIU's Indiana District Council; well regarded by union's members, was elected international vice-president in 1931 and international president and secretary-treasurer in 1945; the MPBPHIU was a small union, and Kelsay worked assiduously to sustain and expand it; during his presidency membership increased substantially; also played an active role in the American Federation of Labor metal trades department and became its second vice-president; after World War II, initiated a program whereby the MPBPHIU provided occupational rehabilitation services to injured veterans, a program that was cited as outstanding by the U.S. government; killed in an automobile accident in Indianapolis, Ind., September 25, 1948; *Who's Who in Labor* (1946); *The American Federationist* (October 1948).

Donald G. Sofchalk

KENIN, Herman David   (1901–1970). Born in Vineland, N.J., October 26, 1901; son of Samuel Benjamin, a member of the Cigarmakers' Union, and Anna (Gordin) Kenin; Jewish; married Maxine Bennett on July 31, 1936; two children; attended Reed College, 1920–1921, and Northwestern College of Law in Portland, Oreg., 1924–1926, 1930–1931; admitted to the Oregon bar in 1931; became a professional musician while attending college and joined Local 99 of the American Federation of Musicians (AFM) in 1920; during the 1920s and 1930s, headed a band that played hotel and night club dates on the West Coast; elected president of AFM Local 99 in 1936; appointed to a vacancy on the AFM's international executive board in 1943 and subsequently elected to the position; served as an American labor delegate to the advisory committee of the salaried and professional workers division of the International Labor Organization meeting in Geneva in 1949; elected international president of the AFM in 1958 after the resignation of James C. Petrillo (q.v.); was instrumental during his presidency in establishing a pension fund for musicians, gaining Congressional repeal of a 20 percent cabaret tax, and democratizing the structure of the AFM; elected an American Federation of Labor-Congress of Industrial Organizations' vice-president and executive council member in 1963; was one of the leaders in the movement to establish the National Endowment for the Arts and Humanities, served on the advisory committee of the National Cultural Center, and was a member of the National Council of the Arts; died in New York City, July 21, 1970; *Who's Who in America,* 1970–1971; *The New York Times,* July 22, 1970; *AFL-CIO News,* February 23, 1963.

KENNEDY, Thomas   (1887–1963). Born in Lansford, Pa., November 2, 1887; son of Peter, a coal miner killed in a mine accident, and Mary (Boyle) Kennedy; Roman Catholic; married Helen Melley on July 23, 1912, and, after her death in 1953, Evelyn Summers on November 12, 1959; two children; attended Lansford public schools for six years; started work in the mines at age 12 as a breaker boy, then became a mule driver and later a miner; joined the United Mine Workers of America (UMWA) in 1900; elected secretary of UMWA Lansford Local 1738 in 1903, serving until 1910; was a delegate to the UMWA international convention in 1906; served as member of the executive board of UMWA District 7, 1908–1910, and as district president, 1910–1925; served during these 15 years on the Anthracite Board of Conciliation and as the union's chief negotiator for anthracite contracts; served as UMWA international secretary-treasurer, 1925–1947, and as international vice-president, 1947–1960; succeeded John L. Lewis (q.v.) as international president of the UMWA in 1960, but was old and ill by that time; W. A. Boyle (q.v.), chosen acting president in November 1962, ran the union during Kennedy's three-year incumbency; was essentially an able, loyal, and personable union bureaucrat; dominated anthracite negotiations for 50 years and participated in all bituminous negotiations after 1925; served on the advisory committee to the National Recovery Administration, 1933; helped lead the UMWA's fight to force the American Federation of Labor to abandon voluntarism and endorse social security and government responsibility for unemployment; was appointed to the National Defense Mediation Board in 1941, but resigned in protest to the board's captive mines decision; appointed to the National War Labor Board in 1942, but again resigned, this time to protest its application of the "Little Steel Formula"; was a member of the advisory committee of the bituminous coal division and the Solid Fuels Administration for War during World War II; served as chairman of the board of trustees of the Anthracite Health and Welfare Fund, 1945–1963; was active in Pennsylvania Democratic politics and was elected lieutenant governor of Pennsylvania in 1934; was candidate for the Democratic gubernatorial nomination in 1938, but was defeated by the state Democratic machine; was a delegate-at-large to the Democratic National Conventions in 1936 and 1940, serving on the Resolutions Committee; served on a great variety of public and private boards and agencies, including the Pennsylvania State Welfare Commission, the Pennsylvania Emergency Relief Board, and American Coal Shipping, Inc.; died at Hazelton, Pa., January 19, 1963; *United Mine Workers Journal*, February 1, 1963; *National Cyclopaedia of American Biography*, Vol. 52; *Current Biography* (1964); *Who's Who in Labor* (1946); Joseph E. Finley, *The Corrupt Kingdom: The Rise and Fall of the United Mine Workers* (1972); Melvyn Dubofsky and Warren Van Tine, *John L. Lewis: A. Biography* (1977).

John W. Hevener

KENNEDY, William Parker (1892–1968). Born in Huttonville, Ontario, Canada, April 3, 1892; son of William James, a wool weaver, and Margaret (Parker) Kennedy; Lutheran; married Amy Hannah Berglund on January 21, 1913; four children; emigrated with parents to Chicago, Ill., in 1902 and completed elementary school there; desirous of a career in railroading, obtained a job as a "news butcher" selling papers and magazines on the Rock Island line in 1907; became a freight brakeman for the Dakota division of the Great Northern Railway in 1909; joined Wheat Sheaf Lodge 463 of the Brotherhood of Railroad Trainmen (BRT) in Grand Forks, N.D., in 1910; became a switchman in 1911 and eventually joined the Chicago, Milwaukee, and St. Paul Railroad; transferred membership to Minnehaha Lodge 625, Minneapolis, Minn., in 1913 and served as president and local chairman; elected secretary of the BRT's general grievance committee for the Chicago, Milwaukee, St. Paul, and Pacific Railroad in 1920 and a year later was elected general chairman, serving in that capacity until 1935; elected to the BRT board of trustees in 1928 and served as secretary until 1935; elected a vice-president in charge of the BRT's northwestern territory in 1935; was placed in charge of the BRT's super-promotion department, 1944–1946; elected general secretary-treasurer in 1946 and, upon the death of Alexander F. Whitney (q.v.) in 1949, became the general president of the BRT; served as national reporting officer for the Railroad Retirement Board and secretary of the board of trustees of the Home for Aged and Disabled Railroad Employes of America, 1946–1949; retired from union affairs in 1962; was a member of the Minnesota Democratic Farmer-Labor party; died in Minneapolis, Minn., May 14, 1968; Joel Seidman, *The Brotherhood of Railroad Trainmen: The Internal Political Life of a National Union* (1962); *Current Biography* (1950); *Who's Who in Railroading* (1959); *Labor*, January 5, 1963, May 25, 1968.

KIRKLAND, Joseph Lane   (1922–   ). Born in Camden, S.C., March 12, 1922; son of Randolph Withers and Louise (Richardson) Kirkland; married Edith Draper Hollyday on June 10, 1944; five children; attended Newberry College in South Carolina in 1940, then graduated from the U.S. Merchant Marine Academy in 1942; received a B.S. degree from Georgetown University's School of Foreign Service in 1948; joined the National Organization of Masters, Mates and Pilots of America while serving as a U.S. Merchant Marine pilot, 1941–1946; was a nautical scientist in the U.S. Navy Department of Hydrographic Office, 1947–1948; joined the research staff of the American Federation of Labor (AFL) in 1948 and served in that capacity until becoming assistant director of the AFL social security department in 1953; retained latter position after the AFL-Congress of Industrial Organizations' (CIO) merger in 1955; served as director of research and education for the International Union of Operating Engineers, 1958–1960; became executive assistant to President George Meany (q.v.) of the AFL-CIO in 1961; elected secretary-treasurer of the AFL-CIO after the resignation of William F. Schnitzler (q.v.) in 1969; served as president of the Institute of Collective Bargaining and Group Relations, as a director of the American Foundation on Automation and Employment, as a board member of Community Health, Inc., and as a member of the advisory board of the U.S. Merchant Marine Academy; was elected president of the AFL-CIO after the retirement of George Meany in 1979; has served on a variety of public and private boards and agencies; usually supported the Democratic party; Joseph C. Goulden, *Meany* (1972); *Who's Who in America, 1972–1973*; *AFL-CIO News,* May 17, 1969; *Newsweek*, September 6, 1971; *Current Biography* (1980).

KIRWAN, James   (fl. 1903–1913). Born in Terry, S.D.; was a member of the Lead City Miners' Union; played a major part in founding the Western Federation of Miners (WFM); was appointed to replace resigning representative of District 5 (South Dakota) on the WFM executive board in 1903 and was elected to the office the following year; amicable and well respected within the WFM, thus reelected several times; served as acting secretary of WFM in 1906–1908, while then Secretary-Treasurer William Haywood (q.v.) was in jail on charge of the murder of former Idaho governor Frank Steunenberg; was a WFM delegate to the disruptive 1906 convention of the Industrial Workers of the World (IWW), which split over the ouster of President Charles Sherman (q.v.); sided with the WFM moderates in opposition to revolutionary syndicalist faction of the IWW led by William Trautmann (q.v.) and Daniel DeLeon (q.v.); in show-down at 1907 WFM convention, Kirwan and Vice-President Charles Mahoney (q.v.) led the moderates against the radical supporters of the Trautmann IWW; voiced bitter objections to IWW as a detriment to the WFM and supported complete severance from the IWW; despite compromise, the WFM in reality abandoned revolutionary unionism to move toward more conventional unionism; Kirwan was a pragmatist, eschewing both revolutionary action and ideological disputation; continued to exert important influence to keep WFM on the "narrower track" of effective industrial unionism; was a member of WFM executive board until 1910, but remained active in the labor movement for several years afterwards; during the 1913 coal miners' strike against the Colorado Fuel and Iron Company, was elected to a commission established by the Colorado State Federation of Labor, at the suggestion of the governor of Colorado, to investigate state militia's role in the strike zones; *Final Report of the U.S. Commission on Industrial Relations* (1915); Vernon H. Jensen, *Heritage of Conflict: Labor Relations in the Nonferrous Metals Industry up to 1930* (1950); Melvyn Dubofsky, *We Shall Be All: A History of the Industrial Workers of the World* (1969).

Donald G. Sofchalk

KISTLER, Alan Anthony (1920–   ). Born in Pittsburgh, Pa., on October 1, 1920; son of Alan A., a dentist, and Margaret Cecilia (Ward) Kistler, a homemaker; Roman Catholic; married Marie Frances Connolly, a homemaker, in 1948; three children; graduated from Schenley High School, Pittsburgh, in 1938; attended the University of Pittsburgh, 1946–1947, and the University of Chicago, 1947–1951, graduating with the M.S. degree; joined the Hotel and Restaurant Employees' and Bartenders' International Union local in Pittsburgh and was a volunteer organizer in Philadelphia and Pittsburgh, 1941–1942, 1946; was a master sergeant in the U.S. Army during World War II, 1942–1946; after securing a job as a newspaperman, he joined the American Newspaper Guild and became unit chairman of the Pittsburgh branch of the guild; was elected recording secretary and chief steward of Pittsburgh Local Industrial Union 1657, Congress of Industrial Organizations (CIO), 1949–1951; became a member of Local 1147, United Steelworkers of America, CIO, in 1952; went to Washington as an organizer and assistant to CIO executive vice-president Allan Haywood (q.v.) in 1952; was assigned to the American Federation of Labor (AFL)-CIO department of organization after the 1955 merger; in this position, he served as coordinator of the General Electric cooperative organizing program and coordinated organizing campaigns conducted by the brewery workers and the school administrators; was appointed assistant director of the AFL-CIO department of organization in 1962; after the department was reorganized and renamed the department of organizing and field services in 1973, he was named director in 1974 with responsibility of coordinating all AFL-CIO activities at the regional level; elected president of the Human Resources Development Institute in 1975;

active in community affairs, he served as chairman of the Neighborhood Planning Council, Washington, D.C., 1970–1971; was a member of the Greenbelt, Md., city council, 1955–1959, and served as mayor of Greenbelt, 1959–1961; *Who's Who in Labor* (1976); *AFL-CIO News*, March 2, 1974.

KNIGHT, Felix Harrison   (1876–1952). Born in Montgomery County, Mo., December 10, 1876; son of John Robert, a teacher, and Mollie (Moore) Knight; Baptist; married Rose M. Michel on June 24, 1903; after high school graduation, secured employment with the St. Louis Street Railway and joined the Amalgamated Association of Street, Electric Railway and Motor Coach Employees of America; later became a railroad carman and joined St. Louis, Mo., Local 34 of the Brotherhood of Railway Carmen of America (BRCA) in 1902; later the same year was elected financial secretary and chairman of the local protective board; was elected a delegate to the St. Louis Central Trades and Labor Union in 1903; became secretary-treasurer of the Chicago, Burlington, and Quincy Railroad joint protective board in 1903; was appointed assistant general president of the BRCA in 1913, serving until 1934; served as member of the National Railroad Adjustment Board, 1918–1920, and again in 1934; was appointed general president of the BRCA in 1935 after the death of Martin F. Ryan (q.v.) and was elected to the position the following year; became a member of the executive council of the American Federation of Labor (AFL) railway employees department in 1935; elected an AFL vice-president and executive council member in 1936, and during that year served on an AFL executive council committee appointed to mediate dispute with the members of the Committee on Industrial Organizations; served as an AFL fraternal delegate to the British Trades Union Congress in 1939; was appointed an AFL alternate on the Combined War Labor Board in 1942; was chairman of an AFL committee investigating labor conditions in Argentina under Juan Peron's regime in 1946; retired his union positions in 1947; died in Kansas City, Mo., October 13, 1952; Leonard Painter, *Through 50 Years with the Brotherhood of Railway Carmen of America* (1941); Philip Taft, *The A.F. of L. from the Death of Gompers to the Merger* (1959); *The American Federationist* (October 1941); *Who's Who in Labor* (1946); *Labor*, October 18, 1952.

KNIGHT, Orie Albert   (1902–1981). Born in New Hampton, Iowa, September 24, 1902; son of William Leonard, a livestock dealer, and Clara Mae (Ransome) Knight; Baptist; married Evelyn Luella Dokken on January 30, 1925; after high school graduation, began working in a Shell Oil Company refinery in 1926; helped organize Hammond, Ind., Local 210 of the International Association of Oil Field, Gas Well, and Refinery Workers in 1933; elected a member of the Congress of Industrial Organizations' (CIO) international executive council in 1936; served as a CIO staff organizer, 1937–1940; elected president of the Oil Workers International Union (OWIU), a CIO affiliate, in 1940; served as a labor member of the National War Labor Board during World War II; elected a CIO vice-president in 1947 and during the same year was a member of the Committee for the Marshall Plan to Aid European Recovery; became a member of the CIO's committee on Latin American affairs and often served as the CIO's fraternal delegate to the Confederation of Latin American Workers; chaired CIO committee investigating Communist influence in CIO-affiliated unions in 1950; result was the expulsion of two unions, including Harry Bridges's (q.v.) International Longshoremen's and Warehousemen's Union; appointed deputy administrator of the National Production Authority that supervised the mobilization effort during the Korean War; led the first national strike in the United States oil industry in 1952; helped negotiate a merger between the OWIU and the United Gas, Coke and Chemical Workers International Union in 1955 and became president of the renamed Oil, Chemical and Atomic Workers International Union; after merger between the American Federation of Labor and the CIO in 1955, became a vice-president and executive council member of the new federation; was a member of the National Urban League; retired union positions in 1965; a Democrat; died in Sun City, Ariz., on April 16, 1981; Melvin Rothbaum, *The Government of the Oil, Chemical and Atomic Workers Union* (1962); Harvey O'Connor, *History of Oil Workers International Union—CIO* (1950); *Who's Who in Labor* (1946); *Current Biography* (1952); *AFL-CIO News*, May 9, 1981.

KONYHA, William (1915–). Born in Cleveland, Ohio, on May 11, 1915; son of Louis, a carpenter, and Mary (Gabor) Konyha, a homemaker; married Kathryn, a homemaker, in 1973; six children; after graduating from Cleveland's John Hay High School in 1932, he studied at the Max Hays Trade School, 1932–1936; joined Cleveland Local 1180 of the United Brotherhood of Carpenters and Joiners (UBC) in 1932; served as the business representative for the Cleveland District Council of Carpenters, 1939–1951; was elected president of UBC Local 1180 in 1939 and served in that position until 1952; during World War II, he was a chief carpenter's mate in the U.S. Navy Seabees, serving in the South Pacific; attended Chicago Technical College, 1945–1947; appointed general representative of the UBC, working primarily for representation at the atomic energy plant in Waverly, Ohio, in 1952; became an international representative for the UBC in 1952 and held this position until 1970; served as the president of the Ohio State Council of Carpenters, 1960–1971; elected vice-president of the Ohio American Federation of Labor-Congress of Industrial Organizations (AFL-CIO) Council in 1962, serving until 1970; became a general executive board member of the UBC, representing District 3 in 1970; was elected second general vice-president in 1972, first vice-president in 1973, and in 1980 was elected general president of the UBC; was elected an AFL-CIO vice-president and executive council member in 1980; *Who's Who in Labor* (1976); *AFL-CIO News*, October 20, 1979, and August 23, 1980.

KROLL, Fred J. (1935–1981). Born in Philadelphia, Pa., on October 29, 1935; son of Fred C., a member of the International Union of Electrical, Radio and Machine Workers, and Catherine Kroll, a school teacher; Roman Catholic; married Hildegarde Kroll, a homemaker; three children; attended Roman Catholic High School, Philadelphia, 1949–1953; employed as a railroad clerk for the Pennsylvania Railroad, 1953–1969; joined the Brotherhood of Railway, Airline and Steamship Clerks, Freight Handlers, Express and State Employees (BRAC) in 1954; elected chairman of BRAC Local 587 in 1961, serving in that position until 1969; was division chairman, Penn Central System, BRAC, 1964–1969; elected BRAC general secretary-treasurer in 1970, and a year later was elected general chairman of the Penn Central System; after serving as a Brotherhood vice-president for a year, he was elected general BRAC president in 1976; after the election, he was severely beaten by a group of men associated with the son of the outgoing BRAC president, C. L. Dennis (q.v.), who had opposed him in the election; was elected a vice-president and executive council member of the American Federation of Labor-Congress of Industrial Organizations (AFL-CIO) in 1978, becoming the youngest person ever elected to that position; acquired a reputation as an aggressive bargainer, especially in protecting union jurisdiction and increasing job security; won a landmark settlement with the Norfolk and Western Railway in 1978; authored a quarterly newsletter for the Penn Central System; died in Philadelphia, Pa., on July 30, 1981; *Who's Who in Labor* (1976); *AFL-CIO News*, March 4, 1978; *Business Week*, January 22, 1979; *The New York Times*, August 1, 1981; *Time*, August 6, 1979.

KROLL, John Jacob   (1885–1971). Born in London, England, June 10, 1885; son of Mark, a tailor, and Julia Kate (Blumberg) Kroll; Jewish; married Sara Sylvia Raben on January 19, 1920; one child; emigrated with family to the United States in 1886; completed two years of a high school education in Rochester, N.Y.; became a garment cutter in 1900 and in 1903 joined the Rochester Local of the United Garment Workers of America (UGW); while a member of UGW Local 61 in Chicago, Ill., was associated with Sidney Hillman (q.v.) in the 1910 strike against Hart, Schaffner and Marx that ultimately led to organization of the Amalgamated Clothing Workers of America (ACWA) in 1914; after organizing men's garment workers in Chicago for several years, was appointed an ACWA national organizer in 1919 and shortly thereafter became the manager of ACWA's Joint Board in Cincinnati, Ohio; became a vice-president and executive board member of the ACWA in 1928; served as vice-president and then president of the Ohio Industrial Union Council, Congress of Industrial Organizations (CIO), 1939–1952; was manager of the New York Laundry Workers Joint Board, 1942–1944; appointed a regional director (Ohio, Kentucky, and West Virginia) of the CIO's Political Action Committee (PAC) in 1943 and a year later became vice-chairman of PAC; served as a labor advisor to the Office of Production Management, 1943–1944; became assistant director of the CIO's southern organizing drive in 1946 but resigned shortly after his appointment when named director of the PAC after the death of Sidney Hillman in 1946; following the American Federation of Labor-CIO merger in 1955, became co-director with James L. McDevitt (q.v.) of the Committee on Political Education (COPE); resigned as co-director of COPE in 1957; retired from union affairs in 1966; was a member of *Histadrut*, the Zionist labor organization; although a Socialist early in his career, usually supported Democratic candidates; died in Cincinnati, Ohio, May 26, 1971; Terry Catchpole, *How to Cope with COPE: The Political Operations of Organized Labor* (1968); Fay Calkins, *The CIO and the Democratic Party* (1952); *Current Biography* (1946).

KRZYCKI, Leo   (1881–1966). Born in Milwaukee, Wis., August 10, 1881; son of Martin, a laborer, and Kathryn Krzycki; married Anna Kadau on February 3, 1909; four children; after attending Milwaukee elementary schools, began work as a lithographer and joined the Lithographic Press Feeders Union (LPFU) in 1898; served as LPFU general vice-president, 1904–1908; elected to the Milwaukee City Council in 1912 and served until 1916; elected as undersheriff of Milwaukee County on the Socialist party ticket in 1918 and served a two-year term; joined the Amalgamated Clothing Workers of America (ACWA) in 1919 and the following year became a general organizer; elected an ACWA vice-president and member of the general executive board in 1922; was appointed by the president of the Congress of Industrial Organizations (CIO), John L. Lewis (q.v.), to the Steel Workers' Organizing Committee in 1936; served as a CIO organizer in the rubber industry and participated in the strike against Goodyear Tire and Rubber Company in 1936; became president of the American Slav Congress in 1941 and served as national president of the American Polish Labor Council; was a member of the CIO Political Action Committee; was a Socialist in politics; died in Milwaukee, Wis., January 22, 1966; Walter Galenson, *The CIO Challenge to the AFL: A History of the American Labor Movement, 1935–1941* (1960); *Who's Who in Labor* (1946); Thomas W. Gavett, *Development of the Labor Movement in Milwaukee* (1965).

L

LABADIE, Joseph Antoine (1850–1933). Born in Paw Paw, Mich., April 18, 1850; son of a French-Indian interpreter father and a Potawatomi Indian mother; after briefly attending a rural school, was apprenticed to a printer in Indiana in 1866; as an itinerant printer, was subsequently active in the International Typographical Union; settled in Detroit, Mich., by the 1870s; founded the first Noble Order of the Knights of Labor (K of L) local assembly in Michigan in 1878 and, as an organizer for the K of L, was instrumental in expanding state membership to twenty-five thousand; meanwhile, played a major role in establishing the Detroit Council of Trades and Labor Unions in 1880; renewed his support of trade unionism after the K of L's decline, and in 1889 helped to found the Michigan Federation of Labor (MFL), which soon affiliated with the American Federation of Labor; was elected the first president of the MFL and served for two terms; as a talented polemicist, was a pioneer of the labor press in Michigan; ran as a Greenback-Labor candidate for mayor of Detroit in 1878, but was active in the Socialist Labor party in the 1880s, and finally embraced philosophical anarchism as the only ultimate means of eliminating the exploitation of labor; due to ill health, retired from active participation in the labor movement in 1893 and took a job with the Detroit Water Board, but continued to publicize in favor of anarchism; was revered by unionists and radicals as the ''gentle anarchist''; moved with wife to a small farm in 1912 and printed anarchist tracts with her; throughout his career, carefully preserved labor and radical materials, and in 1911 presented this collection of records and literature to the University of Michigan as the original basis for the university's Labadie Collection of Labor Materials, later one of the most important archives of its kind in the United States; especially strong in anarchist literature and manuscripts, but also contains the only large body of Industrial Workers of the World records and a wide variety of trade union sources; died in Detroit, Mich., October 7, 1933; Doris B. McLaughlin, *Michigan Labor: A Brief History from 1818 to the*

Present (1970); R. C. Stewart, "The Labadie Labor Collection," *Michigan Alumnus Quarterly Review* (May 1947).

Donald G. Sofchalk

LANE, Dennis   (1881–1942). Born in Chicago, Ill., in 1881; son of Irish immigrant parents; Roman Catholic; after a few years of formal education, began working in the Chicago stockyards; shortly after becoming a cattle butcher, participated actively in the trade union movement and joined Cattle Butchers' Local 87 of the Amalgamated Meat Cutters and Butcher Workmen of North America (AMCBWNA); discharged as a result of his involvement in the 1904 AMCBWNA strike in Chicago but later reinstated; shortly after returning to work, was blacklisted as a result of spokesmanship for a group of workers presenting a formal grievance to a plant superintendent; worked as a truck salesman and door-to-door vegetable peddler; became an AMCBWNA international organizer; was elected an AMCBWNA vice-president and executive board member in 1913; joined an internal reform group that forced Secretary-Treasurer Homer Call's resignation in 1917 for unpopular policies; replaced Call as international secretary-treasurer, the chief AMCBWNA executive officer; as a tough, dedicated, and resourceful trade unionist, was destined to dominate the international office of the AMCBWNA for the next 25 years; led an organizing campaign among packinghouse workers in the Chicago stockyards and other packing centers that achieved considerable success during World War I; but the organizing effort among packinghouse workers was shattered after the war by employer resistance and the unsuccessful strike of 1921–1922; worked during the lean years of the 1920s and early 1930s to consolidate the AMCBWNA's strength among retail butchers; despite long-time support of the concept of industrial organization in meat processing and sympathy to the cause championed by the Congress of Industrial Organizations, was opposed to secession and kept the AMCBWNA loyal to the American Federation of Labor (AFL); served as an AFL fraternal delegate to the British Trades Union Congress in 1935; died in Chicago, Ill., August 10, 1942; David Brody, *The Butcher Workmen: A Study of Unionization* (1964); *The Butcher Workman*, September 1, 1942.

LANGDON, Emma Frances   (1875–1937). Born in La Grange, Tenn., in 1875; daughter of George E. Parker; Protestant; married Charles G. Langdon, a linotype operator and member of the Typographical Union; one child; moved in 1903 to Victor, Colo., in the Cripple Creek mining district, where she and her husband worked as printers for the *Victor Daily Record*, the official voice of the Western Federation of Miners (WFM) in the district; active in the Victor Typographical Union No. 275; during the Cripple Creek miners' strike of 1903–1904, when the National Guard tried to stop publication of the *Record* by seizing most of its staff and the editor, personally set type and ensured continued publication of the paper; a delegate from the Victor Typographical local to a special convention called in early 1904 by the Colorado State Federation of Labor to protest militia harassment of the striking miners and violation of civil liberties in the Cripple Creek and Telluride districts; accompanied a WFM committee which met with Governor James Peabody to protest his imposition of martial law in the mining districts; a very effective speaker, toured Colorado during 1904 condemning the National Guard and vigilante actions that ultimately defeated the striking miners; meanwhile, warned by militia officers not to return to Victor, moved to Denver, where she wrote *The Cripple Creek Strike: A History of Industrial Wars in Colorado, 1903–04* (1904–1905), while continuing to work at her trade, in part to finance publication of her book; dubbed by other unionists as "Colorado's Joan of Arc," was made an honorary member of the WFM by its 1904 convention; transferred her membership in the Typographical Union to the Denver Local No. 49 at the founding convention of the Industrial Workers of the World (1905); for the next several years worked with the WFM promoting subscriptions to the *Miners' Magazine* and the WFM Women's Auxiliary; meanwhile wrote *Labor's Greatest Conflict: The Formation of the Western Federation of Miners—* [and] *A Brief Account of the Rise of the United Mine Workers of America* (1908), which also includes a short history of the Typographical Union; during these years was an organizer for the Socialist party; in 1912, appointed by WFM president Charles Moyer (q.v.) as an international organizer for the union; quite popular with the rank and file, continued as a key organizer for the International Union of Mine, Mill and Smelter Workers (successor to the WFM), especially among lead and zinc miners and smelter men in Arkansas, Kansas, and Oklahoma, until 1927; the general decline of Mine Mill and the end of the Moyer administration in 1926 probably were the main reasons for her retirement as an organizer; despite her own career in the labor movement and her advocacy of the unity and equality of the sexes in their working-class roles, was not a hard-core feminist, believing that women also had to fulfill their "natural" domestic responsibilities; after the death of Charles G. Langdon, married Oscar A. Oesterle in 1919; died in Denver, Colo., on November 29, 1937; Philip S. Foner, *Women and the American Labor Movement from Colonial Times to the Eve of World War I* (1979); Elizabeth Jameson, "Imperfect Unions: Class and Gender in Cripple Creek, 1894–1904," *Class, Sex, and the Woman Worker,* edited by Milton Cantor and Bruce Laurie (1977); George G. Suggs, Jr., *Colorado's War on Militant Unionism: James H. Peabody and the Western Federation of Miners* (1972).

Donald G. Sofchalk

LAUCK, William Jett   (1879–1949). Born in Keyser, W.Va., on August 2, 1879; son of William Blackford, a railroad official, and Emma (Eltinge) Lauck; Presbyterian; married Eleanor Dunlap on October 1, 1908; two children; after completing his elementary and secondary schooling, he completed his undergraduate education at Washington and Lee University, 1898–1903; was a fellow in the Department of Economics, University of Chicago, 1903–1906, and a professor of economics at Washington and Lee University, 1907–1909; a close friend and confidant of John L. Lewis (q.v.), he became the United Mine Workers of America's (UMWA) chief economist when Lewis was elected to the UMWA presidency; was an arbitrator for various railroad organizations, 1911–1940; served as the secretary of the National War Labor Board during World War I, 1917–1919; was in charge of field investigation east of the Rocky Mountains for the U.S. Immigration Commission, 1907–1946; was a representative on the U.S. Tariff Commission in 1911 and chief economist for the U.S. Industrial Relations Commission, 1912–1916; was a member of the special drafting committee that wrote the National Industrial Recovery Act in 1933; a noted economist and experienced Washington lobbyist, his friendship with Lewis and his position as UMWA economist gave him considerable influence on UMWA and later Congress of Industrial Organizations policies; wrote many of Lewis's speeches; authored *Causes of the Panic of 1893* (1905) and *Political and Industrial Democracy* (1926); co-authored numerous books; died on June 17, 1949; *The New York Times*, June 18, 1949; *Who's Who in Labor* (1946); Melvyn Dubofsky and Warren Van Tine, *John L. Lewis: A Biography* (1977); Carmen B. Grayson, "W. Jett Lauck: Biography of a Reformer" (Ph.D. diss., 1975); W. Jett Lauck Papers, University of Virginia.

LAWRENSON, Jack   (1906–1957). Born in Dublin, Ireland, October 22, 1906; son of Robert, a farmer, and Johanna (Fogerty) Lawrenson; Roman Catholic; married Helen Strough Brown on June 28, 1939; two children; attended the public schools of Ireland and Great Britain, then began a career as a merchant seaman; emigrated to the United States and in 1937 was one of the principal founders of the National Maritime Union of America (NMU); was elected an NMU vice-president and for a short time was placed in charge of the Great Lakes division of the NMU; became a leader of the opposition to the administration of NMU president Joseph Curran (q.v.); was defeated for reelection to an NMU vice-presidency in 1949 during a bitterly contested election amid charges of being "soft" on communism; began a moving and trucking business after his defeat and operated it until his death; authored numerous articles and pamphlets on union affairs; was a member of the American Labor party; died in New York City, October 31, 1957; Joseph P. Goldberg, *The Maritime Story: A Study in Labor-Management Relations* (1958); *Who's Who in Labor* (1946); Helen Lawrenson, *Stranger at the Party* (1975).

LAWSON, George W.   (1876–1959). Born in Chicago, Ill., July 4, 1876; son of Louis, a clerk, and Hannah (Nelson) Lawson; Roman Catholic; married Eleanor Payer on June 8, 1904; one child; attended one year of high school in St. Paul, Minn., then worked for several years as an office clerk; entered a shoe factory ca. 1900 and shortly thereafter became a charter member of the St. Paul local of the Boot and Shoe Workers' International Union; served as the union's financial secretary for many years; was secretary of the St. Paul Trades and Labor Assembly, 1912–1919; became secretary-treasurer of the Minnesota State

Federation of Labor (MSFL) in 1914; lobbied successfully in the legislature for improvement of workmen's compensation and for other labor laws; helped coordinate the 1918 political effort to unseat the administration of Governor Joseph Burnquist because of its anti-union policies; played a key role in 1919 in organizing the Working People's Nonpartisan Political League, which, along with the Farmers' Nonpartisan League, laid the basis for the Minnesota Farmer-Labor party; meanwhile,managed to reconcile his kind of union political activism with the established American Federation of Labor (AFL) policy of political nonpartisanship by insuring that the city central bodies and the MSFL remained structurally distinct from the Farmer-Labor campaign organizations; during the rift between the AFL and the Congress of Industrial Organizations (CIO) in the 1930s, was consistently loyal to the AFL, and in Minnesota promptly executed orders of the AFL executive council to state federations to expel their CIO affiliates; cooperated simultaneously with the radical leadership of the powerful Minneapolis, Minn., Teamsters; was centrally involved in the MSFL's formal endorsement of Hubert Humphrey's candidacy for the U.S. Senate in 1948; was on the board of regents of the University of Minnesota, 1933–1959; after retiring as secretary of the MSFL in 1954, wrote *History of Labor in Minnesota* (1955); died in St. Paul, Minn., September 23, 1959; Solon DeLeon, ed., *The American Labor Who's Who* (1925); Theodore Christianson, *Minnesota: A History*, Vol. 4 (1935).

Donald G. Sofchalk

LAWSON, John Cummings   (1900–   ). Born in Aberdeen, Scotland, September 3, 1900; son of Alfred J., a quarry foreman, and Agnes (Walker) Lawson; Presbyterian; married Lillian Hasall on December 28, 1922; two children; emigrated to the United States as a child and settled in Vermont; acquired a grammar school education prior to beginning work in the quarries of Graniteville, Vt.; joined Branch 4 (Graniteville) of the United Stone and Allied Products Workers of America (USAPWA) in 1918; was elected president of Branch 4 and served in that capacity for 15 years; became a member of the USAPWA international executive board in 1930, serving until 1945; was appointed a USAPWA international organizer in 1934 and shortly thereafter was elected international secretary-treasurer, a position he still holds; was later elected secretary-treasurer of the Vermont State Industrial Union Council (IUC) and held that position until election as IUC president in 1946; was an influential figure in Vermont political affairs and served as member of the State Selective Service Appeals Board, the Vermont Vocational Training Committee, the Vermont Apprenticeship Council, and the executive committee of the National Religion and Labor Federation; retired as president of the Vermont IUC in 1950 to devote full time to his duties as secretary-treasurer of the USAPWA; was a delegate to most of the annual conventions of the Congress of Industrial Organizations (CIO) and the biennial conventions of the American Federation of Labor-CIO; *Who's Who in Labor* (1946); *CIO News*, September 4, 1950.

LEE, Ernest S. (1923–   ). Born in Santo Domingo, Dominican Republic, on April 12, 1923; son of Harry, a general in the U.S. Marine Corps, and Henrietta (Mercedes) Lee; married Eileen P. in 1957; four children; educated at Georgetown Preparatory School, Washington, D.C., 1936–1940, Georgetown University, 1941–1943, Villanova University, Philadelphia, Pa., 1943–1944, and received the B.S. from Georgetown in 1953; won the Silver Star in the Korean War as a major in the U.S. Marine Corps; joined Local 400 of the Retail Clerks International Association (RCIA) and served as the director of RCIA's international affairs department, 1958–1959; was the inter-American representative to the International Federation of Commercial, Clerical and Technical Employees, 1959–1962; became executive assistant to the director of the American Federation of Labor-Congress of Industrial Organizations' (AFL-CIO) department of international affairs, 1962–1963; served as assistant director, 1964–1974, and was appointed director on July 1, 1974; served on the advisory committee of the U.S. Department of Labor's Bureau of Labor Statistics and on the board of trustees of the American Institute for Free Labor Development; *Who's Who in Labor* (1976); *AFL-CIO News*, June 1, 1974.

LEE, William Granville   (1859–1929). Born in La Prairie, Ill., November 29, 1859; son of James W., a carpenter and contractor, and Sylvestra Jane (Tracy) Lee; Congregationalist; married Mary R. Rice on October 15, 1901; worked for his father as a carpenter after completing grammar school; became a brakeman on the Atchison, Topeka, and Santa Fe Railroad in 1879; was later transferred to the Rayton-New Mexico Division and was promoted to conductor in 1880; served as deputy recorder of deeds, Ford County, Kansas, 1884–1888; became a brakeman and switchman on the Wabash Railroad in 1888 and shortly thereafter joined the Missouri Pacific in a similar capacity; joined the Brotherhood of Railroad Trainmen (BRT) in 1890; secured employment on the Union Pacific Railroad as a brakeman and then a freight conductor; organized a BRT lodge in Kansas City and served it as master, chairman of the local committee, and member of the general committee of the Union Pacific; became vice grand master of the BRT in 1895; was elected BRT president in 1909; led the union through its long struggle for an eight-hour day, finally achieved through federal legislation after the threat of a nationwide strike in 1917; staunchly believed in the sanctity of contracts and thus expelled nearly one-sixth of the BRT's general membership in 1920 for unauthorized strikes; was defeated for reelection in 1928, primarily because of old age and ill health, but was chosen general secretary-treasurer; politically was a Republican; refused to cooperate with presidents of other railroad brotherhoods who supported the Progressive party candidacy of Robert M. La Follette in 1924; died in Cleveland, Ohio, November 2, 1929; Joel Seidman, *The Brotherhood of Railroad Trainmen: The Internal Political Life of a National Union* (1962); Walter F. McCaleb, *Brotherhood of Railroad Trainmen, with Special Reference to the Life of Alexander F. Whitney* (1936); *Dictionary of American Biography*, Vol. 11.

LEFFINGWELL, Samuel Langdale   (fl. 1850–1885). Born at Chillicothe, Ohio, of English and Scottish descent; apprenticed early as a printer; in July 1850, he became a member of the Cincinnati Typographical Union; in February 1852, formed a printers union in Columbus, Ohio; in 1856, was made president of the Cincinnati Typographical Union and in July, president of the one at Columbus; joined the Knights of Labor in Indianapolis in July 1875; was commissioned organizer, and organized more than a score of assemblies; represented Indianapolis Trades Assembly at first session of Federal Congress of Trade and Labor Unions*; in 1882, was president of the congress at Cleveland; was delegate to several important sessions of General Assembly Knights of Labor; in September 1885, organized Indiana State Federation of Trade and Labor Unions; chosen president twice; established several labor papers, including the first organ of the International Typographical Union; in August 1847, enlisted for the Mexican War, and served to its close; in August 1861, was commissioned major in the Thirty-first Ohio; at battle of Mills Springs, transferred to Forty-fifth; major in Eighty-seventh; taken prisoner at Harpers Ferry, September 15, 1862; paroled; mustered out, 1863; commanded a regiment in southern Ohio to repel John Morgan; February 1864, enlisted as private in First Ohio Cavalry; at battles of Decatur, Rome, Kennesaw, Marietta, Atlanta; January 1865, assigned to special duty at Sherman's headquarters; honorably discharged, June 11, 1865; George E. McNeill, *The Labor Movement: The Problem of To-Day* (1887); John R. Commons et al., *History of Labour in the United States*, Vol. 2 (1918).

George E. McNeill

LEIGHTY, George Earle   (1897–1973). Born in Phillips, Wis., August 16, 1897; son of George W. and Anna B. (Klein) Leighty; Presbyterian; married Marie E. McDonald on June 15, 1917, and, after a divorce in 1923, Florence L. Gates on August 8, 1953; three children; graduating from the public schools of Phillips, Wis., worked as an agent-telegrapher and in various other capacities for the Chicago, Milwaukee, St. Paul, and Pacific Railroad, 1917–1937; joined the Order of Railroad Telegraphers (ORT) in 1917 and shortly thereafter was elected local chairman, serving until 1942; was chosen deputy president of the ORT in 1937 and general chairman of the Chicago, Milwaukee, St. Paul, and Pacific in 1942; served as vice-president of the ORT, 1942–1946, and was elected president in 1946; elected chairman of the National Employees Negotiating Committee of the 16 non-operating railway labor organizations in 1947, serving until 1965; was a member and for a time chairman of the united labor policy committee set up by the American Federation of Labor, the Congress of Industrial Organizations, and the independent railroad brotherhoods to coordinate union labor policies during the Korean War; served as chairman of the Railway Labor Executives' Association, 1950–1965; retired union positions in 1965; edited the *Railroad Telegrapher* for several years; supported the Democratic party; died in

*Federation of Organized Trades and Labor Unions of the United States and Canada.

Washington, D.C., July 17, 1973; Archibald M. McIsaac, *The Order of Railroad Telegraphers: A Study in Trade Unionism and Collective Bargaining* (1933); *AFL-CIO News,* July 21, 1973; *Who's Who in Railroading* (1959).

LEISERSON, William Morris   (1883–1957). Born in Revel, Estonia, on April 15, 1883; son of Mendel and Sarah (Snyder) Leiserson; both parents were Russian Jews active in the anti-czarist movement; married Emily Nash Bodman on June 22, 1912; seven children; emigrated to the United States with his mother in 1890, settling in New York City; left school in 1897 at age 14 to work in a shirtwaist factory; while working, he attended night classes at Cooper Union and the University Settlement; entered the University of Wisconsin in 1904 and soon became a protégé of John R. Commons (q.v.); helped edit two volumes of Commons's *Documentary History of American Labor* and was a staff member of the Pittsburgh Social Survey; after graduating in 1908, he enrolled in the graduate school of Columbia University where he pursued advanced degrees in economics, earning the Ph.D. in 1911; during these years he also worked as an investigator for the New York Commission on Unemployment and Workmen's Compensation; was appointed deputy industrial commissioner of Wisconsin in 1911, in which capacity he established a network of employment offices; was a founder of the National Association of Public and Private Employment Agencies and an early advocate of unemployment insurance; was a staff member of the U.S. Commission on Industrial Relations, 1914–1915; was a professor of economics, Toledo University, 1915–1918, and Antioch College, 1925–1933; was an active participant in establishing state and federal manpower policy during World War I; was appointed an arbitrator for the Amalgamated Clothing Workers of America (ACWA) newly created Labor Adjustment Board in 1919; in this capacity he helped institutionalize collective bargaining practices in the garment industry; served as chairman of the Ohio Commission on Unemployment Insurance, 1931–1932; was involved in the drafting of the labor codes of the National Recovery Administration in 1933 and was appointed secretary of the National Labor Board which was to supervise code compliance; appointed chairman of the National Mediation Board in 1934 which supervised representation election in the railroad industry; was appointed to the National Labor Relations Board in 1939; in this capacity he attempted to reorganize the board and to reverse a perceived left-wing, Congress of Industrial Organizations bias; with the appointment of fellow-Commons student Harry A. Millis to the board, the left wingers were purged and the board developed a policy much more in harmony with the traditional craft-unionist position of the American Federation of Labor; a critic of the Roosevelt Administration's war-time labor policy, he left the National Labor Relations Board in 1943 and resigned from the National Railway Labor Panel in 1944; thereafter, he became a visiting professor at Johns Hopkins University and spent several years researching and writing *American Trade Union Democracy* (1959), a critical study of internal union governance and policy making; died in Washington, D.C., on February 12, 1957; William M. Leiserson

Papers, State Historical Society of Wisconsin; Michael Eisner, *William Morris Leiserson* (1967); Daniel Nelson, *Unemployment Insurance* (1969); *Dictionary of American Biography*, Suppl. 6; *Who's Who in Labor* (1946).

LENNON, John Brown   (1850–1923). Born in Lafayette County, Wis., October 12, 1850; son of John Alexander, a tailor, and Elizabeth Fletcher (Brown) Lennon; Presbyterian; married Juna J. Allen on April 5, 1871; attended the public schools of Hannibal, Mo., then served a four-year apprenticeship in his father's tailor shop; moved to Denver, Colo., in 1869 and became a merchant tailor; helped organize a Denver tailors' union in 1883 and became its secretary; in 1884 served as president of the Denver local that affiliated with the Journeymen Tailors' Union of America (JTU); while attending the JTU national convention as a delegate from Denver, was elected national president; elected vice-president in 1885 and served as general secretary, 1886–1910; elected treasurer of the American Federation of Labor (AFL) in 1890, serving until 1917; appointed to the Commission on Industrial Relations by President Woodrow T. Wilson in 1913; became a member of the U.S. Department of Labor's Board of Mediators in 1917; was a conservative trade unionist and usually supported the policies of AFL president Samuel Gompers; edited *The Tailors*, 1886–1910; politically was a Democrat; died in Bloomington, Ill., January 17, 1923; John B. Lennon Papers, AFL-CIO Archives, George Meany Labor Studies Center; Philip Taft, *The A.F. of L. in the Time of Gompers* (1957); Charles J. Stowell, *The Journeymen Tailors' Union of America: A Study in Trade Union Policy* (1918); *Dictionary of American Biography*, Vol. 11.

LEONARD, Richard   (1902–1981). Born in New Straitsville, Ohio, February 22, 1902; son of Bryan, a coal miner, and Anna (Thomas) Leonard; Roman Catholic; married Mary Price on July 20, 1922; two children; secured employment in a Chrysler Corporation DeSoto plant, then helped organize the plant workers and was elected president of DeSoto Local 227 of the United Automobile, Aircraft, Agricultural Implement Workers of America (UAW); became UAW welfare director in 1937 and was elected secretary of the Michigan Congress of Industrial Organizations' (CIO) industrial union council in 1938; served as a member of the UAW executive board, 1939–1943, and was director of the UAW's Ford department, 1941–1947; ran unsuccessfully for UAW secretary-treasurer in 1941 and 1943 and for a vice-presidency in 1944, but was elected a UAW vice-president in 1946; defeated for reelection in 1947 by John W. Livingston (q.v.) in a UAW election in which Walter P. Reuther (q.v.) consolidated his control of the union; returned to plant work after his defeat and was again elected president of DeSoto Local 227; attempted for a time to build an anti-administration faction in the local; joined the CIO staff in 1948 and was appointed CIO director for Arizona; became an assistant to President Philip Murray (q.v.) of the CIO in 1950 and served as assistant to Walter P. Reuther during his CIO presidency, 1951–1955; after the merger of the CIO and American Federation of Labor (AFL), was appointed assistant to the president of the AFL-CIO industrial union department and served in that capacity until his retirement in 1972; supported the Democratic party; died on August 3, 1981; Jack Stieber, *Governing the UAW* (1962); Frank Cormier and William J. Eaton, *Reuther* (1970); Jean Gould and Lorena Hickok, *Walter Reuther: Labor's Rugged Individualist* (1972); Nelson Lichtenstein, *Labor's War at Home: The CIO in World War II* (1982); Roger Keeran, *The Communist Party and the Auto Workers Unions* (1980).

LEVIN, Ruben   (1902–1981). Born in Poland on August 2, 1902; son of Benjamin, a temple sexton, and Ida Levin, a homemaker; married Bertha, a homemaker, in 1931; three children; emigrated with his family to the United States in 1904, settling first in Manitowoc, Wis., and then moving to Milwaukee; graduated from Milwaukee High School in 1920; received the B.A. in journalism from the University of Wisconsin in 1926; while a college student, he worked as a reporter for *Capitol Times*, a reformist journal in the Wisconsin progressive tradition; later worked for several Wisconsin daily newspapers and spent several years as a "boomer" news reporter for 11 other newspapers, including the *New York Herald-Tribune*'s European edition published in Paris, 1926–1938; joined the American Newspaper Guild in 1935; joined the staff of *Labor*, a national newspaper sponsored by the railroad brotherhoods, in 1938; served as acting editor of *Labor*, 1951–1953, and became editor and manager in 1953; was one of the founders of Labor Press Associates, the forerunner to Press Associates, Inc.; was a member and past president of the Association of Railroad Editors; received the Sidney Hillman (q.v.) Foundation award for a series of articles exposing the emasculation of federal regulatory agencies in 1956; authored numerous articles in periodicals such as *The Nation, New Republic, Common Sense,* and *Survey* and authored *Little Blue Books*; died in Bethesda, Md., on January 29, 1981; *Who's Who in Labor* (1976); *AFL-CIO News*, January 31, 1981; *Labor*, January 31, 1981.

LEWIS, Alma Dennie   (1889–1962). Born in Colfax, Iowa, January 23, 1889; son of Thomas, a coal miner, and Ann Louisa (Watkins) Lewis; Episcopalian; married Irene (Lindig) Perkins on August 30, 1934; attended the public schools of Lucas, Iowa, then began working in nearby coal mines; served overseas with the 27th Engineers, U.S. Army, during World War I; appointed director of mines and minerals for the state of Illinois in 1924, serving until 1930; served as assistant director general of the U.S. Employment Service, 1930–1934; became assistant to his brother, John L. Lewis (q.v.), president of the United Mine Workers of America (UMWA), in 1934 and served in that capacity for five years; in 1939, was appointed chairman of the newly formed United Construction Workers Organizing Committee, Congress of Industrial Organizations (CIO), which attempted to unionize unorganized construction workers; after the UMWA disaffiliated with the CIO in 1941, transferred his Construction Workers Organizing Committee into UMWA District 50; led an unsuccessful effort to organize New York City taxicab drivers in 1949; was elected president of controversial UMWA District 50 in 1954 and served in that capacity until his death in Washington, D.C., January 24, 1962; was a Republican; Saul D. Alinsky, *John L. Lewis: an Unauthorized Biography* (1949); *National Cyclopaedia of American Biography*, Vol. 50; *Who's Who in Labor* (1946).

LEWIS, John Llewellyn   (1880–1969). Born in Lucas, Iowa, February 12, 1880; son of Thomas H., a coal miner, and Ann Louisa (Watkins) Lewis; Protestant; married Myrta Edith Bell on June 5, 1907; three children; completed three and one-half years of high school in Lucas; at age 16, started work as a coal miner in Lucas and then spent ten years in coal and metal mining in the Western states; mined coal in Lucas and Panama, Ill., from 1907 to 1909; was elected in Panama as president of the United Mine Workers of America (UMWA) local union; elected by District 12, UMWA, Illinois, as a lobbyist for state mine safety legislation in 1909; served as American Federation of Labor (AFL) field representative, 1910–1916; was appointed UMWA chief statistician and business manager of the *United Mine Workers Journal* in 1917, and later the same year was named UMWA international vice-president; served as acting UMWA president in 1919 and became international president in 1920, serving until his retirement in 1960; between 1919 and 1933, while overproduction caused depression of the industry, falling prices and wages, and severe unemployment, won a 27 percent wage increase from the U.S. Coal Commission in 1919 and the shortlived Jacksonville agreement in 1924; engaged in bitter internecine struggles to centralize administrative and bargaining power at the expense of district autonomy, particularly in Illinois and Kansas; defeated John Brophy's (q.v.) bid for the union presidency in 1926 by a vote of 173,323 to 60,661 amid charges of fraud; expelled many of his opponents, including Brophy, Alexander Howat (q.v.), Frank Farrington (q.v.), Adolph Germer (q.v.), and Powers Hapgood (q.v.), from the UMWA, and survived challenges from successive rival unions such as the National Miners Union, the Reorganized UMWA, and the West Virginia Mine Workers; meanwhile, union membership dwindled from approximately five hundred thousand to seventy-five thousand; in 1933, played an important role with UMWA economist W. Jett Lauck (q.v.) in the enactment of Section 7(a) of the National Industrial Recovery Act, and within 90 days of its passage, 92 percent of U.S. coal miners were organized; in December 1935, established the Committee for Industrial Organization (CIO) to organize industrial-type unions in the unorganized mass production industries; after quickly winning contracts with the United States Steel Corporation, Goodyear Rubber Corporation, and General Motors Corporation, CIO unions attained a larger membership than AFL affiliates by the end of 1937; CIO unions, expelled by the AFL executive council, reorganized as a rival federation, the Congress of Industrial Organizations (CIO); in 1936, Lewis, a lifelong Republican, supported the reelection of President Franklin D. Roosevelt, and the CIO contributed $500,000 to his campaign; but backed Republican Wendell Willkie in 1940 because of disillusionment with Roosevelt's attitude toward the "Little Steel" strike, his failure to eliminate unemployment, and his interventionist foreign policy; resigned the presidency of the CIO after Roosevelt's reelection; UMWA withdrew from the CIO in 1942, briefly reaffiliated with the AFL in 1946–1947, and then reassumed its independent status; controversial strikes during World War II won the miners a captive mines agreement and portal-to-portal pay; UMWA strikes in 1946 and 1948 won a royalty on every ton of coal mined and thus helped to finance the UMWA welfare and retirement program, but subjected the mines to federal government seizure and Lewis and his union to fines totaling $2,120,000 for civil and criminal contempt of court; by 1956, the welfare and retirement fund had been used to construct ten hospitals in Southern Appalachia, and by 1969 more than $2.6 million had been disbursed to five million beneficiaries in medical and retirement benefits; open-end agreement worked out by Lewis and the Bituminous Coal Operators Association in 1951 eliminated national strikes from the industry for several years; in 1952, led the campaign for the first Federal Mine Safety Act; resigned the UMWA presidency in 1960 and served until his death as president emeritus at an annual salary of $50,000; also served as chairman of the board of trustees and as chief executive officer of the Welfare and Retirement Fund; died in Washington, D.C., June 11, 1969; John L. Lewis Papers, State Historical Society of Wisconsin; Saul D. Alinsky, *John L. Lewis: An Unauthorized Biography* (1949); James A. Wechsler, *Labor Baron: A Portrait of John L. Lewis* (1944); Robert Cairns, *John L. Lewis: Leader of Labor* (1941); Charles A. Madison, *American Labor Leaders: Personalities and Forces in the Labor Movement* (1950); Charles K. McFarland, *Roosevelt, Lewis and the New Deal* (1970); Irving Bernstein, *The Lean Years: A History of the American Worker, 1920–1933* (1960), and *Turbulent Years: A History of the American Worker, 1933–1941* (1970); Melvyn Dubofsky, "J. L. Lewis," *McGraw-Hill Encyclopedia of World Biography*, Vol. 6 (1973); *United Mine Workers Journal,* June 15, 1969; Nelson Lichtenstein, *Labor's War at Home: The CIO in World War II* (1982); Melvyn Dubofsky and Warren Van Tine, *John L. Lewis: A Biography* (1977).

                                                                                    John W. Hevener

LEWIS, Joseph   (1906–1970). Born in Centerville, Calif., October 1, 1906; son of Manuel S., a farmer, and Mary S (Francisco) Lewis; Roman Catholic; married Marie Narcizo in March 1929, and, after her death, Gladys Florence Goulart on March 28, 1942; two children; graduated from high school, then began working at the Wedgewood Stove Company in Centerville, Calif., in 1924; joined the Centerville local of the Stove Mounters International Union of North America (SMIU) in 1924; was elected president of SMIU Local 61 in Newark, Calif., in 1932; became an international vice-president of the SMIU in 1935 and was placed in charge of the West Coast district; elected international president of the SMIU (now the Stove, Furnace and Allied Appliance Workers) in 1944, serving until 1956; was elected a vice-president of the American Federation of Labor (AFL) union label department in 1952, and became secretary-treasurer of the AFL-Congress of Industrial Organizations' union label department in 1956, serving in that capacity until his death; was a Democrat; died in Inverness, Fla., December 14, 1970; *AFL-CIO News*, December 19, 1970; *Who's Who in Labor* (1946); *Who's Who in America, 1970–1971.*

LEWIS, Kathryn   (1911–1962). Born in Panama, Ill., on April 14, 1911; daughter of John L., United Mine Workers of America (UMWA) president, and Myrta (Bell) Lewis; never married; moved with her family to Springfield, Ill., where she attended the public schools and completed her elementary and secondary education; attended Bryn Mawr College; as a result of obesity—she weighed nearly three hundred pounds—she suffered recurring psychological problems and at times secluded herself from friends and relatives; became her father's personal secretary; was a member of the U.S. delegation to the Pan-American Conference in 1938 and served as labor advisor to the U.S. delegation at the regional conference of U.S. members of the International Labor Organization in 1939; was appointed secretary-treasurer of UMWA District 50 in 1941; was appointed UMWA specialist for foreign labor relations in 1952; extremely possessive and defensive of her father, she may have had an influence on the estrangement between Lewis and Franklin D. Roosevelt as well as Philip Murray (q.v.); suffering one of her fits of depression, she went to New York for treatment and died there on January 7, 1962; Melvyn Dubofsky and Warren Van Tine, *John L. Lewis: A Biography* (1977); Saul D. Alinsky, *John L. Lewis: An Unauthorized Biography* (1949); *Who's Who in Labor* (1946).

LEWIS, Thomas L.   (1866–1939). Born in Locust Gap, Pa., in 1866; was of Welsh ancestry; began work as a breaker boy in the Ohio mines at an early age; a brother, W. T. Lewis, served as master workman of District 135, Knights of Labor; was a founder of the United Mine Workers of America (UMWA); after the resignation of Michael Ratchford (q.v.) in September 1898, opposed John Mitchell (q.v.) for the union presidency but withdrew before a vote was taken; despite Mitchell's attempts at accommodation, including appointment of Lewis's friends as international organizers and, in 1903, placement of the staff of 60 international organizers under Lewis's direction, worked consistently as international vice-president to undermine Mitchell's prestige; participated in the successful organizing campaign in District 16, Maryland, in 1903; efforts to preserve the Central Competitive Field Agreement won in 1897 led to a serious rift with Mitchell who, in 1906, sought sectional agreements to restore the 1903 scale; after Mitchell's resignation in 1908, defeated William B. Wilson (q.v.), the incumbent international secretary-treasurer who had Mitchell's support, for the UMWA presidency; during his incumbency, perfected the technique of appointing international organizers to build a personal political machine and converted the *United Mine Workers Journal* into a house organ to support his continued elections; as a result of these innovations, was able to withstand strong challenges from John H. Walker (q.v.) of Illinois in 1909 and William Green (q.v.) of Ohio in 1910, both of whom lost presidential elections marked by serious charges of fraudulent vote counts; signed agreements over the heads of district officers in Pennsylvania in 1909 and Illinois in 1910, thus helping to create an alliance of district officers that brought about his defeat in 1911; was annoyed by John Mitchell's retention of the American Federation of Labor's second vice-presidency and allied himself with the Socialists at the 1911 convention to force Mitchell to resign from either the National Civic Federation or the UMWA; after an unsuccessful effort to regain power in the UMWA in 1912, secured employment as a labor advisor to an anti-union West Virginia operators' association; was an unsuccessful candidate for Ohio secretary of state on the Republican party ticket in 1912; published a coal trade journal, the *Coal Mining Review*, and helped found the National Coal Association; died in Charleston, W.Va., May 1, 1939; *United Mine Workers Journal*, May 15, 1939; Elsie Gluck, *John Mitchell: Miner* (1929); George S. McGovern and Leonard F. Guttridge, *Great Coalfield War* (1972).

John W. Hevener

LINDELOF, Lawrence Peter   (1875–1952). Born in Malmö, Skane, Sweden, May 18, 1875; son of Anders Peter, a railway superintendent for the Swedish government, and Marie (Larson) Lindelof; Presbyterian; married Marie I. Rodriquez on March 31, 1902; two children; attended the public schools of Malmö, then served a four-year apprenticeship as a painter and interior decorator; emigrated to the United States in 1893; settled in Chicago, Ill., attended night school and, in 1910, took courses in commercial law at the Marshall School of Law; failed to find employment in his trade between 1894 and 1901; traveled throughout the United States working at various jobs; gained employment as a painter and decorator in Aurora, Ill., in 1901 and organized Local 448 of the Brotherhood of Painters, Decorators and Paperhangers of America (BPDPHA); transferred his membership to Local 465, Ottawa, Ill., in 1904 and served as its treasurer until 1909; accepted employment with a Chicago painting and decorating contractor in 1909 and transferred his membership there; was elected in 1910 as chairman of the board of trustees of BPDPHA's newly organized District Council 14; elected secretary-treasurer of District Council 14 in 1912 and served until 1926; during this period, was credited with instituting a model apprenticeship system; moved to Hammond, Ind., in 1927 and affiliated with Local 460; was elected vice-president of the BPDPHA and placed in charge of the union's southern district, comprising 13 southern states; elected general president of the BPDPHA in 1929, and in the same year, became the first vice-president of the American Federation of Labor's building and construction trades department; retired union positions in 1952; was a Republican; died in Lafayette, Ind., in October 1952; Philip Zausner, *Unvarnished: The Autobiography of a Union*

Leader (1941); *National Cyclopaedia of American Biography*, Vol. G; *Who's Who in Labor* (1946).

LINGG, Louis (1864–1887). Born in Mannheim, Grand Duchy of Baden, Germany, on September 9, 1864; son of Friedrich, a lumber yard worker; mother operated a laundry; attended German public schools until age 15; was apprenticed to a carpenter from 1879 to 1882; after completing his apprenticeship, he began to travel extensively while working at his trade; during his travels, he became associated with a number of workingmen's and Socialist societies; his interest in socialism had been stimulated by the disregard with which his father had been treated after an industrial accident crippled him; joined the General Working Men's Society, a Lassallean organization, in 1882; sided with the anarchist faction in the ideological disputes that were dividing European Socialists during the mid-1880s; emigrated to the United States in 1885, settled in Chicago, Ill., and immediately joined the International Brotherhood of Carpenters and Joiners; elected a delegate to the Chicago Central Labor Union in 1886; became an organizer for the Brotherhood in 1886; as a result of his previous association with anarchist movements, he joined the International Working People's Association shortly after settling in Chicago; although he was not present at Haymarket Square on May 4, 1886, when a bomb exploded during an anarchist-organized protest meeting killing a policeman, he was charged with being "morally guilty"; and, after fellow defendant William Seliger became a witness for the state and testified that Lingg had engaged in the manufacture of dynamite bombs, he was sentenced to death; committed suicide by exploding a bomb in his mouth on November 10, 1887, one day before his scheduled execution; Philip S. Foner, ed., *The Autobiographies of the Haymarket Martyrs* (1969); Henry David, *The History of the Haymarket Affair* (1963).

LIPSIG, James (1910–1976). Born in New York City on April 1, 1910; son of Benjamin, a storekeeper, and Bessie (Rabinowitz) Lipsig, a homemaker; Jewish; married Frances Katz, a writer, in 1943; one child; graduated from Townsend Harris Hall High School, New York City, in 1926, College of the City of New York in 1930, and Columbia University Law School in 1933; a friend and close associate of Socialist party leader Norman Thomas (q.v.) for many years, he served as the New York state secretary of the Socialist party, 1936–1938; served as general counsel to the Greater New York Joint Board of the Textile Workers Union of America, 1941–1946; served as a staff sergeant, U.S. Army, 1943–1945; became an attorney for the International Ladies' Garment Workers' Union (ILGWU) in 1946 and two years later was appointed assistant executive secretary of the ILGWU, a position he retained for the remainder of his life; active in a great variety of civic, labor, and Jewish affairs, at various times he served as vice-chairman of the Liberal party legislative committee, on the board of directors of the National Sharecroppers Fund, on the board of directors of the League for Industrial Democracy, on the national executive board of the Workers' Defense League, on the national administrative committee of the Jewish Labor Committee and on the executive committee of the National Jewish Community Relations Advisory Council; a Socialist and member of the Liberal party of New York; authored *Sedition, Criminal Syndicalism and Criminal Anarchy Laws* (1937); died in New York City on December 19, 1976; *Who's Who in Labor* (1976); *The New York Times*, December 20, 1976; *Justice*, December 28, 1976.

LITCHMAN, Charles Henry   (1849–1902). Born in Marblehead, Mass., April 8, 1949; son of William, a shoe manufacturer, and Sarah E. (Bartlett) Litchman; married Annie Shirley on February 5, 1868; attended the public schools of Marblehead and spent two years at Marblehead Academy; completed his formal schooling, then became a shoe salesman for his father; established a shoe factory with his brother and began the study of law; as a result of the depression of 1873, lost the shoe factory and had to give up the study of law; secured employment as a journeyman shoemaker; joined the Knights of Saint Crispin and served as the grand scribe of its grand lodge during 1875–1878; was a member of the Marblehead school committee, 1873–1876; joined the Noble Order of the Knights of Labor (K of L) and served as the head of the Massachusetts District Assembly; was general secretary of the K of L, 1878–1881 and 1886–1888; after running unsuccessfully as a Republican, was elected to the Massachusetts state legislature on the Greenback Labor party ticket in 1878 and served one term; campaigned for Republican presidential nominee Benjamin Harrison in 1888, and was appointed by Harrison as a special agent in the U.S. Treasury Department in 1889, serving until 1893; appointed to the U.S. Industrial Commission in 1900 and served until his death; was a Republican; died in Newark, N.J., in 1902; Don D. Descohier, *The Knights of St. Crispin, 1867–1874* (1910); Gerald N. Grob, *Workers and Utopia: A Study of Ideological Conflict in the American Labor Movement, 1865–1900* (1961); Norman J. Ware, *The Labor Movement in the United States, 1860–1895* (1929).

LITTLE, Frank H.   (fl. 1900–1917). Born in 1879, son of a Cherokee Indian mother and a Quaker father; by 1900, was a member of the Western Federation of Miners (WFM); was one of the militants who left the WFM for the Industrial Workers of the World (IWW) in 1907; was jailed for participation in the famous IWW free-speech struggle in Spokane, Wash., in 1909; organized California agricultural and construction workers, including Japanese and Mexicans, into IWW Local 66 at Fresno in 1910; called for direct action and was arrested after Fresno officials prohibited street speeches; Wobblies, packing the jail and being brutalized and tormented by their jailers, forced the city to grant them free speech; subsequently, Little led free-speech fights in Denver, Colo., Kansas City, Mo., and elsewhere; as a member of the IWW general executive board in 1914, persuaded IWW to plan a coordinated effort to organize migratory harvest workers, thus leading in 1915 to the founding of the Agricultural Workers Organization; was involved in the Mesabi iron miners' strike in 1916; as chairman of the general executive board, strongly supported the centralizers' plan for organization of agricultural and industrial workers into unions controlled directly by IWW head William Haywood (q.v.); was archetype of the Wobbly agitator in his fearlessness, bluntness, uncompromising view of the "master" class, and vehement opposition to American intervention in World War I, but failed to convince IWW general executive board to condone draft resistance; helped lead the Arizona copper strikes of 1917; went to Butte, Mont., earlier a bastion of militant unionism but then kept as open shop by the giant Anaconda Company until a serious mine disaster in June 1917 sparked a spontaneous revival of unionism; Little tried to exploit this situation for the IWW by urging the striking miners to persist, and publicly agitating against the war; was feared by the industry as a person who might prolong the strike and was branded by the press as a seditious traitor; on the night of August 1, 1917, was seized and brutally killed by six men; with several thousand people attending his funeral in Butte, soon became one of the major Wobbly martyrs; despite investigation by Montana attorney general, killers were never identified; but hysteria about seditious activity fueled by the affair led to passage of the federal Sedition Act, used paradoxically to persecute national IWW leaders in 1918; Ralph Chaplin, *Wobbly: The Rough-and-Tumble Story of an American Radical* (1948); James P. Cannon, *Notebook of an Agitator* (1958); Arnon Gutfeld, "The Murder of Frank Little," *Labor History* (Spring 1969).

Donald G. Sofchalk

LIVINGSTON, John William (1908–   ). Born in Iberia, Mo., August 17, 1908; son of Richard Monroe, a farmer, and Mary Alice (Burks) Livingston; married Rubye Britt on May 9, 1931; attended high school for two years, then secured employment with the Fisher Body Division of the General Motors Corporation (GMC) in St. Louis, Mo.; helped organize American Federation of Labor (AFL) federal Union 18386, which later became St. Louis Local 25 of the United Automobile, Aircraft, Agricultural Implement Workers of America (UAW); elected president of federal Union 18386 in 1934; was chairman of Local 25's strike committee during the successful strikes against GMC for recognition in 1936–1937; became a UAW international representative in 1939 and served until elected director of UAW Region 5 and member of the international executive board in 1942; served as vice-chairman and chairman of the national UAW-GMC negotiating committee, 1939–1942; was a regional panel member of the National War Labor Board and chairman of the Kansas City Office of Price Administration Labor Advisory Committee during World War II; became co-director, along with Walter P. Reuther (q.v.), of the UAW's GMC department in 1946; elected a UAW vice-president in 1947, and, at the same time, became director of the UAW aircraft, airline, McQuay-Norris, and piston ring department; appointed director of the UAW's agricultural implement department in 1948; named to the National Wage Stabilization Board in 1951; chaired a 12-

member UAW delegation to visit various European countries in 1950 as guests of the British Amalgamated Engineering Union; later in the same year, presided in Paris over initial meeting of the automotive and truck department of the International Metalworkers Federation; became sole director of the UAW's GMC department in 1952; retired his UAW vice-presidency in 1955 and became director of organization of the newly merged AFL-Congress of Industrial Organizations, serving in that capacity until retirement in 1965; appointed director of union relations of the National Alliance of Businessmen in 1968; usually supported the Democratic party; Frank Cormier and William J. Eaton, *Reuther* (1970); Jack Stieber, *Governing the UAW* (1962); *Current Biography* (1959); Nelson Lichtenstein, *Labor's War at Home: The CIO in World War II* (1982); Roger Keeran, *The Communist Party and the Auto Workers Unions* (1980).

LLOYD, Thomas John   (1895–   ). Born in Spanish Forks, Utah, November 13, 1895; son of William E. and Isabelle (Spens) Lloyd; married Ethel M. Foyer; three children; at age 12, while still attending school, began work as a helper in a slaughterhouse in Mammoth, Utah; completed a high school education, then started working full-time as a meat cutter with the Mammoth Supply Company, continuing in that capacity until 1917; served with the U.S. Navy during World War I, 1917–1919; after the war, in 1919–1921, became head meat cutter for the Valley Supply Company in Utah; after securing employment as a retail butcher with Stanford Market Company in Salt Lake City, Utah, in 1921, joined Local 537 of the Amalgamated Meat Cutters and Butcher Workmen of America (AMCBWNA); was store manager of the Stanford Market Company, 1921–1931; elected president of Local 537 in 1924; served as its secretary (chief administrative officer), 1931–1933; became an international vice-president of the AMCBWNA in 1933; was appointed director of the AMCBWNA's packinghouse workers' department in Chicago, Ill., in 1956; after the death of Earl W. Jimerson (q.v.), was elected international president of the AMCBWNA in 1957; helped negotiate a merger between the AMCBWNA and the United Packinghouse Workers of America in 1968; retired from union positions in 1972; David Brody, *The Butcher Workmen: A Study of Unionization* (1964); *AFL-CIO News*, November 9, 1957; *Who's Who in America, 1972–1973*.

LONDON, Meyer   (1871–1926). Born in Suwalki, Russia, December 29, 1871; son of Ephraim, an intellectual and social radical, and Rebecca (Berson) London; Jewish; married Anna Rosenson in 1890; one child; received both a public and private education; emigrated with his family to the United States in 1891, settling in New York City; attended law school there at night and admitted to the bar of the state of New York in 1898; joined the Socialist Labor party (SLP) and in 1896 received its nomination for the New York assembly; broke with SLP leader Daniel DeLeon (q.v.) in 1897 and became associated with the newly organized Social Democratic party; was one of the founding members of the Socialist party of America in 1901; was a leading figure in the movement to organize the needle trades and served them as legal counsel for nearly three decades; supported strikes, participated in negotiations, and was an inspiring and effective speaker in behalf of trade union causes; was a leader of the New York City garment workers' strike of 1910; elected to the U.S. Congress on the Socialist party ticket from New York's Ninth Congressional District in 1914 and served two terms before being defeated for reelection in 1918, primarily as a result of his opposition to American intervention in World War I and his vote against the declaration of war; reelected in 1920, but defeated in 1922 after his congressional district had been radically gerrymandered; during three terms in Congress, supported a variety of labor and social reforms, including anti-lynching measures, old-age pensions, and child labor reforms; was involved in numerous Jewish organizations, notably the Workmen's Circle; died as a result of an automobile accident in New York City, June 6, 1926; Melech Epstein, *Profiles of Eleven* (1965) and *Jewish Labor in the U.S.A., 1914–1952*, 2 Vols. (1953); Harry Rogoff, *An East Side Epic* (1930); *Dictionary of American Biography*, Vol. 11.

LONG, Bob G.   (1927–   ). Born in Vinita, Okla., on September 1, 1927; son of Art L. and Pearl Long; married Sharon Long, a homemaker, in 1966; two children; graduated from Vinita High School in 1946; after completing a four-year term of service in the U.S. Air Force, he took a job in the rubber industry and joined Local 318 of the United Rubber, Cork, Linoleum and Plastic Workers of America (URW); was elected president of Local 318 in 1955, serving in that position until being appointed an international URW field representative in 1962; meanwhile, he served as recording secretary of the Ottawa, Craig and Delaware County Labor Council, 1955–1961; served as assistant to the director of URW District 4, 1967–1970; was appointed a special URW representative in 1970 and two years later was selected by URW president Peter Bommarito (q.v.) to serve as his assistant and advisor; became organizing director of the URW in 1977; arguing that Bommarito was "more of a showman than an administrator" who had lost touch with rank-and-file workers, he challenged the incumbent in the 1978 URW elections; although the reform ticket lost by a 60–40 percent margin, the strength of the opposition forced the URW leadership to reassess its bargaining approach—particularly demands for increased local autonomy— and Bommarito retired three years later and was replaced by Milan O. Stone (q.v.), who defeated another reform candidate for the URW presidency; *Business Week*, September 18, October 30, 1978; *Chemical Week*, October 21, 1981; *Who's Who in Labor* (1976).

LOVESTONE, Jay   (1898–   ). Born Jacob Leibstein in Lithuania in 1898; Jewish; married; emigrated to the United States with his family in 1908 and changed his name to Jay Lovestone; attended public schools in New York City and then graduated from the City College of New York; became a left-wing Socialist during his college days and, in 1919, was one of the founders of the

American Communist party; became the editor of the party's theoretical journal and served as its first general secretary; a vigorous participant in the factional struggles that disrupted the Communist movement during the 1920s, he found himself on the losing side and was ousted from office at the 1928 Communist International Congress; thereafter he led a small group of anti-Stalinist "Lovestonites"; attracted by Lovestone's knowlege of Communist tactics and procedures, David Dubinsky (q.v.), president of the International Ladies' Garment Workers' Union (ILGWU), appointed him to his union's international affairs program, and, in 1943, he became director of international affairs for the ILGWU; participated in the ILGWU's efforts to assist European labor leaders escape from Axis countries and in the recruitment of many of them into the Office of Strategic Services; became a close personal friend of American Federation of Labor (AFL) secretary-treasurer George Meany (q.v.) during the early 1940s and when, in 1944, the AFL took a leading role in the establishment of the Free Trade Union Committee (FTUC) in opposition to the Communist-dominated World Federation of Trade Unions, he became its executive secretary; after the FTUC was reorganized as the International Confederation of Free Trade Unions in 1949, he became its director and retained that position until 1963 when he was named director of the AFL-Congress of Industrial Organizations (CIO) department of international affairs; a virulent anti-Communist by midcentury, he actively cooperated with the U.S. Central Intelligence Agency—which subsidized FTUC activities—in its European and Latin American anti-Communist activities; participated in the organization of the American Institute for Free Labor Development (AIFLD) in 1961 and developed its program to counter Communist influence in Latin America, train labor leaders, and promote American-style union programs such as credit unions, banks, and the like; paticipated in the organization of the African-American Labor Center which was to do in Africa what AIFLD was doing in Latin America; retired as director of the AFL-CIO department of international affairs in 1974, but continued his association with the AFL-CIO as a consultant and a lecturer on international affairs at the AFL-CIO Labor Studies Center; Ronald Radosh, *American Labor and United States Foreign Policy: The Cold War in the Unions from Gompers to Lovestone* (1969); Philip Taft, *Defending Freedom: American Labor and Foreign Affairs* (1973); *AFL-CIO News*, June 1, 1974; Eleanora W. Schoenebaum, ed., *Political Profiles: The Truman Years* (1978), and *Political Profiles: The Eisenhower Years* (1977); Nelson Lichtenstein, ed., *Political Profiles: The Kennedy Years* (1976), and *Political Profiles: The Johnson Years* (1976); Harvey Klehr, "Leninism and Lovestoneism," *Studies in Comparative Communism* (1974); Harvey A. Levenstein, *Communism, Anticommunism, and the CIO* (1981); Bert Cochran, *Labor and Communism: The Conflict that Shaped American Unions* (1977).

LUCIA, Carmen   (1902–   ). Born in Calabria, Italy, on April 3, 1902; daughter of Raefaelio J. and Angela (Rizzo) Lucia; Presbyterian; married Leo Kowski in 1931; one child; completed a sixth grade education in Catholic schools in Rochester, N.Y., and completed high school at the Rochester Business Institute; attended Bryn Mawr Summer School for Women Workers in 1927 and 1930; first served as a spokesman for the Amalgamated Clothing Workers of America (ACWA) in a 1924 Rochester strike; secretary to Abraham Chapman, ACWA Rochester vice-president, 1925–1930; became an organizer for the Independent Neckwear Workers in 1930; organized for the ACWA in 1934; became an organizer for the United Hatters, Cap and Millinery Workers' Union (UHCMW) in 1934 and continued her association with the Hatters until 1974; under the mentorship of Max Zaritsky (q.v.), she rose to the position of vice-president and member of the UHCMW general board in 1946; served on the board of the Affiliated Summer School for Workers in Industry, Inc., and the Bryn Mawr Summer School for Women Workers; was active with the Georgia Workers' Education Service, vice-president of the National Young Women's Christian Association, a member of the Industrial Workers Recreation Association and the League of Women Voters, and during World War II chaired the Atlanta Committee for United War Relief; she supervised the UHCMW's southern organizing drive and chaired the Georgia Federation of Labor's organization committee; because of these activities, she was appointed a member of the American Federation of Labor's southern policy committee; in 1950 she traveled to France as a delegate for the U.S. Department of State's Economic Cooperation Administration and designed and helped to establish a program under which French workers would come to the United States and attend labor education classes while working in American industry; retired in 1974; Carmen Lucia Papers, Southern Labor Archives, Georgia State University; *Who's Who in Labor* (1946); *Hat Worker*, September 15, 1951.

Faye Phillips

LUHRSEN, Julius G.   (1877–1956). Born in Des Plaines, Ill., April 1, 1877; son of Henry W., a hardware merchant, and Louise (Henningsmeyer) Luhrsen; Evangelical Lutheran; married Josephine Cross on December 23, 1900; two children; while attending grammar school, worked on a farm and studied telegraphy at night; became a telegrapher on the Illinois Central Railroad at age 16; moved somewhat later to the Northern Pacific Railroad and was promoted to dispatcher; despite great employer resistance and blacklisting threats, organized the American Train Dispatchers Association (ATDA) in Spokane, Wash., in 1917; was elected the first president of ATDA and held that position until obtaining a leave of absence in 1938; was executive secretary of the Railway Labor Executives' Association during 1938–1945; named by President Franklin D. Roosevelt to the Railroad Retirement Board in 1945; served on a large number of government boards and agencies during World War II; retired union positions in 1950; was a Republican; died in Chicago, Ill., October 16, 1956; *Who's Who in Labor* (1946); *Labor,* October 20, 1956.

LUNA, Charles   (1906–   ). Born in Celeste, Tex., October 21, 1906; son of Charles and Lillie (Green) Luna; married Opal Lewis on November 29, 1929;

two children; after graduating from high school, secured employment as a yard-man on the Santa Fe Railroad in 1925; joined East Dallas, Tex., Local 671 of the Brotherhood of Railroad Trainmen (BRT) in 1929; was a member of the BRT grievance committee for the Santa Fe Railroad, 1936–1946, and served as chairman of the committee, 1904–1946; worked as a national BRT organizer, 1943–1946; became general BRT chairman of the Gulf, Colorado, and Santa Fe Railroad in 1947, serving until 1954; was a member of the national wage-rules committee in 1949 and 1953; served as chairman of the International Association of General Chairmen, 1951–1955; was elected a BRT vice-president in 1954; served as assistant to BRT president William P. Kennedy (q.v.), 1960–1963, and was elected president in 1963; was a founder and was elected first president of the United Transportation Union (UTU), created by the merger of the BRT, the Brotherhood of Locomotive Firemen and Enginemen, the Order of Railway Conductors, and the Switchmen's Union of North America in 1969; was elected chairman of the Congress of Railway Unions created by the UTU, the Brotherhood of Maintenance of Way Employees, the Brotherhood of Railway and Airline Clerks, the Hotel and Restaurant Employees Union, and the Seafarers International Union of North America in 1969; resigned the presidency of the UTU in 1972; after retiring, as required by the UTU constitution, named vice-president and director of transportation for the Stirling Homex Corporation; Joel Seidman, *The Brotherhood of Railroad Trainmen: The Internal Political Life of a National Union* (1962); *Who's Who in America, 1972–1973; AFL-CIO News,* January 5, 1963, August 14, 1971.

LUNDEBERG, Harry   (1901–1951). Born in Oslo, Norway, March 25, 1901; son of Karl, a small businessman and syndicalist, and Allette (Koffeld) Lundeberg, an official of the Norwegian Labor party; was married and had three children; after completing grammar school education, began work at age 14 as a sailor on sailing ships; during a 19-year period at sea, joined a variety of unions, including the Norwegian and British maritime unions, a Spanish syndicalist union, and the Industrial Workers of the World; decided in 1923 to sail only from the port of Seattle, Wash., and transferred his membership from the Australian Seamen's Union to the Sailors Union of the Pacific (SUP) in 1926; rose to prominence during the West Coast waterfront strike of 1934 as an associate of Harry Bridges (q.v.), the West Coast labor leader; was elected business agent of the Seattle local of the SUP in 1935; became the president of the Maritime Federation of the Pacific in 1936, but resigned shortly because of break with Bridges over personal and ideological differences; became secretary-treasurer of the SUP in 1936; founded and became first president of the American Federation of Labor (AFL)-affiliated Seafarers International Union of North America in 1938; led his union in a series of postwar strikes that provided substantial improvements in wage scales and working conditions; served as a vice-president of the California State Federation of Labor during the 1940s; was an officer of the AFL maritime trades council and, after the merger of the AFL and the

Congress of Industrial Organizations (CIO), became president of the AFL-CIO maritime trades department; was a radical anti-capitalist early in his career, but became a vitriolic anti-Communist in the late 1930s and a conservative Republican in the 1950s; edited the *West Coast Sailors* for several years; died in Burlingame, Calif., January 28, 1951; Joseph P. Goldberg, *The Maritime Story: A Study in Labor-Management Relations* (1958); Charles P. Larrowe, *Harry Bridges: The Rise and Fall of Radical Labor in the U.S.* (1972); *Current Biography* (1952); *Dictionary of American Biography*, Suppl. 6.

LUTHER, Seth (fl. 1817–1846). Born in Providence, R.I., toward the end of the eighteenth century; son of an American Revolutionary War veteran; received very little formal education; was probably a Baptist; after an extensive trip down the Ohio River in 1817, returned to New England and worked as a carpenter; as an early advocate of labor reform, traveled widely in support of the workingmen's cause and was a gifted orator, agitator, and publicist; condemned factory working conditions in an address delivered to striking workers during a ten-hour strike in Boston, Mass., in 1832; after publication and reprinting of the address, won immediate recognition as a leading New England labor agitator; after addressing the second convention of the New England Association of Farmers, Mechanics, and Other Working Men in the autumn of 1832, developed a close working relationship with Dr. Charles Douglas (q.v.), a leading Boston unionist; helped organize, along with Douglas, the short-lived Boston Trades' Union in 1934; represented the house carpenters at the founding convention of the Boston Trades' Union and was elected its secretary; during the Boston ten-hour strike of 1835, coauthored the *Ten Hour Circular*, which had a profound impact on the national ten-hour movement, but despite the circular and other extensive efforts in behalf of the strike, could not prevent its failure; was a delegate to the New York meeting of the National Trades' Union in 1836; addressed the convention on factory conditions and the ten-hour day and served on the ways and means committee; was arrested and imprisoned as a result of activities on behalf of the free suffrage movement in Rhode Island in the 1840s; was still agitating for the ten-hour day, in this case in New Hampshire, as late as 1846; authored several pamphlets, including *An Address on the Right of Free Suffrage* (1833) and *An Address Delivered Before the Mechanics and Workingmen of the City of Brooklyn* (1836); Louis Hartz, "Seth Luther: The Story of a Working Class Rebel," *New England Quarterly* (September 1940); Edward Pessen, *Most Uncommon Jacksonians: The Radical Leaders of the Early Labor Movement* (1967); John R. Commons et al., eds., *A Documentary History of American Industrial Society*, Vols. 5, 6, 8 (1910–1911); *Dictionary of American Biography*, Vol. 11.

LYDEN, Michael J. (1879–1973). Born in Barnikelle, County Mayo, Ireland, in 1879; son of Patrick, a farmer, and Mary Lyden; Roman Catholic; married Mary Jane Burke, a precinct committeewoman, in 1911; was forced by economic necessity to leave school at age 14 to work on the family farm; emigrated to the United States in 1899, settling in Philadelphia, Pa.; worked there as a common laborer; took a job in the Carnegie Steel Works at Youngstown, Ohio, in 1903, and later that year became a streetcar operator; joined the Amalgamated Association of Street, Electric Railway and Motor Coach Employees of America and helped negotiate the Youngstown local's first contract; elected shortly thereafter as president of the local and served in that postiion for 30 years; elected secretary of the Youngstown Labor Congress in 1912, and a vice-president of the Ohio State Federation of Labor (OSFL) in 1924; was a pioneer labor lobbyist in Ohio for such reforms as workmen's compensation; admired Samuel Gompers (q.v.), but was a militant unionist concerned with the welfare of all workers; during the 1930s, helped to organize steelworkers, as well as the crafts, in the Youngstown industrial area; during the bitter "Little Steel" strike of 1937, supported the Steel Workers Organizing Committee; became president of the OSFL in 1935 and served continuously in that post until 1958; in later years, was instrumental in bringing about the merger of the American Federation of Labor (AFL) and Congress of Industrial Organizations (CIO) state bodies to form the Ohio AFL-CIO, and elected its president; resigned from this post in 1960, but remained active in union affairs for another decade as a member of the Greater Youngstown AFL-CIO Council; throughout his career, deeply involved in civic affairs and political organizations; helped found and was secretary of the Federated Improvement Clubs; was an ardent promoter of public libraries and scholarship programs; was very active in local and state Democratic party affairs; revered as the "grand old man" of Ohio labor; died in Youngstown, Ohio, February 12, 1973; *AFL-CIO News,* June 18, 1960; *Steel Labor* (December 1960).

Donald G. Sofchalk

LYNCH, James Mathew   (1867–1930). Born in Manlius, N.Y., January 11, 1867; son of James and Sarah (Caulfield) Lynch; Roman Catholic; married Letitia C. McVey on June 28, 1899; nine children; after attending the public schools of Manlius, became a "printer's devil" in the offices of the *Syracuse* (N.Y.) *Evening Herald* in 1884; joined the Syracuse local of the International Typographical Union (ITU) in 1887 and soon became secretary and then vice-president of the local; elected president of the Syracuse local in 1889 and served two terms; was president of the Syracuse Central Trades and Labor Assembly for seven terms; elected first vice-president of the ITU in 1898 and president two years later; led ITU during a period when it won an eight-hour day, established an old-age pension system, reformed its apprentice educational system, and doubled its membership; resigned in 1914 when appointed New York Commissioner of Labor; was named one of five commissioners of the newly merged New York Department of Labor and New York Industrial Commission; served as a commissioner until 1921; after serving as president of the American Life Society, a mutual insurance company, for one year, was again chosen ITU president in 1924 and served until reelection defeat in 1926; appointed to the New York Old Age Security Commission in 1929; was a Democrat; edited the *Advocate*, a Syracuse labor newspaper, in 1930; died in Syracuse, N.Y., July 16, 1930; Seymour M. Lipset et al., *Union Democracy: The Internal Politics of the International Typographical Union* (1956); Irwin Yellowitz, *Labor and the Progressive Movement in New York State, 1897–1916* (1965); *Dictionary of American Biography*, Vol. 11.

LYON, Arlon Everett (1899–). Born in Thedford, Neb., October 15, 1899; son of Alfred S. and Mable (Wright) Lyon; entered the U.S. Army in 1918 shortly after completing his formal education; after discharge in 1919, secured employment in the signal department of the Southern Pacific Railroad; joined the Brotherhood of Railroad Signalmen of America (BRS) in 1920; elected local chairman for the Southern Pacific Railroad in 1924, serving in that capacity until 1927; became assistant grand president of the BRS in 1927; elected grand president of the BRS in 1934; became a vice-president of the Rail Labor Executives' Association in 1940; served during World War II as an alternate member of the National Labor-Manpower Policy Committee and the War Manpower Commission; was executive secretary of the Railway Labor Executives' Association, 1945–1962; appointed by President John F. Kennedy as the labor member of the tripartite Railroad Retirement Board in 1962, serving until 1969; retired from union activities in 1969; served as a member of the executive committee of the International Transport Workers Federation; *Who's Who in Railroading* (1959); *Who's Who in Labor* (1946).

LYONS, John H. (1919–). Born in Cleveland, Ohio, October 29, 1919; son of John H., international president of the International Association of Bridge, Structural, and Ornamental Iron Workers (IABSOIW), and Elizabeth M. (Sexton) Lyons; married Dorothy Ann Boyen on April 15, 1944; two children; secured employment as an iron worker while working for a B.S. degree in mechanical engineering from the University of Missouri's School of Mines; joined the IABSOIW in 1937; received the B.S. degree in 1942; joined the U.S. Air Force in 1943, serving until 1946; was employed by the General Bronze Corporation, New York City, 1946–1954; became an international representative and general organizer for the IABSOIW in 1954; elected a general IABSOIW vice-president in 1959, and in 1961 chosen international president; became a member of the internal disputes panel and a vice-president of both the American Federation of Labor-Congress of Industrial Organizations' (AFL-CIO) metal trades department and the building and construction trades department in 1961; was appointed to the citizens' advisory committee of the President's Commission on Juvenile Delinquency and to the advisory council of the Bureau of Employment Security in 1962; served as a member of the Taft-Hartley Labor-Management Panel and of the National Advisory Manpower Committee in 1963, as chairman of the labor advisory committee of the President's Committee on Equal Employment

Opportunity in 1964, and on the National Commission on Urban Problems in 1967; elected an AFL-CIO vice-president and executive council member in 1967; *AFL-CIO News*, September 16, 1967; *Who's Who in America, 1972–1973*; Joseph C. Goulden, *Meany* (1972).

M

McANINCH, Elisha H. (1841–1922). Born in Pittsburgh, Pa., on September 9, 1841; son of Elisha H., a hotel owner and "proprietor of an omnibus line" on Pittsburgh's south side, and Martha (Clemens) McAninch; Roman Catholic; married Catherine M. Bracken on January 5, 1865; adopted six children; educated in the Pittsburgh public schools; enlisted as a musician and served as a private in the Seventh Regiment and later the Sixty-third Regiment of the Pennsylvania Volunteers, 1861–1864; spent some time as chief bugler; prisoner of war at Belle Isle and Libby Prison; joined the United Sons of Vulcan in 1867 and was appointed first district deputy in 1875; introduced a resolution admitting helpers to the union, which tripled its numerical strength; representative to the Second Joint Committee on Amalgamation of the ironworkers' unions in 1875 and represented the puddlers on the committee drafting a constitution and bylaws; first district vice-president, Amalgamated Association of Iron and Steel Workers (AA) in 1876; served on numerous scale and conference committees of the AA throughout the 1880s; antagonistic toward AA officer, William Martin (q.v.); served as contract labor inspector in 1892; caterer and musician who was associated with numerous bands and was the leader of the Great Eastern Band of Allegheny for five years; organized the Pioneer Catholic Temperance Society at St. Malachi's Church in 1871; joined the Grand Army of the Republic, Post No. 155, in 1902, and served as post commander in 1908; general superintendent, Columbus Club, 1908; contributor to the *National Labor Tribune*; died in Pittsburgh on May 7, 1922; *Vulcan Record*, 1867–1875; John W. Jordan, comp., *A Century and a Half of Pittsburgh and Her People* (1908).

Sharon Trusilo

MacAULEY, Robert Calvin (fl. 1840–1871). Born in County Antrim, Ireland, February 2, 1840; married; had strong taste for mathematics and wonderful memory; before leaving Ireland could repeat large portions of the Bible and Burns's poems; emigrated at age 9 to Philadelphia, Pa., September 2, 1849; attended Nixon Street School; at 11 was apprenticed to a tailor, whom he shortly left because of the tailor's drunkenness; worked with other tailors for three years; at age 21, started in business; in 1865, joined the brotherhood of the union; in 1866, giving up business, became a foreman, and joined Garment Cutters' Association; was chosen its secretary in 1867, and held the office until its dissolution; about this time joined the Knights of Pythias; was first secretary of Knights of Labor; opened business with a partner, as R. C. Macauley & Co., which in time became the headquarters of the Knights of Labor; was chosen master workman in 1871, succeeding his partner Mr. Stephens; during his administration a second union was formed, Ship Carpenters and Caulkers No. 2; gave up business and became foreman in wholesale clothing house; George E. McNeill, *The Labor Movement: The Problem of To-Day* (1887); David Montgomery, *Beyond Equality: Labor and the Radical Republicans, 1862–1872* (1967).

George E. McNeill

McAVOY, Harold   (1904–1968). Born in Philadelphia, Pa., November 5, 1904; son of Thomas and Mary (Owens) McAvoy; Roman Catholic; married Jean A. Buechner on June 22, 1928; one child; after graduating from high school, attended Hefley Business School; secured employment with the U.S. Postal Service in New York City and joined the New York City branch of the National Association of Post Office and Railway Handlers (NAPORH); elected president of the New York branch shortly after NAPORH's affiliation with the American Federation of Labor (AFL) in 1937; elected NAPORH national president in 1941 and served in that capacity until his death; was a NAPORH delegate to the annual conventions of the AFL, 1942–1952, and to the biennial conventions of the AFL-Congress of Industrial Organizations, 1955–1967; led the NAPORH into a merger with the International Hod Carriers', Building and Common Laborers' Union of America in 1968; died in New York City, December 2, 1968; *Who's Who in America, 1968–1969*; *AFL-CIO News*, December 7, 1968.

McBRIDE, John   (1854–1917). Born in Wayne County, Ohio, July 25, 1854; went to work in the coal mines at age 9; joined the Ohio Miners' Amalgamated Association in 1870, and was elected president in 1883; was elected to the Ohio legislature in 1883 and 1885, but was an unsuccessful Democratic candidate for Ohio secretary of state in 1886; organized the Amalgamated Association of Miners of the United States in 1883, but the six-month Hocking Valley, Ohio, coal strike destroyed it; was one of the founders and was elected president of the National Federation of Miners and Mine Laborers in 1885; served as temporary chairman of the American Federation of Labor's (AFL) founding convention in 1886; unsuccessfully sought the AFL's endorsement for U.S. Commissioner of Labor in 1888; was chosen president of the new National Progressive Union of Miners and Mine Laborers, formed by the National Federation of Miners' leaders and a splinter group of Knights of Labor Assembly 135; led a unity convention with John B. Rae of Assembly 135 and established the United Mine Workers of America (UMWA) in 1890, with Rae as its president;

was himself elected president by 1892 convention after Rae lost strikes in 1890 and 1891 and refused to run for reelection; served until 1895, then resigned to serve a one-year term as president of the AFL; served as UMWA head during the depression of 1893–1897, which resulted in unemployment, falling wages, and desperate straits for miners; an eight-week strike of one hundred thousand miners in 1894 to deplete coal stocks and raise coal prices and wages was destroyed by an influx of non-union Pennsylvania anthracite and West Virginia bituminous coal into the market; during the administrations of McBride and his successor, Phil Penna, UMWA's membership fell from 13,000 to 9,731 and its treasury from $2,600 to $600; lost to Samuel Gompers (q.v.) by 18 votes in his bid for reelection to the AFL presidency in 1895; was a principal organizer of a convention of Ohio trade unionists that endorsed the People's party Omaha platform with the addition of several labor planks and nominated a Populist-Labor state ticket that polled 5 percent of Ohio's vote; purchased the *Columbus* (Ohio) *Record*, a weekly newspaper, in 1896 and edited the paper until moving to Arizona in 1917 due to poor health; died in Globe, Ariz., in October 1917; Philip Taft, *The A.F. of L. in the Time of Gompers* (1957); McAlister Coleman, *Men and Coal* (1943); Charles A. Madison, *American Labor Leaders: Person-alities and Forces in the Labor Movement* (1950); John H. M. Laslett, *Labor and the Left: A Study of Socialism and Radical Influences in the American Labor Movement, 1881–1924* (1970).

                                                                John W. Hevener

McBRIDE, Lloyd   (1916–1983). Born in Farmington, Mo., on March 9, 1916; son of a painter in a steel fabricating plant; married Dolores Neihaus in 1937; two children; attended public schools in St. Louis through junior high school when, at age 14, his father lost his job and he was forced to leave school and go to work, ultimately securing work at a much lower wage at the same plant that had laid off his father; joined the Steel Workers Organizing Committee (SWOC) in 1936 and was a charter member of Local 1295 which negotiated the first collective bargaining contract with the Foster Brothers Manufacturing Company in St. Louis; when Local 1295 called a strike a year later, he helped organize a sit-down to discourage strike breakers and soon thereafter, at age 22, was elected president of Local 1295; also served as SWOC voluntary organizer until 1940 when he was appointed a staff representative and paid organizer; elected president of the St. Louis Industrial Union Council, Congress of Industrial Organizations (CIO), in 1940 and served in that position until 1942 when he was elected president of the Missouri State Industrial Council, CIO; resigned his union positions in 1944 and enlisted in the U.S. Navy; after being discharged from military service in 1946, he was appointed a United Steelworkers of America (USWA) staff representative in Granite City, Ill. (the USWA was chartered by the CIO in 1942, replacing the SWOC); appointed a USWA subdistrict director in 1958 and in 1965 became director of USWA District 34, which had its headquarters in St. Louis and covered southern Illinois, Missouri, Kansas, Nebraska, and Iowa; an aggressive organizer, effective administrator, and tough bargainer, he soon reinvigorated organizing efforts in his district, adding several thousand new members to the union's ranks; while serving as director of District 34, he also, at various times, was involved as secretary and/or chairman of collective bargaining negotiations with ARMCO Steel Corporation and American Steel Foundries; served as chairman of the USWA Foundry and Forgings Industry Conference and the Lead Industry Conference; defeated Edward Sadlowski for the USWA presidency in 1977 after a hotly contested campaign that attracted national attention; a supporter of the collaborationist policies of the retiring president, I. W. Abel (q.v.), he vowed to continue the Experimental Negotiating Agreement with the steel industry as long as, in his opinion, it served the best interest of the membership; after assuming the presidency, he placed his greatest emphasis on job security, a more active political policy, a reinvigorated organizing effort in fabricating industries, and improved working conditions; was elected an American Federation of Labor (AFL)-CIO vice-president and executive council member in 1977; also served on the executive board of the AFL-CIO industrial union department, the board of directors of the American Arbitration Association, the U.S. Department of Labor's labor advisory committee, the Committee for National Health Insurance, the advisory board of the Salvation Army, and the Harry S. Truman Library Institute; served as a vice-president of the American Immigration and Citizenship Conference; served as a delegate to the International Metalworkers Federation meeting in Geneva, Switzerland, and was appointed to the Advisory Council for Trade Negotiations by President Jimmy Carter in 1977; retired his USWA presidency in 1981; a Democrat; died in Whitehall, Pa., on November 6, 1983; *Current Biography* (1979); *Steel Labor* (June 1977); *The New York Times*, February 11, 1977.

McCARTHY, Patrick Henry   (1863–1933). Born in Killoughteen, Newcastle West, County Limerick, Ireland, March 17, 1863; son of Patrick and Eileen McCarthy; Roman Catholic; married Jeanette H. Saunders on January 15, 1905; attended the national schools of Ireland and learned the carpenters' trade before emigrating to the United States in 1880; resided in Chicago, Ill., and St. Louis, Mo., for six years, then moved to San Francisco, Calif., and joined the United Brotherhood of Carpenters and Joiners of America (UBC); organized and became the president of the Building Trades Council of San Francisco in 1894 and the State Building Trades Council of California in 1901; elected a member of the UBC executive board in 1904; was one of the founders and became the first president of the Building Trades Temple Association of San Francisco in 1908; served on the Freeholders Committee that framed the charter for the city of San Francisco prior to his election as mayor in 1909 on the Union Labor party ticket; served a two-year term as mayor; acquired near-monopoly control of the construction industry of San Francisco before being deposed by a coalition of businessmen and financiers in 1922; retired from union positions in 1923 and became involved in the investment banking business; identified himself as a Republican;

died in San Francisco, Calif., June 30, 1933; Robert A. Christie, *Empire in Wood: A History of the Carpenters' Union* (1956); Ira B. Cross, *A History of the Labor Movement in California* (1935); Walton Bean, *Boss Ruef's San Francisco: The Story of the Union Labor Party, Big Business, and the Graft Prosecution* (1952); L. A. O'Donnell, "The Greening of a Limerick Man: Patrick Henry McCarthy," *Eire-Ireland* (Summer 1976).

McCLENNAN, William Howard   (1907–   ). Born in Boston, Mass., on September 11, 1907; son of Samuel T., a school custodian, and Mary (Donahue) McClennan, a homemaker; married Muriel, a homemaker, in 1933; two children; graduated from Boston High School, attended Boston University, and participated in labor programs at the University of Massachusetts, Harvard University, and the University of Connecticut; employed as a manager for United Markets, before joining the Boston Fire Department as a fire fighter in 1942; joined the International Association of Fire Fighters (IAFF) in 1942; elected president of the IAFF in 1968; elected president of the newly chartered American Federation of Labor-Congress of Industrial Organizations (AFL-CIO) public employee department in 1974; elected an AFL-CIO vice-president and executive council member in 1977; served on a number of federal commissions dealing with fire prevention and training and was vice-chairman of the National Commission on Fire Prevention and Control which campaigned successfully for the Federal Fire Prevention and Control Act of 1974; active in a variety of professional and civic affairs, he was appointed director of the National Burn Center, 1972, the Muscular Dystrophy Association, 1968, and served as vice-chairman of the National Committee on Fire Safety, 1970–1972; *Who's Who in Labor* (1976); *AFL-CIO News*, March 5, 1977.

McCREERY, Marie Maud Leonard   (1883–1938). Born in Cedarburg, Wis., on February 24, 1883; daughter of Sylvester S., a stockbreeder and veterinary surgeon, and Anna Reilly Leonard; reared a Roman Catholic; married Rex Irving McCreery, an attorney, on November 28, 1902; one child who died in infancy; divorced in June 1918, after a lengthy separation; married James Walter Walker, a carpenter, on October 17, 1923; no children; divorced in 1941 after another lengthy separation during which she claimed to have been abandoned; after attending Wauwatosa (Wis.) High School for one year, her mother's prolonged illness forced her to leave school and assume household responsibilities; moved to Green Bay, Wis., in 1911, where she helped organize the Brown County Political Equality League and became active in the Wisconsin Woman Suffrage Association; contracted tuberculosis in 1917 and spent several months in a sanitarium; after her release, she dropped her previous Democratic party associations and joined the Socialist party of America; became the women's page editor of the *Milwaukee Leader*, edited by Victor Berger (q.v.), in 1917; joined Newspaper Writers Union No. 9, an American Federation of Labor (AFL) affiliate, and became actively involved in its affairs; actively supported the railroad shop strikes in Milwaukee in 1918 and 1922; became an organizer for the Amalgamated Clothing Workers of America in 1927, covering Milwaukee and Waukegan, Ill.; joined Stenographers, Typewriters, Bookkeepers, and Assistants Union No. 16456, an AFL federal labor union, in 1929; became editor-in-chief of the *New Deal*, a weekly newspaper established by the Sheboygan (Wis.) Central Labor Union, from the pages of which she criticized Franklin D. Roosevelt and New Deal policies; was actively involved in the prolonged strike and boycott against the Kohler Company, a plumbing manufacturer; failing health in 1936 forced her to reduce drastically her organizing and editorial duties; as her health permitted during the next two years she campaigned for the Farmer-Labor Progressive Federation; served as an organizer for the stenographers' union, and worked as an instructor at the University of Wisconsin's School for Workers in Milwaukee; although at various times a Democrat and a supporter of La Follette's Progressive party politics, she was a Socialist during much of her life; died in Milwaukee on April 10, 1938; *Notable American Women*, Vol. 2; Milwaukee *Leader* (April 11–13, 1938); Walter H. Uphoff, *The Kohler Strike: Its Socio-Economic Causes and Effects* (1966); *Dictionary of Wisconsin Biography* (1960).

McCURDY, Joseph Patrick   (1892–1977). Born in Baltimore, Md., March 20, 1892; son of John Andrew, superintendent of parks, and Mary Ellen McCurdy; Roman Catholic; married Genevieve Elizabeth Birrane on February 24, 1938; two children; completed grammar school and took night courses at Baltimore Business College; joined Local 15 of the United Garment Workers of America in 1910; elected business representative of Local 15 in 1925, serving until 1941; served as president of the Maryland State Federation of Labor and the District of Columbia Federation of Labor, 1932–1942; elected president of the Baltimore Federation of Labor in 1933, serving until 1942; was the American Federation of Labor (AFL) fraternal delegate to the Canadian Trades and Labor Congress in 1934; served as a member of the Maryland Unemployment Compensation Board, 1937–1951; appointed to the National Labor Relations Regional Board in 1939; helped draft the Maryland old-age pension law and served on state commissions concerned with workmen's compensation, occupational diseases, and unemployment; served as AFL fraternal delegate to the British Trades Union Congress in 1950; served as vice-president of the AFL union label trades department; elected international president of the UGW in 1950; authored "Reasons Why Labor Should Oppose Prohibition"; politically a Democrat; died in Baltimore, Md., on November 12, 1977; *Who's Who in Labor* (1946); *Who's Who in America, 1972–1973*; *AFL-CIO News*, November 19, 1977.

McDEVITT, James Lawrence   (1898–1963). Born in Philadelphia, Pa., November 3, 1898; son of William Paul, a plasterer, and Sarah Margaret (Hickey) McDevitt; Roman Catholic; married Margaret Winifred Murphy on January 25, 1921, and, after her death, Margaret Mary Toole on January 3, 1953; three children; attended Catholic parochial schools for ten years prior to being apprenticed in the plasterers' trade under the direction of Local 8 of the Operative Plasterers' International Association in 1916; enlisted in the U.S. Army in 1918 and served in France during World War I; became a journeyman plasterer after the war; began a ten-year term as business manager of Local 8 in 1925; also served during this period as president of the Philadelphia, Pa., Building Trades Council and as a member of the city's Building Code Commission and Housing Authority; named area labor relations director of the Works Progress Administration in 1935 and appointed to the Philadelphia Regional Labor Board; served as president of the Pennsylvania State Federation of Labor, 1938–1954; during his incumbency, served on a variety of state agencies, including the State Unemployment Compensation Board of Review, the Philadelphia War Chest, the State Planning Commission, the Displaced Persons Commission, the Advisory Committee on Public Utility Arbitration Law, and the Advisory Council for Private Trade Schools; was appointed director of labor's League for Political Education, American Federation of Labor (AFL), in 1951; after the AFL-Congress of Industrial Organizations' merger in 1955, became co-director with Jack Kroll (q.v.) of the Committee on Political Education (COPE); after Kroll's resignation in 1957, became sole director of COPE; was a Democrat; died in Washington, D.C., March 19, 1963; James L. McDevitt Papers, Labor Archives, Pennsylvania State University; Anonymous, *Fraternally Yours, James L. McDevitt: The Portrait of a Man and a Movement* (1956); Terry Catchpole, *How to Cope with COPE: The Political Operations of Organized Labor* (1968); *Current Biography* (1959); *AFL-CIO News*, March 23, 1963.

McDONALD, David John (1902–1979). Born in Pittsburgh, Pa., November 22, 1902; son of David, a steelworker, and Mary (Kelly) McDonald; Roman Catholic; married Emily Price on August 4, 1937, and Rosemary C. McHugh on January 3, 1950; one child, he went to work at age 15 in a mill office of the Jones and Laughlin Steel Corporation; completed high school in 1920, while employed as a machinist's helper in a National Tube Company plant; as a result of experience in the steel industry, became aware of worker grievances and sympathetic to the trade union movement; in 1923, at age 20, became secretary to United Mine Workers of America (UMWA) vice-president Philip Murray (q.v.); despite completion of the Carnegie Institute Drama program in 1932, decided to remain with the UMWA; in 1936, was named secretary-treasurer of the Congress of Industrial Organizations' (CIO) Steel Workers Organizing Committee (SWOC) by Murray, its chairman; performed adeptly in this key post; with the founding of the United Steelworkers of America (USWA) in 1942, became its secretary-treasurer; was named acting president of USWA by its executive board after Murray's death in 1952; was elected to the position the following year; subsequently became a vice-president of the American Federation of Labor-CIO executive council; gained substantial wage and fringe benefits for USWA members, notably a generous supplemental unemployment benefit program negotiated in 1956, and, after the marathon 1959 steel strike, much-improved pension payments; in order to avoid a repetition of the 1959 conflict, worked with basic steel leaders to create a human relations committee for continuous top-level union-management discussion to resolve differences—especially those arising from automation and foreign competition—in advance of actual contract negotiations; thus, contributed to situation in which there were no basic steel strikes during the 1960s; was unsuccessfully challenged in the mid-1950s by dues protestors who tried to unseat him, and by district directors who resented his centralization of bargaining in the presidency; also began to suffer from criticism that he was too cozy with management and out of touch with union rank-and-file members; was further damaged by results of the 1962 and 1963 contracts, which were negotiated in a slack period when steelworkers were more concerned with job security than wage hikes, and which failed to yield benefits when the industry recovered in 1963–1964; had the USWA constitution altered to permit himself two more four-year terms, but secretary-treasurer I. W. Abel (q.v.) successfully opposed him in 1965; usually supported Democratic candidates, but served on several governmental commissions in both Republican and Democratic administrations; coauthored *Coal and Unionism* (1939) and authored his autobiography, *Union Man* (1969); died in Palm Springs, Calif., on August 8, 1979; David J. McDonald Papers, Labor Archives, Pennsylvania State University; *Current Biography* (1953); John A. Orr, "The Steelworker Election of 1965," *Labor Law Journal* (February 1969); John Herling, *Right to Challenge: People and Power in the Steelworkers Union* (1972).

Donald G. Sofchalk

McDONALD, Joseph Donald   (1895–   ). Born in Clatskanine, Oreg., July 10, 1895; son of James William, a carpenter, and Dora (Aldridge) McDonald; married Louisa May Doucette on April 21, 1920; two children; graduated from high school; eventually became an apprentice butcher and joined Local 143 of the Amalgamated Meat Cutters and Butcher Workmen of North America; was elected secretary-treasurer of Local 143, secretary-treasurer of the Oregon Federated Butchers, and secretary-treasurer of the label trades section of the Portland (Oreg.) Central Labor Council (CLC); was elected a vice-president of the Oregon State Federation of Labor (OSFL) in 1939 and became a member of the executive council of the Portland CLC; served during World War II as a labor member of the advisory committee for the Office of Price Administration in Oregon and as a labor member of the Twelfth Regional Panel of the War Labor Board; elected president of the OSFL in 1942, serving in that capacity until the merger of the American Federation of Labor-Congress of Industrial Organizations (AFL-CIO) in Oregon; after the merger, elected president of the Oregon AFL-CIO; during his years of labor leadership in Oregon, was closely associated with labor-oriented problems growing from wartime and from postwar reconversion conflicts, with the negotiation of the AFL-CIO merger in Oregon, and with successful lobbying efforts in the Oregon state legislature; was a delegate to several AFL and AFL-

CIO conventions; a Democrat; retired union positions in 1967; *Who's Who in Labor* (1946); *AFL-CIO News*, September 30, 1967.

McDONNELL, J. P.   (ca. 1840–1906). Born in Dublin, Ireland, ca. 1840; was reared in a middle-class, Roman Catholic family; became deeply committed to the Fenian movement and was often arrested and imprisoned; converted to Marxian communism in 1869, and was an Irish delegate to The Hague Congress of the International in 1872; shortly after The Hague Congress, emigrated to the United States, settling in New York City; was one of the leaders of the Trades and Labor Council of New York in 1876; after the collapse of the International, aligned himself with its American successor, the Workingmen's party of the United States; became the editor of the New York *Labor Standard*, the official English-language organ of the Workingmen's party; broke with the American Communist movement in 1877 when the Socialist Labor party was organized and committed itself exclusively to political action; meanwhile, moved the *Labor Standard*, of which he had assumed control, to Fall River, Mass., and then to Paterson, N.J.; was one of the principal founders of the International Labor Union (ILU) in 1878, which brought together Ira Steward's (q.v.) eight-hour advocates and Socialist trade unionists in an alliance committed to the organization of the unskilled; was a member of the ILU executive board; was one of the leaders in organizing Paterson textile workers and in the textile strikes of 1878; selected as the ILU delegate to the Trades Congress of England in 1879, but prevented from attending by the collapse of the ILU; twice convicted as a result of allegedly libelous utterances in the *Labor Standard*, one of which referred to strike breakers as ''scabs'' and the other exposing working conditions in a Paterson brickyard; was one of the major organizers of the New Jersey State Federation of Trades and Labor Unions in 1883 and served as its chairman for 15 years; organized the Paterson Trades Assembly in 1884; was given credit for the enactment of the New Jersey Labor Day law, the first such law to be enacted in the United States; joined the Anti-Poverty Association organized by Henry George (q.v.) in 1887; never rejected the class consciousness engendered by his faith in socialism, but during his career became increasingly committed to immediate and practical trade union objectives; died in Paterson, N.J., in 1906; John R. Commons et al., *History of Labour in the United States*, Vol. 2 (1918); Philip S. Foner, *History of the Labor Movement in the United States*, Vol. 2 (1955); Norman J. Ware, *The Labor Movement in the United States, 1860–1895* (1929).

McFETRIDGE, William Lane   (1893–1969). Born in Chicago, Ill., November 28, 1893; son of William F., a teamster, and Wilhelmina (Quesse) McFetridge; Roman Catholic; married Barbara A. Werner on October 22, 1923; one child; attended the public schools of Chicago, Ill., and McFarland, Wis., until 1904 when, at age 13, quit school and became an office boy for the Milwaukee Railroad in Chicago; with the exception of a short period during which he was employed by the American Express Company, worked for the Milwaukee Railroad from 1904 to 1923; eventually promoted to traveling claims agent; during his employment with the Milwaukee Railroad, attended night schools, graduating from high school, prelaw, and law school; accepted employment in 1923 as a confidential secretary, investigator, and trouble-shooter for his uncle, William Quesse, the president of the Chicago Flat Janitors Union, which was Local 1 of the Building Service Employees International Union (BSEIU); organized Chicago school maintenance workers and elected president of the new BSEIU local; was an officer of the Chicago Federation of Labor and served as a vice-president of the Illinois State Federation of Labor, 1939–1950; shortly after his election as a national vice-president of the BSEIU, the union president, George Scalise, was imprisoned for extortion, and he assumed the presidency of the shattered, corruption-ridden international and rebuilt it into a solid, respected union; elected an American Federation of Labor (AFL) vice-president and executive council member in 1940; was one of the committee members who drafted the AFL-CIO (Congress of Industrial Organizations) merger agreement in 1955; became a vice-president and member of the executive council of the new federation; was very active in community affairs in Chicago and was a member of numerous public and private organizations, including the National Conference of Christians and Jews, the National Urban League, and Israel Bond Committee, and served as a member of the fiscal advisory committee of the Chicago Board of Education; was the recipient of numerous awards and honors and in 1957 was selected one of Chicago's 100 outstanding citizens; retired and was named president emeritus of the BSEIU in 1960 and resigned as AFL-CIO vice-president in 1965; was a Republican; died in Chicago, Ill., March 15, 1969; Philip Taft, *The A.F. of L. from the Death of Gompers to the Merger* (1959); *Business Week*, August 18, 1951; *Fortune* (November 1946); *AFL-CIO News*, March 22, 1969; *Who's Who in America, 1966–1967.*

McGAW, Homer L.   (fl. 1845–1884). Born at Bethlehem, Ohio, April 8, 1845; in 1853, entered a country printing office as "devil," and joined in a strike, which was a success; after leaving the army, went through college on the money he had saved in the army and working in coal mines, printing offices, and so on, graduating second in his class; became an accountant in Pittsburgh; before age 21 was made cashier of the East Liberty Savings Bank in Pittsburgh; in 1868, he organized the bookkeepers and salesmen of the city into a union, but it failed; the lessons of the Panic of 1873 caused him, with others of similar views, to open correspondence with Eastern labor leaders, among whom was Uriah S. Stephens (q.v.), founder of the Knights of Labor; McGaw soon organized one of the first assemblies of Knights in his printing office; chosen general insurance secretary of the order in 1883, and reelected several times; chosen master workman of District Assembly 3 in January 1884, held the office for one year; built up within the order an assessment insurance association, which cost its members about a cent a day for an indemnity of $500; retained by the

Trades Assembly of Western Pennsylvania to secure the repeal of the conspiracy laws of the state; George E. McNeill, *The Labor Movement: The Problem of To-Day* (1887).

George E. McNeill

MacGOWAN, Charles J.   (1887–1960). Born in Argyllshire, Scotland, in 1887; married; three children; emigrated with his father, a stonemason and trade unionist, to Canada in 1897 and gained a grammar school education prior to beginning an apprenticeship as a boilermaker on the Grand Trunk Pacific Railroad in 1909; shortly thereafter, joined the International Brotherhood of Boilermakers, Iron Ship Builders and Helpers of America (IBB); emigrated to the United States in 1913; beginning in 1917, served his union and the labor movement in various capacities, including as IBB international representative, as assistant to the president of the American Federation of Labor (AFL) railroad labor department, and as a member of the Railroad Adjustment Board; elected an international vice-president of the IBB in 1936, and served in that capacity until elected international president in 1944; served on President Harry S. Truman's Labor-Management Conference in 1945, and during the same year, served as a labor consultant at the founding conference of the United Nations in San Francisco, Calif.; elected an AFL vice-president and executive council member in 1947, and after the AFL-Congress of Industrial Organizations' (CIO) merger in 1955, retained the same position in the new labor federation until his death; was instrumental in the establishment of the AFL's League For Political Education in 1948; was a delegate to the founding convention of the International Confederation of Free Trade Unions in London in 1949; served as a AFL fraternal delegate to the British Trades Union Congress and the International Transportworkers Federation in Utrecht, Holland, in 1951; was an influential participant in the negotiations between the AFL and CIO that resulted in the 1955 merger; retired as president emeritus of the IBB in 1954; was a Democrat; died in Parkville, Mo., October 25, 1960; Philip Taft, *The A.F. of L. from the Death of Gompers to the Merger* (1959); *AFL-CIO News*, October 29, 1960; Arthur J. Goldberg, *AFL-CIO: Labor United* (1956); *Labor*, November 5, 1960; *The American Federation of Labor News-Reporter*, April 30, 1954.

McGRADY, Edward Francis   (1872–1960). Born in Jersey City, N.J., January 29, 1872; son of James T., an assistant foreman in the Boston, Mass., street department, and Jane (Gawley) McGrady; Roman Catholic; married Mary J. Griffin on October 11, 1897; two children; completed high school in Jersey City, N.J., then moved to Boston where he took evening courses in economics and business management; took a job with the *Boston Traveler* as a pressman in 1894 and joined the Web Pressmen local of the International Printing Pressmen's and Assistants' Union of North America (IPPAUNA); became an organizer for the Web Pressmen's local and in 1907 elected president of the local; served as state superintendent and then acting federal director of the U.S. Employment

Service in Massachusetts; during 1907–1909, served variously as secretary of the IPPAUNA, president of the Boston Central Labor Union, and vice-president and president of the Massachusetts State Federation of Labor; served a two-year term on the Boston Common Council and a two-year term in the Massachusetts House of Representatives; became the American Federation of Labor (AFL) official legislative representative in Washington, D.C., in 1919 and served in that capacity until 1933; appointed deputy administrator of the National Recovery Administration in 1933; served as Assistant Secretary of Labor in the U.S. Department of Labor, 1933–1937; retired from union activities in 1937 and became a vice-president for labor relations of the Radio Corporation of America; during World War II, was a special labor consultant to the Secretary and Undersecretary of War; retired from all business affairs in 1959; was a Democrat; died in Newtonville, Mass., July 17, 1960; Philip Taft, *The A.F. of L. from the Death of Gompers to the Merger* (1959); Bruce Minton and John Stuart, *Men Who Lead Labor* (1937); Elizabeth F. Baker, *Printers and Technology: A History of the International Printing Pressmen and Assistants' Union* (1957).

McGUIRE, Peter James   (1852–1906). Born in New York City, July 6, 1852; son of John J., a department store porter, and Catherine Hand (O'Riley) McGuire; Roman Catholic; married Christina Wolff in 1884; four children; forced by family financial circumstances to quit school at age 11; took odd jobs while attending free night classes at Cooper Union; became an apprentice woodjoiner in 1867 and joined the International Workingmen's Association; was an organizer for the Social Democratic party (later the Socialist Labor party), 1874–1879; credited with successfully sponsoring legislation in the Missouri state legislature establishing one of the first bureaus of labor statistics in the United States; appointed deputy commissioner of the Missouri Bureau of Labor Statistics, but resigned after a short time to take a job as a St. Louis furniture worker; organized St. Louis carpenters; inspired the meeting of 12 carpenters' unions in Chicago, Ill., in 1881, which resulted in the organization of the United Brotherhood of Carpenters and Joiners (UBC); elected the first secretary (the chief administrative official) of the UBC and became the editor of the union's newspaper, *The Carpenter*; wrote the convention call for the Chicago conference of national labor unions that resulted in the formation of the Federation of Organized Trades and Labor Unions of the United States and Canada in 1881; moved the headquarters of the UBC to New York and became involved in the eight-hour-day movement; was one of the leaders of the May Day demonstrations of 1886 and 1890; was one of the founders of the American Federation of Labor (AFL) in 1886 and became its first secretary; in 1889 elected a vice-president of AFL, but forced to resign in 1900 because of poor health and alcoholism; growing opposition to his leadership of the UBC resulted in a contrived charge of embezzlement of funds and his expulsion from the union in 1902; died in Camden, N.J., February 18, 1906; Robert A. Christie, *Empire in Wood: A History of the Carpenters' Union* (1956); Philip Taft, *The A.F. of L. in the Time of Gompers* (1957); Gerald

N. Grob, *Workers and Utopia: A Study of Ideological Conflict in the American Labor Movement, 1865–1900* (1961); David N. Lyon, "The World of P. J. McGuire: A Study of the American Labor Movement, 1870–1890" (Ph.D. diss., 1972).

McLAREN, Louise Leonard   (1885–1968). Born in Wellsboro, Pa., August 10, 1885; daughter of Fred Churchill, a lawyer who was elected to Congress in 1895 on the Republican ticket, and Estella (Cook) Leonard, a schoolteacher; married Myron McLaren, a college professor in 1930; no children; attended Miss Beret's School for Girls, Harrisburg, Pa., graduating in 1904; earned a B.A. from Vassar College in 1907; taught high school in Watertown, N.Y., and at Lock Haven (Pa.) Teachers College before becoming industrial secretary of the YMCA in Wilkes-Barre, Pa.; transferred to Baltimore, Md., in 1918, where she served as metropolitan industrial secretary; appointed national industrial secretary for the South in 1920; during her 25 years in this position, she traveled extensively organizing young women in southern industry; founded the Southern Summer School for Women Workers in Industry in 1927, which she modeled after the Bryn Mawr Summer School for Women Workers; served as the director for the Southern Summer School for the following 17 years; under her direction, the school sought to assist women in adapting to the rigors of industrial life while developing their analytical skills and promoting confidence in their efforts at self-expression; improved employment opportunities accompanying World War II reduced the Southern Summer School's potential constituency, and it held its last regular residence session in 1942; two years later the school was closed and McLaren moved to New York City, where she served as an organizer for the Congress of Industrial Organizations' Political Action Committee during the 1944 elections; after working briefly for the American Cancer Society and the Girl Scouts of America, she obtained a teaching and research position with the American Labor Education Service where she remained until her retirement in 1953; throughout her long career as social reformer and promoter of worker education, she retained a sense of social justice and a commitment to Socialist economic theory; died in East Stroudsburg, Pa., on December 16, 1968; Louise L. McLaren Papers, Catherwood Library, New York State School of Industrial and Labor Relations, Cornell University; *Notable American Women*, Vol. 4; Florence H. Schneider, *Patterns of Workers' Education: The Story of the Bryn Mawr Summer School* (1941); Mary E. Frederickson, "A Place to Speak Our Minds: The Southern School for Women Workers" (Ph.D. diss., 1981).

McLAUGHLIN, Hugh   (1831–1904). Born in St. Johnston, County Donegal, Ireland, on October 28, 1831; son of Patrick McLaughlin, a prosperous road contractor and flax dresser; Roman Catholic; married Mary Hagan in 1854; attended the common schools of Ireland until 1845 at which time he became a timekeeper on the Enniskellen and Londonderry Railroad at age 14; a short time later he joined a company of sappers and miners engaged in an ordinance survey and learned the surveyor's trade; discharged for unknown reasons in 1847, he worked as a farm laborer and a railroad laborer for the next two years; after an unsuccessful two-month sojourn in Scotland in search of employment, he secured a job as a watchman on the Enniskellen and Londonderry Railroad in 1849, a position he held until 1853 when he emigrated to the United States; shortly after arriving in New York, he obtained a job on the Camden and Atlantic Railroad in New Jersey but lost the job after being laid up with bilious fever; for the next six years, he worked, at various times, as a farmer, gardener, and teamster; in 1856 he took a job as an iron puddler and in 1863, after moving to Duncannon, Pa., he joined the puddlers' union, the Sons of Vulcan; moved to Chicago, Ill., three years later from whence he sponsored the emigration of the remainder of his family to the United States; led a campaign to organize iron puddlers in Chicago which led to the chartering of Prairie Forge lodge of the Sons of Vulcan in 1866; was elected a delegate to the national convention of the Sons of Vulcan in 1868 and during that meeting was appointed a deputy for the Sons' fourth district; elected president of the Sons of Vulcan in 1871 and reelected a year later; refused to run for a third term in 1873; during his presidency, he reformed administrative procedures and greatly expanded the union's membership—from 1,900 in 1871 to 3,400 in 1873; although defeated for election to the Illinois state legislature in 1870 on a labor ticket, he was elected two years later on a fusionist Liberal Republican-Democratic ticket; represented the Sons of Vulcan at the organizational meeting of the Industrial Labor Congress held in Cleveland, Ohio, on July 14, 1873, and was elected third vice-president of the organization; was a leader in Brooklyn's Democratic party for many years, and was active in promoting construction of the Brooklyn Bridge and Prospect Park; died in New York City on December 7, 1904; Chicago *Workingman's Advocate*, December 13, 1873; David Montgomery, *Beyond Equality: Labor and the Radical Republicans, 1862–1872* (1967); *Who Was Who*, historical volume; *The New York Times*, December 8, 1904.

McLELLAN, Andrew Currie   (1911–1982). Born in Cowdenbeath, Fife, Scotland, on April 17, 1911; son of Andrew and Christina McLellan; married Gloria Jane (second marriage); two children; after obtaining a common school education in Scotland, he emigrated to Canada where he worked as a butcher and joined the Amalgamated Meat Cutters and Butcher Workmen of North America; served as a master sergeant in the U.S. Army during World War II, serving in New Guinea, the Philippine Islands, and the South Pacific; after the war he moved to Texas where he became the legislative director of the Texas State Federation of Labor (TSFL); served as the Latin American specialist for the TSFL, 1949–1954; was a Central American representative, Inter-American Regional Organization of Workers, 1954–1958, and Inter-American representative, International Union of Food and Allied Workers, 1958–1960; was appointed association Inter-American representative for the American Federation of Labor-Congress of Industrial Organizations (AFL-CIO) in 1960, serving until 1964 when he was elevated to the top position; in this capacity he provided liaison between the AFL-CIO and trade unions in Central America, South America, and the Caribbean; became a member of the board of trustees, American Institute of Free Labor Development in 1965; authored numerous articles on Latin America, politics, and illegal aliens; suffering from emphysema and complications resulting from abdominal surgery, he obtained a court order permitting the disconnection of the life support system keeping him alive and on January 17, 1982, died in Washington, D.C.; *Who's Who in Labor* (1976); *The New York Times*, January 18, 1982; *AFL-CIO News*, January 25, 1982.

McMAHON, Thomas F.   (1870–1944). Born in Ballybay, County Monaghan, Ireland, May 2, 1870; son of James, a flax buyer, and Bridget (Shreenan) McMahon; Roman Catholic; married Catherine E. Murray on October 15, 1891; attended the national schools of Ireland before emigrating to the United States in 1887; joined the Knights of Labor in 1889; hired as a cloth folder and joined Cloth Folders' Local 505, United Textile Workers of America (UTW) in 1901; served as business agent of Local 505, 1904–1912; was a UTW national organizer, 1912–1917; elected a national vice-president of the UTW in 1917 and became president in 1921, serving until 1937; appointed a labor board member of the National Recovery Administration in 1934; was a proponent of industrial organization and a charter member of the Committee for Industrial Organization in 1935; resigned UTW presidency in 1937 and accepted an appointment as Rhode Island state labor director, serving until 1939; usually supported Democratic candidates; authored *United Textile Workers of America* (1926); died in Cranston, R.I., April 22, 1944; Walter Galenson, *The CIO Challenge to the AFL: A History of the American Labor Movement, 1935–1941* (1960); Philip Taft, *The A.F. of L. from the Death of Gompers to the Merger* (1959); Robert R. R. Brooks, "The United Textile Workers of America" (Ph.D. diss., 1935).

McNAMARA, Patrick Vincent   (1894–1966). Born in North Weymouth, Mass., October 4, 1894; son of Patrick Vincent, an Irish laborer and shipfitter, and Mary Jane (Thynne) McNamara; Roman Catholic; married Kathleen Kennedy, June 21, 1921, and, after her death in 1929, Mary Mattee on September 3, 1930; two children; completed high school, then attended the Fore River Apprentice School in Quincy, Mass., 1912–1916; worked as a pipe fitter and foreman for the Bethlehem Shipyard, Fore River, 1916–1919; played semi-professional football, 1919–1920; moved to Detroit, Mich., in 1921 and there worked for various construction contractors for the next several years; joined Local 636 of the United Association of Journeymen and Apprentices of the Plumbing and Pipe Fitting Industry of the United States and Canada (UA) in 1924; elected president of UA Local 636 and served in that capacity until 1954; served as a vice-president of the Detroit Federation of Labor, 1939–1945; during World War II, was rent director for the Office of Price Administration in the Detroit area; elected as one of nine members of the Detroit Common Council in 1946; served as a member of the Detroit Board of Education, 1949–1955; elected as a Democrat to the United States Senate in 1954; was one of the co-sponsors of the Labor-Management Reporting and Disclosure Act of 1959; died in Bethesda, Md., April 30, 1966; *Biographical Directory of the American Congress, 1774–1971* (1971); *AFL-CIO News*, May 7, 1966; *National Encyclopedia of American Biography*, Vol. 1.

McNEILL, George Edwin   (1837–1906). Born in Amesbury, Mass., August 4, 1837; son of John, a Scots-Irish immigrant, and Abigail Todd (Hickey) McNeill; married Adeline J. Trefethen on December 24, 1859; educated in public and private schools; began work in 1851 in the Amesbury woolen mills at age 15; during the next few years, attempted shoemaking and salesmanship; moved to Boston, Mass., in 1856; was an advocate of Ira Steward's (q.v.) eight-hour philosophy, serving as secretary of the Grand Eight-Hour League in 1863–1864, and as president of the Boston Eight-Hour League, 1869–1874; edited and served on the editorial staff of labor newspapers in Fall River, Mass., New York City, and Paterson, N.J.; was a founder and served as president of the Workingmen's Institute, 1867–1869; cooperated with Wendell Phillips in lobbying for the creation of the first state bureau of labor statistics, which was approved by the Massachusetts legislature in 1869; served as the deputy director of the Massachusetts Bureau of Labor Statistics, 1869–1873; wrote a charter for an 1874 labor congress in Rochester, N.Y., which was later adopted as the Declaration of Principles of the Noble Order of the Knights of Labor (K of L); became president of the International Labor Union in 1878; joined the K of L in 1883 and served as treasurer of District 30 (Mass.), 1884–1886; organized the Massachusetts Mutual Accident Insurance Company in 1883; after the rejection of his plan for American Federation of Labor (AFL)-K of L cooperation, resigned from the K of L and joined the AFL; became the editor and proprietor of the Boston *Labor Leader* in 1886 and in the same year, ran unsuccessfully for mayor of Boston on the United Labor party ticket; was an AFL fraternal delegate to the British Trades Union Congress in 1897; edited and contributed to *The Labor Movement: The Problem of To-Day* (1887); authored *The Philosophy of the Labor Movement* (1893), *Eight Hour Primer* (1889), *A Study of Accidents and Accident Insurance* (1900), and *Unfrequented Paths: Songs of Nature, Labor, and Men* (1903); died in Somerville, Mass., May 19, 1906; David Montgomery, *Beyond Equality: Labor and the Radical Republicans, 1862–1872* (1967); Norman J. Ware, *The Labor Movement in the United States, 1860–1895* (1929); John R. Commons et al., *History of Labour in the United States*, Vol. 2 (1918); *Dictionary of American Biography*, Vol. 12.

McNULTY, Frank Joseph   (1872–1926). Born in Londonderry, Ireland, August 10, 1872; son of Owen and Catherine (O'Donnell) McNulty; Roman Catholic; married Edith H. Parker in 1893; emigrated with parents to the United States in 1876; attended the public schools of New York City; adopted the electricians' trade; moved to Perth Amboy, N.J., and there helped organize a local of the International Brotherhood of Electrical Workers (IBEW); elected an international vice-president of the IBEW in 1901 and its president in 1903, serving until 1918; was a committed craft unionist and vigorously fought the efforts of a group of secessionist IBEW unionists to organize on an industrial basis and during his incumbency consolidated the IBEW's control of electrical workers; appointed to a commission established under the auspices of the National Civic Federation that studied public ownership in Great Britain in 1906; appointed acting director of public safety in Newark, N.J., in 1917 and two years later resigned his position in the IBEW to become deputy director of public safety in Newark; became president emeritus and chairman of the IBEW international board of directors in 1919, serving in this capacity until his death; served during World War I as vice-chairman of Railway Board of Adjustment No. 2; resigned in August 1918 to accept appointment to a special commission that visited France and Italy at the request of the President of the United States; retired from the Newark city government in 1922 and ran successfully as a Democrat for Congress from the Eighth Congressional District of New Jersey and served one term; died in Newark, N.J., May 26, 1926; Michael A. Mulcaire, *The International Brotherhood of Electrical Workers* (1923); *Dictionary of American Biography*, Vol. 12; *Journal of the Electrical Workers and Operators* (June 1926); *Who's Who in America, 1926–1927*.

McSORLEY, William Joseph   (1876–1962). Born in Philadelphia, Pa., December 13, 1876; son of a lather; Roman Catholic; married; six children; attended the elementary schools of Philadelphia; began working as a lather at age 14; joined Philadelphia Local 53 of the Wood, Wire and Metal Lathers' International Union (WWMLIU) in 1899 and served Local 53 in a variety of capacities during the following six years; elected international president of the WWMLIU in 1904, and held that office, with the exception of a short period, for 51 years; served on the board of governors of the Structural Building Trades Alliance, 1905–1908; was an American Federation of Labor (AFL) delegate to the Canadian Trades and Labor Congress in 1913; elected a vice-president of the AFL building trades department in 1914; was a member of the labor committee of the Council of National Defense during World War I; elected to the executive committee of the American Construction Council in 1922; served as president of the AFL building trades department, 1927–1932; was an AFL fraternal delegate to the British Trades Union Congress in 1937; represented the AFL at the founding congress of the International Confederation of the Free Trade Unions (ICFTU) in 1949 and was an AFL delegate to the 1955 ICFTU congress in Vienna; retired as WWMLIU president in 1955 and named president emeritus; identified himself politically as nonpartisan; died in Cleveland, Ohio, December 15, 1962; *American Federation of Labor News-Reporter*, November 18, 1955; *AFL-CIO News*, December 20, 1962; Solon DeLeon, ed., *The American Labor Who's Who* (1925).

MAGUIRE, Matthew   (fl. 1850–1898). Born in New York City in 1850; son of Irish immigrants, Christopher and Mary (Stafford) Maguire; Roman Catholic; married Martha McCormick in 1870; educated in public schools; began factory work at age 14; served an apprenticeship as a machinist and joined the Machinists' and Blacksmiths' International Union (MBIU); served as a national officer of the MBIU during the early 1870s; was an active union organizer; joined the Knights of Labor and was actively involved in its activities during the 1880s; espoused the Socialist cause and elected to the Paterson, N.J., Board of Aldermen on the Socialist Labor party (SLP) ticket; was also an unsuccessful SLP candidate for vice president of the United States in 1896 and for governor of New Jersey in 1898; after 1893, edited the *Paterson People*; *Who Was Who in America*, Vol. 4; David Montgomery, *Beyond Equality: Labor and Radical Republicans, 1862–1872* (1967).

John W. Hevener

MAHON, William D.   (1861–1949). Born in Athens County, Ohio, August 12, 1861; son of an itinerant tanner; married; four children; formal education ended at an early age with his father's death; worked as a miner in the Hocking Valley district of Ohio; entered the street-railway service in Columbus, Ohio, in 1888 and shortly thereafter assisted in organizing employees of the Columbus transit system and served the local at various times as president, secretary, and business agent; served two terms as president of the Columbus Trades and Labor Council; attended the organizing convention of the Amalgamated Association of Street, Electric Railway and Motor Coach Employees of America (AAS-ERCME) in 1892 and shortly thereafter became an assistant organizer for the new union in Indianapolis, Ind.; elected general president of the AASERCME in 1893 and led the organization into the American Federation of Labor (AFL); appointed presiding judge of the Michigan State Court of Arbitration in 1898, serving until 1900; served on the executive committee of the National Civic Federation; appointed to the first municipal ownership committee after Detroit, Mich., assumed control of its transit system in 1914; appointed by the AFL to investigate municipal ownership and operation in Europe in 1914 and two years later was an AFL fraternal delegate to the British Trades Union Congress; elected an AFL vice-president and executive council member in 1917 and served until 1922, resigning to run (unsuccessfully) for the United States Congress; appointed to the Federal Electric Railway Commission by President Woodrow Wilson in 1918 and the following year appointed to Wilson's Federal Industrial Commission; served on the National Recovery Administration's Transit Code Authority, 1933–1935; reelected to the AFL executive council in 1936, serving until his death; was an essentially conservative trade unionist who strongly advocated the voluntary arbitration of labor disputes in the street-railway industry; was a Democrat; resigned as AASERCME president, an office he had held for more than 52 years, in 1946 and was named president emeritus; edited *The Motorman, Conductor and Motor Coach Operator* for 11 years; died in Detroit, Mich.,

October 31, 1949; Emerson P. Schmidt, *Industrial Relations in Urban Trans-portation* (1973); *The American Federationist* (December 1949); *Mass Trans-portation* (September 1946); *Who's Who in Labor* (1947).

MAHONEY, Charles E.   (fl. 1904–1914). Was a member of Butte, Mont., Miner's and Smeltermen's Local 74 of the Western Federation of Miners (WFM); became a member of the WFM executive board in 1904; elected vice-president of the WFM in 1905; served as acting president when Charles Moyer (q.v.) was imprisoned during the famous Steunenberg murder case, 1906–1908; served as acting chairman of the schismatic 1906 convention of the Industrial Workers of the World (IWW) and elected by convention to the IWW general executive board; when the radical faction of the IWW, led by William Trautmann (q.v.) and Daniel DeLeon (q.v.), succeeded in having IWW president Charles Sherman (q.v.) deposed in disregard of the IWW constitution, Mahoney led the WFM moderates out of the convention; was determined to prevent the IWW split from tearing the WFM apart and therefore persuaded the executive board to withdraw from the IWW; when the issue was raised at the 1907 convention, the most decisive in the WFM's history, Mahoney rallied the moderates to thwart the radical attempt to continue affiliation of the WFM with the IWW (then led by William Trautmann); called a reactionary by his IWW detractors, but was a capable, militant unionist who supported the radical, direct-action preamble adopted by the WFM in 1907; involved in the Michigan copper miners' strike of 1913, one of the bitterest strikes of the period; along with Moyer, went to upper Michigan seeking to open negotiations with the operators; persuaded the governor of Michigan to propose arbitration of the strikers' grievances, but the industry's persistent refusal to deal with the WFM in any way defeated Mahoney's repeated efforts to arrange a peaceful settlement; reelected WFM vice-president in every election from 1906 to 1914; Vernon H. Jensen, *Heritage of Conflict: Labor Relations in the Nonferrous Metals Industry up to 1930* (1950; Emma F. Langdon, *Labor's Greatest Conflicts* (1908); U.S. Department of Labor, Bureau of Labor Statistics, *Michigan Cooper District Strike, Bulletin 139* (1914).

MAHONEY, William   (1869–1952). Born in Chicago, Ill., January 13, 1869; son of a railroader and farmer; married; one child; completed grammar school in Kansas, then apprenticed as a printer and joined the International Typograph-ical Union in 1887; transferred to the International Printing Pressmen's and Assistants' Union of North America in 1893; became a Socialist ca. 1896; attended the Indianapolis College of Law and was admitted to the bar, but after moving to St. Paul, Minn., in 1905 continued to work in his trade; elected president of the St. Paul Trades and Labor Assembly in 1919; was instrumental in founding the *Minnesota Union Advocate* and edited it until 1932; left the Socialist party believing it to be an inadequate political vehicle, but continued to call for gradual replacement of industrial capitalism by government ownership and production for use; in 1918 began promoting independent political action by organized labor and played the key role in involving labor in the Minnesota Farmer Labor party; with the backing of the State Federation of Labor, organized the Working People's Nonpartisan League in 1919; it cooperated with the farmers' Nonpartisan League in fielding Farmer Labor candidates; after impressive electoral victories in 1922, initiated along with Nonpartisan League Secretary Henry Teigan (q.v.) the merger of the two leagues into a permanent Farmer Labor party, planning to use the Minnesota party as the nucleus for a national Farmer Labor party in 1924; this movement failed when Senator Robert La Follette repudiated it and Communists gained control of its St. Paul convention, but Mahoney continued to play a prominent role in the state party; meanwhile, expounded as editor of the *Union Advocate* Farmer Labor ideology and rallied union members behind its candidates; still favored a national third party, but in 1928 warned Farmer Laborites against trying to launch one until they had created more state movements; by 1931, condemned the major parties for offering only "palliatives" and advocated a new national third party to effect "radical" economic change; in 1932, elected mayor of St. Paul; promised municipal ownership, but was only able to impose regulation on the utility firms; defeated for reelection in 1934, then served for a year as regional member of the National Labor Board; in 1942 entered as a candidate for Congress but withdrew before the election; retired in 1944; died in St. Paul, August 16, 1952; Solon DeLeon, ed., *The American Labor Who's Who* (1925); James Weinstein, *The Decline of Socialism in America, 1912–1925* (1967); Carl H. Chrislock, *The Progressive Era in Minnesota* (1971).

Donald G. Sofchalk

MAILE, Francis ("Pooch")   (1919–1980). Born in Phoenixville, Pa., on November 19, 1919; son of Joseph, a school teacher, and Ellen (Lawlor) Maile, a homemaker; married Marguerite, a director of the United Rubber, Cork, Linoleum and Plastics Workers of America (URW); two children; attended but did not graduate from high school; a voracious reader, he was largely self-educated; was a first sergeant in a U.S. Army Ranger unit during World War II; after the war, he took a job in a B. F. Goodrich plant in Oaks, Pa.; joined URW Local 281 in 1945; served in various positions in Local 281 before being elected president of the local in 1950, a position he held until 1961; was elected to the URW international executive board in 1956 and became international special representative in 1961; was promoted to the newly created position of director of the URW's committee on political education in 1966; one of the most popular leaders in the Ohio and national labor movements, he died after a six-year battle with cancer at Barberton, Ohio, on March 1, 1980; *AFL-CIO News*, March 8, 1980; *Who's Who in Labor* (1976); *Akron Beacon Journal*, March 2, 1980.

MALONEY, James   (1870–1960). Born in Scranton, Pa., September 11, 1870; son of P. W., a salesman, and Mary A. (Duleau) Maloney; Roman Catholic; completed grammar school in Scranton, Pa., then began an apprenticeship as a glass bottle blower; joined the Glass Bottle Blowers Association of the United States and Canada (GBBA) in 1890; served his local union in several capacities and in 1909 elected a member of the GBBA general executive board; elected a GBBA international vice-president in 1917, and in 1925, elected to succeed John A. Voll as international president of the union; as a result of prohibition, by 1924 the GBBA had nearly ceased to exist; inspired a joint legislative lobbying effort of the distilling and brewing industries along with the glass container industry to help win repeal of prohibition; during his incumbency, the GBBA grew from two thousand members to thirty-four thousand and the glass blowing industry in the United States and Canada was effectively organized; was an American Federation of Labor fraternal delegate to the Canadian Trades and Labor Congress in 1935 and to the British Trades Union Congress in 1939; retired as president emeritus in 1946 and succeeded by Lee W. Minton (q.v.); was one of the founders of the Union Labor Life Insurance Company and served as its treasurer for several years; died in Scranton, Pa., January 28, 1960; *The American Federationist* (August 1946); *Who's Who in Labor* (1946).

MALONEY, William E. (1884–1964). Born in Detroit, Mich., June 17, 1884; son of James and Mary (Connelly) Maloney; Roman Catholic; married Helen Goodrich on June 7, 1938; acquired a grammar school education, then began working as an itinerant railroad machinist; moved to Chicago, Ill., about 1907 and gained employment with the Rock Island Railroad; employed by the Southern Pacific Railroad as a machinist, 1908–1912; secured a civil service job as a hoisting engineer in Chicago and in 1919 joined Local 459 of the International Union of Operating Engineers (IUOE); served as a marine engineer with the U.S. Merchant Marine, 1917–1919; while serving as business manager of Local 569, it merged with Local 42, thus creating IUOE Local 150 in 1929; served Local 150 as an international supervisor; elected to the IUOE board of trustees in 1931 and the following year became an international vice-president; elected a vice-president of the Chicago Federation of Labor in 1932, beginning a long term of service in that capacity; during the 1930s, led a vigorous drive to organize workers within the IUOE's jurisdiction in Chicago and the surrounding area; successfully resisted the efforts of underworld figures to gain influence in Local 150 during Chicago's turbulent 1930s, but the moderate wealth gained from real estate investments and his later actions in taking local unions into receivership, moves which violated IUOE policies, led to unproven charges of corruption; elected international president of the IUOE in 1940; as president, greatly expanded the use of international agreements and restored the financial stability of the IUOE, while the membership increased from 58,000 to 294,000; retired as IUOE president in 1958 and named president emeritus; died in Chicago, Ill., January 2, 1964; Garth L. Mangum, *The Operating Engineers: The Economic History of a Trade Union* (1964); *Who's Who in America, 1958–1959*; *AFL-CIO News*, January 11, 1964.

MALOY, Elmer J.   (1896–1970). Born in Pittsburgh, Pa., March 22, 1896; son of William Patrick, a stationary engineer, and Bridget Jane (Tighe) Maloy; Roman Catholic; married Ruth Gilfoyle on April 19, 1922; left high school in 1913 and went to work in the Duquesne Works of the Carnegie Steel Company; served in the U.S. Army in World War I, then returned to the Duquesne Works and, failing to land a job as a millwright, worked as a crane operator in the open hearth; when the U.S. Steel Corporation instituted employee representation plans (ERP) to comply with the National Industrial Recovery Act of 1933, Maloy was elected as open hearth representative; was aggressive and persistent and used the local ERP to extract concessions from management on wages and job classifications; by 1936 the Carnegie-Illinois ERPs had become self-assertive; trying to hold the loyalty of the ERPs in the face of increasing Congress of Industrial Organizations' activity, U.S. Steel agreed to the creation of a central joint committee of ERPs for the Pittsburgh district of the Carnegie-Illinois subsidiaries; now secretly working with the Steel Workers Organizing Committee (SWOC) chairman, Philip Murray (q.v.), Maloy engineered his own election as chairman of the Pittsburgh ERP District Council in late 1936; then went to Washington, D.C., where, after meeting with John L. Lewis (q.v.) and Secretary of Labor Frances Perkins, launched a publicity campaign that discredited the ERP as a bargaining agent; was the first president of SWOC Local 1256; elected mayor of Duquesne, Pa., in 1937, running as a Democrat, and twice reelected; was an international representative of the United Steelworkers of America (USWA) during World War II, serving on the labor division of the War Production Board, organizing in central Pennsylvania, and helping to settle the Canadian steel strike of 1943; beginning in 1947, worked out of Pittsburgh as the USWA's expert on job evaluation; in this capacity, worked to eliminate wage discrimination against black steelworkers in Alabama, and helped end the sectional wage differential in basic steel; retired as director of the USWA Wage Division in 1963; died in Tampa, Fla., April 16, 1970; Labor Archives, Pennsylvania State University; Robert R. R. Brooks, *As Steel Goes,...Unionism in a Basic Industry* (1940); Irving Bernstein, *Turbulent Years: A History of the American Worker* (1970); *Who's Who in Labor* (1946).

Donald G. Sofchalk

MARCIANTE, Louis Paul   (1898–1961). Born in Lutcher, La., August 2, 1898; son of Benjamin, a woodworker, and Marie (Di Maria) Marciante; married Anna Louise Smith on June 30, 1922; four children; before completing high school, became an apprentice at age 16 in the electrical industry; joined Local 269 of the International Brotherhood of Electrical Workers of America in 1915; elected business agent of Local 269 in 1917 and thereafter served as its president for four years; served with the U.S. Marine Corps during World War I; after the war, elected secretary of the Mercer County (Trenton, N.J.) Building Trades Council and served for five years; served as president of the Mercer County Central Labor Union for several years prior to being elected president of the

New Jersey State Federation of Labor in 1934, a position he held for the remainder of his life; appointed to the regional labor board organized under the National Recovery Administration in 1933; was an implacable foe of Communist influence in the labor movement, especially in the Congress of Industrial Organizations, and successfully fought the reunification of the labor movement in New Jersey until his death; served as a member of the Trenton Board of Education, 1936–1948; was considered a powerful figure in state Democratic politics and was sometimes allied with Frank Hague's Jersey City organization; died in Atlantic City, N.J., March 30, 1961; Leo Troy, *Organized Labor in New Jersey* (1965); *The New York Times*, March 31, 1961; *Who's Who in Labor* (1946).

MAROT, Helen   (1865–1940). Born in Philadelphia, Pa., June 9, 1865; daughter of Charles Henry, a bookseller and publisher, and Hannah (Griscom) Marot; Society of Friends; educated at Society of Friends schools in Philadelphia; employed by the University Extension Society, Philadelphia, 1893–1895; became a librarian for the Wilmington, Del., Public Library in 1896; one of the organizers, in 1897, of the Library of Economic and Political Science, Philadelphia, which became a center for radical thought; investigated, along with Caroline Pratt, the Philadelphia custom tailoring trades for the United States Industrial Commission in 1899; did investigative work for the Association of Neighborhood Workers of New York City, and as a result the New York Child Labor Commission was formed in 1902; served as secretary of the Pennsylvania Child Labor Commission, 1904–1905; joined the New York Women's Trade Union League (WTUL) in 1906 and became its executive secretary, a position she held from 1906 until 1913; was a delegate to the first national convention of the WTUL in 1907 and served as the chairman of the WTUL finance committee; helped organize the WTUL strike committee for the 1909–1910 New York garment workers' strike; resigned from the WTUL, then pursued a full-time writing career; served on the editorial board of the *Masses*, 1916–1917; was a staff member of *Dial*, 1917–1919; retired in 1920; authored *Handbook of Labor Literature* (1898), *American Trade Unions* (1913), and *Creative Impulse in Industry* (1918); died in New York City, June 3, 1940; Gladys Boone, *The Women's Trade Union Leagues in Great Britain and the United States of America* (1942); *Notable American Women*, Vol. 2; *Who's Who in America*, Vol. 1.

Marie Tedesco

MARTIN, Harry Leland, Jr.   (1908–1958). Born in Hollandale, Miss., October 28, 1908; son of Dr. Harry Leland, a pastor, and Beatrice Mae (Cockcroft) Martin; Baptist; married Montez Weeks on June 1, 1930, and was divorced in 1940; one child; served as the editor of his high school newspaper and associate editor of the *Mississippi Collegian*, the student newspaper of Mississippi College in Clinton, Miss., from which he graduated cum laude, majoring in English, in 1928; served as assistant principal and coach in both Moorhead City School, Moorhead, Miss., 1928–1929, and Hickory Flat Consolidated High School,

1929–1930; joined the staff of the Memphis, Tenn., *Evening Appeal* in 1930; became amusements editor of the *Memphis Commercial Appeal* in 1936, serving in that position until 1948; was the founder and first president of the Newspaper Guild of Memphis and elected an international vice-president and member of the executive board of the American Newspaper Guild (ANG) in 1938; served as the founding president of the Newspaper Film Critics of America in 1939; was a vice-president of the Tennessee State Industrial Union Council, Congress of Industrial Organizations (CIO), and was a member of the executive board of the Memphis Industrial Union Council, CIO; served during World War II as a petty officer in the U.S. Navy, 1942–1945; elected as an anti-Communist candidate to the presidency of the ANG in 1947, serving until 1953; was appointed by President Harry S. Truman to the United Nations' Freedom of Information Conference in Geneva in 1948; served as an official consultant to the United Nations' subcommittee on freedom of information in 1948; during the same year, appointed a special labor advisor and information specialist to the European Recovery Program; served as vice-president of the International Organization of Journalists, 1948–1949, but resigned from the organization in 1949, because of its alleged Communist domination; was an active participant in the organization of the International Federation of Journalists and during 1952–1954 served as its alternate president and North American vice-president; was a member of the CIO executive board, 1950–1953; became director of public information for the American Red Cross in 1955, serving until his death; was a Democrat and member of Americans for Democratic Action; died in Washington, D.C., December 23, 1958; *Current Biography* (1948); *Who's Who in Labor* (1946); *Who's Who in America, 1958–1959.*

MARTIN, Warren Homer   (1902–1968). Born in Marion, Ill., August 16, 1902; son of an Illinois school teacher; Baptist; married twice; four children; graduated from William Jewell College, Mo., in 1928 and attended Kansas City Baptist Theological Seminary; named to the United States Olympic team in 1924 as the national hop, step, and jump champion but failed to make the trip because of financial difficulties; assumed a Baptist pastorate in Leeds, Mo., in 1931 but after pro-labor comments antagonized some members of his congregation, left the ministry and took a job in a General Motors Corporation Chevrolet plant in 1932; when an American Federation of Labor (AFL) federal local was organized in the plant (later Local 93 of the United Automobile, Aircraft and Agricultural Implement Workers of America [UAW]), he joined and a short time later became its president; was discharged in 1934 and moved to Detroit, Mich., devoting his energies there to organizing automobile workers; after the UAW was chartered by the AFL in 1935 elected its vice-president; elected UAW president in 1936, reflecting the UAW's growing independence of the AFL; led the UAW into the Congress of Industrial Organizations in 1936; during three years as UAW president, was constantly embroiled in bitter and divisive factional conflicts at the same time that the UAW was making significant organizational gains; was a gifted orator with considerable rank-and-file support, but his impulsive and temperamental personality along with serious administrative deficiencies resulted in his downfall in 1939; led a small group of UAW unions back into the AFL but after losing several representation elections resigned as the president of the UAW-AFL; left the labor movement and became a farmer; actively involved in Michigan politics; led a movement in 1958 to reduce UAW influence in the Michigan Democratic party; moved to Los Angeles, Calif., in 1961 and became labor counselor for the Tulare and Kings County Employers Council; died in Los Angeles, Calif., January 22, 1968; Homer Martin Papers, Walter Reuther Library, Wayne State University; Sidney Fine, *Sit-Down: The General Motors Strike of 1936–1937* (1969), and *The Automobile under the Blue Eagle: Labor, Management, and the Automobile Manufacturing Code* (1963); Jack Stieber, *Governing the UAW* (1962); Frank Cormier and William J. Eaton, *Reuther* (1970); Roger Keeran, *The Communist Party and the Auto Workers Unions* (1980); Nelson Lichtenstein, *Labor's War at Home: The CIO in World War II* (1982); Harvey A. Levenstein, *Communism, Anticommunism, and the CIO* (1981).

MARTIN, William (1845–1923).* Born in Calderbank, Lanarkshire, Scotland, on January 7, 1845; son of John, a roller, and Jane (Foster) Martin; Methodist; married Emma Robinson on December 25, 1865; one son; married Melissa Caroline Hopkins, a seamstress, on December 24, 1871; four children; possibly had some grammar school or educated through a Methodist Sunday school; worked "pulling up doors," for the Monkland Iron Company in Calderbank in 1853; later worked as a puddler and, eventually, as a forge roller for Kirk Brothers and Company, New Yard Iron Works, in Workington, Cumberland, England, 1865–1868, and became interested in wage scales while a member of Workington Lodge No. 1, National Amalgamated Association of Iron Workers, 1865–1868; emigrated to the United States in 1868 and became a naturalized citizen in 1874; first worked in a Pittsburgh, Pa., mill, then as a roller in Marietta, Ohio, 1868–1872; held other positions as a roller in Wheatland, Pa., and Youngstown, Ohio, 1872, Columbus (Ohio) Rolling Mill, 1873–1878, and Pittsburgh, 1878–1890; became active in unions while in Columbus, initially as a member and then as secretary, 1873–1874, of the Columbus lodge of the Iron and Steel Roll Hands' Union; later became the grand recording secretary of the union's national lodge, 1874–1876; with David Plant, the Roll Hands' president, was one of the first agitators for an amalgamation of ironworkers' unions in 1874; secretary of both the first and second joint committees on amalgamation of three ironworkers unions in 1875; was a trustee of the national lodge, Amalgamated Association of Iron and Steel Workers (AA) in 1876; became the AA's first national secretary, 1878–1890; served on numerous scale and conference committees of the AA at both the district and national levels, and through them met

*Some of the dates in this sketch could not be verified, but they should closely approximate the accurate date.

with iron manufacturers to set sliding scales; attended the first convention of the Federation of Organized Trades and Labor Unions in 1881; was secretary of the inquiry board during the investigation of John Jarrett's (q.v.) presidency, 1882; was a delegate to the National Tariff Convention in 1883; was a delegate to the 1887–1889 American Federation of Labor conventions and served as AFL second vice-president, 1887–1888, and first vice-president, 1889; was a close and long-time friend of Samuel Gompers (q.v.) and bitterly opposed the aims and ideas of Terence Powderly (q.v.); gave testimony at the hearings held by the U.S. Senate Committee on Education and Labor in 1883; was a member of the auditing committee of the Trades Assembly Political Committee of Western Pennsylvania in 1886; served on the Sixth Ward School Board, Pittsburgh, 1887–1888, and as treasurer of Forbes School in 1887; was a member of the Pennsylvania Revenue Commission in 1889; served as labor manager for Carnegie, Phipps and Company, Pittsburgh, 1891–1893; was associated with three companies which sold petroleum-based mill products, 1893–1898; was a sales agent for the Kansas City Life Insurance Company in 1907; held miscellaneous part-time positions, 1907–1911; became night manager for Reymer Brothers in 1911 and retained that employment for the remainder of his life; was also an inventor who invented a street car fender in 1905, a window lock in 1906, and a street car emergency brake in 1906; was a member of numerous fraternal organizations, including the Odd Fellows, the Elks, The Sovereigns of Industry, and various masonic groups; a Republican; was column editor for AA news in the *National Labor Tribune*, 1880–1890; authored "A Brief History of the Amalgamated Association of Iron and Steel Workers of the United States," *Souvenir of the Eleventh Annual Reunion of the Amalgamated Association of Iron and Steel Workers of the United States, Saturday, June 7th, 1890, at Rock Point, PA* (n.d.); died in Wilkinsburg, Pa., on January 11, 1923; Jessie S. Robinson, *The Amalgamated Association of Iron, Steel and Tin Workers* (1920).

                                                                              Sharon Trusilo

MARTINO, Frank D.   (Francesco   Giuseppe   Domenico   Martino) (1919–   ). Born in Albany, N.Y., on April 9, 1919; son of Benny and Rosina Martino; Roman Catholic; married Phyllis in 1963; two children; graduated from Albany High School in 1937 and later took courses at the Rutgers University Labor School, the Cornell University Labor School, and the labor program at Oxford University in England; served as a first sergeant in the U.S. Army during World War II in North Africa and Italy, 1941–1945; after the war he went to work for Sterling Drug's Winthrop Laboratories in Rensselaer, N.Y., and in 1948 joined Local 61 of the International Chemical Workers Union (ICW); while serving as a shop steward in 1949, he participated in a wildcat strike which was opposed by the local's leadership, and, thereafter, took a more active role in union affairs; was elected president of Local 61 in 1954 and during his tenure he won the first companywide master contract with Sterling Drug and negotiated the first workers' pension plan; was appointed an ICW staff representative to

Region 3, New Jersey, in 1956, and two years later, was elected president of the ICW's Representatives Union, serving until 1970; was appointed Washington director of the ICW in 1963 and served in that capacity until being elected an international vice-president and director of Region 7, St. Louis, in 1970; two years later, he was elected international secretary-treasurer of the ICW; was elected international president in 1975; shortly after assuming the ICW presidency, he initiated a major organizing drive, entitled BOOM (Boost Our Own Membership) and GLO (Get Locals Organized), which was designed to rejuvenate the eighty thousand-member union which had steadily lost membership during the late 1960s and early 1970s; *Who's Who in Labor* (1976); *Chemical Week*, December 17, 1975.

MARTINSON, Henry Rudolph   (1883–1981). Born in Minneapolis, Minn., on March 6, 1883; son of Gunerius, a homesteader and painter, and Karina Martinson; Lutheran; married Lorency Melba Mitchell in 1926; attended public schools in Sacred Heart, Minn.; learned painting and decorating trades from his father; was a graduate of the School of Agriculture, University of Minnesota, in 1905; in 1906, he homesteaded in Divide County, N.D.; later he moved to Minot, N.D., where he was a painter and decorator; was state secretary of the Socialist party of North Dakota and editor of *The Iconoclast*, the party's newspaper, 1916–1918; these activities were carried on while in Minot and northwestern North Dakota, where political discontent was strong; was an organizer in North Dakota and Minnesota for the Nonpartisan League (NPL), a major farm political protest movement that started in North Dakota and spread into the plains and western states, 1918–1919; the Socialist party died in North Dakota when most Socialist leaders, like Martinson, joined the influential NPL; joined a local union in Minot in 1920; moved to Fargo, N.D., shortly thereafter where he became a member of Local 1908, International Brotherhood of Painters and Allied Trades and worked as a painter; served as president and business representative of Local 1908; elected secretary of the Fargo Trades and Labor Assembly in 1925, serving until 1926; politically, he was active his entire life, losing races for the North Dakota state legislature in 1936 and again in 1972 at age 90; was deputy commissioner of labor for the state of North Dakota, 1937–1965, his appointment occurring after state expansion of the Department of Agriculture to the Department of Agriculture and Labor; was recording secretary of the Fargo-Moorhead American Federation of Labor-Congress of Industrial Organizations (AFL-CIO) Trades and Assembly from 1965; served as secretary of the southeast North Dakota district of the Building and Construction Trades Council from 1970; authored a *History of North Dakota Labor* (1970), the only general overview of labor in North Dakota and providing valuable information with his long tenure in the movement; he also wrote three articles about his activities with the Socialist party in North Dakota, homesteading in northwestern North Dakota, and organizing for the NPL, entitled ''Comes the Revolution: A Personal Memoir,'' ''Homesteading Episodes,'' and ''Some Memoirs of a Nonpartisan League Organizer," all in *North Dakota History* (Winter 1969; Spring 1973; Spring 1975) as well as several publications of poetry and stories; an advocate for the rights of farmers and laborers, he appeared in the Cannes award-winning film "Northern Lights" (1978) and narrated "Prairie Fire" (1977), both films concerning the history of the Nonpartisan League and Scandinavian immigrant life in North Dakota; moreover, he was the subject of two later documentary films, "Survivor" (1980) and "Rebel Earth" (1980), dealing with his life and experiences in North Dakota; all films produced by New Front Films, Minneapolis; was a life member of the Sons of Norway; died in Fargo on November 20, 1981; "The Interviews: Henry R. Martinson," *North Dakota History* (Spring 1976); D. Jerome Tweton, *In Union There Is Strength: The North Dakota Labor Movement and the United Brotherhood of Carpenters and Joiners* (1982); *Who's Who in North Dakota* (1955); *Who's Who in Labor* (1976); *The Forum* (Fargo-Moorhead), November 21, 1981.

Bruce L. Larson

MASHBURN, Lloyd Abner   (1897–1963). Born in Greeley, Colo., October 10, 1897; son of William James, a farmer, and Susan (Southard) Mashburn; married Luella Carroll on January 22, 1922; four children; completed high school through correspondence courses and then spent two years in a vocational trade school and one year in a manual arts school; served with the U.S. Marine Corps during World War I; joined Los Angeles, Calif., Local 42 of the Wood, Wire and Metal Lathers International Union (WWMLIU) in 1922; elected business agent in 1933, serving until 1939; during 1939–1950, served in a variety of positions in the Los Angeles labor movement, including assistant secretary and later secretary-treasurer of the Los Angeles Building and Construction Trades Council, secretary of the Southern California District Council of Lathers, president of the Los Angeles Temple Association, president of the Los Angeles Labor Council, and vice-chairman of the United American Federation Political Committee; served during World War II on the Los Angeles division of the Selective Service Board and the War Finance Committee of the War Manpower Commission; was on variety of other public committees, serving as vice-chairman of the Los Angeles City Housing Authority and as a member of the personnel board of the Los Angeles Board of Education; was labor commissioner of the state of California, 1951–1953; served as Undersecretary of Labor in the U.S. Department of Labor, 1953–1954, then became an assistant to the president of the WWMLIU in 1954 and elected international president in 1955; was a Republican; died in Chicago, Ill., December 7, 1963; *Who's Who in America, 1960–1961*; *Who's Who in Labor* (1946); *The New York Times*, December 10, 1963.

MASO, Sal   (1900–1971). Born in New York City, July 25, 1900; son of Salvatore, a merchant, and Amelia (Margiotta) Maso; Episcopalian; married Agnes Calvacca on June 15, 1924; one child; completed high school by taking

night classes, then attended a teachers' college for two years; became a metal
lather and joined the Albany, N.Y., local of the International Union of Wood,
Wire and Metal Lathers (WWMLIU) in 1926; transferred to WWMLIU Local
143 in Paterson, N.J., and served it in various capacities; was in influential
figure in the Paterson and New Jersey labor movements, and served as vice-
president and then president of the New Jersey State Building and Construction
Trades Council, president of the United Building and Construction Trades Council of Paterson, and president of the Passaic County Central Labor Union; elected
a vice-president of the WWMLIU in 1939; was active in civic and governmental
affairs in New Jersey, serving as a member of the New Jersey State Board of
Mediation, the Paterson Housing Authority, the Appeals Board of the Passaic
County Selective Service, and as a commissioner of the Paterson Board of
Education; also served on the New Jersey Governor's Committee on Equal
Employment Opportunity; after the death of Lloyd A. Mashburn (q.v.) in 1963,
elected international president of the WWMLIU, serving until his retirement in
1970; was nonpartisan in politics; died in Paterson, N.J., January 21, 1971;
AFL-CIO News, January 30, 1971; *Who's Who in Labor* (1946).

MASON, Lucy Randolph   (1882–1959). Born in Clarens, Va., July 26, 1882;
daughter of Rev. Landon Randolph, an Episcopalian minister, and Lucy (Ambler)
Mason; Episcopalian; completed her formal education, then worked as a stenographer, 1904–1914; employed by the Richmond, Va., Young Women's Christian
Association (YWCA), 1914–1918; did volunteer work for various service organizations, 1918–1923, and was president of the Richmond Equal Suffrage
League and the Richmond League of Women Voters; during World War I,
appointed by Samuel Gompers (q.v.) as Virginia chairman of the Committee on
Women in Industry of the National Advisory Commission; returned to the YWCA
as general secretary in 1923; joined the Union Label League in Richmond in
1923 and later became a member of the International Ladies' Garment Workers'
Union Label League; left the YWCA in the spring of 1932 and replaced Florence
Kelley (q.v.) as general secretary of the National Consumers' League; helped
organize the Friedman-Harry Marks plant in Richmond for the Amalgamated
Clothing Workers of America (ACWA) in 1935; began her Congress of Industrial
Organizations' (CIO) career in 1937 as southern director of organization for
textiles and clothing, working for Stephen Nance (q.v.) out of the Atlanta, Ga.,
Textile Workers Organizing Committee office; her work with the CIO mainly
involved traveling throughout the South as a trouble-shooter, helping to establish
unions in particularly difficult areas; helped organize numerous textile and clothing plants throughout the South, including Cluett, Peabody, and Company of
Atlanta, organized for the ACWA in 1941; was also involved in the organization
of miners in Ducktown, Tenn., for the International Union of Mine, Mill and
Smelter Workers in 1938, and in Port Gibson, Minn., for the International
Woodworkers in 1944, and in Cuthbert, Ga., in 1947; was instrumental in
convincing the 1938 Southern Baptist Convention to adopt a resolution favoring

collective bargaining; worked in 1944 with Sidney Hillman (q.v.) and Paul Christopher (q.v.) for the CIO Political Action Committee in the Carolinas, Georgia, Alabama, and Tennessee; hired by the southern organizing committee to contact local authorities in areas where the CIO was active or expected to be active in 1946; retired from active union work in 1951; authored *To Win These Rights: A Personal Story of the CIO in the South* (1952); died in Atlanta, Ga., May 6, 1959; F. Ray Marshall, *Labor in the South* (1967); *AFL-CIO News*, May 1959; *Notable American Women*, Vol. 4.; *Dictionary of American Biography*, Suppl. 6.

Marie Tedesco

MATHIAS, Charles G. (1913–   ). Born in Baltimore County, Md., August 17, 1913; son of William T., a steel-mill electrician, and Elizabeth R. (Berger) Mathias; Roman Catholic; married Evelyn on September 11, 1940; two children; attended the public schools of Baltimore and night classes at Maryland Institute and Baltimore Tech; was the organizer and president of the Soap and Glycerine Workers' Union at the Gold Dust Corporation in Baltimore, 1935–1937; served as president of Local 1224 of the Steel Workers Organizing Committee, Bethlehem Steel Company, Sparrows Point, Md., and grievance chairman in several departments, 1937–1941; became the Georgia director for the United Textile Workers of America in 1941; during 1941–1943, served on the plant grievance and bargaining committee of the Atlantic Steel Company in Atlanta, Ga., and as a staff member of the Congress of Industrial Organizations' (CIO) shipyard workers in south Georgia and Florida; served with the U.S. Army during World War II; after the war, became a staff representative and subdistrict director, District 35, for the United Steelworkers of America and still held position in 1974; during 1947–1956, served as secretary, vice-president, and president of the Atlanta Industrial Union Council, CIO, and after the American Federation of Labor-CIO merger in Georgia, served as treasurer of the Georgia AFL-CIO, 1956–1964; was involved during his years of service to the state labor movement in legislative lobbying against right-to-work laws and for unemployment compensation legislation, welfare legislation, and the fluoridation of water; involved in civil rights activities since 1946, opposing pension discrimination against blacks at the Atlantic Steel Company and supporting voter registration and cooperation with the Southern Regional Council; served on the federal Rent Control Board, 1947–1950, and as chairman of the Fulton County (Ga.) Board of Public Welfare; a Democrat; F. Ray Marshall, *Labor in the South* (1967).

Merl E. Reed

MATLES, James J. (1909–1975). Born in Soroca, Rumania, on February 24, 1909; married; one child; emigrated to the United States in 1929 at age 19, found work as a machinist in New York City, and immediately joined and became an active member of the International Association of Machinists (IAM); served alternately as local recording secretary, Metal Workers Industrial Union, 1930–

1931, district secretary, 1932–1933, national secretary, Metal Workers Industrial Union, 1933–1934, secretary of the Federation of Metal and Allied Unions, 1934–1935, and grand lodge representative, IAM, 1936–1937; after the organization of the Committee for Industrial Organization (CIO) in 1935, he began organizing electrical workers along industrial lines and, when the United Electrical, Radio and Machine Workers of America (UE) was chartered in 1937, he was elected director of organization for the new national union, a post he held until 1962; during World War II, he served as a CIO representative on the War Manpower Commission and the War Production Board, 1940–1941, before serving in the U.S. Army, 1943–1946; after the war he was caught up in the issue of Communist influence in the labor movement, raids on the UE membership conducted by more conservative CIO unions, and the non-Communist affidavits required by the Taft-Hartley Act; along with other UE leaders, he refused to sign the non-Communist affidavit (although denying any affiliation with the Communist party) and supported UE's withdrawal from the CIO (a short time later the CIO officially expelled UE as "Communist-dominated" union); in 1952 the U.S. Department of Justice began proceedings to have him denaturalized and deported but the U.S. Supreme Court dismissed the action in 1958; was elected the UE general secretary-treasurer in 1962; a fiery orator and volatile organizer during his early years in the labor movement, he gradually mellowed somewhat and acquired a reputation in and outside the labor movement as a smart, tough, meticulous negotiator whose honesty and integrity were unimpeachable; authored *Automation and the New Technology* and coauthored *Them and Us: Struggles of a Rank-and-File Union* (1974); died in Santa Barbara, Calif., on September 16, 1975, shortly after announcing his intention to retire at the UE's annual convention; James J. Matles Papers, UE Archives, New York City; Eleanora W. Schoenebaum, *Political Profiles: The Eisenhower Years* (1977); *New Republic*, October 11, 1975; *The New York Times*, September 17, 1975; *Who's Who in Labor* (1976); James J. Matles Interview, Pennsylvania State University Oral History Collection.

MAURER, James Hudson   (1864–1944). Born in Reading, Pa., April 15, 1864; son of James D., a shoemaker and policeman, and Sarah (Lorah) Maurer; married Mary J. Missmer on April 15, 1886; two children; acquired only 13 months of formal education in the public schools of Reading; at age 6 began working as a newsboy, then worked as a farm laborer and a factory worker; at age 15 served a machinist apprenticeship; joined the Knights of Labor in 1880 and served as an organizer; joined the United Association of Plumbers and Steam Fitters of the United States and Canada in 1901; entered political life as a Populist and edited a party paper, *The Reading Kicker*, in 1898; joined the Socialist Labor party in 1899, and three years later, the Socialist party of America, serving on its national executive committee for ten years; was an unsuccessful Socialist party candidate for governor of Pennsylvania in 1906; during 1911–1918, served three terms as a Socialist member of the Pennsylvania House of

Representatives, successfully sponsoring workmen's compensation, old-age, and mothers' pension legislation; served as president of the Pennsylvania State Federation of Labor, 1912–1928, during which the organization grew from 267 to 1,400 affiliates representing 400,000 members, the largest and most powerful state labor body in the United States; was the Socialist party candidate for Vice-President of the United States in 1928 and 1932; ran for the U.S. Senate on the Socialist ticket in 1934, but two years later resigned from the party because of its "trend toward Communism"; served on the city council, Reading, Pa., 1928–1932, and later served as finance commissioner; after 1917, served as chairman of the Pennsylvania Old Age Assistance Commission; became president of the Workers' Educational Bureau of America and a member of the board of directors of Brookwood Labor College in 1921; after 1922, served on the national committee of the Conference for Progressive Political Action and as president of the Labor Age Publishing Company, publisher of *Labor Age Monthly*; authored *The Far East* (1910), *It Can Be Done* (1938), and *The American Cossack*, the latter denouncing the Pennsylvania constabulary's strike-breaking activities; died in Reading, Pa., March 16, 1944; *National Encyclopedia of American Biography*, Vol. C; *Dictionary of American Biography*, Suppl. 3; Solon DeLeon, ed., *The American Labor Who's Who* (1925); *The New York Times*, March 17, 1944.

John W. Hevener

MAZEY, Emil (1913–   ). Born in Regina, Saskatchewan, Canada, August 2, 1913; son of Lawrence, an auto worker, and Wilma Mazey; married Charlotte Marshall in 1938; one child; moved with family to the United States in 1915, settling in Detroit, Mich.; graduated from Cass Technical High School, Detroit, in 1931; shortly after graduating became an organizer of unemployed workers for the Detroit Unemployed Citizens League; during 1933, attempted to organize workers in the Briggs Manufacturing Company and the following year was discharged from the Gulf Refining Company after organizing workers in the plant where he was employed; organized workers at the Rotary Electric Steel Company, then returned to the Briggs Manufacturing Company in 1936 but was soon discharged for union organizing activities; became an international representative for the United Automobile, Aircraft and Agricultural Implement Workers of America (UAW) and was assigned to organize the Briggs plant in Detroit; organized Briggs Local 212 in 1937 and served as its president until 1941; involved in the organization of the Ford Motor Company River Rouge Plant in 1941 and directed the negotiations in the UAW's first national labor agreement with the Ford Motor Company; returned as president of Briggs Local 212 in 1943 and remained there until inducted into the U.S. armed forces in 1944; served with the U.S. Army in the Philippines but was transferred to Ie Shima, a small island west of Okinawa, after leading a series of demonstrations protesting the shipping and demobilization program of the U.S. Army; elected to the UAW international executive board in 1946 and made co-director of UAW Region 1, comprising Detroit's east side; elected to the office of secretary-treasurer in 1947, beginning a long and continuing term of service in that capacity; served as acting president of the UAW in 1948 when Walter P. Reuther (q.v.) was disabled due to an assassination attempt; led the UAW in the 1948 strike against the Chrysler Corporation; long an advocate of independent political action; has usually supported Democratic candidates since 1960; Jack Stieber, *Governing the UAW* (1962); Jean Gould and Lorena Hickok, *Walter Reuther: Labor's Rugged Individualist* (1972); Frank Cormier and Wiliam J. Eaton, *Reuther* (1970); Roger Keeran, *The Communist Party and the Auto Workers Unions* (1980); Nelson Lichtenstein, *Labor's War at Home: The CIO in World War II* (1982); Michael D. Whitty, ''Emil Mazey: Radical as Liberal. The Evolution of Labor Radicalism in the UAW'' (Ph.D. diss., 1968).

MEANY, George   (1894–1980). Born in New York City, August 16, 1894; son of Michael Joseph, a plumber, and Anne (Cullen) Meany; Roman Catholic; married Eugenia A. McMahon on November 26, 1919; three children; graduated from public school in New York City, then became an apprentice plumber in 1910; became a journeyman plumber in 1915 and joined the United Association of Plumbers and Steam Fitters of the United States and Canada (UA); elected business agent of the New York Local 463, UA, in 1922; served as a delegate to the New York City Central Trades and Labor Assembly and in 1932 was elected a vice-president of the New York State Federation of Labor (NYSFL); while serving as president of the NYSFL, 1934–1939, devoted much of his time and energy to highly successful lobbying efforts before the New York State legislature, to dealing with the varied circumstances related to the initiation of federal work relief and other labor-oriented programs, and to restoring the membership and finances of the state federation during the depression; served on the New York State Industrial Council and on the State Advisory Council on Unemployment Insurance; elected secretary-treasurer of the American Federation of Labor (AFL) in 1939; somewhat frustrated during the early years of his tenure by the conservative, uninnovative policies of AFL president William Green (q.v.), but after 1948 assumed more and more of the decision-making power from the old and ill Green; during World War II, served as a labor delegate to the National Defense Mediation Board and the National War Labor Board; served as AFL fraternal delegate to the British Trades Union Congress in 1945; became the first director of Labor's League for Political Education in 1948; was a member of the executive board of the International Confederation of Free Trade Unions in 1951; appointed to the National Advisory Board on Mobilization Policy in 1951 and to the Contract Compliance Committee in 1952; after the death of William Green in 1952, appointed by the AFL executive council as acting president and subsequently elected president; devoted considerable time during his first years as president to negotiating a merger with the rival Congress of Industrial Organizations (CIO); after the AFL-CIO merger in 1955, elected president of the new federation; served as a delegate to the general assembly of the United Nations in 1957 and 1959; was a vociferous anti-Communist and devoted much of his own time and influence as well as that of the AFL-CIO to the crusade against Communism; during the 1960s, established firm control over the AFL-CIO, beating down all opposition to his policies, including that of the former president of the CIO, Walter Reuther (q.v.); was a Democrat and exerted considerable influence in the councils of the Democratic party; worked closely with the Democratic administrations of the 1960s; broke a tradition dating back to the AFL-CIO merger by refusing to endorse the Democratic presidential nominee in 1972, George S. McGovern; died January 10, 1980; George Meany Papers, AFL-CIO Archives, George Meany Center for Labor Studies; Joseph C. Goulden, *Meany* (1972); Philip Taft, *The A.F. of L. from the Death of Gompers to the Merger* (1959); Ronald Radosh, *American Labor and United States Foreign Policy: The Cold War in the Unions from Gompers to Lovestone* (1969); *National Cyclopaedia of American Biography*, Vol. J; *Current Biography* (1954); Archie Robinson, *George Meany and His Times: A Biography* (1981); *AFL-CIO News*, January 11, 1980.

MEGEL, Carl J. (1899–   ). Born in Hayden, Ind., December 3, 1899; son of Peter and Lena (Kirsch) Megel; married Marion Stewart in April 1925, and after a divorce in 1947, Beverly Falk in October 1962; two children; received B.A. degree from Franklin College in 1923, then attended the graduate schools of the University of Illinois and De Paul University; served as athletic director in a number of schools, 1924–1935, and then became a teacher in Chicago's Lake View High School, serving in that capacity until 1965; was a trustee of the Chicago Teachers Union, 1943–1946, treasurer, 1946–1948, and vice-president, 1949–1951; served as a delegate to the Chicago Federation of Labor and the Illinois State Federation of Labor, 1948–1952; elected president of the American Federation of Teachers (AFT) in 1952, serving until 1964; was a member of the American Federation of Labor-Congress of Industrial Organizations' education committee, 1952–1964; was a delegate to United Nations Educational, Scientific, and Cultural Organization (UNESCO) conferences, 1952–1961, serving as a member of the UNESCO committee, 1953–1959; appointed a member of the White House Conference on Education in 1955; began a long and continuing term of service as the AFT's congressional legislative representative in Washington, D.C., in 1964; Robert J. Braun, *Teachers and Power: The Story of the American Federation of Teachers* (1972); Stephen Cole, *The Unionization of Teachers: A Case Study of the UFT* (1969); *Who's Who in America, 1964–1965*.

MENDELOWITZ, Abraham (1894–1966). Born in Nikolaev, Ukraine, Russia, March 5, 1894; son of Solomon, a tailor, and Leah (Rubenstein) Mendelowitz; Jewish; married Sarah Chayt on April 1, 1917; three children; received little formal education before emigrating to France; joined the French Foreign Legion during World War I and was wounded in Egypt; emigrated to the United States in 1915 and secured employment in the New York cap and millinery industry; joined Local 1 of the Cloth Hat, Cap and Millinery Workers' International Union (CHCMW) in 1916 and shortly thereafter elected an officer in the local; elected a CHCMW vice-president in 1923; became an executive board member of the influential CHCMW Local 24 in 1924 and in 1934 became a co-manager of the local; after the merger between the CHCMW and the United Hatters of North America, became a vice-president of the newly organized United Hatters, Cap and Millinery Workers' International Union (UHCMWIU) in 1934; was one of the founders in 1936 of the Millinery Stabilization Commission, which provided for labor-management cooperation in the millinery industry; was a vigorous opponent of Communist efforts to take control of CHCMW locals during the 1920s and of similar efforts by racketeers in the 1930s; was a member of the New York Central Trades and Labor Council, the Jewish Hebrew Trades, and Workmen's Circle; elected co-manager of millinery workers union Locals 2, 24, 30, 42, 90, and 92; supported the Liberal party of New York; died in New York City, November 14, 1966; Donald B. Robinson, *Spotlight on a Union: The Story of the United Hatters, Cap and Millinery Workers' International Union* (1948); Charles H. Green, *The Headwear Workers* (1944); *Who's Who in Labor* (1946).

MERRILL, Lewis Robert   (1908–1965). Born in Toronto, Canada, in 1908; son of Phillip and Esther (Kreengle) Merrill; married twice; two children; emigrated to the United States in 1929 after having attended the University of Toronto; worked as a credit and investment analyst; while employed by the New York Credit Clearing House, joined the American Federation of Labor (AFL) Bookkeepers, Stenographers and Accountants' Union, federal Local 12646 in 1930; became an office employee of Local 281 of the New York City Sheet Metal Workers' Union in 1931; elected president of federal Local 12646 in 1936 and in that capacity led the campaign for an international charter from the AFL; began a campaign to organize insurance workers in 1936; after the repeated failure of the AFL to grant an international charter to organize banking, social service, and insurance workers, led much of the membership of federal Local 12646 into the Congress of Industrial Organizations (CIO) in 1937 and served as general secretary of the convention sponsoring committee that led to the creation of the United Office and Professional Workers of America (UPPW); elected the first president of the UPPW in 1937; was a member of the CIO executive board and was a member of the CIO health and welfare committee; negotiated one of the then largest white-collar worker union labor contracts with the Prudential Insurance Company in 1943; often denied Communist party membership, but was a contributing editor to the *New Masses* and a trustee of the Jefferson School of Social Science; ended his association with the *New Masses* and the Jefferson School of Social Science in 1946 and became a critic of Communist influence in the UPPW; resigned as president of the UPPW in 1947, a move apparently prompted by the increased Communist influence in the union; after his resignation, became involved in the distribution of magazines, comic books, and paperback books through supermarket chains, and later became a consultant to publishing firms and an investment and financial advisor to various corporations; was affiliated with the American Labor party until 1946; authored several pamphlets relating to the organization of white-collar workers; died in New York City, June 18, 1965; Harvey J. Clermont, *Organizing the Insurance Worker: A History of Labor Unions of Insurance Employees* (1966); Max M. Kampelman, *The Communist Party vs. the C.I.O.: A Study in Power Politics* (1957); *Who's Who in Labor* (1946); Joseph E. Finley, *While Collar Union: The Story of the OPEIU and Its People* (1975).

MIGAS, Nick   (1914–   ). Born in McKees Rocks, Pa., about 1914; son of a coal miner and member of the United Mine Workers of America; married; two children; graduated from high school in Hammond, Ind., in 1933; secured a job as a stocker in the scrap yard of an Inland Steel Company plant; was subsequently promoted to switchman and then conductor; became active in an independent union in the plant and was elected a department steward; after the organization of the Steel Workers Organizing Committee (SWOC) in 1937, he and his union affiliated with SWOC; after SWOC was chartered by the Congress of Industrial Organizations (CIO) as the United Steelworkers of America (USWA) in 1942, he became a staff member of the new international union; was fired from his union position after supporting George Paterson who unsuccessfully challenged incumbent District 31 director, Joseph Germano (q.v.); returned to the mill and in 1945 was elected president of USWA Local 1010; served as a delegate to national USWA conventions in 1946 and 1948; was physically beaten after opposing the union leadership at the 1948 convention but was subsequently elected to his department's grievance committee and retained that office after efforts were unsuccessful to have him removed from office under anti-Communist provisions of the Taft-Hartley Act; shortly thereafter, he left the steel mills and the union to become a dairy farmer in Wisconsin; a Communist; Alice Lynd and Staughton Lynd, eds., *Rank and File: Personal Histories by Working-Class Organizers* (1973).

MILLER, Arnold Ray   (1923–   ). Born in Leewood, W.Va., on April 25, 1923; son of George Matt, a coal miner, and Lulu (Hoy) Miller, a homemaker; married in 1948; two children; attended public schools in Leewood through the ninth grade before dropping out of school to enter the Cabin Creek coal mines in 1939, at which time he also joined the United Mine Workers of America (UMWA); enlisted in the U.S. Army in 1942; severely wounded during the Normandy invasion, he spent two years in military hospitals before being discharged in 1946; after failing to complete an automotive mechanic training course, he returned to the Cabin Creek mines; became an electrician-repairman for the Imperial Colliery Company in 1962 and held that job until 1968 when arthritis and pneumoconiosis (black lung disease) forced his retirement; thereafter, he unsuccessfully lobbied UMWA officials to recognize black lung as an occupationally related ailment under workmen's compensation; was one of the founders of the Black Lung Association (BLA) in 1969, a grass-roots movement of West Virginia miners that called a three-week protest strike and organized and led a miners' march on Charleston, W.Va., to protest the inattention to the black lung problem; supported Joseph Yablonsky's (q.v.) insurgency campaign against W. A. "Tony" Boyle (q.v.) for the UMWA presidency in 1969, serving as Yablonsky's campaign coordinator in UMWA, District 17, West Virginia; elected BLA president in 1970; after Yablonsky's murder in January 1970, he joined with many other outraged miners to organize Miners for Democracy (MFD), an insurgent organization dedicated to union reform; when the U.S. Department of Labor invalidated Boyle's 1969 reelection, Miller became the MFD candidate for the UMWA presidency in 1972 and easily defeated Boyle in an election supervised by over one thousand federal agents; after assuming office, he immediately initiated measures to democratize union governance and to increase retired miner benefits; to dramatize a UMWA campaign for increased mine safety, he called an industrywide, five-day strike in 1974 to memorialize killed and injured miners; later the same year, he led a 24-day strike before agreeing to a new three-year contract with the Bituminous Coal Operators Association; although personally popular with rank-and-file miners, he lacked the dynamic qualities and administrative skills to establish his leadership effectively over the restless, factionalized union membership; became increasingly reclusive as criticism mounted during a 110-day strike in 1977–1978; failing health and membership unrest led to his retirement in 1979; a liberal Democrat; Joseph E. Finley, *The Corrupt Kingdom: The Rise and Fall of the United Mine Workers* (1972); Brit Hume, *Death in the Mines* (1971); *Current Biography* (1973); *Who's Who in Labor* (1976); George W. Hopkins, "Southern Appalachian Coal Miners and Union Insurgency, 1968–1972," in *Southern Workers and Their Unions, 1880–1975*, ed. Merl E. Reed et al. (1981).

MILLER, Edward S. (1901–   ). Born in Cameron, Mo., June 24, 1901; son of John K., a cigarmaker, and Maxine (Stout) Miller; Christian church; married Blanche Spurgeon on January 9, 1938; graduated from high school, then served with the U.S. armed services during World War I; following the war, eventually secured work as a bartender and joined Kansas City, Mo., Local 420 of the Hotel and Restaurant Employees' International Alliance and Bartenders' International League of America (HREIABIL); was elected secretary-treasurer of Local 420 and quickly regenerated the moribund local; elected president of the Kansas City local joint executive board of the HREIABIL and reinvigorated the union's organizing efforts in Kansas City; began a major drive to organize Kansas City hotels in 1937, and after a divisive 19-day strike, succeeded; was a protégé of HREIABIL president Edward Flore (q.v.); in 1938 successfully opposed the reelection of the corruption-tainted vice-president from the union's fifth district; led a major organizing drive in Chicago, Ill., during the early 1940s, which resulted in large membership gains; appointed secretary-treasurer by the HREIABIL executive board in 1946 and elected to the same position a year later; elected international president after the death of Hugo Ernst (q.v.) in 1954; during his incumbency, the HREIABIL began an expensive but successful effort to organize the hotels and restaurants of Miami Beach, Fla.; was a friend of Kansas City political leader Tom Pendergast and Harry S. Truman and usually supports the Democratic party; retired union positions because of failing health in 1973; Matthew Josephson, *Union House, Union Bar: The History of the Hotel and Restaurant Employees and Bartenders International Union, AFL-CIO* (1956); *Who's Who in Labor* (1946); *AFL-CIO News*, February 10, 1973.

MILLER, Frieda Segelke   (1889–1973). Born in La Crosse, Wis., on April 16, 1889; daughter of James Gordon, a lawyer, and Erna (Segelke) Miller; never married; one adopted child; attended La Crosse public schools; earned a B.A. in liberal arts from Milwaukee-Downer College in 1911; studied labor economics and political science at the University of Chicago and completed all the requirements for the Ph.D. but a dissertation, 1911–1915; received a Doctor of Human Letters from Russell Sage College in 1941; worked as a research assistant in the department of social economy, Bryn Mawr College, in 1916; became executive secretary of the Philadelphia Women's Trade Union League (WTUL) in 1917; represented the WTUL on the advisory committee that set up Bryn Mawr Summer School for Women Workers in Industry in 1920; while traveling in Europe in 1923, she attended the Third International Congress of Working Women; became a factory inspector for the Joint Board of Sanitary Control of the International Ladies' Garment Workers' Union (ILGWU) in 1924; became a research investigator for the New York Welfare Council in 1927; two years later was appointed head of the New York State Department of Labor's Division of Women in Industry; selected by President Franklin D. Roosevelt to represent the United States at the International Labor Organization's (ILO) Inter-American Regional Conference in Santiago, Chile, in 1938; also served on the ILO Advisory Committee on Women Workers and was the first woman elected to the ILO's executive board; appointed New York State's industrial commissioner in 1938 and retained that position until 1942 when she resigned after the election of a Republican governor; appointed a special assistant on labor to the United States Ambassador to Great Britain in 1943; appointed director of the federal Women's Bureau in 1944, succeeding Mary Anderson (q.v.), who had served in that position since it was created in 1920; as director of the Women's Bureau, she created the labor advisory committee which brought trade union women to the bureau for the first time; with the advent of the Republican Eisenhower administration in 1953, she resigned from the Women's Bureau, but continued working for the ILO investigating the status of women laborers in the East and in South America; served as a United States representative to the United Nations for the International Union for Child Welfare, 1960–1967; was a Democrat; died in New York City on July 21, 1973; *Notable American Women*, Vol. 4; *Current Biography* (1945); *Who's Who in Labor* (1946); *The New York Times*, July 22, 1973.

MILLER, Joyce Dannen   (1928–   ). Born in Chicago, Ill., on June 19, 1928; daughter of Reuben L. and Lillian (Resenson) Dannen; divorced; three children; received a Ph.B. from the University of Chicago in 1950 and an M.A. in 1951; joined the Amalgamated Clothing Workers of America (ACWA) in 1952; served as the Pittsburgh, Pa., area education director of the ACWA, 1952–1953; appointed education director for the Chicago board of the ACWA in 1962, serving in that position until 1966; became assistant director of social services for the ACWA Chicago board in 1966 and held that position until 1972, when she became the executive assistant to the ACWA general officers and director of social services; after the merger of the ACWA and the Textile Workers of America in 1976, creating the Amalgamated Clothing and Textile Workers Union of America (ACTWU), she was elected an international vice-president and became ACTWU's director of social services; elected national president of the Coalition of Labor Union Women (CLWU) in 1977; was elected an American Federation of Labor-Congress of Industrial Organizations (AFL-CIO) vice-president and executive council member in 1980, becoming the first woman to sit on the executive council; involved in a broad array of social and labor reform activities, she was a member of the East Coast Coalition of Labor Women, the Labor Advisory Committee of Roosevelt University, the Trade Union Women's Study Program at the Cornell Institute of Labor and Industrial Relations, the National Committee on Working Women, the AFL-CIO committee on civil rights, the National Trade Union Council for Human Rights, the Industrial Relations Research Association, the American Social Benefits Association, the National Organization for Women, and the National Women's Political Caucus; a Democrat, she was a member of the executive board of Americans for Democratic Action; authored "Unions and Day Care Centers for Children of Working Mothers," *Child Welfare* (1971), and "A Look at Day Care," *The American Federationist* (May 1965); *Who's Who in Labor* (1976); *Who's Who of American Women* (1983–1984); *AFL-CIO News*, August 23, 1980; Jana Field, "The Coalition of Labor Union Women," *Political Affairs* (March 1975); Philip S. Foner, *Women and the American Labor Movement from World War I to the Present* (1980).

MILLER, Marvin Julian   (1917–   ). Born in New York City, April 14, 1917; son of Alexander, a salesman, and Gertrude (Wald) Miller, a school teacher; Jewish; married Theresa Morgenstern on December 24, 1939; two children; while attending the public schools of Brooklyn, worked as a newspaper delivery boy, a Wall Street runner, and a clerk at a soda fountain; received a B.S. degree in economics from New York University in 1938 and later took graduate courses at the New School for Social Research; worked briefly as a clerk in the U.S. Department of the Treasury and as an investigator for the New York City Department of Welfare; served with the Wage Stabilization Division of the War Labor Board during World War II; after the war was associated with the U.S. Conciliation Service until 1947; then joined the staff of the International

Association of Machinists; became the associate director of research for the United Steelworkers of America (USWA) in 1950, serving in that capacity until 1960; appointed assistant to USWA president David J. McDonald (q.v.); replaced Arthur Goldberg (q.v.) in 1961 on the tripartite committee created by the USWA and the Kaiser Steel Corporation to manage and improve industrial relations; was a member of the National Labor-Management Panel, 1963–1967; elected executive director of the Major League Baseball Players Association in 1966; quickly became a controversial figure in the sports industry; won important concessions from major league baseball club owners and led players in a 13-day strike in the spring of 1972; a Democrat; retired in 1983; *Current Biography* (1973); *Sports Illustrated*, February 24, 1969; *Sport* (October 1972).

MILLER, Saul   (1918–   ). Born in New York City on September 23, 1918; son of Louis, a metal worker, and Kate (Zizmor) Miller; married Beatrice Elbaum, a labor relations training specialist, in 1945; four children; attended De Witt Clinton High School, New York City, 1931–1935, City College of New York, 1935–1937, and New York University, 1937–1941, from which he received a B.S. degree; served as a staff sergeant in the U.S. Army during World War II, 1942–1945; after the war he became a reporter for the *York* (Pa.) *Gazette and Daily*, 1945–1948, and joined the American Newspaper Guild; employed as a copy editor for the *Richmond* (Va.) *Times-Dispatch*, 1948–1949, and as news editor for the *Jamestown* (N.Y.) *Sun*, 1949–1951; became the director of a small Washington, D.C., news service in 1951 and held that position until being appointed associate editor of the *AFL News Reporter* in 1955; after the merger of the American Federation of Labor and the Congress of Industrial Organizations (AFL-CIO) in 1955, he was named the managing editor of the *AFL-CIO News*; was appointed director of the AFL-CIO publications department in 1958; became executive editor of *The American Federationist* in 1960; when the AFL-CIO merged its departments of public relations and publications in 1980, he was appointed director of the new department of information; a member of the National Press Club; retired from union positions in 1982; *AFL-CIO News*, January 5, 1980; *Who's Who in Labor* (1976).

MILLIMAN, Elmer Edward   (1890–1946). Born in Mount Morris, N.Y., November 22, 1890; son of John, a hotel keeper, and Mary (Ward) Milliman; Roman Catholic; married Esther D. Gumaer on June 7, 1919; two children; graduated from high school, then attended Rochester Institute of Technology until family financial problems forced him out of school; secured work on a section gang of the Delaware, Lackawanna and Western Railroad in 1909; served as the foreman of a construction and maintenance crew, 1910–1919; joined the Brotherhood of Maintenance of Way Employees (BMWE) in 1918; elected general chairman of the Delaware, Lackawanna and Western system division of the BMWE in 1919; served as secretary-treasurer of the national General Chairmen's Association and president of the Eastern District General Chairmen's Association, 1919–1922; elected international secretary-treasurer of the BMWE in 1922, serving until 1940; was an American Federation of Labor (AFL) fraternal delegate to the British Trades Union Congress in 1932; elected a member of the AFL committee on education in 1938; served as chairman of the Association of National Reporting Officers established under the Railroad Retirement Act, 1938–1944; elected international president of the BMWE in 1940; during World War II, was a member of the War Production Board's Railway Labor Executives' Association Committee and a member of the Office of Defense Transportation Advisory Board; served on the Railway Labor Executives' Association, 1940–1946; was a member of the AFL committee on international labor relations; was an official in several voluntary organizations, including vice-president of the Catholic Conference on Industrial Problems, chairman of the Committee on Consumer Cooperatives, and president of the Workers Education Bureau of America; was a member of the national advisory board of the Labor League for Human Rights; died in Detroit, Mich., January 1, 1946; Denver W. Hertel, *History of the Brotherhood of Maintenance of Way Employees: Its Birth and Growth, 1877–1955* (1955); Brotherhood of Maintenance of Way Employees, *Pictorial History, 1877–1951* (1952); *Who's Who in Labor* (1946).

MILNE, J. Scott   (1898–1955). Born in Vancouver, British Columbia, Canada, January 21, 1898; son of Robert and Martha (Steele) Milne; married Doris M. Ford on June 20, 1923; two children; completed his formal education in Canada, then served in the Canadian Army during World War I; after the war, emigrated to the United States, settling in Portland, Oreg.; became an electrical lineman and joined Local 125 of the International Brotherhood of Electrical Workers (IBEW); elected financial secretary and business manager of Local 125 in 1923, serving until 1929; appointed an IBEW international representative in 1929; elected an international vice-president representing the IBEW's ninth district, West Coast division in 1936; served as international secretary of the IBEW, 1947–1954; was an American Federation of Labor (AFL) fraternal delegate to the British Trades Union Congress in 1953; elected international president succeeding Daniel W. Tracy (q.v.) in 1954; became an AFL vice-president and executive council member in 1954; elected president of the International Labor Press of America in 1953; edited the *Electrical Workers Journal*, 1947–1954; died in Portland, Oreg., July 20, 1955; *American Federation of Labor News-Reporter*, March 25, 1954, July 22, 1955; *The New York Times*, July 21, 1955; *Who's Who in America, 1954–1955*.

MINTON, Lee Webb   (1911–   ). Born in Washington, Pa., November 17, 1911; son of Romney, a restaurateur, and Lulu (Bayne) Minton; Christian Scientist; married Helen Irene Thompson on July 31, 1938; two children; completed three years of high school, then attended a business college for a short time; learned the glass-blowing trade and in 1934 joined a Pennsylvania local of the Glass Bottle Blowers' Association of the United States and Canada (GBBA);

served as a local representative and a tri-state representative, then elected to the GBBA executive board in 1938; elected GBBA international treasurer in 1945, vice-president in 1946, and president later in 1946; served as a delegate to the Philadelphia Central Labor Union and the Pennsylvania State Federation of Labor; was an American Federation of Labor (AFL) fraternal delegate to the Canadian Trades and Labor Congress in 1951; elected an AFL-Congress of Industrial Organizations' (AFL-CIO) vice-president and executive council member in 1956; was an AFL-CIO delegate to the International Confederation of Free Trade Unions in 1966; appointed a member of the President's Task Force on Economic Growth for the 70s and served on the board of directors of CARE; retired as president emeritus of the GBBA in 1971; Republican, served as chairman of National Labor for Rockefeller Committee in 1964 and 1968; *Who's Who in Labor* (1946); *Who's Who in America, 1972–1973*.

MITCH, William A. (1881–   ). Born in Minersville, Ohio, April 10, 1881; son of Frederick, a coal miner, and Matilda (Jones) Mitch; Methodist; married Mary Evans on April 9, 1909; three children; went to work in the coal mines and joined the United Mine Workers of America (UMWA) in 1894; served as international traveling auditor of the UMWA, 1913–1914, and as secretary-treasurer of District 11, UMWA, Indiana, 1915–1931; played a leading role in the independent labor party movement in Indiana in 1919; served with John Brophy (q.v.) and Chris Golden on the UMWA's Nationalization Research Committee to investigate the feasibility of public ownership of coal mines in 1912–1923; attended the International Mining Congress in Frankfurt, Germany, in 1922; as president of UMWA District 11 in 1932, conducted a violent strike to resist a 25 percent wage reduction, but was forced to accept a reduction from $6.10 to $4.75 per day; along with William Dalrymple and Walter Jones, an Alabama black miner who had been forced by blacklist to move to Ohio, re-organized District 20, Alabama, which had two locals with 225 members in early June 1933; by July 23, they had organized eighteen thousand members into 85 locals; in February and March 1934, eleven thousand miners struck for union recognition and the dues check-off; on March 14, they signed an Alabama Agreement covering 90 percent of the state's operators and 85 percent of its tonnage, granting the check-off and raising wages from $3.40 to $3.60 per day; served as president of District 20, UMWA, Alabama, from 1933 until at least 1946, and president of the Alabama State Federation of Labor from 1933 until 1937; during the 1936 convention of the state federation, John W. Altman, the federation's general counsel, attacked ''Mitch of Indiana'' for organizing racially integrated locals, with blacks occasionally serving as officers with authority over white miners; appointed director of the southern region of the Steel Workers' Organizing Committee by Philip Murray (q.v.) in 1936; after the American Federation of Labor-Congress of Industrial Organizations (CIO) split, served as president of the Alabama State Industrial Union Council, CIO; William A. Mitch Papers, Labor Archives, Pennsylvania State University; *Who's Who in Labor*

(1946); Solon DeLeon, ed., *The American Labor Who's Who* (1925); F. Ray Marshall, *Labor in the South* (1967); John Brophy, *A Miner's Life* (1964); John H. M. Laslett, *Labor and the Left: A Study of Socialism and Radical Influences in the American Labor Movement, 1881–1924* (1970); Philip Taft, *Organizing Dixie: Alabama Workers in the Industrial Era* (1981).

John W. Hevener

MITCHELL, Harry Leland   (1906–   ). Born near Halls, Tenn., June 14, 1906; son of James Y., a barber, tenant farmer, and Baptist preacher, and Maude Ella (Stanfield) Mitchell; reared a Baptist; married Lyndell Carmack, a teacher, on December 26, 1926, and Dorothy Dowe in October 1951, a social worker who had been associated with the Works Progress Administration, the National Youth Administration, and in 1943 became secretary-treasurer of the Southern Tenant Farmers Union (STFU); three children; graduated from Halls High School in 1924 and shortly thereafter became a sharecropper near Ripley, Tenn.; operated a dry-cleaning business in Tyronza, Ark., 1927–1934; along with 17 others, founded the STFU in 1934 and served as its executive secretary, 1934–1939, 1941-1944; conducted aggressive organizing drives during 1934 when the initial Agricultural Adjustments Administration cotton program provided no guarantees to tenant farmers; led strikes in Arkansas and Tennessee during the spring of 1935, which brought local repression of tenants' civil liberties but national publicity to the STFU; by 1937, thirty thousand tenant farmers and sharecroppers, organized interracially, had been enrolled in the STFU; frequently testified before public and private agencies on agricultural problems in an effort to enlist the aid of federal agencies and national organizations for tenants' and sharecroppers' cause; gradually lost faith in orthodox union tactics after the failure of several strikes and instead emphasized the role of the STFU as a pressure group advocating publicity, new legislation, and law enforcement; however, the STFU executive council favored the union approach, and hence he sought affiliation with the Congress of Industrial Organizations and merged, reluctantly, with the Communist-led United Cannery, Agricultural, Packing and Allied Workers of America (UCAPAWA) in 1937; after numerous quarrels with UCAPAWA president Donald J. Henderson (q.v.) over STFU autonomy, dues, communism, and alleged dual union tactics, withdrew from the UCAPAWA following the Missouri sharecroppers demonstration in 1939; elected president of the STFU in 1944 and led the union into the American Federation of Labor (AFL) under the newly chartered National Farm Labor Union (NFLU); served as president of the NFLU, 1945–1955, and its successor, the National Agricultural Workers Union (NAWU), AFL-CIO, 1955–1960; despite the general failures to achieve the STFU's union-oriented goals during the 1930s, he and others exhibited considerable personal courage, stood up to the power of local planters, gained national publicity for sharecroppers and tenants, and won occasional economic victories; after the NAWU merged with the Amalgamated Meat Cutters and Butcher Workmen of North America in 1960, served his new union as an agricultural specialist and was involved in organizing dairy farm and plant workers, rice mill, sugar plantation, and seasonal sugar mill workers, and menhaden fishermen on the Gulf of Mexico; during his career, also served as a special assistant to the National Youth Administration, as an International Ladies' Garment Workers' Union organizer, and as a consultant to the U.S. Department of Labor and the International Labor Organization; was a Socialist until 1936, then supported the Democratic party; authored *Mean Things Happening in This Land: The Life and Times of H. L. Mitchell, Cofounder of the Southern Tenant Farmers Union* (1979); Donald H. Grubbs, *Cry from the Cotton* (1971); Louis Cantor, *A Prologue to the Protest Movement: The Missouri Sharecropper Roadside Demonstration of 1939* (1969); Joan London and Henry Anderson, *So Shall Ye Reap: The Story of Cesar Chavez and the Farm Workers' Movement* (1970); David E. Conrad, *The Forgotten Farmers: The Story of Sharecroppers in the New Deal* (1965); *Current Biography* (1947); *Who's Who in Labor* (1946); H. L. Mitchell Interview, Columbia Oral History Collection.

Merl E. Reed

MITCHELL, James J.   (1896–1957). Born in Carfin, Lanarkshire, Scotland, November 25, 1896; son of Lawrence, a coal miner, and Rose (Tummons) Mitchell; Roman Catholic; married Mrs. Catherine Hallinan Parker on May 21, 1944; adopted three children; received a grammar school education in Scotland, then began working in the Lanarkshire mines and joined the Lanarkshire Miners and Boilermakers Union; emigrated to the United States as a youth and settled in Lynn, Mass., there gaining employment in the shoe industry; joined the Lasters Shoe local in Lynn in 1932; served as a member of the Lasters Shoe local executive board and negotiating agreement committee, 1933–1936; served as secretary of the Lynn Joint Council of Shoe Workers, 1933–1936; was one of the organizers of the independent United Shoe and Leather Workers Union (USLWU) in 1935 and elected its secretary; following the amalgamation of the USLWU, the Shoe Workers Protective Association, and several other independent local unions creating the United Shoe Workers of America (USWA), which was chartered by the Congress of Industrial Organizations in 1937, elected secretary-treasurer of the new national union and served in that capacity until his death; considered one of the seminal figures in the USWA, was instrumental in its founding, growth, and development; died in Washington, D.C., November 11, 1957; *AFL-CIO News*, November 16, 1957; *Who's Who in Labor* (1946).

MITCHELL, John   (1870–1919). Born in Braidwood, Ill., February 4, 1870; son of Robert, a coal miner and farmer, and Martha (Halley) Mitchell; Roman Catholic; married Katherine O'Rourke on June 1, 1891; six children; attended Braidwood public schools for five years and later studied in evening school; studied law for one year; worked in the coal mines of Illinois, Colorado, New Mexico, and elsewhere, 1882–1890; joined the Knights of Labor in 1885, and the United Mine Workers of America (UMWA) at its founding in 1890; elected secretary-treasurer of District 12, UMWA, Illinois, in 1895; appointed international organizer in 1897 and worked with John H. Walker (q.v.) and Mother Jones (q.v.) in southern Illinois and West Virginia; elected UMWA international vice-president in 1897 and appointed acting international president in September 1898, when President Michael Ratchford (q.v.) resigned; elected and served as UMWA international president, 1899–1908; during his administration, the UMWA increased its membership from 34,000 to 300,000 and its treasury from $12,000 to $900,000; due to his skillful direction of the 147,000-man Pennsylvania anthracite strike in 1902, public opinion swung to the miners' side and the Anthracite Coal Strike Commission, appointed by President Theodore Roosevelt, awarded the miners a 14 percent wage increase and the eight- or nine-hour day; served as fourth vice-president of the American Federation of Labor (AFL), 1898–1900, and as second vice-president, 1900–1914, much to the chagrin of the ambitious Thomas L. Lewis (q.v.), who succeeded him as UMWA international president in 1908; along with AFL president Samuel Gompers (q.v.) and secretary-treasurer Frank Morrison (q.v.), was convicted and sentenced to prison for violating a federal court injunction during a strike at Buck's Stove and Range Company of St. Louis, Mo.; on appeal, the U.S. Supreme Court relieved them of prison sentences; assisted in organizing the National Civic Federation in 1900 and retained his membership until a resolution adopted by a combination of Socialists and followers of retiring President Lewis forced him to resign from the federation or the UMWA; was chairman of the trades agreement department of the National Civic Federation, 1908–1911; served as a member of the New York State Workmen's Compensation Commission, 1914–1915, and chairman of the New York State Industrial Commission from 1915 until his death; served during World War I on several city, state, and regional bodies; died in New York City, September 9, 1919, and was buried at Scranton, Pa., where the UMWA in 1924, erected a statue designed by Philip Sheridan; miners still celebrate the second Monday in April as Mitchell Day; John Mitchell Papers, Catholic University of America; Elsie Gluck, *John Mitchell: Miner* (1929); Charles A. Madison, *American Labor Leaders: Personalities and Forces in the Labor Movement* (1950); *Dictionary of American Biography*, Vol. 7; *National Cyclopaedia of American Biography*, Vol. 24; *Who Was Who in America*, Vol. 1; James O. Morris, "The Acquisitive Spirit of John Mitchell, UMWA President (1899–1908)," *Labor History* (Winter 1979).

John W. Hevener

MITCHELL, Walter L. (1915–1968). Born in Florence, Ala., January 30, 1915; son of Goodlow S. and Exel T. (Hendon) Mitchell; married Ruby A. Jenkins on April 8, 1936, and after that marriage ended in divorce in 1954, Lucille Snowden on December 24, 1955; two children; received the LL.B. degree from the Atlanta, Ga., Law School in 1950 and the LL.M. degree in 1951; attended the University of Georgia, 1951–1952; graduated from high school, then began work as a laborer at the Tennessee Valley Authority (TVA) chemical, phosphates, and nitrates plant in 1933 and eventually was promoted to a position as laboratory analyst; organized TVA laboratory workers into an American Federation of Labor (AFL) federal labor union in 1941 and became the first president of the TVA Council of Office, Technical and Service Unions; served as an AFL organizer, 1942–1944, 1946; elected a vice-president and southern regional director of the newly organized International Chemical Workers Union (ICWU) in 1946, serving in that capacity until 1956; elected international president of the ICWU in 1956 and served in that position until his death; became a vice-president of the industrial union department of the AFL-Congress of Industrial Organizations (CIO) and a member of the executive board of the maritime trades department in 1962; was a delegate to the International Labor Organization's chemical industries committee meeting in Geneva in 1962; served on the national board of Americans for Democratic Action and Citizens' Crusade Against Poverty; was a Democrat; died in New Orleans, La., September 19, 1968; Melvin Rothbaum, *The Government of the Oil, Chemical and Atomic Workers Union* (1962); *Who's Who in America, 1968–1969*; *AFL-CIO News*, September 28, 1968.

MOFFETT, Elwood Stewart   (1908–1973). Born in Williamstown, Pa., April 30, 1908; son of Alfred, a coal miner, and Jennie A. (Showers) Moffett; Methodist; married Hannah P. Ely on January 31, 1931; four children; completed high school, then went to work as an anthracite miner in 1924 and joined the United Mine Workers of America (UMWA); elected president of his local at age 27 and reelected several times; when John L. Lewis (q.v.) reorganized District 50, a small UMWA affiliate in the coal and coke by-products field, into a catch-all union for raiding purposes, Moffett was hired as an organizer in 1942; held various staff posts until appointed assistant to the president of District 50, A. D. Lewis (q.v.), in 1948; became a vice-president in 1958 and president after the death of Lewis in 1962; as president, asserted himself on behalf of District 50, reducing per capita payment to the UMWA and building membership in the chemical industry; his relations with the UMWA became increasingly strained; in 1968 the District 50 executive board acclaimed nuclear generation of power and announced it would organize atomic energy workers; within a month UMWA president W. A. Boyle (q.v.) expelled District 50, denouncing its officers for betraying the parent union and jeopardizing coal miners' jobs; expulsion had little effect on District 50 as it was already in fact an independent union whose membership exceeded that of the UMWA; as a result of a UMWA suit, the union changed its name to District 50, Allied and Technical Workers; instituted staff training conferences, worker-education programs, and union-management conferences; concerned about his union's financial standing and seeking to establish coordinated bargaining in chemicals and utilities, began merger talks with the United Steelworkers of America (USWA) in 1969; defeated vice-president Angelo Cafalo in a race for the presidency in 1970; won a legal battle to prevent a District 50 referendum on merger, then gained members' approval of the merger of his 200,000-member union with the USWA in 1972; became a special assistant to the USWA president after the merger; was a Democrat; died in Washington, D.C., February 22, 1973; *Who's Who in America* (1972); *Wall Street Journal,* March 7, 1968; *Steel Labor* (March 1973).

Donald G. Sofchalk

MOHN, Einar Oliver (1906–). Born in Atwater, Minn., August 27, 1906; son of Christopher, a minister, and Hattie (Hansen) Mohn; Lutheran; married Margaret Flockoi on January 1, 1930; three children; graduated from high school, then studied bacteriology at Augsburg College, Minneapolis, Minn., 1925–1927, and the University of Washington, 1927–1928; worked as a bacteriologist for the Whatcom County Dairyman's Association, Bellingham, Wash., 1928–1933; joined Milk Drivers and Dairy Employees Local 93 of the International Brotherhood of Teamsters, Chauffeurs, Warehousemen and Helpers of America (IBT) in 1933; elected secretary of the Billingham Central Labor Council and served as the chief administrative officer of IBT Local 231, 1934–1937; was one of the principal founders of the Western States Dairy Employees Council and its IBT international representative in 1936; became an IBT international organizer in 1941 and was placed in charge of the southern California district; was a founder of the Western Line Drivers Council in 1944 and was its first vice-chairman; elected president of IBT Joint Council 42 and of Warehouse and Produce Council 846; elected an IBT vice-president in 1952; served as an executive assistant to IBT president Dave Beck (q.v.), 1952–1957; began a long term of service as chairman of the powerful Western Conference of Teamsters in 1957; served on numerous commissions and boards in California, including the Citizen's Advisory Commission of Revision and Updating the California Constitution, 1964–1968, the Governor's Commission on Automation and Technological Developments, 1963–1967, the California Commission on Manpower, 1963–1967, and the Stanford Mid-Peninsula Urban Coalition; was a member of the University of California Board of Regents, 1965–1967; usually supported Democrats in state elections; Donald Garnel, *The Rise of Teamster Power in the West* (1972); Sam Romer, *The International Brotherhood of Teamsters: Its Government and Structure* (1962); Robert D. Leiter, *The Teamsters Union: A Study of Its Economic Impact* (1957); *Who's Who in Labor* (1946).

MOLONY, Joseph Patrick (1906–1977). Born in Ennis, County Clare, Ireland, November 6, 1906; Roman Catholic; married Marguerite Bouchard in 1938; one child; attended school for ten years in Ireland, then emigrated to the United States in 1926; worked in various blue-collar jobs before being employed by Republic Steel at its Buffalo works in 1936; became an organizer for the Steel Workers Organizing Committee during the "Little Steel" strike of 1937; elected director of United Steelworkers of America (USWA) District 4, New York State, in 1942; headed the USWA's Bethlehem Steel negotiating committee for many years; was an unsuccessful rank-and-file candidate for a USWA vice-presidency in 1955, which was the first real contest for an elective international office in the union's history and was an indirect challenge to USWA president David J. MacDonald (q.v.); supported McDonald a year later when a group opposed to increased dues attempted to unseat him; helped launch and manage I. W. Abel's (q.v.) successful bid for the USWA presidency in 1965; elected an international vice-president in 1965 and reelected in 1969; as chairman of the USWA civil rights committee, worked to speed implementation of equal rights policy; presided over changes in the wage policy committee that dispersed authority to ratify wage settlements among conferences composed of local union representatives in basic steel, aluminum, can, and nonferrous mining industries; after the merger of the International Union of Mine, Mill and Smelter Workers and the USWA, became the chief negotiator for several unions with jurisdictions in the copper industry; led a nine-month copper strike, 1967–1968, which established companywide coalition bargaining; as chairman of the USWA constitution committee, helped marshal support for a dues increase and for the creation of a strike fund by special convention in 1968; was knowledgeable and articulate and was widely respected in labor circles as a self-taught intellectual; frequently lectured at colleges and universities; a fervent believer that union leaders should participate in civic affairs, served on numerous public and private boards and agencies; before retiring as USWA vice-president in 1973, was chairman of the nonferrous industry coordinating committee; received the Negro Trade Union Council's award for outstanding work on behalf of civil rights in 1974; a Democrat; died in Sun City, Ariz., on April 7, 1977; Lloyd Ulman, *The Government of the Steelworkers Union* (1962); John Herling, *Right to Challenge: People and Power in the Steelworkers Union* (1972); *Wall Street Journal*, February 28, 1973.

                                                                    Donald G. Sofchalk

MONTGOMERY, Robert ("Henry Jr.")   (1904–   ). Born in Beacon, N.Y., May 21, 1904; son of Henry, a rubber corporation executive, and Mary Weed (Bernard) Montgomery; married Elizabeth Bryan Allen on April 14, 1928 and after that marriage ended in divorce, Elisabeth Grant on December 9, 1950; two children; attended exclusive boys' schools until age 16 but then was forced by his father's death to work as a mechanic on the New York, New Haven, and Hartford Railroad; somewhat later, was an oiler on a Standard Oil tanker; briefly tried to become a writer, then made stage debut in 1924; appeared in a silent film in 1926 and made first sound film in 1929; joined the Screen Actors Guild (SAG) in 1933 and the following year served on the National Recovery Administration committee concerned with the film industry; elected a vice-president of the SAG in 1934 and a year later elected president, serving until 1940; during his incumbency the SAG became a strong organization capable of maintaining a closed shop in Hollywood studios; enlisted in the American Field Service in London in 1940 and a year later was commissioned a lieutenant (junior grade) in the U.S. Navy; discharged from the Navy in 1945 and reelected president of the SAG, serving until his resignation in 1947; was also a member of the Directors Guild of America and Actors Equity Association; was a cooperative witness before the House Committee on Un-American Activities concerning Communist influence in the film industry; began directing films in 1946 and later became a producer and ended his association with the labor movement; was a Democrat early in his career, but usually supported Republican candidates after 1940; Murray Ross, *Stars and Strikes: Unionization of Hollywood* (1941); *Current Biography* (1948); *Who's Who in America, 1972–1973*.

MOONEY, Thomas J.   (1882–1942). Born in Chicago, Ill., on December 8, 1882; son of Bernard, a coal miner, and Mary (Heffernan) Mooney, a rag sorter in a paper mill; reared a Roman Catholic; married Rena Ellen (Brink) Hermann, a music teacher, in 1910; no children; attended both parochial and public schools in Holyoke, Mass., at various times; began working in a Holyoke factory in 1896 at age 14; apprenticed as an iron molder in 1897; became a journeyman in 1901 and joined a local union which in 1902 affiliated with the International Molders Union (IMU); traveled extensively during these years in both the United States and Europe; during his travels, he discussed the concept of socialism with many acquaintances and after observing the suffering that followed the Panic of 1907, he joined the Socialist party in Stockton, Calif.; was a delegate to the California Socialist convention in 1908 and following the convention was invited to join Eugene V. Debs's (q.v.) "Red Special," a railroad train from which Debs conducted his 1908 campaign, and in 1910 attended the International Socialist Congress in Copenhagen; settled in San Francisco, Calif., after his return from Copenhagen and joined the Industrial Workers of the World but was never an active member and soon permitted his membership to lapse; aligned himself with the left wing of the Socialist party and helped publish its newspaper *Revolt*; ran unsuccessfully on the Socialist ticket for superior court judge in 1910 and sheriff in 1911; joined the International Workers Defense League in 1912; was a delegate to the San Francisco Labor Council in 1912; was elected a local delegate to the IMU's national convention in 1912; involved along with Warren Billings (q.v.) in several, sometimes violent, strikes between 1913 and 1916; arrested several times as a result of his activities during a violent electrical workers' strike against the Pacific Gas and Electric Company but was never convicted; along with Billings, he was arrested and convicted of a San Francisco Preparedness Day bombing on July 22, 1916, which resulted in the deaths of ten people; was sentenced to hang but his sentence was commuted to life imprisonment as a result of public protests and the intervention of President Woodrow Wilson; although evidence of suppression of evidence, perjury, and subornation of perjury was clearly present, it was not until 1939 that California Governor Culbert L. Olson finally pardoned Mooney; never a particularly likeable man, he was egocentric and vain and had very few remaining friends at the time of his death, although he was still a martyr-hero to thousands; in ill health at the time of his release from prison, he was often an invalid until he died on

March 6, 1942; Richard H. Frost, *The Mooney Case* (1968); *Dictionary of American Biography*, Suppl. 3.

MOORE, Ely   (1798–1861). Born near Belvidere, N.J., July 4, 1798; son of Moses and Mary (Coryell) Moore; married Emma Conant, who bore him six children, and after her death, Mrs. Clara Baker; attended the public schools of Belvidere, then served an apprenticeship as a printer; later studied medicine in New York City, but, after practicing medicine for a few years, resumed the printer's trade and eventually became a land speculator and political activist; elected the first president of the New York General Trades' Union, a federation of craft unions, in 1833, and became the editor of its organ, the *National Trades' Union*; elected chairman of the National Trades' Union, a federation of labor unions from six Eastern cities, in 1834, and served through 1835; was a popular orator and was able to maintain his influence in the labor movement despite his failure to become actively involved in labor conflicts and his equivocal stand on the important prison-labor issue; elected as a Democrat to the U.S. Congress in 1834 and served until 1839; became the political editor of the *New York Evening Post* in 1838; was president of the board of trade and surveyor of the port of New York City, 1839–1845; appointed as a U.S. marshal for the southern district of New York in 1845; became the publisher and editor of the *Warren Journal*, Belvidere, N.J.; after declining appointments as minister to England and governor of the Territory of Kansas, appointed agent for the Miami and other Kansas Indian tribes in 1853; appointed register of the United States land office in Lecompton, Kans., in 1855 and served until 1860; was a Democrat; died in Lecompton, Kans., January 27, 1861; Walter E. Hugins, "Ely Moore: The Case History of a Jacksonian Labor Leader," *Political Science Quarterly* (March 1950), and *Jacksonian Democracy and the Working Class: A Study of the New York Workingmen's Movement, 1829–1837* (1960); Edward Pessen, *Most Uncommon Jacksonians: The Radical Leaders of the Early Labor Movement* (1967); John R. Commons et al., *History of Labour in the United States*, Vol. 1 (1918); *Dictionary of American Biography*, Vol. 13.

MORAN, John J.   (1897–1968). Born in Cecil, Pa., February 26, 1897; son of Thomas, a miner, and Sara A. (Beagan) Moran; married Martha R. Schwartz on July 9, 1923; one child; graduated from high school, then began working in the coal mines and joined the United Mine Workers of America; learned the telegrapher's trade, and became a member of the Order of Railroad Telegraphers; joined the Federation of Long Lines Telephone Workers (FLLTW) in 1938 and the following year elected FLLTW president; after the FLLTW affiliated with the National Federation of Telephone Workers (NFTW) in 1941, became a member of the executive board of the NFTW; elected a vice-president of the NFTW in 1943; during World War II, was a labor member of the telephone committee and the review and appeals committees of the National War Labor Board, and a labor representative on the Board of War Communications; was a staunch advocate of a strong national union and of affiliation with a national labor federation and was a constant critic of the NFTW's independent status and its allegedly excessive provisions for local autonomy; helped lead the bitter and largely unsuccessful strike of telephone workers in 1947, then left the NFTW and became vice-chairman of the Congress of Industrial Organizations' (CIO) rival Telephone Workers' Organizing Committee; following the NFTW's reorganization into the Communications Workers of America (CWA) and its affiliation with the CIO in 1949, became a vice-president of the CWA and was placed in charge of external organization; became a member of the CIO executive board in 1949; resigned the positions of CWA vice-president and director of organization in 1956 because of ill health; died in Boca Raton, Fla., in September 1968; Jack Barbash, *Unions and Telephones: The Story of the Communications Workers of America* (1952); *Who's Who in Labor* (1946); Thomas R. Brooks, *Communication Workers of America: The Story of a Union* (1977).

MORESCHI, Joseph   (1884–1970). Born in Italy in 1884; Roman Catholic; married; at least two children; emigrated with parents to the United States in 1892 and settled in Chicago, Ill.; gained work as a laborer and joined Chicago Local 1 of the International Hod Carriers', Building and Common Laborers' Union of America (IHCBCLU) in 1912; served Local 1 in several capacities, including as president, and also served as president of the Laborers District Council in Chicago; served as a vice-president and executive board member during 1921–1926, then elected president of the IHCBCLU in 1926, holding position for 42 years; served as an American Federation of Labor (AFL) fraternal delegate to the British Trades Union Congress in 1931; negotiated mergers with the Tunnel and Subway Constructors' International Union in 1929 and the International Union of Pavers, Rammermen, Flag Layers, Bridge and Stone Curb Setters and Sheet Asphalt Pavers in 1937; introduced several innovations during his incumbency, including the institution of a system of regional offices in 1935 to facilitate governing the union, the establishment of a legal department, the creation of a death benefit fund, and the publication of *The Laborer*, a monthly IHCBCLU organ founded in 1947; became the editor of *The Laborer* in 1947; as international president, the IHCBCLU increased its membership from less than 20,000 to more than 500,000; retired union positions and named president emeritus in 1968; died in Hot Springs, Ark., March 11, 1970; Arch A. Mercey, *The Laborers' Story, 1903–1953: The First Fifty Years of the International Hod Carriers', Building and Common Laborers' Union of America (AFL)* (1954); *AFL-CIO News*, March 14, 1970.

MORGAN, Elizabeth Chambers   (fl. 1850–1893). Born in Birmingham, England, in 1850; the daughter of poor factory operatives; married Thomas J. Morgan (q.v.), a machinist and Socialist leader, on January 26, 1868; permitted little formal education because of family financial extringencies, she began working in a mill at age 11; emigrated to the United States with her husband in 1869, settling in Chicago, Ill.; became a Socialist as a result of working-class suffering during the depression of the 1870s; became a charter member of the Sovereigns of Industry in 1874; joined Local Assembly 1789 of the Knights of Labor in 1881 and was eventually elevated to the position of master workman in the assembly; was one of the organizers of Ladies' Federal Labor Union No. 2703 (Chicago), American Federation of Labor (AFL) in 1888; used Local 2703 as a vehicle for promoting protective legislation for women and children workers; served as Local 2703's secretary and as its delegate to the Chicago Trade and Labor Assembly; by 1892 Local 2703 had created 23 AFL-affiliated craft locals of women workers and had become the most important organization of women workers within the AFL; was one of the organizers of the Illinois Women's Alliance in 1888 and was a member of its executive committee; along with the alliance's commitment to women and child labor reform, she wrote an influential report exposing the sweatshop conditions in the Chicago garment industry; her report was used by Florence Kelley (q.v.) and other Chicago reformers to press for factory inspection legislation, resulting in the enactment of the Factory and Workshop Inspection Act of 1893; was the only female delegate to the 1894 national AFL convention, which endorsed her efforts on behalf of working women and children; was nominated for vice-president of the AFL but lost to the incumbent, Peter J. McGuire (q.v.); a Socialist; Thomas J. Morgan Collection, University of Illinois, Urbana; Ralph Scharnau, "Thomas J. Morgan and the Chicago Socialist Movement, 1876–1901" (Ph.D. diss., 1970), and "Elizabeth Morgan, Crusader for Labor Reform," *Labor History* (Summer 1973); Philip S. Foner, *Women and the American Labor Movement from Colonial Times to the Eve of World War I* (1979); Ellen M. Ritter, "Elizabeth Morgan: Pioneer Female Labor Agitator," *Central States Speech Journal* (1971).

MORGAN, Thomas John   (1847–1912). Born in Birmingham, England, October 27, 1847; son of Thomas John and Hannah (Simcox) Morgan, both impoverished nail makers who labored 17 hours a day; married Elizabeth Chambers on January 26, 1868; attended a paupers' school until age 9; learned writing and arithmetic at a Unitarian Sunday school; worked, beginning at age 9, as a nail maker, a printer, a molder in an iron foundry, worker in a thimble factory, and as a machinist and brass finisher; unable to escape poverty, even though wife also worked; emigrated to the United States in 1869, settling in Chicago, Ill.; during the Panic of 1873, experienced along with his wife 15 months of unemployment; became active in 1871 in the labor movement and was elected president of his local union of machinists; studied mechanical drawing at the Athenaeum night school, and while employed in the Illinois Central Railroad carshops during 1875–1895, read law and was graduated from Chicago Law College; in the late 1870s, was a prime mover in the creation of the Chicago Trades and Labor Assembly; when it split in 1884, formed along with other radicals the Chicago Central Labor Union, which endured to 1896; in 1879, guided a special committee of the Illinois General Assembly on a tour of Chicago factories that resulted in the creation of a State Bureau of Labor Statistics; also in 1879, drafted city ordinances patterned after the English factory acts that were adopted by the Chicago Board of Aldermen; in the early 1890s, wrote a program for labor's political action, the heart of which, Plank 10, espoused collective ownership of all means of production and distribution; in 1894, the Springfield, Ill., Populist convention and two Illinois State Federation of Labor conventions adopted most of his program, but rejected Plank 10; was a political radical as early as 1875; joined the Socialist Labor party and was its unsuccessful candidate for mayor of Chicago in 1891; was an unsuccessful candidate on the Social Democratic party ticket for Chicago city attorney, 1903, superior court judge, Cook County, 1903, 1907, and for U.S. Senator, 1909; from 1900 until his death, served on numerous Socialist party city, county, state, and national executive campaign committees; was the editor and publisher of *The Provoker*, 1909–1912; died on December 10, 1912; *Who Was Who in America*, Vol. 1; Eugene Staley, *History of the Illinois State Federation of Labor* (1930).

John W. Hevener

MORREALE, Vincent F.   (1902–   ). Born in New York City, July 29, 1902; son of Michele, a builder and contractor, and Angela Maria Morreale; Roman Catholic; married Marie Sambuchelli on June 21, 1934; two children; attended Fordham Preparatory School and Fordham College; received an LL.B. from Fordham Law School; then served as attorney for the New York City Compressed Air Workers Union, 1930–1934; became the attorney for the International Hod Carriers', Building and Common Laborers' Union of America (IHCBCLU) in 1934; associated during World War II with the government war-construction and ship-building program as a labor advisor and public relations official; assumed the title of general counsel after the position was created by the IHCBCLU in 1946 and became the head of the international's legal department; served frequently as an IHCBCLU delegate to the national conventions of the American Federation of Labor (AFL) and the AFL-Congress of Industrial Organizations; actively involved in numerous civic, political, and religious organizations; supported the Democratic party; authored numerous pamphlets and frequently contributed to the IHCBCLU organ, *The Laborer*; Arch A. Mercey, *The Laborers' Story, 1903–1953: The First Fifty Years of the International Hod Carriers', Building and Common Laborers' Union of America (AFL)* (1954); U.S. Department of Labor, *The Workers' Story, 1913–1953* (1953); *Who's Who in Labor* (1946).

MORRISON, Frank   (1859–1949). Born in Franktown, Ontario, Canada, November 23, 1859; son of Christopher, a Scots-Irish immigrant, farmer, and sawyer, and Elizabeth (Nesbitt) Morrison; Church of Christ; married Josephine Curtis on June 11, 1891, and Alice S. Boswell on August 11, 1908; two children; completed one year of high school, then left school to learn the printing trade; soon thereafter emigrated to the United States and in 1873 secured employment on the Madison, Wis., *Journal*; while working as a compositor on a Chicago newspaper in 1886, joined Local 16 of the International Typographical Union (ITU); admitted to the Illinois bar after attending Lake Forest University Law School, 1893–1894; elected a delegate to the ITU national convention in 1896 and selected to represent the ITU at the national American Federation of Labor (AFL) convention meeting in Colorado later in the same year; elected AFL secretary in 1897, and served in that capacity for more than 40 years; became secretary of the AFL labor representation committee that was organized in 1906 to coordinate political activities; sentenced to six months in prison in 1907 as a result of contempt charges growing out of violations of the injunction issued in the Buck's Stove and Range Company case, but the conviction was later reversed by the U.S. Supreme Court; was a close associate and collaborator of AFL presidents Samuel Gompers (q.v.) and William Green (q.v.) and was one of the leading architects of the American labor movement; was a skillful administrator who efficiently managed the routine affairs of the AFL; retired union positions in 1939 and named AFL secretary emeritus; was a nonpartisan in political affairs; died in Washington, D.C., March 12, 1949; Frank Morrison, AFL-CIO Archives, George Meany Labor Studies Center; Philip Taft, *The A.F. of L. in the Time of Gompers* (1957); Lewis L. Lorwin, *The American Federation of Labor: History, Policies, and Prospects* (1933); *The American Federationist* (April 1949); *Dictionary of American Biography*, Suppl. 4.

MORTIMER, Wyndham   (1884–1966). Born in Karthaus, Clearfield County, Pa., March 11, 1884; son of Thomas George, a miner and Knights of Labor member, and Rachel (Jenkins) Mortimer; reared a Protestant; married Margaret Hunter on December 24, 1907; two children; left school at age 12 and went to work in the Pennsylvania coal fields as a "trapper boy"; joined the United Mine Workers of America in 1900; spent several years in the mines, then worked at a variety of occupations prior to taking employment with the White Motor Company in Cleveland, Ohio; organized the employees of the White Motor Company into American Federation of Labor (AFL) federal Local 18463; became president of the Cleveland Auto Council in 1934; led organizing efforts in Flint, Mich., prior to the successful United Automobile, Aircraft and Agricultural Implement Workers of America (UAW) strike against the Fisher Body Company in 1936; considered one of the most effective UAW organizers and strike leaders; was a vocal critic of the AFL leadership's control of the UAW; elected a UAW vice-president in 1936, serving until 1939; was a leader of the union's left-wing "Unity Caucus" and strongly supported affiliation with the Congress of Industrial Organizations (CIO); led the opposition to UAW president Warren Homer Martin (q.v.) in 1937–1938; moved to Los Angeles, Calif., in 1940 as a UAW organizer assigned to the California aircraft industry; was one of the principal leaders of the 1941 strike against the North American Aviation Company; became a CIO organizer in 1942 but resigned after a short time; returned to Los Angeles and there held a number of minor union positions until his retirement in 1945 from union affairs; authored *Organize! My Life as a Union Man* (1971); was a Socialist, but stoutly denied charges of being a member of the Communist party; died in Los Angeles, Calif., August 25, 1966; Jack Stieber, *Governing the UAW* (1962); Sidney Fine, *Sit-Down: The General Motors Strike of 1936–1937* (1969), and *The Automobile under the Blue Eagle: Labor, Management, and the Automobile Manufacturing Code* (1963); Frank Cormier and William J. Eaton, *Reuther* (1970); Roger Keeran, *The Communist Party and the Auto Workers Unions* (1980); Nelson Lichtenstein, *Labor's War at Home: The CIO in World War II* (1982); Harvey A. Levenstein, *Communism, Anticommunism, and the CIO* (1981); Bert Cochran, *Labor and Communism: The Conflict that Shaped American Unions* (1977).

MOST, Johann Joseph   (1846–1906). Born in Augsburg, Germany, on February 5, 1846; son of Josef Most, a lawyer's copyist, and a liberal, educated mother who died when he was 10 years of age; married briefly and divorced; after an unhappy childhood that left him physically and emotionally scarred as a result of childhood illnesses and a cruel stepmother, he entered the bookbinder's trade at age 17 with only the rudiments of a primary education; after five years of itinerant labor while traveling through central Europe, he joined the International Workingmen's Association in Zurich, Switzerland, and became a zealous Socialist; edited Socialist newspapers in several European cities, 1868–1878; he was imprisoned in Austria (two years) and Germany (three years) for his radical beliefs; was twice elected to the German Reichstag; as a result of his radical activities he was expelled from both Germany and Austria; moved to London in 1878 and established *Die Freiheit*, a weekly Socialist newspaper; became an anarchist in 1880 and the following year was again imprisoned, this time for praising the assassination of Alexander II; emigrated to the United States in 1882, settling in New York City where he reestablished *Die Freiheit*; a powerful orator and brilliant writer, he quickly became the dominant figure in the anarchist movement in the United States and dominated the Pittsburgh, Pa., anarchist convention in 1883 which established the Revolutionary Socialist party; was imprisoned in 1886, shortly before the Haymarket affair in Chicago, Ill., and again after the assassination of William McKinley in 1901, even though by that time he had rejected direct individual action and had offended younger, militant anarchists by criticizing the attempted assassination of Henry Frick; died in Cincinnati, Ohio, on March 17, 1906; *Dictionary of American Biography*, Vol. 13; E. M. Schuster, *Native American Anarchism* (1932); Charles A. Madison, *Critics and Crusaders: A Century of American Protest* (1947); Rudolf Rocker, *Johann Most, Das Leben eines Rebellen* (1924).

MOYER, Charles H.   (fl. 1893–1929). Little known about his early years prior to 1893; as a smelter worker for the Homestake Mining Company at Lead, S.D., in the 1880s, was active in the Lead City Miners' Union, which played a major role in the founding of the Western Federation of Miners (WFM) in

1893; was a member by 1900 of the executive board of WFM District 5, South Dakota; elected president after the resignation of WFM president Edward Boyce (q.v.) in 1902; was a thoroughgoing industrial unionist and influenced the WFM to push for the organization of all types of mine employees; as a result of this policy, the WFM became involved in the bitter Cripple Creek and Telluride, Colo., strikes of 1903–1904; during these strikes, was jailed and denied habeus corpus; was convinced, by the use of the state militia to crush the strikes, of the futility of isolated unionism and the need for a broader, more militant, radical unionism; during this period, became a supporter of the Socialist party; along with his union colleagues William Haywood (q.v.) and John O'Neill (q.v.), participated in January 1905 in the Chicago conference that laid the groundwork for the establishment of the Industrial Workers of the World (IWW) and was offered but declined its presidency; WFM affiliation provided the IWW its only substantial initial membership; involved in one of the most famous and bizarre labor conspiracy trials in 1906–1907, when, along with William Haywood and George Pettibone, he was alleged to be a part of a WFM "inner circle," which was accused of murdering former Idaho Governor Frank Steunenberg; kidnapped along with his WFM colleagues by Colorado officials and turned over to Idaho authorities; indicted for conspiracy to murder; after Haywood and Pettibone were acquitted, the charge against Moyer was dropped; angered by the revolutionaries among IWW leaders and by their tactics and opposition to union endorsement of political parties, therefore led the WFM out of the IWW in 1908; was convinced that the union's reputation for revolutionary agitation made dealing effectively with employers more difficult, hence in 1911 helped reaffiliate the WFM with the American Federation of Labor (AFL) and adopted the trade union goal of time contracts; under his guidance, the WFM substituted a commitment to trade union goals for its radical program; within the AFL, tended to veer away from the Socialists, who supported independent political action, advocating instead AFL nonpartisanship; meanwhile, beset by the IWW policy of destroying locals it could not capture and continued employer hostility, the WFM, which changed its name in 1916 to the International Union of Mine, Mill and Smelter Workers, experienced a steady decline in membership; was unable to revive union strength, especially in the crucial copper industry, and hence along with his executive board was forced to resign in 1926; died in Pomona, Calif., June 2, 1929; Vernon H. Jensen, *Heritage of Conflict: Labor Relations in the Nonferrous Metals Industry up to 1930* (1950); John H. M. Laslett, *Labor and the Left: A Study of Socialism and Radical Influences in the American Labor Movement, 1881–1924* (1970).

Donald G. Sofchalk

MULLANEY, Joseph A.   (1872–1954). Born in New York City, June 11, 1872; Roman Catholic; married; four children; completed grammar school, then at age 15 began an apprenticeship as an asbestos worker at the Asbestos Felting Works in New York City in 1888; joined the New York Salamander Association of Boiler and Pipe Coverers in 1888; became the business agent of the Salamander Association in 1902 and led the association out of the Knights of Labor and into the newly organized International Association of Heat and Frost Insulators and Asbestos Workers (IAHFIAW), which affiliated with the American Federation of Labor in 1904; elected international president of the IAHFIAW in 1912; became a vice-president of the New York State Federation of Labor (NYSFL) in 1912 and served in that capacity until 1954; served for many years as chairman of the resolutions committee of the NYSFL but three times refused to assume the presidency of the NYSFL; served as manager of George Meany's (q.v.) successful campaign to win election as president of the NYSFL in 1934; was the seminal figure in the organization of asbestos workers and was popularly known as ''Mr. Asbestos''; in 1937, elected president of the IAHFIAW for life; appointed to the New York State Committee on Employment of the Physically Handicapped in 1951; was an active participant in New York State Democratic politics; involved in successful efforts to achieve protective legislation for industrial workers; was instrumental in the NYSFL's decision to endorse Alfred E. Smith for president of the United States in 1928; died in Flushing, Queens, N.Y., December 25, 1954; *The American Federationist* (February 1955); *The New York Times*, December 25, 1954.

MURPHY, Vincent   (1893–1976). Born in Newark, N.J., on August 1, 1893; son of Thomas Francis, a leather worker, and Sarah (Gaskin) Murphy; Roman Catholic; married Marie K. McConnell on May 30, 1917; three children; attended Catholic parochial schools in Newark through the seventh grade; because of family financial problems, he became a plumber's apprentice at age 15; joined Local 24 of the United Association of Plumbers and Steam Fitters of the United States and Canada (UA) on November 11, 1913; was elected secretary-treasurer of Local 24, UA, in 1920 and continued in that post for the next 18 years; was elected secretary-treasurer of the New Jersey State Federation of Labor in 1933, a position he held until the merger of the American Federation of Labor (AFL) and the Congress of Industrial Organizations (CIO) in New Jersey in 1961; became chairman of the joint committee for annual labor institutes sponsored by the State Federation of Labor, Rutgers University, and the Workers Education Bureau in 1934; outpolled 48 other candidates in the 1937 elections for a seat in the five-member Newark city commission but was denied the post of mayor, which traditionally had gone to the leading candidate in the city commission elections, because of the opposition of Jersey City boss Frank Hague; after again leading the field in city commission elections in 1941 (and after making his peace with Hague), he was selected as mayor of Newark by his fellow commissioners; was reelected in 1945 but lost his seat in the 1949 elections; was an unsuccessful Democratic candidate for governor of New Jersey in 1943; successfully negotiated a merger of the AFL and CIO in the bitterly divided New Jersey labor movement in 1961 and was elected president of the newly organized New Jersey AFL-CIO Council; during his long career, he was involved in a great variety of civic and labor activities, including the New Jersey Security Advisory Board, the State Unemployment Compensation Commission, the American-Jewish Trade Union Committee for Palestine, and the National Association for the Advancement of Colored People; retired union positions in 1970; died in Spring Lake, N.J., on June 8, 1976; *The New York Times*, June 9, 1976; *Who's Who in Labor* (1946); Leo Troy, *Organized Labor in New Jersey* (1965).

MURRAY, Philip   (1886–1952). Born in Blantyre, Scotland, on May 25, 1886; son of William, a coal miner and for a time president of a local of the Scottish miners' union, and Rose Ann (Layden) Murray; Roman Catholic; married Elizabeth Lavery on September 7, 1910; one son; began working in the mines at age 10 after a few years of public education; emigrated with family to the United States in 1902, settled in western Pennsylvania and there began working in the mines; elected president of a local miners' union in 1904 after a dispute with management that cost him his job; became a citizen of the United States in 1911; elected to the executive board of the United Mine Workers of America (UMWA) in 1912; became president of UMWA District 5, Western Pennsylvania, in 1916 and three years later elected a vice-president of the UMWA; during World War I, appointed to the Pennsylvania regional panel of the War Labor Board and served on the National Bituminous Coal Production Committee, 1917–1918; appointed to the Labor and Industrial Advisory Board of the National Recovery Administration in 1933; assisted in the writing and enactment of the Guffy-Snyder Coal Stabilization Act of 1935; participated in the establishment of the Congress of Industrial Organizations (CIO) in 1938; appointed chairman of the Steel Workers Organizing Committee in 1936 and served in that capacity until it was reorganized into the United Steelworkers of America (USWA) in 1942; elected president of the CIO in 1940 after the resignation of John L. Lewis (q.v.); elected international president of the USWA in 1942; expelled from the UMWA in 1942, because of differences with the temperamental UMWA president John L. Lewis; was critical of many administration policies and programs, but generally supported President Franklin D. Roosevelt and the various productivity programs initiated during World War II; served on the National Defense Mediation Board and several other government boards and agencies during World War II; led major strikes against the steel industry in 1946, 1949, and 1952; was a vigorous critic of the Taft-Hartley Act and was indicted by a federal grand jury on charges of violating its provisions barring political expenditures by unions, but after hearing the case the Supreme Court dismissed the indictment; was an opponent of Communist influence in the labor movement and generally assumed a conservative position in the ideological conflicts within the CIO; was actively involved in public affairs and served on the Pittsburgh, Pa., Board of Education from 1918 until his death; was a member of the executive committee of the National Association for the Advancement of Colored People and a member of the board of directors of the American National Red Cross; was a Democrat;

co-authored *Organized Labor and Production* (1940); died in San Francisco, Calif., November 9, 1952; Philip Murray Papers, Catholic University of America; Lloyd Ulman, *The Government of the Steelworkers' Union* (1962); Charles A. Madison, *American Labor Leaders: Personalities and Forces in the Labor Movement* (1950); John Herling, *The Right to Challenge: People and Power in the Steelworkers Union* (1972); Walter Galenson, *The CIO Challenge to the AFL: A History of the American Labor Movement, 1935–1941* (1960); Irving Bernstein, *Turbulent Years: A History of the American Worker, 1933–1941* (1970); Harvey A. Levenstein, *Communism, Anticommunism, and the CIO* (1981); *Dictionary of American Biography*, Suppl. 5; Nelson Lichtenstein, *Labor's War at Home: The CIO in World War II* (1982).

MURRAY, Thomas A.   (1885–1958). Born in New York City in 1885; Roman Catholic; married Elizabeth Jane O'Keefe; four children; attended grammar school, then became an apprentice bricklayer at age 14; joined the Bricklayers, Masons and Plasterers International Union (BMPIU) after completing his apprenticeship; while working as a bricklayer, took courses at Cooper Union for the Advancement of Science and Art; served as a foreman bricklayer and general superintendent for the Kenwell Construction Company, New York City, 1909–1933; elected chairman of the New York Bricklayers' executive committee for Manhattan and the Bronx in 1933; served as president of the Building and Construction Trades Council of Greater New York, 1936–1943; elected a vice-president of the New York State Federation of Labor (NYSFL) in 1940 and three years later appointed president of the organization after the death of the incumbent, Thomas J. Lyons; served as president of the NYSFL from 1943 to 1958; considered an adept conciliator and was one of the principal leaders in the effort to affect a merger between the American Federation of Labor (AFL) and Congress of Industrial Organizations' (CIO) unions in New York State; was scheduled to become president of the New York State AFL-CIO after the 1958 merger, but died in Albany, N.Y., May 2, 1958; was a Democrat; *The American Federationist* (June 1958); *The New York Times*, May 3, 1958.

MURRY, James Wesley   (1935–   ). Born in Billings, Mont., on February 6, 1935; son of Boyd R., a refinery worker, and Kathleen (Cowan) Murry; married Arlene Rowlan in 1954; five children; graduated from Laurel (Mont.) High School in 1953, and attended Eastern Montana College, 1953–1954, 1958–1960; while employed as a refinery worker in Montana, he joined Local 2443, Oil, Chemical and Atomic Workers International Union in 1956 and served as president of that local during 1965–1966; after becoming director of political education for the Montana State American Federation of Labor-Congress of Industrial Organizations (AFL-CIO) in 1966 and as executive secretary (the highest office) of the state AFL-CIO in 1968, he helped obtain enactment of vastly improved workmen's compensation and unemployment systems, the first Montana minimum wage law, and public employee collective bargaining; as a member of the Montana Constitutional Revision Commission, he helped gain adoption of the new constitution of 1972, considered by many observers to be one of the most liberal and advanced in the nation; a member of the Montana Committee for the Humanities, 1973–1979; since 1968 he has been on the board of control of the Rocky Mountain Labor School; a member of the American Committee for Human Rights in Northern Ireland, 1979; involved in the submission by the Montana AFL-CIO of the resolution which was adopted by the national AFL-CIO in support of the Equal Rights Amendment; a liberal Democrat, he was appointed to the economic advisory committee to Senator Max Baucus in 1981; became a member of the Montana Economic Development Project Steering Committee in 1982; worked closely with the Montana Department of Labor and Industry, including administration of the Technical Assistance and Training grant to improve relations between the department and local unions, and operation of "Project Challenge: Work Again" to assist unemployed workers in finding jobs; *Who's Who in Labor* (1976); Michael P. Malone and Dianne G. Dougherty, "Montana's Political Culture," *Montana: The Magazine of Western History* (Winter 1981).

Donald G. Sofchalk

MUSTE, Abraham Johannes ("A. J.")   (1885–1967). Born in Zierikzee, the Netherlands, on January 8, 1885; son of Martin, a coachman, and Adriana (Jonker) Muste; Dutch Reformed; married Anna Huizenga on June 21, 1909; three children; emigrated with his family to the United States in 1891, settling in Grand Rapids, Mich.; attended a parochial school and public schools in Grand Rapids before training for the Dutch Reformed ministry at Hope College (Mich.) and New Brunswick (N.J.) Theological Seminary; also took graduate courses in philosophy at New York University and Columbia University, and heard William James and John Dewey lecture; after ordination as a minister in 1909, he attended Union Theological Seminary while serving pastorates in New York City; voted for Eugene V. Debs (q.v.) for president in 1912 and gradually drew away from Calvinist dogma to Quaker thought and Christian pacifism; joined the newly formed Fellowship of Reconciliation (FOR) in 1916 and became a Quaker in 1918, after leaving the ministry of the Central Congregational Church in Newtonville, Mass., when his opposition to American intervention in World War I became too controversial; worked with other opponents of World War I to secure better conditions and treatment for imprisoned conscientious objectors; as a representative of a loosely organized group of left-wing pacifists called "The Comradeship," he visited Lawrence, Mass., in early 1919 to offer assistance to striking textile workers, and was asked to serve as executive secretary of the strike committee; after the strike was won, he was elected executive secretary of a new independent industrial union, the Amalgamated Textile Workers of America, 1919–1921; was chairman of the faculty at Brookwood Labor College, a residential workers' school near Katonah, N.Y., 1921–1933, raising funds, teaching, and securing endorsements and scholarships from a number of national unions and state federations of labor; served on the executive committee of the Workers' Education Bureau; joined the American Federation of Teachers and was elected a vice-president in 1923; campaigned for Robert M. La Follette in 1924; became increasingly critical of conservative policies of the American Federation of Labor (AFL) and began writing regularly for *Labor Age* in 1926, advocating industrial unionism and challenging "labor-management coopera- tion"; after Brookwood was attacked by the national AFL leadership in 1928, he initiated the Conference for Progressive Labor Action (CPLA), which was formally organized in 1929 with a program calling for organization of the un- skilled and semiskilled, unemployment and old age insurance, and labor political action; CPLA evolved into the "Musteite" American Workers' party in late 1933, after Muste resigned from Brookwood in the face of his colleagues' objections to increasing identification of the school as a political training ground for the CPLA; led victorious Toledo Auto-Lite strike of 1934, with others from his party, and wrote *The Automobile Industry and Organized Labor* (1936); co- chairman of the Workers' party of the United States, a fusion of the Musteites and American Trotskyists, and visited Leon Trotsky in Norway; but in 1936, he resigned from the Workers' party and returned to radical religious pacifism; director of the Presbyterian Labor Temple in New York City, 1937–1940; ex- ecutive secretary of FOR, 1940–1953; with others, he founded *Liberation* mag- azine in 1956; initiated American Forum for Socialist Education in 1957; became a key leader of the movement to stop the war in Vietnam and traveled to South Vietnam in April 1966 and North Vietnam in January 1967; died in New York City on February 11, 1967; Brookwood Labor College Papers, Walter Reuther Archives, Wayne State University; Nat Hentoff, ed., *The Essays of A. J. Muste* (1967); *Liberation*, September-October 1967; JoAnn O. Robinson, *Abraham Went Out* (1982); Rita James Simon, ed., *As We Saw the Thirties* (1967).

Jon Bloom

MYERS, Isaac   (fl. 1835–1889). Born to free black parents in Baltimore, Md., in 1835; Afro-American; Methodist; received a grammar school education in a private day school; was apprenticed to learn the ship-caulking trade at age 16; within four years, he was supervising the caulking of some of the largest clipper ships built in the Baltimore shipyards; took a job as chief porter and shipping clerk of a wholesale grocery business in 1860; was one of the founders of a grocery cooperative in 1864 but, after differences over store policy, resigned his management of the enterprise in 1865 and returned to the shipyards; lost his job shortly thereafter as a result of a strike of white workers who were protesting the presence of black workers, resulting in the discharge of over one thousand black workers from the shipyard; thereafter, he helped organize a union of black shipyard workers and established the Chesapeake Marine Railway and Dry Dock Company, a black-owned cooperative which soon commanded a major share of the work in Baltimore as well as winning federal contracts; was appointed a messenger to the Baltimore collector of customs in 1866; was appointed a special agent in the U.S. Post Office Department in 1870 and was assigned to supervise mail service in the South; meanwhile, he attended the 1869 meeting of the National Labor Union (NLU) and along with other black unionists was seated after a long, acrimonious debate; was one of the founders and first president of the National Colored Labor Union, the first national federation of black unions, which was organized later in the same year; after the NLU voted to create the Labor Reform party, the National Colored Labor Union broke with the organization and supported Republican candidates; he retired from the postal service in 1879 and opened a coal yard in Baltimore; was editor and proprietor of the *Colored Citizen*, a weekly political journal published in Baltimore in 1882; was appointed U.S. gauger in 1882 and held that position until 1887 when the Democrats came into office; was secretary of the Maryland Republican Campaign Committee in 1888; thereafter remained active in business, labor, and social activities, organizing the Maryland Colored State Industrial Fair Association in 1888, the Colored Business Men's Association, which he organized and served as its first president, and the first Building and Loan Association of Baltimore which he helped organize; was also active in the Masons, wrote a three-act play entitled "The Missionary," and for 15 years served as superintendent of the Bethel A.M.E. School of Baltimore; *The Freeman* (Indianapolis), October 12, 1889, reprinted in Philip S. Foner and Ronald L. Lewis, *The Black Worker: A Documentary History from Colonial Times to the Present*, Vol. 1 (1978); Philip S. Foner, *The Voice of Black America* (1972).

MYRUP, Andrew A.   (1880–1943). Born in Copenhagen, Denmark, March 13, 1880; married; three children; attended the common schools of Copenhagen, then emigrated with his family to the United States in 1893, settling in Racine, Wis.; shortly after arriving, served an apprenticeship as a baker and by 1897 had become a journeyman baker; during the period 1897–1901, traveled around the country working at his trade; after a lengthy stay in California, moved to Chicago, Ill., in 1901 and joined Local 62 of the Bakery and Confectionery Workers' International Union of America (BCWIU); elected business agent of Local 62 in 1904 and a year later became a member of the BCWIU executive board; in 1907, elected international secretary-treasurer (chief administrative officer) of the BCWIU; elected international president when the office was created in the early 1940s; during his long leadership tenure in the BCWIU, was able to gain general application of the 40-hour week, substantial increases in wage scales, and improvement of the intolerable working conditions that had characterized the bakery trade at the turn of the century; was a devoted advocate of the union label and made the label an important instrument in organizing the bakery and confectionery trade; was a delegate to the annual conventions of the American Federation of Labor (AFL), 1907–1943, served on numerous AFL committees, and was a vice-president of its union label trades department; served as vice-president of the Union Labor Life Insurance Company; died in Boston, Mass., October 1, 1943; *The American Federationist* (July 1941); *The American Federation of Labor Weekly News Service*, October 10, 1943.

N

NAGLER, Isidore (1895–1959). Born in Uscie Biscupie, Austria-Hungary (now part of Austria), February 25, 1895; son of Lasser, a businessman, and Bertha (Pohoriles) Nagler; Jewish; married Pauline Lefkowitz on November 23, 1919; emigrated to the United States in 1909; employed as a cutter in the garment industry and joined Local 10 of the International Ladies' Garment Workers' Union (ILGWU) in 1911; elected business agent of Local 10 in 1920; served as general manager of the New York Cloak Joint Board, 1928–1939; became an ILGWU vice-president in 1929; served as an ILGWU delegate to the International Clothing Workers' Congress in London in 1934; resumed leadership of the seriously divided Local 10 in 1939 at the request of the international officers of the ILGWU; elected a vice-president and executive board member of the New York State Federation of Labor in 1942; served as an American Federation of Labor fraternal delegate to the British Trades Union Congress in 1943; served on the state executive committee of the American Labor party (ALP), 1936–1944; ran unsuccessfully as the ALP candidate for borough president of the Bronx in 1937 and for the U.S. Congress a year later; served as a member of the state executive and administrative committee of the Liberal party of New York and as the secretary of the regional appeals' panel of the War Manpower Commission; became general manager of the New York Joint Board of the Cloak, Shirt, Skirt and Reefer Makers' Union in 1952; served as labor advisor to the United States delegation to the International Labor Organization conference in Geneva in 1958; was a vice-chairman of the Jewish Labor Committee; died in New York City, September 21, 1959; Harry Haskel, *A Leader of the Garment Workers: The Biography of Isidore Nagler* (1950); Benjamin Stolberg, *Tailor's Progress: The Story of a Famous Union and the Men Who Made It* (1944); Max D. Danish, *The World of David Dubinsky* (1957); *ILGWU Report and Proceedings* (1962).

NANCE, Alexander Stephens (1895–1938). Born in Bowman, Ga., May 19, 1895; son of John L. and Victoria (Bond) Nance; Baptist; married Frances

K. McMurtrey; four children; attended grammar school, then moved to Atlanta, Ga., at age 15 and began working in various newspaper mailrooms; was a charter member of Atlanta Mailers' Union Local 34, organized in 1911; elected president of Local 34 in 1919; led a mailroom workers' strike against Atlanta newspapers in 1922; was circulation manager of the *Southern Ruralist* in 1924 and served as vice-president and director of the Ruralist Press, Inc., in 1926; elected vice-president of the Georgia State Federation of Labor (GSFL) in 1927, serving until his resignation in 1929; served as the GSFL's legislative representative, 1930–1935; elected president of the Atlanta Federation of Trades in 1930, serving until 1935; during 1933, served on the compliance board of the National Recovery Administration and was a member of the National Labor Board; was an active participant in the textile strike of 1934; served as president of the GSFL from 1935 until 1937, when American Federation of Labor president William Green (q.v.) ordered the GSFL divided; appointed director of the Congress of Industrial Organizations' Textile Workers Organizing Committee (TWOC) in the Southeast, which attempted to organize textile, hosiery, and clothing industry workers; was credited with organizing twenty-five thousand workers during the TWOC's first year of activity and, after his death at the end of that year, was described by Sidney Hillman (q.v.) as a martyr to the campaign; was a prominent community and political figure in Atlanta and Georgia; refused a presidential appointment as postmaster of Atlanta; served as a regional director of the Social Security Board and was instrumental in getting Works Progress Administration funds for the consolidated school at Baconton, Ga., which was named in his honor in 1936; also served with the Community Chest, the Family Welfare Society, the Salvation Army, the Georgia Conference on Social Work, and the Christian Council; was a Democrat; died April 3, 1938; Anonymous, A. *Steve Nance, Labor Statesman and Citizen* (n.d.); Lucy Randolph Mason, *To Win These Rights: A Personal Story of the CIO in the South* (1952); Matthew Josephson, *Sidney Hillman: Statesman of American Labor* (1952).

Merl E. Reed

NEEBE, Oscar   (fl. 1850–1893). Born in New York City on July 12, 1850; married in 1873; three children; son of well-to-do parents who returned to Hesse Cassel, Germany, to assure that their children received a good primary education; returned to New York City at the end of the Civil War and was apprenticed in the gold and silver beating trade; poor health forced him to leave this trade after a short time, and he migrated to Chicago, Ill., where after several weeks he attained work as a bartender in a saloon frequented by workers in the McCormick Harvesting plant nearby; spent a summer as a cook on a Great Lakes freighter before returning to New York in 1868 and becoming an apprentice in a tinsmith shop; lost a job with a milk can manufacturer in 1871 after leading a deputation protesting a stretchout and then being deserted by his fellow workers; moved to Philadelphia, Pa., in 1873 and four years later took his family to Chicago where he worked at his trade until being discharged and blacklisted for organizing activities; unable to secure employment in his trade, he worked as a salesman for the Riverdale Distilling Company from 1879 until 1881; in association with his brother and two other men he founded the Acme Yeast Company in 1881; joined the International Workmen's Association in 1877, and a few years later aligned himself with the anarchist faction of the Socialist movement in the United States; became a member of the managing board of *Arbeiter-Zeitung*, a German-language Socialist newspaper, in 1880; was arrested on May 5, 1886, and charged with murder in connection with the Haymarket Square riot the previous day; was convicted and sentenced to 15 years in prison; was pardoned by Governor John P. Altgeld on June 26, 1893; Philip S. Foner, ed., *The Autobiographies of the Haymarket Martyrs* (1969); Henry David, *The History of the Haymarket Affair* (1963).

NEF, Walter T.   (fl. 1909–1920). Born in Europe of German-Swiss parents; was a member by 1909 of the Industrial Workers of the World (IWW) and organized for them while moving from job to job as a construction worker and logger in Oregon; took part in the Spokane, Wash., free speech fight, but was generally not a "soapboxer," rather a tough, practical Wobbly; in 1910 organized Minnesota timber workers and represented them as a delegate to the 1912 IWW convention; also attempted to unionize the harvest hands of the Great Plains, which the IWW had not attempted in any systematic way; in the spring of 1915, met with several Wobblies from the Midwest and the Far West in Kansas City, Mo., to establish the Agricultural Workers Organization (AWO) and was elected its secretary-treasurer (chief officer); concentrating on the migratories who rode the freight trains to the grain fields, the AWO sought higher pay, a ten-hour day, and decent food and bedding for its members; after initial AWO efforts in Oklahoma and Kansas were very successful, moved AWO headquarters to Minneapolis, Minn., and sent his organizers into the northern grain fields; in accord with AWO policy and his own experience, rejected the practice of propagandizing the harvesters in the cities where they congregated between jobs; instead, recruited job delegates to organize on the trains and in the fields; thus the AWO solved the problem of organizing a very mobile labor force; insisted on a high initiation fee and as membership grew AWO not only maintained solvency but also helped the IWW to build a larger national headquarters in Chicago, Ill.; reelected secretary-treasurer of AWO in May 1916, leader of the IWW's most impressive branch, whose control of the main source of harvesters forced high wages and improved living conditions; by the end of the 1916 season, AWO membership reached twenty thousand, the largest ever attained by a single IWW union; the AWO had enlisted some nonagricultural workers, including loggers and railroad laborers; as the result of a dispute over this with William Haywood (q.v.), Nef resigned in late 1916; became secretary of the Philadelphia, Pa., Marine Transport Workers, an IWW local with a large black membership, which controlled the docks until 1920; convicted in Chicago trial of Wobblies, 1919; died in the 1930s; see his "The Militant Harvest Workers," *International So-*

cialist Review (October 1916); Philip S. Foner, *History of the Labor Movement in the United States*, Vol. 4 (1965); John S. Gamba, *The Decline of the I.W.W.* (1962).

Donald G. Sofchalk

NELSON, Oscar Fred   (1884–1943). Born in Chicago, Ill., September 29, 1884; son of Nels and Johanna Nelson; Lutheran; married Helen Hoyer on April 21, 1909; three children; attended the public schools of Chicago: secured employment in a Chicago department store in 1897 and five years later joined the U.S. Postal Service as a clerk; organized a Chicago local of the United National Association of Post Office Clerks (UNAPOC) in 1903 and elected its president; in 1910, elected president of the National Federation of Post Office Clerks (NFPOC), which had been organized in 1906 by a group of Chicago locals that had seceded from the UNAPOC; served as a vice-president of the Chicago Federation of Labor, 1910–1935; was instrumental as the Washington, D.C., representative of the NFPOC in passage of law fixing eight-hour day for postal clerks; served as chief factory inspector for the Illinois State Labor Department, 1913–1917; appointed commissioner of conciliation in the U.S. Department of Labor in 1917, serving until 1929; attended Webster Night School of Law in Chicago and admitted to the Illinois bar in 1922; elected as a Democrat to the Chicago City Council in 1923, but switched to the Republican party in 1927 and served as a city councilman until 1935; served as chairman of the Republican Central Committee of Chicago, 1934–1936; elected a judge of the Chicago superior court in 1935; died in Chicago, Ill., July 14, 1943; Karl Baarslag, *History of the National Federation of Post Office Clerks* (1945); *National Cyclopaedia of American Biography*, Vol. 33.

NESTOR, Agnes   (1880–1948). Born in Grand Rapids, Mich., June 24, 1880; daughter of Irish immigrant Thomas, a machinist, and Anna (McEwen) Nestor; Roman Catholic; acquired a grammar school education in public and parochial schools, then employed by the Eisendrath Glove Factory, Chicago, Ill., in 1897; led a successful ten-day strike against the Eisendrath Company in 1902 and became president of the newly organized Local 2 of the International Glove Workers Union (IGWU); served as vice-president of the IGWU, 1903–1906; joined the Chicago Women's Trade Union League (WTUL) in 1904 and three years later became a member of the executive board of the national WTUL, serving until 1948; elected secretary-treasurer of the IGWU in 1906 and served until 1913 when elected to a two-year term as president; along with Elizabeth Maloney, lobbied the ten-hour bill through the Illinois legislature in 1909; actively involved in the WTUL publicity campaigns in support of striking garment workers in Philadelphia, Pa., in 1909 and Chicago, 1910–1911; elected president of the Chicago WTUL in 1913 and vice-president of the IGWU in 1915, serving in both positions until 1948; appointed to the Commission on Federal Aid to Vocational Education by President Woodrow Wilson in 1914; served on the

Department of Labor advisory committee established by Secretary of Labor William B. Wilson (q.v.) in 1917; during the same year, appointed to the Industrial Survey Commission by the governor of Illinois; was instrumental in the passage of the eight-hour bill in Illinois in 1937; served as the IGWU's director of education and research, 1938–1948; was a Democrat; authored *Brief History of the International Glove Workers Union of America* (1942), and *Woman's Labor Leader: Autobiography of Agnes Nestor* (1954); died in Chicago, Ill., December 20, 1948; Agnes Nestor Papers, Schlesinger Library, Radcliffe College, and the Chicago Historical Society; Gladys Boone, *The Women's Trade Union Leagues in Great Britain and the United States of America* (1942); Mary E. Dreier, *Margaret Dreier Robins: Her Life, Letters and Work* (1950); Mary Anderson, *Woman at Work: The Autobiography of Mary Anderson as Told to Mary N. Winslow* (1951).

Marie Tedesco

NEWMAN, Pauline   (1891–   ). Born in Russia, October 18, 1891 (birth-date has also been listed as 1887 and 1889); daughter of Meyer and Tillie Newman; Jewish; emigrated to the United States in 1901; served as a general organizer and lecturer for the International Ladies' Garment Workers' Union (ILGWU), 1909–1913; was educational director and inspector for the Joint Board of Sanitary Control for the women's garment industry in New York, 1912–1918; served as an organizer and president of the Philadelphia, Pa., Women's Trade Union League (WTUL), 1918–1923; appointed director of the ILGWU Health Center in New York City in 1923, beginning a long and continuing term of service in that capacity; served as a vice-president of the New York branch of the WTUL and was a member of the national executive board of the WTUL; served as a WTUL delegate to the International Congress of Working Women in Vienna in 1923; appointed to the minimum wage board of New York City in 1933; was characterized as a woman of great tact and efficiency; served as a liaison between the ILGWU Health Center medical staff and local unions during much of her career; was a Socialist in her political sympathies and was a Socialist party organizer and lecturer for the northeastern United States, 1913–1915; later supported the American Labor party and the Liberal party of New York; was a member of the organizing committee to oppose the Equal Rights Amendment in 1938; authored "How Women Forged Early Unions," *Allied Industrial Worker* (August 1976), "We Needed Hope More," *GBBA Horizons* (September 1976), and was a frequent contributor to journals such as *Justice*, the *Cleveland Federationist*, and the *Jewish Daily Forward*; Benjamin Stolberg, *Tailor's Progress: The Story of a Famous Union and the Men Who Made It* (1944); Solon DeLeon, ed., *The American Labor Who's Who* (1925); Louis Levine, *The Women's Garment Workers: A History of the International Ladies' Garment Workers' Union* (1924); Pauline Newman Interview, ILGWU Archives.

Marie Tedesco

NINFO, Salvatore   (1883–1960). Born in Santo Stefano, Camastra, Messina, Italy, May 13, 1883; son of Guiseppe, a tailor, and Raffaella (Martino) Ninfo;

Roman Catholic; married Maria Consentino on July 1, 1904; four children; attended grammar school for five years in Italy; emigrated to the United States at age 16; in 1900, led a New York City strike of diggers on the Lexington Avenue subway, the first Italian-American strike; gained employment in the New York garment district and in 1902 joined Cloak Finishers' Local 9 of the International Ladies' Garment Workers' Union (ILGWU); during 1903–1906, served as an American Federation of Labor organizer with the assignment of organizing Italian workers in various crafts in New York, Philadelphia, Pa., and Boston, Mass.; became a member of the executive board of Local 9 in 1906; elected a delegate to the New York Cloak Joint Board in 1908 and the following year appointed a general ILGWU organizer; elected business agent of the New York Cloak Joint Board in 1910; became an ILGWU vice-president in 1916 and served as first vice-president from 1922 to 1934; elected manager of Italian Cloakmakers' Union Local 48 in 1917; served briefly as acting president of the ILGWU after the resignation of Benjamin Schlesinger (q.v.) in 1923; served as treasurer of the Italian Labor Center, the Italian Chamber of Labor, and the Anti-Fascisti Alliance of North America; became manager of ILGWU Local 145, Passaic, N.J., in 1936; elected to the New York City Council in 1937 on the American Labor party ticket and served until 1943; joined the newly organized Liberal party in 1944; retired as ILGWU vice-president in 1956 and three years later retired from all union activities; contributed many articles on industrial and trade union subjects to *Giustizia*, the official Italian language organ of the ILGWU; died in New York City, January 1, 1960; Benjamin Stolberg, *Tailor's Progress: The Story of a Famous Union and the Men Who Made It* (1944); Louis Levine, *The Women's Garment Workers: A History of the International Ladies' Garment Workers' Union* (1924); *ILGWU Report and Proceedings* (1962).

NOCKLES, Edward N.   (1869–1937). Born in Dubuque, Iowa, September 21, 1869; married; attended the public schools of St. Paul, Minn.; moved to Chicago, Ill., by 1900; became an electrician and joined the International Brotherhood of Electrical Workers Local 134; elected secretary of the Chicago Federation of Labor (CFL) in 1901 and retained office until his death; joined with John Fitzpatrick (q.v.), an ally for more than 30 years, to wrest control of the CFL from the corrupt unionists who had dominated it for years; under their leadership, the Chicago labor movement became one of the nation's most dynamic, succeeding after 1905 in organizing many of the city's clothing, meatpacking, and steel workers; was a close friend of Frank P. Walsh, the noted labor lawyer, and served as Walsh's assistant on the National War Labor Board during World War I; coauthored "Labor's Fourteen Points" with Walsh and Fitzpatrick; demanding a governmental guarantee of the right to organize and bargain collectively, an eight-hour day, and nationalization of utilities, the fourteen points became the basis for the American Federation of Labor's postwar reconstruction program; was a key participant in the formation of the Labor party of Illinois in 1919 and the attempt to launch a national Farmer-Labor party,

1919–1923; was a pioneer in the use of radio broadcasting by organized labor and was instrumental in 1926 in founding station WCFL, "The Voice of Labor," serving it as general manager; was disillusioned by his earlier foray into third-party activity and exerted influence against it in the 1930s, supporting Democrat Mayor Edward Kelly and President Franklin D. Roosevelt; was opposed to domination of the airwaves by powerful network stations and was pressing the Federal Communications Commission to grant more transmitting power to WCFL when he died in Chicago, Ill., February 27, 1937; Illinois State Federation of Labor, *Proceedings* (1937); Barbara Warne Newell, *Chicago and the Labor Movement: Metropolitan Unionism in the 1930s* (1961); Eugene Staley, *History of the Illinois State Federation of Labor* (1930).

Donald G. Sofchalk

NOONAN, James Patrick   (1878–1929). Born in St. Louis, Mo., December 15, 1878; son of Irish immigrants, Thomas P., a farmer, and Bridget (Kemmey) Noonan; Roman Catholic; married Inez M. Mitchell, June 26, 1901; two children; orphaned at an early age; quit school at age 13 and held various manual labor jobs; enlisted as a private during the Spanish-American War and, after being discharged from the army, became an electric lineman in St. Louis, Mo.; joined the International Brotherhood of Electrical Workers (IBEW) in 1901; a year later, elected president of his local union; elected president of the Missouri and Illinois District Council in 1903, and the following year, an international vice-president of the IBEW; became acting president in 1917 when the incumbent, Frank J. McNulty (q.v.), took a leave of absence and elected president two years later; elected a vice-president of the American Federation of Labor (AFL) building trades department in 1922; appointed to the National Board of Jurisdictional Awards for the Building Trades; became an AFL vice-president and executive council member in 1924; during 1921–1924, served on a committee of the President's Conference on Unemployment that was concerned with seasonal fluctuations in the construction industry; appointed the American Labor delegate to the World Power Conference in London in 1924; appointed by Governor Gifford Pinchot to Pennsylvania's Giant Power Board and to the St. Lawrence Waterway Commission by Secretary of Commerce Herbert Hoover; died in Washington, D.C., December 4, 1929; Michael A. Mulcaire, *The International Brotherhood of Electrical Workers* (1923); *Dictionary of American Biography*, Vol. 8; Solon DeLeon, ed., *The American Labor Who's Who* (1925).

NORD, Elizabeth   (1902–   ). Born in Lancashire, England, in 1902; daughter of a coal miner and textile weaver; Episcopalian; began working at the Royal Weaving Company in Pawtucket, R.I., in 1916 at age 14; completed one year of high school through night classes while working as a weaver; attended Bryn Mawr Summer School for Women Workers, 1923, 1924, and Barnard and Vineyard Shore Summer School for Women Workers, 1929, 1930; joined the Textile Workers Union of America (TWUA) in 1928; became a full-time organizer for the TWUA in 1934, concentrating on the organization of southern textile workers, especially in Virginia and Maryland; was one of the leaders of the organizing campaign in Cumberland, Md., in 1935 that organized the Celanese Corporation; became a TWUA assistant joint board manager and, during World War II, was appointed acting manager; worked for the U.S. Department of Labor, 1945–1947; returned to union work in 1947 and was elected joint board manager for several terms; retired in 1978; a Democrat; James Findlay et al., "Oral History Interview with Elizabeth Nord," in *The 20th Century Trade Union Woman: Vehicle for Social Change*; Oral History Project and the University of Rhode Island Oral History Project (1978).

NORWOOD, Rose Finkelstein   (1891–1980). Born in Kiev, Russia, on September 10, 1891; daughter of Henry, a tailor, and Fanny (Schafferman) Finkelstein, owner of a small grocery store; Jewish; emigrated with parents to the United States as a very young girl; married Hyman Norwood, owner of a small tire and battery business on December 25, 1921; two children; began full-time work in 1908 as a telephone operator in Boston, Mass., after leaving high school in her senior year; was a telephone operator and supervisor until her marriage; in 1912 she became a charter member of the Boston Telephone Operators' Union (later Local 1A), organized by the International Brotherhood of Electrical Workers with major assistance from the Women's Trade Union League (WTUL); was a member of the executive board of Local 1A, and a leader of the 1919 New England telephone workers' strike; served as secretary of Local 1A, 1927–1933, when the union was trying to reorganize after total defeat in the 1923 New England telephone operators' strike resulted in its being replaced by company unions; became active in Boston WTUL in 1912 and served on the executive board or as an officer from about 1918 until term as president, 1941–1950; was a member of the National WTUL executive board, 1947–1950; was a member of the first class to attend Bryn Mawr Summer School for Women Workers in 1921; attended Brookwood Labor College in 1928 and 1935; active in the defense of Sacco (q.v.) and Vanzetti (q.v.) and in the interwar peace movement; worked as an organizer for a succession of unions, beginning with the Commercial Telegraphers' Union of America, 1933–1937, for which she organized the Boston Postal Telegraph Company; organizer and business agent of the Laundry Workers International Union, 1937–1939, and led strikes in Boston, Watertown, and Somerville, Mass.; worked with the International Ladies' Garment Workers' Union in the early 1940s on campaigns in Boston and Lowell, Mass.; in 1944, she organized the Boston Public Library for the American Federation of State, County and Municipal Employees; organized women wartime shipyard workers in Portland, Me.; was an organizer for the International Jewelry Workers Union, 1944–1949; joined the staff of the Retail Clerks International Union in 1949, and organized the Jordan Marsh department store in Boston; also participated in campaigns in Pennsylvania and New Hampshire; ended her career in the mid-1950s as an organizer with the Building Service Employees International Union;

with the rise of the Nazi threat in the 1930s, she sponsored talks by German refugees in Boston; during World War II, she was the only woman member of the *Boston Herald* Rumor Clinic, chaired by Gordon Allport, whose purpose was to combat fascist-inspired prejudice and rumors designed to undermine the Allied war effort; as president of the Boston WTUL, provided strike support, supervised a workers' education program, and conceived of the "Books for Workers" plan, through which public libraries supplied books to union halls and factories; as a delegate to the Massachusetts Nutrition Conference during World War II, she argued for measures to provide a balanced diet for workers in defense plants; was a member of the Massachusetts Committee for the Marshall Plan; was active in the Boston National Association for the Advancement of Colored People organization; was a member of the Massachusetts Committee for Hoover in 1928, but actively supported Democratic presidential candidates in all subsequent elections; appointed to the Massachusetts American Federation of Labor-Congress of Industrial Organizations committee on senior citizens in April 1980; died in Boston on September 25, 1980; Rose Finkelstein Norwood Papers, Schlesinger Library, Radcliffe College; Sari Roboff, ed., *Boston's Labor Movement* (1977); *Who's Who in Labor* (1946); *Boston Globe*, September 28, 1980; *Boston Herald-American*, September 27, 1980.

Stephen H. Norwood

NUTT, James Henry   (1848–ca. 1921). Born in Worcestershire, England, on November 19, 1848; son of Thomas, a tin-plate worker, and Ann Nutt; Episcopalian; married Sarah Ward on November 26, 1871; nine children; received some grammar school education; was working in a tin mill by 1857 and later worked in a sheet mill until 1867; emigrated to the United States in 1868; worked in mills in Pittsburgh, Pa., New York State, Delmar, Ohio, and finally as a heater for Brown, Bonnel and Company in Youngstown, Ohio, 1876–1891; became a permanent resident of Youngstown after 1880; was a trustee of the national lodge of the Amalgamated Association of Iron and Steel Workers, 1884–1889; was on several committees that negotiated wage scales with iron manufacturers in the 1880s; was a delegate to the 1887 and 1888 conventions of the American Federation of Labor; was commissioner and later secretary of the Labor Bureau, Mahoning and Shenango Iron Manufacturers' Association, 1892–1906; was an organizer of the Western Bar Iron Association and secretary of that association, 1906–1921; was an organizer of the Western Sheet and Tinplate Manufacturers' Association and served as its secretary, 1912–1921; a Republican, he was elected a Youngstown city councilman in 1884 and served three terms; served as president of the Youngstown City Council, 1889–1890, city commissioner, 1891; was active in securing legislation that introduced public utilities and streetcars to Youngstown; served on the Youngstown Board of Education, 1912–1916; served as city safety director, 1916–1921; was a thirty-second degree Mason and member of the Ancient Order of Nobles of the Mystic

Shrine; died about 1921; *Youngstown City Directories*; James G. Butler, Jr., *History of Youngstown and the Mahoning Valley, Ohio* (1921).

Sharon Trusilo

O

OAKES, Grant Wilson (1905–). Born in Westfield, N.Y., April 18, 1905; son of Fred J., a railroad electrician, and Ellen (Lawson) Oakes; Protestant; married Hazel A. Bacon on February 14, 1931; three children; completed high school; studied electrical engineering for three years in a General Electric Company industrial college, then worked for General Electric for seven years; after moving to Chicago, Ill., in 1928, employed by the International Harvester Company as a skilled experimental mechanic; was one of the Congress of Industrial Organizations' (CIO) organizers of Tractor Local 101 of the Steel Workers Organizing Committee at International Harvester's Chicago works in 1936; became secretary, chairman of the grievance committee, and president of Local 101; headed the Farm Equipment Workers Organizing Committee after it was founded in 1938; elected first president of the CIO-chartered United Farm Equipment and Metal Workers of America (FE) in 1942; maintained a strict no-strike policy during World War II, but led his union in major strikes against International Harvester, Allis-Chalmers, and other farm implement manufacturers immediately before and after the war; was a member of the executive board of the CIO, but often opposed CIO policies and was involved in numerous jurisdictional conflicts with the larger United Automobile, Aircraft and Agricultural Implement Workers Union (UAW); defied a CIO order to merge his union with the UAW in 1949 and the FE's charter was revoked; led the FE into a merger with the United Electrical, Radio and Machine Workers Union (UE), which was expelled from the CIO in 1949 for alleged Communist domination; a disastrous 1952 strike against International Harvester and successful UAW raids resulted in the absorption of the remaining UE-FE membership by the UAW in 1954; was purged, whereas many former FE officials were transferred to the UAW; self-identified as a Democrat; supported Henry Wallace's Progressive party candidacy in 1948 and in the same year ran unsuccessfully on the Progressive party ticket for governor of Illinois; *Current Biography* (1950); *Who's Who in Labor* (1946);

Robert Ozanne, *A Century of Labor-Management Relations at McCormick and International Harvester* (1967).

Donald G. Sofchalk

OBERGFELL, Joseph F.   (1881–1945). Born in Germany, July 26, 1881; son of Robert, a carpenter, and Martha (Strobel) Obergfell; married Erna C. Weier on August 20, 1919; emigrated to the United States while still an infant; attended the public elementary schools in Indianapolis, Ind., then secured employment as a bottler in the brewery industry; joined the International Union of United Brewery, Flour, Cereal and Soft Drink Workers (UBFCSDW) in 1898; served as the business representative of several Indianapolis UBFCSDW locals, 1901–1914; was an officer in the Indianapolis Central Labor Union, 1900–1914, and during the same period served as a delegate to the Indiana State Federation of Labor; elected secretary-treasurer of the UBFCSDW in 1914, and continued in that capacity after being elected international president in 1924; was a member of the Trades Union Liberty League and Labor's Joint Legislative Committee for Modification of the Volstead Law, 1919–1933; elected a vice-president of the American Federation of Labor (AFL) union label trades department in 1922, serving until 1942; represented workers in the bakery and brewing industries on the U.S. Minimum Wage Board; led the UBFCSDW through a long jurisdictional dispute with the International Brotherhood of Teamsters, Chauffeurs, Warehousemen and Helpers of America during the 1930s, which resulted in the UBFCSDW affiliating with the Congress of Industrial Organizations (CIO) in 1942 after the failure of the AFL to resolve the dispute satisfactorily; became a member of the CIO executive council in 1942; died in Cincinnati, Ohio, November 3, 1945; Maurer, Fleisher & Associates, *Union with a Heart: International Union of United Brewery, Flour, Cereal, Soft Drink and Distillery Workers of America: 75 Years of a Great Union, 1886–1961* (1961); Philip Taft, *The A.F. of L. from the Death of Gompers to the Merger* (1959); *Who's Who in Labor* (1946).

O'CONNELL, James P.   (1858–1936). Born in Minersville, Pa., August 22, 1858; son of James, a machinist, and Margaret (Donough) O'Connell; Roman Catholic; married Ellen Gallagher on June 12, 1886; four children; graduated from high school in Oil City, Pa., then began, at age 16, a machinist apprenticeship at the W. J. Innis Engine Works in Oil City; during the following eight years, worked as a machinist in Pennsylvania and Michigan; left the shops in 1882 for two years and enjoyed brief success in the oil business; worked for Fall Brook Coal Company, Corning, N.Y., 1884–1887, before returning to Oil City and working in a railroad roundhouse; joined the Knights of Labor and organized and joined an International Association of Machinists (IAM) local, Lodge 113, Oil City; served as an American Federation of Labor (AFL) fraternal delegate to the British Trades Union Congress in 1889; elected to the IAM general executive board in 1891, and became grand master machinist (president) in 1893, serving through 1911; was a close associate of AFL president Samuel Gompers (q.v.) and was an AFL vice-president and executive council member, 1895–1918; served as president of the AFL's metal trades department, 1911–1934; was a rallying point in the AFL for the conservative, pure-and-simple trade unionists who opposed the Populist-Socialist faction led by his successor as IAM president, William H. Johnston (q.v.); appointed to the Commission on Industrial Relations by President Woodrow Wilson in 1913, and received a similar appointment to the Executive Committee on Labor of the Council of National Defense in 1917; was an opponent of industrial unionism, but expanded the jurisdiction of the IAM and reduced skill requirements; during his presidency, the IAM's Populist-Socialist faction became increasingly powerful and was able to democratize the internal governance structure and endorse the government ownership of railroads and telegraph and telephone companies over his opposition; the crowning success of his career was the Murray Hill Agreement, negotiated in 1900 after a prolonged strike, which provided for a nationwide agreement, the closed shop, the nine-hour day, and other reforms; when employers initiated the nine-hour day in 1901, they maintained the same hourly rates, thus reducing machinists' wages by 10 percent; as a result, fifty thousand IAM unionists went on strike, but employers pooled their financial resources, organized a strike-breaking service, and defeated the strike; the conflict led to a long war against the IAM by employers striving to maintain the open shop; was a Democrat; died in Washington, D.C., October 30, 1936; *Machinists' Monthly Journal* (December 1936); Mark Perlman, *The Machinists: A New Study in American Trade Unionism* (1961), and *Democracy in the International Association of Machinists* (1962); John H. M. Laslett, *Labor and the Left: A Study of Socialism and Radical Influences in the American Labor Movement, 1881–1924* (1970); *Who Was Who in America*, Vol. 1.

John W. Hevener

O'CONNOR, Harvey (1898–   ). Born in Minneapolis, Minn., March 29, 1898; son of James J., a railroad cook, and Jessie (Kenney) O'Connor; Unitarian; married Jessie Bross Lloyd in 1930; two children; completed public high school in St. Paul, Minn., and Tacoma, Wash.; employed as a lumber worker prior to becoming the managing editor of the *Seattle Daily Call*, 1917–1918; became editor of the *International Weekly of Seattle* in 1919; indicted for criminal anarchy in 1919 as a result of his activities associated with the Seattle, Wash., general strike but charges were later dropped; became a reporter, city-news editor, and labor editor of the *Seattle Union Record* in 1921, serving until 1924 when named assistant editor of the *Locomotive Engineers Journal*; served during 1927–1930 as a New York bureau manager for the Federated Press, a leftist news agency; was the managing editor of the *People's Press*, 1936–1937; became the editor of the *International Oil Worker* in 1937; served as publicity director of the Oil Workers International Union, 1945–1948; refused to testify before Joseph R. McCarthy's Senate Permanent Investigating Committee in 1954 and was convicted of contempt of Congress; his conviction was reversed on appeal; indicted for contempt of Congress again in 1959 after refusing to obey a subpoena to appear before the House Committee on Un-American Activities, but the indictment was later dismissed; authored *Steel-Dictator* (1935), *History of Oil Workers International Union, CIO* (1950), *The Empire of Oil* (1955), *World Crisis in Oil* (1962), and other books and articles; Melvin Rothbaum, *The Government of the Oil, Chemical, and Atomic Workers Union* (1962); *Who's Who in Labor* (1946); Solon DeLeon, ed., *The American Labor Who's Who* (1925).

O'CONNOR, Thomas Ventry   (1870–1935). Born in Toronto, Canada, in 1870; son of Stephen, an Irish immigrant and brush maker, and Eileen O'Connor; Roman Catholic; married Bridget Gertrude Carney; six children; moved with parents to Buffalo, N.Y., in 1872; became a marine engineer and tugboat captain and was actively involved in trade union activities; served as president of the Licensed Tugmen's Association of the Great Lakes, 1906–1908; elected president of the International Longshoremen's Association (ILA) in 1908; was an American Federation of Labor fraternal delegate to the British Trades Union Congress in 1910; during his ILA incumbency, ruthlessly crushed unauthorized strikes and prided himself in never having sanctioned a longshoremen's strike; assumed the title of honorary president after resigning from the ILA to become a member of the New York State Industrial Board; appointed vice-chairman of the U.S. Shipping Board in 1921 and became chairman in 1924; although no legal improprieties were ever proven, was often accused as president of the U.S. Shipping Board of being overly solicitous of private shipping interests; served as a member of the advisory council of Lincoln Memorial University; was a Republican; died in Buffalo, N.Y., October 17, 1935; Maud Russell, *Men along the Shore* (1966); Charles P. Larrowe, *Shape-Up and Hiring Hall: A Comparison of Hiring Methods and Labor Relations on the New York and Seattle Waterfronts* (1955), and *Maritime Labor Relations on the Great Lakes* (1959).

O'DONNELL, John Joseph   (1925–   ). Born on January 14, 1925; married; three children; served in the U.S. Navy, 1942–1945, and the U.S. Air Force, 1949–1951; employed by Lincoln Laboratory, Cambridge Research Center, U.S. Air Force, 1952–1956; became a member of the Air Line Pilots Association (ALPA) in 1956, and that same year became a pilot for Eastern Air Lines, Inc.; served as a member of the ALPA board of directors, 1960–1964, and as chairman of the retirement and insurance committee, 1966–1970; was elected ALPA president in 1971, serving in that capacity until 1982; elected an American Federation of Labor-Congress of Industrial Organizations (AFL-CIO) vice-president and executive council member in 1979; for 13 years, he served on local and national ALPA negotiating committees representing Eastern Air Lines pilots; was a member of the AFL-CIO committee on community services and was a labor representative on the United Way board of governors and executive committee; was the ALPA representative to the International Federation of Air Line Pilots, 1970–1982; was a member of the U.S. Department of Labor's policy advisory committee on multilateral trade negotiations; wrote numerous articles for the *Airline Pilot*, the ALPA monthly journal, and authored many presentations submitted to the U.S. Senate and House of Representatives; was defeated for reelection as ALPA president in 1982; *Who's Who in Labor* (1976); *AFL-CIO News*, February 24, 1979.

O'HARE, John   (1904–   ). Born in Armadale, West Lothian, Scotland, June 14, 1904; son of Owen, a coal miner, and Ellen O'Hare; Roman Catholic; married Rosella Cecilia Simonis on October 29, 1938; completed secondary school, then attended night-school classes at Toledo University while working in the tobacco industry; joined Local 196 of the Tobacco Workers International Union (TWIU) in 1935 and shortly thereafter elected recording secretary of Local 196; was a member of the committee on minimum wages for the tobacco industry in 1941; served as a general TWIU organizer prior to being elected international president of the union in 1944; represented the TWIU at national conventions of the American Federation of Labor for several years; retired from union affairs in 1968; a Democrat; *Who's Who in Labor* (1946).

O'HARE, Kate Richards Cunningham   (1877–1948). Born in Ottawa County, Kans., on March 26, 1877; daughter of Andrew, a once-prosperous rancher who became a machinist after being ruined by drought in 1877, and Lucy (Thompson) Richards; a Campbellite Protestant early in life; married Francis Patrick O'Hare, a Socialist lecturer and teacher, on January 1, 1902; four children; divorced in 1928; married Charles C. Cunningham, an attorney and mining engineer, on November 28, 1928; received her primary education in rural Kansas schools and graduated from high school in Burchard, Nebr., in 1894; became an apprentice machinist in her father's shop after graduating from high school and later joined the International Machinists Union; converted to socialism after hearing a speech by ''Mother'' Jones (q.v.) in 1899, she joined the Socialist Labor party in 1899; switched her allegiance to the newly formed Socialist party of America (SPA) in 1901 and attended the International School of Social Economy, a Socialist school in Girard, Kans., later that same year; during the period 1901–1917, she was one of the most traveled and most popular speakers on the Socialist lecture circuit; she was especially popular in the southern Great Plains where she enrolled hundreds of small farmers in the Socialist cause; was also a prolific writer and active supporter of woman's suffrage; ran unsuccessfully as a Socialist candidate for Congress from Kansas in 1910; in 1912, along with her husband, she founded, edited, and published the *National Rip-Saw* (later renamed *Social Revolution* in 1917 and *American Vanguard* in 1922), a St. Louis-based Socialist monthly; was elected to and served on the SPA's national women's committee, 1910–1912; an opponent of American involvement in World War I, she chaired the SPA committee on war and militarism in 1917; was arrested in July 1917, indicted for violating the Espionage Act, convicted, and sentenced to five years in the Missouri State Penitentiary; while in prison, she wrote *Kate O'Hare's Prison Letters* (1919), and *In Prison* (1920); her sentence was commuted in May 1920 and she was given a full pardon later by President Calvin Coolidge; after her release from prison, she resumed her speaking activities and added penal reform to her list of social causes; along with her husband, she organized the Children's Crusade in 1922, a dramatic "march on Washington" composed of the children of still-imprisoned war protestors; her campaign against contract prison labor helped bring about federal legislation banning the interstate transportation of convict-made goods in 1929; with her husband, she joined the Llano Co-operative Colony, a utopian commune located near Leesville, La., in 1922, and there founded Commonwealth College, a workers' school that was moved to Mena, Ark., in 1925 after factionalism disrupted the communal experiment; served as dean of women and a teacher at Commonwealth College, 1925–1928; after her divorce and remarriage in 1928, she moved to California, where her husband lived, and in 1934 supported Upton Sinclair's gubernatorial candidacy and anti-poverty campaign; she devoted much of her time thereafter to penal reform; was appointed assistant director of the California Department of Penology in 1939 and was credited with promoting a reform of the California prison system that made it one of the most enlightened in the United States; authored numerous articles and pamphlets as well as *What Happened to Dan?*, a Socialist novel published in 1904 and reissued in 1911 under the title *The Sorrows of Cupid*; died in Benecia, Calif., in January 1948; *Dictionary of American Biography*, Suppl. 4; Solon DeLeon, ed., *The American Labor Who's Who* (1925); "How I Became a Socialist Agitator," *Socialist Woman* (October 1908); David A. Shannon, *The Socialist Party of America: A History* (1955); James Weinstein, *The Decline of Socialism in America, 1912–1925* (1967); Neil K. Basen, "Kate Richards O'Hare: The 'First Lady' of American Socialism, 1901–1917," *Labor History* (Spring 1980); Hugh Lovin, "The Banishment of Kate Richards O'Hare," *Idaho Yesterdays* (Spring 1978); James R. Green, *Grass-Roots Socialism: Radical Movements in the Southwest, 1895–1943* (1978).

OHL, Henry, Jr.   (1873–1940). Born in Milwaukee, Wis., March 16, 1873; son of Henry, a laborer, and Mary Elizabeth (Dietrich) Ohl; married Anna W. E. Fleischmann on April 7, 1894; three children; attended grammar school, then went to work in the printing trade at age 13; joined both Milwaukee, Wis., Local 23 of the International Typographical Union and the Socialist party in 1901; was an organizer and editor for Local 23, 1903–1909; became an organizer for the American Federation of Labor and the Wisconsin State Federation of Labor (WSFL) in 1914; when the prominent unionist, Frank J. Weber (q.v.), died in 1917, became head of the WSFL, retaining position until his death; also played an influential role in the Milwaukee Federated Trades Council; in the 1930s, helped form the Wisconsin Farmer-Labor Federation, an attempt to unify the Progressive and Socialist parties; was a major leader of the Socialist trade unionists who dominated Milwaukee politics before World War I and was deputy city clerk in Mayor Emil Seidel's administration and served in the Wisconsin Assembly, 1917–1918; his most important contribution was the promotion of worker education; helped establish the Milwaukee Workers College in 1921 and served as a trustee; largely as a result of his efforts, worker-education classes were available in several other Wisconsin cities by 1928; was a member of the Wisconsin University Labor Joint Committee on Education for Workers, 1927–1940; not opposed to industrial unionism, but became involved in a bitter jurisdictional battle with the Congress of Industrial Organizations (CIO) over the organization of Allis-Chalmers workers in Milwaukee during the 1930s; left the Socialist party after it endorsed the CIO in 1937; died in Milwaukee, Wis., October 16, 1940; Solon DeLeon, ed., *The American Labor Who's Who* (1925); *Dictionary of Wisconsin Biography* (1960); Thomas W. Gavett, *Development of the Labor Movement in Milwaukee* (1965).

Donald G. Sofchalk

OLANDER, Victor A.   (1873–1949). Born in Chicago, Ill., November 28, 1873; married Elizabeth Grace Cervenko on May 28, 1902; two children; before completing grammar school, began a career as a merchant sailor and for 14 years sailed primarily on the Great Lakes; joined the International Seamen's Union of America (ISU) (name changed to Seafarers International Union of North America in 1938) in 1899 and served as the business agent of the Sailor's Union of the Great Lakes (ISU-GL), 1901–1903; elected a vice-president of the ISU in 1902; served as a delegate from the ISU to both the Chicago and Illinois federations of labor; elected assistant secretary of the ISU-GL in 1903, serving until 1909 when elected general secretary; became a member of the ISU legislative committee in 1913 and participated in the lobbying efforts resulting in the enactment of the La Follette Seamen's Act of 1914; elected secretary-treasurer of the Illinois State Federation of Labor in 1914, serving until 1949; was a member during World War I of the National War Labor Board and the Illinois State Council of Defense; lost the sight in both eyes in 1919 due to cataracts, but his vision was restored by surgery in 1924; elected secretary-treasurer of the ISU in 1925, serving until 1935; was a member of the Unemployment Compensation Advisory Board of the Illinois state Department of Labor; served as secretary of the American Federation of Labor resolutions committee during the conventions of 1927–1933; appointed to the National Recovery Administration District Recovery Board for Illinois and Wisconsin in 1933; died in Chicago, Ill., February 5, 1949; Barbara Warne Newell, *Chicago and the Labor Movement: Metropolitan Unionism in the 1930s* (1961); Eugene Staley, *History of the Illinois State Federation of Labor* (1930); Joseph P. Goldberg, *The Maritime Story: A Study in Labor-Management Relations* (1958).

O'NEILL, John M.   (ca. 1857–1936). Born ca. 1857; graduated from Niagara University, Buffalo, N.Y.; lived in the Black Hills of South Dakota for a time, then worked as a journalist in various Colorado mining towns during the

1890s and elected to the state legislature; resigned as editor of the anti-union *Butte Miner* in order to support the Western Federation of Miners (WFM); participated as a WFM representative in the founding convention of the Western Labor Union, successfully urging it to adopt a Socialist program; became the editor of the WFM journal, *Miners' Magazine* in 1901; was a competent journalist with an incisive mind, making the weekly journal an exponent of the radical industrial unionism espoused by WFM presidents Edward Boyce (q.v.) and Charles Moyer (q.v.); during 1901–1905, when WFM radicalism reached its peak, used his vitriolic pen to attack Samuel Gompers (q.v.) for allegedly selling out to the capitalists; used the *Miners' Magazine* to promote the proposal for a new radical labor movement, and, along with his close friend Moyer, was a delegate to the founding convention of the Industrial Workers of the World (IWW) in 1905; in the 1906 struggle for control of the IWW between President Charles Sherman (q.v.) and the left-wing DeLeon-Trautmann faction, condemned the former for deposing Sherman; supported Moyer as he moved away from the IWW toward a moderate position and denounced the IWW leadership in the pages of the *Miners' Magazine*; by 1910, pointed out that the WFM's isolation from the rest of organized labor rendered it powerless to cope with the corporations and advocated reaffiliation with the American Federation of Labor; when the *Miners' Magazine* changed from a weekly to a monthly, became editor of the UMWA Trinidad *Free Press* as a result of a friendship that he had struck up with United Mine Workers of America (UMWA) leader Adolph Germer (q.v.); died in Colorado, January 5, 1936; Vernon H. Jenson, *Heritage of Conflict: Labor Relations in the Nonferrous Metals Industry up to 1930* (1950); John H. M. Laslett, *Labor and the Left: A Study of Socialism and Radical Influences in the American Labor Movement, 1881–1924* (1970).

Donald G. Sofchalk

O'REILLY, Leonora   (1870–1927). Born in New York City on February 16, 1870; daughter of John O'Reilly, a printer, and Winifred (Rooney) O'Reilly; never married; one child (adopted); was forced by the premature death of her father to leave school at age 11 and take a job in a collar factory; joined a local assembly of the Knights of Labor but apparently was not an activist in the organization; later the same year, 1886, at age 16, she organized the Working Women's Society, a club whose activities eventually inspired Josephine S. Lowell to found the New York Consumers' League in 1890; became interested and involved in settlement house activities after visiting Lillian Wald's Henry Street Settlement in 1894; joined the Social Reform Club, an organization composed of labor leaders and reformers concerned with industrial working conditions; elected a vice-president of the Social Reform Club in 1897; meanwhile, she continued working a ten-hour day in a shirtwaist factory where in 1897 she organized a local of the United Garment Workers of America; managed a model garment workers' cooperative established by Lillian Wald and Louise Perkins at Henry Street and, after its failure, became the head of workers at Asacog

House, a Brooklyn settlement, a position she held from 1899 to 1902; supervised the machine operating department of the Manhattan Trade School for Girls, 1902–1909; joined the Women's Trade Union League (WTUL) after its founding in 1903 and in 1909 became vice-president of the New York branch; actively participated in the historic New York garment workers' strike in 1909; was one of the founding members of the National Association for the Advancement of Colored People in 1909; chaired a WTUL committee that investigated fire safety conditions after the Triangle Shirtwaist Company tragedy in 1911; joined the New York City Woman Suffrage party and in 1912 was appointed chairman of its industrial committee; served as a delegate to the International Congress of Women meeting at The Hague in 1915 and as a delegate to the International Congress of Working Women which met in Washington in 1919; was an active member of the Socialist party of America; died in New York City on April 3, 1927; Leonora O'Reilly Papers, Schlesinger Library, Radcliffe College; *Notable American Women*, Vol. 2; Alice Henry, *The Trade Union Woman* (1915); Gladys Boone, *The Women's Trade Union Leagues in Great Britain and the United States of America* (1942); Philip S. Foner, *Women and the American Labor Movement from Colonial Times to the Eve of World War I* (1979).

ORNBURN, Ira M.   (1889–1950). Born in Moberly, Mo., November 28, 1889; son of Cyrus P., a farmer, and Sallie J. Ornburn; completed his formal education, then gained employment as a railroad call boy; later became a cigar-maker and joined the Cigarmakers' International Union of America (CMIU); elected secretary-treasurer of the Connecticut State Federation of Labor in 1912, serving until 1923; served as a vice-president of the CMIU during 1918–1926, then elected international president in 1926, serving until 1936; despite the objections of Senator George W. Norris of Nebraska, was appointed to the U.S. Tariff Commission in 1930 and served until 1933; was secretary of the National Labor Legislative Committee for Amendment of the Volstead Act in 1931; appointed secretary-treasurer of the American Federation of Labor's union label trades department in 1934 and continued in that capacity until his death; served during World War II on the labor policy committees of the Office of Price Administration and the U.S. Department of Agriculture; during his association with the union label trades department, created labor-management exhibitions and organized the American Federation of Women's Auxiliaries of Labor; died in Washington, D.C., December 17, 1950; *Who's Who in Labor* (1946); *The American Federationist* (January 1950).

Merl E. Reed

O'SULLIVAN, Mary Kenney   (1864–1943). Born on January 8, 1864, in Hannibal, Mo.; daughter of Michael, a railroad machinist, and Mary (Kelly) Kenney; married John F. O'Sullivan, a labor editor, on October 10, 1894; four children; after finishing the fourth grade in the public schools of Hannibal, she left school and took a job as an apprentice dressmaker; somewhat later she secured a job with a printing and binding company; four years later, when the plant in which she was employed was moved to Keokuk, Iowa, she followed, working there until the plant closed in the late 1880s; after losing her job, she moved to Chicago, Ill., where she obtained work in a bindery; joined Women's federal Union 2703, a directly chartered American Federation of Labor (AFL) federal labor union; appointed the first AFL woman general organizer in 1892 and organized garment workers in Troy, N.Y., and New York City and printing employees, carpet weavers, and shoe workers in Massachusetts; when her organizer commission was not renewed by the AFL executive council in 1893, she returned to Chicago where she once again became active in labor affairs at Jane Addams's (q.v.) Hull House with which she had been involved in her previous organizing activities in Chicago; in association with other Hull House labor reformers, she lobbied in the Illinois state legislature for a state factory inspection law, which was passed in 1893, and for a year served as a deputy to Florence Kelley (q.v.), Illinois chief factory inspector under the new legislation; moved to Boston, Mass., after her marriage in 1894 and quickly became involved in reform activities; was one of the founders and the first executive secretary of the Union for Industrial Progress, an organization of labor reformers that studied working conditions in Boston factories and workshops; meanwhile, she continued voluntary organizing activities, primarily among women workers in the garment, laundry, and rubber industries; along with William English Walling (q.v.), she founded the National Women's Trade Union League (WTUL) during the 1903 annual AFL convention and served successively as secretary and first vice-president during the league's early, formative years; despite the WTUL's reticence, she strongly supported the Industrial Workers of the World's 1912 textile strike in Lawrence, Mass.; became a factory inspector in the Massachusetts Department of Labor in 1914 and served in that capacity until retiring, at age 70, in 1934; interested in social justice reforms of all types, she consistently had supported the activities of social settlement workers; was also an ardent woman suffragist, an active prohibitionist, and a pacifist; died in West Medford, Mass., on January 18, 1943; *Notable American Women*, Vol. 2; Alice Henry, *Women and the Labor Movement* (1923); Gladys Boone, *The Women's Trade Union Leagues in Great Britain and the United States of America* (1942); Allan F. Davis, *Spearheads for Reform: The Social Settlements and the Progressive Movement, 1890–1914* (1967); Mary Kenney O'Sullivan, unpublished autobiography, Schlesinger Library, Radcliffe College; Philip S. Foner, *Women and the American Labor Movement from Colonial Times to the Eve of World War I* (1979).

OSWALD, Rudolph A.   (1932–   ). Born in Milwaukee, Wis., on August 4, 1932; son of Carl J., a tailor, and Ann Oswald, a homemaker; married Mary Ellen, a homemaker, in 1957; four children; attended Holy Cross College, 1950–1954, earning the B.A. degree; was a recipient of a Fulbright scholarship and studied at the University of Munich, Germany, 1954–1955; received the M.S. from the University of Wisconsin in 1958 and the Ph.D. from Georgetown

University in 1965; while attending graduate school he also interned at the American Federation of Labor-Congress of Industrial Organizations (AFL-CIO) department of research during 1958; served as research and education director of the International Association of Fire Fighters, 1959–1963; became an AFL-CIO staff economist in 1963, serving until 1972; was research director of the Service Employees International Union, 1972–1975; rejoined the AFL-CIO as assistant director of the department of education, 1975–1976, and, in 1976, was appointed director of the AFL-CIO department of research; was active on numerous governmental and professional committees, including membership on the Federal Employment Pay Council, 1970–1972, chairman of the labor research advisory committee of the U.S. Department of Labor's Bureau of Labor Statistics and of the U.S. Office of Management and Budget, 1968–1972; was a board member of the National Industries for the Blind, the American Statistical Association Advisory Committee of the Bureau of the Census, 1965–1972, and was a board member of the National Bureau of Economic Research in 1974; authored *Adjusting to Automation* (1969) and several articles in *The American Federationist*, beginning in December 1965; *Who's Who in Labor* (1976); *AFL-CIO News*, November 13, 1976.

OWEN, Robert Dale   (1801–1877). Born in Glasgow, Scotland, November 9, 1801; son of Robert, an industrialist and social reformer, and Ann Caroline (Dale) Owen; married Mary Jane Robinson on April 12, 1832, and, after her death in 1871, Lottie Walton Kellogg on June 23, 1876; instructed by private tutors before attending the Philipp Emanuel von Fellenberg School at Hofwyl, Switzerland, 1820–1823; traveled to the United States with his father in 1825 and shortly thereafter proceeded to New Harmony, Ind., where the elder Owen began his cooperative colony; was unable to perform physical labor, so taught school and edited the *New Harmony Gazette*; after the failure of the New Harmony experiment, accompanied Frances Wright to the Nashoba Community near Memphis, Tenn., which she had founded in 1825; as the Nashoba colony was also failing, returned to Europe in 1827 for further study; returned to the United States and became a naturalized citizen; founded and edited, 1828–1832, the *Free Enquirer* and, in association with Frances Wright, opposed organized religion and supported liberal divorce laws, industrial education, and a redistribution of wealth; participated in the organization of the Association for the Protection of Industry and for the Promotion of National Education, which in 1829 succeeded in replacing the influence of Thomas Skidmore (q.v.) and his agrarians in the New York Working Men's party, but soon its own program emphasizing public education and redistribution of wealth was repudiated by the workers; elected to the Indiana legislature for one-year terms in 1836, 1837, and 1838, and for a two-year term in 1851; elected to the U.S. Congress as a Democrat in 1842 and served two terms; major contributions were a resolution that became the basis for resolving the Oregon boundary dispute and a bill leading to the creation of the Smithsonian Institute; served as a delegate to the Indiana Constitutional Convention in 1850; appointed Chargé d'Affaires in Naples by President Franklin Pierce in 1853 and a year later became Minister Resident, serving until 1858; authored *Threading My Way* (1874); following a period of mental illness, died in Lake George, N.Y., June 24, 1877; Frank Podmore, *Robert Owen: A Biography* (1906); Edward Pessen, *Most Uncommon Jacksonians: The Radical Leaders of the Early Labor Movement* (1967); Richard W. Leopold, *Robert Dale Owen: A Biography* (1940); *Dictionary of American Biography*, Vol. 14; Josephine M. Elliott, ed., *To Holland and to New Harmony: Robert Dale Owen's Travel Journal, 1825–1826* (1969), and *Robert Dale Owen's Travel Journal, 1827* (1978).

P

PACHLER, William J. (1904–1970). Born in Thornwood, N.Y., August 20, 1904; son of John A. and Mary (Reilly) Pachler; Roman Catholic; married Gunhild Swanson on June 17, 1928; four children; graduated from high school and attended a business college for one year, majoring in accounting and business law; secured employment with the New York Edison Company and in 1933 became the spokesman for the Tremont Building employees; after the firm became Consolidated Edison Company, joined Local 829 of the International Brotherhood of Electrical Workers (IBEW) and in 1936 became the local's first chairman for the Rider Avenue plant committee; elected president of Local 829 in 1939 and retained that position in 1940 when the local disaffiliated with the IBEW and became Local 12 of the independent Brotherhood of Consolidated Edison Employees; led Local 12 into the Congress of Industrial Organizations (CIO) in 1945, and when the Utility Workers Union of America (UWUA) was chartered later that year, elected its first secretary-treasurer; was one of the organizers of the National Conference of Secretary-Treasurers and served as its chairman until 1960; elected national president of the UWUA in 1960, serving in that capacity until his death; was a member of the American Federation of Labor (AFL)-CIO ethical practices committee and was one of the authors of the AFL-CIO internal disputes plan, was a member of the administrative committee of the Committee on Political Education, and was a member of the executive board of the industrial union department; was a United States delegate to the International Labor Organization conference in Geneva in 1963; was a Democrat; died in Washington, D.C., May 25, 1970; *AFL-CIO News*, June 6, 1970; *Who's Who in Labor* (1946); *The New York Times*, May 29, 1970.

PADWAY, Joseph Arthur (1891–1947). Born in Leeds, Yorkshire, England, July 25, 1891; son of Morris and Rose Padway; married Lydia Rose Paetow on March 9, 1912; one child; acquired an elementary and secondary education in England before emigrating to the United States in 1905; graduated from Marquette University Law School with an LL.B. degree in 1912 and admitted to the Wisconsin bar the same year; became the general counsel for the Wisconsin State Federation of Labor in 1915 and in that capacity was responsible for writing numerous labor and social-welfare bills enacted by the state legislature; served as a senator in the Wisconsin state legislature in 1925; appointed judge of the Milwaukee County Civil Court in 1925 and elected to a full term the following year, resigning in 1927 to resume his labor law practice; served as a regent of the state teachers colleges of Wisconsin, 1933–1938; became the legal counsel for the American Federation of Labor (AFL) in 1938; was a professor of labor law at Columbus University, Washington, D.C., 1938–1942; as the legal counsel for the AFL and several international unions affiliated with the AFL, was involved in the anti-trust suit brought against the American Federation of Musicians' president James C. Petrillo (q.v.) in 1942 and the contempt charges brought against United Mine Workers of America president John L. Lewis (q.v.) for violating an injunction issued during the 1946 coal strike; was a severe critic of the Taft-Hartley Act; was associated most of his life with the Progressive party of Wisconsin; died in San Francisco, Calif., October 9, 1947; Joseph A. Padway Papers, State Historical Society of Wisconsin; Thomas W. Gavett, *Development of the Labor Movement in Milwaukee* (1965); *The American Federationist* (November 1947); *The New York Times*, October 9, 1947.

PARKER, Julia O'Connor   (1890–1972). Born in Woburn, Mass., on September 9, 1890; daughter of John, a leather currier and member of the Knights of Labor, and Sarah (Conneally) O'Connor, immigrants from Ireland; Roman Catholic; married Charles Austin Parker, a newspaper reporter, in 1925; two children; attended parochial schools in Medford, Mass.; worked as a local telephone operator in Boston, Mass., 1908–1919; in 1912, she joined Boston Telephone Operators' Union (later Local 1A), organized by the International Brotherhood of Electrical Workers (IBEW) with major assistance from the Women's Trade Union League (WTUL); was a member of the nine-woman committee that achieved the union's recognition in negotiations with top national company officials after a threatened strike in 1913; served on the executive board or as an officer of the Boston WTUL almost continuously during 1912–1950, including a term as president, 1915–1918 (the first working woman to attain that office), and on the executive board of the National WTUL, 1917–1926; served as president of Local 1A (the largest union local of telephone operators in the United States), 1918–1920, defeating the candidate of the toll operators' faction led by Anna Molloy, which had dominated the union since 1912; served as president of the IBEW Telephone Operators' Department (TOD), 1919–1938; in 1918–1919, when the telephone service came under federal control, she was the only labor representative on the Ryan Commission, whose purpose was to advise Postmaster-General Albert Burleson on wages and working conditions in the telephone service; in April 1919, she led New England Telephone Operators' Union in a six-day strike to compel action on its long-ignored wage demands; the strike (which the male telephone workers initially refused to join) ended on favorable terms for the workers; was a delegate to the First International Congress of Working Women in 1919; faced with TOD's sharply declining membership and Bell Telephone's effort to form a company union, O'Connor in 1923 called for a strike for a seven-hour day and higher wages in New England, the only region in which the union remained strong; the strike, in which the Molloy faction refused to participate, constituted the last stand of the American Federation of Labor (AFL) in the telephone service; although commanding considerable support in larger Massachusetts and Rhode Island cities, the strike ended in the union's total defeat and replacement by company unions until 1971; made three trips to Europe in the 1920s to study labor conditions; was a member of the national committee of the American Civil Liberties Union, 1920–1939, and a member of the national advisory committee of the Workers' Education Bureau; was associated with the labor division of the Democratic National Committee in the presidential elections of 1932, 1936, and 1940, and in the latter two was director of the women's labor division; was employed as an organizer for the AFL, 1939–1957; in the early 1940s, was based in New York City; worked on AFL's Western Union campaign; in 1943, organized chemical workers in New York state; was an organizer, 1944–1947, for the IBEW and the AFL in Texas, Mississippi, Georgia, and Florida; her work in the South included managing a successful campaign in the Peninsular Telephone Company of Pensacola, Fla.; transferred by the AFL in 1947 from Atlanta to the Boston regional office, where she participated in organizing drives of the International Federation of Professional and Technical Engineers and other unions; died in Wayland, Mass., on August 27, 1972; National Women's Trade Union League Papers, Library of Congress, and Schlesinger Library, Radcliffe College; Solon DeLeon, ed., *The American Labor Who's Who* (1925); *Who's Who in Labor* (1946); *Notable American Women*, Vol. 4; *Boston Globe*, August 29, 1972; IBEW *Journal*, October 1972.

Stephen H. Norwood

PARSONS, Albert Ross   (1848–1887). Born in Montgomery, Ala., June 24, 1848; son of Samuel and Elizabeth (Tompkins) Parsons; married Lucy Eldine Gonzalez on June 10, 1871; two children; was orphaned at age 5 and was reared by a brother in Texas; at age 13, joined the Confederate forces during the Civil War and served for four years; apprenticed to a printer after returning to Texas and in 1868 founded the Waco *Spectator*, a weekly Republican periodical; served with the U.S. Internal Revenue Bureau, 1869–1871; moved to Chicago, Ill., in 1871 and worked as a printer during the depression of 1873–1878 and during this time joined the International Typographical Union, helped organize a branch of the Knights of Labor, and became a member of the Socialist party; ran for public office as a Socialist in Cook County, Ill., in 1877 but was defeated; during the railroad strikes of 1877, gained prominence as a Socialist orator and agitator; became secretary of the Chicago Eight Hour League in 1870, joined the Anarchist, or "Black," International after the ideological fissure in the Socialist party in 1881; became the editor of the *Alarm* in 1884 and was one of the leaders of the eight-hour demonstration held on May 1, 1886; although out of the city when the *Alarm* published a call for a demonstration at Chicago's Haymarket Square on May 4, 1886, to protest the killing of strikers at the McCormick Harvesting Works, was convicted along with seven other innocent anarchists for the murder of seven policemen by a bomb thrown during the demonstration; authored *Anarchism: Its Philosophy and Scientific Basis as Defined by Some of Its Opposites* (1887); executed on November 11, 1887; Albert R. Parsons Papers, State Historical Society of Wisconsin; Lucy E. Parsons, *Life of Albert R. Parsons with Brief History of the Labor Movement in America: Also Sketches of the Lives of A. Spies, Geo. Engels, A. Fischer and Louis Lingg*, 2d ed. (1903); Alan Calmer, *Labor Agitator: The Story of Albert R. Parsons* (1937); Norman J. Ware, *The Labor Movement in the United States, 1860–1895* (1929); *Encyclopedia of Social Sciences*, Vol. 11.

PASCOE, David M.   (fl. 1859–1886). Born in Philadelphia, Pa., October 26, 1859; educated in public schools; at 15 apprenticed to J. B. Lippincott & Company, publishers; served five years; remained journeyman until November 1884, when he assumed control of the *Tocsin*, the labor paper of the city; at age 21, joined International Typographical Union (ITU) No. 2; in 1881, trouble being imminent over an increase in prices, he was chosen to be a member of a conservative committee to meet the employers, and an amicable adjustment was arranged to avoid the threatened rupture; at the Pittsburgh session of the ITU the delegates from No. 2 reported five newspapers unionized within a year, brought about more through the conservative manner in which Pascoe and his co-laborers had acted toward the proprietors than for any other reason; in April 1884, elected secretary of local union, reelected in 1885, declined a third term in 1886; delegate to convention of ITU at Pittsburgh, and chairman of his delegation; youngest man ever selected by the Philadelphia union as its delegate to the central body; elected secretary-treasurer; was an active member of the Central Labor Union, also of Local Assembly 3879 (printers), Knights of Labor, which he organized; during the strike in the carpet trade, in the winter of 1884–1885 he was threatened with imprisonment for his advocacy of the cause of the carpet weavers; George E. McNeill, *The Labor Movement: The Problem of To-Day* (1887).

                                                                      George E. McNeill

PERKINS, George W.   (fl. 1891–1934). Early origins unknown; began working at an early age as a cigarmaker and became involved in the trade union movement; was a dedicated craft unionist and was a constant foe of the Knights of Labor and industrial unionism; closely identified with Samuel Gompers (q.v.) during the formative years of the American Federation of Labor (AFL), being referred to by Gompers as one of the "local (Chicago, Ill.) shock troops of labor," and by others as a member of "Sam's gang"; elected international president of the Cigarmakers' International Union of America (CMIU) in 1891 and served in that capacity until 1926; worked hard for the reelection of Gompers as AFL president after his defeat by John McBride (q.v.) in 1894; opposed AFL support of a general strike during the Pullman controversy; in 1918, appointed by the AFL executive council to its Commission of Reconstruction, which planned the postwar recovery program approved by the 1919 AFL convention and called for industrial democracy; represented United States labor at the International Federation of Trade Unions conference meeting in Zurich in 1918; believed that American labor should stop neglecting the world movement, but distrusted European revolutionary slogans and emphasis on politics; along with others, appointed by the AFL executive council to investigate the Federated Press, a news agency serving labor leftist and radical publications, which was banned by the committee from use by AFL publications; during his incumbency as president of the CMIU, charged by critics with pursuing shortsighted policies with regard to mechanization, leading to a decline of union membership from 51,500 to 12,900 between 1909 and 1929; believed the union had "nothing to fear from machines"; ignored unskilled and women workers and the rise of the large-scale factories; in 1912 the CMIU enrolled only about two-fifths of the total number of cigarmakers and none of the nineteen thousand machine workers or twenty-five thousand team workers; along with Gompers, opposed Socialist-sponsored resolutions to organize women workers at the 1912 CMIU convention and refused to implement a resolution to this effect that was passed; his restrictive membership policy was not abandoned until he left the union presidency; with Gompers's support, the CMIU under his leadership held only infrequent conventions; served during 1926–1934 as president of the AFL union label trades department; died in Washington, D.C., February 5, 1934; Philip S. Foner, *History of the Labor Movement in the United States*, Vol. 2 (1955); Samuel Gompers, *Seventy Years of Life and Labor: An Autobiography* (1925); Bernard Mandel, *Samuel Gompers: A Biography* (1963); Philip Taft, *The A.F. of L. in the Time of Gompers* (1957); Rowland H. Harvey, *Samuel Gompers: Champion of the Toiling Masses* (1935).

Merl E. Reed

PERLIS, Leo   (1912–   ). Born in Bialystok, Poland, on February 22, 1912; son of David, a textile manufacturer, and Anna (Gershowitz) Perlis; Jewish; married Miriam Blatt on December 18, 1937; two children; later married Betty Frances Gantz; graduated from Paterson (N.J.) East Side High School in 1930; employed as a silk twister in a Paterson textile mill after completing his formal schooling; joined the United Textile Workers of America (UTWA) in 1934; became a member of the American Newspaper Guild in 1935; served as labor editor of *The Paterson Press*; worked as an organizer for the UTWA in New Jersey during 1937–1938; became state executive director for Labor's Nonpartisan League of New Jersey in 1939 and a year later became the national director of the league; served as director of organization for the American Labor party of New York in 1940; served as principal labor consultant to the War Production

Board, 1941–1943; was national director of the Congress of Industrial Organizations' (CIO) war relief committee, 1943–1945; became director of the national CIO community service committee, 1946–1955; after the merger of the American Federation of Labor (AFL) and the CIO in 1955, he was appointed director of the newly established AFL-CIO department of community service activities; helped to found CARE and the United Way labor participation department; guided development of many AFL-CIO union labor agencies throughout the country; involved in a wide range of civic activities, serving on committees appointed by Presidents Dwight D. Eisenhower, John F. Kennedy, and Richard M. Nixon; wrote numerous articles and bulletins and served as editor of the *American Labor Party News* and the *Labor's Nonpartisan League News of New Jersey*; a member of the American Labor party during the 1930s and 1940s, he later became a Democrat; retired union offices on February 1, 1980; *Who's Who in Labor* (1946, 1976); *AFL-CIO News*, February 9, 1980.

PERLMAN, Selig   (1888–1959). Born in Bialystok, Poland, on December 9, 1888; son of Mordecai, a yarn spinner, and Pauline (Blankstein) Perlman; Jewish; married Eva Shaber on June 23, 1918, and after her death, Eva's sister Fannie Shaber on August 22, 1930; four children (two from each marriage); after attending local schools, he enrolled in the Bialystok School of Commerce in 1900 and completed his course of study in 1906; thereafter, he went to Naples, Italy, where he intended to study medicine at the University of Naples, but, after striking up an acquaintanceship with William English Walling (q.v.), decided instead to travel to the United States and in 1908 enrolled at the University of Wisconsin; while an undergraduate, he became the protégé and research assistant of John R. Commons (q.v.), the founder of the "Wisconsin School" of labor history; received his B.A. in 1910 and his Ph.D. in 1915; continued to serve on Commons's research staff until 1919 when he received a regular faculty appointment at Wisconsin; meanwhile, he had served as a special investigator for the U.S. Commission on Industrial Relations, chaired by Frank Walsh (q.v.), 1913–1915; wrote the fourth and most influential volume of Commons's *History of Labour in the United States* (1918) in which Perlman broke with his earlier enthusiasm for Marxism and leftist "ideologues" who viewed the laborer as "an abstract man in the grip of an abstract force"; instead, he emphasized practical, job-conscious unionism as the driving force of American labor; Perlman placed all of this into a broader theoretical framework in his monumentally influential *A Theory of the Labor Movement* (1928); a gifted teacher, he also had a major role in the development of the University of Wisconsin School for Workers; was a founder of the Wisconsin Commission on Human Rights in 1947, with which he maintained an association until his retirement in 1959; died in Philadelphia, Pa., on August 14, 1959; Selig Perlman Papers, State Historical Society of Wisconsin; *Dictionary of American Biography*, Supp. 6; *Industrial and Labor Relations Review* (1960); *International Encyclopedia of Social Sciences* (1968); *The New York Times*, August 15, 1959.

PERLSTEIN, Meyer   (1884–1958). Born in Cartyz Bereza, Grodno, Russia, September 15, 1884; son of a tailor; Jewish; married; three children; attended grammar schools in Russia and night school in the United States; emigrated with his family to London in 1905 and the following year to the United States; became a shirt maker in the New York City garment industry; joined Shirtmakers Local 23 of the International Ladies' Garment Workers' Union (ILGWU) in 1909; elected recording secretary of the New York Cloak Joint Board in 1910, serving until 1913; forced to resign from the Cloak Joint Board in 1913 because of internal conflicts and assigned to Philadelphia, Pa., as a general organizer; elected an international ILGWU vice-president in 1916; transferred to Cleveland, Ohio, in 1918 and there headed the union until 1923 and initiated early experiments in production engineering; placed in charge of the ILGWU in Chicago in 1923 and led the fight against William Z. Foster (q.v.) and the Trade Union Educational League's efforts to take over the union there; was a staunch supporter of Morris Sigman (q.v.) administration's opposition to the Communists; returned to New York in 1925 and joined the general staff of the Cloak Joint Board; was disillusioned by efforts to accommodate Communist dissidents in the union and resigned from the ILGWU in 1925; rejoined the union and regained union positions in 1934; appointed director of the Southwestern region of the ILGWU with headquarters in St. Louis, Mo., in 1934, and served in that capacity until his death; usually supported Democratic candidates, but opposed President Franklin D. Roosevelt's third-term candidacy in 1940 and endorsed Republican Wendell L. Wilkie; died in St. Louis, Mo., September 11, 1958; Benjamin Stolberg, *Tailor's Progress: The Story of a Famous Union and the Men Who Made It* (1944); Louis Levine, *The Women's Garment Workers: A History of the International Ladies' Garment Workers' Union* (1924); *Who's Who in Labor* (1946); *ILGWU Report and Proceedings* (1959); Sumner H. Shichter, *Union Policies and Industrial Management* (1941).

PESOTTA, Rose   (1896–1965). Born Rose Peisoty in Derazhnya, Russian Ukraine, on November 20, 1896; daughter of Itsaak, a grain merchant, and Masya Peisoty, a intellectual and cultural leader of the town's Jewish community; Jewish; never married; no children; attended a private girls' school and was tutored at home; later attended Bryn Mawr School for Women Workers, 1933, Brookwood Labor College, 1924–1926, and Wisconsin Summer School for Workers, 1930; became radicalized at an early age and joined the Derazhnya anarchist underground prior to emigrating to the United States in 1913 to avoid family pressures to get married; took a job in a shirtwaist factory in New York City and joined Local 25 of the International Ladies' Garment Workers' Union (ILGWU); helped organize the ILGWU's first education department for Local 25 in 1915; was elected to Local 25's executive board in 1920; during the 1920s, she was active in the defense of Sacco (q.v.) and Vanzetti (q.v.); joined the campaign to prevent a Communist takeover of the ILGWU, and was a volunteer organizer of female garment workers; after becoming a paid ILGWU staff member in 1933, she was sent to Los Angeles, Calif., a notorious anti-union city, to organize dressmakers; her successful organizing drives in Los Angeles earned her a national reputation and in 1934 she was elected an international vice-president of the ILGWU; as a vice-president she traveled extensively throughout the United States and to San Juan, Puerto Rico, and Montreal, Canada, supporting organizing efforts among garment workers; participated in the dramatic auto workers' strikes in Flint, Mich., and rubber workers' strikes in Akron, Ohio, during the 1930s; refused to run for reelection to her position as an ILGWU vice-president in 1942 and returned to her former occupation as a sewing machine operator; meanwhile, she chastised the officers of the ILGWU for their failure to include more women, who provided 85 percent of the union's membership, in the ILGWU leadership hierarchy; such outbursts were not uncommon and had earlier alienated her to some extent from other ILGWU officials (all male) who found her outspoken manner and sensitivity to rank-and-file concerns disconcerting; was active in numerous reform organizations, including the New York chapter of the League for Industrial Democracy, the Workers Defense League, Women's Trade Union League, Jewish Labor Committee, and Workmen's Circle; authored *Bread Upon the Waters* (1945), *Days of Our Lives* (1958), and occasional articles for *Justice*, the ILGWU newspaper; died in Miami, Fla., on December 7, 1965; Rose Pesotta Papers, New York Public Library; *Notable American Women*, Vol. 4; Alice Kessler-Harris, "Organizing the Unorganizable: Three Jewish Women and Their Union," *Labor History* (Winter 1976); *Who's Who in Labor* (1946); *The New York Times*, December 8, 1965.

PETERSON, Eric   (1894–1961). Born in Dalarne, Sweden, September 3, 1894; son of Daniel, a village shoemaker, and Karen Amanda Peterson; Protestant; married Theresa T. on June 1, 1916; three children; at age 8 emigrated with his family to Rawlins, Wyo., a booming railroad center; began work as a bellboy at a boarding house for railroad employees and served a machinist apprenticeship in Rawlins; joined the International Association of Machinists (IAM) during a strike in 1913; held local lodge offices at Rawlins and at Deer Lodge, Mont., working in the latter town for the Milwaukee Road; appointed an international organizer in 1929 and assigned to organize the machinists on the Pennsylvania Railroad, a task that required 20 years; elected a general vice-president in 1940, and elected and served as general IAM secretary-treasurer, 1945–1959; cooperated closely with President Harvey Brown (q.v.), with whom others had personal difficulty, and his successor, President Albert J. Hayes (q.v.); computerized union records and trained and supervised the grand lodge's 24-man financial auditing staff; served in 1957 as a member of a special American Federation of Labor-Congress of Industrial Organizations (AFL-CIO) committee to draft a code for minimum accounting and financial controls for unions that was incorporated into the AFL-CIO's ethical practices code on financial practices; retired to Bradenton, Fla., in 1959; represented the AFL-CIO at the White House Conference on Problems of the Aging in 1961; was an independent in politics;

died in Tampa, Fla., March 3, 1961; *The Machinist*, March 16, 1961; *Who's Who in Labor* (1946); Mark Perlman, *The Machinists: A New Study in American Trade Unionism* (1961).

John W. Hevener

PETERSON, Esther (1906–   ). Born in Provo, Utah, December 9, 1906; daughter of Lars, a school superintendent, and Annie (Nielson) Eggertson; Church of Jesus Christ of Latter-Day Saints; educated in the public schools of Provo; received a B.A. degree from Brigham Young University, Provo, 1927, and an M.A. from Columbia University, N.Y., 1930; married Oliver A. Peterson in 1932; taught physical education at Branch Agricultural College, Cedar City, Utah, 1927–1929, and Windsor School, Boston, Mass., 1930–1936; began teaching in the industrial section of the Boston Young Women's Christian Association in 1930; taught economics at Bryn Mawr Summer School for Women Workers and the Hudson Shore Labor School, 1932–1939; served as an organizer for the American Federation of Teachers, 1936; served for a short time as the New England educational director for the International Ladies' Garment Workers' Union before becoming the director of education for the Amalgamated Clothing Workers of America (ACWA) in 1939, serving until 1945; during World War II, was the ACWA's director of war activities; became the ACWA legislative representative in Washington, D.C., in 1945; accompanied her husband, a foreign service officer, to Europe in 1948 and from 1948 to 1952 worked with the women's committee of the Swedish Confederation of Trade Unions; was a United States delegate to the founding conference of the International Confederation of Free Trade Unions (ICFTU) in London in 1949; associated with the women's committee of the ICFTU, 1952–1957; was a founder and later an instructor in the ICFTU's International School for Working Women in Paris; appointed to head the U.S. Department of Labor's Women's Bureau in 1961 and later the same year became First Assistant Secretary of Labor; served as vice-chairman of the President's Commission on the Status of Women, 1961; appointed the first Special Presidential Assistant on Consumer Affairs in 1964; a Democrat; Esther Peterson Papers, John F. Kennedy Library; Rose Pesotta, *Bread Upon the Waters* (1945); *Current Biography* (1961); *National Cyclopaedia of American Biography*, Vol. 1.

Marie Tedesco

PETRILLO, James Caesar (1892–   ). Born in Chicago, Ill., March 16, 1892; son of an Italian immigrant who was a city-sewer digger; Roman Catholic; married Marie Frullate in 1916; four children; attended the Dante Elementary School in Chicago for nine years but never progressed beyond the fourth grade; began playing the trumpet in 1900 and took free lessons at Chicago's Hull House; organized a four-piece band at age 14 and in 1906 joined the American Musicians' Union (AMU) in Chicago; elected president of the AMU in 1914, serving until 1917, when defeated for reelection; after this defeat, resigned from the AMU and joined Chicago Federation of Musicians Local 10 of the American Federation of Musicians (AFM); elected a vice-president of Local 10 in 1919 and president in 1922; elected to the national executive board of the AFM in 1932, and in 1940, elected national president; shortly after being elected, led the AFM in a 27-month strike against the recording industry that resulted in an agreement whereby the companies paid royalties directly into the AFM treasury on all recordings; was an aggressive, sometimes overly suspicious union leader and often offended the public when attempting to protect musicians from the effects of new technological innovations; elected an American Federation of Labor (AFL) vice-president and executive council member in 1951 and retained the position after the AFL-Congress of Industrial Organizations' merger in 1955; resigned all union positions except for the presidency of AFM Local 10 in Chicago, in 1958; defeated for reelection to the presidency of Local 10 in 1962; a Democrat with considerable political influence in Chicago; Robert D. Leiter, *The Musicians and Petrillo* (1953); Paul S. Carpenter, *Music: An Art and a Business* (1950); J. Gould, "Portrait of the Unpredictable Petrillo," *The New York Times Magazine*, December 28, 1947.

PHILLIPS, James Andrew   (1873–1949). Born in Clay County, Ill., September 10, 1873; son of John Jiles, a farmer, and Nancy (Bouseman) Phillips; Christian Scientist; married Inez Richey on February 22, 1902, and, after her death in 1906, Cecil Black on September 5, 1924; two children; completed public grammar school in Louisville, Ill.; began working as a messenger for the Ohio and Mississippi Railroad at age 15; became successively a brakeman, a switchman, and a conductor on the Illinois Central Railroad; placed in charge of a work train that in 1901 helped build a railroad line through Indian territory, which later became a part of the state of Oklahoma; joined Division 3 of the Order of Railway Conductors (ORC) in 1902; placed in charge of the first passenger train to make the run between St. Louis and Kansas City during the Louisiana Purchase Exposition in 1904; served as the legislative representative of the ORC during the 1911 and 1913 sessions of the Missouri General Assembly; became ORC general chairman of the Chicago, Rock Island and Pacific Railway in 1918; elected an ORC vice-president in 1919 and senior vice-president in 1931; assumed the ORC presidency in 1934; served as a United States delegate to the preparatory technical conference on rail transportation to the International Labor Organization in 1939; served as chairman of the Railway Labor Executives' Association, 1939–1941; retired in 1941 and became ORC president emeritus; earlier in his career identified with the Socialist and Progressive parties, but later usually supported the Democratic party; died in Cedar Rapids, Iowa, December 4, 1949; *National Cyclopaedia of American Biography*, Vol. 38; Solon DeLeon, ed., *The American Labor Who's Who* (1925).

PHILLIPS, Paul L.   (1904–1975). Born in Strong, Ark., August 10, 1904; son of H. E. and Coma (Laughlin) Phillips; Methodist; married Fannie S. Simmons on August 29, 1940, and, after her death in 1963, Kathleen G. Canby on June 14, 1964; two children; attended Louisiana Polytechnic Institute during 1928–1930, then secured employment in the paper-making industry; helped organize a local of the International Brotherhood of Paper Makers (IBPM) at an International Paper Company mill in Camden, Ark., in 1932 and became its first president; served as an international representative of the IBPM, 1937–1941; elected a vice-president of the IBPM in 1942 and an international president in 1948; during World War II, represented labor on the New York area division of the War Manpower Commission; elected first president of the United Paper Makers and Paper Workers, formed in 1957 by the merger of the IBPM and the United Paperworkers of America, Congress of Industrial Organizations (CIO); elected an American Federation of Labor (AFL)-CIO vice-president and executive council member in 1957, serving until 1968; served as vice-president of the AFL-CIO industrial union department, 1957–1968; was a member of the advisory boards of the New York State Committee on Atomic Energy and the National Park Service of the U.S. Department of Interior; was a trustee of the College of Forestry, State University of New York; a Democrat and a member of Americans for Democratic Action; retired from union positions in 1968 because of ill health; died in Leesburg, Fla., on February 6, 1975; Harry E. Graham, *The Paper Rebellion: Development and Upheaval in Pulp and Paper Unionism* (1970); *Who's Who in Labor* (1946); *AFL-CIO News*, January 20, 1968, February 15, 1975; *The New York Times*, February 13, 1975.

PHILLIPS, Thomas   (1833–1916). Born in Whitson, Yorkshire, England, March 22, 1833; son of a farmer; christened in the Church of England, but later became a fervent Methodist; acquired a common school education, then was apprenticed at age 13 to his brother-in-law, an active Chartist, as a bootmaker; joined the Rotherham Union of Bootmakers in 1849, and later the same year, became a member of the Chartist Association; emigrated to the United States in 1852, settling in New York City, there working as a shoemaker; moved to Philadelphia, Pa., later in the same year and soon became actively involved in the anti-slavery movement and in labor-organizing activities among shoemakers; became a naturalized citizen of the United States in 1862; was a vigorous advocate of both producer cooperatives and the Rochdale principle of consumers' cooperation; participated in the organization of the very influential Union Co-operative Association, which failed in 1866 after two years of operation because of undercapitalization and overexpansion; helped organize the Philadelphia Lodge of the Knights of St. Crispin (K of SC) in 1869 and devoted considerable time and effort to building up the organization; involved in the organization of a second K of SC lodge in Philadelphia, Friendship Lodge, and served it as Sir Knight; in 1870, elected Grand Sir Knight of the five Philadelphia lodges; served as an organizer for the Sovereigns of Industry during the early 1870s; joined Section 26 of the International Workingmen's Association and represented it at the 1872 convention of anti-Marxist sections in Philadelphia; was a delegate to the K of

SC convention in Boston, Mass., in 1871, and served on the committee on cooperation; joined Local Assembly 2, of the Knights of Labor (K of L) in 1873 and eventually participated in the organization of Shoemakers Local Assembly 64; elected as Local Assembly 64's delegate to K of L District Assembly 1 and served a three-year term; wrote a K of L column for the Philadelphia *Public Record* for 14 months, ca. 1874–1875; actively involved during 1876 in the Greenback Movement and traveled throughout Pennsylvania organizing Greenback Labor Clubs; was an unsuccessful Greenback and single-tax candidate for mayor of Philadelphia in 1887; as a result of his growing disenchantment with Terence Powderly's (q.v.) leadership, broke with the K of L and organized the Boot and Shoe Workers' International Union and elected its general president in 1889; under his leadership, the new union affiliated with the American Federation of Labor; died in 1916; David Montgomery, *Beyond Equality: Labor and the Radical Republicans, 1862–1872*; John R. Commons et al., *History of Labour in the United States*, Vol. 2 (1918); Norman J. Ware, *The Labor Movement in the United States, 1860–1895* (1929); autobiographical sketch in the Thomas Phillips Papers, Labor Collection, Biography and Papers, State Historical Society of Wisconsin.

PILLARD, Charles Harry   (1918–   ). Born in Buffalo, N.Y., on October 26, 1918; son of Harry Alvin, a railroad engineer, and Elizabeth Frances Pillard; married Helen May in 1944; two children; attended the public schools of Buffalo, graduating from Bennett High School in 1936; after completing his formal education, he became an apprentice electrician and in 1940 joined Local 41 of the International Brotherhood of Electrical Workers (IBEW); was a captain in the U.S. Army during World War II, serving in Europe and the Far East, 1941–1945; was elected business manager of Local 41 in 1952, a position he held until 1968; served as president of the New York State Association of Electrical Workers, 1954–1968, vice-president of the Buffalo port council, maritime trades department, New York, 1955–1968; president of the Buffalo building trades council, 1958–1968; and vice-president of the New York State building and construction trades council, 1959–1968; was elected to the IBEW's international executive committee in 1961; seven years later he was appointed IBEW president and in 1970 was regularly elected to that position; became an American Federation of Labor-Congress of Industrial Organizations (AFL-CIO) vice-president and executive council member in 1976 and soon became involved in a myriad of AFL-CIO activities including vice-president and executive council member of the AFL-CIO building and construction trades department, industrial union department, and metal trades department, executive council member of the AFL-CIO railway employees department, the AFL-CIO economic policy committee, and executive board member of the council of the AFL-CIO union for professional employees; was elected co-chairman of the National Joint Apprenticeship and Training Committee for the electrical industry in 1968; involved in a great variety of civic, government, and trade boards and agencies, he was a member of the

National Council on Alcoholism, the National Health Insurance Committee, the Committee on the Employment of the Handicapped, a member of the advisory board of the Electrical Power Research Institute, a member of several committees concerned with veterans and senior citizens; was given the 1970 Civil Rights Award by the Anti-Defamation League of B'nai B'rith; *Who's Who in Labor* (1976); *AFL-CIO News*, February 28, 1976.

PINE, Max   (1866–1928). Born in 1866 in Liubavitch, Russia; Jewish; married; four children; after his father died in 1869, went to live with an aunt in Wielitch, Russia, and there eventually learned the typesetters' trade; emigrated to the United States in 1890 and secured employment as a knee-pants operator; became an official in the New York Knee-Pants Makers' Union; joined the staff of the *Jewish Labor Forward* in 1897 as a reporter and in other capacities; was the proprietor of a print shop, 1901–1906; ran for the New York State Assembly in 1903 on the Socialist party ticket; served as secretary and executive director of the United Hebrew Trades (UHT), 1906–1909; again operated a print shop during 1909–1916; again became secretary of the UHT in 1916, serving until 1926; served as an organizer during the successful efforts to organize New York City tailors, 1912–1913; was one of the principal organizers of the People's Relief Committee, created to assist in the efforts to provide relief to European Jews after World War I; sent to Poland by the committee in 1919 to assist Jewish war victims and in 1921 sent to the Soviet Union to negotiate assistance for Jewish victims of pogroms; in 1923, was instrumental in the founding of the Geverkshaften Campaign for Palestine, which endeavored to create a bond of friendship between the Jewish labor movement in the United States and Jewish workers in Palestine in the interests of the creation of a Jewish state of Palestine; died in Maywood, N.J., March 2, 1928; Hyman J. Fliegel, *The Life and Times of Max Pine: A History of the Jewish Labor Movement in the U.S.A. during the Last Part of the 19th Century and the First Part of the 20th Century* (1959); *Universal Jewish Encyclopedia*, Vol. 8.

PIZER, Morris   (1904–   ). Born in Russian Poland on February 12, 1904; son of David, a tailor, and Dorothy (Gostinsky) Pizer; Jewish; married Florence Werlinsky in February 1942; one child; acquired a high school education by attending night schools and then attended Jewish Teachers' Seminary for two years; emigrated to the United States in 1921 and worked at a variety of occupations before securing a job as an upholsterer in 1922; joined Local 73 of the United Furniture Workers of America (UFWA) and in 1936 elected secretary-treasurer of Local 73; served as president of the UFWA's Metropolitan District Council 3 and executive secretary of the North Atlantic Council, then elected vice-president of the UFWA in 1943, and three years later elected international president; became a member of the Congress of Industrial Organizations' (CIO) executive board in 1946, serving until the American Federation of Labor-CIO merger in 1955; as UFWA president, stressed the importance of coordinated organizing drives in cooperation with other unions, particularly in the Southeast; retired as UFWA president in 1970; edited the *Furniture Workers Press*, 1946–1970; supported the American Labor party during the 1930s and early 1940s; *Who's Who in Labor* (1946); *Who's Who in World Jewry* (1955); *AFL-CIO News*, May 30, 1970.

Merl E. Reed

PODOJIL, Antoinette (1911–   ). Born in Braddock, Pa., on October 9, 1911; the daughter of relatively well-educated Polish immigrants, her father was a steelworker and her mother a homemaker; Roman Catholic; married; five children; moved with her family to Ambridge, Pa., in 1913 and to Cleveland, Ohio, in 1920; attended high school until age 16 and later enrolled in a variety of college courses; began working at the Cleveland Worsted Mills because of family financial extringencies in 1927 and soon was apprenticed as a weaver; ultimately, she learned and, at various times, performed most of the skills associated with the textile industry; at a relatively young age, she was promoted to a supervisory position; although a supervisor, she helped organize a local of the Textile Workers Union of America (TWUA) in the Cleveland Worsted Mills in 1954 and served as president of the local for ten years; although entering active union work at the relatively advanced age of 43, she quickly proved an effective organizer and soon was placed on the TWUA staff, serving as an international organizer in Pennsylvania, Ohio, and Illinois; served three terms as president of the TWUA's Cleveland Joint Board; after retiring all of her union positions but chairman of the Cleveland Joint Board's pension committee, she devoted much of her time and energy to a variety of senior citizen affairs, including extensive lobbying in Washington, D.C., on behalf of the elderly; was an active member of the Federation of Retired Workers; a Democrat, she served on the executive board of the Cleveland branch of Americans for Democratic Action; Lydia Kleiner, "Oral History Interview with Antoinette Podojil," *The 20th Century Trade Union Woman: Vehicle for Social Change*; Oral History Project and Ohio Labor History Project (1978).

POLICASTRO, Thomas Francis (1919–1977). Born in Providence, R.I., on October 22, 1919; married; one child; graduated from Providence Central High School in 1939 and shortly thereafter joined the United Steelworkers of America (USWA), which was then the Steel Workers Organizing Committee, Congress of Industrial Organizations (CIO); served in a variety of positions in his local union including president; was elected a vice-president of the Rhode Island CIO in 1952 and a legislative representative for the USWA; became a USWA staff representative in 1953; was elected president of the Rhode Island CIO in 1955; in that position, he successfully negotiated a merger with the Rhode Island State Federation of Labor, American Federation of Labor (AFL) in 1958, creating the Rhode Island State AFL-CIO; was elected president of the newly merged state AFL-CIO in 1958; thereafter, he also served as president of the

AFL-CIO New England regional council; a committed civil rights activist, he participated in the 1965 march from Selma to Montgomery, Ala.; involved in a variety of other civic activities, he was founder and president of the Rhode Island Group Health Association, chairman of the Consumers Council, vice-chairman of United Way, and a member of the Governor's Commission on Alcoholism; widely recognized as the most influential leader in the Rhode Island labor movement; died in Providence in August 1977; *Who's Who in Labor* (1976); *AFL-CIO News*, August 20, 1977.

POLLARD, William Edward   (1915–   ). Born in Pensacola, Fla., on September 14, 1915; son of William Edward and Willie Mae Pollard; married Josephine, a homemaker, in 1942; two children; Afro-American; educated at Jefferson High School, Los Angeles, Los Angeles City College, and the University of California, Los Angeles; obtained work as a dining car employee on the Southern Pacific Railroad and in 1938 joined Local 456 of the Hotel and Restaurant Employees and Bartenders International Union (HREBIU); served as general chairman of HREBIU Local 456, 1944–1974; elected a vice-president of the Los Angeles County Federation of Labor in 1959, serving until 1964; joined Local 35 of the American Newspaper Guild in 1964; appointed a staff representative of the civil rights department, American Federation of Labor-Congress of Industrial Organizations (AFL-CIO) in 1964 and during the ten years he held that position he was responsible for liaison between the U.S. Equal Employment Opportunities Commission and the AFL-CIO's affiliated national and international unions; served as vice-chairman of Local 35, 1972–1974; an active participant in civil rights activities, he was a charter member of the California Committee for Fair Employment Practices and served on the employment task force of the Leadership Conference on Civil Rights; became a national board member of the National Association for the Advancement of Colored People in 1971; appointed to the labor advocacy committee of the National Urban League in 1974; appointed director of the AFL-CIO department of civil rights in 1974; *Who's Who in Labor* (1976); *AFL-CIO News*, March 9, 1974.

POLLOCK, William   (1899–1982). Born in Philadelphia, Pa., on November 12, 1899; son of Scottish immigrant parents, Louis, a weaver, and Agnes (Garner) Pollock, a homemaker; Congregationalist; married Anna Mae Keen on February 3, 1919; two children; after completing an elementary education, he attended night school at Philadelphia's Northeast High School; his schooling had been interrupted in 1914 when he took a job as an office boy; later found work as a shipfitter during World War I; when the postwar depression struck, he went to work in the textile industry; joined Local 25 of the United Textile Workers of America (UTWA) in 1920; became business agent for Local 25 in 1931, serving in that capacity until 1937; when the UTWA affiliated with the Congress of Industrial Organizations (CIO) in 1937, he joined the staff of the newly organized

Textile Workers Organizing Committee (TWOC); helped to organize the Textile
Joint Board in Philadelphia and served as its first manager; when the TWOC
was reorganized into the Textile Workers Union of America (TWUA), CIO, in
1939, he was elected the new international union's general secretary-treasurer;
was elected executive vice-president in 1953, and, after the retirement of Emil
Rieve (q.v.), in 1956, was elected general president of the TWUA; was elected
an American Federation of Labor (AFL)-CIO vice-president and executive council member in 1967; retired union positions in 1972; four years after his retirement, his long-time dream of a merger between the TWUA and the Amalgamated
Clothing Workers of America was accomplished, creating the Amalgamated
Clothing and Textile Workers Union of America; died in Ocean City, N.J., on
March 4, 1982; *Who's Who in Labor* (1946, 1976); *The New York Times*, March
5, 1982; *AFL-CIO News*, March 13, 1982; William Pollock Interview, Columbia
Oral History Collection.

POSSEHL, John   (1886–1940). Born in Chicago, Ill., in 1886; son of a
chemical engineer; married; one child; at age 4 moved with his family to Savannah, Ga., and there completed public grammar school; completed his formal
education, then secured employment as a marine fireman and engineer and later
as a pile driver operator; prior to World War I, organized a mixed local of the
International Union of Operating Engineers (IUOE) (then called the International
Union of Steam and Operating Engineers) in Savannah and was elected its
secretary; was an influential figure in the Savannah labor movement and served
as president of the Savannah Central Labor Union, 1914–1919; during World
War I, served as a government mediator in the sugar industry; became an international IUOE organizer in 1919, concentrating on organizing activities in
Texas, Louisiana, Tennessee, and other parts of the South; elected an IUOE
vice-president in 1922 and somewhat later became international secretary-treasurer; elected international IUOE president after the death of Arthur M. Huddell
(q.v.) in 1931; as president, reorganized the structure of the IUOE by dividing
the IUOE into administrative districts, converted organizers into international
representatives, revived the IUOE stationary jurisdiction that had been neglected
by Huddell, rewrote the international constitution, held regular conventions,
reached an important accord with the Associated General Contractors, and generally guided the IUOE successfully through the difficult depression period of
the 1930s; served as first vice-president of the American Federation of Labor's
building and construction trades department; was a Democrat; died in Washington, D.C., September 14, 1940; Garth L. Mangum, *The Operating Engineers:
The Economic History of a Trade Union* (1964); *The American Federationist*
(October 1940); *American Federation of Labor Weekly News Service*, September
17, 1940.

POTOFSKY, Jacob Samuel   (1894–1979). Born in Radomisl, Ukraine, Russia, November 16, 1894; son of Simon, a businessman in Russia and later a

clothing worker in Chicago, and Rebecca Potofsky; married Callie Taylor in 1934, and, after her death, Blanche Lydia Zetland on May 18, 1951; three children; emigrated with family to the United States in 1905; attended the grammar schools in Russia and Chicago and high school in Chicago; became a "floor boy" in a Chicago men's clothing factory in 1908 and joined Pantsmakers' Local 144 of the United Garment Workers of America; took part in the historic 1910 strike against Hart, Schaffner and Marx that eventually led to the organization of the Amalgamated Clothing Workers of America (ACWA); became a shop secretary after the strike and during 1912–1913 served as treasurer of Local 144; became secretary-treasurer of the Chicago Joint Board, ACWA, in 1914; moved to New York City in 1916 to assist in establishing a national office and for the next 18 years was assistant general secretary-treasurer of the ACWA; during the 1930s, devoted his energies to organizing cotton-garment workers in Pennsylvania, New Jersey, Connecticut, upstate New York, and Missouri; became ACWA assistant president in 1934; was an original member of the Congress of Industrial Organizations' (CIO) executive board; served as general secretary-treasurer of the ACWA, 1940–1946; served on the CIO Latin-American affairs committee and the political action committee; led the CIO delegation attending the inauguration in 1946 of Miguel Alemán, president of Mexico, at the invitation of the Mexico Federation of Labor; elected president of the ACWA in 1946 after the death of Sidney Hillman (q.v.); after the merger of the American Federation of Labor (AFL) and the CIO in 1955, became a vice-president and executive council member of the AFL-CIO; was a member of a large number of public and private boards and agencies, including the Jewish Labor Committee, the Labor Management and Manpower Policy Committee of the Office of Defense Mobilization, and the New York City Temporary Commission on City Finances, 1965; voted Socialist until 1932 and thereafter supported the American Labor party, the Liberal party of New York, and the Democratic party; retired as ACWA president in 1972; authored "John E. Williams, Arbitrator"; died in New York City on August 5, 1979; Jacob S. Potofsky Papers, Catherwood Library, Cornell University; Louis Finkelstein, *American Spiritual Autobiographies: Fifteen Self-Portraits* (1948); Jesse T. Carpenter, *Competition and Collective Bargaining in the Needle Trades, 1910–1967* (1972); Harry A. Cobrin, *The Men's Clothing Industry: Colonial through Modern Times* (1970); *Current Biography* (1946).

POWDERLY, Terence Vincent   (1849–1924). Born in Carbondale, Pa., January 22, 1849; son of Terence, an Irish immigrant and teamster, and Margery (Walsh) Powderly; married Hannah Deyer on September 19, 1872, and after her death, Emma Fickenscher on March 31, 1919; attended the schools of Carbondale until age 13 and then took employment as a railroad worker; apprenticed as a machinist in 1866 and worked at that trade until 1877; joined the Machinists and Blacksmiths Union in 1871, becoming an organizer for western Pennsylvania three years later; initiated into the Noble Order of the Knights of Labor (K of L) in Philadelphia, Pa., on September 6, 1876; elected master workman of the

Scranton, Pa., assembly and then corresponding secretary of the reorganized district assembly in 1877; elected on the Greenback Labor party ticket to the first of three two-year terms as mayor of Scranton in 1878; believed that skilled workers should assist in organizing the unskilled and opposed the craft or trade union form of organization; was a critic of the wage system and hoped to see it replaced by the organization of producer cooperatives; served on the committee on constitution of the K of L national convention in 1878; became grand worthy foreman in 1879, and, later the same year, grand master workman, holding the latter until 1893; during his incumbency, usually opposed militant trade-union activity and advocated conciliation and mediation; was removed from office in 1893; admitted to the bar of Pennsylvania in 1894; supported the candidacy of William McKinley in 1896 and was appointed U.S. Commissioner General of Immigration, 1897, serving until 1902; in the following years held several positions in the U.S. Department of Labor; was a lifelong advocate of temperance and land reform; consistently supported the Republican party in his later years; contributed to George E. McNeill, ed., *The Labor Movement: The Problem of To-Day* (1887); authored several pamphlets and wrote *Thirty Years of Labor: A History of the Organization of Labor since 1860* (1889); died in Washington, D.C., June 24, 1924; Terence V. Powderly Papers, Catholic University of America; Harry J. Carman, Henry David, and Paul N. Guthrie, eds., *The Path I Trod: The Autobiography of Terence V. Powderly* (1940); Norman J. Ware, *The Labor Movement in the United States, 1860–1895* (1929); Gerald N. Grob, *Workers and Utopia: A Study of Ideological Conflict in the American Labor Movement, 1865–1900* (1961); Charles A. Madison, *American Labor Leaders: Personalities and Forces in the Labor Movement* (1950); *Dictionary of American Biography*, Vol. 15; Vincent J. Falzone, *Terence V. Powderly: Middle Class Reformer* (1978); S. E. Walker, "Terence V. Powderly, 'Labor Mayor': Workingmen's Politics in Scranton, Pennsylvania, 1870–1884" (Ph.D. diss., 1974); and S. E. Walker, "Terence V. Powderly, Machinist: 1866–1877," *Labor History* (Spring 1978).

POWERS, Bertram Anthony (1922–   ). Born in Cambridge, Mass., in 1922; the son of a civil servant; Roman Catholic; married Patricia, a high school teacher with a Ph.D. in English, in 1942; four children; after attending high school for two years, he dropped out and joined the Civilian Conservation Corps; plagued by a nerve injury in the hip that had been sustained after being hit by a truck several years earlier, he underwent two operations and was hospitalized for six months during 1939–1940; sent to Fitchburg State Teachers College by the Massachusetts Division of Vocational Rehabilitation, where he worked as a linotype operator and acquired training in the printing trades; after a year, he returned to Boston and became an apprentice printer; worked at various printing jobs for the next six years during which he completed his training; joined the International Typographical Union (ITU) immediately upon completing his apprenticeship; moved to New York City in 1946 and joined Local 6, ITU, the international union's largest local; worked as a typesetter on *PM*, a New York newspaper, and the *New York Star* before securing employment with the Sorg Printing Company, a large commercial printer, where he worked until 1953 when he quit to devote full time to union affairs; aligned himself with the Progressive party in the ITU's two-party system and, in 1947, ran unsuccessfully for a seat on Local 6's executive committee; became an alternate member of the executive committee a year later and in 1949 was elected a regular member; elected chairman of the committee in 1951; two years later he was elected vice-president of the local and became one of six trustees who supervised Local 6's pension and welfare fund; was elected president of Local 6 in 1961, and as his popularity among the union's membership grew, he won subsequent elections by ever larger majorities; shortly after his initial election, he entered into divisive contract negotiations over the introduction of automated machinery with the New York Publishers' Association that ultimately resulted in a 114-day strike that literally closed down all major New York daily newspapers; thereafter the issue of automation continued to disrupt labor-management relations in the printing industry; after the demise of several newspapers, he realized that automation was inevitable and began to place greater emphasis on lifetime job security for printers currently employed; fearing a further weakening of the three daily newspapers still being published in New York, he hesitated to call strikes but opted instead to use a variety of job actions to force concessions from employers; a tough, no-nonsense union leader, he maintained an earlier skepticism about employer motives and never hesitated to exercise labor's economic power when he felt it necessary; *New Yorker*, March 7, 1970; *Newsweek*, January 7, 1963; *Current Biography* (January 1974).

POWERS, Frank Bernard   (1888–   ). Born in Clear Lake, Minn., May 13, 1888; son of Bernard, a railroad station agent and telegrapher, and Katherine (Donovan) Powers; Roman Catholic; married Laura Knapp on November 9, 1910, and, after her death, Lillian S. Dewey on July 3, 1941; three children; completed two years of high school in Morris, Minn., then quit school at age 15 and became a telegrapher; later completed high school through night school courses and attended the University of Minnesota's School of Journalism; joined the Commercial Telegraphers' Union (CTU) in 1905 and the Order of Railroad Telegraphers in 1909; became circuit chairman of the CTU's United Press Division 47 in 1912 and three years later elected general chairman, serving until 1919; served as the general chairman of the CTU's Universal Service Division 97, 1919–1921; elected international secretary-treasurer of the CTU in 1921; elected international president in 1928 and served until 1941; was vice-president of the International Labor Press Association of America in 1925 and vice-president of the Eastern Labor Press Conference in 1942; served as the American Federation of Labor fraternal delegate to the Trades and Labor Congress of Canada in 1932; became the CTU's editor and statistician in 1941; a Democrat;

Vidkunn Ulriksson, *The Telegraphers: Their Craft and Their Unions* (1953); *Who's Who in Labor* (1946).

PRESSMAN, Lee (1906–   ). Born in New York City, July 1, 1906; son of Harry, a Russian immigrant, and Clara (Rich) Pressman; married Sophia Patnick on June 28, 1931; two children; graduated from high school in New York City, then attended Cornell University, earning a B.A. degree and becoming a member of Phi Beta Kappa; received an LL.B. degree from Harvard Law School; admitted to the New York bar in 1929; was an associate in a New York law firm specializing in cases involving corporations, receiverships, and labor, 1929–1933; campaigned for the Democratic ticket in 1932, then appointed assistant general counsel for the Agricultural Adjustment Administration of the Department of Agriculture; served as general counsel for the Works Progress Administration and the Resettlement Administration during 1935–1936; joined the Steel Workers Organizing Committee in 1936 and later became general counsel for the United Steelworkers of America (USWA), the Congress of Industrial Organizations (CIO), and the National Marine Engineers Beneficial Association; supported the Roosevelt administration's mobilization effort during World War II; was a member of the CIO delegation that visited the Soviet Union in 1945; assisted USWA president Philip Murray (q.v.) in negotiating a new contract with the United States Steel Corporation in 1947; directed the efforts of the CIO legal staff to analyze and consider ways of circumventing the Taft-Hartley Act; a left-winger during the period after World War II, he was forced to resign as general counsel of the CIO and the USWA in 1948; supported Henry Wallace's candidacy for president of the United States on the Progressive party ticket and himself ran for Congress from a New York district in 1948; appearing before the House Committee on Un-American Activities in 1950, admitted membership in the Communist party; resigned from and repudiated the American Labor party in 1950; left the labor movement and resumed a private law practice, 1948; Lloyd Ulman, *The Government of the Steel Workers' Union* (1962); John Herling, *Right to Challenge: People and Power in the Steelworkers' Union* (1972); Max M. Kampelman, *The Communist Party vs. the C.I.O.: A Study in Power Politics* (1957); *Current Biography* (1947); Harvey A. Levenstein, *Communism, Anticommunism, and the CIO* (1981); Bert Cochran, *Labor and Communism: The Conflict that Shaped American Unions* (1977); Lee Pressman Interview, Columbia Oral History Collection; Melvyn Dubofsky and Warren Van Tine, *John L. Lewis: A Biography* (1977).

PRESTON, George (1864–1933). Born in Lincolnshire, England, November 3, 1864; Methodist; completed a grammar school education at an early age; went to sea for three years; settled in Nottingham, England, and served a machinist's apprenticeship; as soon as age permitted, joined a trade union; was a member of a citizen's committee that secured John Burns's nomination as a Labour party candidate for Parliament from Nottingham in 1885; emigrated to the United

States in 1886, settling in Detroit, Mich.; joined the Knights of Labor Assembly 7750 of Machinists and Blacksmiths; joined the International Association of Machinists (IAM) Local Lodge 82 in Detroit in 1890; was a delegate to the 1895 national IAM convention, which elected him grand (national) secretary-treasurer; reelected to office until July 1917; afterward, held several responsible positions and retired to Bay View, near Elkton, Md., a few years before his death; died in Elkton, Md., February 18, 1933; *Machinists' Monthly Journal* (March 1933); Mark Perlman, *The Machinists: A New Study in American Trade Unionism* (1961).

John W. Hevener

PRICE, George Moses (1864–1942). Born in Poltava, Russia, May 21, 1864; Jewish; married Anna Kopkin on July 22, 1891; two children; educated in the Real Gymnasium (high school) of Poltava; emigrated to the United States, settling in New York City; shortly after arriving in the United States, became a sanitary inspector for the Tenth Ward of New York City, holding position while attending the Medical College of New York University; received the M.D. degree in 1895; worked as an inspector in the Tenement Commission for a year, then joined the New York City Department of Health in 1895; chosen to head the Joint Board of Sanitary Control provided for by the Protocol of Peace that ended the historic 1910 garment strike; served in that capacity for 15 years; under his direction, the Joint Board initiated regular shop inspections, fire drills, and educational campaigns in sanitation and public health; headed the New York Factory Commission's investigation of the tragic Triangle Shirtwaist Company fire of 1911 that resulted in 142 deaths; gained the support of several International Ladies' Garment Workers' Union (ILGWU) locals in 1913 and founded the Union Health Center, the first medical clinic organized to serve the workers of a particular industry; under his direction, the Union Health Center, which emphasized clinical services and outpatient care, quickly became a popular and valuable institution; the Union Health Center was officially taken over by the ILGWU in 1930 and had a large, well-trained staff, which by the time of Price's death had treated well in excess of fifty thousand patients; authored *A Handbook on Sanitation* (1901), *Tenement Inspection* (1904), *Hygiene and Public Health* (1910), and several other pamphlets; died in New York City, July 30, 1942, succeeded as director of the health center by his son, Dr. Leo Price; Benjamin Stolberg, *Tailor's Progress: The Story of a Famous Union and the Men Who Made It* (1944); Louis Levine, *The Women's Garment Workers: A History of the International Ladies' Garment Workers' Union* (1924); Leon Stein, *The Triangle Fire* (1962); *Who Was Who in America*, Vol. 3; *The New York Times*, July 31, 1942.

Q

QUILL, Michael Joseph (1905–1966). Born in Gourtloughera, Kilgarvan, County Kerry, Ireland, September 18, 1905; son of John Daniel, a farmer, and Margaret (Lynch) Quill; Roman Catholic; married Maria Theresa O'Neill on December 26, 1937, and, after her death in 1959, Shirley Garry in 1962; one child; attended the schools of Ireland during 1910–1916, then volunteered for the Irish Republican Army and served during the Irish Rebellion of 1919–1923; emigrated to the United States in 1926 and, after working at various jobs, joined the Interborough Rapid Transit Company of New York City as a gateman; was one of the founders of the Transport Workers Union of America (TWUA) in 1934; elected president of the TWUA and full-time organizer in 1935; after the previously independent TWUA affiliated with the Congress of Industrial Organizations (CIO) in 1937 and was given an international charter, elected president of the new international union and joined the national executive board of the CIO; elected to the New York City Council from the Bronx in 1937 on the American Labor party (ALP) ticket; served one term, then refused to support the ALP's condemnation of the Russo-German peace pact of 1939 and ran unsuccessfully for a council seat as an independent; elected to the New York City Council in 1943 as an independent and, returning to the ALP, reelected in 1945; after serving as a vice-president for several years, elected president of the Greater New York CIO Industrial Union Council in 1947, but resigned a year later (also resigning from the ALP) and led a reorganization designed to eliminate Communist influence; elected president of the reorganized New York CIO council in 1949; became a CIO vice-president in 1950; served on the CIO delegation to the International Confederation of Free Trade Unions in 1949 and 1950; served as the chairman of the confederation's committee on resolutions in 1951; led a 12-day strike against the New York City subways and bus lines in 1965 that paralyzed public transportation in the city; arrested for refusing to obey a court order to end the strike and suffered a heart attack shortly after being imprisoned; was a volatile trade union leader whose rhetoric was often more militant than his actions; usually followed the Communist line early in his career, but in the 1940s became a militant anti-Communist; died in New York City, January 28, 1966; L. H. Whittemore, *Man Who Ran the Subways: The Story of Mike Quill* (1968); *Current Biography* (1953); *Newsweek*, January 17, 1966; *Who's Who in Labor* (1946); Harvey A. Levenstein, *Communism, Anticommunism, and the CIO* (1981); Bert Cochran, *Labor and Communism: The Conflict that Shaped American Unions* (1977).

R

RAFTERY, Lawrence M.   (1895–   ). Born in St. Louis, Mo., February 27, 1895; son of Sylvester T., a painting contractor, and Rosa (Winterbauer) Raftery; Roman Catholic; married Enid Veil King on October 19, 1916; nine children; graduated from high school after attending both public and parochial schools; attended Christian Brothers College School of Art and Interior Decorating; worked as a paperhanger and painter and joined St. Louis Local 115 of the Brotherhood of Painters, Decorators and Paperhangers of America (BPDPA) in 1913; served as a trustee and business agent of Local 115, 1919–1923; became secretary and business agent of the St. Louis Painters' District Council in 1925; was a member of the executive board of the Missouri State Federation of Labor, a member of the advisory board of the Missouri Unemployment Bureau in 1929, and a member of the St. Louis Grand Jury in 1936; elected a vice-president of the BPDPA in 1937 and in 1942 became general secretary-treasurer, serving until 1952; elected BPDPA general president in 1952; after the merger of the American Federation of Labor (AFL) and the Congress of Industrial Organization (CIO), became a vice-president and member of the executive council of the building and construction trades department, AFL-CIO, serving until 1968; elected a vice-president and member of the AFL-CIO executive council in 1958; became BPDPA president emeritus in 1964 and was replaced as president by his son, S. Frank Raftery; a Democrat; Philip Zausner, *Unvarnished: The Autobiography of a Union Leader* (1941); *Who's Who in Labor* (1946); *AFL-CIO News,* August 29, 1964; *Who's Who in America,* 1960–1961.

RAJOPPI, Raleigh   (1905–1982). Born in Milburn, N.J., on February 22, 1905; son of Anthony, a nurseryman, and Katherine (Caruso) Rajoppi, a homemaker; Roman Catholic; married Edna Mildred Hamilton, an executive secretary, in 1941; two children; completed a secondary education at Union (N.J.) High School, in 1923, and attended the New Jersey Preparatory School, 1925–1927; later took extension courses at Rutgers University, 1931, and Columbia University, 1942–1943; joined Local 715 of the United Brotherhood of Carpenters and Joiners of America (UBC) in 1924; was elected president of the New Jersey State Council of Carpenters in 1938, a post he held until being elected president emeritus shortly before his death; active in a variety of local and state agencies and commissions, he was a member of the Commission for the Rehabilitation of Physically Handicapped Persons, 1944, the State Board of Mediation, 1944–1948, the Advisory Council of Disability Benefits, 1949–1952, and chaired the Commission on Vocational Education in Correctional Institutions, 1973–1974; was elected a member of the general executive board of UBC District 2 in 1952; served as a state supervisor of the New Jersey Carpenters Funds Account; was a trustee of the New Jersey Carpenters Pension, Welfare, Apprentice and Vocational Funds; was a commissioner of the State Health Care Facilities Financing Authority and chairman of the Union County (N.J.) Board of Trustees; awarded the Rutgers University Award in 1974 after leading a drive that resulted in a UBC donation of 65 acres of virgin forest land to Rutgers University—named the [William] Hutchinson (q.v.) Memorial Forest; died in Livingston, N.J., on March 17, 1982; *Who's Who in Labor* (1976); *The New York Times*, March 24, 1982.

RAMSAY, Claude E.   (1916–   ). Born in Ocean Springs, Miss., December 18, 1916; son of C. A. and Blanche (Bilbo) Ramsay; married Mae Helen Hillman on June 16, 1941; six children; attended the public schools of Jackson County, Miss., and Perkinston Junior College; completed his formal education, then secured employment with the International Paper Company, working for that firm for 24 years; joined the United Paperworkers of America (UPA) in 1939 and in 1951 elected president of UPA Local 203, serving in that capacity until 1959; served as president of the Jackson County Central Labor Union, 1952–1959; was a participant in the merger discussions between the American Federation of Labor and Congress of Industrial Organizations (AFL-CIO) in Mississippi, and elected president of the Mississippi AFL-CIO in 1959, a position he still held in 1974; possessed dynamic leadership qualities and oratorical ability, and had considerable success in the areas of state legislation, political education, public relations, and race relations; was a persistent critic of Mississippi's Balance Agriculture with Industry program for attracting low-paying, low-profit, garment-type industries; was also critical of the Mississippi press (characterizing it as "the worst in the nation"), Governor Ross Barnett (who "almost ruined our state"), the Ku Klux Klan, and Jackson, Miss., television station WLBI (which was "dominated by the Citizen's Council and other 'Right Wing' influences"); under his leadership, the Mississippi AFL-CIO became an effective foe of extremist groups including white racists, the John Birch Society, and others; served on the board of directors of the AFL-CIO Appalachian Council, as chairman of the AFL-CIO southern advisory committee on civil rights, and on numerous other civic boards and agencies; a Democrat; Richard A. McLemore, ed., *A History of Mississippi*, Vol. 2 (1973); Address by Claude Ramsay to the NDEA

Institute in History, University of Mississippi (1966); Robert S. McElvaine, "Claude Ramsay: Organized Labor and Civil Rights in Mississippi, 1959–1966," in *Southern Workers and Their Unions, 1880–1975*, ed. Merl E. Reed et al. (1981).

Merl E. Reed

RANDOLPH, Asa Philip (1889–1979). Born in Crescent City, Fla., April 15, 1889; son of James William, a minister, and Elizabeth (Robinson) Randolph; Methodist; married Lucille E. Green in 1914; Afro-American; completed a high school education at Cookman Institute in Jacksonville, Fla., then moved to New York City and worked there as an elevator operator, porter, and railroad waiter while continuing his education at the College of the City of New York; was a cofounder of the *Messenger*, a militant, Socialist monthly in 1917; served as an instructor in the New York Rand School of Social Science; ran unsuccessfully as a Socialist for New York secretary of state in 1921; acquired considerable experience in labor organization, then founded and served as organizer and first president of the Brotherhood of Sleeping Car Porters (BSCP) in 1925; after ten years of agitation and strife, negotiated a collective bargaining contract with the Pullman Palace Car Company in 1935; served as a member of Mayor Fiorello La Guardia's New York City Commission on Race in 1935; organized the March on Washington Movement in 1941, which led to the creation of the Fair Employment Practices Committee (FEPC); became co-chairman of the National Council for a Permanent FEPC; appointed to the New York Housing Authority in 1942; was a founder of the League for Nonviolent Civil Disobedience Against Military Segregation in 1947; served as a delegate to the International Confederation of Free Trade Unions in 1951; elected a vice-president and executive council member of the American Federation of Labor-Congress of Industrial Organizations (AFL-CIO) at its merger convention in 1955; was one of the leaders of the 1963 march on Washington; was one of the founders of the Negro American Labor Council and served as its president from 1960 to 1966; as one of the principal black spokesmen within the AFL-CIO executive council, often clashed with President George Meany (q.v.) and the conservative leaders of numerous AFL-CIO affiliates over the discriminatory activities of some international unions, but always remained loyal to the AFL-CIO; a Socialist early in his career, but later supported the Liberal party of New York; retired from union activities in 1968; retired AFL-CIO vice-presidency in 1974 and died in New York City on May 16, 1979; Brailsford R. Brazeal, *The Brotherhood of Sleeping Car Porters: Its Origin and Development* (1946); Jervis Anderson, *A. Philip Randolph: A Biographical Portrait* (1972); Joseph C. Goulden, *Meany* (1972); *New Yorker*, December 2, 9, 16, 1972; *Current Biography* (1951); William H. Harris, *Keeping the Faith: A. Philip Randolph, Milton P. Webster and the Brotherhood of Sleeping Car Porters, 1927–1937* (1977); Benjamin Quarles, "A. Philip Randolph: Labor Leader at Large," in *Black Leaders of the Twentieth Century*, ed. John Hope Franklin and August Meier (1982).

RANDOLPH, Woodruff   (1892–1966). Born in Warrenton, Mo., January 31, 1892; son of Joseph Freeman, a carpenter, and Mary Tracy (Busekrus) Randolph; married Agnes M. Johnson on July 1, 1916, and, after her death in 1947, Helen M. Grist-McKenzie on November 6, 1948; four children; entered the printing trade after graduation from high school and became a typesetter; joined the International Typographical Union (ITU) in 1912; received an LL.B. degree from the Webster College of Law, Chicago, Ill., and admitted to the bar of Illinois in 1921; elected president of Chicago ITU Local 16 in 1927; became secretary-treasurer of both the ITU and the International Allied Printing Trades Association in 1928, serving in that capacity until 1944; served as a delegate to the International Labor Organization conference in Geneva in 1936; elected international president of the ITU in 1944 on the Progressive party ticket of the ITU's two-party system and served until 1958; was vigorous opponent of the Taft-Hartley Labor Act, especially its prohibition of the closed shop contract, and devoted much of his time and his union's resources to combating the provisions of the law; edited the ITU's monthly organ, the *Typographical Journal*, 1928–1944; retired from union affairs in 1958 because of ill health; died in Colorado Springs, Colo., October 24, 1966; Elizabeth F. Baker, *Printers and Technology: A History of the International Printing Pressmen and Assistants' Union* (1957); Seymour M. Lipset et al., *Union Democracy: The Internal Politics of the International Typographical Union* (1956); *Current Biography* (1948); *Who's Who in Labor* (1946).

RARICK, Donald C.   (1919–1968). Born in 1919; Roman Catholic; married Eunice Morrison; one child; served in the U.S. Army during World War II, then took a job in the steel industry of western Pennsylvania and joined the United Steelworkers of America (USWA); was an ordinary steelworker in the United States Steel Corporation's Irvin works at McKeesport, Pa., in 1956 and was a local grievance committeeman and a delegate to the USWA convention; voiced opposition at the convention to a dues increase that was coupled with a raise in the salaries of USWA officers and unsuccessfully demanded a roll-call vote; a few months later, formed along with other local USWA leaders from the Pittsburgh-McKeesport area the Dues Protest Committee; failed to force a special convention to reconsider the dues issue and decided to challenge USWA president David J. McDonald (q.v.) in the international elections of 1957; the first contest for the USWA presidency, his bid reflected dissatisfaction not only with the dues increase but with the gap between the "union aristocracy," led by McDonald, and the rank and file; running without the support of any major USWA official, polled an imposing 223,000 votes to McDonald's 404,000; elected president of his local at the Irvin works in 1958; along with his backers, tried for dual unionism and actions detrimental to the union by the 1959 convention, which was dominated by the McDonald forces; was acquitted of the charges brought against him and tried to revive the protest movement for a larger rank-and-file voice in the USWA in 1961 but was unable to obtain the necessary local union nominations to get on the presidential ballot; supported I. W. Abel's (q.v.) successful campaign for the USWA presidency in 1965, but three years later announced his intention to run against Abel in 1969; was an unsuccessful candidate for the Democratic nomination in the twentieth Congressional District of Pennsylvania; died in McKeesport, Pa., September 17, 1968; Dan Wakefield, "Steelworkers at the Polls," *The Nation*, February 23, 1957; Lloyd Ulman, *The Government of the Steel Workers' Union* (1962); John Herling, *Right to Challenge: People and Power in the Steelworkers Union* (1972).

Donald G. Sofchalk

RATCHFORD, Michael D. (1860–1927). Born in County Clare, Ireland, in August 1860; married Deborah Jordan in December 1884; attended public and evening school; emigrated with his parents to the United States in 1872, settling in Stark County, Ohio; began working in the coal mines at age 12 and became an active trade unionist at age 20; elected president of a United Mine Workers of America (UMWA) local at Massillon, Ohio, in 1890, serving until 1892; served as a general organizer, 1893–1894; served as president of District 6, UMWA, 1895–1896, and as international president of the UMWA, 1897–1898; due to unemployment, wage reductions, and an unsuccessful strike in 1894, union membership had fallen to ten thousand and the treasury contained less than $600, insufficient to pay the American Federation of Labor (AFL) per-capita tax; under his leadership, the UMWA called a 12-week strike in July 1897, involving one hundred thousand miners, which paralyzed all bituminous coal fields except those in West Virginia; as a result of the strike, which was supported by AFL organizers and strike funds, he signed the Central Competitive Field Agreement, covering all important coal-producing states except West Virginia; under the terms of the agreement, the eight-hour day was established throughout the bituminous fields, and coal loading rates were based on the 65¢ per ton rate current in the Pittsburgh district; during his short incumbency, raised the union's membership to thirty-three thousand and increased its treasury holdings to $11,000; the UMWA recovery reinvigorated the entire labor movement following the depression; resigned the UMWA presidency in 1898 to serve as labor's representative on the U.S. Industrial Commission, 1898–1900; served as Ohio's commissioner of labor statistics, 1900–1908, as commissioner of the Ohio Coal Operators, 1909–1912, and as commissioner of the Illinois Coal Operators' Association after 1913; was a partisan Republican and a personal friend of Mark Hanna and William McKinley; died in Massillon, Ohio, December 12, 1927; *Who Was Who in America*, Vol. 4; Elsie Gluck, *John Mitchell: Miner* (1929); Selig Perlman and Philip Taft, *History of Labor in the United States, 1896–1932*, Vol. 4 (1935); McAlister Coleman, *Men and Coal* (1943).

John W. Hevener

REAGAN, Ronald (1911–   ). Born in Tampico, Ill., February 6, 1911; son of John Edward, a shoe merchant, and Nellie (Wilson) Reagan; Christian church; married Jane Wyman on January 24, 1940, and, after that marriage ended in divorce in 1948, Nancy Davis on March 4, 1952; four children; attended Eureka (Ill.) College and majored in economics and sociology; graduated with a B.A. degree in 1932, then became a radio broadcaster and soon acquired a national reputation as a sportscaster; after a successful screen test, made his film debut in 1937; joined the Screen Actors Guild (SAG) in 1941; served with the U.S. Army during World War II and rose to the rank of captain while making training films for the Air Force; became a member of the board of directors of the SAG in 1946; served as a friendly witness before the House Committee on Un-American Activities in 1947, but denied extensive Communist influence in the film-making industry; elected president of the SAG in 1947 and served until 1952; organized the Labor League of Hollywood Voters to support Harry S. Truman's campaign for reelection in 1948; elected chairman of the Motion Picture Industry Council in 1949; during 1954–1962, employed by the General Electric Company as a personnel relations counselor and as host and supervisor of a weekly television program, *General Electric Theater*; reelected president of the SAG in 1959 but resigned a year later after becoming a film producer; during 1962–1965, was the host and an occasional performer in *Death Valley Days*, a weekly television program; during the 1960s, the once liberal Democrat became increasingly conservative, appearing on anti-Communist television programs, supporting the Christian Anti-Communist Crusade led by Dr. Fred Schwartz, campaigning for political candidates connected with the John Birch Society, and serving on the advisory board of Young Americans for Freedom; elected governor of California on the Republican party ticket in 1966 and reelected in 1970; elected president of the United States in 1980; *Current Biography* (1967); *The New York Times Magazine*, November 14, 1965, October 16, 1966; *Look*, November 1, 1966.

REDMOND, John P.   (1892–1957). Born in Chicago, Ill., June 2, 1892; son of John E., a livery business operator, and Anna (Statia) Redmond; Roman Catholic; married Theresa V. Lyons on November 22, 1919; two children; was a high school graduate and completed two years of college work; after concluding his formal education, secured employment with the Chicago Fire Department; joined Chicago Local 2 of the International Association of Fire Fighters (IAFF) in 1912 and served as secretary-treasurer of the local's credit union; while serving as an international organizer, organized more than 150 IAFF locals; elected a vice-president of the IAFF in 1930; served as a general IAFF consultant to local unions concerned with pension funds, minimum wage-maximum-hour laws, civil service legislation, and fire prevention and control; appointed by the executive board to fill the unexpired term of IAFF president Fred W. Baer (q.v.) who died in 1946; elected international president in 1947 and served in that capacity until his death; was a member of the American Federation of Labor-Congress of Industrial Organizations' community service committee; died in Atlantic City, N.J., December 10, 1957; James J. Gibbons, *The International Association of*

Fire Fighters (1944); *Who's Who in Labor* (1946); *The New York Times*, December 12, 1957.

REED, John   (1887–1920). Born in Portland, Oreg., on October 22, 1887; son of Charles Jerome, U.S. marshall for the district of Oregon as well as a prominent and wealthy intellectual, and Margaret (Green) Reed; married Anne Mohan (Louise Bryant) on January 17, 1916; after completing his secondary education in the Portland schools, he enrolled in Harvard College where he was a member of the Cosmopolitan Club, served on the editorial boards of the *Lampoon* and the *Harvard Monthly*, wrote a play produced by the Hasty Pudding Club, and was made ivy orator and poet before graduating in 1910; joined the staff of the *American Magazine* in 1911; impressed by the writings of Lincoln Steffens and Ida Tarbell, his interest in social problems was aroused, and in 1913, he joined the staff of *The Masses*; visited Italy and studied the labor and reform movements there; served as a correspondent with Pancho Villa's army for four months during 1913 and his subsequent articles in the *Metropolitan Magazine* and the *New York World* established his reputation as a war correspondent; after leaving Mexico he traveled to Colorado where he witnessed the industrial warfare in the mining districts that led to the Ludlow Massacre of 1914; returned to the Northeast and was arrested in Paterson, N.J., for supporting striking workers in the silk mills; after the outbreak of war in Europe in 1914, he was sent to Europe by the *Metropolitan Magazine* to report on the war; subsequently, he traveled with the armies of Germany, Serbia, Bulgaria, Rumania, and Russia; was sent to Russia by *The Masses* after the overthrow of the czar; witnessed the October Revolution in Petrograd; was appointed bolshevist consul to the port of New York by Nicolai Lenin; meanwhile, as a result of his articles in *The Masses*, he was indicted for sedition; although in Russia during the first trial on these charges, he appeared at the second trial; both trials ended with hung juries; was called before a U.S. Senate investigating committee in 1919; joined the Socialist party in 1919, aligning himself with the left wing of the movement but was expelled, along with other radicals, at the national Socialist convention in Chicago, Ill., in August 1919; after the left wingers themselves split into two hostile groups, he wrote the manifesto and party platform of the Communist Labor party (CLP) which contested the legitimacy of the rival Communist party led by Louis Fraina (q.v.); edited the CLP organ, *The Voice of Labor*; returned to Russia in a futile effort to gain the endorsement of Soviet leaders for his Communist party faction in the United States; after being imprisoned in Finland when he attempted to return to the United States, he was sent back to Russia where he was stricken with typhus; authored *Sangar* (1912), *The Day in Bohemia* (1912), *Insurgent Mexico* (1914), *The War in Eastern Europe* (1916), *Tamburlaine and Other Poems* (1917), *Ten Days That Shook the World* (1919) and two books that were incomplete at the time of his death, *Red Russia* and *Kornilov to Best-Litovsk*; died in Moscow on October 17, 1920;

Robert A. Rosenstone, *Romantic Revolutionary: A Biography of John Reed* (1981); *Dictionary of American Biography*, Vol. 15.

REUTHER, Roy (1909–1968). Born in Wheeling, W.Va., August 29, 1909; son of Valentine, a steel and brewery worker and trade union leader, and Anna (Stoker) Reuther; reared a Lutheran; married Fania Sankin on July 8, 1944; two children; graduated from high school, then began work as an electrician's helper and joined the Wheeling local of the International Brotherhood of Electrical Workers in 1927; moved to Detroit, Mich., in 1932, and, after attending Wayne University for a year-and-a-half, joined the American Federation of Teachers while studying and teaching at Brookwood Labor College in Katonah, N.Y.; enrolled in the Federal Emergency Relief Administration's (FERA) workers' education teacher-training program at the University of Wisconsin and in 1934 was assigned to the FERA's workers' education program in Flint, Mich.; joined the United Automobile, Aircraft and Agricultural Implement Workers of America (UAW) after beginning work at the General Motors Corporation's (GMC) Chevrolet gear and axle plant in Detroit; became the assistant director of UAW organizing efforts in Flint in 1936; was one of the principal strategists and leaders of the successful efforts to organize GMC plants in Flint; was a charter member and the first president of the Greater Flint Congress of Industrial Organizations' (CIO) Industrial Union Council; during World War II, was an information specialist for the labor division of the War Production Board; appointed director of the UAW citizenship department in 1947; became an administrative assistant to UAW vice-president John W. Livingston (q.v.) in 1948, and administrative assistant to UAW president Walter P. Reuther in 1949; appointed national director of the UAW citizenship-legislation department in 1949; took a leave of absence from the UAW to become chairman of the National Voters' Registration Committee during the 1960 presidential campaign; served as the director of the American Federation of Labor-CIO National Voter Registration and Get Out the Vote campaigns in 1962 and 1964; was a Democrat; died in Detroit, Mich., January 10, 1968; Roy Reuther Papers, Walter Reuther Library, Wayne State University; Sidney Fine, *Sit-Down: The General Motors Strike of 1936–1937* (1969); Jack Stieber, *Governing the UAW* (1962); Wyndham Mortimer, *Organize! My Life as a Union Man* (1971).

REUTHER, Victor George (1912–   ). Born in Wheeling, W.Va., January 1, 1912; son of Valentine, a steel and brewery worker and trade union leader, and Anna (Stoker) Reuther; reared a Lutheran; married Sophia Good on July 18, 1936; three children; graduated from high school in Wheeling in 1928; attended the University of West Virginia in 1929, and Wayne University, 1930–1932; joined his brother, Walter (q.v.), on a three-year world tour in 1933 that included Europe, the Soviet Union, India, and Japan; became a speaker for the Emergency Peace Campaign after his return to the United States in 1935; secured employment in 1936 in the Detroit, Mich., automobile industry at the urging of his brother, Walter, who was involved in organizing automobile workers; participated in the organization of United Automobile, Aircraft and Agricultural Implement Workers of America (UAW) Local 174 in West Detroit in 1936; was one of the leaders of the 1936 sit-down strike at the Kelsey-Hayes Wheel Company plant in Detroit and participated in the General Motors Corporation (GMC) strike in Flint, Mich.; became UAW director of organization in Indiana in 1937 and later the same year became an international representative with the task of organizing the employees of the GMC in Michigan and Indiana; served as a labor member of the War Manpower Commission during World War II and was co-director of the UAW's war policy committee; became the UAW education director in 1946; was a Congress of Industrial Organizations (CIO) fraternal delegate to the London meetings of the Trade Union Advisory Committee of the European Recovery Program and became a co-chairman of the Anglo-American Labor Committee on Productivity in 1948; was severely wounded by an assassin in May 1949, losing sight in one eye; was a member of the CIO committee sent to study trade union and economic conditions in Europe, 1951; appointed in 1951 to head the CIO's European office, which was opened as a result of that study; became an administrative assistant to the president of the CIO in 1953 and the UAW in 1955; was a Socialist early in his career, but later supported Democratic candidates; retired union positions in 1971; authored *The Brothers Reuther and the Story of the UAW: A Memoir* (1976); Victor Reuther Papers, Walter Reuther Library, Wayne State University; Sidney Fine, *Sit-Down: The General Motors Strike of 1936–1937* (1969); Frank Cormier and William J. Eaton, *Reuther* (1970); Jean Gould and Lorena Hickok, *Walter Reuther: Labor's Rugged Individualist* (1972); Jack Stieber, *Governing the UAW* (1962).

REUTHER, Walter Philip (1907–1970). Born in Wheeling, W.Va., September 1, 1907; son of Valentine, a steel and brewery worker and trade union leader, and Anna (Stoker) Reuther; reared a Lutheran; married May Wolf on March 13, 1936; two children; attended high school in Wheeling for three years, then became a tool and die maker apprentice at the Wheeling Steel Corporation; later completed high school and took courses at Wayne University, Detroit, Mich., for three years; moved to Detroit in 1926 after being discharged by the Wheeling Steel Corporation for union activities; employed by several Detroit companies before accepting a job with the Ford Motor Company as a tool and die worker; became a foreman in the tool and die room in 1931; discharged for union activities and unable to find other employment, embarked with his brother, Victor (q.v.), on a three-year world tour, 1933–1935, that included Europe, the Soviet Union, China, and Japan; unable to find employment after his return to Detroit because of his reputation as a labor agitator, became a voluntary organizer for the United Automobile, Aircraft and Agricultural Implement Workers of America (UAW); successfully organized many automobile workers in Detroit's West Side into UAW Local 174 and became its president in 1935; elected to the international executive board of the UAW in 1936; was a leader of the important sit-down strike at the Kelsey-Hayes Wheel Company plant in Detroit in 1936; became director of the UAW's General Motors Corporation (GMC) department in 1939; elected first vice-president of the UAW in 1942; served during World War II with the Office of Production Management, the War Manpower Commission, and the War Production Board; elected president of the UAW in 1946 and the following year the so-called Reuther Caucus consolidated its control of the UAW after defeating the George Addes (q.v.)-Rolland J. Thomas (q.v.)-Richard Leonard (q.v.) faction in union elections; elected a vice-president of the Congress of Industrial Organizations (CIO) in 1946; led the UAW in a number of postwar strikes and in 1948 negotiated a contract with GMC that included an "escalator clause" tied to the U.S. Bureau of Labor Statistic's cost-of-living index; was the victim of an attempted assassination in April 1948 that left him partially disabled; became president of the CIO in 1952 after the death of Philip Murray (q.v.); served on the American Federation of Labor (AFL)-CIO unity committee that negotiated the merger of the two organizations in 1955; became an AFL-CIO vice-president and executive council member and president of its industrial union department after the merger; led the UAW out of the AFL-CIO in 1968 and along with the International Brotherhood of Teamsters organized the Alliance for Labor Action in 1969; was a Socialist early in his career, but usually supported the Democratic party after 1933; died in an airplane crash near Pellston, Mich., May 10, 1970; Walter Reuther Papers, Walter Reuther Library, Wayne State University; Henry M. Christman, ed., *Walter P. Reuther: Selected Papers* (1961); Jack Stieber, *Governing the UAW* (1962); Frank Cormier and William J. Eaton, *Reuther* (1970); Jean Gould and Lorena Hickok, *Walter Reuther: Labor's Rugged Individualist* (1972); Sidney Fine, *Sit-Down: The General Motors Strike of 1936–1937* (1969); Roger Keeran, *The Communist Party and the Auto Workers Unions* (1980); Nelson Lichtenstein, *Labor's War at Home: The CIO in World War II* (1982); Victor G. Reuther, *The Brothers Reuther and the Story of the UAW: A Memoir* (1976); Harvey A. Levenstein, *Communism, Anticommunism, and the CIO* (1981); Bert Cochran, *Labor and Communism: The Conflict that Shaped American Unions* (1977).

RICHARDSON, George J.   (1893–1980). Born in Winchester, Mass., on November 25, 1893; son of John, a blacksmith, and Sarah (McLean) Richardson; Community church; married Gertrude M. Gant on October 22, 1914; three children; after graduating from high school, he joined the Vancouver, British Columbia, fire department in 1913; joined independent fire fighters Local S18 in 1916; was a delegate to the founding convention of the International Association of Fire Fighters (IAFF) in 1918; served Local S18 (which became an IAFF affiliate) as secretary, vice-president, and president during the period 1916–1920; elected international secretary-treasurer of the IAFF in 1920, serving in that position until 1956 when he was named secretary-treasurer emeritus; appointed an American Federation of Labor-Congress of Industrial Organizations

(AFL-CIO) special representative in 1957 on assignments to Europe, Asia, and Latin America; also served as an advisor to the U.S. worker delegation to the International Labor Organization in Geneva, Switzerland; resigned his AFL-CIO position in 1962 and then served as a civil defense consultant with the U.S. Department of Defense until 1972; identified himself as an independent in politics; wrote numerous articles and pamphlets on fire fighting and fire protection; died in Long Beach, Calif., on January 5, 1980; *Who's Who in Labor* (1946); *AFL-CIO News*, January 12, 1980.

RICKERT, Thomas A.   (1876–1941). Born in Chicago, Ill., April 24, 1876; son of Charles and Hannah Rickert; married; attended the public schools of Chicago and a business college; became a cutter in a garment factory; joined the United Garment Workers of America (UGW) in 1895; elected president of the UGW in 1904, beginning a life-long tenure in that position; as a result of dissatisfaction with his leadership, a secessionist movement of dissident garment workers emerged after the 1910 strike against Hart, Schaffner and Marx and culminated in the organization of the rival Amalgamated Clothing Workers of America in 1914; served during World War I on the War Labor Conference Board and its successor the War Labor Board; elected an American Federation of Labor (AFL) vice-president and executive council member in 1918; nominated William Green (q.v.) for the AFL presidency after the death of Samuel Gompers (q.v.) in 1924; was appointed to several federal committees during the early years of Franklin D. Roosevelt's administration, but soon became highly critical of New Deal policies and the Democratic administration; was a conservative trade union leader who had previously established a close personal relationship with Samuel Gompers and became a bitter opponent of the Congress of Industrial Organizations (CIO); in turn was characterized by CIO president John L. Lewis (q.v.) as being "regarded in labor circles as an official entertainer for members of the Executive Council"; served on the unsuccessful AFL-CIO unity committee in 1939; identified himself politically as nonpartisan; died in New York City, July 28, 1941; Joel Seidman, *The Needle Trades* (1942); Walter Galenson, *The CIO Challenge to the AFL: A History of the American Labor Movement, 1935– 1941* (1960); Philip Taft, *The A.F. of L. from the Death of Gompers to the Merger* (1959).

RIEVE, Emil   (1892–1975). Born in the province of Zyradow, Russian Poland, June 8, 1892; son of Fred, a textile machinist, and Pauline (Lange) Rieve; Lutheran; married Laura Wosnack on July 1, 1916; one child; elementary school, then emigrated to the United States in 1904 and began working in a Pennsylvania hosiery mill; joined the American Federation of Hosiery Workers (AFHW) in 1907; elected a vice-president of the AFHW in 1914 and became president in 1929; was a labor advisor for the hosiery industry to the National Recovery Administration, 1933–1935; was a member of the national executive board of the United Textile Workers Union in 1934, and led an unsuccessful national strike of 500,000 textile employees; became executive director of the Congress of Industrial Organizations' (CIO) Textile Workers Organizing Committee in 1939 and left the AFHW to become president of the newly organized Textile Workers Union of America (TWU); became a CIO vice-president in 1939, serving until 1955; appointed to the national committee of the International Labor Organization in 1936; served during World War II as an alternate member of the National Mediation Board and of the National War Labor Board, and on them opposed anti-strike legislation and the "Little Steel Formula" of wage determination; was a U.S. delegate to the Inter-American Conference on Social Security in Santiago, Chile, in 1942; resigned from the National War Labor Board in 1945 and released CIO textile workers from their no-strike pledge of December 1941; visited the Soviet Union in 1945 as a member of the CIO delegation invited by the Soviet trade union movement; was a CIO delegate to the World Federation of Trade Unions, 1945–1947; became an executive council member of the International Confederation of Free Trade Unions in 1949; appointed as a labor advisor to the National Security Resources Board in 1950 and served on the Wage Stabilization Board, 1950–1952; became a vice-president and executive council member of the American Federation of Labor-CIO after the 1955 merger; retired as TWU president in 1956, then served as chairman of the TWU executive council, 1956–1960; served as an AFL-CIO fraternal delegate to the British Trades Union Congress in 1956; became president emeritus in 1960; was an early member of the American Labor party and later supported candidates of the Liberal party of New York and the Democratic party; authored *Free Enterprise for Whom?* (1948); died in Lauderhill, Fla., on January 24, 1975; Walter Galenson, *The CIO Challenge to the AFL: A History of the American Labor Movement, 1935–1941* (1960); Art Preis, *Labor's Giant Step: Twenty Years of the CIO* (1964); *Current Biography* (1946); *The New York Times*, January 26, 1975; *AFL-CIO News*, February 1, 1975.

RIFFE, John Vernon   (1904–1958). Born in Jenkins, Ky., on March 15, 1904; son of Gabriel Riffe, a union carpenter; a Presbyterian and in later years an active participant in the Moral Re-Armament movement; married about 1922 and divorced in 1935, remarried in 1937; four children (one by his first wife); attended grammar school in Jenkins; began work first as a trapper; later became a mule driver at Consolidated Mine No. 4, Jenkins, at age 14, and joined the United Mine Workers of America (UMWA) local almost immediately; elected local union president at age 16 and served in various capacities with the local union for the next 14 years; was appointed an organizer in West Virginia by Van A. Bittner (q.v.), UMWA District 17 president in 1933; established a reputation for physical courage and toughness in UMWA organizing in West Virginia in the 1920s and early 1930s; in 1936, he joined the staff under Bittner, then serving as Midwest regional director of the Steel Workers Organizing Committee (SWOC) in Chicago, Ill.; was among those fired upon by the Chicago police in the 1937 Memorial Day Massacre; through the late 1930s and early

1940s, he served as subregional and district official under Bittner, organizing in Wisconsin, Illinois, and California, among steel and packing house workers; was Bittner's chief aide in organizing seventy thousand Bethlehem Steel workers for SWOC in 1940; during World War II, he organized American Rolling Mill plants in Pennsylvania, Maryland, Ohio, and Kentucky for SWOC and its successor, the United Steelworkers of America (USWA), and served as labor representative on the Cincinnati (Ohio) Regional War Labor Board; was named Bittner's chief assistant in the Congress of Industrial Organization's (CIO) southern organizing drive ("Operation Dixie") in 1946 and in 1950 succeeded Bittner as director; was appointed by new CIO president Walter P. Reuther (q.v.) as CIO executive vice-president in 1953, following the death of Allan Haywood (q.v.); his efforts to implement plans for the reorganization of the CIO's internal structure and organizing functions were weakened by his recurrent illnesses, controversial participation in Moral Re-Armament activities, and conflicts with CIO Secretary-Treasurer James B. Carey (q.v.); assisted Reuther and USWA President David McDonald (q.v.) in the American Federation of Labor (AFL)-CIO merger process; after the merger in 1955, he became USWA international representative; died after a long illness in Arlington, Va., on January 7, 1958; *CIO News*, April 13, 1953; *AFL-CIO News*, January 11, 1958; William Grogan, *John Riffe of the Steelworkers: American Labor Statesman* (1959).

Robert H. Zieger

ROBERTSON, David Brown   (1876–1961). Born in West Austintown, Ohio, May 13, 1876; son of Robert, a merchant, and Jane (Brown) Robertson; Presbyterian; married Edna M. Hayes on September 8, 1907; two children; left the public schools at age 12, but later continued his education through night school and correspondence courses; during 1888–1895, worked in a brick factory and a machine shop; took a job on the Pennsylvania Railroad as an engine wiper in 1895; during 1898–1913 he worked for the Erie Railroad as a hostler, fireman, and engineer; elected general chairman of the Brotherhood of Locomotive Firemen and Enginemen (BLFE) for the Erie Railroad in 1905; elected a vice-president of the BLFE in 1913; became international president in 1922; served as chairman of the Railway Labor Executives' Association, 1926–1932; was chairman of the committee that sponsored the Railway Labor Act of 1926; was strongly opposed to the elimination of firemen jobs on diesel-powered locomotives and negotiated national agreements in 1937 and 1950 providing for the employment of firemen as helpers on diesel locomotives; became BLFE president emeritus in 1953; appointed by Supreme Court Chief Justice Earl Warren to head a commission to study and recommend salary and retirement benefits for members of Congress and the federal judiciary; was a liberal in politics, and identified himself as an independent voter; died in Cleveland, Ohio, September 27, 1961; Robert H. Zieger, *Republicans and Labor, 1919–1929* (1969); *Current Biography* (1950); Solon DeLeon, ed., *The American Labor Who's Who* (1925).

ROBINS, Margaret Dreier   (1868–1945). Born in Brooklyn, N.Y., September 6, 1868; daughter of Theodor, a businessman, and Dorothea Adelheid (Dreier) Dreier; German Evangelical and Congregationalist; married Raymond Robins, head of the Northwestern University settlement in Chicago, on June 21, 1905; completed private secondary school in Brooklyn, then at age 19 became secretary-treasurer of the women's auxiliary of the Brooklyn Hospital; served as chairman of the legislative committee of the Women's Municipal League, New York City, 1903–1904; joined the New York Women's Trade Union League (WTUL) in 1904; after marrying, transferred her membership to the Chicago WTUL in 1905; served as president of the Chicago WTUL, 1907–1913 and of the national WTUL, 1907–1922; was a member of the Chicago Federation of Labor's executive board, 1908–1917; during her WTUL career, often performed publicity work and raised funds for strikers, most notably during the 1909–1910 New York and Philadelphia garment workers' strikes and the 1911 International Ladies' Garment Workers' strike in Cleveland; was active in state labor and political affairs; was a member of the vocational education committee of the Illinois State Federation of Labor in 1914 and chairman of the women in industry committee of the Illinois State Council of Defense in 1917; was instrumental in convening the 1919 International Congress of Working Women in Washington, D.C., and at the Geneva Congress in 1921 elected president of the International Federation of Working Women, serving until 1923; supported William Jennings Bryan and the Democratic party in 1908; supported the Progressive party in 1912, and was a member of the executive committee of the Illinois Progressive party; supported the Republican party from 1916 to 1932, and thereafter supported Franklin D. Roosevelt and the Democratic party; was a member of the Republican National Committee in 1928; appointed to the planning committee of the White House Conference on Child Health and Protection by President Herbert H. Hoover in 1929; reelected to the WTUL executive board in 1934 and in 1937 became chairman of the WTUL's Southern committee; died in Brooksville, Fla., February 21, 1945; Mary E. Dreier, Margaret Dreier Robins Papers, Schlesinger Library, Radcliffe College and State Historical Society of Wisconsin; *Margaret Dreier Robins: Her Life, Letters and Work* (1950); Agnes Nestor, *Woman's Labor Leader: An Autobiography of Agnes Nestor* (1954); Mary Anderson, *Woman at Work: The Autobiography of Mary Anderson as told to Mary N. Winslow* (1951); *Notable American Women* (1971); *Dictionary of American Biography*, Suppl. 3; Barbara Estes, "Margaret Dreier Robins: Social Reformer and Labor Organizer" (Ph.D. diss., 1978).

Marie Tedesco

ROBINSON, Reid   (1908–   ). Born in Butte, Mont., June 7, 1908; son of James, a skilled mechanic and boilermaker and a member of the Western Federation of Miners; in 1914, moved to Alberta, Canada, where his family tried homesteading; returned to the United States during World War I; as a newsboy in Seattle, Wash., witnessed the general strike of 1919; in 1921, returned with his family to Butte, where his father edited a labor newspaper; attended high school in Butte, then went to work in the copper mines; during the early 1930s, along with his father, who had been recently elected secretary-treasurer of the International Union of Mine, Mill and Smelter Workers (IUMMSW), and several other organizers, revived the Butte Miners' No. 1, the key local of the IUMMSW; became financial secretary of No. 1 and in 1935 elected its president; with strong backing of a conservative faction, elected international president of the IUMMSW in 1936; although only 28 years old, was capable, a good speaker, and ambitious; the IUMMSW was one of the founding unions of the Congress of Industrial Organizations (CIO) and by virtue of being president of the IUMMSW, became a member of the CIO executive board and in 1940 a vice-president; was president of the IUMMSW for ten years and during this period the union increased its membership from about twenty thousand to more than ninety thousand; negotiated a merger with the National Association of Die Casting Workers in 1943; in expanding the IUMMSW before and during World War II, gained Communist organizers from within the IUMMSW and from other CIO unions; Communist members alienated his original sup-porters, and by 1946 the union was divided into warring rightist and leftist factions; shortly after being reelected in 1946, resigned after losing majority support of the executive board; elected eastern vice-president of the IUMMSW in 1947 and organized in Canada until deported as a Communist agitator; resigned as vice-president and returned to Butte in 1950; later moved to California and there worked at various blue-collar jobs; was not a member of the Communist party, but was on the left ideologically; was an opponent of U.S. Cold War policies and supported Henry Wallace's Progressive party candidacy for president of the United States in 1948; Vernon H. Jensen, *Nonferrous Metals Industry Unionism, 1932–1954* (1954); Transcript of Reid Robinson Interview, 1969, Labor History Archives, Pennsylvania State University; Bert Cochran, *Labor and Communism: The Conflict that Shaped American Unions* (1977); Harvey A. Levenstein, *Communism, Anticommunism, and the CIO* (1981).

Donald G. Sofchalk

ROLLINGS, John Isaac   (1905–1970). Born in St. Charles County, Mo., July 1, 1905; son of John William, a farmer and Sara Ella (Palmer) Rollings; married Fannie Ocepek on December 6, 1928; no children; completed elementary school, then learned the barber's trade in St. Louis, Mo.; joined St. Louis Local 102 of the Journeymen Barbers, Hairdressers and Cosmetologists' International Union of America in 1925; served Local 102 in several capacities, including secretary-treasurer, business representative, and, during 1931–1937, president; became the state legislative representative for the barber industry in 1928, serving in that capacity until 1953; served as president of the St. Louis Union Label Trades Section, 1935–1937; served during World War II as a member of the Seventh Regional Panel of the War Labor Board and was a member of the St. Louis Advisory Committee and the Price Panel Board of the Office of Price

Administration; elected executive secretary (the chief administrative officer) of the St. Louis Central Trades and Labor Union in 1942, serving until 1953; became the president of the Missouri State Association of Barbers in 1944; elected president of the Missouri State Federation of Labor in 1953; was one of the principal negotiators of the American Federation of Labor (AFL)-Congress of Industrial Organizations' (CIO) merger in Missouri in 1956 and elected president of the resulting Missouri AFL-CIO Council; was a member of numerous public and private boards and agencies; retired from his union positions in 1969 and was named president emeritus of the Missouri AFL-CIO Council; usually supported the Democratic party; died in St. Louis, Mo., in December 1970; Gary M. Fink, *Labor's Search for Political Order: The Political Behavior of the Missouri Labor Movement, 1890–1940* (1974); *Who's Who in Labor* (1946); *AFL-CIO News*, December 26, 1970.

ROMBRO, Jacob (Philip Krantz)   (1858–1922). Born in Zuphran, Wilna Province, Russia, October 10, 1858; son of Baruch and Bella Rosa (Uger) Rombro; Jewish; married Eva Gordon; graduated from a rabbinical seminary in 1879, then spent two years at the Technological Institute of St. Petersburg; after the assassination of Alexander II in 1881, was forced into exile and settled in Paris; while continuing his studies at the Sorbonne, began a productive literary career with a treatise on Spinoza; one of the founders of a short-lived Socialist organization, the Jewish *Arbeiter Verein*; emigrated to London in 1883 and there wrote articles in Yiddish for a weekly Socialist journal, *Der Polischer Yidel*; became the editor of a Yiddish Socialist monthly, *Arbeiter Freund*, in 1885; represented the Jewish workers of London as a delegate to the first International Socialist Congress in Paris in 1889; emigrated to the United States in 1890 and became editor of a new Socialist weekly, the *Arbeiter-Zeitung*, which, after being renamed the *Abend-Blatt*, became a daily and the official organ of the Socialist Labor party; as the editor of the first Socialist paper published in Yiddish, had an extraordinary influence during the formative years of the Jewish labor movement in the United States; at the time of his death, was associated with the *Jewish Daily Forward*; died in New York City, November 28, 1922; Melech Epstein, *Jewish Labor in the U.S.A., 1914–1952*, 2 Vols. (1953); *American Jewish Year Book* (1904–1905); *Dictionary of American Biography*, Vol. 16.

ROMUALDI, Serafino   (1900–1967). Born in Bastia Umbra, Italy, November 18, 1900; son of Romualdo, a shoemaker, and Emilia (Cormanni) Romualdi; Roman Catholic; married Rose Pesci Gioconda on September 4, 1928, and remarried after her death; two children; completed secondary school, then attended an Italian teachers' college; emigrated to the United States in 1923, after actively opposing the fascist regime of Benito Mussolini; continued his opposition to fascism through the Italian language press in the United States; joined the American Newspaper Guild and served as a lecturer for the Rand School of

Social Science as well as several international unions, including the Amalgamated Clothing Workers of America and the United Shoe Workers; joined the editorial and publicity staff of the International Ladies' Garment Workers' Union in 1933; served as an editor of the monthly magazine, *El Mondo*, 1939–1941, and as a labor economist in the office of the co-ordinator of inter-American affairs; as a labor advisor to the Office of Strategic Services in Italy in 1944, involved in the effort to rebuild the Italian labor movement; became the inter-American representative of the American Federation of Labor in 1948; served as assistant secretary general of the Inter-American Regional Labor Organization; became the executive director of the American Institute for Free Labor Development after its organization in 1962; was a vigorous opponent of Communist influence in the labor movements of Latin America and devoted much of his time and energy to the promotion of anti-Communist unions and leaders; retired in 1965, then served as a special consultant on inter-American affairs to the U.S. State Department and as a lecturer at the Cuernavaca Labor College; authored *Presidents and Peons: Recollections of a Labor Ambassador in Latin America* (1967); died while attending a meeting of the Mexican Labor Federation in Mexico City, Mexico, November 11, 1967; Serafino Romualdi Papers, Catherwood Library, Cornell University; Ronald Radosh, *American Labor and United States Foreign Policy: The Cold War in the Unions from Gompers to Lovestone* (1969); *The American Federationist* (March 1948); *AFL-CIO News*, November 18, 1967.

RONEY, Frank   (1841–1925). Born in Belfast, Ireland, August 13, 1841; son of a wealthy contractor; Roman Catholic; married three times; three children; as a young man, became associated with the Fenians and quickly rose to a leadership position in the revolutionary movement to overthrow British rule in Ireland; was arrested and charged with treason and emigrated to the United States to avoid imprisonment; lived in New York City and Chicago, Ill.; then moved to Omaha, Neb., and there secured employment as an iron molder with the Omaha Smelting Workers; joined Iron Molders Union 190 and elected its secretary and then its president; while residing in Nebraska, became active in the affairs of the National Labor Reform party (the political arm of the National Labor Union) and elected president of the Nebraska branch; was laid off as a foundry worker, then hired as a U.S. government teamster and sent to Fort Sedgewich, Wyo.; returned to Omaha, again working as a molder; moved to Utah; worked in the Salt Lake City foundry and, when it failed in 1875, moved to California, there securing employment as a molder with the Pacific Iron Works and then with the Union Iron Works of San Francisco; became a U.S. citizen in 1875; joined the Workingmen's party of California in 1877 and served as the temporary chairman of the party's first state convention, held secretly in San Francisco in January 1878; wrote the platform of the Workingmen's party; broke with the leader of the Workingmen's party, Denis Kearney, then led an opposition faction for a short time before disassociating himself from the party; converted to socialism and joined the International Workingmen's Association (IWA), a forerunner of the Socialist Labor party, but devoted more of his attention to trade union activities; although not a sailor, organized the Seamen's Protective Union in 1880 and was its delegate to the San Francisco Representative Assembly of Trades and Labor Union in 1881, serving as president during 1881–1882; was one of the leaders of the anti-Chinese agitation and helped found the League of Deliverance, serving as its chairman; also led a campaign to advertise the anti-Chinese labels of cigar-and shoemakers, the forerunner of the American labor movement's commitment to the trade union label; blacklisted in his trade as a labor agitator; employed as an assistant to the city engineer of San Francisco, holding the position until a change in the city administration cost him his job; in 1885, was one of the principal organizers of the first iron trades council in the United States, the Iron Trades Council of San Francisco (originally the Federated Iron Trades Council) and served as a member of its executive board; was one of the founders of the Representative Council of the Federated Trades and Labor Organization of the Pacific Coast, an anti-Knights of Labor federation dominated by the IWA, and served as its president, 1885–1887; worked for a short time with the U.S. Immigration Service and at other odd jobs prior to gaining steady employment in the Mare Island Navy Yard, Vallejo, Calif., as a foundry worker in 1898; involved in the organization of the Trades and Labor Council of Vallejo in 1899 and served as its president for one term; in 1909, moved to Los Angeles, Calif., and there took no part in labor activities until 1915, then serving one term as secretary-treasurer of the Iron Trades Council of Los Angeles; after 1916, lived a lonely, poverty-stricken existence; authored *Frank Roney: Irish Rebel and Labor Leader*, edited by Ira B. Cross (1931); died in Long Beach, Calif., January 24, 1925; Ira B. Cross, *A History of the Labor Movement in California* (1935); John R. Commons et al., *History of Labour in the United States*, Vol. 2 (1918); Neil L. Shumsky, "Frank Roney's San Francisco—His Diary: April 1875–March 1876," *Labor History* (Spring 1976).

ROSE, Alex (Olesh Royz)   (1898–1977). Born in Warsaw, Russian Poland, October 15, 1898; son of Hyman, a wealthy tanner, and Faiga (Halpern) Royz; Jewish; married Elsie Shapiro on July 7, 1920; two children; completed secondary school in Warsaw, but because of discriminations against Jews, could not pursue a higher education in Poland; emigrated to the United States in 1913 in pursuit of a medical career; after the outbreak of war in Europe in 1914, his parents could no longer finance his education and hence forced to take a job as a millinery worker; joined the Cloth Hat, Cap and Millinery Workers' International Union (CHCMW) in 1914; became recording secretary of CHCMW Local 24 in 1916; enlisted in the British Army's "Jewish Legion" in 1918, serving in Palestine, Egypt, and Syria; returned to the United States in 1920 and resumed union activities; elected secretary-treasurer of Local 24 in 1923 after a bitter campaign against a Communist-supported opponent; elected vice-president of the CHCMW in 1927 and retained that position in the United Hatters, Cap and Millinery

Workers International Union (UHCMW), which was organized in 1934 after the CHCMW and the United Hatters of North America merged; appointed president of the international by the UHCMW executive board in 1950 and subsequently elected to the post; led a successful strike against the Norwalk, Conn., Hat Corporation of America in 1953–1954; chaired the American Federation of Labor-Congress of Industrial Organizations' appeals committee that expelled the International Brotherhood of Teamsters in 1957; was a vigilant opponent of Communist as well as gangster elements in the labor movement during his long career as a labor leader; was a Socialist early in his career, but became an advocate of labor-management cooperation to ensure stability of the hat, cap, and millinery industry; was an active and influential political leader; helped organize the American Labor party in 1936 and served as state secretary and director of the party, 1936–1944; was one of the founders of the Liberal party of New York, becoming its vice-chairman in 1944; was a delegate to the New York State Constitutional Convention in 1966; served as a presidential elector in the national elections of 1940, 1948, 1964, and 1968; died in New York City on January 4, 1977; Donald B. Robinson, *Spotlight on a Union: The Story of the United Hatters, Cap and Millinery Workers' International Union* (1948); J. M. Budish, *History of the Cloth Hat, Cap and Millinery Workers* (1926); *Current Biography* (1959); *AFL-CIO News*, January 8, 1977.

ROSENBERG, Abraham   (1870–1935). Born in Russia in 1870; Jewish; married; emigrated to the United States in 1883; obtained work as a cloak maker in the New York City garment industry and by 1885, at age 15, became actively involved in union activities; joined the Knights of Labor assembly of dress and cloak makers and, after the failure of the Knights, joined the organizing effort that resulted in the creation of the International Ladies' Garment Workers' Union (ILGWU) in 1900; was elected president of the ILGWU in 1908; assuming the leadership of the union after the industry had been devastated by the Panic of 1907 and the following depression, he nevertheless managed successfully to conduct a waist makers' strike in 1909 and a cloak makers' strike in 1910; the settlement negotiated in the latter strike was based on the famous Protocol of Peace, which provided for the arbitration of labor-management disputes in the garment industry; radical Socialists within the ILGWU ranks objected to the protocol and its anti-strike provisions, and in the 1914 convention, they ousted Rosenberg and his influential secretary-treasurer, John Dyche (q.v.); after his defeat in the 1914 elections, he became a general organizer for the ILGWU, a position he retained until his retirement in 1929; a gentle, warm individual, he always retained his commitment to peaceful collective bargaining and moderate union tactics; a Socialist; authored *The Cloakmakers and Their Union* (1920); died in New York City in 1935; *Encyclopedia Judaica*, Vol. 14; Louis Levine, *The Women's Garment Workers: A History of the International Ladies' Garment Workers' Union* (1924); Benjamin Stolberg, *Tailor's Progress: The Story of a Famous Union and the Men Who Made It* (1944).

ROSENBLUM, Frank   (1888–1973). Born in New York City, May 15, 1888; son of Louis, a clothing worker, and Annie (Karna) Rosenblum; Jewish; married Ida Beispil on September 19, 1924; three children; completed grammar school, then began work in the garment industry and eventually secured employment as a cutter in a Hart, Schaffner and Marx plant in Chicago, Ill.; joined a Chicago local of the United Garment Workers of America in 1910; was one of the founders of the Amalgamated Clothing Workers of America (ACWA) in 1914; became an ACWA vice-president and executive-council member in 1914; appointed director of the Congress of Industrial Organizations' (CIO) Midwest Textile Workers Organizing Committee in 1937 and served in that capacity for three years; elected a CIO vice-president in 1940 and became a member of the executive board; was a member of the CIO Political Action Committee and the union label committee; served as chairman of the finance committee; elected ACWA executive vice-president in 1940 and served until 1946, when elected general secretary-treasurer, beginning a long term of service in that capacity; was a vice-president and member of the executive bureau of the World Federation of Trade Unions, 1948–1949; served on a large number of ACWA boards and agencies; retired in 1972; died in Chicago, Ill., February 9, 1973; Matthew Josephson, *Sidney Hillman: Statesman of American Labor* (1952); Leo H. Wolman, *The Chicago Clothing Workers* (1924); Harry A. Cobrin, *The Men's Clothing Industry: Colonial through Modern Times* (1970).

ROY, Andrew   (fl. 1834–1873). Born in Palace Craig, Lanarkshire, Scotland, on July 19, 1834; son of David and Mary Roy; married Janet Watson on July 21, 1865; entered the mines at age 8 while still attending night school; moved with his parents to Cleland in 1847 where he enrolled in a select night school; emigrated to the United States in 1850 at age 16; worked in the mines of Maryland, People Swash, and Georges Creek; moved to Illinois in 1855 to work in the mines at Du Quoin but was discharged after leading a protest against the unjust weighing of mined coal; worked at various times in Rock Island, Galesburg, Shyboyden, Eureka, Avon, and Placerville, 1855–1860; moved to Arkansas in 1860 and acquired a 40-acre farm; after the outbreak of the Civil War, he enlisted in the 10th Battalion Reserve Corps, Pennsylvania Volunteers; wounded and captured during the war and held as a Confederate prisoner of war for 16 months before being exchanged; underwent several operations to remove bone fragments resulting from his war-time bullet wound; moved to Hubbard, Ohio, where he became a bank official; meanwhile, he studied mine and land surveying and civil and mine engineering; used his knowledge of mine and mine engineering to lead a campaign for improved mine safety legislation; drafted a mine safety bill for the soft coal region of Pennsylvania that was passed by the state legislature after being seriously weakened by amendments; campaigned for similar reform in Ohio and other mining areas; was one of the organizers of the Miners' National Association in 1873; was appointed Ohio state inspector of mines; authored *A History of the Coal Miners of the United States* (n.d.); *Chicago*

Workingman's Advocate, January 17, 1874; David Montgomery, *Beyond Equality: Labor and the Radical Republicans, 1862–1872* (1967).

RUEF, Abraham (1864–1936). Born in San Francisco, Calif., on September 2, 1864; son of Myer, a wealthy dry goods and real estate entrepreneur, and Adele (Heruch) Ruef; Jewish; never married; graduated from the University of California with high honors in 1883 at age 18; attended the Hastings College of Law in San Francisco and was admitted to the bar in 1886; became involved in San Francisco politics during the 1880s, supporting a reform program, but soon aligned himself with the Republican machine in San Francisco; when organized labor created the Union Labor party of San Francisco in 1901 as a result of the use of police power against strikers during a teamster and waterfront strikes, he quickly assumed the leadership of the new party and controlled the selection of its candidates; after the Union Labor party won the mayoral elections of 1901, 1903, and 1906—in the latter instance, the entire Labor ticket won despite a Republican-Democratic fusion—he was indicted and convicted of taking bribes from several utility companies and was confined in San Quentin Penitentiary from 1911 to 1915; with his conviction, the Union Labor party, the only labor party to gain complete control of a city government in the United States, collapsed; after his release from prison, he created another fortune, this time in real estate, but lost it in the depression of the 1930s; died in San Francisco on February 29, 1936; Graft Prosecution Records, Bancroft Library, University of California, Berkeley; Walton Bean, *Boss Ruef's San Francisco: The Story of the Union Labor Party, Big Business, and the Graft Prosecution* (1952); "The Road I Traveled," San Francisco *Bulletin*, April 6, May 21-September 5, 1912; *Dictionary of American Biography*, Suppl. 2; Fred J. Cook, *American Political Bosses and Machines* (1973).

RUSTIN, Bayard (1910–). Born in West Chester, Pa., on March 17, 1910; son of Janifer and Julia (Davis) Rustin; he was an illegitimate child raised by his grandparents; Quaker; Afro-American; attended the public schools of West Chester and in 1928 graduated from West Chester High School; later he studied literature and history at Cheney State Teachers College, Wilberforce University, and, from 1938 to 1941, City College of New York; joined the Young Communist League in 1936 and two years later was sent to New York City as an organizer; during this time he earned a living by singing in various nightclubs, often appearing with Josh White and Huddie Ledbetter; a fervent pacifist, he became disillusioned with the Communists in 1941 and joined the Fellowship of Reconciliation, which he served as field secretary and then race relations secretary until 1953; organized the New York branch of the Congress of Racial Equality (CORE) in 1941; in that same year he served as a youth organizer for A. Philip Randolph's (q.v.) projected March on Washington to protest unfair employment practices in the nation's defense industries; as a result of the threatened march, President Franklin D. Roosevelt set up his federal

Committee on Fair Employment Practices; traveled to California in 1942 to attempt to protect the property of Japanese-Americans who had been incarcerated in work camps during World War II; a conscientious objector, he served two and one-half years in Ashland Correction Institute and Lewisburg Penitentiary during World War II, 1943–1945; became chairman of the Free India Committee in 1945 and later spent six months in India observing and studying Gandhi's movement; helped organize CORE's first "freedom ride" in the South in 1947; became director of A. Philip Randolph's Committee Against Discrimination in the Armed Forces in 1947, which helped convince President Harry S. Truman to issue his executive order in 1948 desegregating the armed forces; was one of the founders of the American Committee on Africa in the early 1950s; became executive secretary of the War Resistors League in 1953; helped organize the bus boycott in Montgomery, Ala., in 1955 and, at Martin Luther King, Jr's., instigation, formulated the initial plans for the Southern Christian Leadership Conference; traveled to England in 1958, where he helped organize the campaign for Nuclear Disarmament's first annual protest march from Aldermaston to London in 1959; helped organize the March on Washington for Jobs and Freedom in 1963; became the executive director of the A. Philip Randolph Institute in 1964 in which capacity he sought to strengthen the ties between the civil rights movement and the American labor movement; a member of numerous public and private boards and agencies, he was also a member of the board of directors of the George Meany Center for Labor Studies; received the American Federation of Labor-Congress of Industrial Organizations' Murray-Green-Meany Award in 1980; politically a Socialist who often supported progressive candidates on the Democratic party ticket; *Current Biography* (1967); *The New York Times*, February 4, 1964; *New York Herald-Tribune Magazine*, July 28, 1964; *Saturday Evening Post*, July 11, 1964; Nelson Lichtenstein, ed., *Political Profiles: The Kennedy Years* (1976), *Political Profiles: The Johnson Years* (1976); Eleanora W. Schoenebaum, ed., *Profiles of an Era: The Nixon-Ford Years* (1979).

RUTTENBERG, Harold Joseph   (1914–   ). Born in St. Paul, Minn., May 22, 1914; son of Charles and Fannie (Weinstein) Ruttenberg; married Katherine Monori on September 23, 1936; two children; moved with family, while still a youth, to western Pennsylvania; during the 1920s, came into contact with the rigors of the miners' lives, including a coal-mine disaster; received a B.A. in economics from the University of Pittsburgh, then worked as a newspaper reporter for a time; by 1934–1935, was deeply involved in advising the rank-and-file militants within the Amalgamated Association of Iron, Steel and Tin Workers who prepared the way for the takeover of that union by the Congress of Industrial Organizations (CIO); was one of several intellectuals recruited by Philip Murray (q.v.) for the CIO's Steel Workers Organizing Committee (SWOC) and became its research director in 1936; in addition to serving as an idea man, acted as an organizer and troubleshooter for SWOC; helped subvert the steel industry's employee representation plans and participated in the "Little Steel" strike of

1937; served during World War II as assistant director of the steel division of the War Production Board; in *The Dynamics of Industrial Democracy*, co-authored with Clinton Golden (q.v.) in 1942, called for union-management cooperation to lower costs and maximize productivity, to be achieved through substitution of an annual system of pay for the established system of hourly wage rates and job classification; resigned from the United Steelworkers of America (USWA) to become vice-president of the Portsmouth Steel Corporation in 1946; established his own steel-fabricating firm in 1951; in order to eliminate the periodic unemployment and unstable annual income resulting from the recurrent steel strikes of the 1950s, urged the USWA to accept a two-year wage freeze in return for a guarantee of annual employment coupled with a reduction in basic steel prices; his concern about strike-induced unemployment was ultimately accepted by the USWA leadership in the Experimental Negotiation Agreement of 1973; authored numerous articles on labor-management policies which appeared in various periodicals; Harold J. Ruttenberg Papers, Labor Archives, Pennsylvania State University; *Harper's* (December 1955); Robert R. R. Brooks, *As Steel Goes, . . . Unionism in a Basic Industry* (1940); *Who's Who in Labor* (1946).

Donald G. Sofchalk

RYAN, Joseph Patrick   (1884–1963). Born in Babylon, N.Y., May 11, 1884; son of James F., a landscape gardener, and Mary (Shanahan) Ryan; Roman Catholic; married Margaret Ann Conners on December 31, 1908; two children; attended St. Xavier's school in the Chelsea district of New York City, completing the sixth grade; worked, beginning at age 12, as a stock boy, clerk, and streetcar conductor; began work on the New York docks in 1912; joined Local 791 of the International Longshoremen's Association (ILA) in 1912 and a year later was elected financial secretary of the local; became a full-time, professional union leader in 1916; elected president of the Atlantic Coast District of the ILA in 1918; during the same year, elected vice-president of the ILA; elected president of the international union in 1927; served as a vice-president of the New York State Federation of Labor for more than 20 years prior to 1946 and served as president of the Central Labor Council of Greater New York and Vicinity, 1928–1938; as a result of conflicts with West Coast ILA locals led by Harry R. Bridges (q.v.), the rival International Longshoremen's and Warehousemen's Union was organized in 1937 and gained control of Pacific ports; headed an American Federation of Labor (AFL) investigation of corruption in the International Seamen's Union (ISU); as a result of the investigation and the AFL-Congress of Industrial Organizations split, the ISU was reorganized into the Seafarers International Union of North America in 1938; elected ILA president for life in 1943; retired after the ILA was expelled from the AFL for corruption in 1953 and named president emeritus with a life-long pension; convicted of violating the Taft-Hartley Act in 1955 by accepting $2,500 from a company employing longshoremen and given a six-month suspended sentence and fined $2,500; the conviction was later overturned on appeal; often brought into conflict with left-

wing unions and unionists because of his obsessive anti-Communism and de-
termined opposition to industrial unionism on the waterfront; during his ILA
incumbency, little militant trade union activity occurred and the ILA became
increasingly dominated by gangsters and racketeers; was a Democrat; died in
New York City, June 26, 1963; Charles P. Larrowe, *Shape-Up and Hiring Hall:
A Comparison of Hiring Methods and Labor Relations on the New York and
Seattle Waterfronts* (1955); Maud Russell, *Men along the Shore* (1966); *Current
Biography* (1949).

RYAN, Martin Francis   (1874–1935). Born in Coldwater, W.Va., October
23, 1874; son of John and Mary (Call) Ryan; Roman Catholic; married Sue Ellen
Myers on April 8, 1904; four children; completed high school, then hired as a
mechanic on the Southern Pacific Railroad in 1894 in Fort Worth, Tex.; was a
charter member of Fort Worth Lodge 23 of the Brotherhood of Railway Carmen
of America (BRCA) in 1899; elected a member of the BRCA executive board
in 1903; elected a general vice-president of the BRCA in 1905, and in 1909,
elected general president, serving until his death; was a member of the American
Federation of Labor (AFL) mission to England, Ireland, Scotland, Wales, and
France in 1918, and, along with Samuel Gompers (q.v.), represented American
labor at the Pan-American Federation of Labor conference in Mexico City in
1924; became a vice-president and member of the AFL executive council in
1923, serving until 1928, when elected AFL treasurer; elected a vice-president
and member of the executive council of the AFL railway employees' department
in 1927; died in Kansas City, Mo., January 17, 1935; Leonard Painter, *Through
50 Years with the Brotherhood of Railway Carmen of America* (1941); Philip
Taft, *The A.F. of L. in the Time of Gompers* (1957); Solon DeLeon, ed., *The
American Labor Who's Who* (1925).

S

SACCO, Nicola   (1891–1927). Born in Torre Maggiore, Italy, on April 22, 1891; son of Michele Sacco, a vineyard and olive orchard owner; reared a Roman Catholic; married in 1912; two children; received a primary school education in Italy before emigrating to the United States in 1908; secured employment as a skilled edger in a Milford, Mass., shoe factory, a job he held, with one exception, until 1920; spent two years in Mexico during World War I, 1917–1918, to avoid the draft; became interested in socialism while working in Massachusetts and ultimately became an advocate of Luigi Galleani's philosophical anarchism; during the red scare that followed World War I, many Galleani anarchists in the United States were imprisoned or deported as dangerous radicals; during this campaign against foreign "reds," the paymaster and a guard of a shoe factory were killed in a robbery on the main street of South Braintree, Mass.; along with Bartolomeo Vanzetti (q.v.), Sacco was charged with the murder, convicted in a trial that reflected more the hysteria of the times than sober justice, and was sentenced to death; several appeals for a retrial were rejected; on June 1, 1927, Governor Alvan T. Fuller of Massachusetts, under considerable pressure, appointed an advisory committee to review the case, and it found the trial fair and the defendants guilty; while their guilt or innocence will probably never be conclusively proven, there can be little doubt that the trial was conducted in a prejudicial manner and that at least a reasonable doubt existed as to their guilt; nevertheless, despite national and international protests, Sacco and Vanzetti were electrocuted in the early morning hours of August 23, 1927; see Bartolomeo Vanzetti; *The Sacco-Vanzetti Case*, 5 Vols. (1928, 1929); Marion Denman Frankfurter and Gardner Jackson, eds., *The Letters of Sacco and Vanzetti* (1928); Felix Frankfurter, *The Case of Sacco and Vanzetti* (1927); *Dictionary of American Biography*, Vol. 16.

ST. JOHN, Vincent   (1876–1929). Born in Newport, Ky., July 16, 1876; son of Irish-Dutch parents; moved around the West with his family, drifting from job to job; settled in Colorado as a prospector and hard-rock miner; by 1901, was president of the Telluride Local of the Western Federation of Miners (WFM) and led the bitter strikes of 1901 and 1903 there; was blacklisted and harassed by state officials and accused of (but not tried for) being an accomplice in the murder of former Idaho governor Frank Steunenberg; was one of the WFM militants and supported the WFM in its important role in establishing the Industrial Workers of the World (IWW) in 1905; as a leader of the faction that sought to commit the IWW to revolutionary industrial unionism, helped wrest control of the national organization from President Charles Sherman (q.v.) at the 1906 convention; as a member of the IWW executive board, went to Goldfield, Nev., and there organized the entire labor force; in 1908, elected general secretary-treasurer (chief national officer) of the IWW, which was nearly broke and had less than ten thousand members; was intelligent, shrewd, and widely respected among Wobblies for his utter dedication to the cause and sustained the IWW as an industrial union dedicated to revolutionary syndicalism; at the 1908 convention, was instrumental in purging all references to political action from the constitution; rather than the renowned ''Big'' Bill Haywood (q.v.), led the IWW during the crucial years in which it recovered, waged free-speech fights, and provided strike leadership during the Lawrence, Mass., and Paterson, N.J., textile strikes; was committed to revolution as the ultimate aim, but, as a former trade unionist, influenced the Wobblies to keep in mind the immediate needs of decent wages and working conditions; was convinced by 1915 that he could do no more for the IWW and resigned as general secretary; in 1917, while prospecting and managing a small mining venture in New Mexico, arrested in the federal government's mass roundup of IWW leaders; although not active in the union since 1915, was convicted and spent several years in federal prison; after being released, resumed his mining activities in Arizona; when his health failed, moved to San Francisco, Calif.; was at one time a member of the Socialist party, but abandoned political action after becoming a Wobbly; authored *The I.W.W.: Its History, Structure and Methods* (1917), an influential manifesto; died in San Francisco, Calif., June 21, 1929; *The Industrial Worker*, June 29, 1929; Elizabeth G. Flynn, *I Speak My Own Piece: Autobiography of ''The Rebel Girl''* (1955); Melvyn Dubofsky, *We Shall Be All: A History of the Industrial Workers of the World* (1969).

Donald G. Sofchalk

SALERNO, Joseph   (1897–1981). Born in Italy on January 3, 1897; son of Guy, a Sicilian immigrant, and Vincenza Salerno; Roman Catholic; married Frances Canner; one child; attended Suffolk Law School for four years and at various times also attended Boston University and the Modern School of Literature and Expression, College of Spoken Work, Brookline, Mass.; settled in Boston, Mass., after immigrating to the United States and secured a job in the garment industry; joined the United Garment Workers of America (UGW) in 1913; when the Amalgamated Clothing Workers of America (ACWA) split off from the UGW, he became one of the ACWA founders in Boston in 1914; led a successful five-month strike of garment workers in Boston; became an international ACWA organizer in 1920, concentrating on the organization of the New England garment industry; left the labor movement in 1928 to attend law school and did not return to union activities until 1934; after the organization of the Congress of Industrial Organizations (CIO) he actively participated in a variety of organizing activities and held numerous offices, including regional director of the Steel Workers Organizing Committee and assistant director, New England Textile Workers Union of America (TWUA), Massachusetts state director, TWUA, and national vice-president of the TWUA; was elected president of the Massachusetts State Industrial Union Council, CIO, in 1940, an office he held until 1948; was elected a national vice-president of the ACWA in 1944; during World War II, he served as chairman of the labor division, United War Fund, chairman of the labor division, American Red Cross, and as a member of the New England War Labor Board, the War Manpower Commission, the War Production Board, and the Massachusetts State Post War Rehabilitation Commission; retired union positions in 1972; was a member of the Greater Boston Industrial Relations Council and the American Arbitration Association; died in Wellesley, Mass., on March 25, 1981; *Advance*, March 1981; *Who's Who in Labor* (1946); *The New York Times*, March 27, 1981; John Gunther, *Inside U.S.A.* (1947).

SARGENT, Frank Pierce   (1854–1908). Born in East Orange, Vt., November 18, 1854; son of Charles Edwin, a farmer, and Mary C. (Kinney) Sargent; married Georgia M. McCullough on October 17, 1881; one child; completed grammar school and attended Northfield Academy, Northfield, Mass., for one year; worked as a textile operative and a farm laborer, then moved to Arizona because of poor health and enlisted in the U.S. cavalry; participated in the campaigns against the Apache Indians, 1878–1880; discharged in 1880, then hired by the Southern Pacific Railroad as an engine wiper; somewhat later, became a locomotive fireman and joined the Brotherhood of Locomotive Firemen and Enginemen (BLFE); elected vice-grand master of the BLFE in 1883 and two years later elected grand master; as grand master during 1885–1902, played a prominent role in the Chicago, Burlington and Quincy strike of 1888 and the American Railway Union strike against the Great Northern Railroad in 1894; appointed to the U.S. Industrial Commission in 1898; declined an appointment as director of the Bureau of Engraving and Printing in 1900; became U.S. Commissioner General of Immigration in 1902; was committed to restricting immigration and was especially critical of the increased immigration from southern and southeastern Europe; as a member of the National Civic Federation, was a confidant of Samuel Gompers (q.v.) and John Mitchell (q.v.) and counseled them during their conferences with President Theodore Roosevelt during the Anthracite Coal Strike of 1902; supported the Republican party; died in Washington, D.C., September 4, 1908; *Dictionary of American Biography*, Vol. 16; *Encyclopedia Americana*, Vol. 24.

SAYRE, Harry DeLoss   (1914–1979). Born in Wabash, Ind., November 26, 1914; son of Loren Burdette, a paper coating machine operator, and Iva May (King) Sayre; married Louise Ethel Van Tilburg on June 18, 1938; two children; graduated from Elkhart (Ind.) High School before taking a job with the American Coating Mills Company in Elkart in 1935; joined the Paper Workers Organizing Committee, Congress of Industrial Organizations (CIO), and served as its financial secretary-treasurer, 1939–1940; moved to Michigan in 1941 where he became an international representative for the United Paper, Novelty and Toy Workers International Union (UPNTWIU); elected international secretary-treasurer of the UPNTWIU in 1942; served on the executive council of the Monroe County Council, Civilian Defense, Monroe, Mich., in 1942; was elected secretary-treasurer of the United Paperworkers of America (UPWA), CIO, in 1946, and was elected president of the UPWA a year later; helped negotiate a merger between the UPWA and the International Brotherhood of Paper Makers, American Federation of Labor (AFL) in 1957, creating the United Papermakers and Paperworkers (UPP); became executive vice-president of the UPP in 1957 and was elected international president in 1968; negotiated a merger with the International Brotherhood of Pulp, Sulphite and Paper Mill Workers in 1972 and was elected senior executive vice-president of the newly chartered United Paperworkers International Union; retired from union activities in 1974; supported the American Labor party during the 1930s and 1940s and then generally supported the Democratic party; died in Ft. Myers, Fla., in July 1979; *Who's Who in Labor* (1946); *AFL-CIO News*, July 14, 1979.

SCARBROUGH, W. Carl   (1935–   ). Born in Henderson, Tenn., May 31, 1935; son of Joseph, a farmer, and Jeannette Scarbrough, a homemaker; married Faye in 1952; two children; graduated from Chester County (Tenn.) High School in 1952; after completing his formal education, he took a job in the furniture industry in Memphis and joined Local 282 of the United Furniture Workers of America (UFW); was elected president of Local 282 in 1962 and during the next eight years expanded the local's membership from three hundred to nearly two thousand; was elected a UFW international vice-president in 1964 and, as a result of this position, was appointed southern regional director of the union at age 29; was elected UFW secretary-treasurer in 1970, and, after serving in that capacity for four years, was elected to the international presidency in 1974 by the UFW executive board after the death of the incumbent, Fred Fulford; edited the *Furniture Workers Press*, the UFW official journal; United Furniture Workers Papers, Southern Labor Archives, Georgia State University; *AFL-CIO News*, March 30, 1974; *Who's Who in Labor* (1976).

SCHILLING, Robert   (1843–1922). Born in Osterburg, Saxony (now part of East Germany), October 17, 1843; Spiritualist; emigrated with his parents to the United States in 1846, settling in St. Louis, Mo.; served an enlistment in the Union Army during the Civil War, then became an apprentice cooper and in 1863 joined the first cooper's union organized in Missouri; elected first vice-president of the Coopers' International Union (CIU) in 1871; moved to Cleveland, Ohio, in 1871 and edited the German-language edition of the *Coopers' Journal*; elected president of the National Industrial Congress in 1874, and a year later, elected president of the CIU; joined the Noble Order of the Knights of Labor (K of L) in 1875; as an enthusiastic advocate of currency inflation, was one of the founders of the Greenback party and served as Ohio state chairman of the party; moved to Milwaukee in 1880 and edited two German-language newspapers, *Der Reformer* and *Volksblatt*; became a state K of L organizer for Wisconsin in 1881 and led the movement to considerable political power in 1885–1886, before ideological conflicts divided the movement; became national secretary of the Union Labor party in 1888 and in 1891 served in the same capacity for the People's (Populist) party, after helping to organize it; during 1892–1900, led the People's party in Wisconsin and several times was an unsuccessful candidate for public office; was opposed to the growing strength of the Socialist party in Milwaukee and successfully negotiated a fusion between Democrats and Populists that temporarily stalled the Socialist initiative; retired from active political participation in 1900 and entered the dairy business; died in Milwaukee, Wis., December 26, 1922; M. Small, "Biography of Robert Schilling" (M.A. thesis, 1953); Thomas W. Gavett, *Development of the Labor Movement in Milwaukee* (1965); *Dictionary of Wisconsin Biography* (1960); *Chicago Workingman's Advocate*, April 11, 1874.

SCHLESINGER, Benjamin   (1876–1932). Born in Krakai, Russian Lithuania (now part of the Soviet Union), December 25, 1876; son of Nechemiah, a rabbi, and Judith Schlesinger; Jewish; married Rae Schanhouse; three children; received a rabbinical education in Krakai prior to emigrating to the United States in 1891; orphaned at age 12; settled in Chicago, Ill., and employed in the garment industry as a sewing-machine operator; served as the secretary of the Chicago Cloakmakers' Union and elected treasurer of the short-lived International Cloakmakers' Union of America in 1892–1893; was one of the founders of the International Ladies' Garment Workers' Union (ILGWU) in 1900; served as business manager of the Chicago Cloakmakers' Union, 1902–1903; elected international president of the ILGWU in 1903, but defeated for reelection the following year; became manager of the *Jewish Daily Forward* in 1907, serving until 1912; again elected president of the ILGWU in 1914; was a member of the general executive board of the International Clothing Workers Federation, 1919–1923; served as an American Federation of Labor fraternal delegate to the British Trades Union Congress in 1922; resigned as ILGWU president in 1923 and resumed association with the *Jewish Daily Forward*; elected vice-president of the ILGWU in 1928 and upon the resignation of the incumbent, Morris Sigman (q.v.), became president for the third time; was a skilled bargainer and negotiator, but had a domineering and exacerbating personality, which reduced his ability for leadership; was a Socialist; authored several pamphlets and during 1914–1917 edited *The*

Ladies' Garment Worker; died in a sanitarium in Colorado Springs, Colo., June 6, 1932; Benjamin Schlesinger Papers, ILGWU Archives; Benjamin Stolberg, *Tailor's Progress: The Story of a Famous Union and the Men Who Made It* (1944); Louis Levine, *The Women's Garment Workers; A History of the International Ladies' Garment Workers' Union* (1924); *Dictionary of American Biography,* Vol. 16; Melech Epstein, *Profiles of Eleven* (1965), and *Jewish Labor in the U.S.A., 1914–1952,* 2 Vols. (1953).

SCHLOSSBERG, Joseph (1875–1971). Born in Koidanovo (now Dzerzhinsk), Belorussia, Russia, May 1, 1875; son of Max, a tailor, and Bessie (Feldman) Schlossberg; Jewish; married Anna Grossman on September 5, 1905; two children; emigrated to the United States in 1888 and, after attending the public schools of New York City for one year, began work as a cloak maker in the New York City garment industry; while involved in the organization of garment workers during the 1890s, joined the Socialist Labor party and edited its Yiddish language journals, *Das Abend Blatt,* 1899–1902 and *Der Arbeiter,* 1904–1911; attended the Columbia University School for Political Science, 1905–1907; supported a group of New York City tailors striking against the wishes of their parent organization, the United Garment Workers of America, in 1913, and led a secessionist movement that resulted in the organization of the United Brotherhood of Tailors (UBT); elected secretary of the New York Joint Board of the UBT; was one of the founders of the Amalgamated Clothing Workers of America (ACWA) in 1914 and elected general secretary-treasurer of the new organization; served as a fraternal delegate to the Congress for Labor, Palestine, 1918, the International Congress of Clothing Workers, Copenhagen, 1920, and the Mexican Federation of Labor, Juarez, 1924; was a charter member of the National Labor Committee for Labor, Israel and elected chairman in 1934; appointed to the New York City Board of Higher Education in 1935, serving until 1963; resigned union positions in 1940 to devote further time and effort to Zionist and community affairs; after the establishment of the State of Israel, joined the Histadrut, the Israel General Federation of Labor; was a director of the American Civil Liberties Union, the American Association for Jewish Education, and the Yiddish Scientific Institute; edited the ACWA weekly *Advance* for several years; authored *The Workers and Their World* (1935); died in New York City, January 15, 1971; Joseph Schlossberg Papers, Catherwood Library, Cornell University; Matthew Josephson, *Sidney Hillman: Statesman of American Labor* (1952); Erma Angevine, *In League with the Future* (1959); Joel Seidman, *The Needle Trades* (1942); Melech Epstein, *Jewish Labor in the U.S.A., 1914–1952,* 2 Vols. (1953).

SCHNEIDER, George John (1877–1939). Born in Grand Chute, Wis., on October 30, 1877; parents were farmers of German derivation; never married; Congregationalist; moved with his family to Appleton, Wis., where he attended public schools and learned the paper-making trade; as a youth and a young man, he worked in paper mills in Wisconsin, Minnesota, Maine, California, and Missouri; became a member of the International Brotherhood of Paper Makers (IBPM) about 1900; selected as a general organizer in 1907; organized paper mill workers throughout the early 1900s, sometimes under direct American Federation of Labor auspices; elected second vice-president of the IBPM in 1909 and kept that position until his death; member of the executive board of the Wisconsin State Federation of Labor, 1923–1939; elected to the U.S. Congress from Wisconsin's eighth District, 1922–1932, as a progressive Republican; continued his active role in IBPM while in Congress; defeated for reelection in 1932 but was reelected in 1934 and 1936; defeated in 1938 for reelection; an early adherent of the Wisconsin Progressive party, formed in 1934, and served as a Progressive in the Seventy-fourth and Seventy-fifth Congresses; served on the post office, civil service, immigration and naturalization, and labor committees of the House; compiled a liberal voting record, generally supporting New Deal legislation; a strong supporter of the Walsh-Healy Act and wage and hour legislation; died during an IBPM convention at Toledo, Ohio, on March 12, 1939; *Appleton* (Wis.) *Post-Crescent*, March 13, 1939; *Dictionary of Wisconsin Biography* (1960); *Biographical Directory of the American Congresses* (1971); Matthew J. Burns Papers, documentary biographical material, June 10, 1958, Archives Division, State Historical Society of Wisconsin.

                                                                  Barbara Bartkowiak

SCHNEIDERMAN, Rose   (1884–1972). Born in Savin, Russian Poland, April 6, 1884 (birthdate is listed as 1882 in *All for One*); daughter of Samuel, a tailor, and Deborah (Rothman) Schneiderman; Jewish; emigrated to the United States in 1890; attended the public schools of New York until age 13, then began work in a New York department store; secured employment as a lining maker in the hat and cap industry in 1899 and four years later helped organize Local 23 of the United Cloth Hat and Cap Makers of North America (UCHCM); served as a delegate to the Central Federated Union of New York City during 1903; was the first woman elected to the general executive board of the UCHCM in 1904; joined the Women's Trade Union League (WTUL) in 1905; became vice-president of the New York WTUL in 1907 and a part-time organizer for the national WTUL in 1908; became a full-time organizer for the national WTUL in 1910 and was elected to its executive board in 1911; served as an International Ladies' Garment Workers' Union organizer, 1914–1916; resumed work with the WTUL in 1917 and was elected its president in 1918; served as a WTUL vice-president, 1919–1926, and as president, 1926–1947; was a delegate to the International Congress of Working Women meeting in Washington, D.C., in 1920; was the only woman appointed to the Labor Advisory Board of the National Industrial Recovery Administration in 1933; investigated the needle trades industry in Puerto Rico for the National Recovery Administration in 1934; was secretary of the New York State Department of Labor, 1933–1944; was a political activist and chaired the industrial section of the Woman Suffrage party of New York

City, 1916–1917; ran unsuccessfully for the New York Senate on the Farmer-Labor ticket in 1920; headed the women's division of the American Labor party; although nominally a Socialist, usually supported Democratic candidates; served on the board of trustees, Brookwood Labor College, 1924–1929; was an honorary vice-president of the United Hatters, Cap and Millinery Workers' International Union; authored, with Lucy Goldthwaite, *All for One* (1967); died in New York City, August 11, 1972; Rose Schneiderman Papers, Schlesinger Library, Radcliffe College; Gladys Boone, *The Women's Trade Union Leagues in Great Britain and the United States of America* (1942); Agnes Nestor, *Woman's Labor Leader: An Autobiography of Agnes Nestor* (1954); Donald B. Robinson, *Spotlight on a Union: The Story of the United Hatters, Cap and Millinery Workers' International Union* (1948); Leon Stein, *The Triangle Fire* (1962); Susan Ware, *Beyond Suffrage* (1981); Gary Endelman, "Solidarity Forever: Rose Schneiderman and the Woman's Trade Union League" (Ph.D. diss., 1978); *Notable American Women*, Vol. 4; Philip S. Foner, *Women and the American Labor Movement from Colonial Times to the Eve of World War I* (1979), and *Women and the American Labor Movement from World War I to the Present* (1980).

Marie Tedesco

SCHNITZLER, William F. (1904–   ). Born in Newark, N.J., January 21, 1904; son of Wilhelm, a metal polisher, and Marie (Weithenwit) Schnitzler; married Edith Eckert on September 12, 1931; two children; after attending the public schools of Newark, N.J., began work at age 14 in an ammunition factory during World War I; after working briefly in a metal grinding shop, became an apprentice baker in 1920; joined Local 84 of the Bakery and Confectionery Workers' International Union of America (BCWIU) in 1924; elected business agent of Local 84 in 1934, serving until 1937; became an international representative in 1941; elected a BCWIU vice-president and financial secretary in 1943; elected to the newly created position of secretary-treasurer in 1946; became the international president of the BCWIU in 1950; replaced George Meany (q.v.) as the secretary-treasurer of the American Federation of Labor (AFL) in 1952; was one of the three AFL delegates meeting with Congress of Industrial Organizations' (CIO) representatives to work out a merger of the two labor federations in 1955; elected secretary-treasurer of the newly merged AFL-CIO; served as a fraternal delegate from the AFL-CIO to the British Trades Union Congress in 1956; attended the International Confederation of Free Trade Unions' (ICFTU) African Regional Conference in 1956 and the Tunis conference of the ICFTU in 1957 as an AFL-CIO fraternal delegate; was appointed to the Labor Advisory Committee by the U.S. Secretary of Labor in 1955; became chairman of the reorganized AFL-CIO civil rights committee in 1961; retired union positions in 1969; usually supports the Democratic party; Joseph C. Goulden, *Meany* (1972); *Current Biography* (1965); *Fortune* (January 1953); *The American Federationist* (November 1952); *AFL-CIO News*, May 10, 1969; *Who's Who in America, 1968–1969*.

SCHOEMANN, Peter Theodore   (1893–1976). Born in Milwaukee, Wis., October 26, 1893; son of Paul, a laborer, and Mary (Bauer) Schoemann; Roman Catholic; married Mary Margaret Furey on October 21, 1925; three children; began to work full-time after finishing elementary schooling in the public schools of Milwaukee; became an apprentice in the plumbing industry and joined Local 75 of the United Association of Plumbers and Steam Fitters of the United States and Canada (UA) in 1914; served successively as recording secretary and business representative of Local 75; was chairman of the credentials committee of UA national conventions, 1928–1932, and chairman of the laws committee in 1942; elected president of the Milwaukee Building and Construction Trades Council in 1932, serving until 1952; during World War II, was a regional labor representative on the War Manpower Commission; after serving as a UA vice-president for several years, became acting president in 1953 after appointment of the incumbent, Martin P. Durkin (q.v.), as U.S. Secretary of Labor; elected UA president after the death of Durkin in 1955; became an American Federation of Labor-Congress of Industrial Organizations' (AFL-CIO) vice-president and executive council member in 1957; appointed chairman of the AFL-CIO committee on education and also served on its committee on economic policy; was a conservative trade unionist; became one of the principal spokesmen for the building trades in the AFL-CIO; served on several public boards and agencies, including posts as vice-president of the Milwaukee Housing Authority, chairman of the Wisconsin Board of Vocational and Adult Education, a member of the Milwaukee School Board and certifying officer for Milwaukee County, and a member of the advisory committee of the Milwaukee civil works administration; a Democrat; retired UA presidency in 1971; died in Milwaukee, Wis., on August 7, 1976; Joseph C. Goulden, *Meany* (1972); *AFL-CIO News*, April 24, August 7, 1971, August 14, 1976; *Who's Who in America, 1970–1971*; *Who's Who in Labor* (1946).

SCHOENBERG, William   (1879–1966). Born in Germany in August 1879; married; two children; after a few years of formal education, became an apprentice machinist and worked at his trade in Germany, Switzerland, and South Africa; was an active trade unionist in both Germany and Switzerland; emigrated to the United States in 1907, settling in Chicago, Ill., and joined the International Association of Machinists (IAM); elected business agent of IAM District 8 in 1913, serving until 1920; served as an IAM international representative, 1920–1933; appointed a personal representative of American Federation of Labor (AFL) President William Green (q.v.) in 1933 and placed in charge of AFL organizing activities in Illinois, Iowa, Indiana, and Missouri; was placed in charge of AFL efforts to organize Portland cement plant employees in 1936; saw these efforts bear fruit in the chartering of the United Cement, Lime and Gypsum Workers International Union (UCLGWU) by the AFL in 1939; elected first president of the UCLGWU in 1939; during his presidency, saw the UCLGWU successfully organize more than 90 percent of the cement plants in the United States and

Canada; retired in 1955 and designated president emeritus; died in Des Plaines, Ill., August 2, 1966; *The American Federation of Labor News-Reporter*, December 31, 1954; *AFL-CIO News*, August 13, 1966.

SCHOLLE, August   (1904–1972). Born in Creighton, Pa., May 23, 1904; son of Henry, a glass worker, and Elizabeth (Danner) Scholle; married Kathleen B. Jones on October 23, 1942; two children; completed one year of high school, then became a glass worker; joined Toledo, Ohio, Local 9 of the Federation of Glass, Ceramic, and Silica Sand Workers of America (FGCSSW)(at the time it was the Federation of Flat Glass Workers; it assumed its current name in 1940) in 1933; while serving as national president of the FGCSSW, 1935–1937, led the union into the Congress of Industrial Organizations (CIO); became a CIO regional director and, while based in Toledo during 1937–1940, helped organize auto and other industrial workers in Ohio and Michigan; served as president of the Michigan Industrial Union Council, CIO, from 1940 until the merger of the CIO and American Federation of Labor (AFL) state bodies in 1958; became president of the AFL-CIO council in the latter year; headed the Michigan CIO Political Action Committee during the 1940s and the Michigan Committee on Political Education (COPE) from 1956; successfully prosecuted a "portal-to-portal" suit to the U.S. Supreme Court in 1946, resulting in millions of dollars in additional wages for affected workers; played a salient role during the 1940s and 1950s in developing a new political strategy whereby unionists involved themselves directly in the organizational structure and electoral machinery of the Democratic party; was instrumental in initiating Michigan labor's voter registration campaigns, especially among the auto workers in Wayne County; was also most responsible for creating, in the late 1940s, the labor-liberal basis of the Michigan Democratic party, thus ensuring the successive electoral triumphs of Governor G. Mennen Williams, 1948–1960; lobbied, with Williams's support, for enactment of a steeply progressive state income tax, but saw the Republican legislative majority prevent its passage; initiated legal action to force redistricting on the basis of the one man, one vote principle, thus aiming to outlaw the rural overrepresentation in Michigan that enabled Republicans to stymie such liberal proposals; through the case of *Scholle vs. Hare* (1959–1962), ultimately brought about equal representation for Michigan cities, and also contributed materially to the U.S. Supreme Court's national application of one man, one vote; served as a delegate to all Democratic national conventions from 1948 to 1964; managed the COPE campaign in a way that was crucial in enabling Hubert H. Humphrey to carry Michigan in the presidential race of 1968; served over the years on numerous public agencies, such as the State Board of Education; was a member of several liberal and civil rights organizations, including the National Association for the Advancement of Colored People; retired from the presidency of the Michigan AFL-CIO in 1971; died in Saginaw Bay, Mich., February 15, 1972; August Scholle Papers, Walter Reuther Library, Wayne State University; Doris B. McLaughlin, *Michigan Labor: A Brief History from 1818 to the Present*

(1970); *AFL-CIO News*, February 19, 1972; *The New York Times*, February 17, 1972; *Who's Who in Labor* (1946); *Who's Who in the Midwest, 1969–1970*.

Donald G. Sofchalk

SCHWAB, Michael   (fl. 1853–1893). Born in Kitringen, Germany, on August 9, 1853; son of a small-trades man; married on June 7, 1884; two children; reared a Roman Catholic; after the death of his parents, he quit school at age 16 and was apprenticed to a bookbinder; after completing his apprenticeship, he joined a bookbinding trade union and began reading Socialist literature; joined the Social Democratic Labor party in 1872; left Wuerrburg, where he had resided for several years, in 1874, and began extensive travels through central Europe, spending much time in Zurich where he continued his studies of Socialist theory; emigrated to the United States in 1879, settling in Chicago, Ill., where he worked as a bookbinder; joined the Socialist Labor party in 1880; later that same year, he began a series of western travels but by the end of the year was back in Chicago where he secured employment as a translator for the *Arbeiter-Zeitung*, a German-language, Socialist newspaper; later became a reporter and assistant editor of the *Arbieter-Zeitung*; joined the anarchist International Working People's Association after it was founded in Pittsburgh, Pa., in 1883; printed notice in the *Arbeiter-Zeitung* announcing the May 4, 1886, meeting at Haymarket Square to protest police violence during a strike at the McCormick Harvesting plant two days earlier; along with eight other radicals, he was later arrested for the murder of a policeman at Haymarket Square, convicted, and sentenced to death; sentence was later commuted to life imprisonment by Illinois Governor Richard J. Oglesby; on June 26, 1893, he was given a full pardon by Governor John P. Altgeld; Philip S. Foner, ed., *The Autobiographies of the Haymarket Martyrs* (1969); Henry David, *The History of the Haymarket Affair* (1963).

SCOTT, Sam H.   (1901–1969). Born in Orange County, N.C., March 1, 1901; son of Edward C., a farmer, and Martha J. Scott; Christian church; married Kathryn C. on January 21, 1943; two children; after graduating from high school, attended Duke University for three years; eventually gained employment in the tobacco industry and joined Local 183 of the International Union of Tobacco Workers (IUTW) in 1933; served as president of IUTW Local 183, 1933–1935; became an IUTW general organizer in 1935, serving in that capacity until 1942; joined the United Stone and Allied Products Workers of America (USAPWA) in 1942 and was appointed its international representative in North Carolina, South Carolina, and Georgia; elected USAPWA international president in 1944; served on the Congress of Industrial Organizations' (CIO) executive board until the 1955 merger with the American Federation of Labor (AFL); represented the USAPWA at the biennial conventions of the AFL-CIO, 1955–1967; served as a vice-president of the North Carolina AFL-CIO for a long period; retired as USAPWA's representative in the Southern region, 1968; was a Democrat; died in Winston-Salem, N.C., January 30, 1969; *Who's Who in Labor* (1946); *AFL-CIO News*, February 1, 1969.

SCULLY, John James Joseph   (1867–1947). Born in South Amboy, N.J., February 10, 1867; son of Stephen, a hotel proprietor and coal shipper, and Mary B. (Kelly) Scully; Roman Catholic; married Mary Ann Coleman on February 8, 1888; received a public and private school education in New Jersey and later attended the U.S. Navy Reserves' Columbia Training University; after completing his formal education, became a marine pilot and in 1890 joined the American Brotherhood of Steamboat Pilots—renamed National Organization of Masters, Mates and Pilots of America (NOMMPA) in 1916; was a member of the eight-hour day committee established in 1890 by American Federation of Labor (AFL) president Samuel Gompers (q.v.) to press for a shorter working day; served as a state and national organizer for the AFL; was an executive officer in the U.S. Navy Reserve and served as the supervisor of a minesweeper training school in New York, 1917–1921; elected secretary-treasurer of the NOMMPA after the war and served in that capacity until 1945; was a regional director of the National Labor Relations Board until 1945; served in several public positions, including two terms as Hudson County, N.J., harbor master, president of the New Jersey State Pilots Commission, and member of a variety of conciliation and arbitration committees; was a Democrat; edited *The Master, Mate and Pilot* magazine until his retirement in 1945; died in Jersey City, N.J., April 5, 1947; *Who's Who in Labor* (1946); *The New York Times*, April 7, 1947.

SEFTON, Lawrence Frederick   (1917–1973). Born in Iroquois Falls, Ontario, Canada, March 31, 1917; son of Harry, an accountant, and Mary (McNeil) Sefton; Roman Catholic; married Elaine Marie Melhuish on July 9, 1943; two children; at age 17, began working as a hard-rock miner in Northern Ontario and soon became recording secretary and organizer for Kirkland Lake local of the International Union of Mine, Mill and Smelter Workers; blacklisted following an unsuccessful strike; moved to Toronto, obtained work in a metal plant, and, in 1942, joined Steel Workers Organizing Committee Local 1039; completed high school while living in Toronto; after serving in the Canadian Army during World War II, was appointed a staff representative of the United Steelworkers of America (USWA); led the USWA campaign to organize workers of the Steel Company of Canada's Hamilton, Ontario, works, the largest Canadian steel mill, in 1946; appointed after this success as senior USWA staff representative for Hamilton and Niagara Peninsula; was elected director of USWA District 6, comprising Ontario and all of western Canada, in 1953; became a vice-president of the newly formed Canadian Labour Congress in 1956; belonged to a small group of district directors indirectly challenging David McDonald's (q.v.) leadership in 1955 by supporting Joseph Molony (q.v.) for USWA vice-president; backed secretary-treasurer I. W. Abel's (q.v.) decision to run against McDonald in 1965; influenced the majority of Canadian locals to nominate Abel, thus significantly strengthening Abel's campaign; as chairman of the Congress of Industrial Organizations' committee on white-collar organization, spoke and wrote widely to dispel the myth that white-collar workers were not receptive to unionization; was a Socialist, but also became deeply involved in support of the New Democratic party of Canada; declined to run again for director in the USWA elections of 1973; died in Toronto, Canada, May 9, 1973; commemorated through the naming of the new USWA Centre in Toronto as the Larry Sefton Building; John Herling, *Right to Challenge: People and Power in the Steelworkers Union* (1972); *Canadian Labor* (June 1965); *Who's Who in Labor* (1946).

Donald G. Sofchalk

SEIDEL, Emil   (1864–1947). Born in Ashland, Pa., on December 13, 1864; son of Otto F., a cabinet maker, and Henrietta S. Seidel; married Lucy Geissel on May 8, 1894; moved to Wisconsin with his parents in 1865 and attended the public schools there until 1877 when, at age 13, he began working at odd jobs before becoming a woodcarver; was one of the organizers of the Wood Carver's Union in Milwaukee, Wis., in 1884 and served as its secretary, 1884–1885; studied woodcarving, modeling, and designing in Germany, 1886–1892; returned to the United States in 1892 and the following year assisted with the German exhibit at the Chicago, Ill., World's Fair Exposition; converted to socialism while living in Germany, he became an active Socialist and was one of the founders of the Socialist party organization in Milwaukee in 1898; was a charter member of the Socialist party of America (SPA) in 1901; was an SPA candidate for governor of Wisconsin in 1902; served as an alderman for the Twentieth Ward of Milwaukee, 1904–1908; defeated for election to the office of mayor in 1908, he was elected an alderman-at-large in 1909; was elected mayor of Milwaukee on the Socialist ticket in 1910, serving until 1912; as mayor of Milwaukee—the first Socialist elected to that position in a major American city—he emphasized honesty, efficiency, and expanded social services but found many of his reform proposals frustrated by anti-Socialist elements at the city and state level; was the SPA vice-presidential candidate in 1912, running on the ticket headed by Eugene V. Debs (q.v.); served as an SPA lecturer and organizer, 1912–1916; was once again elected a Milwaukee alderman-at-large, serving from 1916 to 1920; his vocal opposition to American involvement in World War I often incurred the wrath of local, state, and federal officials; was secretary of the Socialist party of Wisconsin, 1920–1924; went into semiretirement on a Wisconsin farm in 1924, although remaining active in Socialist affairs; was again elected a Milwaukee alderman-at-large in 1932, serving until 1936; died in Wisconsin on June 24, 1947; Solon DeLeon, ed., *The American Labor Who's Who* (1925); *Who's Who in America, 1925–1926*; *Dictionary of Wisconsin Biography* (1960); Thomas W. Gavett, *Development of the Labor Movement in Milwaukee* (1965).

SELDEN, David Seeley   (1914–   ). Born in Dearborn, Mich., June 5, 1914; son of Arthur Willis, a school administrator, and Florence Loretta (Seeley)

Selden; married Bernice Cohen on March 22, 1956, after two divorces; three
children; received a B.A. degree in education from Michigan State Normal
College (now Eastern Michigan University) in 1936 and took a job as a social
studies instructor in a Dearborn, Mich., junior high school; joined the Progressive
Education Association in 1936; joined the Dearborn local of the American Federation of Teachers (AFT) in 1940 and, while serving as the president of the
local, 1940–1943, led the successful efforts to build a strong teachers' union in
the city; received an M.A. degree from Wayne State University in 1940; joined
the U.S. Navy in 1943 and served as a crewman on a destroyer; after the war,
moved to Jacksonville, Fla., and unsuccessfully attempted to pursue a literary
career and to found an experimental college; shortly after returning to classroom
teaching, appointed a full-time organizer by the American Federation of Labor
(AFL) in 1948 and assigned to the AFT; became the AFT's special representative
in New York City in 1953; along with Albert Shanker (q.v.), built United
Federation of Teachers, Local 2, AFT, into a strong, militant trade union; appointed to the newly created post of assistant to the AFT president in 1964,
serving until 1968; served as a delegate to the White House Conference on
Education in 1965; elected president of the AFT in 1968, and during the same
year became a member of the executive board of the AFL-Congress of Industrial
Organizations' industrial union department; was a member of the Urban Task
Force on Education in 1969; sentenced to 60 days in jail for violating an injunction
during the Newark, N.J., teachers' strike of 1970; proved to be a vigorous
proponent of a merger between the AFT and the National Education Association,
but caused considerable divisiveness during the early years of his presidency
through his efforts to reach this objective; defeated for reelection in 1972 and
retired from union affairs; politically a Democrat; Robert J. Braun, *Teachers
and Power: The Story of the American Federation of Teachers* (1972); Stephen
Cole, *The Unionization of Teachers: A Case Study of the UFT* (1969).

SENDER, Toni   (1888–1964). Born in Biebrich, Germany, on November 29,
1888; daughter of Moritz, a department store owner, and Marie (Dreyfuss)
Sender; Jewish; unmarried; attended high school for girls, Biebrich; struggling
against parents' demand for absolute obedience, she left home to attend commercial high school in Frankfurt; after completion of a two-year course, began
work at age 15 in a Frankfurt real-estate office, and joined the Social Democratic
party (SPD); moved to Paris in 1910, taking a position in the office of a metal
company; joined French Socialist party; with the outbreak of war in 1914, she
was forced to return to Germany, where she helped organize opposition to the
war effort, and joined the Independent Social Democratic party (USPD) when
it was formed in 1917; chief editor of *Volksrecht*, USPD's organ for southwest
Germany, 1919–1921; was a leader of the November 1918 revolution in Frankfurt
and was elected to the Frankfurt city council, serving from 1919 to 1924; elected
to the first postwar Reichstag in 1920 and served until the Nazi seizure of power
in 1933; opposed affiliation of the USPD with the Communist International and

rejoined SPD in 1922; editor of the shop council magazine of the metal workers' union, 1920–1933, and of the SPD's women's magazine *Frauenwelt*, 1928–1933; at the invitation of her friend Morris Hillquit (q.v.), she visited the United States for the first time in 1926 and attended the American Federation of Labor (AFL) convention in Detroit; beginning in 1927, she studied economics for five semesters at the University of Berlin; an early fighter against Nazism, she was marked for death by the Nazi secret police and fled in disguise to Czechoslovakia in 1933; edited in Antwerp the Flemish Socialist newspaper, *Volksgazet*, 1933–1935; lectured in the United States in 1934 and 1935, offering Americans one of the first eyewitness accounts of Germany under Nazi rule; settled permanently in the United States in 1936 and became a naturalized citizen in 1943; under the auspices of the American Labor Education Service (ALES) from 1941–1943, she organized and taught classes on American labor to anti-fascist German and Austrian refugees in New York City; in charge of the ALES Teachers' Registry, whose purpose was to put workers' education teachers at the disposal of American unions; worked for the U.S. Office of Strategic Services during World War II; from 1944–1946, she was senior economist with the U.N. Relief and Rehabilitation Administration; represented the AFL, 1946–1950, and the International Confederation of Free Trade Unions (ICFTU), 1950–1956, before the UN Economic and Social Council; was the AFL representative at the sessions of the UN Human Rights Committee in Geneva in January 1948; at the UN she continually demanded an investigation of slave labor in the Soviet Union, which she charged constituted an essential part of the Soviet economy; in 1954, as ICFTU representative, she accused the Franco government of Spain of abolishing free trade unions and torturing labor leaders; at sessions of the UN Commission on the Status of Women in the mid-1950s, she called for equal pay for equal work and equal access for girls to vocational training and education beyond the elementary level; authored *The Autobiography of a German Rebel* (1939); died in New York City on June 26, 1964; Toni Sender Papers, State Historical Society of Wisconsin; *Current Biography* (1950); Wilhelm Sternfeld and Eva Tiedemann, *Deutsche Exil-Literatur* (1970); *The New York Times*, June 27, 1964; *AFL-CIO News*, July 4, 1964; *AFL-CIO Free Trade Union News*, August 1964.

Stephen H. Norwood

SESSIONS, John A.   (1918–1977). Born in Ypsilanti, Mich., on December 7, 1918; married; two children; attended the public schools of Ypsilanti before enrolling in the University of Michigan where he earned the B.A. and M.A. degrees; entered the graduate school of Cornell University, receiving a Ph.D. in English in 1953; was an instructor at the University of Michigan, 1945–1946, and an assistant professor of English at Cornell, 1946–1953; became involved with the trade union movement in 1953 when he served as the executive secretary of the International Ladies' Garment Workers' Union Training Institute and remained in that position until 1961; joined the American Federation of Labor-Congress of Industrial Organizations' (AFL-CIO) department of education in

1961, assuming the position of assistant director; was instrumental in developing the AFL-CIO policy on public education; helped found the National Capitol Labor Historical Society and served as its first president; was a member of the District of Columbia Board of Education, 1964–1970; wrote numerous articles on labor history and education; was co-editor of *Samuel Gompers' Seventy Years of Life and Labor, Writers for Tomorrow*; AFL-CIO president George Meany (q.v.) characterized him as "an able and hard-working staff member whose professional approach was always scholarly, yet responsive to the aspirations of workers and their families"; was a member of the American Federation of Teachers and the American Newspaper Guild; died in Washington, D.C., on April 12, 1977; *Who's Who in Labor* (1976); *AFL-CIO News*, April 16, 1977.

SHANKER, Albert   (1928–   ). Born in New York City, September 14, 1928; son of Morris, a Polish immigrant and newspaper deliveryman, and Mamie (Burko) Shanker, a member of the Amalgamated Clothing Workers of America; Jewish; married Edith Gerber on March 18, 1961; four children (one by a previous marriage); graduated from Stuyvesant High School after attending elementary schools in Queens; earned a B.A. degree in philosophy at the University of Illinois and became active in various Socialist groups at the university; received the M.A. degree in philosophy and mathematics from Columbia University; became a substitute teacher in an East Harlem school in 1952; after transferring to Junior High School 126 in Long Island City, joined the New York Teachers Guild (NYTG); became a member of the union's delegate assembly in 1957 and shortly thereafter elected to the executive board; became an American Federation of Teachers (AFT) vice-president and full-time organizer in 1959; became secretary of the newly founded United Federation of Teachers (UFT), Local 2, AFT, formed through merger of the NYTG with a group of high school teachers; served from 1962 to 1964 as an assistant to the UFT president; became editor of the *United Teacher*, the official organ of the UFT, in 1962; elected UFT president in 1964; led a two-week strike of New York City teachers in 1967, thus leading to conviction for violating a state law prohibiting strikes by public employees and imprisonment for 15 days; led another teacher's strike a year later in opposition to school decentralization believing that decentralization would transfer personnel policies, including the hiring and firing of teachers, to local authorities without safeguards for the employment rights of teachers and would negate collective bargaining provisions affecting those rights; as a result of the 1968 strike, again sentenced to 15 days in jail, this time for defying a court injunction; following merger of the UFT and the New York State Teachers' Association, became the executive vice-president of the newly organized New York State United Teachers; elected AFT president in 1972; served as a vice-president of the New York City Central Labor Council, American Federation of Labor-Congress of Industrial Organizations (AFL-CIO), and the Jewish Labor Committee; acted as a director of the League for Industrial Democracy, and was a vice-chairman of the Liberal party's Trade Union Council; elected an AFL-

CIO vice-president and executive council member in 1973; Stephen Cole, *The Unionization of Teachers: A Case Study of the UFT* (1969); Robert J. Braun, *Teachers and Power: The Story of the American Federation of Teachers* (1972); *Current Biography* (1969).

SHEFFIELD, Horace L., Jr.   (1916–   ). Born in Vienna, Ga., on February 22, 1916; son of Horace L., who became a foreman at the Ford River Rouge production foundry, and Georgie Sheffield; Lutheran; married Mary K. Otto in January 1950; four children; moved with his family to Detroit, Mich., during the 1920s; attended Detroit Institute of Technology, 1936–1940, Wayne State University (WSU), 1948–1949, and the University of California at Los Angeles, 1951–1952; honorary Doctor of Laws degree, WSU, 1972; began work as a general laborer at the River Rouge foundry in 1934; was active in the Metropolitan Detroit National Association for the Advancement of Colored People's (NAACP) youth councils in the late 1930s and early 1940s; served as president of the Westside NAACP Youth Council; joined the United Automobile Workers of America (UAW) and was active in the Ford organizing drives of 1940 and thereafter; led a delegation to the UAW international executive board in 1940 to urge creation of an inter-racial committee (the forerunner of the UAW's fair practices committee established in 1945); was a member of A. Philip Randolph's (q.v.) March on Washington committee in 1941; served as a UAW committeeman, 1940–1942, education director, UAW Local 600 Foundry Unit, 1941–1942, appointed to UAW international staff in 1942, and worked with the defense employment department; named first executive secretary of the Michigan State Congress of Industrial Organizations (CIO) civil rights department in 1943; during the 1944 national elections, he worked with Sidney Hillman (q.v.), director of the CIO Political Action Committee (PAC), and was named Michigan CIO-PAC coordinator; became president of Local 600 Foundry Unit in 1946 and served also in that capacity, 1953–1955; was a member of the national Ford negotiation committee in 1955 that negotiated the first supplementary unemployment benefits; as UAW-PAC national staff representative in 1955, he went to Birmingham, Ala., to assist in voter registration and, for the next 12 years, on assignments including working in the South on civil rights, voter registration, and fund raising—frequently working in concert with American Federation of Labor-CIO Committee on Political Education; founded the Trade Union Leadership Council (TULC) in 1957, a labor-community organization in Detroit and elsewhere seeking expansion of civil rights within the unions and the general community economically and politically; served as TULC administrative vice-president and was frequently the center of controversy within the UAW in the late 1950s, as he pressed the international and Local 600 leadership for more progress in eliminating discriminatory barriers for black workers; worked successfully through TULC and other community organizations—black and white—to promote black and white liberal candidates in Detroit, the state, and the nation; from 1943 on, he was a tenacious advocate of the elevation of a black to the

UAW international executive board (IEB); from 1967 to 1974, he served as administrative assistant to Nelson Jack Edwards, the first black chosen to the UAW IEB (1962); was author of the column, "As I See It," on union political and public affairs for the *Michigan Chronicle*, since the early 1950s; was moderator of the Freedom Forum, a half-hour weekly program on radio station WCHB from early 1961 to the early 1970s; served as administrative assistant to UAW presidents Leonard Woodcock (q.v.), 1975–1978, and Douglas Fraser (q.v.), 1978–1981; retired on March 31, 1981; organized the Detroit Association of Black Organizations (DABO) in February 1979 (it reached 137 affiliates by November 1982); served as DABO president from May 1981; "A Salute to . . . Horace L. Sheffield," "Biographical Sketch of Horace L. Sheffield," and other items in the Horace L. Sheffield Papers, Walter P. Reuther Library, Wayne State University.

Robert H. Zieger

SHELLEY, John Francis (1905–   ). Born in San Francisco, Calif., September 3, 1905; son of Denis, a longshoreman, and Mary (Casey) Shelley; Roman Catholic; married Genevieve Giles in September 1932; three children; after attending both parochial and public schools in San Francisco, became a bakery wagon driver and joined Local 484 of the International Brotherhood of Teamsters, Chauffeurs, Warehousemen and Helpers of America (IBT) in 1929; graduated from the University of San Francisco Law School in 1932; elected vice-president of IBT Local 484 in 1935; elected vice-president of the San Francisco Labor Council in 1936 and the following year became president, serving until 1948; elected to the California State Senate in 1938 and reelected in 1942; was Democratic floor leader in the California Senate, 1942–1946; during World War II, served on temporary duty with the U.S. Coast Guard; ran unsuccessfully for lieutenant governor of California on the Democratic ticket in 1946; elected president of the California State Federation of Labor in 1947 and served until his resignation in 1964; ran unsuccessfully against James R. Hoffa (q.v.) for the IBT presidency in 1957; elected mayor of San Francisco in 1963 and served until 1968; became a legislative lobbyist for the city of San Francisco in 1969; was a delegate to the Democratic party's national conventions of 1940 through 1960; Philip Taft, *Labor Politics American Style: The California State Federation of Labor* (1968); *Who's Who in Labor* (1946).

SHERMAN, Charles O. (fl. 1894–1907). Blacklisted in the Pullman strike of 1894; appointed an American Federation of Labor (AFL) organizer, 1902–1903, by Samuel Gompers (q.v.); during that period, founded and served as general secretary of the United Metal Workers International Union; helped the union raid other AFL affiliates in the metal trades as soon as it was chartered by the AFL; beginning in November 1904, participated in the secret meetings that issued a manifesto calling for the founding of the Industrial Workers of the World (IWW); was representative of the IWW group that Ben Williams (q.v.), editor of *Solidarity*, called "also-rans," craft unionists wishing to return to the union movement out of personal ambition or hope for personal profit; at the IWW's founding convention in 1905, was elected the first and only president; during his one-year administration, appointed incompetent organizers and contracted to purchase union labels and insignia from a firm in which he had a personal financial interest; at the IWW's second convention, in September 1906, saw insurgents led by Daniel DeLeon (q.v.) take control of the convention, abolish the office of president, transfer its powers to the general organizer, and elect William Trautmann (q.v.) to that office; supported by factions within the Socialist party and the Western Federation of Miners, briefly maintained a rival IWW, seized physical control of union headquarters, expelled Trautmann from office, ruled the 1905 constitution still in force and the 1906 convention's actions null and void, published the *Industrial Worker* in Joliet, Ill., requested that all per capita payments be paid to the "legal" organization, and appealed to the courts for injunctive relief; watched his organization collapse in 1907 with the courts ruling in favor of the DeLeon-Trautmann faction and the Western Federation of Miners failing to affiliate and pay per capita tax to either organization; Melvyn Dubofsky, *We Shall Be All: A History of the Industrial Workers of the World* (1969).

John W. Hevener

SHIELDS, James Percy   (1889–1953). Born in Neoga, Ill., June 9, 1889; son of an Illinois farmer; married; one child; attended West Salem (Ill.) High School prior to becoming a fireman on the Michigan Central Railroad at the age of 17; during the following several years worked as a fireman for several Midwestern and Southwestern railroads; became an engineer in 1916 and joined Evanston, Wyo., Division 136 of the Brotherhood of Locomotive Engineers (BLE); was elected chairman of Division 136 in 1926; became vice-chairman of the eastern division of the Union Pacific Railroad in 1931 and chairman the following year; became acting assistant grand chief engineer in 1939, and was elected to the position in 1942; elected grand chief engineer of the BLE in 1950; condemned the government seizure of railroads during labor-management disputes, and also criticized the St. Lawrence Seaway and other competitive fields of transportation; died in Cleveland, Ohio, June 29, 1953; Reed C. Richardson, *The Locomotive Engineer, 1863–1963: A Century of Railway Labor Relations and Work Rules* (1963); *Current Biography* (1951); *Labor*, July 4, 1953.

SIDELL, William   (1915–   ). Born in Chicago, Ill., on May 30, 1915; son of Samuel, a carpenter and cabinetmaker, and Fannie (Freeman) Sidell, a homemaker; married Frankie, a homemaker, in 1936; three children; graduated from Belmont High School, Los Angeles, Calif.; after completing his formal schooling, he apprenticed as a carpenter and in 1939 joined Los Angeles Local 721 of the United Brotherhood of Carpenters and Joiners (UBC); served as business manager, Local 721, 1948–1957; was elected secretary-treasurer of the fifty five thousand-member Los Angeles District Council of Carpenters in 1957 and held that position until being elected to the UBC general executive board in 1963; was a member of the California Governor's Advisory Committee on Housing, 1957–1963, and was a trustee for the Carpenters Health and Welfare Fund for Southern California and the Carpenters Pension Trust for Southern California, 1957–1963; served as second UBC general vice-president, 1964–1969, and first general vice-president, 1969–1972; was elected general president of the UBC in 1972; elected a vice-president and member of the executive council of the American Federation of Labor-Congress of Industrial Organizations (AFL-CIO) in 1972; served on the executive committee of the AFL-CIO building and construction trades department, 1972–1979; also chaired the AFL-CIO executive council's committee on housing, 1972–1979; retired union offices in 1979; *Who's Who in Labor* (1976); *AFL-CIO News*, October 20, 1979.

SIEMILLER, Paul Leroy   (1904–   ). Born in Gothenberg, Neb., September 4, 1904; son of Israel Frank, a soldier and farmer, and Lillie May (Sherman); Baptist; married Thelma Mary East on February 16, 1926; one child; attended the public schools of St. Cloud, Fla.; after completion of his formal education, traveled extensively, working at a variety of odd jobs prior to settling in Atlanta, Ga., to serve an apprenticeship as a machinist; during World War I, served with the U.S. Navy; resumed his travels after the war, working as a machinist for various railroad shops; joined International Association of Machinists (IAM) Lodge 823, Port Arthur, Tex., in 1929; laid off during the depression, but moved to Arkansas and secured employment with the Missouri and Arkansas Railroad; joined Harrison, Ark., Lodge 1093 and served it as financial secretary and then president; became a general IAM representative in 1937 and was assigned to organizing activities on the Pennsylvania Railroad; during World War II, served as a labor member of the Sixth Regional War Labor Board; was an American Federation of Labor (AFL) delegate to the International Labor Organization in 1947; was elected an international vice-president and member of the IAM executive board in 1948 and became a Midwestern supervisor; served as director of the manpower division of the Defense Transport Administration in 1951; elected international president of the renamed International Association of Machinists and Aerospace Workers in 1965; was co-chairman of the American Foundation on Automation and Unemployment in 1966; became a vice-president and executive council member of the AFL-Congress of Industrial Organizations in 1965; belonged to numerous public and private boards and agencies; was a political activist, advocating a large role for organized labor in national elections and in legislative lobbying; supported the Democratic party; retired union positions in 1969; *Current Biography* (1966); *Who's Who in America, 1972–1973*.

SIGMAN, Morris   (1881–1931). Born in Costesh, Bessarabia, Russia, May 15, 1881; son of Samuel, a farmer and lumberjack, and Rebecca (Sikernetsky)

Sigman; Jewish; married Mathilda Sikernetsky on March 17, 1912; received little formal education; after working as a lumberjack, emigrated to London in 1902 and obtained employment in a men's clothing factory; emigrated to the United States a year later and secured employment as a presser in a New York cloak shop; organized the independent Cloak and Skirt Pressers' Union in 1904 and later affiliated it with Daniel DeLeon's (q.v.) Socialist Trade and Labor Alliance; helped it to become one of the original unions comprising the Industrial Workers of the World (IWW) a year later; became disillusioned with the dual union activities of the IWW, and thus led his union into the International Ladies' Garment Workers' Union (ILGWU) in 1908; helped organize the New York Joint Board of Cloakmakers in 1909 and served as its general manager, 1910–1913; served as a vice-president of the ILGWU during the same period; chaired the picket committee during the historic strikes of 1910 that established the ILGWU as the principal bargaining agent for New York garment makers; indicted and arrested in 1914–1915 for murder as a result of incidents occurring during the 1910 strike, but acquitted after spending several months in jail; was secretary-treasurer of the ILGWU, 1914–1915; served as business manager of the New York Joint Board of Cloakmakers, 1917–1921; became first vice-president of the ILGWU in 1920 and president in 1923; resigned in 1928 after successfully conducting a long and divisive struggle to prevent a Communist takeover of the union; retired to a small farm near Storm Lake, Iowa; died there on May 20, 1931; Morris Sigman Papers, ILGWU Archives; Louis Levine, *The Women's Garment Workers: A History of the International Ladies' Garment Workers' Union* (1924); Benjamin Stolberg, *Tailor's Progress: The Story of a Famous Union and the Men Who Made It* (1944); *Dictionary of American Biography*, Vol. 17.

SINEY, John   (1831–1880). Born in Bornos, County Queens, Ireland, July 31, 1831; son of Patrick, a small farmer, and Catherine Siney; Roman Catholic; married Mary Hennessey, and, after her death in 1862, Margaret Behan on November 6, 1876; two children; at age 5, moved with his family to Wigan, Lancashire, England; began working in the cotton mills there two years later and kept working for nine years; became an apprentice bricklayer in 1849, and in his early twenties helped to organize the Bricklayers' Association of Wigan; elected president of the association seven times; emigrated to St. Clair, Schuylkill County, Pa., in 1863, and worked as an anthracite miner until 1868; participated in strikes in 1864 and 1868, the first to win a wage increase and the second to resist a wage reduction; in 1868, founded with 15 other miners and was elected the first president of the Workingman's Benevolent Association of St. Clair to resist wage cuts, settle grievances, provide sickness, accident, and death benefits, and improve intellectual life; chaired a convention of delegates in July 1868, representing twenty thousand anthracite miners that founded the Workingman's Benevolent Association (later the Miners' and Laborers' Benevolent Association) of Schuylkill County; served as the association's president at $1,500 per year until 1874; declined the nomination by the National Labor Union convention in 1869 to be its first vice-president; chaired the founding convention of the Labor Reform party at Columbus, Ohio, in 1872; owned and published *The Workingman* for one year, 1873–1874, at Pottsville, Pa.; chaired a Youngstown, Ohio, convention of 42 delegates from five states in 1873 that founded the first national miners' union, the Miners' National Association (MNA), which gained thirty five thousand members by 1875 but was destroyed by the depression; was elected president of the MNA three times; president of the Independent party in 1875 and vice-president of the Greenback party in 1878; participated in the formation of the Greenback Labor party; became a truck farmer and tavern keeper in St. Clair in 1876; died in St. Clair, Pa., April 16, 1880; Edward Pinkowski, *John Siney: The Miners Martyr* (1963); David Montgomery, *Beyond Equality: Labor and the Radical Republicans, 1862–1872* (1967); Ray Boston, *British Chartists in America, 1839–1900* (1971); Chicago *Workingman's Advocate*, November 22, 1973; Charles E. Killeen, "John Siney: The Pioneer in American Industrial Unionism and Industrial Government" (Ph.D. diss., 1975).

John W. Hevener

SKEFFINGTON, Henry J.   (fl. 1858–1889). Born March 5, 1858, at Marysville, Yuba County, Calif., of Irish parents; moved soon after to Philadelphia, Pa.; educated in Catholic schools; at 13 was sent to Portage City, Wis., to study for priest's orders; after one year returned to Philadelphia; after being apprenticed to several trades, learned trade of shoemaking; joined Shoemakers' Local Assembly No. 64 in winter of 1878; was soon advanced from subordinate offices to be master workman; while in that office, successfully resisted reduction of wages, and helped women employees to recover what had been a large reduction; largely by his efforts, shoemakers got charters as locals of their own; in spring of 1884, organized the Brussels carpet weavers, the first local of that trade in Philadelphia; November 15, 1884, two thousand ingrain carpet weavers voted a strike against reduction of wages; three weeks later, he recruited them all as members of Knights of Labor; in January 1885, was sent to New York to organize shoemakers; worked for over three years to organize his craft nationally; finally founding, in June 1884, the National Executive Council of Shoe and Leather Workers of America, Knights of Labor; was delegate repeatedly to important conventions; clashed with Terence V. Powderly (q.v.) over the chartering of a national trade assembly of shoemakers, after which Powderly sought to have him expelled from the Knights of Labor at its 1888 national convention: when that effort failed, Powderly then sought to have him suspended, but without success; thereafter Skeffington issued a call on February 19, 1889, for a national meeting of boot and shoe worker locals which resulted in the formation of the Boot and Shoe Workers International Union which then affiliated with the American Federation of Labor; Skeffington later became an agent for the William L. Douglas Company of Brockton, Mass., an organized firm which carried the union label on its products; Augusta Emile Galster, *The Labor Movement in the*

Shoe Industry (1924); George E. McNeill, *The Labor Movement: The Problem of To-Day* (1887).

George E. McNeill

SKIDMORE, Thomas (1790–1832). Born in Newtown, Fairfield County, Conn., August 13, 1790; married in 1821; proved a gifted student and, at age 13, was appointed a teacher in the Newtown district school; after teaching there for five years, moved to Weston, Conn., for one year and thereafter taught at Princeton and Bordentown, N.J., Richmond, Va., and Edenton and Newbern, N.C.; moved to Wilmington, Del., in 1815 and began a new career in chemical and mechanical research, concentrating on improvements in the manufacture of gunpowder, wire drawing, and paper making; after moving to New York City in 1819, secured employment as a machinist; actively supported the National Republican party and John Q. Adams in the national elections of 1828; was one of the principal founders of the New York Workingmen's party, and was a leading figure in the Committee of Fifty that formulated the platform of the new party; published *The Rights of Man to Property* in 1829, elaborating the agrarian principles upon which he hoped to build a labor reform movement; was nominated for the New York assembly by the Workingmen's party in 1829 but was narrowly defeated; after being forced out of the Workingmen's party, along with his agrarian reformers late in 1829, organized a new party but never made it successful; briefly published a newspaper, *The Friend of Equal Rights*; was a controversial reformer, often characterized as overly zealous and arrogant, but was nevertheless a legitimate radical leading the Workingmen's party at the time of its greatest power and influence; died in New York City during a cholera epidemic in the summer of 1832; Walter Hugins, *Jacksonian Democracy and the Working Class: A Study of the New York Workingmen's Movement, 1829–1837* (1960); Edward Pessen, *Most Uncommon Jacksonians: The Radical Leaders of the Early Labor Movement* (1967), and "Thomas Skidmore: Agrarian Reformer in the Early American Labor Movement," *New York History* (July 1954); John R. Commons et al., *History of Labour in the United States*, Vol. 1 (1918).

SLAMM, Levi D. (fl. 1833–1850). Born in New York City, ca. 1800; although apparently serving an apprenticeship as a locksmith, was listed as a grocer during the period 1833–1837; began his association with the labor movement as a delegate from the Journeymen Locksmith's Society to the General Trades' Union of New York in 1835; besides serving the General Trades as a director of its journal and corresponding secretary, active on several committees and sponsored resolutions covering a variety of subjects; served during 1835 and 1836 as a delegate to the conventions of the National Trades' Union, acting as corresponding secretary and playing an instrumental role in the formulation of the organization's prison labor policy; was involved, despite threats of imprisonment, in the meetings organized to protest the sentencing of striking journeymen tailors in 1837; increasingly active during the second half of the 1830s in

New York politics; closely identified himself with the reformist, Locofoco Equal Rights party often derisively referred to as "Slamm Bang & Co."; ran as a candidate for the state assembly on the Locofoco ticket in 1837 and shortly after the election was named recording secretary of the Equal Rights party; having seen the Panic of 1837 crush the neophyte labor movement, devoted his energies to politics and to publishing the reformist *New Era* in 1840 and the *Daily Plebeian* somewhat later; joined the Tammany Society in 1842 and thereafter fairly consistently supported the Democratic party; exercised considerable influence on the labor movement, despite some questions raised by others about the sincerity of his commitment to the labor movement and about his political opportunism; Walter Hugins, *Jacksonian Democracy and the Working Class: A Study of the New York Workingmen's Movement, 1829–1837* (1960); Edward Pessen, *Most Uncommon Jacksonians: The Radical Leaders of the Early Labor Movement* (1967); John R. Commons et al., eds., *A Documentary History of American Industrial Society*, Vol. 6 (1910); Frederic Byrdsall, *History of the Loco-Foco or Equal Rights Party* (1842).

SMITH, Stanton Everett   (1905–   ). Born in Wyoming, Ohio, on August 29, 1905; son of Charles Henry, an accountant, and Stella Blanche (Keith) Smith; Baptist; married Nancy Virginia Lea, a teacher, on March 19, 1932; four children; received early education from the McCallie School, Chattanooga, Tenn., 1922–1924; studied at Denison University, Denison, Ohio, 1924–1930, earning the B.A. degree; attended the University of Wisconsin in 1930 and later took courses at the University of Chattanooga while teaching high school mathematics in Chattanooga; joined the American Federation of Teachers (AFT) in 1932; served as president of AFT Local 246, 1932–1939; elected national vice-president of the AFT in 1937, serving until 1946; served as secretary-treasurer of the Chattanooga Central Labor Union, 1941–1956; worked as education director of the southeastern region of the International Ladies' Garment Workers' Union, 1942–1945; elected president of the Tennessee Federation of Labor, American Federation of Labor (AFL) in 1949, serving until 1956; after the merger of the AFL and the Congress of Industrial Organizations (CIO), he was elected president of the Tennessee State Labor Council, AFL-CIO, in 1956, serving until 1960; became the coordinator of state and local central bodies for the AFL-CIO in 1960; helped establish the Southern Labor School operated by 13 southern AFL-CIO state councils and served the school as its secretary-treasurer and president at various times; was also active in community and governmental affairs, serving on the Electric Power Board of Chattanooga, 1935–1940, 1950–1955, on the Chattanooga-Hamilton County Planning Commission, 1945–1955, as a member of the National Policy and Performance Council appointed by the U.S. Department of Housing, Education and Welfare, 1970–1973, and on the executive committee of the President's Commission on Employment of the Handicapped, 1961–1974; became assistant director of the AFL-CIO department of organization and field services on April 1, 1974; retired union position in July 1974; wrote numerous articles for the *American Teacher*; biographical information held by the Southern Labor Archives, Georgia State University; *Who's Who in Labor* (1946, 1976); *AFL-CIO News*, June 29, 1974.

SODERSTROM, Reuben G.   (1888–1970). Born in Wright County, Minn., March 10, 1888; son of John F., a minister and shoe merchant, and Anna (Ericson) Soderstrom; married Jeanne M. Shaw on December 2, 1912; two children; after completing the seventh grade, moved to Streator, Ill., and secured work in a glass factory at age 12; became an apprentice printer a few years later and, in 1910, joined the International Typographical Union; soon became president of his local union; was president of the Streator Trades and Labor Assembly, 1913–1920; was elected in 1916 to the Illinois Assembly as an independent Republican; served in that capacity for 16 years and authored or promoted many bills, including the Illinois Anti-injunction Act of 1925 and measures to assist disabled and disadvantaged women and children; as chairman of the house education committee in the 1920s, advocated massive state aid for education; became president of the Illinois State Federation of Labor in 1930, a position retained until 1958; elected president in the latter year of the newly formed American Federation of Labor-Congress of Industrial Organizations' (AFL-CIO) state body; co-edited the Illinois AFL *Weekly News Letter*; was an AFL fraternal delegate to the Canadian Trades and Labor Congress in 1954; served on wartime governmental boards, sat on various AFL and AFL-CIO committees, and was active in numerous charitable and community service organizations; actively supported the War on Poverty during the 1960s; was a life-long promoter of public education, and in 1969 received a University of Illinois certificate of appreciation for his service to labor education and to the university; due to ill health, retired as president of the Illinois AFL-CIO in 1970, but received the title of president emeritus from the executive board; died in Streator, Ill., December 15, 1970; *Who's Who in Labor* (1946); Illinois AFL-CIO *Weekly News Letter*, December 19, 1970.

Donald G. Sofchalk

SORGE, Friedrich Adolph   (1828–1906). Born in Bethau bei Torgau, Saxony (now part of East Germany), November 9, 1828; son of Georg Wilhelm, a clergyman, and Hedwig Klothilde (Lange) Sorge; married; two children; after private tutoring from his father, attended the Franckeschen Stiftungen at Halle; as a result of participating in revolutionary activities in 1848, incarcerated for a short period; after released from prison, moved to Geneva and taught music; forced to leave Geneva in 1851, and moved to Liège; worked there in a carpentry shop and taught German in a private school; arrived in London in 1852 after being forced to leave both Belgium and Germany; emigrated to the United States later in the same year and supported himself as a musician and music teacher in New York City; joined a New York Communist society in 1858; supported the anti-slavery wing of the Republican party during the Civil War; during 1868, was a member of the executive committee of the Union for German Freedom and Unity, secretary of the Secularists, and a member of the *Soziale Partei*; joined the International Workingmen's Association (IWA) in 1869; attended The Hague convention of the IWA in 1872; became general secretary of the IWA after its headquarters moved to New York; along with Otto Weydemeyer, represented the North American Federation of the IWA in 1876 at a Philadelphia conference designed to unify the American labor and Socialist movements; joined with Ira Steward (q.v.) in the Boston Eight-Hour League in 1877, and organized textile workers in New Jersey the following year; was an intimate friend of Karl Marx and Friedrich Engels, and became the most authoritative spokesman for Marx in the United States; died in Hoboken, N.J., October 26, 1906; David Montgomery, *Beyond Equality: Labor and the Radical Republicans, 1862–1872* (1967); G. M. Stekloff, *History of the First International* (1928); Morris Hillquit, *History of Socialism in the United States* (1903); *Dictionary of American Biography*, Vol. 17; Miriam Frank and Martin Glaberman, "Friedrich A. Sorge on the American Labor Movement," *Labor History* (Fall 1977); Philip S. Foner, *American Socialism and Black Americans from the Age of Jackson to World War II* (1977).

SPIES, August Vincent Theodore   (1855–1887). Born in Landeck Castle, central Germany, in 1855; son of a forest district government administrator; educated by private tutors for a career in government service and later studied at the *Polytechnicum* in Cassel; after the death of his father, he emigrated to the United States in 1872, joining relatives in New York City where he became a furniture upholsterer; moved to Chicago in 1873, and a few years later he opened a small upholstery shop; became involved in radical activities and joined the Socialist Labor party in 1877; deeply offended by the anti-worker violence that occurred during the Railroad Strike of 1877, he joined the "lehr und Wehr Verein," an armed workingmen's group; became the manager and editor of the *Arbeiter Zeitung*, a German-language workingman's newspaper which had begun publication in Chicago in 1872; used the columns of the *Arbeiter-Zeitung* to expose corruption in city government and the police department, and, as a result, earned the enmity of local officials; was a delegate to the Congress of the Revolutionary Socialist meeting in Chicago in 1881 and the Congress of the International Working People's Association (Black International) meeting in Pittsburgh in 1883; although never active in organizational affairs, was a member of the Knights of Labor and the Ameri-Kanische Turner Bund; a vigorous orator frequently called upon to speak during labor disturbances, he traveled extensively to promote socialist causes; was invited to address a group of lumber shavers, who were participating in the general strike for the eight-hour day, near the McCormick Harvesting Works outside Chicago on May 2, 1886; during his address a work shift ended and fighting soon broke out between strikers and strike breakers; police intervened, killing four strikers and injuring many more; horrified by the carnage, Spies issued a "Revenge Circular" in which he urged workers to arm themselves and appear "in full force" at Haymarket Square the next evening to protest police brutality; during the meeting a bomb exploded, killing a policeman and injuring several others, whereupon the police opened fire on the protestors, killing at least one and wounding many more; Spies was charged with murder, tried, and convicted in June 1886 in a trial that represented a gross perversion of justice; was executed in Chicago on November 11, 1887; Philip S. Foner, ed., *The Autobiographies of the Haymarket Martyrs* (1969); Lucy E. Parsons, *Life of Albert R. Parsons with Brief History of Labor Movement in America: Also Sketches of the Lives of A. Spies, Geo. Engel, A. Fischer and Louis Lingg*, 2d ed. (1903); David Henry, *The History of the Haymarket Affair*, rev. ed. (1963).

SPRADLING, Abe L.   (1885–1970). Born in Woodford County, Ky., June 19, 1885; son of Abe L. and Annie E. (Gilvin) Spradling; married Lula May Hutton in September 1907, and, after her death in December 1910, Mary A. Jones on October 3, 1931; one child; after completing his formal education in the public schools, became a motorman for the Cincinnati Traction Company in 1903; joined Division 627 of the Amalgamated Association of Street, Electric Railway and Motor Coach Employees of America (AASERMCE) in Cincinnati and in 1915 was elected secretary-treasurer of the local; became an international AASERMCE vice-president in 1927 and was elected to the international executive board in 1935; served as an assistant to international president William D. Mahon (q.v.), 1936–1944; elected international president of the AASERMCE after the resignation of Mahon in 1946; elected an American Federation of Labor-Congress of Industrial Organizations vice-president and executive council member during the 1955 merger convention; served as a director of the Union Labor Life Insurance Company; resigned union positions because of failing health in 1959; died in Cincinnati, Ohio, May 22, 1970; Emerson P. Schmidt, *Industrial Relations in Urban Transportation* (1937); *AFL-CIO News*, May 30, 1970; *Who's Who in America, 1958–1959*.

STANLEY, Miles C.   (1925–1974). Born in Dunbar, W.Va., in 1925; married; three children; after completing a high school education, he went to work as a machinist and joined a local of the International Association of Machinists and Aerospace Workers; served in the U.S. Army during World War II; after the war he joined Local 3715 of the United Steelworkers of America (USWA) and quickly rose through the union ranks, being elected president of the local in 1946; served in this position until 1956; during this time he also served as president of the Kanawha Valley Industrial Union Council and as executive secretary-treasurer of the West Virginia Congress of Industrial Organizations (CIO); helped negotiate the merger of the West Virginia State Federation of Labor, American Federation of Labor (AFL) and the CIO in 1957, creating the West Virginia AFL-CIO; was elected president of the merged AFL-CIO in 1957 and retained that position for the remainder of his life; served as a special assistant to AFL-CIO President George Meany (q.v.), 1965–1967, in which capacity he was instrumental in the establishment of the Hawaii AFL-CIO; also served with the U.S. worker delegation to the International Labor Organization; served as chairman of the AFL-CIO Appalachian council, a manpower training and placement program covering a 12-state region; died in Charleston, W.Va., on May 3, 1974; Evelyn L. K. Harris and Frank J. Krebs, *From Humble Beginnings: West Virginia State Federation of Labor, 1903–1957* (1960); *AFL-CIO News*, May 11, 1974; *The New York Times*, May 5, 1974.

STARR, Mark   (1894–   ). Born in Shoscombe, Somerset, England, April 27, 1894; son of William, a miner, and Susan (Padfield) Starr; reared as a Methodist; married Helen Grosvenor Norton on May 31, 1932; one child; after graduating from grammar school in 1907, began work as a builder's laborer, he recalled, "at 4 shillings for 56½ hours" a week; entered the coal mines a year later working as a powder monkey, a carting boy, and a hewer; attended night school during 1913–1914, while working in the mines, and the following year was awarded a two-year scholarship to the London Labour College by the South Wales Miners' Federation; imprisoned as a conscientious objector during World War I; won an extension of Labour College scholarship for two years following the end of the war; his first book, *A Worker Looks at History*, was published by the Plebs League in 1919; instructed miners in economics and history for the South Wales Miners' Federation and then became a lecturer and divisional organizer for the British National Council of Labour Colleges, 1921–1928, and during the same period became active in the Esperanto movement; Labour party parliamentary candidate, Wimbledon, 1924; emigrated to the United States in November 1928 to teach a course in economic geography at Brookwood Labor College, joining the full-time Brookwood faculty in 1931 and serving as extension director during 1933–1934; appointed education director of the International Ladies' Garment Workers' Union in 1935, serving until 1960; became the focus of a public controversy when the New York Board of Education rejected the recommendation that he be appointed director of a newly established adult education program; labor consultant for the Office of War Information in Britain, 1943, and for the American Military Government in Japan, 1946; active in Local 189 of the American Federation of Teachers (AFT), a local of teachers in the field of workers' education, serving as its chairman or president during various years in the 1940s and 1950s; a vice-president of the AFT, 1940–1942; chairman of the Liberal party for Queens County, New York, and candidate for Congress on the Liberal ticket in 1946 and for numerous local offices; appointed by President Harry S. Truman to the National Commission on Higher Education, 1946–1947; served as an expert on workers' education for the International Labor Organization in Singapore, 1960–1961, Tanganyika, 1961–1962, and East Africa, 1962–1963; became the United Nations' representative of New York Universala Esperanto-Asocco and chairman of the Esperanto Information Center in New York City in 1965; author of *Trade Unionism: Past, Present and Future*

(1923), *A Worker Looks at Economics* (1925), *Lies and Hate in Education* (1929), *Labor in America*, with Harold U. Faulkner (1944), and several primers on labor for high school students, including *American Labor: Its Aims and Methods* (1952), *Labor and the American Way* (1953), and *The American Labor Movement* (1972); Mark Starr Papers, Tamiment Library, New York University; Brookwood Labor College Papers, Walter Reuther Archives, Wayne State University; *Who's Who in Labor* (1946).

Jon Bloom

STEINBOCK, Max   (1917–1975). Born in New York City on February 18, 1917; son of Herman and Bertha (Beresner) Steinbock; Jewish; married Mildred M. Wolsky on June 26, 1941; two children; after completing his elementary and secondary school education in New York City, he attended Cooper Union Art School; joined Local 338 of the United Retail, Wholesale and Department Store Union (RWDSU) in 1940 as an organizer; served in the U.S. Army Air Force during World War II; after the war he became assistant publicity director of the Labor League for Human Rights of the American Federation of Labor; was executive director of the New York County Liberal party, 1946, 1947; became the editor of Local 338 *News* in 1949; appointed editor of the *RWDSU Record* in 1954 and became administrative assistant to RWDSU president Max Greenberg (q.v.); elected a vice-president of the International Labor Press Association (ILPA) in 1965 and in 1973 was elected president of the ILPA; also served on the board of directors of the Workers' Defense League and served on the executive committee of the American Trade Union Council for Histadrut; widely regarded as one of the most capable editors in the labor movement, he made the *RWDSU Record* one of the outstanding labor newspapers in the United States; died in Washington, D.C., on June 17, 1975; *AFL-CIO News*, June 21, 1975; *The New York Times*, June 19, 1975; *RWDSU Record*, June 1975; *Who's Who in America, 1974–1975*.

STEPHENS, Uriah Smith   (1821–1882). Born in Cape May County, N.J., August 3, 1821; Baptist; educated for the Baptist ministry, but indentured to a tailor during the 1837 depression; taught school for a short time; moved to Philadelphia, Pa., in 1846 and worked as a tailor for several years; left Philadelphia in 1853, traveling through the West Indies, Central America, and Mexico, and then spent five years in California; returned to Philadelphia in 1858 as a reformer and abolitionist; supported the Republican candidacies of John Fremont in 1856 and Abraham Lincoln in 1860; helped organize the Garment Cutters' Association in 1862; after the failure of the Garment Cutters' Association, became a co-founder of the Noble Order of the Knights of Labor (K of L) in 1869; as a member of several secret fraternal societies, became much impressed with tradition, secrecy, and ritualism and incorporated those principles into his concept of labor organization; also opposed the wage system, favoring cooperation instead, and advocated a single all-embracing organization of the "producing classes''; was elected master workman when 20 K of L assemblies organized District Assembly 1; ran unsuccessfully for Congress on the Greenback Labor party ticket in 1878 from Pennsylvania's Fifth District; elected grand master workman of the K of L in 1878; resigned his office in the K of L the following year due to illness and to differences over the wisdom of his emphasis on secrecy; died in Philadelphia, Pa., February 13, 1882; Norman J. Ware, *The Labor Movement in the United States, 1860–1895* (1929); Gerald N. Grob, *Workers and Utopia: A Study of Ideological Conflict in the American Labor Movement, 1865–1900* (1961); David Montgomery, *Beyond Equality: Labor and the Radical Republicans, 1862–1872* (1967).

STEWARD, Ira   (1831–1883). Born in New London, Conn., March 10, 1831; married Jane (Henning) Steward in 1880 after the death of his first wife, Mary B., in 1878; self-educated; became a short-hours advocate while serving a 12-hour-day apprenticeship as a machinist in 1850; joined the Machinists and Blacksmiths International Union after being discharged from his machinist's job because of his agitation for shorter hours; secured a resolution at the 1863 national convention of the Machinists demanding an eight-hour-day law; organized the first independent eight-hour organization, the Workingmen's Convention (later renamed the Labor Reform Association), in Boston, Mass., in 1864; played a prominent role in the organization and affairs of the Grand Eight Hour League and its successor, the Boston Eight Hour League; served as titular head of numerous eight-and ten-hour leagues; successfully advocated an effective ten-hour law for women and children in the Massachusetts legislature in 1874; was a co-founder with J. P. McDonnell (q.v.) of the International Labor Union in 1878; also served as an organizer; was a pamphleteer whose theories strongly influenced his generation of labor leaders; believed that eight hours of labor was a vital first step in achieving a fundamental redistribution of wealth that would eventually result in the decline of capitalism and the inauguration of a cooperative commonwealth; emphasized the eight-hour solution and thus often came into conflict with reformers propagating more broadly conceived programs of social reform; his disciples George McNeill (q.v.) and George Guntan carried his theories into the American Federation of Labor; died in Plano, Ill., March 13, 1883; Ira Steward Papers, State Historical Society of Wisconsin; David Montgomery, *Beyond Equality: Labor and the Radical Republicans, 1862–1872* (1967); Norman J. Ware, *The Labor Movement in the United States, 1860–1895* (1929); John R. Commons et al., *History of Labour in the United States*, Vol. 2 (1918); *Science and Society* (Spring 1956); *Dictionary of American Biography*, Vol. 18.

STEVENS, Alzina Parsons   (1849–1900). Born in Parsonsfield, Me., on May 27, 1849; daughter of Enoch, a farmer and small manufacturer, and Louise (Page) Parsons; divorced; no children; was forced at age 13 to leave home and go to work in a textile factory because of the death of her father, which left the family destitute; entered the printing trade in 1867, working as a proofreader and typesetter; moved to Chicago, Ill., in 1872 and joined Typographical Union No. 16; organized and became the first president of Working Woman's Union No. 1 in 1877; moved to Toledo, Ohio, in 1882 and for the next several years worked successively as a proofreader, compositor, correspondent, and finally editor of the *Toledo Bee*; joined the Knights of Labor, helped organize, and became the first master workman of Joan of Arc Assembly, a mixed Toledo local assembly composed of women; served as a delegate to the Knights of Labor District Assembly 72 in Toledo; was elected district master workman in 1890; attended the annual Knights of Labor national conventions in 1888, 1889, and 1890; represented northwestern Ohio labor unions at the national Populist party convention in 1892; returned to Chicago where, after co-editing a short-lived newspaper devoted to social and economic reform, she became a resident at Jane Addams's (q.v.) Hull House; leaving the Knights of Labor, she helped organize several American Federation of Labor locals in Chicago; appointed assistant factory inspector in Illinois (under Florence Kelley [q.v.]) by Governor John P. Altgeld in 1893; became increasingly involved in child labor reform and along with other Hull House reformers helped push a more effective child labor bill through the Illinois state legislature in 1897; a woman of great drive and ambition, her campaign for child labor reform was further motivated by the memory of a lost finger in an industrial accident while she herself was a child; became the first probation officer in the newly created Cook County Juvenile Court in 1899; died in Chicago on June 3, 1900; *Notable American Women*, Vol. 3; Alice Henry, *The Trade Union Woman* (1915) and *Women and the Labor Movement* (1923).

STOKES, Rose Harriet Pastor   (1879–1933). Born in Augustowo, Suwalki, Russian Poland, July 18, 1879; daughter of Jacob and Anna (Lewin) Wieslander; Jewish; married a millionaire, James G. P. Stokes, on July 18, 1905, and, after that marriage ended in divorce, Isaac Romaine in 1927; moved with her family to London in 1872, and there, from ages 7 to 9, received her only formal education at the Bell Lane Free School; emigrated with her family to the United States, settling in Cleveland, Ohio, in 1890; shortly after began work in a Cleveland cigar factory; moved to New York City in 1903 and became a feature writer for the *Jewish Daily News*, already a publisher of some of her poems; became a member of the Socialist party of America (SPA) and active in the Intercollegiate Socialist Study Society headed by her husband from 1907 to 1917; participated in the 1912 New York restaurant and hotel workers' strike; in association with her husband, helped found the short-lived National party in Chicago, Ill., in 1912; withdrew from the SPA in July 1917 because of its opposition to American entry into World War I; convicted in March 1918 for violating the Espionage Act, but saw the conviction overturned on appeal in 1920; rejoined the SPA in February 1918; became increasingly radical and aligned herself with the SPA's left wing; remained with this group when it seceded from the SPA in September 1919 to form the Communist party of America (CPA); wrote for *Pravda* and the *Daily Worker* during the 1920s; elected an American delegate to the Fourth Congress of the Communist International in Moscow in 1922, and was elected to the central executive committee of the Workers' party; served as a reporter for the congress's Negro Commission; authored numerous poems, an unpublished autobiography, and a feminist play, *The Woman Who Wouldn't* (1916); translated with Helena Frank the Yiddish *Songs of Labor* (1914); died in Frankfurt-am-Main, Germany, June 20, 1933; *Dictionary of American Biography*, Vol. 8; *Notable American Women* (1971); James Weinstein, *The Decline of Socialism in America, 1912–1925* (1967).

Marie Tedesco

STOLBERG, Benjamin (1891–1951). Born in Munich, Germany, on November 30, 1891; the adopted son of Michael and Rada Stolberg, chocolate manufacturers; Jewish; married Mary Malvina Fox on January 7, 1925, and was divorced in 1929; one child; shortly after graduating from the Realgymnasium in Munich in 1908, he emigrated to the United States, where for a brief time he studied medicine at Washington University, St. Louis, Mo.; during the next five years, 1909–1914, he roamed the country, working as an itinerent laborer and often staying at settlement houses; enrolled at Harvard University in 1914 and completed the requirements for a degree in philosophy in 1917; received an M.A. in sociology from the University of Chicago in 1919; while a student at Chicago, he lived at Jane Addams's Hull House; was a lecturer on social work at the universities of Oklahoma and Kansas, 1919–1921; served as head of vocational placement, Chicago public school system, 1921–1922; was acting editor of the *Journal of the Brotherhood of Locomotive Engineers*, 1922–1923; meanwhile, he wrote articles, many of them concerning the labor movement, for such publications as the *Chicago Tribune*, *The Nation*, the *New Republic*, and the *New York Evening Post*; moved to New York City in 1923 and thereafter devoted most of his time to freelance journalism; was an associate editor of *Bookman*, 1928–1929, and reviewed works of nonfiction for the *New York Evening Post*, 1932–1933; during the 1920s and early 1930s, he espoused Socialist views but became increasingly critical of the conservative leadership of the American labor movement while at the same time denouncing the sectarianism of the Communist left; was chairman of the New York branch of the League for Industrial Democracy, 1925–1927; became an increasingly harsh critic of Democratic liberalism and the New Deal, and so wrote *The Economic Consequences of the New Deal* (1935); was a defender of Leon Trotsky during the mid-1930s, traveling to Mexico City with John Dewey and others on a commission of inquiry that exonerated Trotsky, but thereafter moved steadily to the right, attacking the Congress of Industrial Organizations as Communist-dominated in *The Story of the CIO* (1938), denouncing Franklin D. Roosevelt and the New Deal as "state capitalism" and "totalitarian liberalism," and throwing his support to such conservative figures as Robert A. Taft and Herbert Hoover; authored *Tailor's Progress: The Story of a Famous Union and the Men Who*

Made It (1944); died in New York City on January 21, 1951; Benjamin Stolberg Papers, Columbia University; *Dictionary of American Biography*, Suppl. 6; *The New York Times*, January 22, 1951.

STONE, Milan O.   (1927–   ). Born in Rock Falls, Wis., on June 11, 1927; son of Oscar, a farmer, and Thelma (Hysen) Stone, a homemaker; divorced; four children; after graduating from Eau Claire (Wis.) High School in 1944, he served in the U.S. Navy, Pacific theater, 1944–1946; after the war, he secured a job in the rubber industry and joined Local 19 of the United Rubber, Cork, Linoleum and Plastic Workers of America (URW) in 1946; served as a time study engineer for Local 19, 1956–1963; elected vice-president of Local 19 in 1959; served on the Eau Claire Area Council, American Federation of Labor-Congress of Industrial Organizations (AFL-CIO), 1960–1963; elected to the executive board of the Wisconsin AFL-CIO Council in 1960, serving until 1964; served as a URW time study engineer, 1963–1972; was a URW special representative, 1972–1974; elected director of URW District 4 in 1974, and in 1977 became a URW vice-president; after the retirement of URW President Peter Bommarito (q.v.) in 1981, he was elected to the URW presidency; although lacking the toughness, flair, and tough-nosed approach to bargaining of his flamboyant predecessor, he was characterized as a careful, plodding union leader whose style might be appropriate to the troubled condition of the American rubber industry; among his major objectives was to replace volatile three-year contract talks with ''on-going negotiations'' and to investigate the possibilities of a merger with the United Automobile, Aerospace and Agricultural Implement Workers of America; *Chemical Week*, October 21, 1981; *Who's Who in Labor* (1976).

STONE, Warren Stanford   (1860–1925). Born in Ainsworth, Iowa, February 1, 1860; son of John, a farmer, and Sarah (Stewart) Stone; married Carrie E. Newell on October 15, 1884; after completing high school, attended Western College, Iowa; began work as a fireman on the Rock Island Railway in 1879; became an engineer in 1884 and eventually joined the Brotherhood of Locomotive Engineers (BLE); served as secretary-treasurer and chairman of the adjustment committee of his local union; appointed grand chief engineer of the BLE after the death of Peter M. Arthur (q.v.) in 1903, and a year later elected to the same position by the delegates to the BLE's national convention; strongly supported the agitation that successfully led to a legislated eight-hour day for railroad workers; although an essentially conservative trade union leader, was a strong advocate of government ownership of the railroads; served as treasurer of the Conference for Progressive Political Action that sponsored the Progressive party candidacy of Robert M. La Follette in 1924; involved the BLE during his presidency in cooperative banking and a wide variety of financial ventures, most of which failed during the early years of the Great Depression; served as a member of the Industrial Peace Committee administering the Nobel Peace Prize; became a director of the Cooperative League in 1923; died in Cleveland, Ohio, June 12, 1925; Reed C. Richardson, *The Locomotive Engineer, 1863–1963: A Century of Railway Labor Relations and Work Rules* (1963); Erma Angevine, *In League with the Future* (1959); *Encyclopedia of Social Sciences*, Vol. 14.

STRASSER, Adolph   (fl. 1871–1939). Born in Austria-Hungary (an area now part of Hungary); emigrated to the United States in 1871 or 1872; helped organize the Social Democratic party in 1873 and the Socialist Labor party in 1877; participated in the 1872 eight-hour strikes and helped organize those New York cigarmakers excluded from membership in the Cigarmakers' International Union of America (CMIU); joined Local 15 (English-speaking), led by Samuel Gompers (q.v.), and guided a successful drive to merge that group with Local 85 (German-speaking) and the Bohemian cigarmakers; founded the United Cigarmakers, open to all regardless of sex, and fought to liberalize the CMIU constitution and to legitimize local membership policies; after the United Cigarmakers received a CMIU charter as Local 144 in 1875, became financial secretary while Gompers was elected president; was elected international president of the CMIU in 1877, serving until 1891; during the early 1880s, sided with Gompers in his refusal to turn Local 144 over to the democratically elected Progressive (Socialist) faction and instead illegally expelled the Progressive president, Samuel Schimkowitz, and disastrously disrupted the union; meanwhile, saw the Progressive defectors joined by other secessionist Socialists to create in 1882 a new union larger than Local 144; maneuvered CMIU committees and the annual convention to maintain control of Local 144 as part of the Gompers machine; fought against the Knights of Labor (K of L) and its District Assembly 49 for giving support to the Progressives, and permitted CMIU members to scab against Progressive strikers in the early 1880s; fearing K of L encroachment, demanded that the K of L cease organizing the trades and in 1886, with four others, issued a call for the Columbus (Ohio) Convention that organized the American Federation of Labor (AFL) in December of that year; testified, in 1883, before the U.S. Senate Committee on Education and Labor against the Pacific Coast migration of Chinese who competed with cigarmakers; opposed the Gompers-inspired proposal for the use of initiative and referendum in CMIU elections, and thus resigned his CMIU presidency in 1891; later accepted the proposal after voting was made compulsory; was opposed to independent political activity and to the Socialist Plank 10 at the 1894 AFL convention; appointed to the newly created AFL legislative committee in 1895 to promote congressional action favorable to labor; named by the AFL executive council in 1904 to arbitrate jurisdictional disputes between brewery workers, who favored industrial unionism, and the craft-oriented firemen and engineers; saw his activities result in revocation of the charter of the Brewery Workers' Union in 1907; served as a CMIU organizer in Pennsylvania, 1909–1910; from 1892 to 1913, he served the CMIU as a lecturer, organizer, auditor, and troubleshooter; also worked as a lecturer for the AFL and during 1903–1905 helped settle jurisdictional disputes; ended his union activities in 1914 and became a real-estate agent in Buffalo, N.Y.; lived in Chicago, 1918–1929, and in 1930 moved to Daytona Beach, Fla.; died in Lakeland, Fla., on January 1, 1939; Philip Taft, *The A.F. of L. in the Time of Gompers* (1957); Bernard Mandel, *Samuel Gompers: A Biography* (1963); Roland H. Harvey, *Samuel Gompers: Champion of the Toiling Masses* (1935); Philip S. Foner, *History of the Labor Movement in the United States*, Vol. 2 (1955); Samuel Gompers, *Seventy Years of Life and Labor: An Autobiography* (1925); *Cigarmakers Official Journal* (1909–1910); Patricia A. Cooper, "Whatever Happened to Adolph Strasser?" *Labor History* (Summer 1979).

Merl E. Reed

STULBERG, Louis   (1901–   ). Born in Bogria, Russian Poland, April 14, 1901; son of Benjamin, a coal dealer, and Jeannette Stulberg; Jewish; married Bebe Friedman on February 17, 1929; one child; after emigrating to Toronto, Canada, began work as a junior cutter in a dress shop and at age 14 joined Local 83 of the International Ladies' Garment Workers' Union (ILGWU); graduated from Harbord Collegiate Institute in Toronto; emigrated to the United States in 1919; while working in the garment industry in Chicago, Ill., completed high school and attended the University of Chicago for one year; played professional baseball for two years with the Memphis Chicks of the Southern Association; served as an ILGWU general organizer for the Midwest, 1924–1927; after moving to New York, affiliated with ILGWU Local 10 and from 1929 to 1945 served as its business agent and assistant manager; became assistant general secretary of the ILGWU in 1945 and an international vice-president two years later; served as manager of New York Undergarment and Negligee Workers' Union, Local 62, ILGWU, 1947–1956; became executive vice-president after the position was created by the ILGWU executive board in 1956; served until his election as general secretary-treasurer in 1959; elected president of the ILGWU after the retirement of David Dubinsky (q.v.) in 1966; elected shortly thereafter as a vice-president and executive council member of the American Federation of Labor-Congress of Industrial Organizations (AFL-CIO); was appointed a United States delegate to the United Nations by President Lyndon B. Johnson in 1968; served as AFL-CIO fraternal delegate to the British Trades Union Congress in 1972; was appointed a fellow of Brandeis University; has usually supported the Democratic party; retired from union affairs in 1975; Louis Stulberg Papers, ILGWU Archives; Max D. Danish, *The World of David Dubinsky* (1957); Benjamin Stolberg, *Tailor's Progress: The Story of a Famous Union and the Men Who Made It* (1944); *AFL-CIO News*, May 3, 1975.

SUFFRIDGE, James Arthur   (1909–   ). Born in Knoxville, Tenn., February 2, 1909; son of Chester Arthur, a retail merchant, and Angie (Dodson) Suffridge; Methodist; married Georgia Nutting on November 18, 1928; two children; after graduating from high school in Oakland, Calif., worked at a variety of odd jobs, including those of wholesale jewelry salesman in northern

California and route boss for a wholesale bakery in St. Louis, Mo.; later took courses at the University of California, Berkeley; became a counter clerk for an Oakland grocery store in 1931 and later promoted to store manager; joined Oakland Food and Drug Local 870 of the Retail Clerks International Protective Association (RCIA) in 1934; was elected secretary-treasurer, the chief administrative officer, of Local 870 in 1936; served as president of the California State Council of Retail Clerks and as financial secretary of the Oakland Central Labor Union; elected international president of the RCIA in 1944 and became the chief administrative officer of the union after the retirement of Secretary-Treasurer C. C. Coulter (q.v.) in 1947 (his title was secretary-treasurer, 1947–1955, and president thereafter); during World War II, was a member of the regional board of the Office of Price Administration and a panel member of the Oakland division of the War Labor Board; created an organizational division within the RCIA in 1945 that stimulated major organizing successes; became an American Federation of Labor-Congress of Industrial Organizations (AFL-CIO) vice-president and executive council member in 1957; served as a member of the executive board of the AFL-CIO industrial union department and was a vice-president of the union label department; retired as president emeritus of the RCIA in 1968 and became chairman of the union's executive board; a Republican; edited the RCIA organ, *Advocate*, 1947–1968; Michael Harrington, *The Retail Clerks* (1962); Albert A. Blum et al., *White-Collar Workers* (1971); George G. Kirstein, *Stores and Unions: A Study of the Growth of Unionism in Dry Goods and Department Stores* (1950); *Saturday Evening Post*, March 16, 1957.

SUGAR, Maurice (1891–   ). Born in Brimley, Mich., in 1891; son of Kalman and Mary (Berman) Sugar, both immigrants from Russia (Lithuania); father owned general store near timber camps; moved to Detroit, Mich., in 1900 and graduated from Central High School in 1919, working his way through school; obtained the B.S.L. from the University of Michigan Law School in 1912; was *Law Review* editor; joined the Intercollegiate Socialist Society that year and the Socialist party of America (SPA) in 1913; Socialist activism brought him into contact with the large International Typographical Union local in Detroit, a city dominated by open-shop proponents; early labor cases largely concerned injunction and picketing violations; quickly became the main lawyer for the Detroit Federation of Labor; was a delegate to the SPA St. Louis emergency convention in April 1917; convicted of draft resistance, disbarred, and jailed (November 1918–September 1919) in 1918; became a left winger but did not join any part of the splintered left after 1919; reinstated to the bar only in 1923 (with the aid of Frank Murphy); regained his role as the main American Federation of Labor lawyer in Detroit; also joined the International Labor Defense; active in unemployed councils during the 1930s, especially mortgage foreclosure and bank depositors' cases; wrote the famous depression ballad, ''The Soup Song''; was the lawyer for arrestees in the wake of the Ford Hunger March of February 1932; was the lawyer for the Auto Workers' Union (Briggs strike of

1933), then for the Mechanics Educational Society of America (Tool and Die Strike of 1934); major critic of the National Labor Board and the Wolman Auto Labor Board; simultaneously developed a reputation as a defender before the law of immigrants and blacks; urged to run for Recorder's Court in 1935 by the Detroit Federation of Labor, his campaign generated wide sympathy for the labor movement (for the first time in the black community) and almost gained him the office; ran for city council later in the year, finishing one place short of election after vicious red-baiting attacks in the local press; became the main lawyer for the fledgling United Automobile Workers (UAW) in 1936, though not trusted by Homer Martin (q.v.); together with Lee Pressman (q.v.), he handled the legal work for the Flint Sit-Down (January-February 1937); was the main conduit to Governor Frank Murphy and a key strike strategist; was the lawyer in several of the Detroit sit-down strikes that followed and wrote extensively arguing for the legality of the sit-down tactic; authored the song, "Sit-Down"; founder and charter board member of the National Lawyers' Guild; lawyer for the unity caucus against Homer Martin in the debilitating factional struggle within the UAW, 1938–1939; with George Addes (q.v.), UAW-Congress of Industrial Organizations secretary-treasurer, Sugar wrote and served as key interpreter of the democratic UAW constitution of 1939; organized the UAW legal department and became general counsel the same year; devised and implemented the legal strategy, based on the "unclean hands" doctrine, that contributed fundamentally to the organizing victory at the Ford Motor Company in April-June 1941; key advisor to Addes and R. J. Thomas (q.v.) on a host of issues throughout the formative years of the UAW; by the war years, he was generally regarded as one of America's outstanding labor lawyers; his association with the so-called Left faction led by Addes put him at odds with Walter Reuther (q.v.) and, when the latter became president in 1946, Sugar was cast in the role of campaign coordinator for the majority of the executive board opposing Reuther; the great factional struggle, unfolding in an increasingly anti-labor and Cold War atmosphere, ended in defeat for Sugar and his allies; he had hardly begun the fight against the Taft-Hartley Act before he was removed from his post in December 1947; retired from active practice shortly thereafter; Maurice Sugar Collection, Walter P. Reuther Library, Wayne State University.

Christopher Johnson

SULLIVAN, David   (1904–1976). Born in Cork City, Ireland, May 7, 1904; son of Stephen and Margaret (Fouhy) O'Sullivan; Roman Catholic; married Catherine Connaire on February 12, 1930; five children; received a secondary education in Ireland before emigrating to the United States in 1925; after arriving in New York City, took a job as an elevator operator; became a naturalized citizen in 1932; was one of the founders of New York City Local 32B of the Building Service Employees International Union (BSEIU) in 1934; was elected secretary-treasurer of Local 32B in 1938 and became president in 1941, serving until 1960; during his association with Local 32B, saw it become one of the largest local unions in the United States; was elected an international vice-president of the BSEIU in 1941; elected international president of the BSEIU in 1960, serving until 1971; during his 12-year incumbency, watched the BSEIU experience a 70 percent increase in membership; was elected a vice-president and executive council member of the American Federation of Labor-Congress of Industrial Organizations in 1967; served as chairman of the labor advisory committee of the Office of Economic Opportunity, as a member of the National Advisory Council on Economic Opportunity and the advisory committee of the National Institute on Labor Education, and on numerous other public and private boards and agencies; was the recipient of the Equal Opportunity Award presented by the National Urban League in 1961; retired as president of the BSEIU in 1971 and was named president emeritus; usually supported the Democratic party; died in New York City on January 23, 1976; Local 32B, Building Service Employees International Union, *"Going Up!": The Story of 32B* (1955); *Who's Who in America, 1972–1973*; *AFL-CIO News*, March 20, 1971; *AFL-CIO News*, January 31, 1976.

SULLIVAN, James William   (1848–1938). Born in Carlisle, Pa., March 9, 1848; son of Timothy and Elizabeth (Hagan) Sullivan; married Lillian Stewart in 1877; left high school shortly before his scheduled graduation to become a printer's apprentice; moved to New York City in 1882 and soon became foreman of the proof room of *The New York Times* and joined the International Typographical Union; during 1887–1889, edited the *Standard*, a weekly newspaper published by Henry George (q.v.) to propagate his land reform proposals; served as a member of the advisory council of the Ethical Culture Society's People's Institute in 1897; elected president of the Central Federated Union of New York City in 1913; as a close friend and advisor of American Federation of Labor (AFL) president Samuel Gompers (q.v.), accompanied Gompers on a tour of Europe in 1909, assisted in the editing of *The American Federationist*, and defended the AFL from Socialist attacks; became an active member of the National Civic Federation, serving on several of its commissions and committees and, as the head of one such commission, returning an unfavorable report on the British system of compulsory health insurance; sailed to Europe in 1916 on an AFL mission to arrange for labor representatives in the postwar peace conference; served during World War I as an assistant to Gompers on the Advisory Commission of the Council of National Defense; was one of the principal American advocates of direct legislation and was able to convince much of the labor movement of its importance; authored *Direct Legislation by the Citizenship through the Initiative and Referendum* (1892) and *Markets for the People* (1913); died in Carlisle, Pa., September 27, 1938; Marguerite Green, *The National Civic Federation and the American Labor Movement, 1900–1925* (1956); *Dictionary of American Biography*, Suppl. 2; Samuel Gompers, *Seventy Years of Life and Labor: An Autobiography* (1925).

SULLIVAN, Jere L. (1863–1928). Born in Willamansett, Mass., January 3, 1863; son of a civil engineer working in the paper industry; Roman Catholic; attended the public schools of Willamansett and, for a short time, Catholic parochial schools; after completing grammar school, worked as an itinerant waiter for several years; while serving as a Knights of Labor organizer in 1885, helped to organize a local assembly of waiters in St. Louis, Mo., which was to become Local 20 of the Hotel and Restaurant Employees' International Alliance and Bartenders' International League (HREIABIL); after moving to Salt Lake City, Utah, joined Local 6 and served as its delegate to the second national convention of the HREIABIL meeting in Chicago, Ill., in 1893; after returning to St. Louis, elected an international vice-president in 1899 and later the same year became secretary-treasurer of the HREIABIL, serving in that capacity until his death; generally regarded as the dominant figure in the early history of the HREIABIL, having assumed the leadership of a union that had nearly been destroyed by bitter factional conflicts and turned it into a solid, unified international union; died in Cincinnati, Ohio, July 27, 1928; Matthew Josephson, *Union House, Union Bar: The History of the Hotel and Restaurant Employees and Bartenders International Union, AFL-CIO* (1956); Jay Rubin and M. J. Obermeier, *Growth of a Union: The Life and Times of Edward Flore* (1943); Solon DeLeon, ed., *The American Labor Who's Who* (1925).

SWANSON, Samuel E. (1902–1972). Born in Chicago, Ill., on May 24, 1902; son of Nils W., a Swedish immigrant and stationary fireman, and Johanna (Ness) Swanson; married Eleanor Christine Hyatt on September 6, 1929; four children; Methodist; while living with an uncle on a northern Minnesota farm, completed the eighth grade; at age 15, he went to work as a migratory harvester in the wheat fields; joined the Industrial Workers of the World in Minot, N.D.; after working in Minnesota logging camps and as a laborer on the Mesabi Range, employed as an underground contract miner on the Vermillion Range, at Ely, Minn., 1927–1940; when the Steel Workers Organizing Committee (SWOC) began organizing the iron miners in 1937, he helped establish SWOC Local 1664 at Ely; as a United Steelworkers of America (USWA) international representative, he participated during 1942–1943 in the negotiation of the initial contract with the Oliver Iron Mining Company; as secretary of the Iron Range Industrial Union Council (the Congress of Industrial Organizations' central body on the Iron Ranges), 1940–1947, formulated the council's case during World War II for federally sponsored development of the Mesabi's extensive deposits of taconite, a rock of low iron content requiring costly processing, to provide employment when the high-grade ore was depleted; meanwhile, he became the representative in charge of Hibbing, Minn., subdistrict office of the USWA, District 33; sought to obtain wage rates and fringe benefits for the iron miners comparable to those in basic steel, which were incorporated into the 1952 contracts with the mining firms; after the mining industry modified its insistence on tax concessions before expanding taconite mining and processing, he campaigned for the 1964 taconite tax amendment (guaranteeing that the taconite industry would not be taxed at a higher level than other industries in the state); adoption of the amendment prompted the mining industry to construct several taconite processing plants, including U.S. Steel Corporation's giant Minntac facility; thus creating thousands of new jobs on the Mesabi during the late 1960s and early 1970s; strong supporter of Hubert H. Humphrey and other Democratic farmer-labor candidates; retired as USWA representative in 1967; died in an auto accident in Salt Lake City, Utah, on March 26, 1972; transcripts of oral history interviews in the Minnesota Historical Society, St. Paul; *Who's Who in Labor* (1946).

Donald G. Sofchalk

SWARTZ, Maud O'Farrell   (1879–1937). Born in County Kildare, Ireland, May 3, 1879; daughter of William J., part owner of a flour mill, and Sarah Matilda (Grace) O'Farrell; Roman Catholic; married Lee Swartz, a printer, in 1905; after attending convent schools in Germany and France, became a governess in Italy; emigrated to the United States in 1901; became a proofreader for a printing firm in New York City in 1902; shortly after becoming a member of the national Women's Trade Union League (WTUL), joined Local 6 of the International Typographical Union in 1913; served as secretary of the New York WTUL, 1917–1921; was a WTUL delegate to numerous conferences, including the 1919 First International Congress of Working Women held in Washington, D.C., the 1919 American Federation of Labor convention, the 1921 Second International Congress of Working Women in Geneva, and the 1922 Pan-American Congress, in Baltimore, Md.; was the American vice-president of the International Federation of Working Women, 1921–1923; served as compensation advisor for the New York WTUL during 1922; succeeded Margaret Dreier Robins (q.v.) as president of the National WTUL in 1922 and served in that capacity until 1926; became the secretary of the New York State Department of Labor in 1931, serving until 1937; died in New York City, February 22, 1937; *Notable American Women* (1971); Solon DeLeon, ed., *The American Labor Who's Who* (1925); Rose Schneiderman and Lucy Goldthwaite, *All for One* (1967); Gladys Boone, *The Women's Trade Union Leagues in Great Britain and the United States of America* (1942).

Marie Tedesco

SWEENEY, John J.   (1934–   ). Born in New York City on May 5, 1934; son of James, a bus driver, and Agnes Sweeney; married Maureen Power, a school teacher, in 1962; two children; after completing his primary and secondary schooling in New York, he enrolled in Iona College, New Rochelle, N.Y., and graduated with a B.A. in 1955; was appointed to the research department of the International Ladies' Garment Workers' Union in 1958; joined the research department of Service Employees International Union (SEIU), Local 32B, in 1961; became assistant to the president of Local 32B in 1966 and in 1973 was elected president of the local; meanwhile, he was elected to the SEIU executive board in 1972 and an international vice-president in 1973; was also elected president of the New York City Joint Council 11 in 1973, executive secretary of the SEIU New York State Council in 1974, executive vice-president of the eastern conference of SEIU unions in 1975; was also elected a vice-president of the New York City American Federation of Labor-Congress of Industrial Organizations (AFL-CIO) and was a member of the advisory committee of the New York State AFL-CIO committee on political education; negotiated a merger of Local 32B and Local 32J in 1977, creating the fifty five thousand-member Local 32B-32J; was elected international secretary-treasurer of the SEIU in January 1980 and international president in June 1980; while still living in New York, he was active on a variety of civic boards and agencies, including trustee, Iona College, member of the New York State Manpower Council, the Pre-Post Retirement Committee, Community Service Committee, the New York City Council on the Environment, and Community Action Progress, City of Yonkers; was appointed an AFL-CIO vice-president and executive council member in 1980; *AFL-CIO News*, January 5, August 23, 1980; *Who's Who in Labor* (1976).

SWEENEY, Vincent D.   (1900–1967). Born in Pittsburgh, Pa., March 3, 1900; son of Philip, a steelworker, and Anna Sweeney; Roman Catholic; married; graduated from Donora (Pa.) High School and received a journalism degree from Notre Dame University in 1922; after editing a small Pennsylvania newspaper, worked for the International News Service, becoming editor of its New York bureau; beginning in 1925, spent a decade with the Pittsburgh *Press*; in order to cover New Deal labor policy and union activity, gave up his post as Sunday editor of the *Press* to become its labor reporter and analyst; recruited by Chairman Philip Murray (q.v.) as public relations director of the Steel Workers Organizing Committee (SWOC), set up by the Congress of Industrial Organizations (CIO); within a month started *Steel Labor*, a monthly distributed free to steelworkers as part of the initial SWOC campaign; later in 1936, began to edit *Steel Labor*, soon developing it into a very readable, informative, and balanced union journal; among the upper echelon staff personnel at United Steelworkers of America (USWA) headquarters, was one of those on whom President Murray relied most; worked closely with Murray as an adviser on USWA matters, a general trouble shooter, and a speechwriter; served in a somewhat similar capacity after David J. McDonald (q.v.) became president in 1952; as when serving Murray, again carefully avoided publicity about himself; helped to establish USWA's program of summer institutes on university campuses after USWA began to develop worker education; was a member of the American Newspaper Guild and the National Press Club; authored *The United Steelworkers of America: Twenty Years Later, 1936–1956* (1956); retired due to ill health in 1961; died in Uniontown, Pa., May 20, 1967; Robert R. R. Brooks, *As Steel Goes, . . . Unionism in a Basic Industry* (1940); *Who's Who in Labor* (1946).

Donald G. Sofchalk

SWINTON, John   (1829–1901). Born in Edinburgh, Scotland, December 12, 1829; son of William and Jane Swinton; after acquiring a few years of formal education, apprenticed to a printer in 1841 at age 13; emigrated to Canada in 1843 and, while living in Montreal, became a journeyman printer; moved to New York City in 1850 and secured work as a printer; attended Easthampton Seminary in Massachusetts and New York Medical College, but did not receive a degree; became involved in the abolitionist movement of the 1850s, and participated in John Brown's raid at Osawatomie, Kans., in 1857; served as chief of *The New York Times* editorial staff, 1860–1870; began working for the *New York Sun* in 1870 and became chief editorial writer in 1875; as a result of the labor conflicts of the 1870s, became an ardent champion of the emerging labor movement; ran as the Socialist Labor party candidate for mayor of New York City in 1874; established in 1883 and served as the editor of *John Swinton's Paper*, described by one authority as "the best labor paper in the country's history"; ran unsuccessfully for the New York State Senate on the Progressive Labor party ticket in 1887; resumed his position as an editorial writer for the *New York Sun* after the failure of his own paper in 1887; although totally blind by 1889, continued his work as a journalist until his death; authored *John Swinton's Travels* (1880) and *Striking for Life* (1894); died in Brooklyn, N.Y., in 1901; John R. Commons et al., *History of Labour in the United States*, Vol. 2 (1918); Norman J. Ware, *The Labor Movement in the United States, 1860–1895* (1929); Gerald N. Grob, *Workers and Utopia: A Study of Ideological Conflict in the American Labor Movement, 1865–1900* (1961); *Encyclopedia of Social Sciences*, Vol. 14.

SWISHER, Elwood Denver   (1913–   ). Born in Jenningston, W.Va., March 24, 1913; son of Francis Columbus and Kate Flossie (Lantz) Swisher; Methodist; married Blanche S. Sneed on August 28, 1934, and Gladys E. Simmons on December 25, 1938; four children; received a public school education in Elkins, W.Va.; after completing high school became an overhead crane operator for a subsidiary of the Union Carbide and Carbon Company and joined Local 89 of the United Gas, Coke and Chemical Workers International Union (UGCCW); elected treasurer and vice-president of Local 89 in 1943 and served until becoming a UGCCW international representative in 1945; became a member of the executive board in 1948 and in 1952 elected UGCCW president; was a member of the Congress of Industrial Organizations' executive board and served on its community services committee and the committee on power and atomic energy and resources development; after the merger of the UGCCW and the Oil Workers International Union in 1955, creating the Oil, Chemical and Atomic Workers International Union, became administrative vice-president of the new union; was a delegate to the International Labor Organization conference in Geneva in 1953; served as a vice-president of the American Federation of the Physically Handicapped; Melvin Rothbaum, *The Government of the Oil, Chemical, and Atomic Workers Union* (1962); Harry Seligson, *Oil, Chemical and Atomic Workers: A Labor Union in Action* (1960); *Who's Who in America, 1960–1961*.

SYLVIS, William H.   (1828–1869). Born in Armagh, Indiana County, Pa.,
November 26, 1828; son of Nicholas, a self-employed wagonmaker, and Maria
(Mott) Sylvis; Methodist; married Amelia A. Thomas on April 11, 1852, and,
after her death in 1865, Florrie Hunter; five children; due to family poverty,
received no formal education; apprenticed at age 18 to a Pennsylvania founder
and became a journeyman molder; failed in an effort to set up a foundry, then
spent several years as an itinerant molder before finding a permanent job in
Philadelphia; during a strike called by a recently established molders' local in
1857, joined the union, soon becoming its secretary; recognizing the need for a
national organization to protect molders in an emergent nationwide market and
against founders' trade associations, persuaded his union, then the largest of the
molders' locals, to propose a national union; elected to issue the call in 1859
that resulted in the founding convention of the Iron Molders' International Union
(IMIU) in 1860; was a Douglas Democrat in 1860; helped recruit a company of
molders for the Pennsylvania militia in which he served; was alarmed by the
decline of the IMIU during the war and left the militia to revive the union;
elected president in early 1863; traveled throughout the country on meager financial resources in 1863, reviving existing locals and forming many new ones;
during the next few years made several innovations, including the issuance of
union membership cards, the imposition of high dues, and the creation of a
centralized administration, which transformed the IMIU into the largest and most
effective trade union of the era; opposed in principle to strikes, but deftly managed
those which were necessary; was a co-founder of the National Labor Union
(NLU) in 1866 and conceived of it as a vehicle for the promotion of producer
cooperatives, the eight-hour day, and currency reform to liberate labor from
exploitation by the wage system and the "money power"; elected president of
the NLU in 1868; combined a commitment to sweeping social reforms with a
skill as a practical trade unionist, allowing him to exercise a remarkable influence
over the labor movement during his brief career of leadership; was convinced
by 1868 that neither major party had labors' interests at heart and hence advocated
that the NLU function as a workingmens' party; died on July 27, 1869, in
Philadelphia, Pa.; NLU, split by dissension over whether it should become a
labor party, declined rapidly after his death; J. C. Sylvis, *The Life, Speeches,
Labors, and Essays of William H. Sylvis* (1872); Reed C. Richardson, *Bulletin
31*, New York State School of Industrial and Labor Relations, *Labor Leader
1860's* (1955); Jonathan Grossman, *William Sylvis: Pioneer of American Labor*
(1945); Charles A. Madison, *American Labor Leaders: Personalities and Forces
in the Labor Movement* (1950); David Montgomery, *Beyond Equality: Labor
and the Radical Republicans, 1862–1872* (1967).

Donald G. Sofchalk

T

TAHNEY, James P. (1897–1970). Born in Chicago, Ill., in 1897; Roman Catholic; married; three children; completed secondary school, then hired by the Chicago and North Western Railroad as an air brake repairman; during 1915–1934, continued to work in the repair shops of the Chicago and North Western and eventually promoted to the position of yard foreman; after the enactment of the National Industrial Recovery Act in 1933, along with a group of like-minded railroad supervisors organized Lodge 1 of the American Railway Supervisors Association (ARSA) in 1934; elected the first president of the ARSA, and, in 1936 retired from railroad when the ARSA presidency was made a full-time, salaried position; although leading a comparatively small, independent, national union with a limited jurisdiction, was able successfully to extend the ARSA's organization to most of the nation's railroads and many of its airlines during his long incumbency, 1934–1970; was an effective negotiator as well as organizer and gained substantial increases in wage scales, improved work rules, and employment security; died in Chicago, Ill., August 26, 1970; Chicago *Tribune*, August 27, 1970; *Labor*, September 5, 1970.

TALBOT, Thomas W. (1845–1892). Born on a South Carolina farm, April 17, 1845; at age 10, went to work in a shoe factory; began a machinist apprenticeship in the North Carolina Railroad machine shops at Florence, S.C., in 1865, and worked as an engineer for the firm until 1874; opened his own machine shop, but later returned to Florence to work in the Wilmington, Columbia, and Augusta Railroad shops; joined the Knights of Labor, and, serving as a master workman and state organizer, organized 11 assemblies; unsuccessfully attempted to organize a machinists' union in Florence; moved to Atlanta, Ga., to work for the Eastern Tennessee, Virginia and Georgia Railroad in 1888 and established the first local union of the future International Association of Machinists; on September 10, 1888, called for the founding of a national Order of United Machinists and Mechanical Engineers of America for the purpose of resisting wage reductions, providing insurance against unemployment, illness, accident, and old age, and to identify craft skill and reputable character; at the first convention of the National Association of Machinists (NAM), held in Atlanta, Ga., in 1889, unanimously elected grand master machinist (national president) and was reelected the following year at Louisville, Ky.; guided NAM in establishing 101 local lodges, of which 41 were in the South, 40 in the Midwest, and 17 in the Far West; the union was originally confined to southern railroad machinists, but within two years, as it organized job machinists in the North and West, economic issues superseded social ties as the unifying factor; resigned shortly after his reelection in 1890 because of "matters of personal concern"; murdered in Florence, S.C., in February 1892, by two youths, one of whom he had recently horsewhipped for insulting a member of his family; Mark Perlman, *The Machinists: A New Study in American Trade Unionism* (1961); the Southern Labor Archives, Atlanta, Ga., has the records of Machinists Lodge No. 1.

John W. Hevener

TEIGAN, Henry George   (1881–1941). Born in Forest City, Iowa, on August 7, 1881; son of Anders Olson and Brita (Monson) Teigan; Lutheran; married Ethel L. Herbert-Reamer on March 29, 1941; two children; attended Iowa public schools and Luther Academy in Albert Lea, Minn., and Central College in Pella, Iowa; graduated from Valparaiso (Ind.) University in 1908; was a teacher in rural Iowa schools, 1900–1904, Des Lacs, N.D., 1909–1910, and Logan, N.D., 1912–1913; served as secretary of the North Dakota State Socialist party, 1913–1916; moved to Minneapolis, Minn., where he became active in the labor movement while serving as secretary of the National Nonpartisan League, 1916–1923; served as secretary to U.S. Senator Magnus Johnson, 1923–1925; was editor of the *Farmer-Labor Advocate* and the *Minnesota Leader*, 1923–1933; elected to the Minnesota state senate in 1933, serving until 1935; edited the *Minnesota Leader*, 1935–1937; elected to the U.S. Congress from the Third District of Minnesota in 1937 on the Farmer-Labor party ticket; served one term; was an unsuccessful candidate for reelection in 1938 and 1940; meanwhile, he resumed his editorial work; died in Minneapolis on March 12, 1941; *Who Was Who*, Vol. 1; *Biographical Directory of the American Congress, 1774–1977*; George W. Lawson, *History of Labor in Minnesota* (1955).

TETLOW, Percy   (1875–1960). Born in Leetonia, Ohio, December 16, 1875; son of William, a miner, and Ann (Hadfield) Tetlow; Methodist; married Sadie M. Carrier on July 3, 1900; three children; completed public grammar school in Leetonia and at age 12 began working in the coal mines at Washingtonville, Ohio; later, during 1900–1901, attended Scranton (Pa.) School of Mines, taking courses in mine engineering; joined the Knights of Labor and was one of the charter members of the United Mine Workers of America (UMWA) in 1890; served as a private in the U.S. Army during the Spanish-American War; elected a subdistrict president, District 6, 1901–1911; served after 1911 at various times as an international representative, president of District 17, West Virginia, and as UMWA statistician; was a member of the Ohio Mine Commission in 1909 and the Constitutional Convention of Ohio in 1912; elected to the Ohio state legislature in 1913; during his service in these capacities, was a champion of mine safety and workmen's compensation legislation; served with the American Expeditionary Force in France and Belgium during World War I; was the first director of industrial affairs of Ohio, serving during 1921–1922; was a member of the International Mining Congress held in Paris in 1927; served by presidential appointment on the National Bituminous Coal Commission, 1935–1943, and during 1938–1943 chaired the commission; after World War II, was instrumental in the creation of the UMWA welfare and retirement fund and as a special UMWA staff representative, helped organize and administer the program until his death; was a member of numerous veterans' organizations, becoming a charter member of the American Legion in 1919; was a Republican; died in Columbus, Ohio, November 19, 1960; J. W. Hess, ed., *Struggle in the Coal Fields: The Autobiography of Fred Mooney* (1967); Robert Cairns, *John L. Lewis: Leader of Labor* (1941); *National Cyclopaedia of American Biography*, Vol. 50; *Who's Who in Labor* (1946).

THIMMES, James Garrett   (1896–1955). Born in Hemlock, Ohio, October 4, 1896; son of Philip, a coal miner, and Cora Belle (Hayden) Thimmes; Protestant; married Thelma Rosalie Runyan on December 2, 1917; five children; was forced by family poverty to leave high school at age 15, gaining employment in a pottery; employed subsequently in several steel mills in the Ohio Valley; served with the U.S. Army Infantry overseas during World War I; moved to Chicago, Ill., in 1924 and became president of Lodge 59, Amalgamated Association of Iron, Steel, and Tin Workers (AA); was one of the delegates to the 1936 AA convention who pressured the union leadership into cooperating with the Congress of Industrial Organizations (CIO) in launching the Steel Workers Organizing Committee (SWOC); after two years on the SWOC staff in Chicago, was assigned to organize steelworkers in California; named director of United Steelworkers of America (USWA) District 38, California, in 1940; became president of the California Industrial Union Council, CIO; served during World War II on the California War Manpower Commission and Reemployment Commission; selected by the USWA executive board to serve the unexpired term of Clinton Golden (q.v.) as international vice-president in 1946, thus becoming the first steelworker to serve as an international USWA officer; elected vice-president by membership referendum in 1953; at the 1950 USWA convention, chaired the constitutional committee that recommended that vacancies in international offices be filled by election; was a Democrat; died in Los Angeles, Calif., January 16, 1955; Lloyd Ulman, *The Government of the Steelworkers' Union* (1962); Vincent

D. Sweeney, *United Steelworkers of America: Twenty Years Later, 1936–1956* (1956); *Who's Who in Labor* (1946).

Donald G. Sofchalk

THOMAS, Norman Mattoon (1884–1968). Born in Marion, Ohio, November 20, 1884; son of Welling Evan, a minister, and Emma (Mattoon) Thomas; Presbyterian; married Frances Violet Stewart on September 1, 1910; five children; attended the public schools of Marion, Ohio, then attended Bucknell College for one year and entered Princeton Theological Seminary; after graduation, worked for two years in New York City's East Side Settlement; became an assistant pastor at Christ Church, New York, in 1910; after extensive world travel, ordained as a Presbyterian clergyman in 1911; in the same year appointed pastor of the East Harlem Church and chairman of the American Parish; joined the Socialist party and resigned his pastorate during World War I, when church elders criticized his outspoken opposition to the war; became secretary of the Fellowship of Reconciliation, an anti-war organization, in 1918 and became editor of its organ, *World Tomorrow*; was one of the founders of the American Civil Liberties Union (originally the National Civil Liberties Bureau); participated in the strike of textile workers at Passaic, N.J., in 1919; became an associate editor of *The Nation* in 1919, and resigned his editorship of *World Tomorrow*; with Harry W. Laidler, helped organize the League for Industrial Democracy; was a long-time participant in the strikes conducted by the Southern Tenant Farmers Union during the 1930s; was a pacifist and opposed American involvement in World War II, often speaking against the war under the auspices of the America First Committee and the Keep America Out of the War Congress; was a candidate on the Socialist party ticket for several New York offices, including governor and state senator, and for mayor of New York City; ran as a Socialist for president of the United States in each election during 1928–1944; was a critic of United States foreign policy following World War II and was especially vocal in his opposition to U.S. involvement in the Vietnam War; authored *The Conscientious Objector in America* (1923), *America's Way Out: A Program for Democracy* (1930), *As I See It* (1932), and several other books and pamphlets; died in New York City, December 19, 1968; Norman Thomas Papers, New York Public Library; Harry Fleischman, *Norman Thomas: A Biography, 1884–1968* (1969); Charles O. Gorham, *Leader at Large: The Long and Fighting Life of Norman Thomas* (1920); Bernard K. Johnpoll, *Pacifist's Progress: Norman Thomas and the Decline of American Socialism* (1970); Murray B. Seidler, *Norman Thomas: Respectable Rebel* (1961); *Current Biography* (1944).

THOMAS, Rolland Jay (1900–1967). Born in East Palestine, Ohio, June 9, 1900; son of Jacob William, a railroad worker, and Mary Alice (Jackson) Thomas; married Mildred Wettergren on August 7, 1937; one child; graduated from high school in Hubbard, Ohio, then attended Wooster College in Wooster, Ohio, for two years; forced to end his college education because of financial difficulties;

took a job in the engineering department of the Bell Telephone Company and then in 1923 became a metal finisher in a Detroit, Mich., Fisher Body plant; became a welder in Detroit Chrysler plant in 1929 and in 1934 joined the American Federation of Labor (AFL) federal labor union that later became Chrysler Local 7 of the United Automobile, Aerospace, Agricultural Implement Workers of America (UAW); elected president of Chrysler Local 7 in 1936 and the following year elected a UAW vice-president; appointed president of the UAW by its executive board in 1939 and a few months later formally elected to the position; served during World War II as a labor member of the National War Labor Board and as a member of the President's Labor Advisory Committee; elected a Congress of Industrial Organizations' (CIO) vice-president and served as secretary-treasurer of the CIO Political Action Committee; defeated for reelection as UAW president by Walter P. Reuther (q.v.) in 1946, but elected first vice-president; defeated for the office of vice-president in 1947, then became the assistant director of organization for the CIO; became an assistant to President George Meany (q.v.) after the 1955 merger of the American Federation of Labor (AFL) and the CIO; appointed an AFL-CIO trouble-shooter in 1963; retired from union activities in 1964 because of ill health; usually supported the Democratic party; died in Muskegon, Mich., April 18, 1967; R. J. Thomas Papers, Walter Reuther Library, Wayne State University; Jack Stieber, *Governing the UAW* (1962); Jean Gould and Lorena Hickok, *Walter Reuther: Labor's Rugged Individualist* (1972); Frank Cormier and William J. Eaton, *Reuther* (1970); Roger Keeran, *The Communist Party and the Auto Workers Unions* (1980); Nelson Lichtenstein, *Labor's War at Home: The CIO in World War II* (1982); R. J. Thomas Interview, Columbia Oral History Collection; Harvey A. Levenstein, *Communism, Anticommunism, and the CIO* (1981); Bert Cochran, *Labor and Communism: The Conflict that Shaped American Unions* (1977).

THOMPSON, Mary Gordon   (1885–1973). Born in Dundee, Scotland, July 14, 1885; daughter of James A., a shoemaker, and Margaret (Young) Gordon, a textile worker; married James Thompson, a hod carrier and English immigrant, in Ludlow, Mass., on September 25, 1905; divorced in 1917; two children (one with James Thompson and one with Robert Fechner, later director of the Civilian Conservation Corps, with whom she lived after divorce); became a textile worker at age 11 in Montrose, Scotland; emigrated to America alone in 1903, later followed by family, and settled in Ludlow, where she found work as a jute spinner; continued as a textile worker until age 30; became president of Spinners' local in Ludlow and its delegate to the Springfield, Mass., Central Labor Union; a fiery speaker, led several strikes in Ludlow; active in women's suffrage movement; lived for a time with Mabel Gillespie, secretary of the Boston Women's Trade Union League (WTUL) in Boston; attended the WTUL's Training School in Chicago in 1916, a program which combined four months of academic training with eight months of field organizing; assigned to field work in Philadelphia, Pa., and then went to Cumberland, Md., where she organized laundry and garment workers and was jailed during a textile workers' strike; in 1918, assisted in organizing women at the Bethlehem Steel works in New Castle, Pa.; under the auspices of the Boston WTUL and the Massachusetts Suffrage Association's Industrial Committee in 1920, undertook an educational campaign among English-speaking textile workers in Fall River and New Bedford, Mass., to overcome opposition to raising the compulsory school age from 14 to 16; in early 1920s, was an organizer for the white goods and neckwear workers' unions; a leader of the "Children's Caravan" which toured Massachusetts campaigning for the Child Labor Amendment in 1924; served as president of the Boston WTUL, 1925–1941, in which capacity she provided strike support, served on a citizens' committee to organize black maids and Pullman porters in Boston, and directed Boston WTUL's soup kitchen and unemployment center for women workers during the depression; organizer and business agent, 1934–1936, of International Ladies' Garment Workers' Union local of white goods workers in Boston; during general textile strike in 1934, led picket line of one thousand workers at Sayles Mill in Rhode Island; in 1936 toured the Soviet Union as a member of the "May 1st Trade Union Delegation" sponsored by the Friends of the Soviet Union, and returned impressed with textile working conditions and child care services for working mothers; a member of the United Textile Workers' Union (UTW) for over 20 years, she paid her dues to a small American Federation of Labor local after the UTW affiliated with the Congress of Industrial Organizations (CIO), charging that the CIO leadership was "primarily interested in self-aggrandizement"; a strong supporter of Franklin D. Roosevelt; after retiring as president of the Boston WTUL, served as executive secretary of Springfield, Mass., chapter of Russian War Relief during World War II; owned an antique shop in Wilbraham, Mass., 1947–1957; died September 19, 1973, in Stafford Springs, Conn.; *Springfield Union*, September 21, 1973; Schlesinger Library, Radcliffe College.

Stephen H. Norwood

THORNE, Florence Calvert   (1877–1973). Born in Hannibal, Mo., on July 28, 1877; daughter of Stephen, a storekeeper and teacher, and Amanthis Belle (Matthews) Thorne; was born and raised a Baptist but later converted to the Roman Catholic faith; never married; no children; graduated from Hannibal High School in 1896; attended Oberlin College, 1897–1898, and then took a job in the Eastman, Ga., public school system; returned to Hannibal and taught history, English, and civics, 1902–1912; meanwhile, she matriculated at the University of Chicago where, in 1909, she was awarded the Ph.B.; enrolled in the University of Chicago Graduate School in 1910; while working on a thesis on the American Federation of Labor (AFL), she met Samuel Gompers (q.v.) and accepted his invitation to spend the summer of 1911 conducting research in the AFL files at the organization's Washington, D.C., headquarters; was appointed assistant editor of *The American Federationist* in 1912, beginning a 40-year association with the AFL; became Gompers's confidential assistant during the period 1912–

1917; and occasionally wrote speeches for him while assuming most of the editorial responsibilities for *The American Federationist* (although Gompers continued as nominal editor); during World War I, she was appointed to the subcommittee on women in industry of the advisory committee of the Council of National Defense; left the AFL in 1918 to assume the assistant directorship of the U.S. Department of Labor's Working Conditions Service in the War Labor Administration; in this position she strived to improve labor-management relations in war industries while also seeking to improve working conditions; assisted Samuel Gompers in the writing of his memoir, *Seventy Years of Life and Labor: An Autobiography*, which was published in 1925; returned to the AFL and *The American Federationist* in 1925 and became an administrative assistant to the new AFL president, William Green (q.v.); organized a voluntary research staff in 1926 to accumulate unemployment statistics from local unions and in 1933 the AFL formally constituted a research department; was appointed director of the AFL research department in 1933 and continued in that capacity for the next 20 years; as director of the research department during the depression years of the 1930s, she provided research assistance to national and local unions useful in the negotiation of National Recovery Administration industrial codes and in lobbying for such social legislation as social security, unemployment compensation insurance, and child labor regulation; served as a member of the Federal Advisory Commission for Employment Security and as a labor advisor to the International Labor Organization during World War II; retired in 1953 after George Meany (q.v.) assumed the AFL presidency; authored *Samuel Gompers: American Statesman* (1957); died in Falls Church, Va., March 16, 1973; many of Thorne's papers are located in the AFL Papers at the State Historical Society of Wisconsin; *Notable American Women*, Vol. 4; Bernard Mandel, *Samuel Gompers: A Biography* (1963); Philip Taft, *The A.F. of L. in the Time of Gompers* (1957); *The New York Times*, March 17, 1973.

TIGHE, Michael F. (1858–1940). Born in Boonton, N.J., March 10, 1858; son of a blast furnace worker; Roman Catholic; married Elizabeth Leonhart on August 15, 1879; one child; moved, after his father was blacklisted for union activities, with his family to West Virginia; left school at age 10, when his father's death forced him to seek employment; hired by the Wheeling Iron and Nail Company and eventually became a puddler and a member of the Sons of Vulcan; joined the newly founded Amalgamated Association of Iron, Steel, and Tin Workers' (AA), Wheeling (W.Va.) Lodge 5 in 1877 and elected its president; was an organizer for AA and the Amalgamated Street Car Workers and was president of the Ohio Valley Trades and Labor Assembly, 1896–1899; was assistant secretary and field organizer for the AA, 1899–1911, a period during which his union was driven out of basic steel; served as secretary, then elected international president in 1918; favored an industrial approach, but was a cautious, conservative business unionist, preoccupied with protecting the interests and jurisdictional claims of the AA; during the great steel strike of 1919, ordered

AA members back to work in order to protect existing AA contracts, a policy that caused resentment within the American Federation of Labor (AFL) National Committee for Organizing Iron and Steel Workers; during the 1920s, AA membership dwindled to insignificance; under the impetus of the labor provisions of the National Industrial Recovery Act of 1933, the AA made a comeback in basic steel, spearheaded by a militant rank-and-file faction that challenged his leadership; was able to subdue these insurgents, but could not sustain momentum in organizing; was under internal and external pressures to accommodate himself to an effective organizational strategy and hence faced an acute dilemma; John L. Lewis's (q.v.) proposal that the AA affiliate with the Congress of Industrial Organizations (CIO) in a joint steel-organizing drive was attractive in that Lewis promised to respect the AA's jurisdiction, but Tighe was reluctant to act independently of the AFL executive council in spite of its contempt for his leadership and unwillingness to accord AA broad industrial jurisdiction; was ill and incapable of resolving the impasse and hence authorized the AA executive board to use its own discretion; the board's acceptance of the CIO proposal gave the Steel Workers Organizing Committee (SWOC) the jurisdictional legitimacy it sought for its campaign; was named a member of the SWOC and resigned as AA president in December 1936, and lived in retirement in Pittsburgh, Pa.; was a Democrat; died in Pittsburgh, Pa., August 5, 1940; David Brody, *Labor in Crisis: The Steel Strike of 1919* (1965); Irving Bernstein, *Turbulent Years: A History of the American Worker, 1933–1941* (1970); *The Amalgamated Journal*, August 8, 1940.

                                                                                   Donald G. Sofchalk

TIPPETT, Thomas   (1890–1979). Born in Peoria, Ill., on October 27, 1890; son of John Champion, a coal miner, and Ellen (Hart) Tippett; raised a Presbyterian; married Mary Voeseke in 1910; one child; worked for several years as a coal miner in Illinois and oil worker in California; became interested in the Tom Mooney (q.v.) case and spoke all over the United States on behalf of freedom for Mooney, possibly as a representative of the International Workers' Defense League in 1919; took night classes at the University of Chicago and worked as an organizer for the Amalgamated Clothing Workers of America, the steel strike of 1919, and the Farmer-Labor party in 1920; was a correspondent and business manager for the Federated Press; as education director for Subdistrict 5, District 12, United Mine Workers of America, ran classes in economics, labor problems, drama, and a variety of other subjects along a circuit of coal camps and small towns in southern Illinois's coal region, 1924–1927; his program became widely known in the workers' education movement, and he went to Brookwood Labor College in 1927 as director of extension, with responsibility for reaching unorganized workers, particularly in the South; attended courses at Columbia University and taught economics at Barnard Summer School for Women Workers, 1928; a trip to the South for Brookwood in 1929 led to his involvement in organizing striking textile workers in Marion, N.C., and was the basis for his classic account of the "Piedmont Revolt," *When Southern Labor Stirs* (1931) and a play, *Mill Shadows*, which Brookwood students and faculty took on tour under his direction in the spring of 1932; when six strikers were shot and killed by police in Marion, he was part of a United Textile Workers delegation to the governor of North Carolina to demand an official investigation; did relief and publicity work for independent miners' unions in Illinois and West Virginia, 1930–1932; sided with A. J. Muste (q.v.), Brookwood's director, in a faculty dispute in 1933, and soon thereafter left Brookwood; wrote a novel about coal mining in Illinois, *Horse Shoe Bottoms* (1935), based on the life of his father; between 1936 and 1947, he was employed in New York and Washington, D.C., by the Works Progress Administration, Division of Research, National Youth Administration, and Office of Price Administration, where he was head of the rent control program; left the government to become director of education for the International Association of Machinists, 1947–1956; moved to Seattle, Wash., and worked as education director of the Aero Mechanics Union, Machinists Lodge 751, 1956–1961, running programs for shop stewards and the general membership at Boeing Aircraft; he knew Mother Jones (q.v.) personally and wrote the entry about her in the *Encyclopedia of the Social Sciences*, Vol. 8 (1933 edition); was also co-author, with Katherine H. Pollak, of *Your Job and Your Pay: A Picture of the World in Which We Work* (1931); died in Seattle, Wash., March 26, 1979; Brookwood Labor College Papers, Walter Reuther Archives, Wayne State University; Solon DeLeon, ed., *The American Labor Who's Who* (1925); Theresa Wolfson, "Tom Tippett and the School He Keeps," *American Labor World* (July 1926).

Jon Bloom

TOBIN, Daniel Joseph   (1875–1955). Born in County Clare, Ireland, in April 1875; son of John, a general storekeeper, and Bridget (Kennelly) Tobin; Roman Catholic; married Annie Elizabeth Reagan in August 1898 and, after her death, Irene Halloran on October 31, 1922; six children; attended the schools of Ireland before emigrating to the United States in 1890; hired by a Boston sheet-metal factory, but continued his education in a Cambridge (Mass.) night school; became a driver and motorman for a Boston street railway company in 1894; became the driver of a delivery truck for a meatpacking firm and joined Local 25 of the International Brotherhood of Teamsters, Chauffeurs, Warehousemen and Helpers of America (IBT), which had been organized in Boston in 1900; elected business representative in 1904; elected the general president of the IBT in 1907, holding position until 1952; served during World War I on President Woodrow T. Wilson's Industrial Conference; elected American Federation of Labor (AFL) treasurer in 1917 and served until 1928; served as delegate to the International Federal Trade Union Conference in 1919 and as an AFL delegate to the Pan-American Labor Conference in 1920; elected an AFL vice-president and executive council member in 1933, serving until 1952; served as a vice-president of the AFL's building trades department, 1933–1952; served as an American delegate to the International Labor Organization in 1939 and as an AFL fraternal delegate to the British Trades Union Congress in 1911, 1938, and 1942; was an administrative assistant to President Franklin D. Roosevelt in 1940; traveled to England at the request of Roosevelt in 1942 to investigate the conditions of labor, capital, and government; was a Democrat and served as chairman of the labor division of the Democratic National Committee during the campaigns of 1932, 1936, 1940, and 1944; edited the *Teamsters Magazine,* 1908–1952; retired from union positions in 1952; died in Indianapolis, Ind., November 14, 1955; Sam Romer, *The International Brotherhood of Teamsters: Its Government and Structure* (1962); Robert D. Leiter, *The Teamsters Union: A Study of Its Economic Impact* (1957); *Current Biography* (1945); *National Cyclopaedia of American Biography,* Vol. G; *Dictionary of American Biography,* Suppl. 5.

TONELLI, Joseph P.   (1908–   ). Born in Grove City, Pa., on February 26, 1908; married; two children; moved to New York City in 1928 and began working in the paper products industry; Roman Catholic; helped organize and served as president of Local 243, International Brotherhood of Pulp, Sulphite and Paper Mill Workers (IBPSPMW), Bronx, mid-1930s; was appointed international organizer in 1939; was the key figure in the international union's efforts in New York City from 1939 through the 1940s in organizing the converter paper industry and in battles against the Congress of Industrial Organizations (CIO); in 1942, he was named chairman of the Greater New York Organizing Committee of IBPSPMW; elected international ninth vice-president in 1944; was frequently under attack by union dissidents in the late 1950s and early 1960s for alleged improprieties in negotiations and handling of finances but was vindicated in convention votes; elected president of IBPSPMW on September 17, 1965; appointed to the Social Security Advisory Board by Lyndon Johnson in 1964; appointed to the Adirondack Park Agency by Governor Nelson Rockefeller; was appointed to the New York State Racing Commission by Rockefeller in 1972 and was appointed chairman of the commission by Governor Hugh Carey in 1976; appointed to the Air Quality Advisory Board, Environmental Protection Agency, by Richard Nixon and to the Advisory Committee on Trade Negotiations and the White House Conference on Handicapped Individuals by Gerald Ford; active in United Nations support and Israel fund-raising endeavors; fostered the merger of IBPSPMW and the United Papermakers and Paperworkers into the United Paperworkers International Union in 1973 and became the first president of the new organization; elected an American Federation of Labor (AFL)-CIO vice-president and executive council member in 1973; served as vice-president of the AFL-CIO industrial union department; during his period of ascendancy, the paper industry unions' membership growth leveled off and defections among West Coast and Canadian locals further eroded union strength; pled guilty to federal charges of embezzling $350,000 in union funds in 1978 and was sentenced to three years in prison; supported Democrats generally but endorsed Richard Nixon for a second term in 1972 and had close ties with Nelson Rockefeller in

New York State; Robert H. Zieger, *Rebuilding the Pulp and Paper Workers' Union, 1933–1941* (1984); Harry E. Graham, *The Paper Rebellion: Development and Upheaval in Pulp and Paper Unionism* (1970); *The New York Times*, July 20, December 7, 20, 1978.

Robert H. Zieger

TOTTEN, Ashley Leopold   (1884–1963). Born in St. Croix, Virgin Islands, October 11, 1884; son of Richard W. and Camilla C. Totten; Lutheran; married Nellie Violet Victoria on March 20, 1924; two children; Afro-American; graduated from high school in the West Indies, then emigrated to the United States in 1905; eventually hired as a sleeping car porter with the Pullman Palace Car Company; elected by the New York Central District in 1924 as a delegate to a wage conference called by the officials of Pullman under the auspices of its employee representation plan; in 1925 was one of the principal founders, along with Asa Philip Randolph (q.v.), of the Brotherhood of Sleeping Car Porters (BSCP) and was immediately discharged by Pullman, becoming an assistant organizer for the new union; elected international secretary-treasurer of the BSCP in 1930, serving in that capacity for more than 30 years; was a founder and elected first president of the American Virgin Islands Civic Association in 1932; became the national reporting officer of the Railroad Retirement Board in 1937; during World War II, was a member of the Labor Arbitration Panel of the War Manpower Commission and was chairman of Selective Service Board No. 55; appointed by President John F. Kennedy as a director of the Virgin Islands Corporation in 1961; served as an executive board member of the League for Industrial Democracy, the American China Policy Association, and the Welfare Defense League; was a member of the Liberal party of New York; died in St. Croix, Virgin Islands, January 26, 1963; Brailsford R. Brazeal, *The Brotherhood of Sleeping Car Porters: Its Origin and Development* (1946); Jervis Anderson, *A. Philip Randolph: A Biographical Portrait* (1972); F. Ray Marshall, *The Negro and Organized Labor* (1965); Herbert R. Northrup, *Organized Labor and the Negro* (1944).

TOWNSEND, Robert, Jr.   (fl. 1807–1843). Born on the British prison ship, *Jersey*, during the American Revolution; son of Robert Townsend, Sr., a New York merchant and coffeehouse owner, who, under the alias Samuel Culper, Jr., served as a spy for General George Washington during the American Revolution; his mother died in childbirth, and hence he was reared by two prominent Brooklyn ladies; listed as a member of the Tammany Society of New York City in 1807 and as a house carpenter in 1825; became actively involved in the New York Workingmen's party after the 1829 elections; elected president of the Workingmen's state convention in 1830 and two years later chosen vice-president of the Antimasonic state convention; switched political allegiance to the Whig party in 1834 and became an anti-Tammany spokesman; did not participate in the New York house carpenters' strike of 1834, but joined and became president of the Journeymen House Carpenters of New York City; attended the preliminary meetings and helped organize the New York General Trades' Union (GTU) and served it as treasurer; offered a resolution during the GTU convention in July 1832, proposing the issuance of a call for a national trades union convention; served as a carpenters' delegate to the first convention of the National Trades' Union (NTU) in 1834 and read a controversial resolution favoring political action to bring about social reform; resigned from the NTU in the fall of 1834, thus ending his short-lived formal association with the trade union movement; during the early summer of 1836, actively supported journeyman tailors convicted of conspiracy; became associated with the Locofoco movement in 1836 and presided over the state convention that created the Equal Rights party; refused the new party's nomination for lieutenant governor, but nominated for the New York Assembly by both the Locofocos and the Whigs and elected, serving one term; presided over the second Locofoco state convention in 1837 and again nominated for the assembly, losing to the Whig candidate in the general elections; appointed city sealer in 1839 and served in that capacity until becoming city weigher of merchandise in 1843; Walter Hugins, *Jacksonian Democracy and the Working Class: A Study of the New York Workingmen's Movement, 1829–1837* (1960); John R. Commons et al., eds., *A Documentary History of American Industrial Society*, Vol. 6 (1910), and *History of Labour in the United States*, Vol. 1 (1918); Philip S. Foner, *History of the Labor Movement in the United States*, Vol. 1 (1947).

TOWNSEND, Willard Saxby   (1895–1957). Born in Cincinnati, Ohio, December 4, 1895; son of William, a contractor, and Beatrice Townsend; Episcopalian; Afro-American; married Consuelo Mann on October 1, 1930; one child; graduated from high school in 1912 and somewhat later studied premedicine for two years at the University of Toronto; received a degree in chemistry from the Royal College of Science in Toronto and an LL.B. from Blackstone College of Law in Chicago, Ill.; worked as a redcap at Cincinnati's Union Depot, 1914–1916, and as a dining car waiter on the Canadian National Railroad, 1921–1925; served as a teacher in Texas, then was a redcap on the Great Northern Railroad, 1930–1936; served during World War I as a first lieutenant in the U.S. Army in France; was a founder of the American Federation of Labor (AFL) Labor Auxiliary of Redcaps in Chicago in 1936 and became its first president; organized an independent Brotherhood of Redcaps in Chicago in 1938 and, when the organization was given an international charter by the Congress of Industrial Organizations (CIO) in 1942 as the United Transport Service Employees of America, elected its president; became a member of the CIO executive board in 1942; elected a vice-president of the National Urban League in 1940; was a member of the board of directors and executive committee of the American Council on Race Relations in 1944; served on the CIO committees on Latin American affairs and housing and community development and on the committee to abolish discrimination; served as a CIO fraternal delegate to the Cuban Fed-

eration of Labor in 1944; was a labor advisor to the International Labor Organization conference in Mexico City in 1946; served as a member of the committee
of the World Federation of Trade Unions to study conditions in Japan, China,
Korea, the Philippines, and the Malayan states in 1947; was a CIO delegate to
the International Confederation of Free Trade Unions in 1952; elected a vice-
president and executive council member of the AFL-CIO at the merger convention in 1955; was a vice-president of the National Association for the Advancement of Colored People, a trustee of Hampton Institute, and a director of the
American Labor Education Service, also serving on numerous other public and
private boards and agencies; co-authored *What the Negro Wants* (1944) and
authored *Full Employment and the Negro Workers* (1945), *Japanese Handbook:
Trade Union Practices* (1948); died in Chicago, Ill., February 3, 1957; *The
American Federationist* (March 1957); *Current Biography* (1948); *AFL-CIO
News*, February 9, 1957; *Who's Who in Labor* (1946).

TRACY, Daniel William   (1886–1955). Born in Bloomington, Ill., April 7,
1886; married; completed his formal education and eventually moved to Houston,
Tex., in 1910; adopted the electrician's trade; joined Local 716 of the International Brotherhood of Electrical Workers (IBEW) in 1913; worked as a lineman
and wireman in Texas and Oklahoma, 1913–1915; elected business manager of
IBEW Locals 716 and 66 in 1916; became an IBEW international vice-president
in 1920; appointed international president of the IBEW in 1933 and later elected
to the position; was a U.S. delegate to the International Labor Organization
(ILO) conference in Geneva in 1935 and served as a labor advisor to Secretary
of State Cordell Hull during the Pan-American Conference in Lima, Peru, in
1938; was a staunch critic of the Committee for Industrial Organization (CIO)
and strongly supported the suspension of the CIO unions by the American Federation of Labor (AFL) executive council in 1936; resigned as IBEW president
in 1940 after being appointed Assistant Secretary of Labor, serving in that
capacity until 1946; served as labor director of the ILO during 1946; became
IBEW international president for the second time in 1947; during the same year,
elected an AFL vice-president and executive council member and also a vice-
president of the AFL metal trades department; served as an AFL delegate to the
AFL-CIO united labor policy committee in 1950; became IBEW president emer-
itus in 1954; was a Democrat; died in Washington, D.C., March 22, 1955; Philip
Taft, *The A.F. of L. from the Death of Gompers to the Merger* (1959); Walter
Galenson, *The CIO Challenge to the AFL: A History of the American Labor
Movement, 1935–1941* (1960); *The American Federationist* (September 1955);
The American Federation of Labor News-Reporter, March 25, 1955.

TRAUTMANN, William E.   (fl. 1900–1917). Born in New Zealand of German-American parents in 1869; became a radical unionist while living in Germany; emigrated to the United States in the late 1890s; and settled in Ohio;
became an organizer for the Brewery Workers Union (BWU); in 1900, elected

to BWU's executive board and became editor of its journal, *Brauer-Zeitung*; was a well-versed Marxist and began advocating syndicalism; meanwhile, joined the Socialist party of America and was a national committeeman from Ohio; when the BWU clashed with the American Federation of Labor (AFL) over a jurisdictional matter in 1902, made a scathing attack on the AFL leaders, accusing them of dividing the workers and selling out to the capitalists; took the initiative in calling the secret conference of radicals that laid the groundwork for the founding of the Industrial Workers of the World (IWW) in 1905 and was influential in formulating its Industrial Union Manifesto; relieved of his posts with the BWU as a result of these activities; as general secretary-treasurer of the IWW and a member of its first general executive board, headed the faction that opposed political action; in 1906, joined with Daniel DeLeon (q.v.) to depose IWW president Charles Sherman (q.v.), which caused a split resulting in the withdrawal of the Western Federation of Miners; with Vincent St. John (q.v.), took advantage of the direct-actionists' control of the 1908 convention to oust DeLeon from the IWW and to eliminate the political clause from the constitution; was an effective polemicist and organizer, but was an indifferent administrator; in 1908, replaced by St. John as secretary-treasurer; elected as a general organizer; in 1909, led the McKees Rocks, Pa., steel strike, the IWW's first successful effort among Eastern United States immigrant workers; was aware of their plight and convinced they could be organized, and enlisted several thousand in an IWW local at McKees Rocks; called an IWW convention of the Pittsburgh district to unionize throughout the district, but his efforts failed to create permanent steelworkers' unions; subsequently tried to establish the IWW among Akron, Ohio, tire and Detroit, Mich., automobile workers, and helped direct the great Lawrence, Mass., textile strike; became disillusioned with the IWW's preoccupation with direct action and joined Daniel DeLeon's Detroit IWW, an adjunct of the Socialist Labor party, in 1913; during World War I, became involved in the Works Council Movement; Melvyn Dubofsky, *We Shall Be All: A History of the Industrial Workers of the World* (1969); Philip S. Foner, *History of the Labor Movement in the United States,* Vol. 4 (1965); Patrick Renshaw, *The Wobblies* (1967).

Donald G. Sofchalk

TRAVIS, Maurice Eugene   (1910–   ). Born in Spokane, Wash., April 24, 1910; son of Charles Franklin, a salesman, and Lotus (Clark) Travis; married Ursula Vinca Dexter; one child; during the 1930s and 1940s, was a business agent for a United Steelworkers of America (USWA) local in California and a member of the California State Industrial Union Council, Congress of Industrial Organizations (CIO); was purged from the USWA in 1944 and became an international representative for the International Union of Mine, Mill and Smelter Workers (IUMMSW); appointed executive assistant to the IUMMSW president, Reid Robinson (q.v.), in 1946; chosen vice-president in the 1946 election that brought the dissension between the left- and right-wing factions to a head, resulting in the secession of a large faction of Connecticut brass workers; was a member of the Communist party and, with other IUMMSW officials, allegedly coordinated union policies with top members of the Communist party; became international president of the IUMMSW after Robinson's resignation in 1946; urged to resign or be removed from the presidency by a CIO special committee set up to investigate the disputed 1946 election; at a special IUMMSW convention in 1947, resigned as president, nominating John Clark (q.v.); became secretary-treasurer as part of the arrangement leading to his resignation from the IUMMSW presidency; along with Clark, consolidated the left-wing control of the IUMMSW, thus offsetting the secessionist movement; helped defend the IUMMSW against the CIO's accusation of Communist domination, thus paving the way for the expulsion of the union in 1950; taking advantage of charges that he and others had run roughshod over the rank and file, the USWA tried unsuccessfully to capture the crucial Butte, Mont., and Anaconda, Mont., IUMMSW locals in 1954; in 1949 publicly resigned his Communist party membership, because the IUMMSW needed to avail itself of National Labor Relations Board procedures to fend off raiding; in 1956, however, indicted along with 13 other IUMMSW leaders for conspiring to falsify the non-Communist affidavits of the Taft-Hartley Act; the case, which involved two trials and several appeals, was dismissed in 1967 by a U.S. district court; left his union post in the late 1950s and retired in California; Vernon H. Jenson, *Nonferrous Metals Industry Unionism, 1932–1954* (1954); F. S. O'Brien, "The 'Communist-Dominated' Unions in the U.S. since 1950," *Labor History* (Spring 1968); *Who's Who in Labor* (1946).

Donald G. Sofchalk

TRAVIS, Robert Carroll   (1906–1979). Born in Toledo, Ohio, February 7, 1906; son of Fred F. and Esther L. Travis; Lutheran; married Sophie Beaudel on July 24, 1940; one child; graduated from high school, then took a job in a General Motors Corporation (GMC) Chevrolet plant in Toledo; was one of the founders of United Automobile, Aerospace and Agricultural Implement Workers of America (UAW) Local 14 in Toledo in 1935 and shortly thereafter elected president of the local; became president of the UAWGMC Council in 1936; was director of organization for the UAW in Flint, Mich., in 1936 and led the successful sit-down strikes against GMC in 1936–1937 that helped the UAW organize the automobile industry; became an international representative of the United Farm Equipment and Metal Workers of America (FE) in 1939 and was one of the leaders of FE's strike against the International Harvester Company in Chicago, Ill., in 1941; during the early 1940s, rejoined the UAW in Illinois, affiliating with the allegedly Communist-controlled Amalgamated Local 453; served as a member of the labor advisory council of the Metropolitan Chicago division of the Office of Price Administration and a member of the Regional Labor Panel of the War Labor Board during World War II; elected president of the Cook County State Industrial Union Council, Congress of Industrial Organizations (CIO), and a vice-president of the Illinois CIO Council, serving until 1947; was a member of the policy committee of the Illinois CIO Political Action

Committee; often associated with radical causes; was a member of the Board of Directors of Abraham Lincoln School, a writer for the *Chicago Star,* and a sponsor of the American Peace Mobilization; edited the *Legislative Guide*, the organ of the legislative committee of the Illinois State Industrial Union Council, CIO; identified himself as a Democrat; died in Los Angeles, Calif., on November 19, 1979; Sidney Fine, *Sit-Down: The General Motors Strike of 1936–1937* (1969); Frank Cormier and William J. Eaton, *Reuther* (1970); Max M. Kampelman, *The Communist Party vs. The C.I.O.: A Study in Power Politics* (1957); Roger Keeran, *The Communist Party and the Auto Unions* (1980).

TREVELLICK, Richard F.   (1830–1895). Born on St. Mary's, one of the Scilly Isles off the coast of England, May 20, 1830 (birthdate has also been listed as May 2, 1830); son of peasant farmers of Cornwall; Methodist; married Victoria in 1858; five children; as a young man, worked as a ship's carpenter and as a seaman in Southampton, England; acquired a reputation as a labor agitator while advocating an eight-hour day in Auckland, New Zealand, and Melbourne, Australia, during 1852–1854; arrived in New Orleans, La., in 1857 and shortly thereafter became president of the Ship Carpenters' and Caulkers' Union and led a successful effort to win a nine-hour day; moved to Detroit, Mich., in 1861 and became the first president of the Detroit Trades' Assembly and the Michigan Grand Eight Hour League: national Union of Ship Carpenters and Caulkers in 1865; attended the Congress of the National Labor Union (NLU) in 1867 as a delegate from the Detroit Trades' Assembly and the Michigan Grand Eight Hour League; elected a NLU delegate to the International Workingmen's Association in 1867 but was unable to attend because of financial difficulties; served as president of the NLU in 1869 and during 1871–1872; served as an organizer and lecturer for the Knights of Labor, 1878–1895; besides his lifelong agitation for eight-hour legislation, fought the blacklist, the importation of Chinese contract labor, and the racial exclusion clauses contained in many trade union charters; was one of the first labor lobbyists and successfully lobbied an eight-hour day act for federal mechanics and laborers through the U.S. Congress in 1868; was a founder of the Greenback Labor party, serving as temporary chairman of the national Greenback Labor party in 1878 and as chairman in 1880; died in Detroit, Mich., February 15, 1895; Richard F. Trevellick Papers, Joseph A. Labadie Collection, University of Michigan; Obediah Hicks, *Life of Richard F. Trevellick, the Labor Orator* (1896); David Montgomery, *Beyond Equality: Labor and the Radical Republicans, 1862–1872* (1967); Doris B. McLaughlin, *Michigan Labor: A Brief History from 1818 to the Present* (1970); *Dictionary of American Biography*, Vol. 18.

TROUP, Augusta Lewis   (ca. 1848–1920). Born in New York City, ca. 1848; daughter of Charles and Elizabeth (Rowe) Lewis; Roman Catholic; married Alexander Troupe on June 12, 1874 (date of marriage has also been listed as June 12, 1872); seven children; attended Brooklyn Heights Seminary and Sacred

Heart Convent School in Manhattanville, N.Y.; became a reporter for the *New York Sun* in 1866; served an apprenticeship as a typesetter on the *New York Era* and shortly thereafter joined the *New York World* as a typesetter; was one of the participants in the initial meeting of the Working Women's Association founded by Elizabeth Cady Stanton and Susan B. Anthony in 1868; later in the same year, became the first president of the Women's Typographical Union (WTU), which evolved from the Working Women's Association; after the WTU was recognized and granted a charter by the International Typographical Union (ITU) in 1869, attended the ITU's 1870 national convention and elected corresponding secretary; after marrying, left the WTU which, torn by dissension and discord because of the failure to win wage rates comparable to those obtained by men, eventually disbanded in 1878; moved to New Haven, Conn., in 1874 and became a reporter for her husband's newspaper, the *New Haven Union*; died in New Haven, Conn., September 14, 1920; George A. Stevens, *New York Typographical Union No. 6: A Study of a Modern Trade Union and Its Predecessors* (1913); George A. Tracy, *History of the Typographical Union* (1913); *Notable American Women* (1971); Eleanor Flexner, *Century of Struggle: The Women's Rights Movement in the U.S.* (1959); Philip S. Foner, *Women and the American Labor Movement from Colonial Times to the Eve of World War I* (1979).

Marie Tedesco

TURNER, Frederick   (fl. 1846–1884). Born in England in 1846; emigrated to the United States in 1856, settling in Philadelphia, Pa.; completed public high school in Philadelphia; practiced the gold-beating trade and joined the Noble Order of the Knights of Labor (K of L); organized Local Assembly 20, consisting of gold-beaters, in 1873; shortly thereafter, organized the first K of L assembly in New York, Local Assembly 28, and, along with James L. Wright (q.v.), the first local in Scranton, Pa., Local Assembly 88, in 1875; served as secretary of District Assembly No. 1, general secretary-treasurer of the K of L, and two terms on the K of L general executive board; was a member of the "Home Club," an inner ring that controlled New York District Assembly No. 49 and opposed many of Grand Master Workman Terence V. Powderly's (q.v.) policies; lobbied the U.S. Congress in support of the Foran bill to restrict contract labor in 1884; because of his activities in the K of L during the 1870s and 1880s, blacklisted in his trade; became an independent grocer; Norman J. Ware, *The Labor Movement in the United States, 1860–1895* (1929); Gerald N. Grob, *Workers and Utopia: A Study of Ideological Conflict in the American Labor Movement, 1865–1900* (1961); *Journal of United Labor*, Vol. 4 (July 1883).

TURNER, J. C.   (1916–   ). Born in Beaumont, Tex., on November 4, 1916; son of James C., a building tradesman, and Lydia Turner, a homemaker; a Roman Catholic convert; married Mary Pauline, a homemaker, in 1934; five children; received a B.A. from Catholic University of America; joined Washington, D.C., Local 77 of the International Union of Operating Engineers (IUOE) in 1934; was elected business manager of Local 77 in 1940, retaining that position until 1971; served as the Maryland State Federation of Labor and the District of Columbia Federation of Labor secretary and vice-president, 1948–1957; was vice-president of the Washington Building and Construction Trades Council, 1952–1965; elected second vice-president of the Maryland State and District of Columbia American Federation of Labor-Congress of Industrial Organizations (AFL-CIO) councils in 1957 and held those offices until 1972; elected president of the Greater Washington Central Labor Council, AFL-CIO, in 1958, serving until 1972; served as president of the Washington Building and Construction Trades Council, 1965–1968; elected an IUOE international vice-president in 1956, serving until 1973; meanwhile, he was elected IUOE secretary-treasurer in 1972; elected international president of the IUOE in 1976; elected an AFL-CIO vice-president and member of the executive council in 1977; active in a variety of governmental and civic activities, he served as a labor member on the Unemployment Compensation Board, District of Columbia, 1958–1968, and the Minimum Wage and Industrial Safety Board of the District of Columbia, 1944–1948; the recipient of numerous awards for civic activity, including the League of Women Voters Man of the Year in 1959, the Humanitarian Award, City of Hope, 1960, Equal Opportunity Day Annual Award, 1962, and the Whitney Young, Jr., Memorial Award, Urban League, 1973; an active Democrat, he served as vice-chairman of the District of Columbia Democratic Committee, 1952–1960, and was a Democratic national committeeman in 1960; wrote numerous articles for *The American Federationist; Who's Who in Labor* (1976); *AFL-CIO News*, December 13, 1975, May 17, 1977.

U

UHL, Alexander (1899–1976). Born in New York City on June 11, 1899; son of Gustav and Julia (Thalman) Uhl; Episcopalian; married Gladys Beauchamp on January 31, 1948 (second marriage); after completing his primary and secondary education in the public schools of New York City, he enrolled at the City College of New York; after graduating with a B.A., he enrolled in the Columbia University School of Journalism; began his journalism career as a reporter with the *Newark Star Eagle*, 1921–1922; joined the Associated Press (AP) in 1923; was Madrid, Spain, bureau chief for AP and covered the Spanish civil war, 1935–1938; served as foreign editor for *PM*, 1940–1948, and was stationed in Europe during World War II; moved to Washington, D.C., after the demise of *PM* and was employed as a writer for the Public Affairs Institute; was a co-founder in 1954 of Press Associates Inc. (PAI), a news service for labor newspapers and became its editor; was a member of the American Newspaper Guild, the National Press Club, and the Overseas Press Club; an enthusiastic supporter of the labor movement, he provided the labor press, in George Meany's (q.v.) words, "with national news, full of insight and value to union members who look to their union paper for facts about the labor movement"; retired as editor of PAI in 1975; a Democrat; returned to Madrid where he was working on a book about the Spanish civil war at the time of his death, August 24, 1976; *AFL-CIO News*, August 28, 1976; *Who's Who in America, 1974–1975*.

V

VALENTINE, Joseph F. (1857–1930). Born in Baltimore, Md., May 13, 1857; Roman Catholic; married; no children; became an apprentice molder at an early age, and went to San Francisco, Calif., as a journeyman in 1880; immediately joined the International Molders Union (IMU) and elected president of his local within a few months; in 1885, helped found a city central council of metal craftsmen, the first such body formed in the United States; emerged as an exceptionally capable leader in handling the bitter San Francisco molders' strike of 1890; as a result, elected first vice-president by the IMU convention of 1890; was responsible for administering the pioneering conciliation agreements of 1891 with the Stove Founders Trade Association and of 1899 with the National Founders' Association; although the latter broke down in 1904, the IMU under his guidance sustained its trade interests; became president of the IMU after the resignation of Martin Fox (q.v.) in 1903; elected a vice-president and executive council member of the American Federation of Labor in 1905 and a vice-president of the metal trades department, reorganizing it on a sounder basis in 1908; as IMU president, maintained the established policy of not opposing the introduction of labor-saving technology; was a militant craft unionist and consistently tried to avoid strikes; however, staunchly supported strikes when vital union interests were at stake; acquired a reputation for firm but fair dealings with unionists and employers; during his term, the IMU executive board tightened up its policy of prohibiting unauthorized strikes; supported the California unions' anti-Chinese agitation, but later succeeded in pressuring several Southern locals to admit black molders; under the strain of interminable years of service to the labor movement, forced to resign union positions in 1924 because of ill health; died in San Francisco, Calif., February 7, 1930; Frank T. Stockton, *The International Molders Union of North America* (1921); Philip Taft, *Organized Labor in American*

History (1964); Robert E. L. Knight, *Industrial Relations in the San Francisco Bay Area* (1960).

                                                                    Donald G. Sofchalk

VAN ARSDALE, Harry, Jr.   (1905–   ). Born in New York City, November 23, 1905; son of a union electrician; Roman Catholic; married Mary (Molly) Casey in 1922; four children; attended an experimental high school for gifted children for two years before quitting school to take a job; worked in a variety of occupations, then, like his father, adopted the electrician's trade and joined New York City Local 3 of the International Brotherhood of Electrical Workers (IBEW); served in several minor positions in the union, then became embroiled in the efforts to frustrate the attempts of both Communists and racketeers to gain control of Local 3; as a result of the ensuing conflicts, arrested on an assault charge in 1932, but released; the following year, again charged and convicted of assault and sentenced to 6 to 12 years in prison; however, the conviction was reversed on appeal; became business manager of Local 3 in 1933 and held that position until 1968, when succeeded by his son; became the financial secretary of Local 3 in 1968; negotiated a seven-hour day for the members of Local 3 in 1933; in 1940 the work day was reduced to six hours and in 1962 to five hours; elected president of the Greater New York Central Trades and Labor Council in 1957 and two years later, after the American Federation of Labor-Congress of Industrial Organizations' (AFL-CIO) merger in New York City, became president of the New York City Central Labor Council, AFL-CIO; helped organize New York City taxi drivers in 1965 and later became president of Local 3036 of the New York City Taxi Drivers Union; served as international treasurer of the IBEW and was a member of the executive board of the Greater New York Building and Construction Trades Council; in addition to serving on numerous federal, state, and local government boards and agencies, was a director of the Lincoln Center for Performing Arts, a trustee of the Carnegie Hall Corporation, and a trustee of the National Urban League; a Democrat; *Reader's Digest* (January 1956); *The New Yorker*, March 16, 1968; *Current Biography* (1969).

VAN KLEECK, Mary Abby   (1883–1972). Born in Glenham, N.Y., on June 26, 1883; daughter of Robert Boyd, Episcopal minister, and Eliza (Mayer) van Kleeck; Episcopalian; never married; no children; educated in the public schools of Flushing, N.Y., and graduated from Flushing High School in 1900; received a B.A. from Smith College in 1904; conducted research on girls employed in New York City factories and tenement child labor for the College Settlement Association and served as industrial secretary of the Alliance Employment Bureau, 1905–1906; was appointed director of the Russell Sage Foundation's department of industrial studies in 1910 and served in that capacity until 1918 and again from 1919 to 1948; taught at the New York School of Philanthropy, 1914–1917; served on the New York Mayor's Committee on Unemployment and as president of the Intercollegiate Bureau of Occupations, 1915; an influential figure in Washington, D.C., during World War I, she served as the director of the women's branch of the Ordnance Department of the U.S. Army for the industrial service section; in that capacity she established standards for female employment in war industries that were adopted by the War Labor Policies Board; served on the War Labor Policies Board, 1918–1919; was appointed director of the U.S. Department of Labor's women in service division; returned to her position at the Russell Sage Foundation after the war, where she concentrated on employer-employee relations, the development of unemployment statistics, the involvement of labor in management, and the evolution of company towns; served on the President's Conference on Unemployment, 1921, and the Committee on Unemployment and Business Cycles in 1922–1923; involved in the establishment of the National Interracial Conference which met in Washington, D.C., in 1928; served as associate director of the International Industrial Relations Institute, 1928–1948; drafted a report on the economic position of women for the International Labor Organization in 1936; joined the executive committee of Hospites, an organization that assisted Nazi Germany refugees during the 1930s; served as president of the Second International Conference on Social Work which met in Frankfurt-am-Main, in 1932; appointed to the federal advisory council of the U.S. Employment Service in 1933 but resigned after one day, protesting New Deal policies she believed detrimental to organized labor and favorable to big business; became increasingly critical of American capitalism after World War I and by the 1930s had become a militant Socialist; joined Soviet-American friendship societies and traveled to the Soviet Union during this period; retired from the Russell Sage Foundation in 1948 and campaigned for Henry A. Wallace and the Progressive party ticket; ran unsuccessfully for the New York state senate as a candidate of the American Labor party in 1948; subpoenaed by Joseph McCarthy's Senate Permanent Subcommittee on Investigations in March 1953 because of her radical sympathies; continued advocating a variety of social reform until retiring to Woodstock, N.Y., in 1972 at age 88; authored *Women in the Bookbinding Trade* (1913), *Artificial Flower Making* (1913), *Working Girls in Evening School* (1914), *Wages in the Millinery Trade* (1914), *A Seasonal Industry* (1917), *Miners and Management* (1934), and co-authored *Technology and Livelihood* (1944); also wrote numerous articles for publications such as *Atlantic Monthly, The Survey, Daily Worker, Soviet Russia Today*, and *New Masses*; died in Kingston, N.Y., on June 8, 1972; Mary van Kleeck's Papers, Smith College, Wayne State University, and the National Archives; *Notable American Women*, Vol. 4; *Who's Who in America, 1972–1973*; Solon DeLeon, ed., *The American Labor Who's Who* (1925); *The New York Times*, June 10, 1972; Philip S. Foner, *Women and the American Labor Movement from World War I to the Present* (1980).

VANZETTI, Bartolomeo   (1888–1927). Born in Villafalletto, Italy, on June 11, 1888; son of Battista, an affluent farmer, and Giovanna Vanzetti; reared a Roman Catholic; never married; after completing a primary and secondary education in Italy, he emigrated to the United States in 1908 after the death of his mother; shortly after arriving in New York City, he began to travel extensively working at various odd jobs to support himself; settled in Plymouth, Mass., in 1915; lived in Mexico during 1917–1918 to avoid World War I conscription; along with Nicola Sacco (q.v.), he was a convert to Luigi Galleani's theories of philosophical anarchism; was working as a fish peddler at the time of his arrest for the murder of a shoe factory paymaster and guard in a robbery in South Braintree, Mass., on April 15, 1920; convicted along with Sacco of the crime in a trial notable primarily for the prejudicial manner in which the trial judge conducted the proceedings and the general public hysteria over the menace of radicalism that characterized the red scare years of 1919–1920; his eloquent defense of his radical beliefs in numerous letters and at his sentencing trial reveals an idealist of keen intelligence and deep convictions who did not fit the profile of a murderer for profit; despite numerous rejected appeals, the appointment of a gubernatorial advisory committee, and worldwide protests, he was executed on August 23, 1927; see Nicola Sacco; *The Sacco-Vanzetti Case*, 5 Vols. (1928, 1929); Marion Denman Frankfurter and Gardner Jackson, eds., *The Letters of Sacco and Vanzetti* (1928); Felix Frankfurter, *The Case of Sacco and Vanzetti* (1927); *Dictionary of American Biography*, Vol. 16; Fred Somkin, "How Vanzetti Said Goodbye," *Journal of American History* (September 1981).

VLADECK, Baruch Charney (Baruch Nachman Charney)   (1886–1938). Born in Dookorah, Minsk, Russia, in January 1886; son of Wolf, a merchant, and Broche (Horowitz) Charney; Jewish; married Clara Richman in 1911; three children; received a few years of formal education in a Russian yeshivah; prior to emigrating to the United States in 1908, was active in the revolutionary movement in Russia and in 1901 was imprisoned the first of several times as an agitator; after arriving in the United States, spent four years traveling, lecturing, and studying; became the manager of the Philadelphia office of *Jewish Daily Forward* in 1912; studied the English language and American history at the University of Pennsylvania; moved to New York City in 1915 and two years later elected to the New York City Board of Aldermen on the Socialist party ticket, serving until 1921; was a moderate in the internal conflicts of the Socialist movement and usually supported the party's right wing when forced to make a choice; became the general manager of the *Jewish Daily Forward* in 1921 and served in that capacity until his death; appointed by Mayor Fiorello La Guardia to the New York Housing Authority in 1934; was one of the original sponsors of the American Labor party (ALP) in 1936 and elected to the New York City Council on the ALP ticket in 1937; served as chairman of the Jewish Labor Committee, 1934–1938, was a director of the Hias during 1916–1938 and was a member of the executive committee of the American Civil Liberties Union; died in New York City, October 30, 1938; B. Charney Vladeck Papers, Tamiment Library, New York University; Melech Epstein, *Jewish Labor in the U.S.A., 1914–1952*, 2 Vols. (1953); Solon DeLeon, ed., *The American Labor Who's*

Who (1925); *Dictionary of American Biography,* Suppl. 2; *American Jewish Year Book*, Vol. 41; *Universal Jewish Encyclopedia*, Vol. 10.

VORSE, Mary Heaton   (1874–1966). Born in New York City, October 9, 1874; daughter of Hiram Heaton, a well-to-do Massachusetts innkeeper, and Ellen (Blackman) Heaton, scion of an old New England family; Episcopalian; married Albert W. Vorse, a writer, in 1898; two children; and after Albert died, Joseph O'Brien, a journalist, in 1912; one child; and subsequent to O'Brien's death in 1915, married for two years to the radical leader, Robert Minor; due to her parents' lengthy sojourns in Europe, educated there; the Provincetown, Mass., home which she and Albert Vorse purchased in 1907 became a mecca for the writers and performers who later founded the famous Provincetown Players; after her second husband's death, went to work as a full-time journalist as a means of supporting herself and her children; aroused by the miserable lives of the mill families while covering the Lawrence textile strike of 1912, she concentrated increasingly on reporting on industrial strife from the workers' viewpoint; although she covered other events, such as the womens' peace movement, the Bolshevik Revolution, and the rise of Nazism, her forte was labor journalism—publishing innumerable articles in such magazines as *The Outlook, Harper's,* and *The Nation* and several books about major strikes she witnessed; *Men and Steel* (1920) portrays the steelworkers' strike of 1919; *Strike: A Novel of Gastonia* (1930) is a slightly fictionalized account of her experiences as a reporter and as an organizer for the left-wing National Textile Workers' Union; *Labor's New Millions* (1938), perhaps her most substantial book, describes and analyzes the Congress of Industrial Organizations' industrial union movement, which she interpreted as being basically the drive of powerless workers for economic security and dignity through collective bargaining, despite its overtones of class struggle; reported on several major strikes of the 1930s, including the General Motors' sit-down (stressing the role of the United Automobile Workers' women's auxiliaries) and the "Little Steel" strike of 1937; always eager to write from firsthand experience, twice hit by bullets during the steel strike violence; despite association with numerous radicals, never joined any radical political organizations; while generally sympathetic toward union leadership, she identified more closely with ordinary workers and their interests; continued during the 1940s and 1950s reporting on labor affairs, pointing out the accommodation of major industries to powerful unions and exposing corruption in the East Coast longshoremen's union; was the recipient in 1962 of the United Automobile Workers' Social Justice Award; authored *A Footnote to Folly: Reminiscences* (1935); died in Provincetown, Mass., on June 14, 1966; Mary Heaton Vorse Papers, Walter P. Reuther Archives, Wayne State University; Murray Kempton, *Part of Our Time: Some Ruins and Monuments* (1955); *Notable American Women,* Vol. 4.

                                                                    Donald G. Sofchalk

W

WALKER, John Hunter (1872–1955). Born in Binny Hill, Stirlingshire, Scotland, April 27, 1872; married; one child; emigrated to Braidwood, Ill., with his parents in 1881; at age 9, began working in a coal mine in Coal City, Ill., and two years later enrolled in the Knights of Labor; subsequently joined the Miners' Federation, the Mine Laborers, and the United Mine Workers of America (UMWA); organized UMWA Local 505 at Central City, Ill., in 1896; assigned to work with John Mitchell (q.v.) and Mother Jones (q.v.) in organizing miners of southern Illinois and West Virginia in 1897; served as a member of the executive board, vice-president, and, during 1905–1913 and 1930–1933, president of District 12, UMWA, Illinois; as district president, played a leading role in obtaining the Miners' Qualification Law and the Shot Firers' Law; also worked for a workmen's compensation law and was largely responsible for affiliating the Illinois miners with the State Federation of Labor in 1908, which, by 1911, became the nation's largest state federation; served as president of the Illinois State Federation of Labor from 1913 until 1930, when the American Federation of Labor (AFL) executive council demanded his resignation for participating in the Reorganized United Mine Workers; was an active, but moderate, member of the Socialist party in his early years and defended John Mitchell (q.v.) from Socialist attack for his membership in the National Civic Federation; supported U.S. entry into World War I and participated in the conference of the American Alliance for Labor and Democracy in 1917, which endorsed the war; participated in the founding of the National Farmer-Labor party at Chicago, Ill., in November 1919, and elected vice-chairman; chosen national chairman in 1920 and ran unsuccessfully for governor of Illinois on the National Farmer-Labor ticket; was a consistent defender of district autonomy within the UMWA and nearly defeated Thomas Lewis (q.v.) for the international presidency in 1909; ran unsuccessfully against John White (q.v.) and Frank Hayes (q.v.) for the UMWA presidency in 1916 and 1918; along with Frank Farrington (q.v.), also a member of the international executive board, opposed confirmation of John L. Lewis (q.v.) as international vice-president; charging that Lewis had suspended the union constitution by neglecting to convene a national convention; in 1930 called, along with other opponents of Lewis, the Springfield convention to reorganize the UMWA; was designated to be president of the Reorganized UMWA, but Oscar Ameringer (q.v.) managed the election of Alexander Howat (q.v.) as president and Walker as secretary-treasurer; as a result of the Springfield convention and the attempted reorganization of the UMWA, forced to resign as president of the state federation by the AFL executive council; succeeded Harry Fishwick as president of District 12, UMWA in 1930; after a three-month strike in 1932, forced to sign an Illinois agreement reducing daily wages from $6.10 to $5.00, which the rank and file rejected four to one; at that point, the international president, John L. Lewis, took over the negotiations, signed the same agreement, destroyed the referendum ballots, and announced it ratified; in February 1933, Lewis destroyed district autonomy in the last important bituminous district by assuming the district debt, appointing a provisional government, and naming William Sneed to replace Walker as district president; retired from active union work in 1945; died in Denver, Colo., August 28, 1955; John H. Walker Papers, University of Illinois; *The New York Times,* August 29, 1955; Eugene Staley, *History of the Illinois State Federation of Labor* (1930); Irving Bernstein, *The Lean Years: A History of the American Worker, 1920–1933* (1960); John H. M. Laslett, *Labor and the Left: A Study of Socialism and Radical Influences in the American Labor Movement, 1881–1924* (1970); Melvyn Dubofsky and Warren Van Tine, *John L. Lewis: A Biography* (1977).

John W. Hevener

WALLING, William English   (1877–1936). Born in Louisville, Ky., on March 14, 1877; son of Willoughby, a physician, and Rosalind (English) Walling; married Anna (Strunsky), a Socialist writer, in 1906; was educated in private schools in Louisville and Edinburgh, Scotland, where his father was attached to the U.S. consul; received a B.S. from the University of Chicago in 1897; after a short stint at Harvard Law School, he enrolled in the graduate school of the University of Chicago where he studied economics and sociology; beginning in 1900, at age 23, he devoted the remainder of his life to the labor movement and working-class reform; was an Illinois state factory inspector, 1900–1901; resided at the University Settlement in New York City, 1901–1905; was one of the founders of the Women's Trade Union League in 1903; traveled to Russia in 1905 to study the revolutionary movement there and upon his return wrote *Russia's Message* (1908); was one of the founders of the National Association for the Advancement of Colored People in 1909; became active in radical politics but did not join the Socialist party until 1910; meanwhile, he stirred a new wave of factionalism in Socialist circles when, in 1909, he accused several right-wing Socialists, including Victor Berger (q.v.) and Morris Hillquit (q.v.), of conspiring to convert the party into a reformist labor party; resigned from the Socialist party in 1917 because of unhappiness with its anti-war stance; after the war, he became a full-time American Federation of Labor (AFL) employee, writing articles for *The American Federationist* and speeches for AFL officials; ran unsuccessfully for Congress as a Democratic/Progressive in 1924; became the executive director of the Labor Chest, an anti-fascist organization that sought to provide relief for workers in fascist-controlled countries; disillusioned by the Russian Revolution and the autocratic policies pursued by the new Soviet government, he gradually reverted to the reformist position to which he had adhered before his romance with left-wing socialism; authored numerous books and articles, including *The Larger Aspects of Socialism* (1913), *Progressivism—And After* (1914), and *American Labor and American Democracy* (1926); died in Amsterdam, Holland, on September 12, 1936; *Dictionary of American Biography*, Suppl. 2; Anna Strunsky Walling et al., *William English Walling: A Symposium* (1938); *The New York Times*, September 13, 1936; William English Walling Papers, State Historical Society of Wisconsin.

WALSH, Francis Patrick   (1864–1939). Born in St. Louis, Mo., on July 20, 1864; son of James, a coal and feed merchant, and Sarah (Delany) Walsh; Roman Catholic; married Katherine M. O'Flaherty on October 21, 1891; nine children; moved with his family to Kansas City, Mo., in 1867 where he was forced to leave school at age 10 to help support the family after the death of his father; worked variously as a Western Union messenger, factory operative, and railroad accountant; learned shorthand and became a court reporter; meanwhile, he read law in a local attorney's office and was admitted to the bar in 1889; became a skillful trial lawyer and an active participant in Kansas City Democratic politics; allied himself with the anti-Pendergast wing of the party; held numerous city offices including chief assistant corporation counsel, 1892–1894, a member of the Tenement Commission, 1906–1908, and president of the Board of Civil Service, 1911–1913; an ally of progressive governor Joseph W. Folk, 1905–1909, he contributed to the progressive reforms instituted during the Folk years and, in 1908, helped organize the Kansas City Board of Public Welfare which won him a national reputation among reformers; organized a bureau of social service within the Democratic National Committee in 1912; was appointed by President Woodrow Wilson in 1913 as chairman of the Commission on Industrial Relations which was created by the U.S. Congress to investigate the causes of the industrial violence that had plagued the nation during the early years of the twentieth century; under his direction, the commission's findings proved quite sympathetic to organized labor; was appointed co-chairman, along with William Howard Taft, of the National War Labor Board in 1918; devoted much of his time after World War I to the promotion of Irish independence and civil liberties causes; was involved in the legal defense efforts of such celebrated defendents as Thomas J. Mooney (q.v.), William Z. Foster (q.v.), Nicola Sacco (q.v.), and Bartolomeo Vanzetti (q.v.); was appointed to the New York State Commission to Recodify the Public Service Law by Governor Franklin D. Roosevelt in 1929, and in 1931, Roosevelt appointed him chairman of the State Power

Authority; was elected the first president of the National Lawyers Guild, a liberal alternative to the American Bar Association, in 1936; was a founder and the first chairman of the Catholic Citizens Committee for Ratification of the Federal Child Labor Amendment, 1936–1939; although usually a Democrat, he refused to support the national ticket in 1920 and endorsed Robert M. La Follette's Progressive party candidacy for president in 1924; supported Alfred E. Smith in 1928 and organized the National Progressive League for Franklin D. Roosevelt in 1932; died in New York City on May 2, 1939; Frank P. Walsh Papers, New York Public Library; *Dictionary of American Biography*, Suppl. 2; Graham Adams, Jr., *Age of Industrial Violence, 1910–1915* (1966); *Who Was Who in America*, Vol. 1; *The New York Times,* May 3, 1939.

WALSH, Richard Francis   (1900–   ). Born in Brooklyn, N.Y., February 20, 1900; son of William and Catherine (O'Toole) Walsh; Roman Catholic; attended public school in Brooklyn, then became an apprentice electrician in the Fifth Avenue Theater, Brooklyn, in 1917 and joined Local 4 of the International Alliance of Theatrical Stage Employees and Moving Picture Operators of the United States and Canada (IATSE); served as an electrician in the Metropolitan Theater, 1923–1936; elected president of the IATSE Local 4 in 1924 and served until 1926, when elected business agent, serving in that capacity until 1937; became an IATSE international vice-president in 1934; again elected president of Local 4 in 1939 and elected international president of the IATSE in 1941; served as the American Federation of Labor (AFL) fraternal delegate to the Trades and Labor Congress of Canada in 1948 and the British Trades Union Congress in 1952; became an AFL-Congress of Industrial Organizations vice-president and executive council member in 1955; served as a director of the Union Labor Life Insurance Company; a Democrat; retired union offices in 1974; Murray Ross, *Stars and Strikes: Unionization of Hollywood* (1941); *Who's Who in America, 1971–1972*; *Who's Who in Labor* (1946); *AFL-CIO News,* April 6, 1974.

WARD, Cyrenus Osborne   (1831–1902). Born in western New York on October 28, 1831; son of Justus, a farmer and construction worker, and Silence (Rolph) Ward; married Stella A. Owen on October 25, 1857; with his parents and nine siblings (including brother Lester Frank Ward), he moved to St. Charles, Ill., in 1834; became a skilled machinist and a violinist who traveled extensively throughout the Midwest with a concert company; opened a hub factory in Myersburg, Pa., in 1858 in partnership with a brother-in-law; after his enlistment during the Civil War was rejected, he became a machinist in the Brooklyn Navy Yard; during this period, his interest in labor problems grew and he became an active publicist, writing numerous articles and making speeches about labor conditions; traveled extensively in Europe after the war and met most of the leaders of the emerging international labor movement, including Karl Marx; wrote a series of articles for the *New York Sun* about labor conditions and the development of the labor movement there; after returning to the United States, he resumed his work as a machinist and his active involvement in labor reform causes; his being a lecturer, writer, organizer, and general agitator resulted in much employment instability, and he ultimately decided to devote all his time to labor reform; accelerating his work as a publicist, he established his own printing plant in 1878, published his first book, *A Labor Catechism of Political Economy*, and numerous pamphlets and journals, and became the associate editor of *Man*, a reformist journal; appointed to the federal Geological Survey in 1884, he was transferred shortly thereafter to the Bureau of Labor, where he worked as a translator and librarian; published his highly influential *A History of the Ancient Working People* in 1889 (second volume in 1900) which aroused considerable attention because of his sympathetic treatment of the history of working people; while employed by the Bureau of Labor, he wrote numerous bulletins and pamphlets; died in Yuma, Ariz., on March 19, 1902; *Dictionary of American Biography*, Vol. 19; G. K. Ward, *Andrew Warde and His Descendants, 1597–1910* (1910); *The New York Times*, March 21, 1902.

WARD, Martin Joseph   (1918–1982). Born in Chicago, Ill., on September 25, 1918; son of Martin Joseph, a pipe fitter, and Catherine Ward; Roman Catholic; married Winifred Marion in 1940; seven children; attended Lindblom High School, Chicago, 1932–1936, and Washburne Trade School, Chicago, 1937–1942; served in the U.S. Navy during World War II; began an apprenticeship in 1937 in the same local as his father, No. 597 of the United Association of Journeymen and Apprentices of the Plumbing and Pipe Fitting Industry of the United States and Canada (UA); after completing military service during World War II, he became an apprentice instructor for Local 597 and in 1948 became a business representative; served as the local's assistant business manager, 1950–1952, and became manager, 1952–1958; was appointed assistant general secretary-treasurer of the UA in 1958 and was elected general secretary-treasurer in 1966; was appointed assistant to the UA general president in 1969; was appointed acting general president of the UA by the union's executive board in June 1971 and later that year was unanimously elected president by the UA convention; was elected a vice-president and executive council member of the American Federation of Labor-Congress of Industrial Organizations (AFL-CIO) in 1972; became very active in AFL-CIO affairs, serving on the operations committee of the Committee on Political Education as well as the economic policy committee, the housing committee, and the civil rights committee; also served as a vice-president of the AFL-CIO building and construction trades and industrial union departments and on the board of directors of the AFL-CIO Mortgage Investment Trust; through the years, he developed a deep interest in international labor affairs and took an active role in the formulation of AFL-CIO policy positions; was an advisor to the U.S. worker representative to the International Labor Organization, served as chairman of the AFL-CIO executive council's standing committee on international affairs, and was on the board of trustees of the American Institute for Free Labor Development, the African-American Labor Center, the Asian-American Free Labor Institute, and the Human Resources Development Institute; commenting on Ward's rigid anti-Communist stance in international affairs, AFL-CIO President Joseph Lane Kirkland (q.v.) declared, "in the far-flung parts of the world, generations of workers yet unborn will fare a little better because Marty gave so unstintingly of himself in pursuit of free trade unionism"; died in Washington, D.C., on October 9, 1982; *AFL-CIO News*, October 16, 1982; *Who's Who in Labor* (1976).

WATT, Robert J.   (1894–1947). Born in Scotland, July 16, 1894; son of Alexander, a garment worker, and Helen (Robertson) Watt; Roman Catholic; married Janet Learmonth on April 28, 1917; two children; attended grammar school for six years, then served a four-year apprenticeship in the painting, paper hanging, and house decorating trade; emigrated to the United States in 1912 and took employment in a Lawrence, Mass., paper mill while continuing his education in night schools; became involved in trade union activities in 1914; served during World War I as a private with the Canadian Army in France, 1917–1919; resumed trade union activities after the war and in 1925 elected president of the Lawrence Central Labor Union, serving until 1930; served as a vice-president of the Massachusetts State Federation of Labor (MSFL), 1926–1929; was secretary-treasurer of the MSFL, 1930–1938; was the permanent American Federation of Labor (AFL) delegate to the International Labor Organization, 1936–1947; appointed to the Massachusetts Unemployment Commission in 1936 and served for two years; appointed a labor member of the commission created by President Franklin D. Roosevelt in 1938 to study labor conditions in Great Britain and Sweden; appointed a labor member of the National Defense Mediation Board in 1942 and an alternate labor member of the National War Labor Board; was a committed anti-Communist and devoted much of his energy to the task of keeping the Soviet Union out of international labor federations with which the AFL was affiliated; was an independent in politics; died aboard the liner *Saturnia* enroute to New York City, July 23, 1947; Philip Taft, *The A.F. of L. from the Death of Gompers to the Merger* (1959); *Current Biography* (1945); *The American Federationist* (August 1947).

WATTS, Glenn Ellis   (1920–   ). Born in Story Point, N.C., on June 4, 1920; son of George Dewey and Nelli Viola Watts; married Bernice Willett, a homemaker, in 1941; three children; graduated from high school in 1938 and then enrolled in Wilson Teachers College in Washington, D.C., matriculating there until 1941; took a job as a telephone company installer in 1941 and joined the local affiliate of the National Federation of Telephone Workers which in 1947 was reorganized, becoming the Communications Workers of America (CWA); worked as a service engineer, 1944–1948; elected president of CWA Division 36 in 1948, serving in that position until 1951 when he was elected director of CWA District 2; served as the assistant to CWA president Joseph A.

Beirne (q.v.), 1956–1965, executive vice-president, 1965–1969, and CWA secretary-treasurer, 1969–1974; after the retirement of Beirne in 1974, he was
elected international president of the CWA; later in the same year, he was elected
a vice-president and member of the American Federation of Labor-Congress of
Industrial Organizations (AFL-CIO) executive council; involved in bargaining
negotiations with the Bell System for many years, he developed the pattern
system of bargaining with different operating companies before national bargaining was achieved in 1974; was a member and officer of numerous civic and
labor reform organizations including the Home Rule Committee for the District
of Columbia, board of trustees for the American Institute for Free Labor Development, AFL-CIO, governing board of Common Cause, board of trustees of
the National Planning Association, board of directors of the Washington Housing
Association, and the Health and Welfare Council of the National Capital Area;
was also actively involved in various community fund-raising groups, including
United Givers Fund, Community Chest, YMCA, United Way, and the National
Urban Coalition; an active participant in the affairs of the Democratic party, he
was elected a member-at-large of the Democratic National Committee in 1974;
Who's Who in Labor (1976); *AFL-CIO News*, November 9, 1974; Thomas R.
Brooks, *Communication Workers of America: The Story of a Union* (1977).

WEAVER, George Leon Paul   (1912–   ). Born in Pittsburgh, Pa., May
18, 1912; son of George J., a maintenance worker, and Josephine (Snell) Weaver;
married Mary Frances on September 7, 1941; Afro-American; graduated from
high school, then attended Roosevelt University in Chicago (then YMCA College), Columbia University, and the Howard University Law School; joined the
United Transport Service Employees (UTSE) in 1940; served as chairman of the
grievance committee and was a member of the executive board of UTSE Local
603; became assistant to the international president of the UTSE and a member
of the general executive board in 1942; appointed director of the Congress of
Industrial Organizations' (CIO) committee to abolish discrimination in 1942;
appointed assistant secretary-treasurer of the CIO in 1945; named special assistant
to the chairman of the National Security Resources Board in 1950; after the
American Federation of Labor (AFL)-CIO merger in 1955, appointed executive
secretary of the AFL-CIO civil rights committee; was a delegate to the 1957 and
1958 conferences of the International Labor Organization (ILO); served as an
assistant to the president of the International Union of Electrical, Radio and
Machine Workers, 1958–1961; appointed Assistant Secretary of Labor for international affairs by President John F. Kennedy in 1961 and became the permanent U.S. representative to the ILO and chairman of the U.S. delegation;
elected chairman of the ILO board of governors in 1968; appointed special
assistant to Director General David A. Morse of the ILO in 1969; a Democrat;
George L. P. Weaver Papers, Walter Reuther Library, Wayne State University;
Fortune (February 1951); *AFL-CIO News*, October 21, 1961, October 4, 1969;
Who's Who in Colored America (1950); *Who's Who in Labor* (1946).

WEBBER, Rev. Charles Clarence   (1892–1982). Born in Osborne Mills, Mich., on August 28, 1892; son of Charles Louis, a flour miller, and Clara (Schneider) Webber, a homemaker; Methodist; married Ardelle P., an attorney in 1917; one child; graduated from Ann Arbor High School in 1910 and the University of Michigan in 1915; attended Boston University School of Theology, 1915–1919, and the Union Theological Seminary, 1919–1920; later earned a master's degree in sociology from Columbia University, 1927–1929; served as the superintendent of the Northside Community Center, Denver, Colo., 1920–1922; organized and served as the first president of the Denver Labor College, 1921–1922; became the pastor of the Church of All Nations, New York City, in 1923 and served in that position until joining the faculty of the Union Theological Seminary in 1926; became an organizer for the Amalgamated Clothing Workers of America (ACWA) in Richmond, Va., in 1935 and terminated his relationship with the Union Theological Seminary the following year; served as a ACWA national representative, 1943–1953; elected president of the Virginia Congress of Industrial Organizations (CIO) Council in 1946, serving until 1953; was appointed director of the Upper South CIO Political Action Committee in 1952 and a year later became national field representative of CIO's religion and labor committee; appointed assistant director of the CIO community relations department in 1955 and, after the merger of the CIO and the American Federation of Labor (AFL), he was appointed the AFL-CIO's national representative for religious relations, a position he held until 1962 when he became a consultant on labor and religion; was involved in a great variety of social, civic, and religious activities, including the National Association for the Advancement of Colored People, the White House Conference on Aging, and the White House Conference on Children and Youth; authored "Religion and Labor," AFL-CIO (n.d.), "Economic Value in a Judeo-Christian Society," AFL-CIO (n.d.), "The Death of a Union," *The American Federationist* (September 1959), and "A Religious Agitator," *Textile Labor* (1968); died in New York City on March 21, 1982; *Who's Who in Labor* (1976); *The New York Times*, March 22, 1982.

WEBBER, Clyde Mayo   (1919–1976). Born in Sloam Spring, Ark., on December 9, 1919; married; one child; became a member of the American Federation of Government Employees (AFGE) in 1949; elected a national vice-president of the AFGE, representing District 13 which included five western states; elected executive vice-president of the AFGE in 1966 and national president in 1972; was elected a vice-president and member of the executive council of the American Federation of Labor-Congress of Industrial Organizations (AFL-CIO) in 1975; represented the AFGE on the Federal Pay Council and the Prevailing Rate Advisory Commission, a government group recommending pay schedules for federal workers; also served as the treasurer of the AFL-CIO public employees department; died in Silver Spring, Md., on June 15, 1976; *Who's Who in Labor* (1976); *AFL-CIO News*, June 19, 1976.

WEBER, Frank Joseph   (1849–1943). Born in Milwaukee, Wis., August 7, 1849; son of Joseph, a German-American coal miner, and Marie Engel (Niemeyer) Weber; married Augusta Streich on December 27, 1877; three children; educated in the Milwaukee, Wis., public schools; during the 1860s and 1870s, employed as an able seaman, teacher, and ship's carpenter; joined a seaman's union in 1868 and, within a few years of its founding, the Knights of Labor in 1869; helped organize several different trade union locals in Milwaukee and in 1887 helped found the Federated Trades Council (FTC); was instrumental in the founding of the Wisconsin State Federation of Labor in 1893 and, having declined to run for president, served it as a general organizer until 1917; during the 1890s, was an American Federation of Labor (AFL) organizer in West Virginia and in the Gulf ports; served as secretary of the Milwaukee FTC during 1902–1934 (upon his motion the office of president had been abolished in 1893); was a leading unionist and a Socialist and had a key role in creating the working coalition of the Milwaukee FTC and the Social Democratic party; elected to the state assembly five times between 1907 and 1925; worked with progressive reformers, including John R. Commons (q.v.), to secure enactment of workmen's compensation and other labor legislation; also promoted vocational schools; rejected the anti-war policy of Victor Berger (q.v.) and helped swing the Milwaukee FTC to support the AFL's pro-war American Alliance for Labor and Democracy in 1918; served during World War I on the Waukesha County Council of Defense; in spite of his membership in the Socialist party, was a conservative trade unionist in several respects; during the 1920s, deplored the lethargy within the labor movement; widely respected as the "grand old man" of the Wisconsin labor movement; retired in 1934; died in Milwaukee, Wis., February 4, 1943; *National Cyclopaedia of American Biography*, Vol. 36; Edwin E. Witte, "Labor in Wisconsin," *Wisconsin Magazine of History* (Winter 1951); Thomas W. Gavett, *Development of the Labor Movement in Milwaukee* (1965).

Donald G. Solfchalk

WEBER, Joseph N.   (1866–1950). Born in Neu Beschenowa, Hungary, June 21, 1866; son of Joseph and Katharine (Wasmer) Weber; married Gisela Liebhodt on September 22, 1891; after a few years of formal education in Hungarian normal schools and gymnasiums, toured the United States at age 14 as a clarinetist in a boy's band; stayed in the United States at the end of the tour and secured employment as a clarinetist at the Tabor Opera House in Denver, Colo.; was one of the organizers of the Denver Musical Union and served the organization as president and secretary; later served as vice-president of the Portland (Oreg.) Musical Union and as president of the Cincinnati (Ohio) Musical Union; participated in the organization of the American Federation of Musicians (AFM) in 1896 and in 1900 elected its president; elected an American Federation of Labor vice-president and executive council member in 1930, serving in that capacity until his death; was credited with building the AFM from a weak trade union with six thousand members into a mature collective-bargaining organization with a membership in excess of one hundred seventy thousand; retired as AFM president in 1940 due to poor health and was named president emeritus; died in New York City, December 12, 1950; Robert D. Leiter, *The Musicians and Petrillo* (1953); *The American Federationist* (July 1940 and January 1951); Solon DeLeon, ed., *The American Labor Who's Who* (1925); *Who's Who in America, 1938–1939*.

WEIHE, William   (1845–1908). Born in Baldwin, Pa., January 21, 1845; married Philopena Ohlinger; two children; after his family moved to Pittsburgh, Pa., went to work in an iron mill at age 15; later, as a "boiler" on a puddling furnace, joined the union of his trade, the Sons of Vulcan, and served as an officer of his local; when the Sons of Vulcan joined with several other unions to form the Amalgamated Association of Iron and Steel Workers (AA) in 1876, became a member of its executive committee; elected a trustee of AA in 1879; became president of AA in 1884 when John Jarrett (q.v.) resigned; was conservative like most AA leaders, but tried to adjust his union to the mechanization in the emergent steel industry; as president, helped AA substantially increase its membership so that it became one of the American Federation of Labor's (AFL) largest affiliates; was elected a vice-president of the AFL in 1890; was elected a member of the Pittsburgh common council in 1896; also was instrumental during his presidency in substituting the eight-hour day for the twelve-hour day in sheet mills; attempted to expand the base of the AA, which was concentrated in the old iron mills, and established several lodges in the Homestead Works of the Carnegie Steel Company; unsuccessfully sought to compromise the issue when the Homestead manager, H. C. Frick, reduced the tonnage scales of the skilled in 1892; the ensuing strike, famous for its dramatic violence, not only destroyed the AA locals at Homestead but marked the beginning of a general AA decline; defended craft interests against the expanding Knights of Labor in the spring of 1886 and later in that year was one of the trade unionists who issued the call for the founding convention of the AFL; resigned as AA president in 1892, but remained active in trade union affairs; helped organize western Pennsylvania for the United Mine Workers during its strike of 1897; was a member of the arbitration committee that settled the strike with Carnegie, Phipps and Co. in 1899; elected to the Pennsylvania state legislature as a Democrat in 1882, but later became a Republican; was deputy immigration inspector and a member of the board of inquiry at Ellis Island from 1896 until his death; died in Pittsburgh, Pa., August 24, 1908; John A. Fitch, *The Steel Workers* (1911); Philip Taft, *The A.F. of L. in the Time of Gompers* (1957); *National Labor Tribune*, August 27, 1908; George E. McNeill, *The Labor Movement: The Problem of To-Day* (1887).

Donald G. Sofchalk

WEIR, Stan   (1921–   ). Born in Los Angeles, Calif., in 1921; mother was a dressmaker and father left household shortly after Stan's birth; married in 1945;

two children; attended public schools, graduating from high school in 1940; attended Los Angeles Junior College and after one term transferred to the University of California, Los Angeles; after completing one year of college, he became an apprentice seaman in the merchant marine and was accepted as a U.S. merchant marine cadet and midshipman in the Naval Reserve in 1941; resigned his position as a midshipman, joined the Sailors Union of the Pacific (an affiliate of the Seafarers International Union), and became a merchant sailor; was a union activist who was often elected a deck delegate on the ships he worked; a dedicated rank-and-file working-class organizer, who emphasized local autonomy and local issues, as a result of which, he was often in trouble with established union leaders; led a campaign to organize Standard Oil of California's tanker fleet in 1943–1944; as a result of conflicts with union leaders, especially over the Sailors Union of the Pacific's racial policy which condoned segregation, he ended his career as a merchant sailor in 1945 and took a job as a Ford assembly line worker in the San Francisco Bay Area and joined the United Automobile Workers Union; returned to Los Angeles in 1951 and joined an International Brotherhood of Teamsters' local while working as a truck driver; in 1954, he led a rebellion in the industrial laundry wagon drivers' local with which he was affiliated, charging collusion between management and the local union secretary and was discharged; after working at several odd jobs during the following year, he took a job with a General Motors assembly plant in 1955; four years later he became a longshoreman in the San Francisco Bay Area where he was hired as a "B-man," which was a class of registered longshoremen that paid a special form of dues to the International Longshoremen's and Warehousemen's Union (ILWU) but were not admitted as members and took whatever jobs were rejected by "A-men"; became the spokesman for B-men grievances against the ILWU and its president, Harry Bridges (q.v.); when B-men were admitted to full union membership in 1963, he was expelled along with several other activists who had criticized Bridges's policies; several years later, he became an instructor at the University of Illinois; a member of the Socialist Labor party; authored *USA: The Labor Revolt* and *Class Forces in the 1970s*; Alice Lynd and Staughton Lynd, *Rank and File: Personal Histories by Working-Class Organizers* (1973).

WERKAU, Carlton William   (1907–   ). Born in Clifton, Ill., September 25, 1907; son of William, a merchant, and Jeannette Cecilia Werkau; Methodist; married Viola Cecelia Litkey on January 4, 1930; completed two years of high school, then left school to work full time; joined the Illinois Union of Telephone Workers in 1926, and, for a time, served as its president; joined the Communications Workers of America (CWA) (then the National Federation of Telephone Workers) in 1939, and, after having served as acting secretary for several months, elected international secretary-treasurer in 1943; joined the Indiana Union of Telephone Workers in 1942; served as a trustee for the village of Bedford Park, Ill., 1941–1947; credited with transforming the CWA into an efficient, businesslike organization, establishing the economic policies and practices that ensured its financial solvency and stability; a Democrat; Jack Barbash, *Unions and Telephones: The Story of the Communications Workers of America* (1952); *Who's Who in Labor* (1946); Thomas R. Brooks, *Communication Workers of America: The Story of a Union* (1977).

WHARTON, Arthur O.   (1873–1944). Born on November 9, 1873; during the 1880s, served a machinist apprenticeship in the Santa Fe Railroad shops and eventually joined the International Association of Machinists (IAM); served as general chairman of District 5, Missouri Pacific Railroad, in 1903; during the early 1900s, was secretary of the IAM's Southwestern section; after signing a satisfactory joint agreement with 26 Southwestern railroads in 1910, led a successful ten-month strike against the Missouri Pacific and one or two other railroads that refused to sign the agreement; in 1911, elected president of the Federation of Federations, a combination of shop-craft unions that dominated the American Federation of Labor's (AFL) railroad employees' department; during 1918–1920, was labor advisor to the Lane Commission that dealt with railroad employees' wages and to its successor, the Railroad Administration's Board of Wages and Working Conditions, which formulated and administered wage and working condition standards for all classes of railroad employees; in 1920, appointed labor advisor to the U.S. Railroad Labor Board; upon William H. Johnston's (q.v.) resignation in 1926, appointed international president as a compromise between conflicting IAM factions; elected to the position in 1927 and served continuously until 1939; as a vice-president and executive council member of the AFL, led the campaign in the executive council to withhold AFL affiliates' support from Brookwood Labor College, believing it had fallen under Communist domination; was a moderate conservative and led a reaction to the progressive policies of Johnston and called on the membership to be less visionary and concentrate its efforts on securing immediate material benefits; reorganized and consolidated the IAM's strength in the 1920s and 1930s, while its membership declined; was an adamant foe of industrial unionism and became the AFL's "archpriest of craft exclusivism"; despite his dislike for industrial organization and the Congress of Industrial Organizations, realized that the IAM would have to expand its concept of organizing or lose its jurisdiction in the airframe industry; forced into semiretirement in Tucson, Ariz., in 1936 by acute bronchial asthma; formally resigned in 1939; died in Tucson, Ariz., December 21, 1944; *Machinists' Monthly Journal* (February 1945); Mark Perlman, *The Machinists: A New Study in American Trade Unionism* (1961), and *Democracy in the International Association of Machinists* (1962); John H. M. Laslett, *Labor and the Left: A Study of Socialism and Radical Influences in the American Labor Movement, 1881–1924* (1970).

John W. Hevener

WHARTON, Hunter Poisal   (1900–1980). Born in Martinsburg, W.Va., on October 20, 1900; son of John Jacob, a railroad conductor, and Annie Lee

Wharton, a homemaker; married Lydia M., a homemaker, in 1925; no children; was educated in public and private schools in Martinsburg and in 1922 graduated from Carnegie Institute of Technology; joined Local 66 of the International Union of Operating Engineers (IUOE) in Pittsburgh, Pa., in 1926; was elected business agent of Local 66 in 1930 and continued in that position until 1950; during these years, he served at various times as secretary of the Pittsburgh Building and Construction Trades Council and as an IUOE international representative; became assistant to the general president of the IUOE in 1950; was elected a trustee of the IUOE in 1955 and a vice-president in 1957; was elected general secretary-treasurer of the IUOE in 1958 and general president in 1962; became an American Federation of Labor-Congress of Industrial Organizations (AFL-CIO) vice-president and member of the executive council in 1965; served as chairman of the AFL-CIO committee on education and on the international affairs, civil rights, and occupational safety and health committees; served as a vice-president of the AFL-CIO building and construction trades department and of the metal trades department; also served, at various times, on the board of directors, the board of trustees, and the executive committee of the National Safety Council; was a member of numerous government commissions; retired in 1975 and was named president-emeritus of the IUOE; died in Rockville, Md., on November 14, 1980; *AFL-CIO News*, November 22, 1980; *Who's Who in Labor* (1976).

WHITE, John P.   (1870–1934). Born in Coal Valley, Ill., February 28, 1870; Roman Catholic; worked as a coal miner in Coal Valley; moved with his family to Iowa, working there in the coal mines; joined the United Mine Workers of America (UMWA); served UMWA District 13 as secretary-treasurer, 1899–1904, and president, 1904–1907 and 1909–1912; elected international vice-president of the UMWA in 1907, serving until 1909; elected and served as international president, UMWA, from 1912 to 1917, resigning to serve as labor consultant to Dr. Harry A. Carfield, chairman of the National Fuel Administration during World War I; after the war, took a management position with the Haynes Powder Company and thereafter occasionally served as a field agent for the UMWA; presided over the Colorado coal strike of 1913–1914, which was marred by the Ludlow Massacre; pledged to unite warring factions within the UMWA during the first two years of his administration and restored harmony and re-plenished the union treasury, which was later depleted by the Colorado strike; during his administration, helped revise the union constitution to call for the six-hour day, a minimum age of 16 for employment in the mines, old-age pensions, workmen's compensation, and the prohibition of membership to National Civic Federation members and Boy Scout leaders; the 1912 convention resolved that the American Federation of Labor organize industrial-type unions, and the radical faction, led by Adolph Germer (q.v.), attempted to endorse the Socialist party as the political arm of the working class; was a political conservative and was accused of attempting to purge Socialists from positions of power in the Illinois district; won the eight-hour day and recognition of mine committees in the anthracite field and universal run-of-mine wage base in the bituminous field; appointed John L. Lewis (q.v.) as the union's chief statistician and business manager of the *Journal*, sinecures from which Lewis rose to the union presidency; died in Des Moines, Iowa, September 21,1934; *United Mine Workers Journal*, October 1, 1934; George S. McGovern and Leonard F. Guttridge, *Great Coalfield War* (1972); McAlister Coleman, *Men and Coal* (1943).

John W. Hevener

WHITFIELD, Owen H. (1892–   ). Born in Jamestown, Miss., in 1892; Protestant; married; several children; attended Okolona College in Mississippi for two years; Afro-American; worked as a railroad fireman and minstrel show tap dancer, then became a sharecropper on a plantation near Charleston in Missouri's southeastern Bootheel region in 1928; while sharecropping, began preaching in several rural black churches; joined the Southern Tenant Farmers Union (STFU) in 1937 and organized black and white sharecroppers in the Bootheel; was charismatic and an excellent speaker, and was an effective union organizer who followed the principle of nonviolence; organized more than 20 STFU locals with a total membership of five thousand; became a STFU vice-president in 1937; was a labor reformer who sought gains for sharecroppers beyond wage increases; favored government intervention over union-led strikes as the most effective means of ameliorating the living conditions of sharecroppers; was not a Communist sympathizer, but strongly supported the merger of the STFU with the Communist-led United Cannery, Agricultural, Packing and Allied Workers of America (UCAPAWA) (the STFU's association with the UCAPAWA was short-lived, and the two unions split in 1939), and in 1937 became a member of the UCAPAWA executive council; elected a UCAPAWA vice-president in 1938; planned in late 1938 the demonstration of Bootheel sharecroppers driven off the land by planters who kept government parity checks for themselves; led the sharecroppers' campout along U.S. Routes 60 and 61 in January 1939, involving 330 families and 1,307 persons; forced to flee the Bootheel shortly thereafter because of lynching threats by planters; organized the St. Louis Committee for the Rehabilitation of the Sharecroppers, which raised money and purchased land for sharecropper resettlement; made a national speaking tour in January 1939, on behalf of the sharecroppers and the STFU, but became disillusioned because of the STFU's inability to provide financial aid to campers; helped form the Missouri Agricultural Workers Council, UCAPAWA, and led the organizing drive to capture STFU locals in the belief that a union affiliated with the Congress of Industrial Organizations could achieve greater gains for the sharecropper; threatened new campout demonstrations in January 1940, as Bootheel planters removed more sharecroppers, thus effectively halting further evictions; appointed by Missouri Governor Lloyd Stark as sharecropper spokesman on a six-member landlord-sharecropper committee supported by the state government and Bootheel planters; went to Washington, D.C., in early 1940 and received promises of aid from the Farm Security Administration, Works

Progress Administration, and the U.S. Housing Authority; left the labor movement in 1944, joining the People's Institute of Applied Religion; his goal of improving economic conditions of Bootheel sharecroppers ultimately failed, but the campout demonstrations changed political and social attitudes in Missouri to the advantage of the sharecroppers; Louis Cantor, *A Prologue to the Protest Movement: The Missouri Roadside Demonstration of 1939* (1969).

Merl E. Reed

WHITNEY, Alexander Fell (1873–1949). Born in Cedar Falls, Iowa, April 12, 1873; son of Joseph Leonard, a minister, and Martha Wallin (Batcheller) Whitney; Presbyterian; married Grace Elizabeth Marshman on September 7, 1893, and, after her death in 1923, Dorothy May Rowley on July 2, 1927; three children; left high school in 1888 and became a news agent on the Illinois Central Railroad; served as a brakeman on several midwestern railroads during 1890–1901; joined G. F. Boynton Lodge 138 of the Brotherhood of Railroad Trainmen (BRT) in 1896; elected master of the general grievance committee of the Chicago and North Western Railway, BRT, in 1901; elected vice-president in 1902 and secretary-treasurer in 1903 of the newly organized Western Association of General Committees of the Order of Railway Conductors and BRT; became a member of the BRT board of grand trustees in 1905 and two years later elected vice-president; elected general secretary-treasurer in 1928 and later the same year became president of the BRT; served as chairman of the Railway Labor Executives' Association, 1932–1934; was one of the principal sponsors and advocates of the Railroad Retirement Act passed by the U.S. Congress in 1935; appointed by President Franklin D. Roosevelt as a delegate to the Inter-American Conference for the Maintenance of Peace in 1936; along with Alvanley Johnston (q.v.) of the Brotherhood of Locomotive Engineers, led his union into a national railroad strike in May 1946 but was forced after two days to end the strike because of the threat of drastic punitive legislation; was a liberal in politics and usually supported Democratic candidates for public office; authored *Main Street, Not Wall Street* (1938), and *Wartime Wages and Railroad Labor* (1944); died in Cleveland, Ohio, July 16, 1949; Walter F. McCaleb, *Brotherhood of Railroad Trainmen, with Special Reference to the Life of Alexander F. Whitney* (1936); Joel Seidman, *The Brotherhood of Railroad Trainmen: The Internal Political Life of a National Union* (1962); Charles A. Madison, *American Labor Leaders: Personalities and Forces in the Labor Movement* (1950); *Current Biography* (1946); *Dictionary of American Biography,* Suppl. 4.

WILKINSON, Joseph (fl. 1856–1887). Born in Ireland, March 23, 1856; left school at the age of 12 to learn the tailor's trade; emigrated to the United States in 1872, and became actively engaged in the labor movement in New York City; with J. P. McDonnell (q.v.), of the *Paterson Labor Standard*, Adolph Strasser (q.v.), and others, he founded the Amalgamated Trade and Labor Union of New York City, and agitated for the enactment of beneficial labor legislation in New York State, such as the establishment of a Bureau of Labor Statistics, the abolition of prison convict-contract labor, reduction of the hours of labor, and the abolition of the manufacture of cigars in tenement houses; the latter measure after being passed was decided unconstitutional by the court of appeals; when the call was issued in 1884 for a convention in Chicago of the Journeymen Tailors Union of America, he was elected by an almost unanimous vote to represent the New York union; in the convention he was prevailed upon to accept the secretaryship of the national union, and was unanimously reelected at the convention held in Baltimore, in August 1885; though busily engaged in the labor movement, he still found time to improve his mind by study; he attended the evening high school in New York for three successive winters, and also belonged to the literary class attached to the Cooper Union; was a delegate to the 1887 convention of the American Federation of Labor; was a protectionist and also an advocate of aid and sympathy to Irish nationalism; George E. McNeill, ed., *The Labor Movement: The Problem of To-Day* (1887); Charles J. Stowell, *The Journeymen Tailors' Union of America: A Study in Trade Union Policy* (1918), and *Studies in Trade Unionism in the Custom Tailoring Trade* (1913).

George E. McNeill

WILLIAMS, Benjamin Hayes   (1877–1965). Born in Monson, Me., March 15, 1877; son of Thomas Huxley, a Welsh quarry worker, and Carrie Williams; married Rose Gerhart on February 27, 1914; at age 11 was put to work in his half-brother's print shop in Nebraska; later, while working as a farm hand, completed high school; in 1900, entered Tabor College, Iowa, graduating in 1904; in 1905, went to Butte, Mont.; evolutionary theory, Bellamy's utopianism, and Marxian socialism shaped his intellectual growth; in Butte, his association with Thomas J. Hagerty (q.v.), a founder of the Industrial Workers of the World (IWW), influenced him to devote himself to union movement; agitated for the Socialist Labor party (SLP) and organized western timber workers for the IWW, 1905–1907; was a delegate to the 1907 IWW convention and elected to its general executive board; assigned as organizer for the eastern United States; was gradually convinced that industrial action must precede political agitation and attacked the program of SLP leader Daniel DeLeon (q.v.), playing a key role in ousting him from the IWW in 1908; gave up his general executive board post in 1908 and helped publish the *Industrial Union Bulletin* until its demise in 1909; was attracted by the IWW-led steel strike and went to New Castle, Pa., where in December 1909, along with a local Wobbly, C. H. McCarty, founded *Solidarity*; became its editor, expanding its circulation to several thousand, and began publishing Wobbly tracts; in 1913, moved *Solidarity* to Cleveland, Ohio, where it became the official organ of the IWW; for several years *Solidarity*'s press published the bulk of the pamphlets, songbooks, and leaflets that were crucial for Wobbly agitation and rank-and-file morale; was a disciple of Marx and Darwin and combined their ideas to argue that evolution was creating a working-class structure parallel to concentrated industrial capitalism; held that industrial capital was more advanced in the United States, making U.S. workers unique in their potential for great class cohesiveness; admitted that the IWW's initial appeal was its ability to improve the workers immediate lot and insisted that through participation they would achieve solidarity and recognize the need for industrial organization to usher in the cooperative commonwealth; principally advocated direct action, the strike, and the slow-down; urged that the IWW concentrate on eastern rather than western workers; favored centralization of the IWW, but when William Haywood (q.v.) insisted on moving *Solidarity* to Chicago, Ill., quit as editor in 1917; returned as editor in 1920 and used the position to advocate IWW cooperation with other radical groups to seize control of industry; was rebuffed by the 1921 convention and left the IWW; participated during the 1930s in the Technocracy movement and continued to be active as a radical in Ohio until his death in 1965; see his "Trends toward Industrial Freedom," *American Journal of Sociology* (March 1915); Warren R. Van Tine, "Ben H. Williams" (M.A. thesis, 1967); Melvyn Dubofsky, *We Shall Be All: A History of the Industrial Workers of the World* (1969).

Donald G. Sofchalk

WILLIAMS, Elijah ("Lige") Henson   (1895–1972). Born in Bienville Parish, La., August 16, 1895; son of William Henson, a farmer, and Martha Anne Price; Baptist; married Annie Laurie Canfield on November 26, 1946; no children; attended the public schools of Bienville Parish, then eventually learned the barber's trade and joined Shreveport, La., Local 161 of the Journeymen Barbers, Hairdressers and Cosmetologists' International Union of America; served as secretary-treasurer of Local 161, then elected president of the Louisiana State Federation of Labor in 1933 and served in that capacity until declining to run for reelection in 1956; was a regional organizer for American Federation of Labor (AFL) president William Green (q.v.) and served as director of AFL Region 16 prior to the merger of the AFL and the Congress of Industrial Organizations (CIO); appointed director of AFL-CIO Region VII in 1956 and continued in that position the remainder of his life; was an advocate of a constant labor offensive and witnessed the creation of most of Louisiana's craft unions; was instrumental in joining local groups into central bodies; as AFL-CIO regional director, helped organize New Orleans, La., hotel workers and Pascagoula, La., shipyard workers; was a Democrat and played an important role in building labor's political power in Louisiana; during the 1950s, was a member of the Louisiana State Democratic Central Committee; died in Shreveport, La., March 17, 1972; *AFL-CIO News*, March 25, 1972; E. H. Williams' Folder, Southern Labor Archives, Atlanta, Ga.

Merl E. Reed

WILLIAMS, Roy Lee   (1915–   ). Born in Ottumwa, Iowa, on March 22, 1915; grew up in Kansas City, Mo., where in 1935, at age 20, he became a trucker; joined Kansas City Local 41 of the International Brotherhood of Teamsters (IBT) and during the period, 1948–1954, served as business agent for several midwestern locals; was elected president of Local 41 in 1954; the following year he became a trustee of the central, southeastern, and southwestern states' pension funds; was appointed spokesman for the IBT negotiating committee in 1967; elected an international vice-president of the IBT in 1971 and director of the Central Conference of Teamsters, IBT, in 1976; meanwhile, he had been indicted three times for violations of the provisions of the Landrum-Griffin Act and embezzlement of union funds but was never convicted; amid charges of mismanagement, he, along with several other union officials, was removed as a trustee of the 3.3 billion-dollar central states pension fund and they were replaced by independent trustees in 1977; in 1981 his ties with alleged underworld chieftian Nick Civella were investigated by a congressional committee; became acting president of the IBT after the death of the incumbent, Frank Fitzsimmons (q.v.) in 1981 and later that year was regularly elected to the IBT presidency; was convicted in 1982 of conspiring to bribe U.S. Senator Howard Cannon of Nevada with a Las Vegas land deal in return for Cannon's support in helping defeat federal deregulation of the trucking industry; *Business Week*, June 8, 1981; *U.S. News and World Report*, May 25, 1981; *Fleet Owner*, July 1981; *Who's Who in America, 1982–1983*; Steven Brill, *The Teamsters* (1978).

WILSON, Boyd L.   (1886–   ). Born in Linn, Mo., on May 31, 1886; son of Benjamin and Josephine Wilson; married; one daughter; Afro-American; graduated from Sumner High School, St. Louis, Mo., and completed two years of college in St. Louis; became a union organizer among black barbers in St. Louis in 1929, an activity that led him to attend a national convention of the American Federation of Labor in Indianapolis, Ind.; hired to organize workers at the Scullin Steel Company in St. Louis by the Steel Workers Organizing Committee of the Congress of Industrial Organizations (CIO) in 1938; was remarkably successful in bringing the predominantly black labor force of Scullin Steel into the CIO; when, in 1942, a group of black steelworkers expressed concern to the president of the United Steelworkers of America (USWA), Philip Murray (q.v.), about the absence of blacks in the union hierarchy, he responded by appointing Wilson as his personal representative to handle black affairs within the union and with employers; helped to adjudicate the grievances of black workers who staged a work stoppage to protest unfair promotion practices at the Carnegie-Illinois steel plant in Clairton, Pa., in 1944; was asked by Murray, as head of the CIO, to serve on the CIO committee for the elimination of racial discrimination; although making several attempts to educate union officials about the special grievances of black members, he met with obstacles; along with other blacks, he worked successfully to get a civil rights department established within the USWA, but this effort resulted in the appointment of two white officials who "knew absolutely nothing about the Negro problem"; although until 1955, neither Murray nor his successor David McDonald (q.v.) appointed Wilson to participate in the

USWA's civil rights division, he nonetheless served as a liaison between the USWA and various black groups; during the 1950s, he was a member of the board of directors of the National Urban League; helped the Urban League of Pittsburgh, Pa., improve its industrial relations department; joined A. Philip Randolph (q.v.) and others in 1959 in starting the Negro American Labor Council; retired in 1966; John G. Spiese interview with Wilson, October 23, 1967, Labor Archives, Pennsylvania State University; Dennis Brunn and Dennis C. Dickerson interview with Wilson, St. Louis, Mo., March 28, 1974; *F.E.P.C. Records, Region III*, Clairton, Pennsylvania File, Box 598, National Archives; *Pittsburgh Courier*, February 19, 1955, July 23, 1960.

Dennis C. Dickerson

WILSON, D. Douglas   (fl. 1895–1915). Was the first regularly elected editor of the International Association of Machinists' (IAM) official organ, the *Machinists' Monthly Journal*, serving from 1895 until his death in 1915, and established its basic format; as editor of the *Journal*, solicited general discussions of political and economic philosophy, articles on technical developments in the trade, regular reports from the national vice-presidents, sporadic reports from local business agents, letters from the membership, and editorial comment on current issues; because his moderate Socialist views were frequently at odds with those of President James O'Connell (q.v.), carefully balanced the *Journal*'s function as mouthpiece for the national administration and voice of the rank and file; averaging 96 pages per issue and costing the union thirty-four thousand dollars annually, the *Journal* attained a level of, in Mark Perlman's estimate, "a machinists' version of *Harper's* or *Scribner's* magazines"; President O'Connell recommended to the 1911 convention that the union reduce expenses by limiting the *Journal* to eight pages and selling it by subscription rather than mailing it to all members; a convention committee reported that on the basis of the *Journal*'s educational, economic, and social value and the devotion of its readers, it constituted the IAM's "richest asset"; as general vice-president and editor, with President O'Connell and Hugh Doran, participated in the famous Murray Hill collective bargaining agreement between the IAM and the National Metal Trades Association; died in 1915; Mark Perlman, *The Machinists: A New Study in American Trade Unionism* (1961).

John W. Hevener

WILSON, James Adair   (1876–1945). Born in Erie, Pa., April 23, 1876; son of Scottish immigrants James, a blacksmith, and Mary (Adair) Wilson; Methodist; married Elsie Schaeffer on June 21, 1905; two children; attended the public schools of Erie, Pa., then became a pattern maker and joined the Pattern Makers League of North America (PMLNA); elected president of the Erie (Pa.) Central Labor Union in 1900 and appointed legislative representative of the Pennsylvania State Federation of Labor; elected president of the PMLNA in 1902; was the American Federation of Labor (AFL) fraternal delegate to the British Trades

Union Congress in 1906; appointed during World War I by President Woodrow Wilson as the chairman of a U.S. delegation designed to encourage trade union movements in allied European nations to cooperate with their governments in prosecuting the war; became an AFL vice-president in 1924 and at the same time appointed a vice-president of the AFL metal trades department; appointed by President Franklin Roosevelt as a labor advisor to the World Monetary and Economic Conference in London in 1933; served as a member of the Public Works Administration's board of labor review; resigned his trade union offices in 1934 and became labor counselor to the International Labor Office in Geneva, Switzerland; during World War II, was an AFL alternate on the Defense Mediation Board and served on a variety of War Labor Board panels; died in Washington, D.C., September 3, 1945; Solon DeLeon, ed., *The American Labor Who's Who* (1925); *National Cyclopaedia of American Biography,* Vol. 33; *The American Federationist* (September 1945).

WILSON, William Bauchop   (1862–1934). Born in Blantyre, Scotland, April 2, 1862; son of Adam, a miner, and Helen Nelson (Bauchop) Wilson; Presbyterian; married Agnes Williamson on June 7, 1883; 11 children; emigrated with parents to the United States in 1870, settling in Arnot, Pa.; received a common school education in Scotland; began working in the Pennsylvania coal mines at age 9; elected secretary of a local miners' union in 1877 and secretary of a local Greenback club the following year; joined the Knights of Labor in 1878 and during 1888–1894 served as a district master workman; was a member of the district executive board of the American Association of Miners and Mine Laborers, 1884–1885; was an unsuccessful candidate for the Pennsylvania state legislature on the Union Labor party ticket in 1888 and shortly thereafter became a supporter of the Populist party; was one of the founding members of the United Mine Workers of America (UMWA) in 1890 and was a member of the UMWA general executive board, 1891–1894; appointed to the Pennsylvania commission that in 1891 revised state laws relating to coal mining; broke with the Knights of Labor in 1894 and helped organize and became general master workman of the Independent Order of the Knights of Labor, a short-lived attempt to reestablish the original principles of the Knights of Labor; was prominently involved in the coal strikes of 1899 and 1902; served as international secretary-treasurer of the UMWA, 1900–1908; elected as a Democrat to the U.S. Congress in 1906 and served as chairman of a special committee to investigate the effect of the Taylor system and other methods of scientific management; served as an American Federation of Labor fraternal delegate to the British Trades Union Congress in 1910; appointed as the first Secretary of Labor by President Woodrow Wilson in 1913 and served until 1921; as Secretary of Labor, reorganized the Bureau of Immigration and Naturalization, developed agencies to mediate industrial disputes, and organized the U.S. Employment Service to handle the problems of wartime deployment and transfer of workers; during World War I, was also a member of the Council for National Defense; served as president of the International Labor Conference of 1919; was a member of the Federation Board for Vocational Education, 1914–1921; in 1921, served on the International Joint Commission, created to prevent disputes between the United States and Canada regarding the use of the boundary waters; after 1921, engaged in mining and agricultural pursuits near Blossburg, Pa.; ran unsuccessfully as a Democratic candidate for the U.S. Senate in 1926; died on a train near Savannah, Ga., May 25, 1934; R. W. Babson, *William B. Wilson and the Department of Labor* (1919); Christopher Evans, *History of the United Mine Workers of America*, 2 Vols. (1918–1920); McAlister Coleman, *Men and Coal* (1943); Arthur S. Link, *Woodrow Wilson: The New Freedom* (1956).

WINDT, John   (fl. 1830–1844). Born in New York City early in the nineteenth century; was of German-Irish descent; became a journeyman printer and an agnostic as a young man; joined the New York Typographical Society in 1830; when the journeymen printers struck for a wage increase in 1831, organized and became an official in the Typographical Association; continued as a journeyman printer until establishing his own printing shop in 1835; became an active participant in the New York Workingmen's party in 1834 and elected secretary of the Workingmen's General Committee; shortly thereafter, however, transferred his allegiance to the Democratic party when it championed labor's cause; was an "ultra antimonopolist" and aligned himself with the anti-Tammany slate of reformers within the Democratic party and became a leader of the Locofocos; nominated for the New York Assembly by the anti-Tammany slate in 1835; during the following two years, published the reformist organ *Democrat*, participated in Locofoco affairs, and ran unsuccessfully for alderman and assemblyman; became a leader of the minority "Rump" faction of the Locofocos that opposed reunification with Tammany Democrats; played a prominent role in the unemployment demonstrations during the Panic of 1837; during the 1840s, became an advocate of the land-reform ideas of George Henry Evans (q.v.) and published the *Working Man's Advocate*, served as secretary and treasurer of the National Reform Association, and ran unsuccessfully for Congress on the Reform Association ticket; his printing shop was a center for reformist activities and publications until his death in the 1870s; Walter Hugins, *Jacksonian Democracy and the Working Class: A Study of the New York Workingmen's Movement, 1829–1837* (1960); John R. Commons et al., *A Documentary History of American Industrial Society*, Vol. 7 (1911); Helene S. Zahler, *Eastern Workingmen and National Land Policy, 1829–1862* (1941); Philip S. Foner, *History of the Labor Movement in the United States*, Vol. 1 (1947).

WIPISINGER, William Wayne   (1924–   ). Born in Cleveland, Ohio, December 10, 1924; son of a journeyman printer; married; five children, attended a Cleveland elementary school and West Technical High School before dropping out after the tenth grade; enlisted in the U.S. Navy in 1942 and served as a diesel mechanic until 1945; after the war, he returned to Cleveland where he worked as an automotive mechanic; joined Lodge 1363 of the International Association of Machinists (IAM) in 1947; quickly becoming active in the affairs of Lodge 1363, he served successively as a shop steward, recording secretary, and, in 1948, was elected president of the thirteen hundred-member local; appointed the IAM grand lodge representative in the Cleveland area in 1951; was transferred to IAM headquarters in 1958 from where he organized truck and automobile mechanics; also served in the union's air transport department, functioning as a troubleshooter for the IAM president, Albert J. Hayes (q.v.); in 1965 he was appointed automotive coordinator for the renamed International Association of Machinists and Aerospace Workers, assuming responsibility for coordinating the activities of the union's 120,000 automobile and truck repair mechanics; elected an IAM general vice-president in 1967, at which time his responsibilities were expanded to include railroad and airline workers, and, in 1977, he was elected president of the IAM, the American Federation of Labor-Congress of Industrial Organizations' (AFL-CIO) third largest affiliate; later the same year, he was elected an AFL-CIO vice-president and executive council member; shortly after assuming office, he launched a vigorous campaign to restore and expand the IAM's declining membership, restoring the confidence and loyalty of the IAM membership, and reversing the deteriorating economic position of machinists; his activism and rhetorical radicalism soon brought him into conflict with the AFL-CIO leadership, including George Meany (q.v.), whose reelection in 1978 he opposed, and Meany's successor, Lane Kirkland (q.v.); a self-styled Socialist and member of the Democratic Socialist Organizing Committee, he nevertheless pursued the traditional pragmatic collective bargaining tactic and has usually supported liberal Democratic candidates for public office; moreover, he is a vice-president of Americans for Democratic Action and a member of the finance committee of the Democratic National Committee; served as a trustee of the National Planning Association, a council member of the New York State School of Industrial and Labor Relations at Cornell University, and was the founder of the Citizen/Labor Energy Coalition; supported Edward Kennedy's campaign for the Democratic presidential nomination in 1980 and walked out of the Democratic National Convention that nominated Jimmy Carter; *Current Biography* (1980); *Who's Who in Labor* (1976); *Fortune*, June 5, 1978.

WOLCHOK, Samuel   (1896–1979). Born in Bobruisk, Russia, September 20, 1896; son of Moses, a carpenter, and Doba (Grazel) Wolchok; Jewish; married Bella Delman on December 31, 1917; two children; emigrated with his family to the United States in 1912; took a job in the New York garment industry as a suspender maker and joined the International Ladies' Garment Workers' Union; attended the Manhattan Preparatory School, 1916–1917; during World War I, joined the U.S. Army and served in France with the Sixth Division's Eighteenth Machine Gun Battalion; after the war, became a clerk in a New York City dairy store and joined the New York local of the Retail Clerks International

Protective Association; between 1922 and 1937, served as the New York local's financial secretary, vice-president, president, and secretary-manager; after the local was suspended in 1937 because of criticism of American Federation of Labor policies, organized a secessionist movement that eventually resulted in the formation of the United Retail, Wholesale and Department Store Employees of America (URWDSE) under the auspices of the Congress of Industrial Organizations (CIO); elected president at the first national convention of the URWDSE; became a member of the CIO executive council in 1938 and during 1938–1939 served as vice-president of the New York State Industrial Union Council, CIO; served during World War II as a labor member of the New York regional panel of the War Labor Board, the Regional War Manpower Employment Practices Committee, and the New York State Permanent Fair Employment Practices Committee; led his union in the historic strike against Montgomery Ward and Company during World War II; took an indefinite leave of absence and ultimately resigned his union offices after the provisions of the Taft-Hartley Act intensified existing divisions in the URWDSE over Communist influence; member of the executive board of the Liberal party of New York and executive board member of Americans for Democratic Action; died in January 1979; George G. Kirstein, *Stores and Unions: A Study of the Growth of Unionism in Dry Goods and Department Stores* (1950); Michael Harrington, *The Retail Clerks* (1962); *Current Biography* (1948).

WOLFGANG, Myra Komaroff   (1914–1976). Born in Montreal, Canada, May 20, 1914; daughter of Abraham and Ida (Ipp) Komaroff; married Moe F. Wolfgang, an attorney, on August 31, 1939; two children; after graduating from high school, she worked as a waitress in Detroit; became a union organizer during the early years of the depression and at age 23 was leading strikes and directing organizing drives in many of Detroit's major hotels and restaurants; led an eight-day sit-down strike at Woolworths during the mid-1930s and negotiated the store's first union contract; was a delegate to the American Federation of Labor (AFL) conventions of 1935, 1936, representing Detroit and Wayne County Federation of Labor; helped establish soup kitchens during sit-down strikes of automobile workers during the late 1930s; was manager of the domestic and personal service department of the U.S. Employment Service, 1938–1940; a member of the Hotel and Restaurant Employees' and Bartenders' International Union (HREBIU), she served her union in a variety of capacities: secretary-treasurer of Detroit Local 705, secretary-treasurer of the Detroit Joint Executive Board of the HREBIU and at the time of her death was an international vice-president responsible for a five-state area; was also a founding member of the Coalition of Labor Union Women in 1974; during the founding convention, she brought the thirty two hundred delegates to their feet by declaring, "You can call Mr. Meany [George] and tell him there are 3,000 women in Chicago and they didn't come to swap recipes"; a staunch proponent of labor legislation, she fought for passage and then for improvements in Michigan's minimum wage law among the other reform measures; the recipient of numerous awards, she received Michigan State University's Distinguished Citizen's Award shortly before her death; died of cancer at age 61 in Detroit, April 12, 1976; *AFL-CIO News*, April 17, 1976; *Who's Who in Labor* (1946); *Time*, April 26, 1976; *The New York Times*, April 13, 1976; Jean Maddern Pitrone, *Myra: The Life and Times of Myra Wolfgang* (1980).

WOLFSON, Theresa   (1897–1972). Born in Brooklyn, N.Y., on July 19, 1897; daughter of Adolph and Rebecca (Hochstein) Wolfson, Russian-Jewish radicals who had emigrated to the United States shortly before her birth; married Iago Galdston, a psychiatrist, on July 19, 1920; two children; divorced in 1935, she married Austin Bigelow Wood, a psychologist, in 1938; educated in the New York City public schools and graduated from Brooklyn High School; received a B.A. from Adelphi University in 1917; while a student at Adelphi, she helped organize a local chapter of the League for Industrial Democracy (then the Intercollegiate Socialist Society) in 1916; after graduating, she served as a volunteer health worker for the Meinhardt Settlement House in New York City; became a field agent and investigator for the National Child Labor Committee in 1918, serving until 1920; during this period, she also joined the New York Consumers' League campaign for minimum wage legislation and the eight-hour day; enrolled as a graduate student in economics at Columbia University and investigated the working conditions of sewing machine operators as a thesis topic; received her M.A. in economics in 1922; after completing her Ph.D. in 1924, she served as the education director for the International Ladies' Garment Workers' Union's Union Health Center, 1925–1927; during the late 1920s, she taught at Bryn Mawr Summer School for Women Workers, lectured at Brookwood Labor College, and conducted classes for the Union Labor Education Committee of the Union Neckwear Workers' Union and the Cap Makers Union, among other union-sponsored schools; accepted a regular appointment at Brooklyn College (then the Brooklyn branch of Hunter College) in 1928, where she taught economics and labor relations until her retirement in 1967; during the 1930s, she taught in summer schools for office workers and the white-collar workshops sponsored by the American Labor Education Service; served on the War Labor Board, 1942–1945, as a public panelist; joined the American Arbitration Association after the war and in 1957 was a co-recipient of the League for Industrial Democracy's John Dewey Award for her arbitration and mediation activities; a consistent supporter of the concept of industrial democracy, she believed that along with education the participation of women and the unskilled in American unions would revitalize democratic ideals in the labor movement; authored numerous articles and co-authored *Labor and the N.R.A.* (1934) and *Frances Wright, Free Enquirer: The Study of a Temperament* (1939); after her retirement in 1967, she taught in the Sarah Lawrence College continuing education program until her death in Brooklyn on May 14, 1972; *Notable American Women*, Vol. 4; Solon DeLeon, ed., *The American Labor Who's Who* (1925);

The New York Times, May 15, 1972; Theresa Wolfson Papers, Catherwood Library, Cornell University.

WOLL, Matthew (1880–1956). Born in Luxembourg, January 25, 1880; son of Michael and Janette (Schwartz) Woll; Roman Catholic; married Irene Kerwin in 1899, and after her death, Celenor Dugas; two children; emigrated to the United States in 1891; attended the public schools of Chicago until 1895, then apprenticed to a photoengraver; entered the night school of Kent College of Law, Lake Forest University, in 1901 and admitted to the Illinois bar three years later; elected president of the International Photo-Engravers Union of North America (IPEU) in 1906; served as an American Federation of Labor (AFL) fraternal delegate to the British Trades Union Congress in 1915 and 1916; served on the War Labor Board during World War I; became an AFL vice-president and executive council member in 1919; because of other duties, resigned as president of the IPEU in 1929 and became first vice-president; served as the president of the AFL's union label trades department, director of the AFL's legal bureau, and chairman of the AFL standing committees on education and social security and international relations; was an AFL delegate to the International Federation of Trade Unions meeting in Warsaw in 1937 and to the International Labor Organization's conference in Oslo in 1938; during the controversy between the AFL and the Committee on Industrial Organization (CIO), usually supported the craft organizing concept, but attempted to project himself as a conciliator; was considered one of the most conservative leaders in the U.S. labor movement and was a vitriolic anti-Communist; served on the National War Labor Board during World War II; became a vice-president and executive council member of the AFL-CIO after the 1955 merger; was president of the Union Labor Life Insurance Company from 1925 until 1955 and then became general executive chairman of the company; at various times, edited both the *American Photo-Engraver* and *The American Federationist*; authored *Labor, Industry and Government* (1935); usually supported the Republican party; died in New York City, June 1, 1956; Philip Taft, *The A.F. of L. from the Death of Gompers to the Merger* (1959); Walter Galenson, *The CIO Challenge to the AFL: A History of the American Labor Movement, 1935–1941* (1960); *Current Biography* (1943); *The American Federationist* (July 1956); *Dictionary of American Biography*, Suppl. 6.

WOOD, Reuben Terrell (1884–1955). Born in Springfield, Mo., August 7, 1884; son of Henry Nicholas Buruley, a college professor, and Martha Wood; Baptist; married Mary Ellen Eshman on December 31, 1936; no children; received six years of formal education in the public schools of Springfield, Mo., and some private tutorial instruction; apprenticed as cigarmaker in 1901 and shortly thereafter joined the Springfield local of the Cigarmakers' International Union; served in several positions in the Springfield labor movement during 1902–1912, including president of the Springfield Central Union; elected president of the Missouri State Federation of Labor (MSFL) in 1912 and served continuously until 1953; during World War I, was a member of the state advisory board of the U.S. Fuel Administration and also served on the Missouri division of the U.S. Food Administration; was national legislative representative of the Brotherhood of Maintenance of Way Employees in 1919–1920; was a Socialist during the early years of his career and served as chairman of the Missouri branch of the Conference for Progressive Political Action (CPPA) in 1922; appointed to the executive committee of the CPPA and served on credentials committee of the 1924 Progressive party convention in Cleveland, Ohio, that nominated Robert M. La Follette for president of the United States; elected to the Seventy-third Congress as a Democrat in 1932, and, during four terms in the U.S. House of Representatives, consistently supported New Deal legislation; was a member of the House labor committee and played an important role in the enactment of labor legislation, especially the National Labor Relations Act and the Fair Labor Standards Act; defeated for reelection in 1940; was a member of the Missouri Constitutional Convention in 1944; was a politics-oriented, militant trade unionist and often disagreed with the apolitical, craft-conscious policies of the national American Federation of Labor leadership; retired from his union positions in 1953 and was named MSFL president emeritus; died in Springfield, Mo., July 16, 1955; Gary M Fink, *Labor's Search for Political Order: The Political Behavior of the Missouri Labor Movement, 1890–1940* (1974); *Biographical Directory of the American Congress, 1774–1971* (1971); *Who's Who in Labor* (1946).

WOODCOCK, Leonard Freel   (1911–   ). Born in Providence, R.I., February 15, 1911; son of Ernest, a manufacturer's representative, and Margaret (Freel) Woodcock; reared as a Roman Catholic; married Loula Martin on May 28, 1941; three children; raised in Northampton, England, after his father was interned in Germany during World War I; attended British schools including the prestigious Chipsey preparatory school; returned with family to the United States in 1926 and settled in Detroit, Mich.; attended Wayne University and the Walsh Institute of Accountancy, 1928–1930; became a machine assembler at the Detroit Gear and Machine Company and joined a plant union that in the late 1930s became a local of the United Automobile, Aerospace and Agricultural Implement Workers of America (UAW); served as educational director for the Wayne County Industrial Union Council, Congress of Industrial Organizations, for two years; became a UAW staff representative in 1940 and served in that capacity until 1944; appointed first administrative assistant to UAW president Walter P. Reuther (q.v.) in 1946; became director of UAW Region 1D in 1947; elected a UAW vice-president in 1955 and assigned the responsibility for the UAW's General Motors and aerospace departments; assumed the office of UAW president after the death of Walter P. Reuther in 1970 and elected to the office in 1972; led the UAW in an eight-week strike against the General Motor's Corporation in the autumn of 1970; is a member of several reform-oriented organizations, including the Urban League, the American Civil Liberties Union, and the National Association for the Advancement of Colored People; became a member of the Wayne State University board of governors in 1959; is a liberal in politics and usually supports Democratic candidates for public office; retired in 1977; Leonard F. Woodcock Papers, Walter Reuther Library, Wayne State University; Jack Stieber, *Governing the UAW* (1962); Jean Gould and Lorena Hickok, *Walter Reuther: Labor's Rugged Individualist* (1972); Frank Cormier and William J. Eaton, *Reuther* (1970).

WRIGHT, James Lendrew   (1816–1893). Born in County Tyrone, Ireland, April 6, 1816; Protestant; son of Scots-Irish parents; emigrated with his family to the United States in 1827, eventually settling in Philadelphia, Pa., where the family evidently prospered; graduated from the Mount Vernon Grammar School, then attended Charles Mead's private academy; served a six-year apprenticeship as a tailor; joined the Tailors' Benevolent Society of Philadelphia in 1837; opened a tailor shop in Frankfort, Pa., in 1847; served as the manager of a prosperous Philadelphia clothing store from 1854 until losing his job in the 1857 depression; along with Uriah S. Stephens (q.v.), organized the Garment Cutters' Association in 1862 and for several years served as the president of the organization; in 1863, helped organize the Philadelphia Trades Assembly and elected treasurer; was one of the seven original founders of the Noble Order of the Knights of Labor (K of L) in 1869 and was credited with naming the organization; served as the temporary chairman of the 1876 conventions that created a national labor organization; became politicized as a result of the violent strikes of the 1870s and ran unsuccessfully for Pennsylvania state treasurer on the United Workingmen ticket in 1877, and the following year ran unsuccessfully for state secretary of internal affairs on the Greenback-Labor party ticket; thereafter forsook politics; continued his activities on behalf of the K of L for the remainder of his life; led a caucus calling for a return to secrecy and other "original principles" of the Order in 1889 in opposition to the leadership of Terence V. Powderly (q.v.); died in Germantown, Pa., August 3, 1893; Norman J. Ware, *The Labor Movement in the United States, 1860–1895* (1929); David Montgomery, *Beyond Equality: Labor and the Radical Republicans, 1862–1872* (1967); John R. Commons et al., *History of Labour in the United States*, Vol. 2 (1918); *Dictionary of American Biography*, Vol. 20.

WURF, Jerry   (1919–1981). Born in New York City, April 18, 1919; son of Sigmund and Lena (Tannenbaum) Wurf; Jewish; married Mildred Kiefer on November 26, 1960; three children; attended the public schools of New York City, then earned a B.A. degree from New York University in 1940; worked in a New York City cafeteria, 1940–1943; became an organizer for Local 448 of the New York Hotel and Restaurant Employees in 1943; appointed administrator of Local 448's welfare fund in 1947; served as an organizer in New York for the American Federation of State, County and Municipal Employees (AFSCME),

1947–1948; became executive director of AFSCME District Council 37 in 1959, serving in that capacity until 1964; defeated Arnold S. Zander (q.v.), founding president of the AFSCME, in a closely contested election in 1964; elected a vice-president and executive council member of the American Federation of Labor-Congress of Industrial Organizations (AFL-CIO) in 1969; served as a vice-president of the AFL-CIO industrial union department and as a member of the executive board of the maritime trades department; served on a variety of public and private boards and agencies and was a member of the executive board of the Americans for Democratic Action, the Jewish Labor Committee, the Leadership Conference on Civil Rights, and Common Cause; a Democrat; died in Washington, D.C., in December 1981; Leo Kramer, *Labor's Paradox: The American Federation of State, County and Municipal Employees, AFL-CIO* (1962); *Who's Who in America, 1972–1973*; Joseph C. Goulden, *Jerry Wurf: Labor's Last Angry Man* (1982); *AFL-CIO News*, May 2, 1964, December 19, 1981.

WYNN, William H.   (1931–   ). Born in South Bend, Ind., on July 17, 1931; son of William A. and Ellie Wynn; married Bonnie Jean, a homemaker, in 1963; two children, graduated from Riley High School, South Bend, in 1949; joined South Bend Local 37 of the Retail Clerks International Association (RCIA) in 1948, even before graduating from high school; was elected business agent of Local 37 in 1954 and held that position for five years before being appointed an organizer for RCIA District Council 12 in 1959; served as director of the RCIA's Northwest Division for three years, 1966–1969, before becoming assistant to the international president in 1969; served as director of the RCIA Central Division, 1971–1974; was elected an international vice-president in 1974 and served in that capacity until the death of the international president, James T. Housewright (q.v.) in 1977; was elected by the RCIA's executive board to fill the vacancy created by Housewright's death and was subsequently elected to a regular term; *AFL-CIO News*, October 1, 1977; *Who's Who in Labor* (1976).

Y

YABLONSKI, Joseph A. (1910–1969). Born in Pittsburgh, Pa., March 3, 1910, son of a coal miner who was killed in a mine accident in 1933; married Margaret Rita Wasicek; three children; at age 15, began work as a coal miner and joined the United Mine Workers of America (UMWA); elected a local union president in 1934; served on the executive board of District 5, UMWA, Pittsburgh, 1934–1942; served on the international executive board, UMWA, 1942–1969; elected president of District 5 in 1958, serving until 1966 when President W. A. Boyle (q.v.) forced him to resign under threat of placing the district in trusteeship; supported Boyle over insurgent Steve Kochis for the union presidency in 1964, but secretly supported an insurgent for election to the national executive board; defeated by George Titler, a Boyle supporter, when in 1966 the international executive board filled a vacancy in the union vice-presidency; was a power in local Democratic politics and appointed by Boyle to direct Labor's Nonpartisan League, the union's political organization; without the union's support, succeeded in adding pneumoconiosis (black lung) to the list of compensated industrial diseases in Pennsylvania in 1965; challenged Boyle for the union presidency in 1969, charging the incumbent administration with neglecting miners' health and safety, collusion with coal operators, and dictatorial union administration; pledged a restoration of district autonomy and democracy, an end to nepotism, mandatory retirement of union officers at age 65, an aggressive campaign to improve miners' health and safety, and an increase in royalties and benefits from the welfare and retirement fund; meanwhile, Boyle increased pensions by 30 percent and promised to double royalties to finance a further increase to woo the votes of more than forty-thousand voting union pensioners; Boyle also pledged to increase wages from $33 to $50 per day, to support a stringent federal mine safety bill, and to seek a guaranteed annual wage; on December 9, defeated by Boyle by a vote of 81,056 to 45,872; along with his wife and daughter, Yablonski was murdered in his Clarksville, Pa., home on December 31, 1969, by Paul Gilly, Claude Villey, and Aubren Martin; the assassins were employed by Gilly's wife, Annette, her father, Silas Huddleston, retired president of a Tennessee UMWA local, William Prater, secretary-treasurer of District 19, and, according to an affidavit made by William Turnblazer, president of District 19, he and President Boyle; all were convicted; a federal court invalidated the 1969 election, and in December 1972, Arnold Miller (q.v.), an insurgent, defeated Boyle; *The New York Times*, January 6, 1970; Brit Hume, *Death in the Mines* (1971); Stuart Brown, *Man Named Tony: The True Story of the Yablonski Murders* (1976); Arthur H. Lewis, *Murder by Contract: The People Versus Tough Tony* (1975); Joseph E. Finley, *The Corrupt Kingdom: The Rise and Fall of the United Mine Workers* (1972).

John W. Hevener

YOUNG, Coleman Alexander   (1918–   ). Born in Tuscaloosa, Ala., on May 24, 1918; son of William Coleman, a barber and tailor, and Ida (Jones) Young, a schoolteacher; married Marion McClellan on January 1947, divorced eight years later; married Nadine Baxter, February 1955, divorced one year later; no children; Afro-American; at age 5, he moved with his family to Detroit, Mich., where his mother ran a small tailor shop and his father worked as a Post Office guard; attended the otherwise all-white St. Mary's Catholic School, and Detroit's Eastern High School; hired into the Ford Motor Company's River Rouge plant in Dearborn, Mich., in 1937 and was subsequently fired after several confrontation's with Harry Bennett's in-plant police; as executive secretary in the Michigan Division of the National Negro Conference, he worked closely with the United Automobile Workers of America's (UAW) Ford organizing committee during the successful campaign of 1940–1941; active in the 1941–1942 campaign to defend black access to public housing; drafted into the U.S. Army in 1942; graduated from the Air Corps' officer candidate school; arrested with 60 other black officers on April 5, 1945, for entering the whites-only officers' club at Freeman Field near Seymour, Ind.; charges were dropped and the Army soon after prohibited racially segregated facilities; returned to Detroit in 1946 and became an organizer for the Congress of Industrial Organizations' (CIO) United Public Workers; elected director of organization by the Wayne County CIO convention in 1947 and installed as the first black member of the county CIO's executive board; lost the position 18 months later when Walter Reuther (q.v.) won control of the county organization and removed left-wing opponents; helped form the National Negro Labor Council in 1950 and served as the organization's only national organizer; subpoenaed to appear before the House Un-American Activities Committee in February 1952; won election as a delegate to the Michigan Constitutional Convention in 1961; won election to the Michigan Senate in 1964 and served two subsequent terms; won election as Detroit's first black mayor in 1973 and was subsequently reelected in 1977 and

1981; August Meier and Elliott Rudwick, *Black Detroit and the Rise of the UAW* (1979); Kirk Cheyfitz, "The Survivor," *Monthly Detroit* (February 1981).

Steve Babson

YOUNG, Kenneth   (1927–   ). Born in New York City, October 20, 1927; son of Lawrence E., a retail buyer, and Rosalie M. Young, a remedial reading teacher; married Charlotte H., a homemaker, in 1951; three children; after attending New York public elementary schools, he graduated from New Rochelle High School in 1944; enrolled in Antioch College in 1944 but had his college education interrupted by military service, 1946–1947; received a B.A. from Antioch in 1950 and later earned a degree in journalism from New York University; after leaving Antioch, he began a life-long involvement in the American trade union movement; joined the American Newspaper Guild in 1951; became director of research, education, and publicity for the Insurance and Allied Workers Organizing Committee, Congress of Industrial Organizations (CIO) in 1951, serving in that position until 1955; after the organizing committee was chartered as the Insurance Workers of America in 1955, he served it in the same capacity until 1957; served as assistant director and then director of publications and public relations for the industrial union department of the American Federation of Labor (AFL)-CIO, 1957–1963; was publicity director for the International Union of Electrical, Radio and Machine Workers (IUE) and editor of its newspaper, the *IUE News*, 1963–1965; served as the AFL-CIO's legislative representative, 1965–1971; became assistant director of the AFL-CIO department of legislation in 1971 and was promoted to director of the department in 1978; became executive assistant to AFL-CIO President Lane Kirkland (q.v.) in 1979; a strong supporter of civil rights activities, he also sought to develop other legislative alliances to further the labor movement's reformist goals; *Who's Who in Labor* (1976); *AFL-CIO News*, December 2, 1978, December 22, 1979.

YOUNGER, Maud   (1870–1936). Born in San Francisco, Calif., on January 10, 1870; daughter of William John, a dentist, and Annie Maria (Lane) Younger; Episcopalian; never married; educated in private schools; inherited a sizeable fortune from her maternal grandfather and during her young adult years settled into a comfortable upper-class social life that included much travel abroad; visited College Settlement in New York City in 1901 to "see the slums" and remained there for the following five years, an experience that profoundly altered her life; her experiences at College Settlement converted her to a strong proponent of protective labor legislation for women, trade unionism, and women's suffrage; took a job in a New York restaurant chain in 1906 to gain first-hand knowledge of women's working conditions and joined the waitresses' union; published an article in *McClure's* magazine in 1907, vividly describing her experiences as a waitress; returned to San Francisco in 1908 and once again took a job as a waitress; locally renowned as the "millionaire waitress," she took a leading role in the organization of a San Francisco waitresses' union and was elected its first president; served three terms as a delegate to the San Francisco Central Trades and Labor Council; campaigned vigorously for an eight-hour law for women and secured a California State Federation of Labor endorsement of the measure which was passed by the state legislature in 1911; at the same time she also campaigned extensively for a women's suffrage amendment to the California constitution and organized a Wage Earners' Equal Suffrage League to mobilize the support of working women for the reform; the enactment of the amendment in California greatly spurred the women's suffrage movement throughout the United States; returned to New York in 1912 and quickly became involved in a dress- and shirtwaist makers' strike being conducted by the International Ladies' Garment Workers' Union; a member of the National Women's Trade Union League (WTUL), she also campaigned for protective legislation for working women in the District of Columbia; although continuing her efforts in behalf of the WTUL thereafter, she devoted an increasing amount of her time and energy to the women's suffrage campaign; became an associate of Alice Paul in the activities of the Congressional Union, a militant organization of women's suffrage proponents, and gave the keynote address at the founding convention of its successor, the National Woman's party in which capacity she lobbied for women's rights in the Congress of the United States; served as a member of the advisory committee of the federal Women's Bureau for several years, a period during which she was also active in the National Consumers' League; broke with many of her former reformist allies in 1923 by helping initiate and actively campaigning for an Equal Rights Amendment that many women feared would threaten hard-won, existing protective legislation; died in Los Gatos, Calif., on June 25, 1936; *Notable American Women*, Vol. 3; *National Cyclopaedia of American Biography*, Vol. 2; *The New York Times*, June 28, 1936.

Z

ZACK, Albert J.   (1917–   ). Born in Holyoke, Mass., on November 22, 1917; son of Charles S., a newspaperman, and Mary C. Zack, a hospital administrator; married Jane N. in 1939; after completing his primary and secondary education in Holyoke, he worked for a number of New England daily newspapers as a reporter and a copy desk editor as well as occasional stints as a radio news broadcaster; joined the American Newspaper Guild while working for the *Springfield* (Mass.) *Daily News* in 1946 and was an active participant in a long, 16-month strike against that newspaper, an experience that strengthened his commitment to organized labor; was appointed public relations director for the Ohio Congress of Industrial Organizations (CIO) Industrial Union Council and was elected secretary-treasurer of the Franklin County (Columbus, Ohio) Industrial Union Council in 1948; became assistant director of public relations for the CIO in 1952 and, after the merger of the American Federation of Labor (AFL) and the CIO in 1955, became the assistant director of public relations for the AFL-CIO; was appointed public relations director of the AFL-CIO in 1957; the "voice" of the AFL-CIO for 22 years, he was credited by AFL-CIO President Lane Kirkland (q.v.) with effectively transmitting organized labor's message to the American public during a period characterized by "conflict rather than accord, failures rather than gains, and inertia rather than progress"; a member of the National Press Club; retired union positions in 1980; *AFL-CIO News*, January 5, 1980; *Who's Who in Labor* (1976).

ZANDER, Arnold Scheuer   (1901–1975). Born in Two Rivers, Wis., November 26, 1901; son of Arnold, a saw filer, and Anna (Scheuer) Zander; Protestant; married Lola Miriam Dynes on June 15, 1929; three children; graduated from the University of Wisconsin in 1923 with a B.S. degree in civil engineering, then worked as a draftsman for the Wisconsin Telephone Company, 1923–1924, a bridge draftsman for the Baltimore and Ohio Railroad, 1925–1927, and a structural steel draftsman for the Manitowoc Shipbuilding Corporation, 1927–1928; received an M.S. degree in city planning from the University of Wisconsin in 1929 and became secretary of the League of Wisconsin Municipalities; awarded the Ph.D. degree in public administration from the University of Wisconsin in 1931; became the chief examiner of the Wisconsin State Civil Service Department's Bureau of Personnel in 1930, serving until 1934; helped found the Wisconsin State Employees' Union and elected its executive secretary in 1933; was one of the founding members of the American Federation of State, County and Municipal Employees (AFSCME) and elected its first president; was a member of the Labor Advisory Board of the National Youth Administration; served during World War II as a labor consultant to the War Manpower Commission and the U.S. Civil Service Commission; served as an American Federation of Labor (AFL) fraternal delegate to the Trades and Labor Congress of Canada in 1943 and the British Trades Union Congress in 1947; was an AFL advisor to the American delegation to the International Labor Organization conference in 1945 and was a delegate to the Tjanstemannens Centralorganisation conference in Stockholm in 1949; served as vice-president of the World Congress of Professional Employees in 1951; became a member of the AFL-Congress of Industrial Organizations' (CIO) general board after the 1955 merger; was chairman of the AFL-CIO committee on consumer cooperatives; defeated for reelection in 1964 in a closely contested election against Jerry Wurf (q.v.); served as president of United World Federalists, 1966–1967; became a lecturer at Wisconsin State University, Green Bay, Wis., in 1968; was a member of numerous public and private boards and agencies, including the American Civil Liberties Union, the National Association for the Advancement of Colored People, and the International Labor Press of America; edited *The Public Employee* for several years; a Democrat; died in Green Bay, Wis., on July 17, 1975; Arnold S. Zander Papers, State Historical Society of Wisconsin; Leo Kramer, *Labor's Paradox: The American Federation of State, County, and Municipal Employees, AFL-CIO* (1962); *Current Biography* (1947); *Who's Who in America, 1972–1973*; *Who's Who in Labor* (1946); *The New York Times,* July 21, 1975; *AFL-CIO News,* July 26, 1975; Joseph C. Goulden, *Jerry Wurf: Labor's Last Angry Man* (1982).

ZARITSKY, Max   (1885–1959). Born in Petrikov, Russia, April 15, 1885; son of Morris, a rabbi and wealthy lumberman, and Anna Zaritsky; Jewish; married Sophie Pilavin on November 21, 1909; acquired the equivalent of a high school education, then left home at age 15 and moved to Vilna, supporting himself there by tutoring the children of wealthy families; witnessed a three-day pogrom against students, liberals, intellectuals, and Jews in Kiev in 1905, then left Russia, eventually emigrating to the United States; settled in Boston, Mass., and in 1907 joined the Cloth Hat, Cap and Millinery Workers' International Union (CHCMW); elected secretary of the Boston Cap Makers' Local in 1908 and three years later became assistant general secretary of the CHCMW and the protégé of the union's leader, Max Zuckerman; elected the first general president of the CHCMW after the office was created in 1919; served as secretary-treasurer of the Needle Trades' Workers Alliance in 1923; resigned the presidency of the CHCMW in 1925 as a result of internal conflicts between right- and left-wing forces in the union; again elected president in 1927; in 1934, elected secretary-treasurer of the United Hatters, Cap and Millinery Workers' International Union (UHCMWIU), formed by the amalgamation of the United Hatters of North America and the CHCMW; was one of the original members of the Committee for Industrial Organization (CIO) formed in 1935; elected president of the UHCMWIU in 1946; withdrew from the CIO in 1937 after unsuccessfully attempting to mediate the conflicts between the American Federation of Labor and the CIO; was an advocate of labor-management cooperation to promote the hat, cap, and millinery industry; along with David Dubinsky (q.v.) and Sidney Hillman (q.v.), was one of the principal founders of the American Labor party in 1936; joined the Liberal party of New York in 1944; retired from his union positions in 1950; died in Boston, Mass., May 10, 1959; Donald B. Robinson, *Spotlight on a Union: The Story of the United Hatters, Cap and Millinery Workers' International Union* (1948); Walter Galenson, *The CIO Challenge to the AFL: A History of the American Labor Movement, 1935–1941* (1960); Marx Lewis, *Max Zaritsky at Fifty: The Story of an Aggressive Labor Leadership* (1935).

ZIMMERMAN, Charles S. (1896–   ). Born near Kiev, Russia, November 27, 1896; son of Ben Zion and Leah Zimmerman; Jewish; married Rose Prepstein on November 23, 1925; one child; attended Russian schools and completed the equivalent of two years of high school; emigrated to the United States in 1913; secured employment as a knee-pants worker in a New York garment factory and joined the United Garment Workers' Union; later became a member of the Amalgamated Clothing Workers' Union after its formation in 1914; took employment in a waist-making factory in 1916 and joined the International Ladies' Garment Workers' Union (ILGWU); shortly thereafter, became secretary-manager of Dressmakers' Union Local 22 of the ILGWU; became an organizer for the Joint Board of the Dress and Waistmakers' Union in 1924; was a member of the Communist party during much of the 1920s, and therefore was expelled from the ILGWU in 1925, but was reinstated in 1931; headed the joint action committee of the left-wing ILGWU locals that led the unsuccessful cloak strike of 1926; elected an ILGWU vice-president in 1934; served as head of the Trade Union Council of the American Labor party; later joined the Liberal party of New York and became a member of the administrative and state executive committees; was a member of numerous public and private boards and agencies, including Americans for Democratic Action and the National Council for a Permanent Fair Employment Practices Commission; appointed chairman of the American Federation of Labor-Congress of Industrial Organizations' civil rights committee in 1957; elected president of the Jewish Labor Committee in 1968; retired as general manager of the ILGWU Dress Joint Council and New York

Dress Joint Board in 1972; Charles S. Zimmerman Papers, ILGWU Archives; Louis Levine, *The Women's Garment Workers: A History of the International Ladies' Garment Workers' Union* (1924); Benjamin Stolberg, *Tailor's Progress: The Story of a Famous Union and the Men Who Made It* (1944); Walter Galenson, *The CIO Challenge to the AFL: A History of the American Labor Movement, 1935–1941* (1960).

ZONARICH, Nicholas A.   (1908–1979). Born in Portage, Pa., on October 6, 1908; son of Nicholas B., a miner, and Rose Zonarich, a homemaker; married Anna in 1929; three children; left school after completing the sixth grade to work in the coal mines; employed as a farm laborer, 1927–1929; secured a job as a laborer and press operator at the New Kensington, Pa., plant of the Aluminum Company of America in 1929; helped organize a federal labor union among the workers of the Kensington plant in 1932; elected president of the newly formed International Aluminum Workers of America, Congress of Industrial Organizations (CIO) in 1937, and served in that position until 1944 when the Aluminum Workers merged with the United Steelworkers of America (USWA); became an international representative for the USWA in 1944; an effective organizer, he participated in numerous organizing campaigns and was credited with organizing over 100 locals; appointed organizational director of the American Federation of Labor-CIO (AFL-CIO) industrial union department in 1960; was a member of the U.S. Department of Labor's Missile Sites Labor Commission, 1961–1968; was an active participant in numerous civic and fraternal activities; retired union positions in 1977; died in Washington, D.C., on August 13, 1979; *Who's Who in Labor* (1976); *AFL-CIO News*, August 18, 1979; Nicholas A. Zonarich, Interview, Pennsylvania State University Oral History Collection.

Appendices

Appendices

Appendix I
Union Affiliations

The alphabetic listing of unions is followed by those labor leaders affiliated or identified with each particular union. State and local unions are listed separately at the end of the appendix. Those individuals listed in italic letters had a significant impact on the union, whereas for those listed in regular type, the union was not their most significant union affiliation. Where it did not create unnecessary confusion, the most recent title of the particular union was used.

Actors and Artists of America, Associated

Dullzell, Paul   Heller, George
Gillmore, Frank

Actors' Equity Association

Derwent, Clarence   *Gillmore, Frank*
Dullzell, Paul   Montgomery, Robert

Agricultural Workers' Union, National

Chavez, Cesar E.   *Mitchell, Harry L.*
Galarza, Ernesto

Air Line Pilots Association, International

Behncke, David L.
O'Donnell, John J.

Amalgamated Transit Union

(See *Street, Electric Railway and Motor Coach Employees of America, Amalgamated Association of.*)

American Federation of Labor

Baer, John M.   *McBride, John*
Brown, Irving J.   *McDevitt, James L.*

Cruikshank, Nelson H.
Delaney, George P.
Evans, Christopher
Fenton, Francis P.
Frayne, Hugh
Frey, John P.
Gompers, Samuel
Googe, George L.
Gray, Richard J.
Green, William
Jewell, Bert M.
Keenan, Joseph D.
Lennon, John B.
Lovestone, Jay
Lucia, Carmen

McGuire, Peter J.
Meany, George
Miller, Saul
Morgan, Elizabeth
Morrison, Frank
O'Sullivan, Mary K.
Padway, Joseph A.
Parker, Julia O.
Ryan, Martin F.
Schnitzler, William F.
Sender, Toni
Thorne, Florence C.
Tobin, Daniel J.
Woll, Matthew

American Federation of Labor-Congress of Industrial Organizations

Baer, John M.
Barkan, Alexander E.
Biemiller, Andrew J.
Bonadio, Frank
Christopher, Paul R.
Conway, Jack T.
Cruikshank, Nelson H.
Daniel, Franz E.
Davis, Walter G.
DeNucci, George
Donahue, Thomas R.
Ellickson, Katherine P.
Georgine, Robert A.
Goldfinger, Nathaniel
Graham, Sylvester
Gray, Richard J.
Green, John
Haggerty, Cornelius J.
Kehrer, Elmer T.
Kirkland, Josesph L.

Kistler, Alan A.
Kroll, John J.
Lee, Ernest S.
Leonard, Richard
Livingston, John W.
Lovestone, Jay
McDevitt, James L.
McLellan, Andrew C.
Meany, George
Miller, Saul
Oswald, Rudolph A.
Perlis, Leo
Schnitzler, William F.
Session, John A.
Thomas, Rolland J.
Webber, Charles C.
Williams, Elijah H.
Young, Kenneth
Zack, Albert J.
Zonarich, Nicholas A.

American Labor Union (Western Labor Union)

Boyce, Edward
Crouch-Hazlett, Ida

Hagerty, Thomas J.
O'Neill, John M.

Automobile, Aerospace and Agricultural Implement Workers of America, United

Addes, George P.
Bieber, Owen F.
Conway, Jack T.
Delorenzo, Anthony J.
Frankensteen, Richard T.

Mazey, Emil
Mortimer, Wyndham
Reuther, Roy
Reuther, Victor G.
Reuther, Walter P.

Fraser, Douglas A.
Gosser, Richard T.
Jeffrey, Mildred
Leonard, Richard
Livingston, John W.
Kehrer, Elmer T.
Martin, Warren H.

Sheffield, Horace L., Jr.
Sugar, Maurice
Thomas, Rolland J.
Travis, Robert C.
Weir, Stan
Woodcock, Leonard F.
Young, Coleman A.

Bakery and Confectionery Workers' International Union of America

Myrup, Andrew A.
Schnitzler, William F.

Barbers, Hairdressers and Cosmetologists' International Union of America, Journeymen

Birthright, William C.   Williams, Elijah H.
Rollings, John I.

Blacksmiths, Drop Forgers and Helpers, International Brotherhood of

Horn, Roy

Boilermakers, Iron Shipbuilders, Blacksmiths, Forgers and Helpers, International Brotherhood of

Calvin, William A.   MacGowan, Charles J.
Jewell, Bert M.

Bookbinders, International Brotherhood of

Haggerty, John B.

Boot and Shoe Workers' International Union

Phillips, Thomas
Skeffington, Henry J.

Boot and Shoe Workers' Union

Anderson, Mary   Lawson, George W.
Billings, Warren K.

Brewery, Flour, Cereal, Soft Drink and Distillery Workers, International Union of United

Feller, Karl F.   Trautmann, William E.
Obergfell, Joseph F.

Brick and Clay Workers of America, The United

Kasten, Frank

Bricklayers, Masons and Plasterers International Union of America

Bates, Harry C.   Gray, Richard J.
Bowen, William J.   Murray, Thomas A.

Bridge and Structural Iron Workers, International Association of
Lyons, John H.

Building Service Employees' International Union
  (See *Service Employees International Union, AFL-CIO.*)

Cannery, Agricultural, Packing and Allied Workers of America, United
Henderson, Donald J.
Whitfield, Owen H.

Carpenters and Joiners of America, United Brotherhood of

Campbell, Patrick J.   *Konyha, William*
Cosgrove, John T.   Lingg, Louis
Crull, John   *McCarthy, Patrick H.*
Duffy, Frank   *McGuire, Peter J.*
Huber, William   *Rajoppi, Raleigh*
Hutcheson, Maurice A.   *Sidell, William*
Hutcheson, William L.

Cement, Lime and Gypsum Workers International Union, United
Schoenberg, William

Chemical Workers Union, International
Martino, Frank D.
Mitchell, Walter L.

Cigarmakers' International Union of America

Azpeitia, Mario   *Ornburn, Ira M.*
Barnes, John M.   *Perkins, George W.*
Bower, Andrew P.   *Strasser, Adolph*
Gompers, Samuel   Wood, Reuben T.

Clothing Workers of America, Amalgamated

Arons, Milton   Jeffrey, Mildred
Bellanca, Dorothy J.   *Kazan, Abraham E.*
Blankenhorn, Ann W. C.   *Kroll, John J.*
Blankenhorn, Heber H.   *Krzycki, Leo*
Blumberg, Hyman   Lucia, Carmen
Daniel, Franz E.   McCreery, Marie M.
DeLeon, Solon   *Miller, Joyce D.*
DeNucci, George   *Peterson, Esther*
Dickason, Gladys M.   *Potofsky, Jacob S.*
Ervin, Charles W.   *Rosenblum, Frank*
Finley, Murray H.   Salerno, Joseph
Golden, Clinton S.   *Schlossberg, Joseph*
Hillman, Bessie A.   Tippett, Thomas
Hillman, Sidney   Webber, Charles C.
Hollander, Louis   Zimmerman, Charles S.

Clothing and Textile Workers Union, Amalgamated

DuChessi, William M.   Miller, Joyce D.
Finley, Murray H.

Coalition of Labor Union Women

Miller, Joyce D.
Wolfgang, Myra K.

Commercial Telegraphers Union

Allen, William L.   Norwood, Rose F.
Doherty, William C.   Powers, Frank B.

Communications Workers of America

Beirne, Joseph A.   Watts, Glenn E.
Crull, John L.   Werkau, Carlton W.
Moran, John J.

Congress of Industrial Organizations

Brophy, John   Krzycki, Leo
Cannon, Joseph D.   Leonard, Richard
Carey, James B.   Lewis, John L.
Christopher, Paul R.   McLaren, Louise L.
Daniel, Franz E.   Mason, Lucy R.
DeCaux, Leonard H.   Murray, Philip
Ellickson, Katherine P.   Nance, Alexander S.
Germer, Adolph F.   Perlis, Leo
Goldberg, Arthur J.   Pressman, Lee
Goldblatt, Louis   Reuther, Victor G.
Goldfinger, Nathaniel   Reuther, Walter P.
Graham, Sylvester   Riffe, John V.
Hapgood, Mary D.   Weaver, George L. P.
Hapgood, Powers   Young, Coleman A.
Haywood, Allan S.   Young, Kenneth
Kistler, Alan A.   Zack, Albert J.
Kroll, John J.

Coopers' International Union

Foran, Martin A.
Schilling, Robert

Die Casting Workers, National Association of

Cheyfitz, Edward T.

Directors Guild of America

Montgomery, Robert

District 50, Allied and Technical Workers

Lewis, Alma D.
Moffett, Elwood S.

Dolls, Toys, Playthings, Novelties and Allied Products of the United States and Canada

Damino, Harry

Electrical, Radio and Machine Workers, International Union of

Carey, James B.   Young, Kenneth
Jennings, Paul J.

Electrical, Radio and Machine Workers of America, United

Carey, James B.   *Matles, James J.*
Delorenzo, Anthony J.   Oakes, Grant W.
Fitzgerald, Albert J.   Young, Kenneth
Jennings, Paul J.

Electrical Workers, International Brotherhood of

Brown, Edward J.   *Noonan, James P.*
Bugniazet, Gustave M.   *Norwood, Rose F.*
Docktor, Wallace J.   Pachler, William J.
Fisher, Joseph A.   *Parker, Julia O.*
Keenan, Joseph D.   *Pillard, Charles H.*
McNulty, Frank J.   Reuther, Roy
Marciante, Louis P.   *Tracy, Daniel W.*
Milne, J. Scott   *Van Arsdale, Harry, Jr.*
Nockles, Edward

Elevator Constructors, International Union of

Feeney, Frank

Engineers, International Union of Operating

Delaney, George P.   *Maloney, William E.*
Fitzgerald, Frank A.   *Possehl, John*
Huddell, Arthur M.   *Turner, J. C.*
Kirkland, Joseph L.   *Wharton, Hunter P.*

Farm Equipment and Metal Workers of America, United

Oakes, Grant W.
Travis, Robert C.

Farm Labor Union, National

Galarza, Ernesto
Mitchell, Harry L.

Farm Workers' Union, United

Chavez, Cesar E.
Huerta, Dolores

Farmers Union, Southern Tenant

Mitchell, Harry L.
Whitfield, Owen H.

Federation of Organized Trades and Labor Unions of the United States and Canada

Evans, Christopher
Foster, William H.
Gompers, Samuel

Howard, Robert
Leffingwell, Samuel L.

Fire Fighters, International Association of

Baer, Fred W.
McClennan, William H.
Oswald, Rudolph A.

Redmond, John P.
Richardson, George J.

Fur and Leather Workers Union, International

Gold, Ben
Kaufman, Morris

Furniture Workers of America, United

Pizer, Morris
Scarbrough, W. Carl

Garment Cutters' Association

Wright, James L.

Garment Workers of America, United

Blumberg, Hyman
Hillman, Bessie A.
Hillman, Sidney
Kroll, John J.
McCurdy, Joseph P.
O'Reilly, Leonora

Potofsky, Jacob S.
Rickert, Thomas A.
Rosenblum, Frank
Salerno, Joseph
Zimmerman, Charles S.

Garment Workers' Union, International Ladies'

Antonini, Luigi
Arons, Milton
Arywitz, Sigmund
Barondess, Joseph
Barnum, Gertrude
Bisno, Abraham
Breslaw, Joseph
Chaiken, Sol C.
Cohn, Fannia
Crosswaith, Frank R.
Dubinsky, David
Dubrow, Evelyn
Dyche, John A.
Feinberg, Israel
Gingold, David R.
Giovannitti, Arturo
Heller, Jacob J.
Hillquit, Morris
Hochman, Julius

Lovestone, Jay
Miller, Frieda S.
Mitchell, Harry L.
Nagler, Isidore
Newman, Pauline
Ninfo, Salvatore
Perlstein, Meyer
Pesotta, Rose
Peterson, Esther
Price, George M.
Romualdi, Serafino
Rosenberg, Abraham
Schlesinger, Benjamin
Sessions, John A.
Sigman, Morris
Starr, Mark
Stulberg, Louis
Sweeney, John J.
Thompson, Mary C.

Hyman, Louis
Kazan, Abraham E.
Lipsig, James

Wolchok, Samuel
Wolfson, Theresa
Zimmerman, Charles S.

Gas, Coke and Chemical Workers of America, United

Swisher, Elwood D.

Glass Bottle Blowers Association of the United States and Canada

Eames, Thomas B.
Maloney, James

Minton, Lee W.

Glass, Ceramic, and Silica Sand Workers of America, Federation of*

Scholle, August

Glass Workers Union, American Flint

Cook, Harry H.
Easton, John B.

Glass Workers, Universal Federation of Window

Cline, Isaac

Gloveworkers Union of America, International

Christman, Elisabeth
Nestor, Agnes

Government Employees, American Federation of

Griner, John F.
Webber, Clyde M.

Granite Cutters International Association of America

Duncan, James

Granite-Cutters' Union

Dyer, Josiah B.

Hatters, Cap and Millinery Workers' International Union, United

Greene, Michael F.
Lucia, Carmen
Mendelowitz, Abraham

Rose, Alex
Schneiderman, Rose
Zaritsky, Max

Heat and Frost Insulators and Asbestos Workers, International Association of

Mullaney, Joseph A.

Heaters National Union

Jones, Thomas P.

*Now the United Glass and Ceramic Workers of North America.

Hod Carriers', Building and Common Laborers' Union of America, International
(See *Laborers' International Union of North America.*)

Horse Shoers of the U.S. and Canada, International Union of Journeymen
Fitzpatrick, John

Hosiery Workers, American Federation of
Holderman, Carl
Rieve, Emil

Hospital and Health Care Employees, National Union of
Davis, Leon J.

Hotel and Restaurant Employees' and Bartenders' International Union

Ernest, Hugo
Flore, Edward
Kavanagh, William F.
Miller, Edward S.
Pollard, William E.
Sullivan, Jere L.
Wolfgang, Myra K.
Wurf, Jerry

Industrial Workers of the World

Bridges, Harry A.
DeLeon, Daniel
Debs, Eugene V.
Dennis, Eugene
Dunne, Vincent R.
Ettor, Joseph J.
Flynn, Elizabeth G.
Foster, William Z.
Giovannitti, Arturo
Hagerty, Thomas J.
Hartung, Albert F.
Haywood, William D.
Hill, Joe
Jones, Mary H.
Kirwan, James
Langdon, Emma F.
Little, Frank H.
Lundeberg, Harry
Mahoney, Charles E.
Mooney, Thomas J.
Moyer, Charles H.
Nef, Walter T.
O'Neill, John M.
St. John, Vincent
Sherman, Charles O.
Sigman, Morris
Trautmann, William E.
Williams, Benjamin H.

Iron, Steel, and Tin Workers, Amalgamated Association of

Bacon, Emery F.
Burke, Walter J.
Cope, Elmer F.
Davis, James J.
Gainor, Edward J.
Germano, Joseph F.
Haigler, Carey E.
Harris, David
Hickman, William W.
Jarrett, John
Keil, Edward A.
McAninch, Elisha H.
Martin, William
Nutt, James H.
Thimmes, James G.
Tighe, Michael F.
Weihe, William

Knights of Labor, Noble Order of the

Ameringer, Oscar
Barnes, John M.
Barry, Leonora M. K.
Barry, Thomas B.
Boyce, Edward
Buchanan, Joseph R.
Carlton, Albert A.
Conlon, Peter J.
Dailey, Edward L.
Davis, Richard L.
DeLeon, Daniel
Dyer, Josiah B.E.
Evans, Christopher
Farrington, Frank
Foster, Frank K.
Frayne, Hugh
Hayes, John W.
Howard, Robert
Irons, Martin
Johnston, William H.
Jones, Mary H.
Labadie, Joseph A.
Leffingwell, Samuel L.
Litchman, Charles H.
McMahon, Thomas F.
McNeill, George E.

Macauley, Robert C.
McGaw, Homer L.
Maurer, James H.
Mitchell, John
Morgan, Elizabeth
Mullaney, Joseph A.
O'Connell, James P.
O'Reilly, Leonora
Parsons, Albert R.
Pascoe, David M.
Phillips, Thomas
Powderly, Terence V.
Preston, George
Rosenberg, Abraham
Schilling, Robert
Skeffington, Henry J.
Stephens, Uriah S.
Stevens, Alzina P.
Sullivan, Jere L.
Talbot, Thomas W.
Tetlow, Percy
Trevellick, Richard F.
Turner, Frederick
Walker, John H.
Weber, Frank J.
Wright, James L.

Knights of St. Crispin

Carlton, Albert A.
Dailey, Edward L.

Litchman, Charles H.
Phillips, Thomas

Laborers' International Union of North America

Fosco, Peter
Graham, James D.

Moreschi, Joseph
Morreale, Vincent F.

Lasters' Protective Union of New England

Dailey, Edward L.

Laundry Workers International Union

Beck, Dave
Norwood, Rose F.

Letter Carriers, National Association of

Doherty, William C.
Gainor, Edward J.

Lithographic Press Feeders Union

Krzycki, Leo

Locomotive Engineers, Brotherhood of

Arthur, Peter M.   *Johnston, Alvanley*
Brown, Guy L.   *Shields, James P.*
Davidson, Roy E.   *Stone, Warren S.*

Locomotive Firemen and Enginemen, Brotherhood of

Carter, William S.   Golden, Clinton S.
Debs, Eugene V.   *Robertson, David B.*
Davidson, Roy E.   *Sargent, Frank P.*
Gilbert, Henry E.

Longshoremen's Association, International

Bridges, Harry A.   *Keefe, Daniel J.*
Connors, David M.   *O'Connor, Thomas V.*
Delaney, George P.   *Ryan, Joseph P.*
Gleason, Thomas W.

Longshoremen's and Warehousemen's Union, International

Bridges, Harry A.   Weir, Stan
Goldblatt, Louis

Machinists and Aerospace Workers, International Association of

Brown, Harvey W.   *O'Connell, James P.*
Brown, Irving J.   *Peterson, Eric*
Conlon, Peter J.   *Preston, George*
Friedrick, Jacob F.   Schoenberg, William
Golden, Clinton S.   *Siemiller, Paul L.*
Handley, John J.   *Talbot, Thomas W.*
Hayes, Albert J.   Tippett, Thomas
Johnston, William H.   *Wharton, Arthur O.*
Matles, James J.   Wilson, D. Douglas
Miller, Marvin J.   *Wipisinger, William W.*
O'Hare, Kate R.

Machinists and Blacksmiths, International Union of

Fehrenrath, John   Powderly, Terence V.
Fincher, Jonathan C.   *Steward, Ira*
Maguire, Matthew

Maintenance of Way Employees, Brotherhood of

Carroll, Thomas C.   *Milliman, Elmer E.*
Fljozdal, Frederick H.

Major League Baseball Players Association

Miller, Marvin J.

Marine Cooks' and Stewards' Association, National

Bryson, Hugh

Marine and Shipbuilding Workers of America, Industrial Union

Green, John
Grogan, John J.

Maritime Union of America, National

Curran, Joseph E.
Lawrenson, Jack

Masters, Mates and Pilots of America, National Organization of

Kirkland, Joseph L.
Scully, John J. J.

Meat Cutters and Butcher Workmen of North America, Amalgamated

Belsky, Joseph   *Jimerson, Earl W.*
Clark, Lewis J.   *Lane, Dennis*
Donnelly, Michael   *Lloyd, Thomas J.*
Fraina, Louis C.   McDonald, Joseph D.
Gorman, Patrick E.   Mitchell, Harry L.
Helstein, Ralph

Metal Polishers, Buffers, Platers, and Helpers International Union

Kelsay, Ray

Metal Workers International Union, United

Sherman, Charles O.

Mine, Mill and Smelter Workers, International Union of

Boyce, Edward   Langdon, Emma F.
Cannon, Joseph D.   Little, Frank H.
Cheyfitz, Edward T.   *Mahoney, Charles E.*
Clark, John   *Moyer, Charles H.*
Driscoll, John J.   *O'Neill, John M.*
Graham, Sylvester   *Robinson, Reid*
Haywood, William D.   St. John, Vincent
Howard, Asbury   Sefton, Lawrence F.
Kirwan, James   *Travis, Maurice E.*

Mine Workers of America, United

Bittner, Van A.   *Lewis, John L.*
Boyle, William A.   *Lewis, Kathryn*
Brophy, John   *Lewis, Thomas L.*
Caddy, Samuel H.   *McBride, John*
Cairns, Thomas F.   McDonald, David J.
Church, Samuel M., Jr.   *Miller, Arnold R.*
Davis, Richard L.   *Mitch, William A.*
Farrington, Frank   *Mitchell, John*
Germer, Adolph F.   Moffett, Elwood S

Gibson, John W.
Green, William
Hapgood, Powers
Hayes, Frank J.
Haywood, Allan S.
Howat, Alexander
Jones, Mary H.
Keeney, C. Frank
Kennedy, Thomas
Lauck, William Jett
Lewis, Alma D.

Mortimer, Wyndham
Murray, Philip
Ratchford, Michael D.
Riffe, John V.
Tetlow, Percy
Tippett, Thomas
Walker, John H.
White, John P.
Wilson, William B.
Yablonski, Joseph A.

Miners, Western Federation of

(See *Mine, Mill and Smelter Workers, International Union of*.)

Miners' Association, American

Hinchcliffe, John

Miners and Mine Laborers, National Federation of

Evans, Christopher
McBride, John

Miners' National Association

Roy, Andrew
Siney, John

Molders and Foundry Workers Union of North America, International*

Delaney, George P.
Fox, Martin
Frey, John P.
Mooney, Thomas J.

Roney, Frank
Sylvis, William H.
Valentine, Joseph F.

Musicians, American Federation of

Ameringer, Oscar
Davis, Hal C.
Kenin, Herman D.

Petrillo, James C.
Weber, Joseph N.

National Colored Labor Union

Douglass, Frederick
Myers, Isaac

National Labor Union

Cameron, Andrew C.
Fincher, Jonathan C.
Hinchcliffe, John
Jessup, William J.

Siney, John
Sylvis, William H.
Trevellick, Richard F.

*Now the International Molders and Allied Workers Union, AFL-CIO.

National Trades' Union

Commerford, John
Douglas, Charles
English, William
Ferral, John

Luther, Seth
Moore, Ely
Slamm, Levi D.
Townsend, Robert, Jr.

Needle Trades Workers Industrial Union

Gold, Ben
Hyman, Louis

Negro American Labor Council

Randolph, Asa P.
Young, Coleman A.

Negro Labor Committee

Crosswaith, Frank R.

Newspaper Guild, American

Broun, Heywood C.
Dubrow, Evelyn
Ervin, Charles W.
Kehrer, Elmer T.
Levin, Ruben

Martin, Harry L.
Miller, Saul
Romualdi, Serafino
Young, Kenneth
Zack, Albert J.

Office and Professional Workers of America, United

Helfgott, Simon
Merrill, Lewis R.

Oil, Chemical and Atomic Workers International Union

Knight, Orie A.
Murry, James W.

Swisher, Elwood D.

Oil Field, Gas Well, and Refinery Workers, International Association of

Germer, Adolph F.
Knight, Orie A.

Oil Workers International Union

Knight, Orie A.
O'Connor, Harvey

Packinghouse Workers of America, United

Church, Samuel M., Jr.
Clark, Lewis J.

Helstein, Ralph

Painters, Decorators and Paperhangers of America, Brotherhood of*

Brennan, Peter J.
Lindelof, Lawrence P.

Martinson, Henry R.
Raftery, Lawrence M.

*Now the International Brotherhood of Painters and Allied Trades of the United States and Canada.

Paper Makers, International Brotherhood of

Burke, John P.
Burns, Matthew J.

Phillips, Paul L.
Schneider, George J.

Paperworkers of America, United

Goldfinger, Nathaniel
Phillips, Paul L.
Ramsey, Claude E.

Sayre, Harry D.
Tonelli, Joseph P.

Pattern Makers League

Wilson, James A.

Photo-Engravers' Union of North America, International

Woll, Matthew

Plasterers' and Cement Masons' International Association of the United States and Canada, Operative

McDevitt, James L.

Plumbers and Steamfitters of the United States and Canada, United Association of

Alpine, John P.
Brown, Henry S.
Clark, Hugh D.
Coefield, John
Durkin, Martin P.
Grogan, John J.

McNamara, Patrick V.
Maurer, James H.
Meany, George
Murphy, Vincent
Schoemann, Peter T.
Ward, Martin J.

Post Office Clerks, National Federation of

Filbey, Francis S.
George, Leo E.

Hallbeck, Elroy C.
Nelson, Oscar F.

Post Office Clerks, United National Association of

Nelson, Oscar F.

Post Office Motor Vehicles Employees, National Federation of

Gibson, Everett G.

Post Office and Railway Mail Laborers', National Association of

McAvoy, Harold

Postal Clerks, United Federation of

Filbey, Francis S.
Hallbeck, Elroy C.

Postal Workers Union, American

Andrews, Emmet C.
Filbey, Francis S.

Potters, National Brotherhood of Operative

Duffy, James M.

Printing Pressmen's and Assistants' Union of North America, International

Berry, George L.   *McGrady, Edward F.*
Dunwody, Thomas E.   Mahoney, William
Googe, George L.

Pulp, Sulphite and Paper Mill Workers, International Brotherhood of

Burke, John P.   *Tonelli, Joseph P.*
Burns, Matthew J.

Railroad Signalmen, Brotherhood of

Clark, Jesse   *Lyon, Arlon E.*
Helt, Daniel W.

Railroad Telegraphers, Order of

Griner, John F.   Moran, John J.
Leighty, George E.   Powers, Frank B.

Railroad Trainmen, Brotherhood of

Chesser, Al H.   *Lee, William G.*
Doak, William N.   *Luna, Charles*
Johnson, William D.   *Whitney, Alexander F.*
Kennedy, William P.

Railway, Airline and Steamship Clerks, Freight Handlers, Express and Station Employees, Brotherhood of

Dennis, Charles L.
Kroll, Fred J.

Railway Carmen of America, Brotherhood of

Harrison, George M.   *Ryan, Martin F.*
Knight, Felix H.

Railway Conductors of America, Order of

Fraser, Harry W.   *Johnson, William D.*
Garretson, Austin B.   *Phillips, James A.*
Hughes, Roy O.

Railway Supervisors Association, Ind., American

Tahney, James P.

Railway Union, American

Debs, Eugene V.

Retail Clerks International Association

Coulter, Clarence C.   Lee, Ernest S.
Davis, Leon J.   *Suffridge, James A.*

Greenberg, Max
Housewright, James T.

Wolchok, Samuel
Wynn, William H.

Retail, Wholesale and Department Store Employees of America, United

Davis, Leon
Gibbons, Harold J.
Gibson, John W.

Greenberg, Max
Steinbock, Max
Wolchok, Samuel

Rubber, Cork, Linoleum and Plastic Workers of America, United*

Bommarito, Peter
Buckmaster, Leland S.
Burns, Thomas F.
Dalrymple, Sherman H.

Long, Bob G.
Maile, Francis
Stone, Milan O.

Screen Actors' Guild

Montgomery, Robert
Reagan, Ronald

Seafarers International Union of North America**

Curran, Joseph E.
Drozak, Frank P.
Furuseth, Andrew

Hall, Paul
Lundeberg, Harry
Olander, Victor A.

Service Employees International Union, AFL-CIO

Donahue, Thomas R.
McFetridge, William L.
Oswald, Rudolph A.

Sullivan, David
Sweeney, John J.

Sheet Metal Workers' International Association

Bonadio, Frank
Byron, Robert

Frayne, Hugh

Ship Carpenters and Caulkers, International Union of

Trevellick, Richard F.

Shoe Workers of America, United

Hapgood, Powers
Mitchell, James J

Signalmen of America, Brotherhood of Railroad

Cashen, Thomas C.

Sleeping Car Porters, Brotherhood of

Dellums, Cottrell L.
Randolph, Asa P.

Totten, Ashley L.

*Formerly the United Rubber Workers of America.

**Formerly the International Seamen's Union.

Stage Employees and Moving Picture Machine Operators of the United States and Canada, International Alliance of Theatrical

Brewer, Roy M.
Walsh, Richard F.

State, County and Municipal Employees, American Federation of

Chapman, Gordon W.   *Flaumenbaum, Irving*
Conway, Jack T.   *Wurf, Jerry*
DeLury, John J.   *Zander, Arnold S.*

Steelworkers of America, United

Abel, Iorwith W.   *Migas, Nick*
Bacon, Emery F.   Miller, Marvin J.
Bittner, Van A.   *Moffett, Elwood S.*
Burke, Walter J.   *Molony, Joseph P.*
Cope, Elmer F.   *Murray, Philip*
DeNucci, George   Policastro, Thomas F.
Easton, John B.   *Pressman, Lee*
Germano, Joseph S.   *Rarick, Donald C.*
Goldberg, Arthur J.   *Riffe, John V.*
Golden, Clinton S.   *Ruttenberg, Harold J.*
Haigler, Carey E.   *Sefton, Lawrence F.*
Howard, Asbury   Stanley, Miles C.
Hudson, Hosea   *Swanson, Samuel E.*
Johns, John S.   *Sweeney, Vincent D.*
Kistler, Alan A.   *Thimmes, James G.*
McBride, Lloyd   Travis, Maurice E.
McDonald, David J.   *Wilson, Boyd L.*
Maloy, Elmer J.   *Zonarich, Nicholas A.*
Mathias, Charles G.

Stereotypers and Electrotypers Union of North America, International

Buckley, Leo J.

Stone and Allied Products Workers of America, United

Lawson, John C.
Scott, Sam H.

Stone Cutters' Association of North America, Journeymen

Givens, Paul A.

Stove, Furnace and Allied Appliance Workers of North America*

Lewis, Joseph

Street, Electric Railway and Motor Coach Employees of America, Amalgamated Association of

Knight, Felix H.   *Mahon, William D.*
Lyden, Michael J.   *Spradling, Abe L.*

*Formerly the Stove Mounters International Union of North America.

Tailors, United Brotherhood of

Schlossberg, Joseph

Tailors' Union of America, Journeymen

Lennon, John B.
Wilkinson, Joseph

Teachers, American Federation of

Barker, Mary C.	Muste, Abraham J.
Borchardt, Selma M.	Peterson, Esther
Counts, George S.	Reuther, Roy
Eklund, John M.	*Selden, David S.*
Gibbons, Harold J.	*Shanker, Albert*
Haley, Margaret A.	*Smith, Stanton E.*
Henderson, Donald J.	*Starr, Mark*
Megel, Carl J.	

Teamsters, Chauffeurs, Warehousemen and Helpers of America, International Brotherhood of

Baldanzi, George	*Gibbons, Harold J.*
Beck, Dave	*Hickey, Thomas L.*
Cairns, Thomas F.	*Hoffa, James R.*
Dobbs, Farrel	*Mohn, Einar O.*
Dunne, Vincent R.	Shelley, John F.
English, John F.	*Tobin, Daniel J.*
Fenton, Francis P.	Weir, Stan
Fitzsimmons, Frank E.	*Williams, Roy L.*

Telephone Workers, National Federation of

(See *Communications Workers of America*.)

Television and Radio Artists, American Federation of

Derwent, Clarence
Heller, George

Textile Workers, National Union of

Greene, Prince W.

Textile Workers of America, Amalgamated

Muste, Abraham J.

Textile Workers of America, United

Baldanzi, George	Mathias, Charles G.
Christopher, Paul R.	Perlis, Leo
Gorman, Francis J.	Pollock, William
Greene, Prince W.	*Rieve, Emil*
McMahon, Thomas F.	Thompson, Mary G.

Textile Workers Union of America

Baldanzi, George
Barkan, Alexander E.
Christopher, Paul R.
DuChessi, William M.
Edelman, John W.
Holderman, Carl

Nord, Elizabeth
Podojil, Antonette
Pollock, William
Rieve, Emil
Salerno, Joseph

Tobacco Workers International Union

O'Hare, John
Scott, Sam H.

Train Dispatchers Association, American

Griner, John F.
Luhrsen, Julius G.

Transport Service Employees of America, United

Davis, Walter G.
Townsend, Willard S.

Weaver, George L. P.

Transport Workers Union of America

Gilmartin, Daniel
Guinan, Matthew

Quill, Michael J.

Transportation Union, United

Chesser, Al H.
Gilbert, Henry E.

Luna, Charles

Typographical Union, International

Barrett, Francis G.
Berger, Victor L.
Buchanan, Joseph R.
Cameron, Andrew C.
Cenerazzo, Walter W.
Donnelly, Samuel B.
Foster, William H.
Hayes, Maximilian S.
Howard, Charles P.
Keating, Edward
Labadie, Joseph A.
Lynch, James M.

Mahoney, William
Morrison, Frank
Ohl, Henry
Parsons, Albert R.
Pascoe, David M.
Powers, Bertram A.
Randolph, Woodruff
Soderstrom, Reuben G.
Stevens, Alzina P.
Sullivan, James W.
Swartz, Maud O.
Troup, Augusta L.

Typographical Union, National

Farquhar, John M.

United Hebrew Trades

Feinstone, Morris
Hillquit, Morris

Mendelowitz, Abraham
Pine, Max

Upholsterers' International Union of North America

Hoffman, Sal B.

Utility Workers Union of America

Fisher, Joseph A.   *Pachler, William J.*

Vulcan, Sons of*

Harris, David   *McAninch, Elisha H.*
Hickman, William W.   *McLaughlin, Hugh*

Watch Workers Union, American

Cenerazzo, Walter W.

Women's Trade Union League

Anderson, Mary   Newman, Pauline
Barnum, Gertrude   *Norwood, Rose F.*
Christman, Elisabeth   *O'Reilly, Leonora*
Dreier, Mary E.   *O'Sullivan, Mary K.*
Ellickson, Katherine P.   Parker, Julia O.
Evans, Elizabeth G.   Pesotta, Rose
Hapgood, Mary D.   *Robins, Margaret D.*
Henry, Alice   *Schneiderman, Rose*
Hillman, Bessie A.   *Swartz, Maud O.*
Kehew, Mary M. K.   *Thompson, Mary G.*
Marot, Helen   *Walling, William E.*
Nestor, Agnes   *Younger, Maud*

Wood, Wire and Metal Lathers' International Union

Georgine, Robert A.   *McSorley, William J.*
Haggerty, Cornelius J.   *Mashburn, Lloyd A.*

Woodworkers of America, International

Hartung, Albert F.

STATE AND LOCAL UNIONS

Alabama

AFL-CIO Council
Mitch, William A.

Industrial Union Council
Haigler, Carey E.

State Federation of Labor
Mitch, William A.

*See also Iron, Steel, and Tin Workers, Amalgamated Association of.

California

Los Angeles Building and Construction Trades Council
Haggerty, Cornelius J.
Mashburn, Lloyd A.

Los Angeles County AFL-CIO
Arywitz, Sigmund

Los Angeles Iron Trades Council
Roney, Frank

Los Angeles Labor Council
Mashburn, Lloyd A.

Oakland Central Labor Union
Suffridge, James A.

San Francisco Building Trades Council
Coefield, John
McCarthy, Patrick H.

San Francisco Industrial Union Council
Bryson, Hugh

San Francisco Labor Council
Ernst, Hugo
Shelley, John F.

San Francisco Representative Assembly of Trades and Labor Unions
Roney, Frank

San Francisco, Iron Trades Council of
Roney, Frank

State Building Trades Council
McCarthy, Patrick H.

State Industrial Union Council

Bryson, Hugh	Thimmes, James G.
Goldblatt, Louis	Travis, Maurice E.

State Federation of Labor

Ernst, Hugo	Lundeberg, Harry
Haggerty, Cornelius J.	*Shelley, John F.*

Vallejo Trades and Labor Council
Roney, Frank

Connecticut

AFL-CIO Council
Driscoll, John J.

State Industrial Union Council
Driscoll, John J.

District of Columbia

Federation of Labor
Coulter, Clarence C.   Turner, J. C.
McCurdy, Joseph P.

Washington Central Labor Union
Coulter, Clarence C.

Florida

Jacksonville Central Labor Union
Jewell, Bert M.

Georgia

AFL-CIO Council
Mathias, Charles G.

Atlanta Federation of Trades
Nance, Alexander S.

Atlanta Industrial Union Council
Mathias, Charles G.

Savannah Trades and Labor Assembly
Googe, George L.
Possehl, John

State Federation of Labor
Googe, George L.
Nance, Alexander S.

Illinois

AFL-CIO Council
Germano, Joseph S.
Soderstrom, Reuben G.

Chicago Building Trades Council
Durkin, Martin P.

Chicago Central Labor Union

Morgan, Thomas J.

Chicago Federation of Labor

Anderson, Mary

Donnelly, Michael

Fitzpatrick, John

George, Leo E.

Keenan, Joseph D.

McFetridge, William L.

Maloney, William E.

Megel, Carl J.

Nelson, Oscar F.

Nockles, Edward N.

Olander, Victor A.

Robins, Margaret D.

Chicago Trade and Labor Assembly

Morgan, Thomas J.

Cook County Industrial Union Council

Germano, Joseph S.

Travis, Robert C.

Springfield Building Trades Council

Byron, Robert

Springfield Federation of Labor

Byron, Robert

State Federation of Labor

Byron, Robert

George, Leo E.

Haywood, Allan S.

McFetridge, William L.

Megel, Carl J.

Olander, Victor A.

Robins, Margaret D.

Soderstrom, Reuben G.

Walker, John H.

State Industrial Union Council

Travis, Robert C.

Streator Trades and Labor Assembly

Soderstrom, Reuben G.

Indiana

Indianapolis Central Labor Union

Obergfell, Joseph F.

State Federation of Labor

Obergfell, Joseph F.

State Federation of Trade and Labor Unions

Leffingwell, Samuel L.

Iowa

AFL-CIO Council
Clark, Hugh D.

Dubuque Federation of Labor
Clark, Hugh D.

Kentucky

Louisville Union Trades and Labor Assembly
Gorman, Patrick E.

State Federation of Labor
Caddy, Samuel H.
Gorman, Patrick E.

State Industrial Union Council
Caddy, Samuel H.

Louisiana

State Federation of Labor
Williams, Elijah H.

Maryland

Baltimore Federation of Labor
Filbey, Francis S.
McCurdy, Joseph P.

State Federation of Labor
McCurdy, Joseph P.
Turner, J. C.

Massachusetts

Boston Central Labor Union
Fenton, Francis P.
McGrady, Edward F.

Boston Central Trades and Labor Unions
Foster, Frank K.

Boston Trades' Union
Douglas, Charles
Luther, Seth

Lawrence Central Labor Union
Watt, Robert J.

State Federation of Labor

Fenton, Francis P.   McGrady, Edward F.
Frey, John P.   *Watt, Robert J.*

State Industrial Union Council

Fitzgerald, Albert J.
Salerno, Joseph

Women's Educational and Industrial Union of Boston

Kehew, Mary M. K.

Michigan

AFL-CIO Council

Scholle, August

Detroit Council of Trades and Labor Unions

Labadie, Joseph A.

Detroit Federation of Labor

McNamara, Patrick V.

Detroit Trades Assembly

Trevellick, Richard F.

Flint Industrial Union Council

Reuther, Roy

State Federation of Labor

Labadie, Joseph A.

State Industrial Union Council

Germer, Adolph F.   *Scholle, August*
Gibson, John W.   Sheffield, Horace L., Jr.
Leonard, Richard

Minnesota

Minneapolis Central Labor Union

Dunne, Vincent R.

Minnesota Iron Range Industrial Union Council

Swanson, Samuel E.

St. Paul Trades and Labor Assembly

Lawson, George W.
Mahoney, William

State Federation of Labor
Lawson, George W.

State Industrial Union Council
Helstein, Ralph

Mississippi

AFL-CIO Council
Ramsay, Claude E.

Jackson County Central Labor Union
Ramsay, Claude E.

Missouri

AFL-CIO Council
Rollings, John I.

St. Louis Central Trades and Labor Union
Knight, Felix H.
Rollings, John I.

St. Louis Industrial Union Council
McBride, Lloyd

Springfield Central Labor Union
Wood, Reuben T.

State Federation of Labor
Raftery, Lawrence M.   *Wood, Reuben T.*
Rollings, John I.

Montana

AFL-CIO Council
Murry, James W.

State Federation of Labor
Graham, James D.

State Industrial Union Council
Graham, Sylvester

Nebraska

Grand Island Central Labor Union
Brewer, Roy M.

State Federation of Labor
Brewer, Roy M.

New Hampshire

State Federation of Labor
Burke, John P.

New Jersey

AFL-CIO Council
Murphy, Vincent

Hudson County Central Labor Union
Kavanagh, William F.

Hudson County Industrial Union Council
Grogan, John J.

Mercer County Building Trades Council
Marciante, Louis P.

Mercer County Central Labor Union
Marciante, Louis P.

Paterson Trades Assembly
McDonnell, J. P.

State Building and Construction Trades Council
Cosgrove, John T.

State Federation of Labor
Cosgrove, John T.   *Marciante, Louis P.*
Eames, Thomas B.   *Murphy, Vincent*
Kavanagh, William F.

State Federation of Trades and Labor Unions
Kavanagh, William F.
McDonnell, J. P.

State Industrial Union Council
Barkan, Alexander E.   *Holderman, Carl*
Dubrow, Evelyn

Union County Central Trades
Cosgrove, John T.

New York

AFL-CIO Council

Brennan, Peter J.
Campbell, Patrick J.
Guinan, Matthew

Hollander, Louis
Sweeney, John J.

General Trades' Union

Commerford, John
Moore, Ely

Slamm, Levi D.
Townsend, Robert, Jr.

New York City Building and Construction Trades Council, Greater

Murray, Thomas A.
Van Arsdale, Harry, Jr.

New York City Central Labor Council, AFL-CIO

Davis, Leon J.
Shanker, Albert

Van Arsdale, Harry, Jr.

New York City Central Trades and Labor Council

Feinberg, Israel
Feinstone, Morris
Meany, George
Mendelowitz, Abraham

Ryan, Joseph P.
Schneiderman, Rose
Sullivan, James W.
Van Arsdale, Harry, Jr.

New York City, Construction Trades Council of, Greater

Brennan, Peter J.

New York City Industrial Union Council, Greater

Curran, Joseph E.
Jennings, Paul J.

Quill, Michael

State Federation of Labor

Meany, George
Mullaney, Joseph A.
Murray, Thomas A.

Nagler, Isidore
Ryan, Joseph P.

State Industrial Union Council

Haywood, Allan S.
Hollander, Louis

Jennings, Paul J.
Wolchok, Samuel

State Trades and Labor Council

McDonnell, J. P.

State Workingmen's Assembly

Jessup, William J.

Syracuse Central Trades and Labor Unions
Lynch, James M.

North Carolina

AFL-CIO Council
Scott, Sam H.

State Federation of Labor
Christopher, Paul R.

North Dakota

AFL-CIO Council
Dockter, Wallace J.

Fargo-Moorhead, AFL-CIO
Martinson, Henry R.

Fargo Trades and Labor Assembly
Martinson, Henry R.

Minot Central Labor Union
Dockter, Wallace J.

Ohio

AFL-CIO Council

Cope, Elmer F.	Konyha, William
Johns, John S.	*Lyden, Michael J.*

Columbus Federation of Labor
DeNucci, George

Franklin County Industrial Union Council
Zack, Albert J.

Stark County Industrial Union Council
Johns, John S.

State Federation of Labor
Frey, John P.
Lyden, Michael J.

State Industrial Union Council

DeNucci, George	Zack, Albert J.
Kroll, John J.	

Valley Trade Council, Ohio

Cook, Harry H.

Oregon

AFL-CIO Council

McDonald, Joseph D.

Portland Central Labor Council

Howard, Charles P.
McDonald, Joseph D.

State Federation of Labor

McDonald, Joseph D.

Pennsylvania

AFL-CIO Council

Davis, Hal C.

Erie Central Labor Union

Wilson, James A.

Philadelphia Building Trades Council

Feeney, Frank
McDevitt, James L.

Philadelphia Central Labor Union

Feeney, Frank   Pascoe, David M.
Minton, Lee W.

Philadelphia Mechanics' Union of Trade Associations

Heighton, William

Philadelphia Trades Assembly

Fincher, Jonathan C.
Wright, James L.

Philadelphia Trades' Union

English, William
Ferral, John

Reading Federated Trades Council

Bower, Andrew P.

State Federation of Labor

Bower, Andrew P.   Maurer, James H.
Davis, Hal C.   Minton, Lee W.
McDevitt, James L.   Wilson, James A.

Puerto Rico

Federación Libre de Trabajadores de Puerto Rico

Iglesias, Santiago

Free Federation of Puerto Rican Workers

Capetillo, Luisa

Rhode Island

AFL-CIO Council

Policastro, Thomas F.

State Federation of Labor

Policastro, Thomas F.

Tennessee

AFL-CIO Council

Smith, Stanton E.

Memphis Industrial Union Council

Martin, Harry L.

State Federation of Labor

Birthright, William C.
Smith, Stanton E.

State Industrial Union Council

Christopher, Paul R.
Martin, Harry L.

Texas

AFL-CIO Council

Brown, Henry S.

San Antonio Building and Construction Trades Council

Brown, Henry S.

State Building and Construction Trades Council

Brown, Henry S.

State Federation of Labor

McLellan, Andrew C.

Vermont

State Industrial Union Council

Lawson, John C.

Virginia

State Industrial Union Council

Webber, Charles C.

West Virginia

Kanawha County Industrial Union Council

Stanley, Miles C.

Parkersburg Trades and Labor Council

Easton, John B.

State AFL-CIO Council

Stanley, Miles C.

State Federation of Labor

Cairns, Thomas F.   Keeney, C. Frank
Easton, John B.

State Industrial Union Council

Easton, John B.
Stanley, Miles C.

Wisconsin

AFL-CIO Council

Friedrick, Jacob F.
Stone, Milan O.

Milwaukee Building and Construction Trades Council

Schoemann, Peter T.

Milwaukee Central Labor Union

Grottkau, Paul

Milwaukee Federation of Trades Councils

Biemiller, Andrew J.   Ohl, Henry
Friedrick, Jacob F.   Weber, Frank J.

Sheboygan Central Labor Union

McCreery, Marie M. L.

State Federation of Labor

Biemiller, Andrew J.   Padway, Joseph A.
Brockhausen, Frederick C.   Schneider, George J.

Handley, John J.   *Weber, Frank J.*
Ohl, Henry

State Industrial Union Council

Burke, Walter J.

Appendix II
Religious Preference

The lists in this appendix include individuals who were identified with certain religious groups even though they may not have maintained their affiliations throughout their lives. Religious preferences were not ascertained for approximately one-third of the individuals listed in the *Biographical Dictionary*.

BAPTIST

Bellamy, Edward
Berry, George L.
Bower, Andrew P.
Davis, James J.
Eames, Thomas B.
Fraser, Harry W.
Googe, George L.
Green, William
Griner, John F.
Harrison, George M.
Howard, Asbury
Hudson, Hosea
Knight, Felix H.

Knight, Orie A.
Luther, Seth
Martin, Harry L., Jr.
Martin, Warren H.
Mitchell, Harry L.
Nance, Alexander S.
Siemiller, Paul L.
Smith, Stanton E.
Stephens, Uriah S.
Thorne, Florence C.
Williams, Elijah H.
Wood, Reuben T.

CHRISTIAN

Brewer, Roy M.
Crull, John L.
George, Leo E.
Hoffa, James R.

Miller, Edward S.
Reagan, Ronald
Scott, Sam H.

CHRISTIAN SCIENTIST

Minton, Lee W.
Phillips, James A.

CHURCH OF CHRIST

Morrison, Frank

CHURCH OF JESUS CHRIST OF LATTER-DAY SAINTS
Peterson, Esther

CONGREGATIONALIST
Baer, John M.
Chapman, Gordon W.
Easton, John B.
Jarrett, John
Johnston, William H.

Lee, William G.
Pollock, William
Robins, Margaret D.
Schneider, George J.

COMMUNITY CHURCH
Kelsay, Ray
Richardson, George J.

DUTCH REFORMED
Muste, Abraham J.

EPISCOPALIAN
Frankensteen, Richard T.
Gibson, Everett G.*
Gillmore, Frank
Haywood, William D.**
Holderman, Carl
Hutchins, Grace
Johnston, Alvanley
Lewis, Alma D.
Maso, Sal

Mason, Lucy R.
Nord, Elizabeth
Nutt, James H.
Townsend, Willard S.
Uhl, Alexander
Van Kleeck, Mary A.
Vorse, Mary H.
Younger, Maud

JEWISH
Barondess, Joseph
Baskin, Joseph
Bellanca, Dorothy J.
Belsky, Joseph
Benson, Herman
Bisno, Abraham
Blumberg, Hyman
Breslaw, Joseph
Cahan, Abraham
Chaiken, Sol C.
Cohn, Fannia
DeLeon, Daniel
DeLeon, Solon
Dubinsky, David
Dyche, John A.
Ellickson, Katherine P.
Ernst, Hugo

Leiserson, William M.
Lipsig, James
London, Meyer
Lovestone, Jay
Mendelowitz, Abraham
Miller, Marvin J.
Nagler, Isidore
Newman, Pauline
Norwood, Rose F.
Perlis, Leo
Perlman, Selig
Perlstein, Meyer
Pesotta, Rose
Pine, Max
Pizer, Morris
Price, George M.
Rombro, Jacob

*Reformed.
**Later rejected the church.

Feinberg, Israel
Feinstone, Morris
Gingold, David R.
Gold, Ben
Goldberg, Arthur J.
Goldfinger, Nathaniel
Goldman, Emma
Gompers, Samuel
Greenberg, Max
Helfgott, Simon
Heller, George
Heller, Jacob J.
Hillman, Bessie A.
Hillman, Sidney
Hillquit, Morris
Hochman, Julius
Hollander, Louis
Hyman, Louis
Kaufman, Morris
Kenin, Herman D.
Kroll, John J.

Rose, Alex
Rosenberg, Abraham
Rosenblum, Frank
Ruef, Abraham
Schlesinger, Benjamin
Schlossberg, Joseph
Schneiderman, Rose
Sender, Toni
Shanker, Albert
Sigman, Morris
Steinbock, Max
Stokes, Rose H. P.
Stolberg, Benjamin
Stulberg, Louis
Vladeck, Baruch C.
Wolchok, Samuel
Wolfson, Theresa
Wurf, Jerry
Zaritsky, Max
Zimmerman, Charles S.

LUTHERAN

Abel, Iorwith W.
Anderson, Mary
Bittner, Van A.
Christman, Elisabeth
Dockter, Wallace J.
Germer, Adolph F.
Hayes, Albert J.
Hill, Joe
Kasten, Frank
Kennedy, William P.
Luhrsen, Julius G.

Martinson, Henry R.
Mohn, Einar O.
Nelson, Oscar F.
Reuther, Roy
Reuther, Victor G.
Reuther, Walter P.
Rieve, Emil
Sheffield, Horace L., Jr.
Teigan, Henry G.
Totten, Ashley L.
Travis, Robert C.

METHODIST

Barker, Mary T.
Brown, Guy L.
Caddy, Samuel H.
Calvin, William A.
Carroll, Thomas C.
Christopher, Paul R.
Clark, Jesse
Counts, George S.
Cruikshank, Nelson H.
Eklund, John M.
Fielden, Samuel
George, Henry
Gibson, John W.

Johnson, William D.
Martin, William
Mitch, William A.
Moffett, Elwood S.
Myers, Isaac
Phillips, Paul L.
Phillips, Thomas
Preston, George
Randolph, Asa P.
Starr, Mark
Suffridge, James A.
Swanson, Samuel E.
Swisher, Elwood D.

Graham, Sylvester
Haigler, Carey E.
Helt, Daniel W.
Housewright, James T.
Hutcheson, Maurice A.
Hutcheson, William L.

Sylvis, William H.
Tetlow, Percy
Trevellick, Richard F.
Webber, Charles C.
Werkau, Carlton W.
Wilson, James A.

PRESBYTERIAN

Addams, Jane
Bacon, Emery
Beck, Dave
Birthright, William C.
Cairns, Thomas F.
Commons, John R.
Davidson, Roy E.
Dreier, Mary E.
Duncan, James
Dunwody, Thomas E.
Farquhar, John M.
Fljozdal, Frederick H.
Gilbert, Henry E.
Hall, Burton
Hughes, Roy O.

Kehrer, Elmer T.
Keil, Edward A.
Lauck, William Jett
Lawson, John C.
Leighty, George E.
Lennon, John B.
Lindelof, Lawrence P.
Lucia, Carmen
Riffe, John V.
Robertson, David B.
Thomas, Norman M.
Tippett, Thomas
Whitney, Alexander F.
Wilson, William B.

PROTESTANT

Brown, Harvey W.
Buckmaster, Leland S.
Byron, Robert
Coulter, Clarence C.
Furuseth, Andrew
Giovannitti, Arturo*
Horn, Roy
Huddell, Arthur M.
Jewell, Bert M.
Jimerson, Earl W.

Kelsay, Ray
Langdon, Emma F.
Lewis, John L.
Mortimer, Wyndham
Oakes, Grant W.
Peterson, Eric
Thimmes, James G.
Whitfield, Owen H.
Wright, James L.
Zander, Arnold S.

ROMAN CATHOLIC

Addes, George P.
Alpine, John P.
Antonini, Luigi
Azpeitia, Mario
Barrett, Francis G.
Barry, Leonora M. K.
Bates, Harry C.
Beirne, Joseph A.
Bieber, Owen F.
Bonadio, Frank

Lewis, Joseph
Lyden, Michael J.
Lynch, James M.
McAnich, Elisha H.
McAvoy, Harold
McCarthy, Patrick H.
McCreery, Marie M. L.
McCurdy, Joseph P.
McDevitt, James L.
McDonald, David J.

Boyce, Edward
Brennan, Peter J.
Bridges, Harry A. R.*
Brophy, John
Broun, Heywood C.**
Brown, Henry S.
Buckley, Leo J.
Bugniazet, Gustave M.
Burke, John P.
Burke, Walter J.
Burns, Matthew J.
Burns, Thomas F.
Campbell, Patrick J.
Carey, James B.
Cashen, Thomas C.
Cenerazzo, Walter W.
Chavez, Cesar E.
Clark, Hugh D.
Conlon, Peter J.
Cosgrove, John T.
Crosswaith, Frank R.
Curran, Joseph E.
Damino, Harry
Delaney, George P.
DeLury, John J.
DeNucci, George
Doherty, William C.
Donahue, Thomas R.
Driscoll, John J.
Duffy, Frank
Duffy, James M.
Durkin, Martin P.
Ellis, Christine S.
English, John F.
Feeney, Frank
Feller, Karl F.
Fenton, Francis P.
Fisher, Joseph A.
Fitzgerald, Albert J.
Fitzgerald, Frank A.
Fitzpatrick, John
Flore, Edward
Fosco, Peter
Gainor, Edward J.
Georgine, Robert A.
Germano, Joseph S.
Gilmartin, Daniel

McDonnell, J. P.
McFetridge, William L.
McGrady, Edward F.
McGuire, Peter J.
McLaughlin, Hugh
McMahon, Thomas F.
McNamara, Patrick V.
McNulty, Frank J.
McSorley, William J.
Maguire, Matthew
Maloney, James
Maloney, William E.
Maloy, Elmer J.
Martino, Frank D.
Mathias, Charles G.
Meany, George
Milliman, Elmer E.
Mitchell, James J.
Mitchell, John
Molony, Joseph P.
Mooney, Thomas J.
Moreschi, Joseph
Morreale, Vincent F.
Mullaney, Joseph A.
Murphy, Vincent
Murray, Philip
Murray, Thomas A.
Nestor, Agnes
Ninfo, Salvatore
Noonan, James P.
O'Connell, James P.
O'Connor, Thomas V.
O'Hare, John
Pachler, William J.
Parker, Julia O.
Petrillo, James C.
Podojil, Antonette
Powers, Bertram A.
Powers, Frank B.
Quill, Michael J.
Raftery, Lawrence M.
Rajoppi, Raleigh
Rarick, Donald C.
Redmond, John P.
Romualdi, Serafino
Roney, Frank
Ryan, Joseph P.

*Reared a Roman Catholic.

**Reared an Episcopalian but converted during the 1930s.

Gleason, Thomas W.
Gorman, Francis J.
Gorman, Patrick E.
Gosser, Richard
Gray, Richard J.
Grogan, John J.
Guinan, Matthew
Haas, Francis J.
Hagerty, Thomas J.
Haggerty, Cornelius J.
Haggerty, John B.
Haley, Margaret A.
Hapgood, Mary D.
Hayes, Frank J.
Hayes, Maximilian S.
Hickey, Thomas J.
Hoffman, Sal B.
Huerta, Dolores
Iglesias, Santiago
Jones, Mary H.
Kavanagh, William F.
Kearney, Denis
Keating, Edward
Keefe, Daniel J.
Keenan, Joseph D.
Kennedy, Thomas
Kistler, Alan A.
Kroll, Fred J.
Lane, Dennis
Lawrenson, Jack
Lawson, George W.
Leonard, Richard

Ryan, Martin F.
Sacco, Nicola
Salerno, Joseph
Schoemann, Peter T.
Schwab, Michael
Scully, John J. J.
Sefton, Lawrence F.
Shelley, John F.
Siney, John
Skeffington, Henry
Sullivan, David
Sullivan, Jere L.
Swartz, Maud O.
Sweeney, Vincent D.
Tahney, James P.
Thorne, Florence C.
Tighe, Michael F.
Tobin, Daniel J.
Tonelli, Joseph P.
Troup, Augusta L.
Turner, J. C.
Valentine, Joseph F.
Van Arsdale, Harry, Jr.
Vanzetti, Bartolomeo
Walsh, Francis P.
Walsh, Richard F.
Ward, Martin J.
Watt, Robert J.
White, John P.
Woll, Matthew
Woodcock, Leonard F.

SOCIETY FOR ETHICAL CULTURE
Derwent, Clarence
Sullivan, James W.

SOCIETY OF FRIENDS (QUAKER)
Biemiller, Andrew J.
Cope, Elmer F.
Garretson, Austin B.
Kelley, Florence

Marot, Helen
Muste, Abraham J.
Rustin, Bayard

SPIRITUALIST
Schilling, Robert

SYRIAN ORTHODOX
Johns, John S.

UNITARIAN

Ameringer, Oscar
Christopher, Paul R.
Hallbeck, Elroy C.
Henry, Alice

Herrick, Elinore M.
Kehew, Mary M. K.
O'Connor, Harvey

Appendix III
Place of Birth

This appendix is divided into two groups of persons: those born in the United States and those born in other countries. Na. indicates that the date or place of birth was not ascertained.

UNITED STATES

Alabama

Name	Birthdate	Birthplace
Drozak, Frank P.	December 24, 1927	Coy
Haigler, Carey E.	August 9, 1902	Birmingham
Hall, Paul	August 21, 1914	Na.
Howard, Asbury	1907	Autaugoville
Mitchell, Walter L.	January 30, 1915	Florence
Parsons, Albert R.	June 24, 1848	Montgomery
Young, Coleman A.	May 24, 1918	Tuscaloosa

Arizona

Name	Birthdate	Birthplace
Chavez, Cesar E.	March 31, 1927	Yuma

Arkansas

Name	Birthdate	Birthplace
Birthright, William C.	May 27, 1887	Helena
Phillips, Paul L.	August 10, 1904	Strong
Webber, Clyde M.	December 9, 1919	Sloam Spring

California

Name	Birthdate	Birthplace
Andrews, Emmet C.	August 3, 1916	San Francisco
Beck, Dave	June 16, 1894	Stockton

Name	Birthdate	Birthplace
Lewis, Joseph	October 1, 1906	Centerville
Reuf, Abraham	September 2, 1864	San Francisco
Shelley, John F.	September 3, 1905	San Francisco
Skeffington, Henry J.	March 5, 1858	Marysville
Weir, Stan	1921	Los Angeles
Younger, Maud	January 10, 1870	San Francisco

Colorado

Name	Birthdate	Birthplace
Mashburn, Lloyd A.	October 10, 1897	Greeley

Connecticut

Name	Birthdate	Birthplace
Delorenzo, Anthony J.	May 7, 1915	Stamford
Douglas, Charles	ca. 1800	New London
Driscoll, John J.	December 11, 1911	Waterbury
Gibson, Everett G.	December 28, 1903	Wallingford
Skidmore, Thomas	August 13, 1790	Newtown
Steward, Ira	March 10, 1831	New London

Florida

Name	Birthdate	Birthplace
Azpeitia, Mario	November 22, 1899	Key West
Pollard, William E.	September 14, 1915	Pensacola
Randolph, Asa P.	April 15, 1889	Crescent City

Georgia

Name	Birthdate	Birthplace
Barker, Mary C.	January 20, 1879	Atlanta
Dunwody, Thomas E.	August 1, 1887	Lafayette
Googe, George L.	July 25, 1900	Palaky
Griner, John F.	August 7, 1907	Camilla
Hudson, Hosea	April 12, 1898	Wilkes County
Nance, Alexander S.	May 19, 1895	Bowman
Sheffield, Horace L., Jr.	February 22, 1916	Vienna

Illinois

Name	Birthdate	Birthplace
Addams, Jane	September 6, 1860	Cedarville
Barnum, Gertrude	September 29, 1866	Chester
Brown, Edward J.	November 20, 1893	Chicago
Bryson, Hugh	October 4, 1914	(rural)
Burke, Walter J.	September 14, 1911	Antioch
Christman, Elisabeth	September 2, 1881	Chicago
Crouch-Hazlett, Ida	ca. 1875	Chicago

Name	Birthdate	Birthplace
Crull, John L.	August 4, 1901	Geneosea
Davidson, Roy E.	July 4, 1901	Fairmount
Dennis, Charles L.	June 21, 1908	Beardstown
Durkin, Martin P.	March 18, 1894	Chicago
Farrington, Frank	1873	Fairburg
Georgine, Robert A.	July 18, 1932	Chicago
Germano, Joseph S.	February 12, 1904	Chicago
Gibson, John W.	August 23, 1910	Harrisburg
Goldberg, Arthur J.	August 8, 1908	Chicago
Haley, Margaret A.	November 15, 1861	Joliet
Hallbeck, Elroy C.	May 15, 1902	Chicago
Hapgood, Powers	December 28, 1899	Chicago
Horn, Roy	March 10, 1872	Warsaw
Howard, Charles P.	September 14, 1879	Harvel
Jimerson, Earl W.	September 2, 1889	East St. Louis
Kasten, Frank	January 13, 1878	Dolton
Keefe, Daniel J.	September 27, 1852	Willowsprings
Keenan, Joseph D.	November 5, 1896	Chicago
Kennedy, Thomas	November 2, 1887	Lansford
Lane, Dennis	1881	Chicago
Lawson, George W.	July 4, 1876	Chicago
Lee, William G.	November 29, 1859	La Prairie
Leighty, George E.	August 16, 1897	Phillips
Lewis, Kathryn	April 14, 1911	Panama
Luhrsen, Julius G.	April 1, 1877	Des Plaines
McFetridge, William L.	November 28, 1893	Chicago
Mahoney, William	January 13, 1869	Chicago
Martin, Warren H.	August 16, 1902	Marion
Miller, Joyce D.	June 19, 1928	Chicago
Mitchell, John	February 4, 1870	Braidwood
Mooney, Thomas J.	December 8, 1882	Chicago
Nelson, Oscar F.	September 29, 1884	Chicago
Olander, Victor A.	November 28, 1873	Chicago
Petrillo, James C.	March 16, 1892	Chicago
Phillips, James A.	September 10, 1873	Clay County
Possehl, John	1886	Chicago
Reagan, Ronald	February 6, 1911	Tampico
Redmond, John P.	June 2, 1892	Chicago
Rickert, Thomas A.	April 24, 1876	Chicago
Shields, James P.	June 9, 1889	Neoga
Sidell, William	May 30, 1915	Chicago
Swanson, Samuel E.	May 24, 1902	Chicago
Tahney, James P.	1897	Chicago
Tippett, Thomas	October 27, 1890	Peoria
Tracy, Daniel W.	April 7, 1886	Bloomington
Ward, Martin J.	September 25, 1918	Chicago
Werkau, Carlton W.	September 25, 1907	Clifton
White, John P.	February 28, 1870	Coal Valley

Indiana

Name	Birthdate	Birthplace
Bacon, Emery F.	May 1, 1909	Indianapolis
Buckmaster, Leland S.	March 30, 1894	Geneva
Clark, Jesse	November 21, 1901	Terre Haute
Cope, Elmer F.	July 24, 1903	Elwood
Debs, Eugene V.	November 5, 1855	Terre Haute
Gainor, Edward J.	August 1, 1870	Greencastle
Givens, Paul A.	October 11, 1891	Indianapolis
Hoffa, James R.	February 14, 1913	Brazil
Kelsay, Ray	July 8, 1888	Marion
Megel, Carl J.	December 3, 1899	Hayden
Sayre, Harry D.	November 26, 1914	Wabash
Wynn, William H.	July 17, 1931	South Bend

Iowa

Name	Birthdate	Birthplace
Brown, Guy L.	August 22, 1893	Boone
Clark, Hugh D.	May 18, 1913	Lamotte
Clark, Lewis J.	April 23, 1902	Centerville
Eklund, John M.	September 14, 1909	Burlington
Garretson, Austin B.	September 14, 1856	Winterset
Hayes, Frank J.	1882	What Cheer
Jeffrey, Mildred	December 29, 1911	Alton
Knight, Orie A.	September 24, 1902	New Hampton
Lewis, Alma D.	January 23, 1889	Colfax
Lewis, John L.	February 12, 1880	Lucas
Nockles, Edward N.	September 21, 1869	Dubuque
Stone, Warren S.	February 1, 1860	Ainsworth
Teigan, Henry G.	August 7, 1881	Forest City
Whitney, Alexander F.	April 12, 1873	Cedar Falls
Williams, Roy L.	March 22, 1915	Ottumwa

Kansas

Name	Birthdate	Birthplace
Counts, George S.	December 9, 1889	Baldwin City
Dunne, Vincent R.	April 17, 1889	Kansas City
Fraser, Harry W.	June 7, 1884	Topeka
Keating, Edward	July 9, 1875	Kansas City
O'Hare, Kate R.	March 26, 1877	Ottawa County

Kentucky

Name	Birthdate	Birthplace
Gorman, Patrick E.	November 27, 1892	Louisville
Riffe, John V.	March 15, 1904	Jenkins
St. John, Vincent	July 16, 1876	Newport

Name	Birthdate	Birthplace
Spradling, Abe L.	June 19, 1885	Woodford County
Walling, William E.	March 14, 1877	Louisville

Louisiana

Name	Birthdate	Birthplace
Marciante, Louis P.	August 22, 1898	Lutcher
Williams, Elijah H.	August 16, 1895	Bienville Parish

Maine

Name	Birthdate	Birthplace
Buckley, Leo J.	February 4, 1899	Lewiston
Stevens, Alzina P.	May 27, 1849	Parsonsfield
Williams, Benjamin H.	March 15, 1877	Monson

Maryland

Name	Birthdate	Birthplace
Douglass, Frederick	February 1817	Tuckahoe
McCurdy, Joseph P.	March 20, 1892	Baltimore
Mathias, Charles G.	August 17, 1913	Baltimore County
Myers, Isaac	1835	Baltimore
Valentine, Joseph F.	May 13, 1857	Baltimore

Massachusetts

Name	Birthdate	Birthplace
Alpine, John P.	ca. 1868	Boston
Bellamy, Edward	March 26, 1850	Chicopee Falls
Blankenhorn, Ann W. C.	September 1, 1891	Provincetown
Burns, Thomas F.	June 19, 1906	Holyoke
Carlton, Albert A.	1847	Lynn
Cenerazzo, Walter W.	July 21, 1913	Somerville
Chamberlain, Edwin M.	November 7, 1835	Cambridge
Dailey, Edward L.	October 6, 1855	Danvers
Dullzell, Paul	June 15, 1879	Boston
English, John F.	April 14, 1889	Boston
Fenton, Francis P.	March 11, 1895	Boston
Fitzgerald, Albert J.	1906	Lynn
Foster, Frank K.	December 18, 1855	Palmer
Foster, William Z.	February 25, 1881	Taunton
Haggerty, Cornelius J.	January 10, 1894	Boston
Hapgood, Mary D.	February 21, 1886	North Brookfield
Huddell, Arthur M.	June 15, 1869	Danvers
Hutchins, Grace	August 19, 1885	Boston
Kehew, Mary M. K.	September 8, 1859	Boston

Name	Birthdate	Birthplace
Litchman, Charles H.	April 8, 1849	Marblehead
McClennan, William H.	September 11, 1907	Boston
McNamara, Patrick V.	October 4, 1894	North Weymouth
McNeill, George E.	August 4, 1837	Amesbury
Parker, Julia O.	September 9, 1890	Woburn
Powers, Bertram A.	1922	Cambridge
Richardson, George J.	November 25, 1893	Winchester
Sullivan, Jere L.	January 3, 1863	Willansett
Zack, Albert J.	November 22, 1917	Holyoke

Michigan

Name	Birthdate	Birthplace
Bieber, Owen F.	December 28, 1929	North Dorr
Bommarito, Peter	May 17, 1915	Detroit
Conway, Jack T.	December 20, 1917	Detroit
Frankensteen, Richard T.	March 6, 1907	Detroit
Hutcheson, Maurice A.	May 7, 1897	Saginaw County
Hutcheson, William L.	February 7, 1874	Saginaw County
Kehrer, Elmer T.	January 11, 1921	Brighton
Labadie, Joseph A.	April 18, 1850	Paw Paw
Maloney, William E.	June 17, 1884	Detroit
Nestor, Agnes	June 24, 1880	Grand Rapids
Selden, David S.	June 5, 1914	Dearborn
Sessions, John A.	December 7, 1918	Ypsilanti
Sugar, Maurice	1891	Brimley
Webber, Charles C.	August 28, 1892	Osborne Mills

Minnesota

Name	Birthdate	Birthplace
Frey, John P.	February 24, 1871	Mankato
Helstein, Ralph	December 11, 1908	Duluth
Martinson, Henry R.	March 6, 1883	Minneapolis
Mohn, Einar O.	August 27, 1906	Atwater
O'Connor, Harvey	March 29, 1898	Minneapolis
Powers, Frank B.	May 13, 1888	Clear Lake
Ruttenberg, Harold J.	May 22, 1914	St. Paul
Soderstrom, Reuben G.	March 10, 1888	Wright County

Mississippi

Name	Birthdate	Birthplace
Martin, Harry L., Jr.	October 28, 1908	Hollandale
Ramsay, Claude E.	December 18, 1916	Ocean Springs
Whitfield, Owen H.	1892	Jamestown

Missouri

Name	Birthdate	Birthplace
Baer, Fred W.	August 16, 1884	Kansas City
Buchanan, Joseph R.	December 6, 1851	Hannibal
Chesser, Al H.	February 26, 1914	Pettis County
Daniel, Franz E.	April 4, 1904	Osceola
Dobbs, Farrel	July 25, 1907	Queen City
Gilbert, Henry E.	October 5, 1906	Ethel
Haggerty, John B.	1884	St. Louis
Harrington, Michael	February 24, 1928	St. Louis
Harrison, George M.	July 19, 1895	Lois
Housewright, James T.	November 23, 1921	Wesco
Johnson, William D.	October 18, 1881	Brookfield
Knight, Felix H.	December 10, 1876	Montgomery County
Livingston, John W.	August 17, 1908	Iberia
McBride, Lloyd	March 9, 1916	Farmington
Miller, Edward S.	June 24, 1901	Cameron
Noonan, James P.	December 15, 1878	St. Louis
Ornburn, Ira M.	November 28, 1889	Moberly
O'Sullivan, Mary K.	January 8, 1864	Hannibal
Raftery, Lawrence M.	February 27, 1895	St. Louis
Randolph, Woodruff	January 31, 1892	Warrenton
Rollings, John I.	July 1, 1905	St. Charles County
Thorne, Florence C.	July 28, 1877	Hannibal
Walsh, Francis P.	July 20, 1864	St. Louis
Wilson, Boyd L.	May 31, 1886	Linn
Wood, Reuben T.	August 7, 1884	Springfield

Montana

Name	Birthdate	Birthplace
Boyle, William A.	December 1, 1904	Bald Butte
Graham, Sylvester	September 1, 1899	Sheridan
Murry, James W.	February 6, 1935	Billings
Robinson, Reid	June 7, 1908	Butte

Nebraska

Name	Birthdate	Birthplace
Brewer, Roy M.	August 9, 1909	Cairo
Jewell, Bert M.	February 5, 1881	Brock
Lyon, Arlon E.	October 15, 1899	Thedford
Siemiller, Paul L.	September 4, 1904	Gothenberg

New Hampshire

Name	Birthdate	Birthplace
Bagley, Sarah	April 29, 1806	Candia
Collins, Jennie	1828	Amoskeag
Flynn, Elizabeth G.	August 7, 1890	Concord

New Jersey

Name	Birthdate	Birthplace
Arons, Milton	January 3, 1917	Newark
Barkan, Alexander E.	August 8, 1909	Bayonne
Beirne, Joseph A.	February 16, 1911	Jersey City
Cline, Isaac	January 12, 1835	Winslow
Cosgrove, John T.	September 11, 1873	Elizabeth
Dubrow, Evelyn	May 6, 1912	Garfield
Eames, Thomas B.	November 20, 1882	Williamstown
Edelman, John W.	June 27, 1893	Belleville
Grogan, John J.	March 26, 1914	Hoboken
Hall, Burton	November 16, 1929	South Orange
Kavanagh, William F.	September 2, 1878	Jersey City
Kenin, Herman D.	October 26, 1901	Vineland
McGrady, Edward F.	January 29, 1872	Jersey City
Moore, Ely	July 4, 1798	Belvidere
Murphy, Vincent	August 1, 1893	Newark
Rajoppi, Raleigh	February 22, 1905	Milburn
Schnitzler, William F.	January 21, 1904	Newark
Scully, John J. J.	February 10, 1867	South Amboy
Stephens, Uriah S.	August 3, 1821	Cape May County
Tighe, Michael F.	March 10, 1858	Boonton

New Mexico

Name	Birthdate	Birthplace
Huerta, Dolores	April 10, 1930	Dawson

New York

Name	Birthdate	Birthplace
Arywitz, Sigmund	1914	Buffalo
Barry, Thomas B.	July 17, 1852	Cohoes
Benson, Herman	July 9, 1915	New York City
Billings, Warren K.	1893	Middletown
Bloor, Ella R.	July 8, 1862	Staten Island
Bowen, William J.	1868	Albany
Brennan, Peter J.	May 24, 1918	New York City
Broun, Heywood C.	December 7, 1888	Brooklyn
Brown, Irving J.	November 20, 1911	New York City
Bugniazet, Gustave M.	1878	New York City
Campbell, Patrick J.	July 22, 1918	New York City
Chaiken, Sol C.	January 9, 1918	New York City
Commerford, John	Na.	Brooklyn
Conlon, Peter J.	September 23, 1869	Brooklyn
Connors, David M.	June 2, 1914	Buffalo
Curran, Joseph E.	March 1, 1906	New York City
Davis, Walter C.	November 27, 1920	New York City
DeLeon, Solon	September 2, 1883	New York City

Name	Birthdate	Birthplace
DeLury, John J.	September 30, 1904	New York City
Donahue, Thomas R.	September 4, 1928	New York City
Dreier, Mary E.	September 26, 1875	Brooklyn
DuChessi, William M.	November 29, 1914	Amsterdam
Ellickson, Katherine P.	September 1, 1905	Yonkers
Ettor, Joseph J.	October 6, 1885	Brooklyn
Evans, Elizabeth G.	February 28, 1856	New Rochelle
Feeney, Frank	April 22, 1870	New York City
Fehrenrath, John	June 29, 1844	Rochester
Finley, Murray H.	March 31, 1922	Syracuse
Fisher, Joseph A.	May 1, 1896	New York City
Fitzgerald, Frank A.	September 5, 1885	New York City
Flaumenbaum, Irving	September 9, 1909	Brooklyn
Flore, Edward	December 5, 1877	Buffalo
Gillmore, Frank	May 14, 1867	New York City
Gleason, Thomas W.	November 8, 1900	New York City
Goldblatt, Louis	June 5, 1910	New York City
Goldfinger, Nathaniel	August 20, 1916	New York City
Gray, Richard J.	December 6, 1887	Albany
Greenberg, Max	August 6, 1907	New York City
Helfgott, Simon	November 15, 1894	New York City
Heller, George	November 20, 1905	New York City
Henderson, Donald J.	February 4, 1902	New York City
Herrick, Elinore M.	June 15, 1895	New York City
Hickey, Thomas L.	1893	New York City
Holderman, Carl	January 15, 1894	Hornell
Jennings, Paul J.	March 19, 1918	Brooklyn
Jessup, William J.	February 7, 1827	New York City
Lipsig, James	April 1, 1910	New York City
Lynch, James M.	January 11, 1867	Manlius
McGuire, Peter J.	July 6, 1852	New York City
Maguire, Matthew	1850	New York City
Martino, Frank D.	April 9, 1919	Albany
Maso, Sal	July 25, 1900	New York City
Meany, George	August 16, 1894	New York City
Miller, Marvin J.	April 14, 1917	New York City
Miller, Saul	September 23, 1918	New York City
Milliman, Elmer E.	November 22, 1890	Mount Morris
Montgomery, Robert	May 21, 1904	Beacon
Morreale, Vincent F.	July 29, 1902	New York City
Mullaney, Joseph A.	June 11, 1872	New York City
Murray, Thomas A.	1885	New York City
Neebe, Oscar	July 12, 1850	New York City
Oakes, Grant W.	April 18, 1905	Westfield
O'Reilly, Leonora	February 16, 1870	New York City
Pachler, William J.	August 20, 1904	Thornwood
Pillard, Charles H.	October 26, 1918	Buffalo

Name	Birthdate	Birthplace
Pressman, Lee	July 1, 1906	New York City
Robins, Margaret D.	September 6, 1868	Brooklyn
Rosenblum, Frank	May 15, 1888	New York City
Ryan, Joseph P.	May 11, 1884	Babylon
Shanker, Albert	September 14, 1928	New York City
Slamm, Levi D.	c. 1800	New York City
Steinbock, Max	February 18, 1917	New York City
Sweeney, John J.	May 5, 1934	New York City
Troup, Augusta L.	c. 1848	New York City
Uhl, Alexander	June 11, 1899	New York City
Van Arsdale, Harry, Jr.	November 23, 1905	New York City
Van Kleeck, Mary A.	June 26, 1883	Glenham
Vorse, Mary H.	October 9, 1874	New York City
Walsh, Richard F.	February 20, 1900	Brooklyn
Ward, Cyrenus O.	October 28, 1831	Western New York
Windt, John	Na.	New York City
Wolfson, Theresa	July 19, 1897	Brooklyn
Wurf, Jerry	April 18, 1919	New York City
Young, Kenneth	October 20, 1927	New York City

North Carolina

Name	Birthdate	Birthplace
Scott, Sam H.	March 1, 1901	Orange County
Watts, Glenn E.	June 4, 1920	Story Point

North Dakota

Name	Birthdate	Birthplace
Dockter, Wallace J.	May 1, 1925	Drake
Hughes, Roy O.	September 24, 1887	Portland

Ohio

Name	Birthdate	Birthplace
Abel, Iorwith W.	August 11, 1908	Magnolia
Baker, E.R.P.	February 1, 1834	Fairfield County
Biemiller, Andrew J.	July 23, 1906	Sandusky
Blankenhorn, Heber H.	March 26, 1884	Orrville
Cashen, Thomas C.	September 15, 1879	South Thompson
Commons, John R.	October 13, 1862	Hollansburg
Cruikshank, Nelson H.	June 21, 1902	Bradner
Doherty, William C.	February 23, 1902	Glendale
Feller, Karl F.	August 6, 1914	Dayton
Fox, Martin	August 22, 1848	Cincinnati
Gosser, Richard T.	December 13, 1900	Toledo
Green, William	March 3, 1873	Coshocton
Hayes, Maximilian S.	May 25, 1866	Havana
Konyha, William	May 11, 1915	Cleveland

Name	Birthdate	Birthplace
Leffingwell, Samuel L.	Na.	Chillicothe
Leonard, Richard	February 22, 1902	New Straitsville
Lyons, John H.	October 29, 1919	Cleveland
McBride, John	July 25, 1854	Wayne County
McGaw, Homer L.	April 8, 1845	Bethlehem
Mahon, William D.	August 12, 1861	Athens County
Mitch, William A.	April 10, 1881	Minersville
Robertson, David B.	May 13, 1876	West Austintown
Smith, Stanton E.	August 29, 1905	Wyoming
Tetlow, Percy	December 16, 1875	Leetonia
Thimmes, James G.	October 4, 1896	Hemlock
Thomas, Norman M.	November 20, 1884	Marion
Thomas, Rolland J.	June 9, 1900	East Palestine
Townsend, Willard S.	December 4, 1895	Cincinnati
Travis, Robert C.	February 7, 1906	Toledo
Wipisinger, William W.	December 10, 1924	Cleveland

Oklahoma

Name	Birthdate	Birthplace
Dickason, Gladys M.	January 28, 1903	Galena
Long, Bob G.	September 1, 1947	Vinita

Oregon

Name	Birthdate	Birthplace
McDonald, Joseph D.	July 10, 1895	Clatskanine
Reed, John	October 22, 1887	Portland

Pennsylvania

Name	Birthdate	Birthplace
Baldanzi, George	January 23, 1907	Black Diamond
Barnes, John M.	June 22, 1866	Lancaster
Bittner, Van A.	March 20, 1885	Bridgeport
Bonadio, Frank	March 19, 1904	Pittsburgh
Bower, Andrew P.	May 14, 1869	Apollo
Brown, Harvey W.	October 28, 1883	Dow
Brown, Henry S.	October 24, 1920	Pittsburgh
Cannon, Joseph D.	October 26, 1871	Locust Gap
Carey, James B.	August 12, 1911	Philadelphia
Coefield, John	June 18, 1869	Petroleum Center
Coulter, Clarence C.	June 4, 1882	Venango County
Davis, Hal C.	February 27, 1914	Pittsburgh
Donnelly, Samuel B.	November 7, 1866	Concord
Easton, John B.	September 26, 1880	Allegheny County
Ervin, Charles W.	November 22, 1865	Philadelphia
Filbey, Francis S.	July 4, 1907	Wrightsville
Fincher, Jonathan C.	1830	Philadelphia

Name	Birthdate	Birthplace
Fitzsimmons, Frank E.	April 7, 1908	Jeannette
Foran, Martin A.	November 11, 1844	Choconut
Frayne, Hugh	November 8, 1869	Scranton
George, Henry	September 2, 1839	Philadelphia
Gibbons, Harold J.	April 10, 1910	Taylor
Golden, Clinton S.	November 16, 1888	Pottsville
Hayes, John W.	December 26, 1854	Philadelphia
Helt, Daniel W.	September 24, 1883	Shamokin
Johns, John S.	March 4, 1915	Beaver Falls
Kelley, Florence	September 12, 1859	Philadelphia
Kennedy, Thomas	November 2, 1887	Lansford
Kistler, Alan A.	October 1, 1920	Pittsburgh
Kroll, Fred J.	October 29, 1935	Philadelphia
Lewis, Thomas L.	1866	Locust Gap
McAninch, Elisha H.	September 9, 1841	Pittsburgh
McAvoy, Harold	November 5, 1904	Philadelphia
McDevitt, James L.	November 3, 1898	Philadelphia
McDonald, David J.	November 22, 1902	Pittsburgh
McLaren, Louise L.	August 10, 1885	Wellsboro
McSorley, William J.	December 13, 1876	Philadelphia
Maile, Francis	November 19, 1919	Phoenixville
Maloney, James	September 11, 1870	Scranton
Maloy, Elmer J.	March 22, 1896	Pittsburgh
Marot, Helen	June 9, 1865	Philadelphia
Maurer, James H.	April 15, 1864	Reading
Migas, Nick	ca. 1914	McKees Rocks
Minton, Lee W.	November 17, 1911	Washington
Moffett, Elwood S.	April 30, 1908	Williamstown
Moran, John J.	February 26, 1897	Cecil
Mortimer, Wyndham	March 11, 1884	Karthaus
O'Connell, James P.	August 22, 1858	Minersville
Pascoe, David M.	October 26, 1859	Philadelphia
Podojil, Antonette	October 9, 1911	Braddock
Pollock, William	November 12, 1899	Philadelphia
Powderly, Terence V.	January 22, 1849	Carbondale
Rustin, Bayard	March 17, 1910	West Chester
Scholle, August	May 23, 1904	Creighton
Seidel, Emil	December 13, 1864	Ashland
Sullivan, James W.	March 9, 1848	Carlisle
Sweeney, Vincent D.	March 3, 1900	Pittsburgh
Sylvis, William H.	November 26, 1828	Armagh
Tonelli, Joseph P.	February 26, 1908	Grove City
Weaver, George L. P.	May 18, 1912	Pittsburgh
Weihe, William	January 21, 1845	Baldwin
Wilson, James A.	April 23, 1876	Erie
Yablonski, Joseph A.	March 3, 1910	Pittsburgh
Zonarich, Nicholas A.	October 6, 1908	Portage

Rhode Island

Name	Birthdate	Birthplace
Luther, Seth	Na.	Providence
Policastro, Thomas F.	October 22, 1919	Providence
Woodcock, Leonard F.	February 15, 1911	Providence

South Carolina

Name	Birthdate	Birthplace
Carroll, Thomas C.	May 22, 1894	Donalds
Christopher, Paul R.	February 14, 1910	Easley
Kirkland, Joseph L.	March 12, 1922	Camden
Talbot, Thomas W.	April 17, 1845	(rural)

South Dakota

Name	Birthdate	Birthplace
Kirwin, James	Na.	Terry

Tennessee

Name	Birthdate	Birthplace
Berry, George L.	September 12, 1882	Lee Valley
Langdon, Emma F.	1875	La Grange
Mitchell, Harry L.	June 14, 1906	Halls
Scarbrough, W. Carl	May 31, 1935	Henderson
Suffridge, James A.	February 2, 1909	Knoxville

Texas

Name	Birthdate	Birthplace
Bates, Harry C.	November 22, 1882	Denton
Carter, William S.	August 11, 1859	Austin
Dellums, Cottrell L.	January 3, 1900	Corsicana
Luna, Charles	October 21, 1906	Celeste
Turner, J. C.	November 4, 1916	Beaumont

Utah

Name	Birthdate	Birthplace
Haywood, William D.	February 4, 1869	Salt Lake City
Lloyd, Thomas J.	November 13, 1895	Spanish Forks
Peterson, Esther	December 9, 1906	Provo

Vermont

Name	Birthdate	Birthplace
Barrett, Francis G.	November 25, 1892	Rutland
Burke, John P.	April 21, 1884	North Duxbury
Sargent, Frank P.	November 18, 1854	East Orange

Virginia

Name	Birthdate	Birthplace
Davis, Richard L.	December 24, 1864	Roanoke
Doak, William N.	December 12, 1882	Rural Retreat
Mason, Lucy R.	July 26, 1882	Clarens

Washington

Name	Birthdate	Birthplace
Dennis, Eugene	August 10, 1905	Seattle
Travis, Maurice E.	April 24, 1910	Spokane

West Virginia

Name	Birthdate	Birthplace
Church, Samuel M.	September 20, 1936	Matewan
Cook, Harry H.	February 28, 1883	Wheeling
Dalrymple, Sherman H.	April 4, 1889	Walton
Duffy, James M.	June 28, 1889	Wheeling
Keeney, C. Frank	Na.	Kanawha County
Lauck, William J.	August 2, 1879	Keyser
Miller, Arnold R.	April 25, 1923	Leewood
Reuther, Roy	August 29, 1909	Wheeling
Reuther, Victor G.	January 1, 1912	Wheeling
Reuther, Walter P.	September 1, 1907	Wheeling
Ryan, Martin F.	October 23, 1874	Coldwater
Stanley, Miles C.	1925	Dunbar
Swisher, Elwood D.	March 24, 1913	Jenningston
Wharton, Hunter P.	October 20, 1900	Martinsburg

Wisconsin

Name	Birthdate	Birthplace
Addes, George P.	August 26, 1910	La Crosse
Baer, John M.	March 29, 1886	Black Creek
Behncke, David L.	1897	(rural)
Burns, Matthew T.	November 6, 1887	Appleton
Chapman, Gordon W.	September 5, 1907	Tomah
George, Leo E.	January 3, 1888	Medford
Haas, Francis J.	March 18, 1889	Racine
Handley, John J.	August 5, 1876	Horicon
Hartung, Albert F.	June 18, 1897	Cataract
Hayes, Albert J.	February 14, 1900	Milwaukee
Krzycki, Leo	August 10, 1881	Milwaukee
Leighty, George E.	August 16, 1897	Phillips
Lennon, John B.	October 12, 1850	Lafayette County
McCreery, Marie M. L.	February 24, 1883	Cedarburg
Miller, Frieda S.	April 16, 1889	La Crosse
Ohl, Henry, Jr.	March 16, 1873	Milwaukee

Oswald, Rudolph A.	August 4, 1932	Milwaukee
Schneider, George J.	October 30, 1877	Grand Chute
Schoemann, Peter T.	October 26, 1893	Milwaukee
Stone, Milan O.	June 11, 1927	Rock Falls
Weber, Frank J.	August 7, 1849	Milwaukee
Zander, Arnold S.	November 26, 1901	Two Rivers

District of Columbia

Name	Birthdate	Birthplace
Borchardt, Selma M.	December 1, 1895	Washington
Delaney, George P.	February 20, 1909	Washington

Puerto Rico

Name	Birthdate	Birthplace
Capetillo, Luisa	1880	Arecibo

Virgin Islands

Name	Birthdate	Birthplace
Crosswaith, Frank R.	July 16, 1892	St. Croix
Totten, Ashley L.	October 11, 1884	St. Croix

COUNTRIES OTHER THAN THE UNITED STATES

Australia

Name	Birthdate	Birthplace
Bridges, Harry R.	July 28, 1901	Melbourne
Henry, Alice	March 21, 1857	Richmond

Austria

Name	Birthdate	Birthplace
Berger, Victor L.	February 28, 1860	Nieder-Rehbach

(For individuals born between 1867 and 1919, see *Austria-Hungary*.)

Austria-Hungary

Name	Birthdate	Birthplace
Ellis, Christine S.	1908	Tinj, Yugoslavia
Ernst, Hugo	December 11, 1876	Varasdin
Nagler, Isidore	February 25, 1895	Uscie Biscupie
Strasser, Adolph	Na.	Na.

(For individuals born before 1867, see *Austria* or *Hungary*.)

Canada

Name	Birthdate	Birthplace
Allen, William L.	April 17, 1896	Comnock, Ontario
Calvin, William A.	February 5, 1898	St. John, New Brunswick

Name	Birthdate	Birthplace
Cheyfitz, Edward T.	September 13, 1913	Montreal, Quebec
Johnston, Alvanley	May 12, 1875	Seeley's Bay, Ontario
Johnston, William H.	December 30, 1874	Westville, Nova Scotia
Kennedy, William P.	April 3, 1892	Huttonville, Ontario
Mazey, Emil	August 2, 1913	Regina, Saskatchewan
Merrill, Lewis R.	1908	Toronto, Ontario
Milne, J. Scott	January 21, 1898	Vancouver, British Columbia
Morrison, Frank	November 23, 1859	Franktown, Ontario
O'Connor, Thomas V.	1870	Toronto, Ontario
Sefton, Lawrence F.	March 31, 1917	Iroquois Falls, Ontario
Wolfgang, Myra K.	May 20, 1914	Montreal, Quebec

Denmark

Name	Birthdate	Birthplace
Brockhausen, Frederick C.	May 20, 1858	Fredericia
Myrup, Andrew A.	March 13, 1880	Copenhagen

Dominican Republic

Name	Birthdate	Birthplace
Lee, Ernest S.	April 12, 1923	Santo Domingo

Estonia

(See *Russian Estonia*.)

Germany

Name	Birthdate	Birthplace
Ameringer, Oscar	August 4, 1870	Achstetten
Engel, George	April 15, 1836	Cassel
Fischer, Adolph	Na.	Bremen
Germer, Adolph F.	January 15, 1881	Welan
Grottkau, Paul	1846	Berlin
Lingg, Louis	September 9, 1864	Mannheim
Most, Johann J.	February 5, 1846	Augsburg
Obergfell, Joseph F.	July 26, 1881	Na.
Schoenberg, William	August 1879	Na.
Schwab, Michael	August 9, 1853	Kitringen
Sender, Toni	November 29, 1888	Biebrich
Spies, August V. T.	1855	Landeck Castle
Stolberg, Benjamin	November 30, 1891	Munich

(See also *Saxony*.)

Hungary

Name	Birthdate	Birthplace
Friedrick, Jacob F.	January 31, 1892	Perjamos
Weber, Joseph N.	June 21, 1866	Neu Beschenowa

(For individuals born between 1867 and 1919, see *Austria-Hungary*.)

Iceland

Name	Birthdate	Birthplace
Fljozdal, Frederick H.	December 19, 1868	Na.

Ireland

Name	Birthdate	Birthplace
Barry, Leonora M. K.	August 13, 1849	Kearney
Boyce, Edward	November 8, 1863	County Donegal
Devyr, Thomas A.	1805	County Donegal
Duffy, Frank	1861	County Monaghan
Fitzpatrick, John	April 21, 1871	Na.
Gilmartin, Daniel	September 22, 1911	Na.
Greene, Michael F.	January 1, 1884	Kilclohor, County Clare
Guinan, Matthew	October 14, 1910	County Offaly
Jones, Mary H.	May 1, 1830	Cork City
Kearney, Denis	February 1, 1847	Oakmount
Lawrenson, Jack	October 22, 1906	Dublin
Lyden, Michael J.	1879	Barnikelle, County Mayo
Macauley, Robert C.	February 2, 1840	County Antrim
McCarthy, Patrick H.	March 17, 1863	Killoughteen, County Limerick
McDonnell, J. P.	ca. 1840	Dublin
McLaughlin, Hugh	October 28, 1831	St. Johnston, County Donegal
McMahon, Thomas F.	May 2, 1870	Ballybay, County Monaghan
McNulty, Frank J.	August 10, 1872	Londonderry
Molony, Joseph P.	November 6, 1906	Ennis, County Clare
Quill, Michael J.	September 18, 1905	Kilgarvan, County Kerry
Ratchford, Michael D.	August 1860	County Clare
Roney, Frank	August 13, 1841	Belfast
Siney, John	July 31, 1831	Bornos, County Queens
Sullivan, David	May 7, 1904	Cork City
Swartz, Maud O.	May 3, 1879	County Kildare
Tobin, Daniel J.	April 1875	County Clare
Wilkinson, Joseph	March 23, 1856	Na.
Wright, James L.	April 6, 1816	County Tyrone

Italy

Name	Birthdate	Birthplace
Antonini, Luigi	September 11, 1883	Vallata Irpina
Damino, Harry O.	January 6, 1893	Catania
DeNucci, George	February 14, 1902	Na.
Fraina, Louis C.	October 13, 1892	Galdo
Giovannitti, Arturo	January 7, 1884	Campobasso
Hoffmann, Sal B.	April 5, 1899	Aversa
Lucia, Carmen	April 3, 1902	Calabria
Moreschi, Joseph	1884	Na.
Ninfo, Salvatore	May 13, 1883	Santo Stefano

Name	Birthdate	Birthplace
Romualdi, Serafino	November 18, 1900	Bastia Umbra
Sacco, Nicola	April 22, 1891	Torre Maggiore
Salerno, Joseph	January 3, 1897	Na.
Vanzetti, Bartolomeo	June 11, 1888	Villafalletto

Latvia

(See *Russian Latvia*.)

Lithuania

(See *Russian Lithuania*.)

Luxembourg

Name	Birthdate	Birthplace
Woll, Matthew	January 25, 1880	Na.

Mexico

Name	Birthdate	Birthplace
Galarza, Ernesto	August 15, 1905	Jalcocotan, Nayarit

The Netherlands

Name	Birthdate	Birthplace
Muste, Abraham J.	January 8, 1885	Zierikzee

New Zealand

Name	Birthdate	Birthplace
De Caux, Leonard H.	October 14, 1899	Westport
Trautmann, William E.	1869	Na.

Norway

Name	Birthdate	Birthplace
Furuseth, Andrew	March 12, 1854	Romedal
Lundeberg, Harry	March 25, 1901	Oslo

Poland

(See *Russian Poland*.)

Rumania

Name	Birthdate	Birthplace
Matles, James J.	February 24, 1909	Soroca

Russia

Name	Birthdate	Birthplace
Barondess, Joseph	July 3, 1867	Kamenets-Podolsk, Ukraine
Baskin, Joseph	October 20, 1880	Minsk

Name	Birthdate	Birthplace
Belsky, Joseph	March 22, 1902	Odessa
Bisno, Abraham	1866	Belaya Tserkov
Breslaw, Joseph	April 18, 1887	Miskifky
Cohn, Fannia	April 5, 1888	Minsk
Davis, Leon J.	November 21, 1907	Pinsk
Feinberg, Israel	December 25, 1887	Berdichev, Ukraine
Gold, Ben	September 8, 1898	Bessarabia
Heller, Jacob J.	August 21, 1889	Na.
Hillman, Bessie A.	May 15, 1889	Grodno
Hochman, Julius	January 12, 1892	Bessarabia
Hyman, Louis	June 17, 1884	Witebask
Kaufman, Morris	September 1884	Minsk
Kazan, Abraham E.	December 15, 1888	Kiev, Ukraine
London, Meyer	December 29, 1871	Suwalki
Mendelowitz, Abraham	March 5, 1894	Nikolaev, Ukraine
Newman, Pauline	October 18, 1891	Na.
Norwood, Rose F.	September 10, 1891	Kiev, Ukraine
Perlstein, Meyer	September 15, 1884	Cartyz Bereza, Grodno
Pesotta, Rose	November 20, 1896	Derazhnya, Ukraine
Pine, Max	1866	Liubavitch
Potofsky, Jacob S.	November 16, 1894	Radomisl, Ukraine
Price, George M.	May 21, 1864	Poltava, Ukraine
Rombro, Jacob	October 10, 1858	Zuphran, Wilna
Rosenberg, Abraham	1870	Na.
Schlossberg, Joseph	May 1, 1875	Koidanovo, Belorussia
Sigman, Morris	May 15, 1881	Costesh, Bessarabia
Vladeck, Baruch C.	January 1886	Dookorah, Minsk
Wolchok, Samuel	September 20, 1896	Bobruisk
Zaritsky, Max	April 15, 1885	Petrikov
Zimmerman, Charles S.	November 27, 1896	Kiev, Ukraine

Russian Estonia

Name	Birthdate	Birthplace
Leiserson, William M.	April 15, 1883	Revel

Russian Latvia

Name	Birthdate	Birthplace
Bellanca, Dorothy J.	August 10, 1894	Zemel
Hillquit, Morris	August 1, 1869	Riga

Russian Lithuania

Name	Birthdate	Birthplace
Blumberg, Hyman	November 25, 1885	Legum
Cahan, Abraham	July 7, 1860	Podberezye
Dyche, John A.	1867	Kovno

Name	Birthdate	Birthplace
Goldman, Emma	June 27, 1869	Kovno
Hillman, Sidney	March 23, 1887	Zagare
Lovestone, Jay	1898	Na.
Schlesinger, Benjamin	December 25, 1876	Krakai

Russian Poland

Name	Birthdate	Birthplace
Dubinsky, David	February 22, 1892	Brest Litovsk
Feinstone, Morris	1878	Warsaw
Fosco, Peter	May 13, 1892	Na.
Gingold, David R.	December 10, 1896	Volcovisk
Hollander, Louis	February 5, 1893	Wadowice
Levin, Ruben	August 2, 1902	Na.
Perlis, Leo	February 22, 1912	Bialystok
Perlman, Selig	December 9, 1888	Bialystok
Pizer, Morris	February 12, 1904	Na.
Rieve, Emil	June 8, 1892	Zyradow
Rose, Alex	October 15, 1898	Warsaw
Schneiderman, Rose	April 6, 1884	Savin
Stokes, Rose H. P.	July 18, 1879	Augustowo, Suwalki
Stulberg, Louis	April 14, 1901	Bogria

Saxony

Name	Birthdate	Birthplace
Schilling, Robert	October 17, 1843	Osterburg
Sorge, Friedrich A.	November 9, 1828	Bethau bei Torgau

Spain

Name	Birthdate	Birthplace
Iglesias, Santiago	February 22, 1872	La Coruña

Sweden

Name	Birthdate	Birthplace
Anderson, Mary	August 27, 1872	Lidköping
Hill, Joe	October 7, 1879	Gavle
Lindelof, Lawrence P.	May 18, 1875	Malmö, Skane
Peterson, Eric	September 3, 1894	Dalarne

Union of Soviet Socialist Republics

(See *Russia, Russian Latvia, Russian Lithuania, Russian Poland.*)

United Kingdom

Name	Birthdate	Birthplace
Arthur, Peter M.	1831	Paisley, Scotland
Brophy, John	November 6, 1883	St. Helens, England

Name	Birthdate	Birthplace
Byron, Robert	ca. 1880	Lynwood, Scotland
Caddy, Samuel H.	December 9, 1883	Short Health, England
Cairns, Thomas F.	1875	Durhamshire, England
Cameron, Andrew C.	September 28, 1836	Berwick-on-Tweed, England
Clark, John	1888	Sheffield, England
Davis, James J.	October 27, 1873	Thedegar, South Wales
Derwent, Clarence	March 23, 1884	London, England
Duncan, James	May 5, 1857	Kincardine County, Scotland
Dyer, Josiah B.	January 5, 1843	Cornwall, England
Evans, Christopher	1841	England
Evans, George H.	March 25, 1805	Bromyard, England
Farquhar, John M.	April 17, 1832	Ayr, Scotland
Fielden, Samuel	February 25, 1847	Todmorden, England
Foster, William H.	May 3, 1847	Liverpool, England
Fraser, Douglas A.	December 18, 1916	Glasgow, Scotland
Gompers, Samuel	January 27, 1850	London, England
Gorman, Francis J.	1877	Bradford, England
Graham, James D.	February 2, 1879	Greenock, Scotland
Green, John	November 15, 1896	Clydebank, Scotland
Harris, David	1837	England
Haywood, Allan S.	October 9, 1888	Yorkshire, England
Heighton, William	1800	Oundle, England
Hickman, William W.	1826	Wednesbury, England
Hinchcliffe, John	1822	Bradford, England
Howard, Robert	ca. 1844	Northwich, England
Howat, Alexander	1876	Glasgow, Scotland
Irons, Martin	March 1, 1833	Dundee, Scotland
Jarrett, John	January 27, 1843	Elbow Vale, Wales
Jones, Thomas P.	March 24, 1826	Aberammon, South Wales
Kroll, John J.	June 10, 1885	London, England
Lawson, John C.	September 3, 1900	Aberdeen, Scotland
MacGowan, Charles J.	1887	Argyllshire, Scotland
McLellan, Andrew C.	April 17, 1911	Cowdenbeath Fife, Scotland
Martin, William	January 7, 1845	Calderbank, Scotland
Mitchell, James J.	November 25, 1896	Carfin, Scotland
Morgan, Elizabeth	1850	Birmingham, England
Morgan, Thomas J.	October 27, 1847	Birmingham, England
Murray, Philip	May 25, 1886	Blantyre, Scotland
Nord, Elizabeth	1902	Lancashire, England
Nutt, James H.	November 19, 1848	Worcestershire, England
O'Hare, John	June 14, 1904	Armadale, Scotland
Owen, Robert D.	November 9, 1801	Glasgow, Scotland
Padway, Joseph A.	July 25, 1891	Leeds, England
Phillips, Thomas	March 22, 1833	Whitson, England
Preston, George	November 3, 1864	Lincolnshire, England
Roy, Andrew	July 19, 1834	Palace Craig, Lanarkshire, Scotland
Starr, Mark	April 27, 1894	Shoscombe, England

Name	Birthdate	Birthplace
Swinton, John	December 12, 1829	Edinburgh, Scotland
Thompson, Mary G.	July 14, 1885	Dundee, Scotland
Trevellick, Richard F.	May 20, 1830	St. Mary's, Scilly Isles
Turner, Frederick	1846	England
Walker, John H.	April 27, 1872	Binny Hill, Scotland
Watt, Robert J.	July 16, 1894	Scotland
Wilson, William B.	April 2, 1862	Blantyre, Scotland

Venezuela

Name	Birthdate	Birthplace
DeLeon, Daniel	December 14, 1852	Curaçao

Yugoslavia

(See *Austria-Hungary*.)

Not Ascertained

Name	Birthdate	Birthplace
Donnelly, Michael	Na.	Na.
English, William	Na.	Na.
Ferral, John	Na.	Na.
Greene, Prince W.	Na.	Na.
Hagerty, Thomas J.	ca. 1862	Na.
Huber, William	Na.	Na.
Keil, Edward A.	Na.	United States
Lewis, Thomas L.	1866	Na.
Little, Frank H.	1879	Na.
Mahoney, Charles E.	Na.	Na.
Moyer, Charles H.	Na.	Na.
Nef, Walter T.	Na.	Europe
O'Donnell, John J.	January 14, 1925	Na.
O'Neill, John M.	ca. 1857	Na.
Perkins, George W.	Na.	Na.
Rarick, Donald C.	1919	Na.
Sherman, Charles O.	Na.	Na.
Townsend, Robert Jr.	Na.	Na.
Wharton, Arthur O.	November 9, 1873	Na.
Wilson, D. Douglas	Na.	Na.

Appendix IV
Formal Education

Because it often was impossible to determine the exact extent of a person's education, especially at the lower levels, this appendix is largely derived. In some cases, it was necessary to use yardsticks like the number of years of formal schooling or the age at which the individual became a full-time wage earner to determine the extent of his education. It was also difficult to determine the U.S. equivalent of a foreign education. Categories 1, 2, and 3 simply reflect attendance at a particular level and do not necessarily mean that the individual completed that level of education.

Key:

Category 1—Grammar (Gra.)
2—Secondary (Sec.)
3—Special: Vocational (V), Night School (N), Business College (B), Labor College (L), (C) Correspondence (Spc.)
4—College (Col.)
5—B.S. or B.A. (Bch.)
6—M.A. or M.S. (Mst.)
7—LL.B. or successfully passing bar exam (Law)
8—Ph.D. or M.D. (Ph.D.)
9—Unknown (Unk.)

Name	Category	(1) Gra.	(2) Sec.	(3) Spc.	(4) Col.	(5) Bch.	(6) Mst.	(7) Law	(8) Ph.D.	(9) Unk.
Abel, Iorwith W.		X	X	B						
Addams, Jane		X	X			X	X			
Addes, George P.		X	X			X				
Allen, William L.		X								
Alpine, John P.		X								

Name	Category	(1) Gra.	(2) Sec.	(3) Spc.	(4) Col.	(5) Bch.	(6) Mst.	(7) Law	(8) Ph.D.	(9) Unk.
Ameringer, Oscar		X								
Anderson, Mary		X								
Andrews, Emmet C.		X	X							
Antonini, Luigi		X	X							
Arons, Milton		X	X	N						
Arthur, Peter M.		X								
Arywitz, Sigmond		X	X		X					
Azpeitia, Mario		X								
Bacon, Emery F.		X	X		X	X	X			
Baer, Fred W.		X								
Baer, John M.		X	X		X	X				
Bagley, Sarah G.										X
Baker, E.R.P.		X	X		X			X		
Baldanzi, George		X								
Barkan, Alexander E.		X	X		X	X				
Barker, Mary C.		X	X		X	X				
Barnes, John M.		X		C						
Barnum, Gertrude		X	X		X					
Barondess, Joseph		X	X		X					
Barrett, Francis G.		X	X							
Barry, Leonora M. K.		X	X							
Barry, Thomas B.		X								
Baskin, Joseph		X	X		X	X				
Bates, Harry C.		X	X							
Beck, Dave		X	X	C						
Behncke, David L.		X	X							
Beirne, Joseph A.		X	X	N	X					
Bellamy, Edward		X	X		X			X		
Bellanca, Dorothy J.		X								
Belsky, Joseph		X	X							
Benson, Herman		X	X		X	X				
Berger, Victor L.		X	X		X					
Berry, George L.		X								
Bieber, Owen F.		X	X							
Biemiller, Andrew J.		X	X		X	X				
Billings, Warren K.		X								
Birthright, William C.		X	X							
Bisno, Abraham		X								
Bittner, Van A.		X	X							
Blankenhorn, Ann W. C.		X	X		X	X				
Blankenhorn, Heber H.		X	X		X	X	X			
Bloor, Ella R.		X								
Blumberg, Hyman		X								
Bommarito, Peter		X	X							
Bonadio, Frank		X	X							
Borchardt, Selma M.		X	X		X	X	X	X		

Name	Category	(1) Gra.	(2) Sec.	(3) Spc.	(4) Col.	(5) Bch.	(6) Mst.	(7) Law	(8) Ph.D.	(9) Unk.
Bowen, William J.		X								
Bower, Andrew P.		X		B						
Boyce, Edward		X								
Boyle, William A.		X								
Brennan, Peter J.		X	X		X	X				
Breslaw, Joseph		X								
Brewer, Roy M.		X	X							
Bridges, Harry A. R.		X	X							
Brockhausen, Frederick C.		X								
Brophy, John		X		L						
Broun, Heywood C.		X	X		X					
Brown, Edward J.		X	X					X		
Brown, Guy L.		X								
Brown, Harvey W.		X								
Brown, Henry S.		X	X		X					
Brown, Irving J.		X	X		X	X				
Bryson, Hugh		X	X	B						
Buchanan, Joseph R.		X								
Buckley, Leo J.		X								
Buckmaster, Leland S.		X	X		X					
Bugniazet, Gustave M.		X								
Burke, John P.		X	X							
Burke, Walter J.		X	X							
Burns, Matthew, J.		X		C						
Burns, Thomas F.		X	X							
Byron, Robert		X								
Caddy, Samuel H.		X								
Cahan, Abraham		X	X		X	X				
Cairns, Thomas F.		X	X	C						
Calvin, William A.		X								
Cameron, Andrew C.		X								
Campbell, Patrick J.		X	X							
Cannon, Joseph D.		X								
Capetillo, Luisa										X
Carey, James B.		X	X	N	X					
Carlton, Albert A.		X								
Carroll, Thomas C.		X	X							
Carter, William S.		X	X		X					
Cashen, Thomas C.		X	X							
Cenerazzo, Walter W.		X	X							
Chaiken, Sol C.		X	X		X	X		X		
Chamberlain, Edwin M.		X								
Chapman, Gordon W.		X	X		X	X				
Chavez, Cesar E.		X								
Chesser, Al H.		X	X							
Cheyfitz, Edward T.		X	X		X	X				

Name	Category	(1) Gra.	(2) Sec.	(3) Spc.	(4) Col.	(5) Bch.	(6) Mst.	(7) Law	(8) Ph.D.	(9) Unk.
Christman, Elisabeth		X								
Christopher, Paul R.		X	X		X					
Church, Samuel M., Jr.		X	X		X					
Clark, Hugh D.		X	X							
Clark, Jesse		X		B						
Clark, John		X								
Clark, Lewis J.		X	X							
Cline, Isaac										X
Coefield, John		X	X							
Cohn, Fannia		X								
Collins, Jennie										X
Commerford, John										X
Commons, John R.		X	X		X	X	X			
Conlon, Peter J.		X		C						
Connors, David M.		X	X							
Conway, Jack T.		X	X		X	X				
Cook, Harry H.		X								
Cope, Elmer F.		X	X		X	X	X			
Cosgrove, John T.		X	X							
Coulter, Clarence C.		X	X							
Counts, George S.		X	X		X	X	X		X	
Crosswaith, Frank R.		X		L						
Crouch-Hazlett, Ida		X	X		X	X	X			
Cruikshank, Nelson H.		X	X		X	X	X			
Crull, John L.		X	X							
Curran, Joseph E.		X								
Dailey, Edward L.		X	X							
Dalrymple, Sherman H.		X								
Damino, Harry O.		X								
Daniel, Franz E.		X	X		X	X				
Davidson, Roy E.		X	X		X					
Davis, Hal C.		X	X							
Davis, James L.		X	X	B						
Davis, Leon J.		X	X		X	X				
Davis, Richard L.		X								
Davis, Walter G.		X	X		X	X				
Debs, Eugene V.		X								
DeCaux, Leonard H.		X	X		X					
Delaney, George P.		X	X		X					
DeLeon, Daniel		X	X		X	X		X		
DeLeon, Solon		X	X		X	X				
Dellums, Cottrell L.		X	X							
Delorenzo, Anthony J.		X	X							
DeLury, John J.		X	X							
Dennis, Charles L.										X
Dennis, Eugene		X	X		X					

Name	Category	(1) Gra.	(2) Sec.	(3) Spc.	(4) Col.	(5) Bch.	(6) Mst.	(7) Law	(8) Ph.D.	(9) Unk.
DeNucci, George		X	X							
Derwent, Clarence		X	X	V						
Devyr, Thomas A.		X								
Dickason, Gladys M.		X	X		X	X	X			
Doak, William N.		X	X	B						
Dobbs, Farrel		X	X							
Dockter, Wallace J.		X	X		X					
Doherty, William C.		X		V						
Donahue, Thomas R.		X	X		X	X		X		
Donnelly, Michael										X
Donnelly, Samuel B.		X	X		X					
Douglas, Charles										X
Douglass, Frederick	None									
Dreier, Mary E.		X	X		X					
Driscoll, John J.		X	X		X	X	X			
Drozak, Frank P.										X
Dubinsky, David		X								
Dubrow, Evelyn		X	X		X	X				
DuChessi, William M.		X								
Duffy, Frank		X								
Duffy, James M.		X								
Dullzell, Paul		X								
Duncan, James		X								
Dunne, Vincent R.		X								
Dunwody, Thomas E.		X	X		X					
Durkin, Martin P.		X		V						
Dyche, John A.										X
Dyer, Josiah B.										X
Eames, Thomas B.		X								
Easton, John B.		X		N						
Edelman, John W.										X
Eklund, John M.		X	X		X	X	X			
Ellickson, Katherine P.		X	X		X	X				
Ellis, Christine S.		X								
Engel, George										X
English, John F.		X								
English, William										X
Ernst, Hugo		X	X							
Ervin, Charles W.		X		C						
Ettor, Joseph J.		X								
Evans, Christopher										X
Evans, Elizabeth G.		X	X		X					
Evans, George H.		X								
Farquhar, John M.		X						X		
Farrington, Frank	None									
Feeney, Frank		X								

Name	Category	(1) Gra.	(2) Sec.	(3) Spc.	(4) Col.	(5) Bch.	(6) Mst.	(7) Law	(8) Ph.D.	(9) Unk.
Fehrenrath, John		X								
Feinberg, Israel		X	X							
Feinstone, Morris		X		V						
Feller, Karl F.		X	X							
Fenton, Francis, P.		X						X		
Ferral, John									X	
Fielden, Samuel		X								
Filbey, Francis S.		X	X							
Fincher, Jonathan C.										X
Finley, Murray H.		X	X		X	X		X		
Fischer, Adolph		X								
Fisher, Joseph A.		X	X		X					
Fitzgerald, Albert J.		X	X							
Fitzgerald, Frank A.		X	X							
Fitzpatrick, John		X								
Fitzsimmons, Frank E.		X								
Flaumenbaum, Irving		X	X		X	X				
Fljozdal, Frederick H.		X		C						
Flore, Edward		X	X							
Flynn, Elizabeth G.		X	X							
Foran, Martin A.		X	X		X					
Fosco, Peter		X								
Foster, Frank K.		X	X							
Foster, William H.										X
Foster, William Z.		X								
Fox, Martin		X								
Fraina, Louis C.		X								
Frankensteen, Richard T.		X	X		X	X				
Fraser, Douglas A.		X	X							
Fraser, Harry W.		X								
Frayne, Hugh		X								
Frey, John P.		X	X							
Friedrick, Jacob F.		X								
Furuseth, Andrew		X								
Gainor, Edward J.		X	X							
Galarza, Ernesto		X	X		X	X	X		X	
Garretson, Austin B.		X	X							
George, Henry		X								
George, Leo E.		X	X		X					
Georgine, Robert A.		X	X		X	X				
Germano, Joseph S.		X	X							
Germer, Adolph F.		X	X	C						
Gibbons, Harold J.		X	X	C						
Gibson, Everett G.		X								
Gibson, John W.		X	X		X					
Gilbert, Henry E.		X	X		X					

Name	Category	(1) Gra.	(2) Sec.	(3) Spc.	(4) Col.	(5) Bch.	(6) Mst.	(7) Law	(8) Ph.D.	(9) Unk.
Gillmore, Frank		X	X							
Gilmartin, Daniel		X	X							
Gingold, David R.		X	X							
Giovannitti, Arturo		X	X		X					
Givens, Paul A.		X	X							
Gleason, Thomas W.		X								
Gold, Ben		X								
Goldberg, Arthur J.		X	X		X	X	X	X		
Goldblatt, Louis		X	X		X	X	X			
Golden, Clinton S.		X								
Goldfinger, Nathaniel		X	X		X	X				
Goldman, Emma		X								
Gompers, Samuel		X		N						
Googe, George L.		X	X	V						
Gorman, Francis J.		X								
Gorman, Patrick E.		X	X					X		
Gosser, Richard T.		X		V						
Graham, James D.		X	X	N						
Graham, Sylvester		X	X							
Gray, Richard J.		X								
Green, John		X	X							
Green, William		X								
Greenberg, Max		X	X							
Greene, Michael F.		X								
Greene, Prince W.										X
Griner, John F.		X	X					X		
Grogan, John J.		X	X		X					
Grottkau, Paul		X	X							
Guinan, Matthew		X	X							
Haas, Francis J.		X	X		X	X	X		X	
Hagerty, Thomas J.		X	X		X					
Haggerty, Cornelius J.		X								
Haggerty, John B.		X	X							
Haigler, Carey E.		X	X							
Haley, Margaret A.		X	X							
Hall, Burton		X	X		X	X		X		
Hall, Paul		X								
Hallbeck, Elroy C.		X	X							
Handley, John J.		X								
Hapgood, Mary D.		X	X		X					
Hapgood, Powers		X	X		X	X				
Harrington, Michael		X	X		X	X	X			
Harris, David										X
Harrison, George M.		X								
Hartung, Albert F.		X								
Hayes, Albert J.		X								

Name	Category	(1) Gra.	(2) Sec.	(3) Spc.	(4) Col.	(5) Bch.	(6) Mst.	(7) Law	(8) Ph.D.	(9) Unk.
Hayes, Frank J.		X								
Hayes, John W.		None								
Hayes, Maximilian S.		X								
Haywood, Allan S.		X								
Haywood, William D.		X								
Heighton, William		X								
Helfgott, Simon		X	X							
Heller, George		X	X		X					
Heller, Jacob J.		X	X		X					
Helstein, Ralph		X	X		X	X		X		
Helt, Daniel W.		X								
Henderson, Donald J.		X	X		X	X	X			
Henry, Alice		X	X							
Herrick, Elinore M.		X	X		X	X				
Hickey, Thomas L.		X								
Hickman, William W.										X
Hill, Joe		X								
Hillman, Bessie A.		X	X							
Hillman, Sidney		X	X							
Hillquit, Morris		X	X					X		
Hinchcliffe, John										X
Hochman, Julius			X	C						
Hoffa, James R.		X								
Hoffmann, Sal B.		X	X							
Holderman, Carl		X	X							
Hollander, Louis		X	X							
Horn, Roy		X								
Housewright, James T.		X	X	V						
Howard, Asbury										X
Howard, Charles P.		X								
Howard, Robert										X
Howat, Alexander										X
Huber, William										X
Huddell, Arthur M.		X								
Hudson, Hosea		X								
Huerta, Dolores										X
Hughes, Roy O.		X	X							
Hutcheson, Maurice A.		X								
Hutcheson, William L.		X								
Hutchins, Grace		X	X		X	X				
Hyman, Louis		X		N						
Iglesias, Santiago		X								
Irons, Martin		X								
Jarrett, John										X
Jeffrey, Mildred		X	X		X	X	X			
Jennings, Paul J.		X	X	V						

Name	Category	(1) Gra.	(2) Sec.	(3) Spc.	(4) Col.	(5) Bch.	(6) Mst.	(7) Law	(8) Ph.D.	(9) Unk.
Jessup, William J.		X								
Jewell, Bert M.		X								
Jimerson, Earl W.		X								
Johns, John S.		X	X							
Johnson, William D.		X								
Johnston, Alvanley		X		B						
Johnston, William H.		X								
Jones, Mary H.		X	X		X					
Jones, Thomas P.										X
Kasten, Frank		X								
Kaufman, Morris	None									
Kavanagh, William F.		X								
Kazan, Abraham E.		X	X		X					
Kearney, Denis										X
Keating, Edward		X								
Keefe, Daniel J.		X								
Keenan, Joseph D.		X	X							
Keeney, C. Frank										X
Kehew, Mary M. K.		X	X							
Kehrer, Elmer T.		X	X		X	X	X			
Keil, Edward A.										X
Kelley, Florence		X	X		X	X		X		
Kelsay, Ray		X								
Kenin, Herman D.		X	X		X	X		X		
Kennedy, Thomas		X								
Kennedy, William P.		X								
Kirkland, Joseph L.		X	X		X	X				
Kirwan, James										X
Kistler, Alan A.		X	X		X	X	X			
Knight, Felix H.		X	X							
Knight, Orie A.		X	X							
Konyha, William		X	X	V						
Kroll, Fred J.		X	X							
Kroll, John J.		X	X							
Krzycki, Leo		X								
Labadie, Joseph A.		X								
Lane, Dennis		X								
Langdon, Emma F.										X
Lauck, William J.		X	X		X	X				
Lawrenson, Jack		X								
Lawson, George W.		X	X							
Lawson, John C.		X								
Lee, Ernest S.		X	X		X	X				
Lee, William G.		X								
Leffingwell, Samuel L.										X
Leighty, George E.		X	X							

Name	Category	(1) Gra.	(2) Sec.	(3) Spc.	(4) Col.	(5) Bch.	(6) Mst.	(7) Law	(8) Ph.D.	(9) Unk.
Leiserson, William M.		X	X		X	X	X		X	
Lennon, John B.		X								
Leonard, Richard		X								
Levin, Ruben		X	X		X	X				
Lewis, Alma D.		X								
Lewis, John L.		X	X							
Lewis, Joseph		X	X							
Lewis, Kathryn		X	X		X					
Lewis, Thomas L.										X
Lindelof, Lawrence P.		X	X		X					
Lingg, Louis		X	X							
Lipsig, James		X	X		X	X		X		
Litchman, Charles H.		X	X							
Little, Frank H.										X
Livingston, John W.		X	X							
Lloyd, Thomas J.		X	X							
London, Meyer		X	X					X		
Long, Bob G.		X	X							
Lovestone, Jay		X	X		X	X				
Lucia, Carmen		X	X							
Luhrsen, Julius G.		X		V						
Luna, Charles		X	X							
Lundeberg, Harry		X								
Luther, Seth		X								
Lyden, Michael J.		X								
Lynch, James M.		X								
Lyon, Arlon E.		X	X							
Lyons, John H.		X	X		X	X				
McAninch, Elisha H.		X								
McAvoy, Harold		X	X		X	X				
McBride, John		X								
McBride, Lloyd		X								
McCarthy, Patrick H.		X								
McCauley, Robert C.		X								
McClennan, William H.		X	X		X					
McCreery, Marie M. L.		X	X							
McCurdy, Joseph P.		X	X		X	X				
McDevitt, James L.		X	X							
McDonald, David J.		X	X		X	X				
McDonald, Joseph D.		X	X							
McDonnell, J. P.										X
McFetridge, William L.		X	X					X		
McGaw, Homer L.		X	X		X	X				
MacGowan, Charles J.		X								
McGrady, Edward F.		X	X	N						
McGuire, Peter J.		X		N						
McLaren, Louise L.		X	X		X	X				

Name	Category	(1) Gra.	(2) Sec.	(3) Spc.	(4) Col.	(5) Bch.	(6) Mst.	(7) Law	(8) Ph.D.	(9) Unk.
McLaughlin, Hugh		X								
McLellan, Andrew C.		X								
McMahon, Thomas F.		X								
McNamara, Patrick V.		X	X	V						
McNeill, George E.		X								
McNulty, Frank J.		X	X							
McSorley, William J.		X								
Maguire, Matthew		X								
Mahon, William D.		X								
Mahoney, Charles E.										X
Mahoney, William		X						X		
Maile, Francis		X	X							
Maloney, James		X								
Maloney, William E.		X								
Maloy, Elmer J.		X	X							
Marciante, Louis P.		X	X							
Marot, Helen		X	X		X					
Martin, Harry L., Jr.		X	X		X	X				
Martin, Warren H.		X	X		X	X				
Martin, William		X								
Martino, Frank D.		X	X		X					
Martinson, Henry R.		X	X		X	X				
Mashburn, Lloyd A.		X	X	V						
Maso, Sal		X	X		X					
Mason, Lucy R.		X	X							
Mathias, Charles G.		X	X	N						
Matles, James J.										X
Maurer, James H.		X								
Mazey, Emil		X	X							
Meany, George		X	X							
Megel, Carl J.		X	X		X	X				
Mendelowitz, Abraham		X								
Merrill, Lewis R.		X	X		X					
Migas, Nick		X	X							
Miller, Arnold R.		X								
Miller, Edward S.		X	X							
Miller, Frieda S.		X	X		X	X	X			
Miller, Joyce D.		X	X		X	X	X			
Miller, Marvin J.		X	X		X	X				
Miller, Saul		X	X		X	X				
Milliman, Elmer E.		X	X		X					
Milne, J. Scott		X	X							
Minton, Lee W.		X	X	B						
Mitch, William A.		X								
Mitchell, Harry L.		X	X							
Mitchell, James J.		X								
Mitchell, John		X		N	X					

Name	Category	(1) Gra.	(2) Sec.	(3) Spc.	(4) Col.	(5) Bch.	(6) Mst.	(7) Law	(8) Ph.D.	(9) Unk.
Mitchell, Walter L.		X	X					X		
Moffett, Elwood S.		X	X							
Mohn, Einar O.		X	X		X					
Molony, Joseph P.		X								
Montgomery, Robert		X	X							
Mooney, Thomas J.		X								
Moore, Ely		X								
Moran, John J.		X	X							
Moreschi, Joseph										X
Morgan, Elizabeth		X								
Morgan, Thomas J.		X	X					X		
Morreale, Vincent F.		X	X		X	X		X		
Morrison, Frank		X	X					X		
Mortimer, Wyndham		X								
Most, Johann J.		X								
Moyer, Charles H.										X
Mullaney, Joseph A.		X								
Murphy, Vincent		X								
Murray, Philip		X								
Murray, Thomas A.		X								
Murry, James W.		X	X		X					
Muste, Abraham J.		X	X		X	X	X			
Myers, Isaac		X								
Myrup, Andrew A.		X								
Nagler, Isidore		X								
Nance, Alexander S.		X								
Neebe, Oscar		X								
Nef, Walter T.										X
Nelson, Oscar F.		X	X					X		
Nestor, Agnes		X								
Newman, Pauline		X								
Ninfo, Salvatore		X								
Nockles, Edward N.		X								
Noonan, James P.		X								
Nord, Elizabeth		X	X							
Norwood, Rose F.		X	X							
Nutt, James H.		X								
Oakes, Grant W.		X	X	V						
Obergfell, Joseph F.		X								
O'Connell, James P.		X	X							
O'Connor, Harvey		X	X							
O'Connor, Thomas V.										X
O'Donnell, John J.										X
O'Hare, John		X	X	N						
O'Hare, Kate R.		X	X							
Ohl, Henry, Jr.		X								

Name	Category	(1) Gra.	(2) Sec.	(3) Spc.	(4) Col.	(5) Bch.	(6) Mst.	(7) Law	(8) Ph.D.	(9) Unk.
Olander, Victor A.		X								
O'Neill, John M.		X	X		X	X				
O'Reilly, Leonora		X								
Ornburn, Ira M.		X								
O'Sullivan, Mary K.		X								
Oswald, Rudolph A.		X	X		X	X	X		X	
Owen, Robert D.		X	X		X					
Pachler, William J.		X	X	B						
Padway, Joseph A.		X	X					X		
Parker, Julia O.		X								
Parsons, Albert R.		X								
Pascoe, David M.		X								
Perkins, George W.										X
Perlis, Leo		X	X							
Perlman, Selig		X	X		X	X	X		X	
Perlstein, Meyer		X		N						
Pesotta, Rose		X	X	L						
Peterson, Eric		X								
Peterson, Esther		X	X		X	X	X			
Petrillo, James C.		X								
Phillips, James A.		X								
Phillips, Paul L.		X	X		X					
Phillips, Thomas		X								
Pillard, Charles H.		X	X							
Pine, Max		X								
Pizer, Morris		X	X		X					
Podojil, Antonette		X	X		X					
Policastro, Thomas F.		X	X							
Pollard, William E.		X	X		X					
Pollock, William		X	X							
Possehl, John		X	X							
Potofsky, Jacob S.		X	X							
Powderly, Terence V.		X								
Powers, Bertram A.		X	X							
Powers, Frank B.		X	X		X					
Pressman, Lee		X	X		X	X		X		
Preston, George		X								
Price, George M.		X	X		X				X	
Quill, Michael J.		X								
Raftery, Lawrence M.		X	X	V						
Rajoppi, Raleigh		X	X		X					
Ramsay, Claude E.		X	X		X					
Randolph, Asa P.		X	X		X					
Randolph, Woodruff		X	X					X		
Rarick, Donald C.		X	X							
Ratchford, Michael D.		X		N						

Name	Category	(1) Gra.	(2) Sec.	(3) Spc.	(4) Col.	(5) Bch.	(6) Mst.	(7) Law	(8) Ph.D.	(9) Unk.
Reagan, Ronald		X	X		X	X				
Redmond, John P.		X	X		X					
Reed, John		X	X		X	X				
Reuther, Roy		X	X		X					
Reuther, Victor		X	X		X					
Reuther, Walter P.		X	X		X					
Richardson, George J.		X	X							
Rickert, Thomas A.		X	X	B						
Rieve, Emil		X								
Riffe, John V.		X								
Robertson, David B.		X		N						
Robins, Margaret D.		X	X							
Robinson, Reid		X	X							
Rollings, John I.		X								
Rombro, Jacob		X	X		X					
Romualdi, Serafino		X	X		X					
Roney, Frank		X								
Rose, Alex		X	X							
Rosenberg, Abraham										X
Rosenblum, Frank		X								
Roy, Andrew		X								
Ruef, Abraham		X	X		X	X		X		
Rustin, Bayard		X	X		X					
Ruttenberg, Harold J.		X	X		X	X				
Ryan, Joseph P.		X								
Ryan, Martin F.		X	X							
Sacco, Nicola		X								
St. John, Vincent										X
Salerno, Joseph		X	X		X			X		
Sargent, Frank P.		X	X							
Sayre, Harry D.		X	X							
Scarbrough, W. Carl		X	X							
Schilling, Robert										X
Schlesinger, Benjamin		X								
Schlossberg, Joseph		X			X					
Schneider, George J.		X								
Schneiderman, Rose		X								
Schnitzler, William F.		X								
Schoemann, Peter T.		X								
Schoenberg, William		X								
Scholle, August		X	X							
Schwab, Michael		X								
Scott, Sam H.		X	X		X					
Scully, John J. J.		X	X	V						
Sefton, Lawrence F.		X	X							

Name	Category	(1) Gra.	(2) Sec.	(3) Spc.	(4) Col.	(5) Bch.	(6) Mst.	(7) Law	(8) Ph.D.	(9) Unk.
Seidel, Emil		X								
Selden, David S.		X	X		X	X	X			
Sender, Toni		X	X	V						
Sessions, John A.		X	X		X	X	X		X	
Shanker, Albert		X	X		X	X	X			
Sheffield, Horace L., Jr.		X	X		X					
Shelley, John F.		X	X		X			X		
Sherman, Charles O.										X
Shields, James P.		X	X							
Sidell, William		X	X							
Siemiller, Paul L.		X	X							
Sigman, Morris		X								
Siney, John		None								
Skeffington, Henry J.		X								
Skidmore, Thomas		X								
Slamm, Levi D.										X
Smith, Stanton E.		X	X		X	X				
Soderstrom, Reuben G.		X								
Sorge, Friedrick A.		X	X		X					
Spies, August V. T.		X	X							
Spradling, Abe L.		X	X							
Stanley, Miles C.		X	X							
Starr, Mark		X	X		X					
Steinbock, Max		X	X	V						
Stephens, Uriah S.		X	X							
Steward, Ira		None								
Stevens, Alzina P.		X								
Stokes, Rose H. P.		X								
Stolberg, Benjamin		X	X		X	X	X			
Stone, Milan O.		X	X							
Stone, Warren S.		X	X		X					
Strasser, Adolph										X
Stulberg, Louis		X	X		X					
Suffridge, James A.		X	X		X					
Sugar, Maurice		X	X		X	X		X		
Sullivan, David		X	X							
Sullivan, James W.		X	X							
Sullivan, Jere L.		X								
Swanson, Samuel E.		X								
Swartz, Maud O.		X	X							
Sweeney, John J.		X	X		X	X				
Sweeney, Vincent D.		X	X		X	X				
Swinton, John		X			X					
Swisher, Elwood D.		X	X							
Sylvis, William H.		None								

Name	Category	(1) Gra.	(2) Sec.	(3) Spc.	(4) Col.	(5) Bch.	(6) Mst.	(7) Law	(8) Ph.D.	(9) Unk.
Tahney, James P.		X	X							
Talbot, Thomas W.		X								
Teigan, Henry G.		X	X		X	X				
Tetlow, Percy		X		V						
Thimmes, James G.		X	X							
Thomas, Norman M.		X	X		X	X				
Thomas, Rolland J.		X	X		X					
Thompson, Mary G.		X								
Thorne, Florence C.		X	X		X	X				
Tighe, Michael F.		X								
Tippett, Thomas		X	X		X					
Tobin, Daniel J.		X		N						
Tonelli, Joseph P.		X	X							
Totten, Ashley L.		X	X							
Townsend, Robert, Jr.										X
Townsend, Willard S.		X	X		X	X		X		
Tracy, Daniel W.		X	X							
Trautmann, William E.										X
Travis, Maurice E.		X								
Travis, Robert C.		X	X							
Trevellick, Richard F.										X
Troup, Augusta L.		X	X							
Turner, Frederick		X	X							
Turner, J. C.		X	X		X	X				
Uhl, Alexander		X	X		X	X				
Valentine, Joseph F.		X								
Van Arsdale, Harry, Jr.		X	X							
Van Kleeck, Mary A.		X	X		X	X				
Vanzetti, Bartolomeo		X	X							
Vladeck, Baruch C.		X			X					
Vorse, Mary H.		X	X							
Walker, John H.		X								
Walling, William E.		X	X		X	X				
Walsh, Francis P.		X						X		
Walsh, Richard F.		X								
Ward, Cyrenus O.										X
Ward, Martin J.		X	X	V						
Watt, Robert J.		X		N						
Watts, Glenn E.		X	X		X					
Weaver, George L. P.		X	X		X					
Webber, Charles C.		X	X		X	X	X			
Webber, Clyde M.										X
Weber, Frank J.		X								
Weber, Joseph N.		X								
Weihe, William		X								
Weir, Stan		X	X		X					

Name	Category	(1) Gra.	(2) Sec.	(3) Spc.	(4) Col.	(5) Bch.	(6) Mst.	(7) Law	(8) Ph.D.	(9) Unk.
Werkau, Carlton W.		X	X							
Wharton, Arthur O.										X
Wharton, Hunter P.		X	X		X	X				
White, John P.										X
Whitfield, Owen H.		X	X		X					
Whitney, Alexander F.		X	X							
Wilkinson, Joseph		X								
Williams, Benjamin H.		X	X		X	X				
Williams, Elijah H.		X	X							
Williams, Roy L.		X	X							
Wilson, Boyd L.		X	X		X					
Wilson, D. Douglas										X
Wilson, James A.		X								
Wilson, William B.		X								
Windt, John										X
Wipisinger, William W.		X	X							
Wolchok, Samuel		X	X							
Wolfgang, Myra K.		X	X							
Wolfson, Theresa		X	X		X	X	X		X	
Woll, Matthew		X		N			X			
Wood, Reuben T.		X								
Woodcock, Leonard F.		X	X		X					
Wright, James L.		X	X							
Wurf, Jerry		X	X		X	X				
Wynn, William H.		X	X							
Yablonski, Joseph A.		X								
Young, Coleman A.		X	X							
Young, Kenneth		X	X		X	X				
Younger, Maud		X	X							
Zack, Albert J.		X	X							
Zander, Arnold S.		X	X		X	X	X		X	
Zaritsky, Max		X	X							
Zimmerman, Charles S.		X	X							
Zonarich, Nicholas A.		X								

Appendix V
Political Preference

Listings in this appendix were determined not only by party membership but also by identification with or support of a political party. Because party identification in some cases changed over time, some persons are listed under more than one party. Category 3 includes a number of different Socialist parties; the three major parties were the Socialist party of America, the Socialist Labor party, and the Socialist Workers party. In category 4 the American Labor party and the Liberal party are listed together. When the American Labor party came increasingly under the control of the Communists, most of its members transferred to the newly organized Liberal party. In category 7, anarchist affiliation is indicated by an "A." Political preferences were not ascertained for approximately 20 percent of the subjects.

Key:
Category 1—Democratic party (Dem.)
 2—Republican party (Rep.)
 3—Socialist parties (Soc.)
 4—American Labor party/Liberal party (A/L.)
 5—Self-identified nonpartisan (Np)
 6—Supporter of an independent labor party (LP)
 7—Communist party of America (CPA)

Name	Category (1) Dem.	(2) Rep.	(3) Soc.	(4) A/L.	(5) Np	(6) LP	(7) CPA
Abel, Iorwith W.	X						
Addams, Jane					X		
Addes, George P.	X						
Alpine, John P.		X					
Ameringer, Oscar			X				
Andrews, Emmet C.	X						
Antonini, Luigi				X			
Arywitz, Sigmund	X						
Bacon, Emery F.	X						

Name	Category (1) Dem.	(2) Rep.	(3) Soc.	(4) A/L.	(5) Np	(6) LP	(7) CPA
Baer, Fred W.	X						
Baer, John M.		X				X	
Baker, E.R.P.	X						
Barkan, Alexander E.	X				X		
Barnes, John M.			X				
Barondess, Joseph			X				
Barrett, Francis G.	X						
Barry, Thomas B.	X						
Baskin, Joseph			X				
Bates, Harry C.	X						
Beck, Dave		X					
Behncke, David L.	X						
Beirne, Joseph A.	X						
Bellamy, Edward			X				
Bellanca, Dorothy J.				X			
Belsky, Joseph				X			
Benson, Herman			X				
Berger, Victor L.			X				
Berry, George L.	X				X		
Bieber, Owen F.	X						
Biemiller, Andrew J.	X		X				
Billings, Warren K.			X				
Birthright, William C.	X						
Bittner, Van A.	X				X		
Blankenhorn, Heber H.	X						
Bloor, Ella R.			X				X
Blumberg, Hyman	X			X			
Bonadio, Frank	X						
Bower, Andrew P.			X				
Boyce, Edward			X				
Brennan, Peter J.	X						
Brewer, Roy M.	X						
Brockhausen, Frederick C.			X				
Brophy, John					X		
Broun, Heywood C.			X				
Brown, Harvey W.					X		
Brown, Henry S.	X						
Bryson, Hugh	X					X	
Buchanan, Joseph R.			X				
Buckmaster, Leland S.	X						
Burke, John P.			X				
Burke, Walter J.	X						
Burns, Matthew J.	X						
Caddy, Samuel H.	X						
Cahan, Abraham			X				
Cairns, Thomas F.					X		

Name	Category (1) Dem.	(2) Rep.	(3) Soc.	(4) A/L.	(5) Np	(6) LP	(7) CPA
Cameron, Andrew C.						X	
Cannon, Joseph D.			X	X			
Carey, James B.	X						
Carroll, Thomas C.	X						
Carter, William S.	X						
Cashen, Thomas C.	X						
Chaiken, Sol C.	X						
Chamberlain, Edwin M.						X	
Chapman, Gordon W.	X						
Chavez, Cesar E.	X						
Chesser, Al H.	X						
Christman, Elisabeth	X						
Christopher, Paul R.	X						
Clark, Jesse		X					
Clark, Lewis J.	X						
Commerford, John	X	X				X	
Conlon, Peter J.			X				
Connors, David M.	X						
Conway, Jack T.	X						
Cook, Harry H.					X		
Cope, Elmer F.	X						
Cosgrove, John T.	X						
Coulter, Clarence C.	X						
Counts, George S.					X		
Crosswaith, Frank R.			X	X			
Crouch-Hazlett, Ida			X				
Cruikshank, Nelson H.	X						
Crull, John L.		X					
Curran, Joseph E.				X			
Dalrymple, Sherman H.	X						
Daniel, Franz E.	X						
Davidson, Roy E.	X						
Davis, James J.		X					
Debs, Eugene V.	X		X			X	
De Caux, Leonard H.							X
Delaney, George P.	X						
DeLeon, Daniel			X				
DeLeon, Solon							X
Dellums, Cottrell L.	X				X		
Delorenzo, Anthony J.	X						
DeLury, John J.	X						
Dennis, Eugene							X
DeNucci, George	X						
Devyr, Thomas A.		X				X	
Doak, William N.		X					
Dobbs, Farrel			X				

Name	Category (1) Dem.	(2) Rep.	(3) Soc.	(4) A/L.	(5) Np	(6) LP	(7) CPA
Doherty, William C.	X						
Donnelly, Michael						X	
Donnelly, Samuel B.		X					
Douglas, Charles	X						
Douglass, Frederick		X					
Dreier, Mary E.				X			
Driscoll, John J.	X						
Dubinsky, David			X	X			
Dubrow, Evelyn	X			X			
Duffy, Frank		X					
Duncan, James					X		
Dunne, Vincent R.			X				X
Dunwody, Thomas E.	X						
Durkin, Martin P.	X						
Eames, Thomas B.					X		
Easton, John B.		X					
Eklund, John M.	X						
Ellickson, Katherine P.	X		X				
Ellis, Christine S.							X
Engel, George			X				A
English, William	X					X	
Ernst, Hugo	X						
Ervin, Charles W.			X				
Ettor, Joseph J.			X				
Evans, George H.						X	
Farquhar, John M.		X					
Feeney, Frank		X					
Feinberg, Israel				X			
Feinstone, Morris			X	X		X	
Feller, Karl F.	X						
Fenton, Francis P.	X						
Ferral, John						X	
Fielden, Samuel							A
Fischer, Adolph							A
Fitzgerald, Albert J.						X	
Fitzsimmons, Frank E.		X					
Fljozdal, Frederick H.					X		
Flore, Edward	X						
Flynn, Elizabeth G.							X
Foran, Martin A.	X						
Fosco, Peter	X						
Foster, Frank K.	X						
Foster, William Z.			X				X
Fraina, Louis C.			X				X
Frankensteen, Richard T.	X						
Fraser, Douglas A.	X						

Name	Category	(1) Dem.	(2) Rep.	(3) Soc.	(4) A/L.	(5) Np	(6) LP	(7) CPA
Frayne, Hugh						X		
Frey, John P.			X					
Friedrick, Jacob F.		X		X			X	
Furuseth, Andrew						X		
Gainor, Edward J.		X						
George, Henry		X					X	
Germano, Joseph S.		X						
Germer, Adolph F.				X		X		
Gibbons, Harold J.		X		X		X		
Gibson, Everett G.		X						
Gibson, John W.		X						
Gillmore, Frank		X						
Gilmartin, Daniel		X						
Gingold, David R.					X			
Giovannitti, Arturo				X				
Gleason, Thomas W.		X						
Gold, Ben								X
Goldberg, Arthur J.		X						
Golden, Clinton S.						X		
Goldman, Emma								A
Gompers, Samuel		X				X		
Googe, George L.		X						
Gorman, Patrick E.						X		
Graham, James D.		X						
Graham, Sylvester		X						
Gray, Richard J.			X					
Green, John		X						
Green, William		X						
Greenberg, Max		X						
Griner, John F.		X						
Grogan, John J.		X						
Grottkau, Paul				X				
Hagerty, Thomas J.				X				
Haggerty, Cornelius J.		X						
Haggerty, John B.		X						
Haigler, Carey E.		X						
Haley, Margaret A.							X	
Hall, Paul		X						
Hallbeck, Elroy C.		X						
Handley, John J.				X			X	
Hapgood, Mary D.				X				
Hapgood, Powers				X				
Harrington, Michael		X		X				
Harris, David			X					
Harrison, George M.		X						
Hartung, Albert F.		X						

Name	Category (1) Dem.	(2) Rep.	(3) Soc.	(4) A/L.	(5) Np	(6) LP	(7) CPA
Hayes, Frank J.	X						
Hayes, Maximilian S.			X			X	
Haywood, Allan S.	X						
Haywood, William D.			X				
Heighton, William						X	
Helfgott, Simon				X			
Heller, George	X						
Heller, Jacob J.				X			
Helstein, Ralph	X						
Helt, Daniel W.		X			X		
Henderson, Donald J.							X
Herrick, Elinore M.	X	X		X			
Hill, Joe			X				
Hillman, Bessie A.	X			X			
Hillman, Sidney	X		X	X			
Hillquit, Morris			X				
Hinchcliffe, John	X					X	
Hochman, Julius				X			
Hoffa, James R.		X					
Hoffmann, Sal B.	X						
Holderman, Carl	X						
Hollander, Louis	X			X			
Horn, Roy					X		
Howard, Asbury	X					X	X
Howard, Charles P.		X					
Howard, Robert	X						
Howat, Alexander			X				
Hudson, Hosea							X
Hughes, Roy A.					X		
Hutcheson, Maurice A.		X					
Hutcheson, William L.		X					
Hutchins, Grace			X				X
Hyman, Louis				X			
Iglesias, Santiago			X				
Jarrett, John		X					
Jeffrey, Mildred	X						
Jennings, Paul J.				X			
Jimerson, Earl W.	X						
Johns, John S.	X						
Johnson, William D.	X						
Johnston, Alvanley		X					
Johnston, William H.			X			X	
Jones, Mary H.	X		X			X	
Kasten, Frank		X					
Kaufman, Morris			X				
Kavanagh, William F.	X				X		

Name	Category (1) Dem.	(2) Rep.	(3) Soc.	(4) A/L.	(5) Np	(6) LP	(7) CPA
Kearney, Denis						X	
Keating, Edward	X						
Keefe, Daniel J.		X					
Keenan, Joseph D.	X						
Kehrer, Elmer T.	X						
Keil, Edward A.		X					
Kelley, Florence			X				
Kennedy, Thomas	X						
Kennedy, William P.	X						
Kirkland, Joseph L.	X						
Knight, Orie A.	X						
Kroll, John J.	X		X				
Krzycki, Leo			X				
Labadie, Joseph A.			X			X	
Lawrenson, Jack				X			
Lawson, George W.	X				X	X	
Lee, William G.		X					
Leighty, George E.	X						
Leiserson, William M.	X						
Lennon, John B.	X						
Leonard, Richard	X						
Lewis, Alma D.		X					
Lewis, John L.		X					
Lewis, Joseph	X						
Lewis, Thomas L.		X					
Lindelof, Lawrence P.		X					
Lingg, Louis			X				A
Lipsig, James			X	X			
Litchman, Charles H.		X					
Little, Frank H.			X				
Livingston, John W.	X						
London, Meyer			X				
Lovestone, Jay	X						X
Luhrsen, Julius G.		X					
Lundeberg, Harry		X					
Lyden, Michael J.	X						
Lynch, James M.	X						
McBride, John	X		X			X	
McBride, Lloyd	X						
McCarthy, Patrick H.		X				X	
McCreery, Marie M. L.	X		X			X	
McCurdy, Joseph P.	X						
McDevitt, James L.	X						
McDonald, David J.	X						
McDonald, Joseph D.	X						
McDonnell, J. P.			X				

Name	Category	(1) Dem.	(2) Rep.	(3) Soc.	(4) A/L.	(5) Np	(6) LP	(7) CPA
McFetridge, William L.			X					
MacGowan, Charles J.		X						
McGrady, Edward F.		X						
McGuire, Peter J.				X				
McLaren, Louise L.				X				
McLaughlin, Hugh		X					X	
McMahon, Thomas F.		X						
McNamara, Patrick V.		X						
McNeill, George E.							X	
McNulty, Frank J.		X						
McSorley, William J.						X		
Maguire, Matthew				X				
Mahon, William D.		X						
Mahoney, Charles E.				X			X	
Mahoney, William				X				
Maloy, Elmer J.		X						
Marciante, Louis P.		X						
Martin, Harry L., Jr.		X						
Martin, Warren H.		X						
Martin, William			X					
Martinson, Henry R.				X			X	
Mashburn, Lloyd A.			X					
Maso, Sal						X		
Mathias, Charles G.		X						
Matles, James J.							X	
Maurer, James H.				X				
Mazey, Emil		X					X	
Meany, George		X						
Mendelowitz, Abraham					X			
Merrill, Lewis R.					X			
Migas, Nick								X
Miller, Arnold R.		X						
Miller, Edward S.		X						
Miller, Frieda S.		X						
Miller, Joyce D.		X						
Miller, Marvin J.		X						
Minton, Lee W.			X					
Mitch, William A.							X	
Mitchell, Harry L.		X		X				
Mitchell, John						X		
Mitchell, Walter L.		X						
Moffett, Elwood S.		X						
Mohn, Einar O.		X						
Molony, Joseph P.		X						
Montgomery, Robert		X	X					
Mooney, Thomas J.				X				

Name	Category (1) Dem.	(2) Rep.	(3) Soc.	(4) A/L.	(5) Np	(6) LP	(7) CPA
Moore, Ely	X						
Morgan, Elizabeth			X				
Morgan, Thomas J.			X				
Morreale, Vincent F.	X						
Morrison, Frank					X		
Mortimer, Wyndham			X				
Most, Johann J.							A
Moyer, Charles H.			X			X	
Mullaney, Joseph A.	X						
Murphy, Vincent	X					X	
Murray, Philip	X						
Murray, Thomas A.	X						
Murry, James W.	X						
Muste, Abraham J.			X				
Myers, Isaac		X					
Nagler, Isidore				X			
Nance, Alexander S.	X						
Neebe, Oscar							A
Nef, Walter T.			X				
Nelson, Oscar F.	X	X					
Nestor, Agnes	X						
Newman, Pauline			X	X			
Ninfo, Salvatore				X			
Nockles, Edward N.	X					X	
Nord, Elizabeth	X						
Norwood, Rose F.	X						
Nutt, James H.		X					
Oakes, Grant W.	X					X	
O'Connell, James P.	X						
O'Connor, Harvey			X				
O'Connor, Thomas V.		X					
O'Hare, John	X						
O'Hare, Kate R.			X				
Ohl, Henry, Jr.			X			X	
O'Neill, John M.			X				
O'Reilly, Leonora			X				
Owen, Robert D.	X					X	
Pachler, William J.	X						
Padway, Joseph			X			X	
Parker, Julia O.	X						
Parsons, Albert R.			X				A
Perlis, Leo	X			X	X		
Perlstein, Meyer	X						
Peterson, Eric					X		
Peterson, Esther	X						
Petrillo, James C.	X						

Name	Category (1) Dem.	(2) Rep.	(3) Soc.	(4) A/L.	(5) Np	(6) LP	(7) CPA
Phillips, James A.	X		X				
Phillips, Paul L.	X						
Phillips, Thomas						X	
Pine, Max			X				
Pizer, Morris				X			
Podojil, Antonette	X						
Possehl, John	X						
Potofsky, Jacob S.	X		X	X			
Powderly, Terence V.		X					
Powers, Frank B.	X						
Pressman, Lee	X		X		X	X	X
Quill, Michael				X			
Raftery, Lawrence M.	X						
Ramsay, Claude	X						
Randolph, Asa P.			X	X			
Rarick, Donald C.	X						
Ratchford, Michael D.		X					
Reagan, Ronald	X	X					
Reed, John			X				X
Reuther, Roy	X						
Reuther, Victor	X		X				
Reuther, Walter P.	X		X				
Richardson, George J.					X		
Rickert, Thomas A.					X		
Rieve, Emil	X			X			
Robertson, David B.					X		
Robins, Margaret D.	X	X				X	
Robinson, Reid						X	
Rollings, John I.	X						
Rombro, Jacob			X				
Roney, Frank			X			X	
Rose, Alex			X	X			
Rosenberg, Abraham			X				
Ruef, Abraham		X				X	
Rustin, Bayard	X		X				
Ryan, Joseph P.	X						
Sacco, Nicola			X				A
St. John, Vincent			X				
Sargent, Frank P.		X					
Sayre, Harry D.	X			X			
Schilling, Robert	X						
Schlesinger, Benjamin			X				
Schlossberg, Joseph			X				
Schneider, George J.	X	X					
Schneiderman, Rose	X		X	X		X	
Schnitzler, William F.	X						

Name	Category (1) Dem.	(2) Rep.	(3) Soc.	(4) A/L.	(5) Np	(6) LP	(7) CPA
Schoemann, Peter T.	X						
Scholle, August	X						
Schwab, Michael			X				A
Scott, Sam H.	X						
Scully, John J. J.	X						
Sefton, Lawrence F.	X		X				
Seidel, Emil			X				
Selden, David S.	X						
Shanker, Albert			X	X			
Sheffield, Horace L., Jr.	X						
Shelley, John F.	X						
Sherman, Charles O.			X				
Siemiller, Paul L.	X						
Sigman, Morris			X				
Siney, John						X	
Skidmore, Thomas		X				X	
Slamm, Levi D.	X					X	
Smith, Stanton E.	X						
Soderstrom, Reuben G.		X					
Sorge, Friedrick A.		X	X				
Spies, August V. T.			X				A
Starr, Mark				X			
Steinbock, Max				X			
Stephens, Uriah S.		X				X	
Steward, Ira						X	
Stokes, Rose H. P.			X				X
Stolberg, Benjamin	X	X	X				
Stone, Warren S.						X	
Strasser, Adolph			X				
Stulberg, Louis	X						
Suffridge, James A.		X					
Sullivan, David	X						
Swanson, Samuel E.	X					X	
Swinton, John			X		X		
Sylvis, William H.	X					X	
Teigan, Henry G.	X		X		X	X	
Tetlow, Percy		X					
Thimmes, James G.	X						
Thomas, Norman M.			X				
Thomas, Rolland J.	X						
Thompson, Mary G.	X						
Tighe, Michael F.	X						
Tippett, Thomas						X	
Tobin, Daniel J.	X						
Tonelli, Joseph P.	X						
Totten, Ashley L.				X			

Name	Category	(1) Dem.	(2) Rep.	(3) Soc.	(4) A/L.	(5) Np	(6) LP	(7) CPA
Townsend, Robert, Jr.							X	
Tracy, Daniel W.		X						
Trautmann, William E.				X				
Travis, Maurice E.								X
Travis, Robert C.		X						
Trevellick, Richard F.							X	
Turner, J. C.		X						
Van Arsdale, Harry, Jr.		X						
Van Kleeck, Mary A.				X	X		X	
Vanzetti, Bartolomeo								A
Vladeck, Baruch C.				X	X			
Walker, John H.		X		X			X	
Walling, William E.		X		X				
Walsh, Francis P.		X						
Walsh, Richard F.		X						
Ward, Cyrenus O.				X				
Watt, Robert J.						X		
Watts, Glenn E.		X						
Weaver, George L. P.		X						
Weber, Frank J.				X				
Weihe, William		X	X					
Weir, Stan				X				
Werkau, Carlton W.		X						
Whitney, Alexander F.		X						
Williams, Benjamin H.				X				
Williams, Elijah H.		X						
Wilson, D. Douglas				X				
Wilson, William B.		X					X	
Windt, John		X					X	
Wipisinger, William W.		X		X				
Wolchok, Samuel		X			X			
Woll, Matthew			X					
Wood, Reuben T.		X		X				
Woodcock, Leonard F.		X						
Wright, James L.							X	
Wurf, Jerry		X						
Yablonski, Joseph A.		X						
Young, Coleman A.		X						
Zander, Arnold S.		X						
Zaritsky, Max					X			
Zimmerman, Charles S.					X			X

Appendix VI
Major Appointive and Elective Public Offices

This appendix is divided into three major categories: U.S. government, state governments, and local governments. The year when the individual took office is listed.

UNITED STATES GOVERNMENT

Name	Year	Position
Alpine, John P.	1931	Assistant Secretary of Labor
Anderson, Mary	1920	Director of the Women's Bureau, Labor Dept.
Blankenhorn, Heber H.	1934	National Labor Relations Board
Brennan, Peter J.	1972	Secretary of Labor
Chapman, Gordon W.	1961	Assistant to the Secretary of State
Conway, Jack T.	1964	Deputy Director, Office of Economic Opportunity
Davis, James J.	1964	Secretary of Labor
Davis, Walter G.	1965	Deputy Director, Office of Economic Opportunity
Delaney, George P.	1963	Director, Office of Labor Affairs, Agency for International Development
Doak, William N.	1930	Secretary of Labor
Doherty, William C.	1962	Ambassador to Jamaica
Donnelly, Samuel B.	1908	Public Printer
Douglass, Frederick	1871	Secretary, Santo Domingo Commission
	1877	U.S. Marshall
	1889	U.S. Minister to Haiti
Durkin, Martin P.	1953	Secretary of Labor
Gibson, John W.	1945	Assistant Secretary of Labor
Goldberg, Arthur J.	1961	Secretary of Labor
	1962	Associate Justice, U.S. Supreme Court
	1965	Ambassador to the United Nations
Haas, Francis J.	1933	Labor Advisory Board, National Recovery Administration
	1935	Labor Policies Board, Works Progress Administration

	1935	Special Conciliator, Department of Labor
Herrick, Elinore M.	1933	Regional Labor Board, National Recovery Administration
Jarrett, John	1889	American Consul to Birmingham, England
Keefe, Daniel J.	1909	Commissioner General of Immigration
Leiserson, William M.	1939	National Labor Relations Board
Litchman, Charles H.	1889	Special Agent, Treasury Department
McGrady, Edward F.	1933	Assistant Secretary of Labor
Mashburn, Lloyd A.	1953	Undersecretary of Labor
Miller, Frieda S.	1944	Director, Women's Bureau, Department of Labor
Moore, Ely	1845	U.S. Marshall
Myers, Isaac	1870	Special Agent, Post Office Department
	1882	U.S. Gauger
Nelson, Oscar F.	1917	Commissioner of Conciliation, Department of Labor
O'Connor, Thomas V.	1921	Chairman, U.S. Shipping Board
Ornburn, Ira M.	1930	Member, U.S. Tariff Commission
Owen, Robert D.	1853	Chargé d'Affaires to Naples
	1854	Minister Resident, Naples
Peterson, Esther	1961	Assistant Secretary of Labor
	1964	Special Presidential Assistant on Consumer Affairs
Powderly, Terence V.	1897	Commissioner General of Immigration
Reagan, Ronald	1980	President of the United States
Sargent, Frank P.	1902	Commissioner General of Immigration
Tracy, Daniel W.	1940	Assistant Secretary of Labor
Weaver, George L. P.	1961	Assistant Secretary of Labor for International Affairs
Weihe, William	1896	Deputy Immigration Inspector
Wilson, William B.	1913	Secretary of Labor

UNITED STATES CONGRESS

Name	Year	Position
Baer, John M.	1917	Representative
Berger, Victor L.	1911	Representative
Berry, George L.	1937	Senator
Biemiller, Andrew J.	1945	Representative
Davis, James J.	1930	Senator
Farquhar, John M.	1885	Representative
Foran, Martin A.	1883	Representative
Iglesias, Santiago	1933	Representative (nonvoting)
Keating, Edward	1913	Representative
London, Meyer	1915	Representative
McNamara, Patrick V.	1955	Senator
McNulty, Frank J.	1923	Representative
Owen, Robert D.	1843	Representative

Schneider, George J.	1922	Representative
Teigan, Henry G.	1937	Representative
Wilson, William B.	1907	Representative
Wood, Reuben T.	1933	Representative

STATE GOVERNMENTS

Name	Year	Position
Arywitz, Sigmund	1959	California State Labor Commissioner
Douglass, Frederick	1881	Recorder of Deeds, District of Columbia
Durkin, Martin P.	1933	Illinois State Director of Labor
Friedrick, Jacob F.	1960	Board of Regents, University of Wisconsin
Gibson, John W.	1941	Chairman, Michigan Department of Labor and Industry
Hayes, Frank J.	1937	Lieutenant Governor—Colorado
Holderman, Carl	1954	New Jersey Commissioner of Labor and Industry
Jeffrey, Mildred	1975	Board of Governors, Wayne State University
Kelley, Florence	1892	Illinois Chief Factory Inspector
Kennedy, Thomas	1935	Lieutenant Governor—Pennsylvania
Lynch, James M.	1914	New York Commissioner of Labor
Mahon, William D.	1898	Presiding Judge, Michigan State Court of Arbitration
Martinson, Henry R.	1937	North Dakota Deputy Commissioner of Labor
Mashburn, Lloyd A.	1951	California State Labor Commissioner
Miller, Frieda S.	1938	New York Industrial Commissioner
O'Hare, Kate R.	1939	Assistant Director, California Department of Penology
O'Sullivan, Mary K.	1914	Factory Inspector, Massachusetts Department of Labor
Ratchford, Michael D.	1900	Ohio Commissioner of Labor Statistics
Reagan, Ronald	1966	Governor—California
Schneiderman, Rose	1933	Secretary, New York State Department of Labor
Swartz, Maud O.	1931	Secretary, New York State Department of Labor

STATE LEGISLATURES

Name	Year	Position
Baker, E.R.P.	1873	Representative—Ohio
Barry, Thomas B.	1885	Representative—Michigan
Biemiller, Andrew J.	1937	Representative—Wisconsin
Boyce, Edward	1895	Representative—Idaho
Debs, Eugene V.	1885	Representative—Indiana
Easton, John B.	1927	Representative—West Virginia
English, William	1837	Representative—Pennsylvania
Fincher, Jonathan C.	1877	Representative—Pennsylvania
Green, William	1910	Senator—Ohio
Grogan, John J.	1943	Representative—New Jersey

Helt, Daniel W.	1917	Representative—Pennsylvania
Hinchcliffe, John	1873	Representative—Illinois
Howard, Robert	1880	Representative—Massachusetts
Iglesias, Santiago	1917	Senator—Puerto Rico
Litchman, Charles H.	1879	Representative—Massachusetts
McGrady, Edward F.		Representative—Massachusetts
McLaughlin, Hugh	1872	Representative—Illinois
Maurer, James H.	1911	Representative, Pennsylvania
Ohl, Henry	1917	Representative—Wisconsin
O'Neill, John M.		Representative—Colorado
Owen, Robert D.	1835	Representative—Indiana
Padway, Joseph A.	1925	Representative—Wisconsin
Shelley, John F.	1939	Senator—California
Soderstrom, Reuben G.	1917	Representative—Illinois
Teigan, Henry G.	1933	Representative—Minnesota
Tetlow, Percy	1913	Representative—Ohio
Weber, Frank J.	1907	Representative—Wisconsin
Weihe, William	1883	Representative—Pennsylvania
Young, Coleman A.	1964	Senator—Michigan

CITY GOVERNMENT

Name	Year	Position
Berger, Victor L.	1910	Alderman-at-Large, Milwaukee, Wis.
Foran, Martin A.	1911	Judge, Cleveland (Ohio) Court of Common Pleas
Grogan, John J.	1953	Mayor, Hoboken, N.J.
Hickman, William W.	1878	Deputy Sheriff, Milwaukee (Wis.) County
	1880	County Coroner, Milwaukee (Wis.) County
Kasten, Frank	1929	Mayor, Blue Island, Ill.
McCarthy, Patrick H.	1909	Mayor, San Francisco, Calif.
Mahoney, William	1933	Mayor, St. Paul, Minn.
Maloy, Elmer J.	1937	Mayor, Duquesne, Pa.
Moore, Ely	1839	Surveyor of the Port of New York City
Murphy, Vincent	1941	Mayor, Newark, N.J.
Nelson, Oscar F.	1923	Chicago (Ill.) City Council
	1935	Judge, Chicago Superior Court
Ninfo, Salvatore	1937	New York City Council
Nutt, James H.	1884	Youngstown (Ohio) City Council
	1889	President, Youngstown (Ohio) City Council
	1891	Youngstown (Ohio) City Commissioner
	1916	Youngstown (Ohio) City Safety Director
Padway, Joseph A.	1925	Milwaukee (Wis.) County Civil Court
Powderly, Terence V.	1879	Mayor, Scranton, Pa.
Quill, Michael J.	1937	New York City Council
Seidel, Emil	1904	Alderman, Milwaukee, Wis.
	1910	Mayor, Milwaukee, Wis.

	1916	Alderman, Milwaukee, Wis.
	1932	Alderman, Milwaukee, Wis.
Shelley, John F.	1964	Mayor, San Francisco, Calif.
Vladeck, Baruch C.	1917	New York City Board of Aldermen
	1937	New York City Council
Young, Coleman A.	1973	Mayor, Detroit, Mich.

Index

Community College of the Air Force, 177

Community Health, Inc., 336

Community Service Committee, 539

Community Service Organization, 150, 308, 327

Conference for Progressive Labor Action, 164, 255, 429

Conference for Progressive Political Action, National, 322, 400, 531, 594

Congress for Labor, Palestine, 504

Congress of Industrial Organizations: affiliation with, 107; conflict with AFL, 302; creation of, 353; executive board of, 85, 97, 126, 152, 157, 219, 224, 266, 268, 290, 338, 392, 403, 419, 442, 465, 469, 494, 554, 591; expulsion from, 145; general council for, 254; leaders' education, 46; marital status of leaders, 44; national publicity director, 179; non-Communist oaths, 97; nonpartisanship, 23; office manager, 206; official of, 484; opposition to, 310; organization of, 40, 58, 304; organizing campaigns, 173; political action committee, 116, 137, 165, 224, 262, 274, 296, 301, 320, 329, 340, 341, 381, 398, 494, 515, 547; religious affiliation, 22; southern organizing committee of, 247; mentioned, 7, 8, 54, 57, 109, 116, 119, 123, 125, 126, 128, 129, 130, 132, 137, 139, 141, 143, 144, 158, 166, 167, 172, 254, 256, 346, 540

Congress of International Working People's Association, 524. *See also* Black International

Congress of Racial Equality, 495–496

Congress of Railway Unions, 152, 184, 364

Congress of the Revolutionary Socialist, 524

Congress of Working Women, Third International, 1923, 406

Congressional Medal of Honor, 214

Conlon, Peter J., biography of, 162–163

Connally, John, 131

Connecticut: AFL-CIO, 194; Blue Cross, 183; fire and safety committee, 183; state federation of labor, 449; state industrial union council, 194

Connecticut Nutmeg, 129

Connors, David M., biography of, 163

Consolidated Edison Corp., 224

Construction Workers Organizing Committee, CIO, United, 352, 353

Consumer Cooperatives, Committee on, 409

Consumer Federation of America, 316

Consumers Council, 467

Contract Compliance Committee, 401

Controcorrente/Countercurrent, 278

Conway, Jack T., biography of, 163–164

Cook, Harry H., biography of, 164

Cook County (Ill.) Commissioner, 230

Cook County (Ill.) Industrial Union Council, 245, 557

Cook County (Ill.) Juvenile Court, 529

Cookman Institute in Jacksonville, Fla., 477

Coolidge, Calvin, 175, 446

Cooper Union, 350, 380, 427, 584

Cooper Union Art School, 527

Cooperative League, 122, 143, 327, 532

Coopers International Union, 217, 229, 503

Coopers' Journal, 229, 503

Cope, Elmer F.: biography of, 164–165; mentioned, 59

Cordwainers, National Association of, 209

Corey, Lewis, 234. *See also* Fraina, Louis C.

Cornell University: Institute of Labor and Industrial Relations, 407; labor school, 394; mentioned, 112, 301, 332, 472, 513

Cosgrove, John T., biography of, 165–166

Coshocton Progressive Miners Union, 264

Cosmopolitan Club, 481

Cotton Belt Railroad shops, 162

Coulter, Clarence C.: biography of, 166; mentioned, 534

Governor's Committee on Area Schools, Iowa, 156

Governor's Committee on Employment of the Handicapped, Iowa, 156

Graham, James D., biography of, 262–263

Graham, Sylvester, biography of, 263

Grand Eight Hour League, 142, 384, 528

Grand Island (Neb.) Central Labor Union, 125

Grand Trunk Pacific Railroad, 379

Grand Valley State College, Personnel and Labor Advisory Council, 112

Granite Cutters International Association, 199

Granite Cutters' National Union, 198, 202

Grape boycott, 151

Gray, Richard J., biography of, 263–264

Great Britain, U.S. Ambassador to, 406

Great Eastern Band of Allegheny, 369

Great Northern Railroad, 178, 309, 321, 335, 501

Greater New York United Order of American Carpenters, 197

Greater Washington Central Labor Council, AFL-CIO, 560

Green, John, biography of, 264

Green, Lloyd, 109

Green, William: biography of, 264–265; mentioned, 39, 141, 199, 262, 263, 401, 422, 432, 485, 507, 549

Greenback-Labor movement, 343, 358, 464, 470, 503, 520, 528, 558, 588

Greenberg, Max: biography of, 265–266; mentioned, 527

Greene, Michael F., biography of, 266

Greene, Prince W., biography of, 266–267

Grinell Company, 53, 87

Griner, John F., biography of, 267–268

Grogan, John J., biography of, 268

Grottkau, Paul, biography of, 268–269

Group Health Association of America, 91

Guffy-Snyder Coal Stabilization Act of 1935, 426

Guinan, Matthew, biography of, 269–270

Gulf, Colorado, and Santa Fe Railroad, 364

Gulf Refining Co., 400

Gypsy Moon, 60

Haas, Francis J., biography of, 271–272

Habar, William, 51

Hagerty, Thomas J.: biography of, 272–273; mentioned, 60, 61, 584

Haggerty, Cornelius J., biography of, 273

Haggerty, John B., biography of, 273–274

Hague, Frank, 391, 425

Haigler, Carey E., biography of, 274

Haiti, 192

Haley, Margaret A., biography of, 274–275

Hall, Burton, biography of, 275–276

Hall, Clifton and Schwartz, 275

Hall, Paul: biography of, 276; mentioned, 195

Hallbeck, Elroy C., biography of, 276–277

Hamilton Grange School, New York City, 186

Hamilton Watch Workers Union, 147

Hampton Institute, 555

Handley, John J., biography of, 277

Hanna, Mark, 479

Hannibal and St. Louis Railroad, 320

Hanson, Florence, 121

Hapgood, Mary D., biography of, 277–279

Hapgood, Powers: biography of, 279–280; mentioned, 57, 58, 277, 353

Harbord Collegiate Institute, Toronto, 533

Harding, Warren G., 153, 175, 178

Hardy, George, 190

Harlan County, Ky., 139

Harlin, Robert, 306

Harper Brothers publishers, 318

Harper's, 567

Harpers Ferry, 349

Harrington, Michael, biography of, 280–281

Harris, David, biography of, 281

About the Editor-in-Chief

GARY M FINK is Professor of History and Chairman of the Department at Georgia State University. He is the author of *Labor's Search for Political Order*; *Labor Unions*; *Organizing Dixie* (with Philip Taft); and *Prelude to the Presidency*, all but the first published by Greenwood Press, and numerous articles appearing in professional journals.